THE OXFORD HANDBOOK OF

MUSICAL
REPATRIATION

THE OXFORD HANDBOOK OF

MUSICAL

REPATRIATION

Edited by

FRANK GUNDERSON
ROBERT C. LANCEFIELD
BRET WOODS

OXFORD
UNIVERSITY PRESS

OXFORD
UNIVERSITY PRESS

Oxford University Press is a department of the University of Oxford. It furthers
the University's objective of excellence in research, scholarship, and education
by publishing worldwide. Oxford is a registered trade mark of Oxford University
Press in the UK and certain other countries.

Published in the United States of America by Oxford University Press
198 Madison Avenue, New York, NY 10016, United States of America.

Library of Congress Cataloging-in-Publication Data
Names: Gunderson, Frank D. | Lancefield, Robert C. | Woods, Bret D., 1978–
Title: The Oxford handbook of musical repatriation / edited by Frank
Gunderson, Robert C. Lancefield, and Bret Woods.
Description: New York, NY: Oxford University Press, [2019] |
Includes bibliographical references and index.
Identifiers: LCCN 2018037868 | ISBN 978–0–19–065980–6 (hardcover)
Subjects: LCSH: Music—Repatriation. | Sound recordings in ethnomusicology.
Classification: LCC ML3799.2 .O95 2019 | DDC 780.9—dc23
LC record available at https://lccn.loc.gov/2018037868

1 3 5 7 9 8 6 4 2

Printed by Sheridan Books, Inc., United States of America

CONTENTS

Acknowledgments

THE idea for putting together an edited volume on the topic of musical repatriation has been brewing since the early 2000s, and it came together most cogently in 2004, with a panel at the Society for Ethnomusicology's international meeting in Tucson, Arizona. Titled "Reconnections: Archived Musical Memories Re-Embodied in the Field," the panel featured Frank Gunderson, Daniel Reed, and Nikos Pappas, with a response by Robert Lancefield. Feedback from this conference led to conversations over several years between Frank Gunderson and Bret Woods about editing a collected volume of chapters geared toward an open dialogue about repatriation, archives, and current scholarship. Since then the project has grown in scope, and in the spirit of those earlier dialogues came to include Robert Lancefield as a co-editor, and as a contributor by way of including his influential 1998 article, "Musical Traces' Retraceable Paths: The Repatriation of Recorded Sound."

The editors express their deepest and most heartfelt thanks to the authors, who responded to this project with great enthusiasm and patient diligence. Thanks also to David Cobb and Mia Gormandy, graduate students at Florida State University, for their assistance in compiling data searches at various stages throughout the term of this project. We are particularly grateful to Anna-Lise Santella at Oxford University Press for stewarding this project through to completion, and to Indiana University Press for their permission to reprint Robert C. Lancefield's article from the *Journal of Folklore Research* 35 (1): 47–68.

About the Editors

Frank Gunderson is Associate Professor of Ethnomusicology at Florida State University. His research interests include African and African diasporan history, musical labor, sonic repatriation, biographical approaches, human rights, and documentary film. He is an active member of the African Studies Association (ASA), the American Anthropological Association (AAA), and the Society for Ethnomusicology (SEM). He is editor of the SEM academic journal *Ethnomusicology*, and has also served as the journal's film, video, and multimedia review editor. He has published articles and reviews in *Africa Today, History and Anthropology, Soundings*, and *African Music*, and has twice been a guest editor of the journal *World of Music*.

Robert C. Lancefield leads digital work at the Davison Art Center, Wesleyan University. A former president of the Museum Computer Network (MCN), the organization for people who do digital work in museums, Lancefield chairs the American Alliance of Museums (AAM) Council of Affiliates. Rob's Wesleyan University MA thesis considered the repatriation of recorded sound and the cultural meanings of intangible cultural documentation. His PhD dissertation examined how ideas about musical bodies and voices lent false credence to ideas of orientalized difference. Formerly a professional musician and recording engineer, Rob performed widely with Talking Drums, a US ensemble of Ghanaians and Americans.

Bret Woods is an ethnomusicologist, author, filmmaker, and theoretician whose work explores music, media, and narrative through the lenses of mediology, anthropology, and social genre theory. Their main areas of focus are digital media studies, narratives and languages, performance and dissemination (through engagement of community and technology), and traditional musics. Bret is an active proponent of "ethnomediology," their approach to studying expression and interaction mediated through access to archives, digital technologies, and the Internet. Bret's research explores engagement in and negotiation of traditions globally and locally through contemporary media.

CONTRIBUTORS

Gage Averill (PhD 1989, University of Washington) is dean of the Faculty of Arts at the University of British Columbia. An ethnomusicologist specializing in music of the Caribbean and North America, he served as president of the Society for Ethnomusicology, 2009–2011. *Four Parts, No Waiting: A Social History of American Barbershop Harmony* (Oxford 2003) won book prizes from the Society for Ethnomusicology and the Society for American Music. *A Day for the Hunter: a Day for the Prey: Popular Music and Power in Haiti* (Chicago 1997) received a best book by the Association for Recorded Sound Collections. *Alan Lomax in Haiti, 1936–37* was named an Outstanding Project (2010) by the Clinton Global Initiative, earning two Grammy nominations. Professor Averill has consulted for the Ford Foundation, the National Endowment for the Arts, the Smithsonian Institution, the Organization of American States, and the Fulbright Foundation, and for films, festivals, and copyright cases.

Michael B. Bakan is professor of Ethnomusicology at Florida State University. His more than fifty publications encompass topics ranging from Indonesian *gamelan* music and early American jazz history to neurodiversity and disability studies. They include the widely used textbook *World Music: Traditions and Transformations*, now in preparation for its third edition with McGraw-Hill and also available in Chinese translation; the monograph *Music of Death and New Creation*, which was reviewed in *The Times* (London) as one of the two "most significant publications on Balinese music in almost half a century"; and his forthcoming book with Oxford University Press on the ethnomusicology of autism. Bakan serves as series editor for the Routledge Focus on World Music Series. As a percussionist, he has performed with George Clinton, John Cage, Rudolf Serkin, the Toronto Symphony, and leading Balinese gamelan ensembles, and he appears on the forthcoming Parliament album *Medicaid Fraud Dog*.

Lisa Osunleti Beckley-Roberts, assistant professor of ethnomusicology at Jackson State University, earned her doctorate in ethnomusicology and masters degrees in ethnomusicology and harp performance at Florida State University, after having received her bachelor of arts degree in harp performance from Dillard University in New Orleans, Louisiana. Her research interests include Africana spiritual traditions and the role of music within them, the creation of sacred space through music, music and memory, and Africana music and dance traditions. She is also an accomplished performer who has been principal harpist with the Valdosta Symphony Orchestra and the Central Florida Symphony Orchestra while also performing with the neo-soul and hip-hop performers of Tallahassee Nights Live. She has published in *Ethnomusicology*, *Journal of Africana*

Studies, and *Worlds of Music*, and she has presented at conferences of professional organizations including the African Studies Association, Caribbean Studies Association, and African and Diasporic Religious Studies Association.

Craig Breaden has been audiovisual archivist at the David M. Rubenstein Rare Book and Manuscript Library at Duke University since 2012. From 2006 to 2012 he was head of Media and Oral History at the Richard B. Russell Library for Political Research and Studies at the University of Georgia. He holds a BA in history from Texas Christian University, an MA in history from Utah State University, and an MS in library science from the University of North Carolina at Chapel Hill.

Patricia Shehan Campbell is Donald E. Peterson Professor of Music at the University of Washington, where she teaches courses at the interface of education and ethnomusicology. She has lectured on the pedagogy of world music and children's musical cultures throughout the United States, in much of Europe and Asia, and in Australia, New Zealand, South America, and eastern and southern Africa. Campbell was designated the Senior Researcher in Music Education (American-national) in 2002 and is 2012 recipient of the Taiji Award and the 2017 Koizumi Prize for the preservation of traditional music through educational practice. She is chair of the advisory board of Smithsonian Folkways and consultant in repatriation efforts for the recordings of Alan Lomax to communities in the American South. Her recent works include co-authorship of *Redefining Music Studies in an Age of Change* (Routledge, 2017), *The Musically Vibrant Classroom: Music for Elementary Classroom Teachers* (W. W. Norton, 2017), and as editor, a six-volume series on *World Music Pedagogy* (Routledge, 2018).

Rona Goonginda Charles (Ngarinyin and Nyikina) is a cultural consultant and researcher based in the Kimberley region of Western Australia. Charles has been engaged as a consultant across a range of disciplines including archaeology, ethnomusicology, and land conservation and management and has played a key role in native title negotiations and management for several groups. Collaborating on ARC-funded projects with Sally Treloyn since 2009, Charles co-leads the Junba Project, has presented at conferences and seminars in Cairns, Melbourne, Perth, Sydney, Ottawa, and Toronto, and has co-written several papers and chapters on *junba* and research collaboration. Charles is currently a project officer at the Wilinggin Aboriginal Corporation.

Beverley Diamond, ethnomusicologist, is professor emerita at Memorial University of Newfoundland, where she founded and directed the Research Centre for the Study of Music, Media, and Place (MMaP) from 2003 to 2015. She has contributed to Canadian cultural historiography, to feminist music research, and to Indigenous studies. Her research has explored constructs of technological mediation, transnationalism, and, most recently, concepts of reconciliation and healing. Publications include *Native American Music in Eastern North America* (Oxford University Press, 2008) and co-edited anthologies: *Aboriginal Music in Contemporary Canada: Echoes and Exchanges* (McGill-Queen's University Press, 2012) and *Music and Gender* (University of Illinois

Press, 2000). Diamond has been recognized with a Trudeau Fellowship (2009–2012), fellowship in the Royal Society of Canada (2008), Order of Canada (2013), and the Social Sciences and Humanities Research Council of Canada Gold Medal (2014). She is a past president of the Society for Ethnomusicology.

Brian Diettrich (PhD, University of Hawai'i at Mānoa) is senior lecturer in Ethnomusicology at Victoria University of Wellington, New Zealand. His research has focused on Oceania and especially the Federated States of Micronesia (FSM). Brian is a co-author of *Music in Pacific Island Cultures: Experiencing Music, Expressing Culture* (Oxford University Press), and his publications have appeared in numerous journals and edited collections. Brian is currently chair of the Study Group on Music and Dance of Oceania, of the International Council for Traditional Music. He has regularly undertaken collaborative, community, and educational projects in Micronesia, including the repatriation of historical sound recordings. Brian previously taught music for several years at the College of Micronesia–FSM, at both the Chuuk and National Campuses.

Andrea Emberly is an ethnomusicologist and assistant professor in the Children, Childhood, and Youth program at York University. Her work focuses on the study of children's musical cultures and the relationship between childhood, well-being, and musical arts practices. At present she is focused on three major research projects in collaboration with communities in several countries: sustaining endangered initiation schools for girls in Vhavenda communities in South Africa (SSHRC Insight Development); using repatriation of archival materials as a means to maintain musical traditions and generate curriculum for young people in five countries (Australia, Canada, South Africa, Uganda, USA) (SSHRC Partnership Development); and the relationships between language, music, and education in remote Aboriginal communities in the Kimberley region of Western Australia (ARC Linkage).

Judith Gray came to the Library of Congress in 1983 to work on the Federal Cylinder Project in the American Folklife Center, helping to document, preserve, and later disseminate copies of early recordings to their communities of origin. She is now coordinator of reference services for the Folklife Center. She has served on the board of the Society for Ethnomusicology and chaired its archiving interest group, and she was a member of the team that developed the statement of ethical principles for the International Association of Sound and Audiovisual Archives.

Robin R. R. Gray is Ts'msyen from Lax Kw'alaams, BC, and Mikisew Cree from Fort Chipewyan, AB. She honors her culture, which also includes being a dancer and singer in Lax Kxeen, a Ts'msyen dance group. Dr. Gray is a community-based researcher, social justice activist, and interdisciplinary scholar whose work intersects the broader fields of anthropology and Indigenous studies. Her research explores the politics of Indigeneity in settler colonial contexts with a focus on knowledge production, decolonization, Indigenous rights and governance, and access and control of Indigenous cultural heritage. Dr. Gray holds a BAS in interdisciplinary studies from Bennett College for Women, and an MA and PhD in sociocultural anthropology from the University of Massachusetts Amherst. She has conducted and been involved in many community-based, ethnographic research projects with, by, and for youth and Indigenous communities addressing policy issues related to health, education, arts and culture, social engagement, and repatriation.

Frank Gunderson (PhD in ethnomusicology, Wesleyan University) is associate professor of ethnomusicology at Florida State University. He is editor of the journal *Ethnomusicology* (2018–2022) and has published articles and reviews in *Africa Today, History and Anthropology, Soundings, World of Music,* and *African Music.* His work with the Northwest "outsider" musician Travis Roberts culminated in the award-winning film *Human Skab* (co-directed with Bret Woods, SnagFilms, 2012). He does research in East Africa, produced the CD *Tanzania: Farmer Composers of North West Tanzania* (Multicultural Media, 1997), and co-edited with Gregory Barz the book *Mashindano! Competitive Music Performance in East Africa* (Mkuki na Nyota Press, 2000). His book *"We Never Sleep We Dream of Farming": Sukuma Labor Songs from Western Tanzania* (Brill Academic Press, 2010) was the 2009–2011 winner of the Society for Ethnomusicology Kwabena Nketia Book Award for best African music monograph. His most recent book is *Rhumba Kiserebuka! The Legacy of Tanzanian Musicians Muhidin Gurumo and Hassan Bitchuka* (Rowman and Littlefield, 2018).

Edward Herbst has researched music, dance, and theater in Bali since 1972 with support from the Andrew W. Mellon Foundation, Henry Luce Foundation, Asian Cultural Council, Fulbright Senior Research Scholar Program, Ford Foundation, Fulbright-Hays (while earning a PhD in ethnomusicology at Wesleyan University), and Indonesian Institute of Sciences (while earning a BA in music and anthropology at Bennington College). As a composer and vocalist he has received numerous grants from the National Endowment for the Arts Opera–Musical Theater, Theater, and Multidisciplinary Programs; Trust for Mutual Understanding; New York State Council on the Arts; and Massachusetts Cultural Council. Herbst chaired the Society for Ethnomusicology's Ethics Committee and is currently research associate in the Anthropology Department at Hunter College. He was commissioned by Sardono Kusumo's Indonesian dance theater to collaborate as composer and solo vocalist on *Maha Buta* in Switzerland and at Mexico's Festival Cervantino and for Sardono's film, *The Sorceress of Dirah*, in Indonesia.

Catherine Ingram is a postdoctoral fellow at the Sydney Conservatorium of Music, University of Sydney, and visiting expert with the Chinese Music Ecology Research Team, Shanghai Conservatory of Music. Since 2004 she has conducted extensive research on Kam musical culture, and her doctoral dissertation (2010) and forthcoming monograph both focus on the contemporary performance of Kam big song. Her numerous publications center on Kam minority music while also encompassing issues concerning gender, the environment, language-music connections, digital fieldwork, anthropological studies of "tradition," and notions of intangible cultural heritage. She is co-author of *Environmental Preservation and Cultural Heritage in China* (Commonground, 2013) and co-editor of *Taking Part in Music: Case Studies in Ethnomusicology* (Aberdeen University Press, 2013).

Michael Iyanaga (PhD in ethnomusicology, UCLA) is assistant professor of music and culture at the Universidade Federal do Recôncavo da Bahia (Brazil) and an associated researcher of the Modern Moves project, King's College London. Prior to his teaching post in Bahia, Dr. Iyanaga taught at the College of William and Mary, the Universidade Federal da Paraíba, and UCLA. As a scholar, Dr. Iyanaga focuses on Afro-Catholic musical practices in Brazil and the wider Atlantic world while also examining broader issues of method, theory, and intellectual history in ethnomusicology and anthropology. His award-winning publications have appeared in academic journals and books in both the United States and Brazil. Outside of the academy, Dr. Iyanaga has also been active in Brazil's public sector, serving on different arts-related committees and playing important roles in state-sponsored cultural heritage research projects.

Elizabeth "Lyz" Jaakola is a musician and educator and an enrolled member of the Fond du Lac band of Lake Superior Ojibwe in Cloquet, Minnesota. She teaches music education and American Indian studies at Fond du Lac Tribal and Community College. She performs and composes in many styles and genres, including traditional Anishinaabe music, jazz, blues, and opera. She has performed as close to home as Duluth, Minnesota, and as far away as Italy for the Rome Opera Festival. Her Native-based compositions have also been heard on radio and television, and she has arranged many Native pieces for solo and choral performance. Lyz is always striving to promote Anishinaabe music and education through her collaborations, performances, and composition.

Birgitta J. Johnson is a jointly appointed associate professor of ethnomusicology in the School of Music and the African American studies program at the University of South Carolina. Her research interests include music in African American churches, musical change and identity in black popular music, and community archiving. She has published articles in the *Black Music Research Journal, Ethnomusicology Forum*, and the *Grove Dictionary of American Music*. She has forthcoming works on music in African American mega-churches, Beyoncé gospel covers, and gospel music research resources in *Liturgy, Popular Music and Society*, and *Oxford Bibliographies in African American Studies*, respectively. Her current manuscript project is titled *Worship Waves, Navigating Identities: Music in the Black Church at the Turn of the 21st Century*; in it she describes how societal and economic changes as well as emerging new media cultures have had an impact on music-making and worship in black Protestant churches in the post-soul era.

Grace Koch is a visiting research fellow at the Australian Institute of Aboriginal and Torres Strait Islander Studies (AIATSIS) and a visiting senior Research fellow at the National Centre for Indigenous Studies, Australian National University. She has been a consultant for the Central Land Council in Alice Springs, Northern Territory, providing documentation for five Aboriginal land claims in Central Australia. Her monograph

We Have the Song So We Have the Land explores how traditional song and ceremony serve as legal evidence for proof of ownership of clan lands in Australia. Repatriation of early recordings from the AIATSIS collections has been an important focus of her work. She has published nationally and internationally on ethics of managing Indigenous collections, analyses of Indigenous music, and audio archiving.

Robert C. Lancefield leads digital work at the Davison Art Center, Wesleyan University, where he led the policy development and implementation of DAC Open Access Images in 2012. Rob currently chairs the American Alliance of Museums (AAM) Council of Affiliates and is a former president of the Museum Computer Network (MCN), the organization for people who do digital work in museums. Lancefield's Wesleyan University MA thesis (1993) considered the repatriation of recorded sound through a survey of archives and a case study of certain recordings of Navajo music, focusing on the multiple cultural meanings of intangible cultural documentation. His Wesleyan PhD dissertation in ethnomusicology (2004) examined how ideas about the musical body and voice lent false credence to dominant US ideas about orientalized difference, and he curated the traveling exhibition *Performing Images, Embodying Race* on related visual culture. Formerly a professional musician and recording engineer, Rob performed widely in the 1980s with Talking Drums, an ensemble of Ghanaians and Americans.

Matthew Dembal Martin (Ngarinyin and Wunambal) is a *manambarra* elder and singer in the Kimberley region of Western Australia. Following a long career as both a stockman working on various cattle stations in the far north and a dancer in the *junba* tradition, Dembal followed his father, the composer Scotty Nyalgodi Martin, as a lead singer of *junba*. Martin has co-led the revitalization of *junba* in the Mowanjum community in recent years, reclaiming records of *junba* from archives and supporting young people to learn the art of *junba* singing. He has spoken at conferences and public talks in Darwin, Melbourne, and Perth, and has co-authored several papers and chapters on *junba* with Sally Treloyn on dance and well-being, and on repatriation.

Jason McCoy received his PhD in musicology from Florida State University. His dissertation focused on the political music of Simon Bikindi, the role it had in inciting genocide, and justification for its censorship in post-genocide Rwanda. He currently lives in Fort Worth, Texas, and teaches at Dallas Baptist University and the University of North Texas.

Peter McMurray is an ethnomusicologist and media artist with interests in Islam, technology, and voice. He is currently a junior fellow at the Harvard Society of Fellows, where he is completing a book/documentary film project, *Pathways to God: The Islamic Acoustics of Turkish Berlin*. He is the assistant curator of the Milman Parry Collection of Oral Literature at Harvard and along with David Elmer is co-editing a collection of essays, *Singers and Tales in the 21st Century*, forthcoming with the Harvard Center for Hellenic Studies. Beginning in fall 2017 he served as lecturer in the Faculty of Music at Cambridge University.

Maurice Mengel is a doctoral candidate at the University of Cologne. From 2004 to 2010, he worked in the Ethnomusicological Department of the Ethnological Museum in Berlin, also known as the Berlin Phonogram Archive. He is writing his dissertation with Lars C. Koch on the history of a Romanian ethnomusicology archive. Apart from the history of ethnomusicology inside and outside Romania, he is interested in the methodology of ethnomusicology and in music and politics.

Richard Moyle's research spans fifty years and incorporates the results of more than ten years of fieldwork in locations in Polynesia and Australia. His books include landmark volumes on the music of Samoa and Tonga, a trilogy on the Aboriginal music of Central Australia, bilingual volumes of oral tradition in three Polynesian languages, and an ongoing series on the music, language, and rituals of the Polynesian outlier of Takū. He taught ethnomusicology for almost thirty years at the University of Auckland, where he was also director of the Archive of Maori and Pacific Music and director of the Centre for Pacific Studies. Although retired, he holds honorary positions at the University of Auckland (Honorary Research Professor, Centre for Pacific Studies) and the Queensland Conservatorium of Music (adjunct professor).

Carlos Odria is a guitarist and musicologist. In 2014, he earned the PhD in musicology from the Florida State University College of Music, where he was the recipient of the Carol Krebs Research Fellowship and the Moellership Grant, awarded by the FSU Center for Leadership and Civic Education. He has presented his research at regional and national conferences. His publications include an article in *Ethnomusicology*, an entry in the *Greenwood Encyclopedia of Latin American Popular Music*, and a forthcoming article in *Mundos Interiores*. Currently, he is an associate lecturer at the University of Massachusetts Boston.

Christopher Orr is recently completed a Doctorate in Musicology at the Florida State University College of Music. His research focuses on the contemporary performance of Algerian *sha'bi* music among the Algerian diaspora in Paris, France. His work examines this music's continuing relationship to oral narratives of immigration and identity construction, along with the evolution of performance practices. In 2016 and 2017, Chris conducted dissertation fieldwork in France as a Chateaubriand Fellow in the Humanities and Social Sciences. He has presented his work at academic conferences in both France and the United States. His other publications include an entry in the *SAGE Encyclopedia of Music and Culture*. An active musician, Chris also teaches private piano lessons and co-leads the FSU Middle East Ensemble, Aziza, as an oud player.

Elizabeth Whittenburg Ozment is an assistant dean in the College of Arts and Sciences at the University of Virginia. Her primary research interests include the sounds of remembrance, public history, and musical expressions of cultural trauma. Her current project explores multimedia memorials and racialized ways of hearing US Civil War history, with forthcoming publications in the *Palgrave Handbook on Race and the Arts in Education* and the *Journal of the Scholarship of Teaching and Learning*. She serves as the media review editor for the Society for American Music *Bulletin* (2016–2019), and her own articles and reviews may be found in the *Journal of American Folklore, Civil War History, Interdisciplinary Humanities,* the *SAGE Encyclopedia of Ethnomusicology,* and the *New Grove Dictionary of American Music and Musicians.* She received a BM from James Madison University, an MM from the University of North Carolina–Greensboro, and a PhD in Musicology/Ethnomusicology from the University of Georgia.

Alex Perullo is a professor of anthropology, african studies, and music at Bryant University. He received a Fulbright Scholar Award to live and conduct research in London as part of the School of Oriental and African Studies (SOAS), University of London, and was named a Centenary Scholar at SOAS. In addition to articles and reviews, Perullo has published two books on African music economies and is currently working on a new manuscript titled *These Rights Are Ours: Ownership, Property, and Law in African Music.* That project is being completed in conjunction with a five-year fellowship that Perullo received from the Framing the Global project, a partnership between Indiana University's Center for the Study of Global Change and Indiana University Press, funded by the Andrew W. Mellon Foundation.

Jennifer C. Post is currently lecturer at University of Arizona School of Music and senior honorary research fellow at University of Western Australia. Recent and forthcoming publications include articles in the journals *Ethnomusicology Forum* and *Yearbook for Traditional Music,* in the edited collection *Current Directions in Ecomusicology* (A. Allen and K. Dawe, eds., Routledge, 2015), in *Research, Records and Responsibility* (A. Harris, et al., eds., Sydney University Press, 2015), and in *Music and Sustainable Cultures* (T. Cooley and G. Barz, eds., University of Illinois Press, forthcoming). An edited collection, *Ethnomusicology: A Contemporary Reader,* volume 2, was published by Routledge in 2018 and a forthcoming monograph, *Wood, Skin and Bone: Musical Instrument Production and Challenges to Local and Global Ecosystems,* is under contract by University of Illinois Press. Her fieldwork in western Mongolia with Kazakh mobile pastoralists focuses on the impact of social, economic, and ecological change on musical production.

Timothy B. Powell (1959–2018) was a faculty member of the Religious Studies Department at the University of Pennsylvania and a consulting scholar at the Penn Museum. Tim earned his PhD from Brandeis University in 1995. Throughout his career he served as the director of Educational Partnerships with Indigenous Communities (EPIC) in the Penn Language Center and founded the Center for Native American Indigenous Research (CNAIR) at the American Philosophical Society, where he continued to serve as a consulting scholar. Powell's publications include "Digital Knowledge Sharing: Forging Partnerships between Scholars, Archives, and Indigenous Communities" and the edited volume *Beyond the Binary: Reconstructing Cultural Identity in a Multicultural Context* (Rutgers University Press). Over the years, Tim successfully applied for and directed more than three million dollars in grants to support digital repatriation in Indian Country.

Carolyn M. Ramzy is an assistant professor of ethnomusicology at Carleton University. Her broad research interests include musics of the Middle East, the performative politics of belonging, and religious nationalism with specific attention to Egypt's Coptic Christians. Prior to her time at Carleton, she was a fellow at the American Research Center in Egypt (ARCE) and a consultant for the US Library of Congress. She has published articles in *Ethnomusicology, Ethnos Journal of Anthropology*, and the *International Journal for Middle East Studies*.

Daniel B. Reed is Laura Boulton Professor of Ethnomusicology and associate professor in the Department of Folklore and Ethnomusicology at Indiana University. Reed's publications on the subjects of West African music and mask performance include the CD-ROM *Music and Culture of West Africa: The Straus Expedition* (Indiana University Press, 2002); the multimedia web resource *Mask, Music and Dance Performance in Western Côte d'Ivoire* (EVIA Digital Archive, 2009); and numerous book chapters, museum catalog entries, and articles in journals such as *Ethnomusicology, Africa Today*, and *The World of Music*. Reed's first book, *Dan Ge Performance: Masks and Music in Contemporary Côte d'Ivoire* (Indiana University Press, 2003) was co-winner of the Royal Anthropological Institute's Amaury Talbot Prize; his second book, *Abidjan USA: Music, Dance and Mobility in the Lives of Four Ivorian Immigrants*, was published by Indiana University Press in 2016.

Trevor Reed (Hopi) is an associate professor of law at Arizona State University's Sandra Day O'Connor College of Law. He received a JD from Columbia Law School and a PhD in ethnomusicology from Columbia's Graduate School of Arts and Sciences. He teaches courses in federal Indian law and copyright law and conducts research in the area of indigenous intellectual property rights. Reed is a Harlan Fiske Stone Scholar and a recipient of the Ford Foundation predoctoral Fellowship. As an outgrowth of his research, Reed co-founded the Hopi Music Repatriation Project, which assists members of the Hopi Tribe in locating, asserting rights to, and finding meaningful ways to reintegrate Hopi intellectual properties housed in archives, museums, and governmental institutions back into local communities.

J. Christopher Roberts is lecturer and coordinator of music teacher preparation at the University of Washington. He holds degrees from Swarthmore College (BA, history) and the University of Washington (MA, PhD, music education), with research and clinical interests in children's musical cultures, world music education, and the nature of children's interest in music. Recent articles have appeared in publications including the *British Journal of Music Education* (2016), *Journal of Research in Music Education* (2013, 2015), *Oxford Handbook of Social Justice in Music Education* (2015), *Oxford Handbook of Children's Musical Cultures* (2013), and *Bulletin of the Council for Research in Music Education* (in press). An elementary music teacher for twenty years, he currently directs the Kodály Levels Program of Seattle.

Hiromi Lorraine Sakata is professor emerita of ethnomusicology at UCLA, where she served as associate dean in the UCLA School of the Arts and Architecture and professor in the Department of Ethnomusicology until her retirement. Before joining the UCLA faculty, she was on the faculty of the University of Washington, where she served as professor and head of the Ethnomusicology Division in the School of Music. She has conducted extensive field research in Afghanistan and Pakistan and is the author of numerous publications including *Music in the Mind: Concepts of Music and Musician in Afghanistan* (Kent State University Press, 1983, and Smithsonian Institution Press, 2002), *Afghanistan Encounters with Music and Friends* (Mazda Publications, 2013), and "Looking Back on 50 Years of Fieldwork in Afghanistan and Pakistan" (*Asian Music* 48). She was made an honorary member of the Society for Ethnomusicology in 2012.

Anthony Seeger is an ethnomusicologist, anthropologist, audiovisual archivist, and musician. His ethnographic research has focused on the Indigenous peoples of the Amazon region of Brazil, especially the Suyá/Kĩsêdjê. He has also written about audiovisual archives, intellectual property, and other subjects that are part of repatriation processes. He has been involved in audiovisual repatriation projects since 1982. In addition to his teaching duties, he was director of the Indiana University Archives of Traditional Music (1982–1988), curator of the Folkways Collection and founding director of Smithsonian Folkways Recordings at the Smithsonian Institution (1988–2000), and faculty director of the UCLA Ethnomusicology Archive (2007–2012). He has served as president of the Society for Ethnomusicology and the International Council for Traditional Music and was a co-founder of the Research Archive Section of the International Association for Sound and Audiovisual Archives. He has been a fellow of the American Academy of Arts and Sciences since 1993.

Laurel Sercombe worked as archivist for the ethnomusicology program at the University of Washington from 1982 until her retirement in 2016. In 1998 she received a predoctoral Smithsonian Research Fellowship and in 2001 received her PhD with the dissertation *And Then It Rained: Power and Song in Western Washington Coast Salish Myth Narratives*. She has lectured for classes in ethnomusicology, library and information science, and American Indian studies, and designed a course on sound archiving. Her publications include "Native Seattle in the Concert Hall: An Ethnography of Two Symphonies" (*Ethnomusicology* 60); "The Story of Dirty Face: Power and Song in Western Washington Coast Salish Myth Narratives," in *Music of the First Nations: Tradition and Innovation in Native North America* (University of Illinois Press, 2009); and "'Ladies and Gentlemen . . . the Beatles': *The Ed Sullivan Show*, CBS TV, February 9, 1964," in *Performance and Popular Music: History, Place and Time* (Ashgate, 2006).

Carla Shapreau is a senior fellow in the Institute of European Studies at the University of California, Berkeley, where she is conducting research regarding music-related losses during the Nazi era and their twenty-first-century ramifications. The results of her research will be published by Yale University Press in a forthcoming book. Shapreau also is the curator of the Salz Collection of Stringed Instruments in the Department of Music and a lecturer in the School of Law, where she teaches a course on art and cultural property law. Co-author of *The Ferrell-Vogüé Machaut Manuscript* (Oxford: DIAMM Publications, 2014; 2015 Claude V. Palisca Award, American Musicological Society) and

Violin Fraud—Deception, Forgery, Theft and Lawsuits in England and America (Oxford University Press, 1997), Shapreau has written and lectured broadly on the topic of cultural property. She also is a violin maker.

Lauren E. Sweetman holds a PhD in ethnomusicology from New York University and a BMus and MA (ethnomusicology) from the University of Toronto. Her doctoral research, funded by New York University, SSRC, SSHRC, and the Wenner-Gren Foundation, investigated the relationship between Māori performing arts, indigenous rights, and health through an ethnographic case study of a Māori-led forensic psychiatric unit. Lauren is particularly invested in collaborative, advocacy-based research, and she has experience in the nonprofit sector as the former assistant director of the Paradigm Shift Project, a Canadian charity that works to advance education on social and environmental justice issues through the production of short documentary films. Lauren also served as the editor of the Student Newsletter for the Society for Ethnomusicology, and is currently a visiting scholar at Ngā Pae O Te Māramatanga, the Māori Center for Research Excellence at the University of Auckland.

Diane Thram (PhD in ethnomusicology 1999, Indiana University) is an associate professor and director of the International Library of African Music (ILAM), a research archive attached to the Music Department at Rhodes University. She came to ILAM/ Rhodes University in 1999 and served as senior lecturer in ethnomusicology through 2005. She has published numerous articles and book chapters from her research on the therapeutic efficacy of music-making in the Indigenous religions of the Shona and Xhosa in Southern Africa and also from her research on media control in Zimbabwe. As director of ILAM, she has relaunched its accredited academic journal, *African Music*; secured funding for professional cataloging, digitizing, and creation of web access to ILAM's holdings; and directs the National Arts Council– and National Heritage Council–funded ILAM research and repatriation initiatives, the ILAM-Red Location Music History Project, and the ILAM Music Heritage Project SA. Designed to repatriate music from ILAM's Hugh Tracey Collections through the South African schools, the ILAM Music Heritage Project SA is creating and publishing African music education textbooks for grades 7–9 and 10–12.

Peter G. Toner is a social anthropologist and ethnomusicologist at St. Thomas University in Fredericton, Canada, with research interests focusing on music in relation to sociality, poetics, ritual, and cultural change. He has conducted two years of field research with Yolngu musicians in Arnhem Land in northern Australia, including doctoral research in Gapuwiyak, NT, on ritual music and sociality, and a postdoctoral project based on the digitization and repatriation of hundreds of hours of archival music back to their Yolngu communities of origin. Since 2005 he has also conducted research on folk music and cultural identity in Atlantic Canada.

Sally Treloyn is a senior lecturer in ethnomusicology and intercultural research at the University of Melbourne. Treloyn specializes in dance-song traditions of the Kimberley, where she has conducted research since 1999, and more recently the Pilbara in Western Australia. Treloyn's research focuses on issues of music endangerment, resilience, sustainability, and vitality; repatriation and dissemination of recordings as tools for revitalization; and intercultural collaboration and research ethics. Treloyn is currently an Australian Research Council Future Fellow for the project "Singing the Future: Assessing the Effectiveness of Repatriation as a Strategy to Sustain the Vitality of Indigenous Song" and directs research at the Wilin Centre for Indigenous Arts and Cultural Development.

Janice Esther Tulk is senior research associate for the Purdy Crawford Chair in Aboriginal Business Studies at Cape Breton University, where her research focuses on wise business practices in Indigenous contexts. She also conducts research into Indigenous expressive culture, particularly among the Mi'kmaq in Newfoundland. Tulk has published in *MUSICultures, Newfoundland and Labrador Studies, Ethnologies, Culture & Tradition, Canadian Folk Music, Journal of Aboriginal Economic Development,* and various anthologies. She is co-editor of *Indigenous Business in Canada: Principles and Practices* and producer/author of the CD/book set *Welta'q "It Sounds Good": Historic Recordings of the Mi'kmaq.*

John Vallier is an archivist and ethnomusicologist at the University of Washington (UW). He studied anthropology at UC Santa Cruz and ethnomusicology at UCLA. At UW he curates the Ethnomusicology Archives and teaches on a range of topics, including Seattle music, remix studies, and sound/video archives. He has written articles for European Meetings in Ethnomusicology, Oxford University Press, the Music Library Association, the International Association of Sound and Audiovisual Archives, and others. Before coming to UW, he was the ethnomusicology archivist at UCLA and a drummer for various projects.

Laura Wagner is the Radio Haiti project archivist at the Rubenstein Rare Book and Manuscript Library at Duke University. She has published several pieces of nonfiction, as well as a novel for young adults about the aftermath of the 2010 Haiti earthquake. She has a PhD in anthropology from the University of North Carolina at Chapel Hill, and a BA from Yale University.

Holly Wissler is an applied ethnomusicologist who shares her time between Cusco, Peru, and Austin, Texas. She has developed various music projects with the Quechua Q'eros community in the southern Peruvian Andes and the Harakmbut Wachiperi community in the Cusco Amazon region, and she has authored articles and documentaries about her work, in Spanish, English, and Quechua. In Peru she works as a local expert and guide for National Geographic, the Smithsonian Institution, the Amazon Conservation Association, Wilderness Travel, and US university study-abroad programs. She has taught classical flute with the Suzuki Association of Peru and served as the Peru director of the Center for World Music. She holds a PhD in ethnomusicology from Florida State University. Most recently Holly was adjunct professor in ethnomusicology at the University of Texas, Austin, where she moved with her adopted deaf son from Q'eros, who now attends the Texas School for the Deaf.

Bret Woods is an ethnomusicologist, author, filmmaker, and theoretician whose work explores music, media, and narrative through the lenses of anthropology, mediology, and social genre theory. Their main areas of focus include digital media studies and the intersections of archives, access, narratives and languages, performance and dissemination, and traditional musics. Bret has conducted ethnographic fieldwork throughout North America, primarily in Cape Breton, Nova Scotia, and southeastern Colorado, as well as throughout northern and coastal Florida and the Pacific Northwest. Bret has played with varied Irish trad communities since 2004, and also plays drums and electronics with the punk band Human Skab, with whom they have extensively performed, recorded, and filmed since 2009. Bret is an active proponent of ethnomediology, his approach to studying expression and interaction mediated through access to archives, digital technologies, and the Internet. Their research explores engagement in and negotiation of traditions globally and locally through contemporary media.

Kirsten Zemke is a senior lecturer in ethnomusicology in the School of Social Sciences at the University of Auckland, New Zealand. Her specialty areas in teaching and research are hip-hop culture, Aotearoa hip-hop, Pasifika pop musics, gender and music, intersectional identities, and popular music history. Born in the United States, she moved to New Zealand in 1981 and spent the next decades studying and making music until finishing her PhD on rap music in Aotearoa in 2000 and taking up a position at the University of Auckland. She tries to integrate her teaching and learning with the wider community by being actively involved with music events and artists, and she currently has two regular ethnomusicology feature radio programs.

Pathways and Trajectories: A Guide to the Organization and Use of This Book

Frank Gunderson and Bret Woods

In addition to the individual archival and repatriation topics explored in each of the projects treated in this Handbook—and in the spirit of problematizing repatriation as an act—each of these chapters crosscuts a specific set of issues relevant to audiovisual archives, and in so doing explores the implications of repatriation from different perspectives and intersecting dialogues. As we explore in the introduction with both language and subjects, the chapters in this Handbook stand on their own and help to situate relationships to one another that cannot be reduced into generalizations. The editors have sequenced the chapters in the Handbook so that they may be read beginning to end as a representative body of ongoing work in the field. The connections between chapters have been further organized as described in what follows to represent dialogues between themes, a symbolic multitude of relationships. Because collecting and returning audiovisual archives is an activity at the core of many fields of study, the chapters have widely interdisciplinary overtones. Our goal in organizing the chapters is to enable the reader to experience the complexity of these intersecting themes, not to gloss over that complexity in favor of a more traditional narrative.

These intersections will develop in the mind of each reader. Rather than trying to force each individual chapter into one specific category, the chapters are organized in a way that demonstrates—as does archival research—the utility of how dialogues about repatriation can intertwine. One effective way to envision these intersecting modes of thought focuses on various "pathways" one might follow through this Handbook. The concept of a pathway—largely inspired by interactive game theory—denotes a collected focus of analytical attention in the field of archival research, a meta-category akin to a frame or an overall theme. The foremost pathway of this Handbook is found in the primary organization of all chapters, a pathway that reverberates throughout the whole of musical repatriation (and hence the title, *The Oxford Handbook of Musical Repatriation*). When narrowing one's focus toward specific aspects of repatriation and archival research, additional organizations and sequences begin to emerge. With that in mind we have laid out four other pathways that associate certain chapters into groups. These pathways of dialogue are not meant to be exclusive or exclusionary, or to "define" certain aspects of the field; rather, they encourage the reader to maintain a focused thematic premise while engaging a group of chapters.

In each of our four suggested pathways we have outlined three "trajectories" that organize the flow of chapters within that pathway. In this context, a *trajectory* refers to the directional approach through which one can explore the related issues and intersecting voices of the chapters within a pathway. Trajectories encourage an ordered flow throughout a pathway that will help to surface how the authors' voices articulate aspects of archival theory and repatriation that may be related to the reader's own research or interests.

We hope this approach to structuring this interdisciplinary Handbook may blur boundaries and acknowledge that at the heart of each archive and repatriation project are people—people who are inseparable from what has come to be known as "intangible cultural heritage." Each category speaks to a broadly conceived issue present in repatriation in the digital age. Scholarship depends on the evidence collected in the archive, and it depends on exploring different modes of thought that lead to a broader awareness and understanding of the intersecting voices and imagined subjects, meanings, and efficacy of each mode of thought. Much in the same respect, we envision the chapters in this Handbook to be an archive—an archive that articulates repatriation and the way in which repatriation intersects multiple fields in contemporary scholarship and practice. We hope that readers can use these pathways and trajectories to enhance their ability to articulate a conversation that resonates within a specific sphere of repatriation. Note that each main *pathway* heading encompasses three general *trajectories* as described in what follows.

Pathway 1: Animating Sonic Archives

This pathway represents repatriation scholarship from some of the largest extant folklore and heritage collections to date. Several contributors present their current work with the monumental collections of John Blacking, Laura Boulton, Francis Densmore, Alan Lomax, Milman Perry, Hugh Tracey, and others,[1] exploring new avenues for community activism, access, and distribution. If considered as texts, audiovisual archives are often the voice of identity as well as the sole connection between communities and their own cultural heritage. This pathway demonstrates that archives speak with a strong voice, a locus for a vibrant dialogue of present identity with past cultural heritage.

The "Retracing Pathways, Returning Collections" trajectory specifically explores the traditional mode of archival "belonging," and the general stories of returning collections to their original communities. Often during this classic sense of repatriation, the collection itself—the audiovisual materials or sound files—is valued intrinsically for the potential it has in representing cultural subjects. In "Memory, Listening, and Performance," the song of the archive and the efficacy of evoking its substance ring out in a personal space, showing how animating sonic archives can have lasting worth not only for remembering traditional practices but also for providing a poignant communal sense of identity among groups often marginalized and underrepresented by a mainstream culture. Finally, chapters in the "Research and Influence" trajectory highlight works that animate archives through research, uncovering useful information that was stored away and was not previously known at large. This process is exemplified in Kay Kaufman Shelemay's article "The Ethnomusicologist and the Transmission of Tradition" (1996). In it, Shelemay notes how her fieldwork and recordings have become an important catalyst for song and music revival among Syrian Jews in Brooklyn. "Clearly, the Syrian music project had left more of a trace than recordings of music and oral histories in an archive. Six years after its inception, it had been absorbed into the fabric of both community activities and individual memories" (1996, 42). Moreover, the chapters in this trajectory explore how privilege is the core resource that allows researchers to spend hundreds of hours immersed in an archive, and such privilege facilitates imagining cultural expressions differently. Rather than romanticizing the role of a researcher or any agent or repatriation, sometimes archival work and repatriation can have a less than positive influence, creating and perpetuating inequitable power structures and complicating the role of the archive for a multitude of subjects. In any case, researchers—simply by engaging with archives—coalesce an imaginative sense of preserved traditions; their research with archival traditions then articulates that sense in ways that might not have become relevant or noticed otherwise.

PATHWAY 2: CURATION AND MODES OF ACCESS

This pathway focuses on the archive itself—the tangible collection of intangible heritage—as well as the archival practices that contribute to the validity of collections, often through accessibility. As audiovisual archives have worth through the cultural sounds and practices they can evoke, keeping collections in lasting physical health is often viewed as the strongest imperative for archivists. Beyond ensuring that archives can preserve and animate sonic heritage, access is equally vital. This pathway demonstrates that negotiating how various publics can use archives has deep and lasting social and cultural implications.

The "Preservation Practices" trajectory in this pathway includes chapters that explore digitization and modes of equity involving preservation. Additionally, the pragmatic aspects of how to curate archives is implicit in several chapters of this Handbook. This suggests that preserving and maintaining control over an archive can be an embedded goal of repatriation, despite how "returning" seems to suggest otherwise. The trajectory titled "Media and Transmission (Film, Radio, and the Internet)" features chapters that demonstrate the influence of broadcast networks over culture and expression. Media outlets are curators of massive archives, and by means of where and how they circulate those materials, they wield immense power over subjects who engage with archives. As media networks become larger and more influential (and their collections grow in size and scope), their potential to reach a multitude of diverse subjects increases—but so, too, does the tendency toward a homogeneous representation of the archive's content. Broad and open access to audiovisual archives is a goal in many instances of repatriation, but much of that access comes in the form of shifting materials into a standardized, public arena (for example, YouTube has become the standard location for accessing audiovisual materials for numerous institutions and media outlets). Finally, the chapters in the trajectory titled "Distribution, Equitable Access, and Censorship" build on these themes in the overall pathway of Curation and Modes of Access by exploring the circuitous nature of thinking about equity in its relationship to distribution. This can include the distribution of funds due to a grant. Governments and institutions may fund elaborate repatriation projects as a mode of diplomacy or legitimacy. However, the equitable imagination can also obscure pragmatic modes of capital gain under the mantle of repatriation.

PATHWAY 3: POWER RELATIONS

This pathway focuses on ownership and dissemination in the digital era—not the ramifications of dissemination for cultural subjects, but the complex dynamic of power itself in negotiating access to archival materials. While social concepts such as "sharing" and "access" are being broadly reconceptualized due to digital technologies, where does that leave institutionalized collections of intangible cultural heritage? This pathway reveals the tragic complexity of negotiating where power rests, as well as the unfortunate reality that repatriation is not always the most effective way to equalize power relations for audiovisual archives and the subjects documented within.

In the "Hegemony, Ideology, and Acknowledging Privilege" trajectory, chapters converge to articulate the distinct kind of power that is embedded in the social imagination in recent history. Broadly imagined, the political framework of the twentieth century has left problematic and inequitable distributions of resources, as well as ideologically charged extensions of power and privilege. The chapters in this trajectory endeavor to acknowledge privilege and understand equitable power relations. The goal of the trajectory is not necessarily to localize solutions for inequity, but rather to identify power structures, understand their efficacy, and work toward transparency in archival relations.

In the "Policies and Institutions, Laws and Governance" trajectory, chapters contribute to ongoing conversations about developing legal strategies to reconnect communities to their own archives and to provide reparation and support. In some cases, policies or laws benefit some groups more than others, and so amending these regulations is intertwined with the ethics of repatriation and archival practices. Policies and laws form the basis for method, and when they become sustainably useful for anyone in a jurisdiction, they contribute to a stable sense of identity for the institutions and governing bodies who enforce them. This trajectory also includes chapters that demonstrate repatriation work funded by institutions or governments, and explores the intersection of these spheres of influence. For example, sometimes institutions rely on government funding to embark on their own repatriation work, or governmental departments might mandate that institutions open or close access to archives. Finally, the chapters in the "Ownership and Intellectual Property" trajectory explore personal connections to archival materials and the complex tasks involved in giving them back when ownership is disputed or unclear. More than enforcing a definition of "ownership" or of the Western notion of "intellectual property," this trajectory demonstrates that power extends from subjects—and that a subjective voice can sometimes also extend from the archive. Audiovisual archives have the potential, when animated, to speak for themselves, articulating their own connections, boundaries, and belonging. This not only is inspirational in undertaking repatriation but also is a guiding ideology for future sustainable archival practices.

PATHWAY 4: RECLAMATION AND SUSTAINABILITY

This pathway introduces a host of developments regarding repatriation projects that stem from individuals and communities reasserting their rights to control archival materials. Reclamation can sometimes take the form of assigning equitable ownership, but it also seems to redefine the very concept of ownership in the Western sense of the term. Authors demonstrate how reclamation and sustainability in the digital world require less emphasis on the physical or tangible location of archives; rather, archival practices in this sense find equity in negotiating the rights over access and reproduction. This pathway demonstrates new conceptual space for archival return as more than simply "giving back," and it situates repatriation in an interactive realm of use and representation.

In the "Pedagogy, Advocacy, and Agency" trajectory, authors introduce methodologies for repatriation as educators and as advocates for cultural heritage. This pathway contains new and poignant projects that boldly address "preservation" and explore what it means to construct and share "knowledge." Returning specialized heritage archives to families and communities who have previously been excluded or alienated from the distribution of that heritage empowers subjects to perform and reshape archives and the traditions they preserve. Teaching can be a direct method of repatriation in this sense. Likewise, pedagogy is a modality of activism and sustainability itself, in that working with youth to reinforce traditions fosters an interest and reciprocity in interacting with archival materials. Advocacy and agency are intertwined with connecting subjects to heritage and encouraging ongoing, self-driven modes of preservation.

Chapters in the "Dialogue and Collaboration" trajectory involve co-authored works, or works that deal with multiple agencies working to find homes for collections. Most repatriation projects require collaboration, but the chapters in this trajectory demonstrate new ways to consider dialogical collaborations that challenge conventional frameworks of control over where archives are made relevant. Sonic heritage as a living tradition requires collaboration to stretch beyond legal and ethical negotiations, and this trajectory listens to the changing voice of archives and where they resonate. Extending from this idea, the "Re-Imagining Ongoing Pathways" trajectory includes chapters that build on new methodologies and expand on the imagination of the archive and of repatriation in the twenty-first century. Scholarship has come a long way toward equity and sustainability, and as archives continue to be made amid the proliferation of digital culture and global capital, these chapters offer important perspectives about working with community organizers, broadly imagining communities through dynamic and changing lenses, and creating ways to redefine heritage and help sustain traditions through their use and agency—without reducing their value into narrow assumptions about how they define presumed cultural subjects.

These pathways and their trajectories are the means by which the editors have related different facets of repatriation throughout this Handbook, and have organized these themes so that no one category represents repatriation more than any other. Much as the Table of Contents organizes all the chapters into one overall flow while they stand individually, each pathway may be read as its own grouping—as a "Table of Contexts" that draws certain chapters into proximity around a common set of themes. We encourage readers to explore these pathways in interactive ways, keeping them in mind while navigating through the Handbook, and crafting their own pathways as themes continue to emerge now and into the future of musical repatriation.

CHAPTER PATHWAYS AND TABLES OF CONTEXTS

Pathway 1: Animating Sonic Archives

Trajectory: Retracing Pathways, Returning Collections

Trajectory: Memory, Listening, and Performance

Pathway 2: Curation and Modes of Access

Trajectory: Preservation Practices

Trajectory: Media and Transmission (Film, Radio, and the Internet)

Pathway 3: Power Relations

Trajectory: Policies and Institutions, Laws and Governance

Pathway 4: Reclamation and Sustainability

Trajectory: Pedagogy, Advocacy, and Agency

Trajectory: Dialogue and Collaboration

Trajectory: Reimagining Ongoing Pathways

NOTE

1. The John Blacking Collection is housed at the University of Western Australia and at Queen's University in Belfast, Ireland. Laura Boulton's collections span the Columbia University Center for Ethnomusicology, which holds the Laura Boulton Collection of Traditional Music; the Harvard University Archive of World Music, where her liturgical music collection is found; the Archive of Folk Culture at the Library of Congress, which holds the wax cylinders, aluminum discs, and reel-to-reel tapes of Boulton's field recordings of traditional vocal and instrumental music worldwide; the Smithsonian Institution Film Archives, containing the originals of her film footage from 1934 to 1979, including collaborative films

with the National Film Board of Canada; Smithsonian Folkways, with the originals of recordings Boulton made for Folkways Records; Indiana University's collection, "The Laura Boulton Collection of World Music and Musical Instruments" at the Mathers Museum of World Cultures; and the remaining recorded materials and correspondence held at the Indiana University Archives of Traditional Music. The Francis Densmore collection and the Jesse Walter Fewkes Collection are housed at the US Library of Congress. The Alan Lomax Collection is entrusted to the Association for Cultural Equity (ACE) at Hunter College in New York City. The Milman Perry Collection of Oral Literature is at the Harvard University Library. The Hugh Tracey Collection is housed at the International Library for African Music (ILAM) in Grahamstown, South Africa.

REFERENCE

Shelemay, Kay Kaufman. 1996. "The Ethnomusicologist and the Transmission of Tradition." *Journal of Musicology* 14 (1): 35–51.

PATHWAYS TOWARD OPEN DIALOGUES ABOUT SONIC HERITAGE

An Introduction to The Oxford Handbook of Musical Repatriation

FRANK GUNDERSON AND BRET WOODS

SCOPE OF THE HANDBOOK

THE *Oxford Handbook of Musical Repatriation* comprises thirty-eight chapters from contributors working in regions all over the world.[1] The Handbook highlights studies exploring sonic repatriation in its broadest sense in the twentieth and twenty-first centuries. "Sonic" or "musical" repatriation refers primarily to the return of audio-visual archival materials to the communities from which they were initially recorded or collected. Repatriation is overtly guided by an ethical mandate to "return," providing reconnection and Indigenous control and access to cultural materials—but as the chapters in this collection reveal, there are more dimensions to repatriation than can be described by simply "giving back" or returning archives to their "homelands." It is our goal with this Handbook to provide a dynamic and densely layered collection of stories and critical questions for anyone engaged in archival work and repatriation projects—a body of thoughtful explorations that demonstrate through contemporary examples how negotiating ownership of and access to sonic heritage crosscuts issues involving (and challenges assumptions regarding) memory, identity, history, power, agency, research, scholarship, preservation, performance, distribution, legitimacy, commodification, curation, decoloniality, and sustainability.

Sylvia Nannyonga-Tamusuza and Andrew Weintraub have framed repatriation as "the process of returning cultural knowledge encoded in sound to the source or origin

xliv   FRANK GUNDERSON AND BRET WOODS

as well as presenting it in a format that is accessible to the communities to which it is returned" (2012, 207). In this Handbook, Tony Seeger defines repatriation as "the return of music to circulation in communities where it has been unavailable as a result of external power differences—often the result of colonialism, but also including differential access to wealth and technology, educational training, and other factors." This involves returning to circulation musics that were taken under conditions of duress such as war, slavery, migration, marginalization, or poverty. Sometimes this includes placing field recordings, recordings of performances, and other research documents into the hands of informants, research collaborators, or their families and communities.

A host of scholars from various fields, including Richard Keeling (1984), Anthony Seeger (1986), Robert Lancefield (1993, 1998), Grace Koch (1995), Judith Gray (1996), Carol Muller (2002), Peter Toner (2003), Barre Toelken (1998), Don Niles (2004), Don Niles and Vincent Palie (2003), Linda Barwick (2004), Shubha Chaudhuri and Anthony Seeger (2004), Ray Edmondson (2004), Beverley Diamond (2007), Gage Averill (2009), John Vallier (2010), Noel Lobley (2011), Carolyn Landau and Janet Topp-Fargion (2012), Sylvia Nannyonga-Tamusuza and Andrew Weintraub (2012), Andrew Weintraub (2009), Aaron Fox (2013), Sally Treloyn and Andrea Emberly (2013), and Diane Thram (2014), among others, have demonstrated in recent years the importance of reconsidering archives as extensions of living traditions, challenging modernist assumptions of intellectual and cultural property and ownership. Their work sets a precedent for musical repatriation, while also problematizing the historically transactional nature of returning archives. In this Handbook, we hope to build on these interdisciplinary directions by providing a dynamic space for critical analysis of archives and musical repatriation.

Scholars who engage in archival research and repatriation projects participate in many activities relevant to this Handbook, including the following:

- Assessing to whom musics might be "returned," especially in cases where the recorded musicians are deceased.
- Searching for and contacting recorded and archived musicians' progeny.
- Documenting what happens to musics after they have been returned to their primary communities.
- Implementing housing and sustainability procedures for repatriated collections, bypassing "siloization" and inaccessibility.
- Facilitating and engaging intergenerational communities via exposure to returned traditions.
- Facilitating translocal and interregional repatriation.
- Investigating heritage ownership, provenance disputes, global/local intellectual property, and cultural property rights.

- Negotiating the return of collections having secret or guarded traditions, or having been recorded under false pretense.
- Digitizing analog archives and implementing progressive preservation policies.
- Enabling the evocation and revival of traditions due to exposure to returned collections.
- Finding ways through ethical dilemmas concerning repatriation, and challenging colonial frameworks of archival ownership and control.

It is our hope that readers engaged and interested in these and related activities can make direct use of the themes and ideas collected in this Handbook.

The scope of this book also aims to add nuance to the function of the "handbook" itself. In his lecture "Gains of the English Language," the Dublin-born poet and Anglican archbishop Richard Chenevix Trench found the word "handbook" to be an "ugly and unnecessary word," a word that had been "called back from its nine hundred years of oblivion" into the modern era (Trench 1905, 75). Despite his disapproval, this compound word imported via German scholarship has since become entrenched in our literate society as a veritable "how-to" sort of archival reference. In the vernacular, even beyond its vocational use, "handbook" tends to evoke its own authority as a definitional type of reference, a collection of generalizable facts about a topic. Even though most readers, academic or otherwise, can entertain a healthy, skeptical nuance when engaging facts and references, handbooks retain a certain presumed authority on a subject—especially for the many people in the world outside of the academy, people for whom handbooks may serve as official guides. This authoritative tone is an unfortunate one for scholarly references, especially for anyone hoping to articulate narratives about the voices and practices preserved in audiovisual archives, due to the complexity of meanings and subjects evoked through collecting or animating archives in varied spaces. It may seem self-evident that archives (and repatriation) intersect with multifaceted issues that cannot be adequately generalized in conventional or authoritative modes of writing. Still, we feel compelled to note that the chapters collected here to form a "handbook" of references about repatriation and archives should be given mindful attention, but they should not be considered as intending to articulate rigid definitions of "repatriation" in contemporary scholarship. Because of the complex, subjective potential of audiovisual materials, there is no standard form of archival repatriation; and for that reason, this "handbook" does not propose narrow conclusions, but broadly and dynamically problematizes the multitude of intersecting, interdisciplinary issues it engages. The primary way we support this multivalent approach is by setting aside any conventional structuring of the Handbook into definite sections. Rather, we provide readers with a set of dynamic pathways they might explore through the lenses of several themes relevant to contemporary repatriation and archival scholarship.

THE ARCHIVE, REPATRIATION, AND CULTURAL HERITAGE

Much like Trench's own fascination with the life, worth, and usage of words such as "handbook," "fatherland," "mother-tongue," and "folk-lore" (Trench 1905, 75)—words, incidentally, that also resonate strongly within the ideology in which archival research and preservation were born—there is a deeply rooted sense of enchantment connected to audiovisual archives. Since the advent of mechanical recording technology at the end of the nineteenth century, the preserving (and correlated fetishizing) of ephemeral cultural expressions—historically generalized as "folklore," more recently referred to as intangible cultural heritage—has been a widespread preoccupation. As a result of the distribution of resources and technologies at the turn of the last century, this preoccupation has been largely a Western one. More than serving simply as static and tangible references, however, audiovisual archives in many collections have served a direct role of representation—the "lore" of "folks," the heritage of others, the evidence of cultural research. Tangible archives of intangible heritage have served as a source of social, cultural, and in some cases financial capital for as long as collections have been imagined as such. Technologies and methodologies for preservation have changed drastically over the course of the last century, but the sense of fascination with archival materials has not diminished.

Moreover, as preservation and access technologies have improved, the broad fascination with audiovisual archives has grown, as has the need to problematize further their life, worth, and usage. This has been the general impetus for negotiating where archives "belong," and doing the work of returning them there—and this lasting and complex concern is the overarching topic of the chapters in this Handbook. But the characteristic quality of audiovisual archives is that, like words, in their static and preserved existence they are in a quantum state. They must be evoked, animated, brought into meaningful use in order to become fully realized. That they have such widespread use and potential reveals a far more complicated task for repatriation than simply returning collections to their sites of excavation. "The basic tool for the manipulation of reality is the manipulation of words. If you can control the meaning of words, you can control the people who must use the words" (Dick 1995 [1978]). In much the same way, control over the subjective use and animation of the heritage preserved within archives has an enduring influence on the subjects who use them as well as on those who are represented within them. Just as with using words, locating, engaging, and returning audiovisual archives has broad, intersecting social implications.

Archives are used not only in specialized research but also in numerous communities as an actualization of cultural practice and remembrance. Like other forms of memory, audiovisual recordings found in archives have played important roles in community self-determination, the preservation of cultural heritage, and both the revival of older traditions and the creation of new ones. The powerful presence and voice with which archives speak can in some cases precipitate the social and cultural value they possess, and this is why articulating who has the rights or control over archival materials is of such lasting social importance. This is especially relevant where the commodification of audiovisual archives is concerned; commercialized recordings can be consumed as de-contextualized curiosities and provide revenue to archival institutions. As technologies have shifted digitally in the twenty-first century, questions of user rights and access as they facilitate repatriation—or render it moot—are important to contemplate. Past discussions of heritage have led to our current, bifurcated designation between "tangible" and "intangible" cultural materials, a binary similar to the Cartesian representation of orality and literacy in much twentieth-century scholarship.[2] Just as orality and literacy are not static polarities, but rather a spectrum of expression, it is useful to place tangible and intangible heritage on a continuum that respects how the two modes of heritage intersect. Tangible heritage conventionally includes physical collections such as instruments, sculpture, bones, and other cultural artifacts, while intangible heritage is relegated to expressions typically ephemeral in nature, such as stories, songs, dance, and oral histories. Much as we find utility in blurring the boundaries between oral and literate culture, we should notice that the value and potential of heritage is evoked through both the physical and metaphysical aspects of audiovisual archival materials.

Archives, however, also can engender a false sense of cultural reality for numerous subjects. In a way, archives do comprise evidence of a displaced heritage—typically following the nineteenth- and twentieth-century modernist practices of preserving traditions that have fallen (or are falling) victim to assimilation, or are at risk of being forgotten in the wake of technological and social change. The one-dimensional (though not necessarily simple) story arc that often emerges from the archive is that, if not for colonization in the first place, these traditions would have continued "undisturbed," within their "natural" and local, Indigenous cultural spaces. Thus, any people forced into a present-day, postcolonial social relationship should ensure that they extend the privilege of preservation to disenfranchised or endangered Indigenous communities—or, to use the terminology of the United Nations Educational, Scientific, and Cultural Organization (UNESCO), that they work to "safeguard intangible cultural heritage without freezing," a slightly paradoxical way to demonstrate an institutional archival authority's responsibility to encourage a preserved traditional practice to operate actively within an Indigenous population (UNESCO n.d.). But what are the institutional or broadly global capital goals of this directive? Who decides the prospects of endangered cultural practices, and how are they imagined to be safeguarded? Here the role of archives and the subjective heritages they preserve should be carefully thought through.

A more dynamic version of this story often falls in the multifaceted camp of repatriation, where responsibilities over these archives and how to "give them back" depend on the situation, and depend on arguing equitable concepts of ownership and control. But the brutal ambiguity of colonization that Marx (ineloquently) contemplated[3] is relevant here in that heritage archives are the valued results of colonial modes of global capital. Disregarding the Eurocentric, romanticized stories of differences and expectations between colonizer and the colonized, we are still left with media—and interacting with it challenges any supposedly universal reality of what heritage is, who it "belongs" to, and how it is dynamically imagined from subject to subject. Intermingled with the uses of heritage in archives we find many lingering assumptions about the locality of culture and meanings of diversity.

To understand repatriation as an academic pursuit, one cannot disregard the "collection" obsession allied with music research that began perhaps as far back as the late eighteenth century, but was enlivened as a scientific pursuit with the advent of recording technology, continuing well into the twentieth century. An exemplar of such expedition-style collection is found in the work of Jesse Walter Fewkes, a zoologist-turned-ethnologist who was one of the first field researchers to employ the wax cylinder recorder in his work among Indigenous peoples of North America, among them the Passamaquoddy, the Zuni, and the Hopi. In a telling letter dated March 20, 1890, and addressed to fellow scholar A. C. Haddon, Fewkes articulated his preference, method, and predictions for using the phonograph:

> I have myself done something in the study of our North American Indian folklore, and will be able in a short time to send you a paper on the use of the phonograph in this study. I have made researches on the legends songs etc of the Passamaquoddy Indians the survivors of those who once inhabited New England. I have been able to get them to talk and sing into the instrument in their native language, and to tell their stories on those magic cylinders of wax where they are indelibly fixed forever. I think I am the first to use this instrument for this purpose and it seems to me to offer most wonderful possibilities in this line of research. In a lecture which I gave on this subject I was able to repeat their songs so that they were perfectly audible in a large audience room. The phonograph will I think give a more scientific turn to the study of Folk Lore for it will give an exact record of the stories exactly as the Indians tell them with their exact pronunciation.
>
> (Fewkes, quoted in Clayton 1996)

Of course, Fewkes and his contemporaries studied culture preserved on recordings and removed from its context as a method of objective research. Fewkes contributed numerous recordings to archives now mostly housed in the Smithsonian, with which a number of other scholars have conducted research and authored academic papers. Following the collection of recordings by colonial expeditions throughout the world, sound archives became places to deposit, study, compare, and represent heritage as learned expertise. Unfortunately, Indigenous community access to such recordings throughout the twentieth century was essentially impossible, as technology was limited and materials were often housed in archives at elite institutions in locations far from the communities from which they were taken. Wax cylinders could not adequately be copied, and by the time later twentieth-century technologies offered easier, more reproducible recordings, there was not necessarily an immediate impetus to convert wax cylinders to another medium unless a direct research need demanded it. Furthermore, copying analog recordings in those days was laborious, costly, and often untenable, in most cases resulting in poor transfers with low signal-to-noise ratios. In many early twentieth-century cases, making recordings available to Indigenous communities was simply not considered. Apart from the technological limitations and costs of reproduction,[4] scholars whose expeditions collecting music and other cultural performances resulted in voluminous archives had no ideological incentive to provide Western technology or resources to Indigenous communities. Treating isolated communities and their cultural practices as "primitive" and "natural" meshed with a scholarly penchant toward imagined objectivity and noninterference that obscured the agency of Indigenous peoples, marginalizing their stake in control over the archives that their own collaboration had made possible.

Toward the latter part of the twentieth century, new, more equitable approaches for making, documenting, and archiving recordings, as well as the importance of getting approvals from the people researchers record, have become of primary importance. Archivists, scholars, and community advocates have worked to increase access to recordings, and their efforts have inspired a heightened interest in cultural heritage. Interest in archival sound recordings from cultural heritage communities, the principled responsibility of sound archives to encourage access to their collections, and the increasing technological capabilities of archives all have led to dramatic changes in archival policies. With the advent of digital sound technologies, the potential of sound archives expanded in unprecedented directions; with increased access to recordings and a heightened interest in more public consumption of cultural heritage, digital technology provided virtually unhindered platforms for reproduction and distribution. Though digital technologies did not single-handedly inspire new archival methods, in a real sense, digital technologies have completely revolutionized the way archives exist, and where they belong.

The first digital recordings on compact discs (CDs) were introduced to the market in 1982, topping record sales by 1988 (Ritchie 2012, 9). The digital era inspires new questions regarding traditional notions of preservation and the use of archives. Digital technologies and the Internet have played a role in fostering awareness about archives in local communities; not only do people know they can access archived recording traditions, they now clearly expect to access them. Multiple copies of recordings can be now made with zero loss of fidelity. Musical repatriation has been conceived more broadly of late, envisioning the archive as more than an *object* of return; in addition to the return of sound recordings, musical repatriation is an act that can involve offering access to heritage through music education, musical instruments, texts, films, and digitized materials via the Internet. Moreover, repatriation has come to include the practice of sharing knowledge and insights imagined throughout the course of ethnographic fieldwork. This also includes granting access to the materials that field research inspires, such as literature, film, and recordings, and the shared experiences, resources, and connections made by students, scholars, teachers, and musicians.

Perspectives in Musical Repatriation
and Praxis

According to the *Oxford English Dictionary*, the English word "repatriation" goes back to an early seventeenth-century usage applied to living bodies. The word itself is derived from the Latin verb *repatriare*—literally, "back to one's fatherland"—which throughout the nineteenth century became subsumed in the wake of nationalism to mean "returned to one's own country." Contemporary political constructions of shared national identity are increasingly complex, even while still clinging to the ideological assumptions of nationalism as belonging to "one people." For example, the meaning implied by Donald Trump during his campaign for the US presidency—to "repatriate" illegal migrant workers back to their countries of origin (Gross 2015)—is consonant with the original use of the term as applied to "bodies," and with the common use of "repatriation" in long-established discourses about immigrants, refugees, and displaced people. This sense of the word is couched in the same rhetoric that legitimizes repatriation of property and personhood, but it is not within this Handbook's scope of "repatriation."[5]

Since the 1970s in particular, repatriation has come to refer to ongoing efforts by museums, in collaboration with tribal leaders[6] and Indigenous activist groups, to return and rebury human remains within home communities according to customary practice. These activities apply to cultural artifacts as well (Brown 1998). They have taken on more urgency in recent decades, especially with the passing of the Native American Graves Protection and Repatriation Act (NAGPRA) of 1990, to the point where offices of repatriation have been opened in some major museums in order to deal with these requests and initiate such projects.[7] Audiovisual archives entail different kinds of complexity than more static artifacts, in that they are records of living traditions, actual subjects' voices and practices that can be heard, seen, and experienced. Still, the urgent need to return certain tangible heritage to its sources has also applied to musical repatriation.

Audiovisual archives, though in many circles still considered "a dark place where one sends things that are no longer needed" (Seeger 2001, 41), have played a significant role in the emergence of ethnomusicology as an intellectual endeavor, in the formation of theory and methodology in the field, and in the continued development of the field as repatriation and fieldwork are practiced and reimagined. In the later part of the twentieth century, archivists working with audiovisual materials began initiating projects whereby the return of collections became politically, ethically, even morally imperative (Keeling 1984; Lancefield 1993; Koch 1995; Gray 1996). As discussed by Averill in this Handbook, the responsibility to repatriate music is qualitatively different from that to return human remains or cultural artifacts, because rarely are the original media or digitized copies of tapes, discs, or videotapes considered essential to community or national identity in and of themselves. Thus, a consensus is often reached that originals should be safely stored in climate-controlled facilities and with redundant backup storage, as long as access to the content can be adequately controlled and maintained based on the wishes of the communities involved. It is important to note, however, that among certain audiovisual archivists, even in the digital era the distinctive gap between "copy" and "original" carries over into their preferred usage of the term "repatriation" itself, whereby only originals are considered "repatriated," and copies are "redistributed."[8]

The assumptions about how and why repatriation is needed in many cases is slow to escape the same modernist and Eurocentric notions of where people and their cultural "body" of expressions belong. Scholars do well to think critically in negotiating this space as they engage and curate archives. It is useful, for example, to contemplate and question the motivations behind contemporary archival practices and repatriation. Particularly with sound and audiovisual archives, heritage exists in the form of living traditions, not as static "bodies" that require transport, collection, and curation. The development of a recent language archive called Wikitongues[9] provides an example of how changes in archival practices renegotiate public and private senses of space, and might eventually challenge the need for any localized control over collections. The motivation behind Wikitongues' mission almost directly mirrors UNESCO's goals of safeguarding heritage. Wikitongues' core agenda, as noted on its website, states: "In the next eighty years, 3,000 languages are expected to disappear. We won't let that happen" (n.d.). The method the site advertises for the organization's preservation of language (and thus culture) follows the same very modern notions of diversity. "Humanity is at stake. As a result of climate change, globalization, and humanitarian crises, half the world's cultures are expected to disappear in eighty years" (UNESCO n.d.). Like UNESCO's mandate, Wikitongues' own goals to provide an archival cultural exchange that represents the diversity of subjects in our world—the very measure of what "humanity" is thought to be—involve extensive archival practices intended to create a public space of interaction where diversity can be localized and consumed, and thus reified and shared. The inspiring and charitable nature of Wikitongues' work notwithstanding, it is precisely this penchant for direct activism that deserves critical thought regarding repatriation and archival practices. How does the growth and practice of the Wikitongues archive resist the nature of language loss and cultural homogeneity? Does the creation of a Creative Commons public media space, which depends on and perpetuates global capital, in any way undermine the goals and mandates of the organization? Does the consumption of endangered language and culture (intangible cultural heritage) contribute to its specialized status or does this constitute a trivialization (or a perpetuated exoticization) of non-Western languages (and by extension, the people who speak them)?

Scholars with access to communities and their cultural expressions (typically those not represented in mainstream media) might be able directly to benefit people through repatriation projects, but the ease with which some people have access to archival technologies as compared to others facilitates a strong pull toward continuing to create and manage archives from the "outside in," often out of the antiquated need to "preserve" marginalized cultural expressions (unfortunately while embodying forces that contributed to their marginalization in the first place). Creating, curating, and repatriating archives are acts that do not simply provide ways to preserve culture and address social change; we must keep in mind that it was the creation of archives under the mantle of preservation, coupled with the imagined and actual kinds of difference and distance between researcher and subject, that led to the need, broadly speaking, for repatriation projects. Repatriation should not be imagined, monolithically, as the instantly corrective path for archives past, present, or future.

The restorative assumptions embedded within repatriation persist, however, and reconnecting to archives evokes a deep sense of cultural importance for many people involved. There was a cultural imagination already at work by the time Bob Dylan's iconic album coined the evocative phrase, "Bringing It All Back Home."[10] The tropes of "home" and "belonging" reveal the lasting nineteenth-century presuppositions that categorically delineate cultural subjects into distinct, generalizable groups presumably connected to definable locales. When subjects who have been displaced from a previously established homeland can return to or otherwise reestablish a systemically recognized place to which they definitively "belong," there is often room for communal healing, restoration, and growth. Romanticized notions of diversity should be considered critically, however. How long does it take to establish a sense of homeland? What concept of home is at work? Can subjects have multiple homes? Who guides various publics in their decisions regarding belonging? Do subjects need to remain where they "belong" in order to embody a distinctive identity? The proliferation of subjects and expressions in the digital world encourages us to consider a shift in perspectives regarding home and belonging, and regarding the role of archives in articulating distinctive identities. Since the birth of HTML and the web, the public imagination has become increasingly mediated through archival modes of interaction that thrive on shared access and reproducibility. This has, in many instances, prompted institutions to redefine their specialized statuses and broaden their accessibility in order to legitimize continued public interest.

Especially since, as Carolyn Landau and Janet Topp Fargion have told us, "We're all archivists now," thinking about the agency and resources that grant access to archival materials must be a goal in scholarship (2012). We depend on the archive, but treating the archive less as a dominant reference and more as a living and changing subject can help us rethink how and why archives take shape. Incorporating technologies that mediate everyday life changes general notions of how to listen and interact with others in varied communities. For example, another recent archive with an open approach is StoryCorps.[11] Like Wikitongues, the archive is user-driven and is a collection of consumable stories that brings other users to the site out of an interest in listening. Their goals, however, are somewhat different. StoryCorps seems not to be interested in preserving a record of generic subjects, but rather in focusing on the diversity of stories that subjects tell. "StoryCorps' mission is to preserve and share humanity's stories in order to build connections between people and create a more just and compassionate world" (n.d.). They go on to point out that their goal is "to remind one another of our shared humanity, to strengthen and build the connections between people, to teach the value of listening, and to weave into the fabric of our culture the understanding that everyone's story matters" (StoryCorps n.d.). The subjects of the archive contribute their voices under a broad assumption that all voices are different but that fixating on or consuming those differences is not the goal. They work not toward "recovery" or "preservation" out of a sense of loss, but rather envision their archive as a resource that supports continued connection and exploration.

Creating and interacting with archives is no longer a specialized activity; digital technology has significantly transformed our cultural sense of what constitutes and legitimizes heritage and the archive. Perhaps these transformations can help us challenge and explore assumptions about diversity and the impetus to preserve rarified traditions under the established Western and scholarly imaginations through and beyond the archive. Digital technologies have become incorporated into the global public conversation, and they offer an alternative model for how audiovisual recordings mediate dynamic expressions. Even when working with people and communities who do not have ready access to the Internet, it is important to rethink and reframe the goals and the very nature of archival preservation and repatriation.

NOTES

1. Though geography is not an organizational rubric in this Handbook, its chapters represent a wide range of geographical areas. These include North America (12), South America (3), the Caribbean (2), Africa south of the Sahara (6), North Africa and the Middle East (2), Greater Europe (5), Australia and the Pacific Islands (6), and Asia (3).

2. See Ong (1982).

3. See Avineri (1968) and Jean (1991).

4. Around 1925, the general transition into electric sound reproduction opened new, more sustainable possibilities for recording and playback. Earlier acoustic recordings were made on wax cylinders of differing sizes and shapes, with deviations that made consistent recording, playback, and plausible duplications impossible. Later in the 1940s, magnetic tape virtually transformed (even deconstructed) the notion of reproducibility, making copies and sampled segments not only widely possible but also relatively easy and broadly accessible.

5. As well as being widely used to refer to the return of people to their countries of origin, "repatriation" in another sense has long been used to denote the return of funds to a corporation's home country; both of these usages are outside the scope of the term's use in this Handbook. See also Sean Williams, "Trump's Corporate Tax Repatriation Plan May Have a Fatal Flaw," *Motley Fool*, December 24, 2016, accessed March 16, 2017, https://www.fool.com/retirement/2016/12/24/trumps-corporate-tax-repatriation-plan-may-have-a.aspx.

6. Although still in use in the United States, the English term "tribe" has come into disfavor elsewhere in the world because of its association with oftentimes dubious, forced, and inaccurate ethnic boundary demarcations practiced by former colonial powers over subjugated territories.

7. Of particular note here are the Office of Repatriation at the Smithsonian National Museum of Natural History in Washington, DC, and the Office of Repatriation at the Field Museum (formerly, Field Museum of Natural History) in Chicago.

8. Personal communication between Frank Gunderson and Judith Gray, September 27, 2013. Library of Congress, Washington, DC. See also Sakata, Sercombe, and Vallier, this Handbook.

9. Wikitongues is a Brooklyn-based nonprofit organization creating a growing, user-driven archive that collects recordings of individuals from around the world speaking their individual dialects of languages to a camera, complete with notes about idioms and oral histories that accompany examples of language. Most of the archive is hosted on YouTube. The site is largely Anglocentric in its translated framework. This makes sense as it was founded in New York, but it is still surprising considering the scope of the whole organization (indeed, it is interesting that there is currently no option to use the site in different languages). Still, the archive, which started in 2014, is now host to videos of thousands of individual language speakers.

10. A staggering number of academic papers, books, presentations, and films have used "bringing it all back home," "taking it all home," or similar phrases, especially in the last few decades as communications and media have shifted to digital ones.

11. StoryCorps (storycorps.org) began in October 2003 with a recording booth installed in Grand Central Terminal in New York City, in which anyone could visit and record a story. Since then their archives have expanded and have a strong presence on the Internet, with means of access including a phone app that you can download and use to upload a story to their archive. Stories can be uploaded in any language (though their site is only in English), and uploaded with tags and metadata under several different permissions.

References

Averill, Gage. 2009. *Alan Lomax in Haiti, 1936–37, Recordings for the Library of Congress*. 10-CD and DVD boxed set of recordings (audio and film) with Alan Lomax's journal edited by Ellen Harold. Harte Records, the Library of Congress, and the Association for Cultural Equity.

Avineri, Shlomo. 1968. *The Social and Political Thought of Karl Marx*. Vol. 619. Cambridge: Cambridge University Press.

Barwick, Linda. 2004. "Turning It All Upside Down . . . Imagining a Distributed Digital Audiovisual Archive." *Literary and Linguistic Computing* 19 (3): 253–263.

Brown, Michael. 1998. "Can Culture Be Copyrighted?" *Current Anthropology* 39 (2) (April): 193–222.

Chaudhuri, Shubha, and Anthony Seeger, eds. 2004. *Global Perspectives on Audiovisual Archives in the 21st Century*. Salt Lake City: Seagull Books.

Diamond, Beverley. 2007. "Reconnecting: University Archives and the Communities of Newfoundland." In *Folk Music, Traditional Music, Ethnomusicology*, edited by Anna Hoefnagels and Gordon E. Smith, 3–12. Newcastle, UK: Cambridge Scholars.

Dick, Philip K. 1995 [1978/1985]. "How to Build a Universe That Doesn't Fall Apart Two Days Later." In *The Shifting Realities of Philip K. Dick: Selected Literary and Philosophical Writings*, edited by Laurence Sutin, 259–280. New York: Pantheon.

Edmondson, Ray. 2004. *Audiovisual Archiving: Philosophy and Principles*. Paris: UNESCO.

Fox, Aaron A. 2013. "Repatriation as Re-Animation through Reciprocity: Laura Boulton's 1946 Iñupiaq Recordings and the Future of the Music Archive." In *Cambridge History of World Music*, edited by Philip V. Bohlman, 522–554. Cambridge: Cambridge University Press.

Gray, Judith. 1996. "Returning Music to the Makers: The Library of Congress, American Indians, and the Federal Cylinder Project." *Cultural Survival Quarterly* 20 (4). https://www.culturalsurvival.org/publications/cultural-survival-quarterly/returning-music-makers-library-congress-american-indians (accessed April 7, 2017).

Gross, Terry. 2015. "America's Forgotten History of Mexican American 'Repatriation.'" *National Public Radio*. September 10. http://www.npr.org/2015/09/10/439114563/americas-forgotten-history-of-mexican-american-repatriation (accessed March 14, 2017).

Jean, Clinton M. 1991. *Behind the Eurocentric Veils the Search for African Realities*. Amherst: University of Massachusetts Press.

Keeling, Richard 1984. "The Archive as Disseminator of Culture: Returning California Indian Music to Its Sources." *Phonographic Bulletin* 38: 44–54.

Koch, Grace. 1995. "This Land Is My Land; The Archive Tells Me So: Sound Archives and Response to the Needs of Indigenous Australians." *International Association of Sound Archives*, 6: 13–22.

Lancefield, Robert C. 1993. "On the Repatriation of Recorded Sound from Ethnomusicological Archives." MA thesis, Wesleyan University.

Lancefield, Robert C. 1998. "'Musical Traces' Retraceable Paths: The Repatriation of Recorded Sound." *Journal of Folklore Research* 35 (1): 47–68. Also reprinted in this Handbook.

Landau, Carolyn, and Janet Topp Fargion. 2012. "We're All Archivists Now: Towards a More Equitable Ethnomusicology." *Ethnomusicology Forum* 21 (2): 125–140.

Lobley, Noel. 2011. "Recording the Vitamins of African Music." *History and Anthropology* 22 (4): 415–429.

Muller, Carol. 2002. "Archiving Africanness in Sacred Song." *Ethnomusicology* 46 (3): 409–428.

Nannyonga-Tamusuza, Sylvia, and Andrew N. Weintraub. 2012. "The Audible Future: Reimagining the Role of Sound Archives and Sound Repatriation in Uganda." *Ethnomusicology* 56 (2): 206–233.

Niles, Don. 2004. "Reclaiming the Past: The Value of Recordings to a National Cultural Heritage." In *Archives for the Future: Global Perspectives on Audio Visual Archiving in the 21st Century*, edited by Anthony Seeger and Shubha Chaudhuri, 196–206. Calcutta: Seagull Books.

Niles, Don, and Vincent Palie. 2003. "Challenges in the Repatriation of Historic Recordings to Papua New Guinea." In *Music and Dance of Aboriginal Australia and the South Pacific: The Effects of Documentation on the Living Traditions*, edited by A. M. Moyle, 59–78. Sydney: University of Sydney.

Ong, Walter J. 1982. *Orality and Literacy*. London: Methuen.

Oxford Living Dictionaries. n.d. "Repatriate." *Oxford Living Dictionaries: English*. Oxford: Oxford University Press. https://en.oxforddictionaries.com/definition/repatriate (accessed March 16, 2017).

Ritchie, Donald. 2012. "Introduction: The Evolution of Oral History." In *The Oxford Handbook of Oral History*, edited by Donald Ritchie, 3–19. Oxford: Oxford University Press.

Seeger, Anthony. 1986. "The Role of Sound Archives in Ethnomusicology Today." *Ethnomusicology* 30 (2): 261–276.

Seeger, Anthony. 2001. "Intellectual Property and Audiovisual Archives and Collections." In *Folk Heritage Collections in Crisis*, 32–47. Washington, DC: Council on Library and Information Resources.

StoryCorps. n.d. "Our History." https://storycorps.org/about/ (accessed April 20, 2017).

Thram, Diane. 2014. "The Legacy of Music Archives in Historical Ethnomusicology: A Model for Engaged Ethnomusicology." In *Theory and Method in Historical Ethnomusicology*, edited by D. Hebert and J. McCollum, 283–310. Lanham, MD: Lexington Books.

Toner, Peter G. 2003. "History, Memory and Music: The Repatriation of Digital Audio to Yolngu Communities; or, Memory as Metadata." In *Researchers, Communities, Institutions, Sound Recordings*, edited by Linda Barwick, Allan Marett, Jane Simpson, and Amanda Harris, 1–19. Sydney: University of Sydney.

Toelken, Barre. 1998. "The Yellowman Tapes, 1966–1997." *Journal of American Folklore* 111 (442): 381–391.

Treloyn, Sally, and Andrea Emberly. 2013. "Sustaining Traditions: Ethnomusicological Collections, Access and Sustainability in Australia." *Musicology Australia* 35 (2): 159–177.

Trench, Richard Chenevix. 1905. *English Past and Present*. London: Routledge.

UNESCO. n.d. "What Is Intangible Cultural Heritage?" http://www.unesco.org/culture/ich/en/safeguarding-003 (accessed April 20, 2017).

Weintraub, Andrew N. 2009. "Introduction." In *Music and Cultural Rights*, edited by Andrew Weintraub and Bell Yung, 1–18. Urbana: University of Illinois Press.

Vallier, John. 2010. "Sound Archiving Close to Home: Why Community Partnerships Matter." *Notes* 67 (1): 39–49.

CHAPTER 1

···

MUSICAL TRACES' RETRACEABLE PATHS

The Repatriation of Recorded Sound

···

ROBERT C. LANCEFIELD

It is a pleasure to see this text from late in the last century resurface in such excellent company. It first appeared in 1998 in the Journal of Folklore Research, *in a thematic issue derived from a series of sessions at the 1996 conference of the American Folklore Society. Under the rubric "International Rites: Heritage, Property, Policy," those sessions included one titled "Who Owns the Lore?"—the question my article (now, chapter) below takes as its leaving-off point.*

The article built in part on a small, rich lode of insightful writing by scholars who include several contributors to this Handbook. With work on musical repatriation and intersecting topics having evolved in deeply relevant ways over the two decades since it was first published, it seemed useful for the essay to appear here as a scene-setting backdrop: a 1990s snapshot of some ways of thinking about the repatriation of recorded sound. I stand by its emphasis on how important it is for people who create or collect documents of cultural practice, and those who care for such collections, to conceive of stewardship in the most inclusive ways. This can be especially true when researchers or institutions transport collections into repositories far removed in some way (geographic, social, economic . . .) from the communities in which they made those mediated traces of cultural practice. I am grateful to Indiana University Press for permission to reprint this article from the Journal of Folklore Research,[*] *and to Frank Gunderson and Bret Woods for the invitation to have it join this Handbook's conversation—a new conversation, but also the latest moment in a long discussion that began more than forty years ago and will, I hope, continue.*

—Robert C. Lancefield, 2018

WHO "owns" traces of the lore? Taken on so general a level, this variant of one of the organizing themes of this special issue has no answer, or innumerable answers. Any

[*] Journal of Folklore Research 35 (1): 47–68. Copyright © 1998 by the Folklore Institute, Indiana University. Reprinted with permission of Indiana University Press.

well-grounded reply to such a question must be sensitive to the specific contexts of a particular case, and thus any sweepingly inclusive statement about the ownership and appropriation of documents of cultural practice could be only deceptively simple. But despite the impossibility of ever putting such unanswerable queries to rest, these questions are vital because of the endless discussions they provoke. These conversations foreground crucial issues worthy of constant reflection. With the aim of contributing to one such stream of open-ended dialogue, this article examines a cluster of practices and programs centered on the transcultural movement of traces of "humanly organized sound" (Blacking 1973, 3)—the repatriation of recorded sound from ethnomusicological archives.[1]

In the past two decades many archives have returned copies of field recordings to people in the communities whose music they document. This can raise difficult ethical questions. Some are similar to those central to the repatriation of objects from museums, while others arise because recordings are replicable replicas of intangible and fleeting sounds. Often of central concern are histories of ethnographic collection and other interactions between members of predominantly "collecting" and "collected" cultures; changing conceptions of archives' social roles, responsibilities, and opportunities; and contending ideas of individual and group ownership of music. For example, a common question about recordings of now-deceased musicians is, "To whom should copies of this tape actually be 'returned'?" The dynamic heterogeneity of most communities can render this pragmatic problem exquisitely complex. As ever, context is everything. And, as ever, nothing—especially nothing intercultural—is simple.

In this article the term "repatriation" and the shorthand word "return" refer to any conveyance of copies of sound recordings made and deposited as scholarly documents from archives to people who feel that the sound is part of their heritage.[2] The reference to "copies" may elicit a common question about the repatriation of sounds, especially if framed subconsciously in the broader discourse on the return of objects: "What about demands for the return of original, on-location field recordings?" In scattered cases concerning ceremonial music from Native American peoples, community members have indeed requested all extant master and copy recordings of certain collections. These requests can be driven by fears of inappropriate access to highly restricted songs (in some instances recorded without informed consent) and can serve as concrete gestures of opposition to the dominant US society's appropriation of many aspects of Native American culture. But references in the literature to this kind of request are surprisingly few. Community members more often seem content to have copies in formats more user-friendly than phonograph cylinders or fragile, half-century-old acetate tapes. So even after repatriating collections, archives usually continue to care for the original master recordings, sometimes protected by access restrictions more finely tuned than they were before institutional dialogue with the copies' recipients.

The idea of repatriation "to people," not necessarily to geographic place, marks the importance of connections between individuals as well as institutions, and acknowledges many communities' heterogeneity and translocality. Some communities' spatial discontinuities are partnered with discontinuities of oral transmission, which can render archival collections all the more important for creative reinventions of group identity. Arjun Appadurai has stated in a different context:

> As group pasts become increasingly parts of museums, exhibits, and collections, both in national and transnational spectacles, culture becomes less what Pierre Bourdieu would have called a habitus (a tacit realm of reproducible practices and dispositions) and more an arena for conscious choice, justification, and representation, the latter often to multiple and spatially dislocated audiences.
>
> (Appadurai 1996, 44; see also Bourdieu 1977)

Archival holdings can be helpful to members of such translocal—in some cases, forcibly translocated—communities. These recorded traces of a communal past can be invaluable to people struggling to craft their own self-reinvention in new locations. But repatriated sound can be equally important as an affirmative marker of continuity. This was true for some Native American recipients of tapes from the American Folklife Center's Federal Cylinder Project. In Judith Gray's words:

> Many anticipate that the recordings will help them reclaim something that has been lost. Occasionally this is the case. More often those who are knowledgeable in the traditions of their communities find it possible to sing along with the recordings, and thus receive verification that, despite all the acculturation pressures over the years, the traditions, the songs, *have* survived. And this is a source of considerable pride.
>
> (Gray 1991, 34)

Often archival recordings are significant in diverse ways, although potential recipients do not always value or desire these traces of their community's musical past (Seeger 1997).

The reference to recordings made "as scholarly documents" may evoke the distinct histories of some folklore and some ethnomusicological collections, despite the overlap of the present-day disciplines of folklore studies and ethnomusicology. With notable exceptions on both sides of this hazy disciplinary divide, perhaps a few more early folklore recordists than (proto-) ethnomusicologists would have answered the question "Who are we collecting for?" with, in part, "The People," not only a pure "Science." But no mode of twentieth-century scholarly field recording has been entirely free of appropriative ideas of salvaging, for outside perusal, traces of putatively dying cultural practices—or, on the other hand, free of individual recordists who placed at the center of their mission the yet-unborn descendants of the people whose voices they documented. Thus, repatriation can constitute a realization of concerned collectors' hopes; or some small, distinctly limited redress for certain acts of cultural appropriation enabled by colonial power; or both. This multiplicity of possible readings is true of many of the intercultural processes addressed in this group of "International Rites" studies. As Margaret Mills noted in her response to the conference panel at which an earlier version of this article was read, a discourse of an ostensibly "transcommunal Science" has long enabled the appropriative displacement of documents of "allegedly nonproprietary knowledge" such as traditional music. Mills then observed that despite these origins, certain acts of displacement have proven in the long run to be "enabling" to local communities as well.[3] (Neither I nor Mills, I believe, would argue that this affords any retroactive alibi for past appropriations, but simply that it refigures in important ways our present understandings of their varied outcomes.) In the case of repatriated sound, this type of positive fallout can span a vast continuum of relationships between field recordings' histories and their present-day effects. At times it can constitute a completely unintended and unforeseen turnabout of a researcher's unconcerned appropriation of the creations of supposedly "vanishing peoples"; at others, it can finally requite a recordist's fervent desire to be of some (nonpaternalistic) service to people she or he worked among, respected, and came to know.[4]

Any mention of repatriation invokes complexly interwoven histories of collecting and return. Because many ethnomusicological collections of sounds and anthropological collections of objects share an appropriative provenance, archives and museums inhabit at times commensurate—though seldom equally conspicuous—locations in present-day landscapes of cultural politics. Many collections of both kinds were deposited as cultural specimens alienated from their sources for the use of outside researchers, and many such institutions now are engaged in processes of return. Discussions of repatriation from museums have had more press, in part because some have been deeply contentious. This potential for conflict is easily understood. If a unique object is given back, it no longer can be in the museum that once held it. Unlike collected objects, field recordings in a tangible sense are mere carriers for traces of past events. Considered strictly as material things, original recordings seldom were actually owned by the music-makers they document, and few people aside from archivists tend to value these things as objects. Rather, their cultural value inheres in (or is constructed from) the replicable sounds they carry. This renders irrelevant some issues, but raises others. For instance, the very replicability that allows a recording both to be kept in an archive and to be returned can raise sometimes well-founded fears of uncontrolled copying upon its reentry into a community.

The weight of history and the intensity of present-day discussions link the repatriation of recorded sound to diverse scholarly writings. Before proceeding further, a brief sketch of a few important streams of allied work will give a sense of this study's discursive bearings. Anthony Seeger has written lucidly on issues central to the intercultural flow of recordings. His thinking informs this article in many ways, most directly as set forth in "The Role of Sound Archives in Ethnomusicology Today" (Seeger 1986; see also 1991a and 1996, 89). As for case studies, the best-documented programs are those of the American Folklife Center and of the Australian Institute for Aboriginal and Torres Strait Islander Studies.[5] Germane to this article's emphasis on repatriation as a global process are accounts of the systematic efforts of the Institute of Papua New Guinea Studies to acquire, from distant repositories in many nations, copies of early recordings of Papua New Guinea music (e.g., Niles 1992). Essential writings not primarily concerned with recordings include Messenger's (1989) and Greenfield's (1996) books on displaced objects and cultural property issues; Clifford's (1988) and Appadurai's (1996) rethinkings of mediated cultural flows; and two Smithsonian Institution Press compilations of essays on museum collection and exhibition (Karp and Lavine 1991; Karp, Kreamer, and Lavine 1992).[6] The literatures these writings represent provide much of the background to the following interpretation of questionnaire findings.

In the fall of 1992 I sent a questionnaire to eighty-one sound archives. Twenty-eight of these archives were located in the United States and fifty-three were in twenty-eight other countries (see the appendix to this article for more quantitative detail than is provided below).[7] These were known primarily as archives of ethnomusicology, folklore, and oral history. These categories blur in regard to many archives' institutional identities, and become even hazier in regard to their collections. While a numerical breakdown would be misleading, this order broadly represents the sample's weighting. Forty-six archives from eighteen countries replied—twenty from the United States and most of the rest from Europe. This distribution maps rather well the historical geography of technologically mediated culture-collecting, reflecting its dominant trajectory toward North America and Europe. These continents' predominance in the sample may be due as well to factors including archivists' English-language competency (the questionnaire was monolingual), my access to contact-person and address information, and comparative levels of understaffing. (Though many such institutions throughout the world struggle with overwork and inadequate funding, these constraints may have been less of a limiting factor for some archives in richer countries.) Thirty-eight respondents met the basic requirements for inclusion in the study by (1) stating that their collections included noncommercial recordings, (2) completing the questionnaire as requested, and (3) following its usage of the term "repatriation." (It should be emphasized that this usage includes the return of recorded sound in the form of copies, not only the quite rare physical return of original tapes.)

Three-fourths of these thirty-eight respondents said that, before depositing their recordings, some collectors had left copies with the people they had recorded. In recent decades this has become increasingly common practice as one aspect of a more generally reciprocal, late-twentieth-century conception of field research relationships (cf. Seeger 1987, 23; 1996). The recipients of such copies can range from individual performers to national archives of countries where research recordings are made. This latter mode of comparatively "local" institutional deposit is now required as a matter of course under the terms of a growing number of research permits, grants, and visas.

About two-thirds of the thirty-eight archives were currently involved in repatriation or in discussions preparatory to it, and seventy-one percent already had returned some recordings. The rest of this interpretive summary is based on this last group, which comprised twenty-seven respondents. Over eighty percent of the twenty-seven had returned recordings of music; about half, of folklore; and one-third, of other cultural sound, including oral history and linguistic recordings. Most of the recordings were noncommercial. The first years of repatriation ranged from 1952 to 1992, with a mean and median in the mid-1970s—a time when many institutions and communities began to negotiate major shifts in their relationships (cf. Karp and Lavine 1991; Karp, Kreamer, and Lavine 1992). Percentages of holdings returned, in terms of collections or tapes, reflected the archives' huge variance in size, funding, sponsorship, and types of holdings. These percentages ranged from well below one percent to seventy-five percent or more, with medians of five to eight percent. The number of communities to which institutions had repatriated ranged from one to hundreds. Notable here are the respondents' disjunct readings of "community," which varied from a count of families to a Canadian archive's "precisely one"—"the francophones." This comment, and the implicit invocations of regional politics of identity evident in replies from national archives in several other countries, serves as a useful reminder of just how contingent concepts of "repatriation" and "community" are, and thus how culturally situated this study's analytical vantage point is.

Over half of the archives had repatriated within their state or province. About three-quarters had returned recordings to other parts of their countries, and a bit under half to other countries located—in aggregate—on five continents. Although many people in the United States hear about repatriation chiefly of Native American recordings, it's a thoroughly global phenomenon. This is more conspicuous in the domain of objects than in that of recorded sound. One recent example (among many) is the journalistic visibility of the return of certain Cambodian sculptures from their possessors in Britain, the United States, and Thailand.[8] In recent decades human-made objects removed from a huge number of countries, many of them in Asia, Africa, and South and Central America, have wended their way homeward—or at least have been requested or demanded by the cultural descendants of their former owners. The scope of these transnational processes can be seen in a list—almost an alphabet—of the locations of some successful claimants: Algeria, Burma, Ecuador, Egypt, Ethiopia, Ghana, Greece, Guatemala, Honduras, Iceland, India, Indonesia, Iraq, Kenya, Laos, Mexico, New Zealand, Nigeria, Panama, Papua New Guinea, Peru, the Solomon Islands, Syria, Turkey, Uganda, Vanuatu, Yemen, Zaïre, and Zimbabwe (Greenfield 1996, 261–266). Much of this highly visible—though markedly intermittent and contested—repatriative flow of objects departs from the historical centers of gravity of colonial, neocolonial, and postcolonial acquisition and returns to sites closer to the people (communities, cultures, nations) from whom collectors from afar once expropriated these things. Recorded sound also retraces originally appropriative paths not just within, but across the boundaries and borders of continents and political states—paths these sounds first traveled as specimens in years past, and along which they return as much more than specimens in the twentieth century's later decades (cf. Niles 1992).

Regrettably, in many cases conspicuous acts of well-justified repatriation of objects are dwarfed by the number of seemingly grounded claims for return that have as yet gone unheeded and by the countervailing smuggling of culturally foundational objects out of their originating countries.[9] This reciprocally unbalanced flow of objects seems analogous in some ways to the accelerating appropriation of "traditional" musics by media producers in more capitalized countries (cf. Feld 1994, 1996). One discrepant aspect of the shared global extent of the return of objects and of sounds illustrates a more general disjuncture between these modes of repatriation. While recorded sounds are sometimes repatriated to people no longer residing physically in the community where the recordings were made, this seems (impressionistically) not so often true of the repatriation of tangible things. Just as sounds are not wedded to a single physical carrier, their return seems less bound to a particular geographic place. This tractability to translocal return is enabled indirectly by the ability of replicable recordings to exist in multiple places at the same time, counterposed to the inevitable unilocality of unique objects. As noted above, the inability of replicas of objects to embody the full depth of their cultural meaning can be central to contentious discussions about their return. Consequently, the often conflictual nature of these discussions may render the connective aura of an object's original location indispensable to arguments for its repatriation.

More than two-thirds of the twenty-seven archives had taken part in community-initiated processes. Just over half had participated in those spurred by depositors or by the repository itself. A slight majority said that some researchers had been directly involved. Close to half reported some indirect involvement on the part of recordists, and about a quarter reported no such involvement, sometimes because the depositors had died. Community members had visited over eighty percent of the archives. As discussed below in regard to a group of visitors from the Navajo Reservation to the Wesleyan University World Music Archives, such visits can provide exceptionally rich experiences for all present.

Over eighty percent of the twenty-seven archives had returned recordings to individuals. Close to ninety percent had repatriated to institutions. Sixty percent had worked in this way with local archives. Lesser numbers had done so with organizations such as libraries, community centers, and schools. Two-thirds had learned new things about their collections from recipients, illustrating how these processes—often thought of as a simple return of what once was taken—can be more than just unidirectional acts of giving back. Although at times repatriation is exactly that sort of one-shot compensatory gesture, at other times it can initiate and underlie more sustained future cooperation between repositories and communities (cf. Gray 1991, 34–35).

Ten of the twenty-seven archives had conveyed tapes to people who no longer lived where the recordings were made. Four of the ten had repatriated to immigrants. Others had returned recordings to refugees, to people who had moved within a country, or to people who had undergone "forceable removal to reserves." This underscores the importance of conceiving of repatriation as a return to people, not to place *per se*. Here the metaphor of appropriative paths retraced bears further elaboration. Many of these paths of return lead not only to their sites of geographic origin, but branch out to now-translocal communities of immigrants, refugees, the diasporic and the dispossessed, leading "back" to people's new homes in places where the sounds have never actually been heard before.

Twenty-eight archives answered questions focused on ethical issues. To my initial surprise, only nine said that the prospect of returning recordings had raised questions about how they were collected, and only ten stated that questions had come up about whether repatriation might make access less restricted than concerned community members might wish. Eighteen said questions had, however, been raised about depositors' restrictions, demonstrating their importance. Enshrined in deposit agreements, access restrictions often provide archives with their only means of trying to protect the people documented in their holdings. Some archives also mentioned such problems as disjunctions between copyright law and traditional music ownership rights, as well as tensions over whether a group or individual should control access (cf. Seeger 1992). Here all manner of intercultural, intellectual property issues surface, many of which confound or recast from the beginning the very notion of music as "property" in the sense propagated by most copyright law (cf. Mills 1996; Seeger 1996, 90–92). These issues can combine to situate some recordings at highly specific, complex junctures of divergent beliefs about authorship, transmission, gender, interethnic power relations, rights of alienation (the authority to convey cultural products to outsiders), and just about any other conceivable cross-cutting category, each defining its own dimension in a dense matrix of concerns. Some recordings are comparatively unfreighted in these ways. Others are so fraught with these issues that they seem not even to inhabit a unique location in such a matrix encompassing other points that represent other tapes from the same cultural group, but rather to construct around themselves uniquely problematic matrices with dimensions all their own. To negotiate mutually acceptable paths through one of these puzzles requires rigorous attention to context. Sometimes conflicting concerns prove to be simply irreconcilable, but satisfactory paths often can be found. (For an ethnomusicologist's reflections on one agonizing and perhaps intractable documentary dilemma, see McAllester 1984.)

Recipients of repatriated recordings had expressed gratitude to most of the questionnaire respondents (though this is certainly not always so—cf. Lee 1992, 29–30). Other community feedback to archives had mentioned both conflictual and cooperative effects of repatriation. Some recipients had told archivists about local disputes regarding the use of sensitive materials. As this illustrates, questions of intra-community access are often important. The gamut of potential problems ranges from the risk of totally uncontrolled access that might violate conditions expressly stated by performers at the time of recording, to the other extreme—the possibility that an individual recipient might sequester tapes in order to deny access to qualified listeners (cf. Gray 1991, 33, on concerns that this might lead to multiple, identical Federal Cylinder Project requests which would have strained the American Folklife Center's resources). On a more positive note, other community members had told of repatriation serving to "prime" local recording or about the use of recordings for teaching or for other approaches to the reconstruction of beleaguered community identity. Repatriation broadened some archives' sense of mission; one respondent said that "it adds a more immediate human dimension, transcending purely scholarly consideration[s]." It also has led to ongoing relationships between archives and communities. These include programs providing technical assistance to community self-documentation projects and a complementary sharing of expertise in the form of community advisory consultation regarding acquisitions and access policies. Such initiatives range hugely in scale, with varying components of technical assistance, sponsorship, and consultation.[10]

These relationships are part of a broad move toward mutually beneficial collaboration between communities and cultural repositories of all sorts. Thus, literature on other types of repositories bears directly, in diverse and suggestive ways, on the topic of cooperative relationships between archives and communities. For example, see Tchen (1992) on the Chinatown History Museum (since renamed the Museum of Chinese in the Americas) and Yoo (1996) on the Japanese American National Museum, both of which have cultivated dialogic relationships with members of the communities represented in their collections and exhibitions. These articles address museums developed and administered largely by members of the ethnic communities they serve (by representing these communities both to themselves and to the larger society), and on whose resources (e.g., private collections and family archives) they often draw. The centrality of outreach programs even for these community-based museums administered by cultural "insiders" helps to undermine any false notion that "local institutions" and "communities" are inherently metonymic for each other. This notion can at times obscure "outside" understandings of community heterogeneity. Some such institutions also are involved in audio recording and archiving. The Japanese American National Museum has served as a (translocal) community partner for self-documentation oral history projects in smaller (comparatively more local) Japanese American communities, defined in ways "geographical, occupational, organizational, or based on a shared experience" (Iki 1996, 7). These examples show how the present study's reliance on the terms "local" and "community" could inadvertently veil a reality of differentiated or nested localities or communities. They also demonstrate that distinctions between "archives" and "museums" are far from absolute.

Finally, for certain questionnaire respondents, repatriation enacted a longstanding sense of responsibility to documented communities. For some, this was a responsibility more valued in the abstract than possible to act upon until recently. In the concise words of one archivist, repatriation "simply reconfirmed our sense of purpose."

This feeling of reconfirmation leads to the story of ethnomusicologist David McAllester's recordings of Navajo ceremonial songs. McAllester began recording Navajo music in 1950, depositing his many collections in Wesleyan University's World Music Archives in Middletown, Connecticut. Over the years, he had left copies of some recordings in Arizona with a singer's relatives who valued them as family documents, but he had had no chance to use recordings to fulfill a central wish of his—and of certain singers with whom he worked. Their hope was that these recorded traces might eventually serve as a means of passing along ceremonial songs to future generations. This was of great concern because of the contemporary lack of prospective students who met the singers' high criteria of integrity, intentions, and seriousness of purpose. By keeping these sounds safe for later conveyance to younger people as yet unknown to the ceremonial practitioners (and perhaps not yet even born), these recordings might let the healing power of some songs outlive their singers, despite the impossibility of unmediated transmission during these people's lifetimes.

In 1991, an opportunity arose for this hope to begin to be fulfilled. A Navajo ceremonial practitioner was deeply interested in learning ceremonial songs that had not survived his community's processes of oral transmission during several difficult mid-twentieth-century decades. This man, related to some of the recorded singers, was roughly the age of their grandchildren's generation. Upon discovering that many of these songs were documented in the ethnomusicologist's collections, he contacted McAllester. After consulting with relatives of several of the people recorded, McAllester began to request copies of certain holdings from the archive. These copies were sent from Connecticut to Arizona, where they remain under the care of a community cultural institution. There they are accessible to the singer, but still protected from any uses that would be likely to contravene the wishes of the original singers. Throughout this process, the archive has worked closely with the collector, the recipient, and several other people from the reservation to strive to return these recordings in appropriate ways.[11]

A visit by the recipients to the archive evoked both a shared concern about appropriate access and a strong sense of the diverse ways of hearing any one collection. Upon being played for our visitors, recordings we'd been dealing with as frozen documents to be cataloged and preserved—albeit beautiful and meaningful ones, in an inevitably distanced way—suddenly were redefined as traces of sound with profoundly real therapeutic value. Before our eyes and ears, sonic traces cataloged as analytical specimens became sources of songs with healing power. What once might have seemed dead things reentered a living tradition. Even as we listened to brief excerpts, our guest began singing along, committing them to memory, knowing immediately how he would use the songs to cure people at home.

This illustrates the total necessity, but at times paradoxically limited utility, of documentation. Information about the recorded singers' wishes and concerns was crucial for access decisions. And since the duration of relevant collections vastly exceeded that of our guests' visit, accurate records were essential in order to make good use of our limited time. (In fact, some time was indeed lost to hunting around in dubs of poorly indexed, earlier twentieth-century materials. This experience stood as an instructive—if embarrassing and frustrating—counterpart to the day's more productive moments spent with better-cataloged holdings.) But beyond their protective and locative functions, more detailed notes turned out to be—well, mostly beside the point that day. While thick files of transcriptions, translations, and fieldnotes were indispensable to us outsiders, they were pretty much irrelevant to our visitors, who generally did just fine with brief indices. They knew, of course, that recordings aren't small bits of objectified sonic reality, but are *made* things—and they easily listened straight through stray artifacts of the recording process.[12] For example, upon hearing one low-energy rendition of a song sung for recording purposes outside of its ceremonial context (sung slowly, in a low pitch register, and with relaxed vocal production, in contrast to the listeners' internalized aural benchmark of actual ceremonial singing), one of our Navajo guests immediately laughed out loud. Shaking his head, he commented to the effect of: "Boy, that could put you right to sleep." In general, our visitors knew full well from the songs themselves what these sounds were, what they once meant, and what to do with them at home to make them mean these things anew, if differently. (My unconfirmed conjecture is that this knowledge was derived primarily from the songs' texts and genre characteristics, as heard by people deeply conversant with other songs from the same large bodies of music.) The archives' local storytelling traditions—our "Tales of Ethnomusicological Ancestors' Adventures in the Field," recounting collection history and ethnographic context—had some passing anecdotal interest. But these documentary tales were largely beside the point once they had served their indispensable functions of aiding, guiding, and at times limiting access.

In repatriating recordings of ceremonial or otherwise restricted music, ethical questions about access are paramount and often thorny. Although the fundamental conceptual concerns that underlie these questions can be broadly similar from program to program, the precise ways in which they're played out in any given case vary tremendously and operate on nowhere near such an abstract level. The path any one repatriation program follows is multiply contingent, determined by complex interactions of diverse individual actors' past and present concerns, fears, and desires, all articulated in a complex space defined by larger social forces ranging from community politics to institutional mandates. For example, repatriation from governmental archives often is bound to follow formal, institutional paths of dialogue and conveyance. As an agency of the US federal government, the American Folklife Center was required by law to begin Federal Cylinder Project dissemination programs by contacting tribal councils (Lee 1992, 26). In some nongovernmental settings, fewer overarching policy requirements limit the efficacious power of case-specific imperatives. Institutions bound less tightly by federal law can give greater weight to desires and concerns stated explicitly by the people recorded, collector/depositors' interpretive readings of these people's implicit wishes, the enthusiastic encouragement or cautious hesitation of the performers' surviving relatives, and the feelings of other community members.[13] The return of some of Wesleyan's holdings of Navajo material instantiates a process enacted under primarily local constraints (doubly local, in this case, to Arizona and Connecticut). For these collections, access decisions are rooted in individual human conscience and connections. These connections include the intricate network of relationships linking the singers, many of whom are now deceased; their relatives; and a collector acting upon a half-century of personal ties and fond hopes by being an active intermediary.

Now, having read this participant's sketch of a case study in repatriation—if you're as skeptical as I am of seemingly happy, intercultural processes enacted between parties in positions historically saturated with power relations as inequitable as those between the dominant US society and Native America, you may well be wondering (as would I!): "What's wrong with this rosy picture?" To my knowledge, the process of repatriating these collections of Navajo song really has gone smoothly to date, though not without occasional tensions arising from contending desires and concerns. (For example, to convey some collections requested by recipients would violate the wishes of singers or their families.) I hope it continues to go at least reasonably smoothly, knowing full well that any act of repatriation is potentially fraught with all the dilemmas with which field recording can inadvertently invest its products. Despite these dangers, the impossibility of foreseeing with certainty the results of intercultural movements of recorded sound need not dissuade one, as Seeger (1991b) has pointed out in a more general context, from making one's best effort. In thinking about repatriation, the hazards arising from contending ideas of music ownership, restricted repertoire, collection history, and contemporary cultural politics shouldn't usually lead—and haven't led, in this case and many others—to paralysis. This activist stance is shared and has been acted upon already by a great many archivists and researchers. Its importance is rooted in the needs of present-day communities, and thus, in turn, in the needs of cultural repositories interested in constructing equitable (perchance sustainable) relationships with the people whose forebears created—and who may themselves continue to create—the intangible contents of archival collections. This stance is grounded equally deeply in the histories of these communities' interactions with cultural outsiders conducting cultural research, histories impossible to relegate only to a distant or proximate past, but which continue through and beyond the present.

Intercultural histories are always being written, and to choose to disavow the hands-on co-writing of their late-twentieth-century chapters would be to freeze many of them at unnecessarily appropriative moments. Every such choice can affect the trajectory of a discipline, a society, or a relationship between societies—which is to say, between some of the people who comprise them. Those of us conducting cultural research or caring for its products must inevitably make tacit or conscious choices between generic disavowal and engagement, and among specific possible courses of engaged action. These latter choices are seldom easy. This is especially true with certain recordings. For example, Seeger has written of those which "should not be made in the first place," such as tapes made surreptitiously or under false pretenses (1986, 271). And Gray has called our attention to the difficulty of repatriating those recordings which, by their very origins, are ethically dubious: "By today's standards, many of the songs now preserved on cylinders would, or should, never have been recorded. . . . But here they all are—part of the heritage of many communities, requiring respect and responsible handling" (1991, 33).

Distant archives do hold alienated recordings of many people's musical pasts—some ethically troublesome by their very nature, but all in need of ethical reflection due (even if for no other reason) to the implications of the plain fact of their displacement. Many of their caretakers have concluded, reasonably, that the reasonable thing to do is to work with community members and collector/depositors to provide appropriate access to them. In an age of growing community self-documentation of present-day musical practice, archives can help people extend their sonic heritage back to the time of their great-grandparents or before—to span in many cases a period of partial breakdowns of oral transmission in traditions under cultural siege.[14] Though the danger of paternalism always lurks (Lee 1992, 25), its inhibitory power is often countered by a dual awareness. First, repatriation need not impose an agenda of local reversion to a purportedly pure, "authentic" practice defined and policed by outsiders, but can simply provide people with traces of their sonic past (if indeed they want them), to do with what they will. Second, a decision not to repatriate carries as heavy an ethical load as a decision to do so. To do nothing is, after all, to do something—and with field recordings, it can be to fail to see that while they are indeed analytical specimens, some also are tangible precipitates of once-evanescent sounds still close to people's hearts. Since the 1970s, a growing number of archivists and researchers have seen and acted upon this as best they can (cf. Seeger 1997).

In these ways repatriation constitutes a tiny—but disproportionately significant— part of the global flow of recorded sound, a flow that in turn is a key component of the encompassing transnational movement of made objects and traces of intangible cultural practices.[15] As a collection of shifting processual strands translocally linking past and present across divides of time, place, and power, repatriation's enactment is complex, its effects unpredictable, its ethical grounding often dauntingly conflicted. Nonetheless, it can enact an ethic of responsibility to the people documented in the collections for which archives care. In this way repatriation can be emblematic of changing relationships among cultural researchers, institutions, and communities, and so can epitomize the expansion—or realization—of the sense of purpose held central by many people who work with recorded traces of cultural sound, whether in the field or the archive.

Appendix: Summary of Questionnaire Findings

Eighty-one questionnaires were sent to archives in 29 countries in 1992–1993; 74 were presumed to have been delivered to their addressees. Forty-six archives responded: 20 in the United States, and 26 in 17 other countries (chiefly in Europe, but also in Australia, Canada, Hong Kong, New Zealand, Papua New Guinea, and Peru). Of these 46 responses, 4 were not tabulated for various reasons. Data from the remaining 42 are summarized below. Many respondents selected multiple answers to some questions and some left occasional questions unanswered; thus, the sums of some of the replies below equal more (e.g., no. 5) or less (e.g., no. 14) than 100%. For a more thorough presentation of methodology and findings, see Lancefield 1993.

A cover letter supplied the questionnaire's working definition of "repatriation": "any conveyance of copies of sound recordings, originally made and deposited as scholarly documents, from archives to people who identify the recorded sound as part of their cultural heritage."

1. *Do your archive's holdings include field, research, or other unpublished (noncommercial) sound recordings? (n = 42)*

    Yes: 90% (38)
    No: 10% (4)

2. *Have any of your depositors left copies of their recordings with the people recorded, before depositing collections in your archive? (n = 38)*

    Yes: 74% (28)
    No: 13% (5)
    Uncertain: 13% (5)

3. *Is your archive currently involved in any repatriation processes, or in discussions preparatory to them? (n = 38)*

    Yes: 63% (24)
    No: 37% (14)

4. *Have sound recordings been repatriated from your archive? (n = 38)*

   Yes: 71% (27)
   No: 29% (11)
   (Those answering "no" were requested to proceed to question 22.)

5. *What types of recordings have been repatriated from your archive? (n = 27)*

   By content:
     Music: 81% (22)
     Folklore: 48% (13)
     Other: 37% (10; including oral history, linguistic recordings, narratives, interviews, ceremonies)
   By accessibility in published form:
     Noncommercial: 70% (19)
     Commercial: 7% (2)

6. *In what year were recordings first repatriated from your archive? (23 answers, from 1952 to 1992, were used)*

   Mean: 1975
   Median: "1970s"

7. *What percentage of your archive's holdings would you estimate have been repatriated?*

   Expressed in terms of collections (16 answers, ranging from 0.01% to 80%):
     Mean: 13%
     Median: 5%
   Expressed in terms of tapes (19 answers, ranging from 0.1% to 75%):
     Mean: 15%
     Median: 8%

8. *To how many communities (or culture groups) has your archive repatriated recordings? (23 answers, ranging from 1 to "100+"):*

   Mean: 18
   Median: 10
   (N.B.: The "communities" respondents referred to here ranged from families to "the francophones"; see the text of the article for more discussion of this.)

9. *Where are the communities to whom your archive has returned recordings? (n = 27)*

   Within your state or province: 52% (14)
   In other regions of your country: 74% (20)
   In other countries: 48% (13)

10. *Who has initiated your archive's repatriation processes? (n = 28)*

    Members of recipient communities: 71% (20)
    Researcher/depositors: 54% (15)
    Your archive: 57% (16)

11. *Have the field researchers who made the recordings been involved in their return? (n = 27)*

    Directly involved: 59% (16)
    Indirectly involved: 48% (13)

Not involved: 26% (7)

Comments included [noted beside a "not involved" response]: "To our knowledge, only two were alive when the project began."

12. *Have members of recipient communities visited your archive? (n = 27)*

Yes: 89% (24)

No: 11%(3)

13. *To whom have recordings actually been repatriated? (n = 27)*

Individuals: 81% (22)

Local archives: 63% (17)

Schools: 26% (7)

Libraries: 33% (9)

Community centers: 37% (10)

Other institutions: 30% (8)

Other institutions included museums, state archives, local radio stations, cultural centers, cultural organizations, tribal governments.

14. *Has your archive learned anything new about your collections from the people to whom recordings have been returned? (n = 27)*

Yes: 67% (18)

No: 22% (6)

Comments included: "Primarily regarding feelings and concerns the communities have regarding access and use of materials."

15. *Have you returned recordings to people who no longer live where the original recordings were made? (n = 27)*

Yes: 37% (10)

No: 52% (14)

16. *How did these people relocate? (n = 10)*

As immigrants: 40% (4)

As refugees: 10% (1)

Other responses included "one town to another," "internal immigrants," "forceable removal to reserves."

17. *Has the prospect of returning recordings raised questions of how they were collected? (n = 28)*

Yes: 32% (9)

No: 68% (19)

Comments included: "Among our own curatorial staff we have many questions regarding the nature of agreements between interviewers and interviewees."

18. *Has anyone raised questions about how returning certain recordings might make them less restricted than community members might want them to be? (n = 28)*

Yes: 36% (10)

No: 64% (18)

Comments included: "One community has expressed concern that some individuals recorded might not want those tapes in tribal archives."

19. *Have questions regarding depositors' restrictions on the uses of recordings been raised?*
   (n = 28)

   Yes: 64% (18)

   No: 36% (10)

   Comments included: "It's been suggested that restrictions should have been imposed—by us or depositor. In one case sacred songs were recorded + tribe let us know that not everyone should hear them."

   "Primarily by Museum staff, as we have little concrete information on the nature of the recordings, their sensitivity, understandings at the time the recordings were made."

20. *Have you had any interesting feedback from recipient communities? (n = 28)*

   Yes: 57% (16)

   No: 43% (12)

   Comments included: "They see audio tapes as one of their most valuable resources in establishing their identity—particularly in places where language and culture have almost been lost."

   "Primarily regarding appropriate use, and interpersonal difficulties in handling and dealing with sensitive material within the communities."

   "Most collections returned have helped to prime further recordings locally, which may or may not come to us."

   "Just many thanks."

21. *Has involvement in repatriation processes affected your archive's sense of mission, or your understanding of your own role? (n = 28)*

   Yes: 43% (12)

   No: 57% (16)

   Comments included: "It adds a more immediate human dimension, transcending purely scholarly consideration[s]."

   "More inclined to consult potentially interested parties prior to making an acquisition."

   "A shift from philological musicological to socio-musicological, context-oriented, qualitative approaches."

   "Yes, positively."

   "We have always placed a high priority on returning/depositing materials in the communities from which they came."

   "It has simply reconfirmed our sense of purpose."

22. *Do you know of other archives in your area that have repatriated recordings? (n = 38)*

   Yes: 16% (6)

   No: 84% (32)

Additional general comments included:

   "Most of our 'repatriation' has been done informally during our own recording work—i.e., leaving copies of early, historic recordings with the groups concerned."

   "There are issues pertaining specifically to federal agencies that have a bearing on what is and isn't possible in this arena."

   "We are still a young archive, looking to build up our collection. . . . We have discussed the possibility of repatriation and there is support for doing so in theory, but not financial support at this time."

"Especially curious to know if communities are requesting repatriation of tapes in the sense of getting the originals to prevent access by outsiders. We have numerous tapes in native languages, with little written documentation on content, but suspicions that much is sensitive. It seems that many communities are not of one mind on the 'appropriate use' issue, very difficult to resolve."

NOTES

I'm delighted to acknowledge that this study benefited greatly from the varied and indispensable contributions of many people, including Marth Becktell, David Begay, Avery Denny, Ellen D'Oench, Jim Farrington, David McAllester, Margaret Mills, Kay Kaufman Shelemay, Mark Slobin, and all of the questionnaire respondents, who are too numerous to thank here individually. It is reprinted in this Handbook with changes only to its citation and reference formats and to several small matters of consistent style in this new publication context, while preserving its sense of present-tense embeddedness in the 1990s as a contextual backdrop for the Handbook.

1. An earlier version of this article was presented as part of the panel "International Rites II: 'Who Owns the Lore?'" at the 1996 meeting of the American Folklore Society (Pittsburgh, October 17). That some passages of this article are cast in a voice primarily addressing cultural researchers and archivists is not meant to exclude other readers, but reflects its tailoring to this publication's primary readership. This also underlies the article's stress on the actions of collector/depositors and archives' staff, an emphasis which is by no means intended to deny or underestimate the equally important agency of community members in the dialogical processes discussed here.

2. "Heritage" is a theoretically loaded term. In this article it refers generally to practices that community members feel to be somehow intrinsic to their group past and their present selves, rather than to performative constructions fabricated purposely as spectacle for cultural outsiders. (Although these categories overlap, this study's examination of the relationship between archival recordings and the idea of musical heritage focuses more on affect and affinity than on spectacle.) This broad construal of "heritage" is more useful here than would be certain more precise analytical usages used elsewhere to good effect (e.g., Kirshenblatt-Gimblett 1995). The latter would be essential conceptual tools for any study focused on how communities use repatriated materials, a topic only touched upon here.

3. Mills was chair and respondent for the panel (see note 1, above). The broad resonance of her statement is palpable in a recent newspaper account of the potential return of a tree grown from botanical specimens clipped (probably surreptitiously) in British Columbia some twenty years ago. The specimens were taken from a rare golden spruce sacred in Haida tradition; the 160-foot tree was killed in January 1997, apparently as a lone individual's act of protest (Anthony DePalma, "Vancouver Journal: The Tale of a Tree, in Which Science Meets Soul," *New York Times*, February 1, 1997, A4).

4. This tacitly elides those recordists who are community members, but does not do so unwittingly. This is because collections made by "insider" researchers seldom are spatially expropriated in ways that lead to their repatriation. In regard to the unforeseen, cf. Clifford (1991, 214) on the "unanticipated ends" of one "dominant practice of collection" of tangible objects.

5. See Gray (1989, 1991, 1997) and Lee (1992) on the American Folklife Center's Federal Cylinder Project, and Koch (1985, 1989, 1997) on Australian programs (see also Keeling 1984 on a large regional program, the California Indian Music Project). Various essays in

Moyle 1992 address these and other programs. Not coincidentally, these two most visible, large-scale archival repatriation processes were undertaken by governmental repositories with the appreciable (though highly contingent and susceptible to fickle legislative whim) resources available in times of political plenty to cultural agencies sponsored by national governments. Archivists at both institutions have inherited huge collections documenting the music of indigenous people suppressed (or worse) in various ways at various times by other arms of the very governments under whose auspices the archives now exist.

6. Also essential is the literature on the collection and repatriation of human remains, which opens out onto an even vaster terrain of vexed ethical issues and acrimonious debate. This literature is not discussed or cited here for reasons of space and because writings on made objects often provide analogies more immediately apposite to this study. For selected references to some of this literature, see Lancefield 1993, 114–116, 137–138 nn. 36–39.

7. See my MA thesis (Lancefield 1993, University Microfilms [ProQuest] no. 1354933) for more on the questionnaire's methodology and findings (259–308, 418–438) and on the case study of the return of certain collections of Navajo ceremonial music from the Wesleyan University World Music Archives (309–402). The thesis, upon which parts of this article are based, also contains a fairly lengthy list of references that situate the repatriation of recorded sound in relation to other global cultural flows.

8. See, for example, three recent *New York Times* articles: Seth Mydans, "Phnom Penh Journal: Treasures Trickle Back to a Plundered Cambodia," December 20, 1996, A4; Alan Ridings, "A Wondrous Trove of Khmer Art," February 17, 1997, 15–16; Carol Vogel, "Tracing Path of Artworks Smuggled out of Asia," April 23, 1997, C9, C14. While most of the objects at issue in this example were expropriated not in the earlier parts of this century but by more recent postcolonial smuggling, the fact of their return (and its visibility) remains broadly apposite. These cases also remind us that there is no neatly periodizable, firm equivalence between colonialism/postcolonialism and appropriation/repatriation.

9. See Greenfield (1996) on this illegal component of the international traffic in art. Also prominent in the 1990s in the domain of repatriated objects are cases arising not from colonial or postcolonial extraction, but from World War II—most visibly, the complex array of claims connecting Germany, Russia, and the United States.

10. Cf. Koch (1997, 40–41) and Gray (1997, 43) for recent examples of this.

11. This account of the case study is based on my participation in the process from 1991 to 1994 (making tape copies for return, assisting recipients visiting the archive, and traveling to Arizona with the depositor to return tapes as one aspect of a reciprocal visit). Findings from this participant observation are supplemented by information from interviews conducted in 1993 with several key participants and from documents in Wesleyan University World Music Archives files. The naming of only the collector reflects deference to the sensibilities of all concerned and absolutely should not imply that his individual identity, subjective views, or personal agency are more significant than those of the other participants in this process.

12. This observation can't be generalized to all analogous situations (cf. Seeger 1987, 97–100, on his experiences playing earlier recordists' tapes for Suyá people). Documentation can be crucial in more thoroughgoing ways for present-day community listeners who are further separated, by time or discontinuity of transmission, from the practices documented in archival materials. And, without implying that outsiders' forms of knowledge—despite their frequent utility—should automatically take epistemological precedence over those of community members, documentation can be useful when the effects of inadvertent

technological alteration of recorded performances happen to coincide with aesthetic or ideological values held by their subsequent listeners (as in the case Seeger relates, cited above).

13. This governmental/nongovernmental distinction is not a hard binary typology. Any effective repatriation project must be acutely sensitive to recordings' specific contexts, as are those of the Australian and American archives mentioned here. For example, whether or not a program's course is constrained to governmental channels, depositor agreements are indispensable navigational aids. (See Koch 1985, 20–21, for a detailed account of one government repository's deposit agreement procedures.) And at times the greater discretionary latitude afforded non-state institutions can simply provide access to more rocks upon which to founder.

14. For an ethnographic example of community self-documentation, see Seeger on some Suyá people's use of cassette recorders (1987, 22; 1991a, 44–45).

15. See Appadurai (1996); cf. Feld (1994, 1996) on issues of appropriation in "World Music" and "World Beat," the most prominent—and not coincidentally, intensely commodified—musical component(s) of this global cultural flow at present.

REFERENCES

Appadurai, Arjun. 1996. *Modernity at Large: Cultural Dimensions of Globalization*. Public Worlds 1. Minneapolis: University of Minnesota Press.

Blacking, John. 1973. *How Musical Is Man?* John Danz Lectures. Seattle: University of Washington Press.

Bourdieu, Pierre. 1977. *Outline of a Theory of Practice*. Translated by Richard Nice. Cambridge Studies in Social Anthropology 16. Cambridge: Cambridge University Press.

Clifford, James. 1988. *The Predicament of Culture: Twentieth-Century Ethnography, Literature, and Art*. Cambridge, MA: Harvard University Press.

Clifford, James. 1991. "Four Northwest Coast Museums: Travel Reflections." In *Exhibiting Cultures: The Poetics and Politics of Museum Display*, edited by Ivan Karp and Steven D. Lavine, 212–254. Washington, DC: Smithsonian Institution Press.

Feld, Steven. 1994. "From Schizophonia to Schismogenesis: On Discourses and Commodification Practices of 'World Music' and 'World Beat.'" In *Music Grooves: Essays and Dialogues*, Charles Keil and Steven Feld, 257–289. Chicago: University of Chicago Press.

Feld, Steven. 1996. "pygmy POP: A Genealogy of Schizophonic Mimesis." *Yearbook for Traditional Music* 28: 1–35.

Gray, Judith. 1989. "Early Ethnographic Recordings in Today's Indian Communities: Federal Agencies and the Federal Cylinder Project." In *Songs of Indian Territory: Native American Music Traditions of Oklahoma*, edited by Willie Smyth, 49–55. Oklahoma City: Center of the American Indian.

Gray, Judith. 1991. "The Songs Come Home—The Federal Cylinder Project." *CRM: Cultural Resources Management* 14 (5): 32–35.

Gray, Judith. 1997. "Returning Music to the Makers: The Library of Congress, American Indians, and the Federal Cylinder Project." *Cultural Survival Quarterly* 20 (4): 42–44.

Greenfield, Jeanette. 1996. *The Return of Cultural Treasures*. 2nd ed. Cambridge: Cambridge University Press.

Iki, Darcie. 1996. "Asking Questions, Changing Lives: The Value of Oral History." *Japanese American National Museum Quarterly* 11 (2): 3–7.

Karp, Ivan, Christine Mullen Kreamer, and Steven D. Lavine, eds. 1992. *Museums and Communities: The Politics of Public Culture*. Washington, DC: Smithsonian Institution Press.

Karp, Ivan, and Stephen D. Lavine, eds. 1991. *Exhibiting Cultures: The Poetics and Politics of Museum Display*. Washington, DC: Smithsonian Institution Press.

Keeling, Richard. 1984. "The Archive as Disseminator of Culture: Returning California Indian Music to Its Sources." *Phonographic Bulletin* 38: 44–54.

Kirshenblatt-Gimblett, Barbara. 1995. "Theorizing Heritage." *Ethnomusicology* 39: 367–380.

Koch, Grace. 1985. "Who Are the Guardians? Problems in Retrieval at an Ethnographic Sound Archive." *Phonographic Bulletin* 43: 17–23.

Koch, Grace. 1989. "The Music Tape Archive of the AIAS Library." *Australian Aboriginal Studies* (Journal of the Australian Institute of Aboriginal and Torres Strait Islander Studies) 1989 (1): 50–53.

Koch, Grace. 1997. "Songs, Land Rights, and Archives in Australia." *Cultural Survival Quarterly* 20 (4): 38–41.

Lancefield, Robert C. 1993. "On the Repatriation of Recorded Sound from Ethnomusicological Archives." MA thesis, Wesleyan University.

Lee, Dorothy Sara. 1992. "Historic Recordings and Contemporary Native American Culture: Returning Materials to Native American Communities." In *Music and Dance of Aboriginal Australia and the South Pacific: The Effects of Documentation on the Living Tradition*, edited by Alice M. Moyle, 24–39. Sydney: University of Sydney.

McAllester, David P. 1984. "A Problem in Ethics." In *Problems & Solutions: Occasional Essays in Musicology Presented to Alice M. Moyle*, edited by Jamie C. Kassler and Jill Stubington, 279–289. Sydney: Hale and Iremonger.

Messenger, Phyllis Mauch, ed. 1989. *The Ethics of Collecting Cultural Property: Whose Culture? Whose Property?* Albuquerque: University of New Mexico Press.

Mills, Sherylle. 1996. "Indigenous Music and the Law: An Analysis of National and International Legislation." *Yearbook for Traditional Music* 28: 57–86.

Moyle, Alice Marshall, ed. 1992. *Music and Dance of Aboriginal Australia and the South Pacific: The Effects of Documentation on the Living Tradition*. Oceania Monographs 41. Sydney: University of Sydney.

Niles, Don. 1992. "Collection, Preservation, and Dissemination: The Institute of Papua New Guinea Studies as the Centre for the Study of All Papua New Guinea Music." With discussion. In *Music and Dance of Aboriginal Australia and the South Pacific: The Effects of Documentation on the Living Tradition*, edited by Alice M. Moyle, 59–78. Sydney: University of Sydney.

Seeger, Anthony. 1986. "The Role of Sound Archives in Ethnomusicology Today." *Ethnomusicology* 30 (2): 261–276.

Seeger, Anthony. 1987. *Why Suyá Sing: A Musical Anthropology of an Amazonian People*. Cambridge Studies in Ethnomusicology. Cambridge: Cambridge University Press.

Seeger, Anthony. 1991a. "After the Alligator Swallows Your Microphone: The Future(?) of Field Recordings." In *Essays in Honor of Frank J. Gillis*, edited by Nancy Cassell McEntire et al., 37–49. Discourse in Ethnomusicology 3. Bloomington, Ind.: Ethnomusicology Publications Group.

Seeger, Anthony. 1991b. "Singing Other People's Songs." *Cultural Survival Quarterly* 15 (3): 36–39.

Seeger, Anthony. 1992. "Ethnomusicology and Music Law." *Ethnomusicology* 36: 345–359.

Seeger, Anthony. 1996. "Ethnomusicologists, Archives, Professional Organizations, and the Shifting Ethics of Intellectual Property." *Yearbook for Traditional Music* 28: 87–105.

Seeger, Anthony. 1997. Prefatory note to "Returning Music to the Makers: The Library of Congress, American Indians, and the Federal Cylinder Project," by Judith Gray. *Cultural Survival Quarterly* 20 (4): 42.

Tchen, John Kuo Wei. 1992. "Creating a Dialogic Museum: The Chinatown History Museum Experiment." In *Museums and Communities: The Politics of Public Culture*, edited by Ivan Karp, Christine Mullen Kreamer, and Steven D. Lavine, 285–326. Washington, DC: Smithsonian Institution Press.

Yoo, David. 1996. "Captivating Memories: Museology, Concentration Camps, and Japanese American History." *American Quarterly* 48 (4): 680–699.

CHAPTER 2

....

REFLECTIONS ON RECONNECTIONS

When Human and Archival Modes of Memory Meet

....

DANIEL B. REED

THIS chapter draws on my experience as director of the Indiana University Archives of Traditional Music (ATM)[1] to explore intersections of human and archival modes of memory in moments of archival repatriation.[2] I recount two repatriation experiences— one in which I traveled to West Africa to repatriate media recorded in 1934 (around which this chapter is centered), and a second involving Assiniboine sisters from Saskatchewan rediscovering a lost song in the ATM's listening library (with which the chapter concludes). Human and archival histories are mutually informative, and as such, moments when people bring the two modes together also can become moments of new memory creation. Repatriation, understood as a meeting point of human and archival memory, can be deeply meaningful because archives are *extensions of humanity*. When the two modes of memory, archival and human, are brought into conversation, the result can be powerful, augmenting the potency and value of each.

Carol Muller's 2002 article "Archiving Africanness in Sacred Song" opens with two quotes: the first, "When a griot dies, it is like a whole library burning down" (here attributed to Tunde Jegede, though this is so common a West African folk expression that it could be attributed to many); and the second, "The public image of the archive is all too often of a dark place where one sends things that are no longer needed" (Seeger 2001). These quotes evoke two different modes of memory storage and retrieval: a human mode—fluid, oral, messy, and selective—and an archival mode—static, mediated, tangible, and often authoritative, but decontextualized and partial. Key to understanding the relationship between the two is that while the human mode is to some extent archival (cf. Muller 2002), the archival is thoroughly human. Both human and archival modes of memory are framed and selective. Human memories, framed by the subjectivity of the person remembering and the space/time context of that remembering, tend to highlight certain elements of past experiences over others (most pronounced in the phenomenon of "selective memory"). Archival memory is framed in many respects: by the historical context, research paradigms and subjective interests of the person(s) who made the original recording, by the recording medium, and by the archival process itself (creating collections, adding metadata, making copies, etc.). People use both modes to preserve and produce histories, histories that are different yet overlapping.

In her compelling article, Muller notes that scholars tend to relegate societies that favor oral communication to the epistemology of "memory," while reserving "archiving" conceptually for societies with "technologies of repetition" such as recording devices (2002, 409). She advocates a more inclusive notion of "archiving" that not only would apply to institutions with media collections but also would encompass certain compositional practices of peoples who favor, and excel in, oral transmission. I appreciate the anticolonial sentiment of Muller's claims, and yet, the two examples of repatriation I discuss in this chapter offer an opportunity to reconsider Muller's model. The first example, which conforms with Muller's model, involves West African griots (singular *jeli*, plural *jeliw*), whose expressive practices function as a kind of embodied archive. By contrast, the second example concerns an Assiniboine family for whom, in the absence of a technological archive, a recording and the memory it preserved would have been lost. While Muller effectively employs "archiving" to address both technological and compositional practice, I want to reclaim "memory" as a concept flexible enough to encompass two different types of storage and retrieval—the archival and the human—that share a great deal in common but are distinct in certain ways as well. Following Astrid Eril, a proponent of "cultural memory studies," I consider "the role the arts and other media play in shaping the way people around the world think about the past" (2011, 5). In this brief chapter, I think about *my* memory of past experiences of repatriation, those moments when human and archival memory danced together in ways that, I assert, get at the heart of the importance of audiovisual archives in human life.

A Return to West Africa
to Find Konkoba

In 1934, Laura Boulton, along with several other participants in the Straus Expedition,[3] documented a mask performance called *Konkoba* (literally, "great/large wilderness"; see Figure 2.1) in the village of Bankumana, French Sudan (now Mali), in West Africa. Years ago, while researching and writing the CD-ROM *Music and Culture of West Africa: The Straus Expedition* (Gibson and Reed 2002), I found the film, photos, and audio recordings of Konkoba to be among the most intriguing documents in the collection of Straus Expedition materials in the Indiana University ATM.[4] In the brief but tantalizing film footage, the enormous Konkoba mask performer glides across the performance space under a huge baobab tree, while several smaller children's masks called *gbonni*[5] dance alongside him. An ensemble consisting of five wooden xylophones (*bala*) forms

FIGURE 2.1 Performance of mask spirit Konkoba, Bankumana, French Sudan, 1934.

Photograph by Frank C. Wonder of the Straus Expedition, courtesy of the Indiana University Archives of Traditional
Music and the Field Museum of Natural History.

a semicircle beneath the tree, playing interlocking patterns that accompany a song. The
footage briefly features a lead musician, El Hadj Kabiné Kouyaté, a *jeli* or griot,[6] who alternately sings a melismatic melody and improvises solo patterns on his *bala*.

My interest piqued, I scoured the scholarly literature for references to Konkoba.
Apart from a brief but informative report by Halim el-Dabh and Frank Proschan (1979),
I found nothing but short descriptions and brief mentions (e.g., Boulton 1969). Still,
I discovered just enough to kindle even greater interest. Konkoba, I learned, is a griot
(*jeli*) phenomenon. One of the "castes" of the *nyamakala* social system of Mandé peoples in West Africa, *jeliw* are best-known for their praise singing, the perpetuation of
oral history, and, especially, for being consummate musicians. Across the vast stretch
of West Africa where *jeliw* are found, their social roles are remarkably consistent. Of
great significance is the fact that the *jeli* job description does not include mask performance, nor the mystical beliefs—involving nature worship, power objects, and other
indigenous religious attributes—associated with Konkoba. This mask thus represents
a striking exception to typical *jeli* social roles. Moreover, *jeliw* have been Muslim for
centuries, and the presence of Islam is felt in Konkoba performance. That Konkoba
performance interweaves indigenous religious beliefs and practices with Qur'anic
song texts and Islamic amulets sewn into the mask performer's clothing only served to
heighten my curiosity.

Given my interests in West African mask performance and negotiations of religious boundaries (Reed 2003), I had for some time wanted to conduct follow-up research on Konkoba, and during the summer of 2003, I finally found the opportunity

to do so. I also envisioned an opportunity for repatriation. Equipped with VHS copies of the Boulton film footage and information from colleagues who had witnessed and/ or documented Konkoba performances in southwestern Mali in recent years, I arrived in the Malian capital of Bamako to begin my search for the present-day location of this mask and its performers. Given that Konkoba performances had occurred on numerous occasions in southwest Mali between 1934 and the present day, I assumed that I would find performers somewhere in the region between Bamako and the Guinea border. This assumption, however, proved false. Accompanied by research assistants Bakary Sidibé and Fadjine Koné, I traveled to numerous villages where either I knew a performance had taken place or I had heard that Konkoba was in residence. At every such community, I heard the same story, "Yes, Konkoba was here in (1934, 1984, and other years), but it was performed by the Kouyaté family of Siguiri, Guinea." So, we eventually accepted that a trip across the border to Guinea would be necessary.

In a Land Rover, we made the arduous, dirt-road trip across the Mali/Guinea border, eventually landing in the small city of Siguiri. There, to our astonishment, we found the Kouyaté family, including not only descendants of performers from the 1934 event in Bankumana, but also an individual named Sekou Kouyaté, who had danced as one of the child *gbonni* performers at this same performance in 1934. Sekou, now in his eighties and one of the heads of the large Kouyaté family, served as our host for a weeklong stay during which we conducted numerous interviews and video- and audiotaped several performances, including one by the Konkoba mask itself.

ARCHIVAL MEMORY: THE STRAUS EXPEDITION

With permission from the Smithsonian Human Studies Film Archives, which holds the rights to the film, I gave the VHS repatriation copies of the original film to the family. This brings up yet another important distinction between human and archival memory. Unlike memory in its oral form, archival memory is commodified, and thus becomes ownable, and owned. My purpose in this chapter is not to discuss intellectual property issues, but the colonialist nature of the extraction of expressive culture from its original context to the Global North where it is transformed into something of "value" is undeniable. The neocolonial perpetuation of such intellectual property regimes resulted in complicated relationships between and among archives as sound and visual media objects were passed from one archive to another. As scholars change jobs and take collections with them, or new agreements are made with descendants or other stakeholders, archival collections sometimes physically move and/or copies of collections become dispersed across multiple institutions. In such cases, archival memory is transferred as commodified goods, though ownership of those goods might or might not be transferred along with the exchange of goods, depending on whether the original archive chooses to maintain its vested "interest." So it was that, in order to avoid breaking the law, I obtained permission from an institution hundreds of miles away from the particular commodified version of archival memory I wanted to repatriate.

Archival memory recalls that Boulton documented Konkoba in 1934 while in West Africa with the Straus Expedition, a multidisciplinary field study conducted under the auspices of the Chicago Field Museum of Natural History with funding from the Carnegie Corporation and the wealthy benefactor Sarah Lavenburg Straus (for whom the expedition was named). The Straus Expedition was in many respects typical of its time. More intent on documenting, in a geographic sense, music and ritual of a given area than on studying any musical practice in any depth, Boulton profited from the Straus Expedition to record the music of twenty-one ethnic groups across a vast stretch of what was then French and British colonial West Africa.

With a hired support staff of nine Africans and an American research team including an ornithologist, a taxidermist, a music collector, and a photographer, traveling in three vehicles across eight thousand miles of Africa in just eight months, this was an expedition in the truest colonial sense of the word (Gibson and Reed 2002). Each evening when the party would stop to rest, the African support staff—hired at the outset of the trip in Dakar—hunted, prepared food, made fires, set up tents, made beds, boiled water, and drew baths. Laura Boulton's husband, the ornithologist Rudyerd Boulton, led the team, which also included the photographer Jack Jennings and the taxidermist Frank C. Wonder. Laura Boulton's study of music was thus only one aspect of this colonial-style expedition, whose primary objective was the documentation of rare birds.

Epistemologically, the Straus Expedition exemplifies a popular social evolutionary paradigm in which African people and their musics were conceptualized as "natural history." Archival documents related to the Straus Expedition in the ATM collection—such as correspondence, grant applications, newspaper clippings, and promotional materials for lectures, as well as commercial releases of field recordings—together paint a picture not just of a research paradigm but more fundamentally of representations of Africa and Africans soaked in a colonialist mentality, an imaginary of Africa as a social evolutionary category: The Primitive. The *Chicago Daily News* announced the Straus Expedition's return with "Weird Music from African Jungles" (October 25, 1934), a headline that not only exoticized but also misrepresented the expedition, which traveled mostly across arid regions and spent little time in rainforest environments. Accompanying this article was a photograph of Boulton displaying "primitive" and "native" instruments used by "African tribesmen" to "make strange music in the jungles." A large entourage led by a team of Westerners across a colonial landscape, the Straus Expedition, as represented through archival materials, evokes that time in history when peoples were sorted according to social evolutionary categories that placed "functional" Native American and African "artifacts" in natural history museums, in contrast to "beautiful" European "art" that hung on the walls of elite fine art institutions.

HUMAN MEMORY: JELIYA

Human memory, in the form of members of the Kouyaté family, paints a different picture of one brief moment of the eight-month expedition. Generally, West African *jeliw* or griots such as the Kouyatés are particularly skilled in the domain of human memory storage and retrieval. They did not need me to remind them of this nearly seventy-year-old event; to a person, they could recall (to greater or lesser extents) significant elements of the story. In interviews, I learned a great deal more about the 1934 event that Boulton documented in Bankumana, Mali. For example, the ATM had no documentation about why this event had taken place, or how Boulton had come to document it. Again, there was nothing in the archival materials to suggest that the performers were not themselves from Bankumana. Thanks to the Kouyatés, I learned that it was not only the "Westerners" who were mobile, moving significant distances across African space; the Konkoba performers were also on the move.

Sekou Kouyaté told me that, in 1934, the father of Modibo Keita—a leading colonial-era politician who in 1960 would become Mali's first president—died.[7] His funeral was a major regional event, so much so that the Kouyaté family walked 200 kilometers to Bamako to offer condolences and perform for the occasion. While walking back home to Siguiri, Sekou's older brother became ill, forcing the group to stop for a rest at Bankumana, where they encountered Boulton and the rest of the Straus Expedition crew. At Bankumana, the Kouyatés were asked to perform for the chief, Nankon Kamara. When Boulton requested to document the event, the family agreed. While the expedition's mode of travel—cars—were certainly highly unusual in 1934 rural West Africa, the Kouyatés had seen cars before (and in fact rented one to ease their journey back from Bankumana to Siguiri). Cameras and recording gear, on the other hand, were a new experience for the *jeli* family. A chance encounter of two groups of people on the move, the interactions between the Kouyatés and Boulton were limited and brief. After that day in 1934, the Kouyatés knew nothing of the results of their interactions with Boulton until I arrived sixty-nine years later.

As I show in what follows, the Kouyatés, via the mediated, archival mode of memory, were able to remember the 1934 event in a new way. Meanwhile, I was able to learn much more about Konkoba, its role in the Kouyaté family's lives, and the roles of music in its performance, both satisfying personal curiosity and adding to the archival record. Laura Boulton's documentation of this collection was terse but thorough in the basic categories of documentation required at the ATM, that which we staff members would summarize as "who/what/when/where." However, perhaps because of the sheer volume and the rapid pace at which she collected, Boulton's documentation is notoriously slight and, at times, erroneous.

Boulton had identified not just the mask, but also the song performed while the mask danced in front of the huge tree in Bankumana, as "Konkoba." Having encountered in my studies of West African mask performance few examples of song titles identical to the names of masks for which they are performed, I was mildly skeptical. When I asked Mamoudou Kouyaté about the song, however, I learned Boulton had gotten it right. "That is the Konkoba song," Mamoudou told me. "That song is one that is dedicated exclusively to the Konkoba." "So," I asked, "you play that . . ."—Mamoudou finished my sentence—" . . . when the Konkoba is ready to come out." His next action demonstrated, though, that this song can also be played in other contexts, and in other ways. Grinning, Mamoudou pulled out a steel-string acoustic guitar and began to play the Konkoba *bala* pattern transposed for the instrument's six strings. He and several other members of his family then proceeded to sing an elegant, tranquil rendition of "Konkoba" that I experienced as seven minutes of bliss.

In retrospect, I thought about the technique so common in folk music of playing multiple variants of the same song.[8] A tradition that encourages variation encourages its own perpetuation, as it can be performed by a wider range of people on a greater range of instruments, perhaps even in a larger number of contexts. Audiovisual archives make a normal practice of copying originals, generally aiming for some degree of redundancy to ensure long-term preservation. Though different from the principle of 1:1 conversion with no alteration of the original that is key to archival media preservation practice, the Kouyatés' flexible oral tradition also results in the practice of some degree of redundancy. Again, repetition and variation—a principal common in much West African musical performance—is at hand. *Jeliw* recount epics, again and again, never the same way twice, with improvisation resulting in variation of many kinds that affect an epic's length, narrative detail, and musical expression. Likewise, during the roughly one-hour performance involving the Konkoba mask that I observed in Siguiri, the elder Sekou Kouyaté told and retold the story of my arrival from America, each time adding or deleting different details, choosing different metaphors, emphasizing different elements of the story. This is an effective technique, as the whole family assembled that day heard and reheard this story, in variant forms. Each of them is a *jeli*, each will presumably remember their own version of the story. The memory will not be lost but will be preserved in great varying redundancy in the multiple carriers of Kouyate individual's memories.

Jeli oral tradition is a living, breathing, dynamic form of memory storage and retrieval, an embodied mode of memory production that remains close to the family's chest. Though probably less effective than archival memory at capturing precise memories, such as the expression on an elder's face as he sang, the Kouyatés' human memory mode needs no repatriation, as it is ever and always home, not subject to the whims of outsiders, not departing with the agent of colonial power with expensive recording gear and Model T cars only to vanish for generations before returning like a ghost.

While Boulton had accurately noted "*Konkoba*" as the name of both mask and song, the meaning of this word was missing in the archive. My background in northern Mandé languages enabled me to make at least a literal translation: "*konko*" means "bush" or "wilderness," while "*ba*" is a suffix that can mean "big," "great," "most powerful," and related meanings depending on context. When I asked Sekou and Mamoudou Kouyaté what "Konkoba" means, their various responses added nuance and depth to my understanding of the name. "Master of the Bush," "Head of the Griots," "King of the Griots," "King of the Bush"—Sekou Kouyaté offered all of these translations, some of which (those including the word "griot") glossed conceptual territory missing from my literal translation. These translations are significant, however, because they get at an important element of the Siguiri Kouyaté family's identity. Both Sekou and Mamoudou Kouyaté stressed that the Konkoba mask—something unique to their family among *jeli* families—renders them special, more powerful, more important than other *jeliw*. Only the "Konkoba Kouyatés" have access to power that comes through the mask from the *jinns*—those spirits mentioned in the Qur'an that some Muslims believe have the capacity to inhabit and influence the corporeal realm.

Mask spirit performance and related mystical beliefs and practices are generally not associated with *jeliw*. Within the *nyamakala* "caste" social structure of northern Mandé people, the blacksmiths, or *numuw*, more so than *jeliw*, are best known for their mastery of such mystical powers. When I asked Sekou Kouyaté about this issue, he confirmed, "In the Maninka world, [mystical power] is not part of the *jeliw*." But then he added, "in the category of *jeliw* of Kouyaté, Konkoba places them on the same level as the nobles." Here Sekou makes an interesting connection I could not have predicted. Clearly, Konkoba distinguishes his family from other Kouyaté *jeliw*. However, instead of making them more like another category of *nyamakala*—the blacksmiths—Konkoba in Kouyaté's mind makes them more like the nobles (*horon*)—a farming caste wholly separate from and outside the category of *nyamakala*. *Nyamakalaw* generally have ambiguous status in Mande life; revered for their arts and their critical contributions to society, they are nonetheless looked down on as "beggars" who must rely on the financial support of others to survive. Associating his family with nobles is an assertion of higher status on the part of Kouyaté.

ARCHIVES MATTER

While over the course of the week in Siguiri I came to learn much about this family, its mask, and the 1934 performance in Bankumana, it was the first day of our encounter, when I shared the 1934 film with them, that mattered most. In a hotel room with no electricity nor means to play the VHS copy I had brought for them, all of us too eager to wait, I decided instead to show them digital files of the Boulton Konkoba footage and audio recordings of the same event on my battery-powered laptop. These digital files came from the commercially released CD-ROM (Gibson and Reed, 2002), based partly on Straus Expedition archival materials, that I had helped create to benefit the ATM.[9] In addition to narrated, multimedia presentations and interactive exercises, the CD-ROM includes digitized files of all the raw archival materials used in the creation of the product. Among those who watched Boulton's film were Sekou Kouyaté and several descendants of performers, including Mamoudou Kouyaté—the son of the principal *jeli* in the 1934 footage. Being professional oral historians, the Kouyatés remembered the story of this performance well, but in sixty-nine years they had never seen the film or photos or listened to the audio recordings. Power was out across the whole city of Siguiri. In the dark hotel room lit only by my laptop screen, we watched and listened together, and the family was deeply moved. At turns laughing, hollering, shaking heads, and jumping up to identify people on the screen, the Kouyatés were thrilled to witness this document of their own history (Figure 2.2). I silently observed Mamoudou as he watched his charismatic, long-deceased father in his prime singing and playing the *bala*. I listened to the laughter and cries of astonishment as the elderly Sekou Kouyaté pointed to the screen, identifying one of the little baboon *gbonni* masks as himself. Family members in the flesh reunited with representations of their lost loved ones. The sentiment in the room was palpable.

Among the thousands of items associated with the Straus Expedition in the ATM vault are those few that preserve the archival memory of the Konkoba performance in Bankumana, French Sudan, in 1934. These include several photographs, several seconds of silent film footage, several pages of cryptic yet critical documentation, and

FIGURE 2.2 El Hadj Kabiné Kouyaté playing the *bala* xylophone, Bankumana, French Sudan, 1934.

Photograph by Frank C. Wonder of the Straus Expedition, courtesy of the Indiana University Archives of Traditional Music and the Field Museum of Natural History.

several brief narrative passages scattered across pages of Boulton's memoir, *The Music Hunter*, as well as liner notes of the Folkways commercial release of select Straus recording excerpts, promotional flyers for Boulton lectures with repurposed photos, and the like. Archival memory, rooted in tangible media, is specific and precise, but partial and decontextualized. Beautiful black-and-white photographs capture performative moments—like the look on the face of the *jeli* Kabiné Kouyaté while he played, his chiseled features, his high cheekbones; the way his *bala* was constructed back in 1934; who was seated next to him, who was not; the specificity of his clothing, and of the way he held his mallets while he sang in spaces between phrases played on the *bala*. Human memory tells us who he was, who his descendants are. It tells us the story of how he ended up in Bankumana that day in 1934, and about his *jeli* family. It tells us about Konkoba. What does its name signify? Why did it dance that day in 1934? What is its value in the lives of this one family—the Kouyatés—who maintain it as a family practice, generation after generation?

Archival memory resides in decontextualized data removed from the contexts of living, human experience, in facts such as the name of the mask, the date, the name of the principal performer, the location—all carefully preserved in Laura Boulton's documentation of her collection. Likewise, the sound, removed from the context of West African space in 1930s time, is carried away on an aluminum disk to an archive where, deemed highly valuable and often authoritative, it is extracted again and transferred to an open reel tape, where it rests until new practices remove it yet again, breaking it apart into numbers—zeros and ones—masterfully reassembled as a sonic object in digital form. Archived sounds contain precise memories, but only partial ones. The sound archive preserves something static and specially framed, what Robert Lancefield described as "traces of past events" (1998, see also this Handbook). These preserved traces are *mediated*, by the researcher framing and capturing image and sound, by the particular recording devices used to capture the memories; the whole ethnographic enterprise is affected by macro-level contexts—the academic concerns and larger social and cultural zeitgeist of the time. This is all the more reason why sound archival collections are inherently partial historical records.

And yet, those historical traces found in sound archival collections are preserved in tangible forms that often have great meaning as historical documents—not just for academic communities but also and even more importantly for the communities where the recordings were made. Something of El Hadj Kabiné Kouyaté's unique personality survives in the scratchy sound of his voice on Boulton's aluminum disc recording, just as in moving images, something about the way he turns his head as he prepares to sing a phrase captures forever something of his charisma. Tangible and precise, archival memory elicited a slight smile of recognition on the face of his son Mamoudou as he watched the film. Years later, *my* memory of this moment of human reconnection remains vivid, and I find myself wondering if the same is true for Mamoudou Kouyaté. Were new memories created at this moment when archival memory and human memory met?

"Our grandfathers
are smiling on us today"

"This is the song we thought we had lost!" exclaimed Joan McArthur to her sister Sara, her face alight with emotion and excitement. On this spring morning in 2002, Joan, Sara, and about a half-dozen other Assiniboine people from Saskatchewan and Montana were visiting the ATM in Bloomington. Their visit, organized by staff at Indiana University's American Indian Studies Research Institute (AISRI), was motivated by the stark reality that the Assiniboine language had at that time fewer than fifty fluent speakers left. The Assiniboine visitors had come to the ATM in search of linguistic materials to assist them both in improving their Assiniboine proficiency and in teaching their language in schools.

In the ATM listening library, the McArthur sisters were searching for recordings to use in their language revitalization effort when Joan stumbled on a familiar melody. She was listening to a CD copy of a wax cylinder recording of Nakota peoples (Assiniboine speakers) made circa 1930 by Felix Cohen at the Fort Belknap Indian Reservation in Montana. Suddenly, Joan heard the beginning of a ritual New Year's song that had been a part of their local repertoire until their father's passing four years prior. This song "was sung by our dad every New Year's Eve when the clock struck 12 a.m.," Sara later told me. "This was an important family gathering for us." When their father died in 1998, the family and community thought they had permanently lost the song, particularly its words in the endangered Assiniboine language. However, Joan's happy accident in the ATM listening library brought the song, and an important piece of familial and cultural memory, back to life.

Later that afternoon, as the Assiniboine group said their goodbyes and headed toward the door, AISRI staff member Linda Cumberland, who had organized their visit, overheard Joan say to Sara, "Our grandfathers are smiling on us today." I later asked Sara what Joan had meant by this comment. Sara responded, "This is something we say at moments when we sense that there is a greater purpose to everything we do." Later that week, with a CD repatriation copy of this nearly eighty-year-old recording in hand, the sisters returned home to Saskatchewan, where they relearned the song.

Research archives like the ATM serve numerous populations, including educators, researchers, students, and the public. No aspect of archival work is more meaningful, however, than serving the communities whose recorded heritage archives have been given the great responsibility, and great honor, of preserving. At large archives like the ATM, the rediscovery of a lost song, story, or other form of expression is not terribly unusual. But my experience with the McArthurs, which occurred less than a year after I had assumed the directorship, was my first experience witnessing it firsthand. Seeing Sara's and Joan's excitement and joy when they rediscovered this song was deeply inspiring. The sisters rediscovered a song, and I rediscovered a perspective that made the scores of meetings, miles of e-mail, the seemingly endless tasks such as budget construction, grant writing, research, and dealing with physical facility problems not just more tolerable but also terrifically alive with meaning.

In that instant when the MacArthur sisters found their father's lost song, infusing human with archival memory, I felt in a visceral way the import of the archival mission, and more generally, why archives matter. In writing reports, grant applications, lectures, and publications during my time as director, I proudly described archival work as the "preservation of cultural heritage," and moments such as the one I have just shared as the "repatriation of cultural heritage." Looking back, those words, though not inaccurate, fail to express fully the existential relationship of archives to people. Again, archives matter because archival recordings are *extensions of our humanity*. As such, archives can be profoundly meaningful to individuals connected—via family, community, or otherwise—to the people and practices preserved on the recordings. As a respondent to Robert Lancefield's 1992–1993 survey of archives wrote, "Repatriation . . . adds a more immediate human dimension" to the archival mission, "transcending purely scholarly consideration" (quoted in Lancefield 1998, 55, also reprinted in this Handbook).

Emotional moments such as when the Kouyatés first watched the sixty-nine-year-old film of their family and when the McArthur sisters found a roughly seventy-year-old recording of their father's song might best be described not just as archival repatriation, but also as *human reconnection*. Archival collections can be part of the processes of human life, as alive as human memory (Seeger 2001). These two stories of reconnection demonstrate that the materials stewarded by audiovisual archives have the potential to grow more valuable with the passing of time. These reconnections were as powerful and potent as they were partly because roughly seven decades separated their recording and their repatriation/reuse. On this issue, Seeger writes, "100 years after their publication, few articles in the *Journal of American Folklore* or *American Anthropologist* are of more than minor interest. The recordings made by some of these authors, however, often continue to be very exciting to scholars, musicians, and members of the communities in which they were recorded. Over time, it may be the collections we have made, rather than what we have done with them, for which we are most gratefully remembered" (Seeger 1988).

Notes

1. I served as director of the ATM from 2001 to 2007.
2. Both cases discussed in this article are examples of a type of repatriation that differs from the return of actual original objects, such as artifacts, often repatriated by museums. Rather than repatriating the original recordings, the ATM gave copies of original recordings to members of the communities where the recordings were made. To ensure their perpetuity into the future, the original recordings remain physically preserved in the climate-controlled vault in Morrison Hall on the Indiana University–Bloomington campus and digitally preserved in Indiana University's mass data storage system.
3. See *Resound* 21 (1/2) (January–April), 2002.

4. Indiana University Archives of Traditional Music Accession #92-313-F. Recordings made during the Straus Expedition were commercially released by Folkways (Boulton 1958).

5. The research assistant Bakari Sidibé claimed that the appropriate name of this mask is "*ngonni*," meaning "little baboon."

6. For more thorough accounts of *jeliya*, or the art of being a *jeli*, see Charry (2000) or "Jeliya" in Gibson and Reed (2002).

7. My interviews with members of the Kouyaté family alternated between Maninkakan (or Malinké) and French. The Maninkakan passages were translated with the help of Bakary Sidibé, who also translated during interviews into French when necessary (I was more proficient in Bamanankan and Jula; this was my first field experience in a Maninkakan setting). All French translations are mine alone.

8. Indeed, a defining characteristic of standard definitions of folklore is the existence of multiple variants of form. Moreover, it is common specifically in the *jeli* tradition not only for families that play the *bala* but also for those who play the twenty-one-string harp-lute *kora* to transpose songs for the guitar (see Charry 2000).

9. This CD-ROM, *Music and Culture of West Africa: The Straus Expedition*, was created with funding from the US National Endowment for the Humanities and published by Indiana University Press. All proceeds from the product's sale were by contract donated directly to the ATM in support of its mission. The film, photographs, and audio recordings of the Konkoba Kouyaté family constituted less than 5 percent of the materials used in the making of this product. Nonetheless, reflecting on this experience, I note my collusion in a neocolonial process that used 1934 recordings of the Kouyatés and many others to benefit the ATM, a relatively powerful institution in the Global North. Although the ATM's operating budget was woefully inadequate to fully support its mission of preserving and disseminating recorded heritage it housed, and outside funding was essential to its sustainability, this CD-ROM in some respects perpetuated the neocolonial intellectual property regimes of earlier archival practice.

References

Boulton, Laura 1958. *African Music*. Sound disc. New York: Folkways Records FW 8852.

Boulton, Laura. 1969. *The Music Hunter: The Autobiography of a Career*. New York: Doubleday.

Charry, Eric. 2000. *Mande Music: Traditional and Modern Music of the Maninka and Mandinka of Western Africa*. Chicago: University of Chicago Press.

El Dabh, Halim, and Frank Proschan. 1979. "Les Traditions du Masque et de la Marionette dans la République de la Guinée." Subventionné par le Smithsonian Institution Foreign Currency Program, le Smithsonian Institution Folklife Program et par Puppeteers of America.

Eril, Astrid. 2011. "Introduction: Why 'Memory'?" In *Memory in Culture*, edited by Astrid Eril, 1–12. London: Palgrave Macmillan.

Gibson, Gloria, and Daniel B. Reed. 2002. *Music and Culture of West Africa: The Straus Expedition*. CD-ROM. Bloomington: Indiana University Press.

Lancefield, Robert C. 1998. "'Musical Traces' Retraceable Paths: The Repatriation of Recorded Sound." *Journal of Folklore Research* 35 (1): 47–68. Also reprinted in this Handbook.

Muller, Carol A. 2002. "Archiving Africanness in Sacred Song." *Ethnomusicology* 46 (3): 409–431.

Reed, Daniel B. 2003. *Dan Ge Performance: Masks and Music in Contemporary Côte d'Ivoire*. Bloomington: Indiana University Press.

Seeger, Anthony. 1988. "On Changes and Continuities." *Resound* 7 (2) (April), 2–3.

Seeger, Anthony. 2001. "Intellectual Property and Audiovisual Archives and Collections." In *Folk Heritage Collections in Crisis*, 32–50. Washington, DC: Council of Library and Information Resources (May).

CHAPTER 3

MUSIC ARCHIVES AND REPATRIATION

Digital Return of Hugh Tracey's "Chemirocha" Recordings in Kenya

DIANE THRAM

THIS chapter considers issues in the restudy and repatriation of digital copies of field recordings of music heritage obtained during the colonial era, specifically from Kenya. It is based on experience working with the Hugh Tracey Collection preserved at the archive and research center he founded in 1954 in South Africa known as the International Library of African Music (ILAM). It begins with a brief synopsis of Tracey's early life and his work documenting both traditional and popular music throughout sub-Saharan Africa over four decades from 1929 to 1972. It then discusses the reasons why, with digital conversion and online access to the collection accomplished,[1] the digital return and restudy of Tracey's field recordings became the ethically responsible thing for ILAM to do.[2] With consideration of the multilayered aspects of his project, it is argued that Tracey's embrace of the colonial worldview—with its inherent paternalism, racism, white privilege, and the implicit exploitation of the musicians he recorded—created the need for the digital return of his field recordings as an act of reciprocity and archival ethics for ILAM. The need to correct errors in existing documentation gives rise to the aim to restudy his recordings at the time of their digital return.

Data from Hugh Tracey's field journals and the fieldcards he inscribed for his three recordings of a Kipsigis song titled "Chemirocha" (literally, "Jimmie Rodgers") is presented along with information on how he disseminated these recordings commercially at the height of Jimmie Rodgers's international popularity. Airplay of "Chemirocha III" in Kenya from its release in 1952 and contemporary musicians' adaptions on YouTube are briefly discussed as evidence of the ongoing popularity of the recording. This is followed by a narrative account of the launch of the "Pilot Project in Restudy and Repatriation of the International Library of African Music (ILAM) Hugh Tracey

Field Recordings" with the return of his 1950 recordings of Kipsigis and Luo music in Kenya in August 2014. A discussion of how this work has subsequently informed on-going efforts to digitally return Tracey's field recordings in other locations, and why this work is ethically mandated for ILAM and ethnomusicology field collections in general, concludes the chapter.

Hugh Tracey and His Archive

Hugh Tracey (1903–1977) arrived in Southern Rhodesia in 1921, at the age of eighteen, from Devonshire, England, to work on his brother's tobacco plantation.[3] There, working in the fields, he learned the Karanga dialect of the Shona language and developed a profound respect for African music and how it functions in social life. This led to his passion to research, document, disseminate, and preserve African music over the next four decades. Writing in 1973 of his lifework assembling his archive, he says, "The history of this collection of authentic African music, songs, legends and stories . . . dates back to the early 1920s when I first sang and wrote down the words of African songs I heard in the tobacco fields of Southern Rhodesia" (1973, 3).

Tracey's project began in 1929, when he took a group of Karanga men to Johannesburg to be recorded by Columbia Records recording engineers in South Africa from London, thus producing the first recordings of indigenous music from Southern Rhodesia. In discussions with the composers Gustav Holst and Ralph Vaughn Williams at the Royal College of Music in London in 1931, Tracey was told not to worry about his lack of formal education in music. They advised him to accumulate as many recordings and as much documentation about them as possible and to let the transcription and analysis come later (Tracey 1973, 4). And, that is exactly what he did. That same year he received a Carnegie Fellowship to do a survey of the music of Southern Rhodesia. From June 1932 to July 1933, Tracey recorded over six hundred items on aluminum discs and took photographs of musicians and their instruments as further documentation. Using his specially made, tempered-steel tuning forks that did not react to temperature or humidity, he measured the intervals played to determine the scales used on each instrument he encountered.[4] With the Carnegie project completed and no prospects for further funding, Tracey moved to South Africa to work for the South Africa Broadcasting Company (SABC Capetown, 1934–1935; SABC Durban, 1936–1947). He discovered Chopi *timbila* xylophone orchestras in 1940 and gained international attention by publishing the monograph *Chopi Musicians: Their Music, Poetry, and Instruments* with Oxford University Press in 1948.[5]

Tracey moved to Johannesburg in 1947 to pursue African music research full-time with an agreement that he would supply Eric Gallo,[6] owner of Gallo Recording Company, with field recordings for commercial release in return for support for his recording excursions. This arrangement continued until Tracey acquired support from the Nuffield Foundation after a 1953 lecture tour in the United Kingdom. The Nuffield Foundation grant, matched by donations from gold, copper, and diamond mining companies of the Congo, Rhodesia, and South Africa, allowed him to establish ILAM as an independent research institute and archive in 1954 in Roodeport on land donated by Gallo (Tracey 1973, 4–5).

From 1939 to 1970 Tracey mounted nineteen field excursions to create his substantial archive of thousands of recordings of the music of eastern, central, and southern Africa,[7] a photograph collection of approximately eight thousand images, and seventeen self-produced films. To dispel the misconception that Tracey recorded only "traditional" African music, it needs to be noted that he also recorded popular music, such as *taarab* and jazz orchestras; and he "discovered" the famous Congolese guitarist Jean Bosco Mwenda. Tracey released two major LP series from his field recordings, *The Sound of Africa* (SOA; 218 LPs with a total of 3,036 tracks)[8] and *The Music of Africa* (MOA; twenty-five LPs), aimed at a general audience. The monumental SOA series, created with funding from the Ford Foundation and distributed to sixty university libraries throughout the world, and publication of ILAM's journal, *African Music*, plus Tracey's books and lecture tours in Europe and the United States established his and ILAM's international reputation.

COLONIAL REPERCUSSIONS— ETHICAL CONSIDERATIONS

With the advent of postcolonial awareness, there is an increasingly audible cry to decolonize ethnomusicology, the discipline, and by extension the collections housed in archives that were collected during the colonial era. Hugh Tracey's project was a knowledge project, a preservation project, and a commercial project that on many levels exploited its subject and subjects—the music and the musicians he recorded. His experience in outdoor broadcasting helped him become an exceptionally good field recordist. He was also a researcher, a writer, a producer of radio shows, a filmmaker, an engineer, an artist, and a businessman.[9] Sadly, Tracey never accomplished the transcription and analysis he was told by Holtz and Vaughn Williams to let come later, because he was unable to secure funding for the "African Music Codification and Textbook Project" he tried to launch in 1969.[10]

In what follows, Tracey's attitudes and methods in carrying out his project are briefly discussed.[11] Tracey's project was conditioned by his colonial worldview, his need for funding, and the rationale that he needed to preserve African music for future generations of Africans because they did not understand the need or have the ability to do it themselves. From extensive research of Hugh Tracey's documents and publications for his doctoral thesis, Lobley concludes:

As well as intending to archive and preserve styles of music, his recordings were meant to remain alive and useful, being reflective of a living and evolving art form. . . . In 1966 the *New York Times* reported how keen Tracey had been to stress that he was interested in the continuity and vitality of African musical expression, and not merely in the preservation of a receding or decaying form (Lobley 2010, 110–111). Tracey ultimately wanted his musical examples to be used as the basic data for textbooks to help ensure the future transmission of indigenous music, but in the short term he wanted his records to be used, firstly by African audiences, and secondarily by world audiences (ibid., 220).

In a letter to the Rockefeller Foundation in 1958, Tracey stated that the purpose of his work was:

> to circulate recordings of the best and most representative items of contemporary African music for immediate use in radio programmes and in industrial or municipal localities where facilities exist for transmission, thus enabling a large proportion of the African community to experience the music of their own race, of which they would otherwise be almost totally ignorant, living as they do in small circumscribed communities.
>
> (letter to Robert W. July, assistant director, October 1, 1958)

Tracey's wish for his music to be used in "industrial or municipal localities where facilities exist for transmission" relates to his promotion of his recordings in the industrial sector as a method to pacify workers in the face of growing agitation by the oppressed demanding independence from their oppressors—the colonial governments (cf. Coetzee 2014). Although a few mining compounds bought his recordings, the reality was that the workers were not interested in listening to recordings of the music they had left behind when they came to urban centers for employment. This led Tracey to turn to funding sources such as the Ford Foundation to carry on with his work.

As Coetzee observes (2014, 1), "Tracey operated in social contexts which were structured primarily in terms of race. His project was practically positioned within, and oriented towards, political systems based on racial inequality." And as Coetzee concludes (2014, 205), "there should be full acknowledgment of the ways in which Tracey's methods and assumptions conspired with broader forces of inequality to *exclude* those he claimed were his project's beneficiaries." The commercial release of his field recordings is perhaps the most obvious way his intended beneficiaries were excluded, to the extent that none of the musicians he recorded—with the possible exception of Jean Bosco Mwenda—realized any financial gain from the recordings. It was the capitalist Eric Gallo with his recording company who enjoyed financial gain while Hugh Tracey enjoyed support for his field excursions. These examples are intended to show why Tracey's colonial legacy is part and parcel of why there is an ethical obligation to carry out the restudy and digital return of his field recordings.

TRACEY'S KIPSIGIS RECORDINGS

On September 15, 1950, Hugh Tracey made thirty field recordings of Kipsigis music in Kapkatet, near Kericho, in the Sotik District of Kenya. The recordings comprise thirty-four songs in total, and among them were three recordings of "Chemirocha," a humorous popular song that originated in the region.[12] The first two of the "Chemirocha" recordings were sung by Kipsigis men, the third by Kipsigis girls. All three were accompanied by *chepkong* (also known as *chepkongo*), a laced six-string bowl lyre. Hugh Tracey's comments in his fieldnotes for September 15, 1950, about his recording session with the Kipsigis read:

> *Kericho*
> A most enjoyable day with recordings from 11:30 to 11:30. We bought various provisions for the next few days at Vera's, phoned Miss Holmes, and went off to Kapkatet to meet the Kipsigis—25 miles back along the tarred road there is a small model village with carpenter, blacksmith, and other tradesmen established in small workshops. We picked out the covered market in case of rain which comes every afternoon and did heavily from 3–5 and intermittently all the evening.
>
> We recorded 30 items in all—the first 16 from the locals and the rest from a party which were brought up by lorry from a village or district 20 miles south. The music was utterly simple but charming in many ways. They have two modes, one for a 5 string lyre and one for a six, both are pentatonic but different, and tunes which fit the one will not fit the other they say. There were a dozen lyres which are the instrument of the district. Bought one, and also a frame lyre, i.e. the frame looks like a wishbone with the cross bar which can be played held to the ear or the tooth, or with an ext. resonator such as a box or a bucket. They sang a song for milking goats, love songs, dances, among others. We had short breaks for food but otherwise were at it hard all the time. The people were jolly and chatting. One group of older men came with spears, long bladed, with caps of black ostrich feather baubles on their tips—and collars of ostrich feathers, over their heads, supported half way down their head at 45 with the mouth just showing (Figure 3.1). It was a blessing we had only tarred road to traverse at the end of our long day.
>
> (Hugh Tracey field journal, September 15, 1950)

Tracey's "technical" field journal from his 1950 East Africa recording excursion contains two pages dated September 15, 1950, with lists of measurements of pitches possible on four different Kipsigis lyres. The third field journal, prepared by an interpreter/translator from Kericho named arap Towett,[13] lists the item number, song title, musicians, and instruments played, with information identical to that on Tracey's fieldcards. In addition, Towett wrote a brief English translation of each song's lyrics. The pages of his entries are not dated, but it is likely this work was done the same day the recordings were made in Kapkatet, since Tracey wrote this comment on a

FIGURE 3.1 Kipsigis men with long-bladed spears with black ostrich feather baubles on their tips and ostrich feather hats worn at a 45-degree angle described by Hugh Tracey in his field journal, Kapkatet, September 15, 1950.

Photograph courtesy of International Library of African Music.

fieldcard: "Arap Towett was the name of the Kipsigis interpreter who translated all his peoples' songs for us" (Hugh Tracey fieldcard 27.1, September 15, 1950).

On the handwritten fieldcard for "Chemirocha I," Tracey says in his remarks:

> The main theme of this song is affection for the Kipsigis country. He also asks why the white man should have taken over the country which incidentally, they themselves took from others in the past. He comes, he says, from Sotik nearby. The name "Chemirocha" is their pronunciation of "Jimmy Rodgers" whose gramophone records were the first to be heard in the district. It is now synonymous for anything strange and new.[14]

He entered that the performers were Bekyibei arap Mosonik with Cheriro arap Korogorem, and credited the composer as "Folk" (Hugh Tracey fieldcard 27.34, "Chemirocha I," September 15, 1950). The journal of Tracey's interpreter/translator, arap Towitt, states the meaning of the lyrics as,

> The singer says he likes and he applauds those places sweet to him. He asks why Europeans came to enslave us. He praise his friends. He says he belongs to Sotik, the name of the place where he lives.

This, and the other two recordings of "Chemirocha" appear in the July 1952 catalog of the African Music Transcription Library, published by Gallo (Africa) Limited. At the time

(1948–1953), Tracey was funded for his field excursions by Gallo in return for managing the African Music Transcription Library and releasing his field recordings thought to be most commercially viable as 78 rpm shellac discs on Gallo's labels.[15]

On his fieldcard for "Chemirocha II," Tracey lists the performers as "Charondet arap Ng'asura with Kipsigis men" and enters Ng'asura as the composer [presumably of the lyrics]. In his remarks, he says:

> Chemirocha the mystical singer (based on Jimmy Rodgers the American guitarist) is at Kericho they say, why, he is said to have visited a friend of his at Ituna! The similarity of the two instruments, the guitar and the local lyre has given rise to the legend of this wandering player whose records have been heard but whose presence is a mystery. The young men having sung this version of Chemirocha said that it was really their sisters' song, but they were too shy to sing it. Eventually the girls were persuaded to sing and gave us the next version.
>
> (Hugh Tracey fieldcard 27.1, "Chemirocha II," September 15, 1950)[16]

A group of unnamed Kipsigis girls gave Tracey the "next version"—"Chemirocha III"—a haunting and captivating recording which is no doubt one of the best known and most widely circulated recordings Hugh Tracey ever released (Figure 3.2). On

FIGURE 3.2 Kipsigis girls singing for Hugh Tracey with male onlookers crowding around. Kapkatet, September 15, 1950. Two of the young men wear modern sunglasses while two others wear European narrow-brimmed felt hats, showing that local youth were appropriating not only Jimmie Rodgers's music but also fashion from Western culture.

Photograph courtesy of International Library of African Music.

the fieldcard for "Chemirocha III," Tracey credits the *chepkong* lyre player Chemutoi Ketienya as the composer (presumably of the lyrics). In all three versions recorded, the lyrics sung are different, but the rhythmic accompaniment for the melody by the lyre player and the melody itself are similar.

Tracey's remarks on the fieldcard for "Chemirocha III" (Figure 3.3) are:

> The mysterious singer and dancer, Chemirocha, has been turned into a local god Pan with the feet of an antelope, half beast, half man. He is urged by the girls to do the leaping dance familiar to all Kipsigis so energetically that he will jump clean out of his clothes—The name Chemirocha is based upon the guitarist Jimmy Rodgers.
>
> (Hugh Tracey fieldcard 27.5, "Chemirocha III," September 15, 1950)

Tracey published "Chemirocha III" in South Africa with Gallotone Record Company (GB 1476 T.) as a 78 rpm shellac record in 1952. This record was a hit in Kenya and beyond.

Below are the lyrics from Tracey's recording transcribed and translated from Kalenjin into English:[17]

Iyaya Jambo 'Mirocha (*vocables* Hello Jimmie Rodgers)
Ololo chepchoni marindet (*vocables* The dress will come off)
Imarmar kot kobut sulualit (Dance until your pants fall off)
Simarmar kot kobut katija (Dance until the skirt falls off)

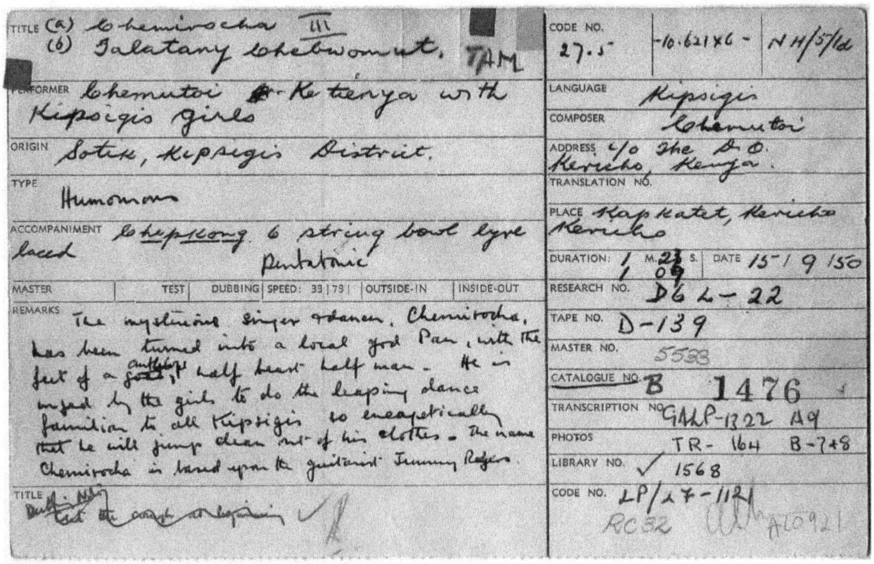

TITLE (a) Chemirocha III
(b) Jalatany Chebwomut. TAM
PERFORMER Chemutoi Ketienya with Kipsigis girls
ORIGIN Sotik, Kipsigis District.
TYPE Humorous
ACCOMPANIMENT Chepkong 6 string bowl lyre laced pentatonic
MASTER | TEST | DUBBING | SPEED: 33 | 78 | OUTSIDE-IN | INSIDE-OUT
REMARKS The mysterious singer & dancer, Chemirocha, has been turned into a local god Pan, with the feet of a antelope half beast half man. He is urged by the girls to do the leaping dance familiar to all Kipsigis so energetically that he will jump clean out of his clothes. The name Chemirocha is based upon the guitarist Jimmy Rodgers.
TITLE

CODE NO. 27.5 | -10.621×6- | NH/5/6d
LANGUAGE Kipsigis
COMPOSER Chemutoi
ADDRESS c/o The D.O. Kericho, Kenya.
TRANSLATION NO.
PLACE Kapkatet, Kericho Kericho
DURATION: 1 M. 23 S. 1 09 | DATE 15/9/50
RESEARCH NO. D6L-22
TAPE NO. D-139
MASTER NO. 5533
CATALOGUE NO. B 1476
TRANSCRIPTION NO. GALP-1322 A9
PHOTOS TR-164 B-7+8
LIBRARY NO. ✓ 1568
CODE NO. LP/27-1121
RC32 AL0921

FIGURE 3.3 Hugh Tracey's fieldcard for "Chemirocha III."

Image courtesy of International Library of African Music.

Haloo Chemirocha (Hello Jimmie Rodgers)
Ololo chepchoni marindet (The dress will come off)
Iya, Jambo 'Mirocha, (Hello Jimmie Rodgers)
Ololo chepchoni marindet (The dress will come off)

Ololo we Chemirocha (3x) (Oh, Jimmie Rodgers)

Haloo Chemirocha, (Hello Jimmie Rodgers)
Imarar kot kobut sulualit (Dance until your pants fall off)
Simarmar kot kobut katija (Dance until your skirt falls off)
Ololo chepchoni marindet (The dress will come off)
Iyeye Chemirocha (Jimmie Rodgers)

Iyaya Jambo 'Mirocha (Hello Jimmie Rodgers)
Ololo chepchoni marindet (The dress will come off)
Ololo Chemirocha (Jimmie Rodgers)
Ololo chepkongo marindet (The dress will come off)
Ololo chemongen ukweli (Don't know the truth)

Ololo lyoo Chemirocha (Jimmie Rodgers)
Lyee Chemirocha (Jimmie Rodgers)
Ololo we chepchoni marindet (The dress will come off)
Imarar kot kobut sulualit (Dance until the pants fall off)
Si mara kot kobut marindet (Dance until the dress falls off)

Iyeye Chemirocha (Jimmie Rodgers)
Ololo Jambo 'Mirocha (Hello Jimmie Rodgers)
Chito kobeber, tiondo kobeber (2x) (Half human, half animal/beast)

Haloo Chemirocha (Hello Jimmie Rodgers)
Ololoo chepchoni marindet (The dress will come off)
Ololoo (vocables)

With the advent of LP technology, "Chemirocha III" was released in the United Kingdom by London (London LB 826) on MOA no. 2, *Kenya*, in 1953, with many of Tracey's other recordings from Kenya on the same disc. Later, in 1958, the same compilation was released by Decca in the United States, with a new album cover but the same album title (Decca LF 1121). It also appeared in the undated South African MOA release "Musical Instruments 1 Strings" (MOA 27, track 9). Finally, eight Kipsigis recordings, including all three versions of "Chemirocha," constitute Side B of the Hugh Tracey SOA album AMA.TR-164. AMA.TR-165 (Side A, eleven tracks; Side B, eight tracks) is made up entirely of his Kipsigis recordings; AMA.TR-166, Side A, consists of seven tracks of Kipsigis recordings. Thus, all thirty-four Kipsigis songs Tracey recorded were published.[18] The numerous releases of his Kipsigis recordings attest to Tracey's commitment to dissemination of his field recordings, both locally and globally, at a time when very few recordings of African music were available for airplay or purchase, although the recording industry was establishing itself in Africa. There are no paper traces at ILAM that document income after publication expenses for ILAM from sales of the SOA or MOA series.[19]

Rodgers and the Popularity of "Chemirocha"

"Chemirocha III" by Kipsigis girls became an iconic hit song in Kenya and beyond. Why were Kipsigis girls singing a song about Jimmie Rodgers in 1950? Why was the 1952 Gallotone release of Tracey's recording a hit in Kenya and so popular internationally? Why is it still so popular now, both in Kenya and internationally?

Born in Mississippi, Jimmie Rodgers (1897–1933) became, according to the historian Bill Malone (1985), the first country singing star (Figure 3.4). Known as the "Father of Country Music," he was also called "America's Blue Yodeler," due to his trademark yodels sung at the end of stanzas in his blues songs. "The Singing Brakeman" was another moniker; he had worked on the railroad until age twenty-seven, when he quit because he had tuberculosis. Although already performing since age thirteen, he turned to music full-time to make a living after quitting the railroad. A singer, songwriter, and guitarist, Rodgers had a very appealing voice and released over one hundred highly entertaining recordings that found favor with people everywhere over the scant six years of his rise to stardom after his first hit on the Victor label in 1927, a blue yodel titled "T for Texas." He soared to fame both at home and abroad, with "T for Texas" selling almost half a million copies in the next two years. His appeal can be attributed to his unique and catchy "blue yodel" style and his easy-to-understand lyrics that often told stories with humorous twists. Rodgers became an icon of American country music with his songs about traveling, tough times, and love even though he was influenced by blues, Tin Pan Alley pop songs, and jazz (Ownby 2004). His recordings were popular everywhere, including Africa.

Hugh Tracey says in the first few seconds of his *Music of Africa* release of "Chemirocha III" that the Kipsigis heard Jimmie Rodgers because of a recording left behind by a missionary. But it is also likely that, in the Kenya Colony of the British Empire, they heard him on British colonial radio, as radio arrived in Kenya by 1938 and Rodgers was extremely popular in Britain. In response to a request for information about the amount of airplay "Chemirocha" has had on Kenyan radio since its release by Tracey in 1952, my Kalenjin research consultant, Kiplagat Kwambai, provided the following information:

> Kenya Broadcasting Company (KBC) music library records show "Chemirocha" was very popular at the media house in the late 50's and 60's when KBC, formerly known as Voice of Kenya (VOK), played "Chemirocha" as a way of celebrating Kenya's

FIGURE 3.4 Jimmie Rodgers in a publicity pose with his Weymann "Jimmie Rodgers Special"
guitar.

Courtesy, Country Music Hall of Fame® and Museum.

diverse culture during and after independence in 1963. The song was played twice
a day in both VOK English service on a programme called Kenya Folk Songs and
VOK Kiswahili service on "Musiki Kiasili" (trans. traditional music). Later in 1975,
a separate studio, KBC Kisumu, began broadcasting in all the major languages from
Western Kenya. Each language was dedicated 2–3 hours each day made up of news,
music and interviews. During the Kalenjin time, "Chemirocha" featured prominently. The song is actually a household sensation among the Kalenjin-speaking
people. In 2005, private vernacular radio stations were set up throughout Kenya.
Kalenjin has Kass FM and Chamgei FM. Both run programmes with traditional
segments where "Chemirocha" is often on the playlist as it reminds people of the very
first recorded music of the Kalenjin. "Chemirocha" has been on Kenyan airwaves
since its release in the 1950's and is still being aired through the many vernacular stations now broadcasting in the country.

(K. Kwambai, e-mail correspondence, February 1, 2017)

Thus it is clear that local residents knew the song when we arrived in Sotik with digital copies from Hugh Tracey's archive to return to them.

Brief mention must be made of the song's present popularity among non-Kenyan contemporary artists who put their interpretations up on YouTube. Perhaps it is the haunting quality of the voices of the Kipsigis girls together with Jimmie Rodgers's legendary status and the perceived quirkiness of a recording coming out of Kenya in 1952 that sings about Jimmie Rodgers as a half man/half beast, dancing until his clothes fall off. Whatever the reasons, the song holds an appeal. A Google search brings up a YouTube version of "Chemirocha" by the Icelandic artist Kria Brekkan posted on August 12, 2008, on "Porch of the Mystics" (https://porchofthemystics.wordpress.com/2008/08/12/chemirocha/). Commentary on the site refers to the "sacred mystery of the original" and calls the song a "Chemirocha hymn." Further, someone wrote the following about the villagers' reaction after hearing Jimmie Rodgers sing a blue yodel:

> Convinced that such strange sounds could not come from a human, the voice was attributed to a centaur-like spirit they called Chemirocha. This half-man half-antelope is honored in fertility rites where young Kipsigi maidens dance seductively to the Jimmie Rodgers records, begging him to join them in a leaping dance in hopes that Chemirocha will jump completely out of his clothes.

Among the responses is one from Kipkorir Pius Cheruiyot on December 4, 2011, that says, "I'm proud to be from Kapkatet. actually Chemirocha is a mispronunciation of Jimmy Rodgers."

A second interpretation, on a site called "The Lake,"[20] is by a South African group called Bye Beneco. Here the commentary reads:

> Chemirocha is not only a song that comes from the Kipsigi tribe in Kenya but it also tells the story of how the American yodler [sic], Jimmy Rodgers (Chemirocha), became a God like symbol for the tribe. Bye Beneco have done their own rendition of the beautiful "worship" song that creates another interesting context.

The above examples show that contemporary pop artists and people reacting to their YouTube videos have some knowledge of what Hugh Tracey said in his documentation and translation of his recording of "Chemirocha" by the Kipsigis girls; perhaps they accessed his comments on the Internet or heard his comments on his release of the recording. On the field card for the "Chemirocha III" recording, Tracey wrote, "The mysterious singer and dancer, Chemirocha, has been turned into a local god Pan with the feet of an antelope, half beast, half man. He is urged by the girls to do the leaping dance familiar to all Kipsigis so energetically that he will jump clean out of his clothes—The name Chemirocha is based upon the guitarist Jimmy Rodgers" (Hugh Tracey fieldcard 27.5, "Chemirocha III," September 15, 1950). The YouTube commentary that suggests Jimmie Rodgers, the centaur-like half man, half antelope, is honored in fertility rites reflects stereotypes of Africa, not anything said by Tracey. There is no suggestion in

Tracey's documentation that "Chemirocha" was ever anything beyond a humorous pop-ular song created locally for entertainment. Tracey often compared what he encountered in Africa with what he knew from his own European culture. His suggestion that "Chemirocha" had been "turned into a local god Pan" stems from the song lyrics calling him half-man, half beast; not from anything spiritual about the song. Likewise, the in-terpretation that Chemirocha is a "God-like symbol for the tribe" and calling the song a "Chemirocha hymn" and a "worship song" have no basis in Tracey's documentation of how the song was performed by its originators. What's more, ILAM's return of the recordings to Kipsigis musicians in Sotik District where they were created revealed only that "Chemirocha" is a light-hearted song sung with great pleasure and that, because of its continued popularity and regular airplay, it has become a symbol of Kipsigis identity.

ILAM's Opportunity

Early in 2014, Tabu Osusa, a popular *benga* (Kenyan rhumba) singer, songwriter, music promoter, producer, and founding director of the Ketebul Music recording studio in Nairobi, contacted me for assistance with a Singing Wells project to document and re-vitalize performance of indigenous music of Uganda that would include support for the construction of traditional instruments. Osusa cofounded Singing Wells (www.singingwells.org) with Abubillah Music Foundation's director, Jimmy Allen, in 2011. The project was being sponsored by the Abubillah Music Foundation. Having vis-ited ILAM during the height of the cataloging and digitizing of its collections in 2008, Osusa was familiar with Hugh Tracey's field recordings and the Tracey instrument col-lection. He wanted to know if ILAM had information on where the various Ugandan instruments Tracey recorded were acquired, and he asked whether ILAM could share this information with the Singing Wells project team. This led to e-mail correspond-ence and a three-way Skype conversation in which I told Jimmy Allen about ILAM's desire to repatriate Hugh Tracey's recordings to their communities of origin and asked whether there was any chance for us to collaborate since we were doing similar work. Allen responded:

> There is every opportunity to collaborate and everything we do is inspired by Hugh Tracey's initial work. We would be very proud to help you in any way we can and the Abubilla Music Foundation, which I lead, should be able to help.
>
> (J. Allen, e-mail correspondence, February 10, 2014)

In the ensuing months, plans were made to carry out digital return of Hugh Tracey's Kipsigis (Rift Valley) and Luo (Lake Victoria region) recordings with the costs of the fieldwork funded by the Abubillah Music Foundation. Launching ILAM's pilot project would never have been possible without the support from the Abubillah Foundation.

Tabu Osusa and his crew at Ketebul were sent MP3s of the recordings and scans of Tracey's fieldcards in advance to provide essential information about locations and names of musicians recorded to use for their preliminary fieldwork. Tabu called on our Kipsigis "fixer," Kiplagat Kwambai, better known as "50 Cows" (his nickname from his years as a radio personality for Kenya Broadcasting), who grew up in the Sotik region, to assist. He and the Ketebul videographer Patrick Ondiek spent several days in the Kericho area working from the performer's names listed on Hugh Tracey's fieldcards to, with help from residents, locate appropriate community organizations and surviving musicians recorded by Tracey and/or their family members. Our team for the fieldwork to the Kipsigis, in addition to 50 Cows and Patrick, were Hunter Allen, videographer; Steve Kivutia, sound man; student assistant, Will Baxley; and radio journalist Ryan Kailath.[21] A minivan and driver were hired by Ketebul to provide transport including the second segment to return the eighty-two recordings Tracey made in 1950 and 1952 in the Lake Victoria region among the Luo.

RETURN OF THE KIPSIGIS RECORDINGS

After a day in Nairobi making copies of the metadata notebooks[22] for the Kipsigis and Luo recordings and buying jewel cases for the CDs I had carried in my luggage from South Africa, we were on our way to the Rift Valley on Monday, August 4, 2014. It took seven hours to get to Bomet, the county seat of the region, so the fieldwork did not begin until Tuesday morning, August 5. Under the direction of 50 Cows, we first went to the Department of Culture and Social Services to meet the Bomet County minister of culture, Patricia Lesoi. With this meeting, the digital return of Hugh Tracey's Kipsigis recordings began. Minister Lesoi was thrilled to receive the recordings and metadata booklet and told us she wanted our help to establish an archive of Kipsigis heritage in her department. I suggested the possibility of staging a Kipsigis music festival to launch the new stadium being built in Bomet, with local musicians performing the music recorded by Hugh Tracey. Her enthusiasm extended to bringing a group of traditional musicians to meet with us when we returned to Bomet from our fieldwork that evening.

Next, we met up with Paul Rotich, leader of the Kamua Musicians Association, in front of his shop called MaKiche Sounds Production. During their visit to Bomet a couple of weeks before, Paul had helped 50 Cows and Patrick locate the various people we were now going to visit. There was a small crowd gathered in front of his shop. Paul introduced us to two female vocalists, Elizabeth Bet and Chebaibai, who were especially interested in the recordings. As our purpose for being there was explained, Elizabeth told us that she was a girl about eight years old when Hugh Tracey came to Kapkatet and she remembered the day, although she was too young to sing with the girls for the "Chemirocha III" recording. She was very excited that the old Kipsigis songs were coming back to the community. She remembered them all and was thrilled to have the recordings so she could sing along with them and relive the music of her youth.

With the introductions and explanations of why we were there completed, we all headed out to the home of Philip arap Charondet, a grandson of Charondet arap Ng'asura, the deceased lead singer on "Chemirocha II." Rotich and his entourage led the way in his station wagon with his shop's name and images of a saxophone and guitar painted on it. The vocalists, Elizabeth and Chebaibai, changed into Kipsigis traditional attire of animal-hide robes worn over their shoulders, beaded skirts, and cowry shell necklaces and headgear when we arrived in Sotik village. We explained our purpose to Philip, showed him the CD of Kipsigis recordings, and told him about how his grandfather sings on the first five tracks on the CD and that we were there to give it to him.

Philip and others who had gathered to welcome us listened to "Chemirocha II" and the other recordings by Ng'asura from the laptop of our soundman, Steve. Philip had access to a CD player among his family members, so he was pleased to receive a CD with recordings neither he nor anyone else in his village had ever heard before. Group photos were taken, and it seemed that everyone was surprised and very pleased this had happened. Philip knew the song "Chemirocha." He told us that his grandfather traveled a lot with his music and because he was a musician, the people in the village gave him the nickname "Chemirocha"—he was their own Jimmie Rodgers.

Next we drove to Kipkewa village, not knowing we were going to meet then-eighty-eight-year-old Cheriyot arap Kuiri, one of the Kipsigis men who sang with Ng'asura on "Chemirocha II." My fieldnotes recounting the moment of our meeting read:

> 5/08/2014, Kipkewa Village in Sotik area
> The highlight today was our visit to Cheriyot arap Kuiri, b. 1926, who sang on Chemirocha II. Now 88 years old, he remembered very well the day the group of Kipsigis men were called by the chief to go and sing for Hugh Tracey. They didn't know what that white man was doing there, but a large crowd gathered—he made the recordings and then he was gone. We played "Chemirocha II" from Steve's laptop, he got up to dance and sang along. When I gave him the CD, he read the song titles and names of musicians on the CD liner and asked me in English, "how am I going to make the sound come out of this thing?" No one in his family has a CD player. Paul said he could get a radio that can play the music from a memory card for 1,000 shillings.

These encounters, and especially finding a musician still alive who was recorded by Tracey, made that first day of fieldwork exciting and rewarding for everyone involved. To see Cheriyot arap Kuiri light up with the sound of the music, then sing along and get up and dance, was an entirely special moment (Figure 3.5).

Wednesday, August 6, began with the recordings being presented at Chebirir Primary School, not far outside Bomet. The local school was built by community parents and had no electricity. The recordings were given to the principal, Mrs. Lily Chumo, along with a metadata notebook with information about each recording. This happened as part of the school's closing ceremony with all 198 pupils, eight teachers, and the school board members present. With 50 Cows serving as translator, our purpose was explained, with

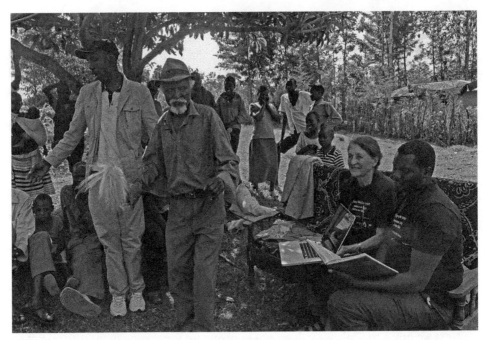

FIGURE 3.5 Paul Rotich and Cheriyot arap Kuiri dancing to "Chemirocha II" playing from the laptop, Kipkewa village, August 5, 2014.

Photograph courtesy of ILAM/Singing Wells.

me emphasizing that we want the recordings to get to schoolchildren throughout the region, and it was all right for Mrs. Chumo to make copies and give them to other schools. Students sang and danced for us in traditional attire. Mrs. Chumo told me that travel to a nearby school with electricity would be necessary in order to use the CD, so Paul Rotich agreed to transfer the music to a memory card and get a battery-powered radio for Mrs. Chumo on our behalf.

After the school visit we traveled a long way on a rough gravel road to get to Chemaitany village, the home of the widow and two sons of the late Bekyebei arap Mosonik, who sang on "Chemirocha I" and five other songs recorded by Tracey. Again, there was no electricity. Mrs. Mosonik listened to "Chemirocha I" and other songs sung by her late husband with earphones from the laptop (Figure 3.6), while Paul Rotich rigged up a car battery to a radio, which served as an amplifier for the recordings on the laptop to play through a large speaker that Rotik was carrying in his car as part of his band's equipment. This allowed the music to be played at high enough volume for everyone to hear and respond to by singing and dancing. Hearing her late husband sing on "Chemirocha I" and then unaccompanied on "Udo udo ee" (a song he sang all his life to calm the female goats to get them to suckle their kids [Hugh Tracey fieldcard 26.2]), Mrs. Mosonik commented her husband always got emotional when he sang that song, and hearing him sing it now made her feel like she was with him again.

FIGURE 3.6 Widow of "Chemirocha I" vocalist, Bekyebei arap Mosonik, listening to her late husband sing from the laptop, Chemaitany village, August 6, 2014.

Photograph courtesy of ILAM/Singing Wells.

A group of local musicians called Koilonget Band played "Chemirocha" and some other Kipsigis songs for us on a six-string lyre with a metal resonator and an accordion. CDs were given to the musicians in the band as well as the Mosonik family members, consisting of two sons, a daughter, and Mosonik's widow. Paul Rotich's ingenuity in finding a solution to the low volume of the laptop speakers saved the day (Figure 3.7). Knowing we were leaving the next morning, Rotich staged a special show with his MaKiche Band at a Bomet nightclub that evening to celebrate our success. The Bomet County culture minister, Patricia Lesoi, joined us in the celebration.

The discovery of a local interpretation of why Chemirocha was thought to be half beast/half man came on Thursday, August 7, when we traveled to Kapkatet to visit Josiah Kimutai arap Sang, the son of the paramount chief who called the local musicians to perform for Hugh Tracey on September 15, 1950. Josiah welcomed us by singing a Kipsigis song while accompanying himself on guitar. Then he explained his understanding of the story behind the "Chemirocha III" song lyrics that describe Chemirocha as half man/half beast.[23] Many have wondered about Hugh Tracey's comment that the singers had turned Chemirocha into a local version of the god Pan. It seemed to me to be an example of his tendency to draw comparisons with European culture. Why would Kipsigis have any knowledge of the god Pan?

Josiah was just an eight-year-old boy when Hugh Tracey came to Kapkatet. He did not remember the event and guessed that he might have been off playing somewhere.

FIGURE 3.7 The sound system rigged up by Paul Rotich, the excellent facilitator of our village visits. He plugged the laptop into a radio powered by a car battery to send the sound to the speaker, giving enough volume for everyone to hear the recordings. Chemaitany village, August 6, 2014.

Photograph courtesy of ILAM/Singing Wells.

However, he knew the song "Chemirocha"; he sang it and then translated his understanding of the lyrics into English for us. When asked why Chemirocha is thought of as half man/half beast, he had an immediate answer. It had to do with the missionaries teaching villagers to pray with their eyes shut and to eat the body and drink the blood of Jesus Christ. What is more, British colonial officials would round the villagers up and take them to the clinics they had built to donate blood for the war effort. The people thought this very strange. What did they do with the blood? Are these white people, the colonialists, cannibals? It must mean they are half man/half beast. Jimmie Rodgers was white—he must be half man/half beast.[24]

Two young local musicians present during the interview were especially excited about receiving the recordings. They promised to use them to revitalize interest in Kipsigis music among their friends and youth of the community. Eventually, Josiah offered to take us to see the Kipsigis Cultural Museum in the heart of Kapkatet, across the road from where he thinks Hugh Tracey may have made the recordings. The modest museum, containing artifacts such as Kipsigis musical instruments and traditional clothing, was established by a local historian in 2008. A primary school teacher and her students were just leaving as we arrived at the museum; I wished I could have somehow given them the recordings because we were not getting to as many schools as I had hoped.

LEARNING FROM RETURNING "CHEMIROCHA"

Lessons learned from the above scant three days in the Kipsigis community where Hugh Tracey made his recordings back in 1950 include: the return of the recordings to artists and their family members, schools, and culture organizations was met with enthusiasm; the cost of doing this work makes it impossible for ILAM without external funding; not enough time was available for restudy of the original field recordings; and play-back devices with USB ports and rechargeable batteries should be given to recipients in communities with no electricity. Subsequently, the return of recordings in Malawi (May 2016) was on USB memory sticks with inexpensive radios with rechargeable batteries and USB ports given to recipients without CD players, to assure they could listen to the music. CDs were given to those who had access to CD players. In general, CD technology is being replaced by listening from cell phones, and MP3s played from portable devices. Finally, the work needs adequate funding to allow time for restudy to be done much more systematically.[25]

I was encouraged when in late October 2016, out of the blue over two years later, I received a phone call from Joseah Bet, Elizabeth Bet's son. He was calling on his mother's behalf to thank me for the CD I had given her. We proceeded to talk at length via WhatsApp. Joseah wants to promote the Kipsigis music of the past; he fears it is dying out. I sent him a link to watch the documentary *Lost Songbooks*, which includes footage of his mother, but his network connection does not have adequate bandwidth. It has since been sent to him on DVD, with a promise that copies of the DVD will be given to Paul Rotich and any others interested. He lives in Bomet. I told him about the Bomet County minister of culture, Mrs. Patricia Lesoi, and my suggestion that we collaborate to stage a Kipsigis Music Festival in the new stadium being built. He said the stadium is almost finished now and he would contact her to see if he can work together to make this happen. This positive feedback suggests people want to do things with the recordings to promote retention of their music culture. But lack of funding is always an issue.

THE ETHICAL MANDATE

Repatriation efforts have been ongoing at ILAM since 2009, when cataloging and digital conversion of the Hugh Tracey Collection was completed. A first initiative was to host a Digital Heritage Workshop at ILAM in December 2008, supported by the African Studies Center, University of Michigan, Ann Arbor. Participants accomplished the workshop's aim of developing guidelines for the reproduction, sale, and repatriation of digital heritage.[26] The first two recommendations of the "Guidelines for Repatriation of Digital Cultural Heritage" (2009, 180) state:

Individuals, groups and institutions in possession of digital cultural heritage should make the best attempt to repatriate it to its communities of origin.

Non-original owners of the heritage are ethically bound to repatriate it in an appropriate format for its owners.

The digital divide[27] remains a stark reality in rural Africa, although cell-phone technology that allows Internet access is breaking this down. Direct transfer of the recordings from a laptop to an individual's cell phone is an option—but unfortunately, many potential recipients of the recordings do not have phones with the capacity to store large audio files. Funding is needed to develop effective means of digital return and to support grassroots work in local communities for projects designed to engage interested youth with their musical heritage in creative ways. This cannot be accomplished without bilateral cooperation between ILAM and culture organizations in the communities of origin.[28]

Finally, questions remain: is the return of field recordings to their sites of origin accepted as an ethical responsibility? Can it become standard archival practice for music archives with collections of ethnomusicological field recordings? Is it standard practice for trained ethnomusicologists to archive their field recordings and/or return copies of them to the people whom they recorded? Is it the researchers' responsibility to carry out the return or the archives' responsibility?[29]

Conclusion

It is encouraging that many music archives are moving away from existing mainly for scholars and into sponsorship of proactive projects in music sustainability.[30] It suggests that the use of field collections for music sustainability projects and the digital return of historic field recordings is spreading in ethnomusicology as a discipline (cf. Titon 2009, Topp Fargion 2012). Given the colonial legacies of Hugh Tracey and his collection, to share his recordings by moving them out of the archive and into the public sphere in as many ways as possible is a responsibility that became central to ILAM's practice as soon as the collection had been cataloged and digitized and made accessible online. The most direct, uncomplicated reason why digital return to source communities is the ethically responsible thing for ILAM to do is because, with present-day technology, it is possible. It is ethically mandated as a "better too late than never" reciprocal gesture that will potentially assist in the sustainability of the music Tracey recorded. Combining restudy of the original recordings with their return is a goal because of the many errors in their existing metadata. This is, of course, a daunting task due to the sheer size and geographic scope of the collection.

The "Chemirocha" story, with its ramifications seen more clearly with the benefit of sixty-five years of hindsight and the insights that postcolonial awareness affords, makes one wonder whether the work of returning historical field recordings to their communities of origin can provide an ethic that aims and works to decolonize ethnomusicology—and an ethic for the work of ethnomusicologists (and whatever others) presently creating field recordings not only for their own research purposes, but in the interest of fostering sustainable music. It is necessary for ILAM to repatriate copies of Tracey's field recordings to their source communities as a gesture toward reconciling the implicit exploitation of the musicians he recorded due to standards (or lack thereof) in the recording industry during the colonial era. For ILAM, the return of Tracey's recordings to their source communities and descendents of musicians he recorded is a gesture toward redress not only of the collector Hugh Tracey's colonial legacy but also of ethnomusicology at large.

Although there are ethnomusicologists and anthropologists who employ an ethic of reciprocity as basic to their practice in carrying out field research, and there are archives preserving collections of field recordings created during the colonial era that are carrying out digital return of those recordings to researched communities as a reciprocal gesture (cf. Fox 2013), it cannot be assumed to correct the legacy of ethnomusicology and anthropology unless it becomes standard practice. Herein lies our challenge.

NOTES

1. Online access to the Hugh Tracey Collection has existed from the ILAM website via its online catalog since late 2008, when cataloging and digital conversion was completed. This fact is mentioned here in order to correct B. Edwards (2016, 274), who states, "the vast majority of Tracey's collection must be consulted onsite." Researchers no longer have to physically come to ILAM to access the collection. The online catalog, with numerous search options, offers metadata and a thirty-second audio clip of each Hugh Tracey recording. Digital files of the recordings and the document archive are available from ILAM for research purposes on request.

2. For discussions of ethical issues in audiovisual archives practice, repatriation of field recording collections, and how these issues extend to applied (advocacy and/or engaged) ethnomusicology and practice in ethnomusicology as a discipline in general, see Lancefield (1993, 1998), Mills (1996), Seeger (1996, 2008), Averill (2003), Titon (2009, 2011), Topp-Fargion (2009, 2012), Harrison et al. (2010), Vallier (2010), Thram (2010, 2011, 2014, 2015), Harrison (2012), Dirksen (2012), Grant (2012), Lambrechts (2012), Fox (2013), and Swijghuisen Reigersberg (2016), to name a few.

3. Leonard Tracey was given his tobacco farm in Southern Rhodesia as a land grant from the British government as compensation for a leg injury he incurred serving in World War I.

4. From this work Tracey compiled a detailed report on his research, including prints of photographs for each instrument documented and technical documentation of the intervals played by each wind instrument, and so forth. The manuscript of this report, archived at ILAM, was meant to be submitted for publication as a book after it was approved by the Carnegie Institute. Unfortunately it was withheld by the director of native development, Harold Jowitt, who objected to Tracey's criticism of missionary practices therein. Ironically, Jowitt had helped Tracey get the Carnegie grant. Scans of the

manuscript instrument images and chapter on flutes and pipes were published by ILAM in the *For Future Generations* (2010) exhibition catalog.

5. B. Edwards (2016, 272) remarks on Vail and White's 1970s field research in Mozambique that enabled their restudy of Tracey's interpretations of Chopi song lyrics found in *Chopi Musicians* (1948), saying, "Noting that Tracey's annotations on the mid-century recordings 'range from the whimsical and patronizing to the completely erroneous,' Vail and White review his archive, retranslating song lyrics and providing more careful contextualization of the ways Chopi and Sena-Podzo music represents the nuances of power, migration, and labour under Portuguese colonial rule."

6. Eric Gallo established South Africa's first recording company, "Gallo Recording Studios," in 1932 and incorporated the company as "Gallo Africa." In the 1950s, with his company commercially successful, Gallo was in a position to support Hugh Tracey's field excursions and the African Music Unit that Tracey managed from 1947 to 1954 when he established ILAM.

7. An accurate count of the number of individual items recorded by Hugh Tracey has not been determined because the recordings are archived in multiple formats. For instance, users of ILAM's online audio search will find multiple copies of various songs when they search the online archive depending on the various media onto which Hugh Tracey transferred his field recordings when he returned from his field excursions. Thus one may find that the same song from the original field recording exists on an acetate disc, a vinyl test pressing, a commercial 78 rpm record, and in the Sound of Africa (SOA) series, and there will be a digital file from each source.

8. The last eight LPs in the SOA series are field recordings made by Andrew Tracey added after the original release with 210 LPs.

9. Tracey engineered the prototype for the Hugh Tracey *kalimba*, which he manufactured at his African Musical Instruments company, founded in 1954, the same year he founded ILAM. In addition to operating this business aimed at providing instruments for teaching African music in public schools, he had a commercial chicken farm on his smallholding in Krugersdorp to generate income for his living expenses.

10. Tracey's "African Music Codification and Textbook Project" sought to recruit researchers from throughout Africa to be trained at ILAM to record the indigenous music of their home region. Their recordings were to be deposited in a "tome" at ILAM. Transcriptions from the recordings were to be used in creating region-specific textbooks to "fulfil one of the basic aims of the Project, namely to bring African music into the field of African education in the broadest sense" (Tracey 1969, 7).

11. Tracey did not conceive of himself as an ethnomusicologist—he was twenty-five years into his project by the time the term was coined. His lack of a university degree meant he was not given credence as a scholar by early musicologists working in sub-Saharan Africa such as Klaus Wachsmann in Uganda or Percival Kirby and David Rycroft in South Africa. However, Nketia's assessment is that Hugh Tracey was foremost among scholars of the colonial period who felt their study of folk music necessarily and ethically demanded attention to music education. He reports that Tracey saw African music as an artistic heritage that needed to be preserved and he worked tirelessly to promote recognition of its value (1998, 51).

12. Kipsigis is one of several ethnic groups in the Sotik District with distinctive dialects of the Kalenjin language. In keeping with the Kipsigis dialect, "Jimmie" was changed to "Chemi" and "Rodgers" to "Rocha." The song title was recorded by Tracey as one word, "Chemirocha," and that usage is retained here.

13. In Kalenjin *arap* means "child of." In the case of the translator, Towett, no first name is given, he is only referred to as arap Towett or simply Towett.
14. Though Tracey spelled Rodgers's name as "Jimmy," the official spelling was "Jimmie."
15. From the late 1940s to early 1950s, before the advent of LP discs, Gallo (Africa) Ltd. published a large number of Hugh Tracey's field recordings on 78 rpm shellac discs. From these Gallo releases, 675 discs containing over 1,350 items from 102 language groups are preserved in ILAM's archive (Lobley 2010, 87).
16. From the *African Music Transcription Library Catalogue* (AMTL) entries, "Chemirocha I" was released on the Trek and "Chemirocha II" on Gallotone labels sometime late in 1951 or early in 1952.
17. The transcription and English translation of the lyrics are by the Kalenjin research consultant, Kiplagat Kwambai.
18. Presently, both the MOA series and SOA series are available from ILAM in CD format and from online vendors in their original album compilations or as single tracks. "Chemirocha III" is also available on the *Kenyan Songs and Strings* CD [SWP030] in the Historical Recordings by Hugh Tracey Series.
19. P. Coetzee, whose PhD thesis, "Performing Whiteness; Representing Otherness: Hugh Tracey and African Music," is based on Hugh Tracey's textual traces archived at ILAM, found no financial records from Tracey's publication of the SOA and MOA series. His son, Andrew Tracey, thinks that if there was income over and above publication expenses it was used for ILAM operations (personal communication, January 21, 2017). The point here is that Tracey did not enrich himself from sale of the recordings.
20. "Bye Beneco/Chemirocha," *The Lake.* http://thelake.co/?p=801bye-beneco-chemirocha/.
21. Kailath narrates a National Public Radio (NPR) *Weekend Edition* feature on the return of Hugh Tracey's "Chemirocha" recordings, aired on June 28, 2015, http://www.npr.org/2015/06/28/417462792/in-a-kenyan-village-a-65-year-old-recording-comes-home. An online article authored by Kailath on the return of the "Chemirocha" recordings appears at http://www.atlasobscura.com/articles/chemirocha-how-an-american-country-singer-became-a-kenyan-star.
22. The field notebooks consist of an index with each song title and artists names in the order they appear on the CD or memory stick being returned, scans of the fieldcards for each recording with blank pages for taking notes when playing the recordings for recipients, and scans of the sketches and fieldnotes in Hugh Tracey's and his wife Peggy's field journals.
23. To see Josiah arap Sang relate in his own words the reasons why Jimmy Rodgers was thought to be half man/half beast watch "LOST SONGBOOKS—Returning Hugh Tracy's recordings to Kenya" (https://www.youtube.com/watch?v=Gi8xeDrsQTs&feature=youtu.be), a brief documentary film produced by Hunter Allen from video documentation of the project fieldwork.
24. For an ethnographic study of the widespread stories of colonialists as vampires, see *Speaking with Vampires: Rumor and History in Colonial Africa* by Luise White (2000), based on research in Kenya, Uganda, and Zambia.
25. To date, Hugh Tracey's Tanzania, Kenya, Uganda, Swaziland, Zambia, and Zimbabwe field recordings have been digitally returned to universities and/or national archives in those countries. Selected Shona mbira recordings (through a postdoctoral project in Zimbabwe) and Xhosa, Pedi, and Tswana recordings have been returned through two ethnomusicology MMUS thesis projects in South Africa and Botswana in 2014–2015. Tracey's Chopi xylophone recordings were returned to *timbila* composers and musicians in Mozambique

through a PhD student from SOAS in 2015–2016. ILAM's Pilot Project was launched July 27, 2014, with the return of Tracey's Wagogo recordings at the Gogo Music Festival in Chamwino, Tz, and the Zanzibari recordings on August 2 to the Dhow Countries Music Academy in Zanzibar. This was followed by return of the Kipsigis and Lou recordings in Kenya during August 3–15, 2014. Follow-up restudy and return of the Zanzibari recordings to descendants of musicians and a local taarab orchestra took place in June 2015. Tracey's recordings from Mombasa and Malindi (1950, 1952), southern Malawi (1949, 1950, 1958), and Natal Province (formerly Zululand) in South Africa (1939, 1955, 1972) were returned in February, May, and November 2016, respectively.

26. The "Guidelines on Reproduction and Sale of Digital Heritage" and "Guidelines for Repatriation of Digital Cultural Heritage" are available for download from the ILAM website: www.ru.ac.za/ilam. They can also be found as Appendix 4.1 and Appendix 4.2 in Thram (2015b, 82–85) and in *African Music* 8 (3) (2009): 179–181.

27. The term "digital divide" refers to those who have Internet access versus those who do not have Internet access.

28. Although ILAM has not been funded as yet for such work, it is encouraging that ILAM is collaborating with Andrea Emberly on her 2017–2018 project, "Connecting Culture and Childhood: Implications of the Repatriation of Archival Recordings for Children and Young People," funded by the Canadian SSHRC. The project enables return of the John Blacking field recordings of Venda music in South Africa, some of which are archived at ILAM and development of educational materials from them in the local communities with local participants.

29. For statistics gathered in the early 1990s on repatriation conducted by music archives and/ or researchers who deposited their field recordings in said archives, collected through a questionnaire circulated by Robert Lancefield in 1992–1993 to which forty-six archives from eighteen countries responded, see Lancefield (1993, 418–438; 1998, 60–63).

30. ILAM has worked toward getting Tracey's recordings out of the archive into schools in South Africa and beyond through the "ILAM Music Heritage Project SA." This project was initally viewed as a form of repatriation intended to fill the need for materials for teaching African music in classrooms that continues to exist, just as it did in the 1960s, when Tracey conceived his African Music Codification and Textbook Project. Tracey's project and the ILAM Music Heritage Project SA both aimed to fill a need for materials to teach African music—not only Western music—in the schools. Having the collection cataloged and digitized made the latter possible to achieve. The "For Future Generations" traveling exhibition, likewise intended to get Tracey's recordings into the public sphere, has reached the general public and countless school children through museum outreach and education programs. For descriptions of ILAM's "For Future Generations" traveling exhibition and the "ILAM Music Heritage Project SA" that created two music education textbooks illustrated with Hugh Tracey's historic images and field recordings, see Thram (2015, 2014) and Thram and Carver (2011) and the ILAM website: www.ru.ac.za/ilam.

References

Averill, Gage. 2003. "Ethnomusicologists as Public Intellectuals: Engaged Ethnomusicology in the University." *Folklore Forum* 34: 49–59.

Coetzee, Paulette. 2014. "Performing Whiteness; Representing Otherness: Hugh Tracey and African Music." PhD thesis, Rhodes University.

Digital Heritage Workshop Participants. 2009. "Guidelines for Reproduction and Sale of Digital Heritage" and "Guidelines for Repatriation of Digital Heritage." Digital Heritage Workshop, International Library of African Music, Grahamstown, South Africa. December, 2008. *African Music* 9 (3): 179–181.

Dirksen, Rebecca. 2012. "Reconsidering Theory and Practice in Ethnomusicology: Applying, Advocating, and Engaging beyond Academia." *Ethnomusicology Review* 17. http://ethnomusicologyreview.ucla.edu.

Edwards, Brent. 2016. "The Sound of Anticolonialism." In *Audible Empire Music, Global Politcs, Critique,* edited by R. Radano and T. Olaniyan, 269–291. London and Durham, NC: Duke University Press.

Fox, Aaron A. 2013. "Repatriation as Reanimation through Reciprocity." In *The Cambridge History of World Music,* edited by Philip Bohlman, 522–554. Cambridge: Cambridge University Press.

Grant, Catherine. 2012. "Rethinking Safeguarding: Objections and Responses to Protecting and Promoting Endangered Musical Heritage." *Ethnomusicology Forum* 21 (1): 31–51.

Harrison, Klisala. 2012. "Epistemologies of Applied Ethnomusicology." *Ethnomusicology* 36: 505–529.

Harrison, Klisala, Elizabeth Mackinlay, and Svanibor Pettan, eds. 2010. *Applied Ethnomusicology: Historical and Contemporary Approaches.* Newcastle upon Tyne, UK: Cambridge Scholars.

Hentoff, Nat. 1966. "Recordings: Hugh Tracey, Collector of African Integrities." *New York Times,* May 29, 1966.

Kailath, Ryan. 2015a. "In a Kenyan Village a 65-Year-Old Recording Comes Home." http://www.npr.org/2015/06/28/417462792/in-a-kenyan-village-a-65-year-old-recording-comes-home (accessed November 12, 2016).

Kailath, Ryan. 2015b. "How an American County Singer Became a Kenyan Star." http://www.atlasobscura.com/articles/chemirocha-how-an-american-country-singer-became-a-kenyan-star (accessed November 12, 2016).

Lambrechts, Lizabe. 2012. "Ethnography and the Archive: Power and Politics in Five South African Music Archives." PhD thesis, Stellenbosch University.

Lancefield, Robert C. 1993. "On the Repatriation of Recorded Sound from Ethnomusicological Archives." MA thesis, Wesleyan University.

Lancefield, Robert C. 1998. "'Musical Traces' Retraceable Paths: The Repatriation of Recorded Sound." *Journal of Folklore Research* 35 (1): 47–68. Also reprinted in this Handbook.

Lobley, Noel. 2010. "The Social Biography of Ethnomusicological Field Recordings: Eliciting Responses to Hugh Tracey's *The Sound of Africa* Series." PhD thesis, University of Oxford.

Malone, Bill C. 1985. *Country Music USA.* Austin: University of Texas Press.

Mills, Sherylle. 1996. "Indigenous Music and the Law: An Analysis of National and International Legislation." *Yearbook for Traditional Music* 28: 57–86.

Ownby, Ted. 2004. "Jimmie Rodgers: The Father of Country Music." Mississippi History Now. http://mshistorynow.mdah.state.ms.us/articles/39/jimmie-rodgers-the-father-of-country-music (accessed January 19, 2017).

Seeger, Anthony. 1996. "Ethnomusicologists, Archives, Professional Organizations, and the Shifting Ethics of Intellectual Property." *Yearbook for Traditional Music* 28: 87–105.

Seeger, Anthony. 2008. "Theories Forged in the Crucible of Action: The Joys, Dangers, and Potentials of Advocacy and Fieldwork." In *Shadows in the Field: New Perspectives for*

Fieldwork in Ethnomusicology, edited by Gregory Barz and Timothy J. Cooley, 271–288. Oxford: Oxford University Press.

Swijghuisen Reigersberg, Muriel. 2016. "Policy Formation, Ethics Statements and Ethics in Ethnomusicology: The Need for Increased and Sustained Engagement." *Collegium* 21: 83–102.

Thram, Diane, ed. 2009. "Guidelines for Repatriation of Digital Cultural Heritage." *African Music* 8 (3): 179–181.

Thram, Diane, ed. 2010. *For Future Generations: Hugh Tracey and the International Library of African Music*. Grahamstown: International Library of African Music.

Thram, Diane, and Mandy Carver. 2011. "African Music for Schools: Repatriating ILAM Field Recordings through Music Education Textbooks." In *Readings in Ethnomusicology: A Collection of Papers Presented at Ethnomusicology Symposium 2011*, 87–91. Dar es Salaam: University of Dar es Salaam.

Thram, Diane. 2014. "The Legacy of Music Archives in Historical Ethnomusicology: A Model for Engaged Ethnomusicology." In *Theory and Method in Historical Ethnomusicology*, edited by D. Hebert and J. McCollum, 283–310. Lexington, KY: Rowman and Littlefield.

Thram, Diane. 2015a. "Challenges Facing African Music Archives." MusicinAfrica portal. September 15, 2015. http://musicinafrica.net/challenges-facing-african-music-archives; translated to French: http://musicinafrica.net/les-d%C3%A9fis-auxquels-font-face-les-archives-de-musique-africaine.

Thram, Diane. 2015b. "Performing the Archive: Repatriation of Digital Heritage and the ILAM Music Heritage Project SA." In *African Musics in Context Institutions, Culture, Identity*, edited by T. Solomon, 67–85. Kampala, Uganda: Fountain.

Titon, Jeff Todd. 2009. "Music and Sustainability: An Ecological Viewpoint." *World of Music* 51 (1): 119–137.

Titon, Jeff Todd. 2011. "The Curry Lecture: Applied Ethnomusicology." sustainablemusic.blogspot.co.uk/search?updated-min=2011-01-01T00:00:00-05:00&updated-max=2012-01-01T00:00:00-05:00&max-results=20 (accessed October 16, 2016).

Topp-Fargion, Janet. 2009. "'For My Own Research Purposes': Examining Ethnomusicology Field Methods for a Sustainable Music." *World of Music* 51 (1): 75–93.

Topp-Fargion, Janet. 2012. "Connecting with Communities: Building Sustainable Models for Audiovisual Archiving into the Future." In *Ethnomusicology in East Africa: Perspectives from Uganda and Beyond*, edited by Sylvia Nannyonga-Tamusuza and Thomas Solomon, 49–59. Kampala, Uganda: Fountain.

Tracey, Hugh. 1933. "Shona Music: Carnegie Research 1932–33." Unpublished typescript. ILAM.

Tracey, Hugh. 1948. *Chopi Musicians: Their Music, Poetry, and Instruments*. London: Oxford University Press.

Tracey, Hugh. 1950. Unpublished field journal, 1950 recording excursion to Kenya.

Tracey, Hugh. 1969. *African Music Codification and Textbook Project: A Primer of Practical Suggestions for Field Research*. With Gerhard Kubik and Andrew Tracey. Roodeport, South Africa: International Library of African Music.

Tracey, Hugh. 1973. "Introduction." In *Catalogue the Sound of Africa Series*. Vol 1. Roodeport, South Africa: International Library of African Music.

Vallier, John. 2010. "Sound Archiving Close to Home: Why Community Partnerships Matter." *Notes* 67 (1): 39–49.

White, Luise. 2000. *Speaking with Vampires: Rumor and History in Colonial Africa*. Oakland: University of California Press.

CHAPTER 4

··

RETHINKING REPATRIATION AND CURATION IN NEWFOUNDLAND
Archives, Angst, and Opportunity

··

BEVERLEY DIAMOND AND JANICE ESTHER TULK

THIS chapter reflects on a series of repatriation projects that the Research Centre for Music, Media, and Place (MMaP) at Memorial University undertook since 2003 in Canada's easternmost province, Newfoundland and Labrador, a place that has long been recognized for its vibrant Anglo-Irish oral traditions but less known for Indigenous songs and stories. Since 2004, MMaP has been producing archival CDs in a series titled "Back on Track." The series aims to recover historically and culturally significant documents for public use; augment cultural content in the schools; promote and disseminate the culture of the province and beyond to local, national, and international audiences; stimulate new artistic work that builds on earlier traditions; and contribute to policy development relating to cultural diversity. Indigenous content was a priority for us, both because of our personal research interest and because of the relative neglect of Indigenous audio sources prior to our series. Overall, our challenge was to consider how any archival project that sought to bring back music from the past constructed a present and future relationship to that past. Before describing how these projects enacted different aims in relation to that overall challenge, to processes of collaboration, and to strategies of representation, we situate our work in relation to the concept of repatriation. We[1] then describe cogent issues that emerged in the production of the series with a more specific focus on one case study.

The concept of "repatriation" is both multivalent and culturally diverse in its application. The term was first used to describe the return of prisoners of war to their homelands and has also described the movement of valuable property, artwork, documents,[2] or money back to their country of origin. The return of human remains to their families/communities and nations is an important form of repatriation.[3] The "patria" of "repatriation"—the homeland—is common to the various applications although such initiatives (certainly most of those in ethnomusicology) are often more locally focused. Each of these has an element of "reparation" for theft or past (usually violent) wrongdoing.[4] For this reason, repatriation is most often used in North America and by international organizations such as UNESCO to describe initiatives to return human remains in museums or other institutional collections, as well as objects and cultural knowledge (intangible cultural heritage) to Indigenous people from whom these things were stolen in the context of colonization. Here the valence of "patria" has connotations of Indigenous sovereignty and self-governance.

The Memorial University Folklore and Language Archive (MUNFLA), which houses much of the material that we work with in the projects described here, was established by the American folklorist Herbert Halpert, who engaged both colleagues and students in collecting the rich oral and physical creative culture of rural people in the province. Of course, this pattern of "mining" the premodern regions for their lore is congruent with the practices of colonialism that underpin the early history of many academic enterprises. A crucial question raised by our projects is whether our broader application of the concept of "repatriation" obfuscates the very specific genocidal institutions such as residential schools and racist attitudes inflicted on Inuit and First Nations people, or whether the broadening of repatriation to include marginalized settler communities actually serves to nuance the inequities of colonialism in productive ways.

In ethnomusicology, the use of the term "repatriation" has become increasingly prevalent in the twenty-first century. Earlier projects that are clearly repatriation in nature if not in name, such as the Library of Congress's Federal Cylinder Project initiated in 1979, are often described as "preservation" initiatives (see Gray and Lee 1985). To our knowledge, most audio recording repatriation has involved Indigenous material. A number of projects have had a high profile at conferences and in print publications (including the current Handbook, of course).[5] Australia has been far ahead in its longstanding mission to return archival recordings to Aboriginal and Torres Strait Islander communities as Barwick, Marett, and Simpson (2003) have described and in articulating the urgent need for this activity, particularly since the 2002 Garma Statement on Indigenous Music and Dance (www.aboriginalartists.com.au/NRP_statement.htm). The motivations to repatriate traditional Indigenous knowledge and culture are most often described in terms of cultural sustainability (or "re-animation," as Aaron A. Fox describes it), human rights, and Indigenous resurgence. While these are laudatory aims, it is important to consider, as Treloyn and Charles (forthcoming) have honestly and thoroughly discussed, how the weight of colonial violence remains in the process of negotiation, making this a "discomfort zone." They write, "It is the experience of many that *something is* taken when a song is recorded and when that recording is transported away. This concern is not remedied by simply ensuring that communities have access to the end products of research" (2015, Ms). Those most heavily involved in repatriation initiatives are undoubtedly museums and archives, but universities are among the institutions engaged in the processes as well.

The projects described in this chapter differ in at least two ways from most other repatriation initiatives. First, we extend the concept of repatriation beyond Indigenous people to settler communities that also experienced colonialism, albeit differently.[6] In part, our projects recognize contexts where the Indigenous/settler distinction is not clear. In some communities, such as Makkovik, where we produced a community history in sound, most residents have both Inuit and European ancestry. While many mixed-descent citizens in Labrador are now affiliating with the Métis, who are recognized in Canada as Aboriginal, this is a recent shift in self-identification. In part, our projects explore how Indigenous and settler musicians have both contributed to certain musical genres, such as hymns, or fiddle and accordion music. Some Coastal Labrador Inuit, for instance, embrace Moravian hymnody as theirs and they have indeed composed repertoire in the style and Indigenized the performance practice. Our Canada-wide project on fiddle and accordion repertoires, discussed later, includes a substantial proportion of Aboriginal tracks, again complicating any tendency to map genre onto inventions of "racial" categories. While the institutionalized racism[7] that Indigenous people experience has been undoubtedly more profoundly injurious than any "inequity" experienced by settlers, we suggest that an extension of the idea of repatriation may actually highlight and nuance these different forms of colonialism and stylistically distinct (though generically similar) performance practices, rather than eliding them or implying assimilation.

A second way our project differs from many repatriation initiatives is in its intentional blurring of the lines between repatriation and curation. Unlike projects where entire collections of recordings have been returned to their communities of origin, ours focuses on smaller corpuses of material in order to produce commodities that might circulate more widely than archivally repatriated sources. The selections of what to include on our CDs were generally made by university specialists sometimes (but not always) in consultation with practitioners and community representatives. Once selections were made, extensive interaction with the collectors, singers, composers, and/or their descendants enabled rich reconstructions of historical contexts, social practices, and individual experiences that related to the music. In most cases, then, the "curation" process involved a "repatriation" of memory—lost histories and intergenerational resonances—that simply returning old recordings might not accomplish. We suggest that repatriation of recorded sound without repatriation of the histories that are preserved only in the oral tradition or in silent memories is partial and incomplete. Again, of course, the blurring of the lines between repatriation and curation raises questions about the construction of memory across time and the potential of new (but unacknowledged) agendas that shape that memory.

THE GLOBAL CONTEXT

In the late twentieth and early twenty-first centuries, audio and video recording has become a realm of both angst and opportunity for a variety of reasons. Archivists, culture-bearers, scholars, and other individuals are aware of the fragility of old recordings, the shelf life of which, as Anthony Seeger has noted, is far less than that of human memory. Fragility, in itself, however, did not produce the groundswell of interest in archival materials that we have seen in the digital era. Within the academy in the past decade, Ronda Sewald's (2005) call for more attention to historic recordings, arguing that they had too long been "scorn[ed] . . . as impossibly encumbered with the baggage of colonialism," paralleled increased attention to history (as seen by the creation of a Special Interest Group on Historical Ethnomusicology within the Society for Ethnomusicology) and to technological mediation. The digital era with its infinite capacity for reproducibility stimulated new types of research, more collaborative styles of research relationships (see Seeger 2004), and a rapid increase in repatriation initiatives. Communities worldwide have learned where their heritage collections are housed, and this has understandably created an expectation that materials should be returned to their original locales. Academics have, by and large, embraced the importance of returning resources to communities in which they were created and collaborating with knowledgeable culture-bearers to identify, correct, and expand documentation. While the "recirculation" of audio materials is not without certain challenges, particularly in the realm of intellectual property, where such matters as group ownership and moral rights have taken a prominent role in public discussion and policy considerations of UNESCO and the World Intellectual Property Organization (WIPO), the advantages of access seem often to trump some of the problems of appropriation. Of course, digitization also offers hope for audio recordings at risk as digital copies may be, if not more permanent, at least more easily transferable to changing formats.

Repatriation has, in turn, led to renewed interest in the preservation of public memory. Compilations such as Seeger and Chaudhuri's *Archives for the Future: Global Perspectives on Audiovisual Archives in the 21st Century* (2004), or the recent *Ethnomusicology Forum* issue "Ethnomusicology, Archives and Communities: Methodologies for an Equitable Discipline" (2012), document the impact of what is now often called "proactive archiving" (Landau and Topp Fargion 2012, 126). The projects described in the following sections are proactive in that they explicitly seek to stimulate memories and discussion and to facilitate the reentry of music into active performance repertoires. We are aware, however, as Paul Connerton argues in *How Modernity Forgets* (2009), that ease of access to information often goes hand in hand with less emphasis on the embodiment of memory, either individually or socially.

REPATRIATION AT THE RESEARCH CENTRE FOR MUSIC, MEDIA, AND PLACE (BD)

The specific projects that we describe here emerged from a commitment to community engagement by the MMaP, which Beverley Diamond established as a Canada Research

Chair[8] in Ethnomusicology at Memorial University of Newfoundland (MUN) in 2003. This commitment was consistent with the mandate of the university itself, which, unlike most other North American institutions, was chartered to respect the "special obligation" it has to the people of Newfoundland and Labrador. The establishment of other MUN units such as the Leslie Harris Centre of Regional Policy Development (Harris Centre) and the Office of Public Engagement are also consistent with this charge.[9] More specifically, MMaP staff were repeatedly told by community members, some of whom served on a community advisory group or the executive committee of the MMaP, that they wanted easier access to the extensive audio recordings (more than 40,000) of the Memorial University of Newfoundland Folklore and Language Archive.[10] We decided, then, that website projects, the creation of a digital database for the archive's well-annotated "Song Title Index," and an archival CD series were high priorities.[11] With no designated project funding from the university, we had to apply regularly to a wide variety of sources[12] to keep the initiatives going. Graduate student assistantships for community collaborations were relatively easy to obtain, and these served simultaneously to support students in our graduate program and give them professional experience while cementing relationships with a number of community organizations who cosponsored some of the assistantships.

The biggest website project (see Diamond 2007 for further information), to date, was the presentation of the American folklorist MacEdward Leach's Newfoundland collections from 1950 and 1951, the earliest audio recording collections (along with those of Kenneth Peacock) made in the province. The site has more than six hundred audio tracks, full song texts as presented by the collector,[13] song notes, biographies of singers, and brief community descriptions as well as a biography of Leach and a reprint of a significant article on the history of collecting in Newfoundland by the folklorist Peter Narváez. The impact of the site has been uniformly positive. Among the dozens of e-mails we have received, we particularly enjoy those that describe happy memories of earlier generations or thank us for enabling younger generations to hear the voice of a grandfather they never knew. Both teachers and singers report searching for repertoire or song histories. A redesign and overhaul of the site (www.mun.ca/folklore/leach) was being planned in 2017. A website on the Songs of Placentia Bay was launched in 2015 as a collaboration between the Town of Placentia, the Placentia Historical Society, and MMaP. The Placentia partners initiated the project as a complement to an exhibition on singers (or their descendants) who were resettled from islands in Conception Bay in the 1960s and their songs.

The CD projects were, at first, research center initiatives, but as time went on, they were sometimes initiated by community organizations/individuals (like the Placentia website project) who approached MMaP requesting collaboration. While each CD project was shaped uniquely both by its subject matter and by the nature of community involvement, all of the series items were created with some shared principles: (1) Each one was intended to stimulate public discussion about a topic that we deemed to be of mutual interest to academics, artists, and audiences. (2) While song notes were created, as with any CD project, the culture-bearers were given special attention, since the biographies of amateur performers are so often missing in CD liner notes about "folk music," even in contexts such as Newfoundland, where composers are carefully recognized in traditional performance contexts and where performance lineages are often acknowledged in live contexts as well. (3) In an attempt to convey social context as well as the diversity of expressive genres, we chose, in some cases, to include both spoken word and musical performance, although the latter predominates. (4) The documentation should exceed the extent and depth of CD liner notes. As a result the "booklets" that accompany each CD range from 40 to 160 pages. The series[14] consists of the following eight volumes published to date, with one more in production:

> *"It's Time for Another One": Folksongs from the South Coast of Newfoundland.* Traditional songs from the communities of Ramea and Grole, collected in the 1960s by Jesse Fudge. Produced by Beverley Diamond in collaboration with Jesse Fudge. 2004.

> *Newfoundland & Labrador Folklore: A Sampler of Songs, Narrations, and Tunes.* Selection of noteworthy items from the MUNFLA collection, made by folklore students supervised by Peter Narváez. Produced by Peter Narváez. 2005.

> *Saturday Nite Jamboree.* Two radio broadcasts from a program of historic significance in the late 1960s, brought to MMaP by a community member. Produced by Neil Rosenberg. 2007.

> *Welta'q—"It Sounds Good": Historic Recordings of the Mi'kmaq.* Recordings from archives and personal collections across Canada. Produced by Janice Esther Tulk. 2009.

> *From the Big Land: Music of Makkovik Featuring Gerald Mitchell.* Both old and new recordings from archival and out-of-print sources. Initiated by Makkovik resident Joan Andersen. Produced by Beverley Diamond in collaboration with Labrador advisors Joan Andersen, Tim Borlase, Martha MacDonald, and Gary Mitchell, 2011.

> *Bellows and Bows: Historic Recordings of Traditional Fiddle & Accordion Music from across Canada.* Double CD set with 160-page book. Produced by Sherry Johnson in collaboration with regional, community-based advisors. 2012.

> *Soufflets et archets: Enregistrements historiques de musique traditionelle pour violon et accordéon du Canada.* Double CD set with 160-page book. Produced by Sherry Johnson; translation by Luc Journe. 2014.

> *Mentioned in Song: Song Traditions of the Loggers of Newfoundland and Labrador.* Produced by Ursula Kelly. 2015.

A forthcoming volume will present the Moravian-taught music in Inuit communities in Labrador.

The *Welta'q* CD is discussed in detail by the producer Janice Esther Tulk in the second part of this chapter. First, Diamond offers some further comments on various forms of community collaboration; on our approach to what Jason Stanyek (2010) has labeled the "intermundane" worlds of voices past and voices present; and on our attempts to stimulate crosstalk between academics, artists, and audiences by challenging some prevalent narratives about Newfoundland and Labrador culture.

While community collaboration is assumed to be positive, our MMaP experience indicates that there are many kinds of collaboration, and issues are neither simple, straightforward, nor inevitably benign. There is a two-way learning curve for both researchers and community members. When our "Back on Track" series was initiated, there was a "wait and see" attitude within some communities, rooted in a long history of what was perceived in some instances as university intransigence[15] or even exploitation. We were reminded on several occasions that the material in our university archives had been given by the people of the province to the university. This language of the "gift," then, clearly indicated a relationship that had reciprocal responsibilities. One prominent traditional singer observed that "they" would let me know if I screwed up. While I had "returned" copies of research materials to communities in the past, there was a difference here because the relationship, albeit with a "come-from-away,"[16] was long-term and live-in. Furthermore, while earlier initiatives had involved copying recordings for individuals or schools, the current projects included professional multimedia production with legal implications as well as sales that generated a modest amount of revenue. Arrangements for the revenue varied. In all cases, we paid a fee to singers or their descendants (as well as the legal copyright holders where we could find them) that was equivalent to a mechanical rights fee, since we were licensing individual tracks from either archival or rare and out-of-print commercial sources. In this way, as in a number of related repatriation initiatives,[17] we wished to extend the principles of copyright to oral tradition bearers, in addition to the collectors who had fixed, and hence legally owned, the recordings. In instances where the project was initiated by MMaP, the remainder of the revenue was used for subsequent productions, but in instances where community members proposed a project to us or were more directly involved (as in the case of *Welta'q* described later, or *From the Big Land*, the first project initiated by a community) other revenue-sharing arrangements were agreed on. Experience taught us that it was wise to state in our agreement letters that we were not seeking copyright but rather asking permission to license audio.

Collaboration took many forms, some more incidental and some more direct. In the course of contacting families for permission to use tracks, we inevitably attempted to verify information and, as a result, gathered richer layers of documentation, photographs, written stories of song composition, and information about new generations of tradition bearers. For some projects, we sought specific expertise; the booklet for *Saturday Nite Jamboree*, for instance, includes a history of early radio in Newfoundland and Labrador, authored by the producer Neil Rosenberg, who interviewed several participants from some of those broadcasts in the 1950s and 1960s in the course of research for the CD booklet. Tulk describes specific expertise for the Mi'kmaw CD *Welta'q*.

From the Big Land was initiated by Joan Andersen, director of the White Elephant Museum in the coastal Labrador community of Makkovik, who approached us about collaboration. She participated energetically in the documentation of the community's history, interviewing elders and some youth, soliciting photographs, and compiling all the data she gathered for display in the local museum. Diamond made two trips to Labrador, one to meet with the Labrador advisors who knew the region much better than she, and one to work with Anderson on some of the local interviews and data gathering. We also hosted Makkovik musicians in St. John's in order to record new tracks at the request of featured performer Gerald Mitchell, and commissioned a Labrador studio to make one further new recording of a Gerald Mitchell composition sung by his nephew and grand-niece. Deciding the scope of the Makkovik project involved negotiation. While the community initially wanted simply to honor Gerald Mitchell, the earliest commercially recorded singer from Labrador, who is now in his late seventies, I was eager to draw on other rich collections[18] of traditional song. We included very little archival audio (two tracks) on the CD, but the booklet does reflect MMaP's interest in a broader approach to the history of music in this small community, a history that was marked by many social upheavals in the course of the twentieth century, events that were described vividly by interviewees and cited in the booklet.

The final CD in the series, concerning the logging industry in the province, demonstrates how song *is* history. *Mentioned in Song* was initiated by Ursula Kelly (the daughter of a logger, now a professor of education and cultural studies), who found a wealth of previously unknown songs that document changes in the logging and paper-making industries, unionization, tragic accidents and fires, the hitherto neglected roles of women ("lumberjills") and Indigenous loggers, and the contribution of Newfoundland and Labrador loggers to the World War II effort in Europe. The CD was introduced to various communities with a semidramatized performance of prose/poetry readings from diaries or other sources authored by loggers as well as contemporary live performances of some of the songs. The project has resonated deeply with local communities and generated requests for other projects that unearth the folklore of other nonseafaring (or partially seafaring) occupations that have had little attention hitherto.

The largest nationwide project to date, *Bellows and Bows*, involved area experts. While the producer Sherry Johnson is well informed about Canadian fiddle traditions throughout most of the country, she felt that certain regions including the far north and various ethnocultural communities required close community knowledge. Furthermore, we agreed that this double album should present not necessarily the nationally renowned performers but those who were locally esteemed though not always well known beyond their communities. We secured funding to offer an honorarium to regional experts (generally one per province) to help with the selection of recordings and to write notes about tunes and performers for their area. Many of them, in turn, relied on community members for detailed information, fact verification, and so forth. We also turned to scholars of specific ethnocultural communities (in particular Métis, Polish, and Ukrainian) for further assistance and track suggestions. The result is a compendium that could only have been created with teamwork. We insisted that this "national" project had to be bilingual, a commitment that involved further fundraising for the translation of the book (and a year's delay in the publication of the French edition).

One strategy that MMaP developed,[19] albeit initially without a deep awareness of the historical nuances, was to bring past and present voices together, at times by engineering an arrangement involving archival audio and newly recorded material, and at other times, by juxtaposing both old and new sources on a CD by commissioning new performances that rearticulate old repertoires for new contexts. At one level this strategy insists on a history that is layered and diverse and valorizes both the earlier voices and the contemporary ones. Jason Stanyek and Benjamin Piekut's theorization of the capacity that audio recording has for presenting a commingling of past and present pertains. They describe audio recordings that are "intermundane" (between the worlds of the dead and the living) as "a mutually effective co-laboring" (2010, 14). While MMaP's archival initiatives are hardly like the 1991 Grammy-winning performance of "Unforgettable" by Natalie and a virtual Nat Cole about which they write, our combination of past and present voices also raises questions about "the poetics of modern bereavement" and "the interanimations of voice, body, and identity" (17). What resonated strongly with our work was their observation that the juxtaposition of dead and alive defies any ascription of certainty about "a direction of temporal flows" and insists that "being recorded means being enrolled in futures (and pasts) that one cannot wholly predict nor control" (18). Certainly, Robert Childs would never have predicted that his voice would be pitch-matched with Pamela Morgan's and complemented by Graham Wells's accordion riffs on our first CD, or even more radically and controversially, that Gordon Kendall's ballad would be layered with electronic sounds, excerpts of political speeches, or rap delivery in what is effectively a new composition by Glen Collins and Monique Tobin. On the other hand, Gerald Mitchell was well aware that he was alive at two different points in history when we produced the CD *From the Big Land*. His youthful voice on some tracks, replicated from his LP recorded in the early 1970s, contrasts markedly with his aging voice on several newly recorded tracks. He was a bit shocked when he first heard the latter. However, this vivid aural representation of time enlivens his "identity" in a new way, making audible his long life in Labrador. The sounding of the passage of time complements and animates the memories of his earliest days on the American army base in Goose Bay, his drawings for the local magazine *Them Days*, and the DIY processes of making a recording in Labrador over three decades earlier, all experiences described in the CD booklet. In other instances, the contrasts between past and present are less explicit, but they still evoke thoughtful reappraisal of relationality. What does it mean, on *Bellows and Bows*, that fiddlers from an earlier generation who are no longer living sit next to the newest compositions of an Inuk in Nunavut, or that the back rooms of fiddle contests and parlor performances sit side by side with studio-made tracks? What does it mean, on *Welta'q*, that a traditional Mi'kmaw *ko'jua* dance could be adapted as a fiddle tune? The past has always "leaked" into the present, but our reflection on the "co-laboring of living and dead" (27) is particularly apt for understanding the potential impact of proactive archival reissues.

I return, however, to the challenge of generating discussion among academics, artists, and audiences, a challenge that was central to MMaP's repatriation vision, and one that could be only partially realized by the explicit juxtaposition of past and present performances on the CDs. Here the accompanying booklets were key. The text of each attempted to raise new issues or recast old ones. The first CD (*It's Time for Another One*) took on the very old issue of what might be the same or different about traditional rural and modern urban performance styles and aesthetics. While "covers" are old news, the newly commissioned performances on that CD were complemented by interviews about *why* the "modern" performances were done the way they were. For Jim Payne, a simple retelling of the story was still modern, albeit with a vocal style informed by contemporary "folk" traditions and a guitar retuning appropriate for large public venues. For Pamela Morgan, "modern" was continuity and dialogue with the past, a continuation of the participatory ethos of small outport communities perhaps. She used digital technology to pitch-match her voice with that of the older singer Robert Childs and added Irish-tinged accordion playing (by Graham Wells) to recast the old tune. For Glen Collins, the modern was a stark contrast where electronics and rap and old news clips came together with the voice of a singer from fifty years ago to constitute a deep reflection on the implications of social change, offered with respect to the past but without compromise.

On *Newfoundland & Labrador Folklore*, Peter Narváez challenged the perceived uniformity of Newfoundland "tradition" by including repertoire that reflected popular music and immigrant influences, including post–World War II American popular music. Rosenberg emphasizes the interpenetrations of tradition and media in the earliest generation of country musicians who performed weekly on *Saturday Nite Jamboree*. On *Welta'q*, Tulk implicitly raises issues about the silences of colonial history, the import of hymns in the Mi'kmaw language, and the influences of media in isolated communities. She alludes to these and discusses other issues in the case study below. Similarly, the history of Makkovik reflects how music was a response to quite extreme social changes, including military installations and the forced removal of Inuit from further north to a community stressed for housing and space. Earlier histories had emphasized the animosity between Inuit and settler there, but, relative to earlier studies of the community, our research found a more reflective attitude and more stories about how music functioned as a form of mediation in Makkovik. Diversity returns as a central theme in Sherry Johnson's book for *Bellows and Bows*. She questions gender inequities and demonstrates how fiddling served many communities not simply in their social life but also in their presentation of distinctive ethnic identities. In the broader scope of ethnomusicology, none of these "narratives" are surprising or innovative, but in the cultural discourses of Newfoundland and Labrador, they have played a role in opening conversation about cultural futures in dialogue with very rich cultural pasts.

REPATRIATING FIELD RECORDINGS FOR EDUCATIONAL USE: THE STORY OF *WELTA'Q* (JET)

The Mi'kmaq are a First Nations people whose traditional territory encompasses Nova Scotia, Prince Edward Island, New Brunswick, the Gaspé Peninsula of Quebec, and parts of Newfoundland in Canada, as well as northern Maine in the United States of America. They were among the first Indigenous peoples in Canada to experience co-lonial encounter due to their location in the northeast and entered into treaties with the British in the 1600s and 1700s. As a result, there has been a significant impact on traditional practices and knowledges. Many Mi'kmaq-specific traditions are in de-cline or have been lost, often replaced by localized forms of intertribal traditions such as powwow (Tulk 2008, 2012). Not surprisingly, then, throughout my research with Mi'kmaw singers between 2002 and 2008, I was repeatedly asked whether I knew of any recordings that could be shared to help revive and revitalize cultural expressions, particularly on the island of Newfoundland. Equally strong was the desire for educa-tional materials that could be used in schools. While I responded to each request as best I could, directing individuals to resources and contacts, it was not until 2007 that I was able to address their concerns in a meaningful way. That year, I became the first project coordinator for the MMaP at Memorial University. I was given the opportunity to pro-duce a regional CD devoted to music of the Mi'kmaq.

The reflections that follow highlight the processes of consultation and negotiation that led to the production of Welta'q. While I provide an overview of a variety of challenges encountered in the project, such as locating the next-of-kin of deceased singers and securing permission from families, collectors, and institutions to include selections, I also describe issues that emerged as a result of the desire to "go beyond" repatriation to create an educational resource that would serve both the Mi'kmaw community and the non-Aboriginal communities that surround them. In particular, I engage with issues of textual and musical transcription, choice of orthography, and translation. In so doing, I illuminate the benefits and challenges of mobilizing our research for the communities with whom we work, as well as the role of technology in revitalizing and sustaining Aboriginal cultures and languages while creating culturally sensitive and appropriate content for use in classrooms.

Selecting Content That "Sounds Good"

Welta'q—"It Sounds Good": Historic Recordings of the Mi'kmaq (2009) brings together twenty-four tracks of music and storytelling drawn from archives and personal research collections across Canada. The extensive notes that contextualize each selection are informed by seven years of archival and ethnographic research in and with Mi'kmaw communities throughout the Atlantic provinces. The CD is accompanied by a sixty-page booklet that, in addition to liner notes, includes textual and musical transcriptions of the songs, translations of Mi'kmaw texts, discussion of Mi'kmaw musical instruments and dance styles, and a selected discography for further research. Featuring artwork by the artist Jerry Evans, a Mi'kmaw from central Newfoundland now living in St. John's, this CD is designed to help disseminate, promote, and recognize Mi'kmaw culture.

With funding from the Leslie Harris Centre of Regional Policy and Development at Memorial University and ethics approval from Mi'kmaw Ethics Watch at Cape Breton

University, I began the process of identifying recordings in institutions and private collections across Canada for possible inclusion on the CD. In each case, it was necessary to assess the quality of the recording, its appropriateness for the project, and its availability. Recordings housed at the Beaton Institute (Cape Breton University), the Centre d'études acadiennes (Université de Moncton), the Canadian Museum of History (Ottawa), MUNFLA (Memorial University of Newfoundland), and MMaP (Memorial University of Newfoundland) were reviewed to produce a master list of potential tracks.[20] Within these collections were recordings made by important ethnographers working in Mi'kmaw territory, such as Helen Creighton and Franziska von Rosen, as well as student ethnographers and public radio hosts such as Bill Doyle and Wendy O'Connor.

Because I wanted the CD to represent the various experiences and genres of Mi'kmaw music, I employed a broad notion of what might be included, such as traditional music, powwow music, hymn-singing, fiddle music, anthems, occupational songs, and family music. Further, given that the Mi'kmaw term most often heard in relation to music— welta'q—actually means "it sounds good" and can apply to a variety of expressive culture, including storytelling, I was open to spoken-word selections as well.

Along with a broad representation of musical and spoken-word genres, there was an effort to highlight the cultural contributions of important tradition bearers. Among them were Sarah Denny, who led the revitalization of traditional Mi'kmaw songs in Eskasoni; Lee Cremo, who was an accomplished fiddler recognized as "Best Bow Arm in the World"; and the Birch Creek Singers, who brought the big drum and powwow repertoire to Mi'kmaw territory (the history is much more recent than that of powwow traditions described in Ellis, Lassiter, and Dunham 2005). The only limitation we imposed from the beginning was that the project should not compete with those of contemporary Mi'kmaw musicians, so recordings that were already commercially available or being rereleased by Mi'kmaw recording studios were not included in the compilation. For example, we chose not to include recordings of George Paul (Red Bank, New Brunswick) and particularly his Mi'kmaw Honour Song, because he produces his own CDs, which are available for purchase throughout Mi'kma'ki. This decision is by no means a reflection on his importance as a tradition bearer.

Finally, in keeping with previous practices in the "Back on Track" series, contemporary recordings were considered for inclusion on the CD. When research demonstrated that there are no archival recordings of Mi'kmaw flute, we commissioned a new flute recording by Paul Pike[21] to complement the narrative of Mi'kmwesu, a flute-playing trickster in Mi'kmaw culture. We also added a newly recorded intertribal song by the Friendship Centre Drum Group (First Light Centre) to the selections under consideration, as it might demonstrate current music-making practices of Aboriginal peoples in urban areas.

Once this tentative track list was assembled, I began collecting new information on each recording, identifying the social, cultural, and historical context for as many as possible. I also located supporting illustrative materials, such as photographs and a map, with the help of the MMaP team. Given the educational goals of the series, it was important to ensure that such materials would be available for the various tracks under consideration. I then consulted with research participants about what should be included and music teachers about how materials should be presented to be useful in a classroom setting. I presented the project at an international colloquium on Indigenous intellectual property,[22] gaining valuable insight from attendees who were also practitioners or producers of similar ethnographic initiatives, and in a graduate-level music education class, benefiting from the practical experience of the music educators in the class.[23] I also had conversations with Lindsay Marshall (Chapel Island), then principal of Mi'kmaq College Institute at Cape Breton University, and Stephen Augustine (Elsipogtog), then curator of ethnology at the Museum of Civilization and now dean of Unama'ki College[24] at Cape Breton University. In particular, the input of the music educator Brenda Jeddore, who has taught in Conne River for her entire career, was invaluable for understanding how various selections would intersect with curriculum outcomes in music, social studies, and religion.

Permissions

Once the track list was finalized, it was necessary to obtain the appropriate permissions to include selections on *Welta'q*. Of course, there were challenges with the availability of some of the recordings identified for inclusion. For example, some archival collections are closed for preservation purposes while deteriorating magnetic tape awaits digitization. This situation is exacerbated by the chronic underfunding of such institutions across Canada. Other challenges related to the original terms of use and restrictions related to recordings, which made some unavailable at the time of the project. These factors influenced the final track list and, indeed, three tracks were removed from the project in the final stages of production when an agreement could not be reached with one collector.

While the legal obligation for appropriate permissions was to collectors and institutions, ethically we felt it necessary to contact the singers or their next of kin to obtain permission. It was particularly challenging to locate families given that some recordings were poorly documented by the original collectors and that significant time had passed. In one case, we were seeking the next of kin of a singer recorded sixty-five years earlier. We relied on our network of consultants to locate individuals and obtain their mailing addresses and then sent letters requesting permission. Singers and/or their next of kin were provided with an honorarium and a copy of the CD once it became available. In one case, we discovered that the deceased performer had two families, so we sought the permission of both and provided honoraria to both. In the end, we located the families of all but one singer, Peter Michaels, who was recorded in Middleton, Nova Scotia, in 1956.

Archival Recordings as Educational Resources

To ensure the project could be used for its intended educational purposes, transcriptions and translations were necessary. We began with musical transcriptions. Initially, we created descriptive transcriptions, but we later realized that they were too complex for educational purposes given their complicated key signatures and rhythms. After much consideration, we made the decision to transpose the transcriptions where necessary to make them easier to read. Some of the complexities were also simplified. As a result, the transcriptions sometimes are more prescriptive in nature or serve as skeletons or guides to those using the collection. The greater challenges, however, were around the transcription and translation of the lyrics for songs and the story of Mi'kmwesu.

The first challenge was finding a translator willing to work on the project. One translator had prepared translations of similar recordings in the past and felt that there was no need for the recordings on *Welta'q* to be translated again. However, there are slight differences between versions of songs and particular performances of songs, and we wanted to represent exactly what was on our recordings (not the generally accepted version of a song). After several attempts, we found two Mi'kmaq-speakers who understood our concerns and were willing to work on the project.

Transcription was the first task. Representing Mi'kmaq in a written form is complicated by the existence and use of several different orthographies throughout Mi'kma'ki. While newer orthographies such as Smith-Francis have been developed, older orthographies such as Metallic, Rand, and Pacifique are still used throughout Mi'kma'ki. We selected Smith-Francis for two reasons: it was the orthography most familiar to our translators, and it was officially adopted by the Mi'kmaw Grand Council in 1982.

Once transcriptions of songs and the story of Mi'kmwesu were available, the task of translation began. Here there were challenges on a number of points. To begin with, Mi'kmaq is a verb-based language in which gendered pronouns do not exist. Some of the words contained in the transcriptions are archaic forms or no longer part of the living language, and could not be translated. Many vocables, which may have had semantic meaning in the past, are no longer translatable, but have meaning in performance through the emotion they convey (Francis, in Christmas 1980, 11–12). Further, our translators struggled with finding the happy medium between denotative and connotative meanings of words in an effort to create translations that would make sense. There were also very localized interpretations of particular lyrics by the translators living in Potlotek (Chapel Island), Nova Scotia. To ensure that the best translation possible was achieved, a third Mi'kmaq-speaker and educator located in Listuguj, Quebec, who was familiar with several orthographies and regional dialects, reviewed the translations and edited them for clarity and to ensure they conformed to the Smith-Francis orthography. We did not attempt to make "singable" translations. The meaning of some translations, particularly the religious hymns, remains veiled to some extent, as in "Ave Maria" (track 18). The connection of these lyrics to the Joyful Mysteries contemplated while reciting the Holy Rosary (Catholic faith) has only recently been made. Moreover, in some cases, culture-bearers using the collection have been able to clarify particular phrases and lines. For example, Stephen Augustine pointed out that the word for flute is a derivative of "root" that implies it is rotting away inside. He also made a connection to a Rand legend in which a piece of root sticking out of the ground makes a whistling sound as a result of the wind blowing (perhaps the origins of the flute). Of course, one of the challenges we face with a fixed medium like a CD and booklet is the inability to update documentation easily as more and more culture-bearers interact with content and increase the body of knowledge surrounding various selections.

The Legacy of Welta'q

Welta'q was launched at Memorial University in St. John's, Newfoundland on October 1, 2009—Mi'kmaq Treaty Day. Since then, over seven hundred copies have been sold. Proceeds from the sale of the CD were given to cultural organizations in the communities from which the recordings were drawn. Family members and consultants were invited to suggest recipient organizations, which included an elder's lodge, a powwow committee, a local school, a local choir, and the Mi'kmaq Resource Centre in Sydney, Nova Scotia. The organizations have been grateful for the revenue received, which has enabled further cultural engagement and revitalization in communities. For example, the family of Chief Peter Jeddore in Conne River asked that their share of the proceeds be given to the Se't Anewey First Nations Choir at St. Anne's School in Conne River. The money was used to purchase moccasins for the choir members' regalia. Since we were unable to locate the family of Peter Michaels, a share of the proceeds is donated to the Mi'kmaq Resource Centre at Cape Breton University. It is a repository of documents and materials related to Mi'kmaw history and culture, accessible to community members, students, and researchers (in person or via media), and funds were used to expand the resources available.

Welta'q, then, has made an impact in communities by providing financial resources for cultural revival and revitalization initiatives identified as important by community members themselves. Further, it has recovered recordings that are not easily accessed for community and public use by making them available on CD, providing much needed Nation-specific resources to augment education and further stimulate cultural production. It is anticipated that this collection will help to acknowledge and promote the many different musical expressions of the Mi'kmaq through time and space, tracing a musical record of culture from precontact to intercultural exchange and innovation. Further, it is hoped that *Welta'q* will celebrate and promote cultural diversity in Newfoundland, where the Mi'kmaw heritage of many has been hidden for decades. In many ways, this CD is a direct response to the province's call for the inclusion or augmentation of cultural content in the education system, which is seen to produce "creative, critical thinkers, students with a lifelong appreciation of the arts and heritage and citizens with a strong sense of cultural stewardship" (Newfoundland and Labrador 2006, 27). *Welta'q*, like other CDs in the "Back on Track" series, increases heritage content in schools and builds capacity through the increased availability of heritage resources.

CONCLUSION

The Internet, with its great potential for interactivity, will no doubt be a platform for other projects in the future. But even in the early twenty-first century, rural Newfoundland still has uneven and inadequate access to the Internet. Commodities may have more longevity in such contexts. While the "Back on Track" CD series will rapidly become a "period piece" as CDs are replaced by other forms of audio transmission, the extensive print documentation for the series (booklets ranging from 40 to 160 pages) may ensure future utility.

Unlike most repatriation initiatives, our projects were clearly curated. While this would seem to violate a fundamental principle of repatriation—namely, the provision of complete collections to communities with recognition that they should control the use of the material—our approach has had certain benefits. By searching many archives (as in the case of *Welta'q*, for instance), we enabled communities to know more about the locations in which their intangible cultural heritage resided. By consulting them about the choice of material to be published as well as the individual and social histories of specific songs, we involved communities in the decision-making and the production process. Most importantly, we managed to repatriate histories and personal memories as well as audio.

The question of expanding the concept of repatriation beyond Indigenous communities is more vexed. As the Garma Statement in Australia states, Indigenous music, dance, and ceremony are "the core of (Indigenous) culture," and "the foundation of personal and social well-being." The return of material that currently lives in archives is not simply a matter of justice but an urgent element of Indigenous recovery and resurgence.[25] Negotiations and preparations to return Indigenous material need to be conducted in each community context with care and commitment. Specific Indigenous repatriation initiatives, then, are of the utmost importance.

Our expansion of the term, on the other hand, acknowledges the mixing of culture (as well as bloodlines) and the contributions of Indigenous people to local industries as in the case of our logging song project and to specific musical genres, as in the case of fiddle and accordion music. These Indigenous as well as settler contributions have hitherto rarely been acknowledged or made public.

We do not discount the strong opinions of settler populations, however, that the university failed to give back the collections made in the name of folklore. We do not discount the economic marginality of all rural Newfoundlanders, not simply in earlier times, but even at present when, for instance, modern services are less available than in larger centers. The very trajectories of modernity defined both Indigenous and rural populations as premodern and enacted colonial violence.

For the time being, we know that our curatorial initiatives have successfully recirculated some parts of the rich oral traditions of Newfoundland and Labrador and have generated new performances and wider conversation.[26] Like all who undertake archiving projects, we reflected carefully on the processes and social implications of intervening in the creation of public memory. We were aware that the unique history of twentieth-century Newfoundland and Labrador has often shaped the stories that are told about its culture. The shifts in governance—from status as an independent nation to a return to a colonial position under a Commission of Government, and finally to its current position as a province within Canada—have given rise to spirited expressions of nationalism and independence at times. The economic roller coaster and hard life of a sea-bound people dependent on declining fish stocks, changing technologies, and increasingly global markets have similarly influenced expressive culture. Both the loss of their country and the loss of a way of life have been prevalent themes in the public and academic spheres. The narratives Newfoundlanders and Labradorians tell about themselves, however, are sometimes oversimplified into pre- and post-Confederation periods, divided by the contested joining with Canada in 1949, and represented by a simplistic binary of traditional and modern lifeways (Overton 1996). Traditional, honest rural life in the outports was romanticized, in particular, in the 1970s and 1980s[27] and increasingly seen to be "undermined by industrialization, the welfare state, urbanization and the introduction of North American values in the period since World War II" (Overton 1996, 49). Newfoundland nationalists often claimed traditional music as a mark of identity. One objective, particularly relevant for the *Welta'q* project that Tulk described earlier, but pertinent for all of the productions discussed in this chapter, was to trouble the homogeneity of such settler narratives by presenting Aboriginal history, including its colonial shaping and social relationality, as a significant dimension of the past, present, and future of Newfoundland and Labrador.

NOTES

1. Beverley Diamond writes about the issues relating to the series as a whole, while Janice Esther Tulk focuses on the *Welta'q* case study.
2. In Canada, for instance, the transfer of the British North America Act from Great Britain to the authority of the Government of Canada in 1982 is often described as repatriating the constitution, although it is more accurately "patriating" the constitution.
3. The US Native American Grave Protection and Repatriation Act (NAGPRA) is one of the most far-reaching programs to return bodies in museum and other institutional collections to be finally buried in the Indigenous communities to which they belong.
4. The most recent application of the term "repatriation" by Donald Trump to describe his initiative to bring industry and the finances they generate back to the United States differs in this respect.
5. The US Library of Congress's Federal Cylinder Project produced catalogs of Indigenous North American recordings and arranged for the return of material to a number of First Nations, often collaborating with communities to arrange for appropriate ceremony to

mark these returns (see Gray and Lee 1985). The ethnomusicology faculty at Columbia University have spearheaded repatriation initiatives in Alaska Inuit and Hopi communities (Fox 2014, 2015; Reed, this volume). Noel Loebley has led initiatives to return collections housed in the Pitt Rivers Museum (Oxford) to their homelands in various African countries. The Australian National Recording Project for Indigenous Performance builds on earlier (and continuing) repatriation initiatives by the Australian Institute of Aboriginal and Torres Strait Islander Studies (AITSIS) and the still active PARADISEC Project based at the University of Sydney. Stephen Wild, Linda Barwick, Allen Marrett, Aaron Corn, and Sally Treloyn are among the ethnomusicologists involved with these initiatives. See also Nannyonga-Tamusuza and Weintraub (2012) and Moon (2016). Online initiatives are proliferating throughout the world.

6. Newfoundland was a British colony (1583), then enjoyed responsible government (1907), then became a colony again when economic constraints demanded assistance by a British Commission of Government (1934), and finally a province of Canada (1949). For most of its history post-1949, when provincial status began, the province has been economically depressed, and lacking in many of the services enjoyed elsewhere.

7. The most widely known were the residential schools that assimilated and abused Indigenous children for more than a century and systematically attempted to destroy knowledge of Indigenous languages, spiritual traditions, and other cultural underpinnings.

8. The Canada Research Chairs program was established by the federal government in Canada and, although run by granting agencies, was funded independently. To hold one of these chairs was, to me, a significant ethical responsibility as well as an opportunity not simply to conduct my own research but also to engage in projects that benefit communities in the region of my university and in other regions where I work.

9. At the same time, I insisted that MMaP should engage nationally and internationally. Initiatives that brought international artists/scholars together were our organization of a symposium on Indigenous Music and Dance as Cultural Property: Global Perspectives, 2008, support for the North Atlantic Fiddle Convention meeting in Newfoundland in 2008, and hosting of the World Conference of the International Council for Traditional Music in St. John's in 2011.

10. The history of this significant archive has been described in Rosenberg (1991) and Fulton (2002).

11. In recent years, the MUN library's Digital Archives Initiative has posted the "Song Title Index" as well as some other audio collections.

12. The funding sources ranged from provincial (the J. R. Smallwood Foundation, the Harris Centre's Applied Research Fund, the Institute for Social and Economic Development) to national ones (the AV Preservation Trust, Canadian Heritage). Where collaborators had access to other university funds as in the case of producer Sherry Johnson for *Bellows and Bows*, we were grateful when the research funds could be complemented.

13. Regrettably not verified or corrected in some cases.

14. The series producer has been Beverley Diamond for each item except *Bellows and Bows*, on which Diamond and Kati Szego collaborated as series producer, and *Mentioned in Song*, for which Diamond and Meghan Forsyth were series producers. The job of the series producer has been to produce transcriptions, assist with the preparation of the booklet content, clear copyright, and contact families of performers. Volume producers have sometimes taken over the family contacts and transcription duties.

15. Many referenced the cancellation of a successful public outreach program known as "MUN Extension Services" that engaged communities in media and other projects between 1959 and 1991.
16. A local expression for anyone who is not born a Newfoundlander or Labradorian. Diamond is a "come-from-away," while Tulk is a Newfoundlander.
17. For example, the PARADISEC project at the University of Sydney, Australia.
18. Particularly the folklorist Kenneth Goldstein's collection of 1980.
19. Here Diamond takes responsibility because this strategy was not uniformly supported or received without controversy.
20. Though not an archive, MMaP does hold the extensive field recording collection of Beverley Diamond, as well as those recordings made by her collaborators on the SPINC project in the 1980s.
21. Pike is a Newfoundland Mi'kmaw musician who plays with the Alaska-based band Medicine Dream. See Tulk (2003, 2004).
22. Indigenous Music and Dance as Cultural Property: Global Perspectives in Toronto, Ontario, May 2–4, 2008, http://www.mun.ca/indigenousIP/.
23. Contexts of Music Education (Education 6502), taught by Dr. Andrea Rose and Ki Adams, Memorial University, St. John's, Newfoundland, October 11, 2008.
24. Mi'kmaq College Institute became Unama'ki College in 2010.
25. www.aboriginalartists.com.au/NRP_statement.htm.
26. Among the attention that the CD series received was a one-hour CBC interview in 2014 by host Jamie Fitzpatrick with Beverley Diamond on *The Performance Hour*.
27. These decades are sometimes described as the cultural "renaissance" in Newfoundland. See Gwyn (1976), Overton (2000).

References

Barwick, Linda, Allan Marett and Jane Simpson, eds. 2003. *Researchers, Communities, Institutions and Sound Recordings*. Sydney: University of Sydney Press.
Christmas, Ben. 1980. "Chants and Customs." *Cape Breton's Magazine* 25: 9–12. Transcribed and translated by Bernie Francis.
Diamond, Beverley. 2007. "Reconnecting: University Archives and the Communities of Newfoundland." In *Folk Music, Traditional Music, Ethnomusicology*, edited by Anna Hoefnagels and Gordon E. Smith, 3–12. Newcastle, UK: Cambridge Scholars.
Ellis, Clyde, Luke E. Lassiter, and Gary H. Dunham. 2005. *Powwow*. Lincoln: University of Nebraska Press.
Fox, Aaron A. 2014. "Repatriation as Re-Animation through Reciprocity." In *The Cambridge History of World Music*. Vol. 1 (North America), edited by P. Bohlman, 522–554. Cambridge: Cambridge University Press.
Fox, Aaron A. 2015. "The Archive of the Archive: The Ethics of Ownership and Repatriation of Indigenous Field Recordings." https://www.youtube.com/watch?v=VAJ5UJB3gGg (accessed January 21, 2017).
Fulton, Patricia. 2002. "The Memorial University, Folklore and Language Archive." 30 (1): 23–28.
Gwyn, Sandra. 1976. "The Newfoundland Renaissance." *Saturday Night* 91 (2): 38–45.

Landau, Carolyn, and Janet Topp Fargion. 2012. "We're All Archivists Now: Towards a More Equitable Ethnomusicology." *Ethnomusicology Forum* 21 (2): 125–140.

Moon, Jocelyn. 2016. "Uploading Matepe: Online Learning, Sustainability and Repatriation in Northeastern Zimbabwe." In *Applied Ethnomusicology in Institutional Policy and Practice*, edited by Klisala Harrison, 190–209. Helsinki: Helsinki Collegium for Advanced Studies.

Nannyonga-Tamusuza, Sylvia, and Andrew Weintraub. 2012. "The Audible Future: Reimagining the Role of Sound Archives and Sound Repatriation in Uganda." *Ethnomusicology* 56 (2): 206–233.

National Recording Project for Indigenous Performance. 2002. "Garma Statement on Indigenous Music and Dance." www.aboriginalartists.com.au/NRP_statement.htm.

Newfoundland and Labrador. 2006. *Creative Newfoundland and Labrador: The Blueprint for Development and Investment in Culture*. St. John's: Government of Newfoundland and Labrador.

Overton, James. 1996. *Making a World of Difference*. St. John's: ISER Books.

Overton, James. 2000. "Sparking a Cultural Revolution: Joey Smallwood, Farley Mowat, Harold Horwood and Newfoundland's Cultural Renaissance." *Newfoundland Studies* 16 (2): 166–204.

Rosenberg, Neil. 1991. "MUNFLA: A Newfoundland Resource for the Study of Folk Music." In *Studies in Newfoundland Folklore: Community and Process*, edited by Gerald Thomas and J. D. A. Widdowson, 154–165. St. John's: Breakwater Books.

Seeger, Anthony. 2004. "New Technology Requires New Collaborations: Changing Ourselves to Better Shape the Future." *Musicology Australia* 27 (1): 94–110.

Seeger, Anthony, and Shubha Chaudhuri, eds. 2004. *Archives for the Future: Global Perspectives on Audiovisual Archives in the 21st Century*. Calcutta: Seagull Books.

Sewald, Ronda L. 2005. "Sound Recordings and Ethnomusicology: Theoretical Barriers to the Use of Archival Collections." *Resound. A Quarterly of the Archives of Traditional Music* 24 (1–2): 1–11, 24, (3–4): 1–10.

Stanyek, Jason, and Benjamin Piekut. 2010. "Deadness: Technologies of the Intermundane." *Drama Review* 54 (1): 14–38.

Treloyn, Sally, and Rona Googinda Charles. Forthcoming. "Music Endangerment, Repatriation and Intercultural Collaboration in an Australian Discomfort Zone." In *Transforming Ethnomusicological Practice*, edited by Beverley Diamond and Salwa el Shawan Castelo Branco.

Tulk, Janice Esther. 2003. "Medicine Dream: Contemporary Native Music and Issues of Identity." MA thesis: University of Alberta.

Tulk, Janice Esther. 2004. "Awakening to Medicine Dream: Contemporary Native Music from Alaska with Newfoundland Roots." *Canadian Folk Music Bulletin* 38 (3): 1–10.

Tulk, Janice Esther. 2008. "'Our Strength Is Ourselves': Identity, Status, and Cultural Revitalization among the Mi'kmaq in Newfoundland." PhD diss., Memorial University of Newfoundland.

Tulk, Janice Esther. 2012. "Localizing Intertribal Traditions: The Powwow as Mi'kmaw Cultural Expression." In *Aboriginal Music in Contemporary Canada*, edited by Anna Hoefnagels and Beverley Diamond, 70–88. Montreal: McGill-Queen's University Press.

CHAPTER 5

REPATRIATING THE ALAN LOMAX HAITIAN RECORDINGS IN POST-QUAKE HAITI

GAGE AVERILL

INTRODUCTION

Ogou Fè
Ogou Badagri
Pa jodi mwen sou lanmè
M byen pre
M pasa rive!

Ogou Fè
Ogou Badagri[1]
We've been at sea so long [literally: it's not just today that I am at sea]
I am so near
[Yet] I cannot get there! [arrive]

THESE lyrics are from a song recorded in Carrefour Dufort, Haiti, in 1937 in the house of Gustav Tanice, whom we see in his doorway in the accompanying photograph (Figure 5.1). On the recording, Mr. Tanice can be heard singing the "call" line (or *voye*, i.e., "throw") with response lines (*ranmase*, "gather in") from the congregation. Recorded by the legendary American folklorist Alan Lomax, this song was figuratively at sea and in exile from Haiti for over seventy years, along with 1,500 other recordings stored on aluminum discs, six films, and accompanying ephemera, all gathered during Lomax's five-month "expedition" to Haiti in 1936–1937. The recordings had been held in the Archive of Folk Culture (AFC) at the Library of Congress. After these were rediscovered in 1999 by Todd Harvey, curator of the Alan Lomax Collection at the AFC, I was fortunate to

FIGURE 5.1 Gustav Tanice, photographed in the door of his house where he organized a Vodou ceremony for the deity Ezili during a visit by Alan and Elizabeth Lomax and Revolie Polinice.

Photograph courtesy of Elizabeth Lomax, courtesy of the Library of Congress
Archives of Folk Culture, Washington, DC.

have been asked by Alan Lomax's daughter, Anna Lomax Wood, an anthropologist and president of the Association for Cultural Equity (ACE), to curate, edit, and annotate these recordings for public consumption.[2]

I knew what an extraordinary project this was for the scholarship on Haitian music, but I was less clear about what it could mean for Haiti, for Haitians, and for Haitian music and culture to have these sounds—severed from their context of production for decades—return to Haiti and circulate freely again. But I did recognize that the voyage of this extraordinary collection of recordings away from and back to Haiti would raise important issues regarding the ethics, poetics, and the problematics of musical repatriation.

KATHERINE DUNHAM
AND THE DIGITAL *GOVI*

In 2003, only a few years after I had agreed to take on the project, I was asked to introduce the famed African American dancer Katherine Dunham at a program at the University of Chicago. She was going to speak about her property in Haiti, the Plantation Leclerc, which she had owned and stewarded for many decades.

Although Ms. Dunham had spent a year in Haiti in 1935–1936, preceding Alan Lomax by six months, and although she had participated in a Vodou temple or *peristil* in Pont Beudet, where Alan Lomax subsequently made many recordings, I had not thought to bring together these connections in my prepared remarks. Just a few minutes before I went onstage, however, in looking through files on my laptop, I realized I had over 200 recordings from Pont Beudet, many of which featured the friends that Ms. Dunham had written about with affection, including Manbo (priestess) Téoline Marseille and her friend Cecile Esperance and even Cecile's common-law American expatriate husband, the infamous Vodou initiate Doc Rieser. In fact, it could be said that I had in my possession a digital soundtrack of her year in Haiti.[3]

I walked over to Ms. Dunham where she sat backstage in her wheelchair, and I asked if she would mind if I played some of these recordings. She consented enthusiastically, having never heard them and expressing shock that they existed. I opened my talk, as I had planned, by singing a song whose opening line is "Na rive nan lakou-a" (we arrive in the courtyard/community), about the dearth of people with profound spiritual knowledge, people the song calls *granmoun*, or "great/revered people." I used the song to talk, in contrast, about the reverence in which Katherine Dunham is held in Haiti for her longtime dedication to Haitian culture, her *granmoun* status. After my introduction, I disregarded many of my prepared notes and commented instead on the overlap of Lomax's and Dunham's travels in Haiti, playing two recordings, the first being a song sung by Cecile and Théoline called "Mesyedanm Bonswa" ("Good Day Ladies and Gentlemen"). The second recording was of a ceremonial song called "Tiyèt Marsey, Na Gade Ounfò" ("Little Théoline Marseille, We Will Protect the Temple"). As she rose out of her wheelchair to stand at the podium, Ms. Dunham turned to me in tears, and said to me, and to the audience, pointing at my laptop computer: "You know young man, that's a *govi* you have there, a digital govi."

The *govi* that she referred to is a clay jug or pot that one finds in Vodou temples or clustered on household altars (*badji*) believed to contain portions of the souls of ancestral family members. I was stunned by the meaning she had invested in my sound files, and thought about her remark often in the years that followed, especially during the period in which the Lomax project stalled due to issues with the original record label. For me, Ms. Dunham had opened another window into how these recordings could be perceived: as traces of ancestral voices from a distant past, the spiritual residue of grandparents and great-grandparents—of *granmoun*—who might have otherwise left no material traces of their lives, beliefs, passions, or life's work. Few families in Haiti have many tangible reminders of their ancestors—typically what remains are only stories. Ms. Dunham's remark heightened the ethical obligation to see to the repatriation of these sounds to Haiti, not just for the generalized repair of social and cultural memory and continuity, which are important in a country that has seen such strife and dislocation, but also for the familial and personal links to the past. I came to feel a deep obligation to those living and those passed away to see this project through, and moreover to try to do the best job possible to honor and to recognize the performers and the vibrant culture they represented.

A Note on Musical Repatriation

In an article I wrote on applied or engaged ethnomusicology (Averill 2003), I argued that the ethical obligation to participate in wider forms of research dissemination and public scholarship is much broader than the reciprocal relationship to communities in which fieldwork was undertaken. The commitment by researchers to share their research with—and provide service to—their communities has roots in the French Revolution, in the approach of Marx and his followers to the role of the intelligentsia, in the emergence of the progressive movement in the United States, in the requirements that land-grant universities serve their communities, and in the ideological transformations that rocked the global academy in the 1960s and 1970s. The rising expectations for universities and researchers to act in the public's interest contrast with an ideal of the university dating from the early modern period as existing apart from and protected from the issues affecting society.

But musical repatriation, a form of public scholarship and applied ethnomusicology, does have roots in the ethics of reciprocity between scholars and communities in and with which they work. Repatriation has emerged as a key issue in ethnographic work over the last five decades, during which the nature of ethnography and of ethnographic collecting/archiving came under sustained critique. Anticolonial movements, decolonization, and the concomitant rise of postcolonial studies in the academy progressively destabilized the notion that the Western academy occupied a privileged position from which to document, analyze, and archive the rest of the world. It was no longer possible to justify a unidirectional flow of knowledge from the Global South to the Global North. Whatever would take the place of colonial models of information gathering (the resource extraction model, proceeding from periphery to core) had to reject the fiction that people at some distance from Western academies should function as passive objects of scrutiny. Postcolonial ethnographic practices came to incorporate reciprocal commitments as well as collaborative and dialogic methodologies to make sure that the relationships with researchers were seen to benefit communities and that the latter were increasingly engaged in the design of ethnographic research projects.

Concerns over repatriation, specifically, emerged first and most viscerally in Indigenous communities, many of which had suffered the removal of ancestral remains for study in Western institutions and for museum display. Across the globe, agreements have been reached to repatriate remains, often with elaborate protocols to welcome ancestors home and to reinter remains properly in accordance with local religious beliefs and practices. The practice was extended to the repatriation of material culture, such as the potlatch regalia of Indigenous Canadian Pacific Coast peoples or the archeological heritage of classical Mediterranean civilizations that had been removed to European and North American museums (Roehrenbeck 2010).

Underlying these changes was the post facto recognition that peoples—and the contemporary nation-states that claim to represent them—have rights to human remains, collective cultural heritage, physical person(s), and biological code, and in certain formulations also to local flora/fauna, ideas, religious and other beliefs, music, and even language. Questions over rights to various forms of patrimony have become more pronounced in the face of commercial exploitation by cultural, pharmaceutical, agricultural, touristic, and other industries with global reach. How these rights should become enshrined in law, and how they are negotiated across considerable cultural differences, is the source of ferment in the global community.[4] Nonetheless, ethnographers who generate or who work on archives need to be conversant with the relevant range of local concerns and expectations, transnational laws and conventions, institutional research ethics protocols, and state-of-the-art archival methods to meet the highest contemporaneous ethical, moral, legal, and technical standards.

The ethical obligation to repatriate music and performance is qualitatively different from that of returning human remains or ritual media, because rarely are the artifacts—tapes, discs, videotapes—considered sacred or essential to community or national identity *in and of themselves*; rather they are the media that store and transmit such expressions. Thus, a consensus is often reached that originals should be safely stored in climate-controlled facilities and with redundant backup storage, as long as access to the content can be adequately controlled and maintained based on the wishes of the communities involved.

Haiti historically had not been a signatory nation to any copyright conventions that could have affected the use and dissemination of the recordings. In addition, the recordings gathered by Alan Lomax in Haiti in 1936 and 1937 had been deposited in the Library of Congress with no stated restrictions on their use. For most of the recordings, at least those involving small groups or individuals, Lomax paid a small fee to the performers for the rights to record and to deposit the materials in the Library of Congress. Although reproduction and dissemination rights were not clearly obtained as far as I can tell, there would be no way by which they could be cleared seventy years later. It is likely that all the original performers were deceased by the time we released these recordings, and the geographic range of the recordings and the difficulty of locating individuals in Haiti would have made it impossible to locate even a tiny fraction of surviving family members to obtain permission.

Haiti has been one of the more challenging places in the hemisphere to protect invaluable original media of any sort. For example, during the chaotic transitional period often called *dechoukay* (uprooting) that followed the end of the Duvalier dictatorship in the late 1980s, many museums, libraries, and other institutions were ransacked. Fires and natural disasters (hurricanes, floods, and, of course, the recent earthquake) have destroyed many collections as well as the facilities that house them. And climate control is almost impossible to guarantee in a country where the electrical supply is predictably unreliable.

With no question of repatriating the original physical media (the aluminum discs, notebooks/papers, and films), our efforts have been devoted to repatriating the content of the media: the sounds and the data/texts. Our initial goal (what I am calling Phase 1) was to produce a collection of the best of the recordings, what eventually became *Alan Lomax in Haiti, 1936–37: Recordings from the Library of Congress* (Harte Recordings, 2009), which I refer to informally throughout the rest of this chapter as the "Haiti Box Set." But from the beginning of this project, I was absorbed by the question of how to make these recordings useful to Haitians, and the subsequent phases have been dedicated to putting the cultural resources of the Alan Lomax recordings in the hands of contemporary Haitian musicians, cultural activists, and lay music devotees in order to enhance Haitian historical and cultural identity.

There were at least two issues that made the repatriation of the Lomax collection to Haiti rather unique. The first was an epochal natural disaster (the Haiti earthquake of January 12, 2010) concurrent with the start of our repatriation initiative and the various changes to the initiative that it ushered in. Another is that the repatriation project was the result of a complex cast of actors, including the Library of Congress in Washington, DC, where the recordings were held; the Association for Cultural Equity in New York, which stewards and promotes the work and legacy of Alan Lomax; myself as the academic lead and curator with my colleague Louis Carl Saint Jean; and the Green Family Foundation, which funded and led the postpublication repatriation process, in the persona of Kimberley Green, its president. There were others involved too (producers of the Haiti Box Set, audio engineers, a film company, and so forth). This chapter thus focuses in, ultimately, on how complex multiactor repatriation efforts can be implemented under difficult circumstances.

PHASE 1: THE RECORDINGS AND THE BOX SET

I have written about the nature of Alan Lomax's Haiti expedition and its relationship to the other ethnographic projects in Haiti in the years following the departure of the US Marines (Averill 2008). Other ethnographers in Haiti in the period included Melville and Frances Herskovits (and Herskovits's graduate student, George Simpson) as well as artist-ethnographers such as author Zora Neale Hurston, dancer/choreographer Katherine Dunham, and novelist Harold Courlander. I argued that Haiti loomed large in the imagination of intellectuals working on African American culture in the wake of the Harlem Renaissance, and that, as an independent black republic since 1804 and one understood to be the "most African" nation in the hemisphere, Haiti raised the hopes of scholars that they might better understand questions of African retentions and of the longer-term impact of slavery on African Americans through ethnographic work in Haiti. Many visitors to Haiti had been intrigued by the sensationalist travelogue reportage and memoirs written about Haitian Vodou and zombies (*zonbi* in Kreyol) during the occupation.

Lomax's ethnographic praxis differed from that of his contemporaries in Haiti in his devotion to sampling the auditory culture of the Haitian people—that is, to recording and collecting. Herskovits, Simpson, and Dunham all made a small number of recordings, and Herskovits and Simpson also made some black-and-white films, but these were subsidiary documentation of their core ethnographic work. Courlander, although writing about music, relied on the transcriptions from singers made in Western notation by the Haitian violinist Arthur Lyncée Duroseau, although later he did make a few recordings of drumming that were notated by the comparative musicologist Dr. Franz Boas. For Alan Lomax, the recording was not the by-product of ethnography or a documentation of such, but his modus operandi. His written materials (logs, journal, etc.) served primarily as supporting documentation for the recordings.

Although there were a few options for mobile recording technology in the mid-1930s, Lomax chose the dual turntable unit manufactured by the Lincoln Thompson's Sound Specialties Company because of its capacity to capture complex overtones and the high-intensity sound of drum ensembles. For best results, he had a new amplifier installed along with a new cutting head to enhance the capacity for drum sound. The unit contained a disc cutter, pickup (reproducing head), battery, and vacuum tubes, and the apparatus could record on 10-inch or 12-inch uncoated/raw aluminum discs. Each side could hold up to about eight minutes of sound, but the recordings made near the inner edges of the disc were often too variable in speed to be usable. Batteries ran out at times, and so the speed of the recordings changed, and by later standards, the raw aluminum recordings made for an unacceptable amount of surface noise ("hiss, pop, and click"). Even with the new amplifier, there was considerable damping in the lower frequencies. On the positive side, the aluminum proved to be so durable that the recordings are as good today as they were in 1936.

Working with a studio engineer at the Library of Congress, I and a staff member from ACE helped select styli for the discs, standardized a numbering system for the two different forms of digital transfer storage media (there was already a classification system that Lomax used at the time of the recordings as well as a separate acquisition numbering system for the Archives of Folk Culture), and then let the studio engineer carry out the rest of the digital transfer.

Not until December of 2008 were we ready to get moving energetically on the first stage of the project. Rounder Records, the original label working with ACE, had been replaced by Harte Records, a San Francisco–based label with a track record of producing box sets for the high-end market. Steve Rosenthal's multi-Grammy winning Magic Shop had been hired to reengineer the sound, boosting bass frequencies and removing as much surface noise as possible. The resulting sound was much closer to what Alan Lomax heard, and it provided an acceptable listening experience for contemporary audiences. Nonetheless, there was no doubt acoustically that these were historical recordings.

After we had a full set of digital files prepared of the audio and audiovisual recordings, I faced a tight timeline of five months to produce the first draft version of the box set, including the selection and "track charting" of ten CDs of recordings and an accompanying book of interpretive notes, song texts, and their English translations. Alan's niece, Ellen Harold, edited Lomax's rich but fragmented fieldnotes into a second book to be included in the box set. The projected work period was, oddly, more or less the same five months (December through April) that Lomax spent in Haiti.

I first coded all the recordings in the audio database based on their genre—Vodou ceremonial, rara, *twoubadou* (troubadour), children's songs, stories, work songs, and so forth. I also indexed the recordings by sound quality, coding whether they were acoustically acceptable for publication (possibly with some truncation at the beginning or end), whether they were marginal, or whether under no circumstances could they be rendered listenable for a public audience.

I concluded that stories (*kont*) would require too much translation and would not appeal to an English-speaking audience, and so, sadly, these were left for future projects. From the remaining higher quality recordings, I began to assess where we had sufficient strength to create thematized CDs for the box set. I settled on an overall arc that might best be described as starting in urban and secular spaces, moving progressively to the rural and sacred. This organizational conceit provided the average listener with more familiar sounds in the first few recordings, sounds that could serve as a bridge to more difficult material.

On the first CD, I wanted people to hear Alan Lomax himself, recorded in his hotel upon arriving in Haiti. I also wanted to include recordings he made of his friend, Zora Neale Hurston, singing African American game songs. My goal was to allow listeners to understand that this was a set of recordings made by a real human being, a visitor to Haiti, a researcher of folk songs possessing broad musical curiosity and his own motivations and priorities. The first disc also introduces us to Lomax's first month in Haiti, in which he recorded a classical pianist and jazz bands at an elite club and met members of the Haitian ruling elite, even while he sought out his first Vodou ceremonies.

In later tracks, I wanted to highlight a single performer, and so I chose a young woman named Francilia (Figure 5.2) from Carrefour Dufort whom Lomax hired to keep house and whom he recorded extensively. And finally, given that Lomax was the first to record an entire Vodou ceremony (or at least much of every song sung), I wanted to devote one of the discs to that ceremony. The Francilia disc and the one devoted to the ceremony were my means of breaking up the genre-based compilation feel of the rest of the discs.

I spent those five months intensively reexperiencing the material that Lomax heard in his headphones through my own headphones, reading his journals, interpreting his handwriting, listening to lyrics, and translating them along with my colleague Louis Carl Saint Jean. I engaged in detective work to try to put together the dates, journals, receipts, recordings, and logs to retrace Lomax's footsteps and to interpret the journey. When we could not understand lyrics or meanings, Louis Carl would sometimes call older relatives in his family's hometown of Fonds-des-Nègres, Haiti. He played songs over the phone to elicit additional insight on the places, meanings, and context of the recordings, and

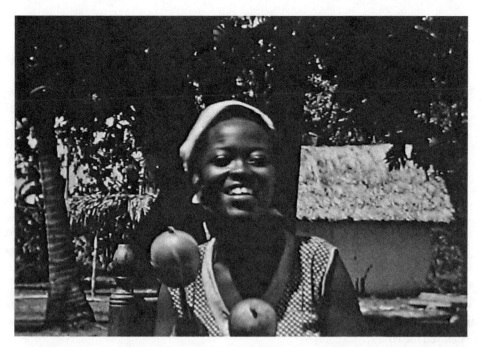

FIGURE 5.2 Francilia, playing *tcha-tcha* (gourd rattles), while singing one of scores of songs she recorded for Alan Lomax.

Photograph courtesy of Elizabeth Lomax, courtesy of the Library of Congress
Archives of Folk Culture, Washington, DC.

sometimes his relatives would run down the street to find someone else to listen and help interpret. By September we had an edited version of the entire set ready for formatting, pressing, and production. After its publication in November, the Clinton Global Initiative declared the Haiti Box Set an "Outstanding Project for 2010," and the combination of the name Alan Lomax (greatly respected by music journalists) and the issues in Haiti before and after the earthquake generated a large volume of media attention.[5]

PHASE 2A: HAITIAN REPATRIATION
AND THE 2010 EARTHQUAKE

With funding and support from the Green Family Foundation, we planned to reintegrate the collection to Haiti.[6]

The initial design was straightforward:

- Produce Kreyol and French translations of the entire box set
- Create a sampler disc for airplay on Haitian radio stations in French and Kreyol

- Design school modules, working with music educator Patricia Shehan Campbell, and translate them into French and Kreyol
- Install listening stations featuring the entire archive at major cultural centers in Haiti
- Distribute box sets at libraries, schools, and cultural centers in Haiti
- Work with a Haitian cinema group to shoot a film documenting the interaction of the historical sounds in the present day
- Introduce the project to musicians and others who might make use of the materials for performance or inclusion into rituals
- Identify any living descendants of the performers in the communities in which Lomax had worked

We launched the initiative with two events in Brooklyn (Figure 5.3) and one scheduled for Miami to generate interest and excitement among Haitians living in the diaspora as well as journalists and music collectors in North America. I planned to arrive in Haiti on January 9, 2010, to prepare for the repatriation effort and to participate in the broadcast by the University of Toronto radio station, CIUT-FM, of the Port-au-Prince Jazz Festival. However, the radio broadcast link was canceled due to technical problems, so I delayed the trip.

Only three days after I was supposed to arrive, the *tranblemanntè* (earthquake) hit central Haiti, registering 7.0 on the Richter scale and centered just southeast of

FIGURE 5.3 Key members of the team that produced the Haiti Box Set: Gage Averill, Ellen Harold, Anna Lomax Wood, and Louis Carl Saint Jean at the launch event at a Brooklyn club in December 2009.

Léogâne. Much of the worst damage, and by far the largest concentration of casualties and fatalities, was in the capital city, Port-au-Prince, but St. Marc, Léogâne, Jacmel, the Central Plateau, and Petite-Goâve were all hard struck. Among the tens of thousands of buildings destroyed were the Presidential Palace, the National Cathedral in Port-au-Prince, Holy Trinity Cathedral, and the National Assembly, as well as the hotel that served as headquarters for the UN's Stabilization Mission to Haiti (MINUSTAH) and some army barracks. With MINUSTAH and the army severely compromised by the loss of life and with the government in disarray, the people of Haiti were largely left to themselves to cope with the damage and devastation in the first days after the earthquake.

On the cultural side, much of Haiti's most iconic architecture was in ruins; art centers and galleries were reduced to rubble with massive damage to art works (those that had not been destroyed were exposed to the elements, theft, or further damage from aftershocks); halls, schools, and concert venues had been destroyed. It is not an exaggeration to say that much of Haiti's cultural heritage—especially its visible, tangible, and material culture—was obliterated or in imminent danger. Even its performance-oriented culture (e.g., music ensembles, theater troupes, folkloric groups) lost instruments, theaters, performance halls, training schools, and master artists. Some musicians and artists were among those living in tent cities without access to the means of a livelihood. And Carnival, the principal annual festival for performance (and income) for musicians, was canceled.

Amid the shock and grief and the need to rally the globe to assist with an emergency response, I concluded that the repatriation effort had lost any possible priority for the country and for our funders, and I expected that we would have to delay for a year or even many more. However, within the week, we heard from the Green Family Foundation that the repatriation effort was more pressing than ever. They argued that having lost so much of its cultural inheritance, the nation needed reminders of its cultural strength and richness. It needed the means to help restore pride and hope in an otherwise bleak reality, and both Haiti and the world also needed antidotes to the vision of Haiti as simply a recipient nation and hemispheric basket case. Our funders encouraged us to get back to work on a transformed repatriation plan in a vastly altered landscape.

As part of our funders' efforts to raise funds and consciousness, I was asked to choose music from the box set for radio and television public service announcements (PSAs) with voiceovers by Naomi Watts, Ben Stiller, Sean Penn, and others. Box sets were distributed to fundraising events as give-away items and as prizes. Our producer announced that 25 percent of the cost of the Haiti Box Sets would go to disaster relief. Carts were prepared with selections from the Haiti Box Set for play over Haiti's few functioning radio stations.

In the earlier days of the project, I had imagined that the repatriation effort would be a more typical one: I would apply for some grants, spend time in Haiti with Haitian colleagues, travel to the places Lomax visited, deliver box sets, and talk to Haitian musicians about how best to disseminate the recordings. But the post-quake team that was assembled, with the lead taken by the Green Family Foundation, was a large one, including myself; Anna Lomax Wood of the Association for Cultural Equity; Kimberly

Green, president of the Green Foundation and her team, which included logistics/ security; our studio engineer; other producers of the box set; members of Fastforward Haiti (working on a film about the project); and an independent news journalist preparing a minidocumentary on the initiative for the Public Broadcasting System.[7]

My flight to Haiti for our April events was unlike any other that I had taken in twenty-five years of working in Haiti. Typically, a flight would be largely made up of Haitian expatriates, some heading home for the first time and bringing boxes of gifts, along with Haitians coming back from visiting relatives in the United States. In April 2011, the flight was packed with Americans on their way to assist in some portion of the relief effort, many of them associated with one or another church and wearing matching T-shirts.

The ride from the airport, usually an exercise in frustration due to mega traffic jams and the ubiquitous potholes in the streets, now had slowed to molasses, with many streets still filled with debris, lots of additional vehicles operated by nongovernmental organizations (NGOs), and an ongoing absence of army and police. In our travels around the city, we visited my old home at the L'Ecole Ste. Trinité, next to the Holy Trinity Cathedral, where I often stayed while conducting early fieldwork between 1987 and 1993. The cathedral had collapsed entirely (Figure 5.4), bringing down with it a famous series of murals. Many of the smaller buildings of the school were being rebuilt, and we talked with students and teachers (Figure 5.5). My old room was entirely visible

FIGURE 5.4 The ruins of the Holy Trinity Cathedral show the devastation of the earthquake on many heritage buildings.

Photograph courtesy of Gage Averill.

FIGURE 5.5 The students at the attached school, the L'Ecole Ste. Trinité gather in front of some of the temporary buildings being used as their school, widely considered Haiti's best school for musical instruction.

Photograph courtesy of Gage Averill.

in the remaining section of the building where the outer wall no longer existed. We visited Quisqueya University, which had been relocated into tents on a new site, and where debris was being cleared for construction. Many of our interactions captured both the horrific devastation in the city and the inspiring dedication of the Haitian people to rebuild and move on with their lives.

That night we gathered for food and music with a Haitian musicologist and some friends of the project in Haiti. We launched officially in Haiti the following night with a special event at Café des Arts, a popular performance venue in Pétion-Ville. The audience—which included government ministers, ambassadors, shop owners, musicians, intellectuals, and activists—was introduced to the project, listened to a Vodou jazz band, watched the first films from the Fastforward Haiti collective, and engaged with the question of how this set and the entire corpus of recordings could be of assistance under the circumstances after the earthquake. A panel (Figure 5.6), including myself along with Joel Widmaïer (a well-known musician/radio producer and old friend), Anna Lomax Wood, our recording engineer Warren Russel-Smith, and musician and cultural activist Djalòki (Jean Luc Dessables), presented perspectives on the project and took questions from the audience (Figure 5.7).

A cultural activist and radio deejay in the Léogâne area who had heard about the project brought together two local Vodou societies in the Léogâne area, one a Petwo-Kongo

FIGURE 5.6 The panel discusses the Haiti Box Set at the Café des Arts in Pétion-Ville, Haiti. Left to right: Jean Luc "Djalòki" Dessables, Joel Widmaïer, Gage Averill, Anna Lomax Wood, and Warren Russel-Smith.

Photograph courtesy of Kimberly Green.

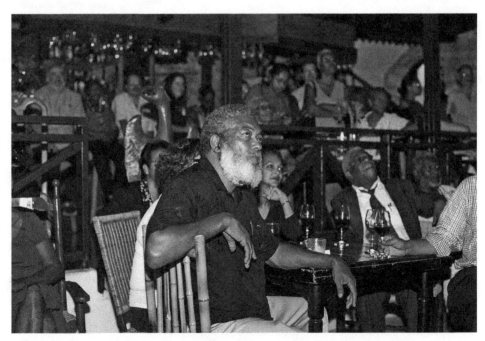

FIGURE 5.7 Audience members at the panel discussion of the Haiti Box Set at the Café des Arts in Pétion-Ville, Haiti.

Photograph courtesy of Gage Averill.

society and the other a Rada group.[8] They held a ceremony under a great *mapou* tree (a tree sacred to Haitian Vodou) welcoming the voices of the ancestors back to Haiti (Figures 5.8 and 5.9). A *delko* (car battery) served as the power source for a portable CD system with speakers. After the ceremony, I played songs from the box set recorded in the Léogâne area that would likely be familiar to contemporary *Vodwizan-yo* (practitioners, servants of the spirit), but then moved to rarer, more archaic, or atypical songs from regional sacred societies. Tears began to flow, and many of the older *ounsi* (initiates) began to nod their heads, with their lips forming the words to songs they had not heard in many decades.

Someone close to the repatriation effort, an owner of a mango exporting company, had located a descendent of one of Lomax's interlocutors. You may remember the picture of Gustave Tanis at the start of this chapter, a prominent figure in Carrefour Dufort, leaning against the doorway of his house at a Vodou ceremony for Ezili, goddess of love and desire. Our colleague had located his daughter, who can be seen in Figure 5.10. We presented her with the box set, showed her films of her father from the ceremony in 1937, and played recordings made by the Lomaxes. Madame Tanice wept, in part for having met the daughter of the man from the United States whom she had heard about and who recorded her father those many years ago, remarking that it felt like meeting a long-lost sister. Afterward she fed the entire team from her street cart,

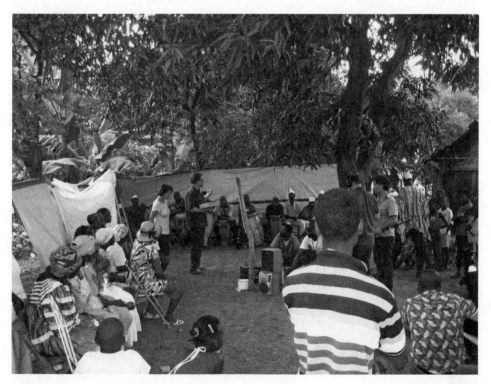

FIGURE 5.8 Gage Averill discusses the recordings with the initiates at the Vodou ceremony in Léogâne, with Anna Lomax Wood standing behind him.

Photograph courtesy of Kimberly Green.

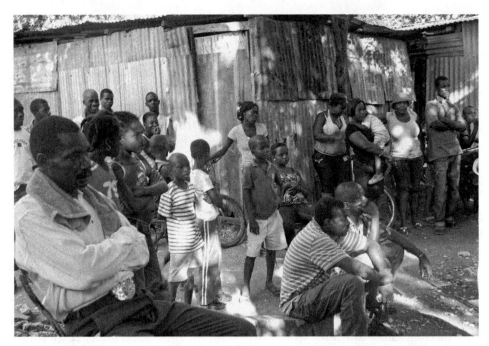

FIGURE 5.9 Community residents not participating in the ceremony gather to listen.
Photograph courtesy of Gage Averill.

refusing payment for the *gwiyo* (fried pork), *pikliz* (hot vegetable relish), and *banann peze* (fried plantains).

We were away from Haiti in May but returned there in June for the second round of repatriation-related activities. As I noted above, the Green Family Foundation had contracted with a Haitian film collective, Fastforward Haiti, to document the repatriation project. They had already filmed many prominent Haitian artists and cultural specialists listening to and responding to Lomax's historical materials. These films, along with the original film shorts made by Elizabeth and Alan Lomax, became part of the shows they presented in slums and in tent cities around Haiti. The shows, which were called "Sinema anba Zetwal" (Cinema under the Stars), consisted of educational shorts dealing with human rights, culture, hygiene, environment, and gender equity, interspersed with live acoustic roots music, raffles, theatrical skits, and performances by local groups. After the films had been shown in Cité Soleil and in a tent city in Pétion-Ville, the Cinema and repatriation teams together headed to Léogâne, near the epicenter of the quake, where we pitched tents and where the cinema team began to erect the massive screen and sound system in a nearby cow field.

I visited the following day with Max Beauvoir, perhaps the best known of Haiti's many Vodou priests (now deceased), and his daughter, Rachel Beauvoir-Dominique, an anthropologist. The two of them told me how they had sat for three days listening to the set after a friend shared it with them. This had been important to Max, Rachel said, because

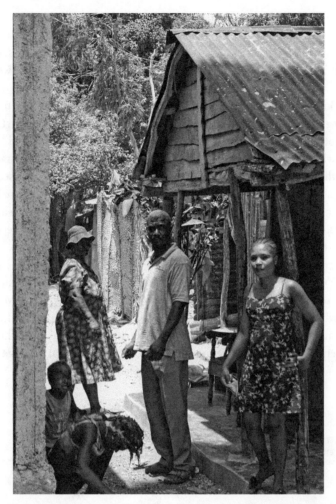

FIGURE 5.10 Madame Tanice (at right) stands by her family's house, which was the setting for a ceremony recorded by Alan Lomax in 1937.

Photograph courtesy of Gage Averill.

he had become alarmed and depressed by an eerie flood on his property that occurred every day in the midafternoon following the earthquake. Combined with an almost complete collapse of his business, which was based on visitors to his temple compound, he was deeply troubled. But both he and Rachel had spoken of their hope that these songs could pass again into ceremonial use.

Max raised a couple of concerns over my interpretations of the recordings and critiqued a part of the musical soundtrack to the six films included in the box set. Because Alan and Elizabeth Lomax had not recorded music simultaneously while they recorded film, I had been dependent on using Lomax's suggestions for accompanying tracks, and he had recommended *banda* drumming for a sequence from a Petwo-Zandò ceremony. Spiritually, Max pointed out, *banda* (associated with the Gede family of deities and with ceremonies focused on death) would not be at all appropriate—and likely counterproductive—in the Petwo context. He also suggested that the common interjection in Vodou songs, *anye o*, had a spiritual interpretation that I missed. I recall this conversation because it suggested so well the next level of interpretation we could reach when information on the recordings could be crowdsourced, and not dependent on the limits of my knowledge and experience of Haitian music as well as that of my colleagues.

The night of the concert in the cow field arrived (Figure 5.11). As part of the show, the films shot by Alan and Elizabeth Lomax in Léogâne were screened. The Léogâne region was where Lomax had shot all of his original films and made many hundreds of his recordings. For many attendees, it was the first time they had seen their own region represented in film. Soon after the start of Lomax's film of a *rara* parade from 1937 (Figure 5.12), a woman jumped up in the second row and began screaming repeatedly, "*Se gran-papa mwen!*" (That's my grandfather!). We began to witness the familial connections, the very personal link to performers from seventy years ago.

Over the course of our trips to Haiti between April and late June, we met with the minister of culture, with the rector of one of Haiti's two main universities (Inivesite Kiskeya/Quisqueya University), and with a prominent musicologist. We showed and played recordings to prominent musicians, priests, and culture brokers; helped present some of the material to large Haitian audiences in marginalized neighborhoods and tent cities; and generated positive coverage globally for Haiti's cultural heritage. However, in comparison to our original goals, there was much left to do.

FIGURE 5.11 Musicians perform at the start of the *Sinema anba Zetwal*.

Photograph courtesy of Gage Averill.

FIGURE 5.12   A still frame from a rara parade filmed by Elizabeth Lomax in Léogâne in 1930.

Photograph courtesy of Elizabeth Lomax, courtesy of the Library of Congress
Archives of Folk Culture, Washington, DC.

PHASE 2B: GRAMMY AWARDS AND THE NEW ORLEANS JAZZ & HERITAGE FESTIVAL

Only a week after I returned from Haiti, I took up a new job as dean at the University of British Columbia and found myself pulled away, like most of the rest of the team, from day-to-day engagement with the repatriation effort. On December 1, 2010, I awoke to the news that the Haiti Box Set had been nominated for two Grammy Awards, one for best box set and the other for best album notes.

The Grammy nods sparked a new round of media attention for the recordings and the repatriation project, and importantly it constituted a good-news item about Haiti, which were in short supply. The reconstruction of Haiti had proven to be a slow and tortuous process. Clearing away the debris from the earthquake was still underway, largely undertaken by two private companies in Haiti (a bottled water company and a telecom company). UN troops had accidentally introduced cholera into Haiti in October of 2010, and the outbreak had become a widespread epidemic. With a peak of perhaps 12,000 NGOs working in Haiti after the earthquake, funding had quite often been spent inefficiently and without sustained impact. Tent cities still dotted the urban areas of central

Haiti, and replacement housing was only slowly becoming available. And in a pattern too common following major disasters, many nations had failed to follow through on their promises of funding for reconstruction; so some good news from the cultural front was welcome.

The team that had traveled together to Haiti reunited for the Grammy weekend, and we met up first for lunch with Gray Davis, former governor of California. Many of us were also attending the various events surrounding the awards ceremony, as well as the awards ceremony itself. Our awards were part of the pretelecast ceremony that took place in the Los Angeles Convention Center, adjacent to the Staples Center (where the telecast was held later in the evening). In comparison to the telecast show, the pretelecast awards are a decidedly low-budget affair, but hosts Bobby McFerrin and Esperanza Spalding kept the proceedings entertaining. We did not win, by the way (losing to the Beatles for best box set), but the awards did permit us to reconsolidate the group involved with the box set and its repatriation.

In the spring of 2011, the repatriation effort, through the Green Family Foundation, was partnered with the New Orleans Jazz & Heritage Festival to explore the links between Haiti and New Orleans, soon after major disasters in both locales. The festival featured a Haitian Pavilion, Haitian concerts at the festival (Ti-Coca, Emeline Michel, and Boukman Eksperyans), and a pair of panels on which I spoke. A listening station, designed and built by Haitian artisans, was installed in Haiti Pavilion; handicrafts were on display and for sale (with the launch of a new line of Haitian furnishings and fashion for sale in Macy's department stores); and performances, videos, and educational materials were pulled together in a demonstration of the potential of the project to tour and to support festivals and exhibits.

PHASE 3: COMING HOME

Health issues within the team, some strained relationships among team members, my new job, and a host of other issues pushed a figurative pause button on subsequent phases of the repatriation effort, but in 2017 the initiative resumed again with updated goals. Anna Lomax Wood and Jorge Arrevalo of the Association for Cultural Equity asked me and my colleague Louis Carl Saint Jean to catalog and annotate the entire collection of over 1,500 of Lomax's recordings for a web-based database. The software serving as a platform for the digital archive will have a wiki-like function, allowing a moderated access by the public to create, add to, edit, and revise the data concerning the recordings.

We are also collaborating with the Association for Cultural Equity with funding from the Green Family Foundation (working with Kimberly Green and Mireille Charles) to bring all of the recordings to multiple repositories in Haiti, as well as to the communities and families from whence they were recorded. The original box set has sold out and is out of production, so we are currently unable to distribute hard copies of the project, but we are discussing a new edition as well as a digital version of the original Haiti Box for enhanced global access, and we will distribute DVDs with Internet-independent play-back systems to each of the communities. We also plan to finish producing and begin disseminating the school lesson plans based on the Haiti Box Set in schools throughout Haiti, working with colleagues at Florida International University (with its Digital Library of the Caribbean) and the Haitian-based Anseye Pou Ayiti (Teach for Haiti), a group devoted to recruiting and training teachers to improve educational outcomes in Haiti.

I also hope to make the recordings more accessible to musicians and storytellers and to see the songs and stories circulate anew. Already, I have worked with the Audio/Ciné Institute in Jacmel, which sponsors the band Lakou Mizik. The band has recorded a session featuring versions of songs sung by Francilia from the Haiti box set, and we are discussing other songs to be retrieved and performed. In upcoming visits to Haiti, we hope to work out more sustained use of the recordings by musicians, cultural organizations, museums, schools, and universities. We also hope to create strong access points in the major communities in which Alan and Elizabeth Lomax and Revolie Polinice recorded performances (Plaisance, Pont Beaudet and the Plateau Central, Léogâne, and the greater Port-au-Prince region).

Finally, the next stage of the repatriation project will also need to establish a richer set of collaborative relationships and North-South partnerships with educational institutions, archives, digital consortia focused on heritage, NGOs, cultural organizations and more. The fragility of cultural heritage, which was so evident in the wake of the earthquake (and in the wake of Hurricane Katrina in New Orleans) argues for concerted international efforts to preserve cultural memory.

We are living in what certainly should be an archival golden era, and an era in which repatriation of musical archives should be both second nature *and* easily accomplished by digital means. The digital revolution allows us to make impeccable copies of documents and recordings and to disseminate them instantly all over the world. But many of the world's great archival treasures sit on people's home shelves, or in boxes in their basements or attics, sometimes forgotten and subject to data deterioration and environmental damage. Ethnographers engaged in the great enterprise of understanding and translating human culture through intercultural dialogue have an obligation to seek out, preserve, interpret, digitalize, repatriate, and make available these kinds of resources. This obligation is at its heart an exercise in reclaiming our past, honoring our ancestors, and preserving our humanity.

The initiative for repatriation of the Alan Lomax Haitian recordings has demonstrated anew how difficult it can be to reach people and to accomplish a repatriation effort in a country as rural as Haiti and with such inadequate infrastructure, even before the quake. And the earthquake of 2010 reminds us of the unexpected events and hurdles in the way of a project like this. Our efforts had to be maximally flexible and resilient, responding to a constantly changing situation and to problems such as the unreliability of the power supply, the low level of literacy, and the breakdown in security. Coups and violent political transformations, and even peaceful and democratic transfers of power, such as recently took place in Haiti (following the prolonged election season of 2015–2017), can result in the wholesale replacement of public servants, who may be the contacts that repatriation efforts rely on. Ethnomusicologists, who may confront political, economic, and social upheavals in their ethnographic work, need to bring the same worst-case-scenario planning to their repatriation efforts.

But Haiti's difficulties and its post-quake trauma also suggest how powerful a tool musical heritage can be in establishing pride, enhancing morale, recovering from social and collective trauma, and nurturing a positive sense of collective identity. It is often precisely the same nations, typically in the developing world—nations that have experienced more than their share of calamities and that have also experienced the greatest amount of social and cultural upheaval—that therefore have the most desperate need to achieve shared cultural memory and identity.

Although the repatriation effort for the Alan Lomax Haitian recordings may have been particularly complex in its cast of characters, repatriation of musical archives will almost always involve funding agencies, government officials, local cultural brokers, Western-based archives, and other constituencies. This kind of work requires that ethnomusicologists exercise abilities in building and sustaining teams and teamwork, whether they are the leaders of those initiatives or one among many actors. There may be multiple agendas at play, some of which might conflict at times with academic goals and objectives, and ethnomusicologists working in these kinds of projects will need to balance goals, negotiate outcomes, provide vision, persuade if necessary, and attend to the complex ecosystem of personalities necessary to achieve collective and collaborative work at a high level.

By bringing cultural archives back into circulation, we are seeding countless future possibilities for epiphanies, growth, development, and discovery. We cannot predict what people will make of these resources, but we can take comfort in knowing that new sets of opportunities will emerge from people who are inspired on a personal level. The repatriation of the Alan Lomax Haiti recordings has brought me face to face with so many of these small and personal human dramas: the older Vodou initiates and priests nodding their heads in remembrance of sacred choruses heard as children, priests debating and critiquing my notes by adding layers of sacred interpretation and theology, and people who encountered their parents or grandparents in the recordings of Alan Lomax. All these experiences have become part of the odyssey of this digital spirit *govi* returning to the descendants of those whose music and stories it captured.

Notes

1. Ogou is a Vodou warrior deity who derives from the Nago nation in Haiti, constituted in Haiti by descendants of Yoruba-speaking slaves, associated in Catholicism with Saint Jacques the Elder (Saint Jacques Majeur). Yet Ogou is also known in the plural, as a family or set of deities: Ogou Fè/Feray, Ogou Badagri, Ogou Batala, Ogou Achade, and many more, each with his own distinct personality and set of associations, symbolisms, and meanings. Ogou Badagri, for example, is skilled at diplomacy.

2. The Association for Cultural Equity, founded by Alan Lomax, has as its mission to "stimulate cultural equity through preservation, research, and dissemination of the world's traditional music, and to reconnect people and communities with their creative heritage."

3. See *Island Possessed* (Dunham 1969).

4. The Berne Convention for the Protection of Literary and Artistic Works (1886) was the original interstate regulatory mechanism, joined in 1952 by the UN's Universal Copyright Convention, largely aimed at states that had not joined the Berne Convention. The World Trade Organization's 1994 TRIPS Agreement (the Agreement on Trade Related Aspects of International Property Rights)—which ventures into plant varieties, food/drink appellations of origin, biological patents, and more—created a much more comprehensive system of protections. UNESCO has developed its *Representative List of the Intangible Cultural Heritage of Humanity* (with no representation from Haiti, I should note), the product of the Convention for the Safeguarding of Intangible Cultural Heritage. UNESCO held conventions in 1970 and 1978, and established the Intergovernmental Committee for Promoting the Return of Cultural Property to Its Countries of Origin or Its Restitution in Case of Illicit Appropriation.

5. For example: A review in the *New York Times*, by Jon Pareles (November 28, 2009); a review and interview in the *Wall Street Journal*, by John Jurgenson (November 27, 2009); "Spirit of Haiti Comes to Life in a Box Set from Alan Lomax," by Fernando Gonzalez (*Miami Herald*, November 22, 2009); National Public Radio's "Tell Me More" (October 12, 2009); *BBC World Service* interview (September 30, 2009); "'Lomax in Haiti' Requires Time and Understanding," by Dave Hoekstra (*Chicago Sun Times*, February 7, 2010); "Haiti's Hidden Treasures," by Will Friedwald (*Wall Street Journal*, February 4, 2010); "Alan Lomax's Haitian Time Capsule: A 10-Disc Box from the '30s Captures a Troubled Nation in Transition," by Tad Hendrickson (*Village Voice*, February 2, 2010); "*Gesang nach dem Beben*: Einblicke in eine kosmopolitische Kultur: Die frühen Aufnajmen des Musikforschers," by Frank Zawatski (*Die Zeit*, February 6, 2010).

6. Former President Bill Clinton, when first brought on board, remarked that he considered this to be "Haiti's Buena Vista Social Club," referring to the Cuban recordings that helped launch a nostalgic revival for old time Cuban *son*. To my thinking, this was a *very* different kind of project than BVSC, which was a contemporary recording and touring project involving an older generation of Cuban musicians, but I agreed that it was likely that the Haiti Box Set would spur interest in Haitian music.

7. The piece appeared as "Haiti's Lost Music," online at *Need to Know* at PBS, August 30, 2010.

8. These would be considered the two main branches of Haitian Vodou, although in practice, the situation is much more complex.

References

Averill, Gage. 2003. "Ethnomusicologists as Public Intellectuals: Engaged Ethnomusicology in the University." *Folklore Forum* 34 (1/2): 49–60.

Averill, Gage. 2008. "Ballad Hunting in the Black Republic: Alan Lomax in Haiti, 1936–37." *Caribbean Studies* 36 (2) (July–December): 3–22.

Averill, Gage. 2009. *Alan Lomax in Haiti, 1936–37: Recordings for the Library of Congress*. 10-CD and -DVD boxed set of recordings (audio and film) with Alan Lomax's journal edited by Ellen Harold. Harte Records, the Library of Congress, and the Association for Cultural Equity.

Dunham, Katherine. 1969. *Island Possessed*. Chicago: University of Chicago Press.

Roehrenbeck, Carol A. 2010. "Repatriation of Cultural Property—Who Owns the Past? An Introduction to Approaches and to Selected Statutory Instruments." *International Journal of Legal Information* 38 (2): article 11.

CHAPTER 6

....

"WHERE DEAD PEOPLE WALK"

Fifty Years of Archives to Q'eros, Peru

....

HOLLY WISSLER

My heart opened. I am happier now. It's as if I have been reunited with my mother.

—Santusa Suqlle, Q'eros woman, 2012, upon viewing 1974 footage filmed by John Cohen of her deceased mother

ARCHIVAL return, like music-making, can be about human connection, deep relationship, and remembrance among all involved, community members and researchers alike. While community archives are a wealth of useful information, it is the people who must transmit, express, live, and embody the returned material, so that the archives can take on meaning and affect lives. Archives are not alive; rather, it is in the active individual and community sharing of archives that serves to stir the memories of the elders and hearts of the youth, help them know their heritage, and even cause them to feel grateful and proud. This is the story of the return and public showing of fifty years of audiovisual archives to the Quechua community of Q'eros in 2010, their spontaneous reactions, and their use of the archives today.

INTRODUCTION: ANDEAN VERTICAL ECOLOGY AND ITS IMPACT ON MUSIC-MAKING

....

Before the Spanish invasion of the Inca Empire in 1532, Andean, Amazonian, and coastal groups adapted to and were linked through a highly organized exchange of products from the many biodiverse regions of modern-day Peru, supporting the largest empire of ancient America.[1] The historian David Cahill explains that soon after the incursion of the Spanish conquistadors, the vast economic network of production in the vertical ecologies was eradicated quickly. He states:

> This system, so ingenious in conception and practical in execution, was effectively destroyed within a few decades of conquest, by dislocation, civil war, depopulation and the ethnographic obtuseness of the new Spanish rulers and administrators. It survived in a few areas, randomly and by chance.
>
> (Cahill 1994, 330)

He then adds in a footnote: "There is a faint echo of it today in the Q'ero community of the Paucartambo province of southern Peru."[2] Cahill's footnote highlights the unique position and renown of the Q'eros' use of their vertical ecology today, which has a direct impact on their musical expressions.

The Q'eros' territory spans from an altitude of 15,000 down to 6,000 feet, and it has provided the Q'eros population with nearly all of the goods they need for self-sustainability, resulting in less need for travel over long distances for trade (see map in Figure 6.1). A crucial factor is that their territory is located on the eastern watershed of the Andes, so their highest altitudes receive the cloud humidity that rolls in from the lower Amazon regions and supports rich grasses for their llamas and alpacas. In addition, the Q'eros did not suffer relocation into reduction communities (*reducciones de indios*, settlements for Spanish control caused by the forcible relocation of Indigenous Andean populations) created by Spanish authorities from the 1570s onward.[3] This relative isolation and sustainability of the Q'eros since pre-Hispanic times has fostered the retention and continued practice of their music and other traditions, which are inextricable expressions of their space, time, and worldview. Today the Q'eros are often popularly idealized as the quintessential Andean people, an embodied "echo" of the past, situated opposite a rapidly changing present.

The Q'eros cultural and ethnic group[4] consists of some three thousand people, formed into five communities that, since 2005, call themselves the Q'eros Nation (see maps in Figures 6.2 and 6.3).[5] Much of my research was in the largest of the five Q'eros communities that pertains to the whole Q'eros Nation, called Hatun (big) Q'eros, with some research in the smaller Q'eros community of Hapu. The Q'eros are a transhumant society that follows the seasonal migration of their livestock between higher and lower pastures.[6] The community of Hatun Q'eros is dispersed among four river valleys, extending from the high *puna* zone, for raising llamas and alpacas for meat and fleece, to the *qheswa* zone for varieties of tubers, and down to the *yunga*, or *monte* cloud forest zone, for corn, bamboo, and other lowland crops. It is typical for a Q'eros family to have a home in all three areas, for working the zones seasonally (see Figure 6.4).

Q'eros' songs express their interdependent relationship to their land and animal resources, and with the mountain gods (*apus*) and Mother Earth (Pacha Mama) that hold vital influence over all livelihood. Q'eros' *pukllay taki* are about revered animals and birds,

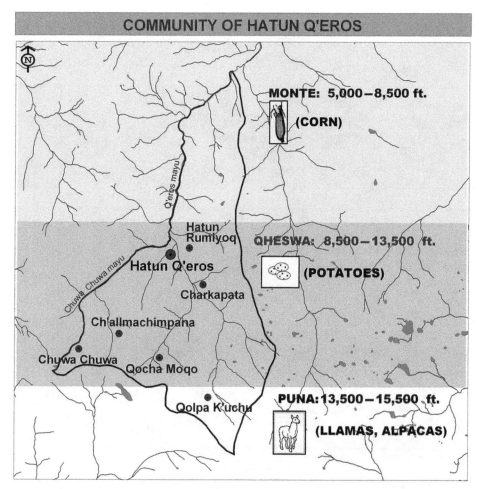

COMMUNITY OF HATUN Q'EROS

MONTE: 5,000–8,500 ft.

(CORN)

QHESWA: 8,500–13,500 ft.

(POTATOES)

PUNA: 13,500–15,500 ft.

(LLAMAS, ALPACAS)

Q'eros mayu

Hatun
Rumiyoq

Hatun Q'eros

Chuwa Chuwa mayu

Charkapata

Ch'allmachimpana

Chuwa Chuwa

Qocha Moqo

Qolpa K'uchu

FIGURE 6.1 Map of the community of Hatun Q'eros. The six high-altitude annexes belonging to the Q'eros community are indicated, as well as the community center of Hatun Q'eros.

Map courtesy of ACCA (Asociación para la Conservación de la Cuenca Amazónica), Cusco, Perú. www.acca.org.pe, 2009. Detail of maps by Sandro Arias (ACCA).

and sacred, medicinal plants and flowers in all three zones. All songs fortify Q'eros' identity and community ties, and the continued reciprocal relationship (*ayni*) between the people, their animals, and the *apus* and Pacha Mama. The animal fertility songs are also the vehicle for the expression and working out of deep loss and grief among family members.

The Q'eros are popularly associated with the Incas because of their expression of pre-Hispanic lifestyle and traditions, and their proximity to the ancient Inca capital of Cusco.[7] They are often called the "Last *Ayllu* [family group] of the Incas."[8] The Q'eros were named "cultural patrimony" in 2007 by Peru's Ministry of Culture, the first and only "people" to receive such status in Peru, and in 2010 the Ministry of Culture named their songs cultural patrimony as well. In 2006, the Q'eros were chosen to be *the*

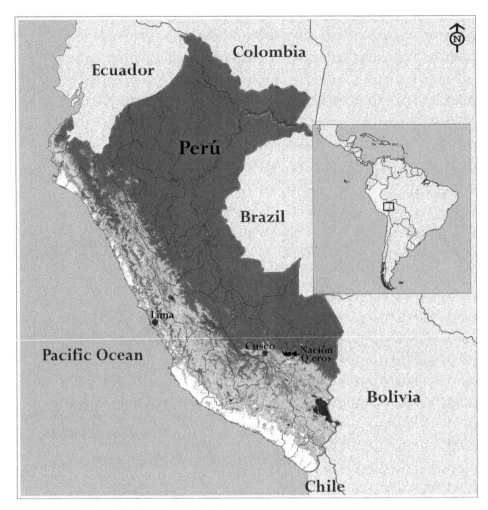

FIGURE 6.2 Map of the Q'eros Nation in Peru.

Map courtesy of ACCA, Asociación para la Conservación de la Cuenca Amazónica,
Cusco, Perú. www.acca.org.pe. 2009. Detail of maps by Sandro Arias (ACCA).

representative Indigenous Andeans to meet in a public forum with the Dalai Lama on his South American tour. Because of this international renown, the Q'eros have been the subject of study and documentation by many international researchers and filmmakers over the past fifty years, and more recently are sought out internationally by people who want to learn from and participate in their spiritual knowledge as it pertains to their connections with the mountain gods and mother earth. For such national and international renown, including association with the Inca Empire, the Q'eros have had little to no access to the numerous audiovisual recordings and publications that have been internationally produced about their culture.

Q'eros lifestyle and traditions are rapidly undergoing unprecedented changes, notably permanent migration out of Q'eros that is more prevalent than ever in their history, with

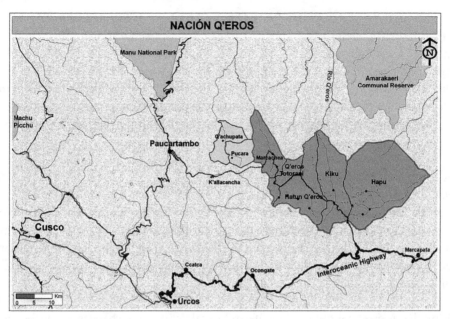

FIGURE 6.3 Map of the Q'eros Nation with nearby regions and cities. The heavy line through the Q'eros Nation is the new road system, under construction through the Q'eros communities.

Map courtesy of ACCA (Asociación para la Conservación de la Cuenca Amazónica), Cusco, Perú. www.acca.org.pe, 2009.

FIGURE 6.4 Typical Q'eros homes, in the high puna zone with llamas and alpacas, 2005.

Photograph by Holly Wissler.

approximately 30 of the 140 families of Hatun Q'eros having migrated to the large city of Cusco, drawn to modern amenities and in search of better education for their children.[9] In part, outward migration is a reaction to ecological changes that cause significant life-style challenges, such as glacial melting and less water, which reduce the quality of high-altitude grasses, and therefore make herds less healthy. This is coupled with the fact that the population of Hatun Q'eros has tripled in the past one hundred years, and therefore so has their animal population, which causes overgrazing and competition in the now lesser quality pasture areas.

The new interoceanic highway that connects the coasts of Peru and Brazil, completed in 2011, heralded the construction of a subsidiary road that arrived at the edge of the Hatun Q'eros community in 2013. In 2016, this new access road, which leaves zig-zag scars through once-pristine pastures, now penetrates through three of the four valleys in Hatun Q'eros and has introduced considerable lifestyle and diet change. For example, since 2010, the Q'eros choose not to cultivate their corn and other crops in their lower cloud-forest territory, and the access trails into the *monte* are now overgrown. Instead, with more vehicle mobility and dependence on the cash economy than ever before, they now purchase corn from nearby markets to make *chicha* (corn beer), the ceremonial drink that is essential to Quechua life and ritual. With these changes, I consider 2010 to be the historic end of Q'eros' autosustainability provided by the preeminent pre-Hispanic use of Andean verticality, which is now giving way to capitalist dependence on and interaction with the cash economy. Most Q'eros are gratified and relieved to have such easy road connection with urban areas, such as Cusco, and feel relief in their work and travel loads, as well as new opportunities available to them.

The Q'eros' changing relationship to their land and resources naturally has an impact on the songs that express this relationship. The Q'eros population in Cusco no longer sings their songs, since all songs are related to seasonal rituals of their land and animals. *Sara taki*, the corn harvest song, is no longer sung since their corn planting and harvest stopped in 2010. Also, there is a whole body of songs that are replete with Q'eros history and known only by the older generation. One such song is *Pariwa*, about high-altitude flamingos[10] that used to live in Q'eros' lakes, as described in a 1922 article by the large landowner of Q'eros' territory at that time.[11] This bird has not appeared in Q'eros for decades, perhaps due to ecological changes in habitat. The emigrated Q'eros who live in cities without their animals no longer hold animal fertility rituals that were vital for animal reproduction. Each animal type has its own ritual and ritual song dedicated to that animal: the Indigenous male/female llamas and alpacas, as well as the European-introduced cattle and sheep. This too is a whole body of songs and rituals that the emigrated youth of Q'eros are not learning; since the practice of these distinctive traditions is not being passed on to the current youngest generation of Q'eros immigrants, therefore, these songs and practices associated with these songs are endangered to this particular Q'eros demographic.

In addition, the Q'eros no longer create new songs since about the mid-twentieth century.[12] The song creation process used to be in the hands of the *alcalde*, or the newly elected authority in charge of carnival that year. He would sing the landscape on his two-day return from the district capital, Paucartambo, where he had just received this *cargo*. Now he receives his *cargo* at the newly established town council (*consejo menor*) in Q'eros,[13] no longer journeying by foot to Paucartambo and singing the earth's topography, flora, and fauna en route as before. Instead, the newly elected carnival officials select a song from the existing pool of *pukllay taki* (carnival songs), so that songs from the same small song group are rotated, and that group is becoming smaller over time due to popular choice.[14] These significant and rapidly increasing changes in the Q'eros communities over the past half-century naturally affect their song practice and production, and its decline, and make the return of their archives even more poignant.

The Q'eros use their strong identity and unification to assert their own choices, such as outward migration, discontinuance of the corn harvest, and insistence on and help with the building of the road from the provincial municipality of Paucartambo, thus inducing change and loss of song production. They own their choices, and I commend the older parents who choose the hard work necessary to move from their home territory where their livelihood is at arm's length to then transition into having to make money for the first time.

During my years of research, I experienced perhaps the tail end of the Q'eros' preroad, somewhat-isolated period. When I began my research in 2003, the interoceanic highway had not been built, so I traveled ten hours on windy, dirt roads on top of dramatic cliff drop-offs, and then hiked two days over two high mountain passes to arrive in Q'eros' territory. When the filmmaker and musician John Cohen did his work in Q'eros in the 1950s, 1960s, and 1970s, he took one week to get into Q'eros. This contrasts radically with today's reality of some Q'eros who now live in Cusco, own their own vehicles, and drive six hours to their home community on the weekend for soccer matches and return on Sunday night. The matches and prize-giving ceremonies—just like school anniversaries and many other events—are supported by solar-powered microphones and loudspeakers, with speeches and music for all. This was not the case as recently as 2010, when to return and show audiovisual archives of the Q'eros to the Q'eros, we needed to carry in our own gasoline-powered generators, computers, and screen to set up what I call an ambulatory movie theater across the Andes.

RETURN OF FIFTY YEARS OF AUDIOVISUAL ARCHIVES TO THE Q'EROS

During my first four years of fieldwork in the two communities of Hatun Q'eros and Hapu (2003–2007), one complaint expressed by community members was that they never see or receive the materials produced by the stream of researchers and filmmakers who have visited over the years, and that we must surely be "making a lot of money" from such publications. In accordance with the Q'eros' noble and direct nature, they openly expressed this resentment to me in our numerous private and public discussions about my documentary production of the yearly cycle of Q'eros musical rituals, *Kusisqa Waqashayku/From Grief and Joy We Sing* (2008, www.qerosmusic. com). Questions arose: "How will we see it?" "How much money are you making?" In response, I promised to show them my finished documentary and committed to returning all profits and donations made from the documentary to the community.[15] I had no idea how I would do this, since the community had neither electricity nor equipment for viewing and listening, yet in the moment, on the spot, I knew it was a promise I had to fulfill.

In later planning stages, I decided that the logistical feat of showing my documentary in Q'eros merited the presentation and return of as many audiovisual materials about their communities that I could locate, to all demographics of the Q'eros region—the men, women, children, and elders. This documentation pertains to them, and they have the right not only to see it, but to own their own copies. I had garnered many close relationships in Q'eros over the years, and my care for these people as individuals and community—in other words, respect for their request and rights—was the primary motivation for archival return. Research ethics and my belief that research products should be returned to them were also a strong motivation, but in retrospect, it was my love for the people and their open door to me that propelled me forward. I wanted to rectify their complaints about never having seen or heard any of the material about them that they know is out there in the world, much of which I had access to and owned myself. I then began collecting as much archival material as I could and planning a mass showing of it all. In comparison to past researchers in Q'eros, I had the advantage of living in Peru year-round, and could collect archives and orchestrate a return, unlike the many international researchers who return to their home countries soon after completing fieldwork, and become involved in job and family obligations that do not allow the time for such an undertaking in the country of research.

In September 2010, I led an expedition—funded mostly by private donations from supportive friends, and partially by the Andres del Castillo museum in Lima—which was a moving cinema across the high Andes.[16] The expedition totaled thirteen days, with showings in eight different locations in numerous valleys across the Q'eros Nation. We traversed six mountain passes, each over 15,000 feet above sea level, with a support team of ten people and twenty horses that carried generators, gasoline, projectors, laptop computers, electric cables, cameras, tents, and food, along with a large, bulky screen hoisted over the shoulder and carried by my *compadre* Jacinto Huamán. With this entourage (see Figure 6.5), we walked about a half day to reach the next location, and then after lunch took a few hours to set up the generator, cables, screen, projector, and speakers, according to the rudimentary circumstances of the stone and dirt-floor building designated for that night's showing. In dark homes and community buildings packed with some forty or fifty people sitting on the floor and standing against walls, we projected photos and video documentaries that spanned fifty-five years of Q'eros life. The showings began at about 7:00 p.m. and finished at around midnight.[17]

FIGURE 6.5 All crew involved: technical assistants, cameramen, cooks, wranglers, 2010.

Photograph courtesy of Paul Yule.

I showed the archive collection in chronological order, beginning with the oldest photos, which were two highly stylized Cusco studio photographs of a Q'eros man from approximately 1910 (date unsure).[18] Most of the photos were from the now-legendary Cusco University expedition in 1955,[19] when an interdisciplinary team of professors and students, headed by the anthropologist Oscar Núñez del Prado, traveled to Hatun Q'eros as the first "outsiders" to enter the then-isolated community with a research intent.[20] I collected photos from the three surviving members of that expedition, Mario Escobar Moscoso (geographer), Luis Barreda Murillo (archeologist, who died on May 22, 2009), and Demetrio Túpac Yupanqui (journalist for *La Prensa* newspaper, Lima, which sponsored the original expedition). The US musician and filmmaker John Cohen's three documentaries about Q'eros' music and textiles followed the opening photograph showing session: *Q'eros, the Shape of Survival* (1979, with footage from 1976); *Peru Weaving: A Continuous Warp* (1980, with footage from 1976); and *Carnival in Q'eros* (1990, with footage from 1989).[21] Cohen, a friend, mentor, and colleague, had been to Q'eros multiple times beginning in 1955; his last two visits with me were in 2005 and 2015. I played some of Cohen's older song recordings, one in particular about *bayeta* (typical Andean woven cloth used to make skirts, shirts, tunics, pants),[22] which was recorded in 1964, has not been sung for decades, and is unknown by the younger generation. I closed every evening with the Quechua version of my 2008 documentary about Q'eros musical rituals, entitled *Kusisqa Waqashayku/From Grief and Joy We Sing*. Including the 1910 photos, the showings, then, spanned nearly a century of archival material about Q'eros.

I purposely made my documentary trilingual in Quechua, Spanish, and English, for various audiences in Q'eros, Peru, and the United States. It was particularly important to me, and the Q'eros, that they have their own version accessible in their mother tongue of *runasimi*,[23] an editing option that was available to me in 2007 via DVD multilingual design, and not available to Cohen in the earlier days of expensive filmmaking. Even though Cohen's films had narration in English, it did not seem to matter; it was truly the visual that reached the hearts of many, and often in profound ways. I was struck by how the audiovisual medium instantly reached and had an on-the-spot emotional impact on Q'eros people of all ages. The immediacy of the projected image and sound caused spontaneous and continuous boisterous reaction. Every night's viewing was raucous with commentary, laughter, and vocal expression, so that often even the Quechua narration and dialogue of my film was not audible over nonstop response and commentary (see Figure 6.6).

At the end of each showing at every location I handed over to the community leader, in formal public presentation before all viewers, an archive package of DVDs containing the above-mentioned documentaries, song recordings, and photographs, along with two books: *Hidden Textiles of Peru: Q'ero Textiles* (Cohen and Rowe, 2002, in English) and *Q'eros, el último ayllu inca* (Flores Ochoa and Núñez del Prado, editors, 2005, in Spanish). I also contributed hard-copy photo albums of communal rituals from my own work from 2005 to 2009.[24] I knew at the time that the literal handover of

FIGURE 6.6 People attentive to projected movies on screen, 2010.

Photograph courtesy of Paul Yule.

archives was merely a moral and affective gesture, and that due to lack of electricity and equipment, most would not be able to make use of the returned documentaries, except for the books—they loved to finger through them and marvel at the photographs. Five short years later, they would have more viewing access with the onset of technology in Q'eros. Today, most of the Q'eros annexes (family groups in contiguous valleys) have shifted from no electricity to solar-panel-generated electricity. A few of the schools—particularly the new, and only, secondary school in the annex of Qocha Moqo—are able to view the documentaries on laptop computers. Even so, at the time of archive handover I felt that the gesture of return was well received, often with formal silence during the bestowal and rounds of applause afterward. For many, it was like viewing "home movies" that they never knew existed and just the viewing alone had inestimable value.

"Where Dead People Walk"

The evening showings were often quite touching and personal, as many Q'eros excitedly recognized living and deceased family members. Many had never seen a moving image before, much less images of their deceased relatives projected on a large screen with good sound. My *comadre* Juliana Apasa Flores commented that the movies were "*wañuq purishanku*"—"where dead people walk." People pointed animatedly to the screen, commenting on a weaving design or article of clothing they no longer weave or wear. There were many beautiful, spontaneous outbursts, for example during a scene from Cohen's 1979 film *The Shape of Survival* when a man and a young boy walked together with their llamas and alpacas. The older man standing beside me exclaimed, "There goes my uncle!" Then he gasped, pointed to the little boy walking next to him, and said, "That is me!" He was grinning from ear to ear.

A great boon was that many people in the 1955 photographs were identified. None of the photos I had collected from the surviving members of the 1955 Cusco University expedition were labeled. The elders reacted in boisterous identification and exuberance, as each subsequent photo would appear. Our spontaneous, continuous conversation was exhilarating. I would ask, "Who is this?" and someone would inevitably respond with the person's name and familial relationship, sometimes lovingly adding a little anecdote. Gina Maldonado, my Quechua tutor and principal assistant in song-text transcription during my dissertation fieldwork, and I rapidly took notes, documenting identification in the moment of discovery. The excitement, and even joy was palpable and we could hardly keep up with our notations. For example, an important identification was a 1963 photo of two of the three Q'eros leaders who made the historic journey to Lima on a plane—a momentous event in those days—to meet with President Belaúnde (see Figure 6.7). When the photograph came on the screen, the president of one of the annexes blurted out, "That is my father!" Alipio Quispe had identified his father, Turibio Quispe, who died in 1996. On this visit to the large capital city, his father and two others

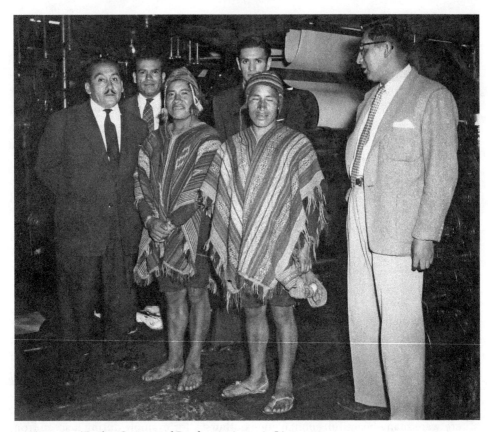

FIGURE 6.7 Turibio Quispe and Prudencio Apasa in Lima, 1963.

Photograph courtesy of Demetrio Tupac Yupanqui.

began the legal transactions of the community's land purchase from the Peruvian government, which had been sold to the government by the *hacendado*, or large landowner.
The resulting 1964 purchase was the first, and only, case in all Peru of an Andean community who fully owned their land title before the agrarian reform of 1969.[25] These two
men are therefore heroes of Q'eros recent history and were now being remembered by
subsequent generations, and made known to the younger generation, as they viewed the
photo on the screen.

My 2008 documentary begins with an interview with Vicente Apasa Huamán, the
third member of the group who flew to Lima in 1963 with the now-identified Turibio
Quispe and Prudencio Apasa in the 1963 photo. In this interview, Vicente talks about the
abuses of his people under the *hacendado*. He relays the infamous story, which was also
published by the folklorist Efraín Morote Best of the 1955 Cusco University expedition,
about the horrendous day—a fateful Wednesday—when many Q'eros men were forcibly
lined up and their single, long braid, a marker of Indigenous identity, was hacked off.[26]
It was my discovery of an older song that is now rarely sung, called "Sortija," that led
me to interviews with Vicente. "Sortija" is about the early twentieth century when the

landowner forced the Q'eros to make long trips to a high pass near the Bolivian border to trade their agricultural goods for silver from the Bolivian mines. Vicente's daughter, my *comadre* Juliana, who first sang the song for me and commented that the films are "where dead people walk," introduced me to her father. Vicente then provided a wealth of history about the *hacienda* days. He was lucid until he died in 2007, at the time my documentary was being edited. In this way, I linked my documentary showing at the end of the evening and the interview with Vicente, the third member of this triumvirate who flew to Lima to purchase the land from the Peruvian president, with the other two heroes in the 1963 photo that was shown at the start of the evening. The evening thus came full circle, through photos and moving images, of the past fifty years of Q'eros history (see Figure 6.8).

One of the most curious and perplexing reactions for me, and for the friends who came along as work staff on the trip, was the nearly continuous laughter throughout the screening of my documentary, but not during Cohen's older documentaries. Laughter flowed, even during the wrenching scenes of grief-singing, when brother and sister Victor and Juana Flores sing their grief about the recent deaths of their spouses through improvised text in the fertility song for the female llamas and alpacas.[27] I spent time analyzing this oddity with my Cusco friends first, but it was Gina Maldonado, my Quechua tutor originally from a Quechua community, who gave an insider's interpretation. Gina believed that the laughter was an expression of *identification* with their

FIGURE 6.8 Vicente Apasa Huaman in Wissler's documentary, 2010.

Photograph courtesy of Paul Yule.

contemporaries on the screen. This was later confirmed when I asked the Q'eros directly, and they responded, simply, "We laugh because we are happy to see ourselves; we are enjoying." Indeed, the laughter was not that of nervousness of disconcertedness, nor of ridicule; rather, it was an expression of pure joy and fascination. I sensed that their constant and contagious laughter has a different meaning and perception than I am used to and conditioned to in my own social world. Indeed, many times I have been startled and at first offended by the unabashed laughter from my *comadres* in Q'eros when I sing with them, dressed as a Q'eros woman, in carnival and animal fertility ritual. I have come to know that their laughter is not a laughing *at*—but a *delighting in* and *sharing with*. The Q'eros seemed to react more with observation, awe, nostalgia, and commentary during Cohen's prior documentaries that showed an earlier Q'eros with people who are no longer alive, and customs that have changed. This contrasted with the identification and joy at viewing my current documentary, expressed through laughter as they viewed themselves and present life on the screen.

HEALING GRIEF
THROUGH DOCUMENTARY VIEWING

One family benefited from fifty-five years of documentation, as John Cohen and I had worked inadvertently with this same family. I only discovered this well into my own fieldwork, during discussions with John and study of his photos and films. John first photographed Raymundo Quispe Chura in 1956 as a six-year-old boy, and up through the production of his film *Carnival in Q'eros* (1990) (see Figure 6.9). Raymundo was one of the first Q'eros I began to work with in 2003, yet when I met him, I did not know of his previous work with John. In preparation for John's return to Q'eros with me in 2005 after a sixteen-year absence, I asked Raymundo if he remembered John photographing and filming him from the 1950s–1980s, and he said that he did not. Yet, after I projected John's movies and left copies, thereby making his name known throughout the Q'eros region, I heard Raymundo say proudly that he remembered and had worked with John for a long time. Perhaps seeing the photos and the footage triggered his memory, combined with the power of suggestion, which helped Raymundo to suddenly remember the now well-known John Cohen. In any case, the introduction and presentation of old Q'eros images never before seen had a changing impact on Raymundo's perspective and memory.

Raymundo Quispe Chura's niece, Santusa Suqlle Quispe, was the single individual who I believe was most profoundly moved and changed by viewing old family images—in this case, John Cohen's 1979 film *Peruvian Weaving*, with footage shot in 1976. In the same photo from 1956, we see Raymundo Quispe Chura with his older sisters, Nicolasa on the middle and Andrea on the right. Nicolasa, who had died over thirty years ago, was featured as primary weaver in the film. An especially lengthy scene shows Nicolasa weaving an intricate design seated on the ground, with her eight-year-old daughter,

FIGURE 6.9 Raymundo, Nicolasa, and Andrea Quispe Chura, 1956.

Photograph courtesy of John Cohen.

Santusa, sitting closely at her side. When this scene suddenly appeared on the screen, Santusa, now in her mid-forties, covered her face in shock as she saw her mother, who died when she was twelve, projected in a large, "live" image before her. I watched as Santusa froze with her hand on her face, tears rolling down, continuing to take in the full scene. When the film ended, I walked over and sat next to her, took her hand, and asked her how she was. She responded, simply and directly as the Q'eros tend to do, *llakisqa, kusisqa*—sad and happy. The next day she watched the same documentary again at another location, and I observed that she was calm, with a tranquil smile, now knowing and expecting that she would see her mother on the large screen.

In October 2012—that is, two years after this mass showing—I invited Santusa over to my home to watch the 1976 footage of her mother again (see Figure 6.10). I gave Santusa her personal copy of this particular film since she is one of the many in the Q'eros diaspora who live in Cusco, and therefore she has access to television and a DVD player. She was riveted, viewing the scene once again in the privacy of my living room. She requested that we watch it numerous times, during which she reflected on her childhood out loud, remembering other family members and recounting her mother's life. Santa's joy was evident, as if she had worked through deep sentiment: "My mother is talking, as if she were alive in this moment; my heart opened. I am happier now. It's as if

FIGURE 6.10 Santusa Suqlle Quispe watching her mother on TV screen, 2012.

Photograph by Holly Wissler.

I have been reunited with my mother. It brought me happiness" (personal communication October 12, 2012; translation from Quechua by author).

She recalled her experience of two years earlier, seeing her mother for the first time with her fellow community members in the mass viewings in Q'eros:

> Now in your home is the first time I could really see my mother. The other times there were lots of people around and I couldn't really see. There was a lot of distraction, and people didn't take me into consideration. They didn't seem to think that seeing my mother might be important for me, so I felt excluded.
>
>   (personal communication October 12, 2012; translation from Quechua by author)

Santusa added that she felt sadness that there was no discussion or processing after the viewing in Q'eros, and this added to her feelings of exclusion. She helped me see the complexity and problematic aspects of staging mass viewings in her description of these two painful experiences when she saw the footage for the first time: first, the grief and shock of seeing her mother, who had died over thirty years earlier when she was a little girl, and second, feeling that her fellow community members did not recognize or acknowledge the impact this had on her, resulting in more hurt and feeling alone. A group discussion afterward might have helped ameliorate difficult emotions, thoughts, and reactions, and create more of a sense of sharing—not only in Santusa's case but also perhaps in others as well. Public discussion in Q'eros holds its own complexities and breaches of intimacy. While the people live communally, it is my experience that they are very private about personal matters. At the very least, it would have been more sensitive of me to inform Santusa ahead of time, privately, that we would view many sequences with her mother. However, the fact that I had hours of material and limited time in each viewing location, combined with my logistical and social responsibilities, and not knowing until the last minute who would show up, put a constraint on holding discussion and processing with many people, like Santusa, who would have seen a deceased family member on the screen. In this way, the showings were very raw, candid, real, and emotional.

It was evident to me that Santusa healed the grief of her childhood loss through continued viewings of her deceased mother on the screen. I witnessed her move from shock and tears in 2010 to feeling uplifted and grateful, and that she had an "open heart," two years later. When she left my home in 2012, she was beaming. She stated, "This experience has been like *hamp'iy* (medicine) for me. I am protected by my mother now, by her wisdom, for all her knowledge about weaving." The last thing she said as she left with her personal DVD copy was "my daughter will be very happy to see her grandmother."

Francisco Apasa Flores, an important community member who was the first president of the newly formed Q'eros Nation (Nación Q'eros) in 2005, also commented, like Santusa, that he felt "happy and sad" when he saw his deceased father, Mariano Apasa, a well-known ritual specialist, negotiate the "alpaca deal" in exchange for Cohen's filming his 1990 film *Carnival in Q'eros*. He expressed animatedly that the people "laughed with joy to see our customs all big on the screen." He pointed out the loss of some traditions (clothing, songs) that he witnessed in the older films, which prompted his opinion: "Twenty years from now I don't want to see our traditions lost like we saw in the movies last night. I hope we are still making our own clothes and practicing our customs. These movies are a great help, they are *ayni*."

Ayni is an ancient concept that governs Andean societies, based on reciprocity among community members and the continual offering to the spirit powers of the earth in return for individual and community welfare. During the peak of my fieldwork in Q'eros (2005–2007), I was constantly negotiating the *ayni* I needed to give the community in exchange for documentation, participation, and just plain being there.[28] Often these negotiations were lengthy, tedious, and tension-filled because the Q'eros are very careful in their negotiations about who and how an "outsider" can be in the community, particularly during festival times. In my first years in Q'eros I never fully knew if I would be granted permission for documentation and participation until it happened, but this dynamic shifted as I began to sing with the Q'eros women in every ritual throughout the year, wearing Q'eros clothing. At first many were skeptical, even disapproving of my documentary production, assuming I was profiting greatly from the proceeds; however, the fact that in 2010 I returned the profits and donations ($4,500) from my documentary sales, which they used to build their town council building, cemented our already well-bonded relationship. In community assembly during the handover of the documentary profits, many commented, "No one has ever done this before." I began to experience a completely opposite reaction to the idea of documentary production during this archive return when suddenly many, like Francisco Apasa Flores, expressed, "You made a documentary with certain people in the community. It is time now to make another one, with us." Suddenly many requested that we make many more documentaries, as if it were easy to do! I reflected on the years of struggle I endured in justifying one documentary, and on how something that was once a delicate, walking-on-eggshells endeavor had suddenly become the popular request. The Q'eros had experienced archival viewing directly and were now the owners with their own copies. The value of this immediate seeing and hearing of their history had taken hold, and they were suddenly requesting that more of the same be made.

Francisco continued his expression of what the viewings had provoked in him:

> We don't see these customs in any other place. We have a lot of strength, and a lot of poverty too. Our life is like that of the Incas. The Incas left their children, and we are here, we have been the people of Q'eros since ancient times. The Spanish arrived to brainwash and kill, we heard about this, but we served like soldiers. The ancient *altomisayoqs* [high ritual specialists] spoke well with the *apus* [mountain gods]. The killers arrived and the *apus* said you are not going to kill the Q'eros.
>
> (personal communication, September 10, 2010; Quechua translation by author with Gina Maldonado)

When the Q'eros Nation was formed in 2005 as an act of Q'eros solidarity and identity, and Francisco was elected as the first president, the nation voted to include the five communities that still practice Q'eros customs, such as clothing, ritual practice, and singing songs. These five communities intentionally excluded three Q'eros-origin communities who have assimilated into *mestizo*, or *misti*, culture by the outward signs such as wearing Western clothing and speaking Spanish.[29] Francisco stated, "We decided not to include them because they are no longer Q'eros."

This singular political and social act of excluding specific Q'eros communities who no longer practice their customs shows the importance of external signs of Q'eros culture to the people of the Q'eros Nation—signs that are prevalent in Cohen's and my documentaries. In this regard, the return of the archives took on a meaning of a larger historical scope that went beyond the remembrance of family members, healing deep wounds, and the important political roles community heroes played in the securing of their land title. As Francisco articulates, the archives stimulated a consciousness about the place of Q'eros in Andean history, and brought to light the specialness of their customs and identity that is connected to both Inca and current-day identity. This was possible because the Q'eros are, and have been, aware of their specialness, and many emphasize this unique identity in their interactions with foreign travelers, often as a means toward capital gain.[30] Many of the children were jolted into awareness about their inherited traditions amid the emotional and spontaneous reactions of their elders. The youth heard heated discussions and reactions about customs they no longer practice, thus sparking an awareness of the real possibility of loss. At that singular point in time, the presentations sent waves through the community about the importance of their people, specific individuals, and community-wide customs, so that there was a palpable cognizance of, and pride in, what it means to be uniquely Q'eros. The viewing of the archives played a role in not forgetting.

Conclusion and Current Archive Use in Q'eros

I am an advocate for the potency that the return of the archives to the Q'eros communities has generated on the grassroots and the most intimate levels, such as the example of one woman reconciling with the thirty years of pain felt over the death of her mother. I believe there was an inherent power in the viewing and return of the archives directly to the *people and community* of origin, versus deposit in an outside institution. The arduous return of the archives literally to their own homes and into their own hands was a gesture of great esteem about who they are, and they were not asked to awkwardly fit into the system of the "other"—the urban, Spanish-speaking world that has dominated Andean culture for centuries, by viewing the archives outside of their own community. This allowed the Q'eros to laugh and comment boisterously, identify elders out loud, heal old wounds, and share and feel the value of the documentation among generations on their own turf, and to ask for more of the same.

Communal viewing and listening to the materials in their birthplace created a community connection and exuberant remembrance that resonated emotionally among all. Many Q'eros implicitly expressed profound satisfaction that past documentation was being shown, and was returned firsthand, to the community that had collaborated in the documentation to begin with. Gina Maldonado, who was already familiar with Q'eros culture and many of the people present at the showings as a result of our work together, summarized:

> It was the first time they could see themselves, hear themselves. There was much laughter, dialogue, and commentary about the scenes. Voluntarily they said, "I want to be interviewed. Are you going to make more documentaries?" They felt valued and respected to be convened in their own language, in the doors of their own homes, called to come to "the movies." The ones who convoked were known people to them, and that is why it was not just another mockery. Late at night, when the presentation was over, they did not want to leave. They were very awake, wanting to see more.
>
> (personal communication, August 20, 2016)

As Gina suggests, the act of taking the movies directly *to them* and inviting them to the event in their language, often by door-to-door announcement, is much different than, say the many presentations of and about Q'eros culture that are staged by the Ministry of Culture in Cusco, which many Q'eros are invited to attend. The same could be said of the premiere of my documentary in Cusco at the public institution ICPNA (Peruvian–North American Institute). In these cases, presentations are staged for the general Cusco public, in Spanish, with some Q'eros in attendance and quite often participating through the awkward staging of singing songs; but the Q'eros are always the minority. They must adjust to an urban system that is not their own. Indeed, presenting the archives in their own homes showed that they were valued, esteemed, and comfortable, and they could react, respond, and converse out loud. None of the Q'eros who attended the Cusco premiere of my documentary felt free to laugh and respond during the showing as they did in Q'eros; rather, like the urban majority, they sat quietly.

Gina continued:

> There was honesty on both parts: the researcher who "kept her word" and the Q'eros who could be honest in their opinions due to today's advanced mediums of communication making it possible for younger generations to see works realized in the past. These presentations showed respect towards the Quechua people, the Andean, the agriculturalist, the weavers, and pastoralists, men and women alike.

Hannah Rae Porst, director of the nongovernmental organization Willka Yachay, which sponsors the only high school in the entire Q'eros Nation (located in Qocha Moqo, the central-most valley of Hatun Q'eros), stated:

> Cohen's and Wissler's films allow the Q'eros people to become more aware of the beauty and depth of their culture and to understand and appreciate the historical context of their lives. Since 2012, students in Qochamoqo have watched John Cohen's and Holly Wissler's documentaries several times during the year. Teachers often play the films on a projector as part of their curriculum and, more informally, students have gathered to watch the films on laptops after school. They'll huddle around a small screen together and revel in seeing their forebears and glimpses of their community's past. One of the most important missions of Willka Yachay's Colegio Etnico is to enable our students to revitalize their community's cultural identity. Our students, their teachers and village elders are in the process of creating a museum. Cohen's and Wissler's films will be curated and always available for community members and future generations to watch and understand their past so they can build their future.
>
> (personal communication, August 23, 2016)

Porst's work with the Colegio Etnico, the ethnic high school, is now able to make these archives available to students, and anyone, right there in Q'eros, as valued tools used in support of identity revitalization. The primary goal of the Colegio Etnico is to focus on traditional knowledge, invite elders to guide learning, and not adhere to the national government public school curricula, which often includes materials that are simply not applicable to Q'eros' life. Decisions are made by consensus, so that the control of the archives is community managed. This school exists in only one annex of Q'eros and only serves a small portion of the population; nevertheless, it is a start toward

Q'eros-run archive control. This small, community-run archive in a local school contrasts with the possibility of a Spanish-language institution in an urban center that would require effort for the Q'eros to travel to and negotiate. The mere existence of and access to the documentation esteems who the Q'eros are, sends that message to them, and values the Q'eros in a larger context as Andean agriculturalists, weavers, and pastoralists, as Gina stated.

John Cohen, now in his mid-eighties, and I have experienced a wonderful journey that started with my asking him, years ago, "Tell me about Q'eros," evolving into mutual sharing of ideas and interpretations, to some poignant, educating disagreements, to John now asking me, "So, tell me what is going on in Q'eros today." He has stated that my in-depth work has helped him to understand his own work more fully, and his set the bedrock for mine. We both fell in love with Q'eros, the people and how they live, and have had our lives changed as a result. In 2015, John discussed the meaning for him, as researcher and friend of the Q'eros, to have had his three documentaries and one book returned to them:

> They recognized relatives, family, and friends who had died long ago. Their response caused me to breathe a deep sigh . . . for it fulfilled an impossible promise I had made to myself (and to them), of returning my vision of Q'eros to their community.
>
> Throughout this long fifty-year endeavor, an unfulfilled disturbing question has grown within me. From the start in 1956, I was always asking myself how could my work help them, to ease them from poverty, to improve their lives, to give them something back. But nothing got back to Q'eros.
>
> Repatriating cultural goods has become a hot political and cultural issue. Reawakening feelings, family and rituals through music and films gets closer to the heart of the matter. I have always considered myself as an artist first, and this new exchange with the Q'eros is gratifying beyond words.
>
> (personal communication, August 13, 2014)

While the Q'eros are experiencing modernization probably faster and more violently than ever before in their history, they still practice many of their traditions, so they rejoiced in both their past and present. While viewing, they learned about their past, within a flourishing, yet changing, present. Pride was palpable, and perhaps they feel there is nothing at stake if they no longer sing the old songs, or weave the older designs, because they do sing and weave the current ones. This contrasts strikingly with my return of song archives to the near-extinct Amazonian Wachiperi group, also in 2010, who indeed no longer sing their songs and have lost the context; nearly everything about their practiced traditions is on the verge of extinction, including their language.[31] The Q'eros archives were enjoyed as a continuance of, and homage to, their living expressions of culture, while the Wachiperi felt a loss and urgency, and the need to do something about it. The contrast in reaction between experiencing the archives through viewing and listening with the Q'eros and the Wachiperi was pronounced: the celebration and enjoyment of changing tradition, versus the pain and loss of listening to a dead one.

The Q'eros do not usually sit around and talk about, revel in, or celebrate their culture, past and present. The archival showings and return were a great jolt of communally shared consciousness about their Q'eros-ness, boisterously articulated, connecting family and community with palpable pride and celebration. On a grassroots level, even the momentary experience of this is worth the archival return.

Notes

1. The ethnohistorian John Murra provided groundbreaking research on the cultivation of and far-reaching web of trade in these multiple ecosystems, which he seminally termed "vertical ecology" (Murra 1972, 1980).
2. The orthography of Q'ero and Q'eros is both interchangeable and debatable. For a complete discussion, see Wissler (2009a, 8–10).
3. The purpose of the colonial Spanish Empire was to gather native populations into centers called "Indian reductions" in order to Christianize, tax, and govern them more effectively.
4. I specify ethnicity because even today the Q'eros marry within their own ethnic group. While this is changing slowly, intermarriage is still rare.
5. Q'eros was once an entire geographic region composed of eight Q'eros cultural communities, with their corresponding *ayllu* groups, today called annexes. The eight communities are Kiku, Hapu, Totorani, Marcachea, Hatun Q'eros, Pucara, Q'allacancha, and Qachupata. Hatun Q'eros is the largest of all these communities, consisting of approximately 24 percent of the total Q'eros population of approximately 3,000. The Q'eros Nation (La Nación Q'eros), an association formed in 2005 by the Q'eros in response to current political forces, consists of five of these communities banding together in a single statement of identity and solidarity (see maps in Figures 6.1 and 6.2).
6. For detail of the Q'eros, and Andean, pastoral transhumant societies, see Webster (1972, 1980, 1981, 1983).
7. The Incas were the ethnic group located in the Cusco valley region that gained power and expanded widely in the 15th century to incorporate many Indigenous groups and form the largest empire in the history of the Americas, until the Spanish invasion in 1532. There is evidence of Inca presence in Q'eros territory. See Luis Barreda Murillo (2005 [c. 1955]).
8. For in-depth discussion of how the Q'eros and their Inca identity and use by the Q'eros in identity negotiation, see Wissler (2009, 35–41).
9. The Q'eros have primary schools through the sixth grade, and only one high school available to them, founded by the nongovernment organization Willka Yachay (www.willkayachay.org).
10. The Chilean Flamingo/flamenco chileno (*Phoenicopterus chilensis*).
11. A 1922 article by the current large landowner (*hacendado*) of Q'eros territory at that time, Luis Yábar Palacio, describes the fauna and provides detailed descriptions of rituals and festivals in Q'eros during his time as *hacendado* (see Yábar Palacio 1922).
12. I have deduced this from interviews with many Q'eros elders and analysis of John Cohen's recordings of Q'eros songs, dating from 1964, which only include the songs still sung today that are now part of the standard song stock (with the exception of one). There is a 1958 description by the Cusco folklorist Efraín Morote Best of the process of creation of new songs, so it is sometime mid-twentieth century when this process stopped, and gave way to a cycling of existing songs. See Efraín Morote Best (2005 [1958]).

13. The town council, which registers births, deaths, marriages, and deals with legal documents of the community, was established in 1998.

14. In my work I recorded seven active *Pukllay taki*, and eight *ñawpa taki*, or songs from before that are no longer sung.

15. See Wissler (2009b). This article serves as prelude and background context to the 2010 return of my documentary, and other archives, to the Q'eros.

16. See a three-minute YouTube excerpt of this return, titled "Return of Archives, Q'eros, Wissler," https://www.youtube.com/watch?v=XGQL087NYhk.

17. As part of prelogistical planning, I took one week in June 2010 to literally walk through the whole trip and stay overnight at all presentation sites in order to officially announce the dates and purpose of the showings. Radio contact between Cusco and Q'eros was unreliable, and the community way of announcing any official presentation is to talk, in person, to the community beforehand. Nowadays there is (unreliable) satellite telephone and Internet for communication.

18. By the Cusco photographer Luis Figueroa Aznar.

19. Universidad Nacional de San Antonio de Abad, Cusco (UNSAAC).

20. The team consisted of Oscar Nuñez del Prado, social anthropologist and expedition leader; Mario Escobar Moscoso, geographer; Efraín Morote Best, folklorist; Josafa Roel Pinead, ethnomusicologist; Manuel Chávez Ballón, archeologist; Luis Barreda Murillo, assistant archeologist; Demetrio Roca, assistant folklorist; Malcom Burke, photographer; Demetrio Túpac Yupanqui, journalist, *La Prensa*. See Flores Ochoa and Nuñez del Prado (2005). This publication commemorates the fifty-year anniversary of this expedition, with articles covering a fifty-year span, beginning with articles from this expedition and my article about two Q'eros' festivals and modernization as the most recent.

21. For information about John Cohen's music, films, and photography, see http://www.johncohenworks.com/home.html.

22. This song is track 34 of the CD *Mountain Music of Peru*, 1991 [1964], Smithsonian/Folkways CD SF 40020. Reissued in 1991 with additional material.

23. *Runasimi*, or "mouth of the people," is the name the Indigenous Andean people, or *runa*, use for Quechua. The term "Quechua" is a Spanish word, derived from the name of the ecological zone, *qheswa*, where the *runa* grow multiple varieties of potatoes.

24. Of the over one thousand field photos I took, I made a selection from the communal ritual of carnival and other community meetings to return via photo albums that community members could easily access and enjoy. Many of the photos I took in the field were of private rituals and leisure time, for particular families who would not like these disclosed publicly. Private life is guarded and normally not shared, so it would not have been appropriate for me to include private photos in the public archives.

25. Peru's agrarian reform was instigated in 1969 by General Juan Velasco's military government to essentially expropriate big estates from the large landowners and hand them over to the peasant population who lived on and worked these lands, as well as to nationalize foreign enterprises. The leftist ideology was progressive, yet ended essentially in economic disaster.

26. See Efraín Morote Best (2005 [1958]).

27. See Wissler 2009b for description of filming and editing this particular grief-singing scene.

28. Some of the *ayni* I gave to the community included medicine for extermination of the external parasites of the llama and alpaca herds; the organization and building of a

much-needed permanent bridge to connect the potato and corn zones; securing funds and collaboration to build a primary school, to name a few.

29. *Mestizo* is a charged and difficult term to define. *Misti* is the term the Q'eros, and many Quechua speakers, call *mestizos*. Originally, in early colonial Peru, the term was based on racial background, and a *mestizo* in postconquest years was literally the offspring of a Spanish man or Spanish born in colonial Peru (*criollo*) with an Indigenous woman, so that the blood was "mixed." Nowadays the term is more of a cultural reference. A *mestizo* is an Andean person who has incorporated influences such as education in Spanish, Catholicism, speaks Spanish as well as Quechua, and wears factory clothes (pants, shoes, jackets), to name a few examples. So a Q'eros person can change from *runa* (person) to *misti*, by change of lifestyle.

30. To their credit, the Q'eros use their identity of a connection to an "Inca past" in interactions with tourists, particularly tourists seeking spiritual interactions and guidance, to sell textiles and spiritual offerings. For a full discussion of the history and use of Q'eros/Inca identity, see Wissler (2009a, 35–41).

31. See Wissler (2015) for description of archive return to the Wachiperi Amazonian group.

REFERENCES

Barreda Murillo, Luis. 2005 [c. 1955]. "Arqueología de Hatun Q'ero Ayllo." In *Q'ero, el último ayllu inka*, 2nd ed., edited by Jorge Flores Ochoa and Juan Núñez del Prado, 39–56. Lima: Instituto Nacional de Cultura y Universidad Nacional Mayor de San Marcos.

Cahill, David. 1994. "Colour by Numbers: Racial and Ethnic Categories in the Viceroyalty of Peru, 1532–1824." *Journal of Latin American Studies* 26 (2): 325–346.

Cohen, John. 1979. *Q'eros, the Shape of Survival*. New York: Cinema Guild. Film.

Cohen, John. 1980. *Peru Weaving: A Continuous Warp*. New York: Cinema Guild. Film.

Cohen, John. 1990. *Carnival in Q'eros*. Berkeley, CA: Berkeley Media LLC. Film.

Cohen, John. 1991 [1964]. *Mountain Music of Peru*. Smithsonian/Folkways CD SF 40020. One compact disc. Reissued with additional material.

Cohen, John, and Ann Pollard Rowe. 2002. *Hidden Threads of Peru: Q'ero Textiles*. London: Merrell.

Flores Ochoa, Jorge, and Juan Núñez del Prado, eds. 2005. *Q'ero, el último ayllu inka*. 2nd ed. Lima: Instituto Nacional de Cultura y Universidad Nacional Mayor de San Marcos.

Morote Best, Efraín. 2005 (1958). "Un nuevo mito de fundación del Imperio." In *Q'ero, el último ayllu inka*, 2nd ed., edited by Jorge Flores Ochoa and Juan Núñez del Prado, 287–310. Lima: Instituto Nacional de Cultura y Universidad Nacional Mayor de San Marcos.

Murra, John. 1972. "El control vertical de un máximo de pisos ecológicos en la economía de las sociedades andinas." In *Visita de la Provincia de León de Huánuco en 1562*, edited by John Murra, 427–476. Huánuco, Peru: Universidad Hermilio Valdizán.

Murra, John. 1980. *The Economic Organization of the Inca State*. Greenwich, CT: JAI Press.

Webster, Steven. 1972. "The Social Organization of a Native Andean Community." PhD diss., University of Washington.

Webster, Steven. 1980. "Ethnicity in the Southern Peruvian Highlands." In *Environment, Society, and Rural Change in Latin America*, edited by D. A. Preston, 135–154. New York: Wiley and Sons.

Webster, Steven. 1981. "Interpretation of an Andean Social and Economic Formation." *Man* 16 (4): 616–633.

Webster, Steven. 1983. "Native Pastoralism in the South Central Andes." *Ethnology* 12 (2): 115–133.

Wissler, Holly. 2009a. "From Grief and Joy We Sing: Social and Cosmic Regenerative Processes in the Songs of Q'eros, Peru." PhD diss., Florida State University.

Wissler, Holly. 2009b. "Grief-Singing and the Camera: The Challenges and Ethics of Documentary Production in an Indigenous Andean Community." *Ethnomusicology Forum* 18 (1): 33–49.

Wissler, Holly. 2015. "Andes to Amazon on the River Q'eros: Indigenous Voice in Grassroots Tourism, Safeguarding, and Ownership Projects of the Q'eros and Wachiperi Peoples." In *The Oxford Handbook of Applied Ethnomusicology*, edited by Svanibor Pettan and Jeff Todd Titon, 398–450. New York: Oxford University Press.

Yábar Palacio, Luis. 1922. "El ayllu de Queros (Paucartambo)." *Revista Universitaria* 38: 3–26. Cusco, Peru.

CHAPTER 7

AUDIOVISUAL ARCHIVES

Bridging Past and Future

JUDITH GRAY

THE statement of ethical principles of the International Association of Sound and Audiovisual Archives[1] recognizes three basic archival tasks (acquiring materials, processing and preserving them, and making them accessible) and eight potential roles (creators of content, performers, recordists, intellectual property owners, depositors, archivists, technicians, and users) that may intersect in the course of those archival tasks. Repatriation and dissemination activities that look to revived or new uses of older materials are dependent on all of those factors, precisely because of the complex histories and present realities that affect audiovisual archives. Archives remain at the midpoint, curating collections of recordings and related documentation—collections that each have a history (sometimes convoluted and problematic), that each require reformatting in the present to remain accessible, and that each carry the potential for renewed use in communities of origin. The histories both of documentary recording itself in the Americas and of dissemination efforts in the United States nearly a century later seem to begin with Native American materials and to expand outward from there. I will be using the word "dissemination" throughout this discussion of these activities, since that was the term in use during the Federal Cylinder Project (FCP) that will be the basis for much of the following. Unlike what museums were doing when repatriating one-of-a-kind objects to Native communities, for example, we were not returning original cylinder recordings to the community, but rather copies in a format accessible at the time. Queries sent to us then and now focus on the recorded contents rather than on the cylinder itself, the artifactual carrier of the sound.[2]

To our knowledge, Jesse Walter Fewkes was the first ethnologist to experiment with cylinder recordings as a tool for ethnographic fieldwork. The success of his March 1890 experiment among Passamaquoddy people in Maine (followed by rapid publication of his results in two journals [Fewkes 1890: *Journal of American Folklore*, 257–280; *Science*, 267–269]) was mirrored in the numerous documentation projects around the world in the next three decades—from Tierra del Fuego to Greenland, from the upper reaches of the Amazon to multiple Pacific Islands. Within the Americas, documentation projects using wax-cylinder technology between 1890 and 1920 were primarily focused on indigenous peoples from the Omaha people of Nebraska to the Huichol of Mexico to the Ona and Yahgan people at the southern tip of South America; comparatively few recordists in the Americas were working in Euroamerican or African American contexts in the early decades.

The earliest sound archives were those established in research institutions in Vienna in 1899 and Berlin in 1900. Both the Phonogrammarchiv of the Austrian Academy of Sciences and the Berliner Phonogramm-Archiv gathered recordings made by many ethnologists including those working in the Americas, creating collections that enabled comparative research in acoustics, musical practice, and psychology. In the Americas, recordings were initially gathered primarily in universities and museums with active fieldwork programs and ethnology expeditions, though occasionally by private individuals (Gray 2003, 58–61). In the United States, many of the museum audio collections in particular eventually made their way to universities or to institutions such as the Library of Congress.

Outreach from such archives was relatively limited. University collections were accessed by faculty and students; recordings in public institutions could be accessed via research trips to their locations or, in some cases, via phonoduplication requests (if the institution had that capability to make copies). Publications about such archival collections ranged from catalog lists to sampler albums including those produced by the Library of Congress starting in 1933.

Increasing awareness of the values of cultural diversity in and around the American bicentennial may have contributed to a much more focused sense in US institutions in the 1970s of the importance of making archival materials available to the communities of origin. And when US audiovisual archives began deliberate dissemination activities, their initial focus was principally on recordings of indigenous peoples. Of the approximately ten thousand field-recorded wax cylinders in the archive of the American Folklife Center, at least three-fourths are from tribal communities, so from its beginnings in 1977, the FCP was primarily concerned with preserving, documenting, and disseminating those recordings.

The 1980 annual meeting of the Society for Ethnomusicology in Bloomington, Indiana, included a panel titled "The Federal Cylinder Project: Early Field Recordings and the Ethnomusicologist." Panel participants Erika Brady, Ron Walcott, and Maria LaVigna were all members of the Cylinder Project staff. They addressed early recording techniques and limitations and, ultimately, "the problems facing the latter-day ethnomusicologists in recording and cataloging these cylinders, as well as the light these recordings shed on the field of ethnomusicology in former years."[3] One element of the project that was not explicit in the abstracts, but which became apparent in the presentations and following discussion, was that here, at last, was a project in which a principal goal was to work with the communities where the recordings had been made, to make the recordings accessible to members of those communities, and to abide by community wishes with regard to the process. I came away thinking, "Finally! Finally there's a project with some hope of producing genuine collaborations between a federal agency and Native communities."

Three years later, I was fortunate enough to join the American Folklife Center's FCP team, just at the moment when enough preservation and cataloging of early cylinder recordings had occurred to enable the team to begin its formal multitribal dissemination work. From that time until the present, I have been involved with the many ethnographic audiovisual collections located in a large, tax-funded federal agency with all of its attendant requirements and realities. The following, then, describes circumstances that will not necessarily be characteristic of or relevant to other types of archives and their parent institutions.

When I arrived at the library, a multiyear documentation-dissemination-presentation project with the Omaha Tribe of Nebraska was still in progress, with periodic visits in the first half of the 1980s by Folklife Center staff to the Macy, Nebraska, community, and with trips by various elders and the tribal historian to Washington, DC. It was apparent, however, that this process could not serve as a model for the return of the many different tribal recordings in the center's archive. We had neither the funding nor the staff to maintain such intensive work and travel, given the number of communities involved, so we needed to explore other possibilities.

While some work was already underway, for example, within the Smithsonian Institution to make historical photographs available to and in a southwestern pueblo, protocols for handling sound recordings were not yet spelled out. To that end, in the summer of 1983, the American Folklife Center convened a group of Cherokee, Seneca, Kiowa, and Santa Clara tribal cultural specialists who all had experience in bridging differing organizational realities of large cultural institutions and tribal governments. They were asked to help the center come up with realistic guidelines for possible dissemination of sound recordings to tribal communities.

One of the first realities of the process that our advisors identified was the need for a federal agency to operate via "the front door." We needed to start by approaching the recognized tribal government, even in instances where we knew that the recordings from that community probably belonged to a particular clan or specific ceremonial society, etc. Similarly, as a federal agency, we needed to inform the relevant congressional delegation of our approach to that tribal nation.[4] Apart from those initial contacts, however, we always tried to find ways to inform the specific rights holders, if those were discoverable to us, or urged the people in the tribal offices to make such connections for us, and we definitely asked to be placed in touch with any designated cultural specialists in the community.

Another reality concerned the audio format to be returned. In the mid-1980s, while the preservation standard for audio recordings was analog tape on 10-inch open reels, the most used—and thus accessible—format in Native communities was the audiocassette. So that was the format to be used in the dissemination context.

While we were principally offering copies of early recordings and whatever relevant cataloging information we had been able to locate, we also prepared information packets containing materials such as suggestions for storage and use of recordings, bibliographies of cultural heritage revitalization publications, information on archival training opportunities, and the like. But, based on the counsel of our advisory team, we only offered these varied resources. What happened next was almost always to be the decision of the community.[5] Did they in fact want to have the recordings? Did they want the supplemental types of information? Did they want a member of the FCP team to visit, to make public or private presentations regarding the recordings? Did they want the recordings mailed to them? Did they want any publicity surrounding this?

In the following four to five years, three of us on the Cylinder Project staff (plus a contractor hired to do the work in the Pacific Northwest and Alaska[6]) contacted and, in most cases, subsequently visited approximately one hundred communities. We gave presentations to tribal councils, to groups of elders, to schoolchildren, to culture committees, to individuals. These presentations took place in libraries, gymnasiums, cultural centers, tribal museums, meeting rooms, restaurants, private homes, and sometimes even at large public events like powwows. In some locations, our visits were publicized, and we were asked to provide interviews to the press and on radio; in other cases, there were simply one-on-one meetings.

The overall process of dissemination, of course, was inevitably shaped by the realities of the collections here in the American Folklife Center's archive, some of which have already been alluded to. The "coverage" of tribal recordings is anything but consistent: while the archive includes recordings from more than 140 tribes (and many more individual communities), one tribe's material may consist of a single cylinder lasting anywhere from two to six minutes, while another tribe is represented by multiple collections lasting several hundred hours. In some cases, material in the American Folklife Center is also found in other repositories, but the two or more repositories may not each have *exactly* the same set of recordings; in some instances, what is available at the American Folklife Center is only a subset of a larger collection elsewhere (a reality particularly true of many California collections). Further, while the sound recordings from many early ethnographic collections eventually came to the Library of Congress, more often than not the documentation such as fieldnotes, transcriptions, and translations for those recordings has remained elsewhere and must be tracked down separately (unless we have been able to secure photocopies, for example, or unless the documentation has been lost entirely).[7] And the collections contain only those genres in which the collectors were interested. In the late nineteenth to early twentieth centuries, ethnographers who created audiovisual documentation focused more often on what they saw as disappearing ceremonies and practices rather than on day-to-day activities. Given the limits of early audio technology,[8] most ethnologists opted not to record spoken narratives (which could be taken down via phonetic dictation), focusing instead on songs from those ceremonies. Thus, stories, personal narratives, social dance songs, "work" songs, or genres such as songs for or by children are almost certainly unrepresented (or, at any rate, underrepresented) in the collections that we were trying to make available to the communities of origin. By the same token, the majority of early documentary recordings that are available for dissemination are in fact of songs.

The bulk of this type of dissemination—initiated by deliberate outreach from the archive to specific communities—was over by the early 1990s, when designated funding for the FCP was over, and when the staff members who had been most directly involved had either left the center or the library itself or, in my case, were assigned to other tasks. While several volumes of cylinder-by-cylinder cataloging had been published, other collections were still incompletely described, and henceforth detailed cataloging could occur only in isolated instances as questions arose about specific collections.

But the same period was marked by new activities and collaborations that reshaped types of dissemination work on the part of multiple federal agencies. One of the first signs was the National Park Service report titled *Keepers of the Treasures: Protecting Historic Properties and Cultural Traditions on Indian Lands*, published in May 1990 (Parker 1990). This report on tribal preservation funding needs, requested by the US Senate, was based on consultations with tribes and discussions with Native American organizations, historic preservation officers and advisors, and other federal agencies. The conclusion of the report was that "Indian tribes must have the opportunity to participate fully in the national historic preservation program, but on terms that respect their cultural values, traditions, and sovereignty," and noted that the principles stated in this context had much broader applicability.

Simultaneously, the Park Service was able to establish the Historic Preservation Fund tribal grant program. In fiscal years 1990 and 1991, almost $1,250,000 was directed to cultural heritage projects by Indian tribes and Alaska Native groups for projects including "oral history, language retention, historic properties survey, computerized databases, ethnobotany, and documentation of song and ceremony by audio and video recording" (Parker 1991, 3). The number of proposals for these grants was large; as one of the reviewers in that first year, I received five full photocopier-paper boxes filled with proposals, requesting amounts of support many times over the available funding. What was evident in the process and in subsequent discussions was that the focus of cultural preservation was truly shifting to the communities themselves, to their recognition of what types of preservation activity they deemed most important—and many of the proposals they were submitting pointed to direct documentation of cultural traditions (frequently involving music) by members of those communities in addition to trips to archives in search of existing documentation. Several of us affiliated with archival institutions helped draft suggested guidelines for cultural documentation projects, in order to help point grantees toward reliable equipment and a realization of the resources necessary to assure long-term sustainability of any documentation created. Our hope was that such suggestions coupled with the funding might help create or bolster infrastructure within communities wishing to take on these self-documentation projects and retrieval of archival materials.

Training in documentation and archiving skills became a matter of increasing interest, and that was an area in which the federal agencies had experience that could be shared. Disseminating this information and these sets of skills became as important in some respects as disseminating actual cultural documentation. The National Park Service, which traditionally had provided training in historic preservation activities and regulations, also produced a brochure for distribution to tribal cultural specialists showing which federal agencies could provide what additional services, including technical assistance for cultural documentation efforts. Meanwhile, the Smithsonian Institution's Office of Museum Programs, and specifically the American Indian Studies Program created in 1990, provided fellowships for tribal members to come to Washington to study museum techniques and to visit other cultural institutions there with tribally relevant holdings. And in 1992 the partners at the Smithsonian, the Park Service, and the American Folklife Center collaborated on a two-week field school covering documentation and archiving skills for tribal community teams brought to Washington.

The early 1990s, then, were marked not only by an initial assessment of the dissemination process but also by these new collaborative efforts with other federal agencies and tribal communities. I had the opportunity to reflect on processes and issues of dissemination in an article titled "The Songs Come Home: The Federal Cylinder Project," published in an issue of CRM: The Journal of Heritage Stewardship (Gray 1991, 32–35).[9] The editor, Patricia Parker, titled that issue "America's Tribal Cultures: A Renaissance in the 1990s." And indeed, the volume pointed to an array of then newly evolving consultations between federal/state agencies and tribal communities as well as revitalization efforts in Pojoaque Pueblo, at Ak-Chin, and in communities in Alaska.

Since the early 1990s, dissemination of Native American field recordings has more often been a response to specific requests from communities and specific individuals within those communities rather than what might constitute an unsolicited approach to tribal governments. Our tasks in the contemporary setting are to listen, to understand what is being sought, and to provide links to relevant materials where we are able to do so. Outreach in this climate has taken the form primarily of presentations in contexts where we find cultural specialists who may then subsequently choose to contact us in search of relevant materials. This includes the now-annual conferences of the Association of Tribal Archives, Libraries, and Museums, and an array of gatherings of tribal representatives in Washington, DC. As more and more attention is being paid to endangered languages, additional opportunities for sharing information about relevant resources have arisen; we have, for example, served as one of the Washington hosts for Breath of Life Archival Institutes for Indigenous Languages, in which teams from fifteen or more communities learn archival research techniques to assist their local language-revitalization efforts. (While the songs on field recordings may be only partially texted, and those words may belong to rituals rather than to the vocabulary of daily life, the early recordings still constitute a treasured resource.)

This form of dissemination, in some respects, may appear to be more passive than active. And yet it may have more lasting impact than the earlier efforts. As tribal communities have become more intentional about cultural preservation and revitalization activities, they are more often contacting us when their archival infrastructure is in place, or when a specific project is underway—that is, when the timing is right for them rather than just for us.

And timing has definitely been a factor in identifying who is able to access what materials. For example, the dissemination of audio recordings in the early 1980s to the Omaha people in Nebraska permitted elders to present tribal-heritage LPs or cassettes (the appropriate technology for the time) to graduating high school students. But the initial mounting of an Omaha music collection on the Library of Congress website in the late 1990s may not have increased access to the recordings *within* the Omaha community, given fewer computer resources there at that time. So while the website (created with specific assistance from knowledgeable elders and tribal consent) facilitated dissemination of tribal recordings to the world at large, it did not necessarily increase access within the home community at that particular moment.

Current timing issues may have more to do with community decision-making regarding policies—e.g., the person(s) or organization(s) to be entrusted with the care of audiovisual collections received from archives—or with pragmatic issues such as access to server capacity for long-term storage of digitized materials. However, in digitizing such collections, the archive is making a commitment to the permanent preservation of those materials and thus to sustained availability of the recordings to communities.

We have, for example, a large collection that came to us as a result of a specific tribal request in 1990. That collection has since been digitized here, while the access copy that the tribe made before sending the collection to Washington is no longer playable within the community. But there has been no consensus about where the digital files that we can supply should be placed; contacts initiated by tribal librarians, tribal museum people, and various tribal council members have not fully resolved the issue. So we need to wait, since that decision is not up to us.

Archival dissemination, however, is not limited to indigenous communities and individuals, or people in one's own country. Increasingly, as we are able to create online catalog records that search engines can find, we are being approached by people from all parts of the world in search of recordings curated here. The greatest number of these inquiries is from descendants of the individuals who had been recorded at some point. We are trying, where possible, to provide one free copy of the recordings to the family member who contacts us, asking that person to serve as the family contact if we are subsequently approached by other relatives or descendants of the person who had been recorded—very small-scale dissemination.

We have come to view these inquiries, in particular, as opportunities not only to provide increased access but also, in many cases, to find out more about the people who had been recorded—ideally to turn an anonymous voice on a tape recording into an actual person with an individual history and known context. In some cases, family members have sent us photos of the person as well as biographical information, and occasionally family stories of the time when the recordings were made. In these ways, there has been reciprocal dissemination *of information*, from the archive to the family/community and vice versa.

Of course, we are not in a position to assess people's assertions of their relationships to specific persons whose recordings are in the archive. In some instances we have witnessed, for example, members of a family do not acknowledge kinship with others who claim it, and they may be unwilling to collaborate on providing access to the recordings to each other. Sometimes this results in multiple phonoduplication requests at full cost for the same set of recordings.

Perhaps all archives holding ethnographic, unpublished audiovisual documentation have encountered competing claims of rights to certain songs or genres. Different members of the same community, the same ritual society, or the same family may have very different views about ownership and about who gets to make decisions. Or groups may claim rights to a specific ritual, a claim that is disputed by other practitioners of the same ritual. This was decidedly an element in the earlier, more formal FCP type of dissemination, from a federal agency to tribal leadership. While those of us involved in the 1980s efforts were definitely trying to communicate with other parts of traditional communities, the mandate to approach via "the front door" sometimes put the dissemination effort squarely in the middle of such competing claims. While we did not ask for specific follow-up from communities we visited, anecdotal accounts that came our way suggest that some contested recordings sooner or later became unavailable, neither the time nor the mode of dissemination being suitable right then for ongoing use of the recordings within the community. But the memory of such recordings and of their former presence in the community is still occasionally mentioned in correspondence with us. And if the next generations of rights-holders wish access or restrictions, our goal is to assist.

In any case, what this particular archive is experiencing today is more frequent dissemination-via-collaborations—collaborations directly with families and communities as well as with nonprofit organizations and individual researchers who work with specific communities. In the 1980s and 1990s, archival recordings here were regularly being sought by record labels, film/documentary producers, and so forth, for direct publication to a broad audience (presuming that permissions could be obtained from the rights-holders). Today, the requests for recordings are often targeted specifically for communities of origin; these tend to come more from individuals and nonprofits working with those communities, or from archival institutions situated there. Such is the case, for example, with the boxed set of Haitian recordings collected by Alan Lomax, the originals of which are held in the Library of Congress, that were used by Lomax's Association for Cultural Equity (ACE) in repatriation and cultural preservation activities in Haiti in the years following the massive 2010 earthquake.[10] Recent requests, coming to us via scholars working directly with community nonprofits and archives or tribal families, involve recordings from particular Greek and Caribbean islands and the Pacific Northwest. The recordings *will* be made available once again in the communities of origin as a result of such partnerships.

The impact of collaborative work between an archive and partners more closely affiliated with specific communities is perhaps no more clearly demonstrated than in our recent project with the Michigan recordings made by Alan Lomax in 1938—recordings of nearly 125 performers from approximately 30 communities in the lower and upper peninsulas of the state, with songs sung in an array of languages including Croatian, Finnish, French Canadian, German, Hungarian, Irish, Italian, and Polish. Partners in the overall project were the American Folklife Center; the Michigan Traditional Arts Program of the Michigan State University Museum; the Center for the Study of Upper Midwestern Cultures, University of Wisconsin; and ACE. Letters were sent to next-of-kin (where that information could be found, either by American Folklife Center staff or our partners in the Upper Midwest), informing people of what materials are available, and seeking permission for publication in some cases. Some public programming took place, with presentations (including restored film footage from the field trip) in several communities. Publicity generated by the project reached additional family members, some of whom have since contacted us in search of copies of their family member's recordings.

Currently, we are engaged in an updated and collaborative dissemination project with the Passamaquoddy Tribe of Maine. During the early 1980s, as part of the FCP, the community first received analog copies of the wax-cylinder recordings mentioned earlier—recordings of two Passamaquoddy men, Noel Josephs and Peter Selmore, that had been made in Calais, Maine, in March 1890 by the archeologist/ethnologist Jesse Walter Fewkes. Tribal linguists and educators have worked with those songs and narratives in the intervening years. But now, thanks to new technology, the Library of Congress has new and somewhat clearer transfers of the recordings. Digital file copies of those new transfers are now in Maine, and community members are annotating them for use both for themselves and for the larger world using the Local Contexts open source platform and TK ("traditional knowledge") labels.[11] The overall project also involves the Peabody Museum at Harvard, the National Anthropological Archives, and scholars at New York University and Washington State University. The work may lead to one or more websites enriched by community understandings of content. We see this project as a pilot for future dissemination activity and shared learning.

When an archive has preserved a recording and is able to make it accessible to community members or to descendants—when people actually hear the voices of the past—it has frequently been our observation that listeners' faces are filled with recognition and pride. But, as noted, what happens after that may or may not result in information available to the archive. While some audiovisual archives may interact with communities and individuals on a longer-term basis, that is not an option for all such archives, nor may it be needed or desired by those seeking the recordings. What people do with those recordings is up to them.

Unfortunately, audiovisual archives generally cannot easily control misuses made of archival recordings, once those have been disseminated or made available broadly on the web. After the Omaha Music website had gone up, we heard that someone was selling CDs on eBay that had been made by downloading recordings from the site. Sometime after that, we stumbled on a briefly lived "educational packages" website that had also downloaded and repackaged material from several of our collection websites, hoping to sell them to teachers. In our case, we know that this often stems from the belief that anything published by federal agencies or on federal websites is public domain and may be repurposed for any use, including commercial ones. But while the work of federal employees is public domain, that is not the case for the non–federally produced items on, for example, recordings or websites. Those who grant us rights to put their performance, words, photographs, and so forth, into print or digital publications are not giving away their own rights for other types of uses. We try to inform the entities making unauthorized copies that there are additional rights to be considered, but since we are not the rights-holders, that information is not always heeded.

When songs return to a community, nonmusical consequences may be as (or even more) significant than any musical ones. While we have heard of one instance where a single song that had been lost to its tribal community became the occasion for the revival of a dance, at least in one year, we know of more instances where a newly available recording represents the reclaiming of personal/family/community history. In some instances, this may be a function of the burgeoning interest in genealogy. It may not be important, in such contexts, for a recorded and archived song to be absorbed into a currently active repertory. The important factors seem to be the song's very existence and the voices of specific singers.

An archive seeking to make recordings available to communities of origin necessarily looks both to the past and to the future: to history, to current practice, and to goals to be achieved. Archives like ours sometimes find that they hold materials obtained in circumstances and by strategies that would be questionable, if not outright unethical, by today's standards—realities from the past that can make such recordings problematic for current community members who may or may not wish to have the recordings made more readily available, either within or outside the community. But in institutions that are supported by local, state, or federal tax dollars or even private funding, there may be requirements to make materials generally accessible; in this context, strategies for privileging communities of origin may simply not be feasible on some levels while entirely practical on others. And there is the ongoing situation arising from the fact that when ethnographic recordings were transferred from one institution to another (due, in many cases, to the lack of playback equipment for some formats), rights over those recordings were only occasionally transferred. So anyone seeking to obtain copies of such recordings, even for the community of origin, must sometimes secure rights from one or more institutions before the current repository is allowed to create such copies. This is another manifestation, as it turns out, of the complex histories of archival recordings.

UNESCO has recognized the importance of preserving recordings that cumulatively add depth to our understanding of the past, having now established an annual World Day for Audiovisual Heritage on October 27. Language in the day's 2010 announcement included this observation: "Audiovisual documents have transformed society by becoming a permanent complement to the traditional written record."[12] But older recordings are particularly vulnerable to the effects of changing technology and the subsequent obsolescence of equipment (and the loss of skills in using and maintaining the older formats). Thus, the permanent responsibility and the costs of preserving documentation require a Janus-like stance on the technical side as well as in regard to the content of any recordings: to accomplish its tasks, an audiovisual archive must have knowledge of the past in order to honor its long-term commitments—assuring that community access is possible, if not now for some reason, then in the future.

Notes

1. http://www.iasa-web.org/ethical-principles.
2. Only once in my entire time at the Library of Congress have I heard someone express even a passing wish for the original cylinders.
3. Abstract book for the 1980 SEM Silver Anniversary Meeting, pp. 90–91. The meeting included several sessions devoted to studies of Native American music. Richard Keeling's abstract (p. 33) for one such study, titled "Indian Music in California: Retrospect and Prospect," included an observation about an important audiovisual archive: "This report focuses on the unique opportunities for investigation provided by sound recordings in museums and repositories, notably the Audio Archive of UC Berkeley's Lowie Museum of Anthropology. This collection, *seldom used*, includes some 3000 sound recordings" [emphasis added]. Keeling began a dissemination project with these recordings around this time, but as his abstract indicated, in 1980 these recordings, like those in other archives, were not particularly available to communities of origin.
4. In one instance, our action of informing a senatorial office of our forthcoming visit to tribal communities within his state led the senator to invite tribal chairs or their delegates to come to Washington for a ceremony, in which he was able to participate, in the Library of Congress. At the ceremony, the Folklife Center presented copies of the relevant cylinder recordings to the respective tribal representatives; in one case, however, the archival recordings from a specific community were minimal (under three minutes), so the person had made a long trip for little material. And ultimately a Cylinder Project staff member still went to the state and visited those communities at their request, taking along an additional set of recordings in the event the ceremonial presentation copies were unavailable for community use.
5. The principal exception to tribal-community choice was location. Some of the recordings were from Canadian First Nations communities, and the realities were such that we could only mail out those recordings rather than promise any on-site visit.
6. She also facilitated the return by mail of the Canadian materials to the respective communities there.
7. One of the major services we have been able to provide in and around the dissemination of audio recordings has been information we are able to accumulate about the locations of related materials in repositories around the country or even beyond US borders.
8. Four-inch wax cylinders typically held around three minutes of material; six-inch Dictaphone cylinders could hold six to seven minutes, though some collectors used very slow recording speeds in order to record for as long as twelve minutes on a single cylinder. In either case, of course, the cylinders are bulky; documenting a lengthy ceremony required the recordist to have large boxes of cylinders.
9. See also the related article, "Returning Music to the Makers: The Library of Congress, American Indians, and the Federal Cylinder Project," *Cultural Survival Quarterly* 20 (4) (Winter 1996). https://www.culturalsurvival.org/publications/cultural-survival-quarterly/returning-music-makers-library-congress-american-indians.
10. See http://www.culturalequity.org/features/haiti/ce_features_lomaxinhaiti-cgi.php.
11. http://www.localcontexts.org. See also the abstract of a presentation on the project given at DPLAFest 2016: https://dplafest2016.sched.org/event/6EAz/wax-works-in-the-age-of-digital-reproduction-the-futures-of-sharing-nativefirst-nations-cultural-heritage.
12. http://www.unesco.org/new/en/communication-and-information/access-to-knowledge/archives/world-day-for-audiovisual-heritage/world-day-for-audiovisual-heritage-2010/.

References

Fewkes, Jesse Walter. 1890. "A Contribution to Passamaquoddy Folk-Lore." *Journal of American Folklore* 3 (11): 257–280.

Fewkes, Jesse Walter. 1890. "On the Use of the Phonograph in the Study of the Languages of American Indians." *Science* 15 (May 2): 267–269.

Gray, Judith. 1991. "The Songs Come Home: The Federal Cylinder Project." *CRM: The Journal of Heritage Stewardship* 14 (5): 32–35.

Gray, Judith. 1996. "Returning Music to the Makers: The Library of Congress, American Indians, and the Federal Cylinder Project." *Cultural Survival Quarterly* 20 (4) (Winter). https://www.culturalsurvival.org/publications/cultural-survival-quarterly/returning-music-makers-library-congress-american-indians.

Gray, Judith. 2003. "Archiving Sound." In *Songcatchers: In Search of the World's Music*, by Mickey Hart with K. M. Kostyal. Washington, DC: National Geographic.

Parker, Patricia L. 1990. *Keepers of the Treasures: Protecting Historic Properties and Cultural Traditions on Indian Lands: A Report on Tribal Preservation Funding Needs Submitted to Congress by the National Park Service, United States Department of the Interior/Prepared by National Park Service, Interagency Resources Division, Branch of Preservation Planning.* Washington, DC.

Parker, Patricia L. 1991. "American's Tribal Cultures—A Renaissance in the 1990s." *CRM: The Journal of Heritage Stewardship* 14 (5): 1, 3.

CHAPTER 8

....

ARCHIVES, REPATRIATION, AND THE CHALLENGES AHEAD

....

ANTHONY SEEGER

INTRODUCTION

....

WHAT happens when an individual or an institution returns recordings to the individual, community, or region where they were originally recorded? To whom are they made available, and how? Does the return have any impact on people's lives or their creative activities? Does it improve the relationship between those who return and those who receive and use them? We know from experience that simply sending copies of recordings to a local institution or individual is no guarantee that the music will be available to local scholars, musicians, and the general public (Gray 1996; Graham 1995; Nannyonga-Tamusuza and Weintraub 2012; Lancefield 1998). We also know that even when recordings are accessible to the community in which they were made there may be little interest in them. Since the 1980s, however, efforts at returning recordings to communities have increased dramatically, as have publications that describe the process. There are now enough descriptions of the active reintroduction of previously unavailable recordings to the artists and communities from which they came to be able to hazard some generalizations about the process.

I avoided the term "repatriation" in that first paragraph because the word itself requires definition. Here I use "repatriation" to refer to the return of music to circulation[1] in communities where it has been unavailable as a result of external power differences—often the result of colonialism, but also including differential access to wealth and technology, educational training, and other factors. In this way, repatriation would be applied to the process whereby an audiovisual archive in North America sends copies of early recordings of indigenous Brazilian music recorded by a North American researcher and inaccessible to members of that community back to them to use as they please within the limits of their own internal knowledge structures and any national regulations such as copyright. I would not use the term "repatriation" to describe one member of a community teaching a song or giving a recording to another member of his or her community. Even though there might be social hierarchy, such as a high-status elder teaching a song to a low-status youth, this difference is due to an internal hierarchy that does not deserve the term "repatriation" because the reentry into recirculation is within the same community or group. Further, the mere act of downloading a file from the Internet is not repatriation unless there is an intentionality to return to circulation in its being uploaded in the first place. The distinction is not perfect, but I believe the term "repatriation" is only one of the ways music reenters circulation, and reserve its use to where external hierarchies are involved.

Although there is considerable variation in the approaches to and the results of repatriation of music long unavailable to members of a local community, several factors are important in the more recent successful projects. First, there must be a motivated individual, community, or institution that thinks the material to be returned to them is significant and important and wants it. Second, there is usually a highly motivated intermediary who can work with the institutional repositories or private collectors to locate appropriate items for return to an individual, group, or nation where they were originally recorded (or were usually performed in the case of recordings made elsewhere). In certain cases, the same person exercises the first and second functions, but so far they have mostly been different individuals or organizations. Third, the best projects are culturally sensitive to local attitudes about the materials and technologically savvy about culturally appropriate ways to make the recordings available again and engage with community groups to make the return successful. Fourth, some financial support is usually required. Finally, some successful projects have much broader goals, of which the return of recordings is only a part; these often have objectives of linguistic or cultural sustainability.

The concentration of early recordings of the world's music in Europe and North America is certainly a result of colonial power and technological dominance. Many early collectors did not make efforts to send copies of their collections to the people they recorded. On the other hand, they had not taken the sounds, but rather a recording of them, and in most cases the performers could continue to perform them. There is a difference between a recording and a physical artifact or skeletal remains in many cases, for taking the latter removes them permanently from their source.[2] The cultural value of ethnographic recordings tends to increase as they age, because the traditions ceased to be performed, or performed in the same way as previously (Seeger 1986).

If power and technology were partly responsible for the amassing of recordings by the colonial powers, the push for repatriation is also partly the result of shifts in power and technological acumen in the world today. In addition to obvious shifts of economic and political power, specific technological changes have also made the repatriation of collections easier and more fruitful than in the past. Digital technology, global communications systems, inexpensive personal recording and playback devices, and increased recognition of the importance of musical performance to other aspects of social life have all contributed to making the fruitful return of recordings to their original makers more common. Researchers in the past were not necessarily blind to the potential significance of their recordings for the communities they studied, but changes in attitudes and technology have enabled us to return them in ways never before imagined. For example, in 1972 I could not return my audio recordings to circulation among the Suyá/Kĩsêdjê. The Brazilian Indian society I made recordings of had no machines to play back any copies of recordings I might have sent them, no access to money for the imported technology, or for batteries, or to maintain it. Not one of them could read a list of contents of any audiotape reels I might have sent them in any language. Nor was there regular delivery of mail or packages to the village. Forty-five years later, in 2017, digital technology is widely available in the community and wi-fi is available near the bilingual school. The younger generation speaks and reads Portuguese as well as Kĩsêdjê, and all my audio recordings fit onto a single pen drive. I had my tapes digitized and the music is now accessible to some (in principal all) members of the community. The leaders have requested that I not post their music to the Internet for others to download. They wanted it returned to circulation among themselves, but not beyond unless they approved it. I always thought they should be able to use the recordings I made, but it took about forty years for that to be fully feasible. And my experience is only one example among many of how technology has enabled repatriation. The rest of this chapter details the impact of technology, communications, and ethical considerations on how the process has improved.

TECHNOLOGY

The earliest device that both recorded and played back sound was the wax cylinder recorder/player that developed from the invention of recording sounds onto tinfoil by Thomas Edison in 1877. The first known ethnographic field recordings were made by Jesse Walter Fewkes in 1890. Most field recordings prior to 1930 (and many later ones) were incised onto soft wax cylinders on wind-up devices that used a horn for recording and playback.[3] A significant advantage to these devices was that they required no electrical power and could fairly easily be packed on a mule or in a steamer trunk. Originally conceived as primarily a business machine for dictation, the acoustically recorded wax cylinders had a short duration (recording about four minutes maximum) and required the person recorded to be close to the recording horn. They could be erased and used for new recordings by shaving off the top layer of wax. While commercial cylinders and discs were manufactured in the millions, the soft wax cylinders were extremely difficult to copy in the pre-electric era. The electrical microphone and disc cutter came later and discs were easier to copy than the acoustic cylinders had been.

Erika Brady's book *A Spiral Way: How the Phonograph Changed Ethnography* (Brady 1999), gives an excellent account of the development and early use of recordings by anthropologists, linguists, folklorists, and by extension ethnomusicologists during the first half of the twentieth century. Among her observations are that many ethnographers made the recordings for the purpose of linguistic or musical transcription onto paper. Most researchers were aware of the shortcomings of their recordings and rarely cited them in their publications—even where they may have transcribed selections from them for publication. In this period, most of the dissemination of research was through print media. The sound recordings were simply a tool to enable accurate transcriptions for study and publication. Yet in spite of their instrumental use, many ethnographic wax cylinders were saved and eventually ended up in audio-visual archives at the Library of Congress, Indiana University, the Lowie Museum of Anthropology, and in smaller numbers at other museums, archives, and libraries in the United States, and the Berlin Phonogrammarchiv, the British Library, the Vienna Phonogram-archiv, and other European institutions. In these the recordings were available to researchers. In most cases the idea of making them available also to to their communities of origin only came later. This was partly because it was unfeasible to do so and partly because it was not part of the envisioned use of research recordings.

Most field recordings during the first half of the twentieth century were made on recording devices that were not found widely in the local communities. This made returning copies of the music to local communities very difficult. Wax cylinders were difficult to copy; acetate discs were easier to copy but fragile, and many disc players required electricity. Wire recorders were relatively scarce. Most reel-to-reel tape recorders, used between 1950 and the 1990s, were heavy, required power or many batteries, and were not found in many homes. It was time-consuming and costly to make one copy of the original tapes; making dozens of them would have been a major effort. Scholars who were concerned about the need to leave materials that could be consulted where they had been recorded tended to select a single institution for deposit. For example, in the 1950s Alan Lomax left copies of the recordings he made in Spain in the national library (Judith Cohen, personal communication). A good example of an initially failed attempt at repatriation is the case of Klaus Wachsmann's recordings in Uganda. He wanted his recordings to be available at the University of Kampala, in Uganda, but did not achieve that in his lifetime. According to Nannyonga-Tamusuza and Weintraub, the British Institute of Recorded Sound eventually sent tape copies of Wachsmann's recordings to the Uganda Museum in Kampala. But the museum had no machines on which to play them, and they eventually became unusable due to inadequate storage (2012, 207). This is a classic case of sending the tapes but not thinking through how they can be used and made broadly available. Both unobtainable technology and difficult communications were part of the problem.

It is probably hard for readers of this chapter to imagine how difficult it was to communicate and return recordings as late as the early twenty-first century in many parts of the world. My own research in Brazil provides an example of the problems. If I wanted to send a written communication to a member of the Suyá/Kĩsêdjê community in the Xingu Indigenous Park in Mato Grosso in the 1970s, it was not productive. There was no regular postal service, and no one in the community could read. If I tried to send them an audiocassette with a message and music through a colleague traveling nearby who could find someone to give it to them, I had no guarantee the cassette would ever reach them. It was also possible that there would be no working cassette player in the village to play the cassette. If there were a player, it was quite possible that there would be no batteries for it—the Suyá/Kĩsêdjê were not part of the money economy, and there were no stores or electricity near their village. At the time there were also no two-way radios. While not all research is done in such isolated places, many parts of the globe could be visited, but only with great difficulty communicated with later.[4]

The Federal Cylinder Project, 1979–1990

Although folklorists and anthropologists had recognized that it could be useful to make researcher recordings available in their home communities since the 1930s, and Alan Lomax had called attention to the need to ensure that the opportunities of the emerging media were available to all peoples (Lomax 2003 [1959], 186), a significant milestone in institutional repatriation projects was the Federal Cylinder Project at the Library of Congress.

Initiated by the Library of Congress in 1979, the Federal Cylinder Project was a large-scale repatriation[5] project for wax-cylinder recordings. It entered its repatriation phase in the mid-1980s. Aware of the possible ethical and practical issues surrounding the return of the early recordings, project staff members contacted or visited over one hundred American Indian communities to discuss the return of the collections. Judith Gray, in a short article reflecting on the project, reported that many of the cylinders contained sacred songs. By today's standards many of the songs should never have been recorded. Despite prior consultations, reception of the materials varied. Some communities found the collections to be haphazard in the disparate song genres in them. "Also, sometimes their enthusiasm waned when members of the community actually heard the recordings. Cylinder recordings do not gain charm and patina like old photographs do" (Gray 1996, 44). The project staff engaged in extensive consultations and collaborative work to address the concerns of indigenous communities regarding the materials to be returned. "If disappointment [in the materials or their sound quality] was great enough, if we had not reached those most interested in trying to work with the cylinder recordings, or if there was some controversy attached to the recordings themselves or to the fact that they were coming back, the cassettes [audio cassettes were at the time the most popular format for accessibility] might simply remain on the shelf, untouched, after being presented to the community—or they might disappear completely" (Gray 1996, 44). In spite of the staff efforts, the result was sometimes no different from the return of Wachsmann's recordings to Uganda (Nannyonga-Tamusuza and Weintraub

2012). In other cases, however, communities used the recordings as part of oral history projects with elders or to reinforce traditions that were rarely being practiced. Sometimes the returned recordings provided stimulus for individual projects and tribal events.

Despite the difficulties encountered by the Federal Cylinder Project, it was possible because of the relatively advanced communication systems in the United States even before the Internet—telephones, postal services, a highway system, electricity, broad access to cassette playback machines, and the high level of fluency in English of most community members. This was not the case in many other parts of the world at that time.

In Brazil, for example, even sending recordings directly to a community did not guarantee wide access, though it could result in some unexpected uses. In 1998 the anthropologist and linguist Laura Graham described her attempt to return copies of her recordings to the Xavante indigenous group in Brazil. After her dissertation fieldwork, she sent copies of the speeches of a deceased Xavante leader famous for the eloquence of his oratory and the wisdom of his thinking back to the village. Years later, when she returned to the village, she asked how they had liked the tapes she had sent. "What tapes?" the elders replied. No one admitted to knowing anything about the tapes she had sent. But something else had happened: one of the sons of the late leader claimed to be speaking with the ghost of his father. As proof, he would recite what his father had said. And, yes, the words and cadences sounded just like his father! It turned out that he had received the tapes but had not told anyone. He was using them to learn his father's speeches and to promote his own claims to political leadership. Talking with ancestor spirits is an old Xavante tradition; no one suspected that the chief's son might be using a new technology to facilitate the process (Graham 1995, 227–236).

The Suyá/Kĩsêdjê response to receiving digital copies of my own recordings in 2010 surprised me. Some of them listened to the recordings and were grateful. One of the chief's sons said that his father had never told him some of the origin myths he had recorded for me, and they helped him understand the stories he knew. There was great consternation when a group of men listened to my recording of a ceremony in which they had performed. They discovered what they considered to be a major error in their performance. They thought the error could have been responsible for a series of subsequent misfortunes—deaths, poor harvest, accidents—and were quite upset about it (Marcela Coelho de Souza, personal communication). If I had not returned the recordings they would never have known of the error. There was sadness as well—hearing the voices of deceased men and women saddened their kinsmen. They are not comfortable looking at photos or hearing the voices of the dead. But there was also appropriation of them for new uses. For example, a Suyá/Kĩsêdjê filmmaker used some of my recordings as background singing in a short film and used a longer segment in another where a woman I had recorded could no longer remember the details of a story.

Overall, the Suyá/Kĩsêdjê were pleased to have the copies available in the village, but the responses to hearing them were not overwhelmingly positive. I suspect this would often be the case.

A Different Method
of Repatriation: Institutionalization

Around the same time the Federal Cylinder Project started to return recordings to American Indian communities, another form of repatriation was taking shape in India. A group of US-based ethnomusicologists who specialized in the music of India, spearheaded by ethnomusicologist Nazir Jairazbhoy, of the University of California–Los Angeles (UCLA), decided to undertake repatriation in a different way. Instead of simply depositing copies of tapes in an existing Indian institution, many of which struggled to maintain their audiovisual archives, they decided to establish a new institution that would collect and house the recordings of Indian music made by scholars and located outside of India. They established the Archives and Research Centre for Ethnomusicology (hereafter ARCE) in Pune and New Delhi in 1982. It was set up as part of the American Institute of Indian Studies (AIIS), which supported foreign research in India and had a headquarters in New Delhi as well as Chicago, Illinois. Dr. Shubha Chaudhuri has been its director for many years. In addition to acquiring copies of recordings from scholars and archives abroad for use in India (literally repatriation), ARCE obtained copies of many AIIS researchers' recordings before they left India at the end of their research grants. ARCE is one of the relatively few archives in South and Southeast Asia whose storage and cataloging meet international standards. It is also a research center in name and in fact. It has undertaken its own research expeditions and has extensive collections of commercial as well as field recordings, a library, a clippings service, and public listening and viewing facilities. It has become an important training institution for Indian archivists and researchers as well as non-Indians. ARCE has worked with regional and community archives to ensure preservation while at the same time enabling local access to the recordings (Seeger and Chaudhuri 2015). ARCE is an example of a different kind of repatriation. Rather than returning a single collection to a single community, it was created with a mission of audiovisual archiving and research that transcended a particular community or region. Audiovisual archives have been established at research and governmental institutions in a number of countries that have similar missions to those of ARCE. Among these are audiovisual archives/research centers in Australia, Cuba, Ghana, Hong Kong, Indonesia, Peru, the Philippines, South Africa, Sudan, and elsewhere (for early twenty-first-century descriptions of some of these see Seeger and Chaudhuri 2004, 118–245).

ANOTHER ALTERNATIVE
TO REPATRIATING RECORDINGS: TRAINING
IN DOCUMENTATION AND PRODUCTION

The return of recordings requires that they be taken away by an outsider and stored. Prior to digital formats, the original had the best quality and every subsequent copy, and copy of a copy, sounded worse. But it is also possible to train members of communities to document their own traditions and keep the original themselves. Ethnomusicologists and anthropologists have been involved with this for decades. I stumbled into it some-what accidentally. Given the difficulty of sending copies of my recordings to the Suyá/ Kĩsêdjê, I tried to provide them with the means for recording their music for themselves. When they became available and batteries less difficult to obtain, I gave some people I was working with inexpensive audiocassette recorder/playback machines. Although somewhat inferior in sound quality to reel-to-reel tapes, they were much easier to use and less difficult to obtain tapes and batteries for. After 1975, the Suyá/Kĩsêdjê recorded their own ceremonies, which taught me what they thought was important in them. I would either trade blank tapes for their recorded ones or copy them onto my recorder using a cable to minimize loss of sound quality. Some of them developed extensive collections of recordings. In 1980, Wetag Suyá had a large collection of cassettes. These included his recordings of Suyá/Kĩsêdjê music, recordings of other indigenous groups he had exchanged recordings with, some political speeches of indigenous leaders, and a few cassettes I had sent to him. He carefully wrapped the tape recorder and cassettes in cloth to keep the insects out and traded artifacts for batteries. Nonliterate, he identified the otherwise identical boxes by inserting different wallet-sized calendars with women's portraits on one side—then widely available in Brazil—and remembered which music was, for example, in a box with a red-haired woman with big eyes on it. He also learned from the tapes. One night I heard novel flute music coming from the men's house and found him sitting there with his tape recorder, quietly listening to a tape of the flute music of another tribe and then playing the melodies on a flute he had made.

What I failed to do was to help the Suyá/Kĩsêdjê create a strategy for long-term pres-ervation. Most of their tapes were playable for a while but then were damaged by mold and insects to the extent they would not play—like many other community recordings around the world. In 2015, I brought them a couple of transfer decks to make MP3 files out of the remaining cassettes. They could then load them onto their modern listening devices. However, for longer-term recirculability a more comprehensive plan is required involving digital transfer and long-term file storage.

Some Brazilian organizations have developed archival strategies for the preserva-tion of indigenous recordings. A Brazilian nongovernmental organization called Vídeo nas Aldéias (Video in the Villages) was established in 1986 to train indigenous peoples in Brazil in the use of video cameras and editing decks (Araújo 2011). In addition to training videographers in many different groups, the organization produced an excellent collection of DVDs, many of them with subtitles in several languages (http://www.videonasaldeias.org.br/2009/index.php), the organization stores the masters and some out-takes in archival storage and has plans for their digitization. The Museum of the Indian (Museu do Índio) in Rio de Janeiro, part of the Fundação Nacional do Índio (FUNAI), has developed an excellent program for recording and safeguarding indigenous music and speech.

In addition to these methods of keeping recordings in the places where they were made by training members of a community in documentation, it is possible to encourage "archiving" through performance. The body is itself an archive, as Diana Taylor has eloquently argued (Taylor 2003; see also Muller 2002), and recordings by themselves do not contain enough information to restore a forgotten tradition. A large body of corporeal and oral traditional knowledge surrounds most musical performances. Audiovisual recordings in archives only become significant when transmission by any other means has ceased.

WHEN IS THE BEST TIME
TO RETURN RECORDINGS?

When is the best time to return recordings? The simple answer is when there is an individual or organization in the region where they were recorded that is interested in having and using them for their own purposes. It may be this only happens once in a while; at other times there may be little interest in the past. I trace my understanding of this to Karl Marx's observations in *The 18th Brumaire of Louis Bonaparte*. He suggests that the interest in the past is heightened at moments of large social changes:

> The tradition of all dead generations weighs like a nightmare on the brains of the living. And just when they seem to be occupied with revolutionizing themselves and things, creating something that did not exist before, precisely in such epochs of revolutionary crisis they anxiously conjure up the spirits of the past to their service, borrowing from the names, battle slogans, and costumes in order to present this new scene in world history in time-honored disguise and borrowed language.
>
> (Marx 2006 [1852], 1)

The revolution of 1848 aside (Marx's analysis is detailed and scathing), I think he is wrong about the negative role of looking to the past in transformative times. He is right that in moments of profound change people frequently look to the past. However, they often do so to create a future different from both that past and the present—a future that may include aspects of their past but arranged in new ways for new purposes, not to reproduce them. Audiovisual recordings, like food and clothing styles, can be especially useful resources for people in transformative times. Written histories are usually created by the powerful and victorious, but the original audiovisual documents in archives often include the voices and images of the less powerful and of the oppressed. It is the wisdom, language, and artistry on those recordings that can be used to create a future that is not based on the story of the victors and powerful alone.

The best time for returning collections is when some people in the community are ready to use them. This may be one of the reasons why the Library of Congress found such varying responses to the recordings they returned to the American Indians. Some were not interested in using the past at the time the recordings were offered. When I directed the Indiana University Archives of Traditional Music, long before most archive catalogs went online, we received a letter from some members of the Fox indigenous group. They said they had forgotten some of the songs in a ceremony. They knew that someone had recorded their grandparents singing, but did not know who or where the recordings were. They asked if we had them. We did, and we sent them a copy of the cylinders. They wrote back later to say they had relearned the songs. Thanks to the foresight of the collector and the careful preservation of the cylinders, the sounds were available when they were wanted. Archives are, to a degree, the repositories of the tools for self-determination of groups like the Fox. When they wanted to relearn the songs for whatever purpose they wanted, those songs were available. Archives hold them until people are ready to use them; if they have done their job right the materials are now more easily found, and the sounds will be more easily accessed by the originating communities. If they have not preserved the contents and annotated them in a meaningful way, there can be deception all around (Seeger 2002).

In the digital era, it might not be necessary to wait for a letter from the Fox. It might be possible for archives or scholars simply to post their recordings online and let people discover them and return them to circulation. This approach assumes two things, however: first, that public access to the music would be considered appropriate by the individuals or communities recorded, and second, that the Internet will not change in ways that make them inaccessible in the future. Neither of these should be taken for granted. The next section addresses the ethical issues of the return of recordings.

ARCHIVES, RETURN, AND ETHICAL REPATRIATIONS

The keys to successful repatriation are a highly motivated member of, or organization within, a community with a vision of how the repatriated materials might be used. This person often works closely with an intermediary person or institution with the language skills to contact distant archives and other holders of material to be returned as well as the skills required to obtain grant funding. Where the former sees the availability of the materials as an opportunity, the intermediaries often see the possibility of working with members of a community as a way to rectify to a degree some of the injustices of a difficult history of colonial encounters. At the same time, the return of its holdings can transform the role of the institution holding the collections. Examples of careful, collaborative, and in different ways successful repatriation are to be found in many parts of the world. Some of them are described elsewhere in this Handbook. Here are just a few that have come to my attention.[6]

Repatriation projects in Australia have been especially important for Australian Aboriginal populations, since land title is intricately linked to song traditions in many places (Koch 2013). The Australian Institute of Aboriginal and Torres Straits Islander Studies has collaborated with many repatriation projects. The Pacific and Related Area Archive for Digital Sources in Endangered Cultures (PARADISEC) has created an impressive online resource and set of practices for archiving and sharing oral traditions in Australia and beyond. Kimberly Christen has reported on innovative software being developed to enable communities to manage the return and use of traditional materials within their own standards of knowledge and learning that she calls "respectful repatriation" (Christen 2011). Australian scholars have also devoted considerable time to documenting repatriation processes and their implications not only for the communities involved but also for the researchers themselves. Two recent examples are Clint Bracknell's dissertation (2015) on Nyungar songs from western Australia and Reuben Brown's dissertation on the repatriation of ancestral bones and the role of a song tradition in Western Arnhem Land (2016). Bracknell is a musician and member of the Nyungar community, which gives his work an important perspective on the song processes he describes and the institutions where information was stored. Brown carefully supports his conclusions with thirty-seven audio and visual examples and 350 pages of appendices meant to be of use to members of the community as well as scholars.[7] But Australia is far from being unique in its reflexive efforts to return materials to communities sensitively and in a way community members find useful.

A special issue of *Ethnomusicology Forum*, "Ethnomusicology, Archives and Communities: Methodologies for an Equitable Discipline," features seven case studies from North America, Europe, Africa, and the Pacific Islands. Although the cases are very different from one another, each demonstrates the importance of an intermediary, interested members of the community, and considerable planning. Many of the examples in this volume demonstrate the importance of these as well. The project of making the only surviving pre–World War II commercial recordings of Balinese music and dance available to contemporary Balinese, developed by Edward Herbst (see also his chapter in this Handbook), is an outstanding example of collaboration between a US scholar and Balinese scholars, musicians, and dancers to assemble hard-to-find materials and make them widely available to the public in Indonesia and to scholars everywhere. It has stimulated the revision of the histories of some Balinese traditions and inspired artists to create new works and change their performance styles. Funded by a number of foundations as well as self-funded, and involving the collaboration of several audiovisual archives and collectors around the world, the project is an excellent example of a large-scale collaborative project with many different outcomes.

THE DOCUMENTARY DECEPTION

As ethnomusicologists collaborate more and more with local community members to produce audiovisual documents that the community expects to be available in the future, we may be promulgating a future deception. Many existing analog recordings will self-destruct before they have been digitized. And many of the digitized recordings, or born-digital recordings we are making today, will scarcely survive our collaboration. File formats are constantly changing, and some of them will be difficult to migrate to other platforms in the future. When earlier business models fail and companies have to downsize, their older materials are often the first to be jettisoned (this was repeatedly the case in the US recording industry). In addition, a simple typo can erase large amounts of data, and there are constant threats to data from hacking and sabotage. Physical archives have been destroyed in twentieth-century wars; digitized archival collections could be among the "collateral damage" of twenty-first-century cyberwarfare. The future of our digital storage devices and services is in doubt. Vint Cerf, at one time a vice president of Google, stated in an interview with the *Guardian* newspaper:

> "We are nonchalantly throwing all of our data into what could become an information black hole without realising it. We digitise things because we think we will preserve them, but what we don't understand is that unless we take other steps, those digital versions may not be any better, and may even be worse, than the artefacts that we digitised," Cerf told the *Guardian*. "If there are photos you really care about, print them out."

(quoted in Maffeo 2015)

While this warning is more about the difficulties future ethnomusicologists and communities may encounter as they attempt to obtain copies of digital and digitized recordings, avoiding digital obsolescence and loss must be part of any long-term access project now and in the future. So far, digital formats have had relatively short life cycles, and the Internet is very new.

CONCLUSION

Returning musical recordings to members of the communities where they were originally recorded is—like almost all human interactions—a rather complex process. It requires a happy confluence of local interest, available intermediaries, cooperative institutions and collectors, and sources of funding. As ethnomusicologists become more involved in this process, we will discover new methods and unexpected successes and drawbacks. That we will be involved in such projects seems inevitable.

In their introduction to the special issue of *Ethnomusicology Forum*, "Ethno-musicology, Archives and Communities: Methodologies for an Equitable Discipline," Carolyn Landau and Janet Topp Fargion state that the issue explores

> the potential of the use of archival recordings to provide a more equitable and en-during outcome for the benefit of cultural heritage communities as well as for eth-nomusicological scholarship. As such, we argue for a fairer ethnomusicology, in which access to knowledge—often encapsulated in recordings—is facilitated for all, with ethnomusicologists taking responsibility for their own part in this important process.
>
> (Landau and Fargion 2012, 125)

The title of their introductory essay is "We're All Archivists Now: Towards a More Equitable Ethnomusicology." Today, the responsibility for returning, or maintaining, musical traditions in circulation is at once a professional responsibility and a profes-sional opportunity to restructure our relations with the people with whom we work. Landau and Fargion suggest that by participating in collaborative projects with individuals and communities, ethnomusicologists and archives can create a more equi-table discipline and also facilitate the recirculation of music through channels of inter-ested people. Archives, as well as most of the heirs of researchers, cannot usually return music to communities effectively because they do not have the researcher's local know-ledge or access to the language and specialists within communities. Until recently, most researchers would not have considered returning music to be part of their professional work. But if we are all archivists—those of us who work in archives, those of us who re-search music, and those of us who have been or are being recorded by researchers—then we are to a degree all part of an enriching process in which music and knowledge about music are transmitted over time both through local oral traditions and also through technologically mediated forms of tradition through recordings.

Digital technology requires us all to be archivists to a much greater degree than ever before. Ethnomusicologists' computers are filled with music, photographs, and infor-mation that have to be organized in order to be retrievable and stored somewhere safe for backup. These born-digital materials need as much care in their organization and secure backup as earlier formats, and archives today struggle to accommodate the im-mense amounts of data ready for deposit. Many of the musicians we work with are also archivists in the sense that their own digital devices house thousands of music files and they are actively adding to their collections. The term "repatriation" in the born-digital era may not make much sense because most researchers share their recordings before they leave what is called "the field" and "the field" is no longer distant—it may be as close as a computer or the smartphone in a pocket.

Regardless of their source, if the audiovisual recordings associated with ethnomusi-cological research are to be available at some time in the future when, in the process of profoundly transforming themselves (Marx's term above), people look to their past to forge their futures, we hope the sounds and images can still be found. To achieve this will require deep thought, sensitive collaboration, and hard work.

Notes

1. I first heard repatriation defined as a return of music to circulation ("recirculate") in a conference paper by Janet Topp Fargion (Fargion 2016) and think the concept expresses well what some people think they are doing when they return recordings to communities and individuals who have not been able to access them. This avoids the concept of nationhood or "patria" and also makes it clear that the individuals or community members are ultimately responsible for whether it continues in circulation.
2. The difference between a recording and a physical artifact or remains is not universal. The separation of sound and the performance of it is not everywhere understood and evaluated in the same way. While the two may be very separate in some cases, in others the recordings have a much more enduring relationship to a performance. There is practically no generalization that can stand up to the diversity of beliefs about sound and recordings around the world; I am forced to write in generalities in order to get beyond single cases.
3. The Vienna Phonogrammarchiv developed a disc machine for making field recordings because the discs were easier to transport and to copy than the wax cylinders. But most early ethnographic recordings were made on Edison cylinder machines, sometimes modified to better control velocity.
4. Today there is wi-fi near the village; solar panels recharge batteries, and they have become very savvy users of emerging technology including social media and mobile phones.
5. This is a "repatriation" project in the literal sense, since many of the American Indian communities were separate nations with which the United States had signed treaties. While I often use "return" in lieu of "repatriation" because of the latter term's implications of a "patria," I use "repatriation" in this case.
6. This brief discussion is in no way meant to be even representative of the variety of approaches and projects today. Rather, they are mentioned because of the significance of some of the ideas and descriptions that have been published and are available for viewing by interested readers.
7. In a similar fashion, an ocean away, Lígia Soares separated parts of her dissertation that deal with theory from a transcription of every song in a very long ceremony that her teacher was concerned might be forgotten in another generation. She wrote part of her dissertation for the community of the Ramkokamekra/Canela and part of it for her examining committee, knowing that each might not read carefully the parts not written for them (Soares 2015). Sekaquaptewa, Hill, and Washburn (2015) is an excellent example of a publication intended for both scholars and community members based on recordings of Hopi Katsina songs in US audiovisual archives. This may be an increasing trend in the future.

References

Araújo, Ana Carvalho Ziller, ed. 2011. *Vídeo nas Aldéias 25 Anos: 1986–2011*. Olinda, Brazil: Vídeo nas Aldéias.

Bracknell, Clint. 2015. "Natj Waalanginy (What Singing?): Nyungar Songs from the South-West of Western Australia." PhD diss., University of Western Australia.

Brady, Erika. 1999. *A Spiral Way: How the Phonograph Changed Ethnography*. Jackson: University of Mississippi Press.

Brown, Reuben. 2016. "Following Footsteps: The *kun-borrk-manyardi* Song Tradition and Its Role in Western Arnhem Land Society." PhD diss., Sydney Conservatory of Music, University of Sydney.

Christen, Kimberly. 2011. "Opening Archives: Respectful Repatriation." *American Archivist* 74 (1) (Spring—Summer): 185–210.

Fargion, Janet Topp. 2016. "Taking the Archive Out: Integrating Archive Holdings in a Fragmented Digital World." Paper presented in a plenary session at the 47th annual conference of the International Association of Sound and Audiovisual Archives (IASA), Washington, DC, September 26, 2016.

Graham, Laura R. 1995. *Performing Dreams: Discourses of Immortality among the Xavante of Central Brazil*. Austin: University of Texas Press.

Gray, Judith. 1996. "Returning Music to the Makers: The Library of Congress, American Indians, and the Federal Cylinder Project." *Cultural Survival Quarterly* 20 (4). https://www.culturalsurvival.org/publications/cultural-survival-quarterly/returning-music-makers-library-congress-american-indians.

Koch, Grace, 2013. *We Have the Song, So We Have the Land: Song and Ceremony as Proof of Ownership in Aboriginal and Torres Strait Islander Land Claims*. AIATSIS Research Discussion Paper Number 33. Canberra: AIATSIS Research Publications.

Lancefield. Robert C. 1998. "'Musical Traces' Retraceable Paths: The Repatriation of Recorded Sound." *Journal of Folklore Research* 35 (1): 47–68. Also reprinted in this Handbook.

Landau, Carolyn, and Janet Topp Fargion, eds. 2012. "Ethnomusicology, Archives and Communities: Methodologies for an Equitable Discipline." *Ethnomusicology Forum* 21 (2): 125–140.

Lomax, Alan. 2003 [1959]. "Saga of a Folksong Hunter." In *Alan Lomax, Selected Writings 1934–1997*, edited by Ronald D. Cohen, 173–186. New York: Routledge.

Maffeo, Lauren. 2015. "Google's Vint Cerf on How to Prevent a Digital Dark Age." *Guardian*, May 29, 2015. https://www.theguardian.com/media-network/2015/may/29/googles-vint-cerf-prevent-digital-dark-age.

Marx, Karl. 2006 [1852]. *The 18th Brumaire of Louis Bonaparte*. https://www.marxists.org/archive/marx/works/1852/18th-brumaire/.

Muller, Carol. 2002. "Archiving Africanness in Sacred Song." *Ethnomusicology* 46 (3): 409–428.

Nannyonga-Tamusuza, Sylvia, and Andrew N. Weintraub. 2012. "The Audible Future: Reimagining the Role of Sound Archives and Sound Repatriation in Uganda." *Ethnomusicology* 56 (2): 206–233.

Seeger, Anthony. 1986. "The Role of Sound Archives in Ethnomusicology Today." *Ethnomusicology* 30: 261–276.

Seeger, Anthony. 2002. "Archives as Part of Community Traditions." In *Music Archiving in the World: Papers Presented at the Conference on the Occasion of the 100th Anniversary of the Berlin Phonogramm-Archiv*, edited by Gabriele Berlin and Artur Simon, 41–47. Berlin: Verlag Fur Wissenschaft und Bildung.

Seeger, Anthony, and Shubha Chaudhuri, eds. 2004. *Archives for the Future: Global Perspectives on Audiovisual Archives in the 21st Century*. Calcutta: Seagull Press. http://www.seagullindia.com/archive/archive.pdf.

Seeger, Anthony, and Shubha Chaudhuri. 2015. "The Contributions of Reconfigured Audiovisual Archives to Sustaining Traditions." *World of Music* 4 (1): 21–34.

Sekaquaptewa, Emory, Kenneth C. Hill, and Dorothy K. Washburn. 2015. *Hopi Katsina Songs.* Lincoln and London: University of Nebraska Press.

Soares, Lígia Raquel Rodrigues. 2015. "'Eu sou o gavião e peguei a minha caça': O ritual *Pep-cahàc dos Ràmkôkamekra/Canela e seus cantos.*" PhD thesis, Universidade Federal do Amazonas.

Taylor, Diana. 2003. *The Archive and the Repertoire: Performing Cultural Memory in the Americas.* Durham, NC: Duke University Press.

CHAPTER 9

RETURNING VOICES

Repatriation as Shared Listening Experiences

BRIAN DIETTRICH

There are real stakes in the way we choose to describe the relations among sound, hearing, bodies, and subjects.

—Jonathan Sterne[1]

With field recordings, . . . some . . . are tangible precipitates of once-evanescent sounds still close to people's hearts.

—Robert Lancefield[2]

UKOKIS sang lyrically, his voice melancholic but sweet. Each phrase of the song was carefully ornamented, some with short undulating melisma that emphasized the emotion of his poetry and which is characteristic of the genre *engi*, plaintive love songs from the Pacific island area of Chuuk. The voice of Ukokis crooned from the speakers of my laptop in 2011 from a recording made more than a century ago in early 1907 on wax cylinder by the German ethnologist Augustin Krämer.[3] As I listened closely to this recording in digital format during a class at the College of Micronesia (COM) in the Federated States of Micronesia, Ukokis resonated through the imaginations of the class and through time as a means of engaging sonically with the sung past, but the recording also raised immediate questions. Although characteristic of Chuukese music during the first half of the twentieth century, *engi* are seldom heard today. For those who listened, the old melodic pattern and the largely inaudible poetry from the distorted 1907 sound spurred uncertainty about the voice and its meaning. Wanting to personalize the voice within Chuuk's specific clan and numerous island communities, students expressed a desire to identify with Ukokis. Looking at his image as painted by Elizabeth Krämer (Krämer 1932, plate 1), one student imagined him as a warrior of the past. A middle-aged student added that she recognized the song style as *engi* and related the sound to memories of her father. Still another student questioned what Ukokis was communicating to the class through his song. What was his message that he addressed for us listening today, she asked?

I take this initial question from the class engagement with the 1907 recording of Ukokis to begin a discussion of repatriation as shared experiences with recorded voices. I ask how we might reframe our work with recordings and our ideas about repatriation in ethnomusicology as a social process that considers human relationships as central to its practices. In focusing on experience through listening, I maintain that the repatriation of audio recordings is more meaningful and personal than the mere relocation of sound "objects" and more consequential than the transfer of historical musics and media from the shelves of archival collections. For indigenous communities, recordings comprise the heard voices of friends, relatives, and ancestors who imprinted their voices to posterity, and repatriation thus involves a shared remembering, listening, and learning from these voices. The physical and legal process of returning recordings plays a critical role in the responsibilities and ethics of any repatriation process, but it is the shared experiences that people have together with them that are foundational to understanding the collaborative and reciprocal potential of sound recordings. Recorded voices, like that of Ukokis from Chuuk, are audible visitors from the past, and the subjective reality of hearing, and thus feeling, these voices enables emergent capacities for personal and social engagement. The voice in the room with us, through its accent, its rhythm, and its idiosyncratic sound qualities, is a projection of the person with us. Thus re-sounding these voices is in part returning people, both individual and collective, to our consciousness.

In this chapter I explore the implications of reimagining repatriation as a social and subjective process that moves beyond the collection and transfer of objects, to careful and subjective social engagements with people. I focus on the Pacific Island area of Micronesia, for which I have undertaken a number of repatriation projects, and especially within the islands of Chuuk State in the Federated States of Micronesia. In recalling and examining my experiences in Micronesia and the larger issues that this work has raised, I employ a self-reflexive account at various instances throughout this chapter. Addressing my personal involvement with recordings elides closely with a growing cohort of writers in music who are "sensitively exploring the interconnectedness between their lives and their areas of study," and the "relationships they share with those in their fields of inquiry" (Bartleet and Ellis 2009, 7). Reflexive but critical accounts are closely connected with the cultural and social; they extend beyond their apparent case studies, and they "show a dynamic relationship between the self and their social and cultural context of creation" (Bartleet and Ellis 2009, 9). I ask how a refocus on the *experience* of repatriation and of listening to voices might expand notions of our subjective engagements in ethnomusicology. I contend that a renewed and critical examination of the social aspects of returning voices might facilitate the underlying personal and social realities that are central to our research, and in turn might offer possibilities for future community advocacy in music studies.

TOWARD REPATRIATION
AS SOCIAL EXPERIENCE

Sound recordings have formed a central thread in the history of ethnomusicology and its methodologies. Within the epistemological turn toward applied ethnomusicology and its basis in engagement and collaboration (Harrison, Pettan, and Mackinlay 2010; Harrison 2012) recent work with audio recordings has encompassed issues of access (Barwick 2004; Diettrich 2007b; Thomas 2007; Campbell 2012; Lobley 2012; Nannyonga-Tamusuza and Weintraub 2012; Niles 2012), law and ethics (Seeger 1996; Koch 2004), cultural heritage (Toner 2003; Corn 2008; Landau 2012), and transmission (Hilder 2012). These discussions have repositioned archives from being mere places of preservation to spaces of advocacy (Barwick 2004; Vallier 2010; Brinkhurst 2012; Johnson 2012; Landau and Fargion 2012). Sound recording and archives have thus taken on new meanings in the twenty-first century, especially with decades of recordings available for listening. This renewed emphasis on archival engagement has brought new questions about processes of repatriation.

As a general term, the verb "repatriate" means to "restore (a person) to his or her native land" (*The Concise Oxford Dictionary* 1998). The term evokes the plight of displaced peoples returning home, but it also refers to ongoing interdisciplinary projects to return and bury human remains—especially of indigenous peoples—within home communities and according to customary law. In ethnomusicology, scholars have framed repatriation as the return of recorded media objects or objects of sound (Nannyonga-Tamusuza and Weintraub 2012), projects that elide with the return of visual material culture found in archives and collections internationally. Sound recordings, however, are more than media objects. When played (and heard), the disembodied voices of remembered and forgotten people become much more socially meaningful for listeners than the recorded media itself. This particular social and subjective quality of the heard recorded voice has profound implications for how can we understand repatriation with recorded sound.

Social engagements with "things" have been at the forefront of writing in material culture studies and what has been known as the "material turn" in the humanities and social sciences (Straw 2011; Harvey and Knox 2014).[4] Scholars of materiality have emphasized relationships with and among artifacts and things, their possible agencies, and their transformative capacities and affordances (Hoskins 2006; Bennett 2010; Herle 2012; Ingold 2012; Holbraad 2012). When considering recorded sound as an object, we recall its bound and finite attributes, but replaying and listening to recorded sound offer a heightened capacity for social engagement. The subjective potential of audio recordings is found in the voices themselves, which literally speak and sing to us, and we may respond to them in turn. Listeners may address a recording by the name of the singer or speaker, may join with a recorded singer in song. Listening to recorded voices can bring people together in laughter and tears through shared memories and past experiences. Hearing the recorded voice of a family member who has passed can transport the recorded person from the internal to the external, to the here and now. We feel the sound of a familiar voice as it reaches us and we recall that person vividly through sound. This heightened capacity for recorded voices also presents ethical challenges for the steward-ship of audio media, and this has been understudied. Morcover, the range of responses to, and possible interactions with, recordings identifies a social and interpersonal en-gagement that is more meaningful than has been acknowledged in ethnomusicology.

In listening critically to recorded voices in this chapter I return to the social, human component of repatriation, and I underscore that recordings, especially those of spoken and sung material, hold human voices that speak, sing, and impart to us through sen-sitive listening. Throughout this chapter, I ask how an emphasis on the recorded voice as well as those who listen might present a critical space to explore not only audio recordings but also the social experience of their return and reintroduction. How do re-corded voices literally and metaphorically "speak" or "sing" to us, and how might an em-phasis on these recorded individuals open a space to rethink the ontology and practice of repatriation in ethnomusicology? I view these themes as possibilities for reimagining repatriation from the mundane return of objects to future engagements with individuals and communities.

Listening in the Archives: Recorded Voices at the University of Hawaiʻi at Mānoa

As a first-year masters student at the University of Hawaiʻi (UH) at Mānoa, I was unpre-pared for how a collection of historical sound recordings would become a catalyst for my introduction to the people and musics of Chuuk and for my future work in ethnomusi-cology. I came to Hawaiʻi in 1999 without a particular geo-cultural focus for my studies, but due to a number of circumstances and with encouragement from Jane Freeman Moulin and Barbara B. Smith, I became closely involved with the growing Micronesian community that called Honolulu home. At the same time Smith introduced me to an extensive collection of audiocassette recordings and open reels of Micronesian music deposited years ago in the ethnomusicology archives of the music department. Like many such repositories of ethnomusicology programs, the University of Hawaiʻi ar-chive holds the audio interactions from years of former projects. The recordings that Smith pointed out were from the Micronesian Music Project, a 1979 initiative led by Kim Bailey, a former (and by then deceased) ethnomusicology masters student also at UH.[5]

Searching through the materials I found over one hundred cassette tapes, many with minimal labels and in cases well-worn over time, but the audiotape overall was in fine condition. Most significantly, Smith pointed out a two-inch stack of onionskin papers and mimeographed notes: song poetry and transcripts of radio broadcasts mostly in Chuukese and that documented the collection. Back then I took the materials and the growing catalog I had begun to new friends from Chuuk in Honolulu, and without exception, listeners quickly recognized names and voices, but the collection itself was unknown and its existence elicited many questions. Only years later, with more experience and time spent in careful listening and discussing with others in Chuuk, would I come to understand the cultural and personal importance of this project in the vast number of twentieth-century elders recorded and the range and rarity of the musics included. To a large extent by chance and circumstance, the Micronesian Music Project became in subsequent years a gateway for my coming to terms with the social engagement of shared listening in ethnomusicology, as well as with the capacity of recordings that, in many cases, lay hidden away in archives. New relationships and new realizations would come from listening to these 1979 recordings with others and in Chuuk in subsequent years.

INTERLUDE: LEGACIES
OF SOUND RECORDINGS

The cultural context of my examples in this chapter comes from the Federated States of Micronesia (FSM): a nation of 607 individual islands in a vast area of the northwestern tropical Pacific. Organized west to east into four states of Yap, Chuuk, Pohnpei, and Kosrae, the nation is characterized by diversity in geography, languages, and cultures. The state of Chuuk is the most populous in the FSM, and it has three main languages and several dialects spread over forty-one individual islands. While my discussion here focuses on the home islands in the FSM, Micronesians are increasingly transnational, and substantial communities from Chuuk and the other states reside on Guam, in Hawai'i, and in the continental United States. The colonial administrations of Spain (1886–1899), Germany (1899–1914), Japan (1914–1945), and the United States (1945–1979) each had a role in the creation of several emergent forms of music and dance in the region. Since the early twentieth century, researchers, government workers, and missionaries from Germany, Japan, and the United States have left a legacy of projects that collected and archived the voices of these "small islands." The voices of the people of Chuuk have been central to past recording projects in Micronesia (Diettrich 2007a, 2007a), and they provide ideal case studies for examining the role and meaning of repatriated archival recordings.[6]

As ethnomusicologists, we find ourselves with an abundance of historical recordings from across the twentieth century, though often scattered in archives across the globe. We make new recordings and interpret their meaning just as others will do in the future, but we also find ourselves looking back at these "retraceable paths" (Lancefield 1998) and the archival legacies of those who came before. The Pacific was a sought-after destination for ethnographic salvage research since the late nineteenth-century, and as a result of this interest, the region was a site of numerous past sound-recording projects. Visiting researchers made recordings in Chuuk—for example, in 1907 and 1909–1910, in the 1930s, and continually from the 1950s to the present—thus creating a large corpus of recorded voices and knowledge in sound. The earliest recordings from Chuuk, as well as some of the earliest of any Oceanic music, were made in 1907 by Augustin Krämer. Krämer and his wife, Elisabeth Krämer-Bannow, resided in Chuuk from January to May 1907, and he returned to Chuuk in 1909 and 1910 as part of the Hamburger Südsee-Expedition to conduct ethnographic work and to collect material objects and recorded sound for the Hamburg Museum (Krämer 1932). The men Ukokis, Essep, and Aurfanu (from Uman Island), and the woman Iséni (from Feefen Island), as well as additional unnamed men and women from Tonoas and Toleisom Islands, all committed their voices to the phonograph horn (Krämer 1932).[7] The temporal depth of these early recordings often gives them great value as documents of historical musics, but the sound quality of some examples imposes a sonic barrier in how they are experienced today and the meaning that they impart. Those individuals who sang into the microphones of collectors retain an agency in their choices and the messages that they reveal today to listeners (Diettrich 2007b), while the archival collections of later decades include the voices of some of Chuuk's most commemorated individuals over the past century.

One example is found in a set of early recordings made before World War II—those made by the Japanese music researcher Hisao Tanabe, who traveled to Chuuk and other locations in Micronesia in 1934 (Tanabe 1935, 1968, 1978). Upon arriving in Chuuk, Tanabe was greeted by Koben Mori (1869–1945), an ancestor of one of Chuuk's large and influential families today.[8] Tanabe traveled to Chuuk and elsewhere in Micronesia with the purpose of recording music examples for a larger ethnology project (Tanabe 1935, 1968). Mori at this time had been a resident of Chuuk since 1891 (Peattie 1988), and he was married with children. He regularly greeted visitors from Japan, and he introduced Tanabe to various singers and led a group of men from Toon Island in a traditional call-and-response chant (*emweyir*) used for hauling. Tanabe's recording is the only known recording of his voice. In 2006 I played the recording of Mori for his descendants. Although the sound is slightly distorted, listening to it sparked listeners to offer stories and memories of him passed down from relatives. Mori passed onto Tanabe much ethnographic information about Chuuk, and his recorded voice from 1934 passes on his legacy to listeners today.

After World War II, visiting researchers and officials from the American territorial administration made an increasing number of recordings in Chuuk. Several sets of recordings exist from the late 1950s, such as those by John Brandt, the district sanitarian for Chuuk at the time. In 1963 the American ethnomusicologist Barbara B. Smith traveled to Chuuk and other locations in Micronesia and recorded musical examples at the request of Micronesian students at the University of Hawai'i at Mānoa.[9] In addition to researchers, missionaries also collected recordings, and beginning in the early 1970s the Liebenzell Mission in Chuuk started what would become a very large collection of sound recordings of Christian music at special gatherings and church functions. The largest recording project undertaken in the region was the 1979 Micronesian Music Project, as previously mentioned. With increased access to technology from the 1970s, Islanders began making sound recordings themselves for local purposes. They kept these recordings and passed them on within families. I have come across a range of these recordings in Chuuk, many of them on cassette tape. From the 1980s and with even more access to technology, both residents and visitors made numerous recordings as part of various functions and projects.

Archiving in the FSM has been and is still framed solely through a discourse of preservation and protection, coming in part from the prevailing programs of historical preservation in the nation that have been funded through the US National Parks Service (Mauricio 2006; Hanlon 2011). In most of these FSM institutions, cultural resources are locked away, and although archival materials are still accessible, there has been little emphasis on public or educational engagement with them. Despite the large corpus of recordings available from Chuuk and elsewhere in Micronesia, few institutions have had the resources needed to engage in extensive archiving and repatriation of sound.[10] The state preservation offices in the FSM have had active but small cultural centers, but the emphasis of these institutions has been on cultural sites and visual material culture, rather than on recorded media of intangible resources.

Listening with John: From the Archives to Shared Experiences

On the table in front of us at the College of Micronesia, the recorded voices of elder women from Pollap Island sang out in unison. "Where did you find all of these recordings?" John interjected with excitement in his voice. Back then in 2001, when I first sat with John Sandy, my efforts were focused on documenting and cataloging the recordings of the 1979 Micronesian Music Project, and I was unaware of the deep social and personal engagements that would emerge. John Sandy was an enthusiastic and insightful listener. He was a senior man from the Chuukese outer island of Pollap, an educator, and a recognized cultural expert in chant and dance and other aspects of culture. At the time of our meeting, John was working at the College of Micronesia, Chuuk Campus, in the new cultural studies program. He also led a number of activities on campus, including introductions to traditional ocean voyaging.

Previously in Honolulu, when the historian (and later director of COM) Joakim "Jojo" Peter talked with me about a media archive that he envisioned for Chuuk, we immediately recognized the potential of the 1979 Micronesian Music Project recordings. In my second visit to Chuuk and the FSM, I arrived with copies of these recordings, and Jojo introduced me to John. While archival matters initially framed the work that John and I undertook in making our way through the recorded performances, our focus shifted to more personal matters. Listening to those voices from 1979 produced significant research about music in Chuuk: it brought out stories, recollections, and memories. John was especially interested and moved by the Pollap recordings, most of which contained familiar voices from his network of relations. The time between the completion of the Micronesian Music Project in 1979 and my work in 2001 was short enough that John easily identified people and music documented in the recordings, and also the contexts in which they had been made. But my relationship with John shifted again when we moved on from the historical recordings and began to record and sing between us.

In addition to his cultural expertise, John was a teacher and an avid learner of traditional culture. He explained to me back in 2001 that he thought of himself as an anthropologist: he frequently interviewed other men and women, and he documented and recorded their knowledge in song, which he then incorporated into his own personal archive and his teachings, including at the college. After so many hours of listening to and talking about others, John was surprised that I could not sing very much from these repertories, and he taught me a number of chants—their melodies, rhythms, and poetry as well as something of the deep cultural knowledge embodied in each brief but multilayered example. These sessions resulted in a small set of recordings by John and retained by the Chuuk archive, from which John's voice would come to teach future listeners. My time with John was relatively brief in 2001, and although we set out future plans for when I would return to Chuuk, in the intervening period when I returned to Hawai'i and embarked on doctoral study John sadly passed away. Only later when I returned to Chuuk for a much longer residency and in-depth research would I come to fully appreciate the cultural importance of those listening sessions and the chants that John had taught. The recordings and my ability to sing from John's repertory marked me as someone who had been given a small portion of significant knowledge, and this came to frame my research experiences with both new opportunities and challenges while residing in Chuuk. Most importantly the recordings of John facilitated my meeting his son Elias in Chuuk in 2004, when I brought copies for him during our first meeting. Elias would become a trusted friend and coworker. We bonded over our interests in traditional song, but it was the initial shared, sometimes poignant listening and subsequent discussions of John's recordings—his voice in the room with us—that resonated and facilitated new ideas and experiences.

I offer this brief account to address the multiple paths of experiences with recorded voices and how they can serve as a vehicle for connections across cultural, social, and temporal boundaries. Sound recordings mediated some of my first experiences in Micronesia, both in listening to recordings with friends and colleagues, as well as making recordings. When considered in regard to experience, the repatriation of recordings thus has significant implications for a community-grounded ethnomusicology that foregrounds our experiences and responsibilities with individuals. In focusing on experience, it is my intention to purposely entangle the personal and the cultural, in order to bring out the "complex layers of consciousness, meaning, and significance" of research (Bartleet and Ellis 2009, 8). An emphasis on a shared, close listening suggests that we consider repatriation as a means of returning and remembering voices. The listening experiences that emerge from this refocusing have significant implications for how we might responsibly and critically engage with sound across the space of time.

Learning with Others: Repatriation, Knowledge, and Classroom Experiences

In addition to the personal and social engagements that I have retraced here, the repatriation of audio recordings has a far-reaching capacity for learning and teaching experiences within local communities. The voices of individuals, their recorded knowledge, and our continued engagements with them have a significant role to play in educational programs in music, culture, and language, as well as in fostering knowledge (Campbell 2012; Fox 2013). To understand the implications of repatriation and recordings for educational contexts, in this last section I return to how I began this chapter, and I discuss student engagements with audio recordings in the classroom at the COM in Chuuk.

The repatriation of historical sound materials may involve a means of accessing indigenous cultural knowledge transmitted from those originally recorded. Knowledge transmission in Chuuk has always been closely associated with listening, and this is evident in the relationship between the term "*roong*" (specialized cultural knowledge) and the word "*rong*" (to hear). Songs are a valuable part of knowledge acquisition and transmission not only through informal, everyday experiences but also through specialist information regarding history, politics, and lore (Diettrich 2016). Over the past century, Chuukese men and women sang into microphones various songs of significant cultural value, and many recordings contain examples of *roong*: knowledge of particular specialized domains, such as ocean wayfinding, ensuring harvests, and land stewardship (Diettrich 2018). The relationship between knowledge and listening is especially complicated, however, since indigenous knowledge in Chuuk is shaped by a hierarchy of social and cultural relationships that carefully manages its access (Goodenough 2002; Nason and Peter 2009). Cultural knowledge is thus restricted and selective so that only certain individuals may choose to willingly and openly share according to cultural protocol. At the same time, there is also a pervading feeling, often articulated in Chuuk today, that indigenous knowledge is endangered and the number of people who retain it is quickly decreasing (Diettrich 2015). In this environment, sound recordings offer a means of engaging with cultural knowledge seemingly forgotten, endangered, or no longer accessible, but the cultural protocol that surrounds access to this knowledge is inherently fraught and complex.

Any consideration of audio recordings and cultural knowledge must account for issues of access. For example, knowledgeable men and women in Chuuk reminded me on occasion how, as an outsider but one with connections to international archives and libraries, I retained knowledge and to a certain degree power through *access* to important cultural materials such as historical sound recordings, song texts, photographs, and information in publications. This was and is very different from access by genealogy, but I had never fully appreciated this issue within my positionality as a researcher until my work with Chuukese elders. The resources that filled my bibliographies, including photographs, sound, and video, and that seemed the standard elements of archival research, were the equivalent in some cases to resources compiled and held by elders in their own handwritten books (*puken roong*) and in their personal recordings. Many of my research experiences in Chuuk thus entailed contributing and sharing songs I had gathered from recorded sources. It was not the *form* of the knowledge that was most important, but it was *access* to that knowledge that raised and still raises questions about responsibility and positionality. Attempting to negotiate these issues often highlighted the fragmented understanding that I had of archival resources. Moreover, my sense of responsibility to find a means of greater community access was at times at odds with the local management of knowledge and questions over how publicly and openly some knowledge can or should be made available. These questions were not and are not limited to my experiences from Chuuk, and indeed, the FSM national government is currently undertaking the creation of a national-level archives, and these issues have been under debate in the nation (Nason and Peter 2009; Haglelgam 2009, 2010).

Listening at the College of Micronesia-FSM

The COM is currently the main tertiary education institution in the FSM, and it has campuses in each of the four states as well as a national campus at Palikir on Pohnpei. Except within a small Micronesian studies program and as content in social science classes, indigenous culture does not play a foundational role in the curriculum of COM, which has been organized in part based on US models, and COM's accreditation is governed through the United States. My perspective on COM comes from teaching music for a number of years at both its Chuuk and National campuses. During these experiences, I regularly brought recordings into the classroom in limited ways and within the bounds of a mostly American-centric music curriculum, but in 2011 an opportunity arose to allow a large class of students to engage closely with past recorded voices. With digital copies of recordings available at the Media Studies office of the campus and with encouragement from the college, I organized a syllabus that enabled students to experience and explore musics (and some dance) from throughout Chuuk state through past recordings.

Using a wide variety of examples from the past century, we listened to and discussed the recordings of well-known individuals, explored a variety of musical genres, and provided historical contexts for discussing indigenous music. One example was a set of recordings made during the early American colonial period by John Brandt. On October 31, 1957, Islanders from across Chuuk (then called Truk) came together at the historically sacred site of Wunuungenota on Weno Island (then called Moen) for the first district-wide song competition (*okkuf*). A powerful voice in these recordings is that of Petrus Mailo, the traditional leader of Weno and an elected official who played a prominent role in the early American administration of Chuuk. In the recordings Mailo addresses the importance of cooperation in the new district government, then he directs choral performances by Mwáán village of *kéénún fénú* (songs of the land) that he composed specifically for the occasion and that describes aspects of traditional government. The recordings of Mailo provided a window into the contexts of the postwar period in Chuuk, but they also offered a chance for students to engage with the influence of this important historical figure through his own recorded voice. Following work with historical recordings, the class discussed the value of indigenous musics in the present, and students undertook projects to make their own recordings as a means of learning from relatives, where appropriate.

While this kind of interaction with indigenous musics in the classroom may be taken for granted in educational curricula in other global locations, in the FSM there are as yet few opportunities for exploring local musics and cultural knowledge in tertiary educational contexts. This problem is multifaceted: curricula are set up to engage with mostly Western models (and musics), but cultural parameters often discourage public imparting of some knowledge, while few lecturers feel willing to engage with such material that has never been part of formal "schooling" in the FSM, although many have a personal interest in such matters (Diettrich 2016). In addition, logistical difficulties abound in organizing guest presenters for a diverse body of students from very separate island communities scattered over more than forty islands in Chuuk.

Facing these challenges, and with encouragement from colleagues at COM, it seemed obvious to make careful and selective use of the voices recorded over the past decades as a means of directly and easily engaging with selected local musical practices. The recorded voices of those Chuukese who sang and spoke into microphones over the past decades became a key means of engaging with music and culture in classroom contexts. During the 2011 class, students heard from and discussed well-known leaders, heard songs from a wide range of men and women, and discussed with each other their thoughts and experiences with local performance practices. In addition, the repatriation of audio recordings involves not only "music" but also recorded speech. One of the most helpful recordings was an extended lecture delivered by Kintoki Joseph, a chief of Udot Island in the late 1970s, and a cultural leader and celebrated proponent of Chuukese indigenous expressive arts. Recorded by Kim Bailey as part of the Micronesian Music Project, in the recording Kintoki methodically explained different types of music and dance and their cultural value, referring to them as *éwúche* (precious). The lecture was originally given as an educational resource for broadcast on the local radio in the early 1980s, and as far as I know, no one since has recorded such a detailed lecture in Chuukese. Informal responses from students about their experiences with sound recordings from 2011 ranged widely but focused on:

- Interest in engaging further with indigenous expressive culture at COM.
- Relating the recordings to memories of knowledgeable parents or grandparents.

- Relating the recordings to the widespread notion that indigenous musics are becoming "lost" in Chuuk.
- Expressing how a particular musical practice compared or contrasted with a student's own island community.

In many cases the responses were positional, and students tended to make strong links between recorded voices and situations in their own communities or families. Based on comments by students and other lecturers, the use of recordings was valuable in allowing students to have meaningful experiences with cultural resources. Three unresolved challenges included questions of how further to develop resources so that the use of the recordings is systematized, how to manage the different language and culture groups of Chuuk in the classroom and with limited representative recordings, and how to select recordings for classroom use based on cultural protocol. For example, we did not use recordings dealing with healing and spiritual practices—both carefully guarded aspects of *roong*—since they seemed inappropriate for public classroom contexts and within the widespread Christian contexts of Chuukese communities. But with divergent opinions about these issues, many questions remain about how to determine a focused curriculum in future. Listening experiences with recordings in the classroom at COM also created additional opportunities for their use, as well as opportunities for new recordings to be made and greater student interest in learning about indigenous culture. The classroom experiences from 2011 have also reflected back on the archive, with subsequent discussions in Chuuk about accessibility and further proactive use of these ancestral voices.

RECORDED VOICES AND FUTURE LISTENING EXPERIENCES

In this chapter, I have attempted to reimagine repatriation with audio recordings as collaborative experiences with past voices that engage closely with individuals and present-day communities. In the case of Chuuk, the extensive collections of available recordings have allowed for a wide variety of engagements and experiences, including the incorporation of recordings into classroom listening and learning. In their recent article "We're All Archivists Now," the authors Landau and Fargion have written:

> It is impossible to ignore the role recordings can and arguably should be playing within the discipline of applied ethnomusicology. When one pays attention to the role that collaborative and proactive research can have in bringing these archival by-products to the center, ethnomusicology has the potential to be applicable for the long term good of all peoples.
>
> (Landau and Fargion 2012, 137)

By examining engagements with recordings from beyond the archive and beyond mere objects of sound storage, I believe we move our research practices toward the advocacy, responsibility, and applied potential that scholars have called for in a growing body of work in ethnomusicology.

From my experiences in Micronesia, I contend that shared listening experiences with individuals, with communities, and in personal and educational contexts have much potential for greater collaborative and proactive work with sound recordings. This work also has implications for how we conduct ethnomusicology and for our responsibilities with colleagues and communities, and in facilitating cross-cultural learning. In this chapter I have asked, What is the role of audio recordings in connecting with past voices, both remembered and forgotten? From my experiences in Micronesia, the repatriation of sound recordings seems to be largely about the future of our shared experiences.

ACKNOWLEDGMENTS

Writing this chapter came about in part through recollections and conversations about past experiences, and I acknowledge the generosity, time, and support of John and Elias Sandy (and extended family), Joakim Peter, students and colleagues at the College of Micronesia-FSM, and the many individuals in Honolulu, in Chuuk, and on Pohnpei who have assisted, collaborated, and shared in projects and in close listening over many years. I thank the music department at the University of Hawai'i at Mānoa, the Micronesian Seminar, the College of Micronesia-FSM, and the Chuuk State Historical Preservation Office for assisting with access to materials and sharing work with me over several years. Past research projects have been financially supported by the College of Micronesia-FSM, the Wenner-Gren Foundation, the University of Hawai'i at Mānoa, Victoria University of Wellington, and the New Zealand School of Music.

NOTES

1. Sterne (2003, 346).
2. Lancefield (1998, 59–60).
3. The original recording was made as part of German colonial research by Krämer in Chuuk in 1907 (Ziegler 2006, 383). The *engi* recording is found as Example 210 on *The Demonstration Collection of E. M. von Hornbostel and the Berlin Phonogramm-Archiv* (von Hornbostel 1963). The recording notes from 1963 originally spelled the example as "angi" and documented it as sung by "Ukokia and Vela," but it was actually "Ukokis from Weno [Island]." The song text is found in Krämer (1932, 378). A partial musical transcription is found as Example 21 in Herzog (1932, 401) with the singer incorrectly identified as female.
4. I am unable to provide a detailed accounting of this literature in the space of this chapter. Much of this work originates with the theorizing of Gell (1998). See Straw (2011) for an introduction involving music and Bates (2012) regarding musical instruments.
5. Kim was a specialist on the music of Pohnpei and wrote a master's thesis that attempted to classify the musical genres of the island. The Micronesian Music project focused on Chuuk (then Truk) and Pohnpei (then Ponape) and was undertaken by teams of local collaborators from both areas and with the intention of producing radio broadcast. Issues of local ownership and cultural politics prevented the project from fully reaching its potential on Pohnpei, but in Chuuk radio broadcasts were made. See Diettrich (2007b).

6. I follow Goodenough and Sugita (1980) for the spelling of Chuukese terms, but without the use of initial double consonants.

7. Herzog (1932, 1936) transcribed a selection of the recorded melodies into staff notation, and Krämer (1932) documented and translated some of the accompanying chant texts. The Berlin Phonogramm Archive houses all original recordings. Two commercially released examples—one of a breadfruit-summoning song (*ótoomey*) and one of a traditional love song (*engi*) that opens this chapter—can be heard respectively in *Music! The Berlin Phonogramm-Archiv 1900–2000* (2000) and von Hornbostel (1963).

8. See Peattie (1988) for information on Koben Mori.

9. The Smith recordings are held at the Pacific Collection Library at the University of Hawai'i at Mānoa and digital copies are found at the National Campus Library of the College of Micronesia-FSM on Pohnpei and at the College of the Marshall Islands on Majuro.

10. Five primary institutions in the FSM have held cultural materials, including sound recordings: (1) radio stations, (2) state historical preservation offices, (3) the Micronesian Seminar, (4) the College of Micronesia, and (5) the national archives. Up until its relocation from Pohnpei to Chuuk in 2012, the Jesuit-run Micronesia Seminar (MicSem) was the most extensive archive of cultural resources in the FSM. In recent years, both the Micronesian Seminar and the Yap State Archives have engaged in work to digitize and archive radio station recordings.

References

Bartleet, Brydie-Leigh, and Carolyn Ellis. 2009. "Making Autoethnography Sing/Making Music Personal." In *Music Autoethnographies*, edited by Brydie-Leigh Bartleet and Carolyn Ellis, 1–13. Brisbane, QLD: Australian Academic Press.

Barwick, Linda. 2004. "Turning It All Upside Down . . . Imagining a Distributed Digital Audiovisual Archive." *Literary and Linguistic Computing* 19 (3): 253–263.

Bates, Eliot. 2012. "The Social Life of Musical Instruments." *Ethnomusicology* 56 (3): 363–395.

Bennett, Jane. 2010. *Vibrant Matter: A Political Ecology of Things*. Durham, NC: Duke University Press.

Brinkhurst, Emma. 2012. "Archives and Access: Reaching Out to the Somali Community of London's King's Cross." *Ethnomusicology Forum* 21 (2): 243–258.

Campbell, Genevieve. 2012. "Ngariwanajirri, the Tiwi 'Strong Kids Song': Using Repatriated Song Recordings in a Contemporary Music Project." *Yearbook for Traditional Music* 44: 1–23.

The Concise Oxford Dictionary. 1998. 9th ed. New York: Oxford University Press.

Corn, Aaron. 2008. "The National Recording Project for Indigenous Performance in Australia: Safeguarding Cultural Survival in Remote Australia." *Copyright Reporter* 26: 112–115.

Diettrich, Brian. 2007a. "Across All Micronesia and Beyond: Innovation and Connections in Chuukese Popular Music and Contemporary Recordings." *World of Music* 49 (1): 65–81.

Diettrich, Brian. 2007b. "Listening Encounters: Sound Recordings and Cultural Meaning from Chuuk State, Micronesia." In *Oceanic Music Encounters: Essays in Honour of Mervyn McLean*, edited by Richard Moyle, 47–58. University of Auckland, Department of Anthropology.

Diettrich, Brian. 2015. "Performing Arts as Cultural Heritage in the Federated States of Micronesia." *International Journal of Heritage Studies* 21 (7): 660–673.

Diettrich, Brian. 2016. "Cultural Disjunctures and Intersections: Indigenous Musics and School-Based Education in Micronesia." In *Intersecting Cultures in Music and Dance Education: An Oceanic Perspective*, edited by Linda Ashley and David Lines, 33–48. Switzerland: Springer International.

Diettrich, Brian. 2018. "'Summoning Breadfruit' and 'Opening Seas': Toward a Performative Ecology in Oceania." *Ethnomusicology* 62 (1): 1–27.

Fox, Aaron A. 2013. "Repatriation as Reanimation through Reciprocity." In *The Cambridge History of World Music*, edited by Philip V. Bohlman, 522–554. Cambridge: Cambridge University Press.

Gell, Alfred. 1998. *Art and Agency*. London: Clarendon Press.

Goodenough, Ward H. 2002. *Under Heaven's Brow: Pre-Christian Religious Tradition in Chuuk*. Philadelphia: American Philosophical Society.

Goodenough, Ward H., and Hiroshi Sugita, comps. 1980. *Trukese-English Dictionary*. Philadelphia: American Philosophical Society.

Haglelgam, John R. 2009. "Micronesia in Review: Issues and Events, 1 July 2007 to 30 June 2008. Federated States of Micronesia." *Contemporary Pacific* 21 (1): 114–118.

Haglelgam, John R. 2010. "Micronesia in Review: Issues and Events, 1 July 2008 to 30 June 2009. Federated States of Micronesia." *Contemporary Pacific* 22 (1): 126–130.

Hanlon, David. 2011. "Nan Madol on Pohnpei." In *Made in Oceania: Social Movements, Cultural Heritage and the State in the Pacific*, edited by Edvard Hviding and Knut M. Rio, 121–140. Wantage, UK: Sean Kingston.

Harrison, Klisala. 2012. "Epistemologies of Applied Ethnomusicology." *Ethnomusicology* 56 (3): 505–529.

Harrison, Klisala, Svanibor Pettan, and Elizabeth Mackinlay, eds. 2010. *Applied Ethnomusicology: Historical and Contemporary Approaches*. Newcastle-upon-Tyne, UK: Cambridge Scholars.

Harvey, Penny, and Hannah Knox. 2014. "Objects and Materials: An Introduction." In *Objects and Materials: A Routledge Companion*, edited by Penny Harvey, Eleanor Conlin Casella, Gillian Evans, Hannah Knox, Christine McLean, Elizabeth B. Silva, Nicholas Thoburn, and Kath Woodward, 1–17. London: Routledge.

Herle, Anita, 2012. "Objects, Agency and Museums: Continuing Dialogues between the Torres Strait and Cambridge." In *Museum Objects: Experiencing the Properties of Things*, edited by Sandra Dudley, 295–310. New York: Routledge.

Herzog, George. 1932. "Die Musik auf Truk." In *Ergebnisse der Südsee-Expedition 1908–1910*. Part 2. Ethnographie, B. Mikronesien, vol. 5, part 2, "Truk," 384–404. Hamburg: Friederichsen, de Gruyter.

Herzog, George 1936. "Die Musik der Karolinen-Inseln." In *Ergebnisse der Südsee-Expedition 1908–1910*, Part 2. Ethnographie, B. Mikronesien, vol. 9, part 2, "Westkarolinen," 384–404. Hamburg: Friederichsen, de Gruyter.

Hilder, Thomas R. 2012. "Repatriation, Revival and Transmission: The Politics of a Sámi Musical Heritage." *Ethnomusicology Forum* 21 (2): 161–179.

Holbraad, Martin. 2012. "How Things Can Unsettle." In *Objects and Materials: A Routledge Companion*, edited by Penny Harvey, Eleanor Conlin Caselle, Gillian Evans, Hannah Knox, Christine McLean, Elizabeth B. Silva, Nicholas Thoburn, and Kath Woodward, 228–237. London: Routledge.

Hoskins, Janet. 2006. "Agency, Biography and Object." In *Handbook of Material Culture*, edited by Christopher Tilley, Webb Keane, Susanne Kuechler, Mike Rowlands, and Patricia Spyer, 74–84. London: Sage Publications.

Ingold, Tim. 2012. "Toward an Ecology of Materials." *Annual Review of Anthropology* 41: 427–442.

Johnson, Birgitta. 2012. "Gospel Archiving in Los Angeles: A Case of Proactive Archiving and Empowering Collaborations." *Ethnomusicology Forum* 21 (2): 221–242.

Koch, Grace. 2004. "Voices of the Past Speaking to the Future: Audiovisual Documents and Proof of Native Title in Australia." *IASA Journal* 22: 20–31.

Krämer, Augustin. 1932. "Truk." In *Ergebnisse der Südsee-Expedition 1908–1910*. Part 2. Ethnographie, B. Mikronesien, vol. 5, 384–404. Hamburg: Friederichsen, de Gruyter.

Lancefield, Robert C. 1998. "'Musical Traces' Retraceable Paths: The Repatriation of Recorded Sound." *Journal of Folklore Research* 35 (1): 47–68. Also reprinted in this Handbook.

Landau, Carolyn. 2012. "Disseminating Music amongst Moroccans in Britain: Exploring the Value of Archival Sound Recordings for a Cultural Heritage Community in the Diaspora." *Ethnomusicology Forum* 21 (2): 259–277.

Landau, Carolyn, and Janet Topp Fargion. 2012. "We're All Archivists Now: Towards a More Equitable Ethnomusicology." *Ethnomusicology Forum* 21 (2): 125–140.

Lobley, Noel. 2012. "Taking Xhosa Music out of the Fridge and into the Townships." *Ethnomusicology Forum* 21 (2): 181–195.

Mauricio, Rufino. 2006. "Resource, Research, and Protection: A View from Pohnpei." *Micronesian Journal of the Humanities and Social Sciences* 5 (1/2): 517–520.

Music! The Berlin Phonogramm-Archiv 1900–2000. 2000. Edited by Artur Simon and Ulrich Wegner. Four CDs and book. Mainz, Germany.

Nannyonga-Tamusuza, Sylvia, and Andrew N. Weintraub. 2012. "The Audible Future: Reimagining the Role of Sound Archives and Sound Repatriation in Uganda." *Ethnomusicology* 56 (2): 206–233.

Nason, James, and Joakim Peter. 2009. "Keeping Rong from Wrong: The Identification and Protection of Traditional Intellectual Property in Chuuk, Federated States of Micronesia." *International Journal of Cultural Property* 16: 273–290.

Niles, Don, 2012. "The National Repatriation of Papua New Guinea Recordings: Experiences Straddling World War II." *Ethnomusicology Forum* 21 (2): 141–159.

Peattie, Mark R. 1988. *Nan'yo: The Rise and Fall of the Japanese in Micronesia, 1885–1945*. Pacific Islands Monograph Series 4. Honolulu: University of Hawai'i Press.

Seeger, Anthony. 1996. "Ethnomusicologists, Archives, Professional Organizations, and the Shifting Ethics of Intellectual Property." *Yearbook for Traditional Music* 28: 87–105.

Sterne, Jonathan. 2003. *The Audible Past: Cultural Origins of Sound Production*. Durham, NC: Duke University Press.

Straw, Will. 2011. "Music and Material Culture." In *The Cultural Study of Music: A Critical Introduction*, edited by Martin Clayton, Trevor Herbert, and Richard Middleton, 227–236. New York: Routledge.

Tanabe, Hisao. 1935. "Masharu oyobi Karorin Gunto ni Okeru Ongaku to Buyo." *Japanese Journal of Ethnology* 1 (2): 258–276. Unpublished translation by Janet Roach, n.d., 17 pp., on file at Micronesian Seminar, Kolonia, Pohnpei.

Tanabe, Hisao. 1968. *Nan'yo, Taiwan, Okinawa Ongaku Kikô*. Tokyo: Ongaku no Tomosha. Unpublished translation of chapter 5, "The Truk Islands," by Yoko Kurokawa, 2006, 50 pages. Personal collection of Brian Diettrich.

Tanabe, Hisao. 1978. *The Music of Micronesia, the Kao-Shan Tribes of Taiwan, and Sakhalin*. Recorded by Hisao Tanabe in Micronesia in 1934; sleeve notes and editing by Hideo Tanabe. Toshiba TW-80011. LP.

Thomas, Martin. 2007. "Taking Them Back: Archival Media in Arnhem Land Today." *Cultural Studies Review* 13 (2): 20–37.

Toner, Peter G. 2003. "History, Memory and Music: The Repatriation of Digital Audio to Yolngu Communities, or, Memory as Metadata." In *Research, Communities, Institutions, Sound Recordings*, edited by Linda Barwick, Allan Marett, Jane Simpson, and Amanda Harris, 2–17. Sydney: University of Sydney.

Vallier, John. 2010. "Sound Archiving Close to Home: Why Community Partnerships Matter." *Notes* 67 (1): 39–49.

von Hornbostel, Erick Moritz. 1963. *The Demonstration Collection of E. M. von Hornbostel and the Berlin Phonogramm-Archiv*. Folkways Records, Smithsonian Center for Folklife and Cultural Heritage. LP (and reissued CD). FW04175.

Ziegler, Susanne. 2006. *Die Wachszylinder des Berliner Phonogramm-Archivs*. Textdokumentation und Klangbeispiele. Berlin: Staatliche Museen zu Berlin, Preußischer Kulturbesitz.

CHAPTER 10

"BOULDERS, FIGHTING ON THE PLAIN"

A World War I–Era Song Repatriated and Remembered in Western Tanzania

FRANK GUNDERSON

How should scholars be thinking about and using archives, in relation to musical fieldwork, in the globalized, digitized, hyperreal, interconnected twenty-first century? For many musicologists and ethnomusicologists, still, the research that is done "in the archive" and the research that is done "in the field" are considered (either consciously or unconsciously) as separate, bracketed-off, binary, disconnected realms of labor. Fieldwork is thought of as a synchronic, "here-and-now" endeavor, and archives are treated as afterthoughts, or as static, ossified, "historical" spaces, even "dark places where one sends things that are no longer needed" (Seeger 2001). Granted, this archive/ fieldwork dichotomy may be more stringently entrenched by those who still subscribe to a specific historical musicology/ethnomusicology divide (Savage 2009/2010). However, historically conscious music researchers working in areas around the world are increasingly coming to consider "the archive" and "the field" in a more fluid way: as a part of an active research continuum. This "archive–field" continuum, if you will, is a conceptual terrain where we might assert the premise of doing "fieldwork in the archive" (a place where we listen to, and act on, the voices that we hear there) or doing "archival work in the field" (among our research associates, where we talk about, provoke, and assist in evoking embodied musical memories).

A related query concerns how might we begin thinking of "repatriation" as connected to this "archive–field" continuum, and not just as an "after-fieldwork/after-thought." When we discuss repatriation in ethnomusicology, the primary activity that comes to mind is "giving back"—usually by returning audiovisual media and documentation at the end of a research cycle, or negotiating giving back the original contents (or copies of contents) found in archives to the people from whom they were obtained. These projects and the intentions driving them are all well, right, and ethically necessary. However, we might also conceive of repatriation as a continual, sustained process that unfolds during the research from its inception—a conversation, a dialogue between research associates about traditions and performance practice, a give and take between researchers and the communities they work with, or an evocative activity that helps flesh out songs and stories about songs submerged or perceived as lost. In other words, I advocate for a more naturalized, "reflexive repatriation," one we as researchers might consider building into our own personal "archive–field" continuums.

In this chapter, I contextualize the process of coming to know, through engaging with this "archive–field" continuum, the history of a particular Sukuma song found in a colonial-era archive in Dar es Salaam, Tanzania, a song that was composed by a Tanzanian foot soldier around 1916, during World War I. Thus, on the occasion of this song's centennial, I discuss what I have discovered about its history; and, advocating source transparency, I share my own coming to consciousness about this song, and my involvement in its local and global transmission (Shelemay 2008) through reflexive repatriation. This will demonstrate not only that ongoing, reflexive acts of repatriation provide historical depth to our research as ethnomusicologists but also, more importantly, that such acts are essential in cueing, evoking, assisting, and inspiring memorial traditions for the communities whose music and lives we study.

This story is set in the Sukuma region of western Tanzania (see map in Figure 10.1). The Sukuma homeland, a roughly 130-square-kilometer region just south of Lake Victoria-Nyanza, is home to roughly 20 percent of the population of Tanzania (Grimes 2008).

Sukuma people have historically worked the land as cotton and rice farmers, and live-stock herding has been an important economic asset as well. Rural life there is based on cooperative social networks that include and extend beyond kinship affiliation. These specialized networks include associations that allocate labor in various ways for activities that include hunting, farming, and healing. All Sukuma labor associations in Tanzania have a seasonal recreational component that highlights dance and dance competitions; and depending on who is watching, these "labor" associations have also been called "dance" associations or "dance" societies (Ranger 1975). As I have discussed elsewhere, these dance societies are led by composers known as *baliingi* (sing., *niingi*), and their song culture is a vital aspect of Sukuma intellectual life (Gunderson 2003, 2008, 2010). These societies are significant culture creators and entertainers.

The term *"baliingi"* also has supernatural implications. An important aspect of the *niingi*'s work is their communication with ancestors (*masamva*), assumed by many to be the source of new musical compositions. Ideas about creative musical processes are discussed openly, freely, and often among *baliingi* and their initiates. What is secret are only the specifics of medicine preparation, the open knowledge of which would be harmful if placed in the hands of competitors. It was these voluntary dance associations that caught the attention of British colonial authorities in the 1920s and 1930s. Like the Germans who preceded them (Gunderson 2013), the British were suspicious of the potential threat that organized resistance from local voluntary "secret"

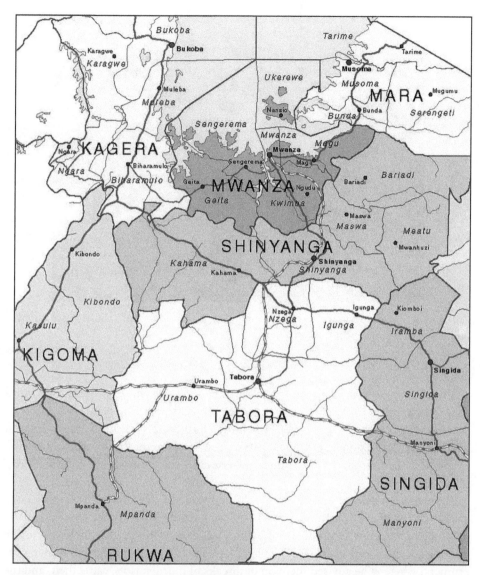

FIGURE 10.1 Northwest Tanzania regional map.

Courtesy of the University of Texas Libraries, University of Texas at Austin.

societies represented. Under particularly intense scrutiny were the *bachweezi* healers and diviners, as well as the many affiliated societies under their considerable influence, who in their work of making medical diagnoses and predictions were also consulted for various predictions about future societal events including war, catastrophes, or political changes (see also Baswezi Report 1930; Bosch 1930; Blohm 1933; Hoesing 2006; Stroeken 2010). Figure 10.2 shows a masked *bachweezi*[1] performer in Kissesa village, Tanzania, in 2004.

FIGURE 10.2 Masked *bachweezi* performer mingling in the audience at a public dance competition, Kissesa village, Tanzania. 2004.

Photograph by Frank Gunderson.

There was great fear about the spread of these societies, and worry that their influence would spread to the chiefs, thus creating top-down political pandemonium via a domino effect (Mwanza 1928). The British thus formed several commissions and put amateur and professional anthropologists and sociologists on the government payroll to monitor these groups. One of these government-paid professional informers was Hans Cory.

The son of a Viennese musical family (Molony 2014), Cory came to Tanganyika as a soldier during World War I, and he then came to oversee several sisal estates. He quickly developed an interest in Sukuma culture and was even initiated into the *buyeye* snake hunting society (Cory 1946). His interests earned him a position with the British government, whereby he advised them on outbreaks of murder, riots, cattle theft, and the proliferation of these secret societies. Cory's work served the aims of the colonial government to prevent social unrest, and to promote the shift from subsistence farming to the production of cheap export crops for a European market. In the end, however, his work with the government commission was half-hearted, as he concluded that the so-called secret elements these societies possessed were harmless. Eventually, in the mid-1950s, Cory's collection was deposited at the University of Dar Es Salaam's East Africa Collection housed in the university library. This archive, reflecting his many diverse interests, consists of typewritten papers, interviews, reports, drawings, paintings, fieldnotes, and song texts (in Kiswahili and Kisukuma), with translations to English and German (Cory n.d.a., n.d.b.). Though Cory published English versions of these texts

(Koritschoner 1937 [he changed his name to Cory after World War II]), the English translations are poor (Songoyi 1990).

In 1994, while working on my doctoral dissertation (Gunderson 1999a, 1999b), I assessed the original materials from the papers in this collection—a collection developed as a result of a discursive practice of surveillance and control (Foucault 1971), because it contained the original Sukuma-language transcriptions and the names of the musicians from whom the songs were collected. It was my intention from the outset to try to use these songs as cues in my interviews with musicians about the history and practice of farmers' music in this region. It was in this collection that I found the song text that I now wish to discuss.

Shiganga Jilikenya ku Mabala ("Boulders, Fighting on the Plain")	
Shiganga jilikenya ku mabala	Boulders fighting on the plain
Bajelemani na Baengeleja	The Germans and the English
Balikiling'himya n'hambo	They run about all over the place
Linguno ya ng'ombe (2×)	Because of cattle (2×)
Simba sana, ng'wana Makoma	Dig deep, child of Makoma
Nhobola yabi ya bangi	Tabora belongs to others
Ya Mabiliji, babalya banhu! (2×)	The Belgians, eaters-of-men! (2×)
Shiganga jilikenya ku mabala	Boulders fighting on the plain
Bajelemani na Baengeleja	The Germans and the English
Balikiling'himya n'hambo	They run about taken to fight
Linguno ya ng'ombe	Because of cattle

According to Cory's meager typewritten notes, the song "Shiganga Jilikenya ku Mabala" ("The Boulders Are Fighting on the Plain") was composed by ng'wana[2] Matonange, sometime during World War I. The song documents a military skirmish between the Germans and the British in the Mwanza region. A note mentioned only that the composer, Matonange, was a foot soldier working for the Germans, and that the song enjoyed some minor popularity as a *beni* song in dance competitions during and immediately after the war, before being collected, transcribed, and archived by Cory.

The German Colonial Army (Schutztruppe) employed African soldiers, known as *askaris*, in its colonies. The askaris were well paid, but harshly disciplined. Eleven thousand askaris and their European officers commanded by Paul Emil von Lettow-Vorbeck managed to resist the numerically superior British, Portuguese, and Belgian colonial forces until the end of World War I in 1918 (Koponen 1988, 133–134). *Beni* was the music most associated with the East African soldier during World War I. Ranger described *beni* as follows:

The *ng'oma*[3] takes its name from its essential musical feature—the attempt to reproduce the effect of a military brass-band, though the elaboration of this attempt might vary from the provision of a full bugle, pipe, and drum detachment to the beating of a single big drum in some rural variants of Beni. The dances done to this Beni music have also varied considerably but all have been based on the idea of military drill. Sometimes the dance took the form of a parade, a procession, a march past; sometimes it took the form of a dance in platoon form; sometimes it took the form of a circling drill step.

(Ranger 1975, 5)

In Cory's notes, there was no indication as to where the composer was from, or what the song was really about. I had decided that I would use this song text, along with dozens of other texts found in this archive, in feedback interviews with musicians in the Sukuma area (cf. Stone and Stone 1981). Initially, I had little luck finding anyone who could remember the song, and due to other research concerns I did not dwell on the matter much. I did, however, have some luck with one elderly singer, Kang'wii'na ng'wana Mihumo (Figure 10.3).[*4] Upon being read the text, he could not recall the melody, but quickly came up with a rhythmic, spoken performance of the text. He claimed that he had learned the song as a youth in the context of beating millet. Based on his analysis and corrections of the idiomatic language used in the song, he was confident that it was from an area found between the Sukuma region and the southernmost neighborly Nyamwezi region, known as Nzega-Shinyanga.

Kangwiina was also able to provide some insight regarding one of the poetic images in the text, that referring to "boulders." The reference to "boulders" has special meaning to Sukuma-area dwellers. Perhaps the most striking feature of the Sukuma landscape are the many surreal glacial deposits of "masses of granite, everywhere tumbled into hills, or piled in solitary grandeur over the rock-strewn plain" (Stokes 1877, n.p.); one example is seen in Figure 10.4. Mentioned often in song, these outcroppings are used as foundations and walls of homes, and they are the cause of irregularly shaped fields for farming. "Boulder" is also an affectionate slang term for a person of strength. The composer Matonange saw the war in purely economic terms, from the point of view of a pastoralist, wryly commenting in the song that the Germans and the British were chasing each other about because of cattle, like "boulders fighting on the plain" (Kangwiina*).

Some six months later (in 1995), upon routine travel to the general area where Kangwiina said he thought the song was from, I showed the song text to another elderly dance leader, ng'wana Makanga. Makanga's only reaction to being shown the song text was simply, "We need to go see my mentor, my dance teacher" (Makanga*). We thus embarked together on a day-long trip to find ng'wana Chiila.

Ng'wana Chiila (Figure 10.5), as it turns out, was a well-known *beni* musician based in south Shinyanga. Chiila, upon being read the text, was ecstatic and immediately recognized this song as one that had been adapted by his own grandfather as a work chorus to accompany village voluntary labor group tasks in the 1940s, labor which included millet threshing, cattle herding, and well digging, as well as the serious labor of millet-beer drinking. He said that he had not heard or even thought about that song since he was a child, nearly fifty years prior. Amid much laughter and tears, the floods

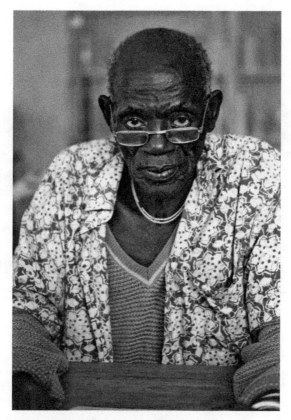

FIGURE 10.3 Kang'wiina ng'wana Mihumo. 1994.

Photograph by Frank Gunderson.

of memory brought forth the melody of the song text Cory had collected, an additional verse, performance practice details, and a few details about the battle documented in the song, as well as a more accurate phonetic transliteration of the text than that found in the Cory Collection notes. Ng'wana Chiila then taught the song to ng'wana Makanga, and I was able to witness and record their quick rehearsal and performance. One can hear in this recording ng'wana Chiila providing ng'wana Makanga with verse cues.

Ng'wana Chiila was unable to tell me anything about the composer, but he could elucidate the meaning of the additional (second) verse not documented in the Cory text.

Third verse of *Shiganga Jilikenya ku Mabala* ("Boulders, Fighting on the Plain")	
Lilongije	It is known only [by]
liKube, liMulungu, baba	Kube, God, baba
liKatabi	Katavi
Liligotola banhu (2x)	That which is knocking the people (2x)

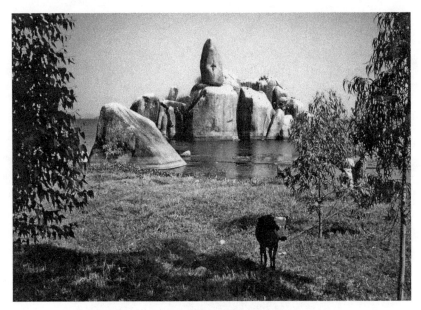

FIGURE 10.4 Bismarck Rock, Lake Victoria-Nyanza, Mwanza.

Photograph by Frank Gunderson.

FIGURE 10.5 Hamala ng'wana Chiila at his home in Ng'wajigiinya village, Tanzania, 1995.

Photograph by Frank Gunderson.

Here, according to Chiila, the "Supreme Creator" is called on using three different local clan names (Kube, Mulungu, Katavi), as only the Creator could know and understand why people were being destroyed in this war. Ng'wana Chiila also reiterated what ng'wana Mihumo had said about the importance of the rock/cattle metaphor. His extended narrative about the song merits quoting in full:

Eee, niimbe ya mapambano ya mimbo ya wakati wa mapambano yale, ya Waingereza na Wagerumani. Eeehe, sababu alikuwa yupo mwimbaji baba yangu, aaa babu ndiye alikuwa upande wa Wajerumani hasa. Alikuwa yeye mwimbaji wa kilimo, kwa sababu kilimo nacho kilikuwa na wimbaji wake kama wana mkusanyiko wa watu ndiyo wanawaambia nje muimbe kwangu, ndiiyo wanaimba sasa. Aliitwa Masanja. Sawasawa. Aliimba hivi . . . Sasa, nieleze basi. Sasa, Wajeremani na Waingereza wakati ule walikuwa wanapigana [Narrator switches to Kisukuma]. Tuhaya giki, "Balikeneja kwa ajili ya ng'ombe." Ku nguno bise twali bafugaji tulina ng'ombe, nguno naboyi twababonaga nubiza nahene baliloga he? Ng'ombe. Sana. Hii giki, "Ban-geleza na Bajerumani balikiliminhya n'hambo ali nguno ya ng'ombe." Ulu bayogelaga ajili ya ng'ombe, maguta. Balye duhu nabo bapejiwe abangi binge. Abubyulya abooyi bikenaja gwenuyo duhu, Ali Nhobola lulu iyene, gakiza maBiliji koyi, ii Nhobola yene kuyulya abangi. Gakiza maBiligiji gangi gakiza iNhobola, Nhobola yabile ya bangi yaMabiliji amalya banhu. Gabalyaga abanhu lya pelanaga gete. Lelo iNhobola hangi yabile yabangi yamabiliji amalya banhu. Iii yali yagabanyiwa insi yise Tabola. Yagabanywa uko kabiligwa uko kabiligwa.

All right, let me sing about the conflict, a song about the time of conflict between the British and Germans. Ahah, because my father was there, a singer, I should say, my grandfather, he was on the side of the Germans, to be exact. He was a farmers' singer, indeed the act of farming requires singers, to bring the farmers together. They told him, "Come, sing to us," then they sang. His name was Masanja. All right, he sang like this [sings song]. Now, let me explain. Now, the Germans and the British at that time were fighting one another. We say, "They were fighting because of cattle." Because we are the cattle herders who have cattle, because we saw them, we knew. Why was it they were doing their witchcraft? For cattle. Very much so. Indeed, like this, that is the way it was, the British and the Germans causing one another to run around, because of cattle. That is why they were arguing, because of cattle, fat. They should only [be the ones to] eat, and others, should be expelled. [They were the ones] who ate, because of fighting there. As for Tabora, the Belgians came there, Tabora was eating others [?]. These others, the Belgians, came to Tabora. Tabora belongs to other people, the Belgians who ate people. They ate people, because they were very angry and fierce. Where the Germans and the British were. Today [at that time] Tabora again belongs to the Belgians, who ate people. Indeed, our country divided up. It was divided up, this side here, and that side there.

Chiila's interpretation overlapped with that of ng'wana Mihumo, however the reference to the Belgians as cannibals was puzzling. Eventually, I took this simply as a literal metaphor regarding the battle prowess of the Belgians, who were siding with the British from their colonial stations in Rwanda and the Congo.

In 1999, after producing and releasing "Shiganga Jilikenya Kimabala" together with several dozen other Sukuma farmers' songs on a CD with Multicultural Media (*Tanzania: We Never Sleep, We Dream of Farming: The Farmer-Composers of Sukumaland*), I visited Tanzania again. I gave hundreds of copies of the CD to all of the musicians and their families involved in making the music on the recording, left the CD on commission for purchase in retail outlets and tourist outlets in and around Mwanza and Dar es Salaam, and performed on-air interviews promoting it with several Tanzanian radio stations. After traveling back to the Sukuma-Shinyanga region, I sadly learned that both ng'wana Chiila and ng'wana Makanga had passed away the previous year. Their families related to me, however, that both singers had revived this song in their song competitions to considerable interest and discussion, particularly in an important state-sponsored "heritage" music festival that took place in 1997.

Upon returning to the United States after that visit, I was contracted to publish my research about this song and others from this period. This led me to revisit World War I history books. I learned that the text reference to *Simba*, as in "Simba Sana," was not a reference to a Disney character, but a Germanized articulation of the Kiswahili—*chimba*, to dig. Thus, "Dig Deep" was a slogan of a far-reaching German education campaign instructing the local askari troops in how to effectively dig trenches and maintain battle-ready competence and discipline. I learned that at Mwanza, the Germans had held their Lake Victoria position until an actual British landing in July of 1914. The German Mwanza forces dug trenches at Seke in the southern Sukuma region and managed to delay the British advance. They finally surrendered their position in September 1916, when the British overran the Seke post and went on to take Tabora in a major victory (Austen 1968, 112), with help from a Belgian unit (the allies of the British) who approached the area from the east, commanded by Charles Tombeur (Tombeur 1968).

I was still most puzzled by the song reference to the widely feared Belgians. I soon learned, however, that the notoriety of the Belgian soldiers was fueled by the word-of-mouth stories of genocidal atrocities committed by King Leopold's personal army in the Belgian Congo (Hochschild 1998). The phrase "eaters of men" most likely refers to the people often cited by both Henry Morton Stanley (1899) and David Livingstone (1870–1871) in their nineteenth-century travelogues: the "BaManyema," African troops in the employ of the Belgians. The Bamanyema were an amalgamated social category associated with immigrants and refugees from the Congo living in Rwanda. Hired by the Belgians as soldiers, they reputedly sharpened their teeth and were widely rumored by their enemies to be cannibals. Beyond this information, I was at a standstill, but I felt at the time that I had compiled enough, and I eventually came to publish what I had learned about this song in a monograph about interpreting Sukuma song (Gunderson 2010).[5]

Several years later, as the result of an invitation to present at a conference in Zanzibar on music, archives, and memory,[6] I had the opportunity and inspiration once again to pick up the trail on this tune. Via online searches for several terms in the third verse, I stumbled on an online historical war-gamers' community that specialized in World War I and East Africa. This online war-gamer contingent was a community of grown men (and a few women) playing with toy soldiers and taking turns sharing their battle moves in chatrooms. Although interested in creating alternative historical battle scenarios and outcomes different from those that actually occurred, these folks were obsessed with the accuracy of names, dates, and places. As it turned out, I hit the jackpot in my discussions with them. After a few initial chatroom queries, I was told that I needed to chat with "WalkerMacDaddy,"[7] who was something of an in-house celebrity with an apparently encyclopedic knowledge about World War I battles in East Africa. After I found him and shared the translated text, it was clear that he understood immediately several points about the third verse that I and my informants knew little about. According to him, "Child of Makoma" referred to Makoma, a notorious marauding Zambian chief who enlisted road pirates, robbers, and disaffected youth, known colloquially as *ruga ruga*, into his private vigilante army. Like the "Manyema," these vigilantes subsequently hired themselves out to both the Germans and the British as soldiers and scouts (Moyd 2014, 67), because they knew the local terrain and could command a price to the highest bidder for their skills. "Child of Makoma" was thus most likely a term of endearment addressing someone who is from this cadre. When I asked "WalkerMacDaddy" what his sources were for this information, he said that he used to spend long hours at the British Library reading unpublished diaries, travelogues, and rare manuscripts in order to collect data and gain further inspiration for his battle scenarios.

At the annual Bulabo Festival in Bujora, Tanzania, in 2014,[8] I had a chance encounter with several traditional healers, chiefs, and governmental administrators (see Figure 10.6) who were from the region where this song had originated. Asking them if they knew what the song meant, or anything about its historical context, they replied, as had ng'wana Kangwiina and ng'wana Chiira, that it was about the British fighting the Germans during World War II (this of course was the world war that they all knew). I took this chance to share with them, line by line, what I knew about the song, and, after singing them a few lines, they finished the song for me, saying they had been hearing it regularly on the radio for about ten years, especially during national and regional political campaigns. I was of course delighted, and soon learned that the government was using the recording I had made with ng'wana Makanga and ng'wana Chiila. It had been receiving periodic election-year airplay on the Mwanza-based Radio Free Africa[9] since 2004. It was being used as the signature soundbite for the government's "get out and vote" campaign, aimed at the rural population in the Sukuma region. When I asked these chiefs about the significance to the government of the line "Shiganga Jilikenya Kumabala," they explained that the image of "the boulders fighting each other on the plain" had nothing to do with familiar rock landscapes, or foreign invaders fighting each other, but referred to significant current events; it meant that "political parties are clashing" and "big eventful change was in the air" (Seni*). After asking the chiefs if they had ever heard the song prior to this radio play, they said that they had not, but that nowadays the song could be heard everywhere: in the villages, being sung (once again) by voluntary farm work brigades, and by competing groups at CCM political rallies.[10] I shared with them what I had come to learn about the song, and they were astonished to hear who the composer was. I learned from

FIGURE 10.6 Left to right: M. Seni, M. Muyanga, T. Mapela, N. Sheli. Bulabo Festival, Bujora
Tanzania, July 7, 2014.

Photograph by Frank Gunderson.

them that ng'wana Matonange had been well-known as a composer in the court of
one of these men's grandfathers (ng'wana Sheli), and that besides being a well-known
beni musician, he was also a leading figure in the secret divination society known
in Shinyanga and Tabora as the *bachweezi* during the 1920s. In a sense this research
had come full circle, as this was the society (see Figure 10.7) that Hans Cory had been
tasked to investigate; and though it was unmarked as such, this would explain further
why he had this text in his collection.

Historical songs in the Sukuma area are considered as "conversations from the past."
Songs are important conduits of ancestral voices, transmitted as first-person narratives
through several generations. In this case, a song associated with long-term memory
lay dormant, awaiting retrieval. The idea of "the body as an archive," explored by Carol
Muller (2002), is evident here. But not all songs stored away in bodily memory are so
easily retrieved; the ravages of time can take their toll. A textual cue, excavated from a
colonial archive, did the trick, helping to bridge long-term memory to recent memory[11]
and bring the memory and song to life. Their subsequent memories and commentary
about the nature of this song, and the chaotic times that inspired it, informed in turn
my own ethnographic and historical interpretation of the song's transmission trajectory and elucidated many historical questions, including those about local memory,
power relations, and knowledge. In this chapter, I have discussed my own ongoing

FIGURE 10.7 *Bachweezi* spirit dancers, Tabora.

From Blohm (vol. 2, 1933).

reflexive repatriation of a specific song over a twenty-year period—a reflexive process in the sense that I have tried to the best of my ability to uncover as much as possible about the song, by engaging with an "archive–field" continuum, and sharing those discoveries in an ongoing relationship with the community of Sukuma musicians from which it came.

ORAL SOURCES

Chiila, "Jiyoga" Ng'humbi Shing'hini (ng'wana). 1995. Farmer, *nfumu* (healer), and *pubha* dance leader. Village of Ng'wajigiinya, Nzega, Tanzania. Interviewed on several occasions, August 15–19.

Makanga, Gembe Ng'honela (ng'wana). 1995. Farmer, *nfumu* (healer), and *pubha* singer. Village of Sayusayu, Shinyanga, Tanzania. Interviewed on several occasions in August.

Mihumo, Kang'wiina (ng'wana). 1994, 1995. Farmer and retired *bunuunguli* dance leader. Village of Isangidjo and Bujora Center, Kisessa, Tanzania. Interviewed on several occasions December 20 and 22, 1994; February 23, 1995.

Seni, Mgema. 2014. Chief (*ntemi*), Kanadi division. Bujora Center, Kisessa, Tanzania. Group interview on July 7.

Sheli (ng'wana). 2014. Healer (*nfumu*), Kanadi division. Bujora Center, Kisessa, Tanzania. Group interview on July 7.

Archives Consulted

Hans Cory Papers, East African Collection, University of Dar es Salaam, Dar es Salaam, Tanzania.
Sukuma Archives, Bujora Cultural Centre, Mwanza, Tanzania.
Tanzania National Archives, Dar es Salaam, Dar es Salaam, Tanzania.
University of Dar es Salaam Library, Dar es Salaam, Tanzania.

Notes

1. Specific Sukuma musical labor genres are named after the labor associations with which they are associated. The *bu-* prefix signifies genre, whereas the *ba-* prefix signifies the people, social groupings, and ethnicities that perform the genre.
2. Ng'wana, literally "child of," is found most often in the context of a personal name, where one differentiates oneself from parents by referring to themselves or others as ng'wana so-and-so ("child of so-and-so").
3. Pan-Bantu term signifying drum(s), dance(s), or any performative event featuring drumming and dancing. In Kiswahili, this is *ngoma* (without an apostrophe, pronounced with a hard "g").
4. Throughout this chapter, an asterisk (*) is used in the inline citations to signify oral sources.
5. This was, in a sense, a larger project employing reflective repatriation. After recording or collecting these songs, I approached musicians and other specialists for further comment. These individuals read or listened to the songs, and then responded in immediate reflection. This process had much to reveal both about the person and about the song itself. Further, I discovered that a song could make a kind of sense to one person, and an entirely different kind of sense to another, and that both could illuminate aspects of deeper meaning. Prior to the interview, I told the collaborators that their discourse about the songs would be published, verbatim. To complete this part of the process, I compared, analyzed, and rendered the commentaries for each song for clarity into an interpretive essay. I further contextualized the song texts, narratives about the songs, and interpretive renderings with supplementary materials collected from extensive archival collections in Tanzania, which included in their holdings local newspapers, film archives, and personal collections. These mission, colonial, and travel accounts were assessed for clues concerning musical practice from the late nineteenth century to the present. I matched interview data and songs with historical references with written records for historical dates. Descriptive and evaluative terms were collected and fed back to subsequent interview sources, with the aim of developing a two-way intersubjective research process that reflected not only the aims of the researcher but also the aims of all parties involved. Historical periodicity was determined on a case-by-case basis. Sometimes, the singer whom I interviewed was the composer of the song, and more exact dating was relatively easy. Usually, however, the singer transmitted texts that the composer had taught to them, or they passed along and transformed texts whose original author was unknown. In other cases, the text or genre itself provided clues to the time of the song's composition.
6. "Memory, Power, and Knowledge in African Music and Beyond," June 10–15, 2015. A conference hosted by the Dhow Countries Music Academy (DCMA), sponsored by the Volkswagen Foundation, Zanzibar Stone Town, Zanzibar, Tanzania.

7. A pseudonym, upon request of the source.
8. *Bulabo*, "flowers" in Kisukuma. This is a local variant of the Catholic Corpus Christi Feast celebration. See also Barz (2004) and Gunderson (1991).
9. 1377 AM. 7-C, Ilemela Industrial Area, Airport Road, Mwanza, Tanzania.
10. *Chama cha Mapinduzi*, or "Party of the Revolution," the ruling political party in Tanzania.
11. Slobin proposes music's tripartite strata in memory consciousness, of "current, recent, and long term, all of which occur simultaneously in the present. The current is always at the forefront of attention, claiming primacy through policy or persuasion . . . the recent is the seedbed of the current . . . the long term operates at another level of memory in this archeology of music cultures" (Slobin 1996, 11).

REFERENCES

Austen, Ralph. 1968. *Northwest Tanzania under German and Colonial Rule; Colonial and Tribal Policies 1889–1939.* New Haven, CT: Yale University Press.

Barz, Gregory. 2004. *Music in East Africa: Experiencing Music, Expressing Culture.* New York: Oxford University Press.

Baswezi Report from P.C. to Chief Secretary, Dar es Salaam. 1930. Baswezi. Secretariat File List Section P1–10 "Police." 19303. Document #1. 4 October. Tanzanian National Archive, Dar es Salaam, Tanzania.

Blohm, Wilhelm. 1933. *Die Nyamwezi: Gesellschaft und Weltbild.* Vols. 1 and 2. Hamburg: Friederichsen, de Gruyter.

Bosch, P. Fr. 1930. *Les Banyamwezi, peuple de l'Afrique Orientale.* Munster: Anthropos Bilbiothek.

Cory, Hans. n.d.a. "Sukuma Songs and Dances." File #191. EAF Z6601 E3. Hans Cory Papers, East African Collection, University of Dar es Salaam, Dar es Salaam, Tanzania.

Cory, Hans. n.d.b. "Sukuma Secret Societies." File #192. EAF Z6601 E3. Hans Cory Papers, East African Collection, University of Dar es Salaam, Dar es Salaam, Tanzania.

Cory, Hans. 1946. "The Buyeye: A Secret Society of Snake Charmers in Sukumaland, Tanganyika Territory." *Africa: Journal of the International Africa Institute* 16 (3): 160–178.

Foucault, Michel. 1971. *The Archaeology of Knowledge and the Discourse on Language.* Translated from the French by A. M. Sheridan Smith. New York: Pantheon.

Grimes, B., ed. n.d. *Ethnologue: Languages of the World.* Ethnologue Database. http://www.sil.org/ftp/ethnologue13/AREAS/AFRICA/Tanz.txt (accessed December 17, 2008).

Gunderson, Frank. 1991. "The History and Practice of Christian Gospel Hymnody in Swahili-Speaking East Africa." MA thesis, Wesleyan University.

Gunderson, Frank. 1999a. "Musical Labor Associations in Sukumaland Tanzania: History and Practice." PhD diss., Wesleyan University.

Gunderson, Frank. 1999b. *Tanzania: We Never Sleep, We Dream of Farming: The Farmer-Composers of Sukumaland.* Music of the Earth series 3013.Wilkes-Barre, PA: Multicultural Media.

Gunderson, Frank. 2003. "From 'Dances with Porcupines' to 'Twirling a Hoe': Musical Labor TRANSFORMED in Sukumaland, Tanzania." *Africa Today* 48 (4): 1–29.

Gunderson, Frank. 2008. "'We Will Leave Signs!': The Inter-textual Song Praxis of Elephant Hunters (*Bayege*) within the Greater Sukuma Region of Western Tanzania." *History and Anthropology* 19 (4): 229–249.

Gunderson, Frank. 2010. *Sukuma Labor Songs from Western Tanzania*. Leiden: Brill Academic Press.

Gunderson, Frank. 2013. "Expressive Bodies/Controlling Impulses: The 'Dance' between Official Culture and Musical Resistance during the Colonial Era in Western Tanzania." *Soundings: A Journal of Interdisciplinary Humanities* 96 (2): 145–169.

Hochschild, Adam. 1998. *King Leopold's Ghost: A Story of Greed, Terror and Heroism in Colonial Africa*. Boston: Houghton Mifflin.

Hoesing, Peter. 2006. "*Kubandwa*: Theory and Historiography of Shared Expressive Culture in Interlacustrine East Africa." MM thesis, College of Music, Florida State University.

Koponen, Juhani. 1988. *People and Production in Late Precolonial Tanzania*. Helsinki: Scandinavian Institute of African Studies.

Koritschoner, H. (later Cory). 1937. "Some East African Native Songs." *Tanganyika Notes and Records* 4: 51–64.

Livingstone, David. 1870–1871. "Manyema Field Diary." Unpublished booklet. DLC 297. Sukuma Archives, Bujora Cultural Centre, Mwanza, Tanzania.

Molony, Thomas. 2014. *Nyerere: The Early Years*. Suffolk, UK: James Currey.

Moyd, Michelle, R. 2014. *Violent Intermediaries: African Soldiers, Conquest, and Everyday Colonialism in German East Africa*. Athens: Ohio University Press.

Muller, Carol. 2002. "Archiving Africanness in Sacred Song." *Ethnomusicology* 46 (3): 409–431.

Mwanza, P. C., to Dar es Salaam Chief Secretary. 1928. Letter. Document 1, "Native Societies." Tattooing of Members and Implications. Native Affairs 20964. August 16. Tanzania National Archive, Dar es Salaam.

Ranger, Terrence. 1975. *Dance and Society in Eastern Africa: The Beni Ngoma*. Berkeley: University of California Press.

Savage, Roger. 2009/2010. "Crossing the Disciplinary Divide: Hermeneutics, Ethnomusicology, and Musicology." *College Music Symposium* 49/50: 402–408.

Seeger, Anthony. 2001. "Intellectual Property and Audiovisual Archives and Collections." In *Folk Heritage Collections in Crisis*, 32–50. Washington, DC: Council on Library and Information Services.

Shelemay, Kay Kaufman. 2008. "The Ethnomusicologist, Ethnographic Method, and the Transmission of Tradition." In *Shadows in the Field: New Perspectives for Fieldwork for Ethnomusicology*, 2nd ed., edited by Gregory F. Barz and Timothy J. Cooley, 141–156. New York and Oxford: Oxford University Press.

Slobin, Mark. 1996. "Introduction." In *Retuning Culture: Musical Changes in Central and Eastern Europe*, edited by Mark Slobin, 1–13. Durham, NC: Duke University Press.

Songoyi, Elias Manandi. 1990. "The Artist and the State in Tanzania." MA thesis, University of Dar es Salaam.

Stanley, Henry Morton. 1899. *Through the Dark Continent*. Vol. 2. London: George Newnes.

Stokes, Charles. 1877. Personal Correspondences of Charles Stokes. October 31, 1877. Zanzibar-Ragei 1878–1880 collection. SABCC.

Stone, Ruth, and Verlon Stone. 1981. "Event, Feedback and Analysis: Research Media in the Study of Music Events." *Ethnomusicology* 25: 215–225.

Stroeken, Koen. 2010. *Moral Power: The Magic of Witchcraft*. New York: Berghahn Books.

"Tombeur" (Charles Henri Marie Ernest). 1968. *Biographie Belge d'Outre-Mer*. Vol. 6. Brussels: Academie Royale des Sciences d'Outre-Mer.

CHAPTER 11

"WE WANT OUR VOICES BACK"

Ethical Dilemmas in the Repatriation of Recordings

GRACE KOCH

INTRODUCTION

THE title of this book, *The Oxford Handbook of Musical Repatriation*, brings up various dilemmas because of the many meanings surrounding the word "repatriation."[1] For example, I am part of a team identifying collections of Indigenous Australian human remains held overseas in museums.[2] Within this context, repatriation means the return of remains to the communities from which they were taken. Thus, the museums and galleries sectors interpret repatriation as the return of actual objects. However, those of us who have worked in information management are concerned with returning the information contained on "objects" consisting of recordings in an audio or video format that will be useful to the people who request them. The physical item containing the recording is, indeed, important, but its actual worth depends on the importance of the information that it contains (Onopkoi 2013). Such "knowledge repatriation" can also be described as the return of intangible cultural heritage (see Russell 2012). In this chapter, I use the term "repatriation" to mean the return of *copies* of recordings, usually in digital form, because they, as well as the originals, hold the same items of sonic heritage.

IMPORTANCE OF RECORDINGS TO INDIGENOUS SOCIETY

The word "liminality" refers to a space that exists between two states of being. If I close my eyes and listen to old recordings of my family made by my father on an old disc-cutting machine, I enter an earlier time where people dear to me, long gone, become present as they speak, evoking feelings and images that can bring me to tears. The recording has captured a unique moment in time, one laden with memories that set a rich personal context, creating a liminal zone between the past and present. There is much literature about how Australian Indigenous people create a liminal space where the creation time, often referred to as the Dreaming, and the present moment combine during the enactment of ceremony and ritual.[3] The anthropologist Ronald Berndt speaks of the holistic nature of the Dreaming as perceived by the Gunwinggu people of western Arnhem Land:

> Just as the essence of Dreaming resides in each human being, male and female, and is activated through ritual, so every element in the natural environment has this same quality—a sacred quality, since sacredness in the Gunwinggu sense is derived from the Dreaming and the spirit beings; it is pervasive, part of life and of living.
>
> (Berndt and Berndt 1970, 226)

For Australian Indigenous people,[4] listening to a recording or viewing a film of a ceremony can offer a threshold experience, hovering between the past and the present. Often a person who knows a ceremony will be aware that the power unleashed by its performance can become embedded in a video or audio recording of that ceremony. For example, in the 1970s, a female staff member from the Australian Institute of Aboriginal Studies (AIAS)[5] happened to be in a room where a film of a ceremony was screening. The male custodians of the ceremony immediately surrounded her, acting to shield her from the potentially harmful spiritual power released by the film.

Recordings can evoke memories, but they can also inspire people to adapt the contents to a contemporary context. The *National Indigenous Languages Survey Report* (NILS), commissioned by the Australian Government in 2005, states:

> The recording of the speech and song of elders . . . provides a way for the following generations to learn and recreate new cultural achievements, both now and in the future. As with any living culture, the results will not be the same as the original but may change in accordance with the times and needs of the new inheritors of the tradition.
>
> (AIATSIS and Federation of Aboriginal and Torres Strait Islander Languages 2005, 22)

We, as managers and archivists, know that the collections we hold are very valuable, but our responsibility becomes almost frightening when we consider the results of deterioration of carriers, format change, and other threats that make preservation vital while the material remains playable. Secure repositories with accurate documentation of their holdings are extremely important, especially in this time of government pressure to disseminate information. The costs for proper care for the collections continue to rise, while funding for the work often does not.

The following section gives some examples of how various Australian institutions and keeping places are addressing the challenges of knowledge repatriation.

REPATRIATION INITIATIVES

With increased contraction of government budgets, public institutions holding cultural collections are coming under pressure to make their holdings available as widely as possible, all the while facing cuts to their budgets. In a press release issued in 2013, Michael Loebenstein, director of the National Film and Sound Archive of Australia (NFSA), stated how people perceive their rights to material in national collections:

> Availability in our current environment is characterised by our users' expectations of being part of a two-way exchange. Instead of "granting access" we are expected to "share" our collections. We live in a "transactional" environment.
>
> (National Film and Sound Archive of Australia 2013a)

Organizations are digitizing their material at a great rate so that items can be accessible online.[6] Initiatives such as the Opening Australia's Archives Open Access Guidelines[7] encourage wide dissemination; the National Library of Australia's online Trove service (http://trove.nla.gov.au/) allows wide-ranging access to listings of its holdings as well as those of most other collecting institutions in the country. With Australian Indigenous material, public institutions are balancing demands to make their collections known with respecting cultural protocols in managing access and dissemination.

In the following section, I describe two national initiatives for repatriation of recordings, then I move on to some other more localized projects.

THE AIATSIS AUDIOVISUAL ARCHIVE

In 1974, ten years after the founding of the AIAS, a conference was held in Canberra, where a group of academics, political figures, and other researchers discussed present and future directions for research in Aboriginal studies. A letter from a group of Aboriginal people who signed themselves as Eaglehawk and Crow[8] questioned the "implied relationship the Institute was to have with Aborigines when it was formed,"[9] and demanded that Aboriginal people be part of the decision-making group for sponsoring and funding research projects (Widders et al. 1974, 1).

In response to this letter and many other requests from Australian Indigenous people, the directions and governance of the Institute have moved toward substantial Australian Indigenous control. The collections—in particular, the sound recordings and the photographs—are now accessed heavily by Australian Indigenous people. The institute's audiovisual archive become one of the world's largest collections of Australian Indigenous cultural information and consists largely of field recordings generated by AIATSIS-funded grants since the 1960s through to 2011. As there are varied conditions of access and use on these, AIATSIS has sought through its website to publicize its Return of Material to Indigenous Clients (ROMTIC) scheme by making up to twenty copies of digitized photographs and audio recordings available free of charge to relatives of people whose images or voices appear within the audio documents. Also, there has been a Community Access Program operating off and on since 1990, whereby AIATSIS staff travel to Australian Indigenous communities, issuing copies of material relevant to the geographic and cultural area.

After years of petitioning the federal government, the executive of AIATSIS, using arguments largely based on concern for the care of its priceless collections, finally succeeded in getting more funding. As part of the Closing the Gap program targeted at redressing some of the inequalities between Australian Indigenous people, the prime minister, Malcolm Turnbull, announced an additional $20 million injection of funds targeted at preserving the collections at AIATSIS, especially the language collections in both print and audiovisual formats.

> This will enable the collection of critical cultural knowledge, and promote an understanding of Aboriginal and Torres Strait Islander cultures, traditions, languages and stories, past and present. It will keep safe this knowledge for all Australians by digitising and protecting it from being lost.
>
> (Turnbull 2016)

A Special Use of Sound Recordings

Two major pieces of legislation created by the Commonwealth of Australia in 1976 and 1993 resulted in the far-reaching recognition of Australian Indigenous rights to land. The Aboriginal Land Rights (Northern Territory) Act 1976 (ALRA) was enacted to provide legal recognition of the Aboriginal system of land tenure within the Northern Territory and to establish a process whereby Indigenous Australian people there could prove their claims to ownership. Later, the Native Title Act 1993 (NTA), enacted by the Commonwealth of Australia, recognized a concept of native title, which was a form of entitlement to land based on Indigenous laws and customs. Native title rights extended to the mainland of Australia and most of its islands, including the Torres Strait to the extreme northeast. Federal Court judges hear native title cases and make determinations based on the validity of the evidence presented to them.[10]

Part of the evidence for land claims has consisted of recordings from AIATSIS. Copies of archival recordings that demonstrate a long-term connection with land under claim have been requested by land councils, native title representative bodies and service providers, Indigenous individuals, consultants, the federal court, and government departments. For example, interviews with elders about their knowledge of the stories, songs, and general history of land under claim as well as actual recordings of performances have been submitted as evidence.

Passing on of cultural knowledge by elders has become an acceptable legal proof of rights to land. The anthropologist Jeremy Beckett, who has worked in the Torres Strait since the 1950s, presented a compelling argument of long-term knowledge continuity based on sound recordings. During one of the court hearings that would ultimately contribute toward the recognition of native title, Beckett described the similarity between songs recorded on wax cylinders by the Cambridge Anthropological Expedition to the Torres Strait in the 1890s and his own recordings from the 1960s.

> [T]he recordings I made from the old men in 1960 were compared by Professor Trevor Jones—professor of music at Monash—with the transcriptions made by Myers (psychologist/musician who was on the 1898 Cambridge Expedition) from Cylinder Recordings . . . and he pronounced the songs virtually unchanged. Now, I think in that case, there is a clear continuity despite the fact that the songs went underground for a period.
>
> (*Mabo v. Queensland* 1986, 2231)

Since then, the wax cylinder recordings from the 1898 Cambridge Expedition have been digitized and copies of these have been repatriated to the various communities in the Torres Strait where they were made. That material, as well as the field recordings made by Jeremy Beckett, has been useful both in serving as legal documentation to land rights and to cultural revitalization in the Torres Strait.

The position of AIATSIS native title research and access officer, which I held for over ten years, involves working with clients to identify items from all parts of the collections that can provide evidence relevant for land claims and arranging copies wherever possible (see Koch 1995). The AIATSIS staff has either prepared documentary evidence, some of which appears on recordings, or supplied other background information to contribute toward the process of claims. An ethical issue arises here because AIATSIS, as a public institution, is responsible for providing information to all clients no matter what position they take regarding a claim.

Recordings made by AIATSIS-funded researchers may contain hidden gems that can strengthen land claims. For example, a linguistic researcher may only have been interested in recording word lists, but Indigenous people often took the chance to pass on their own stories or songs as well. Texts recorded by linguists provide a rich source of evidence of cultural continuity because they may contain oral histories describing the travels of people with their elders who taught them how to take care of specific tracts of land, or of early memories of first contact with white people. Documents tracing the occupation of the land by Indigenous people before the Australian Federation in 1901 can be used as important elements of proof of long-term residence and care for the land under claim. Also, the birthplace or date of birth of an Australian Indigenous person giving a word list may appear on the announcement at the start of a tape. In some cases, claimants whose names have not been included on listings of traditional owners may request copies of recordings where family members speak about genealogical links.

Anthropologists have recorded interviews discussing the general limits of "country" for specific cultural groups. Often their recordings of songs have been tendered as exhibits to the Court. Proof resides in songs because they enshrine the tracks of mythological Creation heroes who traveled over vast distances and established the features of the land. These can be traced on a map; generally the people who own these songs own the land through which they travel (Moyle 1983, 6), and recordings of these "song cycles" can be produced as evidence. Also, listening to recordings by elders who are now deceased can help the owners of the associated ceremonies when they perform them before the court (see Koch 2013).

The growing importance of audio recordings held at AIATSIS in documenting native title claims can be seen by examining statistics for native title requests for audio material during a period of six months in 2008 compared to the same period in 2013. Nearly three times as many clients asked for audiovisual material in 2013, especially Australian Indigenous individuals or consultants who prepare documentation for native title claims.

The National Film and Sound Archive, Australia

Unlike AIATSIS, the NFSA holds mostly published items, but it too has embarked on an ambitious program to repatriate copies of cultural material to relevant Indigenous communities. Reciprocal visits are held each year, both by Indigenous people to the Canberra NFSA headquarters to locate items in the collections and by NFSA staff to Indigenous communities to return copies and to give collection management and preservation advice.

A two-way learning process occurred when Wukun Wanambi, director of the Buku-Larrnnggay Mulka Multimedia Archive and Production Centre at Yirrkala in eastern Arnhem Land, Northern Territory, visited the NFSA in 2008. He searched the collections at the Canberra headquarters and identified the items he wanted digital copies of, mostly films. Later, a team of NFSA staff who had worked with him brought the copies to Yirrkala. He took the staff to the places where the films were made, telling them the stories associated with the sites and adding other contextual elements, thus enriching the documentation and educating users about how his people see the meaning of the landscape. In turn, NFSA staff provided advice on preservation and conservation issues that arise from a hot and humid environment. The Buku-Larrnnggay Mulka archive keeps digital copies of historical material as well as making their own videos and recordings, sometimes repurposing their holdings in very imaginative ways.[11] Their aim is to keep their culture strong and to ensure that their young people know about their rich heritage. I describe the Mulka archive in more detail in the section on localized projects.

OTHER REPATRIATION INITIATIVES

Repatriation of audiovisual material to Australian Indigenous communities involves a variety of formats, such as sound recordings, video, film, and photographs. The first two developments described below have a national focus; these are followed by some localized schemes.

National Indigenous Recording Project

In 2002, the first Symposium of Music and Dance at the fourth Garma[12] festival in Gunyaŋara, northeast Arnhem Land, issued a statement to call on the Australian government to "support and sustain Indigenous performance traditions through the establishment of Indigenous Knowledge Centres" and to recognize the "National Indigenous Recording Project (NIRP) as a National Research Priority" (National Recording Project for Indigenous Performance in Australia 2002).[13] One of the most important strategies for the NIRP was to repatriate copies of sound and visual records to communities.

A series of eleven projects[14] based in the Northern Territory are connected with the NIRP. These concentrate on song styles that are being practiced within a traditional context. Government funding for six of these came through the Australian Research Council Grant scheme, with the rest through the endangered languages program (DoBeS) of the Volkswagen Foundation in Germany,[15] the Hans Rausing Endangered Languages Program[16] at the School of Oriental and African Studies at the University of London, and the University of Sydney. The Junba Project, begun after the initial eleven projects, is also part of the NIRP and is being conducted in Western Australia. I mention it later under the section on localized projects.

The map[17] in Figure 11.1 shows the sites for most of the projects; all work directly with traditional owners, either as local representatives or as full research partners. Some of the aims are to establish local archives and keeping places, to ensure the sustainability of the recordings through time, to train local people to record performances to a high standard, to manage local archives, and to document the recordings so that performers can learn from the information and use it to revitalize their performance practice. Several books and recordings were published, and community-based databases of audiovisual items were created through the activities of the projects.[18]

Ara Irititja Project

In 1994, a group of elders from the Aṉangu Pitjantjatjara Yankunytjatjara (APY) lands of far northwestern South Australia consulted with anthropologists and archival experts to find out how to manage their growing collections of photos and sound recordings, many

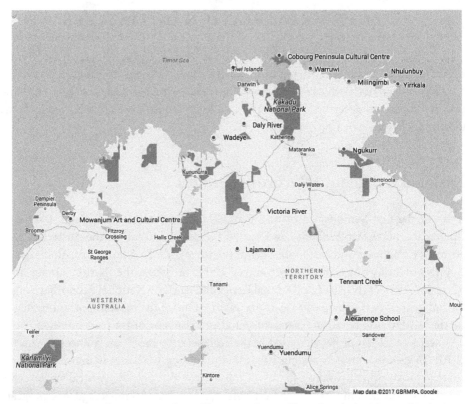

FIGURE 11.1 Map of projects conducted by researchers affiliated with the National Indigenous Recording Project.

of which were from archives, missionaries, and others with historical connections to APY lands. The result was a FileMaker Pro database that enables Australian Indigenous people to manage digitized photographs, sound recordings, videos, and documents in a culturally sensitive way. The English meaning of the term "Ara Irititja" is given on the website http://www.irititja.com as "stories from a long time ago," and, in the beginning, its major aim was to repatriate material of importance to the Anangu (Western Desert) people of Central Australia so that the information it contained could be passed on to future generations. Partnerships with regional and national archives exist so that digital copies of photographs, videos, and sound recordings can be lodged in relevant community centers. In addition, teams of knowledgeable Anangu and others have examined some of the Indigenous holdings of partner organizations in order to provide information on cultural protocols so that the organizations can manage their collections more sensitively in line with the wishes of people in the source communities.[19] For example, the Aboriginal Records Project of the State Library of South Australia has engaged people with specialist knowledge from the Pitjantjatjara Council's Ara Irititja Electronic Archive Project to assess and comment on access conditions for some of the ethnographic collections held in the library. The project design has been so successful that the Northern Territory Library Service uses Community Stories, an interactive form of Ara Irititja, in its library and knowledge centers in remote areas in order to access cultural information that has been repatriated and to add new items relevant to various communities. Land councils, media centers, and history projects in four states and territories have implemented the software as well, and Ara Irititja staff offer training in communities and remote areas to Indigenous people with the responsibility to operate and maintain the database. The original Ara Irititja database was not available on a web-based format, but its successor, a cloud-hosted solution known as Keeping Culture KMS, is now available.[20]

Localized Projects

One of the products of an NIRP project conducted in Belyuen, south of the city of Darwin, is the Belyuen Bangany Wangga workstation.[21] It resulted from a collaborative study between the musicologists Linda Barwick and Allan Marett and the linguist Lysbeth Ford, who sought to create usable platforms for repatriation of archival audio recordings.[22] Originally, the study sought to compare early recordings of performances from the area with present musical practice (Marett 2003). During the research, the Belyuen people showed great interest in all of the source material for the study, so a workstation was established to provide access to community members. An iTunes database was indexed according to individual performer and name (or topic) of each song, as these were the access points most important to community members. In 2001, AIATSIS published a CD titled *Rak Badjalarr* (Marett et al. 2001) featuring the repertoire of the singer Bobby Lane Lambudju. The accompanying booklet presented some of the results of the longitudinal comparative study of songs.

Another research initiative, the Junba Project, led by the ethnomusicologist Sally Treloyn at the Mowanjum Aboriginal Art and Culture Centre in Western Australia, used historical photos and recordings from major collecting institutions as source material for teaching young people to create short films about the song genre *junba*.[23]

An exciting repatriation project for the people of the Great and Little Sandy and Gibson Deserts of Western Australia arose from the recordings, videos, and photographs generated by the Canning Stock Route Project (CSRP) (Mira Canning Stock Route Project Archive 2013). The history of cattle droving through the 2,000-or-more-kilometer Canning Stock Route had been documented mostly from a European standpoint, but the rich and complex knowledge of Australian Indigenous people about the area had not been recorded. The CSRP addressed this need by creating a major exhibition titled "*Yiwarra Kuju*—The Canning Stock Route," comprising paintings, stories, and videos prepared from the perspective of the Indigenous people who lived along the route. Mira, the CSRP archive containing 30,000 unique cultural heritage items in digital form relating to seventeen remote communities along the route, is now available on the Internet at http://mira.canningstockrouteproject.com/browse (accessed May 5, 2016). Unfortunately, the oral histories are only available in print form, but the videos have substantial audio content with subtitles.

In 2000, the Martu Wangka, a group whose land lies along the Canning Stock Route, sent representatives to several national institutions such as AIATSIS and the NFSA to bring back copies of archival film, video, and sound recordings from their area. The Martu Community Access Library is operational in three Martu communities, with plans for three more centers.[24]

Repatriation of archival audio recordings has been important in the reawakening and revitalization of Australian Indigenous languages, especially in the eastern coastal area between Sydney and Brisbane. Because few speakers of the Indigenous languages remain, research on language has relied heavily on archival records and sound recordings. As mentioned earlier in this chapter, the prime minister, in his "Closing the Gap" speech, recognized the special cultural value of such recordings, increasing funding to AIATSIS for their preservation and conservation.

For example, seven local languages are supported by the Muurrbay Aboriginal Language and Culture Co-operative/Many Rivers Aboriginal Language Centre in northern New South Wales. The organization seeks to repatriate both print and archival audio so that grammars and language-learning materials can be developed (Ash et al. 2010, 109–110).

On the other side of Australia, the Wangka Maya Language Centre in Port Hedland, Western Australia, maintains an archive of language recordings consisting of material both created by their own linguists and repatriated from AIATSIS. The center trains local Australian Indigenous language workers to learn more about their languages and to create educational resources. In order to refresh her own knowledge and to practice her transcription skills, one woman, a speaker of Bayungu language, listened to recordings of language elicitation made in the 1960s and 1970s with elderly speakers. This work enabled her, with help from colleagues at Wangka Maya, to create a picture dictionary of the language with an accompanying CD using the early recordings giving samples of the pronunciation of Bayungu (Dixon and Deak 2010, 125–126).

Finally, in this chapter's section on the NFSA, I referred to the Mulka Project. It is a model of organization, knowledge repatriation, and inspiration to the Yolngu people of Eastern Arnhem Land. Its mission is to sustain and protect the local cultural knowledge under the leadership of community members.[25] Its website encourages the return of copies of all text, images, sound, and video recordings related to Northeast Arnhem Land as well as the establishment of partnerships with people and organizations that can train local staff. The project maintains a theater, media lab, project office, and museum staffed by local people, and it records local singers and events. Margaret Yunupingu, a translator and artist at the center, sums up the importance of maintaining identity by using both old and new resources:

> It's important for my people to have their cultures going strong. We don't want our cultures fading away. It's really fun, you know, to see the kids come in and enjoy

themselves. It makes me very proud because the kids are there all the time. I know that they are learning. Sometimes when you are making up a new film or something, the kids are always constantly asking, asking, when are you going to finish that new one, when can we look at that new one? Makes me feel good. And I know my work is very important, you know?

(Humphris 2009)

ETHICAL CONCERNS

Near the beginning of this chapter, I mentioned the tension between the pressure to disseminate copies of recordings and the responsibility to respect Indigenous protocols. Here I would concentrate on some ethical dilemmas existing for staff working within a government institution who deal with requests for recordings from a wide range of clients, some of whom can lay claim to the cultural material on the recordings and others with commercial, academic, or other interests.

To add to the tensions, cultural sensitivities may change over the years. One example of this comes from the earliest recordings held by AIATSIS, made by the Cambridge Expedition to the Torres Strait in 1898. The British Library National Sound Archive wanted to put these on their website as sound files. Among the songs were items from the Malu Bomai rituals that were extremely sacred to the Meriam people of Murray Island. Janet Topp Fargion, the British Library curator for world and traditional music, had repeatedly tried to contact the Meriam elders for permission to use them, but no answer came. Finally, after she made a series of concerted efforts to involve anthropologists and others, the elders gave their permission at the very last minute before the items were scheduled to be put on the web.[26]

In the case of AIATSIS, there has been a growing acknowledgment of the rights of Indigenous people to their cultural property, much of which exists on audio and visual materials. The Act that established the AIAS made no reference to collections, but when it was repealed, the new Australian Institute of Aboriginal and Torres Strait Islander Studies Act 1989 specifically mentioned, in part 10, section 41, "a cultural resource collection" as part of its functions and indicated that information should not be disclosed if it would be "inconsistent with the views and sensitivities of relevant Aboriginal persons or Torres Strait Islanders." How can this provision be operational, especially when there are many Australian Indigenous groups, some of which are in dispute with one another? At present, a risk management approach is the only way to ensure compliance, and clients who want copies of material are required to complete indemnity forms that have been carefully worded to cover most contingencies. In some cases, access versions of audio have been edited to remove some offensive comments and language; but of course, the original archival copies hold the full content. However, what about early recordings that may remain closed to Australian Indigenous clients because of stringent access conditions set by the depositors or because they do not have valid deposit forms?

The AIATSIS, like other archives and libraries around the world, holds recordings that have been collected over many years. When early recordings were made, often there was no idea of the rights of the people being recorded, nor was there any conception about the way the recordings could be used in the future.

In this section, I start with two rather polar examples drawn from two collections of recordings made in the 1960s by grantees of the then AIAS[27] and held in the institute's audiovisual archive.[28]

Closure by the Depositor

Since it was constituted in 1964, the AIATSIS has changed its conditions of deposit for recordings a number of times. In the 1960s, the deposit forms used by the AIAS Sound Archive allowed for four types of access conditions, or options, ranging from completely open access for both copying and listening at the AIAS to closed access requiring all clients to contact the collector directly for either listening or copying. The wording for the closed condition was:

> Option 4: The copies of tapes are deposited in the Institute to ensure preservation. They may not be made available to anyone for any purpose without the written permission of the Depositor or until the Depositor notifies the Institute in writing of a change in the Option under which the material is deposited.
>
> (Australian Institute of Aboriginal Studies 1965–1966)

The deposit forms serve as legal documents within the institute, and compliance with option 4 has proved to be very difficult if the depositors could not be found or if they had died and their heirs could not be located. Some cases arose in which speakers on the recordings or their relatives could not gain access to their own cultural material. In 1987, the deputy principal sent letters to all depositors who had restrictions on their material, asking them if people on the recordings, their relatives, and other Indigenous people with connections to people or languages on the recordings could have access. Almost all of the depositors were happy to accept these new conditions and signed the form.

However, a depositor of language recordings from the Kimberley district of Western Australia wished the closed option to remain, stating his personal commitment to the welfare of the people who had been recorded. He held this position firmly for as long as he lived, although he permitted some non-Indigenous researchers to have access. After he had passed away, AIATSIS staff negotiated with his heirs, explaining the importance of the recordings to Indigenous people. They agreed to transfer ownership of the collection to AIATSIS, thus trusting its care to qualified staff who, bound by provisions of the

AIATSIS Act (1989), understand how best to manage it. The collection moved from a closed status to a more open one.

"Carte Blanche to the World"?

The following example contrasts sharply with the previous one. A depositor wanted all parts of his collection to be freely available against the wishes of people from some of the areas where he had worked. The story touches on many ethical dilemmas.

The anthropologist LaMont West, a grantee of the AIAS in the 1960s, had compiled a remarkable collection of films and sound recordings of language, songs, and ceremonies during his research in Central Arnhem Land and Cape York. Unfortunately, he had not signed a deposit form at all. His extensive field tape report forms contained detailed information about the contents of each recording with some comments about gender and ceremonial restrictions. He then left Australia and became hard to find, although one anthropologist maintained intermittent contact with him. As conditions of access were not clear, the deputy principal of AIAS issued a file note confirming that only the "secret/sacred" parts of the recordings should have restrictions (AIAS 1964).

On March 1, 1988, the depositor contacted the institute requesting that "anyone, whatever their credentials or lack thereof, may use my field materials in any way they fancy with or without acknowledgment. I give the world carte blanche to the legal extent of my right to do so" (West 1988).

His directions did not exempt the material that he had identified as restricted. West's desire for "access to all" conflicted with two provisions of the AIATSIS Act (1989) that stated:

> Section 41. (1) Where information or other matter has been deposited with the Institute under conditions of restricted access, the Institute or the Council shall not disclose that information or other matter except in accordance with those conditions.
>
> Section 41. (2) The Institute or the Council shall not disclose information or other matter held by it (including information or other matter covered by subsection (1) if that disclosure would be inconsistent with the views or sensitivities of relevant Aboriginal persons or Torres Strait Islanders.

Some of those sensitivities became apparent when, in 2001, a group of men from Lockhart River, Queensland, visited AIATSIS and spent at least a week listening to recordings from West's collection that were made in their community. They identified some items that should be restricted, stating that only the appropriate men from their area should be allowed to hear them. West had not indicated that those items were sensitive, so staff could not have realized any potential problems. A file note was included in the documentation to alert collection staff to the wishes of the Lockhart men, thus helping them to comply with the part of the AIATSIS Act that required them to be aware of the views and sensitivities of Australian Indigenous people.

Keeping Problems from Happening Again

This section looks at two developments designed to prevent situations such as the two cases just mentioned. The first comes into play at the point of collection during research. The other concerns ethical practices of management once the recordings have been deposited into an institution. Both offer sets of guidelines applicable to cultural material in any format.

Most importantly, before any recordings are made during research, there should be a clear understanding between the researchers and the people being recorded about the aims of the research, how the recordings will be used, and who will be able to hear them and/or have copies. The *Guidelines for Ethical Research in Australian Indigenous Studies* (GERAIS), formulated at AIATSIS, enumerate fourteen principles that emphasize the importance of two-way respect and communication in all aspects of research. Each of these has a general explanatory section followed by a list of practical means of implementation.

Of most relevance here is Principle 13: Plans should be agreed for managing use of, and access to, research results (AIATSIS 2012, 17). The following is a condensed version of the points in GERAIS that describe the implementation of Principle 13 that can refer to sound recordings:

- identify all people and groups who should be consulted about access strategies
- agree on who holds the rights
- determine the level of community control, and where the originals may be lodged
- clarify which, if any, material should be restricted and how it should be managed

If the above points had been followed, the two situations described at the beginning of this section on ethical concerns would not have arisen.

Following on from GERAIS Principle 13 is the ethical management of Australian Indigenous material. The Aboriginal and Torres Strait Islander Library, Information and Resources Network (ATSILIRN) was founded in 1993 to support staff in collecting institutions who work with Australian Indigenous material. Some of its aims were to inform staff about the special requirements for handling the material, to publicize the importance of it to the wider community, and to influence managers and other people to effect positive change for services to Indigenous Australian clients. The protocols developed by the network have been adopted in various forms by libraries and archives throughout Australia. The section on repatriation states:

> Archives and libraries often hold original records which were created by, about, or with the input of particular Aboriginal and Torres Strait Islander communities. A community may place tremendous importance on particular records and request copies for use and retention within the community. Some records may have been taken from the control of the community or created by theft or deception. In addressing this issue, organizations will:

11.1 Respond sympathetically and co-operatively to any request from an Aboriginal and Torres Strait Islander community for copies of records of specific relevance to the community for its use and retention.

11.2 Agree to the repatriation of original records or the provision of copies to Aboriginal and Islander communities as may be determined through consultation.

11.3 Seek permission to hold copies of repatriated records but refrain from copying such records should permission be denied.

11.4 Assist Aboriginal and Torres Strait Islander communities in planning, providing and maintaining knowledge centers for repatriated records.

(ATSILIRN 2012)

Two of the major professional organizations that cover collection management in Australia, the Australian Library and Information Association and the Australian Society of Archivists, adopted these protocols in 1996. There have been some changes to the original version, especially in relation to operating in a digital environment, but the original principles advocating respect and consultation with Australian Indigenous people remain.

SUMMARY AND CONCLUSION

In this chapter, I have discussed why sound recordings and other material with sonic content are especially important to Australian Indigenous people and have shown how historical material is being used for many purposes, including cultural revitalization and the creation of new artistic expressions.

Within the last twenty years, there have been significant changes in how both audio and video materials containing Australian Indigenous content have been created and managed. Respect for Indigenous viewpoints and consultation with the people whose knowledge is captured in the recordings are vital to the ethical management of this precious heritage.

In the face of increasing pressure from the government for collecting institutions to disseminate material in digital form, all the while cutting financial support, I have shown some examples of how various national agencies and local initiatives have risen to this challenge. I have explored issues of ethics and some dilemmas raised by access to material as well as some remedies in the form of guidelines and protocols.

I end with a quote that echoes some of my own reactions to recordings made of my family. The late Dr. Marika, former council member of the Australian Institute of Aboriginal and Torres Strait Islander Studies, paid tribute to the ethnomusicologist Alice Moyle, who had made many recordings of songs from her homeland in the 1960s.

These are like cultural maintenance and preservation of knowledge in songs. The songs are oral narratives, texts, and oral histories, knowledge and law which have been handed down from father to son about the land immemorial . . . these recordings are like history books to us. . . . I love to listen to the recordings that Alice Moyle made of my father when he was a young man. They bring tears to my eyes when I hear his singing.

(AIATSIS 2005)

Notes

1. The author acknowledges Harold Koch, Cressida Fforde, and Tran Tran for helpful comments in shaping this chapter. Also, the views expressed in this chapter are those of the author and do not necessarily reflect the official policy or position of the Australian Institute of Aboriginal and Torres Strait Islander Studies or of the Australian National University.
2. Australian Research Council Linkage Grant LP13010131 (2014–2017), "Return, Reconcile, Renew: Understanding the History, Effects and Opportunities of Repatriation and Building an Evidence Base for the Future."
3. For some examples of detailed research on this topic, see Bell (2002), Marett (2005), Keen (2006), and Bradley (2010).
4. I use the term "Australian Indigenous people" to refer to both Australian Aboriginal people and Torres Strait Islanders.
5. The Australian Institute of Aboriginal Studies (AIAS) was established by an Act of Parliament in 1964. In 1989, that Act was repealed and was replaced by the Australian Institute of Aboriginal and Torres Strait Islander Studies Act 1989. The 1989 Act broadened its scope to recognize the people of the northernmost part of Australia, the Torres Strait Islanders, and to make formal provision for a cultural collection to be held within the organization. The AIAS became AIATSIS.
6. For example, for national collections, over 42,000 hours of the audio from the oral History and Folklore Collection of the National Library of Australia have been digitized. See http://www.nla.gov.au/corporate-documents/annual-report/2012-2013/director-generals-review (accessed 20/11/2013); 15,348 digital collection items (audio, film, and video) are available online from the National Film and Sound Archive of Australia (NFSA 2012–2013, 37).
7. http://creativecommons.org.au/research/openarchives/opening-australias-archives-open-access-guidelines-version-1 (accessed May 5, 2016).
8. Eaglehawk and Crow are two of the major culture heroes of the Darling River area of southeast Australia and they are names of social divisions of some of the tribes in the area.
9. When the AIAS was founded, its mission was to document all aspects of Aboriginal society as soon as possible because it was believed that most traditional knowledge would be lost within decades. Aboriginal people were seen as objects of study rather than collaborators in research on their culture.
10. For a full description of the differences between the ALRA and the NTA, see Koch (2013, 6–11).
11. See http://yirrkala.com/the-mulka-project (accessed May 5, 2016) for a description of the project along with samples of audio and video productions.
12. The Garma festival in Gukula, eastern Arnhem Land, gives participants four days of immersion in cultural practices and skills of the people of the area, providing programs

of song and dance, art, healing, and other activities. It also sponsors forums for discussion on issues affecting Indigenous people. See http://www.yyf.com.au/pages/?Parent PageID=116&PageID=117 (accessed May 5, 2016).

13. http://www.aboriginalartists.com.au/NRP_statement.htm (accessed May 5, 2016).

14. http://www.aboriginalartists.com.au/NRP_projects.htm (accessed May 5, 2016).

15. See http://dobes.mpi.nl/general/for a description of the DoBeS program. DoBeS is an acronym for Dokumentation Bedrohter Sprachen (Documentation of Endangered Languages) (accessed May 5, 2016).

16. See https://www.soas.ac.uk/linguistics/research/research-clusters/documentation-and-description-of-endangered-languages.html (accessed May 5, 2016).

17. Created by Grace Koch using Google Maps on January 16, 2017. https://www.google.com/maps/d/viewer?mid=1NiMxy1z2piUytDNmma2JQHKmopQ&ll=-16.7851669971 6798%2C130.29438340000002&z=5; https://www.google.com/maps/d/edit?hl=en_US& mid=1HU8A1gCmAzm6Aj3XzP8rDMblO3s.

18. Some of the recordings are Wurrurrumi Kun-Borrk; Kevin Djimarr, *Songs from Western Arnhem Land: The Indigenous Music of Australia*, CD 1 (Sydney: Sydney University Press, 2007); *Jurtbirrk: Love Songs from North Western Arnhem Land* (Batchelor, NT: Batchelor Press, Batchelor Institute of Indigenous Tertiary Education, 2005). Book and recordings are Aaron Corn, *Reflections and Voices: Exploring the Music of Yothu Yindi with Mandawuy Yunupingu* (Sydney: Sydney University Press, 2009); Marett (2005).

19. http://www.irititja.com/about_ara_irititja/partnerships.html) (accessed May 5, 2016).

20. See https://dtc.nt.gov.au/arts-and-museums/northern-territory-library/library-collections/ community-stories for information on the Keeping Culture KMS system.

21. For a listing and discussion of more archivally based projects, see http://www.mybestdocs.com/onopko-h-rmaa2002-indigen-recs.htm (accessed May 5, 2016) and other chapters in this volume.

22. For a portion of the article describing the project, see http://books.google.com.au/books?id=ECYiLo6Sb-MC&pg=PT137&lpg=PT137&dq=sound+recordings+repatriation +Australian&source=bl&ots=ayYVpUl8b8&sig=W-KLZGUtj5-B6q-m3mQoZdyV6o4& hl=en&sa=X&ei=xYdfUpzpMoG-kAXqiYH4BA&ved=0CDUQ6AEwAjgU#v=onepage &q=sound%20recordings%20repatriation%20Australian&f=false (accessed May 5, 2016).

23. See http://www.mowanjumarts.com/keeping-place/youth-engagement/ (accessed May 5, 2016).

24. See the newsletters for *Kanyirninpa jukurrpa* for descriptions of the database rollout at http://kj.org.au/ (accessed May 5, 2016).

25. See http://www.yirrkala.com/themulkaproject/about (accessed May 5, 2016).

26. To hear some of these recordings, go to http://sounds.bl.uk/Search and enter the search term "Haddon" (accessed June 5, 2016).

27. See footnote 6 for a description of the change of the AIAS to AIATSIS.

28. For a detailed discussion of ethics and collection management issues, see Koch (2010).

References

Aboriginal and Torres Strait Islander Library, Information and Resources Network (ATSILIRN). 2012. "ATSILIRN Protocols." http://aiatsis.gov.au/atsilirn/protocols.php (accessed October 10, 2013).

Ara Irititja website. http://www.irititja.com (accessed January 13, 2017).

Ash, Anna, Pauline Hooler, Gary Williams, and Ken Walker. 2010. "Maam Ngawaala: Biindu Ngaawa Nyanggan Bindaayili: Language Centres: Keeping Language Strong." In *Re-awakening Languages: Theory and Practice in the Revitalisation of Australia's Indigenous Languages*, edited by John Hobson Kevin Lowe, Susan Poetsch, and Michael Walsh, 106–118. Sydney, NSW: Sydney University Press.

Australian Institute of Aboriginal Studies. 1964. La Mont West library holdings. File note 64/ 94.

Australian Institute of Aboriginal Studies. 1965–1966. Tape Archive. Contract for deposit of material. File numbers 65/182, 66/486.

Australian Institute of Aboriginal and Torres Strait Islander Studies Act. 1989. https://www.legislation.gov.au/Details/C2012C00085/Html/Text#_Toc313969308 (accessed January 13, 2017).

Australian Institute of Aboriginal and Torres Strait Islander Studies (AIATSIS). 2005. "Musical Connections: Alice Moyle." http://aiatsis.gov.au/collections/collections-online/digitised-collections/musical-connections-alice-moyle (accessed January 13, 2017).

Australian Institute of Aboriginal and Torres Strait Islander Studies. 2012. *Guidelines for Ethical Research in Australian Indigenous Studies (GERAIS)*. Canberra: Australian Institute of Aboriginal and Torres Strait Islander Studies.

Australian Institute of Aboriginal and Torres Strait Islander Studies, and Federation of Aboriginal and Torres Strait Islander Languages. 2005. "National Indigenous Languages Survey Report 2005." Survey report. Acton, ACT: Australian Institute of Aboriginal and Torres Strait Islander Studies. http://arts.gov.au/sites/default/files/pdfs/nils-report-2005.pdf (accessed May 6, 2016).

Bell, Diane. 2002. *Daughters of the Dreaming*. 3rd ed. North Melbourne, Victoria: Spinifex Press.

Berndt, Ronald M., and Catherine H. Berndt. 1970. *Man, Land and Myth*. Sydney, NSW: Ure Smith.

Bradley, John. 2010. *Singing Saltwater Country; Journey to the Songlines of Carpentaria*. Crows Nest, NSW: Allen and Unwin.

Dixon, Sally, and Eleanora Deak. 2010. "Language Centre as Language Revitalisation Strategy: A Case Study from the Pilbara." In *Re-awakening Languages: Theory and Practice in the Revitalisation of Australia's Indigenous Languages*, edited by John Hobson, Kevin Lowe, Susan Poetsch, and Michael Walsh, 119–130. Sydney, NSW: Sydney University Press.

Humphris, Kate. 2009. "Yirrkala Goes Digital." http://www.abc.net.au/local/stories/2009/07/30/2641381.htm.

Keen, Ian. 2006. "Ancestors, Magic and Exchange in Yolngu Doctrines: Extensions of the Person in Time and Space." *Journal of the Royal Anthropological Institute* 12 (3) (September): [515]–530.

Koch, Grace. 1995. "This Land Is My Land: The Archive Tells Me So; Sound Archives and Response to the Needs of Indigenous Australians." *IASA Journal* 6 (November): 13–22. http://www.iasa-web.org/iasa-journal/iasa-journal-nos-6-10 (accessed May 6, 2016).

Koch, Grace. 2010. "Ethics and Research: Dilemmas Raised in Managing Research Collections of Aboriginal and Torres Strait Islander Materials." *Australian Aboriginal Studies* (2): 48–59.

Koch, Grace. 2013. "We Have the Song So We Have the Land: Song and Ceremony as Proof of Ownership in Aboriginal and Torres Strait Islander Land Claims." AIATSIS Research Publications no. 33. Canberra: AIATSIS Research Publications. http://www.aiatsis.gov.au/publications/products/we-have-song-so-we-have-land-song-and-ceremony-proof-ownership-aboriginal-and-torres-strait-islander-land-claims   (accessed May 6, 2016).

Mabo v. Queensland. 1986. 60 ALIR 255.

Marett, Allan. 2003. "Sound Recordings as Maruy among the Aborigines of the Daly Region of North West Australia." In *Researchers, Communities, Institutions, Sound Recordings*, edited by Linda Barwick, Allan Marett, Jane Simpson, and Amanda Harris. Sydney: University of Sydney. http://hdl.handle.net/2123/1511 (accessed May 6, 2016).

Marett, Allan. 2005. *Songs, Dreamings, and Ghosts: The Wangga of North Australia.* Middletown, CT: Wesleyan University Press.

Marett, Allan, Linda Barwick and Lysbeth Ford. 2001. *Rak Badjalarr: Wangga Songs from North Peron Island.* CD. [Canberra]: Aboriginal Studies Press.

Mira Canning Stock Route Project Archive. 2013. http://mira.canningstockrouteproject.com/browse (accessed January 13, 2017).

Moyle, Richard. 1983. "Songs, Ceremonies and Sites: The Agharringa Case." In *Aborigines, Land and Land Rights*, edited by Nicholas Peterson and Marcia Langton, 66–93. Canberra: Australian Institute of Aboriginal Studies.

National Film and Sound Archive of Australia. 2013a. "Cultural Institutions Face Ultimatum: Digitise or Perish." August 5, 2013. http://www.nfsa.gov.au/about/media/releases/2013/08/05/cultural-institutions-face-ultimatum-digitise-or-perish/ (accessed May 10, 2016).

National Film and Sound Archive of Australia. 2013b. "National Film and Sound Archive of Australia Annual Report 2012–13." Annual Report. Canberra, ACT: National Film and Sound Archive of Australia. nfsa.gov.au/about/corporate (accessed November 11, 2013).

National Recording Project for Indigenous Performance in Australia. 2002. "Garma Statement on Indigenous Music and Dance." http://www.aboriginalartists.com.au/NRP_statement.htm (accessed May 6, 2016).

Onopkoi, Helen. 2013. "Evolving Access Solutions—Repatriation of Records to Indigenous Communities." http://www.mybestdocs.com/onopko-h-rmaa2002-indigen-recs.htm (accessed May 6, 2016).

Russell, Maureen. 2012. "Knowledge (or Intangible Cultural Heritage) Repatriation." http://ethnomusicologyreview.ucla.edu/content/archives-and-archiving-knowledge-repatriation (accessed May 5, 2016).

Turnbull, M. 2016. "Speech to Parliament on the 2016 Closing the Gap Report." http://www.malcolmturnbull.com.au/media/speech-to-parliament-on-the-2016-closing-the-gap-report (accessed January 11, 2017).

West, LaMont. 1988. "Letter to AIAS." March 1, 1988.

Widders, Terence, P. Thompson, G. Williams, L. Thompson, B. Bellear, and L. Watson. 1974. "Open Letter concerning the Australian Institute of Aboriginal Studies [and the Significance of Its Conference, May, 1974]." Brickfield Hill, NSW: Eaglehawk and Crow.

CHAPTER 12

....

SHARING JOHN BLACKING

Recontextualizing Children's Music and Reimagining
Musical Instruments in the Repatriation
of a Historical Collection

....

ANDREA EMBERLY AND JENNIFER C. POST

CONSIDERED as a whole, ethnographic collections of musical data amassed by
ethnomusicologists and music collectors in the twentieth and twenty-first centuries can
represent and preserve musical soundscapes and contribute to the development of research practices. As ethnomusicological collections become accessible to individuals,
communities, and institutions beyond the scope of the original collector, their contents
are often repurposed, reimagined, and reinformed—from preserved tangibles to
teaching tools, archaic recordings to digital files, and private collections to publicly
accessible materials. With the growing engagement with repatriation by archives,
individuals, and institutions, these resources, which include field recordings, fieldnotes,
images, and other supporting materials, offer tangible and intangible records of musical
performance, context, and historical data to individuals, scholars, and the communities
that first offered their music for scholarly research.

Collections representing ethnomusicological and anthropological field research
offer evidence of diverse approaches to data gathering and demonstrate how practices
have changed over time. In recent decades, collaborative work in ethnomusicology
and anthropology has defined research trajectories and forged relationships between
ethnographers, individuals, and communities. Goals of socially engaged scholarship
span from scholarly research to advocacy projects maintained entirely by the support of
communities of origin. On the other hand, archival data from the early to mid-twentieth
century indicates that researchers sometimes observed rather than participated in musical events, individuals recorded and interviewed were seen as "subjects" and seldom
identified as collaborators, and permissions for recording and use of gathered data were
not always deemed essential.

As we consider the future of collections now housed in institutional and personal archives assembled by ethnographers who are no longer able to mediate relationships and data, there are critical issues to consider, especially when evaluating materials and determining how they might be treated during repatriation and reuse. This chapter focuses on the John Blacking Collection, housed at the University of Western Australia and Queen's University Belfast, and the complex and sensitive issues surrounding the management of data and the distribution of materials to communities in South Africa where John Blacking did his primary fieldwork during the mid-1950s. The matters of particular significance to be addressed in this chapter have been identified within the context of processing and sharing materials from the Blacking collection to engage communities of origin, scholars, and foreign audiences. We present two case studies related to current collaborative modes of engagement in the field that involve researcher and communities of origin within the context of repatriation and reconnection with Blacking's archival materials. The first area of discussion concerns the use of materials gathered from children who were recorded with limited participant information, and the second the issue of the interpretation and use of historical musical instrument data amassed by Blacking that documents practices that are no longer maintained. Within these two cases we consider the potential value to communities of origin and the impact of repatriation on the contemporary practice of musical arts in South Africa, and in particular, in Vhavenda communities.

Repatriating Historical Ethnomusicological Materials

Recent research on repatriation of historical data from ethnomusicological and anthropological fieldwork offers frameworks for addressing issues related to legacies that had a strong impact on past research. Of particular concern is the social disparity between researcher and "informant" expressed by García when he says, "historically anthropologists treated their informants as spatially and temporally different from themselves" (García 2013, 3). At the same time, García views field materials, especially fieldnotes, as "untapped sources" for information about intellectual history as well as individuals and communities, noting that in some cases the fieldnotes contain significant information not published in ethnographic reports (García 2013). He reflects Seeger's 1986 comments about the diminished role of field materials in ethnomusicological research in general and his call for greater engagement with archival sources. He even more directly echoes the call by Cooley and Barz (2008) for greater self-critical reflection in a postcolonial era of research in ethnomusicology. García addresses the significance of giving agency to individuals and values through the study of fieldnotes, using examples of field data produced in Cuba in 1948 by the anthropologists Bascom and Waterman. Aaron Fox, in his work in Alaska with the

Laura Boulton Collection (especially her 1946 Iñupiat recordings), and Neil Lobley, who worked in South Africa with the Hugh Tracey Collection (recorded throughout sub-Saharan Africa, 1948–1963), have each explored reanimation of fieldwork data in relation to local or source communities. Fox and Lobley both relate to stakeholders as collaborators as they consider the repatriation and reanimation process (Lobley 2012; Fox 2015). The Blacking archive houses an extensive collection of fieldnotes, written both by Blacking and by field assistants such as Victor Ralushai, who was a distinguished professor of indigenous knowledge systems at the University of Venda. These fieldnotes offer a rich history notated by local field assistants, many of whose families had preserved memories of the period when Blacking was present, but access to these materials has never been available. In addition to the fieldnotes, photographs and sound and video recordings document these memories and may provide sources for current researchers in the area to draw on the knowledge of both Blacking and those who made his research possible.

Community members, institutions, and scholars working with historical collections must create new paths of engagement to interpret, preserve, and reengage with artifacts that range from recordings, photographs, and musical instruments to diary entries, fieldnotes, and letters. When a collection such as Blacking's is removed from its context, whether that is a field site, office, or home, it is the reengagement and repurposing of materials that plays a central role in how the collection might be accessed in ways that are meaningful and ethical for communities, institutions, and individuals. A collection amassed over many years from numerous field sites and communities requires sensitive understandings to find pathways for sustainable accessibility. This unpacking and sharing forms the framework for our discussion, and we focus on the issues and ethics that must be considered regarding community, individual, and institution. Our engagement in this process includes ethnomusicological fieldwork, archival analysis, organization, management and research, and exhibition building, all in collaboration with members of Vhavenda communities in Limpopo Province, South Africa.

Historical field data represents various contractual relationships between collectors and individuals or groups. Without a formal contract, simply returning raw materials to a community of origin can lead to marginalized access to a collection outside of its historical context. For example, digital or online copies of raw materials may run the risk of remaining inaccessible to communities of origin. Scholars such as Lobley have attempted varying methodologies for creating paths to access (Lobley 2012). Also, access to materials is often divided between communities of origin (if they are known) and scholarly communities, the latter tending to have greater access to materials housed outside communities, such as the Blacking collections. This artificial divide can lead to questions of how materials are accessed, and by whom. Thus, the archive is only, as Nannyonga-Tamusuza articulates, a "surrogate" (2015, 25) and materials in the collections "are reconstructions of reality through the eyes and ears of the person who made the recording and as such, they only provide one of the many possible renditions of a musical experience" (24). Therefore it becomes necessary, through collaborative community, institutional, and scholarly connections, to create a framework of sustainable accessibility that supports the objectives of those interested in accessing the materials held in historical collections. Through such collaboration, specific issues surrounding ethics and considerations for repatriation, interpretation, and access are raised, and policy, power, and personal relationships can determine how, if, and when collections should be accessed. This multitude of layered issues forms the basis for this chapter. By examining two facets of inquiry into the ethics of accessibility and potentials of repatriation, we explore the intricacies of sharing John Blacking's collection between community, individual, scholar, and institution.

THE JOHN BLACKING COLLECTION

The John Blacking Collection, housed at the University of Western Australia and Queens University Belfast, preserves the work of noted British anthropologist, eth-nomusicologist, ethnographer, teacher, and scholar primarily in Southern and Eastern Africa, Europe, Asia, and the Pacific. John Blacking received his education from King's College, Cambridge, the Musée de l'Homme in Paris, and the University of Witwatersrand in Johannesburg, South Africa. In the 1950s he worked closely with Hugh Tracey at the newly established International Library for African Music (ILAM),[1] which led to his work with Vhavenda communities from 1956 to 1958 and a position at the University of Witwatersrand beginning in 1959. Blacking spent fifteen years based in South Africa (1954–1969) and conducted fieldwork with support from various African and European institutions and organizations.[2] The Blacking archive holds audio, visual, and manuscript field data on music collected in South Africa from Vhavenda communities between 1956 and 1958, in coastal Mozambique during 1955, Zambia in 1957 and 1961, and Uganda in 1965. He also took other short field excursions in Limpopo and KwaZulu-Natal provinces in South Africa during the 1950s and 1960s.[3] The most in-depth information that Blacking has preserved is on music from Venda, where he spent twenty-two months between 1956 and 1958 and returned several times in the early 1960s. Expelled from South Africa in 1969, Blacking joined the faculty at Queen's University, Belfast, where he remained until his death in 1990. Although the archival collections of Blacking's work that exist today include materials from a vast career in the field of ethnomusicology, the bulk of his materials is drawn from his twenty-two months in Vhavenda communities. During his research in Limpopo, South Africa, Blacking focused on Vhavenda children's songs and on girls' initiation ceremonies in-cluding *domba*—a year-long ceremony that is the final stage for young women before marriage. He also collected in-depth information in other areas, including on the pro-duction and use of musical instruments, a subject he demonstrated an interest in during his early work in Malaysia in 1949 and 1950,[4] and as an essential aspect in the study of music in Africa.[5]

One path that researchers working with the Blacking collection have taken is to create a two-part exhibition of materials from the John Blacking Collection at the University of Western Australia and the University of Venda in 2013 and 2014. This process of "sharing John Blacking" with diverse audiences for diverse purposes provides an example of access points for repatriation that began with an exhibition at the University of Western Australia, largely for the university and Perth city museum-going population, followed by an exhibition at the University of Venda that targeted local communities whose families and friends were represented among the images and recordings gathered by John Blacking between 1956 and 1958.

The Australian exhibition explored connections among themes related to the lands and landscapes Blacking reported on during his fieldwork in Eastern and Southern Africa from 1955 to 1966 using images, audio and video recordings, manuscripts, and musical instruments (Post 2013).[6] While the completed exhibition provided access to music and dance practices from Southern Africa for local university and city residents, assembling the exhibition gave scholars and source community members opportunities to respond to calls for collaboration that in some cases resulted in a more in-depth understanding of the local significance of musical practices at the archives site. Preparation for the Australian exhibition also identified primary conservation, access, and communication needs in connection with the collections that played a role in planning and executing the South African exhibition.

The Australian exhibition was also a pilot for an exhibition mounted at the University of Venda in June 2014 (Emberly and Davhula 2014), which focused on Vhavenda images and audio. The collection of photos in the exhibition is still mounted for university and community access. The visual repatriation for this exhibition engaged residents of Vhavenda communities through images taken by John Blacking in the 1950s. This project offered sites for cultural memories through images and sound that represented historical musical practices. By taking initial steps to make materials accessible in any format possible, the goal was to locate individuals, communities, and family members represented in the materials and collaborate on contextualizing and sharing them for present and future use in Vhavenda communities. As a part of this process in regard to engagement with historical collections, the power of nostalgia was invariably generated through access to materials from communities past and present. In addition to the widely acknowledged emotions identified with loss and imagined pasts, the process generated valuable emotional and reflective action that can relate in a beneficial way to a community's effort to reuse and revitalize tradition. The exhibition at the University of Venda has led to further projects that are tasked with the monumental goal of repatriating the entirety of the Blacking collection to communities of origin by forging collaborative relationships between communities, scholars, and institutions. Given Blacking's focus on children's musical cultures, multigenerational collaboration has remained paramount to future repatriation efforts in an attempt to facilitate cross-generational interest in historical musical practices.

REPATRIATING CHILDHOOD

Many of the materials collected by Blacking during his time in Vhavenda communities were from children and young people—some who are still alive—and others whose families now have a vested interest in the collected materials. As with most research at the time, written consent was not obtained for their participation in Blacking's research. Repatriation of materials from the Blacking collection addresses some of these issues directly by supplying access to the relevant materials for discussion, and after that perhaps for dissemination dependent on community decisions regarding materials. Some of the materials contain sensitive recordings, photographs, and video; and thus, before any public display of these materials, appropriate members of communities must review them to consider the impact of dissemination.

Because ethical considerations frame approaches to the study of children's musical cultures, researchers who work with children are presented with complex issues to consider. These may include issues of informed consent and consideration of whether children and young people can consent to engaging in a research project without a clear understanding of the long-term commitment involved when documenting music with video and audio recordings; children being documented at significant (and perhaps vulnerable) life events, such as initiation ceremonies, where music is central; children driving the research decisions and conducting research with other children in regard to snowballing consent when the researcher is not present; and positionality and cultural understandings of the adult/child dichotomy. These ethical issues among others challenge researchers to consider children's participation in research and how to shift away from tokenistic representations of children to informed, child-directed, and child-initiated research participation while balancing issues of consent, access, and dissemination (Greig 2013).

Blacking's early research on children's musical cultures has in many ways laid the path for current trends in ethnomusicology that focus on children's music, not as a simplified version of the dominant adult culture, but rather as comprehensive, dynamic, and child-driven (Minks 2002; Emberly 2014). However, there have been significant shifts in the ways researchers engage with child and youth participants, represent their communities in scholarship, and consider the ethics involved in conducting research with minor-age participants. These shifts indicate how perspectives on childhood depend on the relationship between the researcher and participants, the context of childhood in the community, and global notions of childhood. Blacking's photographs and film recordings represent a power-based relationship between researcher and subject, with the camera often angled down or children being rehearsed to create a scene where they do not acknowledge its presence. In Figure 12.1, a photograph taken by John Blacking during a field research trip in Vhavenda communities from 1956 to 1958, we see a small girl in the shadow of a microphone that she cautiously approaches, we assume to record a song. The documentation does not tell us who she is or what she may be singing, but from the

SHARING JOHN BLACKING 221

image, we read into the relationship between the adult researcher and the child subject. This is juxtaposed with Figure 12.2, a photograph taken by a young girl in Tshakhuma village, Limpopo in 2013. The young "researcher" photographs two of her friends, who are simultaneously photographing her. In this exchange, we note a change in perspective, challenging the viewer to consider who is the researcher and who is the subject. Through active engagement in a research process that frames them as active participants rather than passive actors, children become the viewer and the viewed, offering perspective on their own lives and cultures of childhood that adults may or may not be able to participate in.

Blacking did use children and young people as research collaborators in some ways by asking them to write stories, keep diaries, and provide the materials for transcription and analysis. He published a book on one young woman's story of growing up in a Vhavenda community, *Black Background* (Blacking 1964), and documents from his collection suggest that he asked many young people to share information with him and for translation purposes. Communities can now use these materials to acknowledge the contributions children and young people made to Blacking's historic work knowing that without their participation, documentation, and music, his research would not have succeeded. This recognition of community and individual contribution may support ongoing community frameworks for musical arts education that recognize that the drive for music sustainability must be from both young people and community teachers and leaders.

DRAWING MUSICAL CONNECTIONS BETWEEN THEN AND NOW IN CHILDREN'S MUSIC

Although many scholars have discussed frameworks and issues surrounding repatriation and the complexities of these processes including the "changing conceptions of archives' social roles, responsibilities, and opportunities" (Lancefield 1998, 47; see also this Handbook), there has been limited discussion of materials collected from children and young people and the unique issues this might raise when thinking about repatriation. Children and young people from communities of origin have been unable to access any of the materials from Blacking's collections, the local libraries do not hold copies of his books, scholarship has not been translated into Tshivenda, and there has been limited awareness that a collection of this magnitude has been sequestered away from the communities that provided the bulk of the materials it now holds. Community members have also stressed the importance of access to materials as a tool for teaching given that some of the recordings and transcriptions may be valuable for future sustainment of children's musical practices in Vhavenda communities.

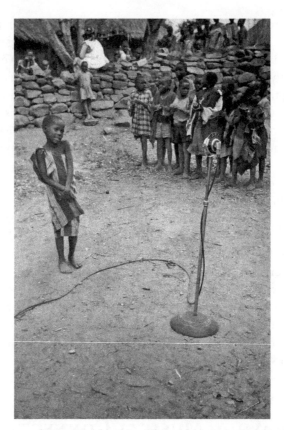

FIGURE 12.1 Girl approaching microphone in a Vhavenda community, c. 1956–1958.
The John Blacking Collection, Callaway Centre Archives, University of Western Australia.

The Blacking materials do have the potentiality to draw connections between historical practices and current musical learning and practices for children and young people
in Vhavenda contexts. Photos, recordings, and documentation support the ongoing
traditions of musical cultures in Vhavenda contexts, with similarities and changes noted
through comparative analysis. Song texts, photographs, and recordings from the collection and from Blacking's published works demonstrate continuity in many areas of
musical performance and highlight the loss of traditions and songs as children's cultural
and social contexts change. For instance, the girls' group dance known as *tshigombela*
is seen in Figure 12.3, a 1950s photograph from the John Blacking Collection, as well as
a similar one (Figure 12.4) of the same dance form in 2009. The dancers in both images
are dancing a section of solo dance known as *u-gaya*, where four dancers come to the
forefront to dance together.[7] The images demonstrate similarities in dress (man's hat,
vest) in addition to the same instrumentation (drums, whistles). The successful integration of *tshigombela* into the school classroom in Vhavenda communities has supported
the maintenance of this particular tradition above others (Emberly and Davidson 2011;
Emberly 2013; Emberly and Davhula 2014) and access to materials from the Blacking

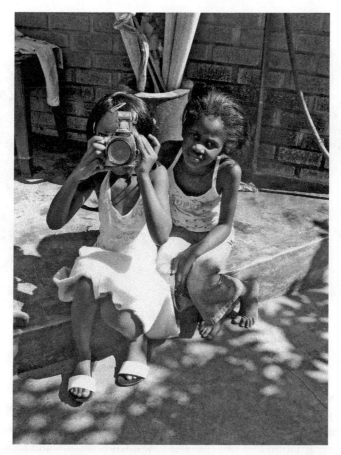

FIGURE 12.2 Vhavenda children in Tshakhuma, Limpopo, South Africa, 2013.

Photograph by Andrea Emberly.

collection support community efforts to drive continued maintenance of traditional musical arts practices in the community (Treloyn and Emberly 2013).

ARCHIVAL PERSPECTIVES
ON REPRESENTATIONS OF CHILDHOOD

As children are encouraged to become more involved in the research process as "active partners and participants in research conducted about them and among them" (Montgomery and Kellett 2009, 47), scholars must acknowledge that their participation in research as active, rather than passive, shifts the ways in which we conceptualize and consider childhood. Given that "archives are far from neutral" (Vallier 2010), the political and power-driven divides between institutions and communities have perhaps

FIGURE 12.3 *Tshigombela* dance, 1950s.

The John Blacking Collection, Callaway Centre Archives, University of Western Australia.

greater impact on children and young people, who have been historically othered in the research process. Distinguishing the unique features of childhood (for example, see Mead and Wolfenstein 1955; Lancy 2008; Montgomery 2009) might further guide our approach to repatriation that can consider how documentation and archival practices represent and engage communities of children and youth. How are children and childhood constructed within this collection, and what are the ramifications for community and public access that may "conflict with present-day cultural and social practices" (Nannyonga-Tamusuza and Weintraub 2012, 216)? This question underscores that repatriation of the cultural capital boxed away in recordings, photos, and documentation must be led by communities of origin, given that the relationship between knowledge and childhood is typically firmly embedded in cultural protocol.

In the case of the Blacking materials, this point is highly sensitive, given that many of Blacking's recordings are of girl's initiation schools, with songs, dances, and information that must only be accessed by those who have gone through the initiation themselves. As such, a consideration of childhood, adulthood, and sacred information must be balanced and led by communities in collaboration with hosting organizations. Through community-led collaboration the outcomes of repatriation can have methodological, theoretical, and practical foci that can benefit children, their local communities, researchers, the international academic community, and beyond.

Initial research with materials from the collection suggests that Vhavenda communities are interested in engaging with historical materials to support musical arts practices for children and young people in the community. With pressures on young

FIGURE 12.4 *Tshigombela dance* (*u-gaya* section) in arts and culture competition at Tshakhuma Primary School, Limpopo, South Africa, 2015.

Photograph by Andrea Emberly.

people to leave rural areas and the dominant presence of a multicultural South African musical sound (Emberly and Davhula 2016), community leaders and young people have indicated an ongoing need for support of Vhavenda musical arts traditions, because, as one young woman noted, "I am proud to be a Venda person, I am proud I know the songs of my culture, it makes me who I am, it makes me a Venda person" (Emberly, personal interview Tshiemuemu secondary school, Tshakhuma, Limpopo July 2009).

As we move away from the historical othering of children and their musical communities, we can move forward with methodological, ethical, and theorectical approaches that aim to present a complex and contextual understanding of children's musical lives that is not solely dependent on the adult perspective. Community access to the Blacking collections could provide a move forward in decolonizing the archive and, as Mbembe argues, be an arena to decolonize the university and the university classroom in order to redistribute different types of knowledges (Mbembe 2015, 6). Although many genres of Venda music continue to be strong, there are certain areas that have suffered—namely, some of those Blacking focused on in his research, such as *domba*.[8] Thus, access to the Blacking collections may provide another system of support for communities aiming to sustain many of the traditions that have been impacted by colonization, education systems, and globalization.

If researchers have reevaluated how to approach the study of childhood and youth, then the outcomes of this examination must be applied and considered for repatriation and archival questions that concern materials collected from and by children and young people. Indigenous knowledge systems that encapsulate and sustain musical traditions do not live within the walls of an archive or within the boxes of an archival collection. The complex colonial histories of how these collections too often come to rest divorced from the indigenous knowledge bearers who, typically uncredited, created them, underscore why, as Masoga suggests, scholars must "research back" (2015, 93) in order to "credit and acknowledge indigenous scholars," because "African musical research should be accountable to African communities." Thus, as Chilisa argues in terms of indigenous research methodologies, the children and young people represented in this particular collection suggest a need for "emancipation from generations of silence" (2012).

REPATRIATING MUSICAL
INSTRUMENT KNOWLEDGE

Making connections between historical practice and current musical interest can be especially difficult when continuity has been all but broken due to material and cultural loss. This is the case with a number of musical instruments once used in Vhavenda communities that are documented in the Blacking collection. Exploring Blacking's field data, his interest in instruments quickly becomes apparent. He includes detailed information not only on Vhavenda instruments but also on other groups in nearby regions. Images, notes, and recordings provide evidence of specific instrument types, such as lamellophones and flutes, which Blacking carefully documented in performance and production. Blacking's data show that he identified instruments as objects that could be measured, their tuning systems notated, the building methods used by makers logged, and their social use briefly described. In the 1950s, musical instrument study still drew primarily on the scientific principles that had characterized early work in comparative musicology. The data on instruments that Blacking gathered represents a style of systematic research that shows little evidence his methods were shared by local instrument makers and musicians. Some of his research on musical instruments was published during his lifetime, but most of his data remains in his archived collections where a researcher will find fieldnotes, logs, images, and recordings as well as diaries containing narrative information he encouraged local Vhavenda children and youth to write, all with information on musical instruments useful for researchers and members of communities of origin (Post 2015).

Considering the repatriation and dissemination of Blacking's South African musical instrument data, several issues emerge that link to larger discussions on repatriating archival information. In the first place, working during the colonial period in South Africa, Blacking engaged with local community members who provided information as subjects rather than as collaborators. His collection includes instrument information identified more with the products of research, such as images and notes accounting for practices related to instrument production and performance, than with the instruments themselves. Also significant, as noted previously, many of the Vhavenda musical instrument practices that Blacking documented in the 1950s have now nearly disappeared in Limpopo, while others that remain have changed in function and production.

Musical instruments, and the narrative and visual information about their production and use, held in historical and contemporary archival collections are rich tangible and intangible cultural resources for researchers and local communities. Recent ethnomusicological study demonstrates that instruments contribute to scholarly knowledge about cultural, economic, and ecological vulnerabilities, adaptation, and resilience through their sounds, images, and stories (Dawe 2011). For communities of origin, historical knowledge embodied in objects, images, and narrative information offers opportunities to consider why cultural changes have taken place and to take action regarding the future use of knowledge of their heritage practices.

When instruments and instrument-related information are separated from locations where they were produced and used in performance, they lose significant connections to ongoing social, cultural, economic, and ecological knowledge. The collectors, museum curators, archivists, and their organizations caretaking instruments take on roles as cultural heritage keepers, not always aware that the heritage they are holding may have changed and even eroded over time in the community of origin. Musical instruments and their musical traditions fade, or even disappear, particularly in socially and politically vulnerable locations that have suffered economic decline, environmental degradation, and therefore cultural loss.

The archived data on musical instruments in the John Blacking Collection demonstrate the ethnographically, archivally, and personally complex terrain in which such materials can be found. The Blacking collection provides considerable access to information on production and use of specific instruments in South Africa. His own in-depth data on musical instruments in Limpopo lands and landscapes in the 1950s includes descriptive, aural, and visual data that includes instrument names, details on construction and materials, names of makers, instrument tunings, repertoires, and performance practice. His information is considerably enhanced with data that he gathered from individuals who authored their own works, offering in some cases firsthand accounts of musical instrument use that have social, cultural, and economic implications.

Understanding Musical Instruments, Cultural Property, and Cultural Loss

Musical instruments represent tangible evidence of cultural practices through which knowledge and traditions have been transmitted over time. When communities have suffered from cultural loss, the repatriation of objects and evidence of their practices can play a critical role in revitalization and reanimation—or simply a reaffirmation of collective regional, local, and family identities (Kuprecht 2014). Archives considering repatriation without an understanding of the complexity of an instrument's social, cultural, economic, and ecological associations may not fully realize the significance of its properties and the implications of its loss within a community of origin.

Blacking's detailed information on Venda[9] xylophones and lamellophones explores the structure of the instruments and their woods, tunings, and playing style, and he chronicles some of their construction techniques. We learn from Blacking that the resonant wood *mutondo* (*kiaat* or wild teak),[10] played a crucial role in the construction of both instrument types. Further research indicates that the wood has multiple uses, not only among Vhavenda communities in Limpopo but also in other regions, where it is used for woodcarving and traditional medicine (Shackleton 2005; Mughovhani 2009, 47). While not addressed explicitly in his notes or publications, a single sentence in a 1956 diary stating, "people can be arrested if found with a piece of *mutondo*," indicates that musicians and instrument makers struggled to access and use the woods they valued—woods that provided the characteristic sound for these idiophones.[11] Today the *mbila mutondo* (*mbila mtondo*), a Venda xylophone that traditionally depended heavily on the *mutondo* tree for its bars, is rarely played today. Preserved in just a few of Blacking's images of performance and instrument making (see Figure 12.5) as well as recordings and film clips, it was probably rare even in the 1950s. Between 1956 and 1965, Blacking made recordings of *mbila mutondo* duets during just two days in the field (in 1956 and 1957), with six pieces and five performers represented.

The *mbira dza madeza* and *mbira tshipai* lamellophones were more widely played during Blacking's research period. The lamellophone had keys typically made from locally sourced metal, such as bicycle spokes. Resonation for the instrument was frequently provided by an added large gourd or paraffin tin (often with attached shells or bottlecaps). The soundboard was most commonly made of *mutondo*,[12] the same hard, resonant, and rare wood used to make the bars for the large *mbila mutondo*. Despite the use of widely accessible recycled metal and a common gourd, the scarcity of the traditional wood used for the soundboard may have constrained its accessibility and use. This instrument is also rarely made or played today.

Combining Blacking's data with contemporary practice provides evidence of degradation of the physical environment that supported instrument making and resulting cultural loss. With the loss of natural resources that spans two generations or more, knowledge about making instruments, and the possibilities for adaptation and innovation, decrease considerably. We begin to understand why the *mbila mutondo* and *mbila madeza* and *mbila tshipai* are seldom made and played today. Blacking's data, including images that demonstrate local use, visual and written evidence of association with known community members, and detailed information on building techniques, may be of value to local musicians and instrument makers and may encourage archives to share information on this now little-known practice.

FIGURE 12.5   Venda *mbila*-making, Limpopo, South Africa, mid-1950s.

The John Blacking Collection, Callaway Centre Archives, University of Western Australia.

Recognizing and Celebrating Local Agency through Musical Instrument Data

The local voices and values of people Blacking worked with provide material that offers other views of musical instruments and their social lives as well. Archival materials in the collections indicate that musical instruments carried a degree of agency in these communities that Blacking himself may not have fully recognized. The wealth of hand-written narrative information he amassed from children and young adults during his work in Limpopo will be highly valued during the repatriation process, but can also be used to enhance collaborative understanding of relationships between musical instruments and local culture. Two school notebooks housed in the Australia collection, signed by Alfred Tshibalanganda (one of Blacking's two primary Vhavenda field assistants),[13] include stories about performance events in Tshivenda language (in one book) with translations into English (in another). One narrative (likely written by Tshibalanganda himself) is a personal story about a *bepha* (a social and cultural practice involving visitation and competition among performers in different communities) in which young people performed *tshikona* in neighboring communities.

The narrative reveals the centrality of music and dance in the lives of a community, the integration of music and musical instruments in social life, and the significance of musical instruments in social and economic success and in reinforcing established power relationships. *Tshikona*, described by Blacking as the "national dance" of the Venda (Blacking 1967, 1973), traditionally takes place under the supervision of local leaders.[14] *Tshikona* is always performed with a *nanga* (flute or pipe) made of the stem of the *musumunu*[15] (bamboo) plant. The type of bamboo used for the *nanga* is grown in one region of Limpopo province on the land of a noted chief; communities report that this species has been difficult to source for several generations. Like the wood for Venda lamellophones and xylophones, access to resources has had an impact on performance at least since Blacking was conducting his fieldwork in the mid-1950s. He noted in 1956 that flutes for *tshikona* in urban areas were made of other materials including metal tubing, hosepipe, curtain rods, or pram handles. Tshibalanganda begins:

> In our district at Gaba I still remember a Tshikona we played in 1954. The Tshikona started while I was at school (at Mphaphuli). When the school closed in June, some boys went to visit in town and some went to the farm to work. But some of my friends and I went home to play Tshikona.
>
> When we reached home, we found that indeed they were busy practicing. And we joined them. People came to see the dancing every day. The old men and women were also busy dancing. One day our headman said to our leader, "Tell my children that I will give them Bepha because they are dancing very nicely." His words were followed with many *mifhululu* (ululation) and *nndaa*. When we boys heard that, flutes were blown in such a way that it was possible they would crack.

Nanga performance involves the production of a single note with multiple flutes playing different pitches to create hocketing or interlocking patterns (See Figures 12.6 and 12.7). In an often-quoted passage, Blacking notes that "tshikona is valuable and beautiful to the Venda, not only because of the quantity of people and tones involved, but because of the quality of relationships that must be established between people and (musical) tones whenever it is performed" (Blacking 1973, 51). The relationship between each performer and the bamboo flute the performer is playing, the role of each piece of bamboo in the community of performers, and the interaction of the flute(s) with one another are also critical to the musical and social success of each event. The *nanga* flute itself has a particular role that has seldom been discussed in depth in the extensive literature about Venda *tshikona* and the practice of *bepha* in which its performance often takes place. Similarly, the *kwatha* (or *phalaphala*), a side-blown horn, plays a role in the discourse as well. The two instruments (*kwatha* and *nanga*) appear to play two social roles: one accompanies social power (the solo horn) and the other represents the interdependence of community. We learn directly from a local resident about these roles as the diarist continues:

> One Sunday we played Tshikona and danced for the whole day. A headman blew his *khwatha* [horn] several times. The headman stood in the middle of the dancers while

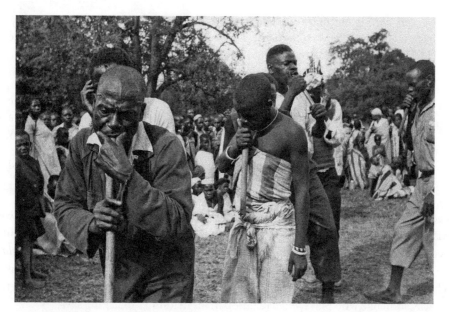

FIGURE 12.6 *Tshikona* with *nanga* (flutes or pipes). The John Blacking Collection, Callaway Centre Archives, University of Western Australia.

FIGURE 12.7 *Tshikona* with *nanga* (flutes or pipes). The John Blacking Collection, Callaway Centre Archives, University of Western Australia.

we were playing our flutes and told us to sit down. He said, "Tomorrow everybody, including girls, should come to the chief's kraal to do work offered to you by the chief." The work was reaping mealies.

There was a signal for them to start tshikona again. We danced for a long time. When we stopped, the headman said, "Everybody must go home with his flute. Because if you leave your flutes here you may not come with us to work. And anyone who does not come tomorrow and stays at home with their flute will be charged a sum [of money] or a hen (due to his absence). If the music does not sound right they will know who is missing.

We asked the headman what time we must come here for our work. . . . He said ["]the khwatha will tell you. I will blow it."

Blacking's own field diary enhances this firsthand account with information on *tshikona* performance practice and tuning of *nanga* flutes.[16] He notes that when two communities meet (ostensibly to compete), they may be able to play together provided the *phala* of the chiefs agree. *Phala* is identified as the keynote in a set of pipes, which can be adapted. While the sound of *phala* is associated with the local chiefs, in fact the tuning can take place by someone who plays *phala* (a flute). In his fieldnotes, Blacking says:

The *phala* is kept in a special place (a small bag) with other flutes. The *phala* is not separate. It is marked with a special sign. If *Phala* is lost you have lost tshikona. How else are you going to begin?

The archival information we have on the *nanga* flute used in *tshikona* reveals its agency and power, its role as a tool for accompanying dance, and its function as an extension of the body. It is an object that continues to have local economic and political value, and is a source of sound central to social networks that carries knowledge about individual presence (and absence). Returning diaries kept by local residents, along with sounds and images that Blacking recorded, may communicate to heritage communities that the resilience of an instrument they value, and the tradition they continue to support, may be tied not only to availability of materials but also to its identification with Vhavenda national identity. The central role *tshikona* musical patterns and social practices play may have encouraged communities to adapt customs in order that key sources for reinforcing cultural identity.

Role of Archives, Museums, and Ethnomusicologists in Musical Instrument Repatriation

Archives and museums play a critical role in the repatriation process, but they can only be effective when they are in a position to understand fully the complexity of the social lives of tangible and intangible materials in historical and contemporary contexts. When Eliot Bates characterizes museums in which musical instruments are stored and exhibited as "mausoleums, places for the display of the musically dead, with organologists acting as morticians, preparing dead instrument bodies for preservation and display" (Bates 2012, 365) he references not only the soundless entities but also the environments in which critical knowledge, such as documents and locally valued sounds, is seldom shared. Without contemporary archivists' and scholars' full knowledge of historical practices and values, partly due to the spatial and temporal separation between the original collector and the local community, instruments are also often without context. What are the best strategies for separating instruments and their documentation from the old framework established in the nineteenth century that identifies instruments as objects to be measured and classified? In a new framework they will be used, shared with contemporary actors, and more effectively understood as "vibrant matter" with complex relationships to people and other objects, nations, economies, and ecologies (Bennett 2010); and most importantly, to be part of a repatriation cycle involving individuals and communities that offered them in the first place.

The ethnographic process of documenting musical instrument production and use has assured that materials, playing style, social life and even relationships to the ecological landscape are well represented in ethnomusicological archives, although it may take considerable sorting and interpretation to identify and use stored data. Identifying sources of information drawn directly from local residents, as in the case of the diaries from local Limpopo children and youth, and recognizing that this information has a greater role in informing the seldom completed work by ethnomusicologists, is critical to the process. Furthermore, when returned to communities, the tangible and intangible musical information connected with instruments will have more value if it is viewed and used as part of an ongoing dialogue about music, sociality, and the physical environment, about instruments and social meaning, and about the complexity of materiality in our understanding of musical performance. Archival projects to repatriate specialist knowledge may benefit from working with ethnomusicologists and other musicians who have access to local systems and peoples as they engage with musicians in regions represented, to negotiate pathways for musical instrument (and related musical) knowledge as it is reengaged and repurposed.

An activist approach to the return and circulation of ethnographic data provides new opportunities, infused with contemporary ideas and ideals. As Lobley says about sound repatriation, "Sound elicitation also modernises academic archival practice, allowing field recorders and curators to move towards a closer understanding of some of the local realities that are important within musical creation, transmission and ownership" (Lobley 2012, 194). Musical instrument information embedded in images, diagrams, stories told by residents, film clips, and sounds, as well as in the instruments themselves, will offer new opportunities for local musicians and instrument makers to take another look at their traditions and make decisions on their own about how they will use it.

CONCLUSION

Circulating recordings can excite and delight people; it can make people shake with pleasure, reduce them to tears of sadness, and inspire them to build and teach an instrument they had almost forgotten. Sometimes it will provoke anger, reinforcing perceptions of disenfranchisement and a lack of shared access to knowledge. (Lobley 2011, 427)

This chapter has explored some of the myriad issues surrounding the repatriation of a historical ethnomusicological collection in relation to ethics, repatriation, and public engagement. Understanding and unpacking these ideas may help shape how future archivists, scholars, and communities engage with archiving and repatriating ethnomusicological collections. These considerations, among many others, inform how those working toward collaborative, accessible, and sustainable access to the Blacking collection aim to frame the repatriation of that rich set of historical materials from a key figure in the field of ethnomusicology.

This chapter has used two case studies to focus on critical issues related to interpretation, use and repatriation of archival data. It has addressed repatriation of materials, but also stressed the consideration and repatriation of knowledge that is embedded in artifacts held in archives. While we focused on children's music and musical instruments, the complexities of a collection as large and diverse as Blacking's provides the opportunity for communities and researchers to unpack a myriad of topics and potential areas for discovery. In order to support Lobley's plea that we take the archive to the people (Lobley 2011, 2012) and that we relate recordings and other materials "more directly to people's daily lives and the ways the chose to absorb and create their own music," repatriation processes must be adaptable to open concepts of repatriation that may extend beyond providing copies of historical materials (Lobley 2011, 425).[17] Engaging with local scholars as well as local community members in leading archival and repatriation processes is central to creating collaborative processes that have the potential for lasting legacy (Alivizatou 2011).

When considering the shifts in ethical approaches to research, lack of information about the location and breadth of a collection, and the complex histories of musical soundscapes, modes of repatriation that are collaborative and creative offer potential avenues for access that is sustainable and meaningful to diverse audiences. One question we have asked about the Blacking collection is whether it is possible to separate the materials from John Blacking as part of the repatriation process, given that each community of origin will have differing views on the importance, value, and need for access to parts of the collection. The volume of the collection also renders individual (or familial) identification impossible, and large communities may have differing views on whether or how the collection should be accessed. In addition, "images are materializations of sociality, which perpetuate indigenous imaginaries and thus contribute to their own reproduction, in one form or another, showing marked resistance to transformation, as much as they are continually transformed" (Geismar 2009, 49). Contextualizing the materials from the collection in their communities of origin is necessary if they are to contribute to meaningful repatriation and scholarly analysis.

The issue of repatriating the Blacking collection is complex, entailing layers of contextualization and ethics concerning the materials in the collection, intellectual and university ownership, and limited access. This chapter has provided insight into the complexity of issues that surround the repatriation of materials with the potential of changing how ethnomusicologists engage with concerns surrounding social responsibility, collection, and documentation. Questions posed by Nannyonga-Tamusuza and Weintraub (2012, 224) in their Music of Uganda Repatriation Project, are extremely relevant in this context—for example: "Where is knowledge located? Where can music of the past be experienced? Whose interests are served by repatriation?" These questions lay the pathway for future engagement with the Blacking collection in order to consider who drives repatriation, whose interests they serve, and for what purpose.

Recently, we have had an opportunity to begin considering further repatriation of materials from the Blacking collection to Vhavenda communities with emphasis on engaging children and young people in the repatriation process. This partnership project relies heavily on community-driven scholarship in collaboration with community leaders, local universities (University of Venda) and archives (ILAM). While the repatriation of the entire collection remains a goal, issues of funding, institutional ownership, and colonial histories remain central. As we move forward with goals of repatriation, we aim to continue to consider collaboration and creativity as the means for achieving long-term access across communities, institutions, and individuals, and to continue meaningful work in ethnomusicology that offers sustainable benefits in the reimagining of a historical collection of materials.

Notes

1. Hugh Tracey began recording music of Southern, Eastern, and Central Africa in 1948, developing his project "from a private research initiative into the African Music Research Unit in 1947, the African Music Society in 1948, and finally ILAM [International Library for African Music] in 1954" (Lobley 2011, 419).
2. Blacking's research among the Vhavenda was supported by grants from the International Library of African Music, the National Council for Social Research of the Republic of South Africa, and the Royal Anthropological Institute in London (Campbell 2000, 340). He worked for Hugh Tracey at the International Library of African Music from 1954 to 1955 and served as lecturer at the University of Witwatersrand from 1959 until 1969.
3. His collection of recordings and images includes documentation of Chopi music in the southern coastal areas of Mozambique; Venda, Pedi, Zulu, Sotho, Tswana, and Tsonga music in Limpopo and KwaZulu Natal, South Africa; Valley Tonga and Nsenga performance in the Zambezi River valley and Petauke districts of Zambia; and music of indigenous groups in Uganda collected during a series of weekend field excursions to record Ganda, Adhola, Acholi, Toro, Kiga, and Karamajong music.

4. See his "Musical Instruments of the Malayan Aborigines: A Short Description of Collections in the Perak Museum, Taiping, the Selangor Museum, Kuala Lumpur and the Raffles Museum, Singapore," *Federation Museums Journal* (Autumn 1954–1955): 35–52.

5. Hugh Tracey's interest in musical instruments probably had an impact on Blacking's work and focus on instruments in different regions.

6. While nearly all the exhibited materials were drawn from the University of Western Australia Collection, some of the musical instruments were acquired for the exhibition by Andrea Emberly in Limpopo during her fieldwork in 2013.

7. *U-gaya* is a section of the group dance known as *tshigombela*. During the *u-gaya* section young solo dancers leave the circle and dance facing each other.

8. *Domba* is one of several initiation schools for young people that signifies the transition from child to adult (for further information, see Du Buisson 1974; Blacking et. al 1980; Blacking and Huffman 1985; Ramabulana 1988; Reily and Weinstock 1998; Mulaudzi 2001).

9. Blacking also recorded information on lamellophones and xylophones among the Nsenga and Valley Tonga in Zambia and the Gwembe, Adhla, Lango, and Acholi peoples of Uganda.

10. The scientific name is *Pterocarpus angolensis*.

11. Blacking fieldnotes held in the University of Western Australia collection.

12. Blacking identifies it as a Transvaal teak tree, and it is also identified as *kiaar*. This is the same wood that Paul Berliner (1978) noted was used for the Shona *mbira*. He noted other woods used as well, including *muzere, suringa, muvanghu, minesenga, mutokota,* and *muvangazi*.

13. Blacking's other assistant was Victor Ralushai.

14. Kruger (2007) enumerates some of the different political and social purposes of the pipe dances and offers a review of literature on tshikona.

15. The scientific name is *Oxytenanthera abyssinica*.

16. Blacking was probably taking notes on a discussion with a local community member.

17. Lobley says about this transition, "Songs that have been reduced to disembodied MP3s and single-line entries in catalogs for use by researchers now came alive through personal interpretations, new performances, and rich and raucous debates" (Lobley 2011, 426).

REFERENCES

Alivizatou, Marilena. 2011. "Intangible Heritage and Erasure: Rethinking Cultural Preservation and Contemporary Museum Practice." *International Journal of Cultural Property* 18: 37–60.

Bates, Eliot. 2012. "The Social Life of Musical Instruments." *Ethnomusicology* 56 (3): 363–395.

Bennett, Jane. 2010. *Vibrant Matter: A Political Ecology of Things.* Durham, NC: Duke University Press.

Berliner, Paul. 1978. *The Soul of Mbira.* Chicago: University of Chicago Press.

Blacking, John. 1964. *Black Background: The Childhood of a South African Girl.* New York: Abelard-Schuman.

Blacking, John. 1967. *Venda Children's Songs.* Johannesburg: Witwatersrand University Press.

Blacking, John. 1973. *How Musical Is Man?* Seattle: University of Washington Press.

Blacking, John, John Baily, and Andrée Grau. 2001 [1980]. *Domba, 1956–1958: A Personal Record of Venda Initiation Rites, Songs and Dances.* Bloomington, IN: Society for Ethnomusicology.

Blacking, John, and Thomas Huffman. 1985. "The Great Enclosure and Domba." *Man London* 20 (3): 542–545.

Chilisa, Bagele. 2012. *Indigenous Research Methodologies.* London: Sage.

Cooley, Timothy J., and Gregory Barz. 2008. "Casting Shadows: Fieldwork Is Dead! Long Live Fieldwork!" In *Shadows in the Field: New Perspectives for Fieldwork in Ethnomusicology,* edited by Gregory Barz and Timothy J. Cooley, 3–24. Oxford: Oxford University Press.

Dawe, Kevin. 2011. "The Cultural Study of Musical Instruments." In *The Cultural Study of Music,* edited by Martin Clayton, Trevor Herbert, and Richard Middleton, 195–205. New York and London: Routledge Press.

Du Buisson, M. A. 1974. "Domba School of the Venda." *Bantu* 21 (11): 4–9.

Emberly, Andrea. 2013. "Venda Children's Musical Cultures in Limpopo, South Africa." In *Oxford Handbook of Children's Musical Cultures,* edited by Trevor Wiggins and Patricia Campbell, 77–95. Oxford and New York: Oxford University Press.

Emberly, Andrea. 2014. "Ethnomusicology and Childhood: Studying Children's Music in the Field." *College Music Symposium* 54: 1–18.

Emberly, Andrea, and Lusani Davhula. 2016. "My Music, My Voice: Musicality, Agency and Childhood in Vhavenda Communities." In "Beyond Pluralizing African Childhoods," *Childhood: A Journal of Global Research* 23 (3): 438–454.

Emberly, Andrea, and Mudzunga Davhula. 2014. *Looking Back, Looking Forward: Vhavenda Musical Life as Documented by John Blacking 1956–1958.* Grahamstown, South Africa: International Library of African Music (ILAM). Exhibition catalog.

Emberly, Andrea, and Jane Davidson. 2011. "From the *Kraal* to the Classroom: Shifting Musical Arts Practices from the Community to the School with Special Reference to Learning *Tshigombela* in Limpopo, South Africa." *International Journal of Music Education* 29 (3): 265.

Fox, Aaron A. 2015. "Repatriation as Reanimation through Reciprocity." In *The Cambridge History of World Music,* edited by Philip Bohlman, 522–554. Cambridge: Cambridge University Press.

García, David F. 2013. "Contesting Anthropology's and Ethnomusicology's Will to Power in the Field: William R. Bascom's and Richard A. Waterman's Fieldwork in Cuba, 1948." *MUSICultures* 40 (2): 1–33.

Geismar, Haidy. 2009. "The Photograph and the Malanggan: Rethinking Images on Malakula, Vanuatu." *Australian Journal of Anthropology* 20: 48–73.

Greig, Anne. 2013. *Doing Research with Children: A Practical Guide.* 3rd ed. London: SAGE.

Kruger, Jaco. 2007. "Singing Psalms with Owls: A Venda 20th Century Musical History, Part Two: *Tshikona,* Beer Songs and Personal Songs." *African Music* 8 (1): 36–59.

Kuprecht, Karolina. 2014. *Indigenous Peoples' Cultural Property Claims Repatriation and Beyond.* Cham, Switzerland: Springer.

Lancefield, Robert C. 1998. "Musical Traces' Retraceable Paths: The Repatriation of Recorded Sound." *Journal of Folklore Research* 35 (1): 47–68. Also reprinted in this Handbook.

Lancy, David F. 2008. *The Anthropology of Childhood: Cherubs, Chattel, Changelings.* Cambridge and New York: Cambridge University Press.

Lobley, Noel. 2011. "Recording the Vitamins of African Music." *History and Anthropology* 22 (4): 415–429.

Lobley, Noel. 2012. "Taking Xhosa Music out of the Fridge and into the Townships." *Ethnomusicology Forum* 21 (2): 181–195.

Masoga, Alfred. 2015. "Music Knows No Boundaries: The Case of Mme Rangwato Magoro." *Southern African Journal of Folklore Studies* 25 (1): 80–100.

Mead, Margaret, and Martha Wolfenstein. 1955. *Childhood in Contemporary Cultures*. Chicago: University of Chicago Press.

Minks, Amanda. 2002. "From Children's Song to Expressive Practices: Old and New Directions in the Ethnomusicological Study of Children." *Ethnomusicology* 46 (3): 379–408.

Mbembe, Achille. 2015. "Decolonizing Knowledge and the Question of the Archive." Public lecture at the Wits Institute for Social and Economic Research (WISER), University of the Witwatersrand (Johannesburg).

Montgomery, Heather, and Mary Kellett. 2009. *Children and Young People's Worlds: Developing Frameworks for Integrated Practice*. Bristol, UK: Policy Press.

Mulaudzi, P. Abraham. 2001. "The Domba Variety: An Initiation Language for Adulthood." *South African Journal of African Languages* 21 (1): 9–15.

Nannyonga-Tamusuza, Sylvia. 2015. "Written Documentation of the Klaus Wachsmann Music Collection: Repatriating the Past to Present Indigenous Users in Uganda." In *African Musics in Context: Institutions, Culture, Identity*, edited by Thomas Soloman, 19–66. Kampala, Uganda: Fountain.

Nannyonga-Tamusuza, Sylvia, and Andrew Weintraub. 2012. "The Audible Future: Reimagining the Role of Sound Archives and Sound Repatriation in Uganda." *Ethnomusicology* 56 (2): 206–233.

Post, Jennifer C. 2013. *Music Dance Landscape Image: John Blacking in Southern and Eastern Africa 1955–66*. Lawrence Wilson Art Gallery, University of Western Australia. Exhibition catalog. Perth: University of Western Australia.

Post, Jennifer C. 2015. "Reviewing, Reconstructing and Reinterpreting Ethnographic Data on Musical Instruments in Archives and Museums." In *Research, Records and Responsibility: Ten Years of PARADISEC*, edited by Amanda Harris, Nick Thieberger, and Linda Barwick, 135–161. Sydney: Sydney University Press.

Ramabulana, Vivian. 1988. "Domba Yesterday and Today." Unpublished master's submission to the Department of Anthropology, University of Venda, South Africa.

Reily, Suzel, and Lev Weinstock, website eds. 1998. *Venda Girls' Initiation Schools by John Blacking*. Belfast, Ireland: Queen's University of Belfast. http://archive.qub.ac.uk/VendaGirls/.

Seeger, Anthony. 1986. "The Role of Sound Archives in Ethnomusicology Today." *Ethnomusicology* 30 (2): 261–276.

Shackleton, Sheona E. 2005. "Bowls, Spoons, and Other Useful Items: The Kiaat Woodcrafters of Bushbuckridge, South Africa." In *Carving Out a Future: Planning for Woodcarving in the 21st Century*, edited by Anthony Cunningham, Brian Belcher, and Bruce Campbell, 81–102. London: Earthscan.

Treloyn, Sally, and Andrea Emberly. 2013. "Sustaining Traditions, Collections, Access and Sustainability in Australia." *Musicology Australia* 35 (2): 1–19.

Vallier, John. 2010. "Sound Archiving Close to Home: Why Community Partnerships Matter." *Notes* 67 (1): 39–49.

CHAPTER 13

....

AUTISM DOESN'T SPEAK, PEOPLE DO

Musical Thinking, Chat Messaging, and Autistic Repatriation

....

MICHAEL B. BAKAN

As a scholar, musician, and advocate for social justice, my work during the past decade has centered primarily on projects involving collaborations with people diagnosed with ASCs, or autism spectrum conditions. Such conditions are more usually referred to as ASDs: autism spectrum disorders.[1] My aversion to the "disorders" portion of that designation points to a basic position of this chapter, that conceptualizing and problematizing autism in terms of disorder, disability, and impairment—and in turn of inability, lack, and loss (Titchkosky 2007, 8)—is both inaccurate and misleading, as well as counterproductive to the best interests of all people: autistic, nonautistic, and otherwise. In taking such a stance, I align myself with autistic self-advocates such as Julia Bascom, who asserts the following:

> Autistic people exist in an unsafe and actively abusive world, but we're more than what happens to us. The autistic community needs to be heard, speaking in our own terms about the items on *our* agenda, on an unprecedented scale, reaching a much broader audience than we ever have been able to before. . . . Autistic brains are different from non-autistic brains—not better or worse, just different. Autistic voices, similarly, can take different forms or styles or express different things through different means than non-autistic voices. These facts are simple and neutral, but regularly obscured and overridden by cultural scripts and fallacies demanding broken, voiceless not-people stranded by huge chasms from the rest of the world in place of everyday autistics. *Simplicity* and *voice* are routinely sacrificed for dehumanization and spectacle. That's not our baggage, but when it's used to silence our voices and complicate our realities, it becomes our business.
>
> (Bascom 2012b, 9–10)

In a very real sense, Bascom's assertion is a call for autistic repatriation. Demanding that autistic voices be heard, loud and clear and speaking on their own terms, constitutes a radical departure from the business-as-usual conversation in the realm of autism discourse. Such discourse has been historically dominated by neurotypical (nonautistic) voices, guided by an implicit assumption of entitlement that leads to the wholesale erasure of autistic points of view. Rather than recognizing "Autism Speaks," the autistic self-advocacy movement is militating for recognition of "Autistic People, Speaking"[2]; rather than resigning themselves to "autism awareness," they are insisting on autism *acceptance*; rather than passively deferring to others' accounts of who they are and what they are all about, they have adopted the rallying cry of the disability rights movement: nothing about us without us. In keeping with such priorities, the following account by the prolific autistic author, scholar, and activist Elizabeth J. Grace conveys how what I am here calling autistic repatriation concerns nothing less than the right to sovereign personhood itself:

> In the early years of the new millennium I was in graduate school with some people who wanted to be school psychologists. I wanted to be an education researcher. We all had to take a required class together from this famous Autism Expert. One day, some of the psych majors came into class chattering excitedly because they had discovered (I think it was) Grandin's *Thinking in Pictures*. "Look, Dr. Famous Person," they said, "we found a book where we can get insider knowledge of what it is like to be a person with autism from the horse's mouth!! She even writes about what it was like for her as a child!!!" I listened, silently, first happy but then biting on my teeth and sitting on my hands as the professor answered. "That's fun and interesting," he said, "but it won't tell you anything. You remember what we learned about Theory of Mind, don't you? By definition, a person with autism does not know what it means 'for life to be like something for someone,' so she cannot possibly get the concept of what it is like to be herself. In order for you to learn things you need to do research. Do you understand?"
>
> (Grace 2012, 142)

An ethnomusicology of autistic repatriation must proceed from the assumption that autistic people not only know what it *is* to be themselves, but are the leading experts at *being* themselves—musically, socially, and in every other way. It must take the position that autistic voices and worldviews not only matter where the subject of autism is concerned, but matter more than all others. An ethnomusicology of autistic repatriation begins from the stance that how autistic people make and experience music, and why it matters to them that they do (Bakan 2014a), is not a point of departure but a point of closure, for it is in what autistic people communicate about their own musical lives—whether in their words, in their music, or in other modes of expression and communication that may as yet escape the comprehension of their neurotypical others—that the deepest forms of ethnomusicological knowledge and insight on the subject of autism are to be gained.

It is to such a form of ethnomusicology—an ethnomusicology of autistic repatriation—that this chapter is dedicated. I write from the vantage point of an ethnomusicologist with both an abiding commitment to ethnography and an unapologetically relativistic stance regarding human diversity. This position compels me to argue on behalf of an approach to engaging with individuals on the autism spectrum, and with the social construct of autism generally, through frameworks of culture and neurodiversity rather than disorder and disability. Neurodiversity, as defined by the autistic scholar Nick Walker, is "the understanding of neurological variation as a natural form of human diversity, subject to the same societal dynamics as other forms of diversity," such as race, gender, ethnicity, or sexual orientation (Walker 2012, 233). Within the paradigmatic framework of neurodiversity, notes Joseph N. Straus (2013, 467), autism is "not a defect or pathology, but rather an aspect of naturally occurring and inherently desirable human variability ... a difference not a deficit." It "is constructed by autistic people themselves through the culture they produce (including writing, art, and music), and its shared features give it cohesion and a distinctive identity" (Straus 2013, 466).[3]

Ethnography and relativism, together with musical experience and music itself, hold considerable potential to leverage a much-needed paradigm shift from pathology to neurodiversity where the consideration of autism is concerned. An ethnomusicology of autism, one that privileges the voices, agency, and culture-making strategies of autistic individuals, is well suited to advancing the kinds of epistemological, humanistic, and pragmatic priorities that such a shift would entail.

Working ethnomusicologically as an advocate for neurodiversity may be seen to contribute to a movement of repatriation within the larger project of autistic self-advocacy. As self-advocates, autistic people are bringing themselves "back" from a colonized condition of disenfranchisement foisted on them historically by a deficit-centric medical-scientific establishment. They are defining who they are and what matters to them on their neurodivergent terms, speaking—or typing, signing, writing, texting, musicking, or otherwise communicating—in their own voices and articulating their own agendas and aspirations, wants and needs, frustrations and concerns, abilities and challenges.[4] This chapter, and the larger ethnomusicological project of dialogue-based ethnography of which it is a part (Bakan 2018), is directed toward the promotion of autistic repatriation.

REPATRIATION, ETHNOMUSICOLOGY OF AUTISM, AND ONLINE DIALOGICAL ETHNOGRAPHY

How might an ethnomusicology of autism best serve to advocate on behalf of cultivating an epistemological landscape in which autistic voices are not just present and heard but also taken seriously in contemporary discourses and debates on autistic personhood, civil rights, and ontology? The inherent integrity and dignity of autistic ways of being have been attacked and marginalized for as long as the term "autism" has been in existence (see Fein 2012; Straus 2013; and Silberman 2015). Reversing that course is an essential move toward autistic repatriation, and to contribute to the documentation and dissemination of autistic voices speaking on their own behalf through ethnography—and also through music and discourses about music—is to engage in a form of advocacy archiving that fosters repatriation. "It starts with the basic, foundational idea that *there is nothing wrong with us*," declares Julia Bascom in her foreword to *Loud Hands: Autistic People, Speaking*. "We are fine. We are complete, complex, human beings leading rich and meaningful existences and deserving dignity, respect, human rights, and the primary voice in the conversation about us" (Bascom 2012b, 10).

This is the premise from which a repatriation-directed ethnomusicology of autism ought rightly to begin—not from the naïve stance that the challenges of living with autism are neither formidable nor profusely heterogeneous and complex,[5] but rather from the position that listening to, learning from, and collaborating with autistic people is a better point of departure than diagnosing, stigmatizing, and trying to "fix," "normalize," or "cure" them. My job as an ethnomusicologist is to understand and engage with autistic people, not to pathologize and change them.

My work from 2011 to 2013 with the Artism Ensemble, a Florida-based, National Endowment for the Arts–funded music performance collective that included several children on the autism spectrum, their coparticipating parents, and professional musicians of diverse musicultural lineages, was consistent with these aspirations. Artism, an outgrowth of its predecessor, the Music-Play Project (Bakan 2009; Bakan, Koen, Bakan, et al. 2008; Bakan, Koen, Kobylarz, et al. 2008), has been the focus of several recent publications (Bakan 2014a, 2014b, 2015a, 2015b, 2016). More significantly for the present study, however, it paved the way toward new vistas of research possibility, including an intensively collaborative project based on my dialogues and interactions with adult autistic musicians and musicologists (Bakan 2018), one of whom, Donald Rindale (a pseudonym), is the focus of this chapter.[6]

The chapter as a whole has two principal objectives. First, it serves as a platform for presenting Donald's insightful and provocative positions on a range of issues relating to autism, advocacy, music, musicology, and philosophy. I avoid the habitual temptation to explain or interpret Donald's words, relying instead on the more-or-less verbatim re-presentation of transcripts from two dialogues we shared in 2013. Related to this priority of re-presentation (as opposed to representation) is my decision to forgo inclusion of a description or definition of what autism is—or of what the autism spectrum is—as I prefer that readers engage with these subjects through the frames in which they emerge in the actual dialogues themselves, and most especially through Donald's articulations and contextualizations of them. That ties to another strategy which goes against disciplinary conventions: my decision *not* to "introduce" Donald here at the outset, neither by way of a biographical sketch nor through a profile of his ascribed, diagnostic identity as a person with an autism spectrum "disorder." Just as I prefer for the reader to engage with Donald's perspectives on autism, music, and the other subjects he broaches in the dialogues in his own words, I am likewise committed to having Donald present his own background story on his life and on living with ASC. This may make for a less convenient reading experience than other approaches would yield—one must read quite far into the dialogues before actually learning what Donald's diagnosis is, how old he is now, and how old he was when he was first diagnosed, for example—but with the payoff of a less author-mediated ground from which to engage with Donald as he engages with and presents himself.[7] Such choices are admittedly risky to make in a scholarly publication, as they respectively dispense with a foundational trope of autism research-based writing, on the one hand, and a cornerstone of ethnographic representation, on the other. They are, however, strategic moves that I consider essential to the program of repatriation and autistic agency facilitation privileged in the chapter overall. Imperfect as they are, they at least orient the work toward Bascom's ideal of making autistic voices the primary ones in conversations about autism, as well as toward alliance with the "nothing about us without us" mantra of the disability rights movement, and of social movements in neurodiversity and autistic self-advocacy that issued in its wake (Fein 2012; Silberman 2015).

The chapter's second key objective is to explore a particular approach to methodology with interesting implications for both repatriation and archiving writ large: online dialogical ethnography. The medium of conversational exchange that Donald and I employed in our dialogues was exclusively electronic (we have, as of this writing, never actually met): our primary medium of exchange was Google Talk (a chat messaging service since discontinued and at present replaced with similar software called Google Hangouts). Online ethnographic interviewing has particular qualities, potentialities, and liabilities generally; these are addressed later in the chapter. It is also a research method with particular implications for the study of autism. The construct of "autism" is inextricable from the conditions of social interaction and communicative exchange that essentially define it. Therefore, the media of interaction and communication involved in ethnographic work with autistic people are not incidental; they are, rather, central to the epistemological, ontological, and pragmatic realities that both prefigure and emerge from the work itself. Repatriation begins with agency and empowerment; giving voice to agency is of key importance, and the medium through which communication happens is definitive. Archiving begins with documentation and dissemination; how voices and ideas are inscribed, especially in the discursive spaces where the voices of autistic people have traditionally been muted, dismissed, or ignored, is likewise definitive. To foreground Donald's views within the context of our dialogical exchange, then, and to situate both his words and their framing dialogue within the chat medium through which they have come to be located in this chapter, serves as a dual enterprise of singular focus. Addressing such issues is my primary purpose in the final portion of the chapter. That part follows the re-presentation of my dialogues with Donald, which are the centerpiece of this chapter.

Introductions

On February 11, 2013, I received an e-mail from someone whose name I did not recognize. Let us call him "Donald Rindale."

> Hello, Dr. Bakan. My name is Donald, and I am a new graduate student and teaching assistant in the Department of Musicology at [Private] University. . . . I have been in contact with [several] members of the FSU Musicology faculty over the past three years regarding [your] Masters and Doctoral programs in Musicology. I had the pleasure of meeting with [one of them] and several FSU students at the American Musicological Society conference in San Francisco back in 2011. Being on the autism spectrum myself, and having recently been made aware of your own extensive research on music and autism, and considering that this is an area in which I am becoming increasingly interested, I am now very much more interested in attending FSU for my Ph.D. studies.
>
> I have attached my current CV to this email to introduce myself and my research activities. It appears that FSU would be an excellent "fit" for me given the historical musicological interests of the faculty members, your own work on music and autism, the excellent placement record of [alumni of] the program, and the presence of opportunities for supplementary certification in Arts Administration and Critical Theory.
>
> I am wondering if we could set up a time to talk on the phone in the near future. Because it has been "a while" since my last communication with FSU, I would certainly appreciate the opportunity to learn about the fellowship/assistantship opportunities, application procedures, and other pertinent matters.
>
> Please let me know if we could arrange something soon. Thank you for your time and consideration.
>
> Sincerely,
> Donald Rindale

I replied that I would be delighted to talk by phone, but Donald did not respond. Some six months went by, and then, on August 24, I was surprised to see a second e-mail from him in my inbox:

> Hello again! I hope you have been doing well these past few months. I was pleased to see an announcement for a lecture that you gave at Columbia University about autism and ethnomusicology. If you wouldn't mind, would you please send me a copy of that presentation? I would love to read that!
>
> Sincerely,
> Donald

In my reply, I told Donald that the Columbia talk paper was still a work in progress— not quite ready for sharing—but I would be sure to send it to him and invite feedback once it was at a more advanced stage. Then I moved the exchange in a new direction, writing:

> At some point, I may also want to interview you in connection with a forthcoming book I'm working on, since I am increasingly writing from a perspective directly informed by autism self-advocacy priorities.
>
> All the best, and good to hear from you!
> Michael

Donald got right back to me to say he would be happy to be interviewed for my project. The next challenge was to figure out what format such an interview might take. Donald was living in Boston at the time, and I was in Tallahassee, Florida. A face-to-face meeting was not a viable option. I had recently been experimenting with chat messaging platforms in my teaching and other contexts. It occurred to me that dialoguing with Donald using Google Talk (now Google Hangout) could work. I proposed this possibility to Donald, suggesting the potential advantage that there would not be "the problem of transference of your words as you wish to express them to my representations of them." Donald agreed that compared to other prospects—phone, Skype—text messaging "might be better, especially if there is a way to preserve the text for ease of quotation" down the road, which Google Talk would indeed provide. We scheduled an October 11, 2013, meeting time for our first Google Talk session, and we did so with a shared, basic sense—albeit one not yet fully articulated by either of us at the time—that "chatting" via text messaging would hold distinctive advantages for both of us in this new, collaborative project. The "why" behind that shared belief is, I think, well captured by Bret Woods in the following comments:

> Chat messaging has its own certain set of qualities desirable to perpetuat[ing] the guise of colloquial speech genres (due to its real-time nature) while offering the potential for agency over utterances not found (or even possible) in other media. Additionally, while one can always find problems of transference with regard to expression in any medium, including "chat," chat offers a realtime hypertextuality that helps a speaker actively dispel many assumptions in real time.[8]

DIALOGUE 1: OCTOBER 11, 2013

D (DONALD): Are you there now?
M (MICHAEL): Yes, I am!
D: Cool. Thanks for your [Google Talk invitation] email! I am available now to chat.
M: Okay. Let's do it. Tell me a little bit about your background and training in music.
D: Sure! As with everyone else, I took classes in general music throughout elementary school, beginning in kindergarten. However, I began serious instrumental study on the trombone when I was in the 4th grade, and maintained that throughout

the rest of elementary school and high school. Halfway through college, I, unfortunately, had to stop playing due to the onset of Temporomandibular Joint Disorder [TMJ]. Also throughout high school, I conducted at rehearsals and concerts quite regularly. In college, I began as a music performance major, but due to my medical difficulties, I switched schools and also switched to an undergraduate major in musicology with a minor in philosophy. I have continued those studies until now.

M: So you don't play music at all anymore?

D: Not really. I have not played trombone in several years, and I only have a rudimentary proficiency on piano, so I don't really get involved with that either.

M: So your musical life is mainly as a listener, analyst, and critical thinker—i.e., musicological.

D: Right now, yes. When I first had to make that change, it was pretty emotionally difficult. However, I found that I have enjoyed the new direction much more than I enjoyed performing, so I guess it was actually a positive change after all.

M: That's good to hear! Prior to that, had you aspired to a professional career in music performance?

D: Oh, yes. It was the only love of my life.

M: I had something similar happen. Chronic pain syndrome (fibromyalgia) that forced me to quit my career as a percussionist for a long time. But I was able to return to performing and now do a lot of it.

D: Well, some of us are not so lucky, unfortunately. But, honestly, if my trombone got run over by a tank, I'd be delighted. I would have no intention of resuming it even if I physically could. It was a wonderful chapter of my life, but that page has long been turned.

M: Yes, life moves us where it does and, if we're lucky, to places we might not have been that are better than those that came before. Sounds like that's the case for you.

D: Yep! And now the same is happening with my transition to law.

M: Oh, tell me about that.

D: I suppose I have been lucky in that every move I have made has been a move "up." Well, after a long period of reflection, I have decided that my talents and skills would be better applied in an area in which I could make a difference, specifically by being much more involved with real people and real problems than I could in musicology. Over the past year or so, law has become increasingly intriguing to me not only in itself, but also as it is a field where the same skills in research, writing, and public speaking which I have cultivated for a long time in musicology could be just as frequently and rigorously utilized.

M: Makes good sense. Do your aspirations in the field of law have anything to do with serving as an advocate for autistic people?

D: I think so. Right now, my interests are quite varied, including constitutional, domestic and international human rights law, the laws of war—maybe those will actually be followed again some day—family law, labor law, etc. I try to do at least 1,000 pages per week of additional reading in law to really get my "gears" going. But sure, I think disability law, generally construed, would be very appropriate in my case. I think there was actually a matter in Florida not too long ago where a court had found that the State simply had to provide medical coverage for various therapies that were necessary for autistic children, so it is nice to see some progress along those lines.

M: Great. Do you self-identify or see yourself as being in alliance with ASAN [Autistic Self Advocacy Network], ANI [Autism Network International], or any of the other autistic self-advocacy organizations?

D: I don't see why not [though I don't know much about them yet]! I guess that once I actually get started, I'll be able to learn more about what organizations are available and can get more involved with them, particularly in the local chapters that would be in my area.

M: Yes, those organizations are doing some very cool things. I can't remember if I mentioned to you a wonderful book called *Loud Hands* that is published by ASAN. [Almost all of] the authors are autistic and it's amazing to read how profoundly different their perspectives, wants, and needs are from what is generally inferred re: autism by the "mainstream," neurotypical society.

D: I can see that. As far as I am concerned, we are like a herd of cats. This is a spectrum, after all, and so there is no one-size-fits-all model of understanding what autism is really like, other than in terms of some of the main, distinguishing characteristics which are more-or-less uniform among everyone so diagnosed. For instance, some can speak, others cannot. Some excel in particular subjects in which others do not, etc.

M: [Right!] It is the diversity of autistic people, like that of any culture, which defines what autism is, not some cookie cutter list of [commonly shared] traits and symptoms.

D: Oh sure. For instance, we have a high-functioning [autistic] professor on our law faculty. Another professor with whom I spoke told me "oh yeah, he's definitely the smartest guy on the faculty." "I know," I said. "We typically are!"

M: LOL! Okay, here's my "main" question. It's a bit complex. Give me a minute to type it out.

D: Sure.

M: My work on the ethnomusicology of autism has gone through a variety of stages and approaches over the years. Now, though, I feel quite clear about where I'm going with it and what I hope for it to achieve. The basic deal is this: Autism is mainly defined in the literature in terms of disorder, deficits, etc. You have the "medical model of disability" with its focus on diagnosis and treatment. Then there's the contrasting social model of disability, wherein the idea is that "disability" doesn't reside in the body (or mind) of the so-called disabled individual, but rather in the lack of understanding and accommodations on the part of society at large (disabling environments, policies, etc.). There are merits to both approaches, surely, and I am particularly sympathetic to the social model approaches. But where I see my own main role residing is in proposing and making manifest a different model again, what I call an ethnographic model of disability [see Bakan 2016]. The basic idea is that as an ethnographer who focuses on music (i.e., as an ethnomusicologist) my goal is not to fix, cure, provide therapy for, diagnose, etc., people with autism. Nor is it specifically to lobby for or build new "environments" that accommodate autistic "disabilities." Rather, it is the same as what it is if I go to Bali to study gamelan music [Bakan 1999] or anywhere else in the world to study whatever music. I want to understand the people whose music is the subject of my investigations, and in turn to understand their music through the lens of their values, experiences, desires, worldviews. Thus, if I'm studying "music and autism" I assume that the autistic people with whom I work are the "experts" in their own cultural traditions, including communication and music, and proceed from that point. I do fieldwork. I observe, I ask questions, I participate in music-making together with my autistic friends. Ultimately, my job is not to figure out what's "wrong" and how it can be made "better" and how music might contribute to that. It is, rather, to say "this is how these particular people, who are labeled autistic, make music and make culture and make community with one another and with their neurotypical counterparts." I'm there to describe and advocate, always assuming that there is no "better" to go for other than cultivating better mutual understanding, and mainly on the side of neurotypicals having a better understanding of autistics.

D: Sounds good.

M: So the question, then, is: As an autistic person, what do you think I, as an ethnomusicologist, can contribute to the cause of autistic self-advocacy? If you were going to continue into a career as a musicologist focusing on the music and musical experiences of autistic people, what would be your primary goals and aspirations, and in what ways can I perhaps be a proxy to driving the kinds of agendas that you would envision for yourself and for other autistic people through musicological inquiry and musical action?

D: This, too, may take a while, but I will hit "enter" periodically so that you can read some of it, rather than just sitting there wondering "where is he!"

M: Okay . . .

D: As far as my interests in the implications of autism for musical listening/ performance/conducting, etc., I have been primarily interested in how it is that, at least in my own case, my neurological configuration actually allows for the particular emotional experiences that I have during particular pieces, even down to minute elements like chord progressions, certain instrumentation-al [sic] timbres, etc. I have never really been interested in the social, interpersonal aspects of musical performance as it relates to autism. In my own case, I never found that I was unable to adequately act as a member of an ensemble because of my own [autistic] profile. In fact, I found ensemble performance to be a welcome refuge from the interpersonal engagements that I had to endure in the outside world. The music did not laugh, or judge, or make nasty comments, or quizzical facial expressions and gestures at the sight of some unexpected behavioral tendencies, among other things. For those reasons, I will always love it, whether I continue in musicology or not. In my own case, I actually do have some kind of capacity for "simulation"—the "technical" term for understanding body language, particularly facial expressions—as it would be incited in others in their dealings with me. I have to credit philosophy . . . for allowing for that. Studying phenomenology in particular, and the sub-field of "philosophy of mind," has allowed me to understand with much greater clarity than before why I am how I am, and why others see me as different in the way that they do. However, just because I discern these things more clearly does not mean that they are somehow not painful for me. For children who are more severely afflicted than myself, they might not be able to realize that others are making fun of them or are adopting a condescending or patronizing disposition towards them. Therefore, they are particularly vulnerable to such hostility, since those who perpetrate it are, presumably, neurotypical and therefore realize they have a "sitting duck." I, however, *am* able to tell such things, and when I realized that their reactions were ones of confusion and derision, that hurt a lot, since I realized how different I am than other people and how I tend to "lose out" on the jovial interactions and social engagements that they take so for granted. Sorry this is so long, but now I will address your question in more detail . . .

M: It's great. Please go on!

D: I am actually going to be writing a seminar paper on the need for musicologists, and intellectual people generally understood, to assume a more public persona. Paul Hollander, Edward Said, and others have written extensively on such matters. In others words, the mental energy and acumen with which we, neurotypical and otherwise, are so fortunately endowed *must* also be applied to assisting "those other people out there" in the "real world." (This is one of the inspirational factors for my switch to law.) I think the same kind of perspective should be practiced by musicologists. There really isn't any reason why it shouldn't be. We are all one people in one world, and if you (hypothetical "you," here) get a five or six year full ride to a Ph.D. program to stroke your beard and think great thoughts, you simply must, as an ethically inclined creature, engage in a more public involvement with the real people and real problems to which I referred. As this relates to autism advocacy, I see this happening in two ways. First, . . . musicologists, and all intellectuals, should become advocates for increased financial and other resources to assist autistic people, particularly as they become ineligible for government resources in many jurisdictions after they reach a certain age. It is simply a matter of human decency and the need to be our brother's keepers, in my view. Second, we can, and should, whether musicologists or not, change the way in which the diagnosis of autism in one's child is received and *perceived*. One of the most profoundly upsetting statements that I hear from parents of autistic children, particularly those rather severely disabled, is that "it was like we were kicked in the gut" when we first heard. You know, the kind of *60 Minutes* or *20/20* interviews where this is discussed and then thoughts for the life he could have had emerge and the tears come and blah blah blah. I can certainly imagine that, when a parent receives such news, there is a period of mourning; mourning for the fact that the desires you may have wanted for him—good level of education and employment, independence, perhaps children of his own—are now substantially or even entirely impeded. Oh, and I am also incensed by people who have killed their autistic children and then themselves in murder-suicides because the conditions became intolerable for the parents precisely *because* of inadequate assistance from the State in caring for its most vulnerable . . . [ellipsis in original]. People have to see children in such conditions, *not* as hopeless people or receptacles of impossible dreams. Instead, they should see those children not merely as dignified beings deserving of their love and attention, but as people who can be "used"—and I don't use that term pejoratively—to advance the cause of disability studies and to inform medical research, public policy and legislation, and other measures aimed at helping them live as full and prosperous lives as possible. It might actually be helpful and encouraging for parents of such children to see their children as "means to an end," insofar as they, and other people's similarly situated children, can be key players in the progress of neuroscience, psychology, etc., so that they and the *next* group of kids *after* them can get the tools that are necessary for them. I think that's it!

M: That's wonderful, Donald. . . . I thank you for your time. . . . Bye for now. Have a great weekend! Nice chatting with you!

D: Thanks, Michael! . . . Please let me know when you'd like to chat again.

M: Will do. Bye.

DIALOGUE 2: NOVEMBER 26, 2013

D: I'm ready whenever you are.

M: Okay. Here I am. How's it going?

D: Doing okay. How are you?

M: Fine, thanks. . . . So, any follow up thoughts since our last conversation?

D: None other than to ask how you found the comments that I made. . . . I was hoping that my comments about how people could use their [autistic] kids as "tools" for further research, such as in some kind of group setting for a big NIH-style research grant, experimental medication, etc., did not come off offensively. Honestly, I do not know what other term I could apply than "tool" for the way I would want more parents of autistic children to view their kids; not as "burdens" to the family, which will or can never be the same ever again, but as "tools" for the process of uncovering the mysteries of the condition to help both themselves and others.

M: [That's] good food for thought[, Donald]. . . . You said some really wonderful stuff in that last conversation, especially the last couple of passages where you were talking about your own phenomenological perspectives on being an autistic musician and what musicologists and others might do in the interests of both accounting and advocating for autistic people, children and otherwise. I was particularly struck by this passage: "I have never really been interested in the social, interpersonal aspects of musical performance as it relates to autism. In my own case, I never found that I was unable to adequately act as a member of an ensemble because of my own profile. In fact, I found ensemble performance to be a welcome refuge from the interpersonal engagements that I had to endure in the outside world. The music did not laugh, or judge, or make nasty comments, or quizzical facial expressions and gestures at the sight of some unexpected behavioral tendencies, among other things. For those reasons, I will always love it, whether I continue in musicology or not."

D: Ah yes, I remember writing that. (Gosh. . . . I wrote that? ☺)

M: Well, maybe you could expand on [it]. It's interesting that you note that "the music didn't laugh" at you; but what about the other musicians? Is there something different about the social environment of music-making that moves musical experience out of the normal mode of social encounter, [which] can often be oppressive for autistics?

D: I think that if there was some kind of special tendency for musical performance to afford that kind of departure from the normal experience, it might not be any greater or less than that afforded by other artistic experiences, like acting or drawing or anything else. For me, at least, musical performance was a method of applying my talents and knowledge towards an art form that I absolutely adored—and at which I did quite well—and provided opportunities to more or less "get away" from the often offensive and upsetting social situations in which I had to operate, social situations, that is, where people were talking to and about me (when their mouths were not occupied by mouthpieces and reeds of various shapes and sizes!). It was a great refuge indeed. It allowed me to demonstrate to people that I was talented, smart, and capable like them, and could do anything they could do, even if I had some shortcomings as far as intimate interaction with them [was concerned].

M: Makes sense. I especially appreciate the line about the other musicians' mouths being otherwise occupied in ways that precluded their using them to be unkind and condescending. What about before or after rehearsals? Did the spirit of goodwill and *communitas* that the shared musical moment facilitated translate [to] outside the bounds of that moment itself? In other words, were musicians with whom you played in the ensembles, by virtue of sharing something meaningful and communicative with you in the making of music, elevated in their consciousness in ways that inspired them to treat you more humanely, more as an equal, than others in your peer group and/or in other situations? Did music form a bridge to other kinds of social connection with fellow musicians?

D: I think that they could have behaved in such a way if I had actually paid attention to it and tried to get them to do so. To be honest, I was so much in my proverbial "own little world" before and after [rehearsals and concerts] that I really did not communicate much at all with anyone else. Were I to [have done] so, I probably would have noticed at least an appreciable degree of collegiality around me.

M: So I'm curious. From these chat exchanges, you strike me as a rather social person. First, you're articulate and a compelling conversationalist; second, you seem very motivated to "keep the conversation going," as it were, which I really appreciate. What is the importance of a "social life" to Donald. I get a sense that there are parallel realities, the one where you revel in the delights of, to quote you, your "own little world," the other where you seem quite intent to reach beyond it, connect, and make an impact, positively so, on the lives of others, whether through these chats, your aspirations in legal studies, etc. In short, what makes you "tick"?

D: Well, I am not as confined in my own "little world" nearly as much as I was even two and a half years ago when I was first diagnosed. I think the main reason for this was taking philosophy courses in phenomenology and learning more and more about that whole perceptual framework. It allowed me to see just how different I was from other, neurotypical people, and also, by implication, to infer what they must think of me and how they must see me. My capacity for "simulation," to [again] use a phrase from philosophy of mind, seems to have correspondingly increased. And so, I actually am finding myself wanting a long-term partner and more relationships in general as a result of this "temptation of normalcy." Ascertaining what "normalcy" is has not always been easy or fun, but at least I have been able to see how other people live, and understand how much different I am from others. Again, that has not always been pleasant; at some times it has been very difficult.

M: How old are you?

D: Twenty-four.

M: So you were diagnosed at about twenty-one?

D: Yep. Right before I turned twenty-two.

M: So all those years that you were actually playing music, you did not "know" you had Asperger's, right?

D: No, I didn't. I didn't know what was wrong.

M: Would it have made a difference to know, in terms of how your musical life might have been pursued, do you think?

D: I don't think it would have made a difference in terms of how I would have pursued my musical life as much as it would just have clarified to me what was wrong and why I was the way that I was, whether in a musical context or not.

M: You've referred twice in the last couple of exchanges to being "wrong": "I didn't know what was wrong," "it would have just clarified to me what was wrong." In the autistic self-advocacy [literature] . . . there is a defiant thread of "There is nothing wrong with me" that permeates the discourse. . . . Do you really feel (as opposed to think) that something is "wrong" with you, or is it more a question of living in a wrong-headed world that won't take you for what you are? I, for one, am finding you to be very much "right" in the way you think, express yourself, etc. Not trying to preach or be Polyanna-ish here, but there is an intriguing mix of emotional sentiments in the way you self-present at times.

D: That reminds me of the website wrongplanet.net.[9] I certainly do feel that it is the case of the world being "wrong-headed" and not taking me for what I am, but when I do feel that way, I do wish that I wasn't this way. Certainly, having this condition has allowed me to apply a rather exceptional degree of focus to academic studies and has facilitated my success in certain professional respects. But if I was afforded the proverbial "pill" or "magic wand" to "take this away," I definitely would.

M: . . . Earlier you alluded to how studying phenomenology/philosophy of mind had sparked in you an awareness of how "different" you were from others and a motivation to find out how and why. Can you take me through a quick synopsis of how that process unfolded?

D: Sure, as best as I can recall. Basically, some kind of connection was forged, or [a] "lightbulb" went "off" in my head, after reading so much of that literature, which made me realize that I was indeed quite different than others and that there must have been something "wrong," i.e., some kind of theretofore unidentified problem by virtue of which I was quite different and unusual in contrast to mostly everyone who I had known, but the name of which I did not know. At that point, I was already clinically depressed and was going to counseling for it, and decided to bring up some of these other concerns. I had learned a bit about autism-spectrum conditions and found that I matched the general descriptions and the specific symptomatologies very closely. Eventually, the psychologist introduced to me the fact that no two people diagnosed with an ASD are really the same and that there was a spectrum of severity and problems associated with the condition generally construed. Then came the affirmation and acceptance of the diagnosis, then the self-imposed mantra that this was one of my "greatest strengths." Then came the realization, through phenomenology and philosophy, that I was truly quite different from everyone else, and the realization of how other people must see me and what they must think about me. Then came a real sadness over the whole thing.

M: So are you moving past that sadness phase at this stage, do you think?

D: I sure hope so. I have work to do and things to accomplish. . . .

M: . . . I do have one more question I'd like to ask, and then we might want to call it a day for now.

D: Sounds good. . . . Sure, ask away!

M: Well, I want to go on a slightly different tack re: the phenomenology of self-type question posed earlier, one that relates specifically to your former musical life. There has been a good deal of literature in which it is suggested that autistic ways of processing music, hearing, etc., are distinctive, that there is a "cultural" dimension of being autistic that defines a particular kind of musicality and way of engaging with music, individual diversities of autistic/Asperger's folks notwithstanding. Retrospectively, can you identify any specific features of your "musicality" [or your approach to musicology] that you link to your Asperger's? . . .

D: Hmm. . . . I do feel that the condition may have some bearing on my love of certain melodic and harmonic progressions, matters of orchestration, timbres, etc., that I [find to be] especially pleasing compared to others. Perhaps there is some kind of neurological anomaly attendant to my condition that allows for those kinds of special experiences, but I'm not sure what it is. . . . And as for my work as a musicologist, I think that the condition was somewhat of a boon in that it allowed me to read and write when so many of my classmates (particularly at the undergraduate level) were out partying. They were having fun; I was doing musicology. ☺

M: Well, there is that, but musicology is fun!

D: I know. ☺

M: Okay. On that note, I must sign off, though to be continued at some future point. If I might take off my "scholar's hat" for a moment, I do want to encourage you to stop thinking about yourself as "wrong" and about your neurological constitution as "some kind of anomaly." You're a cool guy and very likable. The world will catch up; just try to be patient, but most importantly with yourself.

D: Thanks for the advice. Talk to you later!!

M: Okay. Bye for now. Happy Thanksgiving!

D: Happy Thanksgiving to you too!

Medium, Message, and Meaning

The foregoing dialogue transcripts are telling in terms of what they reveal, not just about the two individuals involved in them but also about autism, music, and neurodiversity; salient philosophical, ethical, and musicological issues; and the inherent potential of re-presented dialogue itself as both a productive methodological *and* theoretical tool of ethnomusicological inquiry. Furthermore, these transcripts evidence the value of the medium of chat messaging as a powerful methodological instrument on multiple levels: social, communicative, interactional, archival, and repatriative. The medium may not be the message, but where the prospects of online dialogical ethnography are concerned, it arguably enables the message to be issued more collaboratively and directly, with greater fidelity and fewer restrictions (geographical, economic, etc.), and in a more flexible framework yielding deeper impact than do more conventional modes of ethnographic documentation, representation, and delivery. Moreover, there is a major added bonus for the researcher as well: the elimination of the cumbersome process of transcribing field interviews and the concomitant elimination of the risk of introducing errors or inaccuracies into the transcripts during the process of transcribing (albeit with the risk of reproducing unchecked errors made in the initial chat exchange).

To wit, chat messaging platforms create a complete and immediate archival record of the dialogues they host and do so in a manner that imposes almost no limits on their transferability among conversational partners or possibilities for collaborative editing and development. They facilitate conversations and other forms of interaction across any span of physical distance, and they eliminate travel costs and logistical constraints that would otherwise hinder the viability of many ethnographic projects. They also make it possible to navigate and negotiate *time* in ways that not only live ethnographic field research methods (e.g., live interviews) preclude, but that other communicative media such as phone conversations, video conferencing, and Skype cannot readily accommodate. What I mean by that last point is that when one is engaged in chat messaging, there is a feeling of being part of a live communicative exchange that is happening in the moment (like a live or phone conversation); yet there is also the perpetual possibility of pausing to reflect and critically assess where the conversation is going and how one wants to be a part of it (more like writing in a journal or composing a blog entry). Moreover, there is an implicit phenomenological bracketing of the *words themselves* that defines the exchange as it evolves. Bracketed out are a host of potentially illuminating *and* potentially distracting extralinguistic cues, gestures, and expectations that are inherent to verbal/visual modes of interaction but are largely immaterial in chat messaging (well, there are emojis, but they can only take you so far and tend to be profusely "neurotypical" in their emotive assumptions). These include but are by no means limited to tone of voice, body language, facial expression, eye contact, physical contact (sometimes), and locational proximity.

Such bracketing is a double-edged sword. We lose a lot in the way of contextual framing of the pure linguistic, communicative act, and we potentially lose immediacy too, since thoughts must be translated from their cognition to their written (typed) expression rather than going the more direct route (at least ostensibly given current trends in communicative interaction) from cognition to speech. On the flip side, we gain a lot by not having to filter what is conveyed through various levels of postcommunicative "translation"—for example, by transcribing the interview, or aiming to decipher the "real" intention of the speaker in the midst of potentially conflicting information coming from facial expressions and the like. And at the most basic, pragmatic level, we gain efficiency in our ethnographic process, since the words of our consultants and collaborators, expressed on their terms within a context that merges spontaneous expression with room for critical reflection, are right there before us—again, with no transcription necessary.

We might compare chat messaging as a form of ethnography to listening to recordings as a form of listening. When listening to a recording, we forfeit much of the nuance and context that a live performance (or even a video-recorded performance) of the same music would provide; yet at the same time we may gain a great deal in regard to the quality of the listening experience, since the musicians have had opportunities to craft their performances in accordance with their own aesthetic sensibilities (albeit at the cost of some measure of spontaneous/interactive expression) and since we are able to listen *without* the added sensory, visual, auditory, and social inputs which hearing that same music in live performance would inevitably present.

The ethnographic advantages of chat messaging apply across multiple demographics but arguably hold special relevance in the ethnographic study of autism. People on the autism spectrum face specific and pervasive challenges in several communicative and interactional domains that tend to be foregrounded in conventional "live" ethnographic interview contexts, and by extension in quasi-live communicative media such as Skype. For example, making eye contact during conversations, which is a standard expectation in face-to-face conversational exchange among neurotypical dialogue partners, can be difficult and even stultifying for autistic people. Additionally, ASCs are often associated with so-called *stimming*, or self-stimulatory, behaviors such as hand flapping and body rocking. Since stimming of this type is considered atypical in conversational interactions among neurotypicals, it can raise challenges in interactions involving both autistic and neurotypical individuals: the neurotypical participant may be thrown off or distracted by the stimming of an autistic interlocutor; meanwhile, the autistic conversationalist may feel inhibited from engaging in this natural and often productive form of movement and expression during the conversation, or may at least feel self-conscious in performing his or her customary stims for fear of appearing "weird" or "abnormal." Additional examples could be raised: the approach to and speed of cognitive processing may be markedly different for neurotypical and autistic conversational partners, and vocal cadence, tone of voice, and verbal and nonverbal gestural vocabularies can be very distinct as well.

Chat messaging in a sense levels the playing field in these potentially challenging domains of communicative exchange. Issues of physical behavior and appearance become irrelevant, eye contact becomes a nonissue, and diverse modes and speeds of cognitive processing may be accommodated within the variable tempo acceptable during a chat, where things can move along at a clip akin to that of a standard verbal conversation or be slowed down—or even paused, suspended, or stopped altogether—to allow room for greater reflection, consideration, and introspection. It is often noted that people on the autism spectrum prefer typing-based electronic communications to live, verbal ones. Given the points raised earlier, this seems reasonable enough. In ethnographic studies of autism, therefore, chat messaging may prove to be not merely a substitute for the classic live interview interaction, but rather a superior methodological vehicle for achieving optimal results. That said, Donald Rindale regards the online chat medium as neither advantageous nor disadvantageous for him, as he explained to me in the following mid-December 2013 e-mail exchange:

> M: ... How have you liked this process of using online chat as our main medium of communication? In terms of enabling you to express your views on your terms and in your own words, do you think it has worked better, worse, or the same as a more "conventional" mode of ethnographic discourse, say, live phone conversations or Skype conversations or even (were it feasible) live in-person interviews/conversations would have worked? To that point, do you feel that the fact that you have Asperger's influences your views on the matter—i.e., do you think that not having to deal with verbal conversation, eye contact in face-to-face encounter, and issues of trust vis-à-vis whether your words will be accurately recorded by the "interviewer" might offer special advantages in a context like this for someone on the spectrum?
>
> D: ... I think that the online chat method has worked really well. Other than the inherent advantage of having an actual written record of the exchanges we have had, [though,] I personally don't feel that there is any special advantage of Chatting vs. speaking in person or on the phone. I don't think that the responses I would have given over the phone or in person would have been much different from those that I gave in the Chat. Even as far as issues of facial expressions, eye contact, and other matters of interpersonal communication are concerned, I always try to speak honestly. So, I don't think that the circumstances of an in-person meeting would have altered my answers.

CONCLUSION

Through the medium of chat messaging and the message of Donald Rindale, as made manifest within a particular dialogical context, this chapter offers a slice-of-life vantage point from which to engage with a range of issues relating to music, autism, neurodiversity, philosophical inquiry, social activism, and ethnographic (and in turn ethnomusicological) theory and method. Central to the endeavor has been a goal of autistic repatriation, specifically one that restores the primacy of voice and agency to autistic people themselves in discourses on autism and the autism spectrum. Such repatriation should be regarded as an urgent priority of academic propriety and social justice alike, especially given the profoundly unjust and tragic consequences that have issued in the wake of the customary—if not overtly systematic—muting, discrediting, marginalizing, and maligning of autistic voices and persons across all realms of discourse and public policy historically (see Bascom 2012a and 2012b; Straus 2013; and Silberman 2015).

That such a call for action should come out of a musicological forum on archiving and repatriation seems particularly appropriate. After all, I would contend that it is our skill in listening—careful, critical, engaged, thoughtful, sensitive, and compassionate listening—that defines, first and foremost, who we are and what we do as musicologists when we are at our best. And that is a skill that is as sorely needed as it is in short supply in the domain of inter- and intracultural engagement between autistic people and their neurotypical others.

Such aspirations and ideals do not equate with perfect solutions. The transcripts presented in this chapter, not to mention their framing in other portions of the text, offer up a corpus of ethnographic material that presses us toward unsettling questions of authorship/coauthorship, the ostensible necessity of authorial interpretation and explanation in scholarly writing, and the seeming inevitability of influence that the ethnographer exercises on the subjects of her or his studies. And making such matters all the more unsettling is my refusal personally, hereby asserted, to interrogate them *as* the author in this chapter (except to the extent that I did end up doing that within the dialogues themselves, for better or for worse).

Paradoxically, however, therein may lie the key to how a work such as this, a work of online dialogical ethnography, achieves its measure of repatriation on behalf of autistic and other neurodivergent people, such as Donald Rindale: it allows them to be heard by others speaking for themselves—not perfectly, not with immunity from the voices and influences of their interlocutors, not entirely released from the power of an authorial presence (in this case myself) that ultimately shapes the content and terms of re/re-presentation—but at least, going back to Bascom's words, as what I hope is the "primary voice in the conversation." Autistic people have historically been abused, ignored, and scorned. Even the most verbally adept and eloquent among them—the Donald Rindales of the autistic world, as it were—have been categorically shut out of mainstream discourses as a matter of course, often with no other rationale but for the claim that they *are* autistic and thus ipso facto incapable of generating ideas worthy of serious attention. Dialogues such as the ones Donald and I have shared here compel all who encounter them to acknowledge that Donald knows what he is talking about when it comes to talking about himself, and that in that knowledge is to be found a great and deep source of insight with the potential to benefit not just him or others on the spectrum but all of us, indeed all of humanity.

Collaborating with Donald and with other people speaking (literally or otherwise) from positions of neurodiversity constitutes an act of repatriation wherein the tidy evasions and concealments of diagnostic labeling and its associated practices of human devaluation cannot endure. By the very act of speaking out—not as a voice alone but as a voice in dialogue, not as a case study of neurocognitive disorder but as an exemplar of reasonableness and pragmatic wisdom—Donald retrieves something of what has so often been taken away from him in his life: the respectful attention and listening ears of others. Through such modes of repatriation that privilege the voices and views of autistic people and individuals across the landscape of neurodiverse ways of thinking and being in the world, the capacity of critical inquiry and its sway on the potential for transformative social action are enriched and deepened. And where such repatriation is driven by discourses of and about music, the musicological fields in particular stand to gain much from the broadening of perspectives that neurodiverse points of view may yield.

NOTES

1. In *The Diagnostic and Statistical Manual of Mental Disorders*, 5th ed. (DSM-5) (American Psychiatric Association 2013), three formerly separate "disorders" of the autism spectrum—autism, Asperger syndrome, and PDD-NOS (pervasive developmental disorder—not otherwise specified)—were collapsed into a single diagnostic category: ASD, or autism spectrum disorder. See also Kaufman (2012).
2. The subtitle of the landmark anthology *Loud Hands: Autistic People, Speaking*, which was originally published in 2012 by the Autistic Press of the Autistic Self Advocacy Network (ASAN).
3. Straus's work belongs to a larger body of literature in which musicologists and music theorists are addressing the relationship between music, musical experience, and autism through the lens of disability studies. See also Headlam (2006), Jensen-Moulton (2006), Maloney (2006), Lubet (2011), Straus (2011), and Marrero (2012). On disability studies more broadly, consult *The Disability Studies Reader*, 4th ed. (Davis 2013).
4. See, for example, Williams (1992), Lawson (2000), Shore (2003; of additional interest on account of Shore's professional status as a musician and music educator), Miller (2003), Prince-Hughes (2004), Prince (2010), Biklen (2005), Ariel and Naseef (2006), Tammet (2007), Robison (2007), Mukhopadhyay (2008/2011), Bascom (2012a), and Grandin and Panek (2013). Numerous documentary films, blogs, websites, and other media also contribute to the increasingly present and essential autistic voice of ASC discourse.
5. On the complex heterogeneity of the autism spectrum, see *Loud Hands: Autistic People, Speaking*, and most especially Amy Sequenzia's contribution to that volume, "Non-Speaking, 'Low-Functioning'" (Sequenzia 2012).
6. My online dialogues with Donald Rindale, as re-presented in the present chapter, also serve as the basis for a portion of the fourth chapter of my book *Speaking for Ourselves: Conversations on Life, Music, and Autism* (Bakan 2018), also published by Oxford University Press.
7. I invited Donald to be credited as a coauthor of this chapter. He was initially enthusiastic about the idea, but ultimately declined. This decision was made at the same time that he decided to be represented pseudonymously in the work to help ensure his anonymity. He has, however, reviewed and approved the manuscript at every stage. That said, I take full responsibility for any errors, omissions, or inaccuracies.
8. Bret Woods, personal correspondence with the author, January 9, 2017.
9. WrongPlanet.net self-identifies as "The Online Resource and Community for Autism and Asperger's." The website's main page description states: "Wrong Planet is the web community designed for individuals (and parents/professionals of those) with Autism, Asperger's Syndrome, ADHD, PDDs, and other neurological differences. We provide a discussion forum, where members communicate with each other, an article section, with exclusive articles and how-to guides, a blogging feature, and a chatroom for real-time communication with other Aspies."

References

American Psychiatric Association. 2013. *Diagnostic and Statistical Manual of Mental Disorders.* 5th ed. DSM-5. Arlington, VA: American Psychiatric Publishing.

Ariel, Cindy N., and Robert A. Naseef, eds. 2006. *Voices from the Spectrum: Parents, Grandparents, Siblings, People with Autism, and Professionals Share Their Wisdom.* London and Philadelphia: Jessica Kingsley Publishers.

Bakan, Michael B. 1999. *Music of Death and New Creation: Experiences in the World of Balinese Gamelan Beleganjur.* Chicago: University of Chicago Press.

Bakan, Michael B. 2009. "Measuring Happiness in the 21st Century: Ethnomusicology, Evidence-Based Research, and the New Science of Autism." *Ethnomusicology* 53 (3): 510–518.

Bakan, Michael B. 2014a. "Ethnomusicological Perspectives on Autism, Neurodiversity, and Music Therapy." *Voices: A World Forum for Music Therapy* 14 (3). https://voices.no/index.php/voices/article/view/799/660.

Bakan, Michael B. 2014b. "Neurodiversity and the Ethnomusicology of Autism." *College Music Symposium* 54. http://symposium.music.org/index.php?option=com_k2&view=item&id=10673:neurodiversity-and-the-ethnomusicology-of-autism&Itemid=128.

Bakan, Michael B. 2015a. " 'Don't Go Changing to Try and Please Me': Combating Essentialism through Ethnography in the Ethnomusicology of Autism." *Ethnomusicology* 59 (1): 116–144.

Bakan, Michael B. 2015b. "Being Applied in the Ethnomusicology of Autism." In *The Oxford Handbook of Applied Ethnomusicology,* edited by Svanibor Pettan and Jeff Todd Titon, 278–316. New York: Oxford University Press.

Bakan, Michael B. 2016. "Toward an Ethnographic Model of Disability in the Ethnomusicology of Autism." In *The Oxford Handbook of Music and Disability Studies,* edited by Blake Howe, Stephanie Jensen-Moulton, Neil Lerner, and Joseph Straus, 15–36. New York: Oxford University Press.

Bakan, Michael B. 2018. *Speaking for Ourselves: Conversations on Life, Music, and Autism.* New York: Oxford University Press.

Bakan, Michael B., Benjamin D. Koen, Megan Bakan, Fred Kobylarz, Lindee Morgan, Rachel Goff, and Sally Kahn. 2008. "Saying Something Else: Improvisation and Facilitative Music-Play in a Medical Ethnomusicology Program for Children on the Autism Spectrum." *College Music Symposium* 48: 1–30.

Bakan, Michael B., Benjamin Koen, Fred Kobylarz, Lindee Morgan, Rachel Goff, Sally Kahn, and Megan Bakan. 2008. "Following Frank: Response-Ability and the Co-Creation of Culture in a Medical Ethnomusicology Program for Children on the Autism Spectrum." *Ethnomusicology* 52 (2): 163–202.

Bascom, Julia, ed. 2012a. *Loud Hands: Autistic People, Speaking.* Washington, DC: Autistic Press/Autistic Self Advocacy Network.

Bascom, Julia. 2012b. "Foreword." In *Loud Hands: Autistic People, Speaking,* edited by Julia Bascom, 6–11. Washington, DC: Autistic Press/Autistic Self Advocacy Network.

Biklen, Douglas. 2005. *Autism and the Myth of the Person Alone.* New York: New York University Press.

Davis, Lennard J. 2013. *The Disability Studies Reader.* 4th ed. New York: Routledge.

Fein, Elizabeth. 2012. *The Machine Within: An Ethnography of Asperger's Syndrome, Biomedicine, and the Paradoxes of Identity and Technology in the Late Modern United States.* PhD diss. (Comparative Human Development), University of Chicago.

Grace, Elizabeth J. 2012. "Autistic Community and Culture: Silent Hands No More." In *Loud Hands: Autistic People, Speaking*, edited by Julia Bascom, 141–147. Washington, DC: Autistic Press/Autistic Self Advocacy Network.

Grandin, Temple, and Richard Panek. 2013. *The Autistic Brain: Thinking across the Spectrum*. New York: Houghton Mifflin Harcourt.

Headlam, Dave. 2006. "Learning to Hear Autistically." In *Sounding Off: Theorizing Disability in Music*, edited by Neil Lerner and Joseph N. Straus, 109–120. New York: Routledge.

Jensen-Moulton, Stephanie. 2006. "Finding Autism in the Compositions of a 19th-Century Prodigy: Reconsidering 'Blind Tom' Wiggins." In *Sounding Off: Theorizing Disability in Music*, edited by Neil Lerner and Joseph N. Straus, 199–215. New York: Routledge.

Kaufman, Walter E. 2012. "DSM-5: The New Diagnostic Criteria for Autism Spectrum Disorders." http://www.autismconsortium.org/symposium-files/WalterKaufmannAC2012 Symposium.pdf.

Lawson, Wendy. 2000. *Life behind Glass: A Personal Account of Autism Spectrum Disorder*. London and Philadelphia: Jessica Kingsley Publishers.

Lubet, Alex. 2011. *Music, Disability, and Society*. Philadelphia: Temple University Press.

Maloney, S. Timothy. 2006. "Glenn Gould, Autistic Savant." In *Sounding Off: Theorizing Disability in Music*, edited by Neil Lerner and Joseph N. Straus, 121–135. New York: Routledge.

Marrero, Elyse. 2012. "Performing Neurodiversity: Musical Accommodation by and for an Adolescent with Autism." Master's thesis (Ethnomusicology), Florida State University.

Miller, Jean Kerns. 2003. *Women from Another Planet? Our Lives in the Universe of Autism*. Bloomington, IN: First Books.

Mukhopadhyay, Tito Rajarshi. 2008/2011. *How Can I Talk if My Lips Don't Move? Inside My Autistic Mind*. New York: Arcade.

Prince, Dawn Eddings. 2010. "An Exceptional Path: An Ethnographic Narrative Reflecting on Autistic Parenthood from Evolutionary, Cultural, and Spiritual Perspectives." *Ethos* 38 (1): 56–68.

Prince-Hughes, Dawn. 2004. *Songs of the Gorilla Nation: My Journey through Autism*. New York: Harmony.

Robison, John Elder. 2007. *Look Me in the Eye: My Life with Asperger's*. New York: Crown.

Sequenzia, Amy. 2012. "Non-Speaking, 'Low-Functioning.'" In *Loud Hands: Autistic People, Speaking*, edited by Julia Bascom, 159–161. Washington, DC: Autistic Press/Autistic Self Advocacy Network.

Shore, Stephen. 2003. *Beyond the Wall: Personal Experiences with Autism and Asperger Syndrome*. 2nd ed. Shawnee Mission, KS: Autism Asperger Publishing.

Silberman, Steve. 2015. *NeuroTribes: The Legacy of Autism and the Future of Neurodiversity*. New York: Avery/Penguin Random House.

Straus, Joseph N. 2011. *Extraordinary Measures: Disability in Music*. New York: Oxford University Press.

Straus, Joseph N. 2013. "Autism as Culture." In *The Disability Studies Reader*, 4th ed., edited by Lennard J. Davis, 460–484. New York: Routledge.

Tammet, Daniel. 2007. *Born on a Blue Day: A Memoir (Inside the Extraordinary Mind of an Autistic Savant)*. New York: Free Press.

Titchkosky, Tanya. 2007. *Reading and Writing Disability Differently: The Textured Life of Embodiment*. Toronto: University of Toronto Press.

Walker, Nick. 2012. "Throw Away the Master's Tools: Liberating Ourselves from the Pathology Paradigm." In *Loud Hands: Autistic People, Speaking*, edited by Julia Bascom, 225–237. Washington, DC: Autistic Press/Autistic Self Advocacy Network.

Williams, Donna. 1992. *Nobody, Nowhere: The Extraordinary Autobiography of an Autistic*. New York: HarperCollins.

CHAPTER 14

....

MUSICAL REPATRIATION AS METHOD

....

MICHAEL IYANAGA

INTRODUCTION

FOR ethnomusicologists, the utilitarian aspects of musical repatriation—that is, the transporting, accessing, and disseminating of sound recordings—make it quite different from the loftier theoretical topics that have typically garnered disciplinary attention. Discussions about repatriation tend to revolve around the more immediate and practical issues of ethics, legality, ownership, and distribution. Repatriation, then, seems to engage the kinds of *concrete* concerns with which "applied" ethnomusicology has grappled over the past few decades. Often left out of the conversation, however, is that when treated as a methodological tool, repatriation can also contribute in profound ways to more theoretical concerns in ethnomusicology.

In this chapter,[1] I argue that employing musical repatriation in our fieldwork can help ethnomusicologists write better ethnographies (and, subsequently, theorize more effectively about music and musical people) by giving us a privileged avenue to understand the musical communities with which we work. To illustrate my point, I present an analysis of some of my experiences with musical repatriation in Bahia, Brazil. The examples I present are largely connected to a restudy I conducted there in 2012, which revisited the work done by ethnomusicologist Ralph Waddey on residential patron saint festivals in the 1970s and 1980s (Waddey 1981; Iyanaga 2013a). Consequently, I introduce some basic information regarding my "Waddey restudy" before reviewing some of the important ethnomusicological literature on musical repatriation. I then shift to what constitutes the bulk of this chapter: a detailed explanation of a series of repatriation experiences and some of the important ethnographic lessons learned.

THE WADDEY RESTUDY

From 1975 to the early 1980s, Ralph Waddey, then a PhD candidate in musicology working with Gerard Béhague at the University of Illinois, Urbana-Champaign, conducted extensive fieldwork in the northeastern Brazilian state of Bahia. With the objective of completing a doctoral dissertation on samba, Waddey took his notebook and audio recorder to the state's Recôncavo region (Figure 14.1). Though the intended dissertation never came to fruition, Waddey's hard work resulted in not only lifelong friendships and two landmark articles on samba (Waddey 1980, 1981),[2] but also a formidable home archive of photographs, Super 8 films and VHS tapes, musical instruments, and sound recordings.

Included in his private collection of samba recordings are a handful of recordings of domestic patron saint parties, known as *rezas*. *Rezas* are annual nighttime affairs during which hosts invite friends, family, and neighbors into their homes in order to sing, dance, and eat in honor of a personal patron saint. After intoning the *novena*, which is an hour-long cycle of Catholic a capella prayers sung in unison, the guests then sing rollicking samba for hours while dancing, clapping their hands, and playing musical

FIGURE 14.1 Map showing Bahia's Recôncavo region in the context of Brazil.

Map by Ronald Conner.

instruments.[3] Thus *rezas* nearly always include two distinct musical moments: the novena and the samba.

In 2009, about a year after beginning the research for my doctoral dissertation on Bahian *rezas*, I learned from a mutual friend that Waddey had preserved his field recordings and would likely be quite willing to share them with me. One early morning in March 2010, I wrote Waddey an e-mail to introduce myself and ask whether he did in fact have any *reza* recordings and/or information. His response arrived within a matter of hours and over the course of the day we exchanged a dozen e-mails, most of which were extended discussions about Bahia, patron saints, and samba. His thoughtful e-mails were meticulous and engaging, using a style of writing that was as erudite and fluid as it was humorous and unpretentious. He also revealed himself to be sincere and opinionated, in some cases almost bordering on irreverent.

When he informed me that he had a half-dozen *reza* reel tape recordings, we began discussing the possibility of my visiting him to hear the recordings or, he suggested, we could get together at his home and make digital copies. In April 2011, I was finally able to take a trip to Waddey's New England home. I had never met Ralph Waddey, nor had I even seen a picture of him. Still, it seemed as if I were on my way to visit an old friend. I recognized the gray-haired samba scholar within seconds of seeing him at the train station. Waddey greeted me with a smile and a hug, exuding the same warmth that I had felt by way of our correspondences. As we ambled down the street, we began chatting. He spoke with the same humble erudition that I had grown accustomed to in our e-mail correspondences, but now I could hear his slight southern drawl. Over the course of three pleasurable days, Waddey and I shared stories and spirits as we digitized all of his *reza* recordings.

For circumstantial reasons, Waddey had never been able to return his recordings to the people whose voices had been captured on them. I therefore asked him if, on my imminent return to Bahia, I could deliver copies of the recordings to the original performers. He was delighted by the prospect of giving this little bit back to the people whom he felt had given him so much. Meanwhile, I was excited about the opportunity to act as a courier, seeing this not solely as an ethical endeavor, but also as a chance to initiate a "Waddey restudy." But repatriation is not supposed to be so self-serving, is it?

SOME TRENDS IN
THE REPATRIATION LITERATURE

Historically speaking, ethnomusicological concerns about repatriation began to emerge around the last quarter of the twentieth century,[4] in tandem with a renewed interest in archives, archiving, and modes of dissemination. This should hardly be a surprise, given that archives, whether private or public, are the locations par excellence for the preservation of repatriatable musical things (in this case, sound recordings).

Anthony Seeger, who can be counted among the foremost thinkers on sound archives, has for decades urged ethnomusicologists to consider what archives can offer the world as a whole, noting particularly that repatriation might invert some of the colonial power structures that archives are complicit in maintaining (Seeger 1986, 1996, 2011, 2014). In a pathbreaking article on the subject, Seeger points to the role of the archive in a "post-colonial world":

> If collectors have deposited their recordings in archives, and if the archives have attended to the preservation of the recordings, then we can actively reverse the colonial process and help "repatriate" the recordings. Through repatriation and training we can support the aspirations of the groups that were recorded. We can also give other countries the "means of production" of comparative analysis.
>
> (Seeger 1986, 267)

The tone is decidedly advocative. For Seeger, the leading motivations for repatriating music lie in the aim of subverting the "colonial process."

This ethical imperative in fact seems to underlie most ethnomusicological conversations about repatriation. Yet given cultural restrictions, questions of ownership, and practical (and/or legal) barriers, repatriation rarely seems to be a simple process of taking a recording from an archive and returning it to its "original" source. Consequently, ethnomusicological conversations about repatriation have tended to focus on a handful of somewhat practical preoccupations: (1) to whom sound should be repatriated (whether people, communities, nations, or organizations), (2) what happens in the communities to which sound is repatriated, (3) which recordings should/can be released, (4) how recordings should be disseminated, and (5) who decides ownership (Landau and Fargion 2012, 133–136; Nannyonga-Tamusuza and Weintraub 2012, 208).[5] Overall, then, the concerns tend to be wedged between approaches to repatriation and the effects of such repatriation.

The aftereffects of repatriation have in fact been of great interest to scholars, especially given that the effects of repatriation can never be known beforehand. The recordings may be embraced and used or, conversely, they may also "remain on the shelf, untouched, after being presented to the community—or they may disappear completely" (Gray 1996, n.p.). As such, thinking about repatriation and carrying it out appear to create a sort of reciprocal dialectic between, to employ the classic dichotomy, the "laboratory" and the "field": those in the figurative "lab" discuss the practice and ethics of dissemination to formulate potential approaches, while those in the field generate on-the-ground reports regarding the effects, reports which are subsequently read by lab researchers to rethink dissemination and thus give continuity to the cycle.[6] This recurrent reevaluation very often raises vital concerns, stimulates discussions, and produces revelatory findings.

With its focus on practicality, however, this approach to repatriation unintentionally cleaves it from larger ethnographic inquiries, no doubt exacerbating the distance that is said to separate "applied" ethnomusicology from its "theoretical" counterpart, a mutual exclusivity that is in many ways more imagined than real (see, for example, Seeger 2006; Dirksen 2013; Lühning et al. 2016). Although any attentive scholar involved in repatriation has no doubt seen that "applying" ethnomusicology—whether through repatriation or not—inherently leads to better (that is, thicker) ethnographic analyses and more sensitive theoretical musings, few have detailed explicitly this process. Such silence inadvertently obscures the conversation on repatriation's value as a means of doing fieldwork.

MUSICAL REPATRIATION AS METHOD: SOME IMPORTANT STUDIES

This is not to say, of course, that significant cases of scholars using repatriation in their fieldwork do not exist. In fact, one prominent example comes from the 1980s, when Nazir Ali Jairazbhoy and Amy Catlin-Jairazbhoy conducted a now-classic restudy of Arnold Bake's late-1930s fieldwork in India (Jairazbhoy and Catlin 1990). The project had originally been motivated by a single factor: "to retrace Bake's steps in order to determine the kind and degree of musical change that had taken place in South India during the past forty-six years" (Jairazbhoy 1991, 220). In this context, repatriation was included among the other two somewhat subsidiary purposes of the project: "to acquire more information about Arnold's recordings and his field trip, and to give copies of his recordings to the original performers, their families, or their communities and to leave a copy in ARCE for those interested in further research" (220).

At the same time, however, this repatriation also figured subtly in the couple's study of musical change. Jairazbhoy explains:

> When we played a Bake recording to musicians and asked them, "Do you know this song?" and "Can you sing it?" the answers were often ambiguous.... On reexamining these experiences, it became evident that the outsider's so-called "objective" views of identity and change did not necessarily coincide with those of the individual or the community concerned.
>
> (Jairazbhoy 1991, 222)

Jairazbhoy and Catlin appear to have repatriated the recordings—mainly by way of a listening experience—in a somewhat improvised method for uncovering musical change. Specifically, it served as a means of gaining a better understanding of *emic* (or insider) views regarding musical change: "[A] comparison of the emic interpretations offered by the members of the culture with the etic perceptions of the outside researcher derived from such a Restudy may have much to contribute to the understanding of the society and its values" (Jairazbhoy 1991, 223). For Jairazbhoy, then, this act of repatriation led to important revelations about people and their values.

More recently, and in much more explicit terms, the Brazilian ethnomusicologist Carlos Sandroni has pointed to repatriation as a "scientific imperative." For him, the repatriation of sound recordings obtained during research can be used "as a tool in advancing the research itself" (Sandroni 2005, 49).[7] By way of example, Sandroni recalls how repatriation figured into his restudy of the 1938 Missão de Pesquisas Folclóricas (Mission of Folkloric Research),[8] a pioneering effort led by the renowned Brazilian musicologist/folklorist Mário de Andrade that sought to document "folk" music in Brazil's north and northeast (see Sandroni 2014). As part of this restudy, Sandroni returned cassette tapes of Andrade's recordings to communities that had initially been visited by the Mission, as well as to individuals linked in some way to the musicians heard on the recordings. Reflecting on this experience, Sandroni notes:

> Every time I have had the chance in my research to play for informants the recordings from the Mission's archive . . . the result has been, beyond emotionally impactful (and likely due to this [impact]), an awakening of memories, associations, and comments that revealed themselves to be extremely useful and would be very difficult to obtain by other means. In some cases, such comments clarified aspects of musical practices of the past. In other cases, however, what they brought was the actual "native" conception of their relationship with their "ethnomusicological past," to quote the title of an article by Philip Bohlman.
>
> (Sandroni 2005, 55–56)

Like Jairazbhoy, then, Sandroni discovered that repatriation could elicit "native" (that is, emic or insider) conceptions of music and musical change. Furthermore, for Sandroni, the recordings also facilitated the acquisition of otherwise difficult-to-obtain data. Repatriation, in this case, appears to have helped advance ethnographic research and to construct research relationships more quickly.

To offer one final example, Anthony Seeger has demonstrated that the return of recordings may also be employed to explore musical aesthetics. He reports on the effective use of a historical recording (made in 1960 by Harald Schultz) in his fieldwork with the Kisêdjê (formerly, Suyá) Indians of Central Brazil. Despite the fact that the recording had been altered, making the pitches lower and the tempo slower than they had originally been, the Kisêdjê nevertheless regarded the faulty recording as "beautiful," being "the way the [Kisêdjê] really sang in the old days" (Seeger 2004 [1987], 98). Seeger eventually concludes that the Kisêdjê probably lauded the recording due to its vintage and a general idealization of the past.

However, and perhaps more importantly, the slowed-down recording's lower pitches resonated with Kisêdjê aesthetic preferences regarding the "big throats" of "old men who were good singers" (100–101). Here the Kisêdjê's unexpected positive reaction to the recording allowed Seeger a deeper comprehension of local musical and social values (as well as the relationship between the two). The ethnomusicologist concludes by insisting that recordings ought to be "preserved in publicly accessible locations," as they not only serve "the interests of the people recorded" but "can also be a valuable resource for laboratory-field interaction" (102–103). Although Seeger does not develop his argument any further, his implicit point seems clear: recordings can be used for ethnographic research.

However, because the insights that can be garnered through repatriation vary largely in accordance with the specific fieldwork contexts and our research questions, it behooves us to ask what other types of data might be gleaned by employing repatriation in our fieldwork. Put otherwise, in what ways might repatriation, like transcription, participant observation, bimusicality, and film analysis,[9] constitute an integral method we might call ethnomusicological? My experiences in Brazil suggest that the return of sound recordings can lead to a wide array of revelations, ranging from fundamental metaphors of musical truth to the value of music in religious rituals and local ways of listening and hearing.

SEU MESSIAS, SÃO BRAZ, AND MUSICAL REPATRIATION IN BAHIA

In mid-2011, with my sights set on a "Waddey restudy," I returned to Bahia with the decades-old *reza* recordings and a list of names. I was dismayed to learn that most of the performers whose voices Waddey had originally captured on tape were no longer living. Furthermore, it was difficult to locate people who actually found the recordings meaningful. I therefore decided to change my approach. Rather than search for performers, I began searching for venues: the homes at which the *rezas* had been performed. In other words, since *reza*s are hosted by people at their private residences, even if it was impossible to repatriate the recordings to the main performers, I could at least try to return Waddey's recordings to the devotees who had initially hosted the *rezas*. Consequently, I began my search for the person at whose home Waddey recorded a *reza* for Saint Roch in August 1978. In his brief ethnographic account of the *reza*, Waddey explains that the event took place in São Braz, "a tidewater village dependent almost entirely on fishing," at a house "belonging to a gentleman named Messias" (1981, 264). I thus set out to find the gentleman named Messias who, with any luck, was still living in São Braz.

Repatriation, Take One—January 19, 2012

After much preparation—which included corresponding with Waddey, making numerous copies of the recording, and writing out lists of questions—I decided I was ready to make my trip to São Braz. I was unsure whether Messias was still alive (and if so, if he still lived in São Braz), but Waddey seemed to think that "Messias might well be living" (as he wrote in an e-mail to me from December 2011), so it made little sense for me not to try to find him. It was around noon when I first arrived at the small village of São Braz

(Figure 14.2), so I lunched at one of the few local restaurants and began asking around for the devotee of Saint Roch. I learned not only that he was still alive but also that he lived relatively close to the restaurant at which I was lunching.

I was pointed in the direction of Messias's home and soon found myself standing before a tall wood-and-wire fence, yelling across the open patio to a man resting in the shade of the home's entryway: "Good afternoon! Is this the home of *Seu* Messias?" (I used the honorific "Seu" in addressing the gentleman.) The man assured me it was and signaled for me to open the gate. As I traversed the dirt yard, I could feel the expectations building within me. After all, I was able to locate the healthy, eighty-four-year-old Messias (Manoel Messias Pereira, b. 1927), whom I refer to for the remainder of the chapter as Seu Messias, more than a generation after Waddey first met him!

As I approached the elderly man, securing Waddey's recording in my hand, I nervously bumbled through a string of questions and credentials: "How are you? Are you Seu Messias? I'm here to speak with you. Do you remember Ralph, the foreigner who recorded your *reza* years ago?" With a gentle smile and a nod, Seu Messias motioned for me to enter his home. I lumbered through the entryway and was greeted immediately by his wife, Dona Celina.[10] She was setting the table for lunch and kindly turned to me and asked, "Are you served?" I politely declined the offer, taking a seat at the large wooden table that occupied the spacious front room of the house. As I sat down, Seu

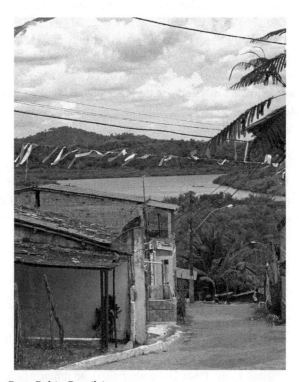

FIGURE 14.2 São Braz, Bahia, Brazil, in 2013.

Photograph by Michael Iyanaga.

Messias unexpectedly began telling me the story of a DVD documentary on Angola-style *capoeira*, the internationally known Brazilian sport/dance/martial art. I soon learned that Seu Messias was a highly respected master, or *mestre*, of capoeira who had been interviewed for the documentary. We then sat in awkward silence as we watched the forty-five-minute DVD, after which Seu Messias shared with me his memories and experiences of capoeira.

After what seemed an eternity, I began trying to encourage Seu Messias to talk about the *reza*, the reason I had come to his home in the first place. Soon the *mestre* began explaining to me the genesis of his devotion to Saint Roch, telling me of his childhood, his pet dog, his parents, his first wife, and his first home. All of these seemingly mundane details were somehow integral to his *reza*, but it would take me quite some time to understand why. Importantly, Seu Messias never actually referred to his *reza* as a "*reza*," calling it instead a "samba." While this terminological substitution is hardly uncommon (given the prominent role of samba at these patron saint festivals), it does reveal samba's centrality at Seu Messias's annual prayer ritual. The *mestre* then briefly touched on his encounter with Ralph Waddey: "My samba was very talked about. He [Waddey] came because it's very big. We have a novena, samba, and on the next day, the 17th [of August], we have capoeira."

The stories the *mestre* had been telling me were no doubt important to him, and they were a good way for me to connect with Seu Messias and learn about his life. But everything seemed only tangentially related to the recording; the restudy seemed to be going awry. Before arriving, after all, I had imagined that we might listen to the recording or at least that our conversation would revolve around the historical recording. But we barely even acknowledged the recording's existence, let alone did we discuss it. In fact, when I first arrived with the CD in hand, the *mestre*'s son suggested we give it a listen, an idea which Seu Messias dismissed out of hand: "Not now." Then, turning to me, he ambiguously justified his response: "Today marks a week that my brother has passed away." He said nothing more and though I did not quite understand, I intuitively knew not to insist. We simply left it at that. As I departed from Seu Messias's house that day, the octogenarian invited me to his annual *reza* for Saint Roch, which would be held at his home on August 16, the saint's official day. Excited to receive such an invitation, I thanked him and told him I would of course be delighted to attend.

Repatriation, Take Two—August 15, 2012

In the Recôncavo, *rezas* tend to be held on official Church-established saints' days. However, people often decide to hold the party earlier or later, a decision that is sometimes made at the last minute. Therefore, without a reliable phone number for Seu Messias, I had to confirm in-person that his bash for Saint Roch would, in fact, occur on August 16. I thus embarked on my second visit to Seu Messias's home, some eight months after first meeting him. I showed up just before noon, braving the incessant winter rainfall so typical of August, and was once again warmly received. Seu Messias cheered my arrival by explaining to a visiting neighbor that I had come back "seventeen years" after my "father" had recorded his "samba." I uncomfortably corrected him, noting that it had in fact been thirty-four years and that Waddey was a friend rather than my father. Unfazed by my attempt to amend the details, Seu Messias simply smiled and invited me into his home.

Accepting Dona Celina's meal offer this time around, I lunched with Seu Messias as we discussed the *reza* (what he referred to as his "samba") that would take place the following day. Soon after we finished eating, Dona Celina insisted that we listen to the historical recording. This time Seu Messias concurred and we sat quietly, listening to the *reza*. The *mestre* used a DVD player hooked up to his television to play the CD. Thus we both sat facing the blank blue screen as the digitized recording buzzed through the television's speakers. Soon after the recording began, Seu Messias's daughter walked into the room. He pointed to the television, springing a question on her: "Who's that?" She answered with a dumbfounded—albeit mostly apathetic—shrug. "It's Lourdes and Dora!" With only mild interest, his daughter asked, "Where's this from?" Raising his arm lengthwise and pointing toward the town plaza, he responded that it was from "the other house" (that is, his prior residence). And smiling, he continued, "It's from before you were alive!" For Seu Messias, the recording's antiquity was one of its most valuable assets.

On that August night in 1978, Waddey started his recorder just a minute or two late. Consequently, the audio abruptly begins at the tail end of the first prayer of the novena. In sequence is a several-second break before the cycle's second prayer. Likewise, the second prayer is separated by a short interval, as is the third prayer, and so on. These breaks—that is, moments without song—are filled with what I initially heard as nondescript chatter. This is common at *rezas*: following any sung text, people regularly hold side conversations about any quotidian issues they have on their minds (Iyanaga 2013b, xvi).

However, it was this apparent "babble" that most piqued Seu Messias's interest. In fact, while the *mestre* sat unmoved and uninterested during the singing, he would lean in toward the television's speakers after each song. Cocking his head sideways in order to expose his ear more fully to the chatter, the octogenarian listened intently and intensely. Then, with a spry exuberance, he would shout out the names of the people whose voices he recognized, reminiscing to me wistfully about those he had outlived.

Waddey's original reel tape recording of Seu Messias's 1978[11] *reza* is hours long. However, due to some technical difficulties, Waddey and I were only able to digitize the first half-hour of the *reza*. The recording, therefore, includes the novena, almost in its entirety (twenty-one minutes), clapped songs (*cantigas*) for Saint Roch (around two minutes), and about six minutes of guitars and percussion warming up before the boisterous improvised samba singing. Consequently, the samba vocals—vital to any samba performance and lasting for hours when originally performed in 1978—were entirely cut out of the digitized recording I repatriated to Seu Messias. This absence did not go unnoticed; the *mestre* lamented repeatedly that the samba was mostly missing from the recording. I assured him I would try to digitize the samba for him, but that it would probably take some time. Regretfully, however, I have been unable to acquire a copy of the complete 1978 recording and thus have yet to make good on my promise to deliver it to him.

Repatriation, Take Three—May 13, 2013

Nearly a year and a half after my first trip to Seu Messias's house, an interesting confluence of events allowed me to visit Seu Messias once again, but this time together with Ralph Waddey (Figure 14.3). Though Waddey had been unable to digitize for Seu Messias the samba from 1978, he did locate a digital copy of a different samba, recorded at Seu Messias's house in August 1982. Therefore, while I could not provide Seu Messias with a copy of his samba from 1978, I could at the very least facilitate his receipt of a different recording of nearly the same vintage.

We arrived in São Braz at around 11:30 a.m. As we entered Seu Messias's home, the now eighty-five-year-old man greeted us with a big smile, a handshake, and a hug, albeit a somewhat stoic one. We were invited to sit at the table, and before we knew it, Waddey and I were being served lunch by Dona Celina. Waddey gave the 1982 recording to Seu Messias and suggested that we all listen to it as we ate. As we listened, I asked Seu Messias about what he was hearing and, as he had done during our prior repatriation experience, the *mestre* pointed out the voices of many of the samba performers, telling us all about the men he could aurally recognize.

FIGURE 14.3 Left to right: Ralph Waddey and Seu Messias at Seu Messias's home in São Braz, Bahia, Brazil, 2013.

Photograph by Michael Iyanaga.

This CD, with nearly two hours of recorded samba, continued playing well after we finished lunch and served as background music for our further topics of conversation. Gradually running out of subjects to discuss with the octogenarian, and thinking that Seu Messias wanted a break from us, Waddey and I decided to take a brief walk outside. To Waddey's and my surprise, as soon as we stepped out into the front yard, Seu Messias turned off the DVD player and began watching television. Rather than allow the 1982 samba to keep playing, as he could no doubt have done, the *mestre* hesitated only seconds before stopping the CD. It was as if he had only been listening to the recording for our sakes, not his.

QUESTIONS RAISED, LESSONS LEARNED

My repatriation experiences taught me quite a bit about *rezas*, but not directly, and certainly not in the ways I had initially imagined. Returning Waddey's recordings to Seu Messias—an act that in itself had far less an impact on the *mestre* than I had anticipated—raised a whole host of new questions that would ultimately lead me to a more comprehensive understanding of the *reza* practice. I explore here some answers to what I believe are three of the most revealing inquiries: (1) How was the death of Seu Messias's brother related to his decision not to listen to the CD?, (2) Why was it the talking on the recording, rather than the singing, that most interested Seu Messias?, and (3) Why did Seu Messias lament not having the 1978 samba but seem mostly bored with the 1982 samba recording? These queries, resulting specifically from my repatriation experiences, might never have arisen through more typical interviews, conversations, and participant observation. After all, how could I ever have thought to ask them?

Let us begin by looking at the first—and for me the most vexing—question. What does a brother's death have to do with listening to a CD? After all, there was no indication that the *mestre*'s brother was on the CD or otherwise responsible for the event. Yet he was linked in deeper ways. Allow me to explain. First, it is important to remember that the CD was a sonic representation of Seu Messias's annual patron saint festival, which, for him, is mainly a "samba" for Saint Roch. Consequently, in the eyes of the *mestre*, I was repatriating a CD not of unison a capella singing—which is in fact mostly what the recording contains (something he could not have known before listening to it)—but rather of rollicking samba.

Still, samba is not just song and dance; it is also emotion. Samba is happiness (that is, *alegria*). This is a "metaphoric utterance" (Rice 2003, 164) that points to a naturalized equivalence between sound/dance and emotion that is central to understanding both samba and happiness in the Recôncavo. Happiness is not somehow "represented" by samba. Rather, the intrinsic link between samba and happiness is such that one serves as a quasi-surrogate of the other. In other words, to perform samba is to put one's own happiness on display. Similarly, in emic terms, happiness is key to defining samba. I have discussed this issue in some detail elsewhere (Iyanaga 2013b, 292–299), so I focus here only on the interconnectedness of happiness, death, and samba.

In the Recôncavo, death is invariably a moment of sadness, a moment of what people term "sentimento," or sentiment. For all intents and purposes, then, death silences samba. That is, because happiness and samba are so closely correlated, a lack of samba is a socially explicit sign of a lack of happiness. In the *reza* context, therefore, happiness and sadness are expressed through samba performance (or the lack thereof). Just as happiness is *socially* displayed and codified in samba performance, so too is personal/familial sadness made social by conspicuously refraining from and effectively silencing samba. And while never described as such, the silencing of samba might best be understood as a form of mourning, as the silencing lasts for a predetermined (though individually variable) period. While this period is most typically a year, for Seu Messias it appears to have only been a few months.

In practical terms, then, if a relative or close friend passes away before a previously scheduled samba performance, that performance will be canceled. I have witnessed this cancellation process innumerable times not only at *rezas* but also at other types of events, both public and private. But there is more, and herein lies the ethnographic lesson I learned with Seu Messias: the happiness is so intrinsically linked to the samba that simply listening to it—even a samba recorded a generation earlier—would disrespect the appropriate "sentiment." When one is in a state of mourning it is socially inappropriate to experience (even if only aurally) the "happiness" embodied so transparently in samba. The point, clear to me only after prolonged reflection, is that Seu Messias's deceased brother deserved "sentiment," even if only in symbolic social terms, and this meant that the samba I brought with me had to be silenced.

In some ways, my second question, regarding the value of mundane chatter, challenges one of the most consecrated dichotomies of classical social science: the division between the sacred and the profane. Whether it is the world according to Durkheim, Turner, Geertz, or Marx, the sacred and its rituals have been definitionally distinct from the "real" world of everyday life. According to this classic view of society, then, the *reza* would be a sacred event distinct from the profane quotidian. Indeed, this is precisely how some have interpreted this Bahian prayer tradition (e.g., Marcelin 1996). Yet upon listening to the recording of this religious moment from 1978, Seu Messias heard something that was much more human than divine. In fact, he could clearly hear the voices and the topics of conversation they expressed, and it was only this "profane" aspect that seemed to matter. For Seu Messias, the *reza* is not just a devotion to a spiritual entity. It is also a precious moment of social interaction, not because it is separate from the profane but because it embraces it. Making Jean and John Comaroff's (1993, xvi) words my own, "[r]ather than being reduced to a species of ceremonial action that insulates enchanted, self-reproducing systems from the 'real' world, then, ritual may be seen for what it often is: a vital element in the processes that make and remake social facts and collective identities."

The abrupt dialogues were precisely what made the recording special; they marked its historicalness in ways that the liturgy never would. This is because of emic understandings of musical continuity and the immutability of the novena. As I have argued elsewhere, as long as the function and intent of each prayer remain unaltered, devotees tend to view the prayers as unchanging from year to year even if some of the texts or melodies are different (Iyanaga 2013a). In other words, independent of the melody or specific text, every song *for* Saint Roch (the Virgin Mary, God, Saint Anthony, etc.) would essentially be treated as "the same."[12] This suggests that when viewed through a broader emic frame, the (unchanging) routine prayer cycle serves as something of a backdrop for the nonroutine, unique conversations between friends and neighbors. Thus for someone seeking to remember the past, which is apparently the only reason Seu Messias would want to listen to this old recording, the "mundane chatter," as I heard it, was much more valuable than the "same" songs he hears annually. Seu Messias was not anomalous. More often than not, when I asked other devotees about their annual festivals, they, like Seu Messias, nearly always focused on the specific people involved in the celebrations.

Therein hid another, subtle methodological lesson: limiting our field recordings of events/rituals to only the *musical* moments because we prejudge them as most valuable can—and often will—produce a recording that misses, from the participants' perspectives, the whole point. If Seu Messias is any indication, then, devotees understand that although the singing at a *reza* can (theoretically) be performed by *anyone*, it never is *just anyone*; rather it is always performed by "someones." That is, attendees at *rezas* are always people who have names and faces, and ultimately matter to the party host in far more intimate ways than a musical ethnographer might ever guess.

So how to explain Seu Messias's disinterest in the 1982 samba recording? Try as I might, I have been unable to articulate this question to Seu Messias as effectively as I would like. But I have gained some insights. In a visit to the *mestre*'s home in early 2017, I tried yet again to bring up the issue. When I asked him, quite directly, whether he preferred the 1978 recording to the 1982 recording, he simply affirmed that he enjoyed them both equally. I thus turned to a different tactic. Upon my arrival at his home earlier that morning, Seu Messias had shown me that he carefully guarded the half-dozen or so CDs comprising the many hours of samba I had recorded at his *reza* in 2012. I asked him if so many hours of samba were not almost too much samba. He grinned and said only, "It's a lot of samba." I insisted on my line of questioning: "Is a recording better when it's shorter or longer?" "Shorter," he immediately responded. "Do you listen to these recordings for the music or the people?" I was leading him a bit, but I could not figure out how else to ask the question. He was again quick to answer: "The people."

The musical content was apparently far less interesting to the eighty-nine-year-old *mestre* than the social content, and made a longer recording merely repetitive. This is because the samba, as with the *novena*, may always be different in its texts and melodies but the function—the songs' defining trait—never is (Iyanaga 2013a, 115–116). Therefore, much like the novena, the only thing that changes from year to year are the performers. Importantly, these samba musicians are rarely female. In fact, gender distinctions tend to underlie the *reza*'s two main musical moments (though this is perhaps more a tendency than a rule): novena:female::samba:male. What is more, while women tend to participate in both moments—in the novena they lead the singing and in the samba they participate as dancers and sing the refrain—men generally make themselves absent during the novena. They stand outside, conversing, or they simply arrive after the novena has finished. Therefore, although the chatter of the 1978 novena gave Seu Messias a good sense of the female presence at that year's event, it could not help him remember the men who attended.

Consequently, just as the conversations from the 1978 recording of the novena mattered most to Seu Messias because they helped him remember the women who were active in his *reza* three decades before, he lamented the lack of samba not so much for the samba itself as for the sonic hints it would give him regarding the men who had performed that year. As such, a few minutes of the 1982 samba recordings were quite sufficient for Seu Messias. He recognized the voices, relished tacitly a few memories of the past, and then grew bored. It seems to me that Seu Messias was not uninterested in the 1982 recording. Rather, after obtaining the information that most interested him, the *mestre* did not feel compelled to continue listening to the samba.

The more important ethnographic point, however, may have been the fact that the recorded samba served a function like that of the recorded novena. This suggests that the two musical moments, which seem so different—one is a capella singing in Portuguese and Latin that follows a strict liturgy while the other is a more spontaneous Afro-Brazilian dance music—in fact function similarly. Both are social celebrations in the name of the saint. In this sense, there is little *conceptual* difference between Catholic prayers and samba dancing. Both are fundamentally, though not exclusively, functional musical modes: the prayers revivify the saint for the year and the samba celebrates that renewed life (Iyanaga 2013b, 62–104).

Concluding Thoughts

Repatriation is thus not just a means of advocacy; it is also a research method. Musical or sound repatriation should be treated not simply as ancillary "applied" or "advocative" work, but as an ethnomusicological method such that repatriating sound is also doing ethnomusicology in the most classic sense. We know that repatriation can return some power—in the form of property and knowledge—to "subjects" who have been unwittingly exploited by our (usually) well-intentioned disciplinary ancestors.[13] Repatriation can just as well help communities remember the past and thus build new futures, often in ways that would be difficult or impossible to predict. In addition, as I have argued in this essay, repatriation can also help ethnographers do better work and write better ethnographies.

Earlier in this chapter, I suggested that concentrating on the methodological benefits of repatriation, rather than on how repatriation can help communities, might seem "self-serving." And while my focus here has indeed been on how repatriation can serve "us" (professional ethnomusicologists),[14] this should not suggest that I do not also recognize how important repatriation can be for communities the world over. And in fact, using repatriation more in our fieldwork may actually stimulate us to look harder for recordings that could be returned to communities. At the same time, though, it would be unwise to forget that repatriation nearly always also benefits (whether implicitly or explicitly) the repatriators. For example, the fact that repatriation is valuable to communities serves as a good, ethical justification for why sound archives are needed (and why archivists should continue to be employed), as well as why funds should be allocated for projects such as the Music of Uganda Repatriation Project, the Federal Cylinder Project, India's Archive and Research Center for Ethnomusicology, and so forth.

My point is that repatriation always serves both sides of the exchange, even if the power dynamics and the benefits vary from case to case. This is precisely why exploring the specific ways in which repatriation has been ethnographically beneficial in any given case may be so useful. Judging by my own case study, together with those I cited earlier, repatriation can (at the very least) facilitate interpersonal interactions, quicken the acquisition of ethnographic data, elucidate music's role in individual and community lives, and draw out emic perspectives regarding musical change, aesthetic tastes, and metaphors of musical truth. But this is only the tip of the iceberg; each instance of repatriation harbors the possibility for novel types of ethnographic insight and new opportunities to engage individuals and communities in conversations about the music that matters to them.

NOTES

1. Parts of this chapter were presented on May 29, 2013, at the biennial Conference of the Brazilian Association of Ethnomusicology (ABET), held in João Pessoa, Brazil. I thank Ralph Waddey and Carlos Sandroni for insightful comments. I also owe a debt of gratitude to Anthony Seeger, whose incisive suggestions on an earlier version of this chapter were, as always, transformative. This chapter was completed with funding from a Fulbright Postdoctoral Award.

2. The importance of this pair of articles is discernable, at the very least, from the number of authors who continue to cite them positively (Zamith 1995; Fryer 2000; Sandroni 2001, 2010; Döring 2004; Lühning 2004; Carmo 2009; Crook 2009; Iyanaga 2010; Nobre 2013). Indeed, the seemingly timeless relevance of Waddey's essays is further underscored by their republication (in Portuguese translation) in the successful dossier submitted to UNESCO for inclusion of *samba-de-roda* on its list "Masterpieces of the Oral and Intangible Heritage of Humanity" (Sandroni and Sant'Anna 2007).

3. The performed instruments generally include *pandeiros* (tambourines), cylindrical membrane drums, guitars, *cavaquinhos* (small, steel-stringed ukuleles), and *violas* (ten-string guitars).

4. The issue of repatriation was an important—albeit less prominent—part of ethnomusicological thought well before the 1980s. And repatriation has always carried with it an ethical tone. According to Robert Lancefield, for instance, the ethnomusicologist David McAllester had most wanted his Navajo recordings to assist the Navajo community by

serving "as a means of passing along ceremonial songs to future generations" (Lancefield 1998, 56).

5. These concerns might be divided into three basic categories: (1) the aftereffects of repatriation (Seeger 1999; Hilder 2012; Kahunde 2012; Landau 2012; Lobley 2012; Fox 2013), (2) ethical and practical issues of dissemination (Gray 1996; Toelken 1998; Brinkhurst 2012; Niles 2012; Averill 2013), and (3) discussions of intellectual property rights (Seeger 1992; Lancefield 1998).

6. One salient example of this "lab"-"field" cycle is discernable in a fascinating experience of the Music of Uganda Repatriation Project, which initiated the repatriation of Klaus Wachsmann's recordings in Uganda: "Recordings were played back for small focus groups. . . . The team used these meetings to disseminate the materials and to help determine the most effective way to disseminate materials in the future. These meetings subsequently shaped the design and direction of the research" (Nannyonga-Tamusuza and Weintraub 2012, 218).

7. I have translated this citation from Portuguese. All subsequent translations are also mine.

8. The results of this restudy were published mainly in the form of a CD titled *Responde a roda outra vez: Música tradicional de Pernambuco e da Paraíba no Trajeto da Missão de 1938* (Sandroni 2004).

9. There are of course other methodological approaches that have become part of ethnomusicology, and this is but a short list. However, my point is that each of these has become, in broad terms, consecrated as an important means of doing ethnomusicology. Arguably, ethnomusicology (as comparative musicology) would never have been born without the methodological use of transcription (of wax cylinder recordings) (Pinto 2005), which continues to be a foundation of ethnomusicological analysis. And participant observation has no doubt been a part of ethnographic research on music at least since the mid-twentieth century, particularly emphasized, for example, by Merriam (1964) in his seminal *The Anthropology of Music.* "Bi-musicality," a term coined and advocated by Hood (1957, 1960), continues to be important in the field even if it is not necessarily designated as such (Baily 2001). Finally, since at least the mid-twentieth century, film has occupied a place of growing importance in the development of new methodological approaches to music (Kubik 1965, 1972; Qureshi 1987; Harbert 2010).

10. In Brazilian Portuguese, as with the term "Seu" for adult males, the honorific title "Dona" is used to recognize adult females (see Iyanaga 2013b, xii).

11. An unpublished recording made by Ralph Waddey in 1978.

12. This is a more complex issue than I can elaborate upon here. It is not exactly that people would not recognize a difference in melody or text. Rather, as long as the function is unaltered (e.g., the opening song, a song to bless the Virgin Mary, a song to ask for the saint's blessing, etc.), people would *say* it is "the same" (Iyanaga 2013a, 115–116).

13. Though it is important not to forget how our scholars have benefited from the recordings they have collected. As Fox (2013, 534) notes, "[a] vast body of field recordings made during the twentieth century, however, ostensibly collected for the purposes of research and other purportedly noncommercial pursuits (preserving 'vanishing' cultures as *national* cultural patrimony chief among them), have nonetheless provided financial and other benefits to collectors and owners of these materials, over long periods of time."

14. It is worth noting that despite ethnomusicology's roots in colonial expansion (Ringer 1991, 191), the field has arguably been important as a counterhegemonic voice within music scholarship due to its "canonic reflexivity" (Bohlman 1992, 118).

References

Averill, Gage. 2013. "Preface: A (Knotted) Stitch in Time, Weaving Connections between Collections." In *Congoma Calling: Spirits and Rhythms of Freedom in Brazilian Jongo Slavery Songs*, edited by Pedro Meira Monteiro and Michael Stone, 7–10. Dartmouth, MA: Laabst.

Baily, John. 2001. "Learning to Perform as a Research Technique in Ethnomusicology." *British Journal of Ethnomusicology* 10 (2): 85–98.

Bohlman, Philip V. 1992. "Ethnomusicology's Challenge to the Canon; the Canon's Challenge to Ethnomusicology." In *Disciplining Music: Musicology and Its Canons*, edited by Katherine Bergeron and Philip V. Bohlman, 116–136. Chicago: University of Chicago Press.

Brinkhurst, Emma. 2012. "Archives and Access: Reaching Out to the Somali Community of London's King's Cross." *Ethnomusicology Forum* 21 (2): 243–258.

Carmo, Raiana Maciel do. 2009. "A política de salvaguarda do patrimônio imaterial e os seus impactos no samba de roda do Recôncavo Baiano." MA thesis, Universidade Federal da Bahia.

Comaroff, Jean, and John Comaroff. 1993. "Introduction." In *Modernity and Its Malcontents: Ritual and Power in Postcolonial Africa*, edited by Jean Comaroff and John Comaroff, xi–xxxi. Chicago: University of Chicago Press.

Crook, Larry. 2009. *Focus: Music of Northeast Brasil*. 2nd ed. New York: Routledge.

Dirksen, Rebecca. 2013. "Reconsidering Theory and Practice in Ethnomusicology: Applying, Advocating, and Engaging beyond Academia." *Ethnomusicology Review* 17. http://ethnomusicologyreview.ucla.edu/journal/volume/17/piece/602 (accessed May 14, 2013).

Döring, Katharina. 2004. "O samba da Bahia: Tradição pouco conhecida." *ICTUS* 5: 69–92.

Fox, Aaron A. 2013. "Repatriation as Reanimation through Reciprocity." In *The Cambridge History of World Music*, edited by Philip V. Bohlman, 522–554. Cambridge: Cambridge University Press.

Fryer, Peter. 2000. *Rhythms of Resistance: African Musical Heritage in Brazil*. Hanover, NH: Wesleyan University Press.

Gray, Judith. 1996. "Returning Music to the Makers: The Library of Congress, American Indians, and the Federal Cylinder Project." *Cultural Survival Quarterly* 20 (4). http://www.culturalsurvival.org/ourpublications/csq/article/returning-music-makers-the-library-congress-american-indians-and-federal (accessed June 22, 2013).

Harbert, Benjamin J. 2010. "Doing Time: The Work of Music in Louisiana Prisons." PhD diss., University of California, Los Angeles.

Hilder, Thomas R. 2012. "Repatriation, Revival and Transmission: The Politics of a Sámi Musical Heritage." *Ethnomusicology Forum* 21 (2): 161–179.

Hood, Mantle. 1957. "Training and Research Methods in Ethnomusicology." *Ethnomusicology* 1 (11): 2–8.

Hood, Mantle. 1960. "The Challenge of 'Bi-Musicality.'" *Ethnomusicology* 4 (2): 55–59.

Iyanaga, Michael. 2010. "O samba de caruru da Bahia: Tradição pouco conhecida." *ICTUS* 11 (2): 120–150.

Iyanaga, Michael. 2013a. "O reestudo e a etnomusicologia brasileira: Três lições teóricas a partir de uma volta à Bahia de Ralph Waddey." *Música e Cultura* 8 (1): 109–120.

Iyanaga, Michael. 2013b. "New World Songs for Catholic Saints: Domestic Performances of Devotion and History in Bahia, Brazil." PhD diss., University of California, Los Angeles.

Jairazbhoy, Nazir Ali. 1991. "The First Restudy of Arnold Bake's Fieldwork in India." In *Comparative Musicology and Anthropology of Music: Essays on the History of*

Ethnomusicology, edited by Bruno Nettl and Philip V. Bohlman, 210–227. Chicago: University of Chicago Press.

Jairazbhoy, Nazir Ali, and Amy Catlin. 1990. *Bake Restudy 1984*. VHS. Van Nuys, CA: Apsara Media for Intercultural Education, 1990.

Kahunde, Samuel. 2012. "Repatriating Archival Sound Recordings to Revive Traditions: The Role of the Klaus Wachsmann Recordings in the Revival of the Royal Music of Bunyoro-Kitara, Uganda." *Ethnomusicology Forum* 21 (2): 197–219.

Kubik, Gerhard. 1965. "Transcription of Mangwilo Xylophone Music from Film Strips." *African Music* 3 (4): 35–51.

Kubik, Gerhard. 1972. "Transcription of African Music from Silent Film: Theory and Methods." *African Music* 5 (1): 28–39.

Lancefield, Robert C. 1998. "'Musical Traces' Retraceable Paths: The Repatriation of Recorded Sound." *Journal of Folklore Research* 35 (1): 47–68. Also reprinted in this Handbook.

Landau, Carolyn. 2012. "Disseminating Music amongst Moroccans in Britain: Exploring the Value of Archival Sound Recordings for a Cultural Heritage Community in the Diaspora." *Ethnomusicology Forum* 21 (2): 259–277.

Landau, Carolyn, and Janet Topp Fargion. 2012. "We're All Archivists Now: Towards a More Equitable Ethnomusicology." *Ethnomusicology Forum* 21 (2): 125–140.

Lobley, Noel. 2012. "Taking Xhosa Music out of the Fridge and into the Townships." *Ethnomusicology Forum* 21 (2): 181–195.

Lühning, Angela Elisabeth. 2004. "Os sons da Bahia: Pesquisa etnomusicológica." *Revista da Bahia* 32 (39): 38–48.

Lühning, Angela Elisabeth, Tiago Carvalho, Flávia Diniz, and Aaron Lopes. 2016. "Ethnomusicological Goals and Challenges in Brazil." *World of Music* 5 (1): 23–53.

Marcelin, Louis Herns. 1996. "A invenção da família afro-americana: Família, parentesco e domesticidade entre os negros do Recôncavo da Bahia, Brasil." PhD diss., Universidade Federal do Rio de Janeiro.

Merriam, Alan P. 1964. *The Anthropology of Music*. Evanston, IL: Northwestern University Press.

Nannyonga-Tamusuza, Sylvia, and Andrew N. Weintraub. 2012. "The Audible Future: Reimagining the Role of Sound Archives and Sound Repatriation in Uganda." *Ethnomusicology* 56 (2): 206–233.

Niles, Don. 2012. "The National Repatriation of Papua New Guinea Recordings: Experiences Straddling World War II." *Ethnomusicology Forum* 21 (2): 141–159.

Nobre, Cássio. 2013. "Samba de viola machete: Considerações sobre tradição e transformação no samba de roda do Recôncavo Baiano." In *Diversidade cultural afro-brasileira: Ensaios e reflexões*, edited by Carlos Alves Moura, 29–44. Brasília: Fundação Cultural Palmares.

Pinto, Tiago de Oliveira. 2005. "Cem anos de etnomusicologia e a 'era fonográfica' da disciplina no Brasil." In *Etnomusicologia: Lugares e caminhos, fronteiras e diálogos*, edited by Angela Elisabeth Lühning and Laila Andresa Cavalcante Rosa, 103–124. Annals of the 2nd National Conference of the Associação Brasileira de Etnomusicologia. Salvador: Contexto.

Qureshi, Regula. 1987. "Musical Sound and Contextual Input: A Performance Model for Musical Analysis." *Ethnomusicology* 31 (1): 56–86.

Rice, Timothy. 2003. "Time, Place, and Metaphor in Musical Experience and Ethnography." *Ethnomusicology* 47 (2): 151–179.

Ringer, Alexander L. 1991. "One World or None? Untimely Reflections on a Timely Musicological Question." In *Comparative Musicology and Anthropology of Music: Essays on the History of Ethnomusicology*, edited by Bruno Nettl and Philip V. Bohlman, 187–198. Chicago: University of Chicago Press.

Sandroni, Carlos. 2001. *Feitiço decente: Transformações do samba no Rio de Janeiro, 1917–1933.* Rio de Janeiro: Zahar.

Sandroni, Carlos, ed. 2004. *Responde a roda outra vez: Música tradicional de Pernambuco e da Paraíba no Trajeto da Missão de 1938.* CD. Recife: Núcleo de Etnomusicologia da UFPE.

Sandroni, Carlos. 2005. "O lugar do etnomusicólogo junto às comunidades pesquisadas: 'Devolução' de registros sonoros como imperativo científico." In *Etnomusicologia: Lugares e caminhos, fronteiras e diálogos*, edited by Angela Elisabeth Lühning and Laila Andresa Cavalcante Rosa, 49–56. Annals of the 2nd National Conference of the Associação Brasileira de Etnomusicologia. Salvador: Contexto.

Sandroni, Carlos. 2010. "Samba de roda, patrimônio imaterial da humanidade." *Estudos avançados* 24 (69): 373–388.

Sandroni, Carlos. 2014. "O acervo da Missão de Pesquisas Folclóricas, 1938–2012." *Debates* 12: 55–62.

Sandroni, Carlos, and Marcia Sant'Anna, eds. 2007. *Samba de Roda do Recôncavo Baiano.* Dossiê IPHAN 4. Brasília: IPHAN.

Seeger, Anthony. 1986. "The Role of Sound Archives in Ethnomusicology Today." *Ethnomusicology* 30 (2): 261–276.

Seeger, Anthony. 1992. "Ethnomusicology and Music Law." *Ethnomusicology* 36 (3): 345–359.

Seeger, Anthony. 1996. "Ethnomusicologists, Archives, Professional Organizations, and the Shifting Ethics of Intellectual Property." *Yearbook for Traditional Music* 28: 87–105.

Seeger, Anthony. 1999. "Happy Birthday ATM: Ethnographic Futures of the Archives of the 21st Century." *Resound: A Quarterly of the Archives of Traditional Music* 18 (1): 1–3.

Seeger, Anthony. 2004 [1987]. *Why Suyá Sing: A Musical Anthropology of an Amazonian People.* Urbana: University of Illinois Press.

Seeger, Anthony. 2006. "Lost Lineages and Neglected Peers: Ethnomusicologists outside Academia." *Ethnomusicology* 50 (2): 214–235.

Seeger, Anthony. 2011. "New Technology Requires New Collaborations: Changing Ourselves to Better Shape the Future." *Musicology Australia* 27 (1): 94–110.

Seeger, Anthony. 2014. "The Reel Living Dead: Tales of Sound from the Archival Vaults in Memory of Elizabeth Travassos." *Debates* 12: 25–33.

Toelken, Barre. 1998. "The Yellowman Tapes, 1966-1997." *Journal of American Folklore* 111 (442): 381-391.

Waddey, Ralph. 1980. "'Viola de Samba' and 'Samba de Viola' in the 'Reconcavo' of Bahia (Brazil)." *Latin America Music Review* 1 (2): 196–212.

Waddey, Ralph. 1981. "'Viola de Samba' and 'Samba de Viola' in the 'Reconcavo' of Bahia (Brazil), Part 2: 'Samba de Viola.'" *Latin America Music Review* 2 (2): 252–279.

Zamith, Rosa Maria. 1995. "O samba-de-roda baiano em tempo e espaço." *Revista Interfaces* 1 (2): 53–66.

CHAPTER 15

....

TEACHERS AS AGENTS
OF THE REPATRIATION
OF MUSIC AND CULTURAL
HERITAGE

....

PATRICIA SHEHAN CAMPBELL
AND J. CHRISTOPHER ROBERTS

TEACHERS are rarely considered to be the influential agents they are in their efforts to share history and cultural heritage to children and youth in their classrooms. Not even when they are regularly engaging in the return of heritage music to young members of the "source culture" through the lessons they have designed are they often seen for their role in promoting and revitalizing cultural expressions. In this chapter, we argue that teachers are repatriating music to their students. Whether or not they are aware of the UNESCO (2003, Article 2) acknowledgment of the repatriation of intangible cultural heritage as a valued and necessary act, teachers are aching to open up the ears and minds of their young students to the world through music meant for listening to, singing, playing, dancing, and creating in new and personal ways but within the style of various cultural expressions. Teachers may not be attuned to the backstory of repatriation as the complex phenomenon it is, involving culture-bearers, collectors, and culture-brokers from the realms of anthropology, ethnomusicology, and folklore in preserving precious artifacts and ideas (Stefano, Davis, and Corsane 2012). Yet without their use of "the 'r' word"—which is not in common usage among teachers—repatriation nonetheless regularly occurs through the music they offer their young students in thoughtfully designed and age-appropriate curricular experiences. We argue and provide evidence to support the position that teachers have been overlooked in their repatriation efforts and impact, and that they are an important component in the preservation and transmission of cultural expressions and artistic understandings. Their repatriative efforts occur along a continuum of children's own musical expressions, those of children in other cultural communities, and the adult music of their heritage cultures. The pedagogical pathways that teachers design and deliver for the music at the core of their lessons are effectively facilitating opportunities for their students to know and respect cultural heritage, both close to and further afield from their immediate musical identities.

ARCHIVED RECORDINGS
AS SOURCE MATERIALS FOR TEACHERS

The preservation of different musical practices is a longstanding effort of music and culture scholars who work to document through recordings the music and spoken word of people in a broad array of the world's cultures. Listeners of every sort, from hobbyists to academicians, and from teachers to their students, have been drawn to archived recordings that entertain, educate, and entice them to know the musical and cultural expressions of their own and other heritages (Milner, 2009). For teachers in search of source materials for their students, archives can appear overwhelming at times but are inarguably rich with potential curricular integration. Teachers can select from among the rich recorded collections of music, dance, and spoken word (poetry, public speeches, and the dramatic arts) and insert these selections into carefully crafted pedagogical plans for the lessons they will facilitate in music as well as in the social sciences and language arts.

Because some teachers with little time on their hands may view archives of recordings as "dark, lifeless places hidden in basements" (Seeger 1986, 89), there is a pressing need to provide pre-service and in-service education that will enable them to seek out and prepare experiences for their students in heritage songs, instrumental music, and stories. With support for full discovery of the nature and substance of both physical and online collections, teachers can identify and adjust material they judge to be appropriate and relevant for repatriating to young students. This leads to their development of effective means by which to share that music and its constituent cultural knowledge. Teachers troll archived collections for the adult-made music of the Civil War, the Silk Road, historic freedom movements, and places in the world that rise to prominence in current events featured on the daily news. Their young students learn about histories of civilizations through song, and about not only inherited traditions from the past but also contemporary rural and urban practices. From wedding music to songs of war, the archived recordings of adult music are important in setting the scenes, telling the stories, and thus ensuring that knowledge of people, places, and times can be known. In many multicultural classrooms, much of the adult-made music selected for lessons serves to connect children to their own lives, and to those of their parents and grandparents. In this sense, then, teachers' use of archived recordings can be taken as a pathway to repatriation when young listeners encounter songs that express their cultural heritage.

While adult music constitutes the clear majority of recorded music, there are nonetheless precious, even priceless, historical recordings of children's musical practices in national and international collections to which teachers have access. Present within the archives of Smithsonian Folkways Recordings, the Library of Congress, and the Association for Cultural Equity are children's songs, singing games, chants, rhythmic and rhymed poetry, stories and dramatizations, instrumental compositions, and even examples of children's jokes, riddles, colloquialisms, and other verbal childlore. Recordings by ethnomusicologists and folklorists of children's expressive practices are found alongside adult-made music within archives associated with university programs, including Indiana University's Archives of Traditional Music, UCLA's Ethnomusicology Archive, and the Ethnomusicology Archives at the University of Washington. In this last archive are found the recordings of children's music of the Venda of South Africa first recorded in 1956–1958 by John Blacking (1967) and "Voices of the First People," a collection of Lushootseed stories and songs for community members from the very young to the experienced and elderly.

Beyond conventional archives, there are also collections of children's music in publications that function as archives, such as the recordings that accompany the African American children's songs in *Step It Down* (Jones and Hawes 1972), the recordings of children's songs from England, Scotland, and Wales associated with the work of British folklorists Peter and Iona Opie (*The Singing Game*, 1985), and the companion website to the *Oxford Handbook of Children's Musical Cultures* (Campbell and Wiggins 2013), with audio and video recordings of children's songs from a sampling of world cultures. Teachers have effectively drawn from these recordings to integrate musical and textual features into curricular studies in music, the language arts, social studies, and even physical education. Their use of these recordings repatriates the songs of children that belong with children, whether as members of a universal "children's culture" or as members of particular communities of children.

The presence and availability to teachers of archived recordings of children is essential to their provision of meaningful repatriative experiences for the young people in their classrooms. In a global view of the child's musical culture, her sonic world comprises music of the children she knows and of the adult community that surrounds her. At the same time, her musical culture is linked to children's music elsewhere in the world, since she is a bona fide member of children's culture and the musical means by which they express themselves in song, chant, rhythmic rhymes, and dance. Thus there is the potential, through the pedagogical application of archived recordings to supplement informal at-home experiences, for teachers to work across a continuum of repatriation acts to bring children into a full-fledged experience of their musical identities within the lessons they design and deliver in schools.

MUSIC-CULTURAL HERITAGE
IN THE CLASSROOM

Three complementary yet distinct dimensions are evident in the repatriation by teachers of intangible cultural heritage in and through music into the classrooms of children and youth. We define them briefly and then proceed to sections that explain, exemplify, and illuminate how music figures prominently in work by teachers to preserve and transmit music that meets the curricular aims of developing an understanding by students of cultural expressions, folklife and folklore, and customs and traditions.

1. *"Close-By" Child-Songs by Children.* The most directly repatriative experience consists of the transmission by teachers of children's music from the children's home culture, or "child-songs" by children and youth, to their young students (Campbell 1991, 2009, 2010). Historic recordings of child-songs from the Caribbean, from Italy and Spain, and from the American South have been taught to children whose families trace their histories to these places and communities (Lomax and Hawes 1997). These child-songs are considered "close-by" by virtue of the musical and linguistic elements that link them to the familiar music of children's home and family culture. As well, they may be songs that are already known by children, or variants of familiar songs. African American child-songs, many with a long and continuing presence in the developmental years of young African American children of a century or more, are frequently pulled by their teachers from archived recordings and introduced to them. They are close-by to some of the repertoire that the children may already know from experiences outside of school. Other "close by" song examples used by teachers in a repatriative manner include Anglo-American child-songs taught to children whose families identify as Anglo-American, and Puerto Rican child-songs taught to children of Puerto Rican parentage, and Chinese child-songs taught to children of Chinese heritage.

2. *Child-Songs from Further Afield.* In many school music programs, as well as in early childhood centers and preschool programs, and in other community spaces in which children are educated, enriched, and nurtured, teachers feature children's music from all corners of the world. Whether this music is performed by adults (Campbell 1991, 2009, 2010) or by children, it offers young students a sense of how children think and behave in ways that are cross-cultural or culture-specific. These child-songs feature children's voices in multiple languages, perpetuating valued folklore beliefs and practices, joining in on seasonal, national, and regional festivities, and working out social relationships, understandings, and skills in playful ways. The singing games, in many cultures, are evidence that children in new and unfamiliar places enjoy gathering in circles, in lines, and with partners,

and find it engaging to pass stones on the pulse while singing, or imitate the movements of a center-circle leader, or enter into a chase around the circle's outside, or rhythmically hand-clap with a partner. Teachers frequently feature child-songs from multiple cultures, often "further afield," in order to multiculturalize their curricular program (Campbell, McCullough-Brabson, and Tucker 1994); they pique children's attention for knowing how these songs compare to the close-by child-songs they already know.

3. *Adult Cultural Heritage Music.* The curricular inclusion by teachers of adult cultural heritage music is standard practice in schools and is particularly prominent in programs geared to children and young teens in elementary and middle schools. Rather than covering all the world's music, teachers frequently match their lesson content to the cultural identities of their students. In neighborhood schools, teachers work together with community volunteers to create curriculum with high relevance to the local cultures, where adult musicians may be invited in to perform local music. In their classroom lessons, music teachers are repatriative in their efforts to offer young students opportunities to know their family heritage music through study units replete with listening and performance. Thus, depending on the community, teachers may teach units featuring a variety of adult cultural heritage music: Filipino *rondalla* and *kulintang* music; polka music from Germany, Poland, and Slovakia; South Asian *bhangra*; jigs and reels from Ireland and Scotland. Teachers may develop lessons of adult-performed music from anywhere in the world, but it is when they tap for curricular use the archived recordings of music (and live musicians) with which their students and their families are associated that they are then engaging in the repatriation process.

"LONDON BRIDGE IS BOUNCIN' DOWN": CLOSE-BY CHILD-SONGS BY CHILDREN

In 1948, Moses Asch founded the Folkways record label (rechristened Smithsonian Folkways Recordings in 1987, once it was purchased by the Smithsonian Institution), and he sought successfully to realize a vision of publishing recordings of music from the far reaches of the world. Music highlighting children's voices and singing their own songs constitutes a valued portion of the Folkways catalog, with a treasury of field recordings released between 1952 and 1980, including *Game Songs of French Canada* (FW 7214) and *Children's Songs and Games from Ecuador, Mexico, and Puerto Rico* (FW 7854). Other albums hold examples of children's musical cultures residing alongside music of adults, with one or two children's songs or singing games found on albums from the US South, Botswana, Japan, and the western Congo. Taken individually and collectively, these recordings provide an opportunity for teachers to provide children access to a range of children's music to a range of children's music from around the world or to focus on one set of recordings from a particular region (Roberts 2013).

For teachers in American schools, recordings from the Folkways archives also provide the opportunity to repatriate American children's musical cultures. Albums such as the 1953 release *1, 2, 3, and a Zing Zing Zing* (FW 7003) and the 1979 album *Songs for Children from New York City* (FW 7858) contain recordings of children's music, some of which are familiar to children even today and others that have not continued to be a general part of children's song repertoire. When a teacher selects a song that lost its cultural currency over the years, then teaches that song to children, it serves as a form of repatriation; without this purposeful intention of the teacher, the song would be lost to time. For example, many kindergarten students enter school knowing "London Bridge," a classic song among English speakers in the United States. A search of the Smithsonian Folkways online archives turns up more than a half-dozen versions of the song, including "London Bridge Is Bouncin' Down," released on *Songs for Children from New York City* (see Figure 15.1 for notation). Many aspects of this song variant are common among children's musical cultures in the United States. The version featured on this forty-year-old recording contains more syncopation than the more well-known variant, the participants do not simply sit and sing but play a game with movement, and the game itself encourages children's creativity in that individual children sing while performing invented movements (Campbell 1991; Marsh 2008; Merrill-Mirsky 1986). In addition, the vocal tessitura on the recording is lower than the vocal range that is typically taught in school settings (Phillips 2014); this is a common performance preference of children who, when left to their own devices to do so, enjoy singing in a deeper chest-centered manner that sounds to them more "mature" (Marsh 2008). On the recording, the tessitura lies low enough for the children so that contemporary Western conceptions of "in-tune singing," a primary goal of music teachers, is not attainable by the children due to the physiological characteristics of their voices.

As such, the performance practice brings up an interesting point for teachers when considering repatriation. Philosophically, acts of repatriation are partly intended to reempower the culture-bearers—in this case, the children. However, the power relationship in the teacher-student relationship is significantly weighted to one side, and teachers, operating in the broader context of school-based settings, have other curricular requirements to meet. In attempting to repatriate this music to them, how much alteration should be made? A teacher with repatriation as a primary motivator might choose to play the recording for the children, model the game, and then lead the children through the game play in the same key. Ultimately, the teacher would turn over game leadership responsibilities to the children, and if they chose to shift to a higher register to facilitate pitch accuracy, it would be a child-based decision. Alternatively, a teacher whose primary focus was conventional skill development might choose to play the game as found on the recording, but raise the pitch to a level where the children would be able to sing with greater pitch accuracy. Music teachers in the United States commonly ask their children to sing in their head voice, the lighter and higher voice that

London Bridge Is Bouncin' Down

FIGURE 15.1 Edet, Edna, collector, 1979. *Songs for Children from New York City* (FW7858). Washington, DC: Smithsonian Folkways. Compact disc.

is found toward the upper end of their range—a singing style that would be highly different from that found on the recording (and, indeed, from most examples of children's self-directed singing game play in the United States). Yet another way for the teacher to balance the pull of the curricula with the desire to respect children's cultural traditions is to select a range in which the students are still able to sing in their chest voice but high enough that they can perform (mostly) in tune. In essence, teachers can try to strike a balance between children's culture and the expectations of what might be considered "music teacher culture." Repatriation does not need to be an all-or-nothing activity, but an act that occurs along a continuum. In this case, the process of teaching a long-forgotten song from the children's culture and providing the chest-voice model can be seen as repatriative. The fact that the teacher selects the range of the song at all may be as a less repatriative act.

In a culturally diverse nation such as the United States, individual teachers may search out historical recordings of child-songs that represent the cultures of some of the children in their classes. If these songs have been lost to the children and are reintroduced into their lives, they serve as forms of repatriation. One case of a Chinese American child illustrates the discovery for the child of her family heritage. In a music curriculum that focused on the development of children's singing skills and repertoire, the music teacher introduced the song "Diou Shou Juan'er" to her first-grade students. The children were primarily of European American heritage, but Rebecca perked up at the sounds of the Mandarin Chinese text and the pentatonic structure of the melody. According to the family, she had arrived home from school with great excitement to share the song with her Chinese grandmother. Then upon walking into music class the following week, Rebecca immediately announced to the teacher, "My grandmother knows that song, but she knows it different!" Rebecca then proceeded to teach her grandmother's version of the game to her classmates and the teacher, and it became the "go-to version" for the rest of the year. Later, Rebecca's grandmother shared memories of the game, discussing pronunciation and alternative game rules.

Brinkhurst (2012) noted that one benefit of repatriation is that it can evoke memories related to the music. In this case, the memories elicited were not Rebecca's, who was born and raised in the United States, but those of her grandmother, who hailed from China. While "London Bridge Is Bouncin' Down" was not retained in children's musical cultures in the United States, "Diou Shou Juan'er" is still well-known in many parts of China. Rebecca's lack of knowledge of the game more likely had to do with the fact of her mother's immigration. By sharing the song with the class, the teacher provided an environment that elicited memories in the grandmother, leading her to share a vital piece of their shared family culture and history. The entire class learned the song and game, but for Rebecca, it was a repatriative experience, in that she learned a cultural heritage children's game that had been lost to her.

For children, the experience of learning a bygone children's song from the family's own cultural heritage is the most directly repatriative act. Children are indeed "multicultural," in that their lives represent both the cultures of their communities and the pan-national experiences of children. For Rebecca, learning the song "Diou Shou Juan'er" allowed her to become reconnected to her cultural roots, while also playing a game that children around the world would find enjoyable. Had the teacher chosen instead to teach a Chinese song typically performed by adults, Rebecca would have made a connection to her cultural heritage, but would not have been as connected to the musical lives of Chinese children.

WOLF SONGS: CHILD-SONGS FROM FURTHER AFIELD

Music teachers, as well as song collectors and folklorists, have long expressed concern that children's singing games are dying out. Well over a century ago, Gomme (1898) worried that industrialization was causing singing games in England to be lost. Today's music teachers fear that the fastidious scheduling of children's lives into fixed study and organized play times, coupled with children's ever-growing fascination with digital devices, have rendered singing games obsolete and lost from children's daily lived experiences. In past years, similar claims turned out to be unfounded, as later scholars determined that researchers have simply failed to look in the right places (Marsh 2008; Campbell and Wiggins 2013). Nonetheless, it is conceivable that the ubiquity of mediated experiences in contemporary society has altered the landscape of children's lives so that the games are indeed fewer in number and less prevalent in their play. Teachers can, in effect, repatriate these singing games by teaching them in the classroom, ensuring that they remain alive, even if the context has shifted.

As a nation of immigrants, the United States continues to face newly arrived families to the country (and to its schools) daily. In some places, pockets of immigrants settle in one region, and one particular immigrant group will populate the schools in that area at greater rates than others. Teachers are wise to choose music that represents regional immigrant culture to bridge the transition for those students into their new school community. More common, however, are schools that contain immigrants from a range of countries; for example, the Tukwila School District in the Seattle area serves children who speak more than eighty different languages (Puget Sound Educational Service District 2014). Tukwila teachers cannot easily find music in available educational resources that represents the range of student diversities.

Repatriation acts can occur in schools of diverse populations by sifting through archives to identify and then teach music that emphasizes distinctions and commonalities across children's musical cultures. For example, children's songs and singing games in which a wolf serves as the main character can be found in many cultures. Historical recordings of children playing wolf-based singing games have been found in Mexico, French Canada, and England, while teachers, parents, and other caregivers have shared versions from countries including Hungary, Greece, and China. Most commonly, the wolf character is a threatening one, an ominous figure who lurks around a group of children, emerging at the end of a song to try to catch innocent youth to eat for dinner. The games are almost all the same: The Wolf sings to the children, telling them that he is preparing to come and "get" them. On the recordings, the tension rises, as the children become more and more excited at the thought of impending doom, with the tempo increasing and the singing volume growing louder. At some point, one that is sometimes preordained and at others is randomly chosen by the Wolf, the Wolf states that he has arrived, and proceeds to chase the children, tagging as many as he can. The field recordings typically end at this point, with children screaming in joy and excitement. In the case of the series of wolf songs, teachers can teach the songs through the recordings, allowing children to learn the language through the performances of culture-bearers. Since the songs come from a range of cultures, a teacher can select a particular song to reflect the culture of a particular student, thereby making the song personally relevant to that child; in that case, the repatriated song is from her or his home culture or ethnicity, not just her or his home culture of children. This collection of wolf songs has been taught to children in American classrooms from the Jersey shore to the Pacific Northwest, in live clinical workshops for teachers and blog posts.

One principal goal of repatriation is to return music that has been lost to the culture-bearers, and to do so in a way that is accessible (e.g., Nannyonga-Tamusuza and Weintraub 2012); and teachers can serve as a successful vehicle through which to transmit singing games. Most recordings in archives were made before video was readily available, and today's children are nothing if not visually oriented. Providing children with field recordings and written descriptions of games is much less likely to lead to adoption by the children. By demonstrating the singing games in class as the children listen to field recordings, teachers provide an opportunity for the material to be repatriated to children in a child-centered way. Further, teachers can incorporate children's opinions and perspectives, asking them to suggest ways to alter the patterns of gameplay to make the games more relevant and fun for them. In this way, older singing games do not remain as historical relics, straitjacketed in time, but become living musical experiences. After teaching a range of singing games from field recordings, teachers can provide children some degree of choice over the games that they play in class, as well, allowing some games to die out because of a lack of interest on the part of the children, while other games flourish and take on new forms. This further serves as a kind of repatriation, as children become the arbitrators of good, deciding how they want to entertain themselves.

Illustration of the repatriation of child-songs from further afield is played out in the work of a teacher's attempt at the curricular integration of French Canadian children's singing games for her children in an elementary school (none of whom were French Canadian). In a summer workshop in which she was enrolled, Anne-Marie Fischer discovered a 1950s recording replete with French-language songs from Montreal. These included songs for jumping rope, bouncing balls, and clapping hands with a partner. Fischer took the results of her research to develop a set of lesson plans for the second-grade students she was charged to teach. Although the children did not know any of the songs that they learned, the game types were familiar to them, through other children's games that they learned in music class or had played on their own, without the assistance of adults. After teaching a jump-rope game and ball-bouncing game from French Canada, Fischer compared them to others that they knew from their own experiences, deepening their understanding of the ways in which children's musical cultures hold similarities across time and place. This case of a teacher's effort to share French Canadian songs to children of different heritages represents a form of repatriation that differs from Rebecca's experience of the Chinese singing game. For Rebecca, learning "Diou Shou Juan'er" allowed her to connect with her status as both a child and as an American of Chinese descent, while the children in Anne-Marie's class connected to the French Canadian songs only in that the experience allowed them to see ties between children's musical cultures.

MISSISSIPPI HILL-COUNTRY MUSIC: ADULT CULTURAL HERITAGE MUSIC

When the folklorist Alan Lomax first recorded fife-and-drum music in Mississippi hill country in 1942, at a Quitman County picnic in northern Mississippi hill country, he did not imagine linkages between children and their adult-cultural-heritage music, nor could he have predicted that this music would find its way into schools some seventy years later. The Senatobia, Mississippi, native Sid Hemphill was performing with his blues-styled string group at that picnic, and the sounds of snare drums and reed flutes made from local river cane stalks were clear testimony of the fusion of the European-flavored snare drum tradition with African polyrhythms. Lomax was intrigued with this adult cultural-heritage music, and he returned to the towns of Como, Senatobia, Tyro, and other small rural settlements in Quitman, Panola, and Tate counties for further recordings of fife-and-drum groups, blues musicians, and spirituals and hymns from African American churches as part of his southern journey in 1959–1960 (Lomax 2002). With video equipment in tow on a third visit to the region in 1978, Lomax, John Bishop, and Worth Long shot their footage of a picnic at which the spirited fife-and-drum music was featured (Szwed 2010).

Over the course of Lomax's three visits in thirty-six years, pieces of African American musically expressive practices emerged to bring to light the distinctive sounds of northern Mississippi legends of song and instrumental capacity, including R. L. Burnside, Napolian Strickland, Otha Turner, and (Mississippi) Fred McDowell. Lomax's recordings of spirituals, hymns, children's songs, blues, and proto-blues forms are preserved within the collections that are maintained online by the Association for Cultural Equity and in physical form at the American Folklife Center of the Library of Congress, Washington, DC. The music of these Lomax collections became nationally and internationally known through radio programs, commercial recordings, and concert tours by the musicians. Fred McDowell's first recording of "You Got to Move," with his wife Fanny McDowell, in Como, Mississippi, was covered in 1971 by the Rolling Stones on their album *Sticky Fingers*. Recordings of R. L. Burnside's acoustic and electric blues were released by Adelphi and Arhoolie Records, introducing his masterful blend of rural and urban blues; these recordings led to Burnside's three tours in Europe, nine appearances at the New Orleans Jazz & Heritage Festival, and a feature spot by Lomax's 1979 documentary film, *The Land Where the Blues Began*. Otha Turner's Rising Star Fife and Drum Band and the Gravel Springs Fife and Drum Band, featuring the multi-instrumentalist Napolian Strickland, performed at weekend "goat picnics" and farm parties. Their syncopated dance music, played on military-style snare drums and cane fifes, was captured on commercial recordings such as *Everybody Hollerin' Goat* and *From Senegal to Senatobia*. The lively music drew listeners to Panola County and raised interest in the plausible relationship between hill-country music and the sounds of enslaved people who had made their forced journey from the African continent in the eighteenth and nineteenth centuries to the farms and plantations of the rural American South. The impression was widespread that the Africanisms in fife-and-drum music, and in other secular and sacred forms, were preserved in rural and remote African American communities in northern Mississippi. Thus came the pilgrimages to hill country by internationally acclaimed musicians who were seeking the origins of the music Lomax had recorded. These included Mick Jagger, Keith Richards, Bill Wyman, and others, who stayed in small-town motels with the aim of meeting the bluesmen, fiddlers, and players of banjo, guitar, and cane fife.

Acts of Repatriation to Communities

More than forty years have passed since the time of the Mississippi video recordings, and the previous journeys by Alan Lomax extend almost eight decades into the past. The northern Mississippi hill-country residents are now two, three, and four generations removed from the musicians whose music is preserved on the archived recordings. The Association for Cultural Equity recognized the need to return the music to the communities of origin and sought ways to connect people, including children and youth, to their musical roots. Repatriation became the appropriate next stage in the process of recording and preserving music, and the folklorist Anna Lomax Wood led the effort to dust off and prepare the archived materials for return and use by people of the Mississippi hill country. Past efforts to repatriate her father's recordings to Scotland, Ireland, Spain, Romania, Italy, Trinidad, Guadeloupe, St. Lucia, Haiti, Grenada/ Carriacou, and various archives in the United States paved the way for doing so with hill-country music. An account of selected repatriation efforts to Mississippi follows, with attention to work in October 2013, the following autumn, and four years in the design and delivery of lessons for use in schools.

Early October is still hot and humid in the hill country of northern Mississippi, but it was deemed a good time for calling together participants to the "All Our Friends Hill Country Blues Celebration." Alice Pierotti, librarian at the Emily J. Pointer Public Library in Como, Mississippi, organized the gathering in 2013 of blues musicians, folklorists, chroniclers, and fans of hill-country music. Joining together for a stretched weekend were the co-organizing civic organizations in Tate and Paola counties, public libraries at Como and Senatobia, members of the Mississippi Blues Commission, University of Mississippi music faculty and staff of the Blues Archives, and curatorial staff of the Association for Cultural Equity. The events were intended to bring together families, too, including children and youth, and so were scheduled from Friday afternoon to Sunday noontime.

The local blues musician Martin Grant kicked off a Friday gathering at the public library in Como, where he demonstrated the traditional crafting of a fife from stalks of river cane. Children and adults sat and stood in rapt attention while Martin hollowed out the inside of a piece of cane of about sixteen inches, and began to mark the holes on the stalk. He adeptly applied a hot iron to burn out the holes, blew in at the mouthhole, and worked his fingers on and off the holes. Martin held his finished fife in transverse position, and the high sounds came out in punctuated fashion, with sharp attacks on short, quick flourishes. Like Otha Turner and Napolian Strickland, Martin did not stand still as he played, but moved subtly from side to side in reflection of the percussive pulse of the fife's melody. There were smiles, nods, and squeals from delighted children and adults who were fixing their fascination on both the cane-crafting process and the rhythmic drive of the brief outbursts of repeating melodic material.

Highlighting the October weekend was the repatriation of Alan Lomax's Tate County audio, video, and photo collections to the Senatobia Public Library. About sixty guests turned out at the Senatobia Public Library on Saturday morning for the repatriation ceremony, mostly relatives and heirs of hill-country artists recorded by Lomax during his visits in 1942, 1959, and 1978. They came as children, grandchildren, great-grandchildren, and other kin to the fife and drum musicians Otha Turner and Napolian Strickland, banjo player Lucius Smith, singers Viola James and James Shorty, and snare drummer Lonnie Young Jr. (son and nephew, respectively, of snare drummer Lonnie Young Sr., and fife-blower Ed Young of the Southern Fife & Drum Corps). Lomax had recorded all of them during his visits, and now their descendants were gathering to commemorate their musical elders. Schoolchildren joined their parents and grandparents, finding their places on folding chairs set up in the library's meeting room for the repatriation ceremony. The event opened with songs and a prayer by the Reverend John Wilkins, a local blues guitarist and himself a notable recording artist. Hal Reed, the grandson of Lucius Smith, had traveled from Bettendorf, Iowa, where he runs the Muddy Waters Blues Club; he was drawn back home to the ceremony to remember his grandfather and to passionately advocate for the inclusion of musical heritage studies in the education of young people.

The repatriation ceremony continued with Anna Lomax Wood's expression of appreciation to the families and their elders for giving time to the documentation projects of her father. She shared audio and video samples from the Association for Cultural Equity collection, and the images played out in the room as an homage to hill-country music and musicians. Small children wiggled to the rhythms they heard, and several singers joined in on some of the familiar church hymns that sounded. Small books of photos and essays, and a DVD of all the digital documentation, were then distributed to enthusiastic families and heirs. There were gasps of recognition, some laughter, and a few tears as those assembled began to recognize their relatives and other familiar people and places that had been featured and chronicled by Lomax and company.

Ninety minutes after it had begun, the repatriation event closed on a hopeful note with the announcement of forthcoming activity in schools to connect the historic music to the youngest generation of heirs of Mississippi hill-country music. Families took note of the future of hill-country music, and nodded their approval in hearing that "a set of lessons have been created" that would support the integration of hill-country heritage in the music, language arts, and social studies curriculum of local Panola and Tate county schools. There were smiles and enthusiastic applause, as families stood up and began to gather for photo opportunities of themselves, other families, fans, and visitors. Hugs, handshakes, and congratulatory pats on the back were traded all around, followed by a mass exodus out of Senatobia Public Library, with hungry children leading the way into the warm midday sun and down Main Street to Coleman's Bar-B-Q.

The return of heritage music to its community of origin had jogged memories, and stories of now-deceased musicians were sailing out in conversations from grandparents to their children and grandchildren. A buoyant spirit prevailed over the veritable feast of beef brisket, catfish sandwiches, baked beans, potato salad, and coleslaw. Then, on into the afternoon, a collective pride in local musical heritage was further evident in the ceremonial unveiling in downtown Como, some eight miles southeast from Senatobia, of an iron plaque of Napolian Strickland. This was the newest of what were then about 170 Blues Trail markers across the state of Mississippi. Sharde Turner, twenty-year-old granddaughter of Otha Turner, led a group of fife-and-drum musicians in a procession to the plaque, and then over to an indoor gallery with chairs set facing an elevated stage. There, families and fans gathered for an afternoon-into-evening time of high-energy performances by local blues musicians. The children danced and drew ever nearer to the musicians (one young boy even crept up to twang the strings of a propped-up electric guitar), while the stories of long-gone musicians continued to be recalled by those who had known "Otha," "Napoleon," "R.L.," and "Fred." Clearly evident in the hearty hooting, the call-outs for favorite blues tunes, and the popping, nodding, patting, and clapping was the collective embrace of the music that had been so strongly associated with the region, that had gone away to inaccessible archives and distant world stages, and that was now returning to the land and people of hill country. The next morning, at Hunter's Chapel, a small yellow-brick church not far from Gravel Springs, Tate County, the prayers rolled forward from families who gave praise and thanksgiving to historic musicians who had been "blessed by God to make the music for all the rest of us in our community." The weekend's aim had been achieved, as the organizing librarian Alice Pierotti had hoped would happen, so that local communities were brought together to recognize the cultural wealth of their history and heritage, to celebrate it, and to feel the pride in the music that had captivated listeners, singers, players, and dancers for generations.

Acts of Repatriation in Schools

Repatriation of hill-country music in schools was inevitable, following announcements and attention to it over the kickoff repatriation weekend. In fact, a set of lessons for the repatriation of Mississippi music traditions to schoolchildren already had been designed and piloted in Seattle, and they were made available on the website of the Association for Cultural Heritage. A cadre of seasoned teachers, graduate students of music education and ethnomusicology, and university professors (including the authors of this chapter) had engaged with the online recordings and films as much as six months earlier to develop pedagogical pathways for teaching and learning music and its cultural meanings. There are twenty-two online lessons featuring music and musicians from the region: Blues by R. L. Burnside and Fred McDowell, fife and drum music with Napolian Strickland and members of the Young family, prison songs from Parchman Penitentiary, hymns featuring Viola James, James Shorty, and other members of local church choirs and congregations, and singing games sung by the Hemphill children. The lessons offer sequential experiences keyed primarily to the primary and middle school grades, although there are also a number intended for use in secondary schools and college, university, and adult education settings. They encompass experiences for developing listening skills, vocal and instrumental skills, awareness and understanding of the musical traditions, and pride in them. While the lessons emphasize learning the music by oral-aural transmission, there is occasional inclusion of Western notation to supplement the traditional process of learning by ear.

Over the week that followed the Como and Senatobia repatriation events in 2013, on a return weeklong trip in 2014, and in online Skype-style exchanges in between and since these visits, I (Campbell) have been involved in repatriating selected hill-country recordings through the education of practicing and prospective teachers—in lectures (and discussion), workshop-oriented participatory experiences, and demonstration classes that feature my teaching of predesigned lessons in elementary and secondary schools. In venues that include the University of Mississippi, Delta State University, and assorted schools and school districts in Cleveland, Como, Oxford, Sardis, and Senatobia, my attention is geared to presenting teachers with an introduction to Lomax's field recordings through multiple sessions that coalesce on the theme, "Return to Hill Country: Musical Riches of a Region." In person and online, we sample lessons as we engage in collective listening to discover and dissect the nuances of local dialects and musical expressions. We join together in recreating the recorded music live through hearty singing, dancing, and rhythmicking activities that feature clapping and stamping. With questions of the music's historical meanings and functions, and with brief biographical sketches of some of the prominent musicians of the region, we come to terms with music's powerful contributions to the making of cultural heritage in hill country. We discuss the challenges of facilitating learning by young students of the local musical treasures, when the instructional resources are crackling recordings from an earlier technological era in which static noise crowds out the clear sounds of real-time performances, even as faded black-and-white photographs and films feature dated clothing and hairstyles of the sort that incite laughter and smart-aleck remarks. We inevitably land on the benefits of bringing to children and youth the historic heritage music of their home territories for the extensive understanding they can develop of themselves, their families, and the people who have built their communities.

Teachers listen, question, deliberate, and recommend moderate redesigns or reshaping of the lessons, and in follow-up exchanges they report on the impact of their activation of pedagogical principles (and the music-cultural material). Teachers work directly with their students, featuring "the goods" of these teacher-education sessions, splicing them into their curricular plans for celebrating Martin Luther King Day and Black History month. Depending on the context of their teaching, they report the "fit" of hill-country music for adding enticement to the state-mandated course in Mississippi history; for teaching musical styles and structures; for studying language and local dialects and their meanings then and now; for transitions through listening, songs, and rhythmic activities between academic school subjects (in elementary schools); and for filling in pieces of an ongoing search by young people for their personal and cultural identities.

My own visits to a handful of Mississippi hill-country schools proved enlightening. The lessons had been piloted with schoolchildren in Seattle, who were in no way affiliated with the music, and not a single child in the pilot classes could claim even a visit to the state of Mississippi (although several children in their "red herring" manner reported that they have been to "the deep south" on family trips to San Antonio, St. Louis, and Disney World). Our interest was in getting beyond questions of what was developmentally appropriate for children and youth in learning encounters at selected grade levels in order to meet the aims of repatriation by way of fostering curiosity and developing a sense of identity and pride in their local history and culture. I gauged the responses by children to R. L. Burnside's "Poor Boy a Long Way from Home" and learned that several had imagined him singing of the family he left in Mississippi because of a job he had to take in Memphis. I realized that long before I made it to step number nine of the lesson for the Parchman work song "Eighteen Hammers," in which children would be invited to emulate the swing of a hammer or a hoe while listening to the recording, that they were already swinging with the pulse in their initial listening. I found out that students sang with conviction the response "Certainly Lord" while listening to the song of the same title that had been recorded in a church in Tyro, Mississippi, in 1959, and that in response to my expression of surprise one girl remarked, "No biggie. This is just like the songs at our church." I discovered that several children had fathers, grandfathers, and uncles who could play blues on slide guitar like Fred McDowell, and that one boy was sure that he had heard "Freight Train Blues" before because it "sounded strangely familiar" in relation to the music his father's friend played on visits to his home. I learned about the meanings that children brought to a song like "Rosie"—that they were sure that she was the girlfriend that was waiting for her man and that "the heavy load" she was carrying were the shoes and clothes that he would wear when he was released from prison (as one boy remarked, "probably he was locked up for something little like stealing cigarettes"). I came to understand that the children's songs that Lomax had recorded in 1942 were still alive, and that second-grade children already knew and could sing with conviction "Red Bird" and "Bumblebee." In every setting, children recognized and could sing "This Little Light of Mine," which appeared to function as an unofficial anthem in the local churches they attended.

It became clear in visits to schools that children had never heard the archived recordings before, nor did they know the names and backstories of the musicians. They felt no particular connection with most of the selections, although a few songs and styles were familiar to them as, living in the region, the music—or musical essence—of several generations ago may still be somewhat present in the nooks and niches of the community. This was all the more reason for repatriation efforts to find their way into schools to provide young students with the systematic exposure, experience, and education that may lead them to an understanding of themselves and their heritage.

The children applied some of their local knowledge to making sense of the music, and they responded to my questions in ways that were analytically clever and inventive. In a tenth-grade English class, we ventured into listening to a recording of "Long John," a work song that Alan Lomax had collected with his father, John Lomax. The chorus came on quickly, and some of the girls were singing "Well, long John, he's long gone" on first hearing and with every return of the chorus. I posted the full set of verses on the screen, and several students were half singing and half speaking the lines as the recording played. One boy offered that the song belonged to slaves, not just working prisoners, and another observed that the song's repetition made sense because "picking cotton takes focus, and simple words and repeated melodies make it easier to multi-task." Within a few listenings to the crackling Lomax recording, a half-dozen boys were sounding out percussive taps and slaps on their metal desktops and chairs. A few used the flats of their hands, and others had metallic pens for "clanging" out their rhythms which, sounding simultaneously, turned into a polyrhythm that aligned with the singing. One girl asked that the recording be turned off ("we don't need no static"), and another responded that "we don't need no old music, we can make our own." At that point, the students took on ownership of the song. They sang in full voice, and slapped and clanged out the rhythmic accompaniment. One boy wiggled his way out of his seat, swaggered to the front of the class, and began hopping and popping while taking the role of lead singer for a verse; the others now waited their turn to sing only the response. He was joined by several of his classmates for another verse in coordinating the movement of their arms, legs, and torsos. The dancers finished with a flourish and a bow, several singers managed a cadential harmony, and the rhythmic percussion closed with a final slap. "This song! Long John! Belongs to second period English!" the lead singer announced. As the students nodded and laughed their affirmation, the English teacher (who had attended one of my teacher lecture-sessions a few days earlier on Mississippi hill-country music) leaned over to me with an apt comment: "Uh-huh. I think you just got yourself a repatriation."

In schools as well as in communities of the Mississippi hill country, the work of repatriation is just beginning, and the activities and outcomes are sporadic and selective. One banner weekend brought folks together for a dynamic though fleeting celebration, and a few weeks of on-site lectures and "cameo-visits" to schools can perk interest but are impermanent and thus removed from a full-scale repatriation. Teachers, a few librarians and civic leaders, and even a few classrooms of young students here and there are briefly touched by the efforts, but there is no evidence of a wholesale commitment to historic musical practices and locally living heritage musicians. The online lessons are there for application by teachers in their classrooms, and an awareness of the treasury of online sources of local Mississippi music and musicians may draw a few children and youth into independent study on their own. It is reasonable to expect that schools in Tate and Panola counties benefited from the burst of energy during that one October 2013 weekend of recognition by families and fans of hill-country music. The colorful events were widely known through coverage by the local media, community librarians have been committing themselves to exhibits and events that follow on their recognition of the area's musical riches, the same funders of the community celebration have supported several of the teacher in-service sessions, and various inroads are in motion by those teachers who have embraced the need for children and youth to be exposed to, or even educated in, the historic and current folkways of their community. For these teachers, the ultimate purpose of teaching adult cultural heritage music is for children to gain a sense of their origins, ancestors, and histories. For an archive waiting to be made useful, teachers with a commitment to their community will find the way through to the repatriation of intangible cultural heritage.

The process of repatriating the Lomax archival material to current residents in Mississippi hill country more closely resembles repatriation as it may be more commonly understood, as multifaceted events with a variety of approaches and outcomes. For the children who learned the musical material through teachers in schools, the particular flavor of the musical selections strongly affected the degree to which the teaching and learning acts were repatriative. Although there are examples of children's musical cultures from Mississippi within the archived collection of recordings by Alan Lomax, most selections that made their way to the children in the experiences described were adult in nature. Degrees of separation exist, then, between the music and the children, when the music that the teacher selects is derived from adult musical cultures. Compared to the Chinese American schoolgirl's experience with "Diou Shou Juan'er," in which the music represented both the culture of children and of her Chinese American family community, the children of Como and Senatobia learned music that represented their community's adult heritage culture.

BIG-AND-LITTLE MUSIC: THROUGH TEACHERS TO CHILDREN

Despite the societal upheaval that is associated with demographic change, technology, and the media, the content of the education of children and youth has changed surprisingly little over the years. Teachers continue to transmit knowledge, facilitate learning, and inspire and encourage the independence of their students to know their world. The active return of music to local communities, of which children are important players, is not new, either (although the rhetoric for making school-community connections to local cultural heritage is there, its realization is infrequent, sometimes random, often isolated). When repatriation is embraced, the use of archived documents may open to live musical engagement and teachers' provision of necessary context for the music and musicians, including biographical profiles of musicians, photos of their instruments, their homes, schools, and churches, and stories of their music in situ.

Repatriation involves the return of cultural knowledge, including music as intangible cultural heritage, and "presenting it in a format that is accessible to the communities to which it is returned" (Nannyonga-Tamusuza and Weintraub 2012, 207). For children, the issue of accessibility looms large as a potential limitation to the effectiveness of repatriation. The classic form of repatriation is to symbolically present hard copies of historical recordings, typically to institutions such as libraries, while simultaneously providing online access so that those with access to the Internet and computers can peruse the materials at their leisure. For children and youth to use and value the materials, and to increase understanding of their meanings, more connections are necessary. Children seldom peruse such websites on their own, reading and listening as adults do. Typically active beings, children are fully ensconced in the here-and-now, and seemingly ancient music appears on the surface to hold little relevance to them.

Teachers step in to fill the gap. By virtue of the knowledge of their individual students as well as their understanding of child development, teachers are able to repatriate in part by building lessons in such a way that children make connections between what they already know and what knowledge is offered through the recordings. They structure activities so that children are able to understand the ways in which these historical recordings reflect some part of their contemporary culture(s). Through lesson plans available on websites such as those of Smithsonian Folkways and the Association for Cultural Equity, experts have done some of this work, and teachers can download lessons for use in their classrooms. However, like politics, "all teaching is local," and effective teachers typically modify the lessons in order to reflect the experiences of the children in their particular classrooms.

We have argued that the types of music appropriate for repatriation to children take three forms. Children participate in multiple musical cultures, both as players in the adult musical cultures of their specific communities and as participants in the musical culture of children, in which the similarities of children's self-selected musical behaviors can be found in cultures across the globe. The most "close-by" approach is for teachers to select recordings of children's music of their home culture, such as a Somali children's song taught in a classroom primarily populated by second-generation Somali American children. A second type of music for repatriation takes a wider view of culture, considering the aspects of children's musical identities that are similar across cultures. This repatriation happens in many classrooms in the United States, where children may learn a subset of musical games recorded in the Caribbean, or in Japan, or in Zimbabwe, observing aspects of the repertoire that resembles the children's music that they know. Finally, children learn music from their home culture, performed primarily by adults, documented by folklorists and various others (such as those recordings made during Lomax's trips to Mississippi), and facilitated by teachers for listening, musically doing, and thinking through what this music means.

These distinctions should not be interpreted as suggesting that teachers' goals vis-à-vis repatriation should always be to teach archived children's music from the culture of their immediate community. Indeed, children's musical growth depends on experiencing the musical genres of adults as well as the experiences of children throughout the world. Only through exposure to a wide range of musics do children expand their soundscapes to become musically literate about the range of musical expression throughout the world, and an active understanding of diverse musical traditions inhabits a central place in the goals of twenty-first-century music education practices. Teaching forgotten children's music from a child's home culture may be the most directly repatriative act, but all three forms of repatriation lead children to connect their contemporary lives to those that came before them, and help them to grow toward adulthood as more culturally competent citizens of the world.

References

Blacking, John. 1967. *Venda Children's Songs*. Johannesburg, South Africa: Witwatersrand University Press.

Brinkhurst, Emma. 2012. "Archives and Access: Reaching Out to the Somali Community of London's King's Cross." *Ethnomusicology Forum* 21 (2): 243–258.

Campbell, Patricia Shehan. 1991. "The Child-Song Genre: A Comparison of Songs by and for Children." *International Journal of Music Education* 17: 14–23.

Campbell, Patricia Shehan. 2009. "Songs by and for Children: A Legacy of Children's Music." *Smithsonian Folkways Magazine*. https://folkways.si.edu/magazine-fall-2009-featuring-childrens-music/smithsonian.

Campbell, Patricia Shehan. 2010. *Songs in Their Heads: Music and Its Meaning in Children's Lives*. 2nd ed. New York: Oxford University Press.

Campbell, Patricia Shehan, E. McCullough-Brabson, and Judith Cook Tucker. 1994. *Roots and Branches: A Legacy of Multicultural Music for Children*. Danbury, CT: World Music Press.

Campbell, Patricia Shehan, and Trevor Wiggins. 2013. "Giving Voice to Children." In *The Oxford Handbook of Children's Musical Culture*, edited by Patricia Shehan Campbell and Trevor Wiggins, 1–24. New York: Oxford University Press.

Gomme, Alice Bertha. 1898. *Traditional Games of England, Scotland, and Ireland*. Vol. 2. London: Thames and Hudson.

Jones, Bessie, and Bess Lomax Hawes. 1972. *Step It Down*. Athens: University of Georgia.

Lomax, Alan. 2002 [1993]. *The Land Where the Blues Began*. Rev. ed. New York: New Press.

Lomax, Alan Elder, and Bess Lomax Hawes, eds. 1997. *Brown Girl in the Ring: An Anthology of Song Games from the Eastern Caribbean*. New York: Pantheon Books.

Marsh, Kathryn. 2008. *The Musical Playground*. New York: Oxford University Press.

Merrill-Mirsky, Carol. 1986. "Girls' Handclapping Games in Three Los Angeles Schools." *Yearbook for Traditional Music* 18: 47–59.

Milner, Greg. 2009. *Perfecting Sound Forever: Aural History of Recorded Sound*. New York Farrar, Straus and Giroux.

Nannyonga-Tamusuza, Sylvia, and Andrew N. Weintraub. 2012. "The Audible Future: Reimagining the Role of Sound Archives and Sound Repatriation in Uganda." *Ethnomusicology* 56 (2): 206–233.

Opie, Iona, and Peter Opie. 1985. *The Singing Game*. New York: Oxford University Press.

Phillips, Kenneth. 2014. *Teaching Kids to Sing*. 2nd ed. New York: Schirmer Books.

Puget Sound Educational Service District. 2014. "The Most Diverse School District in the Nation: A Closer Look at Tukwila School District." https://www.psesd.org/news/the-most-diverse-district-in-the-nation-a-closer-look-at-tukwila-school-district/.

Roberts, J. Christopher. 2013. "A Historical Look at Three Recordings of Children's Musicking in New York City." In *The Oxford Handbook of Children's Musical Cultures*, edited by Patricia Shehan Campbell and Trevor Wiggins, 575–589. New York: Oxford University Press.

Seeger, Anthony. 1986. "The Role of Sound Archives in Ethnomusicology Today." *Ethnomusicology* 30 (2): 261–276.

Stefano, Michelle L., Peter Davis, and Gerard Corsane. 2012. *Safeguarding Intangible Cultural Heritage*. Woodbridge, UK: Boydell Press.

Szwed, John. 2010. *The Man Who Recorded the World*. New York: Viking/Penguin Books.

UNESCO, 2003. Report of the Convention for the Safeguarding of Intangible Cultural Heritage. http://www.unesco.org/new/en/santiago/culture/intangible-heritage/convention intangible-cultural-heritage/.

CHAPTER 16

....

"EACH IN OUR OWN VILLAGE"

Creating Sustainable Interactions between Custodian Communities and Archives

....

CATHERINE INGRAM

INTRODUCTION

....

MUSICAL repatriation, and the possibility of it continuing, depends almost entirely on the establishment of sustainable digital archives.[1] Yet while achieving archival sustainability necessitates using and further developing techniques for sustainable digital data storage, it cannot be fully ensured by technical expertise alone. To achieve sustainability, archives also need to address other issues that include successfully maintaining their financial support, handling and resolving concerns around open access, effectively facilitating streaming or digital online file-sharing, and communicating with stakeholder communities. It is the interactions related to stakeholder communities and archived collections of musical recordings that form the focus of this chapter. Today, such archived recordings still tend to be held in archives that are not located within the stakeholder or originating communities, hence there is often considerable linguistic, geographical, and cultural distance between the two parties.[2]

The maintenance of mutually productive interactions between archives and the often-distant communities from which the data they hold originated—the custodian communities—has a practical importance. Obviously, sustainable archives aim to maintain collections well into the future. However, when an archivist specifies future use of or access to the materials that are deposited, it is not possible to determine how the precise details of all future issues concerning the collection should be handled, and the period over which a fieldworker/archivist can manage a collection is finite.[3] An archived collection must be maintained over a time frame that exceeds the archivist or depositor's lifetime, or in some cases simply exceeds the archivist's engagement with a particular custodian community, involvement in a certain project, or even employment in the field of research. The archive must also have the ability to handle unforeseen kinds of access requests or unforeseen issues in relation to the collection, and the archive needs to respond to access requests in as-yet-unknown technological contexts of the future.[4]

An attempt by archives to develop and maintain an interaction directly with each custodian community offers a solution to this problem, while also working to address ethical concerns of many kinds that can arise when archives are making important decisions about the future of the cultural material of others. Since invariably archives and custodian communities are "each in our own village"—that is, in different physical locations (to use a phrase employed in some Kam minority[5] songs from southwestern China)—this distance is usually first bridged by the fieldworker, who also acts as archivist for the collection (hence the use of the expression "fieldworker/archivist" in this chapter). However, due to the enhanced cultural-rights awareness of many custodian communities and the rapid increases in virtual interconnectedness, long-term dependence on the fieldworker/archivist to fulfill all the requirements of this bridging role is becoming both increasingly impractical and unnecessary.

I begin this chapter from the standpoint that a truly sustainable archive must also promote and support forms of sustainable and unmediated interactions and dialogue between its own organization and custodian communities, and my discussion here works to support this stance. While such an approach to archiving may seem radical or difficult to achieve, the idea has already been highlighted by a number of researchers. Anthony Seeger, for example, states, "The potential for fruitful collaborations between archives and communities whose materials they hold is . . . great, and I believe essential for the future of both" (2004a, 108). Sally Treloyn and Andrea Emberly describe archiving of the well-known Blacking collection after John Blacking's death as requiring consideration of "sustainable repatriation and collaboration with communities of origin" (2013, 174). They also describe Treloyn's work with indigenous communities in northwestern Australia in developing community-based and community-controlled archives that are physically relocated to communities, in part as an effort to enhance community access and circumvent many problems associated with disengagement between communities and archives (168).

In this chapter, I provide examples and describe experiences from my own research to demonstrate how insights from the perspective of the fieldworker/archivist might be used in the process of developing new initiatives that assist in establishing such dialogue and thus archival sustainability. My focus on the fieldworker/archivist viewpoint is not because I privilege the fieldworker/archivist perspective, but rather because the fieldworker/archivist is frequently the one person most exposed to the perspectives and concerns of both cultural custodians and archives. In the following pages, I present and develop insights concerning sustainable custodian-archive dialogue arising from my experience as a fieldworker/archivist who has undertaken extensive research within Kam minority communities in southwestern China over the past fifteen years, and who has been involved in archiving recordings of Kam music. Drawing on my experience,

I propose several new initiatives by which sustainable interactions and dialogue might be achieved, including ways in which archives might better support fieldworker/ archivists to assist in producing more sustainable connections with communities. I agree with Eric Kansa that such initiatives can have benefits beyond the archiving process: "Communities that have access to vital information and are better able to coordinate action are much more likely to be able to assert themselves and guard against cultural misappropriation" (2009, 244).

CONTEMPORARY CONCERNS
OF CULTURAL CUSTODIANS

Since beginning my research about Kam music-making in 2004, I have worked with Kam custodians jointly to create and establish a sustainably archived digital collection of recorded materials with the Pacific and Regional Archive of Digital Sources in Endangered Cultures (PARADISEC).[6] Kam custodians have expressed interest in and enthusiastic support for this preservation of recorded and other materials featuring their own cultural heritage. Their interest has especially grown due to the major sociocultural changes that have occurred within Kam villages over the previous two decades. These include the current absence of most youth from Kam villages for work or study elsewhere, the expansion of Chinese-language education, and a huge increase in television viewing as a popular form of entertainment. These changes have destabilized and, to a large degree, shattered long-existing patterns of musical transmission and norms of village musical performance, resulting in uncertainty regarding the future of much of the music-making featured in the recordings archived in the Kam collection.[7]

To date, the primary focus of the Kam communities I have worked with has been to create recordings that could be viewed by the singers involved on VCDs and DVDs, and which could thereby be preserved for viewing at a later date and by subsequent generations. Many villagers are very proud of the recordings and are keen to play them for others in their own village or elsewhere. The appearance in the videos of singers who have since passed away has also proved to be a great stimulus for making recordings, and for appreciating their long-term value. Sometimes villagers have also given copies of the recordings to friends or relatives in other Kam villages (copies of all recordings made during my fieldwork that were requested by villagers were provided to them). Yet some people in different Kam communities have at times expressed concern about the spread of the recordings, as they did not want singers in other areas to be able to learn all the songs that constituted each village or region's unique repertoire. In a discussion with several Kam song experts on concerns around access to the collection, a number of points were raised:

If Han and foreigners know of our songs, that's definitely good. . . .

> If they know of the songs, it's fine as they don't have the ability to learn the songs. So those people knowing about the songs is just a type of publicity. . . . They aren't able to learn the songs, so they won't say those are their songs. But for Kam people, they are able to learn them, and after they do they will [often] say those song[s] they have learnt are their songs.
>
> (Ingram et al. 2011b, 97)[8]

The long-held Kam view of singing as a valuable form of cultural and symbolic capital has influenced views of songs even when they have been recorded in a digital medium.

As Kam song experts and I have outlined elsewhere (Ingram et al. 2011b), initial discussions with Kam villagers about establishing the archive of recordings have restricted access to the archived recordings to exclude anyone other than myself, PARADISEC personnel, and members of Kam communities.[9] In the discussions I had with individual groups at the time of each recording, and in the discussions I had with village representatives in the region where I produced the greatest number of recordings (and the resultant written agreement), I proposed this restriction. My rationale for doing so was partly because communities never indicated that they were interested in making an archive of recordings that would be available for wider viewing, and also to allay the fears that had occasionally been expressed regarding the possible problems arising through sharing access to the recorded material (and as I had also seen with VCDs and DVDs). The restriction was also suggested so that members of Kam communities could later assume direct decision-making power concerning access when they chose to do so (as noted later, I do not see these decisions to be part of the fieldworker/archivist role). Furthermore, while I knew of the many concerns surrounding unintended usage of musical recordings of cultural heritage (e.g., Feld 1996; Guy 2002; Seeger 2004b), I was not aware of any research to demonstrate that communities had clearly benefited from recordings of their cultural heritage being made widely available to outsiders other than through the creation of commercially available recordings (e.g., Feld 1992; Neuenfeldt 2001; Christen 2005).

Neither during our discussions nor at any time since have any Kam friends or community representatives proposed a more relaxed approach to archival access, so it appears that many people support the restriction. There may well be other reasons for this apparent support: an unfamiliarity with archiving may have led some people to feel that they did not know what access really entailed or who had the power to control it; some may have felt that politeness required them to comply with my suggestions; others may have worried about how state officials would view the archive or the issue of access. However, in the case of the latter, the influence of state organs on village decision-making is complex. For instance, my most recent written agreement with a whole Kam village community was primarily negotiated with—and then subsequently rewritten by—the village party secretary, the most highly placed state representative in the village.

In my conversations and agreements, I did not discuss potential future online access to the material with Kam communities when we talked about access to the recordings, and there were several reasons for this. First, until 2010 the Internet was not widely used in rural Kam areas, so many Kam people had no understanding of computers or the Internet and had no opportunity to visit all the material in the archive before making it accessible to others (except as provided on request on VCDs and DVDs). Even today, familiarity with online media is mainly restricted to Kam youth, who spend little time in their home villages and thus have not had much involvement in producing archived recordings (and may also have only limited experience in Kam musical traditions). Second, during 2004 to 2012, when most of the recordings archived in the collection were made, it had not yet become possible to stream material held in PARADISEC over the web, although streaming was proposed as part of the archive's future developments and is now a feature of the archive. Consequently, at the time the recordings were made and the details of archiving were initially negotiated, villagers could not have had their own experience of online access even if they could find access to the Internet (a point clearly demonstrating my opening assertion that archives may sometimes need to respond to access requests in as-yet-unknown technological contexts of the future that could not have been decided when the collection was deposited).

Third, despite my having developed enough fluency in Kam (a Tai-Kadai family language entirely different from Chinese) to conduct daily life and research almost exclusively in that language and to take part in Kam singing performances, I did not feel confident of my ability to use Kam to discuss clearly the possible implications of wider access to the collection, the nature of a digitally archived collection, or how it could be available on the Internet. Fourth, while archive staff suggested I encourage custodians to allow wider access to the collection (as might be particularly likely through providing online access), it was not essential for cultural custodians to agree to wider access in order for the archive to agree to host the collection.

In June 2011, I initiated and recorded a discussion with four Kam friends who are also respected older "song experts"[10] about Kam views on permitting "fair use"[11] access to the collection (an overview of the discussion was subsequently published as Ingram et al. 2011b). We discussed possible benefits of the wider access to part or all of the collection, as well as concerns that the song experts themselves might have or that they believed were likely to be important for others in their community. My friends generally believed that the main benefit of wider access would be to provide useful publicity for Kam musical traditions. However, discussions of this benefit were always accompanied by concerns over whether or not publicity would rightfully accrue to their own Kam region, and whether wider access might also cause a loss of control over the perceived "possession" of local tradition.

CONTEMPORARY CONCERNS OF ARCHIVES

The archive discussed in this chapter, PARADISEC, shares Kam communities' interest in preserving recordings of cultural and linguistic heritage for future generations. PARADISEC's goal, as described by Nicholas Evans, is to create a special, enduring, digital archive for the languages and cultures of our region—and that includes music, it includes storytelling, it includes a lot of things other than just language itself—which will be a secure repository that will hold things and which ultimately can be accessed by anyone.

(Arnott 2013)

PARADISEC's emphasis is also on the secure preservation of digitized materials, but with a focus also on future community needs:

A founding principle for PARADISEC is that small and endangered cultures need support for locating and reintroducing material that was recorded in the past. Ensuring that the material is well cared for means that it can be made available into the future.

(PARADISEC 2007)

As Nicholas Thieberger and Linda Barwick (at the time of writing, the archive's director and Sydney unit director respectively) explain, PARADISEC is

a practice-based archive, arising from a community of practice who recognized that it was part of our professional responsibility to ensure that the records we create are properly curated into the future. This is a new conception of a data repository, accessioning primary research in the course of fieldwork or shortly after, and building methods and tools to facilitate its deposit and curation. It is unique in its links on the one hand to fieldworkers and to speakers of Indigenous languages and on the other hand to the cutting-edge technologies of Web 2.0 and HTML5.

(Thieberger and Barwick 2012, 251)

PARADISEC places a particular emphasis on digitizing earlier analog field recordings to ensure they are still accessible into the future. It plays a unique and invaluable role within the Asia-Pacific—serving a region containing more than a third of the world's six thousand languages, with most of the languages in this region and their associated cultural expressions being very poorly documented (PARADISEC 2007). Despite the important role assumed by the archive, it faces ongoing concern over funding and lacks a stable source of funds (Arnott 2013). Consequently, it must juggle requirements for performing its important role with these monetary concerns. This necessarily affects the time that staff members have available to deal with issues relating to the archive. My experience indicates that it also seems to have meant that the archive must find ways to demonstrate its relevance and importance within the immediate context—such as by figures regarding the amount of material deposited, rates of access to the material, and other types of immediate impact of the archived material. As Thieberger and Barwick explain, "PARADISEC is a project ahead of its time and so suffers from a lack of vision among funding agencies" (2012, 251).

PARADISEC relies on depositors negotiating access conditions with communities and subsequently informing PARADISEC; while it has no plans to develop direct communication with communities, it does have working relationships with several cultural centers, universities, and other types of agencies in a number of the locations where the collections originate (Harris et al. 2015, 4). With only limited funding, usability of the archive for researchers in a varied range of locations appears to be the access priority, with the directors and a senior staff member stating:

> PARADISEC aims to be as responsive as possible (given our shoestring budget) to the individual needs of researchers, in particular those located in isolated and remote communities who will be the main beneficiaries of the digitized set of materials we have produced over the past decade.
>
> (Harris et al. 2015, 14)

While PARADISEC does not see having relationships with all source communities as practical, it does plan to make the material more easily accessible to members of source communities through lower-cost digital devices. Thieberger states:

> Realistically, an archive like PARADISEC cannot have relationships with the source communities, but it can make a commitment to holding the material and making it as locatable as possible so that local archives can eventually (when they have the capacity) get copies. We can also make the material available in formats that can be accessed via emerging devices (mobile phones and so on). A great advantage of a digital collection with flexible accession procedures is that it lowers the threshold for depositors. We'd like to improve our processes, but can compare them favourably to other repositories we have worked with as researchers.
>
> (Thieberger, personal communication, March 3, 2014)

THE FIELDWORKER/ARCHIVIST PERSPECTIVE WITHIN THE ARCHIVING PROCESS

The fieldworker/archivist has a distinct role within the research and archiving process. S/he must usually undertake most or all of the fieldwork and archiving, and is also generally responsible for developing effective working relationships with both custodian communities and archival staff. Frequently, the fieldworker is also expected to mediate between the concerns and requirements of the two parties—as noted above in the case of PARADISEC, where the fieldworker is usually the depositor and acts on behalf of a community to specify archival access arrangements. While the fieldworker/archivist may be willing to perform such a mediating role, the often differing perspectives and pressures of communities and archives may make it difficult for the fieldworker/archivist to act in a manner that entirely satisfies one or both parties.

Part of this difficulty is also due to both archives and custodian communities developing a range of different concepts of the role of the fieldworker/archivist—none of which may entirely concur with the researcher's own perspective on the scope of his or her role in the archiving process. For example, in my case, some PARADISEC staff encouraged me to discuss with Kam custodians the possibility of permitting wider access to at least some of the Kam collection. They saw the act of representing the views of the archive as part of my role, at least to some degree.

However, my own view of my role was to offer Kam custodians the possibility of archiving the recorded materials and then to operate on behalf of the community in preparing the accessioned materials and communicating with the archive, since the Kam community had no other practical means of performing the latter two tasks. My approach was part of a broader stance of "silent deferral" that I developed during fieldwork. Where possible, I strove to remain silent in decisions or actions regarding Kam cultural matters and to defer the decision-making to my Kam friends and colleagues. Through this method, people began to feel comfortable expressing their opinions to me. They also gained a clear sense that I was interested in helping them to promote Kam culture in the way they saw best, rather than dictating to them how that should be done. As Anthony Seeger points out:

> Colonized peoples and other so-called subaltern populations live in an environment in which others insist on telling them what to do, rarely take the time to understand what they are already doing, and show little respect for their way of life. It is very easy for researchers to reproduce that pattern even while professing to respect the local traditions.

> (Seeger 2008, 279)

In order to fulfill the archive's request, I attempted to explain the views of the archive to selected Kam community members who had important positions of cultural leadership as well as a good understanding of my research approach. In our discussion, I clearly outlined that I was conveying PARADISEC's suggestions rather than presenting my own viewpoint. This was partly what prompted the discussion with four Kam song experts mentioned earlier (published as Ingram et al. 2011b). Because I had established very strong, positive relationships with all four song experts who participated in the discussion, it was possible to raise these issues without misunderstanding. However, I was not sure that I could present the views of PARADISEC so clearly to the broader community without it automatically being assumed that I held the same viewpoint. In other words, actions undertaken on behalf of an archive need to be considered seriously, as they can have consequences for the entire fieldwork project.

These complexities of the fieldworker/archivist role indicate the unique perspective available to the fieldworker/archivist, and consideration of initiatives that work to overcome these difficulties may be useful for developing sustainable custodian–archive interactions. Fieldworker/archivists are perhaps most exposed to the views of both archives and custodians, and thus aware of slippages between the two standpoints. For example, archives may be enthusiastic about promoting forms of open access, but political or cultural issues may make this problematic within custodian communities. Fieldworker/archivists are also mindful of the difficulties they may face in assuming a mediating role between the two parties.

In the remainder of the chapter, I draw on this experience and understanding to suggest new initiatives that might be explored or adapted to improve the situation and, as a result, the sustainability of important cultural archives. While I focus on initiatives relevant to the archiving of musical recordings in a digital, online archive, these initiatives may also be applicable or transferable to other archival contexts.

RECOMMENDED INITIATIVES

The following recommendations that might enhance custodian–archive communication make use of two features integral to sustainable digital archives. First, they use the very audiovisual means that form the basis of the archive. This is helpful because audiovisual materials are accessible without dependence on users' written literacy, and can easily be adapted for different languages by adding subtitles and/or a dubbed voiceover. They also allow viewers to gain an understanding of the content through their own observations.

Second, these recommendations make use of the archive's online streaming capabilities, or can use digital recordable media such as VCDs and DVDs as substitutes where online streaming is not available. There is also future potential for using other e-learning platforms.[12] Online streaming allows the content to reach a broad range of users and promotes familiarity with the online archive interface. However, to facilitate such access most digital archives will need to adapt web interfaces (and the corresponding recordable media substitute) so that users with limited literacy are able to navigate the material—for example, by including features such as clickable images alongside text. As noted by researchers working on the use of information and communications technology (ICT) in late-developing countries, ICT design is often education-, culture-, or gender-exclusive (Norris 2001; Best and Maier 2007), and these exclusivities need to be addressed in order for archives to interact effectively with custodian communities using ICT-mediated methods. The huge surge in mobile phone usage—including mobile broadband usage—within late-developing countries is well documented (International Telecommunication Union 2012) and indicates the importance of pursuing online formats that are readily available on emerging digital devices.

The first recommended initiative involves an audiovisual presentation of the archive to the communities that are the custodians of potentially accessioned materials, with the archive aiming to establish positive initial interactions and directly engage with

communities. At present, archives such as PARADISEC mainly rely on fieldworker/
archivists to describe their organization and services to custodian communities. In the
case of PARADISEC, the archive is introduced through a printed brochure in English,
translations of the brochure into several other languages, and an English-language website. In my fieldwork, it was helpful to me that there was already a translation of the brochure into simplified Chinese, so I could offer a copy to those who were interested and
could read Chinese. However, this Chinese version still excluded a large proportion of
the Kam women I work with, who either are illiterate or have only limited literacy. I did
not introduce PARADISEC to Kam people through its online presence since, at the time
of writing, the Internet had only recently become accessible in a small number of homes
in Kam communities.

A short (perhaps five- to ten-minute) promotional documentary video would be an
excellent way to introduce an archive such as PARADISEC to custodian communities,
especially to communities with relatively low literacy rates. A video would allow custodian communities to see the individuals involved in the archive, and to gain a clear
understanding of the archive and its activities. After viewing such a video, community
members would be better able to make their own evaluations of the potential of the archive and to engage with it in the manner they determine to be most appropriate. Part
of the video could also introduce simple online searching of material contained in the
archive (a CD-ROM or interactive VCD or DVD could be distributed to introduce the
online workings of the archive to offline communities). With the help of a fieldworker/
archivist, a colleague, or a consultant, the video could be dubbed or subtitled in the language of the community and/or the local dominant language, and could be streamed
online from PARADISEC's website as well as being available on VCDs and/or DVDs
(or played in the community by the researcher using alternative projection methods).
The video could also help to outline the archive's relationship with both depositors and
custodian communities, thereby further supporting fieldworker/archivists by clarifying
their position.

The video might conclude with a statement providing information to custodian
communities about how they could contact the archive directly, and explicitly inviting
them to do so. As well as the archive offering standard methods of contact such as mail,
e-mail, fax, and telephone, it could offer the community a means of uploading a written,
audio, or video statement through the website, with options of the statement either remaining private or becoming a public statement that others in the community could
also consult. This would, again, encourage familiarity with the archive and interface,
and it would promote the official nature of the interaction between the archive and the
community.

The development of online contact between the archive and the custodian community is the second recommended initiative. At present, PARADISEC manages its online catalog using an open-source digital media item management system, known as
Nabu,[13] that it developed in 2012, and the system includes the facility for logged-in
users to post comments on individual items. An adaptation of this feature to allow custodian users direct contact with the archive would be helpful, with the facility for the

archive also to respond. Dialogue could use written online correspondence, uploaded audio recordings, and/or even a video blog. The latter would be especially useful for discussions that are intentionally to be made public with open access or access to a certain community with login privileges. Since video quality would not be a crucial issue, webcams or mobile phones could be used to make these recordings. The fieldworker/ archivist, consultants in the field, or other users could again assist with translation if required.

The third recommended initiative involves the archive partnering with researchers or other interested parties to provide more detailed information to both fieldworker/ archivists and communities about certain aspects of archive management and delivery that might require community debate or study. These could include the long-term value of archives, the kinds of materials that communities and researchers might consider archiving, and the benefits and drawbacks of allowing fair-use access to archived materials. Archives regularly deal with these issues in many different contexts, so it seems appropriate that they initiate information-sharing in these areas. Again, to permit the broadest access possible I recommend that this information be shared by producing short videos that are available online or through distributed recorded media, and are dubbed and/or subtitled in target languages. Each film would include interviews with researchers and people from other communities discussing the issue in question and describing their own thoughts and experiences, thereby presenting information for communities so that they could make their own decisions regarding each issue. A video blog could run alongside each topic so that communities could add to the information by posting stories of their own experiences. At regular intervals, each short video could be revised and, where appropriate, sections from material posted by custodian user communities could be incorporated.

This initiative supports communities in developing coordinated action to promote and protect their own cultural heritage, since it provides valuable information for community discussion rather than seeking to impose requests or requirements on communities. It also provides fieldworker/archivists with a useful tool for working with communities who need to hold discussions when such issues arise. It benefits archives themselves in a number of ways: it is a tangible output to show benefactors that the archive is engaged in information-sharing and interaction with communities; custodian responses to the video can help the archive tailor its activities to better meet community needs; and it may result in more communities confidently making parts of their cultural heritage accessible online. It could even be helpful in providing data for further research into these important issues.

Conclusion

The initiatives recommended here build on the longstanding use of educational films— once restricted only to classroom settings, but now increasingly important for providing information in communities with scant resources. Some organizations have pursued this approach for information-sharing and community development. The UK charity Medical Aid Films[14] is one organization that has made very effective use of this manner of information-sharing, and the organization claims that its films have led to greatly improved health outcomes in many countries. In Australia, the government is currently attempting to improve Indigenous health outcomes in northeast Arnhem Land with the twenty-one-part Digital Themed Health Stories, a collaborative effort between remote indigenous communities, Skinnyfish music, and the filmmaker Paul Williams (Sutton Grange Films).[15] Made by and intended for viewing by Indigenous communities, the videos use humor, song, and story to educate about healthy diet and lifestyle choices. Other projects in low-resource settings take the notion of education even further: for example, India's Video Volunteers[16] helps communities gain skills in video making and editing so that they can draw attention to problems that need to be addressed in their own communities.

The initiatives described earlier offer the possibility of working effectively and with relatively little financial outlay to overcome the linguistic, geographic, and cultural divides that often exist between custodian communities and archives. They may benefit custodian groups by sharing knowledge in a way that can empower communities by enabling them to make their own informed decisions regarding invaluable records of cultural heritage, and facilitating equitable and direct contact with archives. As Kansa's (2009) research indicates, when custodian groups have the opportunity to take responsibility for decisions affecting the use of their heritage it can also assist in reducing cultural misappropriation and enhancing community coordination—two factors that would seem essential to the contemporary sustainment of cultural heritage.

The initiatives may benefit archives by providing a better means for handling long-term communication with custodians and changing archival, ethical, and technological environments of the future, as well as potentially improving access to archived materials (which may, in turn, make it easier for archives to demonstrate contemporary relevance and attract funding). They may benefit fieldworker/archivists by ensuring that the both community and archive will continue to have productive dialogue even after the conclusion of the fieldwork or the death of the fieldworker. They allow fieldworker/archivists to assume a more independent and less complicated role in facilitating the interaction of custodian communities and archives, rather than feeling bound to or constrained by either party's requirements.

Support for and attention to sustainable interactions between custodian communities and archives is yet to be fully recognized as an important part of sustainable digital archiving—perhaps because the digital archiving medium is so new and there has been, as yet, limited exploration of the full potential of online archives. Traditional archival models have moved from custodial to postcustodial archiving, where "deep collaborative relationships—horizontal and reciprocal in nature" (University of Texas at Austin Library 2013, 2) are established between major archiving bodies and partner institutions. We can hope that the twenty-first century will be the time for digital archives likewise to develop newer practices that bring even more mutual benefits. The dispersed nature of custodian communities certainly makes it a challenge to develop multiple sustainable relationships. However, growing global virtual interconnectedness offers many exciting new possibilities for overcoming such challenges, if we are willing to experiment and seek them out.

Notes

1. I gratefully acknowledge the many Kam villagers without whose assistance this research could not have been conducted—particularly the residents of Sheeam.
2. Barwick (2004) and Treloyn and Emberly (2013) describe some of the few instances of the management of digital cultural archives or repositories by and within custodian communities.
3. For example, Levin and Süzükei (2006, 41–44) describe Levin being contacted about a new commercial use of a Tuvan recording that he had originally released under license to Smithsonian Folkways, and the concerns Levin faced in deciding the appropriate course of action. Although Levin had not archived the recording, the issues that he had to consider when responding to the request he received via Smithsonian are similar to those that a depositor would need to consider if receiving the same request via an archive.
4. In the case of musical recordings, it is virtually impossible to prevent archived recordings of traditional cultural expression from being used for unintended purposes, and handling even the issues of today seems difficult. As Anthony Seeger notes, "People with the best of intentions can find themselves powerless to reverse exploitative uses of the materials they have acquired on the understanding that they were not to be used for commercial purposes" (2004b, 167).
5. The Kam are known in Chinese as Dong 侗, speak a Tai-Kadai language completely different from Chinese, and are one of China's fifty-five officially recognized minority groups.
6. This research and archiving is detailed in Ingram (2012a, 2012b, 2014) and Ingram et al. (2011b). According to current estimates, the Kam collection with PARADISEC will eventually hold over 180 hours of video recordings and about 130 hours of audio recordings, as well as several hundred digital images (including photographs and scanned fieldnotes). To my knowledge, it is the first and only archive of recordings of Kam musical heritage.
7. I have written in some detail on the musical effects of these changes; see, for example, Ingram (2012a, 2012c), Ingram et al. (2011a), and McLaren et al. (2013).
8. The discussion was conducted in Kam, and is given here in my own free translation.
9. In practice, Kam community members have not yet attempted to access the archive directly, and at present I imagine they would find it easier to enlist my assistance with any such attempt.
10. Song experts (in Kam, *sang ga*) are individuals recognized locally as the most capable Kam song teachers, the most knowledgeable about Kam musical culture, and knowing the greatest number of Kam songs. The song experts I held the discussion with, and who were coauthors of the ensuing publication, were Wu Meifang 吴美芳, Wu Pinxian 吴品仙, Wu Xuegui 吴学桂, and Wu Zhicheng 吴志成.
11. That is, specific deeds (such as the Creative Commons Licence Deeds titled "Attribution-NonCommercial-ShareAlike 3.0 Australia" or in short, CC BY-NC-SA 3.0, and "Attribution-NonCommercial-NoDerivs 3.0 Unported Australia" or CC BY-NC-ND 3.0), whereby the user is free to copy, distribute, and transmit downloaded files, but must agree

that the ways she or he shares the accessed material properly attributes the author, and that the user does not realize commercial gain from the use.

12. A useful leaflet describing a number of alternatives for video screening in low-resource situations where a fixed, online computer system is not present is available from Medical Aid Films (http://medicalaidfilms.org/), a UK-based charity; see http://medicalaidfilms. org/wp-content/uploads/2014/02/Methods-of-screening-MAF-Films-and-Lessons-Learnt-case-studies.pdf (accessed March 10, 2014).

13. See https://github.com/nabu-catalog/nabu (accessed March 13, 2014).

14. See http://medicalaidfilms.org/ (accessed March 15, 2014).

15. See James (2014), Williams (2013), and the Sutton Grange Films website (http://www. sgfilms.com.au/Home/index.html (accessed March 15, 2014).

16. See http://www.videovolunteers.org/ (accessed March 15, 2014).

References

Arnott, Kate. 2013. "Preserving Asia and the Pacific's Cultural Traditions" [televised news report]. *Australia Network News*. Australian Broadcasting Corporation. Last updated October 28, 2013. Available from http://www.abc.net.au/news/2013-10-24/an-preserving-asia-and-the-pacific27s-cultural-traditions/5042756 (accessed February 25, 2014).

Barwick, Linda. 2004. "Turning It All Upside Down . . . Imagining a Distributed Digital Audiovisual Archive." *Literary and Linguistic Computing* 19 (3): 253–263.

Best, Michael L., and Sylvia G. Maier. 2007. "Gender, Culture and ICT Use in Rural South India." *Gender, Technology and Development* 11 (2): 137–155.

Christen, Kimberly. 2005. "Gone Digital: Aboriginal Remix and the Cultural Commons." *International Journal of Cultural Property* 12: 315–345.

Feld, Steven. 1992. "Voices of the Rainforest: Politics of Music." *Arena* 99 (100): 164–177.

Feld, Steven. 1996. "Pygmy POP: A Geneology of Schizophrenic Mimesis." *Yearbook for Traditional Music* 28: 1–35.

Guy, Nancy. 2002. "Trafficking in Taiwan Aboriginal Voices." In *Handle with Care: Ownership and Control of Ethnographic Materials*, edited by S. R. Jaarsma, 195–209. Pittsburgh: University of Pittsburgh Press.

Harris, Amanda, Nicholas Thieberger, and Linda Barwick. 2015. "PARADISEC: Its History and Future." In *Research, Records and Responsibility: Ten Years of PARADISEC*, edited by Amanda Harris, Nicholas Thieberger and Linda Barwick, 1–16. Sydney: Sydney University Press.

Ingram, Catherine. 2012a. "*Eee, mang gay dor ga ey* (Hey, Why Don't You Sing)? Imagining the Future for Kam Big Song." In *Music as Intangible Cultural Heritage: Policy, Ideology, and Practice in the Preservation of East Asian Traditions*, edited by K. Howard, 55–76. Farnham, UK, and Burlington, VT: Ashgate.

Ingram, Catherine. 2012b. "Researching Kam Minority Music in China." In *Encounters: Australia-China Musical Meetings*, edited by N. Ng, 63–80. Bowen Hills, Queensland: Australian Academic Press.

Ingram, Catherine. 2012c. "Tradition and Divergence in Southwestern China: Kam Big Song Singing in the Village and on Stage." *Asia Pacific Journal of Anthropology* 13 (5): 434–453.

Ingram, Catherine. 2014. *Utilising Participation in Musical Ethnographic Fieldwork in Rural China* [blog entry]. Field Research Lab, London School of Economics and Political Science. Last updated February 24, 2014. Available from http://blogs.lse.ac.uk/fieldresearch/

2014/02/24/utilising-participation-in-musical-ethnographic-fieldwork-in-rural-china/ (accessed March 15, 2014).

Ingram, Catherine, with Wu Jialing 吴家玲, Wu Meifang 吴美芳, Wu Meixiang 吴梅香, Wu Pinxian 吴品仙, and Wu Xuegui 吴学桂. 2011a. "Taking the Stage: Rural Kam Women and Contemporary Kam 'Cultural Development.'" In *Women, Gender and Rural Development in China*, edited by T. Jacka and S. Sargeson, 71–93. Cheltenham, UK, and Northampton, MA: Edward Elgar.

Ingram, Catherine, with Wu Meifang 吴美芳, Wu Pinxian 吴品仙, Wu Xuegui 吴学桂, and Wu Zhicheng 吴志成. 2011b. "Discussing 'Fair Use' of Archived Recordings of Minority Music from the Mountains of Southwestern China." *Sustainable Data from Digital Research: Humanities Perspectives on Digital Scholarship (Proceedings of the Conference Held at the University of Melbourne, 12–14 December 2011)*. http://hdl.handle.net/2123/7933.

International Telecommunication Union. 2012. *Measuring the Information Society: Executive Summary* [online report]. Last updated November 9, 2012. Available from http://www.itu.int/dms_pub/itu-d/opb/ind/D-IND-ICTOI-2012-SUM-PDF-E.pdf (accessed March 2, 2014).

James, Felicity. 2014. "Short Films to Deliver Health Messages in Remote Indigenous Communities Where Soft Drink Is Cheaper Than Water" [news report]. Australian Broadcasting Commission. Last updated January 8, 2014. Available from http://www.abc.net.au/news/2014-01-07/short-films-deliver-health-messages-in-remote-indigenous-commun/5189506 (accessed March 15, 2014).

Kansa, Eric. 2009. "Indigenous Heritage and the Digital Commons." In *Traditional Knowledge, Traditional Cultural Expressions and Intellectual Property Law in the Asia-Pacific Region*, edited by C. Antons, 219–244. Alphen aan den Rijn, Netherlands: Kluwer Law International.

Levin, Theodore, and Valentina Süzükei. 2006. *Where Rivers and Mountains Sing: Sound, Music, Nomadism in Tuva and Beyond*. Bloomington and Indianapolis: Indiana University Press.

McLaren, Anne E., Alex English, He Xinyuan, and Catherine Ingram. 2013. *Environmental Preservation and Cultural Heritage in China*. Champaign, IL: Common Ground.

Neuenfeldt, Karl. 2001. "Cultural Politics and a Music Recording Project: Producing *Strike Em! Contemporary Voices from the Torres Strait*." *Journal of Intercultural Studies* 22 (2): 133–145.

Norris, Pippa. 2001. *Digital Divide: Civic Engagement, Information Poverty, and the Internet Worldwide*. Cambridge: Cambridge University Press.

PARADISEC. 2007. *Pacific and Regional Archive for Digital Sources in Endangered Cultures* [pdf brochure]. Last updated September 2007. Available from http://www.paradisec.org.au/08ENbrochureweb.pdf (accessed March 2, 2014).

Seeger, Anthony. 2004a. "New Technology Requires New Collaborations: Changing Ourselves to Better Shape the Future." *Musicology Australia* 27 (1): 94–110.

Seeger, Anthony. 2004b. "Traditional Music Ownership in a Commodified World." In *Music and Copyright*, edited by S. Frith and L. Marshall, 157–170. Edinburgh: Edinburgh University Press.

Seeger, Anthony. 2008. "Theories Forged in the Crucible of Action: The Joys, Dangers and Potentials of Advocacy and Fieldwork." In *Shadows in the Field: New Perspectives for Fieldwork in Ethnomusicology*, edited by G. F. Barz and T. J. Cooley, 271–288. New York and Oxford: Oxford University Press.

Thieberger, Nicholas, and Linda Barwick. 2012. "Keeping Records of Language Diversity in Melanesia: The Pacific and Regional Archive for Digital Sources in Endangered Cultures

(PARADISEC)." In *Melanesian Languages on the Edge of Asia: Challenges for the 21st Century, Language Documentation and Conservation Special Publication No. 5*, edited by N. Evans and M. Klamer, 239–253. Honolulu: University of Hawai'i Press (http://hdl.handle.net/10125/4567).

Treloyn, Sally, and Andrea Emberly. 2013. "Sustaining Traditions: Ethnomusicological Collections, Access and Sustainability in Australia." *Musicology Australia* 35 (2): 159–177.

University of Texas at Austin Library. 2013. *From Custody to Collaboration: The Post-Custodial Archival Model at the University of Texas Libraries* [report]. Last updated January 14, 2013. Available from https://library.stanford.edu/sites/default/files/Univ%20of%Texas.pdf (accessed February 17, 2014).

Williams, Paul. 2013. *Working with Translations: Digital Themed Health Stories* [blog post]. Last updated July 31, 2013. Available from http://www.sgfilms.com.au/Blog/index.php?post_id=4&title=working-with-translations—digital-themed-health-stories (accessed March 15, 2014).

CHAPTER 17

RADIO AFGHANISTAN ARCHIVE PROJECT

Averting Repatriation, Building Capacity

HIROMI LORRAINE SAKATA,
LAUREL SERCOMBE, AND JOHN VALLIER

THE repatriation of sound and video recordings is seen as an essential part of the re-search endeavor as practiced by many ethnomusicologists. It is also one of the ethno-musicology archivist's most sacrosanct functions. From reviving forgotten traditions to inspiring new ones, returned recordings have the potential to have meaningful impact once returned to cultures of origin. As Judith Gray of the Library of Congress, American Folklife Center, notes in relation to repatriation as part of the Federal Cylinder Project:

> Several communities, such as the Kiowa, have used the [repatriated] early recordings as part of oral history projects with elders, stimulating their memories of songs or narrative contexts. On a broader scale, the return of early Omaha recordings . . . has fed into the tribe's ongoing efforts to reclaim cultural material that has been separated from the Nebraska community.
>
> (Gray 1991)

Success, to be sure—but often archivists do not know what impact, if any, repatriated recordings may have had. Again, Judith Gray notes that repatriation results can also be flat-out disappointing:

> Sometimes . . . enthusiasm waned when members of the community actually heard the recordings. Cylinder recordings do not gain charm and patina like old photographs do. Further, some individuals cherished the hope that certain specific songs and narratives were recorded, only to be disappointed to discover that such recordings do not exist.
>
> (Gray 1991)

Beyond mixed results of repatriating recordings or—as is usually the case, returning *copies* of recordings—what can ethnomusicologists and archivists do to benefit the cultures that have made ethnomusicology's very existence possible? Can those whose research involves field recordings work to build the capacity of archives in the developing world? Should we make it a priority to help these archives preserve and provide access to the collections they, not we, possess? If so, what does this shift in priorities mean for archives and ethnography?

Repatriation may involve the return of various kinds of cultural artifacts removed from source communities by researchers and later returned to those communities. For ethnomusicologists, these artifacts are often audio and/or video recordings. The case of the Radio Afghanistan archive, a part of RTA (the National Radio Television of Afghanistan), is not strictly a repatriation project as it does not involve the return of recordings made by outside researchers and removed from that country, but rather a project that aimed more strategically to avert the possibility of a need for repatriation. In this case, music recordings made and located in Afghanistan faced the threat of destruction by a fundamentalist regime, the Taliban. Only after the regime changed in 2001 was it learned that the archivists had hidden the tapes and saved them from being destroyed. At that point, an international organization offered to take the recordings back to their home institution in order to digitize them and return copies back to the archive, but Radio Afghanistan and its archivists refused the offer.

In this chapter, we describe a project that has enabled archivists at Radio Afghanistan to digitize, preserve, and maintain a large cache of unique recordings in their own archive, a project that has given these archivists the equipment and training necessary to continue caring for their collections, thereby avoiding the need for repatriation.

THE STORY AS TOLD BY
HIROMI LORRAINE SAKATA

I first went to Afghanistan in 1966 as an ethnomusicology graduate student to learn something about the music of that country. In January 1967, I had the good fortune to meet Ustad Mohammad Omar, Afghanistan's leading exponent of the *rabab* (a short-neck plucked lute considered the national instrument of Afghanistan) and boldly asked if he would give me private *rabab* lessons. Seeing that I was a guest in his country, he graciously consented. Normally, Ustad Mohammad Omar taught his private students in his home in Kharabat, the old section of Kabul known as the city's entertainment quarters, but because I was his first foreign and female student, he decided to teach me in the more official and respectable workspace of the music studios of Radio Afghanistan. This was my first introduction to Radio Afghanistan and its musicians and staff, and it was where I learned of its respected place and importance in the history of Afghanistan.

Radio Afghanistan

A radio transmitter was first introduced to Afghanistan during the reign of Amanullah Khan (1919–1929) as a part of his effort to modernize the country, but with limited transmission coverage, broadcasting did not last beyond a few years. In 1941, a government radio station was established in Kabul. Known as Radio Kabul, it was administered by the Ministry of Information and Culture. In 1964, the station moved to another location in Kabul and became known as Radio Afghanistan. Today, the station has merged radio and television broadcasting and is known as Radio Television Afghanistan (RTA). From its inception in 1941, advisors from Germany, the United States, Tajikistan, and Uzbekistan provided technical and artistic advice and assistance, including two American advisors who spent time in Kabul: Leo Sarkisian of the Voice of America and Anthony Freeman from the Asia Foundation.

In a population of diverse ethnic and linguistic groups, largely illiterate and without access to other forms of media, Radio Kabul became the unifying voice of the nation, providing programming in the two main languages of Afghanistan, Dari (Persian) and Pashtu. The station employed master musicians who, like other government bureaucrats, enjoyed official sanction, prestige, and support. They developed a musical style combining stylistic elements and melodies from the classical court tradition and regional folk traditions as well as some Western music and instrumentation. This radio style became identified as the national style, the one that all Afghans, both inside and outside the country, identified as their own. Throughout the unimaginable pain and suffering the Afghans have endured in the last thirty-five years, this music has helped them sustain their identity and culture.

In the late 1950s and early 1960s, Radio Kabul was the prime source for international recordings of Afghan music distributed outside Afghanistan. One of the early recordings available in the United States was on the Ethnic Folkways label (now available from Smithsonian Folkways Recordings), *Music of Afghanistan* (FE 4361). It includes studio recordings of some of the most prominent musicians of that era: Ustad Sarahang and Ustad Yaqub Qasimi (classical singers), Ustad Mohammad Omar (*rabab* soloist and leader of the National Orchestra), Hafizulla Khayal (then musical director of the Radio), Madam Parwin (the first amateur female artist to sing on the radio), Awal Mir (Pashtun folk singer), Malang (percussionist), and the Afghan National Orchestra (later known as the National Orchestra of Radio Afghanistan).

Radio musicians also performed for foreign scholars and travelers who came to Kabul to make "field recordings" of Afghan music. A prime example is the recordings made at the station in the early 1960s by Alain Daniélou, historian, philosopher, musicologist, and religious scholar of India, for the UNESCO series *Anthology of Traditional Music of the World.* Recordings such as these were highly influential in defining Afghan music as synonymous with radio music for international listeners.

More recently, the music of Radio Kabul/Afghanistan has served as a resource for Afghan refugee musicians living in Europe and the United States. The memory of working as a singer at Radio Kabul in the 1950s inspired Hossein Arman, with his son Khaled, to form the Kabul Ensemble in Geneva in 1995. Devoted to the performance of traditional Afghan music, it tours widely in Europe. The renowned female radio artist Mahwash received the title of *ustad* from the Ministry of Information and Culture in 1977, a title denoting a high level of mastery and usually reserved for men. When life in Afghanistan became intolerable, particularly for female artists, Mahwash and her family left for Pakistan, where her career as a female singer was also blocked. It was not until 1991, twenty months after leaving Afghanistan, when she and her family moved to the United States, that she was again free to restart her professional singing career. She now tours widely in the United States and Europe, often singing with Hossein and Khaled Arman's Kabul Ensemble. She sings for all the women of Afghanistan, using her voice to represent their voices that have been silenced for so long.

The Radio Archive

In the early 1960s, the station established a sound archive of recordings made for broad-cast, including many of the recordings made by radio musicians in the 1950s. By the end of my first year of fieldwork in Afghanistan, I had made over a hundred recordings of musical examples from various regions of Afghanistan. Not knowing of any other ar-chive there that was dedicated to sound recordings, I offered my recordings to Radio Afghanistan, only to be told that the Radio was not interested in archiving recordings other than Radio Afghanistan studio recordings made primarily for broadcast. It was at this point that I learned of the public/private nature of Radio Afghanistan. It was an official government radio station broadcasting to a public, national audience, but its re-sources were not accessible to the public and were strictly controlled by and for Radio Afghanistan's use only. My access to the music studios of Radio Afghanistan was by invi-tation from my teacher and was strictly monitored.

Throughout Afghanistan's monarchy, its short-lived republic, years of Soviet rule, and civil wars, Radio Kabul, Radio Afghanistan, and later RTA played a central role in the government of Afghanistan through the Ministry of Information and Culture. By the mid-1990s, the archive housed approximately 35,000 hours of historical radio broadcast recordings consisting of political and official commentary as well as music programs. The music tapes alone consisted of 8,500 hours of recordings. During the Taliban regime (1996–2001), television was banned and all music video and recordings were threatened with de-struction. Those of us who worked in Afghanistan prior to the Soviet invasion in 1979 were aware of the existence of the archive and feared that its contents had been destroyed when the Taliban took over the radio station in 1996 and renamed it Radio Shariat.

The Digitization and Training Projects

In late 2002, a year after the fall of the Taliban, I was contacted by a young Afghan American, Farhad Azad, founder and editor of the online journal *Afghan Magazine* (*Lemar-Aftaab*). He had recently returned from Kabul, where he had gone to ascertain the status and survival of Afghan cultural institutions including the archives of RTA. He related the story of the heroic archivists who had risked their lives to hide the archival music tapes in a single room and cover it with a false wall, leaving some copies of tapes exposed in another room as a sacrifice to the Taliban. The Taliban never discovered the hidden tapes, and ironically, instead of destroying the tapes that were left out on purpose for them to find, they demanded that their own chants be recorded over the used tapes so that they could be used for broadcast. The Taliban tapes and cassettes have been cataloged and are a part of the RTA archive, but it is unlikely that these recordings have been aired since the return of RTA. When the Taliban were ousted, the story of the hidden tapes was made public, and Farhad went to see for himself. He took photographs of the archive and a dismal array of broken, defunct equipment used to provide parts for the one or two working reel-to-reel recorders they still used for broadcasting the tapes. Farhad asked if I could help procure more tape recorders to enable RTA to broadcast copies of their archival tapes.

In 2004 I went to Kabul and sought permission from the Ministry of Information and Culture to see the state of the archive for myself and was surprised to find the great attention and care the archivists had given the tapes through the years. They had all been cataloged on index cards and registered in ledger books. Tape contents were written on each tape box, and the location of tapes was posted on each tape shelf. Throughout its forty years of existence, with the exception of the five years the tapes were kept in hiding, the archivists dutifully rewound the tapes periodically to avoid print-through. Critical to the care and preservation of the tapes were devoted archivists like Mr. Siddiq, who is known as "Mr. Computer" for his ability to cite from memory the catalog number of any example in the music collection of 8,500 hours of recordings. The capacity to get things done in Afghanistan is largely dependent on individuals who take personal initiative and responsibility for their actions. Their ability to keep a low profile by working stealthily below the bureaucratic radar allowed archivists like Siddiq to mount and succeed in the plan to hide the Afghan music tapes from the Taliban.

Thankful that the music tapes had survived the threat of destruction by the Taliban, I observed that the collection was still at risk from physical deterioration or destruction from natural disasters. In 2005 I decided to obtain funding for a digitization project for the archive and, with the advice of Laurel Sercombe and John Vallier, and through the auspices of the American Institute of Afghanistan Studies (AIAS), applied for a National Endowment for the Humanities (NEH) preservation and access grant. It was apparent that the Afghan archivists who had risked their lives to save the tapes were not willing to outsource the task of digitizing the tapes to anyone outside of Afghanistan. It was therefore imperative to purchase the equipment and supplies, transport them to Kabul, and train the archivists in their own studios at RTA. The equipment list was long and de-tailed, ranging from highly specialized equipment and supplies such as two ATR open-reel archival tape players and 8,000 Mitsui archival CD-R discs, to common consumer items such as CD jewel box cases that were unavailable in Kabul at the time. The original equipment list included Apple computers, but we quickly changed to Windows-based computers when we learned that there would be no parts or service available for Apple computers in Afghanistan or Pakistan.

In November 2006, the technical consultant Lowell Lybarger, my husband, and I arrived in Kabul and went to the RTA archives to unpack and set up the equipment we had sent, hired an English-to-Dari interpreter, and began the training of six archivists. Lybarger returned in January and April of 2007 for two more intensive periods of training, and I returned periodically to oversee the project in 2007, 2008, and 2010. The RTA archivists took complete ownership not only of the digitizing equipment from the NEH project but also of the digitizing process itself; they eagerly taught other and newer archivists to digitize the materials, thereby ensuring the sustainability of the project even after the end of the grant period.

In May 2007 Taj Mohammad Ahmadzada, who was then the head of the archive, was invited to speak at a conference, "Culture Archives and the State," at Ohio State University. There he met archivists from the Library of Congress, Smithsonian Institution, Indiana University, and others who expressed their eagerness to help in the preservation of the RTA music tapes. This formed the basis of including these institutions along with the University of Washington in another NEH grant to bring the RTA archivists to the United States for an education and training residency.

In January–February of 2008 and again in December of 2008, Shubha Chaudhuri, director of the Archives and Research Centre of Ethnomusicology (ARCE), ran two workshops for the RTA archivists in Delhi, India. Upon the recommendations of ARCE staff, a server and a backup tape drive and tapes for the server were purchased in India and transported to Kabul as accompanied baggage by the archivists. The server sits in a room adjacent to the digitization studio of the archive and has been functioning since 2009; however, the backup tape drive had not been successfully hooked up to the server for lack of technical expertise. The archive's attempt to bring in a technician from the private sector has been complicated by the limited access to RTA for unauthorized personnel. Other technical difficulties and the reluctance of RTA administrators to trust non-RTA personnel to fix equipment have stymied the digitization progress. For example, in 2007 a hard drive containing 326 files crashed. I suggested that they send the hard drive to the United States for data retrieval, but permission was denied. Instead, the archivists were ordered to digitize the lost files over again.

In 2009 Taj Mohammad was replaced by Dost Mohammad as head of the archive. Soon after Dost Mohammad's appointment, one Ampex tape recorder stopped working. An RTA technician alerted me via e-mail, and I contacted the manufacturer in Pennsylvania. The manufacturer, ATR, advised RTA to send them a photograph of the parts on the motherboard that were suspected of malfunctioning and finally recommended that RTA send the motherboard back to them for repairs. Fortunately, the director of RTA had been invited to attend the NEH Summer Education and Training Residency in the United States and personally brought the motherboard with him.

The digitization project culminated in the summer of 2009, when three archivists and the director of RTA came to the United States for an NEH summer residency held at the University of Washington (UW Ethnomusicology Archives and the UW Libraries), Indiana University (Archives of Traditional Music), the Smithsonian Institution (Smithsonian Folkways Recordings), and the Library of Congress (American Folklife Center). During their visit to the Archives of Traditional Music at Indiana University, RTA was offered space on Indiana University's main server to store copies of their preservation files for safekeeping. The director of RTA, a political appointee, refused the offer, citing the lack of copyright laws in Afghanistan as a reason for not making any commitments and added that such an agreement would need the personal approval of Afghan President Karzai. I nevertheless requested that a memorandum of understanding be drafted and presented to the Ministry of Information and Culture and RTA.

In 2010, after months of petitioning both the ministry and RTA to enter the agreement with Indiana University, I was suddenly called to the ministry for the formal signing of the agreement. The signatories were the deputy minister of culture, a political officer from the US Embassy in Kabul, the director of RTA, and me. With the memorandum of understanding duly signed by all parties present, the archivists waited for the director of RTA to permit transfer of the files onto a hard drive that was to be sent to Indiana University by diplomatic pouch. The order never came. Soon after the signing ceremony, the director of RTA left his position and moved to Germany and a new director was appointed. It appears that one of the reasons the director of RTA never gave the archivists permission to send copies of their preservation files to Indiana University's secure server was his unwillingness to take on the personal responsibility of sending the files outside of Afghanistan. The fear of hacking and loss of data has discouraged any attempts to provide Internet access to their materials to date, yet the director of the radio section of RTA is contemplating the sale of their music on CDs or online in the future.

In spite of some of the setbacks (including malfunctioning equipment and changes in personnel) as seen through the eyes of the ethnomusicologists, the digitization project, as seen through the eyes of the RTA archivists, was entirely successful. The archivists now have the equipment and the knowledge to continue digitizing their tape recordings, even after the end of outside funding, and to use CD copies instead of tapes for broadcasting. They now compete with dozens of private radio and television stations operating in Kabul and the provinces. The RTA will surely find its own way to provide access to its music through the Internet. When Siddiq was asked whether he feared loss of the archive if the Taliban were to return, he laughed and said, "No. Because now, I can just put those hard drives inside my jacket and take them somewhere safe."

ISSUES

We now turn a critical eye to the project and address issues arising from our experience in negotiating the diverse perspectives of the project's participants. How is success to be measured in such a collaboration? Whose standards are we using or should we use to determine the success of the project? What prejudgments and expectations do we as ethnomusicologists and archivists bring to the project? If success in our minds is in some way shaped by our orientation as scholars, do our Afghan colleagues share this perspective? Where we find differences that arise from our collaborative efforts, how do we attempt to resolve them?

Several observations about the preceding story may help to focus the issues and address the questions raised by the project:

1. The Radio Afghanistan project as implemented is not a repatriation project since it involves recordings made, archived, and stored in Afghanistan. However, as in repatriation efforts, the aim of the RTA project was local control of cultural heritage, in this case enabled by outsiders providing the necessary training and technology.

2. "Access" and "preservation" have different meanings to the archivists at RTA and the ethnomusicologists involved in the project. As an in-house collection, the RTA recordings need only be accessible for use within the RTA and preserved for its future use there; outside access was deemed undesirable. The ethnomusicologists imagine access for a broader interested audience, including students, musicians, members of the Afghan diaspora, and researchers. Preservation, particularly in the form of digital copies in a secure off-site institution such as Indiana University, is seen by us as a means of safeguarding culture materials, whereas for RTA, this signals a loss of control.

3. Concepts of "ownership" and "responsibility" are determined by personal, cultural, and political factors and may shift over time depending on the individuals involved and perceived self-interest within an organizational or governmental bureaucracy.

4. Basic values concerning the control of cultural property are at the heart of the dilemma posed by the project.

REPATRIATION AND CAPACITY BUILDING

The Radio Afghanistan project was originally inspired by an Afghan American seeking help to upgrade analog tape players at RTA. Since the beginning, Sakata and the other ethnomusicologists involved with the project have aimed to implement what Hennessy describes as a "participatory media project" (Hennessy 2013). In this case, materials deemed at risk had never left their original environment, and it was the environment itself that required attention, at least as the project was first conceived. The project quickly developed into one involving digitization of the large archival collection at RTA, but it continued to be one of capacity development[1] rather than repatriation. The 2003 UNESCO *Convention for the Safeguarding of the Intangible Cultural Heritage* places a high value on capacity building, with emphasis on its implementation at the "national level."

It was clear to the ethnomusicologists that the RTA recordings represent "intangible cultural heritage" of Afghanistan as defined by the UNESCO convention, but it is worth considering whether this is also expressed by Afghans or is a label imposed from the outside to justify a project such as this one. If the project is "participatory" to the extent that there is agreement on this point, then the next consideration is the "safeguarding" of this heritage, defined by the convention as

> measures aimed at ensuring the viability of intangible cultural heritage, including the identification, documentation, research, preservation, protection, promotion, enhancement, transmission, particularly through formal and non-formal education, as well as the revitalization of various aspects of such heritage.

Finding agreement as to the most appropriate form of safeguarding the RTA recordings remains one of the challenges of the Radio Afghanistan project.

PRESERVATION AND ACCESS

The UNESCO *Charter on the Preservation of Digital Heritage* declares, "The purpose of preserving the digital heritage is to ensure that it remains accessible to the public" (Article 2). Both preservation and access have meant something different to the ethnomusicologists involved in the project and to the archivists at RTA and other Afghan stakeholders. From the start, the Afghan perspective was focused on survival and control of materials, while the American perspective was focused on preservation, safe off-site storage, and access.

The RTA archivists initially wanted to upgrade their equipment to broadcast the music over their own airwaves. By digitizing the tape recordings, they could ensure the survival of the content into the future and enhance their broadcast capability. "Access" clearly referred to in-house access for uses controlled by the organization. The implementation of a digitization system, with the on-site server and portable hard drives for backup, served the immediate needs of RTA. Digital copies are now in use for their own TV and radio studios and are also sent to their satellite stations in the provinces.

The ethnomusicologists, meanwhile, looked to digitization not only to facilitate broadcasting but for long-term preservation of the recordings enhanced by secure, off-site storage, in addition to backups at RTA. The ethnomusicologists also looked to digitization as a means of broadening access to the collection. The fear on the Afghan side was that if the recordings were stored off-site, the Radio Afghanistan Archive would lose control of access and of how they would be played and distributed.

Once expressions of intangible culture are documented and realized in digital form, this "digital heritage" and its control, transmission, and circulation present additional challenges as they relate to participatory media projects. Does international policy support endeavors like the Radio Afghanistan project? Article 2 of the charter states:

> Member States may wish to cooperate with relevant organizations and institutions in encouraging a legal and practical environment which will maximize accessibility of the digital heritage. A fair balance between the legitimate rights of creators and other rights holders and the interests of the public to access digital heritage materials should be reaffirmed and promoted, in accordance with international norms and agreements.

According to the UNESCO website, Afghanistan officially ratified the 2003 *Convention for the Safeguarding of the Intangible Cultural Heritage* in the form of "acceptance" (as opposed to full "ratification") so, in theory at least, there is common ground and the basis for a participatory project.

RESPONSIBILITY AND OWNERSHIP: CONTROLLING CULTURAL PROPERTY

Numerous individuals and organizations have a stake in the safeguarding of the RTA recordings. The UNESCO convention stresses the inclusion of "the widest possible participation of communities, groups, and where appropriate, individuals that create, maintain, and transmit such heritage" (Article 15). The Afghan context presents a unique challenge in the negotiation of a truly participatory media project. Among the possible stakeholders one might list are the musicians originally recorded, the descendants of these musicians, RTA, the RTA radio/TV audience, the Afghan population, the Afghan émigré community, and the Afghan government, not to mention the American ethnomusicologists, the NEH (as project funding source), and other non-Afghans interested in the cultural heritage of Afghanistan.

The RTA is a governmental institution with the oversight of the Ministry of Information and Culture, but with a general director (political appointment) and different section heads including radio and television and their staff members (career appointments). Within this bureaucracy, individuals and relationships forged between individuals may hold more weight than their position in the hierarchy. Sakata, noting that Afghans are in general fiercely independent, observes that superiors often have very little persuasion over their subordinates simply by virtue of their positions. Instead, they rely on special relationships with individuals allowing them to save face without forcing the issue. It was individual staff members who took personal responsibility for saving the tapes in the archives from the Taliban and who continue to care for them.

Among other stakeholders, Sakata has personal reasons for her years-long commitment to the Radio Afghanistan project, going back to her field research in Afghanistan in the 1960s–1970s. The project has been one way of acknowledging the personal and professional benefits of that relationship. For her and the other ethnomusicologists, reactions to the Taliban era and the years of US military involvement in Afghanistan have also been motivating factors, arising out of some combination of horror, guilt, and a desperate need to contribute something positive. Whether these impulses are born of Western arrogance and the project represents the imposition of our own values concerning cultural heritage is still unresolved by the participants.

Conclusion

We continue to believe that the Radio Afghanistan project has been beneficial to RTA and to the cause of safeguarding intangible cultural heritage in Afghanistan, even as we examine our motives and our admittedly neocolonial rationalization that "we" know the best solution to "their" problems. As Brown suggests, "When controls are warranted, they should be developed by source communities" (Brown 2014). While we may never resolve our complicated evaluations of and reactions to the project, we have left the larger question of ongoing professional responsibility to the community with which we worked.

Repatriation, though often tricky to implement, is easy to feel good about since it involves returning (or at least sharing) something once taken away but now returned. Even here ethnomusicologists and archivists retain some control, since it is rarely the only copy of a recording that is repatriated. Instances of entirely relinquishing power to a community to decide the fate of its intangible cultural heritage are rare (an extreme case is the highly publicized decision by the folklorist Barre Toelken's chief consultant's wife to destroy Navajo ritual recordings rather than risk their falling into the wrong hands [Toelken 1998]). In our case, the decision to not deposit preservation files at Indiana University was ultimately made by the community.

Pushing beyond repatriation, ethnomusicologists and archivists have much to contribute to genuinely participatory media projects. Funding, technical and technological assistance, and personnel may help in implementing such projects. "Safeguarding" intangible cultural heritage may mean different things in different contexts.[2] True collaboration requires that we be prepared to do less than our professional training and experience dictate (e.g., providing access to files for research), but it may also ask us to do something more (e.g., answering a broader ethical calling to let the community decide). While the researcher's skills of listening, observing, and reporting may be an asset in helping to safeguard the world's music traditions, we also need to stretch as a community—bracketing off our own professional aspirations to add to the scholarly record—and use our skills in ways that are not always rewarded in ivory tower settings.

NOTES

1. For a definition of capacity development building, see the United Nations Committee of Experts on Public Administration, "Definition of Basic Concepts and Terminologies in Governance and Public Administration," United Nations Economic and Social Council, 2006. http://unpan1.un.org/intradoc/groups/public/documents/un/unpan022332.pdf.
2. See Bortolotto's discussion about the shifting notion of safeguarding intangible cultural heritage from what she calls "the old archival approach" to the "new dynamic approach" (2007, 27).

REFERENCES

Bortolotto, Chiara. 2007. "From Objects to Processes: UNESCO's 'Intangible Cultural Heritage.'" *Journal of Museum Ethnography* (19): 21–33.

Brown, Michael F. 2014. "The Possibilities and Perils of Heritage Management." In *Cultural Heritage Ethics: Between Theory and Practice*, edited by Sandis Constantine, 171–180. Cambridge, UK: Open Book. http://www.jstor.org/stable/j.ctt1287k16.17.

Gray, Judith. 1991. "The Songs Come Home: The Federal Cylinder Project." *CRM: Cultural Resources Management* 14 (5): 32–35.

Hennessy, Kate. 2013. "The Intangible and the Digital: Participatory Media Production and Local Cultural Property Rights Discourse." In *Proceedings of Memory of the World in the Digital Age: Digitization and Preservation. An International Conference on Permanent Access to Digital Documentary Heritage, Sept. 26–28, 2012, Vancouver, BC*, edited by Luciana Duranti and Elizabeth Schaffer, 58–68. [n.p.]: UNESCO.

Toelken, Barre. 1998 "The Yellowman Tapes, 1966–1997." *Journal of American Folklore* 111: 381–391.

UNESCO. 2003a. *Charter on the Preservation of Digital Heritage.* http://portal.unesco.org/en/ev.php-URL_ID=17721&URL_DO=DO_TOPIC&URL_SECTION=201.html.

UNESCO. 2003b. *Convention for the Safeguarding of the Intangible Cultural Heritage.* http://www.unesco.org/culture/ich/en/convention.

....

CHAPTER 18

BRINGING RADIO
HAITI HOME

The Digital Archive as Devoir de Mémoire

....

CRAIG BREADEN AND LAURA WAGNER

FROM the early 1970s until 2003, Radio Haiti-Inter was the preeminent independent radio station in Haiti. The uncommonly dynamic agronomist-turned-journalist Jean Dominique was the director of the station and its most iconic voice; his professional partner and life partner, Michèle Montas, ran the newsroom and trained generations of Haitian journalists. For more than thirty years, Radio Haiti served as a beacon of resistance, liberation, and democracy. It broadcast news, interviews and roundtable discussions, in-depth investigative reporting, editorials, performances and cultural commentary (among other types of programming) in Haitian Creole, the language spoken by all Haitian people; promoted national culture; and amplified the voices of the rural and urban masses who had long been excluded from public discourse and political processes. In April 2000, having survived the violent oppression of the Duvalier dictatorship and military rule, Jean Dominique was struck down during a democratic season, assassinated along with station employee Jean-Claude Louissaint in the courtyard of the Radio Haiti station. Not long after an attempt on Michèle Montas's life on Christmas Day 2002, Radio Haiti closed its doors. In 2003, the Academy Award–winning filmmaker Jonathan Demme released the documentary *The Agronomist* about the history of Radio Haiti and the life and death of Jean Dominque.

The Radio Haiti Archive, comprising more than 3,600 audio tapes and accompanying papers, came to Duke University's David M. Rubenstein Rare Book and Manuscript Library in 2013 from Michèle Montas, on condition that the collection be made publicly accessible worldwide, and that digital access to the collection be supported in Haiti. The National Endowment for the Humanities awarded a half-million-dollar grant to Duke in 2015 to process the collection and make it web accessible by late 2017. The core of the team processing the collection is the audiovisual archivist and Radio Haiti project manager, Craig Breaden, and the Radio Haiti project archivist, Laura Wagner, who is

also a writer and cultural anthropologist. Breaden and Wagner bring different professional backgrounds and experiences to the project but share a commitment to bringing
Radio Haiti home. Their differing but sympathetic perspectives reflect the complexity of
a project that tests the technical and descriptive capacities of an institution preparing to
digitally repatriate an archive. The following dialogue was recorded during the summer
of 2016, as the project entered its second year. It has been lightly edited for clarity.

LAURA WAGNER: How did the Radio Haiti Archive come to be at Duke University?
CRAIG BREADEN: I first heard about it from Patrick [Stawski, the curator of the
    Human Rights Archive at the Rubenstein Library], who had talked to Michèle
    [Montas] (Figure 18.1), because a contact of his through the National Coalition of
    Haitian Rights Papers, Jocelyn McCalla, had talked to Michèle and had directed
    her toward Duke as a good place to put the archive. I think she was pretty much
    up in the air at that time about where to put the archive. She followed up with his
    suggestion, but it wasn't with full confidence because it doesn't seem like a natural
    fit. Outside of the fact that we have the NCHR Papers, there's no outward reason
    why they should be here. I think everybody—everybody being Patrick and Kat
    [Stefko, then head of Rubenstein's Technical Services group] and me—we were
    excited about the collection, just from the description of it, and thought—and I'm
    still sort of this way just because I don't have the language and I'm not as familiar
    with the culture as you are, plus I have other collections that I work on, a lot of
    irons in the fire—that even just on the face of it, it's a really great collection. I mean,
    if you're in the archives world you don't have to be super-knowledgeable on this
    subject to look at it and be able to say, "This is really an amazing archive."

FIGURE 18.1 Jean Dominique and Michèle Montas at Radio Haiti in 1995.

Photograph courtesy of Michèle Montas.

LW: Why is that?

CB: Because it's unique insofar as it's big, right? It goes back a long time, and it covers a really super-critical period in recent Haitian history. So it has breadth, and it has depth, and it's not been mined for anything academically. And again, this is taking the view of just an academic archive. There was so much potential there, and when I think about audio, and video too, but even more with audio, and the challenges of an AV archive, I think that these are resources that are often hidden in plain sight. Researchers historically, when they've come up against audio, they almost always ask if there's a transcript. If there's not a transcript they tend not to go any further, so a lot of audiovisual resources get left behind. So if you have an opportunity to bring good description to an audio archive, and see that as an archivist, it's like, "Yeah, we want to do that," because so often those resources don't get used. I saw a lot of value there, because for every audiocassette or audiotape, you'd be talking the equivalent of a box of papers. To me, that's the way I think about it. Or at least a folder or two, you know? If you try to think of, "What's the value of this?" up against papers or more commonly mined resources, first of all, you can't look at it and see what's in it, but it could have just incredible value over the span of a few seconds of time.

LW: Well, that's the optimistic side of how long this project is taking me, and why it takes me so long. Because you can't look at a tape and know what it is. You can know what the title is, and more often than not Radio Haiti was accurate in their titles, but occasionally not. Even so, just looking at that title it doesn't capture most of what's on the tape very often, and it's impossible really to skim it. That makes me feel better: if I think of every recording as being a box, I'm going fast.

CB: I think the other thing that was interesting at the outset was, when a donor approaches, oftentimes you have two different attitudes, and oftentimes they're together at the same time, and one's like, "Oh this is really cool, we can do a lot of stuff with this, look at the value." And then there's another part of you—and we all have different versions of this depending on whether you're a curator or a technical services archivist like me—that's looking for all the arguments against: "Why shouldn't we take this?" Right up front there were probably more arguments against than there were for, because of the technical challenges involved. We knew pretty quickly that whatever we did, we would need to be going for a grant at some point.

LW: What were the arguments against?

CB: The argument against was very similar to the argument for, in my head. It was really big, the technical challenges involved in a foreign language collection, as you now well know, are pretty big, especially because nobody here had the language, so basic discovery of the resources was really difficult. You're left with kind of a hot potato in the sense of, "I can't really do anything with this, you know, what do you think?" Another point against was a very assertive donor, and this is not unusual in an archive, where everybody wants their stuff in line first. It's a natural thing for any donor: they want to give their stuff, but they want their stuff to be attended to. In fact, that's a really good approach for a donor, because the squeaky wheel does get the grease in the archive. For this collection, Michèle didn't donate any money, and we didn't give her any money for it, but she demonstrated how important it was, and that is the value there, the historical importance of it. So, again, different sides of it, we knew we were going to be working with a very assertive donor who expected a lot. Which is great, especially since we were all basically on her side, but also daunting in its way. Then there's the technical challenge of the tapes themselves, the issues they have, resuscitating them, figuring out how you're going to get that done, and thankfully because of the grant we were able to have a lot of that done, so I'm not still scrubbing away with a sponge on a tape box. So just at the outset, the idea of repatriation seemed great, and the way Michèle described wanting to have it cover the earth since digitally we can do it, our response was "Great! Let's put it out there." And then, after that, okay, but technically, as an archive, how do we do that and preserve the recordings, make sure everything drops into place, and we were in this catch-22 position because we want to do that, we don't have a grant yet so we can't really promise we can do it.

LW: So this was when, 2014?

CB: Mid-2013. I remember being on a conference call where I first met Michèle, and we said, "We have the background and the experience to handle these resources, but before we can process it the way it needs to be we really need to get a grant. A big grant." She understood that, and was very cool with donating the collection before we had a budget, and I think after talking more with Patrick—and having Laurent [Dubois, professor of history and romance studies and director of the Forum for Scholars and Publics at Duke University] there was huge interest (?), as somebody at the institution who had this reputation—we showed her we could take care of the materials, that we knew what we were doing in that sense. Added to that, the inventory they provided, which we now know was the product of what it had to be . . .

LW: And it was hugely useful.

CB: With that, we were—and that's a lesson for me here, we were being too optimistic about it.

LW: You mean that the titles would capture the entire content?

CB: Yeah. I mean, we knew that technically it was difficult because we effectively only had a paper copy of the inventory, that is, the electronic document couldn't be easily crosswalked into a spreadsheet. I think there was so much relief that we had that, though, because it's rare to get such a complete inventory, which we were like, "At the very least we have an inventory." And people who are knowledgeable about this subject are going to say, "Okay, I'm going to listen to this tape," and that even if we had just the inventory, we could do one-off digitization as people requested it. Which we do for a lot of our collections. So right off the bat there was a lot of excitement, but we also knew we had a lot of challenges to fulfill Michèle's dream for the collection, which we all wanted—to get it back out there. I would say that the repatriation for an archive is one of the principles of what I do. It's really important to make things accessible, hopefully to make them accessible to the original population or the descendants of the original creators, whoever it might be. And it's important to make it available not only to those specific creators of the content but also to the research community, student community, artistic community, whatever other community. Repatriation is a part of what I do, something I think about. But this was the first time I think I've handled a collection that so explicitly has that part of it. So we got the collection—we'd first started talking about it in early 2013, it might have even been late 2012, and then we started receiving the tapes in October 2013. Then we had the big celebration downtown.

LW: In April 2014.

CB: When we got the tapes, and I saw the big blue bins they were packed in, I was like, "*Oh, yeah.*" And I opened it up, and there was ticker tape, really just shredded paper, packed in there (Figure 18.2), and I thought, "I don't know what's going to come out of this bin, but we'll see." I was impressed when I opened it up, though. They had put a copy of the inventory in each bin, and they were packed snugly enough, so they weren't going to get damaged en route. I had no idea what I was going to find as far as mold, but we knew there would be mold and that it would affect the cost of digitization. That's what I see as the genesis of it. How about you? You first came in contact with the collection not long after we got it.

LW: Probably May or June 2014, when we did the pilot website.[1] I am not an archivist; well, I guess I am called one now. But I'm not an archivist by training or even by temperament, but I had defended my dissertation on April 1, 2014, which coincided with the celebration of the donation of the archive, so I guess it was serendipity.

CB: But you are a capturer of culture . . .

LW: "Capturer of culture"—that sounds very acquisitive. Like some colonial explorer in the jungle with a net.

CB: I think that most people who are involved with history or anthropology, there's a part of them that are naturally archivists, that they save things, they're saving things.

LW: Yeah, I mean I'm a salvager in some ways, a hoarder in certain ways. I don't know; I have a certain attention to detail and ability to keep track of details, which has been useful.

CB: It's a part of your discipline; it's directed.

LW: Okay. I mean I'm interested in anthropology, I'm interested in storytelling, I'm interested in the stories of people's lives, and in my own research how large, macro

FIGURE 18.2 One of the Radio Haiti bins, freshly opened.

Photograph courtesy of Craig Breaden.

issues play out and affect the trajectory and the experiences of people's everyday lives, which is what I like a lot about this collection—it goes beyond the broad strokes, right? You have these major themes that anyone who studies anything related to twentieth-century history would know about. The Duvalier regime, or the coup years in the '90s, or any number of major events. But because it's day-to-day reportage, and interviews and things like that, it's really at a granular level—and they were also talking to not only public figures, you know, politicians and policy makers and public intellectuals and people like that, but they were talking to just a lot of people, period, from different social backgrounds—it really gets at the way these big historical events played out in people's lived experiences, and I like that. And so when you were saying right now about repatriation and bringing the archives back to the creators or the descendants of the creators, in a sense—and this probably sounds a little bit sentimental—but this is Haiti's archive. Certainly it's Jean and Michèle's archive, but it's also the archive of a very large number of journalists and field correspondents and also everybody who participated in it on a daily basis. And participating in it can mean talking on the air, or calling in, but also listening, because it was really about interaction. Radio Haiti (Figure 18.3) matters because people were listening. They weren't talking to themselves; they were talking to people, and the act of listening was part of the participation. So that's what I was thinking about when you were talking about who this belongs to.

LW: The very first time I met Laurent when I was just starting in grad school, he said something like, and it stuck with me, that Haiti is an incredibly intellectual society and it has nothing to do with whether or not people can read or write. Which is to say that it's a place where debate and political conversations and cultural exchanges

FIGURE 18.3 Three Radio Haiti staff members in 1995: Fanfan Mathieu (reporter), Edouarzin Dionisse (technician), and Fritzson Orius (reporter).

are happening all the time and in different kinds of milieux, and it isn't necessarily people who are formally educated or who have a certain kind of formal education. I think in some ways your average Haitian person is more politically aware and analytical than the average American person.

CB: Is there a special significance, do you think, to the archive being audio, in the way it relates to the Haitian Creole language, itself a topic of political discourse?

LW: Sure. Radio Haiti was all about creating a forum where everyone was represented, where everyone's voice mattered, especially those people who had been systematically excluded: the urban poor, poor farmers in the countryside, *Vodouisants*, women, laborers.... And they did it in Haitian Creole in addition to French, in the language that all Haitian people speak and understand, regardless of education or class background.

CB: Does an audio archive have more importance in a culture where you have a Radio Haiti, you have this spirited debate, you have this spirit of talking about these things? The archive might carry a unique value that it might not carry in the United States.

LW: Yes and no. Haiti is also smaller, and Jean Dominique was a uniquely charismatic and powerful figure. A lot of scholars and academics of Haiti, and Haitian scholars, push back against this idea of exceptionalism, which is something we talk about a lot, so I'm loathe to say it is more important in Haiti because "X," but I think it was about context, it was a moment that was a perfect confluence of a lot of things, that radio technology was taking off in the way it was at that moment, and then Jean was a really extraordinarily effective, passionate communicator. He was the right person in the right place at the right time.

CB: One of the things that strike me as being unique about it, too, is that you have the smallness of the country and the population, but there's also this other piece, that broadcasting history covers a fairly narrow window of time. There hasn't been radio for that long. By the time that Jean died, radio was available widely only for about 75 years. And so if we think about it in those terms, Radio Haiti was on the air, well certainly before Jean Dominique owned it, since ...

LW: 1935.

CB: But even if you think about just his tenure there, that's a huge percentage of the entire era of broadcasting. To have that much tape, that much audio, from one station, that did this arts-into-politics thing, I mean, is mind-blowing when you think about it, and given the smallness of Haiti, makes it seem even bigger.

LW: It's a small country that nonetheless has outsized importance, partly because it has come to represent so much to so many people, for good and for bad, and because it is so close to the United States and has its particular history. Radio Haiti is not only about Haiti, and even the things that are about Haiti are applicable in so many other contexts, and are representative of the time globally, regarding what kind of international interventions were happening. The effects of structural adjustment policies, all these things that you see play out in all kinds of different contexts. Haiti is not unique, but in some ways is perhaps exemplary.

CB: It also went off the air not long after the beginning of the 24-hour news cycle, and pervasive Internet. I don't know what the Internet was like in Haiti by the time Jean was killed, but certainly, even here in the United States it wasn't that great by 2000. It wasn't until a couple of years later that you could get media online, audio and video media online, and I think today the context for a place like Radio Haiti online is completely different than what it would have been then, which also makes me think about its impact, its repatriation impact, or the impact we're going to have in taking it back there.

LW: You mean in terms of just how it's going to happen, or the fact that the infrastructure is now, to a degree, there for it to spread in a different way?

CB: Yeah, I think both, there's going to be some balance. When it was in its heyday, there weren't as many competitors in the field, for eyes and ears. You have that now. This information that we're going to give is going to be on an Internet that's much bigger than it was fifteen or sixteen years ago. What's cool about it too is that there are going to be that many more contexts that people can put the information into as they hear it.

LW: Yeah. A lot of the events that are either spoken of in this archive, or often they had real-time recordings of them, are touchstones. There are particular dates, particular moments, often bad ones—a particular massacre, a particular attack, a particular assassination—that people talk about, but through time the memory evolves and can become distorted. There's always distortion, I'm not judging distortion; it's just that something happens through time and narrative and hindsight. And in this archive we have a lot of these events presented without hindsight and without the meaning that was then assigned to them later, and that's very valuable, regarding saying, "Here's what happened." I think that's a unique thing, an important thing, about the whole collection. Also, you see trends evolving, and that's something that certainly I see now, because I'm looking at the whole archive and moving through it and seeing it as a whole. I feel like I have this god's eye view—that's very self-aggrandizing (*laughter*)—I sometimes listen, and I know what happens later, I know what happens to that person, and so the recordings knit themselves into a narrative at the same time. And yet, you can also zoom in on them, and try to divorce yourself from the knowledge you have of what comes later. I want to add something. When I was saying before that in Haiti people talk a lot about politics and have these kinds of debates and exchanges, at the same time there is a lot of silencing, and it's the result of having first gone through almost 30 years of right-wing dictatorship with Duvalier, where if you said the wrong thing not only could you get killed but your whole family could get killed—everybody, down to little kids. There were a lot of cases like that. So that obviously makes people afraid to talk, and then the generation after that I think grew up that way, they were taught never to talk and then things changed, but it was still a very unstable climate in different ways. One thing you get when you listen to all this stuff is, you know, sure, there was Duvalier, Duvalierism, and Macoutes, and after the fall of Duvalier, those Macoutes were still there, even if they were no longer the formal Tontons Macoutes.[2] The mentality of repression was there, and it just sort of changed its face, and so at the same time there is this great tradition of speaking, there's also a history of silence. That's why you hear these stories of people listening to Radio Haiti with the volume really low because you didn't necessarily want your neighbors knowing that that was what you were listening to. That's one of the ways that Jean Dominique was extraordinary and created something that was extraordinary. Because he was probably singularly fearless in certain ways. That's what I've been told. So the question you brought up,

"Is the archive safer here than it is in Haiti?" Probably. Even though that's weird to say.

CB: It's ironic.

LW: It's both ironic and obvious at the same time. It's ironic that something that is such an important part of Haitian national heritage and memory is here, in Durham, North Carolina.

CB: In a country that does not have a good history in Haiti.

LW: Well, *no.* . . . And the US doesn't come across particularly favorably in this very archive. That's ironic; that's funny every time I think about it. If only the US government knew what it was preserving in this archive. I asked Michèle once about what Jean would think about our working on the archive, and she said, "Jean never thought of it as an archive." Meaning, I think, that he never imagined it would end, that at some point this would be some sort of relic rather than a living body of work. For him, it was alive. I think that's what she meant. When I thought of archives before I worked in an archive, on an archive, I thought of something static. And I don't think this *is* static. What we're doing is putting it back into motion. The idea that the physical archive is at Duke, and it's safer here—I remember when I first started, and I thought it was really strange that I was working in a cubicle with all of this stuff, and how far it was from the actual content of what I was listening to which was, you know, tear gas and blood on the streets, and how strange and alienating it is that I'm in this space doing this. And you said, "*Yeah*, it's 'cause it's safer here." You know, it's a miracle that this archive survived the 1980 to 1986 exile of the Radio Haiti journalists—that's probably the biggest miracle, because they didn't know that was going to happen, they didn't have time to pack it up. It just sat there, in the ransacked station. It's a miracle that it survived the coup years, although in that case, they had more time to put things away. It's a miracle that it survived the earthquake, because luckily Jean and Michèle's house was fine, but an awful lot of other buildings, including the old Radio Haiti station building, and many other important sites of national heritage, were destroyed in the earthquake. This all could have been lost in 35 seconds on January 12, 2010. So in a physical sense, yes, it is safer here. And yes, there are people who are still alive, who were never held accountable for some of the things they did, and who would dislike very much to know that these recordings are going to come back to life and their crimes and misdeeds are going to be brought to light again.

CB: I remember that moment, too, when we talked about that, because when I said that, I certainly wasn't trying to pull some "They're safer because they're in the United States, which is safer!" I think part of it *was* probably that, honestly, but part of it, too was that they're safer, they're literally safer here at Duke because you're working on it and I'm working on it. And we both have an experience, or set of experiences, that are very different. But I can name other archives that I've seen of audiotape, in the United States, that don't get treated well and that aren't treated up to standard, and they languish. Usually, every archive has a collection or two like that anyway, just because there are backlogs and whatnot. But there are places that don't know how to describe these things; they don't know how to deal with audio and visual materials. So in that sense I was very literal, like "Here, *at Duke.*" They would have been safe at any number of other archives as well, but we've shown institutionally that we can handle these sorts of things. And I think that's really important. Talking about this process of repatriation, I was thinking of what technically has to happen before that can happen. Because of the idea that there's this science—that's not a good term for it, but—behind preservation, because it's partly science but it's also partly intention, and needing to judge how to treat certain materials. But being able to take an archive of this size and create digital replicas of the stuff, and then being able to preserve it, and then being able to describe it, and then being able to make it fit to go online, and then being able to actually get it online, and get it streaming in such a way that people can then *get* it—we're only halfway down that process. And it's already been an enormous amount of work. And so the idea of repatriation, it doesn't happen without all that other stuff happening too. There are dependencies that go back to the very beginning, when we first started taking tapes out of boxes, and how we approached the description. Because one thing that's important about archival work and the whole spirit behind it was the idea of authenticity. Like, "This is the tape that came from Radio Haiti, we digitized the tape in such a way that we're getting the clearest possible picture of the audio on that tape, and we're presenting it in such a way that you can track this authenticity down the line." So, in doing that and presenting it through the website we're going to present it through, hopefully presenting it through the DLOC [Digital Library of the Caribbean] website, presenting it—it's going to be a little more dicey with the hard drives,[3] because once those hard drives are out of our hands, anything could happen with those files. But the idea is that we're providing some guarantee of authenticity. Which is important, not only if you're a researcher, but if you're a Haitian and you're listening to your own history, it's important to know that this happened. Even if it's just like, "We swear!" we can show a trail of custody, the provenance, the source, which was Jean Dominique. So that's part of where the repatriation starts, at least in my head.

LW: It's been challenging for me because I want us to have the most accessible, user-friendly interface possible for people in Haiti. Understanding that whatever we create will never be as democratic and universal as radio was, but I also want it to be as far from *impossible* as possible if that makes sense. And, far more than I expected coming into the project, it's been a paradigm shift for some of the other people working on creating digital access, because when I say, "Researchers will be fine, that's not who I'm worried about, that's not who I'm thinking about"—you know, researchers who want to use this material will figure it out, and they'll be fine; I don't think of them as the primary audience—and I didn't realize how heterodox that was until I had to keep saying it over and over. (*laughs*)

CB: And it's because we're completely tuned not to hear that. That *is* a paradigm shift, and it's an important one. And I think that's something that you kept saying, and now I'm saying it too, to some degree . . .

LW: Good!

CB: . . . because for so long, and particularly at an archive like Duke—and again, that's also its strength because it's got this sort of juggernaut thing going on. It's very hard; it turns very slowly, but it's got a lot of power. And this is the first time that I've heard of, at least, where we're doing this with one of our archives. Where we're taking it back, trying to take it back to the community from which it came. It's been hard to impress what that means on people. Part of it is super technical. Part of it is our websites can only do so much. If you're our IT department, it's "Well, this is what our websites do. This is the way they function." And that can mean all sorts of things. That can mean we don't have a streaming server. We have a server and people will be able to download the audio, which is great for us. But the red flag goes up at Duke because—copyright, right? And so it could be that there's a famous French song that's smack dab in the middle of a recording, and we start talking about putting all this stuff online, that could potentially have all these copyright issues, it's like right away the red flags go up. And this is partly because of all the other collections we've dealt with, and the things we think about. What I hope is changing is, it's not like—we don't want that to be the guiding issue. We want access to be the guiding issue. And luckily Duke is—they might not be at the very forefront, but they're more progressive in their ideas about sharing information. And part of that was Kevin Smith's doing, our [former] legal adviser, and part of that is also—I think there's a mission at Duke to try to be more progressive than its roots always imply.

LW: (*laughs*) You mean in the library, or at Duke University . . . ?

CB: At the library. We have a very progressive director of the library, the university library, and we have a very progressive director of the Rubenstein Library. But they are also entrenched in library practice, and so they have to weigh their responsibilities across the board. So there's the institutionalized thinking, and we're trying to steer the ship, in this case, to accommodate something. I don't think you can find a similar case here, at Duke, where we've done this.

LW: I truly didn't know any of that coming in, the institutional culture of the library. It's not my—it's not where I grew up. It's not how I was trained. So not only do I want to think outside the box, I don't even know why we *need* the box, half the time. So it's a balance . . .

CB: (*laughs*)

LW: . . . Which has always been my strongest suit: equanimity. (*laughs*)

CB: It's ultimately from those kinds of tensions that good things can come.

LW: Eventually! But I'm also the one who has people in Haiti sending me messages saying, "When's it happening? Can you get me this recording? What about this one?" And I try to accommodate that as much as I can. I also have a lot of people, a *lot* of people who I feel accountable to, many of whom I don't know. Just as the library has a sense of accountability to certain kinds of practices. Radio Haiti and Jean Dominique, it's a huge legacy. And it's mostly a privilege to do it, but it's also a significant weight to know that I'm responsible for that.

CB: I'm glad we were not doing this project ten years ago, because the tools were not even close to what they are now, with social media and everything. I feel like not only can we digitize things more easily and just put them online, but there are so many old, dead-looking web pages out there with various archives on them using HTML that isn't interactive at all. Something I'm thinking about, and you're thinking about even more than I am, with the idea of repatriation, is what that means in a social media context. Repatriation in the context of computers in general, but certainly I think social media in particular, is—you're going to lose, there's a linearity you're going to lose, that came with the recordings being chronologically done, as a set, that if you look at it on the page as part of the archive, it's like, "Oh yeah," it's sort of easy to see. But it hits social media, and people start embedding and sharing and linking, and it just, it's gonna go *whoomp!* What do you think about that?

LW: I think linearity is . . . I'm not going to say "overrated," I think it's—this is sort of an obnoxious postmodern thing to say, but—it's not the only way that time works.

CB: But we're talking about essentially decontextualizing. . . . It doesn't have to be just chronological, but we're supporting decontextualizing the archive when we put it up like that.

LW: But that would happen anyway! No one was going to listen to all of them in order, anyway. People were always going to seek certain topics, certain themes. . . .

CB: But here's my point. That we're going to allow people to pick up an embed code for a recording and put it wherever they want, free of context is something different than maybe we've done before. And in fact, up until last year, we didn't even have embed codes in any of our finding aids or digital collections. It's a fairly recent development, where you can present the information within a completely different web page without ever having to leave that page, or even know where the resource came from. So I think that's interesting. It's way different from say, ten, fifteen, twenty years ago, where this kind of repatriation would be like, "We sent a box of tapes back to the village in Papua New Guinea. . . ."

LW: Right. And, from the point of view of information technology in Haiti, that's changing so much, so rapidly. This definitely couldn't have happened ten years ago, in that sense. It's changed utterly, especially after the earthquake, regarding access, social media, the presence of smartphones that have become—not ubiquitous, but very, very common, and more common among poor people—among people in the Haitian countryside—than a lot of people in the US might think. This is a very accessible technology, and there are certain kinds of data plans, and use of apps and things like that, that didn't exist five years ago. So it's totally changed. And it makes me wonder—things are so much more possible now that I wonder what it'll look like in five years, and how can we, in designing this project, how can we prepare for whatever it's going to look like in five years? How can we know we're on the right path for things to continue to grow and amplify in five years? And that's not really what I do. It's not where my expertise is. . . .

CB: Nor mine.

LW: But I hope to sort of prod the people who can do it.

CB: I think it's fascinating the way that technology is accessed in Haiti, from what you've told me, and how that's going to affect this process. The fact that it becomes . . . I don't know if *transactional* is the right word . . . Like, from what you've told me, people are going to—they pay for a data plan, they would typically take some time to download the recording and then listen to the recording. Is that right?

LW: Not necessarily. So far we've been putting things on SoundCloud, right? Most people in Haiti don't use SoundCloud regularly. Some do, but it's not one of the common apps. But people stream from YouTube, they don't download from YouTube, they stream from YouTube. It might take them a while for it to load . . .

CB: To buffer . . .

LW: Yes. Depending on probably the time of day and how cloudy it is, and, I don't know. People do download songs, but they also send them via messenger app by recording the song as a voicemail and sending it to a friend.

CB: That's so cool.

LW: So there's all these kinds of workarounds and things like that, that are easier, that are faster, that are cheaper. So I don't know how to build this into the places where people already are because that's also a moving target. I do think that the flash drives were a fantastic idea, so: Bravo, Patrick.

CB: We should probably talk about Patrick's idea.

LW: Yeah, we should. Patrick had this great idea to create Radio Haiti flash drives, and you and I made approximately one thousand flash drives, each containing around sixteen hours of Radio Haiti audio that I selected and curated, from the early 1970s through 2002, covering a variety of topics, including really all kinds of things, from Haitian history and the revolution, arts, literature, the rights of rural peasant farmers, the legacy of Duvalierism, the coup years and the aftermath, the assassination of Jean Dominique, and other salient moments of impunity, and other topics. There were twenty-eight or twenty-nine recordings, total. And I distributed them, or rather I gave them to other people to distribute (Figure 18.4). So each USB drive had the *vèvè*, Radio Haiti's symbol, which is a version of a Vodou-style ritual drawing but in the shape of a microphone.[4] And that was the symbol that was on their building and their letterhead. So it's that, and on the other side of the flash drive they have the permanent URL of the finding aid, which for now is almost impossible to access in Haiti because it is so huge, but it is there. And I gave them to grassroots organizations, community organizations, cultural institutions, libraries, schools, things like that, for them to be distributed, and hopefully be copied and shared widely. And people were hugely receptive and excited about this. And I'm still getting requests from people who want one. Even though you can access the content online. So it's a little bit funny, because people

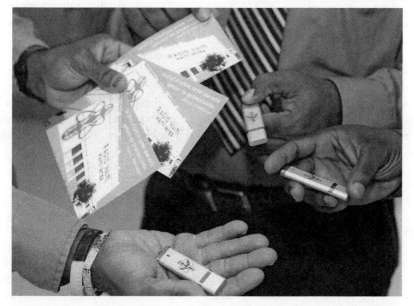

FIGURE 18.4 Radio Haiti flash drives and postcards distributed in Limonade, Haiti.

Photograph courtesy of the MIT-Haiti Initiative.

will e-mail me, so they have the Internet, but they're writing because everyone wants that thing. And—gosh, if we could do it again, that would be great. I think the more we do things like that, the better.

CB: So that was conceived of as kind of a promotional project. Since we had a year to go, we were sort of in between, you had the opportunity to go to Haiti, we thought this would be something where, it would be kind of like a calling card, and we actually did have a calling card, a little postcard that we made to sort of start bringing people in. But the response was pretty amazing. And the interesting thing about it, thinking about the mechanics of delivering the audio back to Haiti, is—it's really interesting how that flash drive, it's in some ways so much better than a web page could be, because it's something they can hold on to, it's here, you just plug it in, it'll work, it's not trying to get this enormous conception of a web page or whatever it's going to be, to work. All the things that have to go into that, all the people that have to work on that to make it happen. It's like, this was you and me, and we just made a bunch of copies of the flash drives, and then we got people together in Haiti and said, "Hey, hand these out!"

LW: Pretty much!

CB: In some ways, that seems much more pre-Internet and much more aligned with a radio station than broadcasting over the web, which seems like it should be more similar. . . .

LW: I think part of it is the allure of the object. It's also that people want that *thing*. And I'm glad that we put the *vèvè* on it. I told you when I handed Michèle her copy she was speechless and emotional to see it. To see this tangible thing, even though you *could* get it online. So I don't know. I feel like in a perfect world, where money and time were no object, I would want to put the whole archive on a flash drive and then make a million of them. And if not a million, several thousand. And just give 'em out.

CB: That was a good project. And . . . it was *you* taking it back, and I think that it wasn't just us sending them in a box or anything, I think that having you there was important as well.

LW: I mean, it was targeted, right? I talked to friends, professional contacts who work in different parts of the country, who were doing either educational work or community work, and said, "Here you go. Distribute these as you see fit." But we could go so much bigger. There are so many other people, other places, other libraries. Everybody—I didn't have enough. Everybody wanted them. And wanted me to come talk about the archive, and present it. I feel like I could do this for ten years, probably.

CB: So we've talked some about how this is kind of a different kind of repatriation.

LW: Yeah, I mean, only because the existing definition of repatriation of archives is—and I didn't really realize this—is grounded in this atonement for colonial sins. The bad old days of anthropology as colonialism's handmaiden, as they say. Going in, extracting, acquiring people's stories or ceremonies or whatever. The cultural life of a community, of a place. And then going away with it, and putting it in some archive in the US or some museum, and it lives on the shelves forever. Sits dormant on the shelves forever. Which is a kind of theft. That isn't what this project is. First, it was an archive before it came to us. It was an archive of Radio Haiti kept

by Radio Haiti, kept by the journalists who had the foresight to do it, and who
recognized the importance of the archive. I should also say that they revisited their
own archives all the time. They would do these commemorations, remembrances
of particular dates or particular people, so a lot of their stuff is them drawing from
their own archives. It was always in their minds. So this is something that was
created by Haitian people primarily for Haitian people, and it was always meant
to be recorded, shared and broadcast. It's not—you hear about some other digital
repatriation of things that were—they may have been public events, or not, but
things that were fairly intimate or sacred. And—I mean, this is intimate and sacred
in its own way, but it was always intended to be something that was publicly, widely
transmitted to as many people as possible. And the fact that Duke is just a stopping
point for it. It's really—we're the amplifier. Because we can digitize it all and make
it all available, and do this, it can reach far more people than it could otherwise.
I don't know. Do you have anything else to say about that?

CB: I was thinking I like the idea of the archive going back to Haiti and other radio
stations in Haiti using the content to create their own programming. I think
that's cool, just like Radio Haiti did with their own programming, just to see that
continue would be super. I think there's . . . "repatriation" as a word just doesn't fit.
There's so much in it that says that we have the power to be able to do that. I don't
feel like it's my choice to be doing it or that it's somehow down to us that we're
doing it. Although it is, mechanically it is. But it's more; it's more . . . I feel like that
term is loaded. That idea of "patrimony." *Noblesse oblige.*

LW: Like we're bestowing.

CB: I mean, I'm proud of it. I'm proud of the work we did, but I'm not doing it for
some aggrandizement of my own self. It's not about that.

LW: But like I said, other repatriation projects have been about atonement, and to be
fair the United States has a lot to atone for in Haiti.

CB: That's good. I like that.

LW: Right? It's a little bit of a counterweight.

CB: I'm not that worried about the theory of it, though.

LW: No. I have other stuff to do.

CB: I have other stuff to do. I'm worried about getting the recordings back to Haiti!
(*laughs*)

LW: I guess we started with talking about memory. There's this untranslatable term
in French, which is *devoir de mémoire*, which translates more or less to "the duty
to remember." But it's talking about a very active process of keeping the memory
alive, and not allowing certain things to fade into oblivion. And it's something
that comes up in Radio Haiti's own archive. When they talk, in the post-Duvalier
moment, about what they are going to do with Fort Dimanche, which was the
infamous political prison under Duvalier. In 1991, you had people talking about,
"Are we going to turn it into a museum? What are we going to do with this
building?" And ultimately, none of that happened for a number of reasons. But
there were these attempts to commemorate the victims of Duvalierist violence,
and of that time, and as the archive unfolds there is more and more to remember.
Victims of the coup years, victims of army violence, victims of conflicts over land,
people who were killed for being in the political opposition, journalists who were

killed, and so on. And so *devoir de mémoire* becomes central to what Radio Haiti was doing. And then, one step further now, we have Radio Haiti's work, and so we are both commemorating and keeping the memory of Radio Haiti itself alive, and also all the things that they themselves were commemorating and trying to keep alive. But it's hard. And it's hard anywhere, especially to remember the less glorious part of our history. And especially when it's personal—when the tragedy isn't abstract, when it's in your own family and your friends and people that you knew. And I think it's especially hard in a place, in any place, in any context where people are caught up in a daily struggle to survive. We see it with the earthquake, even, and it wasn't that long ago. The way that that is already fading into the past and people don't have a choice but to live in the same kind of buildings that collapsed on January 12, and that when—because it's not *if*, it's *when*—another big earthquake happens will collapse again, and the same thing will happen. And yet when it's going to rain *tonight*, when you need somewhere to sleep *tonight*, when you need somewhere for your kids to sleep *tonight* so they can go to school, when you need to *live*, you can't think about that stuff. The same with deforestation in Haiti. Everyone knows you shouldn't cut down trees, that it's bad for the soil, that it leads to landslides. And yet if you have to feed your kids today, and you can cut down this tree and make some charcoal and sell it, that's what you do. So if we're talking about a context like that in Haiti or anywhere else, the extra emotional labor that it takes to actively keep the memory alive is really hard. That's something that I think about as we're doing this project, is, well, *Is it going to work?*

CB: Well at least it would help keep the memory alive.

LW: It's there. Whether or not people engage with it, and remember it, is another question. But it is there—or rather, it will be there.

For More Information

Radio Haiti collection guide: http://library.duke.edu/rubenstein/findingaids/radiohaiti/
Radio Haiti archives on Soundcloud: https://soundcloud.com/radiohaitiarchives/
Radio Haiti pilot website: www.radiohaitilives.com
The project on Facebook: facebook.com/radiohaitiinter/
The project on Twitter: @AchivRadyoAyiti

Notes

1. From 2014 to 2015, Laura worked with Meagan Bonnell, Laurent Dubois, and Sandie Blaise at the Forum for Scholars and Publics to create a trilingual pilot website featuring a curated selection of Radio Haiti audio.
2. The Tontons Macoutes, formally known as the Volontaires de la Sécurité Nationale (VSN), were the militia formed under François Duvalier. After the fall of Jean-Claude Duvalier in

1986 and the dissolution of the official militia, Macoutes and the mentality of Macoutism endured.

3. When the collection is fully digitized and described, we will be giving hard drives containing the entire archive to libraries, archives, and other cultural and educational institutions in Haiti.

4. A *vèvè* is a ritual symbol in Haitian Vodou. Radio Haiti's trademark was a unique *vèvè* designed by the renowned Haitian artist Rose-Marie Desruisseau, representing a microphone.

CHAPTER 19

....

BALI 1928 MUSIC RECORDINGS AND 1930S FILMS

Strategies for Cultural Repatriation

....

EDWARD HERBST

BALI 1928 is an ongoing restoration and repatriation project involving the first published recordings of music in Bali as well as related film footage and photographs from the 1930s.[1] These are the only music recordings made in Bali and released before World War II, a diverse representation of new and ancient genres that were published on 78 rpm discs that quickly went out of print. Our project has resulted in the release and distribution of a collection of five CD and DVD volumes in Indonesia and CDs in the United States.[2]

Our concept of repatriation has at its core the Indonesian *pemulangan kembali* (returning back). But when dealing with cultural repatriation the range of implications expands beyond objects into territory determined by particular and localized circumstances reflecting the community and context within which the material originated. A core principle has been collaboration with Indonesians participating in all facets of the vision, planning, and implementation. In addition to providing tools for performing artists to discover techniques of the past, we have come to realize that through archival media Indonesians can directly access empirical evidence of their cultural history, often in contrast with the representation of earlier times as promulgated by national, regional, and local government, or by culture and arts institutions that may have interests other than historical and cultural accuracy. We are already seeing some evidence that this kind of repatriation can lead to more open discourse.

THE SOURCE: INTERCULTURAL
COLLABORATION IN 1928–1929

The 1928 recording sessions were carried out by Odeon and Beka, subsidiaries of the German conglomerate Lindstrom, and the Russian-born German artist and musician Walter Spies (De Zoete and Spies 1938) has been credited with having chosen and organized the gamelan (instrumental ensembles) and singers.[3] But considerable evidence derived from my field and archival research[4] suggests that the renowned Balinese dance master Ida Boda (aka Ida Bagus Boda) was actually the "A&R man" (artists and repertoire) for the Beka sessions, and that about 50 percent of the extant Beka recordings were made in 1929. Born in the village of Negara, Batuan, in the district of Gianyar (South Central Bali) with family origins in Budakeling, Karangasem (East Bali), he and his family had moved in the 1890s to Kaliungu, Denpasar (South Bali). Ida Boda's extensive network of students and fellow performers enriched the artist pool for the 1928 recordings, most especially the vocal music that constitutes 50 percent of the extant tracks.

Between Odeon and Beka, Spies and Boda (Figure 19.1), almost every genre of gamelan and song was documented. So even from the inception of this project during the nascent Dutch colonial era, Balinese creative agency and indigenous aesthetic preferences led to intercultural collaboration with Westerners.

The Canadian composer and pianist Colin McPhee and his wife, the anthropologist Jane Belo, first heard these 78 rpm discs in New York in the winter of 1930–1931 and were inspired to leave soon after for Bali, where they carried out research over the next eight years. In his memoir, *A House in Bali*, McPhee recalled how in 1931 one frustrated European shopkeeper entrusted to sell the records in Bali smashed his entire inventory in rage at their inability to sell (McPhee 1946). The records have since become extremely rare.

Although it seems clear, judging from a Beka Music Company catalog,[5] that the company recorded a considerable amount of additional music, a decision may have been made not to publish many more once they realized the lack of a market. The recording masters were aluminum plates, most likely stored in Berlin at the Carl Lindstrom factory (the parent company), which was bombed during World War II.

As we reflect on the import of the 1928–1929 collection, it is sobering to acknowledge that—just as two salient examples—the extraordinary singing styles of Ida Bagus Oka Kerebuak and Ni Lemon would have been lost forever had not, as we now assume, Ida Boda brought Balinese sensibilities to the Beka recording sessions. Walter Spies appears to have been responsible for choosing only vocal music accompanied by a variety of gamelan ensembles. Similarly, McPhee limited his research to instrumental music. But singing—whether it be romantic, didactic, spiritual, or humorous—occupies a significant place in the Balinese musical world, and elders have described to us how in earlier times it would evoke deep emotions resulting in goosebumps (literally making one's hair

FIGURE 19.1 Ida Boda as *panasar* (comic narrator) standing on left with Jangér Kedaton, c. 1937–1939.

Photo by Arthur Fleischmann, reproduced courtesy of the Arthur Fleischmann family.

stand on end) and weeping among the audience, making the aural evidence in these recordings all the more significant as expressive culture.

THE INDIGENOUS INCENTIVE
FOR REPATRIATION

Before the idea for our current initiative arose, one small gesture of repatriation led to full engagement and a fifteen-year process. In 1998 Allan Evans, director of Arbiter Records, asked if I would write CD notes for *The Roots of Gamelan*, a sampler of some of the 1928 recordings he had assembled with 1940 recordings of McPhee's "Balinese Ceremonial Music"—transcriptions for two pianos played by McPhee and Benjamin Britten. I wrote these notes while in the United States (Herbst 1999) and soon after brought the CD to Bali.

Upon arriving, I visited the composer Wayan Beratha, son of one of the major composers of 1928, Madé Regog, and we listened together to the many tracks recorded in his village of Belaluan. When Beratha heard one, "Curik Ngaras" (Starlings Kissing), he laughed and said, "I haven't heard this since I was a kid." He urged me for a cassette copy and within a week I received word that he had already taught the composition to a children's gamelan in his village.

Listening together with the Balinese musicologist Nyoman Rembang to selections from the classic *gambuh* repertoire (Figure 19.2) of his native village Sésétan (on a cassette from the UCLA Ethnomusicology Archive), I was moved by his teary eyes. Rembang explained that he had not heard this music since the age of six, before the Japanese occupation in World War II when the gambuh instruments were buried (as was common in Bali to keep them from being seized by the occupiers). Young musicians from a few of the village traditions that had been recorded also implored me to give them cassette dubs.

The overwhelming responses from musicians and singers led toward a commitment to initiating repatriation of all extant recordings from 1928 (and as we discovered, 1929), numbering, upon publication in 2015, 111 sides, each three minutes in duration. Philip Yampolsky provided me with a list of the many 78s he had personally located at archives around the world based on Andrew Toth's earlier discography (Toth 1980). In the 1970s Toth had been the archivist at UCLA's Ethnomusicology Archive, where Colin McPhee had taught briefly and donated his collection. Yampolsky's information led Arbiter and me on a worldwide quest that ranged from Indonesia's National Museums to UCLA, the University of Amsterdam, the Library of Congress, the University of Washington, and numerous public and private collections. The process of gaining permission from each archive and visiting most of the collections has taken us eight years.

Previous to our project, the only recordings available to most Balinese had been of music released by the indigenous cassette industry since the 1970s and the subsequent

FIGURE 19.2 Prabu Manis ("refined prince" on right) and Patih Tua/Rangga ("old minister" on left) and gamelan gambuh of Sésétan, c. 1931–1938.

Photo by Colin McPhee, courtesy of UCLA Ethnomusicology Archive and Colin McPhee Estate.

CD and DVD market. As a result of this and the fact that Balinese music is an aural tradition taught without notation, understanding of artistic roots and creative evolution are most often based on word-of-mouth speculation reflecting intervillage, interregional competitiveness as well as a half century of cultural history defined by the dominant institutions of education and government such as ASTI (Akademi Seni Tari Indonesia), which became ISI (Indonesian Institute of Arts), KOKAR (Konservatori Karawitan Indonesia Bali), now SMKI (Sekolah Menengah Karawitan Indonesia), the high school conservatory of music and dance, Udayana University, and Listibiya (the Council for Development and Promotion of Balinese Culture).

Similarly, hardly any dancers had ever seen film footage of the original creators of twentieth-century dance or of the choreographic techniques and styles of earlier times. Such access now offers everyone insights into the finer details of dance technique as it evolved among a wide range of individual artists, leading to a new understanding of Balinese creative processes.

A DIALOGIC METHODOLOGY

Diverse participants made the key choices that shaped and defined the project. When I began to seek support, one condition for funding made by Philip Yampolsky while a program officer at the Ford Foundation was that my research be carried out with a team of Balinese who could learn my "methodology." I had in fact developed a reflexive and dialogic methodology for my earlier work with Balinese singing, based principally on what I learned to be indigenous Balinese principles and practices of worldly and metaphysical orientation, variation, inner creative process, analysis, and discourse.

Once I arrived for that first "official" visit in 2003, the Balinese performer and scholar Wayan Dibia expressed the opinion that whatever content I would eventually write as the exegesis of the research should be translated in full so that the English and Indonesian language content would be identical. He suggested that presenting the content differently could come across as condescending to both Indonesians and Westerners. This may seem obvious, but its implications have been challenging and far-reaching. A profound feeling of accountability and responsibility accompanied the certainty that all my research findings and interpretations would be read by a broad range of Balinese and other Indonesians.

Balinese culture is endowed with a plethora of artistic and religious practices, local and regional terminologies, and ways of explaining and interpreting sung poetry and literature. Music and dance forms are, even today, performed differently according to locale, and those of the 1920s and 1930s were considerably more diverse than those of today. It seemed incumbent on us to carry out thorough research that would reflect heterogeneous and often contradictory perspectives. Indeed, early in the course of our research for *Bali 1928*, we found a great many versions of events and opinions among the oldest generation, necessitating a dialogic methodology. Even post-publication, we see the breadth and depth of discovery continuing in a process by which further dissemi-nation of the audiovisual materials results in elders previously unknown to us coming forth with new information.

One essential element in the synergy of the repatriation process has been the indig-enous research team composed of practitioners. Our repeated visits with elderly artists were not interviews, but rather open-ended conversations full of humor, camaraderie, and heartfelt, profound memories stimulated by the unprecedented archival materials, as if windows had been opened after many decades. In Balinese artistic, religious, and literary activities, an often-stated guiding principle is *bayu-sabda-idep* (energy-voice-mind), integrating action with communication and conceptualization/thought (Herbst 1997, 121–133). For this reason, many of our research visits involved interactive musical exchanges with our sources. An aspect of this prioritization of practice is that I was oc-casionally challenged to sing at least one Balinese *tembang* (song) before the discus-sion could progress, so as to legitimize my interest in personal and often spiritual topics relating to people's ancestors who performed in the 1920s.

What has kept me (and my Balinese partners) so dedicated to the project has been the madness to our methods—madness in the Balinese sense of being *gandrung* (infatuated, madly in love) with so much of this music and dance of a bygone era which serve as keys to the early twentieth-century creative process.

Between 2003 and 2016—at least once during each visit to Bali—I gave at least fifteen multimedia presentations at the ISI institute and Udayana University, and at confer-ences and seminars in Bali and Java. There was always discussion that included students and faculty with an opportunity for me to answer their questions, providing me with a grasp of what excited and interested them in the materials, ways to present the archival resources to the contemporary community, and a broadened understanding of the ar-chival content through their perspectives and expertise.

One of the first questions to come from a student, and one that we heard often, was why we did not combine the audio from 1928 with the silent films from the 1930s. Of course, video has made audiovisual documentation ubiquitous and taken for granted. I explained that each sound recording captured a particular moment in time, as did each film sequence. If we were to combine them, each unique moment would no longer be discernable. Moreover, if we were to begin altering archival material in this kind of procedure, it would lose its authenticity and value as proof of past practices. As I often suggest, "You cannot argue with your ears." But I continually acknowledge that some Balinese teenager is sure to use a digital device to combine audio and moving image as a personal historical artifact.

Many Balinese scholars and artists suggest that with the empirical evidence we now have in the 1928 recordings and films of seminal masters and innovators, their under-standing of the social dynamics and creative impetus of twentieth-century Balinese aesthetics is far beyond anything previously thought possible. Imagine trying to under-stand the creative evolution of jazz without recordings from the 1920s and 1930s. These circumstances of loss, rediscovery, reacquisition, and revival have broad implications well beyond Bali, with the potential to inspire and inform recovery projects elsewhere.

Another unanticipated aspect of repatriation was our Indonesian-language translations of excerpts from writings by Western scholars and artists who had conducted research in Bali in the 1920s, 1930s, and ensuing decades. Numerous Balinese musicians expressed an interest in what Colin McPhee and others had witnessed, and I realized that very few had actually read such works. These writings by foreigners also offered insights into the music recordings and dance drama film footage while helping Balinese and others conceptualize the "spirit of the time."

REPATRIATION TO AND FOR WHOM?

My initial Indonesian colleagues for this project (Endo Suanda in Bandung, Madé Bandem and Wayan Dibia in Bali) and I determined that merely establishing archives online or in an Indonesian university or library would not provide a sufficiently accessible resource for the broad public. Balinese arts are still spread out in the villages, and many performers are not comfortable in institutional settings, lacking online access beyond their smartphones.

We decided to publish the materials and arrange for them to be sold to the public at extremely affordable prices, and to provide them free to genealogical and cultural descendants of the 1928 and 1930s artists, gamelan clubs, arts organizations, libraries, universities, conservatories, independent teachers, and regional arts centers.

As of this writing, my partner, STIKOM Bali (College of Information Management and Computer Sciences),[6] has given one thousand published sets free of charge to such recipients, with occasional sets sold at the cost of production. STIKOM's circle of experts, led by our Indonesian project coordinator Marlowe Bandem, has been uniquely suited to the task of publishing, video restoration and editing, repatriation, and distribution. They see this project as an unprecedented model for the recovery and use of audiovisual archives, a model that can be replicated throughout Indonesia.[7]

AUDIOVISUAL STRATEGIES
FOR A DISCERNING PUBLIC

Once the project was underway and after several research visits to Bali, the UCLA archive gave permission for us to include their 78s in our CD series—and, amazingly, due to the great vision of the Ethnomusicology Archive's director at the time, Anthony Seeger, to lend us a great many 78 rpm discs. Allan Evans made his own audio transfers in New York. In addition to providing state-of-the-art digital restoration, Evans has successfully brought to fruition original techniques that mechanically explore areas within the groove walls to fully expose sounds otherwise left buried in shellac discs. Evans's new audio restoration Sonic Depth Technology enables us to hear and examine difficult-to-perceive subtleties in the recorded sound.

This enabled us to hear much more clearly, for instance, the drumming patterns, or detect the presence of an instrument, like the *klintong*, a small gong. Such audio information has been essential for my Balinese colleagues to reconceptualize and fully appreciate subtle, kinesthetic aspects of the singing as well as elements that went into the creative evolution of gamelan music in the 1920s, offering, for instance, surprising evidence of techniques for *légong* ("classical" female dance) accompaniment still practiced during the birth of *kebyar*.

Such audible details triggered a difference in attitude in many Balinese musicians. The earliest cassette dubs that I brought to Bali were sometimes taken to be a quaint curiosity of interest as nostalgia. But over the years and stages of audio restoration, performers took the recordings more and more seriously as two-dimensionality gave way to sonic depth and revelatory experience. Similarly, with our digital video restoration of the 1930s films, the original archival footage we acquired was intriguing but not always taken to be instructional as aesthetic keys, sometimes evoking laughs as if it were a Charlie Chaplin film at fast speed. This is common with archival collections due to the difference in frames per second between the early 16-millimeter cameras and later moving-picture technologies.[8]

And even more problematic, but easier to remedy with software, was that many film sequences had right and left reversed.[9] In addition to everyday etiquette for right- and left-hand functions, the unintentional reversal misrepresented the choreography; and in the case of musicians, it would reverse drumming patterns or have a musician holding a mallet with his left hand on a backward gamelan instrument.

Inviting dance masters to watch the films repeatedly along with the video editor allowed us to determine the appropriate speed. Traditionally, Balinese dancers have been taught by teachers employing gamelan *mulut* (mouth gamelan) in which all the instruments of the orchestra are sung at once as vocables representing melody, drum patterns, and the timbres of various instruments. This internalization of music inherent in Balinese dance pedagogy offered direct input from dancers as they viewed the films while singing in the same way they had learned and some continue to teach. And still, even after consulting such a dance master, we occasionally showed a video to a dancer or musician from a particular village whose performers had been filmed in the 1930s, who instructed us to make adjustments to a different speed in accordance with their distinct, local aesthetic.

COLLABORATIVE RESEARCH

The fact that I have been essentially writing for a Balinese readership as much as or more than for international readers, with my extensive notes translated into Indonesian, has led to methodological choices. While trying to be rigorous in the research process by taking into account both Balinese and non-Balinese scholarly sources, my quotes are mostly from firsthand conversations with these near-centenarian musicians, singers, and dancers who offer missing narratives and perspectives often contrary to accepted wisdom. I identify individuals by name and include contrasting opinions in order to give future researchers (Balinese and others) the opportunity to pursue these sources on their own.

The project has been taking place at the last possible moment when these links to the 1920s and 1930s are (or were) still alive, and we wanted to focus on these individuals' perspectives. We have also maintained a healthy skepticism toward written sources, Balinese and foreign, by following up with primary sources whenever possible. As my American singing teacher, Frank Baker, once advised, "Beware hearsay evidence." Balinese friends always laugh and recognize the aphorism when I interpret this as *keto koné* (so they say), a very common expression. Differing from some Indonesian academic tendencies since the 1960s, we see the diversity of local narratives and epistemologies as a cultural asset rather than something to rectify and replace.

An interesting consequence of the fact that these recordings had been unavailable in Bali, or anywhere, until now, is that my Balinese colleagues and I have been similarly dealing with varying degrees of unknowns, necessitating a collaborative research process. One point that I often discussed with my research team is that it is important to stay aware of what you do not know. A little bit of knowledge can be a dangerous thing, creating too much certainty and leaving little room for unexpected experiences and input from others.

Due to the prevalence of status hierarchies within Indonesian society, a related obstacle for indigenous researchers—both students and faculty—is the difficulty of humbling themselves while interacting with nonacademic "village" performers. Even a student from the arts institute or university may be considered to be above, or more "advanced," than "common village artists," making it embarrassing to ask simple questions that are essential for acquiring information and understanding. Sometimes when I posed a question to an elderly artist, a Balinese member of my research team would interrupt to answer the question, providing a generic response that precluded an answer which could reflect some unique, local epistemology, technique, or ethnopoetic terminology reflecting practices in the distant past or specific to that particular artist or locale.

Against Anonymity

A significant and truly moving development in the documentation process has been the degree to which a great many near-centenarian villagers, local artists, and communities have engaged with us in identifying specific locations as well as individual musicians, dancers, actors, priests, and others in the audio recordings, photographs, and film footage from 1928 and the 1930s. Among both young and old, the level of excitement about and anticipation of the publication and dissemination of our archival materials could not have been imagined. We have come to see this as a struggle against anonymity, which is so common on the Internet, but also for intentional and sometimes valid reasons, in many scholarly, particularly anthropological, writings.

One evening amid a temple festival at Pura Kawitan Kelaci I was sitting among numerous extended family members, showing McPhee's film of ritual *gambang* (bamboo xylophone) musicians on my laptop. An elderly woman walked by and stopped to peer at the moving images, laughing and bellowing out that the gambang player on the right was definitely Wayan Pegeg as a young man; she recognized him by the way he tied his *udeng* (head scarf), in those days a form of self-expression that has allowed our sources to identify numerous musicians in the archival films and photographs.

I have realized that in twenty-first-century Indonesia, this kind of recognition of individual artists instills pride and a new sense of cultural identity for young people in these communities, inspiring them to continue or even renew artistic repertoires amid their rapidly modernizing society.[10] Anonymity not only deprives families and cultural descendants of their heritage and history but also marginalizes and homogenizes so that entrenched hegemonies prevail and continue to dominate discourse, authority, and power. Of course, the process of identifying locales and individuals also stimulates deeper and more informed research findings, unanticipated sources and unique narratives leading to richer repatriation results.

In conceiving a strategy for dissemination through online access to visual media, we observed that one shortcoming of many online resources, including those of major libraries, is anonymity. While this is most often unavoidable, as a musical anthropologist I cannot help but view its effect as an expropriation of images (often perceived as exotic) without the dignity of personhood. Particularly unreliable is Google Images, which flood the viewer with machine-selected, unlabeled photos upon initiating a search.

Since our research and documentation is providing us the opportunity to locate the families of artists and ensembles photographed and filmed, we have information to embed into each file as metadata including the name and village of the performers, the photographer, and the name of the archive giving permission for dissemination of each photograph.

As my Balinese partners and I further strategized about how to publish the 105 archival photographs,[11] our assessment of most libraries' online access to photographs left us dissatisfied with the common practice of allowing the download of selected images as only a small file with display dimensions the size of a postage stamp or a business card, often containing erroneous identification. Since our purpose is dissemination and access to images that can be used for study as research tools and as a legacy and source of pleasure and pride for hereditary and cultural descendants, we have chosen to post—on our Indonesian- and English-language websites[12]—larger files that can be reproduced with higher resolution.

We have included similar procedures of embedding metadata in all the archival films included on our DVDs and Bali 1928 YouTube channel to ensure proper identification.

Each video excerpt opens with titles identifying the performer and/or ensembles depicted, with their village and region, as well as the filmmaker (Colin McPhee, Miguel Covarrubias, or Rolf de Maré). At the end of each excerpt, our titles identify and thank the archive that gave permission for the film to be disseminated. At the end of the collection of excerpts for each volume of the series, we identify the production staff, funding sources, and institutional support.

CHALLENGES ENCOUNTERING THE PAST

The ambiguous, allusive nature of Balinese poetry and song has required a more dialogic approach to textual translation, for which a team of eight scholars (including the author of a seminal Balinese dictionary) and "traditional village artists" met regularly to seek consensus on hermeneutics, poetic "grammar," and dramatic and literary content.

This came about after listening together with one Balinese colleague—transcribing, interpreting, and translating the Kawi (Old Javanese) or Balinese verses to Indonesian—only to have a similar session with another expert who disagreed on the words being sung, as well as their interpretation. I decided that a team approach was best, wherein we could discuss many different interpretations and then find consensus. This allowed for seasoned performers' opinions concerning the way specific poetic lines would be enacted within a dramatic context, not just their literal or literary meaning.[13]

Another challenge in transcribing and interpreting the vocal music was due to the historical distance evidenced by a different variety of playful melismatic phrasing and creative shaping of vowels to produce unique timbres (Herbst 1997). And while some of the sung poems remain within the repertoire to this day, Balinese performers have always (even more in earlier times) prided themselves in improvisation, deviating from composed text according to *désa-kala-patra* (place, time, context). This heightened the need for repeated listening and teamwork.

Again and again, listening and discussing the recordings with the oldest generation, we are struck with the degree of improvisation, experimentation, playfulness, and subtle nuance in vocal and instrumental music and dance of the 1920s and 1930s (for comparison, see Supanggah 2011). The most revered exponent of *kebyar* in the 1920s and 1930s was the dancer Ketut Marya (also spelled Mario). There is now a Marya Arts Center in his home city of Tabanan. His close musical partner, Wayan Begeg (1919–2012; see Figures 19.3 and 19.4), enjoyed our many visits and was a great raconteur.

He recalled being invited to an annual Marya festival in which competitions focus on Marya's many dances. Wayan Begeg was an honorary guest, and after the event, the organizer asked him about his impression. Begeg told me and my team that if Marya were up above the *wantilan* (stage) looking down, he would be weeping. He would not

FIGURE 19.3 Gong Kebyar players of Pangkung, Tabanan, 1949. Left to right: I Wayan Begeg, I Wayan Sukra (composer), and I Nengah Rita.

Photo courtesy of Wayan Begeg.

FIGURE 19.4 I Wayan Begeg of Gong Kebyar Pangkung, Tabanan, dancing exuberantly while listening to the *Bali 1928* recordings at his home, 2006.

Still image from video by Edward Herbst.

recognize the dances as his own. Marya did not use a consistent *pakem* (choreography). Begeg told us:

> Marya's style no longer exists. In the old days with Pak Marya dancing and me leading the music, he would say, "When I dance, the music accompanies me. I don't follow the music." The relationship was basically the same as today only now it is more like a contest between gamelan and dancer. With Marya, as a musician I would be watching the spirit of the dance; if it is sad and soft, gentle, we are too; if it is slow, we are slow.

In Wayan Begeg's opinion, this was a creative process more intimate, spirited, flexible, and spontaneous than *kebyar* performance practice today.

Unearthing Local Narratives

Marya is widely celebrated as the genius who created *kebyar* dance beginning in the teens and 1920s,[14] but our research among the oldest generation has led us to understand that many features of his style were preceded by others, unknown or just forgotten, from remote and now marginalized villages in North Bali. With the evidence provided by films, audio recordings, and firsthand encounters with near centenarians, we are all now able to see that the creative trajectory of kebyar occurred in many locales and that Marya used these innovations, bringing them to an extraordinary level of virtuosity and complexity.

One of McPhee's film sequences shows the gamelan of Jineng Dalem on the northern coast, where one-hundred-year-old Gdé Mataram recently identified his father, Gdé Lila, as the ensemble's leader and *trompong* player. The most striking feature of Gdé Lila's performance style was his almost dance-like way of moving the mallets, characterized by slow arcs of his extended arms as well as sliding movements across the bronze kettle-gongs. This elegant style suggests what could have been an innovation among musicians preceding the signature *Igel Trompong* dance created by Marya in the teens and known since the 1960s by the Indonesian name "Kebyar Trompong".

When one Balinese colleague from the south watched the McPhee film, he commented that this style in which a kebyar musician is "almost dancing" the trompong was common in many areas of Bali and not special to the north. However, I recalled a page of McPhee's unpublished fieldnotes from UCLA's Ethnomusicology Archive, in which he states: "NB [North Balinese] musicians seem to think more melodically, more spaciously, more floridly. This can be seen in the elegant gestures of the NB trompong player, whose performance is almost a dance. It coincides with the flamboyant style of the temple carvings." Repatriating McPhee's film in combination with his unpublished notes reveals to Balinese that what had then been an innovation specific to a now-marginalized region, soon after became a ubiquitous feature of modern Balinese dance.

Researching the 1928 recordings of poetic songs from the Brahmana community in Klungkung led us to the families of the singers and a great-grandson of the author of many of the excerpted *geguritan* poems, Anak Agung Gdé Pemeregan, born in 1810. This provided a new understanding that Pemeregan's *Duh Ratnayu*, a poem that remains to this day one of Bali's most popular romantic tales—generally thought of as generic love lyrics adapted by *arja* dance-opera's ever-popular (Chinese) Sampik-Ingtai story—was actually a contemporary account of a tragic, prohibited love affair between first cousins in the royal court of Klungkung during the 1890s. This revelation transforms the song from what has, for almost a century, been expunged from royal chronicles and thought of by the public and Balinese historians to be from the imagination of the poet, into what must have been at the time the equivalent of a scandalous news story, a topical song, and an omen of the collapse of the kingdom to the Dutch.[15]

While it has always been accepted that the earliest manifestations of kebyar style came from North Bali, the creative process has been largely left unexplored due to a lack of evidence. One key opening came when we visited the lion of kebyar composers and master teacher of all of the arts institutes, Wayan Beratha, and played him recordings of the gamelan of long-ignored Busungbiu from North Bali. After one minute into *Legod Bawa*, Beratha laughed and exclaimed in surprise, "*Jayasemara*," the name of his most seminal, influential composition. It was apparent that many of the techniques, key musical phrases, and themes associated with Beratha's compositions of the 1960s were being played in remote Busungbiu in 1928.

When I subsequently visited the musicians in Busungbiu, they explained how their distinctive northern gamelan (with metallophone keys resting on nails rather than suspended and free-ringing as in the south) had been melted down in 1992 to be reforged in the most generic style for performing much of the standard, island-wide repertoire popularized by the Bali Arts Festival and the government arts academy, ASTI. The hegemony these institutions have enjoyed has always been viewed with varying degrees of admiration and resentment in villages outside the Denpasar region. I have repeatedly heard the government slogan "*ABRI masuk désa*"—signifying the military's presence in local communities—jokingly transformed into "*ASTI masuk désa*" to suggest that ASTI had supplanted and disempowered local arts traditions.

But we cannot ignore the fact that ASTI (which became ISI) was founded in 1968, just two years after the anti-Communist massacre of 1965–1966 as Major General Suharto was swept into power as president. ASTI was preceded by KOKAR, the conservatory of performing arts, the founding of which, in 1960 during the Sukarno era, had followed a decade of extreme regional political violence in Bali.[16] The influence of KOKAR, ASTI, and Listibiya (the Council for Development and Promotion of Balinese Culture) functioned as a double-edged sword, with the goal of preserving traditional Balinese arts but ultimately serving to centralize cultural influence and stave off regional animosities through homogeneity and standardization (Aryasa 1984–1985). This has also had an effect of marginalizing regions outside of Denpasar and Gianyar (South Central Bali) and sometimes promulgating a biased version of cultural history.[17]

Soon after, in Busungbiu, we played the CD from my boombox for eighty-year-old Wayan Weker, son of Wayan Patra, the drummer and leader of the gamelan club in 1928. Weker recognized the distinctive musical style but the younger, middle-aged musicians asked me skeptically whether these were indeed recordings of their fathers' gamelan, as they did not recognize the repertoire or the techniques. They asked me, "*Apa ini, kréasi?*" ("What's this, modern music?"), *kreasi* signifying "new creation" and generally associated with the 1980s to the present—not with their grandparents. On the bright side, in 2009 and 2013 I participated in the "Conference on the Musical Identity of Northern Bali" and observed a movement afoot to revive their regional instrumental styles and repertoires.

Beginning in 2006 our team visited the children and grandchildren of singers featured in 1928 and gained insights into their lives and aesthetics, as well as help in interpreting the text of their poetic, romantic, and philosophical songs. In these songs, we have discovered an influence of the Sasak Muslim culture from the neighboring island of Lombok. The Balinese singers (born in the 1870s) made occasional visits to Lombok to perform, teach, and listen, and they were "crazy" about Sasak vocal styles that evince Muslim musical influence. While Balinese music has been present in Lombok, Sasak influence in Bali has not been considered except for one genre, *cakepung*. My research team, including three Balinese singers—I Ketut Kodi, Ni Ketut Suryatini, and Ni Ketut Arini—visited Lombok on two occasions to spend time with the Sasak singer Mamiq Ambar and document the linkages.

DISCOVERING OLD AND NEW PERCEPTIONS AND SENSIBILITIES

The most challenging issue my Balinese colleagues and I have been grappling with is tonality and modal practice. The microtonal singing of 1928 clearly reflects archaic seven-tone gamelan such as gambuh while exhibiting an even wider palette of pitches to the octave. The ambiguities of intonation became profound when I realized that today's most revered singers are enchanted by the subtleties of this 1928 singing but have great difficulty imitating them. This revealed some truth in the music scholar Wayan Sinti's bold accusation in the *Bali Post* newspaper, "The Balinese public's ears have been colonized (occupied) by [modern] gong kebyar tuning."

Investigating the implications of music from such a temporal distance heightens the dialogic, collaborative nature of the research process, with each of us providing resources for the other as various modes of understanding and analysis intertwine. Some prominent Balinese colleagues (nonsingers) hear Ida Bagus Oka Kerebuak (Figure 19.5) and comment that this is a very simple style and today's "way of singing a melody" is more "developed." But most skilled singers I have encountered are in awe of the subtle, complex nuances of tonality and melodic phrasing, and a mastery of breathing and lengthy (melodic) exhalations that reflect the practice of *pranayama* yoga.

FIGURE 19.5 Singer Ida Bagus Oka Kerebuak of Geria Pidada, Klungkung.

Photo courtesy of Geria Pidada, Klungkung.

So the issue becomes one of musical perception, in which new ways of hearing intervals seem necessary in order for many Balinese to penetrate through their own culturally and historically specific processes of music cognition. This leads to the ambiguous terrain of implicit and explicit musical knowledge and practice and explains some of the difficulty Balinese singers experience traversing the years since 1928 and hearing an entirely "new" set of semitones or microtones that are not part of their intuitive, implicit aesthetic. Still, some have already proposed that a new category of competition in the island-wide Bali Arts Festival be established for singing in the older style recorded by Beka between 1928 and 1929.

A striking characteristic of the male singers recorded in 1928 is the relatively high pitch range, so much so that it is not uncommon for listeners to express doubt that the voice is that of a man. Given that many of the voices are in a range rarely heard in Bali today, we can assume a changing aesthetic. One factor to consider is that up until the 1920s and 1930s both female and male dramatic roles were performed by men.

One of McPhee's film sequences was identified by several dance experts as *Jogéd Pingitan* performed by a teenage girl. But we soon discovered it was actually gandrung, the same dance style but performed by a boy named Madé Sarin (Figure 19.6) in female costume and makeup (but also popular for arousing excited erotic interest among men).

FIGURE 19.6 I Madé Sarin, gandrung dancer of Ketapian Kelod, c. 1931–1938.
Still image from film by Colin McPhee, courtesy of UCLA Ethnomusicology Archive and Colin McPhee Estate.

Over the course of many visits our team got to know the elderly Madé Sarin and learned that he and Wayan Rindi of nearby Banjar Lebah were the last of the male gandrung and that the next generations of dancers, beginning with those trained in the 1940s, were always girls. The Japanese occupiers were concerned with protecting the "morals" of their soldiers from homoerotic tendencies, and even after the occupation the male gandrung tradition was not revived, perhaps due to the modern, newly independent nation of Indonesia having had similar circumscribed moralistic considerations.

In Bali today there is a new generation of young men reviving this and other female dance roles, including Madé Sarin's great-grand-nephew, and—thanks to the film restorations—they now have film documentation to inspire and inform their artistic pursuit.

Among the 1928 recordings, four selections offer surprising aural evidence of a singing style for Old Javanese–language classical *wirama kakawin* sung poetry that differs from today's standards (Rubinstein 1992). The vocalists recorded in 1928 were associated with the royal court of Klungkung, which before the Dutch conquest was the literary and spiritual center of Bali. The archival recordings show how the emphasis had previously been on interpretation and meaning of the poetic narrative as well as musicality and beauty. But a formalized and regulated system of counting *guru-laghu* (long and short syllables) is now taken for granted in Balinese universities, arts institutes, and island-wide kakawin competitions, having only been introduced as late as 1958 at Udayana University's Department of Literature.

Upon visiting kakawin experts in the eastern regions of Klungkung and Karangasem, we learned that today's singers in those areas continue to sing in a freer, intuitive, and spontaneous manner when performing for local rituals and ceremonial events, and only conform to the academic guru-laghu rules when participating in the island-wide competitions in Bali's capital city of Denpasar. This dichotomy, illuminated by the 1928 recordings, is explored in my analytic notes that include a broad range of views—often contentious—reflecting our dialogic research methods in diverse geographical regions.

REPATRIATION ON A PERSONAL LEVEL

Our research team has made many remarkable discoveries with help from these previously unavailable 1930s photos and films. A Balinese friend saw one photo I had found in the Claire Holt Collection at the New York Public Library, and told me one of the dancers was a hundred-year-old woman who still lived up the road (Figure 19.7). The next day we visited her, and when she saw the photo she said, "Sing tiang" ("That's not me"). But since I knew she had been in this same group, *Jangér Kedaton,* I asked if she would like to hear some old recordings. When she heard the music from my boombox, she exclaimed, "Niki tiang!" ("That's me!").

FIGURE 19.7 Singer Mémén Redia, aka Ni Wayan Pempen of Kedaton, 2007.

Photo by Edward Herbst.

It became apparent that she was the ten-year-old solo singer for six of the tracks from 1928. She then identified herself on my laptop in circa 1931 film footage shot by Covarrubias (Figure 19.8). Most importantly, she remembered the lyrics to all the songs, correcting our earlier transcriptions. Next, she remembered the 1928 recording session, describing it in detail including the equipment, and the fact that the recording engineers only allowed for one take of each song. If there was a mistake, there was no second take. This provides insight into several tracks including one of Busungbiu's gamelan gong kebyar in which the initial crashing sound of "*byong*" is "loud" but not "together," falling short of the very definition of kebyar.

During my next visit to Bali, I visited the same friend who had led us to Mémén Redia. When I was told that she had passed away and the family and village had already performed the *ngaben* "cremation rituals," I went to my laptop and captured a still image of Mémén Redia from the Covarrubias film when she was still Wayan Pempen at the age of twelve or thirteen. A local photo shop enlarged the image and put it in a big frame, which I brought to her family compound. When her son greeted me at the door, I explained that I heard his mother had died and I thought they would like the photo to remember her by. He answered, "She's still alive—come in and visit her." My friend had heard the loud gamelan sounds of a cremation and assumed it was the "hundred-year-old." I did visit and left them with the photo. Subsequently, on my arrival in Bali the next year, we were in a nearby village visiting an eighty-five-year-old musician, Wayan Rugeh, who had attended countless performances of many of the singers and musicians recorded in 1928, including Mémén Redia. He was the first to tell me that she

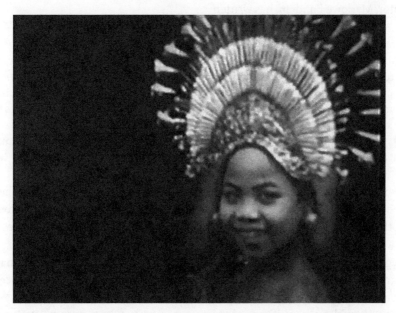

FIGURE 19.8 Ni Wayan Pempen, lead singer for 1928 Jangér Kedaton recordings.

Still image from film by Miguel Covarrubias, c. 1930–1934, courtesy of Rocio Sagaon Vinaver and Djahel Vinaver.

had just died, and her cremation tower featured something that shocked and delighted all her friends and community—a photograph of her as a child. So the premature news of her death provided the opportunity for a unique use of repatriation in a society where early-twentieth-century family photographs are rare.

REVISIONING THE FUTURE
FROM A DEEPER PAST

In July 2015, we held a public launch of the *Bali 1928* series as a seminar, multimedia gallery show (105 archival photographs mounted on walls and five DVDs simultaneously played on monitors) and concert in Bali. Anthony Seeger attended and presented an illuminating talk on repatriation and the importance of archives and access (Seeger 2004 and 2015). His participation served as a UCLA presence, receiving praise and appreciation by Indonesians who could simultaneously read his paper in translation. About two hundred Balinese attendees included dozens of genealogical and artistic descendants of the artists recorded in 1928 and those filmed in the 1930s: their children, grandchildren, and great-grandchildren, all of whom I know and have visited. Each attendee received a copy of the full set of CDs and DVDs (Herbst 2015).

Diverse *Bali 1928* activities have continued since publication and public launch. STIKOM inaugurated a Bali 1928 Archive on campus with all the multimedia materials including 85 (from our digital collection of 155) archival photographs on display. The coordinator, Marlowe Bandem, has written:

> Photographer Rio Helmi's involvement goes beyond simply curating the exhibition—selecting, arranging and presenting; he has also been actively engaged in restoring the quality of the photographs, including carrying out adjustments, cropping and printing the digital files that have been entrusted to Bali 1928 Archives by archive centers around the world. Given the quality of most of the digital files that are no longer in their original format or even high-resolution, printing is no ordinary process. It needs to be carried out using specific archival photographic paper that avoids rapid fading and ensures a long life span.

Helmi used museum-quality, acid-free paper and ink with the expectation that these selected prints will be available for exhibitions in Bali for at least seventy-five years (given they are stored in a climate-controlled space). As to access from archives worldwide, we were provided with digital images taken from glass lantern slides, prints, and negatives. In some cases, negatives no longer exist. Quite a few other images are photographs I took of archival prints on location in the homes of Balinese descendants of the artists of 1928.

Following publication, a new phase began to assure that the repatriated materials are used to maximum potential. Our island-wide activities at universities and regional schools, arts centers, and smaller village venues are acquainting the public with these resources to inform, explain, and elicit dialog and comments, as well as to stimulate further research, reconstruction, revival, and new creation. A common format is *Sinema Bali 1928*, for which we project sixty to ninety minutes of films as I provide spontaneous running commentary (in Indonesian) based on our research encounters, followed by a panel that often includes Professor Madé Bandem, our senior project advisor. At times when I am away from Bali, many of these outreach efforts have been led by Marlowe Bandem and his STIKOM team, taking the form of "STIKOM road shows" as well as *Sinema Bali 1928* screenings.

In summation—even as this repatriation effort continues to evolve—we have engaged in a dialogic process through all phases of conception and action. We paid close attention and responded to the interests, predilections, and needs of the contemporary Balinese community. Expanding the repatriated resources—to include deep involvement with the oldest generation that had firsthand knowledge of the cultural context within which the archival materials were produced—provided a depth of perspective that could be included in the written documentation. All phases of activity were collaborative and involved American, Balinese, and other Indonesian researchers, translators, video editors, graphic designers, website designers, and artistic consultants.

This dialogic methodology has served as a compass for guiding our ever-changing understanding of what was being repatriated, where, and how (Figure 19.9). Experience in Bali and elsewhere has led me to the viewpoint that in so many ways, practice precedes theory, and that the most valuable results derive from open perceptions, intimate engagement, empathy, and a willingness to accommodate and integrate unanticipated influences.

FIGURE 19.9 Elder musicians I Ketut Gina and Mangku Gejer with members of the Gamelan Gong Gedé in the village of Sulahan, Bangli, 2016, identifying musicians in films from the 1930s.

Photo by Komang Ongki.

NOTES

1. As we reflect on the project's achievements, it is clear that such results would not have occurred without a certain serendipitous synergy at key moments, introducing unexpected elements that proved essential. Without the best possible audio restoration provided by Allan Evans, the recordings would not have provided such pleasure or evoked such insight, analysis, and memories among Balinese musicians and singers. If it had not been for Philip Yampolsky's expeditions to so many archives back in the 1980s, we would not have located and assembled such a comprehensive collection. If Anthony Seeger had not been director of UCLA's Ethnomusicology Archive, I cannot imagine us having been allowed to borrow their 78 rpm discs in order to make high-quality transfers in Evans's studio. Without Ketut Kodi and other research team members, the depth of discourse and breadth of perspective would not have reached the level that it has. Without coordinator Marlowe Bandem and the cooperation of STIKOM, the high-quality production and ever-widening dissemination of our published materials would not have been so beneficial to Balinese society. And if the project had begun just a few years later, the older generation would have been gone—and with it an immeasurable treasure of cultural memory, artistic wit and wisdom.

2. Vol. 1: *Gamelan Gong Kebyar*; vol. 2: *Tembang Kuna—Songs from an Earlier Time*; vol. 3: *Lotring & the Sources of Gamelan Tradition*; vol. 4: *Music for Temple Festivals & Death Rituals*; vol. 5: *Vocal Music in Dance Dramas: Jangér, Arja, Topéng & Cepung* (Herbst 2009, 2015; 2014, 2015; 2015a; 2015b; 2015c). Over four hours of films from the 1930s by Colin McPhee and Miguel Covarrubias are on YouTube channel Bali1928.net (also accessible from edwardherbst.net), with more films by Rolf de Maré and Claire Holt included on the DVDs published in Bali. While the YouTube channel is an unprecedented resource, Indonesians benefit by having the DVDs, with their higher resolution and the ability to view the overall flow of each volume, which reflects considerable editing and restoration work by the Indonesian team.

3. One example being Toth (1980, 16–17).

4. Unpublished letters from Bali written by Walter Spies to his mother and to the ethnomusicologist Jaap Kunst, provided by Spies's nephew, David Sandberg.

5. Provided to me and annotated (2002) by Philip Yampolsky, who suggests it was "apparently published in 1932."

6. Sekolah Tinggi Manajemen Informatika dan Teknik Komputer.

7. The Research Foundation of the City University of New York supported the project with funding from the Andrew W. Mellon Foundation and the Henry Luce Foundation. Additional funding has been provided by the Ford Foundation, Asian Cultural Council, a Fulbright Senior Research Scholar Award, and through the generosity of Ray Noren and others.

8. Such early cameras recorded at 16 or 18 frames per second (fps), whereas newer sound-recording cameras introduced in the 1930s ran at 24 or 25 fps. In other words, older films would play back at faster speeds unless their conversion or playback compensated for this difference in frame rate.

9. According to Garry Margolis (personal communication, 2015), who at Colin McPhee's request in the early 1960s at UCLA assembled McPhee's original footage, "The film that runs through the camera has the emulsion side facing the lens and should be viewed with the emulsion facing the projector lens. Contact prints are made with the camera original

emulsion in contact with the print film emulsion, so a contact print should be viewed with the emulsion facing away from the projector lens. If a camera original is viewed with the emulsion facing away from the lens, as is normal for prints, the image will be reversed, left to right."

10. McPhee (1935, 163) wrote idealistically of Balinese music as "an art which, however, is so impersonal that the composer himself has lost his identity." However, Hildred Geertz (2004) challenges the idea of anonymity by showing how individual sculptors in Batuan were known and appreciated during their lifetimes for the art they created for the *pura désa* (community temple), but that because written records were not kept, their identities could be forgotten over time. And Sudéwi (2011, 138) provides a "royal chronicle" from *Babad Dalem Sukawati* describing the creation of légong dance in 1880, with several choreographers listed by name. Also see Herbst (2015, vol. 3, 22–23), online at http://edwardherbst.net.

11. Archival photos taken by Colin McPhee, Walter Spies, Arthur Fleischmann, and others, courtesy of the descendants of the 1920s and 1930s performers.

12. Our Indonesian-language website (Bali1928.net), English-language site (edwardherbst.net), and Arbiter's (http://arbiterrecords.org/catalog/category/world-arbiter/) offer free downloads of the written and visual materials and links to distributors of the musical tracks from the CDs as well as the YouTube channel Bali 1928.

13. All song lyrics with translations are included in the CD notes available as PDF files on the published CDs and as free downloads from the project websites.

14. By today's Balinese performing artists as well as Western writers including Walter Spies and Beryl de Zoete, Margaret Mead, Miguel Covarrubias, and later generations of scholars.

15. Herbst (2014, vol. 2, 55–61); online at edwardherbst.net.

16. See Geoffrey Robinson (1995).

17. Another significant factor influencing homogeneity is the tourist economy, beginning with the opening of the Bali Hotel in 1927 and continuing to the present, with about 4,000,000 Balinese hosting 4,000,000 tourists each year. Hotels and other venues can most successfully market a familiar product, and village ensembles would imitate the commercially successful ones. However, this is not relevant to Busungbiu, which is geographically remote and outside the tourist circuit.

References

Aryasa, I Wayan, et al. 1984–1985. *Pengetahuan Karawitan Bali*. Denpasar, Indonesia: Proyek Pengembangan Kesenian Bali, Departemen Pendidikan dan Kebudayaan.

De Zoete, Beryl, and Walter Spies. 1938. *Dance and Drama in Bali*. London: Faber and Faber. New ed., Kuala Lumpur: Oxford University Press, 1973.

Geertz, Hildred. 2004. *The Life of a Balinese Temple: Artistry, Imagination and History in a Peasant Village*. Honolulu: University of Hawai'i Press.

Herbst, Edward. 1997a. "Baris," "Gamelan," "Indonesia: An Overview," "Balinese Dance Traditions," "Balinese Ceremonial Dance," "Balinese Dance Theater," "Balinese Mask Dance Theater," "Kakul, I Nyoman," "Kebyar," "Légong," "Mario, I Ketut," "Sardono," "Wayang." In *International Encyclopedia of Dance*, edited by Selma Jeanne Cohen. New York: Oxford University Press and Dance Perspectives Foundation.

Herbst, Edward. 1997b. *Voices in Bali: Energies and Perceptions in Vocal Music and Dance Theater.* With accompanying CD. Hanover, NH and London: Wesleyan University Press.

Herbst, Edward. 1999. "The Roots of Gamelan: Bali, 1928." CD notes (24 pp.) for digitally remastered Odeon-Beka 78 rpm recordings as well as Colin McPhee's 1940 piano transcriptions performed by McPhee with Benjamin Britten. New York: Arbiter of Cultural Traditions. http://arbiterrecords.org/catalog/.

Herbst, Edward. 2009, 2015. "Bali 1928—Vol. 1: Gamelan Gong Kebyar." CD notes (75 pp. on PDF and online) for digitally remastered Odeon-Beka 78 rpm recordings. New York: Arbiter of Cultural Traditions and Denpasar: STIKOM Bali. http://bit.ly/2cpQtNM, www.edwardherbst.net, and in Indonesian at www.Bali1928.net.

Herbst, Edward. 2014, 2015. "Bali 1928—Vol. 2: Tembang Kuna—Songs from an Earlier Time." CD notes (116 pp. on PDF and online). New York: Arbiter of Cultural Traditions and Denpasar: STIKOM Bali. http://bit.ly/2cgW3nU, www.edwardherbst.net, and in Indonesian at www.Bali1928.net.

Herbst, Edward. 2015a. "Bali 1928—Vol. 3: Lotring and the Sources of Gamelan Tradition." CD notes (98 pp. on PDF and online). New York: Arbiter of Cultural Traditions and Denpasar: STIKOM Bali. http://bit.ly/2cQHJB2, www.edwardherbst.net, and in Indonesian at www.Bali1928.net.

Herbst, Edward. 2015b. "Bali 1928—Vol. 4: Music for Temple Festivals and Death Rituals." CD notes (119 pp. on PDF and online). New York: Arbiter of Cultural Traditions and Denpasar: STIKOM Bali. http://bit.ly/2d0KpMH, www.edwardherbst.net, and in Indonesian at www.Bali1928.net.

Herbst, Edward. 2015c. "Bali 1928—Vol. 5: Vocal Music in Dance Dramas: Jangér, Arja, Topéng and Cepung." CD notes (92 pp. on PDF and online) for digitally remastered Odeon-Beka 78 rpm recordings. New York: Arbiter of Cultural Traditions and Denpasar: STIKOM Bali. http://bit.ly/2cLveuq, www.edwardherbst.net, and in Indonesian at www.Bali1928.net.

McPhee, Colin. 1935. "The Absolute Music of Bali." *Modern Music* 12 (May–June): 163–169.

McPhee, Colin. 1946. *A House in Bali.* New York: John Day. Reprint, Hong Kong: Periplus Editions, 2000.

Robinson, Geoffrey. 1995. *The Dark Side of Paradise: Political Violence in Bali.* Ithaca, NY: Cornell University Press.

Rubinstein, Raechelle. 1992. "Pepaosan: Challenges and Change." In *Balinese Music in Context: A Sixty-Fifth Birthday Tribute to Hans Oesch,* edited by D. Schaareman, 85–114. Forum Ethnomusicologicum 4. Winterthur, Switzerland: Amadeus Verlag.

Seeger, Anthony. 2015. "Retrieving the Past for a Creative Future: Archives, Repatriation, and the Challenges Ahead." Paper presented in Denpasar, Bali (unpublished). Available at http://edwardherbst.net/wp-content/uploads/2016/06/Anthony-Seeger_Bali-Paper.July-2015.pdf.

Seeger, Anthony, and Shubha Chaudhuri, eds. 2004. *Archives for the Future: Global Perspectives on Audiovisual Archives in the 21st Century.* Calcutta: Seagull Press. Available at http://www.seagullindia.com/archive/download.html.

Supanggah, Rahayu. 2011. *The Rich Styles of Interpretation in Javanese Gamelan Music.* Surakarta, Indonesia: ISI Press.

Toth, Andrew. 1980. *Recordings of the Traditional Music of Bali and Lombok.* Special series no. 4. Society for Ethnomusicology.

CHAPTER 20

....

CINEMATIC JOURNEYS
TO THE SOURCE

Musical Repatriation to Africa in Film

....

LISA OSUNLETI BECKLEY-ROBERTS

They Are We.
Emma Christopher and Sergio Leyva Seiglei, producers. Directed by Emma Christopher.
DVD, 77 minutes. 2013. Distributed by Icarus Films.

Throw Down Your Heart.
Béla Fleck and Sascha Paladino, producers. Directed by Sascha Paladino.
DVD, 97 minutes. 2008. Distributed by New Video Group.

Feel Like Going Home.
Paul G. Allen, Jody Patton, and Ulrich Felsberg, producers. Directed by Martin Scorsese.
DVD, 110 minutes. 2003. Distributed by Columbia Music Video.

Search for the Everlasting Coconut Tree.
Adimu Madyun, Dedan Gills, Belvie Rooks, United Roots, and Tony Jackson, producers. Directed by Adimu Madyun.
DVD, 97 minutes. 2015. Distributed by 393 Films.

WHERE are the places memories exist, where do they come from, and how are they preserved? How does memory contribute to, benefit from, and suffer as the result of repatriation? This chapter is a critical film analysis of four documentaries—*They Are We*, a film by Emma Christopher; *Throw Down Your Heart*, featuring Béla Fleck and directed by Sascha Paladino; *The Blues: Feel Like Going Home*, featuring Corey Harris and directed by Martin Scorsese; and *Search for the Everlasting Coconut Tree*, featuring and directed by Adimu Madyun—all chosen for their exploration of musicians' journeys to the birthplace of their instrument, genre, or message. They are by no means the only films that explore the main themes of this chapter, but each uniquely addresses memory and the need to find and reconnect, via repatriation, with the source of a style of music. Each story is about an artist, or group of artists, who perform music that originates in Africa south of the Sahara. But as each experiences her individual return, she also examines the separation of music and people from Africa in the trans-Atlantic slave trade while creating opportunities for themselves and the descendants of those left in Africa to heal from it.

Though repatriation is usually viewed as a physical return to a group's or an individual's ancestral homeland, this chapter asserts that prior to physical return, and perhaps in lieu of it, the collective memory,[1] of some members of the African diaspora, as retained through artistic endeavors, served as the homeland before physical return was possible. This is not to claim that those memories and the perception of memory as the homeland are without fault. Both real and imagined memories may be romanticized through nostalgia and an expectation that people and places remain static. Nonetheless, blacks in the Americas who are the descendants of enslaved African people sang, danced, and performed *Africa* based on what was passed down through generations, and in those moments, they returned. For many this was the entirety of their repatriation experience. However, those communal reenactments of places and behaviors eventually made possible each of the physical repatriation experiences featured in the films reviewed here.

It is impossible to consider the theme of music and repatriation to Africa in film without mention of *The Language You Cry In: Story of a Mende Song*, produced and directed by Alvaro Toepke and Angel Serrano. This groundbreaking film was one of the first to view music as a way of preserving memory of a homeland and as such how repatriation was made possible. In this documentary, a funeral hymn passed down to members of a sea-island community in Georgia serves as the key to reuniting the members of that community with a Mende village in Sierra Leone called Senehum Ngola. One woman from Senehum Ngola recalls how the funeral hymn became what Carol Muller refers to as a "living archive," in that as her grandmother taught it to her, she told her that the descendants of those stolen from their village would continue to sing it, and one day return to them. When discussing the work of Isaiah Shembe, a South African who was instrumental in establishing a new form of hymn performance practice in South Africa, she states, "What Isaiah Shembe did in that moment was to create a living archive for holding Africanness as a cultural practice in trust for future generations until such time as it would be reconstituted as a force of power and visible social identity" (Muller 2002, 413). Likewise, the films surveyed here are viewed from the perspective that physical repatriation to Africa was achieved because generations of Africans in the diaspora[2] invoked the homeland through collective memory and performance. Moreover, they understood that the archival memory of the homeland culture could be embodied and maintained through the music they performed. The act of remembering and performing was the first stage of their repatriation.

Though there are many forms of memory, those that contribute to group identity are of most interest here. For those who are the descendants of people forcibly removed from Africa, memory—functioning through music—has served as the emotional and spiritual means of repatriation for generations. Until recently, people like me could only dream of going back to Africa to visit the homeland. As such, we returned home through our performances and our collective memories. Now that it is possible for members of the African diaspora to physically return to Africa, there is an opportunity to heal, grow, and expand our understanding of how music has functioned, as a means of repatriation.

THEY ARE WE

They Are We is the story of how a group of Afro-Cubans discovered their ancestral homeland in what is now Sierra Leone and, through great effort, could travel there to reunite with the descendants of the people from which an ancestor was kidnapped during the trade of enslaved people. The reunion was made possible by an anthropologist who heard and recorded songs and dances that were part of an annual celebration held in honor of Saint Lazaro by the Afro-Cubans (referred to as Gangá-Longobá, or Gangá for short). The Gangá, who now live in the town of Perico within the province of Matanzas, Cuba, performed music and dances passed down for generations as a part of a spiritual ritual that continues to take place annually in December. This was an act of collective memory, one in which they as a group performed elements of their African past.[3] Dr. Emma Christopher was fascinated by the Gangá-Longobá's performance in Cuba when she witnessed them. Her curiosity was piqued when she was told that these had been performed, and taught by an enslaved person who was from somewhere in West Africa. Although the performers were not able to identify specifically where the pieces came from, they were clear that the pieces were indeed African and that they used them during an annual celebration in honor of Saint Lazaro. Lazaro and other Catholic saints have long been used in Cuba to cover the worship of African deities.[4]

Christopher showed footage of the Cuban songs and dances to many villagers from different ethnic groups, in varying parts of West Africa, and was eventually able to identify the small, remote area (a part of the Upper Banta chiefdom, a village named Mokpangumba near Banta Mokele in the Moyambe district) where the tradition, historically belonging to part of the Menda healing society, originated. Through work with the governments of both nations, she created an opportunity for the Afro-Cuban performers to visit the village. The documentary detailed the painstaking process of showing the performances to people in Sierra Leone in order to determine from whom it was likely derived. Eventually she received a clue that revealed the music was in the Banta language, which was once widely spoken in the region.

The story of finding the source of the music and dance was remarkable, but overshadowing this was how, through performance, Africans in the diaspora in Cuba collectively "remembered" their homeland and both groups experienced their reunion as healing.

The overt goal of the documentary was connection, through collective memory, of the artistic expression of being African in Cuba among the Gangá and in Mokpangumba, Sierra Leone. While the filmmakers had this aim, they also framed the events to show that performative remembrance had been an integral part of maintaining the connection. The group, therefore, served as a collective or community of "rememberers" who encouraged younger members both to recognize connections between their own actions and those of their ancestors and to identify as a part of a continuum of performers of the tradition. The film suggested that memories have served (and continue to serve) as a source of immense pride and as a basis of identity for members of the Gangá community and for Afro-Cubans at large.

The film included scenes of the Gangá-Longobá community musicians from Cuba as they prepared to travel to Sierra Leone, their reflections about what they expected to encounter once there, and some of their day-to-day behaviors. In these moments, there were demonstrations of behaviors and unities of attitude that could be identified as Africanisms (Holloway 1990, 2). These appeared to have become so deeply entrenched in their identity that it was impossible to separate who they were from who they believe they had been historically as people. For instance, as Alfredo Duquesne, a woodcarver and musician, discussed how and why he carved masks, it became clear that both his methods and his attitude about the work were based in an African worldview about his personal responsibility, legacy, and role within the community. Likewise, each musician viewed her or his role in the ensemble as a continuation of ancestral practices and a part of her or his own cultural identity and generational responsibility.

Perhaps the most notable line from the film is the one from which the title is taken: "They are we!" proclaimed by an excited Sierra Leonean when he saw the video of the Afro-Cubans singing and dancing. That sentiment is what many members of the African diaspora long for. It is representative of the aspiration simply to belong somewhere and to be *from* somewhere. It is an opportunity to have memories, both real and imagined, confirmed and more specifically to connect with their perceived Africanness. In his 1995 article, "Toward a Pan-African Identity: Diaspora African Repatriates in Ghana," Obiagele Lake stated, the "removal of Africans from their cultural roots . . . did not erase Africans' sense of belonging to a broader African people" (Lake 1995, 21–22).[5] Similarly, that removal of Africans did not erase their place within African societies, and time has not relieved the pain over their absence. The proclamation "They are we!" speaks to the value that Africans place on welcoming members of the diaspora back to their homeland. Moreover, the producers of the film provided, through their editing, an opportunity for viewers to understand the mutual value placed on regaining what was lost. People in many of the communities where Christopher showed the footage of Afro-Cubans eagerly responded, tried to help her find what ethnic group the Gangá of Cuba came from, and seemed to want to claim kinship with them. They genuinely were impressed and proud of how "African" the performance was, despite being done in Cuba. One woman who watched with her community as Christopher showed the footage of the Gangá made a plea to the performers to send a picture and not to forget about them in Africa. She said that they wanted to understand her, and the Gangá, more.

There are a few shortcomings in the film. Perhaps because of time constraints, it does not address the history of religious and social climates of Cuba that allowed for this ancestral tradition, as well as Orisha and other African religious traditions, to survive.[6] The opening scenes featuring music, dance, and spiritual possession were identified by Christopher as a festival for Saint Lazarus held annually on December 17. In fact, what was taking place was a celebration of Babaluaye, an Orisha who was historically worshiped covertly by saying that it was a celebration of Saint Lazarus.[7] Additionally, no real attention is given to the fact that the traditional spiritual practices are diminishing in parts of Africa like Sierra Leone because of their oppression by Christian and Islamic evangelical movements. The traditional healer and leader of the society in Mokpangumba, referred to as the Bomusigie, mentions that she has grown discouraged about performing the rituals and the presence of the Afro-Cubans gave her strength, but this is not examined. Rather, there is a brief scene where children were seen and heard singing a Christian hymn. The inclusion of this scene alludes to the way that Christianity may have caused the decline of indigenous spiritual practices, but the absence of a discussion of this matter leaves one wanting to know more.

Nonetheless, *They Are We* is a powerful testament to the strength of memory and the validity of the assertion that music made repatriation possible. One of the featured musicians from Cuba, Alfredo Duquesne, commented that as a result of finding the source of the music he has performed his entire life, and therefore his homeland, "we are not lost after all." The (collective) memory preserved in the songs and dances gave members of the diaspora an active way to maintain their identity and the connection that they had with their ancestral home. Though the religious tradition that the music comes from has been transformed in Sierra Leone due to immense pressure from foreign religions, colonialism, and the sociocultural damage of the slave trade, what the Gangá passed down for generations was an element of their cultural identity that served as a means for repatriation.

THROW DOWN YOUR HEART

In *Throw Down Your Heart*, Béla Fleck visits Uganda, Tanzania, Gambia, and Mali. He describes his motivation for the trip by stating,

> For so long (the banjo has been) associated with a white, southern, stereotype. And, a lot of people in the United States don't realize that the banjo is an African instrument. One way to illustrate it would be to take the banjo back to Africa and research some of the roots of the banjo, but also to just play with some great African musicians and find a role for the banjo in their music.

In each country he visited, Fleck listened to music by local musicians and tried to incorporate his banjo performance with their local styles. Fleck's endeavor to return the banjo to Africa and participate in music there was a repatriation that articulates and shines light on the impact that Africa has had on the development of American identity.

While Fleck says that he wanted to research the history of the American banjo, he does not say why he chose to travel to those specific countries, and his inquiry into the history of the instrument consisted mainly of talking to musicians about their own music traditions. His choice to travel to Gambia and Mali makes sense to Americans who recognize that many Africans brought to America as enslaved people came from West and Central Africa, carrying with them the memory of their music and instruments (to include banjo-related instruments). Fleck's chosen destinations appear to be related to the musicians with whom he is familiar in each of the regions; or, perhaps the choices were dictated by the type of music and musicians with which he was interested in collaborating. Nonetheless, each community he visited presented a unique opportunity for collaboration and observation. Those in East Africa, related to traditions of Nilotic and Nilotic diaspora string playing, likely influenced West African approaches to making and playing the instrument and subsequently impacted early African American performance and construction.[8]

Though it seems Fleck intended simply to illustrate a history of the banjo, and to make music, he achieved a far deeper connection. *Throw Down Your Heart* affirms that music from Africa was remembered among Africans in the Americas and subsequently, perhaps inadvertently, created memories and an American identity for white Americans.[9] The memory, identity, and pride associated with American folk music, which has for the most part excluded the presence of Africa, needs to be shifted in order to include the experiences of Africans in America. Though Fleck does not directly address this in *Throw Down Your Heart*, his commitment to sharing his perception of the origin of the banjo could help to facilitate that shift.[10] Nonetheless, evidence of African influence on the banjo tradition is visible in playing techniques such as the clawhammer or frailing style that is popular in bluegrass music.[11]

Each of the film's cross-cultural exchanges is valuable and produces beautiful, enjoyable music. Moreover, the discussions that ensue between performances illuminate the role of music in preserving the story of composers and performers, and reflecting the society from which it emerges. In one scene filmed in Bagamoyo, on the northern coast of Tanzania, Fleck's guide, John Kitime, tells him about how captured Africans knew from stories that they had been told that if they were brought to that place where the water was endless (the ocean), they would be taken away and never be allowed to return. They responded by saying they would "throw down their hearts." This is the literal meaning of the word "Bagamoyo," which came to be the name of this port. Recognizing that those same people took with them their memories and culture—and, as much as possible, reinvented them wherever they ended up—served as a reminder that music was (and is) a means of repatriation when their physical return was impossible.[12]

FEEL LIKE GOING HOME

Feel Like Going Home, directed by Martin Scorsese, was the first documentary in a seven-part series about the history and context of the blues. Scorsese, a huge fan of the blues, has said that as a result of listening to the blues and recognizing its roots in Africa, he was able to understand better the rock and roll music that he grew up loving (Guralnick et al. 2003, 6). This recognition was likely an impetus to make this documentary, which aims to highlight the African roots of blues music.

In the film, Mississippi bluesman Corey Harris traveled throughout Mississippi and discussed the blues tradition with notable blues performers in that state. As he did this, he highlighted how musicians in the genre have always found a way to negotiate identity and oppression in their coded songs. He also elucidated the regional differences in blues and folk musics in Mississippi and the areas that musicians migrated to and from in Mississippi. He then made the journey to Mali, where he wove those concepts and approaches to making music into the stories, approaches, and aesthetics of musicians there. Viewers learn how the blues singer is, in a sense, the "New World" griot or *djaliya* and how those singers have retained their Africanness via music and its efficacy.[13]

Harris comments at the beginning of the film, "The blues takes you back to the place where it first came to life. There's an old African saying that the roots of a tree cast no shadow, that's how deep the blues goes. If you really listen to the music you understand . . . this is the one thing they could never really take away from black people." He was clear that playing the blues connected him to his ancestors, to his history both in the United States and Africa, and to his calling to preserve that history in ways that allowed the traditions that he is a part of to continue to evolve as a result of his own experiences. While the blues was born in Mississippi, Harris aims to show that the roots of that music are in Africa.

Feel Like Going Home opens with archival footage of a fife and drum ensemble from the hill-country region of north Mississippi that morphs into an idyllic view of the Niger River bank in Africa, and then into more archival footage of men chopping down a tree and singing a work song. This smooth transition introduces the film and offers a glimpse of the story that unfolds over the course of 110 minutes, though the transitions are not always as effortless as in that opening scene. Instead, there are times when the history of the blues, in its many locales, feels disjointed and it is unclear why a new place or musician is introduced and how the artists are related. In the film the beginning of the blues' trip home is told through narration about, and footage of, John and Alan Lomax's collection of ballads. While in many ways that was a wise choice, this footage does not document the beginning of the blues tradition per se and its inclusion as a starting point seems misleading. What the Lomaxes did was to solidify the position of the blues within the American experience and legitimize the classification of blues as an American folk music, symbolically. Lead Belly's original recording, made by the Lomax men while he was in a Louisiana penitentiary, and the artist's subsequent performances in New York upon his release, exposed northern and international audiences (presumably white and black) to the blues. Simultaneously, in the South, the blues continued to change in order to reflect the social and political climate there.

Harris mentions that the Mississippi that John and Alan Lomax encountered in 1941 still exists in rural areas. His allusion to socioeconomic challenges that blacks still face, along with the role that music has played in navigating these challenges, would have been a valuable addition, and the absence of such a statement is felt throughout the film. There is not an implication that all is well, nor one of how bad things are; but there is no acknowledgment of the current state of affairs for blacks in America. The documentary pays no attention to the realities that still make the blues tradition necessary, nor does it acknowledge that the desire to repatriate is rooted in a need to escape those realities.

The film asserts how revolutionary the genre could be, and the relationship between it and the music of African *djeliya* in preserving history and helping people to deal with their world. In a scene at Bettie's Place in Prairie Point, Mississippi, Willie King, accompanied by the Liberators, sings the powerful lyrics of "Terrorized" as couples danced. "Now you talk about terror, what about poor me? I been terrorized all my days. Couldn't walk down the road without somebody wanting to stop and pick on poor me." This is an example of what King refers to as one of his "struggle songs." It is one of many that he wrote and performed in an effort not only to entertain listeners, but also to give voice to the struggle of the disenfranchised black people in America. Moreover, the struggle songs were intended to empower those people. The clip is short, but it is one of the most profound in the film because of the feelings it triggers. Because the blues' social commentary and political efficacy is not yet part of popular culture's understanding of the blues, this was a missed opportunity to delve further into that discussion.

If Mississippi was indeed the land where the blues was born, as *Feel Like Going Home* asserts, then it was conceived in Africa. Over half of the film was set in the American South, mostly in Mississippi, but the power of the time that Harris spent in Africa is immeasurable. The guitarist first arrived in Bamako, Mali, and through his reflections, he explained that both the blues and he as a black American felt at home there. Though the film does not mention it, John Lee Hooker also traveled to Bamako, along with Ray Charles and Otis Redding during the late 1960s. During that visit, Hooker spent a significant amount of time with the Malian musician Ali Farke Toure, whom Harris met with and interviewed as a part of the documentary. After recognizing the similarities between their music styles, Toure began incorporating much of Hooker's guitar technique into his own compositions. This earlier instance of repatriation influenced the music of Mali and musicians who were featured in the film, and it likely influenced more recent developments in the blues in America. The omission of the exchange between Toure and Hooker was an unfortunate oversight because it could have led to a valuable discussion of the ways that blues and Malian music are intertwined and have been in conversation for at least a generation now as the blues has found its way home to Africa. More importantly, that trip was a part of the blues' return to the homeland.

Harris did, however, show that blues musicians were similar to *djeliya* because they saw the music they performed as a gift from the creator that helped and healed the people. That help was given through performances of music and dance that retold stories, gave social commentary in codes, and provided alternative realities. These unities of attitude and the intended efficacy of performance illuminated the fact that each performer is at a particular point on a continuum of the African experience told through music.

Each of the musicians Harris spoke with in Mali discussed the relationship between blues and the music they created and performed. They cited similarities in rhythm (polyrhythm), pitch organization (pentatonicism), themes (loss, love, and sadness), and motivation to perform (sacred callings). Furthermore, each musician said or implied that the blues was rooted in Africa and that it had always been a means of maintaining Africanness by the members of the diaspora. Likewise, nearly all of them spoke in some way about the pain that both African Americans and Africans suffered, and continue to suffer, as a result of the trans-Atlantic slave trade. Ali Farka Toure, during Harris's time in Niafunké, Mali, commented that Africa is the "navel" of Africans in America, meaning that it is the root and homeland from which they can and should draw their strength. This statement is the essence of why there was a need to include a return to Africa in this installment of the history of the blues. Blues musicians provided a communal space within which their audiences could remember elements of their African culture, without completely knowing or acknowledging where they come from, and the music provided a means through which to deal with the trauma of their individual and collective pasts.

SEARCH FOR THE EVERLASTING COCONUT TREE

Similarly, Adimu Madyun, or WolfHawkJaguar as he is known to his fans, is committed to the work of healing trauma. This desire to assist in restoring balance is one of the several focal points of the film *Search for the Everlasting Coconut Tree*, in which he seeks to help young men he mentors at a community center in Oakland, California. He uses the journey of repatriation to deal with multiple issues and that lends a great deal to the beauty of the film. On the one hand, *Search for the Everlasting Coconut Tree* is about Madyun's endeavor to find answers to his mentees' questions about life, freedom, and finding the path to their destiny. On the other, it is equally his personal journey, through music, to an African spiritual tradition. These themes are informed, supported, and envisioned through his music.

Madyun's music is in an American hip-hop/neo-soul style that tells stories about Yoruba deities and his life as a worshiper of them.[14] His music, he explains in the film, came to be a combination of dream journals and his journey to become an Orisha devotee. His desire to embrace this African religion, and the juxtaposed responsibility he felt toward building and supporting community, are themes in his music as well as this documentary. They were the impetus for the physical repatriation to Nigeria but also the basis on which it can be asserted that the return to Nigeria had already happened. Moreover, there is a clear emphasis throughout the film that he and the music he performs are African. While in Nigeria, Madyun is asked to stay there—to which he responds, "I never left!"

As if to give the viewer the impression that he walked into a workout session at a community center, the documentary begins with a gathering of Madyun, community elders, and the young men with whom they work, finishing an exercise routine in which they are directed to "salute your brothers!" They do so with an embrace. They then discuss how they would like to plant seeds within themselves for growth and evolution. In this discussion Madyun tells those gathered that he plans to travel to Nigeria. Madyun talks about his endeavor to someday find "the everlasting coconut tree." He describes it as a source of wisdom that he came to understand as he sat at the feet of elders and learned from them. It was because of his time with elders that he also discovered that his "magic" was music, and those songs eventually led to his invitation to perform at the Orisha World Congress in Nigeria. He explains that while he is there, he plans to find the mystical tree and get answers to their questions. At that point the perspective of the documentary shifts from allowing viewers to observe the events that are happening to having participants speak directly into the camera. Young men, whose ages range from twenty to twenty-three, stand alone, look into the camera, and ask questions about what they see as their most pressing challenges.

In an intentional effort to connect their own community and culture to that of a remembered or reimagined Africa, Madyun speaks about how prior to their departure for Nigeria, there will be a "village celebration" to send them off, and the "village elders" speak to the travelers about what to expect. There is an *ebo*,[15] or spiritual work, that Madyun helps the members of his band (Band of Hunters) perform to protect them on the trip. This was prescribed by his spiritual teacher, his *iya*.[16] The community perceives themselves as African, or rather as an extension of African culture that functions and shares the philosophy of Africans. If the language were not enough to convince the viewer of the symbiotic relationship and the mission of healing by strengthening bonds between African Americans and Africans, this is illuminated by one of the elders who speaks about their separation due to the trans-Atlantic slave trade, saying, "We also feel very sad for what happened! It's wrong that you should ever go home and feel as a foreigner. It's wrong! It's very wrong!"

At vital moments of transition throughout the film, and at times when one of the songs by WolfHawkJaguar explicates a sentiment, graphic depictions of complex ideas are communicated through drawings that come to life through movement and the music that accompanies them. One of the first of these, and perhaps one of the most significant, features a bird flying with a seed in its beak and then dropping it into the earth. This happens and is meant to imply that as the band is traveling to Africa, seeds from America (which had grown from a tree originally in Africa) are returning and some new version of the original will be planted there. When the band arrives in Nigeria, Adekoya Adefunmi gives them a tour of Dr. Wándé Abímbolá's[17] family compound and of Orisha shrines. Adefunmi is a son of the original king of the Oyotunji African village in South

Carolina.[18] Viewers who know the history of the practice of Orisha traditions in the United States by African Americans will recognize the significance of Adefunmi giving the tour in two ways: (1) It is a reminder of the connection between Oyotunji African village and the Nigerian priesthood, and (2) it inspires the realization that African Americans who have become practitioners of the religion (a form of repatriation), regardless of whether they have returned to the geographic homeland of Nigeria, are an intricate part of the survival, growth, and evolution of the religious practice. That is, the practitioners are the seeds and have been returned to the homeland.

Before Madyun and his bandmates search for the everlasting coconut tree, they are scheduled to perform at the Orisha World Congress; however, due to an ironic twist of fate, they are overlooked by mistake. Madyun uses this as an opportunity to discuss the Yoruba concept of *suuru*,[19] or patience, and never loses his temper, although he is upset. He acknowledges that this is simply a manifestation of the Orisha Eshu, the trickster, who he believes is playing a trick on him to teach him a lesson that associated with the quest for the coconut tree. As a result of the mistake, WolfHawkJaguar and the Band of Hunters are invited to perform for the Ooni of Ife, or traditional rule of Ile-Ife, which is the seat of Yoruba power in Nigeria, at his personal palace. Ultimately, the performance plays into the idea of the journey as an opportunity to sow and tend seeds, as illustrated by the bird graphic.

As the film progresses, and the goal of finding the everlasting coconut tree becomes the focus, the tree is found literally and metaphorically. After a physical coconut tree is located, the band members meet a woman who helps answer the young men's questions. Upon returning to Oakland, Madyun, members of his band, and the elders who traveled with them participate in a tree-planting ceremony.

Search for the Everlasting Coconut Tree differs from the other documentaries in this analysis because the people featured within strongly believe, articulate, and view themselves as African prior to their return to Africa. Madyun believes that through his journey to Nigeria and by finding the everlasting coconut tree, he will be a part of a predestined cycle to return to the homeland, actively contribute to Orisha culture there (through his music), and bring healing, discovered in Africa, back to his community. As an artist-activist, he seems committed not only to fulfilling his own destiny to return to the homeland but also to continuing to build and inspire others to remember an African identity in Oakland, California. Like his music, the film mixes elements of Orisha archetypes with contemporary expressions of African American culture. It also asserts that through memory, the people of the African diaspora maintain much of their African identity until they can return.

CONCLUSION

The films surveyed in this chapter all stand as a testament to the ability of participatory collective memories to function as the homeland in the African diaspora until a time when physical repatriation is possible. The descendants of enslaved Africans, motivated by a desire to maintain elements of their culture, use memory in this way for many reasons. Principal among those reasons is an inability, due to financial, social, and political constraints, to physically return. Though the memories, and performance of them, change in ways that better suit their needs in different physical locations, they sustain practitioners and offer the comfort of "home" and aid in the retention of identity. Some are masked so well that they are no longer recognizable as African even to practitioners. This is the case with the banjo, which found its way into Anglo-American folk music. Other collective memories are preserved in a way that expresses the adaptability of African traits, such as storytelling and serving the community through empowering, healing, and providing an alternate reality, which is the case in blues music and Orisha hip-hop. Then there are some that refuse to change except in the slightest ways, like those of the Gangá of Cuba. Nonetheless, these forms of music performance are manifestations of a collective memory of place, culture, and identity. They highlight people's ability to recreate a place described in metaphors, melodic lines, rhythms, instruments, archetypes, and approaches and ideas to and about performance. They are the embodiment of a return, for some period, to the homeland, and they provide the basis on which physical repatriation is possible.

While it seems the return became a sort of resolution in each of these films to the internal conflict caused by the brutal separation of people from their homeland, or that appears to be the hope of each of those journeying "home," we are still left with one issue with which we must contend. Members of the diaspora have yet to achieve a feeling of being completely at home in the Americas. Returning to the source of the musical traditions that we have kept alive in our memory to maintain an aspect of our identity and culture assists in the healing of being descendants of those taken to be enslaved, it is only one step in a larger process that requires more. Perhaps repatriation, and reflection on it, must be followed by more serious inquiry into our collective memory and how it has served us, as well acceptance that it is all a part of a grieving process that will never end—rather it will change.

Notes

1. Collective memory as defined by Alan Confino is "an exploration of a shared identity that unites a social group, be it a family or a nation, whose members nonetheless have different interests and motivations" (1997, 1390). "Memory," as it is used in this chapter, refers to a communal remembrance in the way that Confino defines it and in addition is shown to be a substitute locale for homeland until physical return is possible.

2. In her article, Muller discusses members of the "new African diaspora" as groups of immigrants from Africa that left a more modernized Africa than members of the older or more frequently spoken of African diaspora who were the descendants of enslaved Africans. Because these groups left Africa under very different circumstances, their memories of the homeland and interaction with it are quite different. However, the

phenomenon of the body as an archive or locale of memories that allows members of a diaspora to inhabit "two or more places simultaneously" is mutually true for both groups.

3. The Gangá were performing not only music and dance that was African but also a spiritual tradition associated with their ancestors.

4. Among the deities associated with the Catholic saints are a number of Orisha that are worshiped in Cuba. Orisha are deities of the Yoruba people of Southwest Nigeria. The religious practices of the Yoruba were introduced to Cuba and the Americas through trans-Atlantic slave trade. Many of the religious practices of the Africans who were enslaved and taken to the Americas survived through a complex process of hiding them behind the archetype of Catholic saints.

5. For additional resources on the desire to connect with African identity and African reception of diaspora repatriates, see Uya (1971), Drake (1982), Skinner (1982), and Carmichael (1969).

6. African religious traditions in Cuba survived for several reasons. Most important among these, however, was the fact that the dominant religion of those who were slave owners was Catholic. Because of this, practitioners could hide rituals and worship of their deities behind veneration of the saints.

7. It is evident for many reasons that the Orisha Babaluaye was the center of this celebration. Principal among these was that a participant appears during the celebration wearing burlap, a sash, and a hat in the style indicative of a priest who is possessed by the spirit. Additionally, the way he danced (i.e., the specific style and steps) were those associated with the Orisha.

8. For more information on the transmission of musical styles within Africa, see Gerhard Kubik, "Intra-African Streams of Influence," in *Africa: The Garland Encyclopedia*, vol. 1, edited by Ruth Stone (1998), 293–326.

9. American folk music is a syncretic art form. The banjo, which was initially played by people of African descent in a style reminiscent of how it was played in Africa, contributed significantly to the style. As such, American folk music is equally African and European and is a part of American identity. Unfortunately, for much of American history the influence of blacks on the culture has been ignored.

10. Fleck seemed to recognize that American "folk" music includes all of the folks' influences despite the perceived exclusion of people of color. The resistance to this wider view of folk music was seen in the backlash after Beyonce's 2016 performance at the Country Music Awards with the Dixie Chicks.

11. According to Jay Scott Odell, clawhammer or frailing is a plucking style of playing the banjo that produces a polyrhythmic accent to playing achieved by plucking in a downward motion using the nails of one or several fingers (almost as if striking the string) and then plucking upward with the thumbnail.

12. Enslaved East Africans were trafficked throughout the Indian Ocean and the Arab peninsula.

13. A *djeliya/djali/djeli* is a storyteller who maintains the history of Mande, Mandinka, and Maninka royal families through generations. These ethnic groups are centered in what is now Mali. *Djali* are sometimes referred to as griot, and in the Americas many storytellers choose or are identified by that title.

14. The Yoruba are an ethnic group who are centered in Southwest Nigeria. Orisha devotees are often referred to as "traditionalists" in Nigeria because they have resisted pressure to convert to Islam or Christianity.

15. *Ebo* is a Yoruba word that refers to an offering, sacrifice, or any type of work that has been determined necessary through divination. In this case, the *ebo* was an egg dipped in palm oil that was used both to purify the users and to protect them.

16. *Iya* is Yoruba for mother, but is also used for elder women and particularly for spiritual teachers. For elder men and spiritual teachers, the term *baba* is often used.

17. Dr. Abímbolá is a noted Nigerian academic, scholar of Ifa philosophy, and political figure. His books, articles, and work have been hugely important in the preservation of Orisha shrines in Nigeria, and he has staunchly worked to end persecution of "traditionalists" or Orisha/Ifa devotees.

18. Oyotunji African village was founded near Sheldon, South Carolina, in 1970 by Oba (King) Ofuntola Oseijeman Adelabu Adefunmi I, the first African American to be initiated into the Orisha tradition. The village asserts that it is a sovereign African nation that exists within the United States' borders. As such, it has been a place that has garnered both positive and negative reactions from nonpractitioners, but it remains an important and valuable part of the history of Orisha and Africana religions in America.

19. *Suuru* is Yoruba for patience and is a characteristic of good character and a cool head.

REFERENCES

Carmichael, Stokely. 1969. "Pan-Africanism—Land and Power." *Black Scholar* 1 (1): 36–43.

Confino, Alon. 1997. "Collective Memory and Cultural History: Problems of Method." *American Historical Review* 12 (5): 1386–1403.

Cristopher, Emily. 2014. *They Are We.* DVD. Brooklyn: Icarus Films.

Drake, St. Clair. 1982. "Diaspora Studies and Pan-Africanism." In *Global Dimensions of the African Diaspora*, edited by Joseph Harris, 451–515. Washington, DC: Howard University Press.

Guralnick, Peter, Robert Santelli, Holly George-Warren, and Christopher John Farley, eds. 2003. *Martin Scorsese Presents the Blues: A Musical Journey.* New York: Amistad.

Holloway, Joseph E., ed. 1990. *Africanisms in American Culture.* Bloomington: Indiana University Press.

Kubik, Gerhard, 1998. "Intra-African Streams of Influence." In *Africa: The Garland Encyclopedia of World Music*, edited by Ruth Stone, 293–326. New York: Garland.

Lake, Obiagele. 1995. "Toward a Pan-African Identity: Diaspora African Repatriates in Ghana." *Anthropological Quaterly* 68 (1): 21–36.

Madyun, Adimu, Ayodele, WordSlanger, and Nzinga. 2015. *Search for the Everlasting Coconut Tree.* DVD. Directed by Adimu Madyun. Oakland, CA: 393 Films.

Muller, Carol A. 2002. "Archiving Africanness in Sacred Song." *Ethnomusicology* 46 (3): 409–431.

Odell, Jay Scott. 2014. "Banjo." In *Oxford Music Online.* Accessed February 6, 2017. http://www.oxfordmusiconline.com.

Paladino, Sascha. 2008. *Throw Down Your Heart.* Special edition. DVD. Portland: Old School.

Scorsese, Martin. 2003. *The Blues: Feel Like Going Home.* Volume 1 of *The Blues: A Musical Journey.* DVD. New York: Vulcan Productions and Road Movies Filmproduktion.

Skinner, Elliot P. 1982 "The Dialectic between Diaspora and Homelands." In *Global Dimensions of the African Diaspora*, edited by Joseph E. Harris, 11–40. Washington, DC: Howard University Press.

Toepke, Alvaro, and Angel Serrano. 1999. *The Language You Cry In: Story of a Mende Song*. Online Stream. San Francisco: California Newsreel.

Uya, Okon. 1971. *Black Brotherhood: Afro-Americans*. Lexington, KY: DC Heath.

CHAPTER 21

"*POUR PRÉSERVER LA MÉMOIRE*"

Algerian Sha'bī *Musicians as Repatriated Subjects and Agents of Repatriation*

CHRISTOPHER ORR

MARSEILLE, 2011. Some forty-two weathered, yet cheerful musicians enter the stage of the storied Opéra Municipal. A mixture of French and Arabic wafts through the performance hall as they are welcomed onstage. The musicians have with them *'ūds*, Algerian *mandoles*,[1] *darbūkas* (hand drums), banjos, violins, an accordion, a *qānūn*, a piano, and a string bass. The assortment could resemble an innovative fusion project but in fact consists of seasoned performers of the early popular genre of Algerian music known as *sha'bī*. Most of the men seem quite old, but soon it becomes evident that age has not blunted their musical abilities or their love of performing. They have been gathered together to take part in the documentary film project *El Gusto* (2012). The film follows the efforts of its director, Safinez Bousbia, to reunite the scattered members of a *sha'bī* music conservatory class that had existed in the city of Algiers some fifty years earlier, prior to the Algerian War of Independence and the flight of the group's Jewish members to France. Their premier performance in Marseille as the El Gusto Orchestra was only the first evening in a multiyear world concert tour that would promote *sha'bī* internationally and prompt its resurgence in Algeria.

The premise of the project began when Bousbia, an Oxford architecture student at the time, stumbled upon a small shop in Algiers while looking for an antique mirror. Although born in Algeria, she spent most of her formative years living abroad in Europe and the Middle East before earning advanced degrees in Ireland and the United Kingdom. What began as a short visit to the Algerian capital with a friend became an unexpectedly transformative moment in the life of the soon-to-be filmmaker. As the old shop owner, Mohamad Ferkioui, conversed with Bousbia, he began opening up to her about his time as a *sha'bī* musician under the direction of El Hadj M'hamed El Anka in the 1950s. She was so taken by this man's story that she set out to find and reunite all of the remaining members of this ensemble while documenting the process on film. I argue that the achievement of *El Gusto* is not simply a repatri-ation of individual musicians as documented through the story of the film. Nor is it merely the repatriation of the music itself through the reunion of these musicians, though it does achieve this end. Rather, the film's gravitas owes to the weight of the performers' memories of this period of history, communicated on screen for the first time on such a large scale.

For all of the musicians involved with *El Gusto*, reconnecting with long-lost friends and playing music that had been silenced for half of a century brought forth immense joy but also an onslaught of memories, some of which carried the emotional traumas of a turbulent time in Algerian history. Through several means, the film showcases how *sha'bī* music facilitates particular kinds of collective memory among performers, conflated with the nostalgia of a bygone era.

Two hours into the premier concert at Marseille we arrive at the final number of the evening, and the ensemble shows no sign of slowing down as the musicians launch into the instrumental introduction of the song "Ya Rayah" (Oh, Traveler). Made famous in 1993 by the Algerian popular musician Rachid Taha, the song was first recorded by the Algerian *sha'bī* artist Dahmane El Harrachi, who wrote the song while living in Paris. The song's poignant lyrics speak across the decades to the descendants of Algerian immigrants now present in the audience, most of whom already know the words from Taha's hit version. After the concluding introductory phrase, one of the *'ūd* players, Abdelmadjid Meskoud, settles into the vocal melody with El Harrachi's haunting words to the young Algerian emigrant, "Oh, traveler, where are you going? You'll inevitably grow weary and return. How many naïve ones have gone before you and regretted it?" By now dozens of audience members are dancing in front of the stage, while others clap and sing along to the well-known tune. Many of the audience members are French citizens of Algerian descent, whose parents and grandparents immigrated to the port city of Marseille forty, fifty, or sixty years before. Their exuberant expressions and enthusiastic participation evince a felt sense of coming home, of embracing identity, and of reclaiming a marginalized cul-tural heritage.

Fast-forward five years to 2016. The same group is in concert again, this time in Algiers. Amid the original members, however, one can find several younger musicians as well. They are new additions to the group, chosen from among participants in master classes held ahead of the group's performance. Thanks to El Gusto's ongoing mentorship program, these youths receive individualized, informal training from the group's older members before eventually performing alongside them. Many will travel abroad on the group's upcoming performance tour.

In this chapter, I explore an expanded understanding of repatriation that moves be-yond the idea of returned recordings of sonic cultural heritage to include the reunion of separated individuals who embody a tradition. This alternative understanding of the concept proves particularly relevant for diasporic communities, whose expert practitioners are more likely to be isolated from one another or from contexts that facilitate the tradition's continuation. The narrative of separation and reunion is the fulcrum on which the story of *El Gusto* pivots. Many of the musicians in the film had not performed with one another since their exile to France in the early 1960s. Within the storyline of the film, however, Bousbia presents the reunion of Jewish and Muslim musicians not only as the repatriation of musical culture-bearers but also as the reconstitution of their shared oral history. I arrive at this conclusion through Maurice Halbwachs's foundational theories on collective memory, which suggest that the perpetuation of a memory within a sociocultural group depends on relevant social contexts in which individual recollections may be engaged.

The musicians in the film are brought together from varying degrees of artistic isolation to perform and exchange ideas for the first time in over fifty years. Their shared memories are immediately reignited within the context of this recovered camaraderie. The lively exchanges of cultural history, personal anecdotes, and opinions on musical interpretation during their interactions on film illuminate a unique chapter of musical collaboration in the history of *sha'bī* music just before the War of Independence—a history in danger of disappearing with its aging witnesses scattered on both sides of the Mediterranean. The film's focus on the musicians' anxiety over the disappearance of this memory enhances the overall importance of *sha'bī* music by framing it as a synecdoche of Franco-Algerian history during the mid-twentieth century—a history fraught with societal and institutionalized amnesias on the part of both countries. Set in this light, *El Gusto* as a reunion of individuals expands out to the repatriation of (inter)national memory and cultural knowledge to be reclaimed by younger generations of Algerians as well as immigrants and their descendants living in France.

After examining the film itself, I turn to ongoing activities of the El Gusto Orchestra to show how its initiatives have effectively shifted the positionality of individuals involved from repatriated filmic subjects to empowered agents of repatriation. The opening vignettes in this chapter illustrate this shift. As members of El Gusto become involved with the ensemble's intergenerational educational program, their positionalities transform from passive subjects of embodied cultural knowledge to proponents of the genre's continuation. This empowerment extends to Bousbia's personal efforts to safeguard the rights of *sha'bī* musicians, past and present. Her reclamation of royalty rights on behalf of deceased musicians and their families not only benefits these individuals directly but also improves the viability of a career as a *sha'bī* artist in Algeria. I conclude with possible implications of an extended definition of repatriation both for ethnography and for the power relations between researcher and research participant. By using the El Gusto project as a case study, I hope to enliven the potential for similar projects conducted by ethnographers to act as catalysts of self-empowerment for the interlocutors they seek to document.

THE EMERGENCE OF SHA'BĪ

Algerian *sha'bī* coalesced into a distinct genre in the 1930s and 1940s. It draws from a variety of local and regional traditions, including Moroccan and west-Algerian sung poetry known as *malḥūn*; Sufi devotional chant, or *medḥ*; and the *ṣan'a* Andalusi tradition of Algiers. Literally meaning "popular" or "of the people," *sha'bī* succeeded because its practitioners eschewed what many felt to be the erudite, elitist nature of the Andalusi repertoire. As evinced by their sources, *sha'bī* texts are replete with adulations to God and moral commendations to the listener, while set in a language that is closer to colloquial dialect than the Andalusi body of strophic *muwashshaḥ* poetry (Poché 2005, 92; Glasser 2016, 85). In the decades between World War II and Algerian Independence, the sounds of *sha'bī* orchestras permeated the cafés and narrow streets of the Casbah. Musicians played nightly for loyal patrons, often until the early morning. Accessible and innovative, yet refined and rooted in cultural heritage, *sha'bī* sonically reflected a society increasingly marked by the tensions of foreign influence, a crisis of national identity under colonial rule, and massive demographic shifts resulting in the growth of the country's urban centers (Saadallah 1981, 13).

Early *sha'bī* artists adapted *malḥūn* texts into a musical form modeled after the *ṣan'a* classical repertoire, but in a manner accessible to a wider audience. In contrast to the long, multimovement form of the Andalusi *nūba*, or suite, *sha'bī* songs were organized into shorter renditions of poetic texts that alternated between *bayt* (couplet) and refrain, as well as an improvisatory, unmetered introduction or interlude called *istikhbār*. As the genre developed, artists took more liberties with musical form than typically permitted in Andalusi performance practice by freely employing different melodic and rhythmic modes derived from *ṣan'a* according to the ambience of the performance and the response of listeners (Aous 1996, 17). The instrumentation, while based on the Andalusi orchestra, underwent an expansion of forces with the addition of banjo, violin, guitar, piano, and the signature lead instrument of *sha'bī*, the *mandole* (21). Orchestras typically consist of three to six musicians, with the El Gusto Orchestra as a notable exception. The lead singer accompanies himself on *mandole* while singing the *bayt*. After each couplet, the accompanying instrumentalists reprise the sung melody in a heterophonic texture, along with responsorial vocal interjections.

One of the genre's leading early proponents, El Hadj M'hamed El Anka (1907–1978), is widely celebrated as the veritable originator and unequivocal standard-bearer of classic *sha'bī* music. What is more, he provides a common thread among many of the musicians reunited in the *El Gusto* film who participated in his formalized class at the Conservatory of Algiers and performed with him until the start of the war in the mid-1950s. Therefore, their reunion brought together practitioners whose training and personal experiences place them at the heart of the genre's development.

As an instructor and performer, El Anka sought to elevate the genre to the status of a respectable tradition on the level of Andalusi music. At the same time, he blurred the boundaries between the two by including lighter movements from within the *nūba* corpus in his performances, along with the related colloquial genres *ḥawzī* and *'arūbī* (Glasser 2016, 103). His approach facilitated compositional innovation through improvisation and varied melodic interpretation, an approach influenced in part by his exposure to American jazz (Hadj Ali 2015). He carried forward the innovations of his late mentor, Cheikh Mustapha Nador, with energetic, harmonized arrangements of *malḥūn* and vocal techniques taken from his own knowledge of *medḥ* (Saadallah 1981, 58–60, 63). By the early 1930s, El Anka became widely known throughout Algeria thanks to his regular performance engagements, his exposure on Algerois radio, and a series of recordings produced by Colombia and Algériaphone (70, 72). Those close to him remember him for his finesse of style and prodigious memory of song texts (Mokhtari 2002, 23). Moreover, he was celebrated by a circle of devoted pupils who both emulated and carried forward his contributions to the genre.

REPATRIATION AS PERSONAL RECONCILIATION IN *EL GUSTO*

One way in which *El Gusto* fosters tropes of nostalgia and memory is through its intentional foregrounding of space. The entire film is structured around a guided tour of Algiers, narrated by Bousbia's interlocutor Mustapha Tahmi, who leads the camera crew spatially through his memories of an epoch when *sha'bī* music could still be heard on the streets of the Casbah. Throughout the journey, Tahmi is visibly jarred or simply drawn into silence by the physical reminders of that time gone by. In numerous instances throughout the film, cutaways to other interviewees' encounters with crumbling spaces serve as visual analogies to the fading memories of the aging El Gusto musicians. The deterioration of the Casbah has incited a good deal of consternation around the world, as its architecture was designated a UNESCO World Heritage site in 1992. The scenes with Tahmi deftly analogize the degradation of the physical with the deterioration of the musical legacy of these men, setting up the premise of their reunion as a repatriation of musical and cultural heritage.

Through each segment, Bousbia's interviews with different musicians highlight their shared feelings of nostalgia and loss. Tahmi stops at several closed storefronts and reminisces about a former time when these deserted spaces were filled with outdoor seating, bustling restaurants, and the reverberations of *sha'bī* performances. Looking forlornly at the closed front of a former café, Tahmi sighs and confesses, "All those shops are closed now. We miss that time." Driving down along the docks, Tahmi reminisces fondly of the "*sha'bī* of the streets" that accompanied the eating, drinking, and festivities of evenings spent there. He then takes the film crew to the Algiers Opera House. As the camera circles dramatically around him, he stares out into the hall from the stage, tearing up as the overlaid singing of fellow musician Liamine Haimoun rises up in the film's audio, singing "Djazair Ya Hbibti" (Algeria, My Love). At this point in the film, Bousbia's narrative voice dramatically declares her decision to search out the expatriated members of the ensemble.

In close relation to the film's focus on space, Bousbia highlights the musicians' longing for this time of artistic collaboration between Jews and Muslims before 1962 as a means of hope for restored coexistence. In the film, Tahmi reflects on his sonic memories of the prewar Casbah, particularly during major life-cycle events and holidays, when the musical sounds of Muslim and Jewish celebrations could be heard intermingling through the streets from neighboring houses.

Despite this mutual accord, however, the vast majority of Jews would ultimately leave the country, either during the intervening years of the war or in a final wave of exodus in 1962, when some 100,000 Jews and *pieds-noirs* (European settlers) left the Mediterranean shore on boats bound for France. In the years leading up to the war, Jews were already feeling the tenuousness of their political position, caught between pressures from both sides of the conflict. As French citizens, actively supporting the revolutionary efforts would be considered treasonous. However, as the war progressed, the Algerian revolutionary leadership warned Jewish populations that avoiding active participation in the war effort would jeopardize future Jewish-Muslim relations (Laskier 1994, 330).

Many of the musicians interviewed in the film reflect on the tumultuous period leading up to and during the war between 1954 and 1962. By 1956, the reality of the conflict had come to Algiers in the form of curfews, travel restrictions, and checkpoints around the Casbah (Laskier 1994, 326). Increasing pressures from National Liberation Front (FLN) militants and the realities of curfews made it harder for musicians to find work in a wartime environment. Eventually, musicians were ordered to stop playing and the bars were closed, placing most *sha'bī* musicians out of work. The greatest point of rupture, however, was felt by Jewish musicians, most of whom would soon leave their native country and the Casbah forever.

The rising tensions leading up to the war placed Jewish *sha'bī* musicians—and the Jewish community in general—in an impossible and increasingly dangerous position, and by 1964, virtually all Jews had left the country. The visible pain of this exile on the faces of those interviewed by Bousbia highlights the psychological loss of musical collaborations no longer possible after the war. Luc Cherki, a Jewish musician who fled to Paris, captures the sentiment most succinctly, stating, "When I left Algeria, I took only a suitcase, my guitar, and my *chanson chaâbi*."

COLLECTIVE MEMORY AND ITS REPATRIATION

Beyond Bousbia's intentional framing of nostalgia and memory in the film itself, *El Gusto* provides an ethnographic window through which to theorize the capacity of musical performance to foster bonds of collective memory among relations strained by distances of time and space. The ways in which the members of El Gusto reflect on their time together during the years leading up to 1962 can be interpreted in light of Maurice Halbwachs's thoughts on collective memory and history.

The collective nature of memory, according to Halbwachs's argument, refers to the social framework in which individual recollections must occur in order to subsist as a component of the collective memory of a group. Memories, while located within the recollections of individual people, are recalled and reconstructed in dialogue with others (Halbwachs 1980, 27). Halbwachs speaks of collective memory as contrasted with what he believes to be aims of the historian. According to Halbwachs, the historian looks for demarcations of segmentations in the past marked by radical transformations, whereas individual members of a group form a collective memory during times of stability. In an effort to preserve the identity of the group, its members seek to suppress those aspects that suggest estrangement and boundary, and instead highlight their continuity with the past, even with former generations. Functioning with its own internal memory and identity, a group will fall under the illusion that the changes it has experienced only reveal changes to their relationships to other groups, and not to fractures within the group itself, for this would suggest a chasm forming between themselves and a former—or subsequent—generation (Halbwachs 1950/2011, 147).

Toward the end of the film, Bousbia splices together several comments of musicians relating to their worries about being remembered, about growing older, and about the legacy they will leave behind. Their comments reflect those of Halbwachs when he states, "Since social memory erodes at the edges as individual members, especially older ones, become isolated or die, it is constantly transformed along with the group itself" (1950/2011, 144). His point here may help explain the resolve of one Jewish El Gusto member, the pianist Maurice El Medioni, to never return to his native Algeria (Aidi 2014, 333). Over fifty years after El Medioni and Luc Cherki fled Algiers in 1962, the nation of Algeria they had called home no longer seems recognizable to them. Equipped with the hindsight of over half a century, the two Jewish Algerian musicians now living in France can distinguish the rupture that occurred at that point in their nation's history. That moment stands not just as an arbitrary division of periods in an official national history but also as a real and radical moment of transformation, so much so that the group with which they share their fading collective memory is an entirely different one from the new generations of Algerians who have since come of age. Herein lies the distinction laid out by Halbwachs between memory and a state-sanctioned, national history: a nation only has one "official history," whereby the state asserts a definitive account of its past in an effort to forge a particular national identity. In contrast, however, a collective memory—and the group that harbors it—changes over time, in some cases even splitting into entirely new groups at major points of trauma. The emotional leverage behind Bousbia's film is located in its capacity to showcase the collective memory of these men as an intangible cultural heritage in and of itself. In the process of repatriating individual musicians to one another, the event of the film's release serves as a repatriation of this important, yet repressed chapter of Algerian history back to Algerians and the international community.

MEMORIES OF THE "SILENT GENERATION"

The impact of *El Gusto* as a repatriation of both music and collective memory stems in part from the association of the first-generation Maghrebi immigrants to France as the "Silent Generation." The assignation originates both from this demographic's reticence toward speaking publicly about their life experiences and the concomitant amnesias present within French and Algerian national memories (Leal 2012, 4). This reticence was magnified by their marginal place in French society during the first decades of worker migration. As young men hired for temporary labor and corralled into separate living areas, this generation simply did not have the same visibility in broader French society as their children later would enjoy. The latter's status as French citizens and integration into major French institutions such as the education system made their presence much more poignantly felt than that of their parents. Additionally, fears of urban violence associated with youth of North African descent have dominated public consciousness of the past three decades, often at the expense of their immigrant parents or grandparents (11).

The endeavor to make these silent voices heard finds its precedent in a 1997 televised filmic event when the French network Canal Plus aired a three-part documentary saga titled *Mémoires d'immigrés: L'héritage maghrébin* by the French-Algerian filmmaker Yamina Benguigui. The series traces a historical thread from the initial immigrant "fathers," to the "mothers," or wives who joined them upon family reunification, and finally to their children, whose problematic relationship to their parents' heritage is highlighted in the third and final episode. As Sylvie Durmelat points out, this family-oriented organizational scheme intentionally establishes an alternative chronology that rests on personal, oral narrative rather than official histories of immigration (Durmelat 2000, 208). Durmelat contends that this "familial temporality" is necessary for the emergence of collective memory in the series. Quoting the sociologist Alfred Grooser, she states, "collective memory is less actual memory than transmission via the family, school and the media" (175). Moreover, she argues that Benguigui fulfills the role of a "memory *entrepreneuse*" (a concept developed by the French historian Gérard Noiriel) by functioning as an intermediary who collects individual oral histories and produces a singular collective memory on behalf of the concerned community (173).

Édouard Mills-Affif similarly views the success of *Mémoires d'immigrés* as tied to the way in which it deals with collective memory. He argues that Benguigui avoids the pitfalls of previous projects on the Silent Generation because she successfully walks the tightrope between portraying the immigrant as victim and the immigrant as stigmatized vagrant. In Benguigui's work, individual immigrants are not simply victimized subjects or troubled delinquents, but instead are presented as valued possessors of memory. Furthermore, their memories—and the collective memory assembled through Benguigui's mediatized amalgamation—are showcased in the series as an integral part of French national history (Mills-Affif 2007, 56). In this way, Benguigui's project achieves a move toward social integration based on migrants' own narratives rather than assimilation to a dominant cultural norm.

I argue that Bousbia's direction of *El Gusto* similarly fulfills the role of memory *entrepreneuse* for Algerian immigrants, whose collective memory spans the national histories of both France and Algeria. As with the familial chronology adopted by Benguigui in her triptych, it is the quotidian nature of the *El Gusto* musicians' personal recollections, set against the backdrop of cataclysmic political upheaval, that has the deepest impression on the viewer and enables international audiences to relate to their narratives. The film's plot synthesizes these individual narratives into a catharsis of physical and musical reunion as materialized in the El Gusto Orchestra at the end of the film. This same orchestra, then, embarked on a series of international tours in the years following the film's release, giving the men an unprecedented platform with which to promote their music—and their memories. In the process, their stories are repatriated as oral history to multiple audiences. For third- and fourth-generation children of Maghrebi immigrants, these narratives form a piece of their own cultural heritage. For youth in Algeria, the musicians' recollections during concerts belie a suppressed reality of Muslim-Jewish conviviality and trans-Mediterranean cosmopolitanism that had existed among *sha'bī* musicians and Algerian society more broadly.

From Repatriated Subjects to Agents of Repatriation

Since the release of *El Gusto*, Bousbia has continued to assist several initiatives that further repatriate Algerian music and culture. The El Gusto Orchestra continues to tour internationally. While some of its members have passed away or are no longer able to perform regularly, many still actively engage in intergenerational transmission of this music through the ensemble's activities. Before each performance, the orchestra holds open rehearsals in which youth are invited to participate. Those who show promising talent and a hard-working attitude may eventually be invited to perform as a bona fide member of the group. This process of transmission goes beyond the teaching of musical instruction, however, to encompass a broader transmission of oral patrimony. Over the past three years of this mentorship program, Bousbia has observed that many youths who come to work with the older musicians have grown to appreciate the stories and anecdotes of the older men. Once a part of the orchestra, the new members are given the opportunity to travel with the group on tour. As Bousbia recalls, today's youth, many of whom grew up just after the years of intense violence of Algeria's civil war in the 1990s, do not travel abroad to the extent that the older musicians had during peak years of emigration to France.[2]

Bousbia's personal initiatives with *sha'bī* music have continued the repatriation of this musical heritage in other ways. Through the establishment of her own music publishing company in Algeria, she has worked to reclaim royalty rights of artists who recorded in Algeria. In many instances, Algerian *sha'bī* artists are not paid royalties due to them for the use of their recordings or given credit for original songs, which can end up in anything from television commercials to cellphone ringtones. On one level, she seeks to educate artists about their rights of ownership. Her work also extends to legal action, having won around a dozen cases on behalf of artists who reclaimed their royalty rights to their own master recordings. Bousbia feels that her work has already begun to change the perception of musicians' social status in Algerian society as creative artists.

Lastly, despite the bureaucratic hindrances to date in establishing an institutionalized digital archive in Algeria, Bousbia has persisted in personally collecting sonic cultural heritage as part and parcel of her repatriation of artists' intellectual property rights. Upon her engagement with the families of late artists, many family members unearth any number of treasures from their loved ones, from vinyl recordings to photographs and written notes. Very often, she is able to convert items such as vinyl records and VHS tapes into more durable formats, which she can then give back to each respective family. Her efforts not only aid the individual musicians and their families directly but also complement her broader goal of preserving Algeria's sonic cultural heritage for future generations.

Looking ahead, Bousbia hopes one day to establish an institutionalized and publicly accessible database of intangible cultural heritage of Algerian oral history. In the meantime, many of the El Gusto Orchestra's members continue to promote themselves and the cultural knowledge they possess to the next generation of enthusiasts. Due in large part to the publicity of *El Gusto*, many of the musicians featured in the film have become ambassadors of the music through various mediated avenues. In 2015, El Gusto musicians Rachid Berkani and Liamine Haimoun joined Bousbia in an interview as part of the *Fikra* Conference in Algiers. In a town-hall format with Algerian audience members, the two musicians discussed the growing role of the Municipal Conservatory of Algiers for promoting *sha'bī* classes and facilitating its transmission to younger generations.

The musician, comedian, actor, and author Robert Castel is one of the most well-known members to appear in *El Gusto*, having enjoyed a long and successful career in comedy, film, and television. He now appears separately with his group, "El Gusto du chaâbi," which was recently featured at the Institut du Monde Arabe in Paris. In a promotional interview, he reflects on the interfaith comportment between his father, the famous Jewish Andalusi musician Lili Labassi, and collaborating Arab musicians. Following the success of the El Gusto Orchestra's tours, Castel was motivated to establish his ensemble, consisting of six musicians, to perform Algerian *sha'bī* and the "Franco-oriental" music of his father.[3] Another El Gusto member with a longstanding solo career, Abdelmadjid Meskoud, similarly appeared at the Institute in 2016 under the billing, "The Master of El Gusto." These are but a few of the most recent examples of the opportunities afforded to *sha'bī* musicians in the afterglow of the film.

CONCLUSIONS

In this chapter, I have argued that the documentary film *El Gusto* constitutes a repatriation of individual culture-bearers that empowers the very subjects it documents to become the agents of repatriation. For the musicians involved, the initial film project has brought forth media appearances, live performances, and record deals, all of which provide platforms for them to promote themselves and their art.

The superimposition of individuals and their combined memories through an expanded definition of repatriation places the concept at the center of the emerging subfield of endangered music preservation. In her book *Music Endangerment* (2014), Catherine Grant adapts principles from the field of linguistic preservation to propose a model for evaluating the vitality of a music genre in danger of disappearing (Grant 2014, 111). Several of these principles find correlations in the El Gusto project. In the case of both language and music, the degree of intergenerational transmission plays a decisive role in assuring the perpetuation of cultural knowledge. The transmission of *sha'bī* music from musician to pupil through the orchestra's mentorship program bridges an intergenerational divide and passes on intangible cultural heritage in a manner that maintains the tradition's relevance and accessibility for younger generations. Grant's model also considers the feasibility for musicians to earn a living as a crucial factor in a genre's perpetuation. Bousbia's legal actions on behalf of musicians' intellectual property rights are one step toward ensuring *sha'bī*'s solvency as a profession.

Lastly, Grant cites the importance of the broader community's vested interest in continuing a musical tradition. *El Gusto* has invigorated a newfound public awareness, not only of *sha'bī* music but also of fleeting oral history in Algeria more generally. Bousbia's work with her own personal digital archive, and the hope of one day establishing a publicly accessible one, rides on this awareness. In her talk at the 2014 TEDxCasbah conference in Algiers, she proposes the creation of a foundation with the goal of encouraging sustainable transmission of cultural heritage through the empowerment and education of the public. She states, "The Foundation's vocation is, first, for the preservation of memory by working toward the transmission of this knowledge . . . and secondly, by giving people the means of working with this knowledge" (Bousbia 2014).

Finally, the examination of *El Gusto* demonstrates the potential for ethnographic projects to directly benefit the interlocutors that we, as ethnomusicologists, seek to document, by enabling their own self-advocacy. If ethnomusicology is understood as "the study of how people make and experience music, and of why it matters to them that they do" (Bakan 2015, 116), then I see no better aspiration than the promotion of such self-advocacy among the interlocutors we choose to represent by empowering them to be their own "memory entrepreneurs" and agents of repatriation.

NOTES

1. The *mandole* is a fretted lute invented by the Algerois luthier Mr. Bélido in 1941 at the request of El Anka (Aous 1996, 21).
2. Safinez Bousbia, interview by author, Tallahassee, Florida, August 11, 2016. I express my sincerest gratitude to Safinez Bousbia for volunteering her time, insights, and personal experiences to make this chapter possible.
3. "Robert Castel en concert à l'Institut du monde arabe," March 14, 2016, http://larchemag.fr/2016/03/14/2329/robert-castel-en-concert-a-linstitut-du-monde-arabe/.

REFERENCES

Aidi, Hisham D. 2014. *Rebel Music: Race, Empire, and the New Muslim Youth Culture.* New York: Pantheon Books.

Aous, Rachid. 1996. *Les grands maîtres Algériens du cha'bi et du Hawzi: Diwân Arabe et Kabyle.* Paris: El-Ouns.

Bakan, Michael B. 2015. "'Don't Go Changing to Try and Please Me': Combating Essentialism through Ethnography in the Ethnomusicology of Autism." *Ethnomusicology* 59 (1): 116–144.

Bousbia, Safinez. "*El Gusto*, de la Casbah à New York." Presentation at the TEDxCasbah event in Algiers, Algeria, on January 18, 2014.

Durmelat, Sylvie. 2000. "Transmission and Mourning in *Mémoires d'immigrés: L'héritage maghrébin*: Yamina Benguigui as 'Memory Entrepreneuse.'" In *Women, Immigration and Identities in France*, edited by Jane Freedman and Carrie Tarr, 171–188. Oxford: Berg.

El Gusto. 2012. Directed by Safinez Bousbia. Dublin, Ireland. Quidam Group. DVD.

Glasser, Jonathan. 2016. *The Lost Paradise: Andalusi Music in Urban North Africa.* New York: University of Chicago Press.

Grant, Catherine. 2014. *Music Endangerment: How Language Maintenance Can Help.* New York: Oxford University Press.

Hadj Ali, Bachir. "El Anka et la tradition chaabi." *Maghrebzine*, June 25, 2015. http://maghrebzine.fr/soiree-ramadan/le-guide-lorient-a-paris/el-anka-et-la-tradition-chaabi/. Originally published in *Annuaire de l'Afrique du Nord* 17 (1979): 905–911.

Halbwachs, Maurice. 1950/2011. "From *Collective Memory*." In *The Collective Memory Reader*, edited by Jeffrey K. Olick, Vered Vinitzky-Seroussi, and Daniel Levy, 139–149. New York: Oxford University Press, 2011. Originally published in Jeanne Halbwachs Alexandre, *La mémoire collective: Ouvrage posthume publié.* Paris: Presses universitaires de France, 1950.

Halbwachs, Maurice. 1980. *The Collective Memory.* Translated by Francis J. Ditter, Jr., and Vida Yazdi Ditter. New York: Harper and Row.

Laskier, Michael M. 1994. *North African Jewry in the Twentieth Century: The Jews of Morocco, Tunisia, and Algeria.* New York: New York University Press.

Leal, Rebecca Erin. 2012. "Mon père, l'étranger: Stéréotypes et représentations des immigrés algériens en France." PhD diss., University of Iowa.

Mills-Affif, E. 2007. "Vu à la télé, la saga des immigrés." In *Qui a peur de la télévision en couleurs? La diversité culturelle dans les médias*, edited by Isabelle Rigoni, 39–57. Montreuil, France: Éditions aux Lieux d'Être.

Mokhtari, Rachid. 2002. *Cheikh El Hasnaoui: La voix de l'errance: Essai*. Algiers: Chihab.

Poché, Christian. 2005. *Dictionnaire des musiques et des danses traditionnelles de la Méditerranée*. Paris: Fayard.

Saadallah, Rabah. 1981. *Le chaâbi d'el-Hadj M'hamed el-Anka: Maitre et rénovateur de la musique "chaâbi."* Algiers: Maison des Livres.

CHAPTER 22

REPATRIATING AN EGYPTIAN MODERNITY

Transcriptions and the Rise of Coptic Women's Song Activism

CAROLYN M. RAMZY

INTRODUCTION

IN her first satellite TV program in the early 2000s, the Coptic popular singer Monika Kyrillos did something unusual. She not only sang *alḥān*, an Orthodox liturgical genre reserved for male singers, but also taught her audiences how to sing them using Western music notation and French solfège.[1] Only in her early twenties, her fresh-faced appearance stood in strong contrast to the aging blind cantors (*mu'allimīn*, sing. *mu'allim*), clerics, and religious elite who traditionally taught and disseminated the hymns through a rich oral tradition. While these cantors depended on repetition, mnemonic devices, and chironomy to indicate intricate and melismatic passages, Monika turned to a divide in the television screen and pointed to a transcription of a Coptic hymn.[2] Dictated by her famous father, George Kyrillos, Monika's transcriptions also drew from Ragheb Moftah's collection, sixteen folios of Coptic liturgical transcriptions that were historically collected by a European musicologist, Ernest Newlandsmith (1932) as they were commissioned by the amateur Egyptian collector at the beginning of the twentieth century.[3] Unlike Ragheb Moftah's earlier transcriptions that targeted academic and non-Egyptian audiences, Monika Kyrillos repatriated Western music transcriptions to navigate a modern Egyptian piety and facilitate women's song activism in male-dominated contexts.

Today Monika is an international and satellite star, performing *alḥān* at the Cairo Opera house, hosting her own show on Coptic Christian television, and touring throughout the world. In Egypt and in North America, she continues to teach *alḥān* to mixed audiences and has even shared the stage with one of the highest clerical ranks, a Coptic Orthodox bishop. Kyrillos's rising transnational career marks a significant change in women's participation of the genre, highlighting shifting ideas about women's modern piety, music expertise, and spiritual activism in the Orthodox Church. While women have been traditionally relegated to singing and leading other church choirs that perform the more popular, though comparatively undervalued, colloquial Arabic genre known as *taratīl* and *taranīm*, things have slowly changed.[4] Now, consecrated Orthodox nuns, devoted sisters (*mukarrasāt*), spiritual activists (*khudām*), and many girls sing *alḥān* in youth camps, choirs, and competitions both inside and outside of Egypt.[5] Though women still cannot perform as official cantors (*shamamsa*) in liturgical settings, some have even initiated a Facebook forum advocating for their official consecration as deaconesses in Orthodox Church services.[6]

Following the rise of Monika's careers, first as a singer in her father's group David Ensemble, and now as the director of her own group, David Junior, I examine Coptic Orthodox music culture through a gendered lens. Specifically, I look at how the repatriation of music transcriptions for popular use acts as what Sarah Ghabrial calls a "double bind" for women who perform and teach *alḥān* (2016, 562). As women increasingly sound their presence in the Coptic church, they are often complicit in some of the Church's moral narratives in containing women's bodies, voices, and comportment in the Orthodox community. While the use of Coptic music transcription imparts expertise status to the women who use them, their colonialist genealogies and problematic discourses of modernity also reinscribe Coptic gender hierarchies within modernist narratives of piety and ethnoreligious nationalism that closely mirror that of the Egyptian state. As these music archives and Western music notation increasingly denote the community's sense of modernity and agency as a religious minority in Egypt's Muslim majority nation, I ask: How are women's participation and performance, like that of Monika Kyrillos, entangled in Coptic's heritage-making projects? More importantly, how do women's increased audibility, musical activism, and the use of Western music notation intersect with problematic and postcolonial discourses of a pious modernity (Deeb 2006)?[7] Drawing on Deniz Kandiyoti's work on the role of gender as a both a product and a signifier of "modernity" and "nation" (1991, 1996), and Timothy Mitchell's understanding of modern forms of expertise (2002), I analyze how the renewed interest in Western music notation has allowed Coptic Orthodox women to craft expertise status and legitimize their performances of *alḥān* during a contemporary religious revival. I illustrate how, by singing from and teaching audiences how to read Western music notation, Coptic women are part of larger Church reforms to inculcate a modern Coptic piety and identity that, while appearing to challenge them, may ultimately reinforce Orthodox Church gender hierarchies as they speak to larger politics of Egyptian Christian belonging in contemporary Egypt.

TRANSCRIBING MODERNITY

Transcription scholarship began as a tool of colonial and imperial acquisitiveness. Used by early music scholars of cross-cultural music studies, they reflected a desire to capture exotic sensory experiences in the discipline's predecessor, comparative musicology (Ellingson 1992, 110). Besides gold, jewels, and spices, early conquistadors also brought back musical instruments, notation, music theory manuscripts, and sometimes musicians themselves. When the Renaissance and Enlightenment moved European thinking away from notions of divine law, transcriptions became illustrative of preconceived ethnocentric universalist theories about latent harmony and social development. In other words, scholars assumed that the closer non-European musics sounded to European classical tuning and harmonic structure, the more civilized and "modern" their participants. Importantly, transcription's use as scientific applications of cross-cultural study also validated ethnomusicology as a serious discipline and raised its scholars to expert status. Despite the rise of humanism and interest in comparative transcriptions, early scholars continued to articulate bias toward European classical music as the epitome of science, innovation, and modernity, while non-European musics fell under the rubric of natural and primitive life sounds (Mersenne 1636; Ellingson 1992, 115). Tonometric measurements that forced nondiatonic melodies within a piano's twelve-semitone keyboard, as well as the addition of piano accompaniments, also made early studies particularly vulnerable to orientalist preoccupations with unearthing a kind of harmonic universalism in non-European music traditions (Amiot 1779; Jones 1792; Fletcher et al. 1893; Fillmore 1895; Ellingson 1992).

In Egypt, transcriptions not only pioneered early experiments in music scholarship (Villoteau 1809) but also, close to the mid-nineteenth century, played a critical role in the proselytization of Orthodox Coptic Christianity. More importantly, such musical conversions engendered loyal subjectivities to the British colonial state. Early scholars and missionaries who notated Coptic *alḥān* revealed their intentions of bringing "modernity" and "progress" to new Coptic converts by teaching them basic principles of Western classical music.[8] In the nineteenth century, one French Jesuit priest who taught at a Coptic Catholic seminary in Cairo notated Coptic hymns with the aim to "bring [the hymns] more accuracy" and to provide pedagogical tools for new believers who themselves would become Catholic priests (Badet 1899). Father Louis Badet writes that, to prevent the further decline of the Coptic community's heritage and to ensure the rise of "good cantors," members needed continued Western classical training, followed by rudimentary texts on how to read notation on a music staff:

> It is therefore important to prevent such a loss, and to annotate the liturgical songs of this rite, and to teach them to the students of the Coptic seminaries. Later, when they themselves are priests, they will, in turn, teach them to the schoolchildren. They will then be able to train good cantors for their churches and perhaps succeed in the congregation singing, at least the principal songs, which we would strongly desire.

As it can be seen, the transcription of the Coptic liturgical songs, will not only prevent their decline, but will help in their execution and will bring [them] more accuracy. However, for this work to be durable, it is absolutely necessary for the seminary students to receive some basic elements of music and solfèdge: consequently, they will be given half-hour singing lessons twice a week. It will also be useful for them to learn to play the harmonium, at least for those who manifest special musical abilities.[9]

Here I want to highlight early transcription's autocentric ideologies and how they later transferred into contemporary Coptic Orthodox ideas about a pious modernity.[10] I also wish to emphasize both transcriptions' role within larger efforts to make colonized subalterns legible and, in turn, their lingering effects in postcolonial archives as documents of authenticity and scientific authority.[11] Like early exhibitions that transformed newly discovered civilizations into tangible objects that visitors could view and subsequently touch, transcriptions made Egyptian colonial subjects into something they could hear. In other words, transcriptions came to be numbered among the types of material evidence of Europe's imperial age in Egypt, from the organization of panoramas to the display of merchandise, lectures, guidebooks, and transcribed songbooks.[12] Writing about a British colonial encounter and the machinery of representation, Timothy Mitchell concludes that early explorers and scholars, through this colonizing project, ordered Egypt into something object-like, legible, readable, and like a book (1988: 33). In turn, transcriptions legibly contained popular Egyptian audibility and piety as early as the nineteenth century, and did so through a process that echoes what Mitchell calls "enframing" (44–45). Through written texts and expert studies, imperialist scientists and scholars contained and divided Egyptian oral knowledge, such as *alḥān*, into notation and suffused written texts and transcriptions with notions of "modernity" and production. Such legibility, Mitchell writes, not only produced the world-as-exhibition, but for anxious European experts, it also organized the production of statistical knowledge (46). This standardization easily identified and produced visible social and spatial hierarchies of the conceived chaos of the Egyptian encounter. In other words: just as enframing made Egyptians easier to read, Western music transcriptions also made them easier to hear, though as I argue later, not necessarily more audible.[13]

Europeans were not the only ones to imbue transcription with the power to create the appearances of objectness and scientific validity, and to discipline the order of things. By the early twentieth century, reformist and middle-class Copts educated in European and American missionary schools began to invest the transcription of their oral traditions with a sense of both material and moral authority in larger religious nationalist projects. In 1916, an Egyptian lieutenant named Kamil Ibrahim Ghubriyal was the first Egyptian to publish his own *alḥān* transcriptions in a booklet titled *Al-tawqīʿāt al-mūsīqiyah li-maradāt al-Kanīsa al-Murqusiyya* (The musical notation of the responses of the Church of Saint Mark). He notated *alḥān* with piano accompaniment and harmonization similar to what North American scholars had begun to criticize for their problematic and misleading search of a "latent sense of harmony."[14] Nonetheless, with the anxious aim of preserving his community's moral fabric in the face of "trendy and modern-day living," Ghubriyal targeted women in upper social classes, where he believed that imported popular songs, pianos, and the British colonial culture threatened their religious foundation.[15] In an effort to mirror "ladies' tastes," in which the abilities to read and play Western music played a significant role in marking socioeconomic class, he hoped his orchestrations would extend spiritual hymns into popular Coptic contexts as well as festivals for schoolgirls and schoolboys. Despite his best intentions to disseminate his booklets widely and to install organs in local churches, his project failed for lack of funding, though not without setting a precedent for popularizing religious forms of entertainment and political discourse beyond the community's clerical elite.

Coptic Women, Popular Song, and Religious Revival

Historically, the Coptic church has always been a patriarchal institution in which male deacons, priests, bishops, and ultimately the pope undertake all public leadership and song roles. This status is also reinforced in a Coptic eschatological worldview in which only male cantors and clerics are consecrated to perform important liturgical sacraments and rite-of-passage ceremonies through singing *alḥān*. In their performance, *alḥān* are believed to renew the community's ties between heaven and earth, mirroring a heavenly afterlife of continuous song and praise known as *tasbīḥ*.[16] Women have traditionally served their communities in other ways as parts of larger congregational singing. As contemplative and cloistered nuns who have been initiated into the hierarchies of the Orthodox Church, they regularly perform *alḥān* in the privacy of their convents and their all-women services, with the exception of one cantor and an Orthodox priest who must be present to perform the liturgy (van Doorn-Harder 1995). Active nuns who serve outside of convents regularly attend services both inside and outside their communities near social projects they manage, and live near the retreat centers and orphanages they serve (1995, 38). In their capacity as good wives and Coptic mothers, laywomen also play a critical role as religious educators in the home, hence the popular Egyptian saying "*al um madrasa*" or "the mother is a school."[17]

At the turn of the century, when Egyptians were navigating early nationalist and postcolonial narratives, the Church appropriated secular understandings of domestic femininity and focused on the family as a microcosm of the nation (Armanios 2002; Armanios and Amstutz 2013, 516). The historians Armanios and Amstutz illustrate how, during Pope Shenouda's ministry and the rise of Islamic radicalism in Egypt, popular media such as religious Coptic films continued to call on women to preserve family cohesiveness and keep Copts Coptic as good mothers and good wives (2013, 515). They argue that Coptic "Holy-wood" movies targeted female audiences to reinscribe biologically deterministic views of men and women (515). One notable example is the

Coptic film *Rafiqa the Martyr and Her Five Children* (date unknown), which celebrates the soft-spoken yet determined mother saint who confirmed her children's faith through religious lessons and later died by their side as staunch Orthodox Copts who refused conversion.[18] Armanios also emphasizes that this rhetoric posits men as "naturally predisposed to leadership, activity, and strong work ethic" while women are "naturally nurturing, passive, and receptive,"[19] a position that is further grounded in Orthodox interpretation of biblical scripture where "the man is the head of the woman" (1 Corinthians 11:3). Armanios and Amstutz conclude that through their repeated depiction of women's subjugation, modesty, and piety, religious biopics echo the Church's anxieties about broader modern developments shaping women's lives, as well as reacting to feminist movements demanding women's increased autonomy both within and outside of their religious communities. In turn, despite women's more visible presence in Coptic cinema, gender ideals have only gotten more conservative within the Coptic Orthodox Church, prompting some of the latest protests about divorce and even veiling of Christian women's hair.[20]

In his collection, Ragheb Moftah's efforts to transcribe *alḥān* echoed similar nationalist narratives like those in Orthodox popular media and cinema, though distinctly situated within an indigeneity discourse known as pharaonism (Reid 2015; Goode 2007; van der Vliet 2009). Using pharaonic tropes, these political narratives not only rallied all segments of Egyptian society to contest British colonial authority but also specifically spoke to Copts as the last remaining "modern sons" of the pharaohs.[21] Specifically, these discourses of belonging and exceptionalism also spoke to the shifting interreligious relationships between Egypt's Christians and Muslims. More importantly they reflected the community's ambivalences about the increasing political and social marginalization during Anwar Sadat's presidency beginning in 1970. By emphasizing the community's liturgical music, Moftah's reformist efforts specifically targeted literate and middle-class Coptic male cantors as they fell out of Egyptian public spheres.

Moftah's canonization efforts of *alḥān* facilitated the rise of a vernacular popular genre of Coptic devotional music known as *taratīl* and *taranīm*, a genre that soon blurred the lines between distinctly gendered performances of Orthodox piety. As these popular songs entered the community's religious education, they also paved the way for women's participation in Church settings. While these songs traditionally drew their origins from early European and American missionary encounters in Egypt, they became especially popular among women during the rise of the Sunday School movement. In one of his earliest and undated publications, the movement's founder, Habib Girgis, published pamphlets of Arabic colloquial "spiritual songs" that mimicked translations of American Presbyterian missionary hymns to compete with American evangelical efforts. While Catholic Jesuit missionaries taught newly converted clerics to read their *alḥān* in Western musical notation, American Presbyterians prided themselves on other kinds of literacy efforts: reading the Bible and doing so through song.[22] Many American and later Egyptian missionaries arrived at women's homes with songbooks to facilitate their reading lessons. These books included the now famous *Bahgat al-dhamīr fī nazm al-mazamīr* (The joys of the spirit in the psalter, 1877). To appeal to their audiences who also did not read Western classical music notation, organizations such as the Presbyterian Holy Synod committee relied on familiar and popular Egyptian scales, *awzān* (sing. *wazn*), to teach translated hymns and biblical psalms. Known for short as *Nazm al-mazamīr*, this publication offered the psalms as 433 smaller "spiritual songs" and drew on melodies from translated Presbyterian hymns, Egyptian folk music, British anthems, and even American popular ballads. To help remind singers of the melody, missionaries relied on *awzan* as popular mnemonic devices to make their psalter more accessible.

To compete with these missionary efforts, the Sunday School leader Habib Girgis targeted Coptic Orthodox women. In his earliest publication, *Muftāh al-ʿanghām: Al-taranīm al-urthuduksiyya* (*Melody Keys: The Orthodox Taranīm*, undated), Girgis used indigenous and specifically Orthodox texts and melodies in his pedagogical *taratīl*. In turn, he also based his *taratīl* melodies on familiar Egyptian folk songs, popular songs, and *alḥān* melodies to facilitate women's participation in liturgical services where men traditionally dominated the performance. His earliest dated *taratīl* pamphlet, *Salawāt al-shaʿab athanāʾ al-qudās* (Congregational prayers during the liturgy, 1922), is specifically dedicated to the Coptic Orthodox Women's Society. This elite philanthropic society not only sponsored his efforts and freely disseminated his pamphlets in churches all over Egypt but also reached out to teach women in "lower orders" to read in the name of modernity (Girgis 1922, 1). As most could not read the antiquated Coptic language, Girgis provide simplified Arabic transliterations to encourage women's congregational participation.[23] In his work, he hoped to familiarize them with proper Church etiquette and how to act in deference to both clerical and divine authority. Interjecting biblical scripture, simple songs, and local teachable parables into the text, Girgis instructed his attendees to be mindful of their bodily and spiritual comportment before and after prayer. In one passage, he described how worshipers cross themselves upon entering the church, when and where to seat, and even how to greet other parishioners. The list goes on to address other prohibitions for the church-attending body, such as sitting, standing, seeing, hearing, speaking, and finally singing. As did early Coptic film hagiopics, Girgis's writings emphasized women's comportment and modesty in piety and shifted women's feminist subjectivities as they became increasingly audible as congregants, Sunday School teachers, and musical activists in their community.

MODERNIST PROJECTS AND THE DISSONANCES OF CONTEMPORARY FEMALE PIETY

In her work, Deniz Kandiyoti writes about the tensions and contradictions inherent in the gender agendas of some nationalist projects. She examines how women's imagery, portrayals, and participation can represent vagaries of nationalist discourses, fluctuating from representing women as victims of social backwardness to icons of modernity or privileged bearers of cultural authenticity:

> On the one hand, nationalist movements invite women to participate more fully in collective life by interpellating them as "national" actors: mothers, educator, workers and even fighters. On the other hand, they reaffirm the boundaries of culturally acceptable feminine conduct and exert pressure on women to articulate their gender interests within the terms of reference set by nationalist discourse.
>
> (Kandiyoti 1991, 433)

At the turn of the twenty-first century, Coptic women experienced similar dissonances in how their voices and imagery had been portrayed within their community's religious revival. Armanios further highlights these inherent contradictions for Coptic women, for whom the Church affirmed their assertive role as "spiritual managers" of their homes while also advocating for more docile imagery of "virtuous" and spiritually conscious women (2002). While the Sunday School and Church Upbringing movements have paved various routes for women to emerge as teachers, choir directors, and even satellite sensations to teach *alḥān*, these roles have also been implicated in what Ghabrial calls a "double bind," in which the resistance to one system often entails a complicity with another (2016, 562). Ghabrial illustrates this bind in her study when Algerian women confirm French orientalist imaginary of pathologized Muslim men and infantilized Muslim women when they use the colonial court system to obtain a divorce. In other words, Ghabrial writes, their litigious actions often served to consolidate and subvert paternalist norms in both familial and state contexts. Here, as Coptic Orthodox women like Monika Kyrillos increasingly resist Coptic patriarchy by forging expertise and repatriating Western music notation to teach *alḥān* in male-dominated spaces, they are often drawn up in the Church's moral efforts to contain women's voices and shape a specific pious comportment in the church and beyond.

Monika George Kyrillos began her career at the age of nine, singing in her father's group, David Ensemble. Like many cantors before her, she learned *alḥān* and *taratīl* entirely by ear, since her father did not always transcribe Coptic *alḥān*. Rather, George began his ensemble by composing melodies for the biblical psalms that he felt mirrored canonical *alḥān*, but without *taratīl*'s troubled missionary links. He only learned how to read notation after he entered the Higher Institute of Arab Music studies in Giza, where he was motivated to learn Western counterpoint and harmony because "it matched the highness of God."[24] More importantly, he wanted to render Coptic Church music with a kind of modern expertise and what would become David Ensemble's impromptu mission: to perform Coptic hymns with "a scale of professionalism and scientific way that mixed with a spiritual performance."[25] George began exclusively to notate and orchestrate Coptic *alḥān* when the Egyptian Centre for Culture and Arts (*Makan*) invited him to perform as part of a Parisian "Festival of Sacred Arts" in 1995. Following international acclaim and audiences that preferred the sounds of Coptic *alḥān* orchestrations to his Arabic psalm compositions, Kyrillos returned to Stockholm's "Orient Festival" in June 1997, and in 1998 Monika debuted as a soloist at the Marseille Opera House in Venice. There, she sang the famous Easter hymn "Golgotha," touted by David Ensemble to have direct pharaonic roots that date back almost five thousand years.[26] Since then, she has always been at her father's side, working to preserve Coptic music in notation and disseminating the oral tradition in a modern way to appeal to Coptic youth in her own ensemble known as David Juniors.[27] When George began to deliver pedagogical satellite programming that teaches *alḥān* to general TV audiences in his show *Ma wara al-alḥān* ("What Is the Story behind Alḥān") in 1999, Monika joined his show as part of the choir. Today, she is not only his collaborator and cohost but also regularly hosts her own shows, such as *Naghamāt qibbtiya* ("Coptic Tunes," 2010) and *Hanranim Tany* ("Let's Sing Again," 2016), in which she teaches *alḥān* as well as *taratīl* through Western music notation.

Monika Kyrillos's career as a burgeoning expert and teacher of Coptic *alḥān* reflects what Timothy Mitchell called the "politics of expertise": the formation of Western experiences as a template for universal knowledge and one that has colonial genealogies (2002, 7). The politics of technoscience that reigned in Egypt at the beginning of the twentieth century—precisely the beginning of Coptic music reform—was closely aligned with the politics of national development and claimed to bring the expertise of modern social sciences to transform peasant agriculture and to repair the ills of society (15). Such expertise is deeply marked by socioeconomic class. In a postcolonial context, the anthropologist Walter Armbrust adds that it was middle-class and elite reformers who emerged as the focal point of modernity and nationalist ideology in Egypt (1996, 9), with a particular emphasis on women as advocates and recipients of reform (Ahmed 1992; Zuhur 1992; Baron 1994). In their efforts to imagine a modern nation (and for Copts, a modern Church), middle-class reformists turned their attention to resocializing folk and popular pious practices that did not reflect a Western modernity. This included an effort to textualize tradition performed and transmitted by Church cantors, who traditionally came from lower socioeconomic classes. As she was educated in a private French Catholic school, Kyrillos's upper-middle-class habitus was particularly close to these reformist efforts. Through Cambridge's International General Certificate of Secondary Education (IGCSE) program in Egypt, she not only learned to read and transcribe Coptic *alḥān* into Western notation but also began to articulate the same preservationist anxieties that motivated Moftah and missionary projects to notate *alḥān*. Writing and teaching from a transcription, she insisted in our interview, was a pedagogical way to help people sing more accurately, a notion that closely echoed the French Jesuit Badet's efforts to "bring [the hymns] more accuracy" to newly converted Coptic Catholic clerics.

In her role as a satellite star, Monika Kyrillos has participated in several televised music ensembles on Coptic satellite TV that are beginning to overshadow generations of traditional male cantors from lower socioeconomic classes known as *mu'allimin* (sing. *mu'allim*). As predominantly blind cantors, believed to have heightened abilities to memorize long texts because of their increased dependence on their ears, *mu'allimin* were regarded as the gatekeepers to a Coptic sounded heritage. They also play a critical role in producing the next generation of deacons and priests and in creating a unified music curriculum coming out of the Didymus Institute for the Blind, where they predominantly teach (Gabry-Thienpont, 2017). With the exception of mnemonic devices known as *hazzāt*, with which cantors indicate the rise and fall of melodies and melismas through dashes and dots over hymn texts, *mu'allimin* depend on recordings and oral rote to teach the hymns. Though *mu'allimin* continue to be respected—sometimes even flown out to the diaspora for their services—their status as gatekeepers is slowly diminishing, replaced by contemporary and modernist song projects that efface their lower socioeconomic class and facilitate *alḥān*'s dissemination to today's youth against the backdrop of new technologies, textualization, and images of progress. In Monika's words, "The rhythm of life has changed, and no one has time to learn orally (*yistilim*) from a *mu'allim*." As increasingly educated elites join the ranks of the clergy as teachers and spiritual directors, many upper- and middle-class reformers regard *mu'allimin* as part of an older way of life and one that is increasingly giving away to the speed of modernity. While many of these reforms have yet to be fully instituted in the community, Coptic reformists have managed to do something else: to supplement Church structure and to produce a moral education for the masses (Sedra 2011, 166), one in which women are at the helm.

In her first program, "Coptic Tunes," a young Monika taught her audiences more than to read and sing *alḥān* using French solfège. Rather, in her trademark soft-spoken voice, and sitting against the backdrop of a sound recording studio, she also teaches about a particular middle-class comportment that is Western-inspired while still in keeping with a distinct image of the ideal Coptic woman as docile and spiritually conscious (Armanios 2002, 113). Here, Monika's spiritual expertise is linked with her musical one as she gently teaches a mixed group of young men and women how to sing *alḥān*, subtitled for viewers in English and Arabic. She even uses domestic metaphors—the kitchen knife to cut a whole note in half to make a half note—to simplify Western music notation.[28] Moreover, sitting on the high stool while the other adults sit on the floor, the image on the screen is reminiscent of a Sunday School classroom, or even a young mother teaching her children. The scene highlights Armanios's argument about the spiritual cultivation of Coptic women into "spiritual managers" of their homes, one that echoes similar nationalist narratives at the turn of the century, when intellectual elites called on upper-class mothers and wives to become modern and "scientific managers" of their households. Their role was to produce and to train the future sons of a new and postindependent nation (Abu-Lughod 1998).[29] Six years later, a grown-up Monika sings on her next show, "Let's Sing Again," on Sat-7 TV, an Arabic evangelical satellite channel. This time she does not accompany her father, but rather her new husband in a new rendition that further emphasizes familial and domestic dynamics. Together they lead her group David Juniors, a new choir project designed to teach non-professional and Coptic youth how to read both *alḥān* and *taratīl* through Western music notation.

CONCLUDING THOUGHTS

Early Coptic music transcriptions, undertaken by Christian missionary and European musicologists to Egypt, served two purposes: to proselytize Orthodox Christians and to contain Copts as subjects of their new colonial states. Today, by repatriating these transcriptions for contemporary pious performances, elite Coptic reformists such as Ragheb Moftah have located modernist narratives that frame their indigeneity revivals within colonial imaginaries to set them apart as Egypt's only "modern sons of the pharaohs." Yet, while these narratives speak to larger ambivalences about Coptic belonging in a Muslim-majority nation, they also exclude Coptic "daughters" from conversations of belonging, leaving Coptic women—and specifically nonelite Coptic women—outside of these narratives. Because of her elite class habitus, Monika Kyrillos is an exception. Despite transcription's orientalist genealogies to make Coptic subjects more legible both to the missionary and to colonial empire, she has slowly forged a sonic space for herself and other women through her use of Western music transcriptions. This new expert status, however, is tenuous and perpetuates Coptic women's belonging along narrow maternal, familial lines, and upper socioeconomic class.

While I argue that the transcriptions and canonization of Coptic *alḥān* have reinscribed Orthodox gender hierarchies for women along a reformist middle-class habitus, there are promising shifts afoot. When Monika joined the Coptic Orthodox Diocese Bishop David on stage in an international concert in New York in 2016, something remarkable happened: in David Ensemble's manicured and well-rehearsed rendition of liturgical *alḥān*, it was Bishop David who seemed strangely out of place, perhaps even "out of tune" in a genre that long belonged to a clerical elite. Before his performance, Bishop David gently joked to the audience that he had "practiced" a hymn, now transcribed in Western music notation, that he had performed his whole life to ensure that he "got it right" with the audience. This moment in which a bishop questioned his "in-tuneness" prompted laughs, but it also opened up alternative spaces to see clerics questioning their ultimate and sonic authorities, thanks to the rise of Coptic music experts such as Monika. Importantly, his willingness to share the stage with Monika highlighted how the repatriations of Coptic music transcriptions prompt experiments with modern performances of piety that embrace women's voices in what was exclusively men's domain.

NOTES

1. To watch segments of this show, see http://www.davidensemble.com/english/coptic_tunes. htm (accessed February 12, 2016).
2. For an example of the music notation, see http://www.davidensemble.com/english/ musicnotation.htm (accessed February 12, 2016).

3. Nicknamed the "father of Coptic Music," Moftah spent his life collecting liturgical hymns. Working with an English missionary and violinist, Ernest Newlandsmith, Moftah commissioned sixteen folios of music transcriptions, of which only fourteen made it to the US Library of Congress and Institute of Coptic Studies archives as the Ragheb Moftah Collection of Coptic Liturgical Hymns. Copies of these transcriptions, as well as accompanying recordings, are also housed at the Institute of Coptic Studies in Cairo, Egypt, as well as the German Center for World Music in Hanover, Germany.

4. The Coptic community uses the terms *taratīl* and *taranīm* interchangeably to describe nonliturgical devotional songs that complement the official Coptic liturgical hymnody known as *alḥān*. For the sake of brevity and clarity, I refer to *taratīl* and *taranīm* solely as *taratīl* (sing. *tartīla*).

5. See the Archangel Michael Monastery that hosts young Coptic women to perform and recording Coptic *alḥān*: https://www.facebook.com/archangelmonastery/ (accessed October 8, 2016).

6. https://www.facebook.com/Women-Deacons-in-the-Coptic-Orthodox-Church-645153102218073/?fref=ts (accessed October 8, 2016).

7. Here I am drawing on Lara Deeb's notion of pious modernity in which Lebanese Shi'a Muslims infused public piety through "authenticated" forms of Islam that drew on rigorous textual study inspired by a Western "scientific" rationality.

8. As the historian Beth Baron (2014) observed, it was difficult to proselytize to Egyptian Muslims who were protected both by law and their familial kin, so missionaries focused their efforts on orphaned children and on Coptic Orthodox Christians.

9. For an English translation of Louis Badet's preface, see https://www.loc.gov/item/ihas.200155952/ (accessed October 25, 2016).

10. In his edited work *Questions of Modernity* (2000), Timothy Mitchell problematizes modernity's assumed singular history that Louis Badet assumes here—namely, an autocentric picture of itself as the expression of a universal certainty.

11. For more on the early history of transcription in comparative musicology, see Terr Ellingson's "Transcription" and "Notation" in *Ethnomusicology: An Introduction* (1992).

12. The *Description de l'Égypt* where Villoteau published his first transcriptions of Coptic *alḥān* is a case in point. In their dramatic and oversized volumes, they are one of the earliest and most famous documents to trace Napoleon Bonaparte's expedition to Egypt, with particular attention given to the transcription of classical and religious music (1826).

13. In Villoteau's transcription of a Coptic service, the *savant* blamed his inability to transcribe the "savage and soporific" melodies that shifted and changed between keys on the community's lack of interest in "the sciences and the arts." For an English translation of the section "About the Music of the Copts" in his transcription, see https://www.loc.gov/item/ihas.200155950/ (accessed October 25, 2016).

14. At the turn of the century, a number of scholars emerged to problematize the notion of latent harmony; see Erich M. Von Hornbostel and Otto Abraham (1904), Benjamin Ives Gilman (1908), and Franz Boas (1894).

15. For an English translation of Ghubriyal's entire preface, see https://www.loc.gov/item/ihas.200155976/ (accessed October 25, 2016).

16. For more on the importance of the role of Orthodox priesthood, see Pope Shenouda III's book *The Priesthood* (1999).

17. Laywomen's roles as spiritual activists, choir leaders, and Sunday School educators grew with the rise of the Sunday School movement beginning in 1918. This religious education

revival focused on educating the laity and led to a burgeoning religious renaissance in the 1970s. Known as *Ḥarkit al-Tarbiyya al-Kanāsiyya* (the Church Upbringing movement), this religious renaissance paralleled Egypt's broader Islamic revival, which shifted the country's religious ethos and sensibilities, leading to a dramatic proliferation of performances and displays of public piety. In this revival, women emerged as preachers, teachers, and prominent disseminators of their faith (Mahmood 2005; Hirschkind 2006). In the Coptic community, the Church Upbringing movement would significantly shape Christian feminist subjectivities, giving rise to women's spiritual activism and their increased audibility in the Orthodox Church.

18. The subtitled film may be viewed here: https://www.youtube.com/watch?v=FwARjzX 61Nw (accessed February 12, 2016). Another notable example is *The Bloody Mountain: Our Mother Dolagi and Her Children* (date unknown) located here: https://www.youtube.com/watch?v=m3s1VW8yFoE (accessed February 12, 2016). Another notable example is the film *Rafiqa the Saint and Her Five Children*.

19. Here, Armanios is quoting Kelsy Burke and Amy McDowell's work "Superstars and Misfits: Two Pop-Trends in the Gender of Contemporary Evangelicalism," *Journal of Religion and Pop Culture* 24 (2012): 72.

20. In one instance, one of the nominees for the Coptic papal seat, Bishop Bishoy of Damietta of Egypt, urged Christian women to model Muslim women and dress more modestly. This led to a uproar and protest at the Coptic Patriarchate in central Cairo in May 2012. See Mariz Tadros's article "Egypt's Women Have Had Enough of Being Told to Cover Up," *Guardian*, May 29, 2012; https://www.theguardian.com/commentisfree/2012/may/29/egypt-women-cover-up-coptic (accessed October 25, 2016).

21. At the height of an Egyptian nationalism just a few years later in 1925, Moftah enlisted the help of a British missionary and musician, Ernest Newlandsmith, to notate the Coptic *alḥān* without piano accompaniment. This time, however, Moftah aimed to uncover the hymns' authentic ancient Egyptian links under what Newlandsmith identified as "appalling debris of Arabic ornamentation" (1932, 146). For more on the discursive politics of Moftah and Newlandsmith's collaboration, see my article "Modern Singing Songs of the Pharaohs: Transcription and Orientalism in a Digital Coptic Music Collection," *Ethnologies* (2015). Also, listen to Moftah's introduction to his music collection at https://memory.loc.gov/natlib/ihas/service/coptic/200181952/seg02/audio/0001.mp3 (accessed October 26, 2016).

22. The historian Beth Baron writes about the rise of American Bible women—and later converted Egyptian orphan girls in their care—who entered Egyptian homes to teach new converts, mostly other women, to read the word of God (Baron 1994, 54–59).

23. For more on Habib Girgis's reformist efforts, see Bishop Anba Suriel's "Habib Girgis, Coptic Orthodox Educator and a Light in the Darkness" (PhD diss., Fordham University, 2014).

24. Personal interview, July 17, 2009.

25. See the ensemble mission statement at http://www.davidensemble.com/english/ensemble.htm (accessed October 26, 2016).

26. Ibid. Eighteen years later, Monika and her father debuted a music video for the same hymn. See https://www.youtube.com/watch?v=pIJfjDnoX9M (accessed October 27, 2016).

27. Personal interview, October 9, 2016.

28. https://www.youtube.com/watch?v=1Bd5ZC7ySjI (accessed October 27, 2016).

29. Armanios quotes the historian Ramzi Tadrus's 1910 remark as a case in point: "There is no advancement for the nation except for the advancement of the woman, and there is no advancement for the woman unless she is educated and trained with a proper cultivation

which will giver her a soft disposition and a knowledge of real beauty—that within the self. That is the sort of training which will mould [*sic*] a girl into a mature woman who is able to make the home for her father, brother, husband, and son a flourishing paradise" (Armanios 2002, 114; Tadrus 1910, 49); https://www.youtube.com/watch?v=Y2p2VXvkdjo (accessed October 27, 2016).

References

Abu-Lughod, Lila. 1998. *Remaking Women: Feminism and Modernity in the Middle East.* Princeton, NJ: Princeton University Press.

Ahmed, Leila. 1992. *Women and Gender in Islam.* New Haven, CT: Yale University Press.

Amiot, Joseph M. 1779. *Mémoire sur la musique des Chinois tant anciens que modernes.* (Paris): Nyon L'aîné.

Armanios, Febe. 2002. "The 'Virtuous Woman': Images of Gender in Modern Coptic Society." *Middle Eastern Studies* 38 (1): 110–130.

Armanios, Febe, and Andrew Amstutz. 2013. "Emerging Christian Media in Egypt: Clerical Authority and the Visualization of Women in Coptic Video Films." *International Journal of Middle East Studies* 45: 513–533.

Armbrust, Walter. 1996. *Mass Culture and Modernism in Egypt.* Cambridge: Cambridge University Press.

Badet, Louis. 1899. *Chants liturgiques des Coptes, notés et mis en ordre par le Père Louis Badet, S.J.* Cairo: Collège de la Sainte-Famille, Petit Séminaire Copte.

Baron, Beth. 1994. *The Women's Awakening in Egypt.* New Haven, CT: Yale University Press.

Baron, Beth. 2014. *The Orphan Scandal: Christian Missionaries and the Rise of the Muslim Brotherhood.* Stanford, CA: Stanford University Press.

Boas, Franz. 1894. "Review of Alice Fletcher, *A Study of Omaha Indian Music.*" *Journal of American Folklore* 7 (25): 169.

Deeb, Lara. 2006. *An Enchanted Modern: Gender and Public Piety in Shi'a Lebanon.* Princeton, NJ: Princeton University Press.

van Doorn-Harder, Nelly. 1995. *Contemporary Coptic Nuns.* Columbia: University of South Carolina Press.

Ellingson, Ter. 1992. "Transcription" and "Notation." In *Ethnomusicology: An Introduction*, edited by Helen Myers, 110–152. London: Macmillan.

Fletcher, Alice Cunningham, John Fillmore, and Francis La Flesche. 1893. *A Study of Omaha Indian Music.* Cambridge, MA: Peabody Museum of Archeology and Ethnology.

Fillmore, John Comfort. 1895. "What Do Indians Mean to Do When They Sing, and How Far Do They Succeed?" *Journal of American Folklore* 8 (29): 138–142.

Gabry, Séverine. 2017. "Transmitting Coptic Musical Heritage." In *Copts in Context, Negotiating Identity, Tradition and Modernity*, edited by Nelly can Doorn-Harder. Columbia: University of South Carolina Press.

Ghabrial, Sarah. 2016. "Gender, Power, and Agency in the Historical Study of the Middle East and North Africa." *International Journal of Middle East Studies* 48 (3): 561–564.

Ghurbriyāl, Kāmil Ibrāhīm. 1916. *Al-tawqīʿāt al-mūsīqīyyah lī maraddāt al-kanīsa al-Murqusiyyah* [The musical notation of the responses of the church of Saint Mark]. The Government of Sudan and Egypt.

Gilman, Benjamin. 1908. "Hopi Songs." *Journal of American Ethnology and Archeology* 5:xi–235.

Girgis, Habib. 1922. *Salawāt al-sha'b athna'al-qudās* [The congregation's prayers during the liturgy]. Cairo: Printings House of Awareness on Fagala Street.

Girgis, Habib. n.d. *Muftāḥ al-anghām lil-tarānīm al-Urthūdhuksiyah* [A key to the tunes for Orthodox hymns]. Cairo: Sunday School General Committee.

Goode, James. F. 2007. *Negotiating for the Past: Archaeology, Nationalism, and Diplomacy in the Middle East, 1919–1941*. Austin: University of Texas Press.

Hirschkind, Charles. 2006. *The Ethical Soundscape: Cassette Sermons and Islamic Counterpublics*. New York: Columbia University Press.

Jones, William. 1792. "On the Musical Modes of the Hindoos." *Asiatick Researches* 3:55–87.

Kandiyoti, Deniz. 1991. "Identity and Its Discontents: Women and the Nation." *Journal of International Studies* 20 (3): 429–443.

Kandiyoti, Deniz, ed. 1996. *Gendering the Middle East: Emerging Perspectives*. Syracuse, NY: Syracuse University Press.

Mahmood, Saba. 2005. *Politics of Piety: The Islam Revival and the Feminist Subject*. Princeton, NJ: Princeton University Press.

Mersenne, Marin. 1636. *Harmonie universelle*. Paris: Sebastien Cramoisy.

Mitchell, Timothy, ed. 2000. *Questions of Modernity*. Minneapolis: University of Minnesota Press.

Mitchell, Timothy. 2002. *Rule of Experts: Egypt, Techno-Politics, Modernity*. Berkeley: University of California Press.

Newlandsmith, Ernest. 1932. "Music of the Orient: Recent Discoveries in Egypt." *Musical Standard* 37 (May, June, July) 146; 161–162; 184–185.

Pope Shenouda, III. 1999. *The Priesthood*. Cairo: Dar El Tiba El Qawmiyya.

Reid, Donald Malcolm. 2015. *Contesting Antiquity in Egypt; Archaeologies, Museums, and the Struggle for Identities from World War I to Nasser*. Cairo: American University in Cairo.

Sedra, Paul. 2011. *From Mission to Modernity: Evangelical Reforms and Education in Nineteenth Century Egypt*. New York: Tauris Academic Studies.

Tadrus, Ramzi. 1910. *Al-aqbat fi'l qarn al-'ishrin* [The Copts in the twentieth century]. Vol. 1. Cairo: Jaridat Misr.

van der Vliet, Jacques. 2009. "The Copts: 'Modern Sons of the Pharaohs'?" *Church History and Religious Culture* 89 (1–3): 279–290.

van Doorn-Harder, Nelly. 1995. *Contemporary Coptic Nuns*. Columbia: University of South Carolina Press.

Villoteau, Guillaume. 1809. "Chapitre 5: De la musique des Qobtes" [Chapter 5: About the music of the Copts]. In *Description de l'Égypte: ou, Recueil des observations et des recherches qui ont été faites en Égypte pendant l'éxpédition de l'armée française, publié par les ordres de Sa Majesté l'empereur Napoléon le Grand*. Vol. 2, part 1a, 754–757. 21 vols. Paris: Imprimérie impériale.

Villoteau, Guillaume. 1826. *De l'état actuel de l'art musical en Égypte*. Paris: Imprimérie de C. L. F. Panckoucke.

Zuhur, Sherifa. 1992. *Revealing Reveiling: Islamist Gender Ideology in Contemporary Egypt*. Albany: State University of New York Press.

CHAPTER 23

MEMORY, TRAUMA, AND THE POLITICS OF REPATRIATING BIKINDI'S MUSIC IN THE AFTERMATH OF THE RWANDAN GENOCIDE

JASON MCCOY

MUSICAL repatriation may follow along official, institutional procedures, but it can also result from informal social exchanges that inevitably occur throughout the course of ethnographic field research. In such situations, the one providing reaccess to musical artifacts may not even be aware that they are involved in a process of repatriation, or if they are, repatriation may be a byproduct of more primary research goals. Nevertheless, musical repatriation is ineluctably a political act, bringing to the social foreground the postcolonial disparities of privilege between the provider and recipient, a disparity reflective of larger imbalances of global power between the geopolitical entities that the two represent. The politics are all the more highly charged when musical repatriation proceeds within the contextual aftermath of mass political violence, and the musical artifacts are directly linked to that conflict and its concomitant emotional turmoil. In such cases, the provider may find themselves in an ethical morass.

Such was the case when I began providing recordings of songs composed by the controversial songwriter Simon Bikindi—songs that are now de facto censored in Rwanda—to survivors and witnesses of the 1994 genocide. What follows is a personal account of my experiences, beginning with a brief introduction to the topic, followed by a discussion of the laws related to the censorship of Bikindi's music, the lyrical content of the songs, and the context in which they were composed, pointing out why many Rwandans find them so detestable while others do not. Finally, I will conclude with several ethnographic vignettes that I hope will impress on the reader the ethical conundrum I created for myself in choosing to provide access to Bikindi's music.

"So what do *you* think of Bikindi's music?" inquired the high-level university official[1] in an imperious manner. It was early June 2008. A couple of weeks prior I had arrived in Rwanda for the first time and taken up residency in the southern town of Butare[2] to conduct research on Bikindi's songs and the role they potentially played in inciting genocide. With the help of a friend who was a music instructor at the National University, located just down the road from the guesthouse where I stayed, I set up a meeting with this official so that I could inform him of my research activities and request the school's support should I need it.

"Uh, I'm not really sure," I replied. "That's why I'm here—to talk to people and find out what they think so that I can better understand." I then returned the volley. "Why? What might be the problem?"

The official leveled his gaze at me across the conference table and said in no uncertain terms, "Well, if you were to say his music was okay, then *that* would be a problem."

I had researched the political dynamics in Rwanda enough to know that Bikindi's songs were frowned on by the nation's sole ruling party, the Rwandan Patriotic Front (RPF), and by extension its affiliate public institutions, including the National University. Not only were his songs composed in part to protest the RPF's reinvasion of Rwanda in February 1993, but also they were soon thereafter incorporated by politicians and radio broadcasters into the propaganda campaign used to incite the genocide of the Tutsi minority that was carried out the following year. This was the first time, though, that I had been warned, implicitly or otherwise, by a public official that it would be troublesome if I were to voice or somehow signify approval of Bikindi's music.

Fortunately (I suppose), I did not think Bikindi's music was "okay." I believed his songs were a crucial factor in inciting genocide. Aired numerous times per day on the pro-genocide radio station, RTLM,[3] they provided much of the soundtrack to the massive killing spree that took place from April 6 to mid-July 1994 and that resulted in the murders of an estimated 800,000 Rwandans (Carlsson, Han, et al. 1999). After *génocidaires* finished their day's "work" of hunting down Tutsi and Hutu sympathizers (the genocide was commonly framed as a form of civic labor by the leaders who orchestrated it), they would regularly congregate at local bars, where they would listen to Bikindi's songs on the radio or request the bartender to play a cassette. The songs clearly resonated with them ideologically and provided further rational and emotional thrust to their motives.

It is just that I suspected then, as I do now, that there was good reason to question whether or not inciting anti-Tutsi fear, hatred, and violence was Bikindi's intent. These suspicions were affirmed over the course of seven years of research throughout which I shared the songs with Rwandans who experienced the genocide firsthand, including Bikindi, and listened to their responses. Replete with metaphorical and allusive language, his lyrics provoke an interpretive process that can go in a number of ways. Indeed, I found that Tutsi who were targeted during the genocide and are now supportive of the RPF were certain of Bikindi's malign intentions. Hutu who were neither targeted nor participated in the genocide, yet felt that they were being unfairly and collectively blamed, and thus politically and socially disenfranchised, tended to defend Bikindi or at least have a more neutral view. The four ex-members of his profes-sional troupe, Irindiro Ballet, whom I talked to—one a Twa, one a Hutu, and the other two Tutsi—all defended him, though the two Tutsi did so with some qualifications—namely, that Bikindi was an opportunist who composed partisan songs in order to enrich himself and elevate his status, though he himself had no ill will toward Tutsi.[4] Bikindi, for his part, attested that he tried to use his talents to help restore peace and encourage mutual respect between Hutu and Tutsi. He blamed RTLM's broadcasters for rhetorically contextualizing the songs in a way that caused listeners to interpret a pro-genocide message.

Whatever the case may be, on December 2, 2008, Bikindi was convicted of incite-ment to genocide and sentenced to fifteen years in prison by the International Criminal Tribunal for Rwanda (ICTR), a court mandated by the United Nations to bring to jus-tice those deemed most responsible for the genocide. The prosecution charged him with composing and performing music with the intent of incitement. The judges agreed, but they could not convict him specifically for musical incitement, because Bikindi composed the songs in 1993, and the court's statutes only cover crimes committed in 1994. Bikindi was instead convicted for allegedly making a couple of statements from a moving car equipped with a PA system in which he urged Hutu bystanders to continue killing Tutsi. The judges ruled, however, that it was Bikindi's stature as a popular celeb-rity musician that enabled him to influence people to kill.[5]

Bikindi now bears the distinction of being the only professional musician in the his-tory of modern international law to be convicted of crimes related to mass atrocity. His reputation is that of a heinous war criminal. He is vilified in much of the scholarly and journalistic literature on the genocide, and his music is now de facto censored in Rwanda. There is no law that explicitly prohibits Rwandans from owning and listening to Bikindi's music, rather its censorship is subsumed under several broadly written laws against harboring divisionist, sectarian, or genocidal ideology or disseminating gen-ocide propaganda. Some of these laws carry steep fines and lengthy prison sentences, and the RPF has used them to stamp out political dissent, demanding ideological con-formity for fear of another genocide.

Because of the law's ambiguities, Rwandan citizens must determine for themselves what expressive activities might get them into trouble (Buckley-Zistel 2006; Amnesty International 2010). Owning or otherwise demonstrating an appreciation of Bikindi's music, for instance, might lead to accusations of harboring genocide ideology, particu-larly for Hutu. Even if they are not formally charged, they may still be suspected of such. Therefore, most Rwandans choose to be safe rather than sorry, a censorial referred to here as coerced self-censorship.

Bikindi's music is never played on the radio or television, and it is all but impossible to find his recordings sold in music shops. Of the approximately sixty Rwandans who participated in my research on the reception of Bikindi's music, almost none had heard the songs since the genocide. The only participants who owned such a recording were, of course, Bikindi, and a refugee couple living near my home in the United States, where they were safe from harm. According to them, they received the recording from friends in Canada, who received it from friends in Paris, who happened to find it there in an African music shop.

I then brought the recording back to Rwanda.

When I began sharing the songs with Rwandans fifteen years after the genocide, there were some who found the lyrical content too infuriating and the associated memories too painful, and so they wanted nothing more to do with them. One man whose wife and children had been murdered during the genocide said simply, "Perhaps it is better to let some things die." But others exhibited an eagerness to listen to and engage with the songs again, and several requested recordings. This desire cut across lines of ethnic identity, partisan affiliation, and experiences of the genocide and its aftermath.

Because Rwandan law does not explicitly forbid Bikindi's music, I believed that I had the legal cover not only to share Bikindi's music with willing listeners but to provide recordings to those who requested them. Still, legal justification does not equal ethical justification, and this is the issue I continue to wrestle with: Was I, as a foreigner and a representative of a Western neocolonial power, ethically justified in distributing Bikindi's songs under the nose of a government and a sizable portion of the population that desired their erasure from the nation's collective memory? On the other hand, would I have been ethically justified in refusing to return the songs to people for whom the songs still held profound, personal meaning?

CENSORSHIP AND LAWS AGAINST DIVISIONISM, SECTARIANISM, AND GENOCIDE IDEOLOGY

Laws against genocide ideology and propaganda are articulated by two sets of legal statutes. The first is Law No. 47/2001: On the Prevention, Suppression and Punishment of the Crime of Discrimination and Sectarianism, enacted on December 18, 2001. The second is Law No. 18/2008: Relating to the Punishment of the Crime of Genocide Ideology, enacted on July 23, 2008. Beginning with the first of these laws, Article 1 defines discrimination and sectarianism as follows:

> 1° Discrimination is any speech, writing, or actions based on ethnicity, region or country of origin, the colour of the skin, physical features, sex, language, religion or ideas aimed at depriving a person or group of persons of their rights as provided by Rwandan law and by International Conventions to which Rwanda is party.
>
> 2° Sectarianism means the use of any speech, written statement or action that divides people, that is likely to spark conflicts among people, or that causes an uprising which might degenerate into strife among people based on discrimination mentioned in 1°.

The French version of Article 1(2) is more broadly worded in comparison to the English.[6] It reads, "La pratique du sectarisme est un crime commis au moyen de l'expression orale, écrite ou tout acte de division pouvant générer des conflits au sein de la population, ou susciter des querelles" ("The practice of sectarianism is a crime committed by means of any oral or written expression or act of divisionism that could generate conflict among the population or cause quarrels"). Article 3 of the law attempts to clarify further what constitutes the crimes of discrimination and sectarianism:

> The crime of discrimination occurs when the author makes use of any speech, written statement or action based on ethnicity, region or country of origin, colour of the skin, physical features, sex, language, religion or ideas with the aim of denying one or a group of persons their human rights provided by Rwandan law and International Conventions to which Rwanda is party.
>
> The crime of sectarianism occurs when the author makes use of any speech, written statement or action that causes conflict or that causes an uprising that may degenerate into strife among people.

According to these laws, anything that a person says or does that is somehow related to categories of social differentiation to the extent that it may potentially provoke "conflict," "strife among people," or, according to the French, "quarrels," may result in that person being prosecuted. Article 3, however, makes it a crime to deny an individual or group of persons "their human rights provided by Rwandan law and *International Conventions* to which Rwanda is party." This is self-contradictory in that "international conventions" regarding human rights generally uphold freedom of expression, even if such expression denigrates other groups of people, though this is far from uniform; varying exceptions to this right have been made according to different international conventions and declarations throughout the twentieth century. The question then arises: to what international convention(s) does Rwandan law adhere?

It would seem then that merely possessing and listening to a recording of Bikindi's songs would not constitute a crime. The more likely problem would be when someone plays the songs for others. Article 8 establishes the following as a crime:

> [making] public any speech, writing, pictures or images or any symbols over radio airwaves, television, in a meeting or public place, with the aim of discriminating [against] people or sowing sectarianism among them . . .

Because the RPF considers Bikindi's songs to be an expression of divisionism and sectarianism, playing them for others in public could be legally interpreted as an attempt to spread these ideas, though there must be proof of intent. If a person is convicted of intentionally sowing divisionism and sectarianism, then punishment runs from a fine of 30,000 Rwanda francs (RWF; as of this writing, about $45) to 300,000 RWF (about $450), in addition to a possible prison sentence of between one and five years. If a person's actions are deemed especially egregious, or that person is a prominent public figure, a maximum sentence of life imprisonment may be imposed.

The 2008 Law Relating to the Punishment of the Crime of Genocide Ideology is more severe. Article 2 defines genocide ideology as follows:

> an aggregate of thoughts characterized by conduct, speeches, documents and other acts aimed at exterminating or inciting others to exterminate people based on ethnic group, origin, nationality, region, color, physical appearance, sex, language, religion or political opinion, committed in normal periods or during war.

While this definition could be critiqued, the more troubling issue is found in Article 3, which states:

> The crime of genocide ideology is characterized in any behaviour manifested by facts aimed at dehumanizing a person or a group of persons with the same characteristics in the following manner:
> 1° threatening, intimidating, degrading through defamatory speeches, documents or actions which aim at propounding wickedness or inciting hatred;
> 2° marginalizing, laughing at one's misfortunes, defaming, mocking, boasting, despising, degrading, creating confusion aimed at negating the genocide which occurred, stirring up ill feelings, taking revenge, altering testimony or evidence for the genocide which occurred;
> 3° killing, planning to kill or attempting to kill someone for purposes of furthering genocide ideology.

Penalties for breaking the law on genocide ideology range from a prison sentence of between ten and twenty-five years and a fine of between two hundred thousand and one million Rwandan francs (RWF, roughly $300 to $1,500). The penalties are harsher for "a leader in public administrative organs, political organisations, private administrative organs, or nongovernment organs, a religious leader, or a former leader in such organs." Young children, defined as those under the age of twelve, are not exempt. If found guilty, they are taken to a special learning center for up to twelve months to be re-educated. Older children between the ages of twelve and eighteen are given a sentence equal to half the time as adults.

Article 8 regarding the dissemination of genocide ideology is especially concerning:

> Any person who disseminates genocide ideology in public through documents, speeches, pictures, media, or any other means shall be sentenced to an imprisonment from twenty years to twenty-five years and a fine of two million to five million RWF.

Note here that the law says nothing about intent. Out of ignorance or carelessness, people might share news articles, web links, or for that matter, Bikindi's songs with others, and if authorities determine that those actions constitute a means of spreading genocide ideology, then they could be imprisoned for a minimum of two decades.

THE CONTEXT OF THE SONGS

The two songs that were broadcast the most and were at the center of Bikindi's trial were "Akabyutso" ("The Awakening") and "Intabaza" ("The Alert"). They were produced in March and April 1993, over a year before the genocide and a month after the RPF's reinvasion. This was a time marked by economic ruin, political upheaval, war, and societal collapse—a time that Rwandans refer to as "Igihirahiro," roughly translated as "the time of uncertainty/chaos."[7] The global price of coffee, Rwanda's main cash crop, had been plummeting since the late 1980s, sapping the nation's treasury. As a result, the Rwandan economy grew largely dependent on foreign monetary aid. President Juvénal Habyarimana thus relented to international pressure and allowed for the organization of oppositional parties, though he floundered in his commitment to holding national elections that would threaten to topple his dictatorship and unseat his party, the MRND.[8] Rather than placate Habyarimana's many political foes, the weakly enacted advent of multipartyism resulted in widespread resentment and a wave of mass violence as partisan loyalists took to the streets in order to terrorize the citizenry into supporting their preferred party.

Meanwhile, the Rwandan military (Forces Armées Rwandaises, or FAR) was at war with the RPF. At that time, the RPF was a militarized political operation based in southern Uganda whose members were mostly Tutsi exiles. When the Tutsi-dominated monarchy, under which Hutu were severely oppressed, was overthrown in 1959 and an exclusively Hutu government was installed, hundreds of thousands of Tutsi fled in order to escape reprisal killings and persecution. The largest and most active contingent settled in southern Uganda, where they eventually founded the RPF. The exiles were never fully embraced by their Ugandan neighbors. Rwanda was still their home, and they desired to return. The RPF also sought to end the discriminatory practices against Tutsi that had forced them to flee in the first place. Habyarimana refused them, however, citing overpopulation and poor economic conditions, and so on October 1, 1990, the RPF invaded.

The RPF's attack was initially repelled by the FAR. Delegates from the RPF soon then began meeting with Habyarimana and other MRND officials in Arusha, Tanzania, to negotiate a series of accords that would put an end to armed conflict, enable the return of Rwandan exiles, and reform the government in a way that would allow for RPF representation. Both sides, though, were resistant to compromises, and the accords were never fully implemented by Habyarimana. On February 7, 1993, the RPF broke a ceasefire agreement and attacked again, this time with much more success. They overran much of northern Rwanda and came within twenty kilometers of capturing the capital city of Kigali. Thousands of Rwandan civilians were killed, and hundreds of thousands were displaced from their homes before the RPF and MRND agreed to another ceasefire.

From the perspective of many Rwandans, it appeared that the RPF desired not only to return and share power but ultimately to take over.

The RPF heralded itself as a liberator of Tutsi. Rumors, some of which were likely true, circulated in the press and in political speeches that Tutsi in Rwanda were secretly conspiring with the RPF to restore the monarchy, or something akin to it.[9] A cadre of influential MRND members attempted to exploit the RPF invasion and the rumors of a Tutsi conspiracy as a means to resolve the partisan discord in Rwanda and reinforce their political superiority. They formed a new party, the extremist CDR.[10] Using the press, radio, and political speeches and rallies, they sought to deflect hostility away from themselves and toward a common enemy, one that not only dwelled in plain sight but was politically neutered and offered little resistance. Tutsi made for an easy target.

Bikindi's songs became the anthems of Igihirahiro. During our visit, Bikindi recalled two experiences in particular as his inspiration.[11] The first was a visit to a hospital to see the son of a good friend and journalist. The young man was not politically active, but as he was walking to the market, he was accosted by a group of partisan fanatics and had his eyes gouged out. To Bikindi, this senseless and horrific act committed against an innocent person was indicative of a broader insanity gripping society to which he, as a famous musician, felt compelled to respond. The second experience, occurring soon after this incident, was a grenade attack in Kigali's main bus park, again carried out by partisan fanatics. Bikindi's office was located on an upper floor of a nearby building where he worked for the Ministry of Culture and Youth as a talent scout and festival organizer. When he heard and felt the explosions, he looked out his window to see the carnage below. He then rushed to the scene, where he offered his car to help transport the injured to a hospital.

THE CONTENT OF THE SONGS

Nowhere in his lyrics did Bikindi denigrate Tutsi or advocate violence against them. On the surface, the lyrics called for national unity, transparent elections free of corruption and violence, respect and generosity across the social strata, and support for the FAR in their war with the RPF. However, this was far from the sentimental pablum typical of much patriotic music. His lyrics were lengthy and poetically dense. Bikindi was regarded by his audiences as a genius who could masterfully harness a deep knowledge of history, culture, and language, and underscore it with a sophisticated musical vitality. When I listened to the songs with a linguist at the National University who helped me translate the lyrics, he shook his head and sighed, lamenting, "There will never be another like him."

"Intabaza" unfolds as a mythic narrative in which the protagonist, Mutabazi,[12] travels throughout the whole of Rwanda, and as he does so, he sees that the entire nation is engulfed in misery, animosity, and destruction. The lyrics mention nearly every clan and region, the latter often referred to by older, precolonial names that are no longer commonly used. Rwandan political hierarchies have long been contested along the lines of clanship and region, and so this was a clever rhetorical ploy through which Bikindi hoped to instill in listeners a sense that all were suffering from the consequences of war, poverty, political corruption, and partisan terrorism, and should therefore let go of their parochial concerns in favor of national unity.

Eventually, Mutabazi arrives at the abode of the powerful diviner, Biryaobayoboke, where he is welcomed as an earnest seeker of peace and justice. A divination ritual is performed during which Biryaobayoboke recalls the history of Rwanda, emphasizing especially the harsh treatment of *bene sebahinzi*—"fellow descendants of the father of farmers"[13]—under the monarchy and colonial administration. *Bene sebahinzi* is a common euphemism for Hutu, but Bikindi would remind his audience that almost all Rwandans—Hutu, Tutsi, and Twa—belong to agrarian communities that have been historically marginalized and exploited by central political authorities. In fact, the song specifies that *bene sebahinzi* include all three ethnic groups, culminating in the following dialogue between Biryaobayoboke [B] and Mutabazi [M]:

> **B:** *Bene sebahinzi bagomba kumenya kandi ko abo banyarwanda batuye u Rwanda barimo amoko atatu: Gahutu, Gatwa na Gatutsi.*
> Fellow descendants of the father of farmers must know also that the Rwandans who inhabit Rwanda are composed of three ethnic groups (*amoko*[14]): Hutu, Twa, and Tutsi.
> *Ibyo ntibihinduka rwose.*
> All those things cannot be changed.
>
> **M:** *Ibyo ntibihinduka.*
> Those things cannot be changed.
>
> **B:** *Twese tugomba kwemera ko nta wasabye kuvuka ari umuhutu, umutwa cyangwa umututsi.*
> All of us must realize that no one asked to be born a Hutu, Twa, or Tutsi.
>
> **M:** *None se?*
> And so?
>
> **B:** *Bityo tukemera ko nta wusumba undi.*
> Therefore, we must accept that no one is superior to another.
> *Tukemera ko nta wugomba kuryamira undi kandi ko inyungu za rubanda-nyamwinshi arizo zigomba gushyirwa imbere!*
> We must accept that no one may oppress another and that priority must be given to the benefits of the majority people!
>
> **M:** *Rwose!*
> Indeed!
>
> **B:** *Ayiii . . . ! Ayiii . . . ! Bahamagare rwose bene sebahinzi baze mbahe intsinzi.*
> [Cheering] Call all the descendants of the father of farmers together, for I shall give them the solution.

The "solution" that Biryaobayoboke proposes is for Rwandans to stop fighting among themselves, hold fair and peaceful elections, and respect the results, no matter if it is Hutu, Tutsi, or Twa who are chosen. Naïvely idealistic, perhaps, but hard to criticize—except that other themes woven throughout the work are disturbing in that they could easily be construed as a call for Hutu solidarity in the face of Tutsi adversaries. The trope of *bene sebahinzi* is a deeply culturally embedded euphemism for Hutu. It may not be disingenuous of Bikindi to claim that he intended this to refer to all who farm, but no doubt he was aware of the term's cultural and historical associations to the extent that most audiences would have understood it as an exclusive moniker for Hutu. Moreover, the song attributes Rwanda's problems to "a spirit that attacks from abroad" ("muzimu utera aturutse ishyanga"). This could refer to the RPF who were attacking from Uganda, but many listeners understood it as a reference to all Tutsi. It was widely taught and believed that Tutsi were the descendants of cattle-herding ancestors who arrived in the region of Rwanda and subjugated Hutu farmers who had settled there long before.

Whereas "Intabaza," despite its foreboding imagery, is ultimately a song of triumph and hope, "Akabyutso" is marked by a darker tone. It is commonly known as "Nanga abahutu" ("I despise Hutu"), as this line is often repeated throughout the song. The lyrics chastise Hutu who are foolish and forget Rwanda's history of oppression under the monarchy, who are greedy and selfish, who use flattery, bribery, and corruption to manipulate the political process, who involve themselves in partisan violence, and who do not respect others. Tutsi are never mentioned in the song, but even so critics contend that Bikindi intended to unify Hutu and shame those who were sympathetic to Tutsi or who cooperated with the RPF. Perhaps the most disturbing line states: "Me, I despise a Hutu, a Hutu who receives a coin to kill a person and then kills a Hutu!" ("Njyewe nanga umuhutu, umuhutu uhabwa igiceri akica umuntu kandi akica umuhutu!") Critics charge that Bikindi was instructing Hutu audiences that they should lay aside their political and economic differences and instead come together to kill Tutsi. Bikindi's defense is to point out that Hutu did dominate the political sphere and were therefore ultimately responsible for Rwanda's woes. While key political and media figures at the time were demonizing Tutsi and trumpeting Hutu Power, Bikindi turned the tables around, charging that it was actually Hutu who were the problem. As for the line concerning the killing of a Hutu, Bikindi claims that, indeed, some Hutu were so consumed with money that for even a small amount they would go and kill their own kind. In his trial and in our conversation, he stressed that he believed that the RPF was still the main enemy, which he likened specifically to the abusive monarchy from which it emerged, not to Tutsi in general. In the midst of war with the RPF, he feared that the partisan violence and selfish motives of many politicians and their lackeys would ensure his nation's defeat.

Sharing the Songs with Survivors and Witnesses

In late May 2008, about a week or so after my initial arrival in Rwanda, I met and befriended a Tutsi man named Julius who was a pastor and teacher at a Bible school near

Kigali. He had come to Butare for a week to lead a theological seminar and was staying at the same guesthouse where I lived. The first morning after his arrival, as we were eating breakfast and getting to know one another, I told him of my research. Julius's eyes lit up, and he told me that he would "very much like to hear Bikindi's music." I cued up "Intabaza" on my iPod, handed it to him, and showed him how to use it.

As soon as he hit the play button, he burst into uncontrollable laughter. When he eventually calmed down some, I asked him why he was laughing so. He replied:

> "Ahhh . . . because this music—it takes me back to 1994!"
>
> "You mean . . . back to the war? The genocide?"
>
> "Yes, back to 1994!"
>
> "But Pastor, that was a nightmare. How can you be laughing like this?"
>
> "Yes, it's true, but I was, you know, a young man then. I had just been married. I was in love. This music reminds me of that time, the time of my youth." He then continued listening.

Over the following week, whenever he was not teaching or sleeping, Julius listened to Bikindi's music—even during meals. I asked him several times why he seemed so possessed by it. Here are some of the reasons he provided:

> "This is the music of my youth. We all loved to listen to Bikindi's music back then, to dance to it."
>
> "This is the great music of Rwanda. The older people, we like this kind of music. Younger people don't listen to this anymore."
>
> "*It is my history.*" (He repeated this one a lot.)
>
> "It is like this, you see. Earlier today I was having some trouble finding Bikindi's songs on this device. I was searching through the songs on it, and I saw that you had a song by Donna Summer [the 1975 hit disco single, "Love to Love You, Baby"]. When I was in secondary school, we listened to this song all the time and danced to it. We really liked it. When I listen to Bikindi, it's the same kind of feeling."

One afternoon, Julius told me some of what he went through during the genocide. He and his wife had sent their children to hide with friends while the couple hid at another friend's house. After three days, a group of *génocidaires* came to the house. They did not find Julius but spotted his wife and abducted her. They took her to a nearby mountainside, where they were going to kill her. As it turned out, some of the *génocidaires* were friends of Julius's father, and when they discovered that the woman they had in hand was the daughter-in-law of this man, they convinced the others to let her go.

Julius admitted to being "traumatized" during the ordeal—his words, not mine. He was so numb from despair that he says he fell asleep after his wife was taken, not an uncommon occurrence for people helplessly overwhelmed by terror and grief. He then told me that, in light of his experiences, listening to Bikindi's songs made him "praise God for surviving" the genocide.

When Julius was set to return to Kigali, he asked for a recording of the songs. He said, half-jokingly, that he could play the songs for his neighbors and charge them money to come and listen. I was wary at first of giving in to his request. I wanted to be considerate of Bikindi's intellectual property rights, but more so, I thought that the distribution of Bikindi's music might be an affront to the RPF, under whose authority I was a guest and in whose good graces I wished to remain. As an excuse, I tried to explain to Julius the proprietary nature of Apple products and how this made it difficult to reproduce recordings off an iPod. It was a flimsy excuse—I had the means to get the song files off the iPod and onto a CD—and Julius seemed none too convinced; in fact, he seemed downright crestfallen. And so I relented.

I asked him, "Are you sure it's okay? I would not want you to get in trouble."

"No, no, it's no problem," he reassured me. "I am Tutsi, I am a survivor. No one is going to accuse me of anything."

We visited again the following year. I asked if he was still listening to the songs on a regular basis. He informed me sadly that a cousin of his had stolen the CD and took it back with her to Uganda. So I gave him another one.

It was a somewhat similar experience with Pierre, a Tutsi, and former politician. *Génocidaires* sliced apart his Achilles tendons and beat him to within a sliver of his life. They then murdered his fiancée as he feebly looked on, crippled and pinned to the ground. Pierre endured the rest of the genocide in a nearly abandoned hospital where, at one point, he says he crawled along the floor through the wards begging the few remaining patients to end his life. When we listened to Bikindi's songs together, a sort of placid calm seemed to come over him. Several times he said, simply, "It is good to remember." Near the end of our visit, he asked for a recording. I was glad to oblige. How could I refuse?

Innocent was twelve years old during the genocide. His mother died when he was an infant, and his father was killed during the genocide. When we met, he worked as a custodian and groundskeeper for a small motel, but earlier in life he had been a street boy who survived through begging, low-level thievery, and the mercy of others. Soon after genocidal killing commenced in Butare, *génocidaires* found him along the road and forced him into a car. They then drove him to a clearing at the base of a hill, where he was to be killed along with numerous other Tutsi. Just as he was about to be killed, a United Nations vehicle appeared at the crest of the hill. The *génocidaires* did not want to be seen murdering children, so they took Innocent and the others into the nearby woods. The other children were stabbed to death. Innocent was severely beaten and was also about to be killed when the *génocidaires* noticed seven thousand Rwandan francs (roughly equivalent to $14) protruding from his back pocket, and so, strangely, took the money and set him free. He eventually found sanctuary with an elderly wealthy woman who paid off the *génocidaires* to leave them alone. Other children also hid in the woman's house. When the RPF arrived in Butare to flush out and capture the *génocidaires*, several of the children ran out of the house, thinking that they had been liberated, and were killed in the crossfire. Innocent cites this as perhaps the most agonizing memory of his ordeal.

For some reason, Innocent insisted that he tell me of his experiences of the genocide before he listened and responded to Bikindi's songs. It took two evenings for him to relay his story to his satisfaction. When he finished, I cued up "Intabaza" on my iPod and handed it to him. Innocent did not recognize it. I then switched over to "Akabyutso." At this, Innocent's eyes opened wide and his body stiffened. He began jabbing at my iPod with his finger, exclaiming in English, "This is it! This is the music of genocide!" It was the first time throughout his testimonial that he outwardly displayed much emotion. He explained that in the months leading up to and during the genocide, he would sometimes hang around outside the town's bars, eavesdropping in on the conversation and collecting whatever information might be useful. He told me that he often heard the patrons listening to "Akabyutso" and singing along with it. Innocent continued listening to the song, and like Pierre, he seemed to enter a more tranquil state, his eyes half-closed and his body softly swaying, and like those patrons at the bar, he too began singing along: "Mbwirabumvaaa . . . yeee."[15]

After listening and reflecting for a while, he stated, "Now, as I hear this song, I go back—the memories of that day come back. It makes me really hate Bikindi—someone like Bikindi, who has been created by God, who has been given the knowledge to save the people, to give them a good message. However, later, he changed, and he gave them a message like this. It hurts me so much." Innocent then continued listening and singing along. When he finished, we spent some time discussing possible interpretations of the song, and Innocent's anger seemed to wane as he became more engrossed in his analysis. As the conversation came to a close late in the evening, Innocent said that he wished he could to listen to Bikindi's music again whenever he wanted but didn't have the means. We agreed to give a CD to our mutual friend and interpreter, Paul, who owned a CD player. Innocent then grew silent. After a moment, he looked at me and said, "Ahhh . . . Jason, I am going to sleep so well tonight, like I have not slept in a long time. I feel such peace now."

"So it's good to tell your story then?" I asked him. "Why is it good? Why does it feel good to tell your story?"

Innocent thought for a moment, and then replied, "Because we just keep some things, many things in our hearts. Sometimes you cannot find someone who will believe you when I tell my story. So if you meet someone who you feel you are now capable of telling your story to, it means that you 'move,' you 'move' those things away. It was just hurting me somewhere. So if you find someone to tell about. . . ." He trailed off into silence.

We rose from the table and said our goodbyes. Innocent then wrapped his arms tightly around me. "Thank you, thank you, my brother," he said over and over. He then strolled off down the dirt road toward the motel where he worked and lived, and as he disappeared into the darkness, I heard him humming to himself. Paul then turned to me and said, "It's amazing. He told me that he has never told anyone of his story before, not even me. Here in Rwanda, we don't talk about these things very often."

Before going further, let me clarify that I am in no position to diagnose Innocent, Pierre, Julius, or anyone else as having post-traumatic stress disorder (PTSD) or any psychopathological condition. People who endure traumatic events will deal with them in their individual ways, and just because someone endured a traumatic event does not invariably mean that they will continue to be traumatized, certainly not in the modern clinical understanding of that term. To conclude that these men suffered from PTSD would require far more time, a more personal relationship, and a more controlled environment than I was afforded, as well as formal training and experience. The only claim I make here is that they did endure a traumatic experience and that it continued to affect them. In narrativizing those experiences and listening to and engaging with music associated with them, they seemed to benefit in some therapeutic way. It brought them a small measure of peace and relief. In light of this, I believe it would have been almost cruel of me to deny their request to own Bikindi's songs.

It was often a different case with my Hutu friends. Take Jean-Baptiste, for example. Three of his brothers were imprisoned on suspicion of genocide-related crimes, though charges were never formally filed. They were eventually released when a lawyer friend who was a Tutsi argued their case. A fourth brother was later given a life sentence. I attended his trial with Jean-Baptiste. The year prior, Jean-Baptiste had traveled four hours over cratered, mountainous roads to acquire a recording of Bikindi's songs from me. When we met at the guesthouse, he appeared uncharacteristically nervous; his shoulders were hunched up, and his face was downcast as he furtively glanced about. He took the recording from me and quickly turned around to travel the four hours back home.

When I visited him again the following year to attend his brother's trial, we had dinner one evening with a group of local priests. I was curious to hear what they thought of Bikindi. As we were enjoying our food and beer, I was about to break out my iPod, which I had in my jeans pocket. Jean-Baptiste noticed what I was about to do, stayed my hand under the table, and gave me a quick warning glance. I apologized to him the next day, and he explained that because his brother was on trial, he, his family, and friends were all under suspicion and it was not safe to discuss Bikindi, much less share his music.

Another Hutu friend and Anglican priest, Charmant, also requested a recording. One day, he took me to share Bikindi's songs with some friends of his who worked at the Murambi Genocide Memorial, each of whom had survived the massacre that had occurred on the grounds there. Even though Charmant's friends were Tutsi survivors of the genocide, when we returned to the guesthouse, my closest Rwandan friend and research colleague, Aaron, was waiting for me. He was upset. After Charmant had left, Aaron said that we should not have done what we did. He went on to explain that because Charmant is Hutu, if people found out he had Bikindi's songs and that the two of us were sharing them with others, it could cast aspersions on Charmant, no matter how unfair that might be. Bear in mind that it was Charmant's choice to own the songs, but it was still my choice to present him the opportunity to own them.

Still, Aaron's rebuke confused me. I had also supplied him with a recording, and he regularly shared the songs openly and publicly when we went out together—for instance, when we would relax at the sauna together or meet up with friends at a restaurant or ride the bus. But Aaron is also well connected to the RPF.

Some time later, another Tutsi friend advised me, point blank, not to hand out any more recordings of Bikindi's songs.

These incidents raise critical questions as to how propaganda should be conceptualized. Propaganda is not merely a material object; it is an expressive and interpretive process, its meaning and influence dependent on context, intentionality, and the identities and experiences of those on the receiving end. Nevertheless, under the vagaries of Rwandan law, and with the paranoid, heavy-handed way the RPF operates, I could be accused of disseminating genocide propaganda.

I did not keep track of how many recordings I gave out—not many, maybe a dozen or so. Most of the recipients were RPF loyalists. A few, in fact, were RPF officials, police, and military officers. A couple of local pop musicians wanted a recording, as did my musician friend mentioned at the beginning of this chapter, mainly because he considered Bikindi a master of traditional Rwandan music and wanted to learn more from his musical stylings. This might be a moot point in that, as of this writing, the songs may now be streamed on YouTube. However, in August 2012, the RPF enacted measures that legally enable it to censor Internet content, monitor people's web activities, and read people's e-mails. This includes online activity conducted with mobile phones.[16]

On December 9, 2010, the Ministry of Education enacted a policy requiring all foreign scholars to obtain research permits at least three months prior to conducting field research in Rwanda. Part of the reason for this, no doubt, is to prevent research that might be subversive of the RPF's goal of ideological conformity. By that point, though, I had already concluded my field research. All that was left was to travel to Tanzania and meet with Bikindi in person at the UN Detention Facility. Otherwise, I am almost certain that I would have been denied permission to carry out my research unless I made clear that my purpose was to denounce Bikindi and somehow establish a clear causal link between his music and the genocide. Even then, I have my doubts. The fact of the matter is that political research on Rwanda is currently in a state of crisis. Field researchers especially are caught in a bind between telling the truth as best as they understand it and protecting their friends and research participants, as well as ensuring that they do not hinder opportunities for other scholars, even if the choice to remain silent enables unjust activities and human rights abuses on the part of the government.

Ethnomusicologists are instilled early on with the ethical imperative to make available our scholarly materials and analyses to those who facilitate or constitute the subjects of our work. Musical repatriation, though, is not always a simple, unilateral exchange free of controversy. Especially where political agendas, postcolonial legacies, and entrenched social conflicts are concerned, issues of human rights, rightful ownership, and the agency of providers and receivers are invariably challenged. Since my time in Rwanda, I have often reflected on and questioned my assumption that musical expression—with the understanding that musical consumption is a form of expression—is a sacred, universal right. For now, I do not know if I did the right thing in providing recordings of Bikindi's songs to Rwandans, yet I know that it would have felt very wrong had I not.

NOTES

1. Out of respect for people's privacy and security, I refer to people only in general terms or use pseudonyms.
2. During the redistricting process of 2006, the Rwandan government changed the name of the town to Huye, though most Rwandans still refer to it as Butare.
3. Radio-Télévision Libre des Mille Collines, or Free Radio-Television of a Thousand Hills (though there was never any television component).
4. In fact, Bikindi's second wife, Angeline Mukabanana, is Tutsi.
5. See *Final Judgment. Simon Bikindi vs. The Prosecutor*. Case No. ICTR-01-72-A, International Criminal Tribunal for Rwanda (ICTR), Arusha, Tanzania, December 2, 2008.
6. Rwandan laws are inscribed in both English and French.
7. Most of the following summary reflects a broadly established and conventional account of the political history of Rwanda (e.g., Newbury 1988; Prunier 1995; Des Forges 1999; Mamdani 2001; Melvern 2006). There is much debate, though, concerning the actions of the RPF in the early 1990s. While there is general consensus that RPF soldiers killed many innocent Rwandan civilians, there is fierce disagreement over how many were killed by the RPF, whether casualties were intentional or not, the motives behind the attacks, and who ordered and had knowledge of the attacks (see Prunier 1998; Reyntjens 2004; Lemarchand 2007; Davenport and Stam 2009).
8. Mouvement Républicain National pour la Démocratie et le Développement, or National Republican Movement for Democracy and Development.
9. These rumors and the idea that Tutsi in Rwanda were traitors would especially gain traction after Melchior Ndadaye, the first democratically elected Hutu president of Burundi, was assassinated by Tutsi soldiers on October 21, 1993. However, this occurred more than six months after Bikindi composed "Intabaza" and "Akabyutso."
10. Coalition pour la Défense de la République.
11. Personal interview, May 26, 2011.
12. Literally, "the one who saves."
13. *Bene* is sometimes translated as "brothers and sisters" or "children" (though the proper Kinyarwanda term for "children" is *abana*). The term connotes a sense of familial intimacy through a shared ancestry, thus my translation as "fellow descendants."
14. *Amoko*, the plural of *ubwoko*, once referred to clans but is used now to refer to ethnicity in Rwanda.
15. *Mbwirabumva* roughly translates as "I speak to those with ears," implying "those who understand." This phrase is repeated often in both "Akabyutso" and "Intabaza."
16. *State of Internet Freedoms in Rwanda 2014: An Investigation into the Policies and Practices Defining Internet Freedom in Rwanda*. Collaboration on International ICT Policy in East and Southern Africa (CIPESA), OpenNet Africa. Available at http://www.cipesa.org/?wpfb_dl=179.

REFERENCES

Amnesty International. 2010. "Vague Laws Used to Criminalise Criticism of the Government in Rwanda" [report]. August 31, 2010. Available at http://www.amnesty.org/en/news-and-updates/report/vague-laws-used-criminalise-criticism-government-rwanda-2010-08-31.

Buckley-Zistel, Susanne. 2006. "Remembering to Forget: Chosen Amnesia as a Strategy for Local Coexistence in Post-Genocide Rwanda." *Africa: The Journal of the International African Institute* 76 (2): 131–150.

Carlsson, Ingvar, Sung-Joo Han, and Rufus M. Kupolati. 1999. *Report of the Independent Inquiry into the Actions of the United Nations during the 1994 Genocide in Rwanda* (S/1999/1257). December 16, 1999.

Davenport, Christian, and Allan C. Stam. 2009. "What Really Happened in Rwanda?" *Miller-McCune*. October 6, 2009. Available at http://politics.virginia.edu/wp-content/uploads/2015/11/Stam-Rwanda-VISC.pdf .

Des Forges, Alison. 1999. *Leave None to Tell the Story: Genocide in Rwanda*. New York: Human Rights Watch.

Lemarchand, René. 2007. "Genocide, Memory and Ethnic Reconciliation in Rwanda." In *L'Afrique des Grand Lacs: Annuaire 2006–2007*, 21–30. Paris: L'Harmattan.

Mamdani, Mahmood. 2001. *When Victims Become Killers: Colonialism, Nativism, and the Genocide in Rwanda*. Princeton, NJ: Princeton University Press.

Melvern, Linda. 2006. *Conspiracy to Murder: The Rwandan Genocide*. London: Verso.

Newbury, Catherine. 1988. *The Cohesion of Oppression: Clientship and Ethnicity in Rwanda, 1860–1960*. New York: Columbia University Press.

Prunier, Gérard. 1995. *The Rwanda Crisis: History of a Genocide*. New York: Columbia University Press.

Prunier, Gérard. 1998. "The Rwandan Patriotic Front." In *African Guerillas*, edited by Christopher Clapham, 119–133. Bloomington: University of Indiana Press.

Reyntjens, Filip. 2004. "Rwanda, Ten Years On: From Genocide to Dictatorship." *African Affairs* 103: 177–210. Available at https://doi.org/10.1093/afraf/adh045.

....

CHAPTER 24

NEW FOLK MUSIC AS ATTEMPTED REPATRIATION IN ROMANIA

....

MAURICE MENGEL

INTRODUCTION

....

WHEN I was in Bucharest in the early 2000s, I interviewed several people, none of them music specialists, about folk music (*muzică populară*)[1] from the socialist[2] period (1948–1989). Pascal Troneci, an elementary teacher in his fifties, was one of several people who told me that the folk music played in the state media was "real folk music" (*muzică populară adevărată*). At the same time, I could hardly convince the ethnomusicologists from the Institut de Etnografie şi Folclor in Bucharest, one of the country's most important folk music archives, to talk about this music at all. My impression was that many Romanian ethnomusicologists avoided my questions concerning folk music in the socialist media and that they did not want to be associated in any way with this kind of music. Instead, they insisted that they were specialists for traditional peasant music, which apparently had nothing to do with the folk music of the media.

The observation that there were two separate domains of Romanian folk music is nothing new (cf. Giurchescu 1987; Rădulescu 1997). Marian-Bălaşa, for example, explains that for many decades Romanian ethnomusicologists tended to use the expression *muzică populară* (popular music) exclusively for commercial folk music in the media, and they reserved the term *folclor muzical* (musical folklore) for traditional peasant music (Marian-Bălaşa 2011b, 6). In this chapter, I argue first that the emergence of these two related domains of folk music was the product of socialist cultural policies and second that these policies attempted to repatriate Romanian folk music. My use of the term "repatriation" to refer to socialist efforts to return a transformed folk music to the Romanian people may seem somewhat surprising. Romanian communists did not typically employ the word "repatriation," and today it is not particularly obvious why the communists thought it necessary and important to bring their version of folk music to the people, especially given that traditional music was still alive and well in parts of Romania. Socialist notions of what this music was and who constituted the people were indeed somewhat peculiar, as I will show. However, they affected many people—musicians, arrangers, composers, listeners, even those who attempted not to listen—and shaped the realities of music-making over many decades. Despite their importance, the cultural policies of the socialist state in Romania have largely been ignored by ethnomusicologists to this date.

The policy regime I describe in this chapter—including its central ideas, its means of legitimation, and the structures that enforced it—essentially remained unchanged from the time it was first declared, just after the communists gained full control of the government in early 1948, Nicolae until Ceaușescu was removed from power in December 1989. The variations that did exist over this time span concerned mainly the enforcement of the policy. For instance, there are two more liberal phases, from circa 1955 to circa 1958 and from 1965 to circa 1971, in which the state permitted artists and intellectuals in general a somewhat greater deviation from official positions. Another change concerned the politics of identity and the notion of the nation that was implied in cultural policies. One finds a shift from Marxist-style internationalism, whose adherents at least rhetorically used the adjective "Romanian" to include the country's minorities in the early socialist phase, to an ultranationalist stance after Ceaușescu's proclamation of the July thesis in 1971, when "Romanian" tended to be interpreted more narrowly as an ethnic category, de facto excluding minorities, a stance reminiscent of trends in the 1930s and 1940s.

In the case of socialist Romania, it is perhaps particularly obvious that policies (goals and guidelines) can differ drastically from the realities they help to create. Thus, I not only talk about official policies but also briefly cover related areas, such as the measures taken by the state to implement and enforce its policies, their reception among parts of the population, and some of their effects on ethnomusicologists.

Throughout this chapter I refer to the Institut de Etnografie și Folclor "Constantin Brăiloiu" (The "Constantin Brăiloiu" Institute for Ethnography and Folklore), as it is known today, its ethnomusicologists, and their work as a case study to illustrate my arguments. The institute was initially founded in 1949 by the young communist government as Institut de Folclor (Folklore Institute), which was based on two older archives including Constantin Brăiloiu's Folklore Archive (Prezidiul Marii Adunări Naționale al Republicii Populare Române 1998–1999, 22; Mengel 2007). Over the years, the institute changed its name several times (cf. Marian-Bălașa 2000b, 143–148). For simplicity, I refer to the institute either with its original or its present-day name, omitting the official labels from the 1970s and 1980s.

CULTURAL POLICY AND FOLK MUSIC

As in other socialist countries, the Romanian communists[3] periodically held party conventions to discuss their recent work and to determine the future course of the party.

Just as in other socialist countries, these congresses were largely orchestrated by the secretary general and the politburo, while other party members had only limited influence (cf. Tismaneanu 2004, 193). Often the proceedings were later published. Today, these texts are not particularly reliable if one reads them as they were originally intended: as accurate reports on the party's work and the country in general. Particularly in the 1980s, when the living conditions for most Romanians were extremely dire, it was obvious that the ever bright and optimistic reports did not match reality. Nevertheless, these reports are perhaps unsurpassed as sources on the official public policies of the times.

In Romanian party congresses, cultural policy never played a major role. The speeches at the congresses were mostly concerned with economic issues and the organization and history of the Communist Party. Even science and education in state institutions, as means to improve economic productivity, received considerably more attention than culture and the arts. If culture and the arts were discussed, then it was usually only very generally, collectively as a facet of society (that whole that for Marxists forms the superstructure). Individual arts were only occasionally singled out. In these cases, literature was the art most often mentioned; more rarely, music, musicians, and composers were. To my knowledge, none of the reports ever explicitly discussed folklore or folk music; but just as in Soviet cultural policy, it was understood that the guidelines elaborated for culture and the arts, in general, were to be translated and transferred to all domains of culture, including folklore and folk music. The task of translating general guidelines to specific fields was left to lower-level state institutions. Thus, although the party congresses did not discuss folk music explicitly, they defined the policy cornerstones for folk music.

Most importantly, perhaps, the party congresses left no doubt that the purpose of the party, the state, and all its institutions was to create communism, the classless utopia originally envisaged by Karl Marx (Partidul Comunist Român 1965, 134). Implicit in this assumption was the idea that current Romanian society was in a phase of drastic and ongoing change from an unjust capitalist past through an already significantly different present to a still more different utopian future.

Indeed, Romania went through massive transformations after the Communists took control. In 1948 a new constitution modeled after Soviet examples took effect (Deletant 2012, 410; cf. Tismaneanu 2004, 107). Nationalization of agriculture, forced industrialization, and programs to intensify industry were begun. There were also forced resettlements, usually from villages deemed archaic to cities conceived of as more modern. The Securitate (Romanian secret police) was created in August 1948 and soon became infamous for its violence (Deletant 2012, 413). Thousands of political prisoners were sent to labor camps, where many died (Deletant 2012, 418). Many Romanians remember this early socialist period as especially tough, arbitrary, and terrifying (Giurchescu 2013; cf. Tismaneanu 2004, 20; Deletant 2012, 413). In this as well, Romanian communists emulated contemporary Stalinist policies (cf. Tismaneanu 2004, 107).

Meanwhile, the cultural sector was reconstructed (cf. Iacob 2009, 255, 257–260). Independent institutions became government institutions. For example, the Folklore

Archive (*arhiva de folclor*), which originally belonged to the private Society of Romanian Composers (Societatea Compositor Român), became a state institution in 1949. As the Institut de Folklor, it reported directly to the Ministry of the Arts and Information (Ministeriul Artelor și Informațiilor) (Prezidiul Marii Adunări Naționale al Republicii Populare Române 1998–1999, 21). The Society of Romanian Composers was similarly transformed into the Composers' Union and later into the Composers' and Musicologists' Union, which closely resembled its Soviet counterpart. After its reorganization, the union actively implemented the state's cultural policy, especially under its first president, Matei Socor, who favored a Soviet hard line similar to Andrei Zhdanov's in the USSR (cf. Crotty 2007, 155).

As one can see in the congress reports, the Romanian communists saw themselves—just like their Soviet counterparts—as the vanguard of the revolution, that is, as representatives of the people and as the motor of social change (Partidul Comunist Român 1965, 134). As such, they claimed leadership in all domains of life, including that of the arts and culture. Put simply, the party reserved the right to determine what appropriate art was and scholarship and what should be supported with state funding, and more generally to judge and steer culture, organizing culture and arts much like the planned economy (cf. Iacob 2009, 256).

Cristian Vasile (2009, 264) wonders why in general the Romanian intelligentsia did not resist more after the communists took control and instead submitted to the new regime without too much resistance, even though the communists with their claim of leadership in all domains of life severely curtailed artistic and intellectual freedom. It appears the Stalinist cultural policy regime that the Romanian communists copied from the Soviet Union had already "matured" to an extent where it ensured a relatively high level of compliance. After more than a decade of right-wing authoritarian regimes in Romania before and during World War II, the authoritarian style of the communist politics may not have looked all that new to many intellectuals.

It appears that roughly the same means of policy enforcement were employed in Romania as in other contemporary Stalinist dictatorships. These measures ranged from actual physical violence to censorship and self-censorship and the withdrawal of privileges necessary for a successful career, such as the possibility to publish or perform or the provision of rewards for complicit behavior (Marian-Bălașa 2013). Examples that illustrate the state's treatment of intellectuals include Harry Brauner, the institute's first director, who was imprisoned in 1950 and placed in solitary confinement for many years, although he never questioned the leadership of the party or their policies (Marian-Bălașa 2000a). Crotty and Sandu-Dediu discuss the case of the composer Mihail Andricu, who was publically shamed in a show trial and stripped of economic and symbolic privileges in 1959 because of his "cosmopolitan lifestyle" (Crotty 2007, 166). Sandu-Dediu (2007, 184) argues Andricu was basically judged for listening to Western music with his students and for having friends in the French embassy. Marian-Bălașa remembers a case where his editor changed his text without his approval, adding quotes from Ceaușescu to increase the likelihood of getting the text through censorship (Marian-Bălașa 2013). This last case underlines the fact that intellectuals often anticipated political influence and adapted their products in advance, while also suggesting that authors were not always entirely responsible for the content of their publications.

If the publications of the Folklore Institute are any indication of cultural policy at large, the state interfered massively with cultural institutions, especially in the early phase of socialism in Romania (c. 1948–1954). Under these conditions, the Folklore Institute managed to publish only a limited number of publications, which all ostensibly complied with the hard-line Soviet-style cultural policy of the day. A case in point is the institute's first folklore anthology, *Din Folclorul Nostru* (Beniuc 1953), which quotes Maxim Gorki on page 1 and mixes classic folklore genres such as folk songs, *colinde* (carols), and ballads with new genres (workers' songs and songs praising socialism). During socialism, leading folklorists, such as the institute's second and third directors Sabin Drăgoi and Mihai Pop, declared these new genres officially to be part of folklore (e.g., Drăgoi 1951, Pop 1956). This new and enlarged notion of folklore was a radical break with previous folklore scholarship, when folklore was nearly always limited to the folklife of Romanian peasants. After Joseph Stalin's death, and after Romanian intellectuals had generally accepted the supremacy of the communist state in cultural matters,[4] the state allowed its intelligentsia somewhat greater freedom as long as the socialist project was not questioned (cf. Crotty 2007, 165). In these years, the Folklore Institute published its own journal and dozens of monographs on a much greater variety of topics than in the previous phase (cf. Raliade 1994).

Returning to the party congress, it is noteworthy that in public statements cultural policy was typically described in vague terms. Only occasionally was a specific aesthetic agenda alluded to, as in this quote from one of Ceauşescu's speeches at the 1965 party congress:

> There is no doubt that authors, painters, composers, and all art- and literature-creating people will not stint with work and talent to create new, valuable works, full of revolutionary humanism and powerful social optimism, which will reflect the multifarious impulses and thoughts, wishes, and endeavors of our people, and of their imperturbable trust in tomorrow, in the future of freedom and the independence of our nation in the communist future.
>
> (Partidul Comunist Român 1965, 100; author's translation)

Ceauşescu's reference to strength and his decidedly optimistic outlook on the future are reminiscent of classic Soviet socialist realism. The fact that he explicitly recognized cultural diversity here illustrates the extent of the relaxation in this period: diversity was allowed as long as it complied with the state's general doctrines. Although this thaw did not change the basic distribution of power, which remained in the hands of a few, many Romanians to this day remember Ceauşescu's first years as a more liberal phase.[5] Also, this quote leaves no doubt that the regime believed Romanian culture should be national, rather than international.

In this section, I used reports from Romanian party congresses to outline basic elements of public cultural policy in socialist Romania. I highlighted that the state consciously aimed to transform society, that the Communist Party claimed the right to decide the course of this transition, and that according to Stalin's dictum of the writers as engineers of the soul, intellectuals were encouraged to collaborate in the task of creating a more socialist society—or in the lingo of the Stalinist period, to aid in the creation of the new man (cf. Sandu-Dediu 2007, 179). How folk musicians and ethnomusicologists could contribute to this task was left open in public-policy discourse, but judging by the quote discussed earlier, it should have quickly become clear to everyone involved that the state desired a socialist realist position from its intellectuals.

Socialist Realism and Folk Music

Recently, several observers have argued that the Soviet socialist realism influenced the arts in Romania in general (Cucu et al. 2013), and musical compositions during the early socialist period specifically (Crotty 2007; Sandu-Dediu 2007). However, these observers do not explain several peculiarities in application of socialist realism to Romania folk music: first, although the concept of socialist realism clearly influenced Romanian musical life, the expression itself was rarely if ever used in Romanian discourse. For example, in a discussion between composers about a proposed resolution that would mirror Zhdanov's resolution on music, the term is not used a single time (cf. reprints in Cosma 1995a, 1995b), even though the discussion revolved around the very criteria that make up musical socialist realism. Among these were the rejection of formalism and Western influences in favor of accessibility, the embrace of an optimistic outlook celebrating the proletariat and socialism's achievements, and a generally heroic tone (cf. Zhdanov 2003, 427–428).

In my interpretation, Romanian discourse often, although not always, camouflaged Romania's dependence on the Soviet Union as the quasi-colonizer. This camouflage accounts for discourse in the early period, before the Soviet Union withdrew its army from Romania in the 1950s, but also for later times, when nationalist sentiments were on the rise and Romanians did not like to be reminded of Soviet domination. Accordingly, Soviet names, quotes, and key terms were routinely avoided in large parts of the discourse—for example, in many scholarly articles—while other parts, especially editorials or introductions, often made clear references to Soviet models.

A second peculiarity not yet sufficiently explored in the literature is how the concept of socialist realism applied to the practice of folk music. Perhaps the most evident new trend in Romanian folk music in the early socialist period were the folk orchestras and folk dance ensembles that often performed together and were often organized as a single large ensemble (Popescu-Județ 1995). There had been folk ensembles in Romania since long before the 1940s, such as the *taraf* (pl. *tarafuri*), an ensemble type which in the nineteenth century often featured several violins, *nai* (panflute), *cobza* (a short-neck lute), and in the twentieth century several violins, *țambal* (cimbalom, a stick-struck board zither), accordion, and double bass. However, these older ensemble types, often with a dozen or fewer musicians, were considerably smaller than the new folk orchestras, which in the early socialist period sometimes boasted a membership of over a hundred musicians (Alexandru 2007).

Making the new folk orchestras the central showcase for new folk music was a significant break with earlier traditions in representing Romanian folklore. Up to the socialist period, there had been hardly any Romanian scholarship on ensembles such as *tarafuri*, indicating that they were not perceived as a particularly important part of Romanian folk music. Perhaps the relative omission of *tarafuri* from scholarship was because in the twentieth century they often performed in urban contexts, while Romanian scholarship focused on rural settings. Alternatively, perhaps *tarafuri* were not intensively studied because their musicians—usually referred to as *lăutari* (sing. *lăutar*)—were often Roma, while Romanian scholarship tended to focus on non-Roma Romanian peasants. In any case, around 1950 the folk orchestras were so new that even the most basic questions still had to be debated. Composers, for example, still discussed in 1952 whether Romanian folk music could and should be accompanied using harmony or with instruments at all (Cosma 1995b, 85–86). Similarly, in 1954 the institute's director still had to cite recent research to argue that the music played by *lăutari* could be considered Romanian folk music at all:

> A problem that has occupied and still occupies our musicians is that of the *lăutari* folklore (*folclor lăutăresc*) that is often used in the creations of our composers and [also] broadcasted with preference on our radio stations. To clarify this issue the [Folklore] Institute has intensively researched an important group of *lăutari* from near Bucharest. From this research it was found that the musicians performed folk music (*muzică populară*).
>
> (Drăgoi 1954, 7; author's translation)[6]

Barbu Lăutaru, one of the first folk orchestras in the country, was created during this early experimental phase. Named after a famous nineteenth-century Moldovian *lăutar* who possibly performed for Franz Liszt (Ciobanu 1958, 101–102), the orchestra officially belonged to the Folklore Institute until 1952–1953 (Marian-Bălaşa 2000b, 144). Later it was relocated to a different state institution (Drăgoi 1954, 5; cf. Marian-Bălaşa 1999, 12).

Listening to recordings of the Barbu Lăutaru orchestra, such as *Rapsodia Romina: Monitor Presents the Barbu Lautaru Orchestra* (2007), one can argue that this new style of folk music took an optimistic stance, rather than presenting sentimental, gloomy, or critical reflection. Correspondingly, ritual folk music including laments or the often sad or sentimental genre of *doine* (a type of sung folk music that in Romania is not usually regarded as song although it is sung) were not often performed in socialist Romania, especially in the early period. Instead, the happier folk songs and dance tunes stood in the center of the repertoire, often enriched by newly created genres that would not previously have been regarded as folklore. These included patriotic songs (such as the composition "Hora Unirii") and those that praise the achievements of socialism, as illustrated in the already mentioned collection *Din Folclorul Nostru*.

On socialist stages, folk orchestras were often accompanied by dance ensembles that performed elaborate choreography, typically joining different dances from a particular region together into a single suite (Forner 1995). Gheorghe Popescu-Judeţ and his wife, Eugenia, were among the most successful choreographers for state-run folk dance ensembles in the period between 1949 and 1970. As dancers, they won an international prize for character dance in Prague in 1950, a category sometimes associated with the Soviet choreographer Igor Moiseyev and his fusion of ballet with folk dance elements (Forner 1995; cf. Shay 2002, 57–67). In Romania, Gheorghe Popescu-Judeţ choreographed primarily for the Ciocîrlia ensemble, which officially belonged to the Ministry of the Interior, while his wife, Eugenia, primarily choreographed for the Perinita ensemble (Popescu-Judeţ 1995). There are no detailed analyses of staged Romanian folk music and folk dance from the early socialist period, but it seems that in Romania—as in other countries that were under the influence of the Soviet Union at the time—a Soviet aesthetic was imported that provided a framework for bringing rural traditions to big stages (cf. Silverman 1983, 56, 59; Rice 1994, 176; Buchanan 2006, 244–245).

To give one example of how the Soviet model influenced Romanian staged folk dance, Eugenia recounts how the Russian choreographer Ivan Korilov suggested changes to Gheorghe's dance notation system on a visit to Bucharest in 1950. Specifically, the choreographer wanted them to also notate the work of the passive foot and not only the active one, emphasizing a tendency to more accurate transcriptions (Popescu-Judeţ 1995). It seems likely that this interaction illustrates not only the migration of a single technicality in a specific notation system but also the larger importation of an aesthetic system for staged performances. Anca Giurchescu characterizes Gheorghe Popescu-Judeţ's choreographies as an imitation of Moiseyev's style and recalls that Gheorghe treated folklore as "raw material that had to be collected, selected, and reworked (re-created) to raise its artistic level" (Giurchescu 2013).

Overall, the new style—both in dance and music—featured accessibility for the audience while performers show great technical virtuosity (e.g., relatively simple and symmetrical melodies and dance moves, but at extremely high tempo). Other characteristics include the use of large ensembles in which the performers play or dance together with extreme precision and facility, as well as a fusion of musical material from oral culture with compositional techniques and performance practices from the written culture of art music and ballet dance.

If socialist realism in music meant "all that is heroic, bright, and beautiful" and "musical images full of beauty and strength" (Gorodinsky quoted by Schwarz 1973, 114), then Romanian communists tried hard to create a new folk music tradition that mirrored these features.

REACTIONS

While in the early days the new style of folk music was pioneered mostly by professional folk orchestras (alone or accompanied by a vocalist) and their dance ensembles, the new optimistic and uncritical performance style later spread to other genres of folk music in socialist Romania, transported and promoted by a wide range of state institutions such as the state-run ensembles, the state-run media, and Electrecord, the country's state-owned and only record label. The state also provided facilities for amateurs who wanted to engage in folk music and dance, primarily through community centers (*cămine culturale*) and houses of culture (*case de cultura*), as well as festivals and competitions (cf. Giurchescu 1987, 163–171).

Examples discussed by Paul Nixon (1998, 14–16) and the Romanian ethnomusicologist Speranța Rădulescu (1997, 107–108) suggest that most performances—especially those that reached a large audience—occurred within state institutions (state-run ensembles, concert halls, festivals, competitions, houses of culture, the radio, TV) and that for prizes, for broadcasting, or for bigger stages the state nearly always actively selected those performances that embodied the new style, rather than the more traditional forms of peasant culture.

Rădulescu, born in 1949 and graduated in 1973, remembers that she never heard "traditional peasant music" until she was already employed as a researcher at the Institute for Folklore and Ethnography. Even as a researcher at the institute, she found recordings of such music only after several months of "determined digging in the archives" (Rădulescu 1997, 9). According to her, intellectuals other than ethnomusicologists in general did not know or remember traditional peasant music. Her account suggests that the policies of the socialist state by and large replaced the old traditions of folk music with their new socialist realist counterparts. Rădulescu also leaves no doubt that most intellectuals hated this new folk music that was propagated by the media:

> [T]hese radio stations, eventually joined by television, used [...] to submit us to impressive infusions of "Romanian popular music" and "folklore." Every time I heard this folklore, I turned my set off; I disliked it to the point of nausea. Moreover, nobody in the group that I frequented, made up of musicians and modest intellectuals, showed for it anything but a mixture of disdain and disgust.
>
> (Rădulescu 1997, 8)

Even considering that retrospective recollection is not necessarily a reliable indicator of musical taste, my interviews confirm that Romanian intellectuals nearly always disassociate themselves from folk music of the state, sometimes even to this day. Correspondingly, these observations indicate that the people who did enjoy the socialist folk music tended to be less-educated listeners who looked back to the countryside with nostalgia.

As Giurchescu already observed many years ago, the socialist state attempted to use folk music because of its association with the Romanian nation, to make itself appear to be the legitimate Romanian state (1987, 169). This need for legitimation explains the nearly ubiquitous use of folk culture and folk music by the socialist state: for example, the massive competition and festival Cîntarea României, which involved millions of Romanians every year from the event's inception in 1975 until its termination in 1989 (Giurchescu 1987, 164). Another example is the frequent presence of socialist realist folk music in the newspaper *Scînteia* as the communist mouthpiece, where one finds articles on folk music every few issues. It seems that especially in the last decade of socialist Romania, the association of the socialist state with the nation was rejected by growing parts of the population. People increasingly identified the folk music of the media with the contemporary political system, which lost even more credibility when living standards plummeted during the 1980s.

It is evident that in a Stalinist dictatorship like Ceaușescu's Romania there was little room for resisting official policies without risking drastic punishments. It is perhaps less obvious that in such situations even quite small symbolic actions often became acts of resistance. Sabina Paula Pieslak discusses a musical example of resistance when she analyzes *colinde* (carol) performances by Madrigal, the leading early-music ensemble in socialist Romania. Like other ensembles, Madrigal was controlled by the state. For example, the ensemble was accompanied by Securitate officers on tours outside Romania, and the concert programs had to be approved by state officials (Pieslak 2007b, 225). Usually, the ensemble was not allowed to perform *colinde* because the genre was considered too religious—or, perhaps, because the performance would have been considered too traditional and not socialist realist enough. For a performance outside Romania, however, *colinde* were approved, and recordings of this performance made their way to Romania. Listening to these recordings of *colinde* was illegal and consequently signified resisting the state. Eventually, Madrigal's *colinde* were played during the so-called revolution of 1989 to signify the end of the Ceaușescu regime (Pieslak 2007a, 178; 2007b, 227–232).

Viewed within this context, the Romanian ethnomusicologists did not have much leeway for resistance without the risk of losing their careers or spending time in jail. Many of them occasionally also "serviced" the state in their applied work—for example, by reviewing new recordings in the socialist realist style or participating in folk music juries (cf. Rădulescu 1997, 10; Nixon 1998, figure 1). The institute's ethnomusicologists typically attempted to resist the state by carving out research topics that would pass censorship, but which their colleagues would not associate too much with socialist policies. Such topics included the history of folk music scholarship in Romania—for example, highlighting Anton Pann's and Béla Bartók's contributions (e.g., Pann 1955; Alexandru 1958). Other relatively inconspicuous topics were the study of folk music instruments (Alexandru 1956), although this topic also found practical use in the creation of folk orchestras at the time. Perhaps the most esteemed text genre, and the one with the least obvious political connotations for its perceived objectivity, was the ethnographic monograph, a descriptive anthology that typically would focus on traditional peasant music and cover one or several genres of folk music for a small region (e.g., Comişel 1959). Another strategy of emphasizing relative independence from the state for many ethnomusicologists was to create links to Brăiloiu and prewar folklore scholarship in general, since it was of presocialist origin. I believe that in this context Romanian ethnomusicologists began to interpret adherence to old prewar topics and methods as resisting socialist pressures and hence as a marker of good scholarship, a habit that is still visible in present-day Romania. After an initial innovative period in which ethnomusicologists found new topics that were meaningful to both the new socialist research framework and the presocialist research traditions (mostly from the 1950s and 1960s), conceptual or methodological innovation became rare in Romanian ethnomusicology, while Brăiloiu and other classics in Romanian folkloristics remained continually in fashion.

Conclusions

From the perspective of the communists, traditional folk music as it had developed over generations was not particularly well suited for the transformation of socialist society. As a product of a capitalist period, it was thought to mirror an undesirable economic system and did not in itself deserve any preservation efforts. In fact, there were no significant efforts to preserve traditional culture and folk music in socialist Romania, except perhaps for the passive documentation of traditions by ethnomusicologists and other academics. Nonetheless, as Groys (1992, 37–38) emphasizes for the Soviet Union, within socialist realism artists were encouraged to mine the artistic and cultural traditions of previous centuries to produce new socialist art. True to this idea, in Romania the communists encouraged the same quasi-colonial process: local raw material—here rural Romanian folk music—was "exported" to the cities; "processed" by scholars, composers, and arrangers, and others according to the foreign ideology of a socialist realism; and then finally "reimported" to the Romanian population through state institutions. For the state, the sole value of traditional peasant music, then, was as a resource in the process of making new socialist art.

Essentially, this process is one of repatriation: the socialists removed folk music from its home contexts, "updated" it to reflect the ideals of socialist realism, and then returned it to the Romanian population—and not only to the peasants who had made the presocialist folk music, but to every citizen.

It is not uncommon that the process of musical repatriation changes some of the music's earlier qualities. For instance, socialist repatriation in Romania changed traditions when they were put on stage and broadcast via the media. Since this repatriation was typically organized by the state, dictated from above, and sometimes acted out against the will of communities that still lived the traditions in question, the introduction of the new socialist realist policy regime sometimes destroyed existing traditions. Thus, if the Romanian case is different from other musical repatriations, then perhaps it is because the new socialist folk music sometimes replaced older traditions almost entirely. Another difference is that here the state, as the main agent, used immense resources to make repatriation happen; practically all state institutions, even the secret police, participated in the process.

Despite these resources, the repatriation was clearly not completely successful. Socialism's high expectations of making society more equal and just failed; socialist realist folk music did not gain a substantial audience over time. In the long term, the general appreciation of folk culture even decreased, especially in the final years of the regime. To this day, folk music in Romania is sometimes perceived in political and nationalist ways that resemble the communist and other nationalist periods. This phenomenon becomes perhaps most obvious in the xenophobic reactions to *manele*, a genre of popular music often associated with Roma musicians, in which the old racist ideas of a mono-ethnic Romania resurface (cf. Marian-Bălaşa 2011a, 316). However, perhaps it is noteworthy that the effects of socialist realist folk music—especially in the first few decades—could have been considered a success in a different context. The new policy regime increased access to music education for many Romanians and over the years a substantial number of people enjoyed the state-supported folk music, even finding a musical "home" in this music.

It is noteworthy that ethnomusicologists and music archives had a significant position in this repatriation. Ethnomusicologists were one of the very few groups the socialist state allowed and even encouraged to access and contribute to both domains, the old traditions and the new folk music. Only through this position—which was achieved through expertise gained in the field and in the archive—did they have the authority to authenticate the new traditions for the socialist state, as they did for instance when acting as jurors or writing LP cover texts for popular artists. Although the state was powerful and the dictatorship threatened uncooperative ethnomusicologists with drastic penalties, they did have some freedom to decide their own level of cooperation with the state.

Often when I tried to talk with Romanian ethnomusicologists, musicologists, or musicians about socialist cultural policy in the late 1990s and the early 2000s, I got only vague responses. It was often implied that socialist policies were absurd, that the representatives of the communist state were incompetent in musical matters, and that the whole political talk that was required during the socialist period was *limba de lemn*— literally, "wooden tongue or speech." I took this expression to mean a required, rhetorical, but essentially meaningless bureaucratic exercise. Hence I was surprised when I discovered that the official socialist discourse on folklore and folk music was in itself consistent; that many of the state's measures, which in the accounts of participants seemed arbitrary, were in fact derived from more general policies; and that even these general policies were often grounded in a socialist worldview. In these respects, the socialist cultural policy regime is no different from policy regimes in other political contexts. Socialist cultural policy was not the arbitrary product of a mad ruler; it inherited more from the modern state and the modern mode of governmentality than many people like to hear.

I do not argue in favor of socialist policies, their goals, or the means employed; rather I argue that if one tries to understand folk music in socialist Romania—even the more traditional peasant music in many rural settings—one simply cannot ignore the state without significantly distorting cultural history. Not only was the state the most powerful actor in the cultural domain (via its institutions and their employees), but it also consciously attempted to radically transform society, including the spheres of folklore and folk music, and it invested considerable resources to this end. Outside of Romania, this conclusion may be old hat, given that the state is an important topic in landmark publications of early postsocialist ethnomusicology (e.g., Rice 1994; Slobin 1996). However, until recently there was not a lot of data available to make a similar case for Romania. Unsurprisingly, perhaps, the picture that does emerge for Romania shows parallels to other countries, particularly in Eastern Europe, but also elsewhere in the socialist world. If one focuses less on sound and more on policy, it is obvious that many countries experienced similar trends originating from the Soviet Union, particularly at the beginning of the Cold War.

There is a lesson here that may apply to other musical repatriations. Repatriation often happens within larger ideological frameworks. In Romania, the socialists tried to profit from the people's identification of folk music with the Romanian nation, but ultimately they attained nearly the opposite effect: many people identified new folk music with the socialist state they rejected. Other musical repatriations are similarly embedded in conceptual frameworks—for example, a postcolonial impetus to compensate for the wrongs of the past. The Romanian example suggests that musical repatriations succeed, perhaps even without expensive publicity efforts, when the parties involved in the exchange and the communities they represent share the underlying values of the project's larger ethical dimension and can openly communicate those values to their constituents.

Notes

1. In this chapter I use the English term "folk music" as the translation of Romanian *muzică populară* (lit. popular music) and semantically related terms such as *folclor muzical* (musical folklore) to refer to things that sometimes are described as folk music.
2. I use "socialism" to refer to the political system that existed in Romania from 1948 to 1989 and to label this period. I use "communist" for members of a communist party and anybody officially representing a communist-led state.
3. After a fusion with another party, the Romanian Communist Party (Partidul Comunist Român) was renamed the Romanian Workers' Party (Partidul Muncitoresc Român) in 1948. In 1965 the old name was restored (Tismaneanu 2004, 93, 194).
4. It is not clear whether Stalin's death in 1953 caused any direct changes in Romanian politics. When Nikita Khrushchev announced his program of de-Stalinization in 1956 at the twentieth convention of the Communist Party of the Soviet Union in Moscow, Gheorghe Gheorghiu-Dej, the Romanian secretary general who was present at the meeting, was appalled by Khrushchev's reforms and prevented Romania from taking a similar course (Tismaneanu 2004, 143–148), so that one cannot simply attribute the relative cultural relaxation from the early 1950s in Romania to Stalin's death. However, Khrushchev's reforms

limited the Soviet Union's influence over Romania, as exemplified by the withdrawal of Soviet troops from Romania under his reign. In this respect the first Soviet thaw did change the political climate in Romania significantly, and it allowed Romanian politicians to take a more nationalist position (cf. Tismaneanu 2004, 167).

5. The thaw around Ceauşescu's early years in power in the mid-1960s was both real and superficial. It never limited Ceauşescu's power (Tismaneanu 2004, 193), generally Stalinist policies remained in place, but there were noticeable shifts particularly in the cultural domain and in the connections with Western countries. For example, I remember seeing Rolling Stones albums from this period in record collections in Bucharest. Also, US folklorists visited Romania and Romanian folklorists were allowed to travel to the United States. And only in this period of socialism, Romanian ethnomusicologists published book-length anthologies on some of Romania's minorities (Roma, Tartars).

6. "O problemă care a preocupat şi mai preocupă încă pe muzicienii noştri este aceea a folklorului [sic] lăutăresc folosit adesea în creaţiile compozitorilor noştri şi difuzat cu preferinţă la posturile noastre de radio. Pentru a lămuri această problemă Institutul a făcut o cercetare aprofundată unui important grup de lăutari din apropierea Bucureştilor. Din această cercetare s-a constatat că muzica executata de lăutari este muzica populară."

REFERENCES

Alexandru, Tiberiu. 1956. *Instrumentele muzicale ale popurului romîn*. Bucharest: Editura de stat pentru literatură şi artă (ESPLA).

Alexandru, Tiberiu. 1958. *Bela Bartok despre folclorul romînesc*. Bucharest: Editura Muzicală.

Alexandru, Tiberiu. 2007 (reissue). "About the orchestra (liner notes)." In *Rapsodia Romina: Monitor Presents the Barbu Lautaru Orchestra*. Monitor MFS 377. http://media. smithsonianfolkways.org/liner_notes/monitor/MON00377.pdf.

Beniuc, Mihail. 1953. *Din folclorul nostru: Culegere de texte şi melodii*. [Bucharest:] Editura de Stat pentru Literatură şi Artă.

Buchanan, Donna A. 2006. *Performing Democracy: Bulgarian Music and Musicians in Transition*. Chicago: University of Chicago Press.

Ciobanu, Gheorghe. 1958. "Barbu Lăutarul." *Revista de Folclor* 3 (4): 99–133.

Comişel, Emilia, ed. 1959. *Antologie folclorică din ţinutul Pădurenilor (Hunedoara)*. [Bucharest]: Editura Muzicală. Alcătuită de un grup de folclorişti din cadrul Institului de Folclor, condus de Emilia Comişel.

Cosma, Octavian L. 1995a. "Uniunea compozitorilor şi muzicologilor din România—75 de ani: Arhiva Societăţii Compozitorilor Români." Şedinţa Comitetului din 18 februarie 1934. *Muzica*, n.s., 6 (1): 111–133.

Cosma, Octavian L. 1995b. "Uniunea Compozitorilor şi Muzicologilor din România—75 de ani: Arhiva Uniunii (2)." Rezoluţia din 1952. *Muzica* 6 (3): 73–99.

Crotty, Joel. 2007. "A Preliminary Investigation of Music, Socialist Realism, and the Romanian Experience, 1948–1959: (Re)reading, (Re)listening, and (Re)writing Music History for a Different Audience." *Journal of Musicological Research* 26 (2–3): 156–176.

Cucu, Vasile S., Keith A. Hitchins, Ernest Latham Jr., and David Turnock. 2013. "Romania." *Encyclopaedia Britannica*. Online Academic Edition. http://www.britannica.com/EBchecked/topic/508461/Romania (accessed December 6, 2013).

Deletant, Dennis. 2012. "România sub regimul comunist (Decembrie 1947–Decembrie 1989)." In *Istoria României*, edited by Mihaiş D. D. Bărbulescu, Keith Hitchins, Şerban Papacostea, and Pompiliu Teodor, 407–480. Bucharest: Grupul Editorial Corint.

Drăgoi, Sabin V. 1951. "Noua creaţie populară." *Muzica* 2 (2): 15–19.

Drăgoi, Sabin V. 1954. "Cinci ani de activitate a Institutului de Folclor: O sărbătoare a folcloriştilor noştri." *Muzica* 5 (6): 5–9.

Giurchescu, Anca. 1987. "The National Festival 'Song in Romania': Manipulations of Symbols in the Political Discourse." In *Symbols of Power: The Aesthetics of Political Legitimation in the Soviet Union and Eastern Europe*, edited by Claes Arvidsson and Lars E. Blomqvist, 163–171. Stockholm: Almqvist & Wiksele.

Giurchescu, Anca. 2013. Interview by Maurice Mengel. Electronic communication. October 2013.

Groys, Boris. 1992. *The Total Art of Stalinism: Avant-garde, Aesthetic Dictatorship, and Beyond*. Princeton, NJ: Princeton University Press.

Iacob, Bogdan C. 2009. "Avatars of the Romanian Academy and the Historical Front: 1948 versus 1955." In *Stalinism Revisited: The Establishment of Communist Regimes in East-Central Europe*, edited by Vladimir Tismaneanu, 255–281. Budapest and New York: Central European University Press.

Marian-Bălaşa, Marin. 1999. "Institutul 'Brăiloiu' în contextul evoluţiei etnologiei Româneşti: O istorie prescurtată." *Revista de Etnografie şi Folclor* 44 (1): 9–18.

Marian-Bălaşa, Marin. 2000a. "Harry Brauner: Field Collector, Director, Victim, and Love." *European Meetings in Ethnomusicology* 7:83–192.

Marian-Bălaşa, Marin. 2000b. "Romanian Traditional Identity as Searched by the Brăiloiu Institute." *European Meetings in Ethnomusicology* 7: 127–182.

Marian-Bălaşa, Marin. 2011a. "Manelişti şi antimanelişti (sau despre muzică şi segregare în cultura şi societatea românească)." In *Muzicologii, etnologii, subiectivităţi, politici*, edited by Marin Marian-Bălaşa, 302–322. Bucharest: Editura Muzicală.

Marian-Bălaşa, Marin. 2011b. "Sistematic şi aleator în antologiile şi monografiile etnomuzicale." In *Muzicologii, etnologii, subiectivităţi, politici*, edited by Marin Marian-Bălaşa, 12–47. Bucharest: Editura Muzicală.

Marian-Bălaşa, Marin. 2013. Interview by Maurice Mengel. Electronic communication, November 26.

Mengel, Maurice. 2007. "The Age of Archives in Early Romanian Ethnomusicology: Towards a Paradigm of the Archive between 1927 and 1943." *European Meetings in Ethnomusicology* 12: 146–168.

Nixon, Paul. 1998. *Sociality, Music, Dance: Human Figurations in a Transylvanian Valley*. Göteborg: Göteborg University.

Pann, Anton. 1955. *Cîntece de lume: Transcrise din psaltică în notaţia modernă*. With the assistance of G. Ciobanu. Bucharest: Editura de stat pentru literatură şi artă (ESPLA). Cu un studiu introductiv de Gh. Ciobanu.

Partidul Comunist Român. 1965. "IX. Parteitag der Rumänischen Kommunistischen Partei, 19–24." July 1965. Berlin: Dietz.

Pieslak, Sabina P. 2007a. "A Political History of Romanian Colinde (Carols)." PhD diss., University of Michigan.

Pieslak, Sabina P. 2007b. "Romania's Madrigal Choir and the Politics of Prestige." *Journal of Musicological Research* 26 (2): 215–240.

Popescu-Judeţ, Eugenia. 1995. Interview by Michelle Forner. Archive of Folk Culture, American Folklife Center, Library of Congress. Gheorghe and Eugenia Popescu-Judetz Collection (AFC1990/022-57). Washington, DC, March 28.

Pop, Mihai. 1956. "Problemele şi perspectivele folcloristicii noastre." *Revista de Folclor* 1 (1–2): 9–35.

Prezidiul Marii Adunări Naţionale al Republicii Populare Române. 1998–99. "Decretul nr. 136 din 6 aprilie 1949" (reprint). *Anuar Institutului De Etnografie şi Folclor "Constantin Brăiloiu"* 9–10: 31–32.

Rădulescu, Speranţa 1997. "Traditional Musics and Ethnomusicology: Under Political Pressure: The Romanian Case." *Anthropology Today* 13 (6): 8–12.

Raliade, Rodica 1994. "Bibliografiei 'Revistei de Etnografie şi Folclor (1981–1993).'" *Revista de Etnografie şi Folclor* 39 (3–4): 329–380.

Rapsodia Romina: Monitor Presents the Barbu Lautaru Orchestra in Hora Staccato and Other Romanian Dances. Monitor; Smithsonian Folkways, 2007 (reissue), CD.

Rice, Timothy. 1994. *May It Fill Your Soul: Experiencing Bulgarian Music*. Chicago: University of Chicago Press.

Sandu-Dediu, Valentina. 2007. "Dodecaphonic Composition in 1950s and 1960s Europe: The Ideological Issue of Rightist or Leftist Orientation." *Journal of Musicological Research* 26 (2–3): 177–192.

Schwarz, Boris. 1973. *Music and Musical Life in Soviet Russia, 1917–1970*. New York: Norton.

Shay, Anthony. 2002. *Choreographic Politics: State Folk Dance Companies, Representation and Power*. Middletown, CT: Wesleyan University Press.

Silverman, Carol. 1983. "The Politics of Folklore in Bulgaria." *Anthropological Quarterly* 56 (2): 55–61.

Slobin, Mark, ed. 1996. *Retuning Culture: Musical Changes in Central and Eastern Europe*. Durham, NC: Duke University Press.

Tismaneanu, Vladimir. 2004. *Stalinism for All Seasons: A Political History of Romanian Communism*. Berkeley: University of California Press.

Vasile, Cristian. 2009. "Propaganda and Culture in Romania at the Beginning of the Communist Regime." In *Stalinism Revisited: The Establishment of Communist Regimes in East-Central Europe*, edited by Vladimir Tismaneanu, 367–385. Budapest and New York Central European University Press.

Zhdanov, Andrei. 2003. "Speech to the Congress of Soviet Writers [1934]." In *Art in Theory, 1900–2000: An Anthology of Changing Ideas*, edited by Charles Harrison and Paul Wood, 426–429. Malden, MA: Blackwell.

CHAPTER 25

....

THE POLITICS
OF REPATRIATING
CIVIL WAR BRASS MUSIC

....

ELIZABETH WHITTENBURG OZMENT

INTRODUCTION

....

IN the last few decades, a small segment of white American men across the United States with considerable amounts of leisure time and disposable income have dedicated many resources to researching, purchasing, refurbishing, and performing US Civil War brass music. In doing so, they contribute to the commodification and circulation of a partisan national origin story that celebrates the exceptionalism of a particular American sub-group with whom they identify.

I argue that this performance of Civil War music can be fruitfully conceptualized as an act of repatriation. Although the notion of repatriation has traditionally been limited to returning dispossessed objects to disenfranchised communities, what happens when dominant social groups appropriate that model and use it to engage in cultural reclamation and musical revival?

It is important to distinguish between repatriation and revival, as I employ these terms. Revival is a mimetic process that stimulates heritage by representing cultural practices that proponents associate with the past and believe to be endangered.[1]

My exploration of these issues is informed by ethnographic data collected from 2010 to 2014 from brass band collectors, performers, and audiences at the Cornets and Cannons Civil War Sesquicentennial Music Festival, Gettysburg Remembrance Day Commemorations, Berkley Plantation commemoration of *Taps*, both Shiloh 150th anniversary battle reenactments, an annual Cornet Conspiracy gathering, and nearly a dozen other concerts, reenactments, and observances, all related to Civil War memory. Most informants with whom I had close interactions self-identified as upper middle class, highly educated, white, male American citizens over the age of forty, most of whom were either raised or resided on the East Coast and who had an ancestor who fought in the Civil War.[2] These informants generously shared their time and knowledge with me, and I am grateful for their willingness to contribute their perspectives and many intimate details about their hobby and personal lives. Like other elements of the Civil War reenactment movement, these brass band revivalists are deeply invested in the preservation of Civil War–era history and music. They experience personal pleasure from their hobby and believe it to be their responsibility to preserve the memory of the war. Although most of my informants had never met each other, they sincerely believed in the existence of a close-knit community founded on a shared interest in Civil War brass music. While I respect these hobbyists for their musical skills and uncompromising commitment to their cause, it quickly became apparent that more was at stake in their revival than merely the preservation of musical artifacts.

I focus my analysis particularly on one subgroup of Civil War brass revivalists who collectively own approximately 2,000 Civil War–era instruments, many traceable to period instrument makers, regimental bands, and historical individuals. They call themselves the "Cornet Conspiracy," a name that refers to the competition for instruments that ultimately kindled their friendship.[3] These men found each other while competing for antique brass instruments on eBay. One member of the "Cornet Conspiracy" describes on his blog how he became an eBay relic hunter: "I wanted badly to collect vintage brass . . . but these were the days before the Internet and eBay, and you had to visit a lot of antique stores in Florida before you'd find an old horn of any type. It was largely a matter of luck. . . . My first authentic vintage pocket cornets [were] a J. W. Pepper Gautrot, and a rare Boosey E-flat. This was in the course of collecting all types of vintage cornets which became an obsession just short of addiction, starting in 1998 when eBay hit."[4] Collectors shared with me similar origin stories that highlighted their shift to eBay bidding. "What started this [collecting]? Mark Elrod's *Pictorial History*. First book that turned me on to the keyed bugle. I purchased an instrument on eBay and then learned how to play it. . . . This keyed bugle [pointing to his horn] I bought on eBay and had restored by R—. Now I perform with [three] bands."[5]

A common obsession for Civil War brass music drove these men and other collectors to spend enough time on eBay that their bidding wars became a form of socialization and competitive community-making. As the men began to recognize the usernames of other relic-hunters, they sent threatening eBay messages to each other while bidding on auction lots. Said one collector, "We met through eBay. Seriously, we were sending each other hate-grams."[6] Competition for instruments only intensified their sense of individual and community purpose. While tracking other collectors' bidding histories, they gathered data about each other and discovered themselves to be middle-aged white American men who resided in New York, Ohio, Alaska, Texas, Kentucky, Georgia, and Florida, who share a considerable amount of expendable income, leisure time, and investment in Civil War memory. They traveled in 2001 to Gainesville, Florida, for their first annual meeting to compare their collections, and it was during this gathering that they "conspired" to cooperatively hunt for particular types of objects as a strategy to enlarge their individual and group instrument collections. The fetishes and skills of each man contributed a different expertise to the club.[7] Said one member, "We were fighting over instruments on eBay until we decided it was OK to let each other have instruments if we were able to play them together."[8] This gentlemen's agreement founded an exclusive community that is recognized within the larger brass revival community as including some of the most accomplished collectors and performers of Civil War music.[9]

Brass revivals are not merely about reclaiming objects but also a reaction to a shared sense of lost or missing cultural heritage. As instrument collection and performance realizes the sonic possibilities of these artifacts, intangible expressions of the impulse to repatriate also occur. The correspondence and friendship of the Cornet Conspiracy on eBay eventually led to their collaboration to return American Civil War music to locations (both metaphorical and literal) where they believe that this heritage should reside. Some of their philanthropic efforts include the donation of material musical culture to heritage organizations, museums, and archives, as well as the establishment and managing of performing ensembles. These activities were often conducted with the intent of encouraging descendants of Civil War soldiers to engage with what they believe to be a significant and unique heritage.[10]

The primary strategy by which brass revivalists recreate an audible heritage is to impersonate mid-nineteenth-century military bandsmen in sound and appearance. This is a form of escapism, creating an artificial experience of time and an opportunity to socialize with like-minded people. In a way similar to what Thomas Turino has described in other revivals, "the community isn't imagined but actual; nonetheless, it is sporadic, temporary, and geographically diffuse" (Turino 2008, 161). Although most visible on the East Coast, brass bands and battle reenactments occur concurrently across the United States and abroad. During the 2011–2015 US Civil War sesquicentennial observances, hardly a day passed without a Civil War commemorative event somewhere in the United States, and these heritage events often included brass band performances that announced gendered and racialized reconstructions of an American past.

Conspiracy: The Sounds

Around nine o'clock in the morning on April 20, 2012, eleven casually clad men carried armfuls of instrument cases onto the stage of a Southern concert hall and curiously peeked over their shoulders to size up their competition while piling their arsenal in self-claimed corners. The unsheathing of their instruments revealed E-flat and B-flat cornets, alto and tenor horns, and baritone horns of various shapes, sizes, and lacquer hues.[11] With so many more instruments than there were men on the stage, they transformed the concert hall into a veritable museum of nineteenth-century musical instruments. There was a ritualistic pattern to the way the men removed each artifact from its case, examined its body for imperfections, rolled their fingers over the valves, and then propped the instrument on its side for display. When they seemed satisfied with their exhibits, they turned to each other with handshakes, hugs, and group photographs. They spent nearly an hour asking after each other's families, comparing their instruments, inquiring after the minute details of the design and history of their horns, expressing mock jealousy or contempt for each other's prized possessions, and swapping war stories about the acquisition of their items and of being "sniped" by other collectors who outbid them for prized artifacts.[12] It was at once a fraternal reunion and a confrontation between skilled competitors, a blend of comradeship and rivalry. This was the annual meeting of the Cornet Conspiracy.

By ten o'clock, they transitioned to a formal band rehearsal, and after warming up with a couple of major scales, they arranged their chairs in a semicircle at the edge of the stage, tuned to a cornettist, and rehearsed the *William Tell Overture*.[13] One performer interrupted the rehearsal to deliver a critique, "That's a piece-of-trash horn," which garnered the response, "I don't feel comfortable on it," to which another man replied, "Why don't you go get another one?"[14] The musician in question exited with his devalued horn and returned with a different instrument of the same type. As the rehearsal continued, the musicians frequently paused for critiques, repairs, and inventory exchanges when players encountered intonation problems or uneven tone across an instrument's range, or if the timbre of one horn was too piercing. Seeming to aim for a homogeneous, mellow, and almost muted sound quality, the band spent the first half hour of their rehearsal adjusting the balance and timbre of the ensemble, and appeared most satisfied when they produced an organ-like sound.

They devoted the remainder of their practice time to selecting and rehearsing the repertoire that they would perform later that afternoon in a public open-air concert, reminiscent of Victorian-era gazebo concerts, in front of the concert hall. The musicians agreed that their repertoire should have a Southern theme since they were performing for a Southern audience, but their opinions diverged as to what criteria constituted Southern music. When the lead cornettist suggested that they play an arrangement of "Marching through Georgia" because it had a Southern state in the title, another member declared it to be inappropriate because it was a Union army favorite, but this was quickly rebutted: "But they [the audience] won't know it. They will see the title but won't know the tune." The lead cornettist added, "When they hear it, they'll love it, and it will be[come] Southern."[15]

The series of decisions made by the Cornet Conspiracy during this rehearsal reveals an acute awareness and attention to the active construction of heritage that is at the core of Civil War brass revivals. With each instrument selection, critique of each other's technique, and debate over repertoire, these collectors shaped a "Civil War" music heritage that they, as cultural authorities, presented to a public audience as "authentic" representation of that tradition. The production of "heritage" by Civil War brass band revivals promotes a culture of nostalgia and escapism that promises a beneficial and usable past (Cullen 1995). I posit that it is not the things that they collect but the indexed meanings that are associated with these musical artifacts that are the crux of this revival.[16] These musicians contribute to larger conversations about the meaning of Civil War music and, more generally, of the war. Members of this ensemble believe that nineteenth-century brass music represents a burgeoning national music ethos that was characterized by a blend of European and American popular and art music traditions. Some claim that their interpretation of this music tradition revitalizes the memory and sounds of the common men who participated in this war.[17] The series of instrument, timbre, and repertoire choices made by the Cornet Conspiracy suggests that Civil War memory can be stabilized through music, which is why the sound quality by the Conspiracy band was of vital importance.

While observing their 2012 annual rehearsal, I sat in the concert hall with a senior bandsman who shared with me his insight about Civil War music.[18] He told me that it is not the composition, but the instrumentation that matters. Although he believed that repertoire should correlate to the time period and function of the brass instrument during the war era, it was not important if the audience recognized the melody. What was critical was that individual timbres and ensemble blend be historically accurate, because these sounds aid his imagination process and help him crystallize memories about American history. What mattered was that the ensemble somehow "sounded" like a Civil War–era ensemble, however this is supposed to sound. Many of the musicians with whom I spoke are conscious and attentive to how their preservation and re-presentation of Civil War music directly influences contemporary perceptions of American history. One collector explained, "Music is the best way to create the atmosphere in which a modern audience can start relating to these people that breathed and loved, and had wives and girlfriends, and somehow you start relating to that. Music is the most powerful way to take an audience back to really thinking about these people, and you admire them."[19] To these collectors, music confirms a truth about the past that is not obtainable through history books, and this suggests that music can register unspeakable aspects of the past.

Reconstructing Civil War brass music is an active and physical experience. If, as Diana Taylor proposes, heritage should be considered an embodied practice and the bodily transfer of knowledge, then music becomes heritage through performative acts of collecting, restoring, sharing, and listening (Taylor 2003; see also Rojek and Urry 1997; Smith, 2006). The practices of brass revivalists may be interpreted as transforming commodities into living objects with which practitioners can interact, controlling them through touch, movement, vibrations, and breath. Collectors have described their performances as breathing life back into the metal and when accomplished as an ensemble, the blending of instrumental timbres creates a sonic cohesion that enhances a sense of group homogeneity.[20] The brass collectors described in this chapter value and try to replicate what they call a "sweet" or "warm" sound that they imagine characterized the brass soundscape of mid-nineteenth-century America.[21] Said one collector, "These instruments have such a sweet, melancholy sound that carries well outdoors. The keyed bugle is so good at producing a smooth, legato sound. The most comparable modern brass instrument would have to be the flugelhorn. . . . I know that when I play different pitches from different parts of the horn, it sounds really different in my head. The difference comes from the cutting holes into the metal, so it feels different when the sound is coming out of here [points to a hole in the horn near the mouthpiece] than when the sound is coming out of here [points to the bell]."[22] This aesthetic informs the criteria with which they judge the authenticity of their music and that of others, and this is why the exhibition and critique of instruments during the Cornet Conspiracy rehearsal was significant. The obsession with authenticity makes collecting an ongoing heritage test, and those who pass the scrutiny of other aficionados can become influential cultural authorities.[23]

REVIVAL: A HISTORICIZATION

The "conspiracy band" examined here represents a larger impulse to return Civil War sonic heritage to its "rightful owners." Briefly historicizing this movement will help clarify the political and discursive function of brass revival bands. Long and didactic relationships between Civil War hobbyists and American educational, military, park, and media systems have been instrumental in facilitating and legitimizing this revival. Financial resources and access to archives and performance spaces by employees from these institutions paved the way for other people to participate in Civil War music. One of the first Americans to organize a Civil War reenactment band was Fred Benkovic, who began collecting instruments while serving in World War II, as did Arne B. Larson, a band director whose collection became one of the founding inventories for the National Music Museum.[24] Robert Eliason, a former curator of the Henry Ford Museum Musical Instrument Collection and notable brass historian, collected and performed with the Yankee Brass Band, and this type of public administrator–private collector identity continues to be common among Civil War instrument collectors.[25] The most celebrated Civil War brass music collector is Mark Elrod, a former bugler and historian with the US Army's Old Guard Fife and Drum Corps and "The President's Own" Marine Band, who teamed with Robert Garofalo, Catholic University of America professor/conductor emeritus, to author a two-volume pictorial history of Civil War–era instruments and formed the Heritage Americana Band.[26] As these examples suggest, leaders of the brass heritage revival have often had professional ties to military, educational, and cultural memory (museums) institutions, and their heritage hobby seems to be a natural extension of their professions.[27] Through enactments of cultural heritage, these notable participants began to create communities of like-minded people who shared their passion for history and music.[28] Although it is unclear when the Civil War brass revival originated, it increased markedly in vigor during the 1961–1965 centennial celebrations—a historical milestone that compelled people to revisit and renegotiate the war's contested legacies.[29] At this time, interpretations of the war began to be frequently revitalized through activities known as "reenactments," a selective, scripted performance, a mode of interpretive representation that is similar in content and performance style to "living history."[30] Civil War reenacting, as it developed in the 1960s and continues to the present, is a recreational activity most commonly consisting of men in mid-nineteenth-century military dress with replica firearms partaking in role-playing activities. In this context, the closer a reenactment brings the actor to an affectively *true* experience, the more successful or *authentic* the performance.

When the US Civil War Centennial Commission promoted reconciliationist commemorations that celebrated military heroism at the expense of emancipationist histories to avoid fueling regional and racial tensions during the civil rights movement, the Cuban Missile Crisis, and the Cold War, the arts were elevated as a strategic means of celebrating the war while deflecting analysis of its unresolved social problems. As David Blight maintains, where the memory of the Civil War was concerned, Americans "preferred its music and pathos to its enduring challenges" (Blight 2001, 4; Cook 2007, 34–41). The social insecurity that coincided with the centennial may have signaled a promising future for minorities, but it seemed to the dominant class to signify a world spinning out of control. Rapid cultural change continued in the latter half of the 1960s and into the following decade as the second wave of feminism, the counterculture movement, and antiwar protests threatened patriarchal governance. This correlates with Michael Kammen's assessment that nostalgia becomes more prominent when a community is experiencing cultural anxiety, transition, and a sense of discontinuity with its past, and that "all three of those tendencies became apparent in the sixties and then were manifest during the seventies" (1991, 618).[31]

Reenactments continued after the zenith of the centennial, and as government funding for these activities waned, the privatization of events greatly influenced the development of regional differences in how Civil War reenactments were organized, received, and performed. A large number of participants became extremely devoted to the hobby for various reasons relating to individual and group identity, nationalism, escapism, nostalgia, and profit. For many working- and middle-class white suburban men, the Civil War offered a retreat to a past era when demonstrations of patriarchal power were evident in nearly all forms of public life and could even be heard in the music of brass bands. A burst of collecting, performing, and recording this music during the 1960s laid the groundwork for the movement to restore Civil War sonic heritage in the following decades.[32]

A period of heightened heritage discourse developed during the 1970s and 1980s, while racial, ethnic, and religious diasporic groups developed strategies to defend their distinctive cultural identities in public. Demands for civil rights and refusals to assimilate into the dominant culture by black, Native American, and Chicano nationalists deconstructed the myth of a cohesive American identity and ushered in an era of multiculturalism (Kammen 1991, 620). In recognition of the era's great innovations in social history, museums adopted heritage enactment as a strategy to resist unproblematized representations of linear social progress that focused almost exclusively on narratives constructed around the accomplishments of powerful white men. American heritage and living history museums featuring costumed enactment to supplement or replace more traditional exhibits and collections boomed during the 1970s and 1980s. These museum activities bore similarities to reenactment hobbies in that both presumed it was possible to resurrect the past through performance (Magelssen 2007, xxi). Museum curators and social historians alike strove to balance status quo narratives with ones that

replaced white men with minorities, women, children, and people from lower socioeconomic classes, and which would engage tourists with themes of social conflict and social
cycles (Magelssen 2007, 21). This and other movements to reinsert the lived experiences
of women and minorities into the retelling of American history coincided with an increase in minority museums, archives, and heritage groups. Demands for community
recognition, self-definition, and equal opportunities led to the repatriation of land, material objects, and public displays of minority arts.[33]

These efforts were interpreted by many white Americans as threatening the existing social order, and legislative resistance and the development of reactive political
strategies were two responses the dominant culture used to counteract minority power
movements. There was a return to traditionalist expressions of patriotism in the rhetoric
of conservative politicians, and minority nationalist efforts were confronted by lobbyists
and legislators whose fears of white power erosion influenced new monolinguistic and
anti-immigrant legislation (Kammen 1991, 638). As some white Americans appropriated
the rhetoric and display of "heritage" as a tool to reaffirm their racial and patriarchal
dominance, white heritage organizations exhibited newfound confidence about publicly
celebrating their lineage (Kammen 1991, 644). By framing themselves as an endangered
community under threat by women and minorities, many white men began to reclaim
their historically bestowed power by reconstructing American nationalist narratives
in their image. Not coincidentally, a renewed interest in Civil War history during this
time allowed many people to channel anxieties about cataclysmic social upheaval into
reclaiming and reshaping historical legacies. This past became a source of agency for
contemporary Americans because the manipulation of historical memory seemed to
offer a way to silence minority voices. The 1980s saw renewed interest in reenacting
among middle-class, suburban white men, and this fed into the establishment of a significant share of America's Civil War revival bands. This renewal continued through the
1990s and intensified into the twenty-first century, as eBay and other forms of digital
commerce greatly aided revivalist passions to collect, restore, and trade artifacts, recruit
reenactor-musicians, and disseminate information about Civil War brass music.

RETURN: WHAT WAS LOST?

Here I circle back to examine the types of meaning that can be generated by the return of
Civil War brass music. If heritage is not a product but a meaningful process, then I argue
that this brass revival attempts to reclaim two particular heritage traits: race and gender.
Evidence that the American brass band functions as a signifier of white male heritage is
reflected in the visual and audible performance of this music by revivalists. One way this
community reconstitutes its sonic heritage is through returning individual instruments
with traceable histories to other collected instruments from the same regiment.
Reuniting and reusing these instruments in revival bands, according to participants,
salvages their sonic possibilities. Civil War brass enthusiasts are drawn to a blend

of technical proficiency, military order, and expressive sentimentality that conjures a sensitive soldier-musician archetype with which they may empathize or identify. Preservation and performance of sonic artifacts and, by extension, a soldier-musician archetype by brass band revivalists, thus becomes a form of collective remembering. One member of the Cornet Conspiracy described this process as follows, "You know, I heard this story on NPR about a descendant of those who were in the Holocaust, who plays music on their instruments, and I guess it's kind of similar to that. *It gives you empathy for the owner.* It's the closest I will get to time traveling. It establishes for me almost a spiritual connection with those who played two hundred years ago. That's really why I continue to play."[34]

Significantly, however, this type of memory facilitates deep and powerful ownership of the past while bypassing less desirable aspects of nineteenth-century life such as slavery and war violence. Their efforts are in earnest. The ideologies perpetuated by this form of political activism are too deeply embedded in the heritage production process for most practitioners to recognize.[35] But it is precisely this absence of reflection about the causes and enduring consequences of the Civil War conflict that makes the continuation of this hobby a highly political practice.

What has been "stolen" from the brass band revivalists is not a set of historical instruments but a form of imagined manhood, referred to briefly earlier in the chapter, that may be described as the "citizen-soldier," or what Michael Kimmel terms the "heroic artisan," which is mythologized by the "cult of the fallen soldier."[36] This mythical man is rational, honorable, and exists in a world of other men who judge each other on the basis of bravery, honor, and skill. According to Kimmel, "He is free in a free country, embodying republican virtue and autonomy. And he is white" (1996, 151). This form of masculinity encapsulates a memory of the mid-nineteenth century that disentangles historical actors from the causes and consequences of the war. Furthermore, it reconciles Northern and Southern military histories by focusing on the shared aspects of white American manhood.[37]

Brass bands that function within this discursive framework are exclusive music fraternities that facilitate male bonding and reinforce social privilege by providing space for white men to reaffirm the masculinity of one another and their ancestors.[38] This space hearkens back to the nineteenth-century gendered separation of public and private spheres, by excluding the full participation of women.

Ultimately, Civil War brass music revivals work as a strategy to retrieve lost identities and diminished social entitlements. When during my fieldwork I found myself surrounded by uniformed collector-musicians at a coffee shop in downtown Frankfort, Kentucky, I asked a bandsman why he dons a wool suit and carries a dented horn. He turned to me softly, brushed the hairs of a thick gray mustache away from his lips, and explained in so many words that because schools no longer teach the war as they did, we are losing his past.[39] Our coffee shop chat burned in my mind as one of the fleeting moments when a bandsman deviated from his instrument fact script and engaged deeper questions about the stakes of brass collecting. In other instances Civil War reenactors explained their craft to me as a response to social phenomena including the safety, isolation, and commercialization of ever-expanding American suburbia; the loss of power at home and in the workplace; the perceived threat of nonwhite, non-Christian, non-English-speaking immigrants to Christian family values; the disregard of our nation's founding fathers by the nation's youth; and what they identify in a variety of ways as the feminization of American culture. What has been lost to these men is not necessarily a musical heritage, but their sense of masculinity, a racialized form of gender that they can see and hear in Civil War brass music. Collecting and performing Civil War music creates a site of negotiation across racial and gender social axes to audibly remasculinize themselves, what Kimmel has described in other similar cases as the impulse to "return to the scene of defeat and retrieve lost manhood" (1996, 311). Even Richard Crawford's descriptions of the Civil War brass musician point to this extramusical value: "Indeed, the image of musicians in paramilitary garb signals that artistry is not the only impulse they serve, perhaps not even the primary one" (2001, 272). We may, therefore, consider the celebration of male privilege as part of the aesthetic achievement and appeal of this music tradition.

It may seem as though this revival is no different from men's lodges or wilderness retreats, but what differentiates these revivals is that the repatriation of sonic heritage is a public statement made by a group to promote their vision of the past and to influence the production of a national consciousness. Thus, sonic heritage becomes a resource to support a type of exclusionary citizenship. As David Glassberg notes, certain elements of the past must be remembered while others are forgotten in order to create group cohesion, and therefore all communities are formed at the expense of other groups (Glassberg 1996, 13). Practitioners of brass band heritage celebrate the sounds of the white American Civil War experience while insisting that their rituals have nothing to do with women or people of color. The logic here is that if the rituals in question do not explicitly engage with these issues, then the tradition must only be about music. Thus, the enactment of a perceived sonic heritage becomes cloaked in the politics of its ideology, rendering participants unlikely to interpret their actions as having any political motivation or consequence.

That the "heroic artisan" is imagined to be a white man is important because it reaffirms his primacy in American history narratives. The militant yet unarmed brass musician in military garb becomes emblematic of the "everyman," and his imagined white identity is crucial because if the actors, achievements, and sacrifices associated with this war are remembered as white, then the universal white male emerges as the founding father of the modern nation that is understood to be born from this conflict. Implicit to this heritage crafting is a racial discourse in which whiteness in the United States is affirmed as homogeneous and stable.

Civil War hobbyists facilitate male bonding and legitimize benchmarks for American citizenship entitlements by relying on a contemporary Caucasian framework. Bonding among bandsmen depends on an unspoken understanding of whiteness as biologically visible and indicative of European descent. Despite a rhetoric of authenticity that permeates their sport, Civil War reenactors do not observe the nineteenth-century "variegated" racial hierarchy that regulated unprecedented numbers of immigrants from European nations (including Ireland, Scotland, and Italy) by marking them in stark contrast to Anglo-Saxon Protestants.[40] What during the US Civil War were perceived to be distinctly lesser nonwhite races in the Anglo-Saxon model of whiteness became twentieth-century white ethnicities under the Caucasian paradigm. Americanizing Europeans into a single race during the twentieth-century operated as a citizenship project that historian Matthew Frye Jacobson (1999) describes as a realignment of privilege along the black-white color line during Jim Crow.

The Caucasian model affords white people the privilege to selectively and temporarily position themselves as ethnically exceptional (with-heritage), while retaining the privileges of whiteness that distance them from those who are overdetermined by their (nonwhite) ethnic identity. Caucasian-ism was, and remains, a powerful rhetorical device to build coalitions and claim entitlements through whiteness. This locates the criteria for full American citizenship within a framework of lineage that selectively includes massive migrations of European peoples who are today easily interpreted within the United States as part of the white racial category, yet excludes African, Latino, Asian, and other immigrant groups. The application of such a model to US Civil War memory almost entirely erases the memory of Indigenous American and African American peoples who did not have as much primacy in the war as citizen-soldiers. Paul Shackel contends that patriotic and heritage commemorations are a method to control the past by returning the ideals of cultural leaders and authorities to develop social unity and maintain social inequalities in society (Shackel 2003, 659). When viewed according to Shackel's model, the repatriation of Civil War sonic heritage is really about mediating contemporary relationships between racial, ethnic, and gender groups in the United States.

These actions raise questions about the relationship between sonic heritage and social empowerment. If social power can be harnessed by sounding authority, then music collecting is not only competition for material goods but competition for social prominence. David Lowenthal writes:

> The past is everywhere a battleground of rival attachments. In discovering, correcting, elaborating, inventing, and celebrating their histories, competing groups struggle to validate present goals by appealing to continuity with, or inheritance from, ancestral and other precursors. The politics of the past is no trivial academic game; it is an integral part of every people's earnest search of a heritage essential to autonomy and identity.

> (Lowenthal 1994, 302)

In contemporary performances of Civil War music, we can hear a competition to control the official national narrative, to police the boundaries of national citizenship, to privilege limited interpretations of the past.

Repatriation: New Application

In this chapter, I have argued that musical repatriation can be understood not only as a return of dispossessed objects to subjugated communities but also as a discursive strategy to control representations of past and present identities. Although I recognize the possible danger of applying the term "repatriation" too broadly, I also see the value in using the concept of repatriation as a model for critically examining the complexities of heritage construction. I wish to allow for the possibility that repatriation models can be appropriated by powerful social groups. In this case, Civil War–era brass instruments are treated as fragments of the past to be gathered and strung together by revivalists to restore what they interpret to be an endangered historical truth. The displacement and subsequent return of heritage described in this chapter are not of one nation-state taking from another, but instead, the tracing of a white American musical lineage that testifies for the existence of a unique "Civil War" sonic heritage. Invoking past sounds through music relics is significant because it implies *ownership* of the past, which in this instance involves the privilege of constructing a sonic nationhood, and the entitlement to control social inclusion or exclusion from that representation. As is often the case with musical heritage, here the dominant social group constructs a hegemonic vision of nationhood that legitimizes the continued prosperity of people who occupy privileged social positions. To own implies mastery over something, which is evident in every stage of their music research, purchase, restoration, practice, critique, and public presentation. I argue that the repatriation of Civil War brass band music provides fertile ground for examining the cultural politics of sonic heritage. Trafficking in the return of musical objects and sounds associated with discrete historical events and eras exerts physical and intellectual ownership over the musical past. By studying the resulting representations and justifications for selectively preserving tangible and intangible sonic heritage, we can better understand the values that individuals and communities assign to history, a process robust enough to determine which pasts are remembered or forgotten.

Notes

1. Kirshenblatt-Gimblett (1998, 149); Livingston (1999, 68). Kirshenblatt-Gimblett writes: "Despite a discourse of conservation, preservation, restoration, reclamation, recovery, re-creation, recuperation, revitalization, and regeneration, heritage produces something new in the present that has recourse to the past."
2. Although contextual identifiers resulting from the localities of my data collection remain, to reduce the risk of deductive disclosure, my key informants are identified in this chapter by pseudonyms. Prominent leaders (past and present) of music revivals may be identified by name.
3. They use the term "conspiracy band," to describe a loose community of rival music collectors. While this term may describe numerous bands of collectors, the particular group of collectors uses the term "Cornet Conspiracy" to distinguish themselves from similar clubs. eBay inc (2005); Nussbaum (2009); Faust (n.d.).

4. DeCarlis (n.d.).
5. Josh, interview with author, April 19, 2012, Athens, Georgia.
6. Cornet Conspiracy Brass Band, group interview with author, April 20, 2012, Athens, Georgia.
7. Don, interview with the author, April 20, 2012, Athens, Georgia. There is a symbiotic relationship and money flow within the ensemble among bidders, buyers, and repairmen. Don explained,

> They all collect instruments but specialize in different things. Several members make a living restoring and repairing instruments. That one [man] created the group. They didn't like each other at first until he brought them together. They're from all over the country. That one is an attorney. Some are professional musicians. They really play. Not just this stuff, they play other music too. That one is a jazz player. That one went to Eastman. Several guys in the group make a living repairing these things, because they don't look like that when they first buy them.

8. Josh, interview with author, April 19, 2012.
9. During our group interview, the most pressing concern from members of the conspiracy band was to learn how many instruments each man owned. At one point during our interview, one of the collectors interrupted my questions to start a tally. "I want to know, down the line, how many horns each of us own. . . . There are more instruments between us than any museum has, that I know of. There must be 2,000 some instruments between us." Collector 1: 200, Collector 2: 30, Collector 3: 90, Collector 4: 100, Collector 5: 200, Collector 6: 850, Collector 7: 160, Collector 8: 50–60, Collector 9: 275, Collector 10: 120, Collector 11: 20–30. Cornet Conspiracy Brass Band, group interview with author.
10. The Cornet Conspiracy described here is but one of many Civil War music communities that perform or loan their collections to be performed. These ensembles often model the identity of their ensemble after a documented nineteenth-century ensemble, which is usually referenced by the name of the revival band and the adornment of regimental uniform costumes. There is much overlap in the rosters of these clubs, as most members of the conspiracy band described in this paper are also active members of other Civil War brass revival bands.
11. Nineteenth-century brass instruments possessed different valve combinations, tubing lengths, mouthpiece designs, and bore sizes than standard contemporary Western brass instruments. Differences in instrument design and production are compounded with a natural softening of the metal and a history of dents and repairs that impact the timbre of each instrument.
12. Cornet Conspiracy Brass Band, group interview with author; DeCarlis (n.d.). "Sniped" is one of many militaristic terms these collectors use when describing their hobby. "Sniping" is a colloquial term used by online auction users and researchers to describe a form of late-bidding behavior where the agent submits a bid at the last possible moment during a fixed closing time auction. Of interest to longstanding collectors of similar objects is the anonymity of snipers among other bidders. Increased frequency of sniping is attributable, in part, to companies such as Esnipe, which places last-minute bids for customers. See Axel Ockenfels and Alvin Roth, "Last-Minute Bidding and the Rules for Ending Second-Price Auctions: Evidence from eBay and Amazon Auctions on the Internet," *American Economic Review* 92 (September 2002): 1093–1103.
13. Although the "William Tell Overture" is a nineteenth-century opera overture by Gioachino Rossini and not purposefully composed for Civil War brass bands, wind ensembles from

this era frequently performed arrangements from symphonies and operas. However, this overture's American association with *The Lone Ranger* and other pop culture references may explain its popularity and frequent performance by revival bands.

14. The University of Georgia Symposium on American Band History, open rehearsal with Cornet Conspiracy Brass Band, April 20, 2012, Athens, Georgia.

15. The University of Georgia Symposium on American Band History, open rehearsal with Cornet Conspiracy Brass Band, April 20, 2012, Athens, Georgia.

16. See Smith (2006, 11). She goes on to argue that heritage is the construction and performance of a hegemonic discourse that regulates cultural practices.

17. Cornet Conspiracy Brass Band, group interview with author.

18. Don, interview with the author.

19. Bob, phone interview with the author, January 25, 2012.

20. Josh specifically commented on this, stating that this music tradition "is not dead" because "there are a number of skilled players who keep it alive." Josh, interview with the author, April 20, 2012, Athens, Georgia; Lewis (2015).

21. Cornet Conspiracy Brass Band, group interview with author. The language that brass collectors use to describe their sound is very similar to the nostalgic rhetoric that Gage Averill (2010) found in his study of barbershop quartets.

22. Josh, interview with the author, April 20, 2012.

23. Holyfield and Beacham (2011) call this type of cultural authority a "memory broker."

24. Dudgeon (1993, 118); Historic Brass Society (2009); National Music Museum (n.d.). Benkovic founded the First Brigade Band in 1964, often cited as the first regularly performing Civil War brass revival band.

25. Dudgeon (1993, 118); Herbert and Wallace (1997, 142).

26. For a biographical interview transcript of Elrod's collection and career, see Lewis (2015); see also Elrod and Garofalo (1985), Borowicz (1990, 126), and Dudgeon (1993, 118). Some of the musicians whom I met have played Elrod's instruments, and occasionally described Elrod as a role model.

27. This certainly is not an exhaustive list. Dozens of ensembles and collections have revived interest in US brass heritage. These hobbyists commonly volunteer and perform at museums, parks, and schools. They also create and distribute sound recordings and lend their collections to archives for public display.

28. There were extramusical benefits to these clubs. Bringing together men so similar in interest and status in individual revival bands and at reenactments and festivals has become a form of professional networking. Professional resources, such as access to archives, performance spaces, gigs, equipment, and publicity, help popularize and legitimize the hobby and its participants. Therefore, the status one accumulates within this community of music collectors can extend well beyond the brass world.

29. Crawford (2001, 272–293); McWhirter (2012, 7–32). Music was intricately tied to the processes of representing the Civil War from its very outbreak. The mid-nineteenth-century brass band carried with it a music of European descent and presented progressive stories about speedy changes in instrument designs, amateur music collectives, masculine heroism and competition, and audible homogeneity that appealed primarily to white Americans who envisioned themselves as models of democracy during a period of rapid and uncertain social change. Similar to the reception of brass bands during the nineteenth century, the performance of American patriotic songs and western European themes on European-derived instruments by contemporary musicians dressed in Western

military garb suggests that the American identity is undeniably rooted in a shared western European heritage.

30. Reenactment is one mode of living history performance that Jay Anderson defines as the reasoned attempt to simulate life in another time. See Anderson (1984); Turner (1990, 123).

31. Kammen describes this period in American history as the "heritage syndrome."

32. Druesedow (2003, 240–254); Hamburger (1996, 620–650). Many contemporary collectors cite books and recordings from the centennial as their inspiration to join this heritage movement, the most important recording being Fennell and Gabel (1961), a double album of brass music performed on period instruments with added sound effects and narration.

33. It is important to note that these events took place during the same time that America's post–World War II class system hardened and the country's national economy began to shift toward a global market, and that white anxieties were complex and often displaced in reaction to minority power movements.

34. Josh, interview with author, April 19, 2012.

35. Identifiers that I shared with my informants (including my whiteness, class, nationality, musician-identity, and interest in Civil War historical memory) may have helped facilitate conversations with collectors, musicians, audiences, and nonmusician reenactors. Most of the musicians I met were incredibly articulate in their descriptions of Civil War music, but even my most knowledgeable informants seemed unsettled by questions about diversity. When confronted with uncomfortable questions, bandsmen generally redirected the conversation to their instruments.

36. For discussions of "the cult of the fallen soldier," see Kimmel (1996, 16); Savage (1997, 167); Blight (2001, 38).

37. It would be understandable to assume that the deep North-South regional divisions from which Civil War armies were organized would remain a hotly contested element in the Civil War commemoration and reenactment, but this is not usually the case among white participants. David Blight (2001) identifies three camps of Civil War remembrance: the "emancipationist" vision, in which we conceptualize the war as a struggle over the future of race relations in the United States; the "reconciliationist" vision, in which collective forgetting of racial questions allowed Northern and Southern whites to mourn each other's losses and bond through their shared sense of whiteness; and the "white supremacist" vision of confederate redemption from which Lost Cause mythology blossomed. A primary determinant of which camp one's memory falls into is not determined by ancestral or geographic positioning, but by a conscious decision to either heal the regional divisions between the white North and South or justice for people of color. It should be noted that the ideology articulated by the majority of collectors, bandsmen, and audiences whom I encountered aligned with Blight's reconciliationist vision. Their glorification of a common military experience, laced with themes of courage, pain, and dedication to a cause (whatever it may be) overshadowed deeper examinations of class conflicts and race relations in the United States. Their emphasis on the common noncombative experience of bandsmen is also in keeping with reconciliationist ideology. Memory scholars frequently note that white male Civil War hobbyists tend to be attracted to the rebel character and material scarcity of the confederacy, and often alternate in their collection and performance of Northern/Southern military culture. (See Turner 1990; Horwitz 1998; Blight 2001.) The professional class of these collectors explains a slight, but not divisive, tension

between the reserved presentation of Civil War brass music revivalists and some of the more rambunctious military battle reenactors, who are more numerous and diverse in socioeconomic identity. In my experience with brass collectors, concerns about instrument makers and collection completeness take precedence over regional concerns; however, an instrument is generally interpreted to have added value if it can be attributed to a particular regiment or musician.

38. Kimmel (1996, 291–328). According to Kimmel, these types of masculine hobbies "celebrate cultures with elaborate rituals for men, all the while protesting that such rituals have nothing to do with women. Since the rituals exclude women, they must only be 'about' men and manhood" (319).

39. Ron, interview with author, September 1, 2011, Frankfurt, Kentucky.

40. For more about nineteenth-century American racial categories and the history of how this hierarchy morphed in the public consciousness, see Jacobson 1999. Jacobson argues that three systems that determined whiteness over time in the United States are capitalism, republicanism, and citizenship. He writes, "To trace the process by which Celts and Slavs became Caucasians is to recognize race as an ideological, political deployment rather than as a neutral, biological determined element of nature" (14).

References

Anderson, Jay. 1984. *Time Machines: The World of Living History*. Nashville, TN: American Association for State and Local History.

Averill, Gage. 2010. *Four Parts, No Waiting: A Social History of American Barbershop Quartet*. New York: Oxford University Press.

Blight, David. 2001. *Race and Reunion: The Civil War in American Memory*. Cambridge, MA: Harvard University Press.

Borowicz, Jon T. 1990. "The Mid-Nineteenth Century Brass Band—A Rebirth." *Historic Brass Journal* 2: 123–131.

Cook, Robert. 2007. *Troubled Commemoration: The American Civil War Centennial, 1961–1965*. Baton Rouge: Louisiana State University Press.

Crawford, Richard. 2001. *America's Musical Life: A History*. New York: Norton.

Cullen, Jim. 1995. *The Civil War in Popular Culture: A Reusable Past*. Washington, DC: Smithsonian Institution Press.

DeCarlis, N. n.d. "Pocket Cornets and Me." *Pocket Cornets: The World's Largest Virtual Museum of the Smallest Cornets and Trumpets Ever Made!* http://www.pocketcornets.com (accessed December 12, 2013).

Dudgeon, Ralph. 1993. *The Keyed Bugle*. Metuchen, NJ: Scarecrow Press.

Druesedow, John. 2003. "Music of the Civil War Era: A Discography." *Notes: Quarterly Journal of the Music Library Association* 60: 240–254.

eBay Inc. 2005. "Moving Stories about the Power of All of Us." *The Chatter: The eBay Community Newsletter*. January 2005. http://pages.ebay.com/community/chatter/2005/january/poaoustories.html (accessed December 16, 2013).

Elrod, Mark, and Robert Garofalo. 1985. *A Pictorial History of Civil War Era Musical Instruments and Military Bands*. Charleston, WV: Pictorial Histories Publications.

Faust, William Hull. n.d. *The Musical Instrument Collection of William Hull Faust*. http://www.conicalbore.com/ (accessed December 16, 2013).

Fennell, Frederick, and Martin Gabel. 1961. *The Civil War: Its Music and Its Sounds*. Mercury. LP.

Glassberg, David. 1996. *Sense of History: The Place of the Past in American Life*. Amherst: University of Massachusetts Press.

Hamburger, Susan. 1996. "Musical and Narrative Recordings." In *The American Civil War: A Handbook of Literature and Research*, edited by Steven Woodworth, 620–658. Westport, CT: Greenwood Press.

Herbert, Trevor, and John Wallace. 1997. *The Cambridge Companion to Brass Instruments*. Cambridge: Cambridge University Press.

Historic Brass Society. 2009. "Fred Benkovic (1924–2009)." Obituary. http://www.historicbrass. org/TheStacks/News/News2009/tabid/296/Default.aspx (accessed November 24, 2013).

Holyfield, Lori, and Clifford Beacham. 2011. "Memory Brokers, Shameful Pasts and Civil War Commemoration." *Journal of Black Studies* 42 (3): 436–456.

Horwitz, Tony. 1998. *Confederates in the Attic: Dispatches from the Unfinished Civil War*. New York: Pantheon Books.

Jacobson, Matthew Frye. *Whiteness of a Different Color: European Immigrants and the Alchemy of Race*. Cambridge, MA: Harvard University Press, 1999.

Kammen, Michael. 1991. *Mystic Chords of Memory: The Transformation of Tradition in American Culture*. New York: Knopf.

Kimmel, Michael. 1996. *Manhood in America: A Cultural History*. New York: Free Press.

Kirshenblatt-Gimblett. 1998. *Destination Culture: Tourism, Museums, and Heritage*. Berkeley: University of California Press.

Lewis, Joseph. 2015. "The Development of Civil War Brass Band Instruments into Modern-Day Brass Band Instruments with a Related Teaching Unit for a High School General Music Course." Masters thesis, Bowling Green State University.

Livingston, Tamara. 1999. "Music Revivals: Towards a General Theory." *Ethnomusicology* 43 (1): 66–85.

Lowenthal, David. 1994. "Conclusion: Archaeologists and Others." In *The Politics of the Past*, edited by Peter Gathercole and David Lowenthal, 302–314. New York: Routledge.

Magelssen, Scott. 2007. *Living History Museums: Undoing History through Performance*. Toronto: Scarecrow Press.

McWhirter, Christian. 2012. *Battle Hymns: The Power and Popularity of Music in the Civil War*. Chapel Hill: University of North Carolina Press.

National Music Museum. n.d. "The Arne B. Larson Collection." http://orgs.usd.edu/nmm/ arne.html (accessed October 12, 2013).

Nussbaum, Jeff. 2009. "*Pocket Cornets* by Nick DeCarlis." Review. *Historic Brass Society*. http://www.historicbrass.org/thestacks/bookreviews/bookreviews2009/pocketcornetsby nickdecarlis/tabid/358/default.aspx (accessed December 12, 2013).

Rojek, Chris, and John Urry. 1997. *Touring Cultures: Transformations of Travel and Theory*. New York: Routledge.

Savage, Kirk. 1997. *Standing Soldiers, Kneeling Slaves: Race, War, and Monument in Nineteenth-Century America*. Princeton, NJ: Princeton University Press.

Shackel, Paul. 2003. *Memory in Black and White: Race, Commemoration, and the Post-Bellum Landscape*. Walnut Creek, CA: Alta Mira Press.

Smith, Laurajane. 2006. *Uses of Heritage*. London: Routledge.

Taylor, Diana. 2003. *The Archive and the Repertoire: Performing Cultural Memory in the Americas*. Durham, NC: Duke University Press.

Turino, Thomas. 2008. *Music as Social Life: The Politics of Participation*. Chicago: University of Chicago Press.

Turner, Rory. 1990. "Bloodless Battles: The Civil War Reenacted." *TDR* 34 (4): 123–136.

CHAPTER 26

RADIO ARCHIVES AND THE ART OF PERSUASION

CARLOS ODRIA

"IMAGINE a world populated only by, let's say, two hundred and fifty girls and thirty men. Things would get complicated," said Mr. Gutierrez[1] in his office at the Grupo RPP building in Lima's exclusive area of San Isidro. "An average girl would need to compete fiercely on a regular basis, playing tricks on her gender peers and finding ways to outperform them in any conceivable way. She would really need to devise astute mechanisms to seduce one of the scarce males in town, while the male population, on the other hand, would have the power to choose among and discard several existing options. Well, the radio is *that* girl." With this heteronormative story (and its social assumptions, which are unpacked later in this chapter), Mr. Gutierrez illustrated for me a condensed picture of the dynamics in the radio industry in Peru's capital city. His affable smile, intellectual references, and conversational skills helped me to comprehend the intricacies of business decision-making inside Grupo RPP, the country's largest media corporation, which owns most popular newspapers, TV channels, and radio stations. A dark-skinned and black-haired man in his forties, Mr. Gutierrez possesses the rare ability to function competently in both the creative and the marketing areas of the corporation. He is a successful manager of commercial marketing at Grupo RPP and a copresenter in a morning top-ranked show aired by Radio Oxigeno, one of the class-specific stations owned by the group. "Radio stations are *productos vivos* (living products)," he explained when answering my question about the company's strategies for securing massive audiences in Lima's dynamic cultural landscape. "Our stations are successful because we follow closely the social dynamics of the country and we are always positive about the true nature of our work—that is, that radio, more than a means to distribute music is predominantly a commercial business."

Throughout our conversations, Mr. Gutierrez showed his expertise and his ability to navigate across the two seemingly disconnected worlds that sustain the broadcasting industry. Peppering his conversation with casual jokes and anecdotes taken from local imagery, he portrayed Peruvian radio as a profitable business that nonetheless demands an almost chameleonic ability to read people's mindsets. As he explained it, not only does Grupo RPP reinforce musical trends by building playlists intended to reflect the musical taste of what he described as Lima's stratified society but it also seeks to preserve such stratification by implementing musical trends that encourage listeners to accept racial distinctions. The corporation he belongs to professes the idea that a successful broadcasting business "endures by making hit songs and by betting on large-scale tendencies." Nevertheless, Mr. Gutierrez suggested, these marketing strategies become much harder to accomplish when applied to an ethnically heterogeneous society such as Lima's. The difficulty has led marketing strategists to manipulate playlists in a way that enables them to persuade audiences to assume racialized identities that match expected behaviors.

In this chapter, I build on sonic repatriation studies to explore the dissemination of these "living products" mentioned by Mr. Gutierrez. Grupo RPP marketing specialists such as Mr. Gutierrez have created a range of class-oriented radio stations that air selective playlists; they seek to persuade Lima's audiences to comply with the corporation's hegemonic discourse, as it becomes manifest through the aesthetic composition of the playlists. I use the lens of repatriation studies to review how this type of programming functions as a social technology that allows Peru's influential groups to reinforce the hierarchical organization of the society by promoting race-specific aesthetic concepts in media consumption (Crabtree et al. 2006; Boesten 2010; Thorp and Paredes 2010). In this regard, my use of the term "repatriation" deals with the act of disseminating playlists as dynamic archives (living products) and, more precisely, with the kind of vertical relations that frame and are generated through the process of song dissemination.

At one level, "repatriation" is a term that designates the process of transferring the ownership of an artifact (Jacknis 1996; Ferguson et al. 2000; Mihesuah 2000; Fine-Dare 2002; Fforde et al. 2004; McIntosh 2006). At another level, however, repatriation also encompasses the transaction that engages at least two individuals in handling the ownership of such an artifact. Thus, I understand repatriation not merely as the act of returning, conceding, or disseminating something to a person or community, but as the process by which a power relation between "givers" and "takers" is performed within the transaction. Repatriating artifacts implicates the agency of possessors who are willing to cede their belongings and pass them down. Even though "takers" may exert legal or political pressure to force "givers" to relinquish their items, the process of repatriation may be seen as hierarchical in nature because it presupposes the "taker's" initiative and the "giver's" acceptance or at least partial-passiveness within the power relation. As I will show, Grupo RPP passes down songs and selective playlists from a privileged position. It does so for the express purpose of perpetuating the existing social hierarchy. The corporation uses its infrastructural apparatus and broadcasting abilities to enact the power relations that serve as pillars for its regulatory control over the listenership.

For this reason, I examine their dissemination practices as a social technology that delivers ideological content. An analysis of their broadcasting activities must consider their social agenda and recognize the existence of hegemonic interests that move beyond the implicit cultural or even economic value of the playlist—despite Mr. Gutierrez's assertion that radio businesses are eminently profit-oriented organizations. To be sure,

Grupo RPP's activities not only involve business decision-making within the expected constraints and demands of the market plus the ensuing unequal media distribution scenario. More importantly, their activities originate from a need to preserve their political and cultural authority. Their strategy comprises the construction of a compelling aesthetic sonic discourse that is aired in the airwaves of Lima and massively shapes the auditory lives of thousands of listeners.

Consequently, I also employ the term "repatriation" to refer to the act of passing down playlists that have been selected and compiled through archival editorial policies (Edmondson 2004 , 14). My emphasis is on the social relationships enacted in the forging, dissemination, and consumption of the archives and on the ethical underpinnings of racially driven policies. This perspective calls for the use of a wide-ranging, and to some extent unusual, analytical scope that is not limited to discussing the historicities or particularities of the cultural artifact per se, but that, more broadly, invokes a "critical and reflexive discourse about relations of power in cultural representations" (Nannyonga-Tamusuza and Weintraub 2012, 213). I believe it is important to weight the social dimension that houses, and in fact makes possible, the repatriation of sonic objects. People's relations, power positions, and ideological or ethical manifestations constitute the kernel of the transaction that occurs during an exchange of ownership. Therefore, an analysis of these factors may offer a deeper understanding of the fundamental constructions of the "self" and "other" implicitly performed by parties during repatriation practices. It is imperative to push forward the theoretical envelope of repatriation studies to go beyond the prioritization of material or symbolic objects in order to reevaluate the ambiguous and unquantifiable, yet basic, role of human action and belief in the process, especially as these are expressed when contending with diverse and socially constructed notions of ownership.

CRIOLLO BROADCASTING POLICIES

During my fieldwork in Lima in 2012–2013, which included conversations and interviews with marketing specialists and music programmers in Grupo RPP, I learned about the sonic aesthetic concepts that programmers use to produce audible environments that fit certain demographics of race and class. Grupo RPP's analysts and marketing consultants center their work on developing these kinds of standardized social markers that reflect their hegemonic values. They establish a framework of permitted musical styles and assign it to Lima's various sectors of society. In this way, the corporation's mainstream radio programming has become a mechanism by which Peruvian media investors control the musical preferences of socially disparate audiences in the city.

When referring to the story that portrays Lima's radio stations as an astute girl, Mr. Gutierrez indirectly articulated a patriarchal attitude indicative of both Grupo RPP's executive board and the *criollo* elite to which that board belongs. I use the term "criollo" to denote Lima's ruling conservative minority that comprises mostly white and mestizo

Western-educated circles and holds strong political influence over the Peruvian government. The Peruvian anthropologist José Matos Mar describes this criollo minority as one that centers its influential power on "maintain[ing] control over the state's apparatus and the institutional legality" (1984, 104). Matos Mar points out that criollos "concentrate the direction of political parties, the management of banking system, enterprises, cultural leadership, and ecclesiastic hierarchies" (104), and in this fashion, they maintain a leadership that surpasses the powers and capacities of a democratically elected government. Furthermore, and perhaps more importantly for understanding the connection between radio programming policies and Lima's social organization, Matos Mar states that the criollo elite "develops powerful efforts to preserve and expand the formal order it embodies by 'incorporating' or 'integrating' the rest of the country" to its monopoly of power (105). Then, as a city controlled by criollo structures of domination based on gender, social, and ethnic/racial categories, the Peruvian capital appears as a flimsily assembled edifice of collectivities that confront each other to gain power against the backdrop of the elite's rule (Gandolfo 2006, 6). Within this context of constant struggle, the population moves away from a potential consensus in the political and civic spheres.

To illustrate this situation, I describe here some attitudes that inform everyday relations among contesting groups, as expressed in colloquial narratives. For instance, criollos usually describe the capital city as Lima *provinciana* (provincial or rural Lima). This is a somehow derisive phrase that alludes to a perception of migrant Amerindians as intruders and polluting agents. Lima provinciana also refers to the gradual distortion of the garrisoned Western values that have shaped urban life for decades. By introducing their indigenous practices and modes of socioeconomic organization, Amerindians have drastically (and, according to criollos, negatively) transformed the physical and cultural environment of the capital. Amerindians coming from rural areas in search of economic opportunity have enlarged Lima's demography and geopolitical boundaries to unthinkable limits in mostly unplanned, chaotic ways; perhaps more importantly, migrants have put an end to criollos' idyllic view of Lima as a city that once was dreamed to mirror a European cosmopolitanism: a *Lima de antaño* (yesteryear Lima) in which luxury, dissipation, order, cleanliness, and social influence were markers of progress and modernity enjoyed by the fair-skinned descendants of Spanish conquistadores.

Within the Grupo RPP's editorial policies, the corporation managerial board frames a one-sided conversation with the listenership to normalize the imposition of criollo racial hierarchies. As Mr. Gutierrez indicated, marketing specialists and consultants map out discrete "large-scale tendencies" based on assumptions regarding people's tastes and preferences informed by their socioeconomic/ethnic makeup. Subsequently, radio presenters, disc jockeys, and programmers merely articulate and try to make the corporation's comprehensive outlook on the city's social composition appealing. Nonetheless, programming is underpinned by a discourse about the permissible and ideal order that should reign in the face of what criollos see as the city's ongoing cultural degradation. Grupo RPP's playlists—whether or not their aired material truly fulfills the aesthetic and recreational needs of the audience—constitute archives that articulate a detailed social project.

SONIC AESTHETIC CONCEPTS

While showing me around the modern installations of the Grupo RPP broadcasting building, Mr. Gutierrez explained the different "concepts" behind the seven stations owned by the corporation: RPP Noticias, Radio Capital, Studio92, Radio Oxigeno, Radio Corazón, Radio Felicidad, and La Zona. Each of these stations has an orientation that makes it unique, especially regarding their different market goals and intended audiences. The need to cover a diverse range of listeners in Lima's complex social fabric demands that programmers take pains to articulate the cultural values that professedly define the identity of targeted segments. In doing so, the corporation promotes a criollo imagery that, as the ethnomusicologist Joshua Tucker asserts in his exploration of a satiric radio program aired by Studio92, builds on "the association between musical style and social position" (2010, 554). This type of association identified by Tucker is key to understanding the mechanisms by which the customization of radio playlists expresses criollo notions of cultural and ethnic superiority. Furthermore, the programmers' association of musical style with social position causes members of Lima's socioeconomic sectors to see themselves represented in the stylistic composition symbolized by each station; but this only renders the discourse of the authoritative institution more persuasive. This phenomenon helps to establish a communication loop that positions radio programmers and listeners into an unequal power relation. While striving to develop engaging musical trends, marketing specialists are informed by criollo thought, which then leads audiences to accept subconsciously the corporation's hegemonic ideas. That interaction, in turn, preserves social hierarchies and unequal relations through listeners' sincere belief that their musical taste plays a vital role in making the playlist. However, as I discovered, this belief is unsubstantiated.

"All presenters and disc jockeys embrace and follow the trends that define each of our stations," said Mr. Gutierrez while showing me the surprisingly small size of each "station," which were not more than compact booths decorated with logos and designs representative of their individual concepts. The ten-story building owned by Grupo RPP devotes most of its usable space to house executive and programming activities, while only two entire floors are employed for actual broadcasting. Through the glass windows isolating each station's booth from the corridors, I could see some of the best-known public figures in the country—media celebrities I listened to during my teenage years in Lima. Taking a short pause in their live shows, they would wave their hands and smile at Mr. Gutierrez as we walked by. "People trust opinion leaders," my guide said and added, "Here at RPP we have most of them."

Shortly after this tour, we walked down the stairs, entered his office, and sat down at his desk. I expressed my eagerness to learn more about the minutiae of radio programming.

He immediately started a long conversation about the ideas shaping editorial policies at the corporation. His description was effortless and clear; he knew these policies like the back of his hand. "In radio," he explained, "presenters learn how to manage moods, how to profit from specific moments in order to engage their audiences." Furthermore, by airing content-specific playlists and introducing their personal comments and live responses to the radio listeners in real time (via phone calls and online communications), presenters employ "different narratives and contents to socialize with the people." In this way, as Mr. Gutierrez affirmed, relationships are successfully established between presenters and listeners.

Socioeconomic Levels and Notions of Beauty

To better illustrate the conflation of mood, aesthetic concept, and criollo thought, here I discuss the role marketing consultants play in the editorial process in the corporation. Peruvian media organizations such as Grupo RPP rely heavily on the use of statistical data and analyses provided by marketing consultants. Even though these advisers offer an ostensibly objective analysis of the demographics of Lima's radio listenership, it can be argued that they also perpetuate ramifications of criollo thought by using monolithic social categories to categorize people's consumption preferences. For example, the Peruvian Association of Enterprises and Market Research (APEIM), a leading institution in public opinion research, states that, "depending on the social status of a person or a family, it is possible to infer a series of behaviors or to establish a group of tendencies framing possible behaviors" (APEIM 2005, 2, my translation). Following this assumption, the APEIM and other Peruvian research institutions that advise large media corporations have instituted the use of a "socioeconomic level" parameter (*nivel socioeconómico*) as a major referent in the classification and consequent stereotyping of Peru's social fabric. The APEIM affirms that "to identify the aspects that integrate a socioeconomic level in the population is a dynamic activity that supposes an analysis of the diverse characteristics of persons and families," such as the educational background and occupation of the head of the household, the types of facilities inside homes, the external characteristics of the houses, and the access to health providers (2–3). Through this form of scrutiny, the APEIM concludes, researchers can quantitatively determine how people located within particular levels of society will act and feel in relation to the market's activity.

At Grupo RPP, the use of the socioeconomic level parameter is paramount in designing the aesthetics models for each of its radio stations. Programmers closely follow the cultural implications associated with the five discrete societal sectors recognized by APEIM. These are indexed in a hierarchical scale that goes from "A" to "E," with "A" referring to Lima's most influential and economic-empowered group (white criollos) and "E" to the most disenfranchised one (Amerindians). Radio Oxigeno, for instance, is a genre-specific station that targets an audience located within levels A, B, and possibly upper C, focusing on listeners older than twenty-five but younger than fifty years old. The station's aesthetic concept centers on "attitude-oriented theme"; that is, it aims to reflect the listeners' attitude toward life and existence, as it is inferred according to the cultural parameters corresponding to their socioeconomic level. The featured genres and artists, the presenters' narratives, the colloquial speech tone, the use of Spanish local jargon or its strategic avoidance, and the variety of discussion topics aired in daily shows need to convey a spirit of "intensity and revelry." These feelings are interconnected with expected attitudes toward life held by the targeted audience within the metropolitan population. Grupo RPP assumes that people included in this segment possess a "good attitude" and "optimal social skills" (*mucha calle*). Even though they "rebel" against conformism, they also function well in society, are productive individuals, and do not complain about political or economic national problems. The corporation's hypothesis is that these listeners are not conformists; they maintain their position in society while also allowing themselves to contend with (at least nominally) the status quo. They might belong to prominent and influential families in the city and are professionals who are successfully employed and hold degrees in higher education. As such, this group follows conventional Western notions of progress while recognizing that indigenous Amerindian societies still rely on archaic forms of organization that are detrimental to national progress. Grupo RPP consultants perceive their Radio Oxigeno followers as active participants in the development of social life in cosmopolitan districts such as Miraflores, San Isidro, San Borja, or La Molina, and the corporation also assumes this segment of their audience does not possess an Andean heritage. For these various reasons, Radio Oxigeno is a station that mirrors a politically correct "nonconformist" attitude that supports the continuous renewal of the democratic government. This nonconformism is mirrored and promoted by airing American and British mainstream popular music recorded in the 1970s, 1980s, and 1990s, especially rock and roll and its variants. A top-ranking list published by Radio Oxigeno in December 2013 consists of artists such as Keane, Van Halen, Poison, Guns'n'Roses, Queen, Led Zeppelin, U2, and R.E.M.

Radio programmers at Grupo RPP develop a "strategic vision" that pursues a coherent articulation of their aesthetic concepts. Genre stations are expected to mirror the localized social consciousness of their targeted audiences. For instance, Grupo RPP criollo executives, building on this strategic vision, developed the idea of creating Radio La Zona, a station focused on Lima's young population (twelve to twenty-five years old) who are positioned in socioeconomic levels D and E according to APEIM. Conceptually, La Zona targets an audience that marketing specialists perceive as immersed in cultural and economic transformation. Individuals within these levels struggle not only to survive but also to increase their material capital by studying for technical careers or by becoming entrepreneurs. Many of these young listeners have parents and grandparents who migrated to Lima from rural areas and, due to this, have experienced great difficulty in the process of cultural adaptation. Building from that experience, marketing specialists assume listeners of La Zona learned early in their childhood and adolescence to move away from cultural practices and preferences that would classify them as *provincianos* (backward provincial people). Moreover, specialists believe that La Zona's listeners present themselves as Western-educated or at least aspiring criollos, because they see themselves as mestizos or Amerindians but wish to be recognized as modern citizens with a cosmopolitan and sophisticated taste for international music. Nonetheless, as Grupo RPP further infers, La Zona's segmented audience makes up an idiosyncratic urban culture informed by signs of underdevelopment in the sense that their everyday life is marked by street violence, gang delinquency, criminality, economic instability, and a notable absence of Western standards in education and social etiquette. These are some of the elements that also define life in *la zona*, a colloquial Spanish term used in Lima to refer to a poor and implicitly high-crime neighborhood populated by migrants or uneducated mestizos. A sign of this pigeonholed association between delinquency, rural heritage, education, and musical taste is seen in the appearance of the radio booth of this station at Grupo RPP's headquarters; its walls are painted with street-like, gang-themed graffiti all around. Furthermore, Mr. Gutierrez went on to explain that La Zona presenters are trained to "understand the youth" by mimicking their gang-oriented speech modes. Additionally, to mirror the purportedly shifting consciousness that La Zona's audience presently endures, programmers follow an editorial policy focused on "following the immediate tendency" in musical trends. Ultimately, as Mr. Gutierrez seemed to indicate, there is a level of contempt on the part of marketing specialists that leads them to assume that this targeted audience cannot generate a musical taste of their own. Therefore, programmers need to undertake a sort of pedagogical role when generating a playlist. This authoritative stance can be seen in the type of genres featured in La Zona, which include reggaeton, salsa, and bachata. All three are, in the criollo urban imagery, associated with dance, rhythm, loudness, and ultimately with debauchery and a black or African expressive culture that has been pejoratively rejected by whites and criollos alike (Feldman 2006, 265).

An interesting phenomenon takes place with Grupo RPP's flagship news station, RPP Noticias. This station has the highest listening base in the country (API 2013, 2), regardless of socioeconomic classification. As a news/talk station that promotes immediacy and credibility for its mostly low-income listenership, RRP Noticias showcases commentators, journalists, politicians, writers, analysts, musicians, and comedians who rank as the most trusted public figures in the country. Mr. Gutierrez exemplified this credibility with the following story. According to a recent national poll, Peruvians of all races and social positions consider RRP Noticias the second-most trusted institution in the entire country, outranked only by the Catholic Church. "RRP Noticias builds values," Mr. Gutierrez affirmed, and this is true because "95% of the population accepts all the information and news that it spreads."[2] The consequence of this credibility is that the station's programming—which includes not only the news but also a variety of shows on topics ranging from sports, politics, and Catholicism to cuisine, health, and entertainment—has become an effective means of controlling social opinion. Ultimately, the Peruvian media scholar Jorge Luis Acevedo affirms that, due to its unchallenged national popularity, this station and the corporate group it represents have achieved a concentration of media channels and broadcasted information that successfully leads to an oligarchy limiting political, cultural, and religious pluralism in the country (Acevedo 2011, 2013).

RECONTEXTUALIZING REPATRIATION PROCESSES

Songs and playlists can become an emblematic site of confrontation or agreement. In the case of repatriation initiatives, either when debating or asserting ownership of sonic objects, people formulate hierarchies that structure the dynamics of their dealings around disputed artifacts. In light of the complex exchange of power relations seen in the dissemination of playlists on Lima's airwaves, a thoughtful discussion of repatriation practices does not only encompass a transaction in which archival materials are made available to listeners. Theoretical explorations can be used to fathom postcolonial contemporary societies such as Lima, where media industries have become one of the main arenas for constructing hegemonic and politically empowering and disempowering forms of sociability through selective song circulation.

The ideas spread by Grupo RPP materialize in class-oriented radio stations that emerge as part of a media-driven cultural process. Such a process reshapes the local society and occurs within what may be seen as a partial process of repatriation, in the sense that the corporation's aesthetic concepts articulate segregating categories by including certain songs and excluding others. The means and the goals of archival dissemination correspond here to a unilateral set of editorial decisions concerning the availability of mainstream recordings and the social outcomes that selective distribution achieves. Lima's segmented audiences are not invited to participate in this process of choosing or discovering the musical products they consume; they are simply given the illusion of choosing artists and songs they are expected to like based on their race and positions in the criollo hierarchical model.

Thus, a discourse on repatriation applied to Lima's broadcasting industry concerns the spread of ideology, the shaping of society, and an analysis of power structures. Framing the passing down of playlists as a vertical transaction enables a conversation that moves toward a critical study of the imbalanced social relationships fomented by archival dissemination. Grupo RPP uses marketing strategies that pertain to the central role of the mediascape in establishing and practicing policies embedded with subtexts. An analysis of the process that leads to the formation of their aesthetic concepts sheds light on broader questions regarding the politics of music dissemination, and more importantly, the editorial policies that inform the structuring of the mediascape. For instance, to what extent does the dissemination of sonic archives, carried out by means of mass communication, strengthen hierarchical differences in societies? Does the mere decision to make certain cultural objects (songs, genres, and playlists) available for mass consumption empower or disempower sectors of society at both ends of the repatriation transaction? As seen in the practices of Grupo RPP, in some cases those who disseminate sound objects determine not only the conditions in which these objects are received by audiences but also the subtexts of the item that is handled, subtexts that invariably position the taker in a disenfranchised condition in relation to the giver. Narratives concerning dominant cultural practices, essentialist value judgments, race-based hierarchies, and unyielding notions of the "other" have an impact (although not always entirely consciously) on the making of mass-media policies for music programming. Through this lens, selective song circulation may be seen as a mode of performance that solidifies hegemonic power, because it has enabled Lima's criollo radio programmers and investors to determine the prevalence of certain cultural restrictions. In the case of Grupo RPP radio stations, repatriation behaves as a social technology that has a bearing on the development of vertical social structures (Gandy 2000, 2001). Furthermore, within the broader transnational ambit, media-scape/repatriation practices may be assessed as social technologies that perpetuate the conditions by which stratified and culturally fragmented societies remain disjointed in an era of global communication. The mediascape has become a space for human beings around the world to coexist, communicate, and construct collective realms, and it is problematic to recognize that media tycoons and large corporations usually possess their full control.

PERSUASION

Mr. Gutierrez invited me to chat in his office at Grupo RPP's headquarters. Visibly passionate about the topic, he started philosophizing on the nature of the broadcasting business:

> Our stations seek to produce a comfy space for the audience. As a presenter, I want to pull reality's leg. I want to be considered as just one more friend in the gang, as if the audience and I were in a party listening to music, drinking beer, laughing aloud. Every presenter tries to accomplish that. Some work with emotions and styles, others with formal methods or intuition. In the end, everyone wants to make of the radio a sort of visit, an accepted intrusion that needs to be friendly.

His depiction of radio shows articulates two important points concerning the persuasive aspects of criollo-sponsored programming. First, it points to the use of sonic moods—that is, organic aural contexts defined by particular aesthetics and speech codes that enable presenters to articulate the dominant ideology. Being at a party, having informal conversations, and listening casually to music are social situations in which, according to Mr. Gutierrez, people may remain open to receive and interiorize messages coming from familiar and friendly voices. As Tucker affirms in his critique of radio consumption models in Peru, the use of sonic moods to facilitate the reception of ideology has become media corporations' strategy to inscribe elitist notions about ethnic and cultural stereotypes:

> Rather than attending to a specific message or narrative, [in Peru] listeners use music radio primarily to create a context, whether designing a relaxing home environment via a broadcaster of romantic baladas, or by stimulating a workplace via a loud and lively salsa station. . . . Interaction with radio sound is therefore often transitory and distracted. Nevertheless, embedded in broadcasts are framings and distinctions . . . The relatively unremarked nature of radio is what ensures that its ideological effects become pervasive, naturalized, and hard to disavow.
>
> (Tucker 2010, 559)

This "unremarked nature" of radio narratives in the country opens the possibility for programmers to devise aural environments that persuade listeners by co-creating all-encompassing sonic envelopes, which organically index social class and ethnicity. The pervasiveness of radio aural environments can be seen not only within the privacy of houses or workplaces but also especially outdoors, in the shared and thickly polluted soundscapes of urban Lima. Traveling in Lima's public transportation, for instance, frequently becomes a sort of passive indoctrination in which passengers of *combis* and *custers* (nicknames given to popular small and medium-size public transportation vehicles) involuntarily hear radio programs being played loudly by bus drivers. This involuntary audition is of the utmost importance here when considering that, according to Lima's Management of Urban Transportation an average citizen in Lima "loses" three to four hours every day when traveling in public vehicles.[3]

Grupo RPP stations such as Oxigeno and La Zona broadcast contents that communicate ideas about class and social position articulated through tailored sonic moods, genres, and playlists. Broadcasting editorial policies disseminate generalized notions of "self" and "other" as well as monolithic identity categories. However, rather than seeking to structure society by overtly imposing disparaging fixed categories, radio programmers seek to enable an "accepted intrusion" to ensure the maintenance of a captive listenership. Here it is relevant to reframe Grupo RPP's broadcasting policies through the lens of Michael Burawoy's idea of work as a game. Burawoy's construct will help to understand the way in which persuasive programming techniques deployed by criollo marketing specialists reinforce systems of class control. He uses the "work as a game" concept to discuss the methods employed in "factory regimes" (1985) and argues that modern labor markets devise policies that procure a spontaneous subjugation of workers to the rule of capitalist machinery. This spontaneous subjugation, Burawoy maintains, is achieved by factory management, which persuades workers that extra labor and internal competition inside the factory is a game and not a form of overt exploitation.

THE GAME OF BEING A LISTENER

Burawoy argues that to perpetuate the hegemony of capitalist systems, factory managements have developed a strategy to recontextualize everyday coercive and dehumanizing work environments in the form of a game involving self-realizing competition among workers and managers. In the workers' eyes, Burawoy affirms, the game approach transforms the executive mandate of securing surplus labor—that is, employees' unpaid hours of work—into a bearable and eventually desirable lifestyle. He points out that during his ethnographic experience inside an American factory the promotion of work as a game was "effective in generating consent [from the workers] only because it precluded the *arbitrary* application of coercion (punitive sanctions that ranged from disciplinary procedures to firing)" (1985, 194, his emphasis). Moreover, this modality of human control was developed in the factory because management could simply no longer hire and fire at will due to the growing influence of labor unions in the United States. For this reason, Burawoy lastly asserts, "No longer able to rely on the despotism of early capitalism, management had to *persuade* workers to deliver surplus labor; that is, management had to manufacture consent" (194).

I contend that a similar form of persuasion is enacted by Grupo RPP through its imposed association between music style and social position, in that consultants and programmers work together to devise media contents that give listeners the illusion of being in control of the songs and playlists they listen to when dialing the station of their choice. A case in point is Studio92, Grupo RPP's "youthful station," which targets socioeconomic levels A and B: that is, the most educated and affluent criollo sector of the society, according to leading marketing analysts. This station sets musical trends nationwide and broadcasts a range of English-speaking international pop artists such as Avril Lavigne, Selena Gomez, Pitbull, and One Direction. According to Mr. Gutierrez, Studio92 is defined by an ethos of freshness and cosmopolitanism, conveying a sense of uninhibitedness to its listeners. These characteristics are associated, in criollo thought, with the higher socioeconomic spheres of society that have earned a formal (Western-influenced) education or possess a Caucasian heritage (Cadena 1988; Drinot 2006). Contradictorily, and perhaps for this very reason, the station's most loyal audience comprises young citizens within lower levels B and C (API 2013), consisting of mestizos and sometimes young Amerindians who apparently seek to rework their socioeconomic identity by acquiring a more reputable musical taste to the eyes of criollo elites. Presenters at Studio92 are playful and mischievous; they are "showmen, actors, and famous people who have some recognition in the media." In addition, the inclusion of online social networks such as Facebook and Twitter has become a valuable tool for reaching out to this audience. Through online networking, programmers keep track of audiences' tastes and points of view while promoting an apparent democratization of the playlist. Studio92 followers are encouraged to request their favorite songs and artists by posting messages to the station's Facebook wall, even though, as a Grupo RPP programmer mentioned to me in a private conversation, the broadcasted material within this and other stations is never strongly influenced by public opinion. Rather, playlists circulate day by day, remaining impervious to the likes and dislikes posted on social networking websites. "There is a playlist we all need to respect," this programmer said, and added with some dismay: "Everything repeats itself."

Similar to the factory workers investigated by Burawoy, Lima's followers of popular radio stations such as Studio92 voluntarily become segmented audiences, whose social position and cultural values are both assessed and sanctioned by marketing consultants. The aesthetic sonic concepts broadcast by the corporation help persuade listeners that they will find individual (and apparent) self-realization by becoming engaged radio listeners. The concept of work as a game is played out here as a sincere assumption on the part of audiences that their social identities are well mirrored, nurtured, and understood by disc jockeys who recognize and value the uniqueness of each listener/individual. By extension, Lima's audiences consent in this way to be subjects of the segregation policies enforced by mainstream commercial media—especially by becoming captive audiences of stations that air aesthetic concepts which, at their core, constitute sanctioned discourses about race, social position, and economic power. Building on the radio scholar Oscar H. Gandy's critique of audience segmentation practices, it can be argued that Lima's radio listeners who find themselves positively mirrored by Grupo RPP's stations are being disdained by the workings of a social construction that strips away the diversity of individual complexity to assign "invidious distinctions" (Gandy 2000) among them. In Lima, local radio programming has become an effective way to "divide audiences into racialized segments" and to render them merely "markets or products" (Gandy 2001). In turn, radio archives are disseminated in a way that reinforces a mechanical and repetitive consumption of musical trends and media stereotypes, which are framed by preconceptions regarding the appropriate taste of given ethnic communities.

Through this path of action, the concentration of technical resources that disseminate authoritative (but concealed) discourses about human value enables Grupo RPP to manipulate information and structure musical trends in a way that diminishes listeners' ability to deviate from the dominant ideology. In this sense, the disenfranchised sectors of Lima's society assume a role of subalternity; they actively consume and conform to the sonic aesthetic concepts articulated by media specialists. The term "subalternity" is a much-debated concept but, for the present discussion, I focus on a construct of subalternity that relates to the degree of "deviation" (Spivak 1988, 80; Svensson 2012, 13) that positions cultural forms generated by oppressed or socioeconomically disenfranchised groups *against* or *below* dominant ideologies concerning general notions of beauty, civilization, and knowledge. In this sense, when there is any deviation, the expressive culture of the disenfranchised community has been normalized and disciplined according to the dominant standards. If, on the other hand, expressive forms deviate from the standard discourse, then a sense of impropriety and illegitimacy is cast over these expressions. In this scenario, where one hegemonic discourse sets the norm and determines different degrees of conformity and deviance, the subaltern group (Lima's lower socioeconomic segmented audiences) cannot find effective ways to represent or express their dynamic constitution as a social group. This occurs because most of the variables are controlled and supplied by criollos through massive dissemination of a universalizing discourse. The impossibility of the segmented audience's diverting from the norm by choosing original musical products or even consuming their own leads them to adopt an almost complete conformance with the set of criollo values that so overtly disparages them.

The elite-subaltern relation shaped by a reduced ability to deviate from the norm is equivalent to the vertical relation established in Grupo RPP's dissemination model. In both cases, a disempowered receiver is only able to accept or negate the reception of the cultural artifact. The elite that releases the artifact can control the conditions in which the process is enacted. Moreover, it also regulates exactly which objects are broadcast to accomplish what purposes. The vertical relation that emerges from this procedure exemplifies the role of hegemonic racial discourses that shape Lima's society under criollo media investors. For instance, the elite-subaltern relation is maintained in Lima between "classic Limeños" and "neo-Limeños" (Arellano and Burgos 2010, 77)—that is, between criollos who are perceived as the original bearers of progressive culture and Amerindian migrants who are seen as the defenders of decaying notions of beauty, civilization, and knowledge. In this vertical scale, wealthy classic Limeños inside the Grupo RPP use the airwaves to amplify a discourse based on neocolonial stereotypes that strengthen a sense of class-belonging within lower socioeconomic strata without resorting to direct discriminatory messages, which are difficult to tolerate in a contemporary global society.

In contrast, neo-Limeños are persuaded to become malleable consumers of radio content that is designed based on the assumption that race and taste are interconnected, fixed categories. Even though my research in Lima's peripheral urban areas shows that original expressive forms of culture are rapidly emerging as the product of novel Andean/mestizo sensibilities (Odria 2017), mainstream radio broadcasting is still overpowering audiences' capacity to produce or appreciate alternative musical voices at the macro level. Simultaneously, the concentration of power held by radio corporations is being acknowledged by guilds of local musicians, who have recently led a controversial movement demanding that mainstream radio stations include contemporary Peruvian music of any kind in their daily programming. For instance, the musician and activist Walter Cobos has asserted, "Peruvian music has the right to be aired in the radio"; nonetheless, he maintained, "Radio stations have been repeating the same hits for more than 50 years" and this occurs because "stations simply don't want to broadcast our national music."[4] Even though such movements are advocating for a real democratization of the airwaves by spreading awareness of media corporations' monopoly on the dissemination of culture, the criollo elite's capacity to control political and public opinion remains undiminished.

THAT LIMA IS GONE

Within every aspect of urban life, Lima's Amerindians have disavowed the long-lasting dream of returning the city to its fabled status of *Ciudad de los Reyes* (City of Kings), as it was nicknamed by Spaniards when Lima became the center of political power and commercial trade during the Viceroyalty of Peru (1545–1824). During the rapid demographic changes that characterized the second half of the twentieth century, the dynamic economic activity carried out by rural migrants in the city led to the formation of what has been described as an "informal economy": an innovative mode of production, distribution, and consumption of goods that defied criollos' legally formal apparatus. Lima's informal economy is perhaps one of the most radical cultural developments made by Amerindians, and it has helped them contest the paternalistic and oppressive tutelage of a discriminatory state (De Soto 1988, 4). However, the informal economy has not solved all the relevant issues. Criollos and migrants still perpetuate frictions that reflect their clashing aesthetic ideals. Additionally, the rise of the mediascape has provided criollos with a new platform from which to battle the influence of Amerindian cultures at a massive scale.

On the one hand, the "City of Kings" ideal has been an aesthetic and moral referent for many criollos wishing to re-create an imagined milieu of Western splendor and a pleasure-oriented life ruled by European standards; on the other hand, rural migrants have become by now Lima's majority, constituting 87.3 percent of the total population (Arellano and Burgos 2010, 76). Historically, the tensions that sprang out of the cultural clash between older and newer residents throughout the twentieth century have been expressed, for example, in the state's sponsoring of Western-based educational policies that sought to diminish the relative value of Andean traditions and practices while praising the universal superiority of Western art and culture (Cadena 2010). In everyday social life, urban highlanders have been marginalized because their use of Andean communal models centered, for example, on the formation of self-sustained and self-organized neighborhood organizations (Degregori et al. 1986; Golte and Adams 1990; Zapata Velasco 1996). From the elite's and government's perspective, the incorporation of Andean practices can be harmful to the legitimacy of the modern nation-state. Additionally, it is common to hear phrases in everyday criollo conversations that scorn and look down on migrants' modes of living. As an Amerindian/Mestizo Limeño, I grew up accustomed to phrases that refer to Andean descendants and mestizos as *cholos*, a category that denotes a culturally backward and racially inferior sector of the population. Criollos have traditionally deemed this sector of society extraneous to the city's original European composition. In fact, as a response to their limited economic resources and the institutionalized segregation exerted by urban metropolitan neighbors, most of the incoming migrants settled in shantytowns beyond the margins of the urban territory, where they generated innovative forms of socioeconomic organization combining Andean, national, and transnational practices (Montoya 2010).

Despite their inventiveness and rapid acclimatization to the demands of an oppressive environment, highlanders who moved to the city were perceived as carriers of a static identity that had negative attributes such as primitiveness and antisociality. Uncountable times, I have heard migrants referred to as unhygienic, treacherous, repressed (*reprimidos*), ugly, and racially weak as well as lacking a sense of taste and enjoying dissonant and uncultivated music. These types of descriptions arise from a criollo belief in the superiority of Western standards. The ability for criollos to determine the value of beauty and social practices from a positivistic stance is rooted in a moral conception of the world. As the purported descendants of Spanish conquistadores and heirs of their traditions, Lima's elites proclaim themselves the cultural bearers of tradition and modernity, assuming this dominant role in conjunction with the state's national agenda. Following this, the aesthetic priorities of the criollos—as reflected in their consumption preferences, social etiquette, forms of entertainment, and musical taste—are hoisted as markers of universally accepted quality not only within the strongholds of aristocratic life in metropolitan Lima, but also, and perhaps more importantly here, in the scale of social values that inform the content of the local mediascape that reaches every sector of society.

As seen in Mr. Gutierrez's description of Grupo RPP radio editorial policies, the patriarchal sense of authority inherited by criollos perpetuates and reworks itself using manufacturing forms of political leadership and social influence. It does so seeking to shape or coerce the agency of Andean descendants in Lima. In the present time, this form of regulation is better achieved through mediascape propaganda that imparts and articulates hierarchies based on inherited cultural authority. Simultaneously, criollos face the difficulty of achieving control over the vibrant transformation of Lima's culture by booming Andean migrant communities. Influenced by an ethos of constant innovation, highlanders have learned to adjust quickly as a means of survival. This social dynamism, of course, also affects their aesthetic preferences and consumption practices, a situation that forces radio programmers to maintain a sensitive ear for the inception of trends so genre stations can profit from their captive audiences. Ultimately, processes of archival dissemination, reflected in the customization of radio playlists, have evolved to subsume and, to a large extent, normalize initially diverging musical trends pursued by migrants. It seems that the infrastructural control of the mediascape is finally tipping the scale in favor of the criollos.

CONCLUSION

The act of regulating the dissemination of songs through playlists can enact or indicate modes of unequal power distribution, thus reinforcing a sense of subalternity. In this chapter, I built from repatriation studies to examine the way in which a powerful media corporation regulates radio broadcasting to accomplish precisely that goal. Lima's media investors foment a cultural process that has a bearing in the structuring of society.

As I argued, listeners of Grupo RPP have become passive receivers of songs that articulate ideological contents by means of their premeditated arrangement. Even if listeners have the choice of turning off their devices or listening to another station, in reality, their musical choices have already been determined by a limited range of products and the impact of trending categories propagated by class-specific stations. In a way, by being persuaded, they have already been caught inside a game that only permits variance of limited and predetermined deviations.

In Lima's postcolonial society, the process of disseminating songs or styles at a massive scale is initiated by criollo privileged groups. This prerogative grants them the ability to frame relationships with their listenership at will, shaping the roles of those who release songs and those who receive them. Since listeners of mainstream radio tend to develop a sense of symbolic or affective ownership of the artists and songs they follow, discussing ongoing relationships between audiences and programmers sheds light on the ethical substructures that permeate repatriation processes from the perspective I present here. In other words, at first sight, the ownership of selected mainstream radio songs appears to be fluidly conceded by programmers to their Lima audiences; nonetheless, in reality, the process of passing down the songs itself constitutes the mechanism by which ownership is controlled and negated. This regulating aspect of the broadcasting industry institutes a cultural process that aims to preserve a disarticulated and hierarchized body politic through establishing statistical socioeconomic parameters and developing aural moods to match them. Thus, in order to excavate the ethical intricacies of broadcasting, I used a concept of repatriation that focuses on three interrelated ideas: radio playlists and editorial policies constitute dynamic archives; broadcasting is used to disseminate not only songs but also ideology; and repatriation vertically frames social relations between media investors and listeners.

To return something (an object, a favor) involves a social transaction—that is, the establishment of basic relations that connect at least two individuals with varying cognitive constitutions, socioeconomic backgrounds, or political orientations. Similarly, the passing down of an artifact in a repatriation process also implies a basic relation. I have argued that media investors who disseminate selective playlists handle songs from a position of cultural and economic authority. In this light, criollo tycoons circulate aural contents to establish relations with their audiences, aiming to persuade them to adopt ready-made musical preferences and, through this means, reinforce a system of typological classification. Then, sonic repatriation, broadly understood in the form of a social transaction, can become an operation in which an unequal distribution of power leads to the strengthening of subalternity. Criollo racial discourse, which morphs into radio editorial policies, emerges as a reaction to the arrival of Andean migrants and as a social ideology centered on praising and encouraging conservative musical practices built on an idealized European model.

Such discourse and ideology acquired momentum when the Western-educated class sought to develop distinctive criollo musical expressions to counteract the Andeanization of Lima's soundscape (Llorens 1983, 78). The corollary of this friction is that foremost criollo corporations such as Grupo RPP continue to envision the development of a society in which a fractured population can be easily kept beneath the elite's rule. Broadcasting strategies are deployed to maintain racial hierarchies, actively shaping the representation of social groups within the spectrum of diverse radio aesthetics. The way in which rural migrants and mestizos are negatively "imagined" (Anderson 2006) within this spectrum, as a passive and homogeneous community—arguably lacking the cultural capital to achieve responsible political agency—appears palpable in the segmentation of radio audiences. The verticality needed to mold the process of disseminating sonic narratives, fraught as they are with subtexts of class and race, has forced Lima mainstream media corporations to employ persuasive techniques to reelaborate typecast concepts of beauty and to preserve a given social order.

Notes

1. Unless stated otherwise, all quotes in this chapter come from my interviews and conversations conducted in 2013 with "Mr. Gutierrez," my main informant at Grupo RPP, whose real name I keep confidential. These are my translations from Spanish.
2. I could not corroborate the existence of this poll and the percentages quoted by Mr. Gutierrez.
3. "Proyectos: Concesion de rutas: Problematica," Gerencia de Transporte Urbano, http://www.gtu.munlima.gob.pe/proyectos/concesionrutas_problematica.htm (accessed November 14, 2013).
4. "Percy Cespedez and Walter Cobos: 'Peruvian Music Has the Right to Be Aired in the Radio,'" *Peru.com*, November 12, 2013, http://peru.com/entretenimiento/musica/percy-cespedez-y-walter-cobos-musica-peruana-tiene-derecho-sonar-radios-noticia-128306.

References

Acevedo, Jorge. 2011. "La radio y la televisión en la coyuntura electoral. ¿La mejor regulación es la que no existe?" *La Mirada de Telemo* 6: 1–5.

Acevedo, Jorge. 2013. "La imposible neutralidad: Radios educativas y comunitarias en el contexto de conflictos socioambientales." *Perspectivas* 2: 1–18.

Anderson, Benedict. 2006. *Imagined Communities: Reflections on the Origin and Spread of Nationalism*. London: Verso.

APEIM. 2005. *Niveles socioeconomicos en Lima Metropolitana y Callao*. Lima: Asociación Peruana de Empresas de Investigacion de Mercados.

API. 2013. "Audiencias radiales 2012: Resumen anual." *Market Report* 2 (February).

Arellano, Rolando, and David Burgos. 2010. *Ciudad de los Reyes, de los Chavez, de los Quispe*. Lima: Editorial Planeta.

Boesten, Jelke. 2010. *Intersecting Inequalities: Women and Social Policy in Peru, 1990–2000*. University Park: Pennsylvania State University Press.

Burawoy, Michael. 1979. *Manufacturing Consent: Changes in the Labor Process under Monopoly Capitalism*. Chicago: University of Chicago.

Burawoy, Michael. 1985. *The Politics of Production: Factory Regimes under Capitalism and Socialism*. London: Verso.

Burawoy, Michael. 2012. "The Roots of Domination: Beyond Bourdieu and Gramsci." *Sociology* 46 (2): 187–206.

Cadena, Marisol de la. 1988. "Silent Racism and Intellectual Superiority in Peru." *Bulletin of Latin American Research* 17 (2): 143–164.

Cadena, Marisol de la. 2010. "Indigenous Cosmopolitics in the Andes: Conceptual Reflections beyond 'Politics.'" *Cultural Anthropology* 25 (2): 334–370.

Crabtree, John, ed. 2006. *Making Institutions Work in Peru: Democracy, Development and Inequality since 1980*. London: University of London.

Degregori, Carlos Iván, Cecilia Blondet, and Nicolás Lynch. 1986. *Conquistadores de un Nuevo Mundo: De Invasores a Ciudadanos en San Martín de Porres*. Lima: Instituto de Estudios Peruanos.

Drinot, Paulo. 2006. "Nation-Building, Racism, and Inequality: Institutional Development in Peru in Historical Perspective." In *Making Institutions Work in Peru: Democracy, Development, and Inequality since 1980*, edited by John Crabtree, 5–23. London: Institute for the Study of the Americas.

Edmondson, Ray. 2004. *Audiovisual Archiving: Philosophy and Principles*. Paris: UNESCO.

Feldman, Heidi. 2006. *Black Rhythms of Peru: Reviving African Musical Heritage in the Black Pacific*. Middletown, CT: Wesleyan University Press.

Ferguson, Thomas J., Roger Anyon, and Edmund J. Ladd. 2000. "Repatriation at the Pueblo of Zuni: Diverse Solutions to Complex Problems." In *Repatriation Reader: Who Owns American Indian Remains?*, edited by Davon Abbott, 239–265. Lincoln: University of Nebraska Press.

Fforde, Cressida, Jane Hubert, and Paul Turnbull. 2004. *The Dead and Their Possessions: Repatriation in Principle, Policy and Practice*. London: Routledge.

Fine-Dare, Kathleen Sue. 2002. *Grave Injustice: The American Indian Repatriation Movement and NAGPRA*. Lincoln: University of Nebraska Press.

Gandolfo, Daniella M. 2006. "The City as Its Limits: Taboo, Transgression, and Urban Renewal in Lima, Peru." PhD diss., Columbia University.

Gandy, Oscar H. 2000. "Audience Segmentation: Is It Racism or Just Good Business?" *Media Development* 47 (2): 3–6.

Gandy, Oscar H. 2001. "Dividing Practices: Segmentation and Targeting in the Emerging Public Sphere." In *Mediated Politics: Communication in the Future of Democracy*, edited by Bennett W. Lance and Robert M. Entman, 141–159. Cambridge: Cambridge University Press.

Golte, Jürgen, and Norma Adams. 1990. *Los Caballos de Troya de los Invasores: Estrategias campesinas en la Conquista de la Gran Lima*. Lima: Instituto de Estudios Peruanos.

Jacknis, Ira. 1996. "Repatriation as Social Drama: The Kwakiutl Indians of British Columbia, 1922–1980." *American Indian Quarterly* 20 (2): 274–286.

Llorens, José Antonio. 1983. *Música popular en Lima: Criollos y Andinos*. Lima: Instituto de Estudios Peruanos.

Matos Mar, José. 1969. "Dominación, desarrollos desiguales y pluralismos en la sociedad y culturas peruanas." In *Peru Problema*, edited by José Matos Mar and Augusto Salazar Bondy, 13–52. Lima: Instituto de Estudios Peruanos.

Matos Mar, José. 1984. *Desborde popular y crisis del estado: El nuevo rostro del Perú en la DéCADA de 1980*. Lima: Instituto de Estudios Peruanos.

McIntosh, Molly L. 2006. "Exploring Machu Picchu: An Analysis of the Legal and Ethical Issues Surrounding the Repatriation of Cultural Property." *Duke Journal of Comparative and International Law* 17: 199–221.

Mihesuah, Devon Abbott, ed. 2000. *Repatriation Reader: Who Owns American Indian Remains?* Lincoln: University of Nebraska Press.

Montoya, Rodrigo. 2010. *Porvenir de la cultura Quechua en Perú: Desde Lima, Villa El Salvador y Puquio.* Lima: Fondo Editorial de la Universidad Nacional Mayor de San Marcos.

Nannyonga-Tamusuza, Sylvia, and Andrew N. Weintraub. 2012. "The Audible Future: Reimagining the Role of Sound Archives and Sound Repatriation in Uganda." *Ethnomusicology* 56 (2): 206–233.

Odria, Carlos. 2017. "Seeking a New Path: Pasacalle Activists Practicing Culture in Villa El Salvador, Perú." *Ethnomusicology* 61 (1): 1–30.

Soto, Hernando de. 1988. "Why Does the Informal Economy Matter?" *Estudios Publicos* 30 (Fall): 1–11.

Spivak, Gayatri. 1988. "Can the Subaltern Speak?" In *Marxism and the Interpretation of Culture*, edited by Cary Nelson and Larry Grossberg, 271–313. Chicago: University of Illinois Press.

Svensson, Fredrik. 2012. "Paolo Freire, Gayatri Spivak, and the (Im)possibility of Education: The Methodological Leap in Pedagogy of the Oppressed and 'Righting Wrongs.'" PhD diss., Södertörn University.

Thorp, Rosemary, and Mariza Paredes. 2010. *Ethnicity and the Persistence of Inequality: The Case of Peru.* Basingstoke, UK: Palgrave Macmillan.

Tucker, Joshua. 2010. "Music Radio and Global Mediation." *Cultural Studies* 24 (4): 553–579.

Zapata Velasco, Antonio. 1996. *Sociedad y poder local: La Comunidad de Villa El Salvador, 1971, 1996.* Lima: DESCO.

CHAPTER 27

....

THE BANNING OF SAMOA'S
REPATRIATED MAU SONGS

....

RICHARD MOYLE

THIS chapter focuses on a series of songs recorded in former Western Samoa (now Samoa) and is somewhat unusual in that the recordings ceased to exist in their initial format more than fifty years ago. However, just as live performances of the songs are known to have roused high emotions during the nationalistic activities of the 1920s and 1930s, for which these songs were composed, so too the radio broadcast of digital copies three Samoan generations later generated a set of rapid and intense responses from listeners. Repatriation of the copies initially paved the way for those responses.

The recordings, all 78 rpm discs, carried the New Zealand Broadcasting Service (NZBS) label, indicating that the pressings occurred during the organization's sixteen-year existence from 1936 to 1962 (Peterson 2001, 23), and the 78 rpm format suggests an earlier time within that period. From the beginning of World War I until (Western) Samoa's independence in 1962, the country was administered by New Zealand under a League of Nations mandate, and it is reasonable to assume that the original recordings were made primarily for use in Samoa itself, although their intended purpose and the occasion, location, and date are unknown. The NZBS became the New Zealand Broadcasting Corporation in 1962 and Radio New Zealand in 1995. No broadcasting occurred in Western Samoa between 1933 and 1946 (although it is of course possible that the recordings of the material discussed here occurred during that period). The Radio New Zealand Sound Archive has neither copies nor even documentation of the existence of the recordings, and no other copies of the discs are known to exist. In 1966, while in Samoa undertaking more than two years of research on traditional music, I requested dubs from these discs, then still in use for broadcasting.[1]

Over the next thirty-five years, the dubs were kept in the Archive of Maori and Pacific Music at the University of Auckland. They were also included on an LP of traditional Samoan songs (Moyle 1989) and on a CD devoted to Mau songs (Archive of Maori and Pacific Music 2004). In 2000, the dubs were also included in a large quantity of audio material repatriated to Radio 2AP, but within a few weeks were banned from airing by the minister of broadcasting. To understand the intensity of feeling aroused by the postrepatriation broadcasts of songs created and performed more than sixty-five years earlier, as well as the subsequent ban, it is necessary to examine two topics, the first of which is the cultural potential of Samoan singing.[2]

SAMOAN SONGS AS POLITICAL ARTIFACTS

The act of singing in Samoa was formerly, among other things, a means of opening a direct line of communication with the supernatural world, particularly with those spirits thought to be causing a sickness (Moyle 1988, 72–74) and thereby effecting a cure. But on a more general level, singing was, and is, widely acknowledged as a superior form of verbal utterance: culturally superior in that, unlike other formal forms of utterance, a song performance may not be interrupted, and aesthetically superior in that the performed lyrics have the inherent capacity to generate and sustain a range of emotions, including joy and sorrow, self-pride and humility, courage and anger. One measure of the social significance of any event is the creation of a new song for a single performance at that event but, in part through the widely used structural elements of assonant rhyme and strophes and in part through the skillful blend of the linguistically familiar and the unexpected, some lyrics live on long after the event for which they were originally created.

Songs voicing criticism are of two kinds: spontaneous and planned. Most villages have in living memory encountered a socially competitive situation in which one group sought to assert its superiority at the expense of another, in many cases composing a spontaneous responsorial couplet whose first line was sung by a leader and the second by an ad hoc group, for example:

Nuʻu lāiti e	You puny villages—
Nuʻu laiti faʻafiatele	You puny villages, you speak provocatively
ʻAe ʻā maua sasa maini.	But when I catch you,
	you'll be thrashed till you tingle.
[X] e, sola ʻi lalō	Oh, [X]—flee back down
Tefe pea ʻo le Mālō	Let the Administration circumcise itself.
[X] valevalea	[X] village—is really stupid
Fana le peʻa, lē lavea	They shoot at a flying fox—but fail to injure it
Fuʻe le umu, ʻeleʻelea.	They uncover an earth-oven—but get all dirty.
Tepa ʻiā [X] ʻua mū	Gaze on [X] village: it's burning
Mū pea ia—	Let it burn—
ʻO se nuʻu e faʻatalatū.	That village of impotent boasters.

The second kind of song voicing criticism represents the collective voice of a large so-cial unit, typically a village, and is the subject of group discussion, composition, and rehearsal before performance at a predetermined occasion. By convention, the language of the lyrics is restrained and dignified, and the overall structure may parallel that of a spoken speech (Tuʻi 1987). It is to this kind of song that the old recordings discussed here belong.[3]

A further contextualizing topic is the historical and cultural significance of the song lyrics under discussion, which relate to the nationalistic movement of the 1920s and 1930s known as the Mau.

SONGS OF THE MAU

Field's study of the Mau (1984, 1991) confirms the use of singing to rally support, create and sustain a sense of group identity, and ridicule the opposition. The following are typical:

> [the Administrator] Richardson reported that a group of Mau from Savaiʻi had marched through Apia streets singing what he called "defiant and obscene songs." He said he had identified the responsible chiefs and had ordered them to appear be-fore the Fono a Faipule [Government Council] to explain themselves. As they had refused he would arrest them on breach of the peace charges. But, said Richardson, he would need six extra police from New Zealand.
>
> (Field 1984, 110)

> Shortly after the attempted arrest of [Paramount Chief] Tupua Tamasese, some 300 Mau supporters from Palauli, Savaiʻi, arrived in Apia singing anti-Government songs and making threatening speeches.
>
> (Field 1984, 122)

> Led by [several Mau leaders], they had marched into town, some carrying knives and clubs, chanting:
>
> Samoa! Samoa! The military police are coming,
> **The military police are coming to have a war with us.**
> **We are frightened, we are frightened, O Samoa! O Samoa!**
>
> (Field 1984, 123)

> July 24, 1936. At a mass rally in support of the return of the deported Mau leader O. F. Nelson, "songs against New Zealand were sung and large banners depicting the shooting of Tupua Tamasese were displayed."

Acting-Administrator Turnbull added, somewhat disingenuously, perhaps to cover the dignity of his own position, "It must be said, however, that these songs were sung in very good spirit and must not be taken literally at word value" (Field 1984, 214).[4] For their part, the hastily recruited New Zealanders making up the Samoan Military Police did not help matters, and they responded in kind on at least one occasion:

> Samoa Military Police recruited in New Zealand, . . . on one occasion were heard "singing insulting songs in Samoan."
>
> (Field 1984, 125)

In his contribution to *Remembering the Mau*, the historian Barry Rigby noted (Anonymous 1997, 99):

> Tamasese earned instant and enduring martyrdom. Whereas NZ erects grey stone monuments for its fallen heroes, Samoans remember Tamasese in the words of a well-known song which, in English, goes:
>
> > The machine gun goes rat-tat-tat
> > The chief stopped and said
> > please keep the peace
> > look up to the sky [or God] for solutions
> > allow Britain [New Zealand] to do as she wants.
> >
> > Oh Governor [Prime Minister], you have denied
> > that you did not know of the
> > machine gun, but . . . [we know]
> > that you are responsible for pulling the trigger.

By contrast, the songs I had obtained in the 1960s were of a different kind: long (up to twelve verses) and including the chiefly titles of Mau participants, as well as mythological expressions and biblical references. In short, such songs were the functional equivalent of oratory, which is a prominent element of Samoan chiefly culture. Three examples follow:[5]

'Ua pāpā fana o le Mālō ma le Kōvana	The Government and the Administrator kept firing their guns.
'Ua fola i le ala sui o nofoaga	Representatives of settlements were spread out on the road;
'O le toto 'ua masa'a, Tamasese 'ua alaga	Blood was spilt, and Tamasese stood up.
E leai se peau e laga 'ae te'i 'ua fana	There was even not a wave breaking, but suddenly he was shot;
'Ua masoe i le ala le alofi o 'Ā'ana.	He was wounded on the road at the gathering at 'Ā'ana.

Se'i faitau maia pe fia o le Kōmiti 'ua aulia	Do count for me how many of the [Mau]
'O le sauaga na fai i Apia	Committee were present
'O suafa ia 'ua tusia	After the barbarism perpetuated in Apia:
'Ua sau fo'i ma manuao	Their names have indeed been recorded.
'Ua se'ia vao a le Mau 'o le pule fa'a-vaegā'au	Warships came, and
	The Mau's forests were uprooted during the martial law.
E to'alua 'ua ta fana o le Mau.	And two of the Mau were shot.
Tālofa i le tagi mai ala	Alas for the weeping on the road:
'Ua malepe le fale o le agāga	The very heart of the matter has been wrecked
'O le Kōvana fo'i 'ua na fanafana	Even the Administrator was firing—
Pei lā 'o se Mau fo'i 'ua agasala.	As if a member of the Mau could have been at fault....
'Ailoga 'ā taumate Niu Sila lou māsiasi	New Zealand, doubtless you don't realize your shame
Nusipepa 'o lo'o 'ua alu 'ua so'o le lalolagi	Newspaper accounts are going out, encircling the globe, so
'A 'o fea lau āmio tonu ma lou sasagi?	Where now is your justice and your pride?
Tālofa 'e te lē mamate.	What a pity you didn't all die.

It should be noted that explicit attacks are not the only form of effective poetics: praise of a leader also constitutes implicit criticism of the leader's political opponents.

Enduring interest in the Mau was not confined to Samoa itself but spread to New Zealand, as the numbers of Samoans emigrating there rose and non-Samoan authors and scholars kept such matters of recent history in the public arena. In 1979, Philip J. Parr privately published an analysis of the Mau titled *The Murder of Tamasese*, which had the stated aim, "Fifty years later, let the truth be known!" (Parr 1979, 3). Between 1989 and 1995, the journalist Michael Field and a military historian within the Department of Internal Affairs, Ian McGibbon, exchanged several vituperative letters in Wellington newspapers on issues of responsibility and culpability for the series of events in Samoa culminating in 1929 with the shooting by New Zealand forces of the paramount chief Tupua Tamasese Lealofi III.[6]

In 1994, Victoria University of Wellington's Samoan Studies section held an event at which Field and McGibbon presented in person their contrasting views.[7] In 1991–1992, an oral history–gathering project titled *E le galo le Mau* ("Remembering the Mau")[8] was undertaken among sixteen New Zealand–resident Samoans who witnessed the events of the Mau, and a few academics (including this author).[9] Transcripts of interviews with Mau observers (published in Anonymous 1997) indicate that a few songs continued to be widely known, sung live (e.g., 117, 133–134, 147, 151–152, 163), and played on the radio

(121), and that they continued to be known until the end of the twentieth century. The transcripts also confirm two situations that were to directly affect the repatriation. Samoa itself was not totally united in its opposition to New Zealand administration; individual families, villages, and even whole districts were known to oppose the Mau and its intentions.

RECORDED SONGS OF THE MAU

While living in Samoa in the 1960s, I used to hear on the radio some—perhaps all— of the songs I had dubbed; most had no pre- or back-announcement and were played close to the station's close-down time on a Sunday night as part of the regular broadcast then of older recordings by secular choirs. Although it may have been a function of the Samoan circles in which I moved, I did not hear any adverse comments about the propriety of either the songs themselves or the broadcast of them. During those fieldwork years I also encountered many Samoans who remembered the Mau songs, to the point where the identity and significance of proper names in the lyrics were explained to me and, through constant replay of the dubs, I was eventually able to sing along with middle-aged folk in several villages in the privacy of their homes. I also recorded a few male groups singing Mau songs that were apparently unknown beyond their own village environs and were not among those held at 2AP. In later years, recordings of Mau songs reemerged on at least two occasions in New Zealand. In 1995, John Kneubuhl's play *Think of a Garden* premiered in Auckland. Kneubuhl, a child in Samoa when Tamasese was shot, based his play on the events leading up to the shooting, from the perspective of a family living in American Samoa. I was asked by the play's producer to provide copies of the old recordings to add a sense of realism to some of the staged actions, and for several months thereafter I received a stream of requests from local Samoans for further copies for their own use.

Again in Auckland in 2004, a one-day symposium on the Mau was organized by the University of Auckland's Centre for Pacific Studies. To a packed venue, several speakers—Samoans, historians (including the Department of Internal Affairs historian), authors (including Michael Field), and a former Samoan prime minister (Tupua Tamasese Tuiatua Tupuola Efi)—referred in their presentations to the existence of contemporary songs and their effectiveness in rallying supporters and humiliating opponents of the movement. The archive had issued a CD of all known Mau songs to coincide with the symposium, and these sold well (Archive of Maori and Pacific Music, 2004), and indeed continue to do so.

On both occasions, Samoans' principal reaction to hearing the songs was the expressed desire to have a personal copy and listen to them again. Of course, the point has to be made that such people appeared to come from families and villages that had supported the Mau, although it was known that other families and even entire villages had been opposed. However, at none of the events outlined above were anti-Mau sentiments expressed or explained, and the overall impression was that the distances of time and place sufficed for at least New Zealand–resident Samoans to view the Mau in general and its songs in particular as historic artifacts of ethnic self-identity and nationalistic pride rather than as proclamations of ongoing political passion.

Within Samoa itself, I had on several occasions offered my own recordings, including Mau songs, to 2AP for consideration for broadcast, and from time to time thereafter heard them played. Beyond the choirs' own villages, however, little interest was apparent among my host families.

Before the repatriation, then, there had been more than a decade of interest within New Zealand in the events, personalities, and songs associated with the Mau and presented in publications, dramatic performances, symposia, and at least one undergraduate course. Within Samoa, none of these phenomena occurred, which might have led an outside observer to believe that there existed little to trouble the waters of local politics. However, those still waters belonged to a river continuing to run deep and about to rise.

THE REPATRIATION

On the retirement in 1993 of the founding director of the Archive of Maori and Pacific Music, Mervyn McLean, I took his position as an adjunct to my existing ethnomusicology teaching within the Department of Anthropology. In addition to maintaining correspondence on a personal level with individual Samoans, I also continued to retain more formal links, including as coteacher of a two-week choral conducting course in 1996, and as chief judge in the choir section of the Teuila national performing arts competition in 1997.

A significant part of my own recordings from the 1960s consisted of fables containing short songs. Wearing my archive director's hat, in 2000 I personally repatriated to Samoa many fables and songs from my own collection, as well as the NZBS recordings, having ascertained through correspondence that the materials were of historical significance and would be welcomed back. The handover to the director of Station 2AP was reported in the local newspaper, and covered live on local radio and television. Broadcasts of the materials followed almost immediately. The range of listener responses could not have been wider. Although hardly any of the fable narrators were still alive thirty-five years after they were recorded, their names and storytelling reputations had endured, and descendants rang in to the station to request copies and repeat playings. But the NZBS recordings were quite another matter, because several songs originated from the Mau. As noted earlier, the Mau movement divided Samoa into supporting and opposing forces whose views prompted mass protests, civil disobedience, and violence, culminating in the allegedly accidental shooting by New Zealand soldiers of Tamasese. The high value Samoan culture places on precedent, competitive prestige, and local pride means that all history, regardless of its age, remains alive. Radio 2AP's phones were flooded, some callers demanding that the song broadcasts should be stopped, others that they be repeated. Threats were made against the station manager and the station premises. Eventually, the minister of broadcasting intervened and formally banned all further airings. By late 2002, the recordings had been removed from the station archives and, although rumors abounded, their whereabouts remained, and remain, unknown.

Precisely because the songs composed and sung in the 1920s and 1930s became popular as political artifacts of the Mau and thus highlighted political differences within Samoa, they were banned seventy years later even though those persons advocating continuation or discontinuation of the broadcasts had not personally experienced the Mau itself. Cultural distance may well explain the differing reactions to repatriation of the songs in the homeland and within Samoa's largest expatriate community, in Auckland; but in both locations the primary response was to their lyrical, rather than their musical, content. They were composed not to foreground any musical distinction but to express through poetry and promulgate through musical performance a set of essentially political views of their times and which, despite the passing of more than half a century and thirty-eight years of national independence, encapsulated those views with an enduring potency sufficient to reignite, among the descendants of those from both sides caught up in the Mau, emotional responses similar to those originally generated by their live performances. Although the act of repatriation itself may have been innocuous, public broadcast was evidently not, forcing back into the public arena the political views, both supportive and opposing, that more than two generations of Samoans had preferred to hold private. The subsequent clash of values required an immediate remedy, which was the removal of the cause.

Was the repatriation exercise worthwhile with respect to the Mau songs? I mused over this matter for more than a decade, privately seeking the views of colleagues and Samoans in both Samoa and New Zealand. On one level, it makes sense that the recordings as historical artifacts had every right to reside in the country where they were created; but on another level, public views about these recordings had hardened over three generations of Mau-affected men and women. The public welcomes afforded the repatriated items as a whole had been preceded by formal correspondence with Radio 2AP, and there was nothing to suggest that the gesture would not be appreciated. Moreover, the subsequent decision to broadcast the Mau songs lay with station staff, who presumably followed any existing programming protocol in doing so. A Samoan government-organized display of historical photographs relating to the Mau, held coincidently at around the time of the repatriation, attracted local interest but did not stimulate any passionate displays of pro- or contra-Mau loyalties. Similarly, Mau song lyrics, long accessible on the Internet, had not roused any large-scale demonstrations of past loyalties. However, it was not the songs themselves that generated intense feelings during the period of Mau activities, nor was it those same songs that caused problems in 2000. In the first instance, the reason was the performances of the songs, and in the second it was the broadcast of recorded performances, confirming my earlier point graphically that the act of singing represents a superior form of verbal utterance. Whereas I repatriated the artifacts, the radio station through the act of broadcasting transformed those passive artifacts into culturally active communication tools of the most powerful form known to Samoans. As such, and because the broadcasts were heard throughout the country, the sentiments expressed in the lyrics could not be ignored.

The postrepatriation events also raise issues about the inherent value of audio archives and their contents. Preservation techniques may ensure the integrity of each item as an audible artifact and allow generations of descendants of the original singers, as well as others, to experience the What? Who? When? and How? of the performance. But the artifact is more than a human creation and of itself cannot illustrate the Why? Why did the lyrics use such themes and forms of language? Why was the performance by a choir, and why that particular choir? Why were such songs so emotionally powerful and politically influential? Why was the reaction to their public broadcast so extreme? Enduring fidelity of acoustic reproduction may be an archival imperative, but clearly it was not a priority for Samoan listeners in 2000. As with any emotive situation, there are nuances and complexities here beyond easy explanation or investigation, especially by a non-Samoan, and there are enduring unknowns. What, for example, changed between the 1960s, when radio broadcasts of Mau songs continued regularly and apparently without large-scale protest, and 2000, when more highly charged responses occurred immediately and eventually succeeded in effecting change? Why did the passage of time since the 1960s harden attitudes toward the Mau rather than blurring memories a further two generations more distant?

Some answers suggest themselves. Repatriation was made to a Samoan society in many ways different from that of the era of the songs' original performances and different also from that of the 1960s. The social differences were more of extent rather than kind and considered as improvements (e.g., communications, health, education) and included also elements of cultural protocols and procedures (e.g., kava ceremonies, awarding of chiefly titles, transference of property). But although Samoans then and now readily confirm such changes, and hold varying views on their desirability insofar as they affect themselves, my experience is that they tend to agree that core Samoan social values remained largely unchanged, as summed up in the recently popular phrase *teu le vā* ("preserving the relationship"). Occasions of cultural or social significance call for forms of verbal expression that praise and thereby legitimize relationships (e.g., those of family, village, government), and nowhere more visibly than in group song.

Samoan group songs are created to meet social requirements and expectations relating to specific occasions, usually at the village level, where they are considered as intangible corporate evidence of the genuineness of opinions expressed in the lyrics. As such, they exceed in prestige the other visible form of public verbal expression, oratory, as summed up in the expression *E seua le lāuga 'ae lē seua le pese* ("A speech may [legitimately] be interrupted, but not a song"). Then and now, by far the greatest number of group songs broadcast on Samoa's several radio stations relating to current events receive a single airing either on or soon after the performance date. Songs composed for specific historical events tend to be archived but rarely, if ever, rebroadcast at a later date. In that light, it appears that broadcast of the Mau songs constituted part of the momentum of a novel event rather than reflecting normal radio station practice.[10] Moreover, the strength of attachment of bespoke song lyrics to an event is such that they cannot be reused for any other event and in most cases are discarded and eventually forgotten. It might be argued that, by allowing preservation of the sonic content, the advent of audio (and later video) recordings intruded on this process of natural attrition, opening the way for songs intended to celebrate events from the past to exert new forms of influence on the present. Such recordings eliminated the original and intrinsic performance relevance of time and place and personnel by allowing for unlimited replay opportunities anytime, anywhere, and for anyone—and nowhere more so than via radio broadcast. On the face of it, public broadcast was the catalyst for an identity change in the Mau songs, from private to public, and this fueled an emotional response in some listeners. However, performances of such songs during the period of the nationalist movement itself were public (although selectively so, since they presumably were attended only by supporters). Broadcast, by contrast, was heard indiscriminately, removing the distinction between supporters and nonsupporters, and bypassing differentiated time, place, and occasion. One might further argue that, because the song lyrics focused on essentially divisive issues of the 1920s and 1930s—to support or to oppose the principles and practices of the Mau movement—they retained the potential to do so again when broadcast more than seventy years later. In sum, although the songs themselves remained unchanged, they were the products of a society which itself had sufficiently changed by the time of repatriation as to generate a strong reaction to the juxtaposition of what were considered mismatched relationships. How many individuals voiced their objection to the broadcasts, and who those people were, is not recorded; all that can be said with certainty is that the objections were of sufficient number and strength as to persuade the minister to act in the way he did.

A possible ethical dimension to the repatriation resides in the decision to transfer the recordings from a university repository in Auckland to a government facility in Samoa. As noted earlier, however, the decision constituted a formal repetition of the more informal provision of copies on request by individual Samoans over several decades. For its part, it seems unlikely that the station would have agreed to receive the material, and organize radio, television, and newspaper coverage of the event, knowing that adverse circumstances would result. As noted, reception in New Zealand was very different: the 1991–1992 national data-collecting project, the 1994 debate in Wellington, and the 2004 symposium in Auckland were all Samoan-led exercises intended to better inform fellow Samoans about one segment of their own history, and as educational initiatives, they were evidently well received. By contrast, no comparable initiatives were conducted in Samoa itself. The inherent values of an intangible cultural artifact capable of objective examination and rational discussion outside the country did not survive transplantation to Samoa itself, where culture is experienced in different subjective ways. Geographical distance enabled a degree of social distance, but the corollary also held true. The repatriated songs constituted items taken from their archival time capsule and reintroduced to a Samoan society similar enough for listeners to recognize and understand the lyrics and to appreciate the ongoing social power of those lyrics, but a society also different enough to be unable to accommodate that power within the prevailing milieu. Public exposure was met by a public response, the unplanned outcome of a planned initiative.

NOTES

1. My journal at that time notes that, except for the announcer's booth, Samoa's 2AP radio station premises were not air conditioned, and these discs were stacked on top of a filing cabinet in the station's open-plan main room. Predictably, in the tropical conditions, they had already warped and to keep the needle in the grooves as the disc revolved, it was necessary to weight the stylus head with a coin secured by chewing gum.

2. Coincidently, there is a precedent for the banning of Samoan musical—or, rather, sung—material. The second publication in the Samoan language, a collection of lyrics of sixteen locally composed songs that combined indigenous and Christian philosophies (Anonymous 1847), was later withdrawn from sale and destroyed by its London Missionary Society publisher, a few copies fortunately surviving.

3. Elsewhere (Moyle 1995, 187–193) I have analyzed the lyrics of one such song.

4. Turnbull's view contrasts with two nineteenth-century authors, both long-term residents in Samoa: "Heavy fines cannot keep the poetic fire from indulging in cutting sarcastic songs, and in war time these are more stinging than gunshot wounds" (Pratt 1890, 655). "The Samoans are very sensitive indeed to ridicule, especially in songs, and the composer of a song needs to be careful not to offend them in this respect" (Brown 1910, 423).

5. Translations appear in Anonymous (1997, 169); Moyle (1995, 174–177).

6. Several of these letters are reproduced in Anonymous (1997).

7. The public announcement of the event exhorted readers, "Be there to learn and share your history, if you are Samoan, or to find out what NZ's role was in the South Pacific in the <u>early</u> days of contact if you are not Samoan" (Anonymous 1997, 73, *emphasis in original*).

8. A closer translation is "the Mau will not be forgotten."

9. The project "was funded by an Australian Sesquicentennial Gift Trust Award in Oral History, administered by Historical Branch, Department of Internal Affairs" (Anonymous 1997, 193), and awarded to the Samoan History Association Committee. The collected transcripts and translations, together with newspaper articles and other relevant publications (including Moyle 1995), were compiled into a workbook for use in Samoan studies teaching at Victoria University of Wellington (Anonymous 1997).

10. And there is irony in that at least one of the early Mau songs was recorded by the NZBS in 2AP's own studio.

REFERENCES

Anonymous. 1847. *O viiga e faalelei a'i atu i le atua moni: Na fatuina e le Samoa.* London: Religious Tract Society.

Anonymous. 1997. *O le toe fa'amanatuina o le Mau [:] Remembering the Mau.* Part 2. The Work-Book of Samoan Studies Students at Victoria University of Wellington, Wellington, New Zealand.

Archive of Maori and Pacific Music. 2004. *Songs of the Mau.* CD. Auckland: Archive of Maori and Pacific Music, University of Auckland.

Brown, George. 1910. *Melanesians and Polynesians: Their Life Histories Described and Compared*. London: Macmillan.

Field, Michael J. 1984. *Mau: Samoa's Struggle against New Zealand Oppression*. Wellington: Reed.

Field, Michael J. 1991. *Mau: Samoa's Struggle for Freedom*. Auckland: Polynesian Press. Revised edition of Field (1984).

Moyle, Richard. 1988. *Traditional Samoan Music*. Auckland: Auckland University Press, in association with the Institute for Polynesian Studies.

Moyle, Richard M. 1989. *Samoan Songs: An Historical Collection*. Music of Oceania series, Musicaphon BM30SL2705.

Moyle, Richard M. 1995. "Songs of the Mau." In *New Guinea Ethnomusicology Conference Proceedings*, edited by Robert Reigle, 183–197. Occasional Papers in Pacific Ethnomusicology 4. Auckland: University of Auckland, Department of Anthropology, the Archive of Maori and Pacific Music.

Parr, Philip J. 1979. *The Murder of Tamasese*. [Levin, New Zealand]: Aspect Press.

Peterson, Adrian. 2001. "Radio in Samoa." Radio Heritage Foundation. http://www.radioheritage.net/Story7.asp.

Pratt. 1890. "The Genealogy of the Kings and Princes of Samoa." In *Report of the Second Meeting of the Australian Association for the Advancement of Science*, 655–663. Sydney: Australian Association for the Advancement of Science.

Tu'i, Tātupu Fa'afetai Matā'afa. 1987. *Lāuga: Samoan Oratory*. Suva, Fiji: Institute of Pacific Studies, University of the South Pacific.

CHAPTER 28

....

BELLS IN THE CULTURAL SOUNDSCAPE

Nazi-Era Plunder, Repatriation, and Campanology

....

CARLA SHAPREAU

In 1943, after the removal of church bells from the other occupied countries and even from the Reich, Hitler ordered their removal from Belgium. The Belgians protested, invoking The Hague Regulations, and refused an offer to buy; thereupon the Germans requisitioned the bells against receipt.

—International Military Tribunal, Nuremberg, 1946[1]

THE Nazi era resulted in the largest decimation of bells the world has witnessed (Figure 28.1). The Third Reich seized approximately 175,000 bells in Continental Europe for their strategic raw-material content, to be melted down for the German war machine. This had a dramatic impact on traditional communal soundscapes throughout Europe as silence replaced the ringing of bells, long integral to civic and religious life. Most of these bells were destroyed. The plunder of these musical instruments during World War II was viewed as a war crime at the International Military War Tribunal at Nuremberg in 1945. The seized bells that escaped ruin were discovered by the Allies after the war and were repatriated[2] to their nations of origin, but fell far short in numbers to satisfy the needs of the European population.

Out of this landscape of massive postwar loss grew an unexpected opportunity from the bells that lay on the ground in the thousands in German bell dumps. Created over many centuries, these bells formed a de facto exhibition of Europe's bells, providing a unique moment in the history of campanology.[3] This graveyard of bells spawned intensive studies on the art of historical bell founding, tuning, and art. Mysteries of tuning employed by sixteenth- and seventeenth-century master bellfounders, lost for centuries, were rediscovered, contributing to a new era of bell founding in Europe in the postwar era.

FIGURE 28.1 Plundered bells, Hamburg Harbor, 1944.

Nürnberg, Germanisches Nationalmuseum, Deutsches Glockenarchiv,
"Glockenlager im Hamburger Hafen."

THE REICH OFFICE FOR METALS AND THE LOOTING CAMPAIGN

Bells have long been a target among musical instruments during times of war. Selected not for their musical virtue but for their material, bells are made from metal alloys generally containing roughly 80 percent copper and 20 percent tin, although ingredients may vary regionally.[4] Bell spoils were taken during the Napoleonic campaigns,[5] but not to the extent of the tremendous plunder during World War II. The Nazi seizure of bells throughout the Reich and in occupied Europe was initiated "under a decree of 15th March 1940, in execution of the 'Four Year Plan,'" as part of a nonferrous-metal campaign to meet the needs of Germany's war industries.[6] The Reich Office for Metals (Reichsstelle für Metalle), under the Ministry of Economics, carried out the nonferrous-metal mobilization, which included bells (Figure 28.2).[7] Under a decree of July 17, 1942, the Reich Office for Metals was consolidated into the Reich Office for Iron and Metals (Reichsstelle für Eisen und Metalle).[8]

Germany recognized the historical importance of the bells it confiscated and graded the spoils from "A" to "D," with some national variation. For example, in Belgium "A" bells were cast from 1850 to the present, "B" bells 1790 to 1850, "C" bells about 1700 to

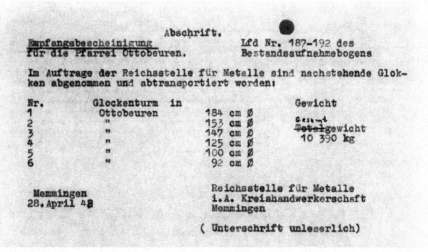

FIGURE 28.2 Reich Office for Metals receipt, 1942. Six bells taken from the Parish of Ottobueren, cast in 1440, 1577, 1864, and 1926.

US National Archives and Records Administration (Reich Office for Metals, receipt, April 28, 1942, NARA, RG260, M1949, Roll 18).

1790, and "D" bells before about 1740.[9] In the Netherlands, category "A" applied to bells cast after 1800.[10] The Germans generally left one small bell for each community,[11] although this was not always the case. For example, the Evangelical Vicar from Budingen, Germany reported, "The Nazis took all the bells, even though the order that *one* bell had to be left for each community, has been known. They took their revenge over the church-community because of its resistance towards the Nazis."[12] Poland reported that many of its older bells from the eighteenth to the fourteenth centuries were taken and never recovered.[13] The "A" bells were melted down first.[14] Some bells were broken up in their source nations for easier shipment to Germany.[15]

In the former Czechoslovakia, as a result of the Munich Agreement on September 29, 1938, Sudetenland was annexed into the German Reich and lost its bells under regulations applicable in the Reich in 1940. In the Protectorate of Bohemia and Moravia, Germany, ordered an inventory of bells in 1940, and under Regulation 414 of November 26, 1941, bell owners were required to register and surrender bronze bells weighing more than 1 kilogram to collecting points, excluding the oldest bells in the "D" category. By 1942 all of Czechoslovakia's "A" bells had been transported to Germany, and "B" and "C" bells were seized in 1942 and 1943. Under instructions from the Reich Office for Metals, approximately 3,000 bells were eventually shipped from Czechoslovakia to Lünen and roughly 6,000 to 9,000 bells were sent to smelters at Norddeutsche Affinerie and Zinnwerke Wilhelmsburg in Hamburg. Slovakia's bells were seized in 1944.[16]

In France, metal reserves were "allocated" to Germany. Among these were "copper cables which are still extensively available below ground from the time of street cars," and residents were expected to "hand over all metal objects made of copper and tin," according to a telegram of April 26, 1941, to the German ambassador to France, Otto Abetz, from his liaison Hans Schwarzmann and G. Schreiber. Regarding French bells, the telegram continued:

> The Reichs Marshall has ordered the removal of church bells which represent the most important and last reserve of copper and tin. The Reich Marshall stressed in this connection, that no church bells would be removed in Germany before all bells had been removed in France. Here the removal will be carried out first in France, then Belgium and if necessary finally in Holland.[17]

Seizures were to begin on May 1, 1941, but after a meeting in Vichy of French officials, it was concluded that such a seizure from households and the removal of church bells would result in opposition by the French population and could not proceed without the use of force. As a result, most of France's bells were spared in light of the French decision to give up statuary and other objects instead of bells.[18] In contrast, after the Reich annexed Alsace-Lorraine, the Reich Office for Metals in Berlin ordered the removal of bells from this region's towers in April 1941.[19] Germany applied the same bell classification in Alsace-Lorraine that it applied to bells in Germany—"A" bells were cast since 1918, "B" and "C" bells were progressively more historically valuable, and "D" were the most valuable.[20] A postwar account by Chaplain Abbot Hoch of Strasbourg confirmed that he had seen "a stock of at least 30 tons of broken bells" on the premises of one scrap-metal dealer in Ulm, Germany; he observed "French bells from the district of Colmar" and "the name of Turkheim and of about ten other Alsatian communities" visible on the broken bells.[21]

In Poland, the Nazi-run Generalgouvernement issued a decree requiring the surrender of bells on August 28, 1941, with a deadline of September 10, 1941, extended into 1942.[22] Bells were collected in Polish depots, including Buski Brzozów and Dunajec, and were sent by train to smelting factories in the Reich, or were first melted into bars in local foundries. A lack of clear paperwork and markings resulted in some confusion as to source of origin: "40 railway freight wagons of bells presumed to be Polish were received . . . 4 of the railway wagons were without recorded place of departure. It is possible, therefore, that some of these bells, especially among those with Cyrillic or Old Slavonic writing, may be from the present USSR area."[23]

Exemptions for Polish bells of historic and artistic importance were difficult to obtain.[24] Many historical bells were seized, such as those from Kraków.[25] The communal impact of bells in the city's soundscape was witnessed and considered by the Polish Jewish songwriter Mordecai Gebirtig, interned in the Kraków Ghetto, who in October 1941 wrote the song "Glokn Klang!" ("Tolling Bells"). In his lyrics Gebirtig remarked, "The bells are tolling—Gling Glong! Gling Glong! Like someone were asking: How long, now? How long? How long, now? How long? Will man be a beast? Will man be so shameless? . . . The bells are tolling—Gling Glong! Gling Glong! Like someone were answering: Not long, now! Not long!"[26] The Nazis seized approximately 22,500 bells from

Poland. Of these, it was estimated in 1948 that only 1,700 bells were "returned or return-able" from Germany.[27]

In the Netherlands, the Reich demanded Dutch bells in July 1942, and in the autumn the first bells were removed from civic and church towers, with transportation to Germany beginning in February 1943.[28] The Dutch anticipated that the nation might have to sacrifice up to 90 percent of its bells, approximately 2,700,000 kilograms in weight. In response, the Dutch State Office for Monument Conservation initiated the largest inventory of bells in the nation's history, carried out in 1939–1940. The inventory included eighty-one carillons[29] and chimes, and 5,950 swinging bells.[30] The Dutch Inspection for the Protection of Art Treasures and Science documented each bell, including its measurements, bellfounder, and year of casting, along with photographs and plaster casts of decorations and inscriptions.[31] The most valuable Dutch bells were marked with the letter "M" for "monument," and the Dutch posted signs in bell towers in Dutch, French, English, and German declaring the bells' protected status. It read:

> Her Majesty's Government having exempted a very limited number of bells from requisition as historical monuments of the greatest importance, instantly beseeches the Commanders of the military forces of foreign powers likewise to respect these bells marked with an M.[32]

In the end, the Germans took about 75 percent by weight of Dutch bells. "A" bells cast after 1800 went first.[33] The Dutch argued that its carillons, "the highest expression of Niederdeutsch culture," should not be taken, and in May 1942 the Nazis agreed to this demand; carillon bells were marked with a "K."[34] But in the summer of 1943, the Germans "ordered the removal of all bells, regardless of category, from the sea-bordering provinces—Zeeland, Zuid-Holland, Noord-Holland (except the city of Amsterdam) Friesland, and Groningen." It was estimated that of the 9,000 bells in the Netherlands before World War II, approximately 6,500 were seized by the Nazis.[35] Before the confiscations, the sound of bells emanated from religious, civil, and private bell towers, in general every fifteen minutes, permeating quotidian life in Dutch communities. Afterward, this sonic landscape had largely vanished.

Seizures in Belgium began in January 1943. Bells made in 1450 and earlier were excluded from seizure, as were carillons if regularly played, although there was a carillon seizure at Saint Peters Church in Leuven. "The largest were broken up to get onto lorries. Gen. Frank S. Ross, USA, found the majority of the bells in western Germany [after the war] and sent them back." Approximately 3,995 bells from categories A, B, and C were confiscated in Belgium.[36] Numerous efforts in various nations were undertaken to save bells from seizure, including burying or otherwise hiding them. In the Netherlands, confiscated bells loaded on board the vessel *Hoop op zegen* bound for Germany appear to have been intentionally run aground in Ijsselmeer in order to save Dutch bells from the smelter.[37] Some bells en route to Germany via rail were "pushed off moving freight trains in Belgium."[38] In October 1943 Germany issued an order to confiscate Belgium's organs for their pipes, estimated to contain 20,000 kilograms of tin, to be commenced on March 17, 1944. Fortunately, this effort was subverted due to strategic advances by the Allied forces.[39]

Among the smallest of bells looted during the Nazi era were those that adorned objects of Jewish religious and cultural life, such as the crown, finials, and breastplate of the Torah scroll, and Besamim spice boxes, generally made of precious metals, largely silver, with designs influenced by local tradition and reflecting Jewish heritage. Many of these objects were damaged or destroyed after their seizure, while others were deposited in storage locations associated with various Nazi agencies such as the Einsatzstab Reichsleiter Rosenberg, the Reich Security Head Office (Reichssicherheitshauptamt), the Gestapo (Geheime Staatspolizei), and others.[40]

Among the Axis nations bell losses also were extremely high. Germany looked to its own bells for needed copper and tin and in late 1941 bells began coming down; approximately 33,750,000 kilograms of bell metal were requisitioned, equivalent to about 102,500 bells. In the Reich as in other nations, the newest bells in the "A" category were generally melted down. [41] Many of the requisitioned German bells were centuries old. For example, bells removed from steeples in Bamberg were considered "singularly precious by reason of age or of art," including many from the fifteenth and sixteenth centuries (Figure 28.3). As noted earlier, bells removed from Ottobeuren were cast in 1440 and 1577; bells requisitioned from Oxenbronn were cast in 1666.[42]

The church resisted the surrender of bells to the Reich. Nazi Minister of Propaganda Joseph Goebbels remarked in his diary on December 12, 1941, "[t]he priests have now found a new way to make things difficult for us," referring to resentment in some districts regarding bell requisitions.[43] In February Goebbels's frustrations continued, "The priests are using the confiscation of church bells to campaign without restraint against the Party. This is totally unjustified because the bells were also taken in the [first] world war. It is not the Party that takes the bells away, it is the Wehrmacht. But the Party is nonetheless charged with enlightening the public of the cause in order to undercut the priests."[44]

In Austria, approximately 6,675 bells were surrendered after annexation.[45] Many Austrian bells were sent to Brixlegg, Illsen,[46] and Hamburg to be melted down.[47] This included three Protestant church bells from Land Salzburg named "Faith," "Hope," and "Bell of the Emigrants," given up on December 3, 1942.[48] "As far as the bells of the city of Salzburg are concerned the information received from the office of the Prince Archbishop indicates that they were brought to Brixleg, Tyrol, and broken up there."[49]

Italy supplied Germany with approximately 50 percent of its bells by weight, with one bell generally left in each tower. The Italian *Ufficio Monopolio* Metalli estimated that about 12,000 bells weighing approximately 5,000,000 kilograms were removed from Italian bell towers during the war. Bell weights, metallic content, shape, and ornamentation were recorded.[50] Bells taken from a number of the Italian communities are recorded in the US and UK National Archives.[51] For example, the German metal refinery, Zinnwerke, Wilhelmsberg, received 1,028,524 kilograms of broken Italian metal from Italian cities from May 27, 1943, through July 7, 1944.[52] This bell metal was transferred by Italy to Germany under contract for refinement and was to be returned to Italy in

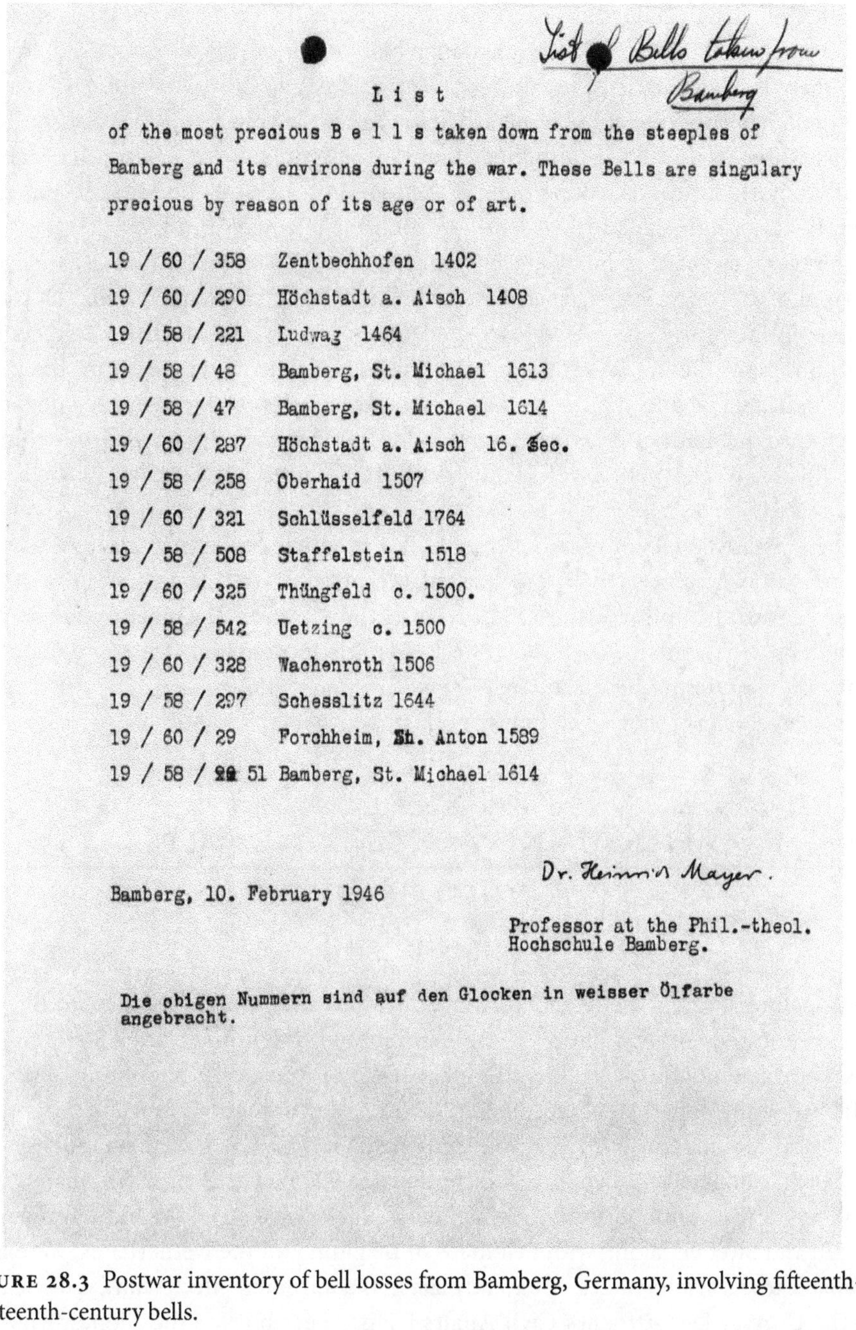

List of Bells taken from Bamberg

L i s t

of the most precious B e l l s taken down from the steeples of Bamberg and its environs during the war. These Bells are singulary precious by reason of its age or of art.

19 / 60 / 358 Zentbechhofen 1402
19 / 60 / 290 Höchstadt a. Aisch 1408
19 / 58 / 221 Ludwag 1464
19 / 58 / 48 Bamberg, St. Michael 1613
19 / 58 / 47 Bamberg, St. Michael 1614
19 / 60 / 287 Höchstadt a. Aisch 16. Sec.
19 / 58 / 258 Oberhaid 1507
19 / 60 / 321 Schlüsselfeld 1764
19 / 58 / 508 Staffelstein 1518
19 / 60 / 325 Thüngfeld c. 1500.
19 / 58 / 542 Uetzing c. 1500
19 / 60 / 328 Wachenroth 1506
19 / 58 / 297 Schesslitz 1644
19 / 60 / 29 Forchheim, St. Anton 1589
19 / 58 / 51 Bamberg, St. Michael 1614

Bamberg, 10. February 1946

Dr. Heinrich Mayer.

Professor at the Phil.-theol.
Hochschule Bamberg.

Die obigen Nummern sind auf den Glocken in weisser Ölfarbe angebracht.

FIGURE 28.3 Postwar inventory of bell losses from Bamberg, Germany, involving fifteenth- to eighteenth-century bells.

US National Archives and Records Administration (Heinrich Mayer, list, February 10, 1946, NARA, RG260, M1949, Roll 18).

ingots. Only 105,949 kilograms of copper were reportedly sent back, with the remainder of the agreement unfulfilled.[53] While Italian bell foundry furnaces ran cold during the war, there is evidence that the Pontifical Marinelli bell foundry in Agnone apparently cast molten bronze into at least one bell in 1943 and this bore a pro-Axis inscription, as discussed below.[54] The bell-founding tradition at Agnone is long-lived; the Marinelli family reports it began making bells in Agnone in 1339, and continues to this day.[55] Agnone also is remembered for its internment camp during World War II.[56]

The Nazis swept through Yugoslavia in the spring of 1941, capturing Sarajevo on April 16 of that year. Yugoslavia's wartime bell loss statistics are uncertain.[57] It was reported, "When the Yugoslavs refused to deliver up their bells, German soldiers were sent to remove them. These the Yugoslavs slew."[58] However, records from the British Zone indicate that 499,566 kilograms of Yugoslavian bell metal were melted during the war.[59] Documentation for other nations is incomplete, including bells from Hungary and Russia. In the nations of Denmark, Luxembourg, and Norway no bells were confiscated.[60]

These massive bell confiscations caught the attention of German cultural property experts, who documented in great detail the physical and acoustical properties of those bells with cultural, historical, and artistic importance. The chief custodian of art monuments in Germany, Dr. Robert Hiecke, reportedly prepared a photographic album of the most culturally significant bells for Reichsmarshall Hermann Göring.[61] The current whereabouts of such an album is uncertain.[62]

The Monuments, Fine Arts, and Archives Divisions

Long before World War II ended, concerns arose over the destruction of fine arts, monuments, and other cultural valuables in Europe, and in the United States this discussion was brought to President Franklin Delano Roosevelt's attention.[63] Roosevelt established the American Commission for the Protection and Salvage of Artistic and Historical Monuments in War Areas on August 20, 1943.[64] Bell data, although incomplete, regarding bells in Belgium, Czechoslovakia, Denmark, Poland, Germany, Spain, France, Italy, Luxembourg, the Netherlands, Norway, Austria, Poland, Portugal, the USSR, and Sweden, along with bell maps of Belgium and the Netherlands, were made available to the armed forces, apparently late in the war; their effect, if any, is unclear.[65]

The US War Department's Civil Affairs Division established the Monuments, Fine Arts, and Archives division (MFA&A), which engaged in wartime and postwar protection and recovery efforts.[66] Britain's MFA&A worked in concert with the United States during and after the war, as did other Allied nations. On April 23, 1945, the British and US MFA&A met to discuss adoption of a standard procedure with regard to protection and registration of looted cultural objects found in Germany.[67] After the war, the

MFA&A was instrumental in discovering, protecting, and returning confiscated and otherwise displaced cultural objects.[68] By September 1948, the United States estimated it had located 1,500 depositories containing approximately 10.7 million objects.[69]

THE ALLIED DISCOVERY
OF GERMAN BELL DUMPS

The bells were being marked with various colours according to their country of origin, and the German bells too could be marked according to their Land of origin. There were now approximately 13,000 bells in the Hamburg dumps.[70]

The Allied Property Control Branches supervised the disposition of bells after the war (Figure 28.4). Anne Olivier Popham, British MFA&A officer and director of the Education Branch, reported in October 1946 that the location of bell dumps in the British Zone of Germany in Hamburg included Freihafen, Reiherstieg Holzlager, Getreidlager, Zinnwerke, Norddeutsche Affinerie,[71] and Schlesische Damischiffarts

FIGURE 28.4 European bells that escaped the smelter, Hamburg, August 1945.

US National Archives and Records Administration (NARA, Photo Archive, RG239).

Gesellschaft. Additional depositories in the British Zone included Kiel, Lünen, Hüttenwerke Kayser, Geschert, nr Coesfeld, Petit u. Gebrüder Edellrock Bell Foundry, Nordkirchen Repository, Kall-Eifel Metalhütte Kall, and Hannover-Stöcken.[72] Other Allied depositories included, but were not limited to, those in Hettstedt, Ilsenberg, Kall, Oranienburg, and Wansleben.[73]

The Allies found the confiscated bells graded by painted numbers that generally identified the country of origin. The bell dumps in Hamburg and Lünen were found to contain mainly B- and C-category bells.[74] The US MFA&A reported of the Hamburg bell dumps, "During the war about 40,000 church bells were brought to Hamburg to be melted down for war material. The majority of these bells were from German churches but some thousands were from churches in allied countries."[75] The bell dump in Lünen was reported to hold approximately 1,650 bells, 372 of which had come from the American Zone.[76] There also were a considerable number of bells reported in the Russian Zone, including at the Hettstedt and Magdeburg depositories.[77]

Popham said of the situation in Hamburg:

> As historical monuments or works of art they [the bells] were supervised by MFA&A. A specialist member of the staff of the Denkmalamt, Schleswig Holstein was continuing her war-time work of inventorising the bells in the Hamburg dumps [Table 28.1], assisted by a member of the Bavarian Denkmalamt. The bells here were being identified and the foreign bells removed area by area. . . .[78]

THE POSTWAR REPATRIATION OF EUROPE'S BELLS

Under the Allied postwar policy of "external restitution," plundered property was repatriated to the presumed country of origin, not to individual owners. It was the responsibility of the source nations to return the repatriated bells to their owners.[79] In the case of bells, there were not enough whole or broken bells to go around, and this resulted in a repatriation process fraught with policy concerns, complications among the four Allied zones of occupation, conflicts involving border disputes, and ownership disputes between nations and private parties, including German churches and German metal refineries.

The US military advisor on cultural matters, John Nicholas Brown, stated with respect to bell reparations, "It is the policy of US Military Government to return identifiable looted or stolen objects to the country of pre-war ownership."[80] The British MFA&A's restitution policy was to first restitute bells to formerly occupied nations and only after this to Germany.[81] The British initially considered Austria's bell claims similar to Germany's, "Austria is NOT a country entitled to restitutions not being an Allied Nation." However, Prince Archbishop of Salzburg, Monsignor Rohracher, appealed

Table 28.1 British Bell Estimate for the Hamburg Bell Dumps, December 12, 1947

Nations	Bells Confiscated	Bells Restituted Whole	Broken Bell Metal Restituted	Bell Loss Total by Weight
Austria	4,173 bells/ 1,669,458 kg	145 bells/40,096 kg	12 kg	1,629,350 kg
Belgium	7,897 bells/ 3,159,100 kg	803 bells/ 587,724 kg	2,943,881 kg	77,495 kg
Czechoslovakia	4,081 bells/ 1,632,503 kg	25 bells/5,840 kg	757 kg	1,625,906 kg
France[1]	1,962 bells/ 784,868 kg	37 bells/25,731 kg	595,259 kg	163,878 kg
Germany	52,813 bells/ 21,125,314 kg	10,373 bells/ 4,196,169 kg	518,399 kg	16,410,256 kg
Hungary	754 bells[2]/ 30,160 kg	1 bell/200 kg	38,395 kg wirebars	29,960 kg
Italy	6,201 bells/ 2,480,537 kg	None; bells delivered broken	1,145,184 kg	1,335,353 kg
Netherlands	4,632 bells/ 1,852,796 kg	301 bells/ 220,163 kg	1,144,540 kg	488,093 kg
Poland	5,892 bells/ 2,356,826 kg	1,063 bells/ 158,108 kg	390,017 kg	1,808,701 kg
Russia	218 bells/8,723 kg	None. All bells delivered broken	8,723 kg	0 kg
Yugoslavia	1,248 bells/ 499,566 kg	19 bells/2,716 kg	446,480 kg	50,360 kg
Totals	89,871 bells/ 35,599,851 kg	12,767 bells/ 5,236,747 kg	7,231,647 kg	23,619,352 kg

[1] Alsace-Lorraine only.

[2] "This lot was delivered as broken bells." Ewan Phillips, memorandum, December 12, 1947, FO 1050/ 1481, TNA.

© 2018 Carla Shapreau. Original data from Ewan Phillips, memorandum, December 12, 1947, FO 1050/ 1481, TNA, National Archives of the United Kingdom, Kew. (Restitution statistics are estimates because not all bells were clearly identifiable.)

this decision to the British and to the pope. The British reconsidered its decision;[82] and by September 1946, they decided that Austrian bells in the British Zone would be inventoried for an immediate return.[83]

Anne Popham said of the British bell policy:

In various places in the British Zone of Germany, but principally in Hamburg, are dumps of Church Bells requisitioned by the Germans as material for war production purposes from Churches in Occupied Countries as well as in Italy, Austria and Germany itself. British Military Government policy has been in the first place to restitute those bells which could be identified as coming from Occupied Allied Countries.[84]

Interzonal transfers of bells were problematic; the Allied Religious Affairs Committee agreed on a quadripartite level to the return of all church bells to their ecclesiastical owners on February 25, 1946.[85] The United States and Britain entered into their own interzonal agreement.

> By an agreement reached between Generals Clay and Robertson in February, 1946, the return to their Zones of origin of certain categories of cultural material displaced during the war from either the US or British Zones to the other, was authorized, and consequent upon this Church bells from Wurttenburg-Baden, Greater Hesse and Bavaria now in dumps in the British Zone are due for return.
>   The problem of the return of bells to their churches of origin both in the British and American Zones is one of considerable complexity and magnitude and for reasons of economy both in finance, labour and transport, is not one which can be dealt with by individual churches.[86]

There was no agreement between the Soviet and French authorities for the interzonal transfer of church bells until spring of 1948, delaying the return of bells to the French and Russian Zones of occupation.[87] Finally, on April 17, 1948, a four-power agreement on the zonal exchange of bells was reached.[88]

The identification of looted property was generally accomplished using foreign missions with national representatives who conducted inspections in the zones of occupation. One of Poland's delegates in the postwar search for missing bells was Dr. Tadeusz Gostyński, who discovered bells in Hamburg's Norddeutsche Affinerie, Zinkenwerke, and Freihafen refineries, as well as in Kupferwerk and Lünen. In addition to the repatriation of whole and broken bells, Poland received German war reparations in the form of 390 tons of bronze slabs.[89] Poland's efforts at restitution and compensation were stalled in 1951 and not restarted until 1991. The Polish Ministry of Culture has continued efforts into the twenty-first century.[90]

Shifting national borders resulting from World War II gave rise to bell ownership disputes. For example, Poland and the German Evangelical and Roman Catholic Church had competing claims to approximately 1,000 seized bells of "great value," which had come from territories east of the Oder-Neisse Line. German territories east of this line had fallen under Polish control at the war's end, and Germans were expelled from this region. After the war, the Allies intended to return these bells to Poland because they had originated there, east of the Oder-Neisse Line. However, German church authorities objected to this plan, citing both canon law and Article 56 of the 1899 Hague Convention, claiming that the bells were the private property of their church communities, now relocated to Germany, west of the Oder-Neisse Line.[91]

The Polish government fought back, with a Polish representative remarking, "The Germans had killed 3,000 priests in Poland during their occupation. . . . Of the 1,500 (approximate) bells Dr. Sostinsky considered that 80% could be readily identified and returned to their churches. Nearly 500 were of mediaeval origin."[92] Poland also pointed out that it was the Polish bishops, landowners, and local congregations that had provided the bells to churches in Poland. In the end, a compromise was struck whereby "some 1000 bells . . . will under this plan be moved from the dump in Hamburg to churches in the Russian Zone, and we shall in exchange get about 400 bells from their [the Russian Zone] dump near Magdeburg."[93] The issue, however, was still being discussed in August 1949, by British and US MFA&A and Religious Affairs Branch personnel, when it was finally decided that remaining bells in Germany should go back to the churches from where they originated, to a reconstructed church, or to the custody of the Polish government in anticipation of reconstruction of the churches.[94]

To satisfy the Allied restitution demands, remaining German bell stocks in the bell dumps were to be drawn on, "while every effort will be made to spare and ultimately return the really important and historical ones, it appears likely that a considerable quantity of the more modern German bells will never see their home towns again."[95] German churches were regularly making requests for the return of their bells, but there were not enough bells to go around.[96] On November 8, 1946, the British and American MFA&A met to decide how to handle the return of German church bells in the US and British Zones.[97] They concurred regarding the existing repatriation procedure and suggested that the German Landesamt für Denkmalpflege maintain a file of requests should partial restitution of bells to German churches come into effect at a later date,[98] with German church bells not returned through church channels, but through German state offices for monument conservation.[99]

Disputes resulting in hostilities broke out after the war over bell fragments, highly valued for use in casting new bells. The tally of broken bells under British administration in Hamburg alone was nearly five million kilograms.[100] One such dispute broke out over bell scrap found in Ulm, Germany, that bore French markings and to which the French Mission for Restitution asserted a claim.[101] A French investigation revealed on May 28, 1945, that about thirty tons of broken Alsatian bells were on the premises of the scrap metal dealer and refiner Neubronner & Sellin, which had purchased the bells from the Reich Office for Metals during the war.[102] Mathäus Wiedemann, the foreman at Neubronner & Sellin, assured the French investigator that none of the bell parts would be "alienated or destroyed."[103]

However, Neubronner & Sellin, in the first half of 1946, manufactured new bells for churches in Württemberg and Bavaria from the bell scrap, stating that it had done so with US approval and that France was untimely in its follow-up. Outraged at the outcome, the chief of reparations and restitution for France wrote to the chief of the French mission for restitution in Frankfurt-Hoechst on August 29, 1946, stating:

> These facts cannot manifest with more evidence the dishonesty of Neubronner & Sellin, as well as their complete contempt of the promise given. I cannot stress

enough the bitterness resented by certain Alsatian parishes in face of the difficulties they are to overcome in order to have their rights respected, and also the impatience with which they expect the return of their bells, or the allowance of bronze required for the founding of new bells. I would very much appreciate if you would take up this urgent matter with the American agencies, so that this injustice will soon be repaired and the German firm cannot profit of their concealment.[104]

This French claim was "closed" on October 18, 1946, with the words, "the bells are no longer identifiable and as such cannot be restituted."[105]

Disputes also broke out between German churches and German refineries that had paid the Reich for bell scrap and wanted compensation for the return of broken bells to German churches. The churches responded that they had been forced to surrender their bells and did not want to have to pay to get whole or broken bells back. Church representatives argued that the refineries should not be permitted to make "a large profit at the expense of the churches out of metal which these firms acquired as a result of enforced confiscation."[106] By September 15, 1949, the Allies turned over this internal German dispute to the German governmental authorities, under applicable German and Occupation legislation. "Owing to the development in the policy of transferring purely internal German affairs to the hands of the Germans, and to the establishment of a German Federal Government, it would not be appropriate to take any further action in this matter. The churches which are interested in this matter must now approach the German Governmental authorities with a view to claiming the metal or compensation for it, in accordance with German Law and any Occupation Legislation which may be appropriate." [107] The British file on the return of church bells was closed on October 14, 1949.

Postwar bell damage statistics are incomplete. A 1948 estimate of bell losses due to Nazi confiscations is listed in Table 28.2. In addition, damage caused by Allied military has been estimated to be, "for Belgium—about 2%, for Czechoslovakia—almost none, for France—more than loss by sequestration, for Netherlands—10%, Austria—1%, German—2.5%, Italy 10%, other countries—not known."[108] England suffered the loss of bells by air attack as well, with London faring the worst.[109] In Lübeck, the destruction is memorialized by the fallen broken bells caused by Allied bombs in March 1942.[110] "In St. Stephen's Cathedral in Vienna, the great bell, made from captured Turkish cannon, fell through several floors when the edifice became ablaze, breaking itself and part of the structure as it dropped. The 'Jeanne d'Arc' in Rouen Cathedral, largest bell in France, was reduced to a gray ash by fire during the latter part of the war. . . . the Parish Church of Berlin, the Garrison Church of Potsdam (both installed by Frederick the Great), and the still older instrument in the Castle of Darmstadt" were destroyed by Allied air attack.[111] But in the wake of the war's catastrophic bell losses a nascent chance for progress arose from the ruins.

Of the Judaica bells recovered by the Allies postwar from Nazi-run repositories such as the Institute for Research on the Jewish Question (Institut zur Erforschung der

Table 28.2 1948 Estimate of Bell Losses Due to Nazi Confiscations Based on 1937 Boundaries

Prewar Bell Totals	Bells Confiscated	Bells Restituted or to Be Restituted	Bells Lost (Not Recoverable as Whole Bells)	Bells Lost, Weight in Kilograms	Bell Loss Totals by Percentage of Weight
Allied Nations					
Belgium: 8,870	5,020	800	4,220	2,790,000	57.3%
Czechoslovakia: 15,000	12,000	560	11,440	2,247,000	74.9%
France: 75,000	3,000	1,340	1,160	1,300,000	4.3%
Netherlands[1] 9,000	6,500	1,840	4,660	1,918,000	55.6%
Poland: 32,785	22,500	1,700	20,800	2,590,000	64.8%
USSR: unknown	unknown	est. 15	unknown	unknown	unknown
Yugoslavia: unknown	unknown	5 known	unknown	unknown	unknown
Axis Nations					
Austria: 7,360	6,675	1,245	5,340	2,225,000	77.4%
Germany: 109,000	102,500	12,500	90,000	27,750,000	74.0%
Italy: 25,000	12,000	1,565	10,435	4,348,000	43.5%
Hungary: unknown	150 known	unknown	150	30 known	unknown
Total: 282,015 bells	170,345 bells	21,570 bells	148,205 bells	45,198,000 kg	

Over 175,000 bells, weighing about 55,000,000 kg were removed from towers in Europe. Of these, over 150,000, weighing upward of 45,000,000 kg, were destroyed.

[1] See also Boogert, "Seven Centuries," 25; Truyen, "A Bell Atlas," 172 ("In September 1946 a final tally was made and ... 4,793 bells weighing 1,872,813 kilos had been melted down").

© 2018 Carla Shapreau. Original data from Percival Price, *Campanology, Europe 1945–47. A Report on the Condition of Carillons on the Continent of Europe as a Result of the Recent War, on the Sequestration and Melting Down of Bells by the Central Powers, and on Research into the Tonal Qualities of Bells Made Accessible by War-Time Dislodgment* (Ann Arbor: University of Michigan Press, 1948), 142–143.

Judenfrage), those in the custody of the US military government were restituted if an owner could be identified, but many were unclaimed or deemed "heirless." These were transferred to the Jewish Restitution Successor Organization or the Jewish Cultural Reconstruction, for dissemination to religious, cultural, and educational institutions as trustees for the true owner and for the purpose of perpetuating the spiritual and cultural heritage of the Jewish people.[112]

WORLD WAR II AND CAMPANOLOGY

The bell confiscations throughout Europe during the Nazi era resulted in a vast congregation of bells in Germany, with ramifications for the field of campanology. This odd landscape provided a "unique opportunity . . . to make measurements that would not have been possible with bells hanging in their towers. . . . [A] number of selected bells were transported from the dumps to the laboratory to be tested in more detail."[113] In addition to acoustical studies, the bells bore an array of ornamentation with significant artistic, historical, and cultural meaning, and these were recorded as "a record in bronze of the artistic taste of the people who ordered them. In the depositories, this art form represented a period of eight centuries. Subjects of decoration varied from saints to monkeys, and inscriptions ranged from the most pious prayers to the most vaunting self-praise of an individual."[114]

Several nations documented their bells before forfeiture, adding to the reservoir of historical information.[115] Of those bells seized, a study was performed in Germany in 1942 by the Kommission für Glockenuntersuchung and continued after the war. Acoustic recordings were made of strike notes, the decay of partials, relative intensities of partials, pitch and place of partials, and full sound. The physical attributes of the bells were recorded, including size, bell wall profiles and thicknesses, weight, ornamentation, metallic alloy composition, and tuning. Some of the research was conducted at the Landesamt für Denkmalpflege in Malente, primarily on B and C bells.[116] A card catalog was created with information on approximately 16,300 bells, with photographs, rubbings of inscriptions and ornamentation, impressed reliefs of artistic details, and plaster casts of ornamentation of figures, medallions, bellfounder's marks, and band motifs.[117]

By the nineteenth century, the art of casting bells had faded, and some say it had been lost:[118] "The 19th century should be dismissed. Certainly, the occasional carillon appeared, but the abominable quality of each resulted in their being melted down long ago."[119] The classical era of bell founding had come in the seventeenth and eighteenth centuries—with master bell makers such as Francois Hemony (1609–1667) and Pieter Hemony (1619–1680) working in the Netherlands, and Andreas Jozef Van den Gheyn (1737–1793) in Belgium—and then vanished.[120] In England, the height of the art of bell founding reportedly took place "from 1660 to 1750."[121] At the end of the nineteenth century and in the early twentieth century, developments in bell tuning were evolving in several nations.[122] Nonetheless, "before the war, the interest in the tuning of early musical instruments was all but non-existent. This changed only after 1945."[123]

After the war, there was renewed interest in emulating the great bells of the seventeenth and eighteenth centuries in connection with satisfying the pressing needs for reconstruction and the recasting of thousands of bells. Modern equipment and techniques expanded avenues for acoustic analysis. It became apparent in the postwar years that some notable historical bellfounders had tuned their bells in the meantone temperament.[124] Heightened government oversight on quality standards for new bells contributed to rising standards in the Netherlands.[125] With the postwar era came breakthroughs in bell tuning and the tone quality, with a significant impact on the field of campanology.[126]

Bells and the Judgment at Nuremberg

The United States, Britain, France, and the USSR entered into an agreement on August 8, 1945, establishing the International Military Tribunal at Nuremberg for the trial and punishment of the major war criminals of the European Axis.[127] Count 3 of the indictment against the defendants for "war crimes," included "violations of the laws or customs of war. Such violations shall include, but not be limited to, . . . plunder of public or private property, wanton destruction of cities, towns or villages, or devastation not justified by military necessity."[128]

The prosecution argued that the plunder of art and other cultural objects, including evidence of bell confiscations, was in violation of international law under the 1907 Hague convention Respecting the Laws and Customs of War on Land.[129] Article 46 of the convention prohibits the confiscation of private property, and Article 56 provides:

> The property of municipalities, that of institutions dedicated to religion, charity and education, the arts and sciences, even when State property, shall be treated as private property. All seizure of, destruction or willful damage done to institutions of this character, historical monuments, works of art and science, is forbidden, and should be made the subject of legal proceedings.[130]

In response, Germany argued that the 1907 Hague Convention was inapplicable under Article 2 to nations not party to the convention. The International Military Tribunal found it unnecessary to decide this issue, holding instead that the 1907 Hague Convention codified existing customary international law, "the convention expressly stated that it was an attempt 'to revise the general laws and customs of war,' which it thus recognized to be then existing but by 1939 these rules laid down in the convention were recognized by all civilized nations, and were regarded as being declaratory of the laws and customs of war which are referred to in Article 6(b) of the Charter."[131] Article 6(b) of the Charter of the International Military Tribunal at Nuremberg established the tribunal's authority to try to punish persons who, acting on behalf of the Axis countries, committed war crimes that included, in part, the plunder of public and private property.[132]

At trial, on January 22, 1946, the assistant prosecutor for the French Republic addressed the tribunal on the issue of bell spoliation in Belgium by the Germans during the occupation. The French were entrusted by the Belgian government to plead its case, and in this capacity, prosecutor said of bell confiscations that "Belgium was in 1939 the

largest producer in Europe of non-ferrous metals, of copper, lead, zinc, and tin." In light
of the Nazis' need for these strategic metals under the Four Year Plan, the occupying
authorities ran a number of salvage campaigns for the war effort, including "the salvage
campaigns for bells."[133] The prosecution proffered evidence of the German seizure in
Belgium of 3,995 church bells, weighing 3,198,333 kilograms, in January 1943 (Figure
28.5).[134]

Regarding the plundering of bells in the Eastern territory, the prosecution's trial brief
on the spoliation of Russia remarked:

> On a decree of the High Command, dated 19 November 1941, the urgent necessity
> of collecting metals, scrap iron and other raw materials in the occupied territories
> for the German armament production was stressed. . . . As part of the program of
> securing metal, it was ordered that church bells should be systematically seized. In
> May, 1942, the opinion was expressed that this program would yield 800 to 1000 tons
> of metal. Payment was to be made by the Reich only for the expense of removing the
> bells; "otherwise, the surrender of the bells is regarded by the Reich as a voluntary
> contribution of the population in the Eastern territory."[135]

In its concluding arguments, the prosecution asserted that "(1) The acts of the Nazi
conspirators as revealed by the evidence are prohibited by the Hague Regulations. . . .
It has been shown above that the Nazis forcibly removed large quantities of machinery,

PARTIAL TRANSLATION OF DOCUMENT ECH–12

Report of Activity of the Department "Protection of Art" of the
Military Administration in Belgium and Northern France, p. 70
*Number of Church Bells Removed in the Provinces of Belgium
and Shipped to the Reich.*

Provinces	Number	Weight
		Kg.
Westflandern (West Flanders)	490	477,954
Ostflandern (East Flanders)	344	346,119
Antwerpen (Antwerp)	421	345,031
Barabant	722	514,009
Limburg	251	202,351
Gennegau	558	447,046
Namur	589	429,032
Luttich (Liege)	498	359,675
Luxemburg	122	77,216
Total	3,995	3,198,433

FIGURE 28.5 Trial exhibit, US chief of counsel for prosecution of Axis criminality, International
Military Tribunal, Nuremberg, 1946. Office of US Chief of Counsel for Prosecution of Axis
Criminality, *Nazi Conspiracy and Aggression*, International Military Tribunal, Nuremberg
(Washington, DC: US Government Printing Office, 1946), 7: 632.

foodstuffs, and raw materials to Germany, including even church bells and the strategic metals contained in the transmission systems of the occupied countries. Articles 52 and 53[136] of the Hague Regulations (the only pertinent provisions) provide no basis for such action."[137]

The tribunal's judgment on Count 3 of the indictment for "War Crimes," provided, in part, that

> public and private property was systematically plundered and pillaged in order to enlarge the resources of Germany at the expense of the rest of Europe. . . . There was in truth a systematic "plunder of public or private property," which was criminal under Article 6(b) of the Charter the International War Tribunal. . . . Raw materials and the finished products alike were confiscated for the needs of the German industry. . . . In addition . . . a wholesale seizure was made of art treasures, furniture, textiles and similar articles in all the invaded countries.[138]

The Nazi plunder of material culture was held to constitute a war crime under Count 3 of the indictment, resulting in convictions at Nuremberg.[139]

Memories of unresolved bell losses are long-lived and have fueled twenty-first-century efforts at historical reconstruction and remediation. For example, Poland's Ministry of Culture and National Heritage published four detailed catalogs of its wartime bell losses in 2000, 2006, 2008, and 2011.[140] "Although over half a century elapsed from the end of the last World War, the problem of wartime losses in the area of broadly conceived culture, which confronts almost all European countries, remains open." While Poland recognizes that many of its bells were "irrevocably destroyed," nevertheless it has attempted through the publication of its bell catalogs to document the history of Nazi-era bell confiscations and has remarked, "One can hope that the present, multifaceted activities will make it possible to describe the losses more fully and will raise the chances for at least partial restitution."[141]

In 2001, about one hundred Czech churches sought compensation for Nazi-era bell confiscations under the 2000 German Foundation Act, associated with Remembrance, Responsibility, and Future, a foundation that primarily dealt with forced labor claims, but also included a remedy for certain property losses.[142] In or about 2004, the Property Claims Commission hearing these bell claims granted modest compensation for the claimants' wartime bell losses under the German Foundation Act. The commission found that the seizures constituted a "Nazi wrong" in the Sudetenland and in the Protectorate and remarked that the 1907 Hague Convention (and in particular Article 56, referenced earlier), while not strictly applicable because Czechoslovakia had not acceded to the convention, were nevertheless generally accepted as a codification of already existing norms of customary international law, citing the decision of the International Military Tribunal at Nuremberg for legal support.[143] The evidentiary role that bell losses played in the legal process provides a haunting example of the role that musical material culture may play in the event of war.

DENAZIFICATION AND BRONZE

After the war, monuments and other materials that glorified the Nazi regime were destroyed as part of the Allied denazification program. The Allied Control Council Directive No. 30 of May 4, 1946, provided that monuments, statues, memorials, insignia, posters, emblems, edifices, and street or other markers with inscriptions that glorified the Nazi regime must be eradicated by January 1, 1947. Some of these objects of material culture were made of bronze.

However, even before this directive was formalized, at least one repatriation decision was made in light of these political sensibilities. One of seven Italian bells found by the British in a salvage dump at Monkeberg near Kiel in the spring of 1946, cast by the Pontificia Fonderia Marinelli in Agnone, bore an inscription supportive of the fascist effort. The British MFA&A decided not to repatriate the bell, stating, "There is no question in my mind after reading this inscription, that it would be a mistake to return the bell, since it is more concerned with the victory than with the morality of a discredited political system."[144]

Similar efforts were made to remove Nazi symbols in public venues after the war. On October 25, 1945, the vicar general of Munich and Freising, Ferdinand Buchwieser, wrote to the US military government in Munich from Rochusstrasse 7, raising the subject of obtaining bell material for casting from such now disfavored Nazi symbols in bronze, asking:

> In these days the bronze sovereign-symbol of the police-barracks, 130 Rosenheimerstr, will be taken down and stored in the courtyard at St. Martin's street. It is said to weigh 16 centweights and to be very appropriate for the founding of church-bells. Having through the 3rd Reich lost almost all our bells we should be very thankful if the Military Government allocated this material to us for the founding of church bells.[145]

The response provided on November 26, 1945, by the branch chief of the US Reparations, Deliveries and Restitution division to the director of the US Office of Military Government for Munich was that "you are authorized to dispose of this and other Nazi insignia in any manner which will destroy them beyond recognition."[146] In addition to the requirements of Allied Directive No. 30, the German population sought metal for recasting their church bells from their surroundings. For example, in Bavaria bronze statues by the Austrian sculptor Josef Thorak, who created Reich-sponsored art, were taken for their bell metal, and in Frankfurt, "citizens have generously responded to an appeal [for bell metal] which sent them gathering up bronze rings from old shell cases."[147] Just as the Reich had viewed Europe's bells as fungible raw materials during the war, after the war these bell shards and other bronze materials were again viewed as raw materials—but now for the casting of new bells.

CONCLUSION

By the time Germany surrendered on May 7, 1945, bell casualties reportedly numbered about 150,000. The gap in the communal soundscape in Europe was enormous. In the Netherlands, "there were only a few places where the elated populace were able to celebrate and confirm the liberation with ringing bells."[148] From the bells that escaped ruin and from broken bells came postwar repatriation, reconstruction, and revitalization of the art of bell founding. Recognition of the importance of protecting and conserving objects of cultural and heritage was heightened in response to this great loss. These values were enforced under international law at the International Military Tribunal at Nuremberg, and again in 2004 by the Property Claims Commission, which ruled on bell claims under the German Foundation Act of 2000. Yet, concern for the preservation of bells continues today. In February 2017, the International Committee of Museums and Collections of Instruments and Music (CIMCIM), a division of the International Council of Museums, adopted the following statement: "CIMCIM recognizes the importance of preserving historical musical instruments outside museums. In particular, CIMCIM stresses the risks facing unprotected organs and bells and supports initiatives to ensure their careful documentation and preservation."[149] The bell remains a symbol of local, regional, and global community. A bell now rings in the autumn equinox with the annual ceremony held at the United Nations headquarters in observance of the International Day of Peace, followed by a moment of silence.[150]

NOTES

1. Office of US Chief of Counsel for Prosecution of Axis Criminality, *Nazi Conspiracy and Aggression*, International Military Tribunal, Nuremberg (Washington, DC: US Government Printing Office, 1946), vol. 1, chap. 11, 1056.

2. "Repatriation" generally refers to the return of cultural or historical artifacts to their country of origin. In contrast, "restitution" is the "act of restoring something taken from another person." *Oxford English Dictionary*, http://www.oed.com/view/Entry/163966?redirectedFrom=restitution#eid. However, the terms "repatriation" and "restitution" are often used synonymously to mean the return of property to individuals, groups or nations. See, for example, US Immigration and Customs Enforcement Information Library, "World War II Cultural Artifact Cases," https://www.ice.gov/factsheets/cultural-artifacts-ww2.

3. Campanology is the "systematic study of bells (Lat. *campana*), especially large hanging bells. The field embraces bell design, manufacture and tuning, hanging and methods of sounding, performance and repertoire, and the history and traditions of bells in their many functions as signal and apotropaic devices, ritual implements, musical instruments (individually and grouped as chimes, carillons, etc.), symbols, and other aspects. In a more limited sense, campanology denotes the study of bell ringing." *The Grove Dictionary of Musical Instruments*, 3rd ed., edited by Laurence Libin (New York: Oxford University Press, 2014), 453.

4. Percival Price, *Campanology, Europe 1945–47: A Report on the Condition of Carillons on the Continent of Europe as a Result of the Recent War, on the Sequestration and Melting Down of Bells by the Central Powers, and on Research into the Tonal Qualities of Bells Made Accessible by War-Time Dislodgment* (Ann Arbor: University of Michigan Press, 1948), 62.

5. Ibid., 78.

6. Kenneth Macassey, memorandum, December 14, 1948, National Archives of the United Kingdom ("TNA"), Kew, FO 1050/1481, RA/006/3; *Trial of the Major War Criminals before the International Military Tribunal* (Nuremberg: International Military Tribunal, 1947), vol. 6, January 22, 1946, 7; see also Ludwig Veit, "Das Deutsche Glockenarchiv im Germanischen Nationalmuseum 1965–1985," in *Lusus campanularum: Beiträge zur Glockenkunde*, edited by Tilmann Breuer (Munich: Bayerisches Landesamt für Denkmalpflege, 1986), 91.

7. See, for example, Reichsstelle für Metalle, memorandum, April 28, 1942, NARA, RG260, M1949, Roll 18, Frames 371–372.

8. *Military Government Guide: The Light Metals Industry in Germany*, War Department (Washington, DC: US Government Printing Office, May 1945), 34–35, NARA, RG 226, M1934, Roll 2.

9. Price, *Campanology*, 5.

10. Wim Truyen, "A Bell Atlas, Research and Cataloguing of Historic Swinging Bells and Carillon Bells," in *45 Years of Dutch Carillons, 1945–1990*, edited by Loek Boogert, André Lehr, and Jacques Maassen (The Netherlands: Nederlandse Klokkenspel-Vereniging, 1992), 168–177, 170.

11. Price, *Campanology*, 5.

12. Vicar Emil Weber, letter, December 7, 1945, NARA, RG 260, M1949, Roll 18.

13. Jerzy Golos and Agnieszka Kasprzak-Miler, *Straty Wojenne Zabytkowe Dzwony Utracone W Latach 1939–1945 W Granicach Polski PO 1945* [wartime losses, historic bells, lost between 1939–1945 within post-1945 borders of Poland] (Poznán: Ministerstwo Kultury I Dziedzictwa Narodowego, 2000), 37.

14. US Monuments, Fine Arts, and Archives (MFA&A), memorandum "Restitution of Church Bells," July 31, 1947, NARA, RG 260, M1927, Roll 12; Veit, "Das Deutsche Glockenarchiv," 92.

15. See, for example, Price, *Campanology*, 130.

16. Ibid., 17–18; Pierre A. Karrer, *ADR and the Law: Developments in the Law* (Huntington, NY: Juris, 2008), 336; Veit, "Das Deutsche Glockenarchiv," 92.

17. Office of US Chief of Counsel for Prosecution of Axis Criminality, *Nazi Conspiracy and Aggression*, vol. 7, Exhibit EC-323, 406.

18. Ibid. On the loss of French statuary, see Kirrily Freeman, *Bronzes to Bullets: Vichy and Destruction of French Public Statuary, 1941–1944* (Stanford, CA: Stanford University Press, 2009), 40–43. See also, Percival Price, *Bells and Man*, Oxford: Oxford University Press, 1983), 232; Kirrily Freeman, "'The Bells, Too, Are Fighting': The Fate of European Church Bells in the Second World War," *Canadian Journal of History* 43 (2008), 417, 432–435.

19. Nuremberg Trial Proceedings, January 22, 1946, vols. 6, 7; Price, *Campanology*, 31.

20. Price, *Campanology*, 74.

21. Chaplain Abbot Hoch, certification, July 31, 1946, NARA, RG260, M1949, Roll 13.

22. Golos and Kasprzak-Miler, *Straty Wojenne Zabytkowe*, 30.

23. Price, *Campanology*, 98.

24. Golos and Kasprzak-Miler, *Straty Wojenne Zabytkowe*, 31, 33–34.

25. Ibid., 163–188 (bells missing from Kraków include those made in 1541, 1546, 1554, 1666, 1703, 1751, 1759, 1760, 1763, 1773, and 1785).

26. Mordecai Gebirtig, "Tolling Bells," lyrics: https://encyclopedia.ushmm.org/content/en/song/tolling-bells (last accessed on April 28, 2019). Translated from Yiddish to English by Dr. Bret Werb. Gebirtig was shot and killed in the Kraków ghetto during a roundup for deportation to the Bełżec extermination camp on June 4, 1942. Biographical Note, *Papers of Mordecai Gebirtig*, YIVO Institute for Jewish Research, http://digifindingaids.cjh.org/?pID=131227 (accessed May 15, 2016). Special thanks to Dr. Bret Werb, musicologist, US Holocaust Memorial Museum, for information regarding Mordecai Gebirtig and his song "Glokn Klang!"

27. Price, *Campanology*, 142.

28. Loek Boogert, "Seven Centuries, Origins and Development of Dutch Carillon Culture up to 1945," in Boogert, Lehr, and Maassen, *45 Years of Dutch Carillons*, 12–25, 24.

29. A carillon is "composed of tuned bronze bells which are played from a baton keyboard" and must have at least twenty-three bells. "Instruments built before 1940 and composed of between 15 and 22 bells may be designated as '"historical carillons.'" World Carillon Federation, http://www.carillon.org/eng/fs_orga.htm (accessed May 15, 2016).

30. Wim Truyen, "A Bell Atlas," 169.

31. Boogert, "Seven Centuries," 24.

32. Ibid., 24 (other Dutch bells were marked "P" for *Prüfung* [examination]), and Truyen, "A Bell Atlas," 170. See also Price, *Campanology*, 39–41.

33. Truyen, "A Bell Atlas," 171.

34. Ibid.

35. Price, *Campanology*, 39–41, 142.

36. Ibid., 5, 12; Office of US Chief of Counsel for Prosecution of Axis Criminality, *Nazi Conspiracy and Aggression*, vol. 7, Exhibits ECH-11 and 12, 631–632.

37. Luc Rombouts, *Singing Bronze: A History of Carillon Music* (Leuven, Belgium: Lipsius Leuven, 2014), 269.

38. Price, *Campanology*, 4–5.

39. Ibid., 6.

40. Julie-Marthe Cohen, Felicitas Heimann-Jelinek, and Ruth Jolanda Weinberger, *Handbook on Judaica Provenance Research: Ceremonial Objects*, Conference on Jewish Material Claims against Germany, 2018, 16–27, 86, 95, 106, http://art-69bd.kxcdn.com/wp-content/uploads//2018/02/Judaica-Handbook-2.20.2018.pdf (accessed May 15, 2016).

41. Price, *Campanology*, 142–143, 74 ("A" bells included "practically all cast since 1918").

42. Dr. Heinrich Mayer, bell list, February 10, 1946, NARA, RG260, M1946, Roll 80; P. Maurus Zech, letter, April 6, 1940, and Town Council of Oxenbronn, letter, June 29, 1945, NARA, RG260, M1949, Roll 18.

43. Joseph Goebbels, *Die Tagebücher von Joseph Goebbels*, edited by Elke Fröhlich (Berlin/New York: de Gruyter, 1993–1996), diary entry December 12, 1941 (Teil II, Band 2), 482.

44. Goebbels, *Die Tagebücher*, diary entries February 5 and 12, 1942 (Teil II, Band 3), 255, 292.

45. Price, *Campanology*, 61–71, 142.

46. Church bells from Upper Austria were removed in March 1941 to the iron works in Illsen for processing, L. B. LaFarge, memorandum, May 10, 1946, NARA, RG 260, M1949, Roll 9.

47. Price, *Campanology*, 61–71.

48. Ibid., 69–70.

49. Vernon R. Kennedy, memorandum, August 11, 1947, NARA, RG 260, M1927, Roll 12.

50. Price, *Campanology*, 130–133.

51. See, for example, Ewan Phillips, memorandum, "Broken Bell Metal—Zinnwerke (Wilhelmsburg)," December 5, 1947, FO/1050/1481 TNA; Italian Mission for Restitution, memorandum, November 19, 1946, NARA, RG260, M1949, Roll 18.

52. Phillips, memorandum, "Broken Bell Metal" (the last shipment is dated January 7, 1945, but these fragments, listed as Italian, were dispatched from or through Schönebeck).

53. Price, *Campanology*, 131.

54. Deputy controller, Religious Affairs Branch (British Element), memorandum, June 25, 1946, FO 1050/1481, TNA (this bell was discovered by the British in May 1946 in a salvage dump at Monkeberg near Kiel).

55. Marinelli Pontificia Fonderia di Campane history, http://campanemarinelli.com/en/ marinelli-campane/storia-fonderia/ (accessed May 15, 2016).

56. Joshua D. Zimmerman, ed., *Jews in Italy under Fascist and Nazi Rule, 1922–1945* (Cambridge: Cambridge University Press, 2005), map no. 2; and Isabella Clough Marinaro, "Between Surveillance and Exile: Biopolitics and the Roma in Italy," *Bulletin of Italian Politics* 1 (2) (2009): 265–287, 272.

57. Price, *Campanology*, 141. Price reports that thirteen French, Italian, and Yugoslavian bells left on the ground in the US Zone after the war were installed in towers in Breunberg, Burgweinstein, Babenhausen, Illsen, Krumbach, and elsewhere in Germany, but these were later returned. Price, *Campanology*, 121.

58. Ibid., 64.

59. Ewan Phillips, memorandum, December 12, 1947, FO 1050/1481, TNA.

60. Price, *Campanology*, 19, 20, 33.

61. Ibid., 74.

62. Dr. Matthias Nuding, Deutsche Glockenarchiv, Germanisches Nationalmuseum, e-mail to author, April 1, 2015.

63. Craig Hugh Smyth, *Repatriation of Art from the Collecting Point in Munich after World War II* (Montclair, NJ: Abner Schram, 1988), 10–19.

64. *Report of the American Commission for the Protection and Salvage of Artistic and Historic Monuments in War Areas* (Washington, DC: US Government Printing Office, 1946), 4–5.

65. William Bell Dinsmoor Papers, 1943–1946, American School of Classical Studies, Athens, Series II, the American Commission—Organization Files, Box 6; Mason Hammond, memorandum, June 16, 1945, NARA, RG260, M1941, Roll 19.

66. The US MFA&A Commission liaised with similar groups abroad, as the "MFA&A work was a joint operation." *Report of the American Commission for the Protection and Salvage of Artistic and Historic Monuments in War Areas* (Washington, DC: US Government Printing Office, 1946), 24–25. In May 1944, Prime Minister Churchill created a British commission to focus on restitution and reparations policy for the postwar period, known as "the Macmillan Committee." Ibid., 27.

67. Ibid., 24; Douglas Cooper, memorandum, April 23, 1945, FO 1046/146/3, TNA.

68. See, for example, Lynn H. Nichols, *The Rape of Europa: The Fate of Europe's Treasures in the Third Reich and the Second World War* (New York: Alfred A. Knopf, 1995); Robert M. Edsel, with Bret Witter, *The Monuments Men: Allied Heros, Nazi Thieves, and the Greatest Treasure Hunt in History* (New York: Center Street, 2009).

69. "Report to the President of the Presidential Advisory Commission on Holocaust Assets in the United States," Staff Report, *Plunder and Restitution: The US and Holocaust Victims' Assets* (Washington, DC: US Government Printing Office, December 2000), SR-97.

70. Anne Olivier Popham, minutes, November 11, 1946, NARA, RG260, M1949, Roll 18.

71. Norddeutsche Affinerie history, "Growth and Destruction during and after World War II," http://www.funding universe.com/company-histories/norddeutsche-affinerie-ag-history/ (accessed May 15, 2016).
72. Anne Olivier Popham, memorandum, October 24, 1946, NARA, RG 260, M1949, Roll 18.
73. Price, *Campanology*, 76.
74. Popham, minutes.
75. Maj. G. Willmot, memorandum, August 7, 1946, NARA, RG 260, M1949, Roll 18.
76. Popham, minutes.
77. Maj. L. G. Perry, memorandum, "Bavarian Bells in North Rhine Region," May 3, 1946, NARA, RG 260, M1946, Roll 80; Kenneth Macassey, draft memorandum, April 26, 1948, FO 1050/1481, TNA.
78. Popham, minutes.
79. Staff Report, *Plunder and Restitution*, SR-139-144.
80. MFA&A, memorandum, August 13, 1945, NARA, RG260, M1949, Roll 13. See also Price, *Campanology*, 12; Maj. Louis Bancel LaFarge, memorandum, August 19, 1946, NARA, RG 260, M1949, Roll 18 ("Readily accessible German owned bells, on tops of heaps, will be returned according to Province, with some priority to Bavarian bells because of interzonal exchange").
81. Lt. Col. A. Jewitt, letter, July 26, 1946, FO 1050/1481, TNA.
82. Chief UK Reparations, Deliveries, and Restitutions Division, memorandum, January 7, 1946, FO/1057/152, "Claims, Austria Church Bells," TNA.
83. Donald King, memorandum, September 9, 1946, FO 1057/152, TNA.
84. Popham, memorandum.
85. Kenneth Macassey, letter, December 15, 1948, FO 1050/1481, TNA.
86. Popham, memorandum.
87. Ibid.
88. Unsigned, file note, April 17, 1948, "Four-Power Agreement on Exchange of Bells," FO 1050/1481, TNA.
89. Golos and Kasprzak-Miler, *Straty Wojenne Zabytkowe*, 33 ("Owing to a misunderstanding among the Polish delegates, the Polish quota was reduced from the original 1559 tons to 390 tons").
90. Ibid., 34, 37.
91. Unsigned, memorandum, February 16, 1948; and MFA&A British Element, memorandum, March 4, 1948, FO 1050/1481, TNA.
92. E. C. Norris, letter, April 21, 1948, FO 1050/1481, TNA.
93. Kenneth Macassey, draft memorandum.
94. Unsigned, meeting notes, August 29, 1949, FO 1050/1481, TNA.
95. Cecil Gould, letter, November 30, 1945, NARA, RG 260, M1949, Roll 18.
96. Dr. Georg Lill, letter, September 2, 1945, NARA, RG 260, M1949, Roll 80 ("Every day we are asked about the fate of the church bells from Bavaria, which are stored in Hamburg"); Georg Brombierständl, letter, November 28, 1945, NARA, RG 260, M1949, Roll 80 ("The Catholic parsonage of Mallersdorf is asking the High Military Government of Hamburg in the name of the Christian community and the Convent of Mallersdorf to release these bells or to make conditions, by which the bells could be returned").
97. Popham, minutes.
98. George E. Seigler, memorandum, November 13, 1945, NARA, RG 260, M1946, Roll 80.
99. Maj. Louis Bancel LaFarge, letter, August 19, 1946, NARA, RG 260, M1949, Roll 18.

100. British MFA&A, memorandum, December 14, 1948, FO 1050/1481, TNA.

101. US MFA&A List of "Repositories Containing French Loot—Württemburg-Baden," NARA, RG 260, M1941, Roll 13 ("All bells broken up and part melted to bronze ingots, rest reserved for making bells for Württemberg and Bavaria").

102. A. Hoch, declaration, "Annex 1," July 31, 1946, NARA, RG 260, M1949, Roll 13.

103. Mathäus Wiedemann, declaration, Annex II, May 28, 1945, NARA, RG 260, M1939, Roll 13.

104. Chief, Reparations and Restitutions Section, letter, August 29, 1946, NARA, RG 260, M1949, Roll 13.

105. William W. Furie, memorandum, October 18, 1946, NARA, RG 260, M1949, Roll 13.

106. Religious Affairs Branch, Roman Catholic Section, Zonal Executive Offices (British Element), memorandum, September 2, 1948, TNA, FO 1050/1481.

107. Sir Alfred Brown, letter, September 15, 1949, TNA, FO 1050/1481.

108. Price, *Campanology*, 142–143, compare ibid. at 119. See also Deutsches Glockenarchive, Nürnberg, http://www.gnm.de/index.php?id=264 (accessed May 15, 2016); Veit, "Das Deutsche Glockenarchiv," 91 et seq.; André Lehr, *The Art of the Carillon in the Low Countries* (Belgium: Lannoo, 1991), 268 (in Belgium a commission was established on May 18, 1943, to protect bells, which included an inventory of bells seized by the Germans).

109. Ernest Morris, *Bells of All Nations* (London: Robert Hale, 1951), 111.

110. A memorial to the shattered bells is preserved in Lübeck, http://www.st-marien-luebeck.com/gedenkkapelle.html (accessed May 15, 2016).

111. Percival Price, "The Bells Came Down," *Michigan Alumnus, Quarterly Review* 55 (10) (December 4, 1948), 17.

112. Property Card, *Institut zur Erforschung der Judenfrage*, Insp. August 11, 1945, RG 260, M1940, Roll 3; Receipt, Office of Military Government (US) for Germany to Joshua Starr, March 8, 1949, NARA, RG 260, M1947, Roll 40. See, for example, eighteenth-century bells for Torah finials, World War II Looted Cultural Treasures, Israel Museum, Jerusalem, https://www.imj.org.il/en/collections/281473 (accessed May 15, 2016).

113. Engelbert Wiegman van Heuven, *Acoustical Measurements on Church-Bells and Carillons* (The Hague: Gebroeders Van Cleef, 1949), 2–3.

114. Price, "The Bells Came Down," 9–18, 16.

115. See, for example, Lehr, *The Art of the Carillon in the Low Countries*, 268; Truyen, "A Bell Atlas," 169.

116. Price, *Campanology*, 101–105, 109, 117–118.

117. Ibid., 101–105, 109, 117–118; Deutsche Glockenarchiv, Germanisches Nationalmuseum (http://www.gnm.de/index.php?id=264, accessed May 15, 2016); this archive holds about 30,000 index cards on approximately 16,300 bells seized by the Nazis from 1940 to 1943, as well as "plaster casts, paper set-offs, graphite rub-offs, roughly 13,000 photo negatives and extensive files," Dr. Matthias Nuding, e-mail to author, January 2, 2014.

118. Van Heuven, *Acoustical Measurements*, 1.

119. Lehr, "Restoration of Historic Carillons," in Boogert, Lehr, and Maassen, *45 Years of Dutch Carillons*, 74–89, 75.

120. See, for example, Morris, *Bells of All Nations*, 34.

121. H. B. Walters, *Church Bells of England* (London: Oxford University Press 1912), 215.

122. André Lehr, "Acoustic Research: Discussion on Physics and Music," in Boogert, Lehr, and Maassen, *45 Years of Dutch Carillons*, 132–145, 132.

123. Lehr, "Restoration," 77.

124. Lehr, "Acoustic Research," 134.

125. Lehr, "Restoration," 76.

126. Van Heuven, *Acoustical Measurements*, 2.

127. The following governments expressed adherence to this agreement: Greece, Denmark, Yugoslavia, The Netherlands, Czechoslovakia, Poland, Belgium, Ethiopia, Australia, Honduras, Norway, Panama, Luxemburg, Haiti, New Zealand, India, Venezuela, Uruguay, and Paraguay. *The Nurnberg Trial*, 6 FRD 69 (Nuremberg: International Military Tribunal, 1946), http://www.uniset.ca/other/cs4/6FRD69.html (accessed May 15, 2016).

128. "Charter of the International Military Tribunal at Nuremberg," *Trial of the Major War Criminals before the International Military Tribunal* (Nuremberg: International Military Tribunal, 1947), vol. 1, art. 6(b).

129. Convention Respecting the Laws and Customs of War on Land and Its Annex: Regulations concerning the Laws and Customs of War on Land (Hague IV). The Hague, October 18, 1907, 36 Stat. 2277 ("The 1907 Hague Convention"). Article 6(b) prohibited, in part, the plunder of public or private property.

130. The 1907 Hague Convention, Art. 56. Germany signed The 1907 Hague Convention on October 18, 1907, and ratified it on November 27, 1909. http://www.icrc.org/ihl.nsf/INTRO/195 (accessed May 15, 2016).

131. *The Nurnberg Trial*, 6 FRD 69, 130 (Nuremberg: International Military Tribunal, 1946).

132. "Charter of the International Military Tribunal at Nuremberg," vol. 1, 1018.

133. *Nuremberg Trial Proceedings*, vol. 6, January 22, 1946, 7.

134. Office of US Chief of Counsel for Prosecution of Axis Criminality, *Nazi Conspiracy and Aggression*, vol. 7, Exhibits ECH-11 and 12, 631–632. See also "US Prosecution's Trial Brief on the Spoliation of Belgium," Donovan Nuremberg Trials Collection, Cornell University Law Library, 6, http://lawcollections.library.cornell.edu/bookreader/nur:00795/#page/8/mode/1up (accessed May 15, 2016).

135. Trial Brief, "The Spoliation of Russia," Section 28.02, 8, citing Exhibit EC 389 Memorandum from Zimmermann to the Reichswirtschafteministerium, May 1942, Donovan Collection, International Military Tribunal at Nuremberg, Cornell Law Library, http://lawcollections.library.cornell.edu/nuremberg/catalog/nur:00896 (accessed May 15, 2016).

136. Articles 52 and 53 of The 1907 Hague Convention provide for requisitions on the basis of necessity for military operations, proportional to the resources of the country, and with eventual compensation.

137. US Chief Counsel for Prosecution, *Germanization and Spoliation*, vol. 1, chap. 13, 1075.

138. *The Nurnberg Trial*, 6 FRD 69, 111, 120–123 (Nuremberg: International Military Tribunal, 1946).

139. *The Nurnberg Trial*, 111, 120–123.

140. Polish Ministry of Culture and National Heritage, Publications, http://kolekcje.mkidn.gov.pl/en/The-Division-for-Looted-Art (accessed May 15, 2016).

141. Golos and Kasprzak-Miler, *Straty Wojenne Zabytkowe*, 32–35. See also Andrzej Jakubowski, Francesca Fiorentini, and Ewa Manikowska, "Memory, Cultural Heritage and Community Rights: Church Bells in Eastern Europe and the Balkans," *International Human Rights Law Review* 5 (2016), 274–306.

142. Czech bell compensation awards were made under the German Foundation Act, the Remembrance, Responsibility, and Future Foundation, http://www.stiftung-evz.de/eng/the-foundation/law.html (accessed May 15, 2016).

143. Pierre A. Karrer, *ADR and the Law*, 327–342; communication with Professor Richard M. Buxbaum, former commissioner, Property Claims Commission, May 31, 2016; e-mail from Dr. Pierre A. Karrer, former chairman of the Property Claims Commission, June 14, 2016.

144. Deputy controller, Religious Affairs Branch (British Element), memorandum, June 25, 1946, FO 1050/1481, TNA (the inscription stated: *Dic deipapae carmen dic caesis dic victoribus dic acta per seacula posteris dic m.liberatricem romana novis virtute fascibos restituta lictoriis in holstem cum irrueret divinim eradicantem cultum romae et nomen et sus inter gentes victricem imperasse unam AD 1943.XX*).

145. Ferdinand Buchwieser, letter, October 25, 1945, NARA, RG 260, M1947, Roll 91.

146. Jacob M. Silvey, memorandum, "Monuments: Munich, Denazification," November 26, 1945, NARA, RG 260, M1946, Roll 91.

147. Hellmut Lehmann-Haup, art investigation officer MFA&A, report, February 25, 1948, NARA, RG260, M1946, Roll 76.

148. Boogert, "Seven Centuries," 25.

149. Dr. Christina Linsenmeyer, CIMCIM secretary, e-mail to author, April 23, 2017.

150. UN News Centre, http://www.un.org/en/events/peaceday/ (accessed May 15, 2016); "Peace Bells Ring for Earth"; International Atomic Energy Agency, http://www.iaea.org/newscenter/news/2006/earthday.html (accessed May 15, 2016).

CHAPTER 29

···

DIGITAL REPATRIATION

Copyright Policies, Fair Use, and Ethics

···

ALEX PERULLO

MANY practitioners and scholars discuss the digital archive as fundamental to de-mocracy, cultural development, nationalism, and the equitable sharing of knowledge.[1] A digital archive can open access to information that, in the past, would often not circu-late beyond the confines of a particular space; it can lead to scholarly and nonscholarly studies on topics that were once hard to locate (Crossen-White 2015); it can provide new opportunities to create interactive resources that link sound, video, and text, often into simple search features; and it has added to the "social life of data," where information circulating from an archive can significantly influence people's understanding and in-terpretation of everyday experiences (Beer and Burrows 2013). Writing in the *Guardian* newspaper about the digitization of 14,000 sound recordings at the Imperial War Museum London, Lynsey Martenstyn notes, "these sound recordings bring history to life, allowing online users to listen to first hand recollections from the men and women who participated in and lived with the effects of war."[2]

Despite potential benefits, many issues arise in the digitization of and widespread ac-cess to cultural documents, including sound recordings. Many communities may not want their histories, cultures, and identities to circulate within the social life of data.[3] Some communities may question the ethical priorities of archives that place material online without consultation of those same communities. Many legal issues may arise should an archive opt to place copyrighted materials freely online. Communities may question the underlying intentions and potential profits—regarding individual jobs and careers—that archives provide using the intellectual wealth of others.[4] And the notion of "bringing history to life" through access to materials creates an idea that people will interpret those materials in a manner relevant, both historically and culturally, to the communities from which they came.

This tension between moving Indigenous knowledge into public view and preserving the rights of Indigenous populations existed long before the emergence of digital archives. Yet the digital archive movement pushes further in encouraging users to see online resources as a panacea for the equitable circulation and sharing of data. It posits a "world is flat" argument that suggests that everyone—either now or in the near future—can make use of the global circulation of online data.[5] This notion, however, is a fallacy, given the restrictions both in terms of access and time that exists in communities around the world to make use of online materials, which raises several potential concerns: what are the legal and ethical responsibilities of an archive? Should archives that contain Indigenous knowledge follow the rules established under contemporary copyright law or under Indigenous systems that may encourage different relations to cultural documents?

In this chapter, I examine three issues involving online digital archives: conflicts with copyright law, notions of fair use, and ethics and equality in the materials being selected for digitization. While there are other issues that can be discussed, including conflicts over Indigenous conceptions of rights and ownership, these three represent dominant concerns in the movement of archives from physical to digital form and from private to public dissemination. Online digital archives include any repository that allows Internet users to access large collections of materials (in the case of this chapter, music), including collections where users need to register or pay for access, as well as those that appear freely online. I focus on scholarly or academic archives rather than massive online resources, such as YouTube. Massive online resources often allow users to break legal and ethical rules discussed here by permitting anyone to post content even when copyrighted. While copyright owners may ask to have that material taken down, YouTube makes it prohibitively difficult to do so; it is far easier to post content than to delete it. However, it should also be noted that many archives opt to use resources, such as YouTube, to deposit materials. The Associated Press, for instance, has placed thousands of hours of archival material, dating back to 1895, on YouTube. Clearly these massive online resources reshape the archival landscape and should be addressed in another essay. Here, however, I focus on academic-oriented archives that aim to place their resources online.

I also argue that academically oriented archives should aim to make information digitally available—under certain restrictions and conditions, with appropriate resources and funding, and with attention to ethical and legal considerations—so that a wide array of people can assess and make use of their materials. Despite concerns that many Indigenous communities may not attain access to materials presented in a digital archive and many misinterpretations may emerge from the online availability of data, restricting access to material within an archive does little to promote awareness of populations or give voice to Indigenous peoples who may not even know that these repositories exist. Additionally, it is through the digital archive that repatriation has increased globally, allowing many to hear, see, and read about materials that address cultural and historical events. By keeping these items protected locally, archival objects become more about privilege and power—where access is only granted to a select few—than the potential openness of digital media. I make this argument despite my concerns about the significant imbalance in access to the Internet globally and, as illustrated later, concerns over legal and ethical issues.

In interviews with artists in eastern Africa, many expressed interest in the circulation of their music or the music from their countries online.[6] Not to appear online, as several artists suggest, was essentially not to exist in the contemporary global circulation of data. Christom Mwingira explains, "I would very much like my music or our [Tanzanian] music to be in a music library as it would allow our music to be heard [globally], and we can become known to other people and to other musicians." He also mentions that it would be a point of national pride to appear in an online archive.[7] Musicians view the potential circulation of data in digital archives as a form of cultural promotion needed to preserve other aspects of cultural identity. The Tanzanian musician and artist Ibony Moalim explains, "This kind of service is too new to our society; we don't have even a single music library in our country."[8] He argues that international archives could preserve the traditions and ideas of African artists into the future in ways that most African countries have been unable to do.

Others may dispute the arguments made by these artists and suggest that online archives never fully repatriate materials to their countries of origin. If repatriation means the return of material to a country of origin, then online archives never fully commit to this task. The music remains preserved on servers and in its original forms in the Western world. In employing digital archives, the physical presence and the official return can only occur through digital conveyance, which raises the question as to whether such as transference of cultural material signifies repatriation. If materials streamed through a website reach an Indigenous community, does that signify repatriation? While it is not difficult to imagine situations in which communities would be disappointed by only being told about digital files online rather than receiving physical copies of their music, the medium of return may cause less controversy than access and willingness to respect community rights. In other words, if a community received songs on a compact disc or in digital format, and they could easily play either, the medium is likely to matter less than the protection of their rights and identities in the preserved materials. The issue is that many communities, particularly those in eastern Africa, do not have easy access to digital music players. Cellphones are widely used across Africa, reaching around 80 percent of adults in Tanzania, Ghana, and Kenya. Many people also play music on their phones. Yet, very few people stream music from these devices, which means repatriation could be rather limited to only those who can afford regular access to the Internet.

Returning to the interviews with eastern African artists, however, these musicians viewed the digital-ness of repatriation positively. If an archive returned sound recordings in physical form, such as on compact discs or cassette tapes, few people would have the means to play those materials. If the archive constructed a building to house equipment to play that material, few people would have the means or the time to travel to the facility. Digital music streamed online is available to many people throughout eastern Africa or has the potential to be more equitable once online access becomes less of a barrier. Alternative solutions, such as loading mp3 players with repatriated music that can be easily shared and distributed, may provide better access to these communities. However, these efforts present their own challenges of fairness and equity in the distribution of such technology. For instance, how would you repatriate to community members that are widely dispersed throughout a region or in different parts of the world?

Despite many imperfections, the digital movement of music online represents an attempt to provide wider access to materials and to promote the music of Indigenous communities. This idea of promotion remains consistently and culturally significant among many eastern African artists consulted in this research. From the common expressions of frustration among many musicians, a theme emerged that they wanted to be treated fairly, rather than be protected or hidden away according to Western notions of ethics. Scholarly notions of ethics frequently treat Indigenous populations differently—as more fragile, remote, undeveloped—rather than as equal, sharing the same rights as those in developed nations. Many artists stated that they would be proud to have their music appear in digital archives, as it would symbolize the importance and value of their music within the global circulation of data. It would also do more to promote African music, according to some, than the pay-to-play schemes that many encounter with local radio stations. Hamza Kalala explained, "I would very much like for the [archives] to put my music on the Internet to promote my music and culture more. And, it is better to do this than to pay radio announcers to play your music when they do not see the benefit of your music."[9] Though Kalala works as a contemporary musician, whereas music deposited in archives often documents songs from previous generations, he emphasized the need to have fees included in the archive structure. These fees would go to pay musicians for their contributions to the archive in much the same way that radio stations pay royalties to artists. In other words, if an American artist in an archive would receive a royalty from their contributions, so too should African artists.

It is beyond the scope of this chapter to examine whether such notions of equality could exist within the global circulation of data. In the case of recorded music, the challenge is to return recordings to communities in ways that will assist those communities and will not take away from existing efforts to promote music within those areas. Even if musicians, Indigenous communities, and others want materials associated with them to be available to a broader public, archives need to carefully weigh potential benefits with many pitfalls. Certainly, budget restrictions represent a major hurdle for many repositories. It is the legal and ethical considerations, however, that may ultimately push archives to maintain their information in private rather than promote open, digital access online.

ETHNOGRAPHIC ARCHIVES AND COPYRIGHT LAW

In 1999, Indiana University, the University of Michigan, and the Mellon Foundation started an initiative to preserve and annotate scholarly field recordings. Many of those who helped to initiate the project, including the ethnomusicologists Ruth Stone and Lester Monts, realized that there was an abundance of materials that never made it into any archive: scholars often left their rare recordings in boxes or in basements to deteriorate; researchers hoarded materials at home as they were afraid placing them in an archive that could limit their own access to those materials; and some individuals may have never realized the inherent value of their field recordings. Over time, as these materials remained in peoples' homes or offices, they would either become unplayable or, on the passing of the scholar, be discarded. Given the inherent value of these research collections, including recordings of songs, ceremonies, and interviews, the group decided to find a way to preserve and provide access to these recordings. They also wanted these recordings to be annotated to provide information about the content of the collections, which could then be useful for future research. The project eventually became the Ethnographic Video for Instruction and Analysis (EVIA) Digital Archive (DA).

For many depositors, the EVIA model proved both exciting and daunting. Scholars needed to submit up to twelve hours of fieldwork videos in their entirety. Scholars could not edit or delete material from any recording, which meant that every mistake—dropped audio, poor camera footage, or shaky images—remained in any submitted footage.[10] The reason for this policy was that one could never tell what would become valuable to other scholars. Dark footage of a music concert may be able to be lightened in postprocessing or a scholar could simply make use of the audio even though the footage would normally not be viewable to a wide audience. Once scholars submitted their fieldwork videos, the EVIA team would create digitally preserved copies and back up everything on mirrored servers.

In addition to providing complete fieldwork videos, scholars needed to use software called the Annotator's Workbench to annotate the videos. To encourage thorough and detailed annotations, scholars would attend a summer retreat at Indiana University, where they would spend days watching their videos, dividing the material up into events, scenes, and actions, and then describing every detail that they believed could be useful. The amount of detail in any piece of recorded footage is astounding, which meant that scholars could spend an entire day describing the details of a few minutes of footage.

While EVIA represented a different approach to archiving, particularly through encouraging a protracted commitment by each submitting scholar, the legal and ethical issues remained similar to many other archives that aim to make recordings available online. In the early organizational meetings, I joined a group of lawyers, scholars, and technology specialists to develop a legal and ethical framework for the Archive. Our task was to conceptualize a process for accepting scholarly materials and for deciding on the best means to fairly provide access to deposited resources.

One of the first issues concerned the rights of composers. Composers have ethical and economic rights to benefit from their original creations. The composer can be a single person or an entire group. Alternatively, the composer can be a community, as is the case with some folkloric traditions. In the commercial release of a recording, the composer and performers can receive various royalties. For instance, if a composer's song appears on a compact disc or is available for download, then the composer receives a mechanical royalty for every copy of the compact disc that is created or for every download of the song that is made. If a service provides streaming access to a song online, then the composer can also receive a mechanical royalty every time the song is played. A composer can also receive royalties from radio stations, restaurants, bars, offices, or live performance venues for the public performance of a song that he or she wrote. Also, if a television or film company uses a composer's song, then they must create a license agreement with the composer and pay a license fee (this is called synchronization rights). These various income streams—mechanical royalties, public performance royalties, and synchronization rights—are all a part of the composer's revenue for creating an original work.

In examining the viability of a digital archive of ethnographic videos, the EVIA DA copyright group found that many scholars did not know the authors of compositions that appeared on their ethnographic recordings. While the researcher could identify performers, the location, and the meaning of the songs, many did not take into account the composers of the works. Even if an agreement had been made with the performers, an ethnographer would also need an agreement with the composer(s) to be able to make the songs accessible online. To complicate matters further, in recordings of festivals, where many groups perform over several hours or days, there could be hundreds of possible composers. It would be practically impossible for an ethnographer to document and attain agreements from all of these individuals. Further, under most copyright acts, the process of combining musical works with moving images requires a synchronization license. In filming a musical performance, an ethnographer films a scene to be "synched" with the music being performed by a band. This process, which can be considered the same as when a movie director uses an artist's song in a film, requires specific permission of the copyright owner. A written agreement from the copyright owner to the ethnographer could then be transferred to a digital archive, which would then give them permission to use the recordings.

The complexity of attaining all of the requisite permissions for using videos in a digital archive was compounded by additional factors. Many communities that performed traditional music did not conceptualize their songs as having a distinct author. Copyright law was created to protect the rights of creators, including composers, authors, and lyricists. There was an expectation that an identifiable author existed with clear separation between the creators of different works. Composing songs in many cultures, however, is not so clear-cut or straightforward. Many cultures accept the borrowing of ideas, melodies, rhythms, and even lyrics from other artists' works to create new music (this was even customary in American popular music but has become more difficult with the strict enforcement of copyright law). Some communities allow songs to be altered or changed within a specific population, but are more restrictive regarding the use of the song by others. Other communities permit anyone to use a song and never identify a single author. Moreover, most commonly, a single author may have created the basic elements of a song, but the song itself was molded and reformed over time by many people. These compositional practices do not fit with conceptions of ownership presented in many contemporary copyright laws, which makes them harder to implement into a digital archive that aims to uphold the standards of intellectual property rights.

To put this issue another way, should an archive abide by both the rules of music found in a particular community and the rules assigned to music through international trade agreements? If "yes," then an archive would need to have an agreement from each participant, performer, and community leader featured in a video, as well as written agreements from composers stating that they agree to the terms of the archive. This means that a very long agreement would need to be signed or verbally consented-to that documented the legal and cultural potential of the recordings for now and into the future. Asking artists to sign lengthy agreements, however, would create ethical problems for many researchers. In each country that we examined—from the United States to France and from Tanzania to Papua New Guinea—many examples existed of artists losing rights to their music after signing previous legal agreements. It was untenable to ask every fieldworker to attain these types of permissions and unethical to require informants to comprehend national and international legal terminology in signing them.

A second issue in examining ethnographic videos for EVIA was that many copyright laws in less developed countries gave the rights to traditional music to a state copyright organization. This means that any legal rights in a traditional recording rest with the state organization rather than a community or individual. In one case in the EVIA DA, the ethnomusicologist Frank Gunderson had hundreds of hours of video of traditional songs of the Sukuma peoples in East Africa. Gunderson's videos clearly identified the performers of songs and the community from which they emerged. In some cases, the composers could be determined, but in other cases, they could not. While the community and individual performers gave Gunderson permission to record and use the songs, the Tanzanian government could have had a say in the administration of rights in traditional music appearing on Gunderson's online videos. This raised the potential need to attain a release from the Tanzanian government in order to use the videos. Since many African countries treat traditional music similarly, this further complicates acquiring permissions.

Finally, even if ethnographers could identity the composers of every song that appeared in an archive, how would the archive or fieldworker find the composers and how would they pay to use their songs? Each song comes from a country with different copyright policies and with different organizations that collect money on behalf of artists. Many artists who appear in ethnographies are not a part of any official collective management organizations. This means that even if a digital archive paid a royalty for the use of songs, the funding might not end up in the composer's hands. To pay composers who had registered with various collective management organizations, the archive would need to hire the services of outside companies to manage the rights of so many composers in so many different countries.

The potential polyphony of rules and rights involving ethnographic videos made developing a clear, comprehensive means for administrating the EVIA DA problematic.

Initial conversations revolved around the potential scenarios that could emerge. We created a list of ethnographic films that could be deposited in the collection, including folk music from Europe, jazz music from North America, and popular music from Africa. Each case presented unique problems in addressing the rights of performers, composers, communities, governments, researchers, and archives.

Ultimately, the EVIA DA group realized that it would be impossible for researchers to attain all requisite permissions. It would also counter the efforts of research where a scholar could become more preoccupied with legal rights than with comprehending the cultural dynamics of communities in which they worked. Keeping in mind that these conversations occurred in a pre-YouTube environment, the group worked to develop a series of legal and ethical steps that would best serve the interests of both the communities documented by researchers and academic scholars. These steps included the following: a thorough vetting process of the materials being deposited into the archive to ensure that the scholar knew the legal and ethical issues surrounding their recordings; attaining written agreements from the scholars depositing the material and, wherever possible, from the communities from which the materials came; a requirement to have end users register with EVIA DA, agree to the terms of the Archive, and then attain approval from the EVIA administrators to use the Archive (registration would remain free in keeping with the open intentions of the Archive); and finally all videos would be streamed, thereby limiting the ability of end users to download or copy material (though we did realize that savvy users could still copy streaming video). Moreover, at any point where someone identified material that should not be a part of the Archive, they could easily submit a request to block or take down problematic content.

Thus EVIA DA was created intentionally with online use in mind and with the aim of maintaining as many safeguards as possible. The intention was to build a dynamic dialogue between communities, ethnographers, end users, and administrators of the Archive to address any issues as they arose and best preserve ethnographic fieldwork videos. The benefits of this approach were that many people made use of and continue to use the hundreds of hours of video in the archive and, thus far, no complaints have been made against any content of the Archive. On the other hand, given the openness of other repositories, the restrictiveness of the EVIA DA appears almost too stringent. For one, users cannot search online for content in the Archive, as it remains housed within a protected environment that users need to know about to find. Though communities can easily gain access to the Archive, it fails to meet the interest of the eastern African artists who want their music to appear online and widely available for people to see and hear.

A strain thus exists between the interest of an archive in protecting legal/ethical concerns and efforts to promote potential interests of communities. While these interests are not always mutually exclusive, the complexity of legal rights in recorded music causes significant concern for administrators of archives. In consulting on several projects since the EVIA DA, many administrators want to move archival resources online but fear repercussions of copyright law. If the archive can argue that the recorded material exists in the public domain—meaning that it is no longer protected by copyright law—then legal concerns become secondary and ethical issues become more significant. Even arguing for public domain, however, can be challenging. As of the first of January 2017, any work copyrighted before 1923 exists in the public domain. In addition, in the United States, works published before 1977 and without a copyright notice, also fall into the public domain. Potentially many ethnographic recordings made before 1977, housed in archives that exist in the United States, can thus claim that the materials are in the public domain. Yet, making the decision on whether a recording has ever had a copyright notice raises many other concerns that often negate the assurance of public domain. In addition, ethically, an archive may decide that Indigenous communities deserve further protections since original copyright protection was rarely afforded to them.

In litigious environments, it is easy to see why administrators become preoccupied with copyright laws eventually arriving at a conclusion that an online archive could be far too challenging and costly. Others may take the opposite response and simply post material online in a manner often common for those outside of academics. It is not hard to see how these archives could be viewed as achieving broader goals of repatriation despite potentially breaking international copyright law or ignoring the interests of communities from which the recordings came. One colleague, for instance, explained to me a decision that he made to not deposit his recordings of ceremonies that contained copyrighted songs to an archive only to find, years later, that someone else had posted very similar recordings on YouTube. Perhaps, this colleague wondered, academics have become too restrictive and insular to provide broader usefulness. In more recent years, many concerns about litigation have been allayed, which I discuss in the later section regarding fair use. Still, any archive should consider legal issues involved in posting materials online even if the main reason is to not hinder the commercial potential of artists attempting to make a career in music.

SOUND ARCHIVES AND COPYRIGHT LAW

Where EVIA aims to maintain scholarly materials, other archives connect both scholarly and commercial interests in music. The Smithsonian Folkways, for instance, considers itself a "nonprofit record company" with a central mission of educating users about music, people, and cultures throughout the world. The organization works mainly with record labels and other archives, such as the Archives and Research Centre for Ethnomusicology (ARCE), to release recordings and documentation to support its mission. The record companies and archives that Folkways works with have, in most cases, already acquired permissions from songwriters, communities, and composers to release their recordings commercially. These permissions provide some assurance to Folkways that they can both commercially release the music and provide royalties to the recordings' rights holders.

Many archives hold music that they could release commercially to generate interest in their collections and gain some financial benefit. To release this material legally, staff at the archives need to find the composer, lyricist, performers, and other individuals who collaborated on each song. Dan Sheehy, former curator and director of the Smithsonian Folkways, explains that it is often far simpler to create new recordings than to try to find the authors of older works that exist in an archive. Nonetheless, Folkways has tried, in many circumstances, to locate the performers and composers of songs that the label wants to release commercially. This has meant talking to other musicians and communities about the whereabouts of an artist, placing advertisements in *Rolling Stone* magazine asking for assistance in locating an artist, and working with families to identity the heirs to a musician's family. This last step can be a challenge, since there are often conflicts with various heirs about who rightfully deserves any royalties. As Sheehy states, "Someone could contact Folkways claiming to be an heir to an artist, but how do we know they are a credible person to make this call? If the recordings come from a community, then we have to ask, what is community and who represents it? These are difficult questions."[11] Folkways now requires families that claim to be an heir to submit a death certificate and a will that shows those who are heirs to an artist's estate.

The prodigious efforts by Smithsonian Folkways to locate rights holders sets the label apart from many other education-based archives. It is not only difficult to locate performers and composers who appear in older recordings but also time consuming and expensive. Most archives are not able to hire individuals to take on these efforts, particularly when the costs of archiving are so great.

Several new archives have emerged that require performers to sign contracts and permit the archive to use their materials. The Singing Wells Project is a nonprofit organization that works to record, archive, and share the music of East Africa. It is imagined as both a repatriation project and a means to promote East African music to a wider audience. The group of engineers, musicians, and producers state that they did not want to become "fossil collectors," where recordings become stored in inaccessible archives.[12] Instead, they wanted to create an archive that was readily accessible and beneficial to anyone who listened or had access to the recorded material. To do this, Singing Wells partners with organizations in African countries—such as a Ketebul, a nonprofit organization based in Kenya—to identify music traditions, record the music of East African artists, and then distribute video and audio recordings online through YouTube and SoundCloud, as well as through album sales and downloads. To secure permission to do this, Singing Wells asks the artists they work with to sign an agreement that lists the compositions recorded and the rights granted to Singing Wells by the artists. The agreement also guarantees the artists royalties on any commercially released recordings.

The challenges faced by organizations such as the Smithsonian Folkways and Singing Wells illustrate some of the issues that prevent or hinder archives from making their materials widely available. The work that goes into identifying rights holders is extensive and costly. The benefits of migrating a music archive to digital form are apparent by looking at the output of these institutions. Smithsonian Folkways, for instance, has over two million impressions per album that they publish. This means that an album appears in the printed press, blogs, radio, downloads, iTunes, YouTube, Spotify, and other sources over two million times per year. Folkways makes available over 45,000 tracks, with a wealth of documentation, liner notes, videos, and other information.

For other archives that work with material still protected by copyright law, and which they also do not have rights and permissions to use, promotion of their materials digitally may involve a combination of factors discussed thus far, including registering end users and selecting only certain items to present online. These archives may also opt to consider how to alter the presentation of archival material in ways that are transformative. A transformation of the purpose, character, and meaning of the archived materials—transformations that could be as minor as making the materials searchable in an online database—could qualify as fair use.

FAIR USE AND ONLINE ARCHIVES

The notion of fair use recognizes that there are certain circumstances in which the reproduction and even transformation of copyrighted works can be done freely and fairly. According to section 107 of the United States Copyright Act, you can reproduce another author's work without needing to provide financial compensation if the work is being used as a part of criticism, news reporting, teaching, scholarship, or research. Most academically based digital archives aim to provide materials that fall under these provisions, which means that, in principle, an archive should be able to claim fair use to protect its interests. Deciding on whether an archive meets fair use or whether anything can be considered fair use, however, means carefully weighing and considering four criteria. In legal cases lawyers would lay out a claim for or against fair use, which the judge would then make a ruling on based on case law and the particulars of the fair use doctrine. While fair use has some basic statutory designations, it exists as a flexible and case-dependent framework. The discussion that follows draws on existing case law and current debates about fair use to better comprehend its application with digital archives.

One criterion used to consider whether something can be considered as fair use is to interpret the amount of the material being used. To claim fair use, the use of the material needs to be brief or limited to a small portion of the original item. When you photocopy a written document, you are permitted to copy a certain percentage of that item. In general terms, a classroom teacher can copy a single chapter of a book if that chapter does not make up a significant portion of the book. An educator or scholar can photocopy a complete book chapter, if it is less than 2,500 words (this would mean copying only the first section of this chapter), or an excerpt from a prose work of not more than 1,000 words or 10 percent of the work. With sound recordings, an educator can only make a single copy of a recording that he or she already owns. Also, the copy can only be used for classroom purposes or research. As should be obvious here, these are rather strict limits on the amount of material that an educator can use even in classroom teaching.

Problematically, most digital archives want to present entire collections of songs, texts, and photographs for anyone to access. This presentation is not necessarily limited to classroom use or even to educational purposes. One could certainly imagine people accessing an archive and listening to recordings for entertainment purposes, which moves beyond an educational or classroom-oriented purpose. More important for fair use, entire songs appear online. They are not excerpts. Digital, online collections include hundreds of songs from various artists that are easily and readily accessible to end users. Based on an initial reading of this facet of fair use, a digital archive would not be able to claim a fair use. Importantly, however, you need to consider the totality of criteria of fair use to decide on a specific case. This means that even if one criterion does not work, the potential still exists to use fair use.

A second criterion is the "purpose and character of the use." This asks whether the use is for commercial or for nonprofit, educational purposes.[13] Although there are many examples of commercially oriented archives, most of the ones that aim to preserve ethnographic recordings do not function with commercial intentions. A few archives do sell music from their collections. The International Library of African Music (ILAM), for instance, which has rights and permissions for the recordings made by Hugh Tracey, repackages and sells recordings in its collection. These recordings generate income for the archive and help to promote the work being done by researchers and staff of the organization. Like most archives that sell music, ILAM has the rights to sell this music based on previous agreements made between Hugh Tracey and the musicians that he worked with beginning in the 1940s. In some cases, the copyright protection in the recordings has expired, so the recordings are in the public domain. Songs and recordings that are in the public domain can be sold, performed, copied, and distributed without financial compensation to the creators of the work. If an archive meets these conditions—either owning the economic rights to the music in their collections or using works for which the copyright has expired—then they can commercially sell that music without considering fair use. In this way, ILAM's recordings can be made commercially available without violating copyright law.

For archives that do not have permissions from creators of works, they need to show that the purpose of providing the work is for its use in scholarship and research. Many archives provide information, biographies, translations, and musical analysis of the songs that appear in their collections. The archive also makes items searchable and includes vital metadata along with archived materials. This added content enhances the educational purpose of the archive and, and it can be used to build a case about the transformative element of an archive. Rather than just presenting entire works for people to listen to, watch, or read, the archive enriches the listener's ability to access and make sense of the materials. This added benefit is an advantage to a fair use argument, as it is not simply the wholesale presentation or copy of a work but also a creative endeavor to make the work available to end users.

In the case of the EVIA DA, the annotation and digitization of hundreds of hours of videos from collectors transforms formerly unrelated materials into a single repository of searchable content. This effort both to describe materials in detail and to provide access to previously unavailable videos, all for educational purposes, supports a claim to fair use. Other cases that have emerged similar to those of an online-digital-music-archive include *Authors Guild, Inc. v. HathiTrust* 12-4547-cv (2d Cir. 2014). The Authors Guild filed a lawsuit against HathiTrust Digital Library, a consortium of many American-based universities that entered into an agreement with Google, Inc., as part of the Google Book project to scan millions of books. HathiTrust argued that the digitization of texts in university libraries by Google was fair use because, among other reasons, the purpose of the digitization effort was noncommercial; the ability to search digital copies enhances scholarship and research; and the capacity to search texts "serve[s] an entirely different purpose than the original works."

In the verdict for the case, the court stated that the full-text searchable database is a "quintessentially transformative use." The circuit judge, Barrington D. Parker, continued, "The result of a word search is different in purpose, character, expression, meaning, and message from the page (and the book) from which it is drawn. Indeed, we can discern little or no resemblance between the original text and the results of the HDL full-text search" (18). In a previous, lower-court ruling the district judge, Harold Baer Jr., further added that the project was in the public interest by promoting science and the useful arts as mandated by copyright law.[14] This idea of the HathiTrust as both transformative and in the public interest reflects the organization's own statements as creating a "cultural record" for the "public good" that supports teaching, learning, and research.[15]

The verdict of the *Authors Guild, Inc. v. HathiTrust* case provides support to many other academic archives that want to place materials online because they transform content and advance teaching, learning, and research. It should be noted, however, that the court ruled in *Authors Guild, Inc. v. HathiTrust* that preservation in itself is not transformative. It is only when that material becomes searchable or has added content that the use of archival materials becomes transformative.

The third fair use criterion addresses the nature of a digital archive. Essentially, this asks whether the material in question is informational, educational, and an added benefit to society. As discussed in the previous fair use points, academic digital archives support content that could benefit various educational initiatives. Even the effort to repatriate sound recordings, a potential purpose of any archive, can be seen as beneficial socially, culturally, and educationally.

Finally, the fourth criterion of fair use addresses the "effect of the use upon the potential market." Would a digital archive take away the commercial benefits from authors or anyone else? By allowing access to field recordings or older commercial recordings to be freely available online, would this deter people from purchasing commercially available recordings? Most digital archives aim to promote materials that are either unpublished or no longer available to the public. Or, they make available rare materials that are difficult to access otherwise. Unlike popular file-sharing services that allow users to easily distribute and download commercially available materials, archives tend to focus on materials that are noncommercial or less commercial. Field recordings, such as those that appear in EVIA DA, are often not high quality and are not organized in the way that an album is, with separate tracks for each song. Rather, the research recognizes the rawness or unedited nature of the material as being insightful to comprehending context, sound, and cultural practices. Without the archives providing access to this music, fewer people would be able to hear and learn about these cultural traditions.

There are scholars, however, who can capture high-quality recordings that they release commercially (many of the examples illustrated above from ILAM, the Smithsonian Folkways, Singing Wells, and even Frank Gunderson's collection illustrate this point). In these circumstances, the use of digital audio recordings in a public archive could hinder the sale of similar music in a local market. It is worth noting that section 108 of the United States Copyright Act, referred to as "Limitations on exclusive rights: Reproduction by libraries and archives," does not provide any exceptions for archives wanting to allow music to be available online. Section 108 does authorize the reproduction of sound recordings for preservation purposes. It also allows libraries to lend music to library patrons. However, section 108 notes that any digital copies cannot be distributed in that format or made available in that format outside the premises of the library or archive" (17 USC § 108(b)(2)).[16] For recordings that might be considered commercially popular, such as recordings of popular music, concerts, or practice sessions, different restrictions might need to be in place as compared to those materials that have less commercial value. Of course, determining commercial value is both challenging and rather subjective, which is the reason that judicial decisions are often needed to determine fair use.

Many online resources now claim fair use even though they overstep the criteria outlined in this section. Educational and scholarly archives that move material online should have a strong case for fair use, yet even these organizations should be cognizant of rights held by composers and other copyright holders. Simply claiming fair use does not absolve organizations from finding the best means to protect content creators, scholars, and the educational mission of an archive.

ETHICS IN THE CIRCULATION
OF INFORMATION ONLINE

On Monday, December 9, 2013, the Drouot auction house in Paris, France, auctioned thirty-two sacred masks of the Hopi Tribe. The masks, referred to as Katsinam masks, represent ancestral spirits, and their sale made headlines based on the ceremonial, cultural, and sacred value of the items. A court case, protests, and pressure from the US Embassy in France to halt the sale of the sacred objects failed to prevent the eventual auction of the Hopi ancestral items.[17] A few weeks later, in January 2014, the Denver Museum of Nature and Science decided to return thirty *vigango*, memorial totems with cultural and spiritual significance of the Mijikenda peoples of Kenya, to the National Museums of Kenya. The decision by the museum to return the items was based on ethical obligations. In a *New York Times* article about the repatriation of the *vigango*, the Denver museum's curator of anthropology, Chip Colwell-Chanthaphonh, commented that while a museum is "not legally required to return cultural property," it had an "ethical obligation to do so."[18] The contrast between the French auction house's approach to sacred items and the repatriation effort of the Denver museum present the broad spectrum of possible outcomes that can occur in dealing with culturally significant items.

In disciplines that entail ethnographic research, scholars have long been aware of the ethical issues that come with research. One of the primary ethical responsibilities in ethnomusicology and anthropology is to "do no harm," which includes weighing "carefully the potential consequences and inadvertent impacts of their work."[19] Of course, conceptualizing the impact of research on local communities represents a significant scholarly challenge. Researchers may not be aware that they are being shown something that is meant to be private. Alternatively, items documented by researchers can transform over time to become sacred or offensive. The challenge of digital archives includes contemplating the many potential ethical issues that can arise from historic materials in a contemporary archive intended for future generations. Living up to such a mandate may be impossible given the dynamic and changing nature of traditions in societies.

For instance, Ronato Rosaldo (1989) famously wrote about playing back recordings of headhunting ceremonies only to be told by his Ilongot informants that he needed to turn the player off since the recording was deeply disturbing to them. The recording reminded them of a sacred ceremony in which they could no longer participate. Cultural changes, particularly those created through the influence of missionaries and Christianity, led to alternative relationships with past traditions and actions. These changes made Rosaldo's recordings unplayable among the Ilongot peoples who had once participated in the traditions. More recent generations of Ilongot may have different reactions to Rosaldo's recordings, given changes to their relationships with headhunting, Christianity, and the state (Yang 2011). Moreover, not every Ilongot would likely agree on the significance and meaning of Rosaldo's recordings or that of anyone else who has documented sacred traditions in the past.

The dynamic nature of cultural traditions and people's responses to them extends beyond just the moment those elements are collected. Several scholars write about the ways that museum collections take on new meanings through interactions with visitors, exhibition producers, and the producing cultures.[20] The same can be said of archives where numerous visitors—particularly in places where those visitors can leave comments—shape people's engagement and understanding of archived items. The potential then is for any archived item to take on new meanings and ethical consideration. Something that may not have been sacred previously can become so over time or through changes in people's relationships with that cultural tradition.

In addition, ethical considerations extend beyond sacred and secret ceremonies. They include statements and actions that may reveal private, offensive, or scandalous information about people to a broader public. In my own research I documented a number of situations that would be disrespectful if posted in an online digital archive. This included married men with mistresses at nightclubs; displays of overt sexuality; comments made by intoxicated individuals who found their way in front of a microphone; and political statements made during interviews with highly regarded artists. In each of these cases potential repercussions could emerge should these items appear in an online digital archive, even though none of the individuals involved stated that I could not release my field recordings. In each case, the people knew that I was filming and documenting the events. Consent one day does not mean that those same individuals would consent in perpetuity. Ethics requires each of us to read thoroughly into a given situation and understand the potential impacts of any choices made with fieldwork materials.

It should also be noted that ethical considerations do not disappear when Indigenous communities run an archive or approve the content of that archive. As Michael Brown discussed in his book *Who Owns Native Culture?*, even archives managed by local communities can encounter problems from those within that community. Brown discussed an archival collection managed by Indian nations in which an archivist for an eastern tribe was "pressured to release a collection of medical records to tribal attorneys" (2003, 32). The archivist refused due to the ease with which people could use the medical records to identify specific community members. Brown goes on to discuss an archivist from a western tribe who only permitted those individuals who were enrolled members of the tribe to access information on cultural practices. Individuals wishing to see religious documents needed to show that they were brought up in local communities (2003, 33). In both cases, archivists restricted sacred or private content even when it was requested by some members of the same tribes or by those who might normally have access to the archives.

In these examples—that of Rosaldo, my own, and those illustrated by Brown—the documentation and recordings have potential impacts on local communities. Where these considerations become more complicated is when someone has been given permission to record, archive, and present information to a broader public but others in that community disagree. If a group of people performs a sacred ceremony, which a researcher records, and all but a few people agree that the researcher can use those materials as she sees fit, should the researcher be able to place that material in an online archive? Perhaps more importantly: how often do researchers attain such clearances by a broad array of individuals involved in performances, festivals, or other similar events? And what happens when an informant changes his mind about material recorded by a researcher?

The current circulation of information online presents opportunities to be more thoroughly critical of the images and sounds that appear in digital archives. Several East African colleagues and friends explained to me that writing about a sacred ceremony is a far less egregious offense than showing a film of those elements to a public audience. Showing that film online for anyone to see further heightens any potential offense. In other words, the more public some recordings become, the more problematic they are for some communities. Making an item more public reduces the control that item's community has over it. However, as stated earlier in this chapter, hiding materials within an archive, even from the communities from which those materials are drawn, may also not benefit those communities.

In addition to considerations of content, digital archives need to be cognizant of the ways materials in the archives are used. Holly Crossen-White describes "citizen historians" who make use of historical documents in digital archives but who may be "less familiar with ethical considerations or perhaps do not make the connections to ethical frameworks that govern other forms of research" (2015, 117). In other words, the growing number of digital archives and the ease of access to information online has spurred a movement of citizen intellectuals sorting through documents and making assessments about the past. These uses of the archives represent a potentially important and useful means to make research more transparent and fair since many people throughout the world can use the documents. Yet, given the openness with which some archives digitize and display information—often permitting personal details and information to emerge—it also causes numerous ethical problems to arise. For instance, Crossen-White notes that searching for information about an individual in multiple digital archives can reveal a life narrative at odds with the ones created by the individual for themselves and potentially harmful to the descendants of that individual (2015, 116).

Ethical concerns are not new to the social sciences and humanities; they are critical considerations for all scholars.[21] Debate continually emerges on both the ethics of those who collected original recordings and the ethics of those who use them now.[22] It is, therefore, incumbent on administrators and depositing scholars to make a thorough assessment of materials in an archive. If sensitive material exists there, then it should not appear in an online digital archive unless several levels of approval have been granted. With the EVIA DA, depositing scholars could block any content deemed culturally sensitive. Those materials would remain in the archive, but they would not be viewable to anyone but the depositor and those with special permission. In addition the EVIA DA also required any user to register with the digital archive in order to grant access to those who want to conduct research on the materials.

Despite these many ethical issues, the promotion of content in an archive should remain a goal of many institutions in part because there is also an ethical need to share materials. This is a key point, since ethically based decisions are often made to restrict data and information. Yet, restricting data can also be unethical, as it privileges certain people who are able to travel to or access an archive. When communities agree to have their music, traditions, and other materials documented, arrangements should be made to return those documents to the communities. This represents a logistical and funding challenge for many institutions, yet plays a major role in fostering relationships, promoting equitable research practices, and participating in the contemporary life of data.

CONCLUSION

One of the questions that this chapter set out to answer was whether an archive could repatriate materials digitally without infringing legal or cultural rights. The best answer is that it depends. While I argue that archives should make efforts to move an archive into public view, which would allow community members anywhere in the world access to historic and culturally important materials, considerations need to be examined including the content of the archive, the desired audience, the safeguards put in place to protect rights holders and communities, and the desires of communities themselves. Many issues exist that make digital repatriation problematic or, at the very least, unsatisfactory in terms of repatriation. There can be little doubt that those who benefit the most from digital archives are often those with the best access to online resources, the time to search through those materials, and the knowledge about the best ways to make use of them. These considerations often limit or eliminate access by the Indigenous community members who were intended to be the recipients of repatriated materials.

Despite these concerns, many individuals interviewed for this project want to see their recordings available online. Repatriation for them means more than being able to access the materials themselves. It means knowing that others can learn about their music, traditions, and works of art. It means having one's art exist in a similar global repository—the Internet—as the work of other artists from around the world. While some of these same artists would like to receive some payments for the circulation of their art, they also want to be part of the social life of data. Copyright is already a nebulous enterprise for many Indigenous communities. There is a lack of trust in the royalty system that, at least from an eastern African perspective, appears to work for those in the West but not for those in developing countries. For this reason, the pride that comes from having one's music—whether historical or contemporary—preserved indefinitely in an online digital archive marks one of the potential benefits to repatriation efforts of sound recordings to Indigenous populations. Nonetheless, paying attention to legal issues, including copyright and fair use, and the cultural rights of Indigenous communities matters significantly in any consideration for online content. While many current websites allow users to post any material, even when copyrighted, the digital archive should aim for strong legal and ethical standards. This will help to ensure a better means for the repatriation of sound recordings.

NOTES

1. See Purcell (2016); Asato and Wertheimer (2015). The comment about the importance of a digital archive for democracy comes from Jerry Handfield, state archivist, Washington State Archives: "In a democracy it is predicated on the fact that the records belong to the people." From the film *The Importance of Digital Archives*, accessed on February 1, 2013, https://youtu.be/UvMbi3xlhlk.
2. Lynsey Martenstyn, "Digital Archives: Making Museum Collections Available to Everyone," *Guardian*, May 3, 2013.
3. In writing about the Maori aspiration to control their own destinies and resources, including information about the Maori peoples, Anahera Morehu asks about relationships that the Maori have with information repositories when materials within those organizations could have been previously stolen or illicitly removed from Indigenous groups (2016, 61).

4. For information about concerns and conflicts in owning and collecting Indigenous knowledge, see Brown (2003) and Callison, Roy, and LeCheminant (2016).

5. The "world is flat" is an idea posited by Thomas Friedman (2009) to argue that a "level playing field" exists in terms of global commerce. Just as the original notion that the world is flat was incorrect, so too is Friedman's.

6. I interviewed artists and producers from Kenya and Tanzania about their interest in archives. These interviews included artists, producers, and composers from a wide array of genres. While my research was on larger issues of copyright law and musical ownership, archiving would frequently come up in conversation. I began these interviews in 1998 and continue to conduct research on subjects related to music, ethics, and the law.

7. Interview with Mwingira conducted in Dar es Salaam, Tanzania, June 11, 2015. The Kiswahili version of Christom Mwingira's comments are as follows: "Napenda sana muziki wangu au wetu usikike katika maktaba za muziki kwa maana muziki wetu ukipata nafasi kusikika tutaweza kujulikana na pia kujuana na wanamuziki wengine."

8. Personal communication with Iboany Moalim, November 16, 2016, Dar es Salaam, Tanzania. Moalim wrote a long letter explaining his opinions and ideas on digital archives in answering my questions.

9. The original Kiswahili of the interview is as follows: "Napenda sana waweke muziki wangu katika internet ili kuweza kujitangaza zaidi kimataifa na ni bora kufanya hivi kuliko kutoa pesa kwa watangazaji wa radio hapa nchi wakidai wanakutangaza bila kuona matunda na faida zake."

10. Most scholars, who recorded either audio or video as part of their research, originally imagined that these materials would only be used for classroom teaching or research purposes. In the pre-YouTube era (before 2005), few people anticipated that their recordings would be widely accessible or, in some cases, even of interest to a broad audience. Video quality sometimes was poor and unstable, indicating a researcher's eye rather than that of a cinematographer.

11. Personal interview with Dan Sheehy, January 13, 2013.

12. For more on the mission of Singing Wells, see http://www.singingwells.org/about-the-project.

13. Many cases argue about the transformative nature of the work as well. This is not particularly relevant here, since archives attempt to preserve material more often than to transform it into something new.

14. *Authors Guild, Inc. v. HathiTrust*, 11 CV 6351 (HB), US District Court, Southern District of New York.

15. See HathiTrust website, accessed October 4, 2016, https://www.hathitrust.org/community.

16. For a useful analysis of digitization and archives, see Hirtle et al. (2009), chapter 6: "The Libraries and Archives Exemptions."

17. In a twist of events, the Annenberg Foundation was able to purchase twenty-one Katsinam masks for the Hopi and three for the San Carlos Apaches in order to return the masks to the tribe. The auction house commented at one point during the sale of the items that they hoped the buyer would save some of the items for other buyers. See Associated Press, "Hopi Tribe Sues Paris Auction House," *New York Times*, December 4, 2013, A8; John M. Glionna, "A Secret Mission to Rescue Tribes' Spiritual Artifacts: How the Annenberg Foundation Saved 24 Hopi and Apache Items Being Sold at a Paris Auction," *Los Angeles Times*, December 22, 2013.

18. Tom Mashberg, "Sending Artworks Home, but to Whom? Denver Museum to Return Totems to Kenyan Museum," *New York Times*, January 4, 2014, C1.
19. American Anthropological Association, "Do No Harm," Ethics Statement, 2012, accessed October 12, 2016, http://ethics.americananthro.org/category/statement.
20. See Karp and Lavine (1991) and Carlson (2013) for discussions of these issues with Ilongot artifacts.
21. For overviews of ethics in anthropology, see Glazer (1996), Fluehr-Lobban (1998, 2002), Kingsolver (2004), and Robin (2004). On ethics in ethnomusicology, see Slobin (1992), Shelemay (2013), and the Society for Ethnomusicology statement: http://www.ethnomusicology.org/?page=EthicsStatement.
22. See, for instance, the debate between Nannyonga-Tamusuza and Weintraub (2012, 2015) and Cooke (2015).

References

Asato, Noriko, and Andrew Wertheimer. 2015. "Exploring the Kyoto Digital Archives Project: Challenging the Funding Model of Digital Archive Development." In *Digital Libraries: Providing Quality Information*, 17th International Conference on Asia-Pacific Digital Libraries, ICADL 2015, Seoul, Korea, December 9–12, 2015, Proceedings, edited by Robert B. Allen, Jane Hunter, and Marcia L. Zeng, 22–32. Switzerland: Springer International.

Beer, David Gareth, and John Roger Burrows. 2013. "Popular Culture, Digital Archives and the New Social Life of Data." *Theory, Culture and Society* 30 (4): 47–71.

Brown, Michael F. 2003. *Who Owns Native Culture?* Cambridge, MA: Harvard University Press.

Callison, Camille, Loriene Roy, and Gretchen Alice LeCheminant. 2016. *Indigenous Notions of Ownership and Libraries, Archives and Museums*. Berlin: De Gruyter.

Carlson, Sarah E. 2013. "From the Philippines to the Field Museum: A Study of Ilongot (Bugkalot) Personal Adornment." Honors Projects, Illinois Wesleyan University. Paper 45. http://digitalcommons.iwu.edu/socanth_honproj/45.

Cooke, Peter. 2015. "A Response to Sylvia Nannyonga-Tamusuza and Andrew N. Weintraub's 'The Audible Future: Reimagining the Role of Sound Archives and Sound Repatriation in Uganda.'" *Ethnomusicology* 59 (3): 475–479.

Crossen-White, Holly L. 2015. "Using Digital Archives in Historical Research: What Are the Ethical Concerns for a 'Forgotten' Individual?" *Research Ethics* 11 (2): 108–119.

Fluehr-Lobban, Carolyn. 1998. "Ethics." In *Handbook of Methods in Cultural Anthropology*, edited by H. Russell Bernard, 173–202. Walnut Creek, CA: AltaMira.

Fluehr-Lobban, Carolyn. 2002. "A Century of Ethics and Professional Anthropology." *AAA Anthropology News* 43 (3): 20.

Friedman, Thomas L. 2009. *The World Is Flat: A Brief History of the Twenty-First Century*. Bridgewater, NJ: Distributed by Paw Prints/Baker & Taylor.

Glazer, Myron Perez. 1996. "Ethics." In *Encyclopedia of Cultural Anthropology*. Vol. 2, edited by David Levinson and Melvin Ember, 389–393. New York: Henry Holt.

Hirtle, Peter B., Emily Hudson, Andrew T. Kenyon, and Cornell University. 2009. *Copyright and Cultural Institutions: Guidelines for Digitization for US Libraries, Archives, and Museums*. Ithaca, NY: Cornell University Library.

Karp, Ivan, and Stephen Lavine. 1991. "Culture and Representation." In *Exhibiting Culture*, edited by Ivan Karp and Stephen D. Lavine, 11–25. Washington, DC: Smithsonian Institution Press.

Kingsolver, Ann. 2004. "Thinking and Acting Ethically in Anthropology." In *Thinking Anthropologically: A Practical Guide for Students*, edited by Philip Carl Salzman and Patricia C. Rice, 71–79. Upper Saddle River, NJ: Prentice Hall.

Morehu, Anahera. 2016. "How to Integrate Mātauranga Māori into a Colonial Viewpoint." In *Indigenous Notions of Ownership and Libraries, Archives, and Museums*, edited by Camille Callison, Loriene Roy, and Gretchen Alice LeCheminant, 57–64. Weitere Ausg. Berlin: De Gruyter.

Nannyonga-Tamusuza, Sylvia, and Andrew N. Weintraub. 2012. "The Audible Future: Reimagining the Role of Sound Archives and Sound Repatriation in Uganda." *Ethnomusicology* 56 (2): 206–233.

Nannyonga-Tamusuza, Sylvia, and Andrew N. Weintraub. 2015. "A Response to Peter Cooke's Response." *Ethnomusicology* 59 (3): 480–482.

Purcell, Aaron D. 2016. *Digital Library Programs for Libraries and Archives: Developing, Managing, and Sustaining Unique Digital Collections*. Chicago: ALA Neal-Schuman, an imprint of the American Library Association.

Robin, Ron. 2004. *Scandals and Scoundrels: Seven Cases That Shook the Academy*. Berkeley: University of California Press.

Rosaldo, Renato. 1989. *Culture and Truth: The Remaking of Social Analysis*. Boston: Beacon.

Shelemay, Kay Kaufman. 2013. "The Ethics of Ethnomusicology in a Cosmopolitan Age." In *The Cambridge History of World Music*, edited by Philip V. Bohlman, 786–806. Cambridge: Cambridge University Press.

Slobin, Mark. 1992. "Ethical Issues." In *Ethnomusicology. An Introduction*, edited by Helen Myers, 329–336. London: Macmillan.

Yang, Shu-Yuan. 2011. "Headhunting, Christianity, and History among the Bugkalot (Ilongot) of Northern Luzon, Philippines." *Philippine Studies* 59 (2): 155–186.

···

CHAPTER 30

MOUNTAIN HIGHS, VALLEY LOWS

Institutional Archiving of Gospel Music in the Twenty-First Century

···

BIRGITTA J. JOHNSON

OFTEN the issue of archives and repatriation is discussed in terms of dichotomous and unequal exchanges between members of a "collecting culture" and "collected culture" (Johnson 2012, 221). However, with the expansion of approaches to archiving that focus on collaborative and proactive archiving, today's collected culture, or more specifically, groups from within a "cultural heritage community," are themselves being considered community archivists. Though lacking access to modern audiovisual facilities, there are groups whose responsibility to a community's music culture extends beyond performance and includes various forms of preservation (e.g., collecting audio and visual recordings and storing sheet music). While collaborative archiving approaches ease hierarchical and power relations involved with collecting and preserving archived audiovisual materials, access to those collected materials can still be an issue that could shackle efforts around repatriation and reinscribe old dichotomies and uneven power relationships. Fortunately, the advent of digital audiovisual archives and/or archives that have digitized their holdings for preservation purposes are now simultaneously engaging in proactive archiving and becoming hosts for user-driven "reactive access" as a result of the broader access cultural heritage communities and general users have to collected and digitized holdings.[1] For example, certain recent African American gospel archiving efforts have focused on collaborative methods and partnerships between institutions and culture heritage communities, and they have also benefited from the rise of digital archiving and online archive and library platforms in the 2000s that partially allow the archive, as a center of knowledge production, to be less geographically bound to one physical location.[2] Just as proactive approaches saw archives working with less hierarchical models of collecting and preservation, digital finding aids, online audio and video playback applications, and social media efforts have made holdings with a particular cultural and communal significance more accessible and available not only to the original owners and culture-bearers but also to other users such as scholars, artists, and students.

Since the mid-2000s, there has been an increase in gospel music archiving by institutions in higher education, community groups, and individual collectors. Just as the formalized study of gospel music was delayed for most of the twentieth century, the pathway to archiving gospel music history outside of museum exhibitions has been relatively unpaved until recently. As we know, gospel music, like blues and jazz, is a vital American-born art form. A confluence of influences from West Africa, Euro-American hymnody, and nineteenth-century African American folk forms, black gospel music is a twentieth-century creation that not only has had an impact on much of the sound of African American Protestant Christian worship. It also has influenced almost every major secular genre of the century, from rhythm and blues and rock 'n' roll to soul, funk, and disco. One of the great challenges of documenting and chronicling gospel music's rich heritage is that it is still very much alive and a part of living culture in a more immediate way than any other African American musical folk form. It is music that is part of a religious heritage that intertwines with an even broader African American cultural heritage. It is a performance tradition that is practiced on a weekly basis in houses of worship all over the country. Moreover, it is still developing and reinventing itself inside and outside of the Christian commercial music industries via professional gospel artists and composers, as well as continuing to influence other genres such as soul, R&B, folk, and hip-hop. To approach gospel music documentation and to pursue the archiving of gospel music traditions in the twenty-first century is much akin to answering Oscar Hammerstein's famed lyric from the *Sound of Music*, "How do you catch a wave upon the sand?" (Rogers and Hammerstein 1959).

When archiving gospel, you encounter common challenges that most archiving efforts face: Which formats and objects to collect? How do you catalog what is collected? What institutions or organizations can assist in or lead the effort over the long term? Over the last decades of the twentieth century, the most pressing of these has become the sustainability of collections. This is not merely an issue of facilities and funding but also one of access to collections and maintaining interest and engagement from the communities we hope institutions are serving locally and nonlocally. The increase of gospel archiving in the twenty-first century owes much to partnership programs and projects that move toward collaboration and thoughtful engagement with community members, who themselves have served as local and amateur archivists of the culture. Whereas traditional approaches to archiving relied on one-way relationships of donating items for preservation and had issues of low access to the public, the three projects highlighted in this chapter engage in collaborative approaches to archiving and documentation and include various levels of reciprocity. And with the developments and advancements of Internet streaming technology, data storage capacity, and dialectic field methods, gospel archiving is moving toward increasing not only how much of the tradition is preserved through recordings, videos, and other ephemera but also how much of the tradition—past and present—is being made accessible to larger and diverse audiences. As Ray Edmondson noted in 2004, "the only limit to proactive access is imagination" (Edmondson 2004, 20). This is a sentiment that has been surely made easier by twenty-first-century advances in digital technology but also efforts of institutions and community partners who are dually invested in traditional preservation as well as continued means of access and engagement with archival holdings beyond warehousing collections and limited geographically bound exhibitions.

Since 2004, three university archive initiatives and collections have engaged in various kinds of partnership and reciprocity with cultural heritage communities within gospel music on local, regional, and national levels. Through university and private streams of funding, archives and libraries at the University of California, Los Angeles (UCLA), the University of Southern California (USC), and Baylor University have contributed significantly not only to preserving gospel music's recorded and ephemeral past but also to documenting its contemporary and current performance traditions via fieldwork projects, and to increased accessibility of audio and visual holdings. This veritable "boom" in institution-backed archiving represents a "mountain high" moment in the documentation, preservation, and research of the African American gospel music tradition. A genre with one foot deeply planted in America's folk musical landscape, gospel music is also a religious genre with long-held ties to the commercial music industry since the 1920s. This makes it particularly daunting to archive the tradition in the past as well as its present-day practices, when balancing the needs of a large and diverse cultural heritage community and the limits of copyright and fair-use policies. Archive initiatives that have been able to traverse these challenges have brought the cause of gospel archiving to the peaks of visibility and broader access. While two of these programs have faced sustainability challenges in recent years, one has expanded its holdings and its impact by partnering with the Smithsonian's National Museum of African American History and Culture, which opened in September of 2016 in Washington, DC. This chapter includes brief overviews of UCLA's Gospel Archiving in Los Angeles Project (the GALA Project), USC's Gospel Music History Archive, and the Baylor University Black Gospel Music Restoration Project (BGMRP), noting the distinctiveness of each archiving initiative and the ways in which they collaborate with culture-bearers, community partners, and collectors to advance shared preservation goals. These overviews also briefly address "valley low" moments that some of these programs have faced due to factors related to funding or limits of technology at the time of the initial projects.

Over the last three decades, researchers have moved toward more relationship-centered field methods and have become more conscious of the ethics and benefits of reciprocity in fieldwork settings (Rice 1997; Shelemay 1997; Hellier-Tinoco 2003). Similarly, some archives have also expanded beyond data collection and sound warehousing approaches and are reviving and strengthening their community presence by pursuing funding and programs that emphasize repatriation, collaborative archiving, and proactive archiving (Lancefield 1998, also reprinted in this Handbook; Seeger and

Chaudhuri 2004; Ruskin 2006; Corn 2007; Vallier 2010; Johnson 2012). This chapter describes three examples of these types of efforts, where collaboration, reciprocity of resources, and institutional/community partnerships are providing variations on many ideas scholars have regarding archive collections and community engagement. The aim of providing these reflective snapshots of gospel archiving in the twenty-first century is to delineate key success strategies as well as limitations of some of these projects, but also to note the significant role advances in technology have played in current and on-going documentation and archiving. Elements and approaches to community engagement that these projects have in common have led to a significant increase in archival holdings for black gospel music across a range of substyles and eras. These increased holdings of audio and video recordings and ephemeral artifacts will inevitably not only have an impact on the preservation and appreciation of the tradition but also bolster a broad range of research efforts and scholarship about African American sacred music as a whole.

The GALA Project

In May 2014, the UCLA Ethnomusicology Archive received a "UCLA-in-LA" grant from the UCLA Center for Community Partnerships to pursue a nine-month, community-engaged archiving project to increase the representation of gospel music in the archive's holdings and collaborate with local musicians, artists, and churches in the Los Angeles community. Building from previous success with a university-funded community archiving project with members of the Filipino community of Los Angeles (AFAMILA) the year prior, the GALA Project was developed by the archive's head archivist at the time, John Vallier, and the ethnomusicology professor Jacqueline Cogdell DjeDje to engage the large gospel music performance community in the city in more collaborate and interactive ways. With that in mind, the GALA Project partnered with one key local organization for gospel music performance and preservation, the Heritage Music Foundation of Los Angeles, founded by the famed composer, educator, and music director Dr. Margaret Pleasant Douroux. Taking advantage of the long, rich, and sometimes overlooked history of gospel music performance and recording based in metropolitan Los Angeles, the GALA Project went beyond the typical processing of donated materials, taking a five-part approach developed in collaboration with the GALA Project's main community partner. The five goals of the project included (1) organize and digitize the large audio collection owned by the Heritage Music Foundation (HMF), (2) develop a strategic plan to assist with HMF's long-term goals of building a center for gospel music in the city, (3) expand LA-based gospel and related music collections in the archive and at HMF, (4) host an end-of-project symposium at UCLA, and (5) establish and maintain a community-based organization (CBO) server in the archive. The nine-month project ended up lasting one year, from June 2004 to June 2005, and it included a major audiovisual field documentation component in addition to the collaborative efforts to digitally and physically house HMF's extensive gospel music collection of recordings, sheet music, and other important ephemera.

The HMF was founded in 1981 by Margaret Pleasant Douroux. In addition to mentoring hundreds of gospel music performers and composers as well as African American church music leaders and music ministers, Douroux and HMF members from all around the country have dedicated themselves to preserving gospel music history and musical traditions of the black church via workshops, conferences, concerts, album recording projects, and the compilation of a large audio collection. I was a graduate student in the Department of Ethnomusicology at the time of the project and was brought in to organize and run the audi-ovideo documentation or fieldwork component of the project as a graduate student assistant. The GALA Project took a team and collaborative approach toward reaching the five goals noted earlier. During the fall, John Vallier led the effort to work with Douroux and her leadership team to draft a strategic plan for HMF. Once completed, the strategic plan could be used by HMF to attract donors and foundations that could assist them in establishing a performance, education, and preservation center known as the Gospel House. Douroux's vision for the Gospel House was to have a monument and performance space dedicated to the legacy of gospel music, similar to how country music has the Grand Ole Opry. Vallier and the archive staff also worked with HMF's event coordinator and administrative assistant, Glenn Ford, to catalog and process HMF's audio collection of just over five hundred items. Ford received training on how to enter information from the recordings' labels or covers into the database that would be later uploaded into the publically accessible finding aid for the Online Archive of California.[3] Most of these were 331/3 rpm LP records, but some were 78 rpm albums—from commercially available records to various independently recorded and produced albums from Los Angeles and San Francisco Bay Area churches. Ford learned about the digitization process and helped with correctly identifying aspects of the metadata associated with noncommercial items in HMF's collection, such as cassette tapes of HMF conferences and Douroux's gospel music history radio show, photographs, and other ephemera in their collection. The largest part of this effort began with Vallier, Ford, and myself gathering all of HMF's decades of recordings and sheet music stored over the years in church office spaces, homes, and a garage in various parts of Los Angeles, and getting the items in shape to be processed by the archive staff and student workers.

In addition to processing and digitizing more than five hundred items that belonged to HMF's community archive, part of the GALA Project was a fieldwork component in which I supervised the recording of every event the HMF held during the grant year. Beyond holding many gospel audio materials, HMF is a very active organization and a virtual reservoir for the performance and development of black sacred music traditions, in addition to the various styles of gospel music. From July 2004 to March of 2005, the fieldwork team and I recorded nine performance and workshop events hosted by the Heritage Music Foundation (see Table 30.1). Some were multiday events, like HMF's Nineteenth Annual National Gospel Music Conference in October 2004 or their two-night Easter Music Workshop in February 2005.

Table 30.1 Events Documented by the Heritage Music Foundation

Event	Date	Location
Praise and Worship Workshop	7/30/2004	Greater New Bethel Baptist Church
Night of Classical Gospel	8/16/2004	Greater New Bethel Baptist Church
19th Annual National Gospel Music Conference	10/20/2004–23/2004	Radisson Hotel LAX / Greater New Bethel Baptist Church
Christmas Sacred Music Workshop	12/1/2004–12/3/2004	Greater New Bethel Baptist Church
Easter Music Workshop	2/17/2005–2/18/2005	Greater New Bethel Baptist Church
Legacy of Gospel Music Festival: Oratorical Contest & Scholarship Award Program	3/7/2005	Greater New Bethel Baptist Church
Legacy of Gospel Music Festival: College Night & GALA Culminating Program	3/14/2005	Greater New Bethel Baptist Church
Legacy of Gospel Music Festival: Margaret P. Douroux's Birthday Celebration	3/21/2005	Greater New Bethel Baptist Church
Legacy of Gospel Music Festival: 3 Mo' Sisters of Gospel	3/28/2005	Greater New Bethel Baptist Church

The fieldwork team included UCLA ethnomusicology graduate students and community members from churches in the city like the Faithful Central Bible Church, and using project funds we paid them for their assistance. For each event, we used two digital video cameras and one digital audiotape (DAT) recorder. In addition to making video and audio recordings of each event, team members assisted in getting signed consent forms from singers and musicians late into the evening, and Jacqueline DjeDje or I took meticulous fieldnotes of each event, which on average lasted two and a half hours. DjeDje often took photographs at events, which were also entered into the GALA holdings. In the spirit of capturing as much gospel music performance in Los Angeles as possible, we also recorded a few non-HMF events. Through the GALA Project, we sent out requests for donations to the project as well as requests to come and record events through ads placed in local African American newspapers, letters sent to African American churches in the city, and connections that Jacqueline DjeDje and I had to the Los Angeles gospel community. This allowed us to capture events by local gospel groups as well as prominent gospel organizations such as the Los Angeles chapter of the Gospel Music Workshop of America. By the end of the project, we had recorded over 325 hours of ethnographic footage to add to the holdings already being processed from HMF's collection. After its materials and metadata had been processed, we also discovered the GALA Project represented the collection with the largest finding aid in the Online Archive of California. Seventeen large archive boxes of materials collected during the project year are kept in the climate-controlled Southern Regional Library Facility, where much of the UCLA Ethnomusicology Archive holdings are located. In subsequent years this has increased due to the continued efforts by DjeDje to encourage other community members to donate materials under the umbrella of the GALA Project. To date, the GALA Project has six other subcollections not including HMF's collection and DjeDje's own subcollection on gospel music in Catholic Churches in Los Angeles.

The project was exciting, and as the year progressed, we got even more enthusiastic responses from people in the community who also valued the tradition and the work HMF was doing over the years. When it came time to hold the end-of-year symposium, it was decided that instead of having the event on the campus of UCLA in Westwood, the better and more logistically manageable option would be to have the event at HMF's home congregation, the Greater New Bethel Baptist Church of Inglewood, California, in conjunction with HMF's month-long Legacy of Gospel Festival in March. In addition to presenting the completed strategic plan to HMF, we were able to share a short promotional video that I had developed with one of the community recordists from the fieldwork team, Kenrick "ICE" McDonald. The eight-and-a-half-minute video took footage from the year's events and organized it around the themes that summarized the scope of traditions GALA documented during the year: "The Word," "The Music," and "The Legacy." The film featured some[4] of the diversity of black sacred music performed during the year such as solo and choral spirituals, traditional gospel, contemporary gospel, and praise and worship music performed by HMF, church choirs, community choirs, and community vocal groups. Excerpts from workshop lectures and sermonettes were also included. The video's ending credits provide the archive identification number and event information for each video featured. A copy of the DVD was presented to Douroux and the HMF staff to be used along with their strategic plan for soliciting foundation funding support in the future. Another copy was entered into the holdings for the GALA Project. As May approached, the archive team and I noted that HMF's collection was large, and we needed more time to complete digitizing it. Fortunately, with the help of a National Endowment for the Arts grant from the Traditional Arts Growth Fund, we got additional funding to pay Glenn Ford as he continued to catalog metadata and digitize albums for an additional month.

While the scope of the fieldwork project was substantial and the music collection of HMF sizable, one limitation of the GALA Project besides not being able to secure additional funding in subsequent years was that it predated many advances in digital recording technology, streaming technology, and online archival platforms. Project funds would only allow for the purchase of consumer-grade video cameras, which at that time were the point-and-shoot versions of camcorders that required external microphones and lighting to reach their best visual quality. There was no funding for such accessories, and during the project year, the popularity and use of DAT recorders started to be phased out in favor of nontape formats like mp3 recorders and WAV file recorders. As much as the GALA Project was an advancement for gospel archiving and a leap forward in multisited ethnographic research in gospel music performance and education, the equipment and technology being used was quickly falling behind the curve.

As it did in another project discussed later, the lack of funding and continued financial support has left the progress of the GALA collection and the move to raise awareness about it to scholars and archival staff. As mentioned earlier, Jacqueline DjeDje continued engaging members of the community, including the Trinity Baptist Church and the gospel radio announcers John and Vermya Phillips, to donate their materials to the archive as named subcollections. The GALA Project was featured in academic articles by John Vallier and myself for *Notes* and *Ethnomusicology Forum*, respectively in 2010 and 2012. I have presented academic papers related to the GALA Project, Margaret Douroux, and gospel archiving at six conferences around the country since 2005. The first was at HMF's 20th Annual National Gospel Music Conference in the fall of 2005. To combine youth education and engagement opportunities, I included trips to the UCLA Ethnomusicology Archive for the Gospel Music Ensemble in UCLA's World Music Summer Institute in June of 2006 and 2007. The institute was a week-long performance intensive that also included lecture and field trip activities. While at the archive, the students got to see GALA Project items and the GALA promotional video. Due to the status of Douroux and HMF in the West Coast gospel community and around the country, a great many musicians, composers, clinicians, and singers were documented by the GALA Project cameras. Unfortunately, some of them have since passed away in the last few years. Among them are the composer-director Stan Lee; composer-director Theola Booker; the mother of organist Billy Preston, Robbie Williams-Preston; and singer-pianist-minister of music, DeWayne Knox. Conversely, some people filmed have developed as artists and have achieved success in gospel and sacred music world; an example of this is Damian Price of Texas. The song he introduced at HMF's New Music workshop, "He's So Freely Passing Out Blessings," was later included in the *Total Praise* hymnal in 2011. Because the GALA film footage is unedited, viewers get to see Price introducing the song, rehearsing singers, and getting articulation and interpretation notes from Douroux for the concert later that week. The film captured during the GALA Project provides not only examples of gospel and black sacred music performance culture but also visual examples of the processes, instructional methods, and skills that ground these still largely oral traditions.

Lastly, one of the GALA Project's main accessibility challenges has been allowing access to some parts of the collection to off-campus users. In addition to copyright issues, at the beginning of the project online streaming platforms like iTunes U and YouTube were either not invented or in their infancy. For almost a decade this very large collection and many of the documented musical events were largely inaccessible to users who did not physically visit the UCLA Ethnomusicology Archive in Los Angeles. Although the GALA Project represented a major "mountain high" moment in the area of gospel archiving, accessibility challenges made for a period of "valley low" activity outside of the efforts of individuals directly involved with the project. Fortunately, through years of effort, UCLA Ethnomusicology archivist and assistant adjunct professor

Maureen Russell was able to have many video recordings in the archive's holdings accepted into the California Light and Sound Collection (CLSC) on the Internet archive. The California Light and Sound Collection is a part of the California Audiovisual Preservation Project, a partnership of seventy-five libraries, archives, and museums developing an online database of film and video and audio recordings documenting California history (Russell 2014a). The first videos accepted in 2014 were from other UCLA Ethnomusicology Archive Collections, but by December of 2015, twenty-seven videos from the GALA Project were accepted into the streaming collection under the umbrella of African American Music. In some cases, the visual footage looks better in its digital form than in its original tape form. This is possibly due to better playback devices such as retina-display-equipped Mac computers as well as higher quality digital transferring techniques and advances in Internet digital streaming that have emerged in the decade since the videos were first captured. And the same metadata included in the finding aid for each item is included in the video interface on the Ethnomusicology Archive Channel in CLSC.[5]

In addition to the GALA holdings for gospel, many of the filmed lecture-demonstrations and guest speakers at UCLA in Jacqueline DjeDje's ethnomusicology courses and symposiums for African and African American music have been put online and made accessible to the public for free through the Ethnomusicology Archive Channel (Russell 2014b). Being able to access GALA Project videos among the rich collection of ethnographic materials may raise the profile of both the collected items and the community partners and participants involved over the course of the year. There is no log-in required to view materials on the channel. Once a person accesses the collection, a simple word or name search will provide videos from the collection to be streamed at no cost to the viewer. If viewers wish to comment, save a "favorite" video, or share the link to a video, they must create a user account, which is also free. Scholars and educators now have a powerful audiovisual resource for research and curriculum development related to gospel music's past legacy and its twenty-first-century present.

THE GOSPEL MUSIC HISTORY ARCHIVE (UNIVERSITY OF SOUTHERN CALIFORNIA)

While its holdings are significantly smaller than GALA's, with roughly 147 items across four subcollections, USC's Gospel Music History Archive resulted from a partnership between the USC Center for Religion and Civic Culture, the Gospel Music History Project (the Black Voice Foundation for Media, History and the Arts), and internal grants received by the USC Digital Library from the Flora Thornton Foundation and the Zumberge Research and Innovation Fund. This grant-supported partnership made possible an individual web presence for the collection and free access to its visual print materials and ephemera via the USC Digital Library's website. The Gospel Music

History Archive began with Daniel Walker, who was a professor in USC's Center for Religion and Civic Culture in the College of Letters and Sciences. While conducting research for a book on the gospel pioneer Arizona Draines, and on the music of the Church of God in Christ in 2002, Walker saw a lack of archival materials related to gospel music and of initiatives that engage church archives from the many rich gospel music centers around the country. By 2007, and further influenced by the loss of much of Thomas Dorsey's music collection in the fire that almost destroyed all of Pilgrim Baptist Church in Chicago a year earlier in 2006, Walker partnered with the librarians Tim Stanton, Matt Gainer, and Giao Luong, to launch the Gospel Music History Archive at USC.

This gospel archive collection represents several layers of institutional partnerships within a university, collaborations between two universities, and participation with community partners such as Kevin Burkhardt's Gospel Memorabilia International of Beverly Hills and the Victory Baptist Church of Los Angeles, California. USC's other university partner is the Archives of African American Music and Culture at Indiana University, Bloomington. Forty-five music-related items from Indiana's archive can be accessed through the USC website. The USC Gospel Music History Archive currently includes mostly paper-based and printed materials, but it is still very rich in historical and musical artifacts. It includes seventy-two items from a historic LA gospel music center, Victory Baptist Church. Founded by the Reverend Arthur Atlas Peters and fourteen others in 1943, Victory was one of the first congregations in Los Angeles to include gospel music in its worship services. By 1950, it was the first black congregation to have a weekly television broadcast featuring the seventy-five-voiced Voices of Victory choir, and it was the congregation from where Martin Luther King Jr. addressed the national media through the church's radio program after the assassination of Malcolm X in 1965. The inclusion of materials from Victory Baptist Church makes the archive a valuable resource not only for gospel music history but also for the long history of African American communities on the West Coast and American civil rights history in general. In an article about the collection, Walker notes, "For me the work is about giving scholars, congregants, filmmakers, journalists, and the general public access to the materials needed [to] paint a more nuanced picture of Black life in America" (Walker 2012).

While USC's collection has a few metadata issues related to assigning the appropriate gospel era or date to recordings, there is much to be learned from it about gospel music in Los Angeles as well as gospel music's role in the broader community outside of sacred services and weekly church worship. For example, one item in the collection is the promotional concert program for the legendary Wings over Jordan Choir. The eight-page document includes photos, sheet music of the choir's songs, and detailed information about the choir and its members, including outreach activities the choir pursued. It contains photographs of choir members awarding scholarships to young people all over

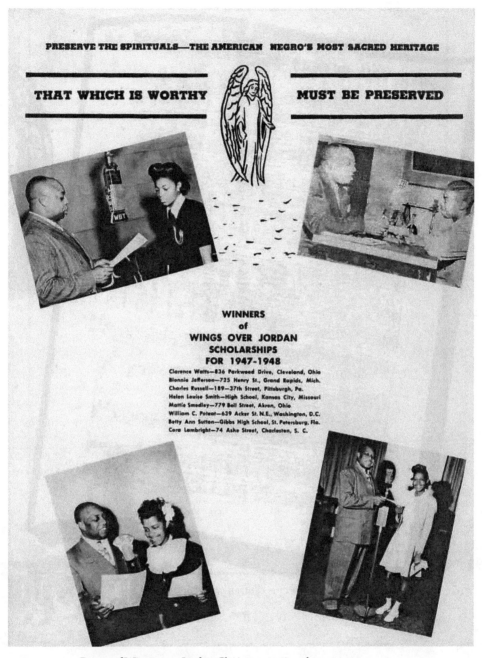

FIGURE 30.1 Page 3 of Wings over Jordan Choir promotional program.

FIGURE 30.2 Cover page of Zion Temple Church program.

the country while on tour after holding a national essay-writing contest for the school year 1947–1948 (Figure 30.1). These pages provide rare visual accounts of community service activities one of the first nationally known, professional black sacred music groups of post–World War II America. This kind of archival documentation also adds to the scholarship that examines the activist and social justice contributions of gospel music artists during the golden era of gospel, approximately 1945 to 1965, which overlaps the broader civil rights movement taking place in America.

Not only does the online archive show the digitized images of each page of the program, which can be zoomed in to note tiny image details, but also the metadata section for each item in the collection includes contact information for the owners of the original materials in cases where USC only holds the digital copies of the materials. Researchers exploring this collection can easily find unique items such as all the official commemorative materials that came with the first-issue US postal stamps of women in gospel (Clara Ward, Mahalia Jackson, Rosetta Tharpe, and Roberta Martin) in 1998, which included gold-plated replicas of the original stamps. Another unique item of note includes a digital copy of the twenty-page Sixth Anniversary program of Zion Temple Church, a nondenominational, interracial Los Angeles church founded by a black woman, Bishop Sara Butler, and pastored by a black woman, the Reverend Geraldine O'Connor. The church still exists today on Vernon Avenue, at the same address seen in the screen capture of the 1946 program in the archive's image interface shown in Figure 30.2. Archival evidence of this nature further supports research that notes the importance of the historic Los Angeles–based Azusa Street Revival to the rise of multicultural churches and women in pastoral roles decades before the rise of civil rights and women's rights movements.

Daniel Walker also conducted interviews with Los Angeles gospel composers and performers to be included in the archiving project's holdings. During its opening in 2012, gospel figures such as the Clara Ward Singers of Los Angeles, the gospel musician and director Rodena Preston, and the gospel radio announcer and narrator Edna Tatum visited the library to preview the collection and give their impressions of seeing the items assembled (Walker 2012). Also in 2012, the archive gained another USC institutional partner in the Pentecostal and Charismatic Research Archive, housed in USC's library system. Walker notes that the collaboration allowed the Gospel Music History Archive to have access to "a substantial set of materials from the Church of God in Christ" (Walker 2012). In this case, "substantial" would be the 1,488 items of that archive's subcollections with the Center for African American Church History and Research in Dallas, Texas,[6] as well as the 346 items of the Dr. Mattie McGlothen Library and Museum of Richmond, California. These institutional collaborations are possible through digital connections that have become much more viable and accessible to more people in the twenty-first century. Library and archive-based digital platforms like the USC Gospel History Archive may become even more crucial in today's economic climate. Walker noted that he and his team experienced "many fits and starts" due to "administrative changes and lack of funding" over the years, but getting the archive to a place where it can be electronically housed in the library system was key to having a platform that can be updated, expanded, and kept accessible to users for free if they have Internet access. Currently, expansion and updating of the holdings has stopped due to the lack of long-term funding; but librarians originally involved with the project, including Tim Stanton, still respond to requests about the collection via the website's e-mail contact portal.

BLACK GOSPEL MUSIC RESTORATION
PROJECT (BAYLOR UNIVERSITY)

The roots of Baylor University's BGMRP date back to February 2005, when journalism professor and former gospel and Christian music editor for *Billboard Magazine*,
Robert Darden, wrote an op-ed piece for the *New York Times* titled "Gospel's Got the
Blues." Darden had just published his book *People Get Ready: A New History of Black
Gospel Music*, and afterward he noted that most the music from gospel's "Golden Age"
was missing, hard to find, or lost. Many scholars and audiences have a good idea of
the sound of the Golden Age, but the actual recorded music—the massive number of
records produced during this era, roughly from 1945 to 1965—is largely unheard today
in its original form. Darden's op-ed got the attention of Charles Royce, a New York
businessman, who asked Darden to create a proposal to digitize this period of gospel's
recorded legacy. Darden contacted Baylor's dean of libraries and vice president of information technology, Pattie Orr, and the staff at the Moody Library; and the rest is now
new-gospel archiving history. The BGMRP is an example of what can happen when all
the crucial pieces of archiving and preservation in the twenty-first century come together: multiple streams of funding, collaboration, state of the art technology, community engagement, and institutional partnerships.

In the lower levels of Baylor University's Moody Library complex, there is a state-of-
the-art facility, the Ray I. Riley Digitization Center, where the BGMRP has digitized,
scanned, and cataloged more than 2,500 previously unavailable 78s, 45s, LPs, and
audiotapes in various formats. Full-time librarians as well as student workers assigned
to the library process, clean, and digitally store the sound recordings as uncompressed
audio files on the project's server. Contributions to the collection have come from other
universities, archives, and mostly collectors. As noted on a printed promotional brochure for the project, "the ultimate goal of the black gospel music restoration project
is to create the definitive on-line encyclopedia of gospel music, making this pivotal art
form forever available to scholars and fans alike." By 2006, the initial moves to make this
goal a reality were underway. Through generous donations and an endowment, audio
donations from various sources, a team of digitizing and library specialists, a thorough
plan for community engagement, and layers of institutional collaborations, the BGMRP
is currently among the largest audio repositories for African American gospel music in
the world.

After the *New York Times* piece had been circulated, Charles Royce was not the
only person to come forward to assist with the gospel archiving initiative financially.
Funding gifts from Harold (a 1951 Baylor graduate) and Dottie Riley of Austin, Texas,
helped to build the Ray I. Riley Digitization Center and the Dottie S. Riley Conference
Room in the Crouch Fine Arts Library. This digitization facility is the nerve center for
the BGMRP due to a large number of audio donations contributed very soon after the
project was announced. Baylor alumna Ella Prichard of the Prichard Family Foundation

was the next to step up to contribute significantly. In addition to donating to the project, funding a listening area inside Crouch Fine Arts Library known as Lev's Gathering
Place (named for her late husband, Lev Prichard III), Ella Prichard and her foundation
started the Lev H. Prichard III Traditional Black Music Restoration Endowed Fund in
2009. These gifts have provided the means to have a digital *and* real-world physical presence, unlike the other projects described earlier. Lev's Gathering Place re-creates a small
chapel space right in the library complete with stained glass, wooden pews, and individual listening stations with audio samples from the collection that can be played on
headphones. Having a dedicated digitization facility on site contributes to the growth of
the Royce-Darden Collection but also to its longevity, as items continue to be donated
several years later. The success of the collection and digitization efforts of the BGMRP
illustrate the crucial role foundation and private funding plays in the growth of gospel
archiving in the twenty-first century. Being able to afford equipment, facilities, staffing,
and marketing and promotion are crucial to making holdings accessible not only to on-
campus users such as students, faculty, staff and guest researchers but also to off-campus
users via public online access to many recordings.

What makes this a partnership program instead of a one-way collecting effort is the
method by which items are given and subsequently returned. The project pays for
the shipping costs, scans and digitizes donations, and then returns the original items to
the owners if they would like them to be returned. Being able to have original recordings
returned has been an attractive feature for donors, as has being able to receive and listen
to digital versions of older audio formats with improved sound quality. In a 2014 presentation by Baylor Libraries Assistant Director of Digital Projects Darryl Stuhr, it was noted
that the bulk of the collection has consisted of 45 rpm records, on which much of the
music of the golden era of gospel was first released. While more popular and nationally
known artists' music also was released on long-playing formats like the LP record, most
regional groups and lesser-known artists primarily recorded for 45 rpm records. Stuhr's
report at the 2014 Pruit Symposium luncheon noted the collection included a little over
twelve hundred 45 rpm records, just under four hundred LPs, and the several 78 rpm
records and various tape formats used between the 1940s through the 1980s. These include 16-inch transcription discs. Even though the collection is primarily related to an
audio preservation project, it includes and welcomes other ephemera such as public relations photos, press packets, newspaper and magazine clippings, and sheet music.

The BGMRP got its largest sound donation, however, from one major gospel music
collector, Robert Marovich of Chicago, Illinois. A gospel historian and the author of
A City Called Heaven: Chicago and the Birth of Gospel Music, Robert Marovich is also
known for his online blog space for gospel music history and gospel music industry
news, *Journal of Gospel Music* at http://journalofgospelmusic.com. Marovich's collection
of approximately nine hundred 45s represents the largest donation by one contributor to
the Baylor project. The digitization staff processes his collection roughly ninety records
at a time, and as of December 2016 they had completed most of the eighteen hundred individual sides the records represent. Having on-site and dedicated facilities has allowed
the project to process numerous items over the years, whereas other archiving efforts

often must share facilities and staff within an institution with other entities and may not even be located on or near campus library facilities.

Another factor that has made the BGMRP a major success is that it has been made accessible on-campus and off-campus for free. Partnering with iTunes U has greatly aided in making public domain music and related metadata accessible to users. For each sound recording available for public use, the metadata includes a digital image of the record's imprint in color.[7] The metadata for each sound recording is thorough,[8] including information such as song title, artist(s), performers, publisher/record label, the original date, format type, composer/arranger, the record label number and matrix number, the digitization date, the digital format (WAV files), and provenance if the school owns a physical copy of the recording. Each entry also includes a rights statement, which asks individuals who know they are the copyright holder for an item to contact the university. Some of the hundreds of songs digitized for the collection are not in the public domain. Due to copyright restrictions, these items are only available for listening by users on campus and those with university-issued credentials. However, researchers and scholars can request access to these and other items by e-mailing the digital collections staff from the collection website to set up an appointment.

With so much information and so many resources available online, the BGMRP also has done well to enhance the collection's visibility and user-friendly platform by having a sharp and visually appealing digital library interface. The project's front page is vibrant and takes full advantage of an archiving project that has its own visual brand and iconography that integrates Baylor's school colors into all graphics. Its graphic design creates interest and excitement around the project and uses 45 rpm record icons to direct visitors to key areas of the project: the audio holdings, the financial endowment page, the request/appeal for sound materials, and an informational page on the history of the project. It also includes links to on-campus and off-campus social media platforms such as Baylor Proud, the Baylor Intranet, Facebook, Instagram, iTunes, Pinterest, Twitter, and YouTube.[9]

The ways the project has incorporated students and staff from the journalism department, library sciences, and music departments continues to be another advantage of this initiative, years after its launch. In addition to the BGMRP's digital library interface, the project has its own blog space, which chronicles current events related to the collection, its donor network, and community engagement efforts. Baylor students and researchers involved with the project contribute to the blog, which is a part of a larger blog space hosted by Baylor University Digital Libraries Collections. Each blog entry is a way to keep public interest in, and awareness of, the collection high, on and off campus. Every time the project is discussed in the media, the library staff receives more phone calls, e-mails, and letters from serious collectors with rare items as well as noncollectors with donations from people's churches, attics, and garages. The project has been featured on NPR's *Talk of the Nation, Fresh Air with Terry Gross*, and *All Things Considered* as well as in newspapers and magazines on the local, state, and national levels. As of October 2016, the collection also had its own short radio show segment on the Waco, Texas, NPR affiliate, KWBU-FM, titled "Shout! Black Gospel Music Moments" and hosted by

Robert Darden. Airing twice a week, it features stories from the golden age of gospel and uses music from the BGMRP's collection. Plans to air the segments at other public radio stations around the country have been announced (Ames 2016).

Another key component to the success of the BGMRP is how community and scholarly engagement was implemented once a representative sample of the audio holdings was digitized and ready to be made public. In November 2013, the theme of Baylor's annual Pruit Memorial Symposium series was "Marching to Zion: Celebrating and Preserving Black Music." The two-day symposium included invited scholars, community members, pastors, and seminarians as well as live musical performances by the Jones Family Singers and the Bells of Joy Quartet on Friday and Saturday, respectively. Instead of formal academic papers, the symposium included a panel discussion on the importance of celebrating black sacred music with Dr. Emmett G. Price III (former associate professor of music and African American studies at Northeastern University), Dr. Dwandalyn Reece (curator of music and performing arts at the Smithsonian Institution National Museum of African American History and Culture), and myself. Robert Darden moderated the panel; the panelists spoke on a variety of issues related to the current state and status of African American sacred music history and preservation, and answered questions important to students, scholars, public servants, and lay persons who participated in the symposium.

The mix of discussion, tours of the BGMRP's new facilities, and crowd-pleasing gospel performances was well received by campus and local communities, and so the Pruit Symposium tapped BGMRP's leaders again to host an even bigger symposium the following year. By October 2014, there was much to celebrate besides the continued growth of the collection and continued financial support. After the 2013 symposium, the Smithsonian Institution curator Dwandalyn Reece announced that the National Museum of African American History and Culture in Washington, DC, then still under construction, would be partnering with the BGMRP's Royce-Darden Collection to provide musical examples for the museum's sound installations (Ames 2013). The 2014 "Marching to Zion" expanded to three days of activities[10] and included formal paper presentations by ethnomusicologists, musicologist, theologians, graduate students, and pastors. In addition to round tables and presentations, the symposium included a Sunday gospel brunch featuring the Jones Family Singers; a hands-on documentation and preserving family records workshop by Deborra Richardson (retired chair and chief archivist for the Smithsonian American History Museum's Archive Center); and a keynote luncheon where Dwandalyn Reece made the official announcement of the Baylor-Smithsonian partnership. There were also key presentations by Baylor's digital libraries staff, Tim Logan and Darryl Stuhr, that chronicled the history of the BGMRP from ideas and logistics to implementation and development. Most of the symposium's daytime activities took place in the newly opened McLane Stadium's press areas and president's suite. The symposium also hosted the book launches of *Readings in African American Church Music and Worship,* volume 2, edited by James Abbington, and Robert Darden's book *Nothing but Love in God's Water,* volume 1: *Black Sacred Music from the Civil War to the Civil Rights Movement*; a free black sacred music sing-along featuring James Abbington and other symposium presenters at Roxy Grove Hall on the first night; and a combined choir performance under the direction of James Abbington on the second night at 7th & James Baptist Church. The symposium's keynote address, "Songs of Life: Living, Love and Struggle," was given by an original civil rights movement freedom singer and black music scholar, Dr. Bernice Johnson Reagon (accompanied by her daughter, singer-musician Toshi Reagon). In addition to drawing more participants from communities in Waco and around the region, the 2014 edition of "Marching to Zion" included collaborations and sponsorship from various Baylor units including the School of Music, the Baylor University Campus Diversity Committee, the Department of American Studies, the Kyle Lake Center for Effective Preaching at Truett Seminary, and the Department of Journalism, Public Relations, and New Media. The depth and breadth of attendees was tremendous, and, once again, all but the Sunday gospel brunch was free and open to the public.

In the months after the 2014 Pruit Symposium "Marching to Zion," the conference participants Darden, Reece, myself, and Robert Marovich participated in two podcasts that addressed the rarer civil rights B-side records of the Royce-Darden collection and African American sacred music history in general for audio podcasts for the Kennedy Center's ArtsEdge program for K–12 students, and another for Public Radio International and Studio 360 discussing the relevance of these recordings and the social contexts for their creation and their importance in the chronicling of American history. However, the crowning institutional partnership for Baylor's BGMRP is its inclusion in the Smithsonian National Museum for African American History and Culture.[11]

Summary

In 1999, gospel singer Yolanda Adams released her seventh album, *Mountain High, Valley Low*. After twelve years of album releases and steadily rising acclaim among gospel listeners, Adams saw meteoric and massive success with the project due to its crossover popularity on R&B radio. The album, and its distribution by major label Elektra Records, partially led the charge of several contemporary gospel artists into secular radio formats and broader mainstream music success during the late 1990s. The song that carried the lyrics of the album's title, "Wherever You Are," represented the perfect collaboration between Adam's powerhouse gospel vocals and the hit-making production juggernauts of Jimmy Jam and Terry Lewis. The lyrics of the song speak about accessibility to the divine. While the song could have easily followed a common gospel songwriting trope of listing the dichotomous aspects of triumphs and hardships believers face, its central message was about accessibility. "Mountain high, valley low, desert heat, arctic cold. Wherever You are, that's where I wanna be" (Adams et al. 1999). In addition to leaning into common religious calls for access to the divine, the lyrics intimate a context where access includes agency on the part of the divine and the believer, a two-way relationship that is proactive and reactive, mutually engaged, and concerned with reciprocity. The three gospel archiving projects described in this chapter remind me of the sentiments raised in Adam's song in a variety of ways.

In a post on the BGMRP's blog, Eric Ames notes the following in a story about the museum preview visit conducted by Pattie Orr, Robert Darden, and others in September of 2016 at the National Museum of African American History and Culture:

> After more than four years of discussions, file sharing, digitization, permissions granting and plenty of logistical conversations, it is truly rewarding to see materials from the BGMRP making their big debut at the NMAAHC. As the project enters its second decade dedicated to collecting, cataloging, preserving and providing access to materials from America's black gospel music heritage, we are truly grateful to be a part of not only Baylor Nation but, in some small way, the history of the nation itself.
>
> (Ames 2016)

Ames's comments laud the importance of contributing to preservation efforts and knowledge production, and they point to the importance of public access to these sites of knowledge production in more tangible and accessible ways and in multiple venues.

Furthermore, his sentiment about being a part of national history through archiving and preservation efforts is a common theme among all the projects described here. In the proposal for the GALA Project, John Vallier raised the following sentiment, "Why archive? It's a pledge to the future. Without archiving, it's easy to forget our past." It became the subliminal mission statement of the project and even repeated by the community partners by the end of the year. The Heritage Music Foundation used the quote on some of their promotional materials, and group members not only got used to signing the archive's video consent forms but also at times assisted project workers with collecting them at larger events or events that went late into the night. Understanding that the GALA Project was a collective effort quickly became evident once the archive's dedication to gospel archiving and long-term collaboration was firmly established among the project's community partners.

The way so many scholars, artists, organizations, institutions, and everyday citizens have come together to collaborate and partner with each other toward the goal of recognizing the importance of gospel music to American culture and history over the last twenty years is a testament to the power of a genre and performance culture that is still often overlooked, understudied, or merely seen as a means to a commercial, pop-related end. Regardless of the relative "valley lows" that issues of longevity may present to some of the projects described here, fewer technical obstacles impede the future of gospel archiving than in the past. In each of these three projects, one can see that as it received more funding and developmental support via more advanced technology and scholars and culture-bearers engaged in more collaborative and access-minded initiatives, the "mountain high" moments increased in the short term and over the long term. It is fortuitous that gospel music is finally being put more consistently at the center of archival efforts in the first decades of the twenty-first century. The culminating triumph and innovation is that gospel music collections are more accessible to even broader audiences on a global scale. Increased accessibility and reciprocity in archiving efforts have led to more efficient and effective portals of knowledge with the ability to produce lasting success at various levels through partnerships and communicative relationships across institutional, geographical, and disciplinary lines.

NOTES

1. Edmondson provides a broader scope for the concept of access. In a 2004 UNESCO report on audiovisual archiving philosophies and principles, he noted access can be "proactive," initiated by the institution itself, or "reactive," initiated by users of the institution (Edmondson 2004, 20).

2. For an earlier and non-US-based example of this kind of collaborative and broader access-oriented digital archiving initiative, see Linda Barwick's work with the PARADISEC (the Pacific and Regional Archive of Digital Sources in Endangered Cultures) (Barwick 2004).

3. The Online Archive of California (OAC, http://www.oac.cdlib.org) provides free public access to detailed descriptions of primary resource collections maintained by more than two hundred contributing institutions including libraries, special collections, archives, historical societies, and museums throughout California and collections maintained by the ten University of California campuses (http://www.oac.cdlib.org/institutions/).

4. Substyles like gospel jazz and gospelized classical music were also documented. For more information on the holdings and documented events of the GALA Project, see Johnson (2012).

5. For a visual example, see this entry taken from a class on spirituals for congregational singing captured on October 21, 2004, at the Heritage Music Foundation's National Gospel Music Conference and Exposition at the LAX Radisson Hotel in Los Angeles, California: https://archive.org/details/calauem_000285.

6. While large, this subcollection also needs to have further developed metadata. For example, it includes many photos and visual ephemera of highly recognizable leaders in the Church of God in Christ, gospel music, and African American politics, but many are unlabeled or marked as "unidentified."

7. See link for a visual example of the digital collections search interface described in the text: http://digitalcollections.baylor.edu/cdm/search/collection/fa-gospel/searchterm/Low!Medium/field/risk!risk/mode/exact!exact/conn/or!and/order/nosort/page/2.

8. The thoroughness of the metadata for these items still should be corroborated in some cases due to the common instance of gospel artists and groups covering the same or similar songs, and record companies assigning writing/arranging credit to the performers and not the original composers. For example, the 45 rpm recording of "The Blood Will Never Lose Its Power" (ID# 59_80) by the Caravans lists the song's composer/arranger as James Cleveland in accordance with the name listed on the records imprint. However, the song and much of the arrangement was composed by Andraé Crouch in the late 1950s and recorded the same year as the Caravan's version in 1964 with Crouch's first group, the Cogic Singers on Simpson Records, a smaller, lesser-known record company than the Savoy imprint, Gospel, for which the Caravans recorded.

9. See link for visual example of the BGMRP's landing page: http://digitalcollections.baylor.edu/cdm/portal/collection/fa-gospel.

10. See here for full schedule and participant list: http://www.baylor.edu/pruit/index.php?id=865215.

11. The NMAAHC opened in September 2016. See Ames (2016) and Goodrich and Fogleman (2016) for fuller descriptions of how BGMRP's audio recordings and ephemera were incorporated in several museum installations.

REFERENCES

Adams, Yolanda, Terry Lewis, James Harris III, and James Wright. 1999. "Wherever You Are" from *Mountain High . . . Valley Low*. Elektra Records 62439-2.

Ames, Eric. 2013. "This Train Is Bound for DC: The Smithsonian-Baylor Digital Projects Group Black Gospel Collaboration Confirmed!" BU Libraries Digital Collections Blog. http://blogs.baylor.edu/digitalcollections/2013/12/16/smithsonian-dpg-collaobration-announcement/ (accessed November 9, 2016).

Ames, Eric. 2016. "The Scene at the Crossroads: A Peek at Baylor's Presence in the NMAAHC." BU Libraries Digital Collections Blog. http://blogs.baylor.edu/digitalcollections/2016/09/22/the-scene-at-the-crossroads-a-peek-at-baylors-presence-in-the-nmaahc/ (accessed October 22, 2016).

Barwick, Linda. 2004. "Turning It All Upside Down . . . Imagining a Distributed Digital Audiovisual Archive." *Literary and Linguistic Computing* 19 (3): 253–265.

Corn, Aaron. 2007. "To Sing Their Voices Eternal: Why We Need a National Recording Project for Indigenous Performance in Australia." *Music Forum* (February–April): 22–25. http://www.aboriginalartists.com.au/MusicForum-Feb07-AaronCorn.pdf (accessed November 12, 2016).

Edmondson, Ray. 2004. *Audiovisual Archiving: Philosophy and Principles*. Commemorating the 25th Anniversary of the UNESCO Recommendation for the Safeguarding and Preservation of Moving Images. Paris: UNESCO.

Goodrich, Terry, and Lori Fogleman. 2016. "Baylor's Black Gospel Restoration Project to Be a Highlight in the Sept. 24 Opening of the Smithsonian's National Museum of African American History in D.C." *Baylor Media Communications*. September 16. https://www.baylor.edu/mediacommunications/news.php?action=story&story=172437 (accessed November 12, 2016)

Hellier-Tinoco, Ruth. 2003. "Experiencing People: Relationships, Responsibility, and Reciprocity." *British Journal of Ethnomusicology* 12 (1): 19–34.

Johnson, Birgitta. 2012. "Gospel Archiving in Los Angeles: A Case of Proactive Archiving and Empowering Collaborations." *Ethnomusicology Forum* 21 (2): 221–242.

Lancefield, Robert C. 1998. "'Musical Traces' Retraceable Paths: The Repatriation of Recorded Sound." *Journal of Folklore Research* 35 (1): 47–68. Also reprinted in this Handbook.

Rice, Timothy. 1997. "Towards Mediation of Field Methods and Field Experience in Ethnomusicology." In *Shadows in the Field: New Perspectives for Fieldwork in Ethnomusicology*, edited by Gregory F. Barz and Timothy J. Cooley, 101–120. New York: Oxford University Press.

Rogers, Richard, and Oscar Hammerstein II. 1959. "Maria." *The Sound of Music*, Columbia Masterworks.

Ruskin, Jesse. 2006. "Collecting and Connecting: Archiving Filipino American Music in Los Angeles." *Pacific Review of Ethnomusicology* 11 (Winter): 1–15.

Russell, Maureen. 2014a. "Highlights from the Ethnomusicology Archive: African American Music." *Ethnomusicology Review*, June 24, 2014. http://ethnomusicologyreview.ucla.edu/content/highlights-ethnomusicology-archive-african-american-music (accessed December 1, 2016).

Russell, Maureen. 2014b. "First Round of Ethnomusicology Archive Recordings now on California Light and Sound." *Ethnomusicology Review*, August 29, 2014. http://ethnomusicologyreview.ucla.edu/content/first-round-ethnomusicology-archive-recordings-now-california-light-and-sound (accessed December 1, 2016).

Seeger, Anthony, and Shubha Chaudhuri, eds. 2004. *Archives for the Future: Global Perspectives on Audiovisual Archives in the 21st Century*. Gurgaon, Haryana, India: Archives and Research Centre for Ethnomusicology, American Institute of Indian Studies; Calcutta: Seagull Books.

Shelemay, Kay Kaufman. 1997. "The Ethnomusicologist, Ethnographic Method, and the Transmission of Tradition." In *Shadows in the Field: New Perspectives for Fieldwork in Ethnomusicology*, edited by Gregory F. Barz and Timothy J. Cooley, 189–204. New York: Oxford University Press.

Vallier, John. 2010. "Sound Archiving Close to Home: Why Community Partnerships Matter." *Notes* 67 (1): 39–49.

Walker, Daniel. 2012. "Gospel Luminaries Encounter Digital Archive." *Commentary*. USC Center for Religion and Civic Culture website. September 4, 2012. http://crcc.usc.edu/gospel-archive-visit/ (accessed October 16, 2016).

Gospel Music Archival Collections Links

The UCLA Ethnomusicology Archive Gospel Archiving in Los Angeles
The Gospel Archiving in Los Angeles (GALA) Collection Home Page
    https://www.ethnomusic.ucla.edu/archive/collections/2004_06/
The Finding Aid for the GALA Project at the Online Archive of California
    http://www.oac.cdlib.org/findaid/ark:/13030/kt2j49q27r/?query=GALA+Collection
GALA Project Fieldwork Videos Available on the Ethnomusicology Archive Channel/
    California Audiovisual Preservation Project
    https://archive.org/details/uclaethnomusicologyarchive
The University of Southern California Digital Library Gospel Music History Archive
    http://digitallibrary.usc.edu/cdm/landingpage/collection/p15799coll9
The Baylor University Black Gospel Music Restoration Project
The Black Gospel Music Restoration Project Main Portal
    http://digitalcollections.baylor.edu/cdm/portal/collection/fa-gospel
Royce-Darden Collection of the BGMRP Landing Page
    http://digitalcollections.baylor.edu/cdm/landingpage/collection/fa-gospel
The Black Gospel Music Restoration Project Blog
    http://blogs.baylor.edu/digitalcollections/category/collections/black-gospel-music-restoration-project/
The Black Gospel Music Restoration Project on iTunes U
    https://itunes.apple.com/us/itunes-u/black-gospel-music-restoration/id431880465?mt=10

CHAPTER 31

"THE SONGS ARE ALIVE"

Bringing Frances Densmore's Recordings
Back Home to Ojibwe Country

LYZ JAAKOLA AND TIMOTHY B. POWELL

THIS is the story of bringing "Frances Densmore's Ojibwe Music" from the Library of Congress back home to the Ojibwemowining Digital Arts Studio (ODAS), directed by Lyz Jaakola, at Fond du Lac Tribal and Community College (FdLTCC). What we hope our story will show is how the songs, so long inaccessible because Densmore recorded them on wax cylinders, come back to life when returned to Ojibwe communities. As Frances Densmore herself wrote in the introduction to *Chippewa Music*, "Chippewa songs are not petrified specimens; they are alive with the warm blood of human nature" (Densmore 1910, 1). This brief account conveys what it means to "wake up" traditional knowledge 116 years after Densmore recorded the songs from 1907 to 1910 at the Leech Lake, White Earth, Lac du Flambeau, Nett Lake, and Red Lake Ojibwe communities in northern Minnesota and Wisconsin.

The authors, Tim Powell and Lyz Jaakola, tell two sides of the same story. Tim, a professor at the University of Pennsylvania, explains the digital component of the repatriation project and explores the theoretical question of how digital objects come to be seen in new ways when situated within traditional Ojibwe-Anishinaabe knowledge systems. Lyz picks up the story in the second half to explain what revitalizing these very powerful songs means to her as a professional musician, a teacher at FdLTCC, and an active member in the community. Given that many of the songs, though not all, are Midewiwin (Grand Medicine Society), Lyz also discusses the proper handling of culturally sensitive materials from an Ojibwe perspective. She also provides examples of how those songs not designated as culturally sensitive are being used to teach traditional Ojibwe values to the upcoming generation.

TIM POWELL: GETTING THE DENSMORE
RECORDINGS FROM THE ARCHIVE
TO THE RESERVATION

Boozhoo ("hello"), my name is Tim. I have been working with the Ojibwe communities of northern Minnesota for the last sixteen years. As the director of Educational Partnerships with Indigenous Communities (EPIC), operated through the Penn Language Center, I am dedicated to returning digitized archival materials to the communities where they originated and to studying how the songs and stories are being used to preserve the language, revitalize traditional culture, and instill traditional values. This case study of "sonic repatriation" examines what it means to take seriously the fact that these songs are, as Lyz observes, "living spiritual beings" and how such awareness can help decolonize the archives.[1]

Defining Digital Repatriation

The area of digital repatriation is still relatively new and has been growing quickly, although its future remains uncertain.[2] The Densmore recordings, interestingly, played a prominent role in the field's origins. Recorded in 1907–1910 on wax cylinders by Frances Densmore, the recordings remained unavailable to Ojibwe-Anishinaabe communities for seventy years. In 1979, the Library of Congress launched the Federal Cylinder Project, one of the first and most important predigital repatriation projects, wherein cassette copies of the wax cylinder recordings were distributed to the Ojibwe communities where Densmore had worked (Gray 1996). These very poor quality recordings—"dubs of dubs," as Lyz calls them—circulated somewhat randomly, hand to hand. The problems Lyz describes in her first encounter with the cassette recordings played a significant role in shaping our efforts to engage in a more effective and culturally sensitive form of repatriation that restores this traditional knowledge to those within the community who are the authorized "keepers" of such knowledge.

While the Federal Cylinder Project was successful at increasing access to the Densmore recordings, the technological limitations of the time led, inadvertently and perhaps inevitably, to a radical decontextualization of these traditional songs. Densmore's ethnographic notes are quite extraordinary, even if much of the material she printed would be considered culturally sensitive by today's standards.[3] The cassettes quickly became separated from Densmore's notes, which detail how the Ojibwe-Anishinaabe knowledge keepers understood the songs. As a result, the repatriation in the form of cassette recordings did not make the kind of impact that is now possible in the digital age.

These earlier problems of unreliable access and decontextualization became the focus of a careful planning process that went on for five years before the songs returned to the communities of origin. In 2009, a National Endowment for the Humanities (NEH) Digital Humanities Start-Up grant brought together elders, teachers, and curriculum developers from White Earth, Leech Lake, and Fond du Lac along with linguists, anthropologists, librarians, and archivists to discuss not just the transfer but also the sustainability of the project, so that the songs would be of use to Ojibwe-Anishinaabe communities for many years to come. In sharp contrast to the open-access policy that defines the success of many non-Native digital projects, the planning phase coordinated efforts to limit access of the Midewiwin songs to the general public and to establishment protocols to assure that the traditional knowledge would be made available to Midewiwin leaders for use in the lodge. In 2014, Lyz and I worked with Larry Anderson, president of FdLTCC, to write a successful NEH Humanities Initiatives for Tribal College and Universities grant to support a project titled "Teaching Ojibwe Values through Stories and Songs: Building a Digital Repository at the Ojibwemowining Center." The grant included funding to pay for repatriating digital copies of Densmore's Ojibwe recordings at a cost of more than $1,000.

To ensure that the songs would not be lost or become inaccessible once the grant concluded, the recordings and ethnographic material were incorporated into a database designed in FileMaker Pro. With the help of Lyz and the IT department at FdLTCC, the FileMaker Pro database was absorbed into the digital archive being built at the Ojibwemowining Digital Arts Studio that Lyz directs. Mirroring the work that Lyz has done to teach her students about the traditional values associated with the songs, I worked with two wonderful younger colleagues, Juliet Gilmore-Larkin and Joshua Garrett-Davis, to teach them how scholars and archivists can adopt some of these same values into digital repatriation projects. We discussed, for example, the concepts of *gwayakochigewin* ("doing things in the right way") and *bimaadiziwin* ("a healthy way of life") that Thomas Peacock writes about in *Ojibwe Waasa Inaabidaa: We Look in All Directions* (Peacock 2009, 112, 90). While those of us in the academy are under intense pressure to publish single-authored articles and monographs, these traditional values teach a sense of humility and a focus on the community, such that we worked hard to put away the academic mindset and to design the database in a way that would honor the ancestors and benefit future generations of Ojibwe-Anishinaabe people. The database, for example, reveals the names of all the Ojibwe-Anishinaabe singers in contrast to the Library of Congress catalog, which describes the "performer" simply as "various artists."[4] To ensure the sustainability of the database for the coming generations, we presented the database to Lyz Jaakola and worked with IT at FdLTCC to ensure it was integrated into their system with safeguards in place to protect the culturally sensitive materials. Ensuring sustainability of digital objects, however, remains a constant challenge. FileMaker Pro is proprietary software and will, inevitably, one day need to be updated, and its content may need to be migrated. In keeping with the values of *gwayakochigewin* and *bimaadiziwin*, we realized the need to maintain a strong relationship with FdLTCC and Lyz Jaakola after the grant's end to study and, we hope, overcome these challenges. Our greatest hope is that the songs will be sung and passed down through the oral tradition, which may yet prove a more reliable system for sustainability, so that these living spiritual beings will play a meaningful role in maintaining the health of Ojibwe-Anishinaabe communities.

To strengthen the relationship between the songs, Densmore's ethnographic notes, and the contemporary oral tradition, the "Teaching Ojibwe Values through Stories and Songs" project created digital videos of contemporary Ojibwe-Anishinaabe knowledge keepers, thus reconnecting the digital recordings to the tribe's rich history of oral storytelling. Although the planned digital exhibit has not yet been completed, I can provide an example of how the videos of elders telling stories can illuminate and enliven Densmore's ethnographic materials. Densmore writes, for example, of the song listed as "No. 115. 'The Approach of the Storm,' sung by Ga'gandac'":

> The Thunder manido' represents to the Indian the mysterious spirit of the storm, and he imagines that this manido' sometimes makes a noise to warn him of its approach. This is his interpretation of the distant thunder which precedes the storm. Hearing this, the Indian hastens to put tobacco on the fire in order that the smoke may ascend as an offering or signal of peace to the manido'. The idea which underlies the song is, "That which lives in the sky is coming and, being friendly, it makes a noise to let me know of its approach." This means much less to the white race than to the Indian.
>
> (Densmore 1910, 130)

The "Thunder manido'" or Animikii ("Thunderbird") is one of the most powerful beings in Ojibwe cosmology. Fortunately, despite Densmore's concern about the "white race['s]" lack of understanding, she nevertheless accurately recorded in English the traditional knowledge Ga'gandac' was willing to share with her.

In the digital exhibit, Ga'gandac's explanation is juxtaposed with a digital video of Dan Jones, the head of the Ojibwe language program at FdLTCC, titled "Blessed by Thunderbirds."[5] The video is part of a series created for the project titled *The Stories and Values behind Ojibwe Words*, inspired by Dan Jones's insightful observation, "You cannot separate the language from the culture; the language is how we convey the values that we have in our society" (Jones 2015). Dan teaches the cultural values associated with Animikiig ("Thunderbirds") by telling a story. Just as Ga'gandac' had been taught, Dan recounts how his father used to wake him up in the middle of the night to burn tobacco when the thunderbirds were passing overhead. Dan then brings the past into the present by telling a story of how lighting had recently struck a birch tree near his home in the Nigigoonsiminikaaning First Nation in Canada. When he told the elders in the community, they all came over to collect pieces of the wood, explaining to Dan that the tree had been "blessed by Thunderbirds." In this way, the songs cease to be simply digital objects and become integrated into community-based efforts to revitalize the language and traditional values for future generations.

What Does It Mean to Recognize Living Spiritual Beings in Digital Form?

"Teaching Ojibwe Values through Stories and Songs" is part of a larger movement going on throughout the Americas to decolonize archives holding Indigenous traditional knowledge. As Jennifer O'Neal writes in her important article, "'The Right to Know': Decolonizing Native American Archives":

> Since the federal government's establishment and collection of these archival records is considered part of colonialism, the act of Native Americans gathering and repurposing these records for their benefit is indeed an act of decolonization.
>
> (O'Neal 2015, 9)

O'Neal goes on to identify the "'archival turn' in ethnic archiving that argues that new non-western perspectives are desperately needed in archival education, practice, and the profession at large" (O'Neal 2015, 15). To provide a culturally specific example of what such a practice might look like, I want to investigate what it means to think about these songs, pictographs, and stories as "living spiritual beings," to borrow Lyz's intriguing phrase. Doing so, I argue, allows us to think in new ways about Western conceptions of digital objects, ownership, and ethics.

To see the songs as living spiritual beings, it is first necessary to restore them to an Ojibwe-Anishinaabe cultural context, to a knowledge system that predates European colonization and continues to thrive in the present day (Treuer 2010). In Ojibwemowin ("the Ojibwe language"), the songs are considered *adizookaanag*. In the introduction to the collection *Centering Anishinaabeg Studies: Understanding the World through Stories*, the editors write, "*Adizookaanag* are generally considered 'traditional or 'sacred' narratives that embody values, philosophies, and laws important to life. They are also *manidoog* (manitous), living beings who work with Anishinaabeg in the interest of demonstrating principles necessary for *mino-bimaadiziwin*, that good and beautiful life" (Doerfler, Sinclair, and Stark 2013). In Ojibwe cosmology, *manidoog* ("spirits") possess the power to shape-shift. This can be seen quite clearly in the case of the living spiritual beings with which we had the honor to work. As the database shows, in the last 120 years these empowered songs have shape-shifted from the oral tradition to pictographs, then, once Densmore arrived, from pictograph to wax cylinders to musical scores. When the living spiritual beings are returned to knowledge keepers and Midewiwin leaders, as Lyz describes later, they return to their original form when they are performed in drum circles and sung. If this epistemological shift seems difficult to comprehend, imagine the difference between listening to the scratchy digital copies of Densmore's wax cylinder recordings and standing just outside a drum circle performing a song, where you can quite literally feel the pulse of these living spiritual beings.

Awareness of such transformative powers allows us to perceive more clearly what still needs to be done to decolonize archival systems of knowledge. Archival metadata (e.g., author, title, publication date), for example, makes it harder to recognize these living spiritual beings by (mis)labeling them as the "Frances Densmore collection of Chippewa cylinder recordings." My point is not to blame the Library of Congress or individual archivists, whom we need as valued allies, but rather to begin a conversation that I hope will continue beyond the margins of this brief analysis, enabling us to think critically about how to better honor and preserve Ojibwe-Anishinaabe traditional knowledge. Recognizing the songs as *adizookaanag*, for example, helps identify a problematic disjuncture between the archival knowledge system and the Ojibwe-Anishinaabe knowledge system, of which these living spiritual beings are a vital part. As the anthropologist Tim Ingold writes in "Rethinking the Animate, Re-Animating Thought," systems like archival catalogs attempt to fix animate beings "within a grid of concepts and categories" that seek "closure rather than openness" (Ingold 2006, 16). What is particularly important about Ingold's writings is not just that he calls for the recognition of living spiritual beings as *beings*, rather than myths or figments of the Indigenous imagination, but also that he invites non-Native scholars and archivists to open themselves up to being "astonished" in an act of what he calls "animistic openness." To do so, Ingold argues, creates the possibility of "rethinking indigenous animism" with the goal of leading "us to propose the re-animation of our own, so-called, 'western' tradition of thought" (Ingold 2006, 19).

To provide a concrete example of how archival systems could productively be opened up to astonishment, it is necessary to understand in what sense the Library of Congress catalog is "closed." Take, for example, the limited sense of temporality that operates in almost every archival catalog. Here the dates associated with the songs are 1907–1910, derived from the implicit logic that the objects being described are the wax cylinders "collected" (captured?) by Francis Densmore, rather than living spiritual beings. To shift the focus from the white anthropologist, Densmore, to the songs as *manidoog* ("spirits") opens up a whole new spiritual timescape. To return to the idea that these living spiritual beings possess the power of shape-shifting—that is, to say they may manifest themselves as wax cylinders or cassettes or digital objects, but these forms do not define their *being*—allows us to see that the cataloging system is closed to recognizing that *adizookaanag* operate on a very different timescape. These *manidoog* have existed since the beginning of time, not 1907, and will continue to animate Ojibwe-Anishinaabeg culture long after the digital objects become obsolete.

The problem with closed systems becomes more readily apparent when one considers how labeling living spiritual beings as the "Frances Densmore collection" comes to be interpreted under US copyright law. Not surprisingly, the law eschews astonishment, causing a vast multitude of difficulties that inhibit the integration of the Western and Indigenous knowledge systems. As Peter Hirtle, Emily Hudson, and Andrew Kenyon write in *Copyright and Cultural Institutions*:

> Federal copyright protection only arises when a work is fixed in a tangible medium of expression.... The requirement that a work must exist in a tangible form can mean that meritorious subject matter—such as improvised music and dance, extemporaneous speeches, oral stories, and so forth—are ineligible for federal copyright protection because they have never been committed to material form.
>
> (Hirtle, Hudson, and Kenyon 2009, 23)

In other words, because Densmore "fixed" the songs in a tangible medium (i.e., recorded them on wax cylinders) she holds the copyright. One could argue that well before Densmore appeared on the scene, the Ojibwe-Anishinaabe had "fixed" the songs in pictographic form. I do not, however, want to be waylaid by debating whether the Supreme Court would be swayed by pictographic evidence and would refer readers interested in the question of traditional knowledge and copyright to the work of Jane Anderson (2005, 2012a, 2012b). I am more interested in striving, as a non-Native scholar, to better understand how understanding the songs as *adizookaanag* can improve digital repatriation projects.

I would ask, in closing, that we consider carefully what the Ojibwe-Anishinaabe elders taught Francis Densmore when they presented these living spiritual beings to her. As Densmore writes of working with a traditional knowledge keeper named Débwawĕn'dûnk:

> At this time tobacco had been provided, which the old chief smoked in silence. When he was ready, he seated himself before the phonograph and again made a speech translated as follows: "I am not doing this for the sake of curiosity, but I have smoked a pipe to the *Mĭdé manidó* from whom these songs came, and I ask them not to be offended with me for singing these songs which belong to them."
>
> (Densmore 1910, 57)

To recognize the songs as *adizookaanag* entails a sense of responsibility and obligation for those involved with digital repatriation projects. Regardless of what US copyright laws decree, we need to acknowledge, as Débwawĕn'dûnk taught Densmore, these songs belong to the *Mĭdé manidó* ("spirits of the Grand Medicine Society"), a knowledge system that remains both valid and viable. As my mentor Larry Aitken taught me, Ojibwe materials in archives and museums are "dormant... [but] still alive... waiting to bring forth the knowledge that ... can teach us many, many lessons" (Aitken, personal correspondence, 2006). And although digitization is usually considered to be part of the Western knowledge system, the lesson I have learned is that the living spiritual beings that were gifted to Densmore possess the power to shape-shift into and out of digital form. We are thus living in a unique historical moment in which digital technology can reconnect *adizookaanag* with Ojibwe-Anishinaabe knowledge keepers and, in doing so, teach both Native and non-Native people about *mino-bimaadiziwin*, that good and beautiful life.

LYZ JAAKOLA: MUSIC IS
A LIVING SPIRITUAL BEING

Boozhoo Nindinawemaaganidoog. Nitaa-nagamokwe indizhinikaaz. Migizi indodem. Anishinaabekwe indaw. Nagaajiiwanaang indoojibaa minawaa Nagaajiiwanaang gabe-gikendaasowiigamigong indanokii. ("Hello my relatives. They call me 'the lady who knows how to sing.' I am Eagle clan. I am an Anishinaabe woman. I live at Fond du Lac reservation and I work at the Fond du Lac Tribal and Community College.")

My story begins a long time ago. I will not start then but I will say this: music in Ojibwe-Anishinaabe culture is more than just an entertainment. Music is a living spiritual being. I have known this my whole life, although my experience with American education ran counter to this fundamental teaching. Making sense of this duality in understanding music became a mode I frequently used growing up on the reservation and studying Western music. Perhaps this is why I understand Frances Densmore's work in a different way than most.

I had known about the work of Frances Densmore since I was fifteen. An instructor at my boarding school mentioned that she knew about the work of an ethnomusicologist from Red Wing, Minnesota, who had extensively published about my tribe, the Ojibwe-Anishinaabe. I then began a long journey. Now, over thirty years later, I feel that I am beginning the journey toward a better fulfillment of my name.

Over the years, I gathered bits and pieces of information about the songs and collection of wax cylinders Frances Densmore had gathered and written about at the beginning of the twentieth century. When teaching at the K–12 Bureau of Indian Affairs (BIA) school, I even asked our tribal council's permission to pursue the repatriation of the Densmore recordings. I felt it was our cultural right to know these songs, and to teach them to our youth. I felt the songs had been held as prisoners of war and they called out to be set free. Although the voice on the other end of the telephone at the Library of Congress, Judith Gray, was sympathetic, I was not successful in acquiring the recordings at that time.

I later found out that a set of cassette tapes was making its way around Indian Country. In the mid-1990s I attended a National Indian Education Conference in Arizona, where I met another Indigenous musician who introduced me to what their tribe was doing with Densmore recordings of Lakota songs and digital systems. It made me even more hungry to know how to work with the Ojibwe song recordings. I called the Library of Congress, again, at that point. The woman I spoke to suggested that there was a way to get the recordings, but it most likely involved a hefty processing fee—a fee that I did not know how to pay.

When I started as adjunct faculty at FdLTCC, I also started working as a cultural consultant and researcher for our local PBS station. I traveled to twenty-one different Ojibwe reservations and urban communities, where I met with many people. In my travels, I was presented with a shoebox full of cassette recordings of some of the wax cylinders of Densmore's "Chippewa Music." The person who gave me the tapes said they were made of dubbed copies of tapes, dubs of dubs. It was fairly common in the later twentieth century for tribal musicians to share traditional recordings via cassette tapes. We operate within a different "copyright" system. The Dakota elder Floyd Crow Westerman called it "Indian copyright," because our system involves cultural protocol and not an impersonal exchange of money.[6] By the time I received the box of cassettes, I had learned enough about the Densmore recordings to know that they potentially contained Midewiwin (Grand Medicine Society) songs—songs that are bound to traditional protocol and carry spiritual power. So, I carefully and graciously accepted these cassette tapes. I brought them home, but I did not dare to listen to them outright, lest I inadvertently access a Midewiwin song, a medicine song, that was not meant for me.

The cassette tapes stayed in the box. My spirit name was found and given to me in my youth by a Midewiwin woman, but that did not make me a Midewiwin. I knew that it was in my future to seek Midewiwin teachings, but I did not feel ready at that time in my life. But now that the recordings were in my care, I felt that I had to prepare myself. Over time, when I needed another nudge, another set of these recordings came to me: a "better" cassette copy. I felt a little more confident, as I had prepared myself somewhat to begin my Midewiwin walk; so in private I dared to place one of the tapes into a cassette deck. I did so, however, with my finger on the eject button—ready to hit eject if this were a Midewiwin song—because of the way the cassettes had come to me, I did not know what was going to play. There was not a list of contents or track list or any way to know which songs were on which tapes.

I had already become familiar with the publications *Chippewa Music I* and *II*, in which Densmore had transcribed, translated, drawn, analyzed, and written anecdotal narratives for each of the songs from her recording sessions. I had listened to the recordings that the American Folklife Center had released. I had heard some ceremonial music, some social songs, some children's songs, and other teachings over my thirty-some years, and so I felt brave enough to pop one of these cassettes into the player.

I pressed play; thankfully the first song I heard I recognized, " 'One Wind' by Kimiwun" from a Folklife Center album, *Songs of the Chippewa* (Densmore 1950). I found that song in the catalog portion of Densmore's book. I made a reasonable assumption that the next song on the cassette would correspond with the next song in the book. According to that catalog, the next song should have been another "social" song. When the recording from the tape continued, it was not the next song in the book. It was not a Midewiwin song, thankfully, but it still was not what it was "supposed" to be. This confirmed my suspicions that listening to the tapes would be like a spiritual "Russian roulette." I asked myself, "Was I up to this risk?" I decided that no, I was not. This new box of eighteen cassettes went lovingly on the shelf, next to the other box of cassette tapes.

A few years had passed when I was invited to a meeting where I met Tim Powell and others who had been involved in working with language, culture, and education with tribal colleges in northern Minnesota. Tim spoke with me about the work that was being done in digital repatriation, and I immediately thought about the Densmore collection. It was almost too much to hope for, and besides, who would go through the work of weeding through those recordings? But the next thing I knew I was holding a flash drive containing some of the digitized Densmore collection of Chippewa music recordings. I did not know what to do with the song files, so I went to an elder, a singing mentor, and asked what she thought I should do. As elders often do, she chose not to "give me the answer" but talked to me about our teachings. During the talk it became clear to me that I should give tobacco, to go through and learn more about Midewiwin so I can do the work I need to do, to fulfill my name and be the Anishinaabe that I am meant to be.

I formally made my intentions to seek Midewiwin instruction known and after receiving some introductory instruction, I began to listen to the tracks on the jump drive. The digitized copies are still not twenty-first-century clear, of course. The wax cylinders could not capture and hold the spirit of these songs, but the digital recordings make it easier to hear and understand the intentions of the songs and the iterations of the words.

As the recordings were becoming more familiar to me, I listened and analyzed. I wanted to share them with "everyone," but I know that in our culture a digital repatriation is a new phenomenon. I began having conversations with people from regional Ojibwe-Anishinaabe communities about what they thought about the recordings, how might FdLTCC Ojibwemowining keep them, share them, use them, and so forth. The reactions have been mixed. Some culture-bearers are not song-keepers and therefore see the collection as interesting but not something they feel adds to their "medicine bundles."[7] Some song-keepers have shown no interest in the Densmore collection database, and others are very interested. I will share one example, one I feel has been the most promising encounter to date.

One of the culture-bearers and song-keepers is a young man of Lac du Flambeau. After talking to him on occasion for about a year, I invited him to campus. This culture-bearer had received a copy of the tapes about the time those were going around in the late 1990s, and he was interested in our collection and database as soon as I mentioned it to him. I gathered that he had experiences similar to mine, in not knowing which songs were which in the cassette recordings. The FdLTCC invited him to come to campus to share teachings through our "Traditional Teachings Today" series, funded by the NEH grant. We gifted him with traditional gifts and tobacco, as is cultural protocol. He shared teachings about craft, hide, floral designs, language, and the cultural significance of each with a group of students and community members.

He also spent time in the Ojibwemowining Digital Arts Studio listening to the Densmore collection and interpreting the recordings. We studied the entries in the database, compared the entries to pages in the book, and listened to about forty songs in total, all of which had been recorded at Lac du Flambeau in 1911. Some of the songs were familiar to this culture-bearer. He sang along with accuracy and enthusiasm, making note of occasional differences in language, rhythm, or melody. Some of the songs were unfamiliar to him, but he did share stories about the singer who had been recorded, since the oral tradition at Lac du Flambeau still carries details about the individuals who had been recorded by Densmore. This session was recorded and transcribed by a Midewiwin student, and it lays the groundwork for future such encounters with song-keepers of the other communities represented in the entire collection.

The culture-bearer was very happy to receive copies of the songs to take back to his home community. He stated on his departure that he would most likely have the new songs memorized by the time he arrived at home, and that he intended to sing them at the next appropriate opportunity. The database made this possible. If we did not have the recordings organized, or the pages arranged the way they are, or the digital technology to listen to the tracks, this encounter would not have had the impact that it did. This made me feel quite accomplished to have helped facilitate that reconnection. It felt responsible and appropriate, and I felt privileged to be able to share with someone who knows the importance and value of these recordings. I know that these songs have begun another part of their life, and I am grateful to have been instrumental in their journey.

During my second sabbatical, I began writing a curriculum called "An Ojibwe-Anishinaabe Music Curriculum," with the intention of aligning lesson plans with grade-level state standards for Minnesota's music educators. The state began adding "new" educational standards specific to Minnesota's American Indian tribes in 2008 with each discipline's scheduled revisions. Educators have been receptive to implementing the standards, but so far there has not been a concerted effort to support the standards with curriculum. As an Ojibwe-Anishinaabe music educator, I have been asked to assist the state's teachers in how they might meet the standards. It was a natural development for me to begin writing a curriculum. In the curriculum I included some nonsacred tracks from the Densmore collection, some tracks of contemporary music, and some newly composed tracks based on the characteristics of Ojibwe music as made evident in the repertoire recorded by Frances Densmore. There are thirteen lesson plans using a variety of musical resources representative of the digital Densmore collection and other songs in the "Ojibwe repertoire," some of which were composed specifically for this curriculum based on examples from the Densmore recordings. In my understanding of Anishinaabe songs, cultural protocol, and "ownership," it has been made clear to me that each song has what we might call a heritage and potential legacy. They come from somewhere, from someone, and to simply make a "cover recording" of some of the songs is not a respectful way to share them. How each song is treated or shared may impact that song and community. There are over five hundred songs in this Densmore collection, and a respectful relationship with each song is desired. These factors were considered when writing the curriculum.

Some of the lesson plans have been used when I have traveled to schools across Minnesota as a music educator, and some are going to be used as FdLTCC launches its four-year teacher education program. There are hopes that this curriculum will be widely accepted when it has been completely vetted and published. Other agencies have also assisted with this curriculum development. The Perpich Center for Arts Education in Minneapolis hosted some educator workshops and Minnesota Public Radio developed some lesson plans based on works that I have provided, including reproductions of older songs from the Densmore collection and newer compositions that were inspired by the songs in the collection.

Another relationship that is developing is a closer tie with the Minnesota Historical Society, where the Frances Densmore Papers are held. I now serve as chairwoman of the

Fond du Lac Band Cultural Resources Advisory Board and I work closely with the newly formed Fond du Lac Reservation Historical Society and the Fond du Lac tribal historic preservation officer. Conversations that for decades have been one-sided are now taking a different and exciting tone, as the state is looking to Indigenous peoples and organizations as valuable and contributing allies, telling our own stories. The Densmore database has helped move this relationship forward.

To reinvigorate the use of the language, it is the ODAS's mission to create new works in the language to share with Ojibwe communities. As has been possible, songs have been written in the style of the "old songs" and performed or recorded for radio play. Students, faculty, and community members have also produced and are working on videos to promote language learning. Some of the language material comes from the Densmore collection or from events and activities that have arisen from having this resource. These recordings are played "in house" over a PA system in the resource center, and some are on YouTube or Vimeo channels.[8]

There have been songs made "in the style" of women's songs in the Densmore collection. These songs have been performed as part of the local repertoire and regular gatherings. The culture-bearers and song-keepers who gather at FdLTCC are often listening to recordings in the Ojibwemowining Resource Center or ODAS Studio when they hold practices or during recording sessions. This space and the recorded resources have created a unique setting for this type of cultural learning to occur. Groups and individuals with local, regional, and/or international touring schedules have listened to and been inspired by the repatriated songs.

One of the songs has been made into a singing game, "Honour Water," which has been available for free as an iPad app since summer 2016. Produced through a partnership between Pinnguaq, Oshkii Giizhik Singers, and Indigenous game developer Elizabeth LaPensee, the game teaches players three songs (all recorded in ODAS) and gauges their singing accuracy, encouraging them to learn Ojibwe language and songs.

Another project that our studio has been involved with is scripting and recording audio phrases for an exhibit at the Duluth Children's Museum. We were approached to assist with the accuracy of language recordings they wanted to include in an exhibit about wild rice, *manomin*. We wrote some phrases, translated them, recorded students and children saying the phrases, and sent the tracks to the exhibit developer. This exhibit was planned to launch in January 2017.

One unexpected outcome of having the recordings and resources on campus is the many opportunities I have had to talk or write about my role in the repatriation of the recordings. I was fortunate to attend and present at an NEH-sponsored panel at the 2015 conference of the Association of Tribal Archives, Libraries, and Museums (ATALM) in Washington, DC. Our session was titled "Models of Collaboration for Access and Use of Native Language Materials," and I was honored to present with professionals in Native American studies, national archives, and museums. I also was invited to speak at the 2016 Western Historical Society Conference in St. Paul, Minnesota, in a session about Frances Densmore and the Colonial/Indigenous Archive. As a two-year tribal college faculty member, I am not often asked to present in such a fashion for colleagues and professionals, so these opportunities were much appreciated.

Although the Densmore collection is not a new resource, its digital repatriation is a new beginning. I am grateful to be involved in such a project and humbled by the work that I do to continue to build these relationships. There is still much to do, and I hope I can continue to do this work in a good way. The songs, and our ancestors who entrusted Frances Densmore with them, are not living. I believe they are dancing in a new era of tribal self-determination that only our traditional Indigenous knowledge can bring.

CONCLUSION

This is Tim, again. To connect the two sides of the story that Lyz and I tell into a more holistic approach, I want to share a few final thoughts. In the first, more theoretical section, I noted the benefits of thinking of the songs not as wax cylinders or digital objects but as living spiritual beings with the power to shape-shift. Lyz then provided examples from the community about how the songs are transforming themselves and transforming Ojibwe-Anishinaabeare people playing and listening to the songs. If the songs were, as Lyz suggests, once prisoners of war, they have now been set free. What always amazes and delights me is how brilliantly communities integrate the songs into contemporary life in ways that digital humanities scholars, like myself, could never dream of. With Lyz's thoughtful care, the songs have shape-shifted into curriculum to help Native and non-Native students to better understand their history and their future. They have inspired contemporary drum circles to create new songs; not "covers" but vibrant variations suitable to be played on tribal radio stations and National Public Radio. And, most importantly, they have been carefully stewarded by Lyz, with guidance from Midewiwin leaders, so that they can be integrated into the ongoing oral tradition that stretches back to precolonial times and forward to the upcoming generations who are eager to learn the language and dance the knowledge. For this we give thanks, *miigwech*.

NOTES

1. Indigenous communities have known for thousands of years that songs are "living spiritual beings." Somewhat remarkably, these same ideas are now being recognized by scholars as animacy (Ingold 2000), vibrant matter (Bennett 2010), and multispecies anthropology (Kirksey and Helmreich 2010). These works have influenced my thought, but I also to acknowledge the Indigenous elders who taught me: Larry Aitken (Leech Lake Ojibwe), Watie Akin (Penobscot), Tom Belt (Cherokee Nation), and Rick Hill (Tuscarora at the Six Nations of Grand River). Some of the songs are considered culturally sensitive because they are associated with the Grand Medicine Society.

2. I am cautiously optimistic about the future of digital repatriation, although I think it is highly unfortunate that some of the major granting agencies that support this kind of work are restricting the use of funding for digitization. As this chapter demonstrates, one does not need a supercomputer or data-mining algorithms to make a meaningful impact in Indigenous communities. To prohibit funds from being used for digitization thus inadvertently widens the digital divide that we should all be dedicated to overcoming and could jeopardize the future of the field.

3. For more on Densmore's methods and interactions with tribes see Jensen and Patterson's *Travels with Frances Densmore: Her Life, Work, and Legacy in Native American Studies* (2015).

4. Library of Congress Online Catalog, accessed February 6, 2017, https://catalog.loc.gov/vwebv/holdingsInfo?searchId=2367&recCount=25&recPointer=1&bibId=16173825.

5. "Blessed by Thunderbirds," accessed December 31, 2016, https://www.youtube.com/watch?v=kVm6KVKeinI.

6. Personal conversation.

7. A medicine bundle is a collection of medicines that one uses to maintain spiritual balance. Medicine may or may not be physical; it could be a song or word.

8. For more on Lyz Jaakola's work on curriculum development and teaching, see Barbara Rice, "Resources for Teaching the Music of Native American Peoples," https://childrensmusic.org/pass-it-on/features/resources-for-teaching-the-music-of-native-american-peoples.aspx, and the "Classical MPR in the Classroom Series," accessed December 31, 2016, http://minnesota.publicradio.org/radio/services/cms/education/native_american_resource_guide.pdf.

References

Anderson, Jane. 2005. "Access and Control of Indigenous Knowledge in Libraries and Archives: Ownership and Future Use." In *Correcting Course: Rebalancing Copyright for Libraries in the National and International Area*. New York: American Library Association and the MacArthur Foundation. http://ccnmtl.columbia.edu/projects/alaconf2005/paper_anderson.pdf.

Anderson, Jane. 2012a. "Intellectual Property and Safeguarding of Traditional Cultures: Legal Issues and Practical Options for Museums, Libraries and Archives." *Heritage and Society* 4 (2): 253–260.

Anderson, Jane. 2012b. "On Resolution / Intellectual Property and Indigenous Knowledge Disputes / Prologue." *Landscapes of Violence* 2 (1): 1–14.

Bennett, Jane. 2010. *Vibrant Matter: The Political Ecology of Things*. London: Duke University Press.

Densmore, Frances. 1910. *Chippewa Music*. Smithsonian Institution Bureau of American Ethnology Series, Bulletin 45. Washington, DC: US Government Printing Office.

Densmore, Frances. 1950. *Songs of the Chippewa: From the Archive of Folk Song*. Washington, DC: Library of Congress.

Doerfler, Jill, Niigaanwewidam James Sinclair, and Heidi Kiiwetinepinesiik Stark. 2013. "*Bagijige*: Making an Offering." In *Centering Anishinaabeg Studies: Understanding the World through Stories*, edited by Jill Doerfler, Niigaanwewidam James Sinclair, and Heidi Kiiwetinepinesiik Stark, xv–xxvii. East Lansing: Michigan State University Press.

Gray, Judith. 1996. "Returning Music to the Makers: The Library of Congress, American Indians, and the Federal Cylinder Project." *Cultural Survival* 20 (4). https://www.culturalsurvival.org/publications/cultural-survival-quarterly/returning-music-makers-library-congress-american-indians.

Hirtle, Peter, Emily Hudson, and Andrew Kenyon. 2009. *Copyright and Cultural Institutions: Guidelines for Digitization for US Libraries, Archives and Museums*. Ithaca, NY: Cornell University Press.

Ingold, Tim. 2000. *The Perception of the Environment: Essays on Livelihood, Dwelling, and Skill*. New York: Routledge.

Ingold, Tim. 2006. "Rethinking the Animate, Re-Animating Thought." *Ethnos* 71 (1): 9–20.

Jones, Dan. 2015. "Blessed by Thunderbirds." http://ojibwearchive.sas.upenn.edu/content/dan-jones/ (accessed February 6, 2017).

Kirksey, S. Eban, and Stanley Helmrich. 2010. "The Emergence of Multispecies Ethnography." *Cultural Anthropology* 25: 545–576.

O'Neal, Jennifer. 2015. " 'The Right to Know': Decolonizing Native American Archives." *Journal of Western Archives* 6 (1). http://digitalcommons.usu.edu/westernarchives/vol6/iss1/2/.

Peacock, Thomas. 2009. *Ojibwe Waasa Inaabidaa: We Look in All Directions*. Minneapolis: Minnesota Historical Society.

Treuer, Anton S. 2010. *The Assassination of Hole in the Day*. St. Paul: Minnesota Historical Press.

CHAPTER 32

......

MOVING SONGS

Repatriating Audiovisual Recordings of Aboriginal Australian Dance and Song (Kimberley Region, Northwestern Australia)

......

SALLY TRELOYN, MATTHEW DEMBAL MARTIN, AND RONA GOONGINDA CHARLES

THIS chapter focuses on the movement and circulation of audiovisual recordings of the public dance-song genre *junba* in Mowanjum, an Aboriginal community in the Kimberley, a region of northwest Australia. In this chapter, we—Treloyn (an ethnomusicologist who has researched *junba* since 1999) and two members of the cultural heritage community, Martin (an elder dancer and singer) and Charles (a cultural consultant and singer)—share narratives and stories that were recorded during the early stages of a project called "Strategies for Sustaining Aboriginal Song and Dance in the Modern World: The Mowanjum and Fitzroy River Valley Communities of Western Australia."[1] As the title suggests, the emphasis of the project was on sustaining song and dance practice, particularly that associated with *junba*. The project was designed as a response to concerns expressed by the elder songman and composer Scotty Nyalgodi Martin† (Matthew Dembal Martin's father) to Treloyn in 2007 that children and young people were increasingly disengaged from the practice of *junba* to the detriment of their social and emotional well-being. At the heart of this concern is the interconnectedness of the practice of *junba*, the health and happiness of people, and the spiritual and cultural health of Country that provides food and life (Treloyn and Martin 2014).[2]

Following a recommendation made in the Garma Statement on Indigenous Music and Dance that repatriation of song recordings to communities of origin should be supported due to the "role [it can play] in the maintenance and protection of tradition" (Garma 2002), and consultation with elders and Indigenous organizations that support the cultural heritage interests of Kimberley peoples (the Mowanjum Art and Culture Centre and the Kimberley Aboriginal Law and Culture Centre), it was determined that the project would involve repatriation of recordings of *junba*. The research aimed to determine the most effective ways of repatriating and disseminating these recordings to support the sustainment of *junba* practices and knowledges. In carrying out the project—known in Mowanjum as "the Junba Project"—we recognized that a research process that supported intergenerational collaboration and knowledge transmission would be a key to achieving this aim. The resultant project involved

- community-led discovery and identification of records of *junba* (including audio, video, and photos) held in the archive of the Australian Institute for Aboriginal and Torres Strait Islander Studies (AIATSIS) and private collections (Treloyn and Charles 2015; Treloyn, Martin, and Charles 2016).
- use of new media tools for discovering, sharing, and producing knowledge about *junba* in collections and the community, such as curating collections for *junba* records for access via digital media libraries and a community-managed digital content management system (Treloyn and Emberly 2013; Treloyn, Charles, and Nulgit 2013), software for digital storytelling projects, CDs, DVDs, and more recently, USBs, Bluetooth, and cloud sharing.
- opportunities to practice *junba* through "on Country" teaching and learning camps and picnics, and engagement and investment by Indigenous organizations within the local and regional community.

We have charted growth in musical and linguistic diversity in the repertory of *junba* performed at the annual Mowanjum Festival between 2010 and 2015, concluding that while many factors inform what and when *junba* dance-songs are performed, these interventions appear to have accompanied, if not supported, the revitalization of *junba* (Treloyn, Charles, and Nulgit 2013; Treloyn and Charles 2015).

During the project we also reflected on the complex intercultural relationships that permeate the work: questions that circle around the involvement of Treloyn (an *almara* "white fella" ethnomusicologist) in the practice, recording, and representation of *junba* beginning in 1999; and contemporary reverberations of colonial acts that have endangered *junba* and its practitioners since the mid-1800s (Treloyn and Charles 2014). Most recently, we have turned to an Indigenous epistemological framework to conceptualize the departure of voices from Country when a recording is moved away to an archive, and their return many decades later when a recording is repatriated (Treloyn, Martin, and Charles 2016).

We have come to understand repatriation as a collection of plural processes that brings personal and political relations (those within the cultural heritage community and those between *almara* researchers and Ngarinyin, Worrorra, and Wunambal singers) from the past into the present.[3] For us, repatriation has generated discourse that allows us to reflect on intercultural relationships within the project team, within the local and regional community in the past and present, and between the cultural heritage community and collecting institutions.

In this chapter, we provide a sample of narratives and dialogues about recordings, processes of repatriation, and their implications that arose in the first few years of the project (to 2014). Our intention is to present readers with a window into our thinking and conversations, and thus create the potential for continued critical discourse that extends to an international audience.

Ambiguous Good(s): An Ethnomusicologist's Story

In 1999 the Ngarinyin Aboriginal Corporation asked ethnomusicologist Linda Barwick to travel from Sydney to the town of Derby, and onward to the small community of Dodnun on Mount Elizabeth Station in the northern Kimberley, to record and document *junba* songs composed and sung by Scotty Nyalgodi Martin†. Barwick, along with Allan Marett, had previously traveled to the Kimberley and met Martin and his singers, conducting research to record and document the songs of the northern Kimberley. I (Treloyn), in my first year of graduate studies at the University of Sydney, had been working to transcribe and analyze recordings that Barwick and Marett had made in Bijili (near Dodnun, Mount Elizabeth Station) and Prap Prap (Drysdale River Station) of performances of several *junba* repertories, including Martin's *jadmi junba* series. I accompanied Barwick on her fieldtrip and then returned to the Kimberley in July 2000 to commence long-term fieldwork to research the *junba* tradition. For two years, I worked with elder Ngarinyin, Worrorra, and Wunambal men and women to record and transcribe known *junba* songs and research their histories and cultural significance. I documented much of this in my doctoral dissertation, which centered on analysis and ethnography of the performance practice and composition of *junba*, and Martin's repertory (Treloyn 2006).

With almost four years elapsing between the time I conducted fieldwork (2000–2002) and the completion of my dissertation, my experience of writing about *junba* was marked by a disjunction, between my lived experience of *junba* and living within its community of practitioners, and the tools of description and language at my disposal. I remained in contact with Martin† and others in the Kimberley, responding to requests for copies of compact cassettes and then CDs, and, in 2008, to Martin's request that I return to help "keep *junba* strong." Having held the internal dissonance between my fieldwork and writing for several years, the prospect of returning and responding to these requests was a great personal and professional opportunity. Following consultations with elders in 2008 and 2009 we commenced the Junba Project.

The project sought to support community-based efforts to keep *junba* strong by harnessing the repatriation, dissemination, and creation of recordings. As noted, the rationale for this approach was based on recommendations made in the Garma Statement on Indigenous Music and Dance, requests for access to recordings from the cultural heritage community, and a handful of reports about the role that repatriated recordings can play in renewal of musical practice in Australia (for example, Marett and Barwick 2003) and elsewhere. I proceeded with the notion that this was a "good" that I might do for both the cultural heritage community and myself. However, I also proceeded with some caution and, through a review of relevant literature, identified a range of concerns that may arise from the reintroduction of records to cultural heritage communities (Treloyn and Emberly 2013). Of particular concern to me were factors that might serve to ossify elements of *junba* practice.

As detailed elsewhere (Treloyn and Martin 2014), singing *junba* is an act of composition, wherein the composer brings together lyrics, melody, and rhythm with the accompanying dance—all associated with the taste and bone of ancestors residing in Country—to stimulate Country and people, making them healthy and happy. *Junba* is core to personal and community identity and social connectedness, and it is considered to maintain both the health of Country and the health of people. According to the ethnomusicologist Catherine Ellis, the power of Central Australian–style singing, of which *junba* is an example, is activated by the "correct interlocking" of musical elements, dance, place, and accompanying ritual/ceremonial action, which she effectively illustrates with interlocking, layered cog-wheels (Ellis 1985, 95). Repertories comprise multiple songs, each with unique, relatively short texts that repeat cyclically and are set isorhythmically (i.e., each repeat has an identical rhythmic setting) throughout each song performance. The length of the song varies according to the progress of accompanying ritual and social activity. Each song in a repertory is set to the same tune, often associated with the taste or scent of the ancestor and Country being celebrated, and this tune expands and contracts to accommodate texts of different lengths. As Ellis explains: "Through correct interlocking the power of the ancestor, being drawn out of the earth by the strength of the song, is present" (Ellis 1985, 109). The composer Scotty Nyalgodi Martin† has described singing as an engine, a "power generator" that "lights up" his community and Country (personal communication, October–November 2011). Hence, as Marett has suggested, musical patterns in Australian song can "make and unmake the world" (Marett 2010, 250).

At the risk of overtheorizing the mechanics of the social efficacy of *junba* musical systems, I was concerned that if a single recording of a single performance of a song were selected and privileged time after time by a listener (due to availability of a single recording or the sound quality of the recording, for example), the variable interlocking of melody and text/rhythm that is intrinsic to the power of the singing may become fixed. Should the listener apply the principles of melodic setting learned from one performance in their setting of other songs in a repertory, the variable interlocking of elements, the expansion and contraction of melody around points-of-fit with rhythmicized text that characterizes the tradition, may be restricted. As one anonymous reader of a funding application indicated, repatriation is not an "unambiguous good." Similar concerns expressed by senior ethnomusicologists in Australia, including Stephen Wild (1992, 13) and Steven Knopoff (2004, 181), ensured that I would come to weave these concerns into the project rather than simply attempt to ignore them.

This being the case however, during the project evidence mounted that such a concern ought not prohibit repatriation. Numerous factors indicated this. First, *junba* musical knowledge is transmitted and acquired implicitly. Knowledge is transmitted and acquired when individual songs are repeated multiple times, each minimally varied, during a performance, over years, and in their correct social, geographical, and spiritual contexts. The collections of recordings repatriated to the cultural heritage community were held in the digital media libraries and burned to CDs in such a way as to accommodate this mode of listening and learning with multiple performances of the same songs included, sung by multiple people, sometimes over several decades. Barwick has outlined how new music technologies have allowed a strengthening of networks and relationships that underpin song performance and production in Wadeye (to the northeast of the Kimberley, in the Northern Territory; Barwick 2017, 170). Second, even if a learner were to prefer just one performance, and this resulted in an ossification of its musical form, simplification of a song form does not necessarily mean that there has been a dissolution of its power. As a study of rhythmic mode in the Wangga-performing community of Wadeye shows, expert singers deliberately reduced the number of complex rhythmic modes used in performances to facilitate maximum participation in dance, and thus enhance personal and group identity (Marett 2007). Third, songs and performances typically are selected on the basis of family connections and Countries of origin, both of which are core to individual and group identity (see also Toner 2003, writing of Yolngu listening). Fourth, as noted, the initial analysis appears to indicate that the repatriation activities conducted in the course of the project may have stimulated a greater musical and linguistic diversity, and larger number of dance-songs in *junba* performance events (Treloyn, Charles, and Nulgit 2013, Treloyn and Charles 2015).

BRING THEM BACK TO COUNTRY: STORIES FROM CULTURE-BEARERS

We begin with a conversation that took place on the evening of June 8, 2011, at a place in Wilinggin (Ngarinyin Country) called Anbada (also known as "Old Station") on the Mount Barnett pastoral lease. Anbada was the site of an historical *bararru* (dance ground) and, looking to the east as the sun goes down in the west, you can see Geyelnggu (Mount Barnett Range) glowing red (see Figure 32.1). We—a group of Ngarinyin from four generations, Treloyn, and visiting ethnomusicologist Andrea Emberly—had gathered for what we called a "*junba* camp" (Figure 32.1). Our intention was to immerse children and young people in *junba*: how to prepare for it, what it means, and how to dance and sing. We held the camp at Anbada, which is aproximately 300 kilometers from Mowanjum and the nearest town of Derby, to ensure that children and young people were free of the distractions, because it is in the heart of Wilinggin, the site of an

FIGURE 32.1 *Yilala* preparing to dance at the Anbada *junba* camp led by Matthew Dembal Martin, June 9, 2011.

Photo by Andrea Emberly.

ancestral *bararru*, and close to the nearby Kupungarri Aboriginal Community where many Ngarinyin live and where many Ngarinyin *yilila* (children) attend school.

The camp, which went for five days, involved a range of daily activities centered on *junba*: clearing the dance ground of grass, constructing the *wurawun* (bough screen) behind which the dancers would prepare, refreshing the paint and weaving on the boards that the dancers carry on their shoulders, harvesting the bark of the paperbark tree (*Melaleuca leucadendra*) to craft *ngardarri* (paperbark headcaps) to be worn by dancers, and collecting *ornmal* (white ochre) for body paint. In the evenings we prepared food, Matthew Dembal Martin and Pansy Nulgit led singing and stories, and we watched video recordings of *junba* performed by Ngarinyin children and recorded by Linda Barwick and Allan Marett at the nearby *bararru* at Bijili (on Mount Elizabeth Station near the Dodnun community) and Prap Prap (also known as Maranbabidingarri, near Drysdale River Station) in 1997 and 1998. The following conversation, recorded as we watched one video (played on Treloyn's laptop, powered from the battery of a motor vehicle) illustrates the nature and pluralism of responses to a recording from the recent past.

>   **Pansy Nulgit (PN):** Where this one *longa*? Where this one *la*? [Where is this performance taking place?][4]

Sally Treloyn (ST): Ah, this one is those Wanalirri boys at Bijili in 1997. . . . They did Nyalgodi's *Jadmi* beforehand.

PN: Ah yeah, I know. . . . That's the boys what bin (that were) dancing. But today nothing, you can't get those pobela [poor fellows] (to dance). (Speaking to children, crowded around the laptop showing the video) Come on we can't see!

Matthew Martin (MM): (Addressing the children watching the video) Get the idea, how they bin learn? This one now (is) Wanalirri (the *junba* dance-song that celebrates the Wanjina named Wanalirri).[5] This mob want to look im (These children need to look at the rock painting of Wanalirri and the dance).

PN: You bella hear im? [Do you boys and girls hear the singers?] Neville (a well-known singer from Derby) singing there.

(A new song commences and singing with a clapstick accompaniment can be heard with the lyrics *gubardwardangu balja gumandangi wurre gowadngerri* . . .)

MM: That's the, what now?

ST: Warm-up song (It is the type of song known as a "warm-up" song, sung while the dancers are preparing to dance)

PN: We never sing that *gubard* (the warm-up song beginning with *gubardwardangu* anymore). *Galanba* (Nulgit states the language term for this type of song—*galanba*)

MM: (Instructing the children who are watching the video what to do when the singers sing this type of song) Stand up one time [Stand still on the dance ground]

Anonymous: (Speaking to child sitting in front of the screen) Move back a bit mummy![6] We want to watch! (pauses) Ah, you right.

PN: (Commending the high quality of the singing) Lucy Ward (a senior, very highly skilled singer), (is) right there! (With sadness in tone of voice) And old girl (a singer who had since passed away).

(M. Martin, Pansy Nulgit, and Sally Treloyn, June 8, 2011, Anbada)

In this conversation, we hear interest from an elder (Nulgit) about the location at which the performance is taking place ("Where this one *longa*?"). In determining this, the watchers glean information about who may be dancing, who may be singing, and what, as the practice and content of *junba* is inseparable from Country. We hear sadness expressed that the participation of young people in *junba* is declining ("That's the boys what bin [that were] dancing. But today nothing, you can't get those pobela"). We become aware that children are enthusiastically crowded around the video that elders are attempting to watch ("Come on we can't see!"). We hear Martin directing children's attention to learn choreography and gestures from the video, to educate them about the Wanjina spirit and Country that is being danced and sung, and about the finer details of performance that they ought to remember ("Get the idea, how they bin learn? This one now [is] Wanalirri. This mob want to look im"). We also hear elders identify singers in the recording, enjoying and exclaiming at their skills.

Martin, tasked with leading *junba* performances and teaching children to sing and dance, had explained to Treloyn how he tells stories and videos to support children to learn how to dance today, in much the same way as children in the past, "the old days," learned from witnessing actual performances "the show":

> [I] tell kids about the DVD. In the old days the old people didn't do that (watch), because there was no DVD. We would see it in the show. We got it from the story (that goes) to the dancing part of it. (The reason is) you got to be told first the story, and when it comes to the show time, you can see it clear—dancing and music playing and when they are singing. That's like the real thing in the dancing and you think back to the story, so you can easily pick it up from there. Especially the young people. Good for the imagination. Just like when you read a book and see it later on.
>
> It (the DVD) makes them think and when it comes to real time (a performance) it comes out clear in their mind now, they can see that thing in the dancing. They think "I hear that song, I can dance it now." And they can hear that song when they (the singers are) singing. When it comes to dancing they know the tune, they know when to stop, when to go. They know how it goes from the spirit.
>
> (Martin in conversation with Treloyn, March 19, 2012, Mowanjum Community)

In the months before the Anbada *junba* camp, Martin explained his motivation for pursuing the return of recordings from archival and private collections to support his teaching/learning efforts:

> We have to get that thing straight. Get it down in computers and, like in CDs, many *junba* (songs and repertories), dancing and singing. That's the special thing for our kids then—our next generation coming up. They got to pick all that (up) like the old people did. They pass it on to generation after generation. Well that's what I'm trying to get now, trying to teach these kids properly you know? Proper way of dancing, proper way of singing, to learn to sing. So if I am not around, well they got a CD there to look at. A picture to see. They can listen to CD, DVD, look at the pictures. That spirit will bring their mind back, and the kids will carry on from there. When they get older, older, older, they'll, sort of, get everything in their mind. Just in case something happens to us. . . . They can have their *junba* but they can (also) have another song, (from) other old people, that (have) all passed away now. They (the old people are) not singing here with us but we have got to keep carrying on how, teaching our children, let them listen. We can show them our dancing, how they dance from old, old songs. . . . DVDs that's the main thing. They can watch the pictures, see the show.
>
> (Martin in conversation with Treloyn, March 15, 2011, Mowanjum Community)

In November 2012, Martin, Charles, and seven other Ngarinyin, Worrorra, and Wunambal ranging in age from twenty-three to seventy visited AIATSIS (a journey of some 5,000 kilometers) with Treloyn, Allan Marett, and a staff member from the Mowanjum Art and Culture Centre, to identify audio and pictorial resources relating to *junba* and organize for their replication and return (Figure 32.2). Charles, speaking with Treloyn at a conference in Melbourne in 2013, recounted her experience:

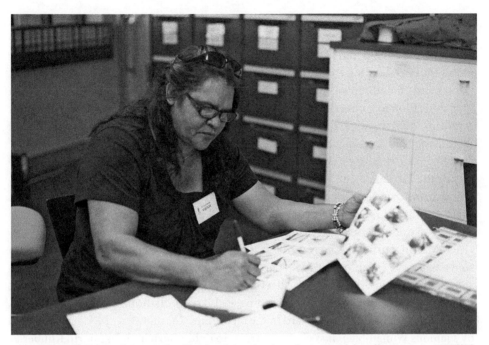

FIGURE 32.2 Rona Goonginda Charles investigating the pictorial collection at AIATSIS, November 29, 2011.

Photo by Katie Breckon.

We went to the archive, Canberra. And I was so amazed. I found lot of the old stuff: a lot of photographs of *junba*, and also my old people (family) that I grew up with and I knew. We were able to go and get copies and bring him back because our Art Centre is establishing an archive. (Because of this) we (are) getting all the archive material from Canberra and maybe Western Australia to put them in our own system in the community.

(Charles in conversation with Treloyn, December 2, 2013, Melbourne; Treloyn and Charles 2015, 196–197)

Reflecting on the trip, Martin explained the cultural and personal significance of the recordings and of the need to bring them to the places—the Country—in which they were recorded.

Matthew Martin (MM): [I]t was good (to) see those old, old things from old people, and the song. [We] pick the song from old, old people. They (the old people) are still there (in the recordings): like the old people are gone but their spirit is still there. What you call that place? (AIATSIS) They (the old people) are still there, they still remain. Can't forget them.
Sally Treloyn (ST): And is that why it is important to bring them back.
MM: . . . (We need to) bring the whole lot back, . . . bring them back to Country.

(Martin in conversation with Treloyn, January 16, 2014, Mowanjum Community; Treloyn and Charles 2015, 197)

Martin explains that the need to move recordings back to Country relates to the presence of spirits—namely, *burrunguma* (the spirits of deceased family members)— singing in recordings and pictured in photos. Key to appreciating the significance of this requires understanding that Country is not simply a geographical place or landscape, it is intrinsic to individual and group identity: people are born from Country, live their lives in relation to Country, and in death return to Country. Spirits of deceased people reside in Country and respond to *junba*. Spirits are emotionally moved by the actions of their living family, and living family is moved by spirits (see Treloyn 2006; Treloyn and Martin 2014). Matthew has previously explained how spirits travel with totems (dance boards used in dance), and with singers and dancers as they travel to perform. Singing and dancing makes spirits, and therefore Country, healthy and happy (Treloyn and Martin 2014). To return copies of recordings and photos to Country and families is to strengthen the bond between living and deceased kin.

For Martin, retrieving the recordings is also a way to recall and, in some cases, learn songs that have fallen out of his repertoire or that, since he was a dancer (and not a singer) for much of his life, he may have never sung before. This is not simply a process of listening to and learning from a recording, it also relies on the presence of spirits ("old, old people") whose voices are heard in the recordings. In August 2012 Martin was asked by a famous Wunambal *junba* dancer to travel to Kalumburu in the far north Kimberley to perform songs that his (the dancer's) deceased father had composed. While Martin was familiar with a handful of the songs, he did not hold enough to maintain an entire danced performance. He requested that we burn CDs of recordings held in the collection at the Mowanjum Art and Culture Centre, made by the teacher Lesley Reilly in 1974 and the ethnomusicologist Raymond Keogh in 1985. From these, he repeatedly listened to and sang along with the recordings, both prior to our departure from Mowanjum and over the long two-day rough road journey to Kalumburu, and he acquired the necessary songs:

> Listening to the songs reminded me of all the old people and it was like they were in me. They were sitting beside me, you know? And I picked them songs up. It was like they was telling me "that way," "sing this song that way." It was like they were telling me which way to sing.
>
> (Martin speaking to Treloyn, January 16, 2014, Mowanjum Community)

Having learned the songs and sung in Kalumburu fulfilling his family duties to perform, Martin also requested that Treloyn prepare multiple CD copies of other repertoires known to have originated in or to be related to family groups who resided there. Once we arrived in Kalumburu, Martin traveled around the community greeting family members, distributing the recordings.

> ST: I remember that we made a little set of CDs with (the songs of) old man
> Wurumalu, Karadada, and Wunanggu (deceased composers with living family

in Kalumburu), all them old man composers, and I remember when we were in Kalumburu you went around handing out those CDs.

MM: Yeah, yeah.

ST: Do you reckon you could say a little bit about why that was important?

MM: That was the family you know, family takes that. You have to give them back the recording, so they can listen to their grandfather, uncle, whatever, father. They listen to the songs. They'll dance, they'll pick it up too. Slowly, some might. If they're wanting to sing the song for themselves. They can pick up the song from their old parents. That's real good that. That's real good, you know, handing it back to the family. . . . It is the Wurnan.

> (Martin speaking to Treloyn, January 16, 2014, Mowanjum Community)

Wurnan sharing binds neighboring and distant groups between clans and individuals of opposite but complementary and interdependent moieties (Redmond 2001). *Junba* repertories are shared and passed from group to group along Wurnan paths. Songs and their associated dances generally move from the people who conceived them and the place where they were conceived, toward the clan and families of the places that are named and depicted in them (Treloyn, Martin, and Charles 2016). The relational sharing ethos of Wurnan also underpins the transmission of songs from generation to generation and continues as groups share their songs with others under the direction of elders and the composer. As Martin explained, this has continued through the transmission of songs and dances via repatriated recordings:

> It's the Wurnan. We have to do it for family. We have to give the families back. We musn't forget about (them), they musn't forget about their family that passed away. They must remember their songs. (When they) see the picture, they will always remember them then. Old people passed away, some of us too young to know. They didn't know (them) but they can look at the picture and the boys when they start singing and they can see how they was, in their days.

> (Martin speaking to Treloyn, January 16, 2014, Mowanjum Community)

Recordings play a role in the continuation of *junba* and Wurnan when children and young people participate in the practice. Just as Ngarinyin have used Wurnan to accommodate incoming settlers and the pastoral industry through the twentieth century (Redmond 2005), similarly Wurnan is used to enfold new technologies in intergenerational song transmission. When children and young people participate, elders and the spirits of deceased family respond by joining them on the dance-ground.

ST: So, anything you want to say about why it's important to bring those old recordings back from Canberra, and how you have been using those old recordings for yourself, to teach kids?

MM: Yeah, well the main thing is learning (teaching) kids, our next generation coming up, before it (the songs and dances) die away you know—(before) the

Culture dies away, the songs, the dancing. . . . [T]o keep it up for them, you know—
keep teaching, learning songs, dancing, get them dance. You seen it.

ST: How do you teach the kids to dance with the old recordings?

MM: Well that's the recording, you go by the words. The meaning you know, the
meaning of the songs and, what it's about—Country or it's about spirits, birds. Just
follow that. Like they copy dancing, how that animal dances. Follow the spirit.
Spirit is always there.

ST: And what does it mean if you have an old recording with old, old people singing
in it and you can hear their voices?

MM: Yeah. It's sort of bringing in to it, you know. Old, old songs, old people, all what
been passed away, like they're bringing the spirit back to you. So you can carry on,
and like you're the teacher for the next generation.

ST: It's like the spirits are helping you do the teaching?

MM: Yeah, it's like the old spirits comes back. You can't see it but you can feel it.

ST: You can feel it.

MM: Yeah, by singing . . . Totems and all those things. Dancing, it brings memories
back too, from the old people. When young people dance, it brings back the
memories of old people. They (the old people that have passed) are teaching them.
It's just like they're happy to dance and you see the young kids running around.
They are willing to dance. The spirit comes back to them.

(Martin speaking to Treloyn, January 16, 2014, Mowanjum Community)

Finally, it is important that we note that in the Kimberley and elsewhere in Australia,
remembrance of family that has passed can bring sadness and sorrow. People may avoid
saying the name of a deceased family member aloud, instead using a kinship term,
and may avoid viewing their image. Nationwide, cultural warnings for Aboriginal and
Torres Strait Islander readers and viewers have become standard whenever there is a
possibility that a person, recorded or pictured, may now be deceased. Aware of this,
Treloyn asked Martin:

ST: And when you hear an old, old recording of old people singing, how does that
make you feel?

MM: Ah, it makes you a bit sad, but you know you feel like getting those old songs
back, so you can have it here from the old people singing to your time.

ST: Why do you feel a bit sad?

MM: (You) feel sad for listening to their voice, the old people's voice. (It) sort of makes
you feel off. But when you start singing it you feel the power coming into you.

ST: Aha.

MM: (It is) like the old spirit coming to you. So you start singing, and you don't
miss a word. You pick those songs up. You listen to it a couple of times maybe,
and you pick it up. (That) thing can't get away from your mind, it stays there. . . .
It comes into your, just like, when a spirit comes into you, you just understand
more, you understand the words. You pick up those words, sing those songs, you
don't forget it. It stays in your brain you don't forget. Like a recording . . . (You) go
by the spirit see—that thing (song) he sings to you. I didn't try it (receiving songs

from spirits in dreams) but I just get songs from the old people what that have passed away. I just get it from listening. . . . Sad, next one you feel happy now. (You) start to sing that old, old songs. . . . You have to explore, carry it out. It's like the spirit comes to you and tells you you are the boss man now. Just like the spirit been leave it up to you now. That *anguma* (spirit of a deceased family member) you know, *anguma*. That *anguma*, you know, he says something to you and tells "carry on."

ST: When you (are) happy for singing a song that you have picked up and that spirit's come and handed it over, do you feel that feeling of *liyan*?

MM: Yeah. That *liyan* make you, sort of, feel happiness come to you more. Start singing the song after the old people come to you. It makes you feel proud. Proud to carry on from the old, old people.

ST: Having those old old recordings in your hands is important.

MM: Yeah that's important yeah, more people to know about the old, old songs.

(Martin speaking to Treloyn, January 16, 2014, Mowanjum Community)

While hearing the voices of deceased family may bring sadness, the presence of spirits and the continuation of the deceased family members songs may bring feelings of happiness, well-being, and connectedness associated with the feeling referred to as *liyan*. In response to a question following a conference presentation in Melbourne in 2013, Charles provided an eloquent example of how *junba* recordings can also support physical and emotional well-being in aged care facilities. Martin's mother, struggling with the transition from her remote community to an aged care facility in Derby, was able to physically move, make eye contact with Charles, rise from her bed, and bathe when Charles played her recordings of *junba* (Treloyn and Charles 2015).

Conclusion

In this chapter we have presented narratives and dialogues to do with repatriating recordings of *junba* to the cultural heritage community in the Kimberley region of northwest Australia. Treloyn outlined her concerns as an *almara* ethnomusicologist as she grapples with the impact that repatriation and her long-term engagement with *junba* practitioners may have on the dance-song practice. We have also provided a sample of narratives and dialogues about recordings, processes of repatriation, and their implications. *Junba* repertories have been shared from group to group across the Kimberley, moving the spirits and Country with which they are laden as they go since time immemorial. In the course of the nineteenth and twentieth centuries this movement of dance and song has enabled Ngarinyin, displaced from their Country, to manage new social and physical environments.

New technologies have provided a further means of moving dance and song: as recordings of *junba* are discovered and replicated from archival collections and transported back to kin and Country; as these recordings are used to support the continuation, teaching, and learning of the practice; as recordings support intergroup efforts to continue Wurnan. Many questions that arise from this technological innovation are yet to be considered. However, in the sample of narratives and dialogues that we have provided in this chapter it can be seen that when songs are moved from archives to communities of origin, children may be moved to dance, and elder singers may be moved to feel happiness and pride.

Notes

1. The research presented in this chapter was supported by the Australian Research Council in partnership with the Mowanjum Art and Culture Centre and Kimberley Aboriginal Law and Culture Centre (LP0990650), and Kimberley Language Resource Centre (LP120200721), as well as the Australian Institute of Aboriginal and Torres Strait Islander Studies. The primary author thanks her coauthors for generously sharing their insights and reflections and patiently reviewing the manuscript. Any errors are the responsibility of the primary author. We also thank the elders and families of Mowanjum, Kupungarri, Dodnun, and Ngallagunda communities. We pay our respects to the members of the Martin family, who recently lost the great composer Scotty Nyalgodi Martin.

2. "Country" is a term commonly used in Aboriginal English and refers to place or places to which individuals and families trace their identity and have hereditary and spiritual ties. The term is capitalized to distinguish it from other uses.

3. Residents of the Mowanjum community identify as Ngarinyin, Worrorra, and Wunambal, three language groups indigenous to the northern Kimberley. The site of Mowanjum community is situated on Nyikina and Warrwa.

4. Treloyn has transcribed the speech of coauthors and others, and has provided written interpretations of these narratives and dialogues. There has been an attempt to preserve the distinctive features of the Aboriginal English employed by the speakers and the "orality" of their discourse (Martin 2003). To assist non-speakers/non-readers of Aboriginal English, Treloyn has minimally normalized transcriptions and provided explanatory notes in parentheses () and translations, glosses, and additional words in brackets [].

5. Wanjina are local ancestral spirits that created the landscape, language, and *junba* in the *lalarn* (Dreamtime). Wanjina spirits are intrinsic to a person's identity, and people are both born from and return to the Wanjina in death. This repertory, composed by the Worrorra composer Watty Ngerdu in the 1950s–1960s, is named after the Ngarinyin "boss" Wanjina spirit and the place known as Wanalirri. The performance was at Bijili—a dance ground site near the community of Dodnun (Mount Elizabeth Station), and the dancers in this video were predominantly from the nearby Ngallagunda Community. The video was recorded by Linda Barwick with Allan Marett in 1997.

6. In Ngarinyin culture, parents and grandparents often address their children and grandchildren by a kinship term, hence here a woman addresses a young child as "mummy."

REFERENCES

Barwick, Linda. 2017. "Keepsakes and Surrogates: Hijacking Music Technology at Wadeye (Northwest Australia)." In *Music, Indigeneity, Digital Media*, edited by Thomas Hilder, Shzr Ee Tan, and Henry Stobart, 156–175. Rochester, NY: University of Rochester Press.

Ellis, Catherine. 1985. *Aboriginal Music: Education for Living—Cross-Cultural Experiences from South Australia*. St. Lucia: University of Queensland Press.

Garma Forum on Indigenous Performance Research. 2002. *Garma Statement on Indigenous Music and Performance*. http://www.garma.telstra.com/2002/statement-music02.htm.

Knopoff, Steven. 2004. "Intrusions and Delusions: Considering the Impact of Recording Technology on the Subject Matter of Ethnomusicological Research." In *Music Research: New Directions for a New Century*, edited by Michael Ewans, Rosalind Halton, and John A. Phillips, 177–186. London: Cambridge Scholars Press.

Marett, Allan. 2007. "Simplifying Musical Practice in Order to Enhance Local Identity: The Case of Rhythmic Modes in the Walakandha Wangga (Wadeye, Northern Territory)." *Australian Aboriginal Studies* 2:63–75.

Marett, Allan. 2010. "Vanishing Songs: How Musical Extinctions Threaten the Planet." *Ethnomusicology Forum* 19 (2):249–262.

Marett, Allan, and Linda Barwick. 2003. "Endangered Songs and Endangered Languages." In *Maintaining the Links: Language Identity and the Land: Seventh Conference of the Foundation for Endangered Languages, Broome, WA*, edited by Joseph Blythe and R. McKenna Brown, 144–151. Bath, UK: Foundation for Endangered Languages.

Martin, Jim R. 2003. "Voicing the 'Other': Reading and Writing Indigenous Australians." In *Critical Discourse Analysis: Theory and Interdisciplinarity*, edited by Gilbert Weiss and Ruth Wodak, 199–222. Hampshire, UK: Palgrave Macmillan.

Redmond, Anthony. 2001. "Rulug Wayirri: Moving Kin and Country in the Northern Kimberley." PhD diss., University of Sydney.

Redmond, Anthony. 2005. "Strange Relatives: Mutualities and Dependencies between Aborigines and Pastoralists in the Northern Kimberley." *Oceania* 75 (3): 234–246.

Toner, Peter. 2003. "History, Memory and Music: The Repatriation of Digital Audio to Yolngu." In *Researchers, Communities, Institutions and Sound Recordings*, edited by Linda Barwick, Allan Marett, Jane Simpson, and Amanda Harris, 2–17. Sydney: University of Sydney Press.

Treloyn, Sally. 2006. "Songs That Pull: Jadmi *Junba* from the Kimberley Region of Northwest Australia." PhD diss., University of Sydney.

Treloyn, Sally, and Andrea Emberly. 2013. "Sustaining Traditions: Ethnomusicological Collections, Access and Sustainability in Australia." *Musicology Australia* 35 (2): 159–177.

Treloyn, Sally, Rona Goonginda Charles, and Sherika Nulgit. 2013. "Repatriation of Song Materials to Support Intergenerational Transmission of Knowledge about Language in the Kimberley Region of Northwest Australia." In *Endangered Languages beyond Boundaries: Proceedings of the 17th Foundation for Endangered Languages Conference*, edited by Mary Jane Norris, Erik Anonby, and Marie-Odile Junker, 18–24. Bath, UK: Foundation for Endangered Languages.

Treloyn, Sally, and Rona Goonginda Charles. 2014. "How Do You Feel about Squeezing Oranges? Reflections and Lessons on Collaboration in Ethnomusicological Research in an Aboriginal Australian Community." In *Collaborative Ethnomusicology: New Approaches* to *Music Research between Indigenous and Non-Indigenous Australians*, edited by Katelyn Barney, 169–186. Melbourne: Lyrebird Press.

Treloyn, Sally, and Rona Goonginda Charles. 2015. "Repatriation and Innovation: The Impact of Archival Recordings on Endangered Dance-Song Traditions and Ethnomusicological Research." In *Research, Records and Responsibility: Ten Years of PARADISEC*, edited by Linda Barwick, Nick Thieberger, and Amanda Harris, 187–205. Sydney: University of Sydney Press.

Treloyn, Sally, and Matthew Dembal Martin. 2014. "Perspectives on Dancing, Singing and Wellbeing from the Kimberley Region of Northwest Australia." *Journal for the Anthropological Study of Human Movement* 21 (1): unpaginated. http://jashm.press.illinois.edu/21.1/treloyn.html.

Treloyn, Sally, Matthew Dembal Martin, and Rona Goonginda Charles. 2016. "Cultural Precedents for the Repatriation of Legacy Song Records to Communities of Origin." *Australian Aboriginal Studies* 2: 94–103.

Wild, Stephen. 1992. "Issues in the Collection, Preservation and Dissemination of Traditional Music." In *Music and Dance of Aboriginal Australia and the South Pacific: The Effects of Documentation on the Living Tradition*, edited by Alice Moyle, 7–15. Sydney: University of Sydney.

CHAPTER 33

....

AFTER THE ARCHIVE

An Archaeology of Bosnian Voices

....

PETER MCMURRAY

THE voices of the dead speak in uncanny ways, preserved by various technologies mediating between past and present.[1] In his posthumous book on oral tradition and the Internet, John Miles Foley describes an experience with a broken link on a multimedia website he had created to explore the oral poetry of Halil Bajgorić, a singer from the town of Stolac, located today in Bosnia-Herzegovina. After describing his media-rich project on Bajgorić's song *The Wedding of Mustajbey's Son Bećirbey*, Foley recounts:

> One day, quite out of the ether, I received an email from a certain Ćamil Bajgorić, who pronounced himself interested in reading [the online poem]. It seems he'd dis-
> covered an online reference to the eEdition while surfing, and was contacting me because the URL wasn't working. . . . Now as a rule, broken links are a dependable source of embarrassment, but in this instance the reported malfunction turned out to be a stroke of good luck. . . . Why? Because Ćamil went on to mention that the guslar (or epic singer) Halil Bajgorić, the performer of the epic he wanted to read and hear, was none other than his own grandfather! He wanted to read and hear the story, of course, but part of his motivation was also, shall we say, genealogical.
>
> (Foley 2012, 141)

Foley uses this exchange to explore the rich parallels between the "pathways" of oral tradition (OT) and information technology (IT): the grandfather in the anecdote, Halil, "himself preliterate, composed his epic without the cognitive prosthesis of the page," while his grandson Ćamil, a "book- and computer-literate resident of Michigan" had in turn "sought to attend that performance via the virtual reality of the Internet" (142). Foley finds it significant that the analog medium of the book, or "the culturally sanctioned vehicle—never figured in the interface between grandfather and grandson" until he mailed a copy to Ćamil (142).

Reading over Foley's shoulder, as it were, we might see other pathways in this anecdote: pathways of the archive, of diaspora, and of temporality. In this chapter, I echo Foley in positioning these issues at the faultlines of digitization—the moment when the analog is rendered almost-immaterial—but I do so not to erase the analog but rather to suggest its perpetual intertwining with the digital. Like Foley, I draw on the history and archives of the Milman Parry Collection of Oral Literature, an archive comprising poems from southeastern Europe and especially the former Yugoslavia that have been inscribed in a number of different ways: as written texts, as sound recordings on various media, and even as photographs. I undertake a sonic archaeology of this archive and particularly what I call its *afterlife*, or the complex web of technologically mediated and in-person encounters it has generated some eighty years after its creation. The ongoing returns, recursions, and repatriations that have marked its history continue today, shaped all the more by the diaspora from Bosnia (and other parts of the former Yugoslavia) since the wars of the 1990s. I focus on two case studies to show, somewhat paradoxically, that precisely *because* global flows of people and media have destabilized traditional geographical ideas of a homeland (i.e., *patria*) and bounded cultural heritage, repatriation becomes ever more vital. In addition, the ongoing flow of people and media associated with this archive similarly destabilizes the archive itself, as well as certain theories of archive—in particular, the otherwise illuminating field of media archaeology. These theories of archives and archaeology have all too often failed to account adequately for questions of power in archival transactions, questions that become increasingly visible (and pressing) in the case of the Milman Parry Collection in light of the transnational flows of archival materials and people between the former Yugoslavia and the United States.

In other words, repatriation calls attention to the uncertain stability of archival projects. This uncertainty pervades not only because repatriation means that objects may continue to move in or out of archives well after those archives have been established, cataloged, and made public; repatriation also unsettles the archive by pointing to the precarity of its formation and the social, political, and technological conditions that produced the archive. As the examples here show, the disintegration of the basic political entities on one end of the Parry collection's production—the former Yugoslavia—makes it difficult to know where the *patria* of repatriation is in the first place: should materials be sent (back) to Serbia or Bosnia? To Texas or some less easily delineated online public? Conversely, repatriation also underscores the cultural stability and political hegemony the United States enjoys, which makes the archive's history after collection rather uneventful by comparison. Repatriation is not only a process of returning archival holdings but also a kind of critique of the entire archival venture. At the same time, the transfer of these holdings in one direction or another (i.e., collecting or repatriating) is a process saturated in technologies whose affordances are also highly contingent. In the case of the Milman Parry Collection, without a custom-made sound recorder (discussed later), these epic songs could not have been recorded in full, a process that produced not just a large repository of recordings but also a kind of imaginary repertoire in the archive that far exceeded any singer's individual repertoire. Similarly, without the specific affordances of the Internet, any act of repatriation would have required choosing partic-ular destinations (again, the question of *which patria*).

Central to my discussion here, then, is the very idea of *archive*: what constitutes an archive, and especially a sound archive? What kinds of power dynamics emerge from it and inflect the knowledge produced from its holdings? And how can the life of an archive be narrated to account for these broader exigencies? Acts of repatriation, while apparently subsequent to the formation and definition of the archive and its scope, will play a critical role in addressing these questions of power and ontology. Drawing on theories of archives and temporality, I suggest here that what comes *after* the archive, especially including acts of repatriation (or decisions not to do so), requires users and curators to rethink what a particular archive is, what it contains, and how those contents interact with the world beyond the archive. Ultimately, I argue that the after-life of an archive demands repatriation, not only as an act of cultural remuneration—a kind of belated payment for the artifacts in question—but also (even for the most self-interested of archives) as a means for self-explication. Precisely *after* the archive, and especially through acts of repatriation, we begin to understand its meaning in the world. In a sense, then, repatriation *precedes* the archive.

While I draw here on several more recent theories of archives and afterness (Derrida 1996, Richter 2011, Ernst 2015), two key publications bookending the 1960s set the tone for addressing these questions in the context of the Milman Parry Collection: Albert Lord's 1960 *The Singer of Tales* (reissued in 2000 with a CD-ROM of audiovisual ar-chival materials) and Michel Foucault's 1969 *L'archéologie du savoir*, or *The Archaeology of Knowledge* (published in English 1972). The former articulates theory about oral utterances based on this particular archive, the latter articulates theory about archives based on general reflections about utterances. In short, Lord was the student of Milman Parry, the archive's namesake, and his book draws on the holdings of the Milman Parry Collection to theorize about the nature of oral poetry. The archive serves as the source material for a broader theory of speech, song, and other discourse. Foucault, in turn, is particularly interested not in making theories out of archival holdings, but in theorizing more broadly what archives themselves do. An archive is not a set of texts or even institutions, but rather "a system of discursivity, in the enunciative possibilities and impossibilities that it lays down" (1972, 129). Archives are sites of cultural power, not only collecting utterances but also creating rules for those utterances. Archival theory since Foucault has followed at least two major directions: one, among historians and anthropologists, observing actual archives and their legacies; the other, among theorists and media scholars, addressing the technological and processual dimensions that set into motion and then perpetuate archives' cultural power.[2] The life history of the Milman Parry Collection and its repatriations bring both those strands together again, showing the particular social, technological, and political contingencies of archive-making and maintenance as well as the possibilities for actively combatting the inertia of archival power through repatriation. Again, this process of repatriation, while appar-ently a geographical gesture, is just as much a temporal and ontological act of rethinking and remaking the archive.

WHEN AND WHERE IS THE ARCHIVE?

The story of the Milman Parry Collection is often told—not incorrectly—as a geograph-ical narrative, marked by a constant flow of people, machines, and recorded media be-tween the United States and the former Yugoslavia. Milman Parry, as is well known, was a scholar of Homeric epic with interests in its genesis and poetics.[3] After completing his doctoral studies at the Sorbonne, he returned to the United States and soon there-after began teaching Classics at Harvard University. In 1933, following up on the urgings of mentors and colleagues at the Sorbonne (particularly the linguist Antoine Meillet and the Slavist/ethnographer Matthias Murko), Parry spent a summer in Yugoslavia, studying a living tradition of epic song. Among the singers he met at that time was Nikola Vujnović, a literate singer who would become his principal assistant in the field. He made arrangements to return for the academic year 1934–1935 (including summers), during which time he recorded thousands of epic and lyric songs with an eye to carrying out a comparative study of how epic singers in Yugoslavia learned and performed their repertoire of songs. Parry died shortly after his return to the United States in December 1935, after which time the massive collection was turned over to his former student and assistant, Albert Lord.

The archive's history becomes more complex yet equally fascinating in its own right as an archival constellation *after* this initial period of recording—of inscription, broadly, since Parry was recording audio but also taking down large numbers of texts by dic-tation or "autograph" (having singers write text themselves), as well as photographing singers and on at least one occasion, filming as well. A web of relations emerged, span-ning the archive at Harvard, American scholars (especially Homerists), and oral poets and scholars in Yugoslavia as well as the surrounding countries. The trans-Atlantic flows of people and media that emerged included some of these notable highlights: re-turn trips by Albert Lord to Albania (1937), Yugoslavia, and especially Macedonia (1950, 1951, accompanied by Miloš Velimirović), and then again repeatedly in the 1960s, with emphasis on Bulgaria (accompanied by David Bynum); the invitation of field assistants and other colleagues from Europe to aid in archival transcription (or reinscription in a different medium), including Parry's assistant, Nikola Vujnović (1937–1938), the Hungarian composer/ethnomusicologist Béla Bartók (beginning in spring 1940), Lord's assistant from the 1950s trips, Miloš Velimirović, who would remain in the United States to pursue a career in musicology; and publications by figures such as Zlatan Čolaković, a prodigious scholar and Fulbright stipendist at Harvard (1984–1988), whose publications in the two decades before his death in 2009 renewed scholarly interest in the archive, es-pecially in the former Yugoslavia (e.g., Čolaković 1992). The flow of media that circulated with and around these people is less well documented, but in many ways represents the central process at work in the narratives that follow.

These movements of individuals overlay on broader movements and cultural shifts: World War II, for example, not only reconfigured much of Yugoslav culture and politics but also necessitated Albert Lord's service in the navy, slowing down his work on the archive; it precipitated Béla Bartók's exile to the United States, where he would die shortly after the war's end in 1945; and it also led to the death of Parry's assistant, Nikola Vujnović, who went missing during the war. The large-scale migrations that have taken place since the wars and political upheaval in the former Yugoslavia, especially in Bosnia (1992–1995), have similarly shifted the terrain from which this collection was recorded. Any attempt to clearly delineate the archive as "here" and the field/recording site as "there" loses coherence quickly.

Going further, however, in the case studies that follow, I suggest that the fundamental question here is one of time rather than place: not *where* is the archive or homeland, but *when*? The art historian Gerhard Richter has argued for the importance of *afterness*, the unique ontological and epistemological status that comes with following something, a state in which the thing-following-after haunts and reshapes the thing itself (2011). What he writes about museums readily applies to archives: "What is a museum [or archive] other than the concretized space in which the after is staged in particular and ever-shifting relations to social, historical, and aesthetics-political force fields of associations, expectations, and imbrications?" (11). Instead, the museum or archive becomes a site not so much of memory but of reading and reconsidering implicit ideas of temporality. Afterness is haunted by but also haunts that which preceded it in an ongoing feedback loop. Jacques Derrida argued that archives are similarly made up not so much by what they contain but by future responses to them, an idea he calls (somewhat opaquely) the "*archivable concept of the archive*" (his italics), which points always already to the future: "It is a question of the future, the question of the future itself, the question of a response, of a promise and of a responsibility for tomorrow. The archive: if we want to know what that will have meant, we will only know in times to come. Perhaps" (36). The archive then becomes something that always precedes us, that entails a future obligation on its users and curators in the (never-ending?) process of its becoming-an-archive. This afterlife of responsibilities encompasses the geographical shifts and contingencies of migrations and other movements, calling for a certain curation, or caring-for-the-soul, of the mediations between disc and voice, between individual and place, between cultures. But in that future obligation also lies the possibility for understanding what the archive had already been. We will only know the archive in times to come—specifically, in times of repatriation.

THE PARRY COLLECTION AS MEDIA: A BRIEF ARCHAEOLOGY

If an archive like the Parry collection entails a particular kind of temporality, such temporality is produced in large degree through an array of technologies that document and affix sung performance. Even before Parry left Yugoslavia in late summer 1935, he was already transcribing material he had. This is clear from the archive itself, in particular through the *pričanje* interviews conducted with epic singers. Parry and Vujnović ask questions about particular words in the poems that had been recorded, suggesting they were likely listening back through them. (Perhaps Parry was taking notes through the course of performance instead of, or in addition to, relistening; Béla Bartók seemed to think that Parry was not doing any transcription, cf. Bartók 1942.) In any case, one of the central challenges that emerged after the return from Yugoslavia in 1935—and one that every archivist knows—is the need for systematic and almost incessant copying, or more precisely transferring, from one medium to another. This transfer took a variety of forms during the early decades of the Parry collection (aluminum disc copied to duplicate aluminum disc, or transcribed to paper notebook or musical manuscript paper; later wire spool copied to tape, or transcribed to various paper formats, etc.) and continues to current efforts to digitize the recordings. Such multimedia inscription and proliferation is, again, an integral part of this archive, but likely part of most archives, especially those involving time-based media that may have a limited shelf-life.

Parry's approach to the question of duplication and inscription in the field was, again, active and multifaceted. He relied on multiple modes of inscribing songs in the field: recording audio, as described thus far; taking down dictations of poems from singers in person (the working method used by previous scholars like the turn-of-the-century collector, Luka Marjanović); collecting dictations at a distance through proxies (Kosta Hörmann's method, and also the method Parry used to gather most women's lyric songs, cf. Vidan 2003); or even having literate singers write their own "autograph manuscripts." This heterogeneous corpus of "texts" or "songs"—neither term adequately covers the entirety of this material—augmented the already heterogeneous documentation from Parry's 1933 trip, for which he used a parlograph, an early dictation machine that recorded to cylinders (Elmer 2013, 342). Adding to this, as mentioned earlier, Parry also took photographs and collected various objects, including a series of picture postcards. While the postcards and many of the photos bear little information about the actual performances in question, some of the photos show singers in what looks like a posed performance, while a few show the actual recording process. (One of these—of Jusuf Smajić, discussed later—is of particular importance to the question of copies and family-mediated sharing.)

The history of the archive that followed has been told most often in conjunction with the articulation and propagation of oral-formulaic theory as described in Albert Lord's *The Singer of Tales* (1960). A broader telling may include Lord's collaborative 1951 publication with Béla Bartók (see Suchoff 2001), as well as the volumes of published poetry in the *Serbo-Croatian Heroic Songs* series beginning shortly thereafter (see Parry and Lord 1954a, 1954b). But if we think archaeologically, other narratives also emerge. My first impulse in writing this chapter was to emphasize that these materials would not have been documented at all without the recording efforts of Parry, Vujnović, and Lord. This is not an archive of looted objects but rather "intangible heritage" that was on the verge of becoming not just intangible but nonexistent.

However, other more interesting archival tales can also be told, including one about the ontology archives and another about the temporality of copying (especially of copying sound). In terms of ontology, the Parry collection is arguably more interesting not because it almost did not exist (i.e., this tradition was dying out, etc.) but because it set out not merely to document but also to create a kind of fictional repertoire. Or rather, a meta-repertoire: the sum repertoire of all singers across all locations (to the degree possible) in the mid-1930s. The archive is an explicitly material instantiation of that imaginary repertoire, which no single singer could have known but might be thought of as an ideal form of "the tradition." In terms of copying and its temporality, however, the archive becomes a massive simulacrum, a series of copies, transfers, and transcriptions, first of sound transcribed on paper or aluminum disc, then later transcribed to paper or typed, then perhaps recorded to reel-to-reel tape for easier access, and then again in the past decade, digitized. The time of these copies is critical: they all began in the sound of performed poetry, making repeatability fraught, if not impossible, even when recorded. (Each playback degrades the recorded medium itself, not to mention the passage of time for any given listener.)[4] The former archive is in the spirit of Lord, a concrete collection of actual objects that determine the possibilities of theory; the latter archive is in the spirit of Foucault or Derrida, an assemblage of inscriptions that stake out the bounds of the utterable within that cultural moment and space. Repatriation would bring these two archival strands together, as copies of these materials would be sent "back" to the former Yugoslavia (but also to Texas, and the virtual nonplace of the Internet), yet that process would ultimately clarify what the concrete objects had been in the first place.

REPATRIATING BOSNIAN VOICES,
I. ONLINE–OFFLINE, TEXAS–HERZEGOVINA

As this brief history has suggested, the timelines of the archive most often do not align with the exigencies of life and history. The examples of repatriation here deal with families of singers or (in my concluding section) scholars who were unable to wait, possibly for many years, to have access to the materials through the archive's website. One example that illustrates the complex temporalities of these media involves the singer Mujo Kukuruzović. One of the "Stolac singers" in the Parry collection, Kukuruzović was in fact from the small town of Gubavica but somehow recorded for Parry in Stolac, a city about fifteen miles away (and farther from Mostar, the cultural capital of Herzegovina). Like Halil Bajgorić, the aforementioned singer who plays such a central role for Foley's work and comes from Stolac, Kukuruzović was a relatively young (Kukuruzović was forty-three when Parry met him, Bajgorić thirty-seven), preliterate farmer. He sang and recorded twelve songs for Parry and apparently left enough of an impression that he recorded on two separate occasions. In more recent years, he has become a figure of increasing stature as scholars—in particular Foley, who was informally given intellectual stewardship by Lord for the Stolac materials in the Parry collection, and the linguist Ronelle Alexander—have devoted more attention to his songs and his speech.

However, interest in the Stolac singers has extended beyond academic circles. In August 2011, Enver Spahalić, a great-great-grandson of Kukuruzović living in Texas, contacted the Parry collection, hoping to find some archival material beyond the limited selections that had already been made available digitally. His great-uncle, Halil, was Mujo's son and was still living in Gubavica. Before long, several relatives were corresponding—by e-mail, a significant note for Derrida (1996, 16–17)—about arrangements to share some of the archival materials with Halil and the wider family. Such requests from scholars are very common, but somewhat less so from families. In this case, my clearest recollection in fulfilling the request was the difficulty of making digital copies of the discs. The analog-to-digital conversion process in a literal sense is straightforward (at least when we, as staff of the Parry Collection, make copies ourselves; not so for the professional-grade transfer done by the university's library). It simply entails playing back an analog recording and capturing the audio on a nearby computer. The trick is the playback itself. As noted, the aluminum discs are often not perfectly playable—many have slight warps, calcium deposits, or poorly cut grooves. Digital transfer becomes a combination of deejaying the disc through various calibrations of the playback apparatus and of audio editing afterward to stitch together the various usable sections of the recording. Two discs, in particular, consumed extraordinary amounts of time, with one of them never properly transferring. And even more troubling archivally, one disc is simply missing—part of a small but significant number of discs that apparently vanished shortly after Lord's death as curatorial succession was being determined.

Two months later, Spahalić and his wife, Selma, traveled to Gubavica. They generously made a smartphone video and sent it to me, a kind of homemade "feedback interview" (Stone and Stone 1981) that highlights the many layers of mediation involved here, but also the irrepressible materiality of sound media, even in a digital age. Like the "Avdo Kino," this video clip runs just about ninety seconds. It comprises two shots, both comfortably domestic and focused on Halil Kukuruzović, Mujo's son and the patriarch of the family. In the first shot, Halil and his wife, Djulsa, sit on a couch, flanked by their sons and grandsons. A laptop lies open on a coffee table, playing back the sounds of Mujo performing *Alija Alagić in Captivity* and serving as a reminder that however immaterial a digital sound file may be, the information it contains must physically displace air to generate sound—in other words, it must materialize in some form, whether via a laptop, CD, or smartphone. Although women are present too—implied by the kiss blown by one of Halil's sons to an invisible niece, and confirmed in later correspondence—the space is in many ways still gendered, enhanced by the return of this highly gendered archive. The family listens intently to the song, with the teenage grandsons even making a good faith effort (though one is clearly more interested in Spahalić while he films). The second shot shows Halil and his wife alone, sitting on a couch at the home of Spahalić's mother (Figure 33.1). Halil addresses the camera to send a message back to the United States:

FIGURE 33.1 Halil Kukuruzović responds to recordings.

Still frame from video by Enver Spahalić.

My good friends, thank you all for providing this material about my father to my nephew. About him, where he was spent his time, and what he was doing. It means a lot to us. Thank you very much!

Ironically, the video file itself (shared via cloud storage) initially would not open and play due to privacy settings, a kind of microcommentary on archival attempts at repatriation and the friction of circulation in general. In corresponding about this complication, we began an exchange about the temporal delays in the whole process, dating back to the formation of the archive itself to our present (sometimes beleaguered) efforts to make these materials available to all. Spahalić wrote astutely: "It is amazing that something that was made 76 years ago can be heard today, no one could believe that anything was saved for all this time and that it can be converted to something that can be played today" (e-mail December 1, 2011). This intertwined (and as described earlier, ongoing) process of saving and converting in order to facilitate contemporary listening is inevitably an experience of deep temporality, as time is produced through sound, then inscribed through sound media, then re-sounded (or resonated) via technical means to be heard again by the ear. Early commentaries on the phonograph pointed to the possibility of hearing the dead; but in a more general sense, people listening to reproduced sound are hearing time, something arguably even less audible than the dead.

As ever, reality flees the archival desire to capture and document. As rich a document as this movie is, the e-mail Spahalić wrote to accompany it is perhaps even more evocative. He responded to my e-mail asking if he had come back yet as follows:

Yes, I came back a couple weeks ago and I was still working on the video for you. The reaction of the family was unbelievable especially after I showed them pictures of Mujo. My great-uncle Halil (Mujo's son) started crying when he saw the pictures. They did not have any pictures of him at all. Now they are already planning to frame these pictures and keep them in the living room on display. I did not want to give them the material until the whole family was there. My great-uncle, three sons and their wives and kids were there. They were sitting and listening amazed for a couple hours, especially the "*Pričanje*" [interview]. . . . I still don't know how to thank you [all] for what you did for us.

(Spahalić e-mail, November 29, 2011)

Expressions of gratitude are meaningful, but I suspect I speak for all curators when I say that the description of Halil Kukuruzović's reaction (not to mention the video Spahalić made) to seeing photos and hearing recordings of his father is even more rewarding.

Several themes emerge from these interactions: the affective power of media; the relative impact of photography, recorded performance, and recorded speech; configurations of family; and even the performative act of bringing back recordings, as Spahalić took the initiative to create a small-scale ritual here with the gathering of family, the presentation of media-as-gift, documentation (both as a kind of historical evidence and gift in return), and so forth. For a variety of reasons, such ritualization becomes an important part of many of these exchanges. I would highlight two ideas that emerge here that have relevance for a broader understanding of an archive. First, an archive, like all documentary projects, is always already failing to capture a total reality. Few archives would claim that they do so, and their fragmentary qualities are in many ways one of their essential characteristics. In this case, Spahalić was unable to, or chose not to, make a video of the family's reaction to the photograph, which in many ways was both more intense and more intimate. We are left with a trace of a trace, a retrospective description of an observation of the reactions of others. Second, time is always passing. He notes that he had been home a couple of weeks, that the family is *planning* (i.e., in the future) to frame pictures, that he waited until the whole family was present, and that they sat listening for hours. Again, time is always passing. However, much as it has been noted that music organizes time, so too does the archive, even more so when the archive consists of such an abundance of time-based media. Foucault's textual archive imposes certain constraints on the potential to make certain statements; here Parry's sonic archive imposes constraints and boundaries on certain experiences of temporality.

The toggling between offline and online media, between analog and digital experience, between absence and presence, culminated the following May, when I had the privilege to travel to Gubavica to meet not only the Kukuruzović family but also the Spahalićs, whom I had never personally met, despite our ongoing correspondence. I traveled from Sarajevo with Mirsad Kukuruzović, a grandson of Mujo's who had been informally researching this material for years, reading Lord, Foley, and others' commentaries on these so-called Stolac singers. I was accompanied as well by Ronelle Alexander, mentioned earlier, as well as the Tuzla-based scholar Mirsad Kunić, whose research and recent book (2012) fittingly focuses on memory and forgetting in Bosnian epic. We mostly came empty-handed but we were present and had an intriguing conversation about Mujo Kukuruzović, poetry traditions in the area, and the family.

Halil and his family revealed a smattering of new information through our conversation: There was a *kafana* just down the street where Mujo and others would perform; he did not make his living from singing but did earn money regularly and was invited to travel as far as Sarajevo and Montenegro; and he was in demand enough that even Christians would invite him to perform at their weddings, asking him simply to "adapt" the songs a little (*"samo prilagodi pjesme malo"*). However, most interesting to me was to hear about the family's listening process. They did not know that the recordings we sent were made in nearby Stolac. Faint environmental sounds can be heard (birds, other voices), and some family members were certain they heard someone call out "Babo" (Grandpa) in the recording, as though it had been done just in front of their home. We had trouble locating this moment in the recording when we listened together, but it raises a question of how archival material should—or could—be listened to. Who is the ideal archival listener? Is there one? Who has expertise about such materials? Since the advent of audio recording and the cultural transformation of psychoanalysis, listening has changed, Barthes argues. Today listening entails "the power (and virtually the function) of playing over unknown spaces," including the unconscious, the supplementary, and the delayed (1985, 258). Barthes goes on to suggest that listening is no longer about particular signifiers and the recognition of those signifiers, but rather a dispersion or "*shimmering* of signifiers," which, when listened to, "ceaselessly produces new ones from them without ever arresting their meaning" (259). The productively imaginative listening by the Kukuruzović family resonates with the kind of dispersal—in this case, geographical, temporal, and psychoacoustical—of signifying that Barthes is exploring. Listening with Halil and his family suggests the rich play of time that emerges from the archive as it is reopened and redispersed.

REPATRIATING BOSNIAN VOICES, II. FAMILY PHOTOS AND SONIC ABSENCE

A year later, I received an e-mail from Indira Jusić, an acquaintance of Enver Spahalić's from Texas. She wrote, "Yesterday was one of the most exciting days of my life, since I found out that you have recordings of my great-grandfather in your collection." Indeed, her great-grandfather, Jusuf Smajić, had fascinated me for several years because of a series of photographs in the Parry collection showing him recording for Parry in September 1934 while sitting in a field near the town of Glamoč, also in present-day Bosnia-Herzegovina. I had seen the pictures countless times because they are some of the few that show Parry's recording apparatus, which no longer exists (at least in the holdings of the Parry collection). In a much darker photo from the same session, Smajić is seen close up, but holding his cane in his lap. After years of seeing the picture, I finally realized that he was using it instead of a *gusle* or a *tambura*, as though he were accompanying himself with it. Jusić and I had a lengthy e-mail correspondence about this absent instrument and the way her father, a skilled singer and multi-instrumentalist, would pick and strum his cane as though it were a lute or other musical instrument.

Her e-mails add so much depth to the biography of this singer, as well as the process of digital transfer and cultural return/repatriation of archival materials, that it is useful to reproduce large excerpts of our correspondence here:

E-mail from Indira Jusić (December 19, 2012)
Yesterday was one of the most exciting days in my life since I found out that you have recordings of my great grandfather in your collection. His name was Jusuf Smajić. I live in Texas, and got your e-mail from Enver Spahalić. I lived with my grandmother and she told me many, many times that her father was a well-known man and was "recorded on a radio before World War II." She was a little girl at the time and obviously did not know what exactly was going on. We came to US in 1996 and she passed away here in 2003. I wish she knew that those recordings were here in USA.

E-mail from Peter McMurray (December 19, 2012)
Thanks so much for your e-mail! It's been a pleasure to get to know Enver and his family—I was fortunate enough to meet some of his relatives in Herzegovina this spring, which was a wonderful experience. Please send him my best regards.

I'm curious how you met Enver? And do you have family still living in the former Yugoslavia? It really is a pity that your grandmother passed away before we connected, but I must say that for the past couple years I've grown particularly interested in the recordings your great-grandfather made for Milman Parry. We have some photographs of him that look like he was using a cane instead of proper *gusle* when he made the recording [see Figure 33.2].

E-mail from Indira Jusić (December 19, 2012)
Thank you so much, I am so overwhelmed at this moment, if I could I would jump through this computer and hug you! I am sorry, it might not be the proper thing to say, but I just want to kiss your hand out of excitement, respect and appreciation. I will write to you soon into more details, I just need to put myself together.

E-mail from Indira Jusić (December 19, 2012)
I have known Enver for many years because we both live in DFW [Dallas-Fort Worth]. I see him once in a while, but we never get to talk that much, maybe that is why I did not know about his great-grandfather's recordings. I saw a video on Facebook that mutual friend put online that was talking about Avdo Medjedović, in which they said that Milman Parry was sent from France to Western Bosnia (where Glamoć is), and from there to Sandžak. My grandmother told me many times how her father "got recorded on radio." Also on a video was a picture of man being recorded. That is when I realized that this is it and I searched Jusuf Smajić and Harvard and that is how I found out. I called this mutual friend that put the video on Facebook and he told me that Enver is in touch with you since his great-grandfather was recorded too.

FIGURE 33.2 Jusuf Smajić with cane, recording for Milman Parry, September 1934.

MPC 0054. Milman Parry Collection, Harvard University.

My mother lives here in Arlington too, and she remembers my great-grandfather. She was in her teenage years when he died. My mother did not live with him, but spend most school breaks with him. My grandmother never referred to her father as being a "guslar," which would be someone using *gusle*. She always told me that he sang "junačke pjesme" [heroic songs]. He used a cane because he had a leg injury and as a consequence he was left with a limp. My mother remembers him using a cane to perform. She said the he referred to it as "keva" not as "stap," which is what they call it nowadays. She remembers after dinner he would tell them, "Kids give me my *keva* and I will sing for you." She also remembers that *keva* had about 3 cracks (but she does not know if my great-grandfather carved them himself) and that he would keep something white in his pocket that he would get out to use on his cane that would serve him almost like guitar pick. (She does not remember any wires on the cane, but the cracks themselves would make sound.) She also remembers he had multiple instruments at home, things like "shargije," "frula," and "gajde" (bagpipe) that he would use to perform.

Here in Dallas–Fort Worth we have a distant cousin that remembers him. There also other grandchildren in Glamoč, Bosnia, and scattered through Europe. I was very close to my grandmother, and her family always amazed me, since even those that were not very educated were very intelligent people. She was a great storyteller of their past and ever since I had my daughter I have felt that I should write these stories down.

I would love to have any recording that you can share with me. I have been to Boston twice, even my grandmother was there once, but we never knew.

E-mail from Peter McMurray (December 20, 2012)
This is really quite amazing to hear. Your great-grandfather sounds like quite the man! And these details about the cane are extremely interesting. There is a whole corpus of stories that I've heard informally about singers who perform without formal instruments—some who rub sticks against one another (more like *gusle*) or who pace the room, and now this with the cane. Another question that interested Parry and Lord (and me, in different ways) is the overlap between the tradition of singing narrative songs (like *junačke pjesme*) and of other traditions. Parry and Lord recorded a lot of singers who sang shorter lyric songs (especially so-called "*ženske pjesme*") but I've often wondered about instrumental music too. So this is fascinating to hear that your great-grandfather was a multi-instrumentalist.

E-mail from Indira Jusić (December 21, 2012)
It is very possible that he used cane as silent *gusle* too with his "*junačke pjesme*," since most of the time he performed for my mom he sang fast, happy songs so she could dance. She also said all the instruments were handmade. My grandmother also told me he would perform *ilahije* and *kaside* too with a group of girls from village when they had a drought. He also sang *mevlud*, since he took on the role of imam in the village after WWII.

My mom was born in 1949, so she remembers him 20 years or more after his recordings. During WWII he moved to a big city for 5–6 years, and probably was influenced by some things there, too. Enver refers to his grandfather as a *guslar*. I never heard anyone ever say anything like that for my great-grandfather, or even mentioned *gusle*, they always said that he sang or he knew "*junačke pjesme*."

I am very curious to find out about this too. I will ask some older members of our family and let you know if they remember anything about cane.

E-mail from Peter McMurray (May 18, 2013)
I've just transferred the three items we have from aluminum disc to digital soundfile. I could send those to you as a CD or just put them online and you could download them and burn them yourself. What do you prefer?

E-mail from Indira Jusić (December 27, 2013)
I went to Bosnia and gave the CDs to my cousins that are still there. They were super excited, and were wondering about the place where it was recorded and about interpreter that is in pictures, etc. Jusuf's granddaughter, who is now in her 70s (the one that he raised and that still lives in Glamoč), is constantly listening to the CDs, and whoever does not like them or does not want to listen to them is nothing less than enemy to her, hehe. Her daughter is visiting us right now, so she told me that story yesterday. . . . [I]f you need any more information I can ask my cousin that is visiting here, since she remembers Jusuf from when he was alive, or her mother back in Glamoč.

A few days later, Indira wrote again with a four-page narrative of Smajić's life, including more details about the difficulties of wartime: World War II for Smajić, and the Bosnian War (1992–1995) for her. Both were war refugees, though Smajić had ultimately been able to move back into his home. Like Enver Spahalić conducting feedback interviews, Indira also took on the role of ethnographer, gathering family history stories from other relatives who were no longer in Bosnia:

E-mailed document from Indira Jusić (January 7, 2014)
There is a distant cousin that lives here in Fort Worth and remembers Jusuf in this post war time [after he moved back to his home after World War II]. I gave him the recordings that you sent me, too. He said that Jusuf would ride on a horse 20 kilometers to his village to come see his father, and then he would perform songs for many people that would gather. He said there would be at least 20 of them listening, and his mother would prepare a pitcher of lemonade and put it in front of Jusuf. He remembers the excitement of those nights. Jusuf became his role model and he said that he would be sad when Jusuf would not come, but since he had memorized some parts of those songs, he would imitate Jusuf [in his place].

Even edited down to this form, this e-mail exchange—in particular the commentaries by Indira Jusić—offers a wide range of material to comment on, from questions of musical instruments in traditional life, village religious life, and the impact of World War II to the potential roles of Facebook in ethnography, the materiality of digital sound recording, multigenerational storytelling, and the mediation of memory. I focus on two aspects briefly: first, the question of archival absences; and second, the ways offline, face-to-face interventions constrain and inflect various forms of digital transfer.

In reflecting on the question of absence, I find that much of the energy in this whole exchange comes from that which is missing: for Indira Jusić, the archive in its entirety as well as memory of her great-grandfather, whom she never met; for me, the missing instrument in a photograph. As so often, one listens (and looks) in the archive for the absent; listening to the recording of Smajić (which I had previously done), one hears *only* the voice. In photographs, it starts to become apparent that something more was happening. But only with the additional biographical information from family is this speculation—that Smajić was *not* a *guslar* but nevertheless an epic singer— confirmed. The absence becomes productive in raising questions, which then prompt other questions (as raised by Jusić and her family): Where was this recording session held? Who else was present? Her speculation, "I will probably never find out," points precisely to the impossible futurity and promise of the archive suggested by Derrida. Indeed, this entire exchange required the passage of time. Had she sought these recordings a few years earlier, I probably would have sent all the same materials but without any questions about the use of the cane-as-instrument. Perhaps this is not the greatest revelation—nothing on the magnitude of Parry's and Lord's theorizing about the origins of Homer—and yet we have learned something that exceeded the initial grasp of the archive, which reminds us of its contingency as well as its thinness (in opposition to a potential "thick" description). In many ways, the collection of interviews in the archive is a treasure trove of ethnographic detail; in other ways, its fixations on singers' experience primarily as bards elides so many other facets of culture. Anthony

Seeger's suggestion (1986) that our archives may be of greater value than our academic theories certainly applies here, not least for its call to repatriate when we can and to plan for unforeseeable future opportunities to repatriate. But this claim to archival primacy fails to acknowledge just how much our archives are in so many ways already a product of our theories—of the things we seek in research—that the two can never be fully disentangled.

In addition to this question of absence is that of presence—specifically human presence, the physical, fleshy encounters that bring an archive, even one that has been (or is being) made digital, into a fully material realm, with all its messiness and resistance to copying. In this exchange, the entire transfer of information and media took place digitally. And yet, it still required considerable physical activity for Jusić to burn CDs, take them to Bosnia, share them with relatives, discuss them, then return to the United States and write to me. And while digital transfer cannot compare with such efforts, it does entail its own (uniquely frustrating) forms of labor to render digital audio from an aluminum disc.[5] The physicality of these interactions is perhaps more pronounced with the earlier instance of return, in which the return was mediated in multiple ways (creating media, sharing it, then having the family make their own media in response), yet Jusić's enthusiastic response that she would like to "jump through the computer" to express her excitement shows the kinds of affective registers that exceed the digital. Paradoxically, where digital communication fails in its communicative capacity, she turns to traditional gestures of respect and affection—kissing the hand—to articulate her sense of this encounter.

More broadly, the encounter with Jusić and the Smajić family via the Spahilić family suggests that the archive is not merely situated in this ecology of interpersonal, on- and offline connections; it forges them. Without an archive—and especially an online one—I would likely never have met Enver Spahalić and the Kukuruzović family or Indira Jusić and the Smajić family. The particular mix of digital interactions was likewise contingent on Spahalić and Jusić knowing one another from face-to-face encounters in Texas. Such encounters are not simply serendipitous; they depend on a broad range of factors tied to (forced) migration and global politics. This confluence of on- and offline encounters *changes* the archive significantly. Had we never been in touch, the Parry collection would have remained, for all intents and purposes, just as complete an archive. The archive was already in its afterlife, so to speak. Indeed, our encounters, however interesting they may be, have not generated new songs—the ostensible focus of the Parry collection's holdings. Yet these encounters have created a kind of "supplement" (to return to Barthes) that facilitates a new mode of listening. To put it another way, our interactions create no new data but offer important new access to metadata about the archive, the poetic traditions it contains, and their contemporary reception. This metadata could not be recovered from some original source recording; it had to be created anew through ethnography. This slow revelation of the archive's contents is in many ways a temporal gesture—the aging of the archive and its repositioning in a new time and place, where migration, international travel, and digital circulation are ever more present.

ACADEMIC AFTERWORD:
FROM ARCHAEOLOGY TO GENEALOGY

The foregoing narrative is rather affirmative; it is archive-positive, so to speak. Archives preserved a repertoire, and that repertoire has since made a positive impact in a few lives. But lurking beneath this glossy surface are weighty questions of politics and power that could be traced in other directions: personal, institutional, academic, and certainly political. In the mid-1990s, Enes Kujundžić, the director of the National Library and Archive, met with the curators of the Milman Parry Collection. They briefly discussed the possibility of creating a copy of the archive to help replenish the Sarajevo national library, which had been destroyed by shelling along with numerous other sites of cultural heritage. These conversations helped nudge the archive to join forces with Harvard's fledgling Library Digital Initiative in 2002, thus leading to the digitization and online existence of these recordings. The project, and even the prospect of sending a copy back to Sarajevo, raises all kinds of intriguing (and vexing) questions. Where should such an archive reside? What are the prospects and limitations of digital copies? What kinds of institutional arrangements best serve the materials in the archive itself, and do those same arrangements best serve the people who created those materials in the first place? And where do families, friends, communities, and larger polities fit into such a discussion?

The answers to these questions are complex, but it seems that the afterlife of an archive and the afterlife of the places and people involved in it are perpetually intertwined. These two case studies exemplify not only the realities of those intertwinings but also the fruits that can come from them. In short, it has proven to be good *for the archive* to be returned, in some form. The archive itself is richer for these encounters. Both Enver Spahalić and Indira Jusić and their families are refugees from the Bosnian War that came with the dissolution of the former Yugoslavia. Their stories are compelling in their own right—and deserve a telling in another forum. But whatever else may be said, they have transformed the archive by reaching out and connecting with the staff, the recordings, the photographs and other holdings, and even indirectly with the physical space, which now is richer (and fuller) with the inclusion of printouts of their correspondence, request forms, and stored copies of the media they have sent back to us.

On a different level, Spahalić, Jusić, and their families have also transformed what the archive can mean. They have transformed the possibilities of theory, to borrow from Foucault once more, from an archaeological approach to a genealogical one. This genealogical existence is both figurative, as Foucault himself (somewhat ambiguously) posited (1977), leaving space for politics and perhaps some individual agency, and also emphatically literal: this genealogy consists of generations of people scattered across new homelands, connecting to their familial past through aluminum discs, reinscribed into digital sound and carried back to Bosnia. An archive cannot retrieve or re-create a homeland, or *patria*, to return to, and the very existence of the Parry collection attests to the nascent possibilities of a multicultural Yugoslavia, while its holdings simultaneously point to its eventual disintegration. But through these returns—these post-patriations, in a sense—the archive can perhaps invigorate individuals' and communities' connections to those pasts and places, however mythical they may have become.

On a personal concluding note, these interactions are gratifying and yet inevitably disappointing. In my undergraduate thesis about meeting other families of other epic singers involved in the Parry collection and bringing them recordings, I noted that the Milman Parry Collection was regrettably inaccessible, especially for those with direct family connections to the archive. In the ensuing years, I worked for more than a decade as a curator in the archive, which has only heightened that sense. While hundreds of recordings have been put online, they represent only a fraction of the materials in the archive. And most people old enough to remember these traditions firsthand are not likely to be browsing around online. If archives and their repatriations are *temporal* processes, it bears remembering that they are also temporal *processes*. That is, repatriation, like the making of an archive, takes time. Such a sentiment sounds defeatist and perhaps self-rationalizing. With each passing year, I realize I am only beginning to sense the time of the archive. And yet perhaps, inadvertently, that temporality also grants some small access to the time of the poetry tradition that gave rise to it, itself the product of sonic processes spanning centuries. In any case, the Milman Parry Collection is a better, more complete archive because of these repatriating gestures, however incomplete they remain.

Notes

1. I thank the members of the Critical Archives Workshop at Harvard's MetaLAB in spring 2014 (Michael Heller, Matthew Battles, Brigid Cohen, Hannah Marcus, Stephanie Frampton, and Ryo Morimoto) for their incisive, collegial thinking about archives and the consequences of the archival turn.
2. For the historical/anthropological thread, see Farge (2013; originally published in 1989 and a key work in the "archival turn"), Steedman (2001), Burton (2003, 2006), Spieker (2008), Stoler (2009), Weld (2014), and Heller (2016). Many of these works also respond to Derrida's *Archive Fever* (1996). My own essay on the sensory capacities of the Parry collection (McMurray 2015) also engages these issues anthropologically. For the media theory thread, see Kittler (1990 [1985]), Huhtamo and Parikka (2011), Parikka (2012), and Ernst (2016), one of several places where Wolfgang Ernst writes about the Milman Parry Collection.
3. For further details on Parry's research and the resulting archival materials, see Lord (2000), Mitchell and Nagy (2000), and Elmer (2013).
4. The temporality of sound and music is a regular point of inquiry for music studies, from Zuckerkandl's discussions in *Sound and Symbol* (1956, 151–256) to Georgina Born's recent work on music as process in "Making Time: Temporality, History, and the Cultural Object" (2015).
5. Kirschenbaum (2007) highlights some of the unseen (or unacknowledged) materialities and costs of digital media and their upkeep.

References

Barthes, Roland. 1985. "Listening." In *The Responsibility of Forms*, translated by Richard Howard, 245–260. New York: Hill and Wang.

Bartók, Béla. 1942. "Parry Collection of Yugoslav Folk Music: Eminent Composer, Who Is Working on It, Discusses Its Significance." *New York Times*, June 28, 1942.

Born, Georgina. 2015. "Making Time: Temporality, History, and the Cultural Object." *New Literary History* 46 (3): 361–386.

Burton, Antoinette. 2003. *Dwelling in the Archive: Women Writing House, Home, and History in Colonial India*. Oxford: Oxford University Press.

Burton, Antoinette, ed. 2006. *Archive Stories: Facts, Fictions, and the Writing of History*. Durham, NC: Duke University Press.

Čolaković, Zlatan. 1992. "South Slavic Muslim Epic Songs: Problems of Collecting, Editing, and Publishing." *California Slavic Studies* 14: 232–269.

Derrida, Jacques. 1994. *Specters of Marx: The State of the Debt, the Work of Mourning, and the New International*. Translated by Peggy Kamuf. New York: Routledge.

Derrida, Jacques. 1996. *Archive Fever: A Freudian Impression*. Translated by Eric Prenowitz. Chicago: University of Chicago Press.

Elmer, David. 2013. "The Milman Parry Collection of Oral Poetry." *Oral Tradition* 28 (2): 341–354.

Ernst, Wolfgang. 2015 [2002]. *Stirrings in the Archives: Order from Disorder*. Lanham, MD: Rowman and Littlefield.

Ernst, Wolfgang. 2016. *Sonic Time Machines: Explicit Sound, Sirenic Voices, and Implicit Sonicity*. Amsterdam: University of Amsterdam Press.

Farge, Annette. 2013. *The Allure of the Archives*. Translated by Thomas Scott-Railton. New Haven, CT: Yale University Press.

Foley, John. 2012. *Oral Tradition and the Internet: Pathways of the Mind*. Urbana: University of Illinois Press.

Foucault, Michel. 1972 [1969]. *The Archaeology of Knowledge*. Translated by Alan Sheridan. New York: Pantheon Books.

Foucault, Michel. 1977. "Nietzsche, Genealogy, History." In *Language, Counter-Memory, Practice: Selected Essays and Interviews*, translated by Donald F. Bouchard and Sherry Simon, 139–164. Ithaca, NY: Cornell University Press.

Heller, Michael. 2016. *Loft Jazz: Improvising New York in the 1970s*. Berkeley: University of California Press.

Huhtamo, Erkki, and Jussi Parikka, eds. 2011. *Media Archaeology: Approaches, Applications, and Implications*. Berkeley: University of California Press.

Kirschenbaum, Matthew. 2007. *Mechanisms: New Media and the Forensic Imagination*. Cambridge, MA: MIT Press.

Kittler, Friedrich. 1990 [1985]. *Discourse Networks 1800/1900*. Translated by Michael Metteer with Chris Cullens. Stanford, CA: Stanford University Press.

Kunić, Mirsad. 2012. *Usmeno Pamćenje i Zaborav: Krajiška Epika i Njeni Junaci*. Tešanj, Bosnia: Centar za kulturu i obrazovanje.

Lord, Albert B. 2000 [1960]. *The Singer of Tales*. 2nd ed. Edited by Stephen Mitchell and Gregory Nagy. Cambridge, MA: Harvard University Press.

McMurray, Peter. 2015. "Archival Excess: Sensational Histories beyond the Audiovisual." *Fontes Artis Musicae* 62 (3): 262–275.

Mitchell, Stephen, and Gregory Nagy. 2000. "Introduction." In Albert B. Lord, *The Singer of Tales*, 2nd ed., edited by Stephen Mitchell and Gregory Nagy, vii–xxix. Cambridge, MA: Harvard University Press.

Parikka, Jussi. 2012. *What Is Media Archaeology?* Cambridge: Polity Press.

Parry, Milman, and Albert B. Lord. 1954a. *Serbo-Croatian Heroic Songs*. Vol. 1: *Novi Pazar, English Translations*. Cambridge, MA: Harvard University Press.

Parry, Milman, and Albert B. Lord. 1954b. *Serbo-Croatian Heroic Songs*. Vol. 2: *Novi Pazar, Serbocroatian Texts*. Cambridge, MA: Harvard University Press.

Richter, Gerhard. 2011. *Afterness: Figures of Following in Modern Thought and Aesthetics*. New York: Columbia University Press.

Seeger, Anthony. 1986. "The Role of Sound Archives in Ethnomusicology Today." *Ethnomusicology* 30 (2): 261–276.

Spieker, Sven. 2008. *The Big Archive: Art from Bureaucracy*. Cambridge, MA: MIT Press.

Steedman, Carolyn. 2001. *Dust: The Archive and Cultural History*. Manchester, UK: Manchester University Press.

Stoler, Ann Laura. 2009. *Along the Archival Grain: Epistemic Anxieties and Colonial Common Sense*. Princeton, NJ: Princeton University Press.

Stone, Ruth, and Vernon L. Stone. 1981. "Event, Feedback, and Analysis: Research Media in the Study of Music Events." *Ethnomusicology* 25 (2): 215–225.

Suchoff, Benjamin. 2001. *Béla Bartók: Life and Work*. Lanham, MD: Scarecrow Press.

Vidan, Aida. 2003. *Embroidered with Gold, Strung with Pearls: The Traditional Ballads of Bosnian Women*. Cambridge, MA: Milman Parry Collection of Oral Literature.

Weld, Kirsten. 2014. *Paper Cadavers: The Archives of Dictatorship in Guatemala*. Durham, NC: Duke University Press.

Zuckerkandl, Victor. 1956. "Time." In *Sound and Symbol: Music and the External World*, translated by Willard Trask, 151–266. Princeton, NJ: Princeton University Press.

....

CHAPTER 34

RECLAIMING OWNERSHIP OF THE INDIGENOUS VOICE

The Hopi Music Repatriation Project

....

TREVOR REED

INTRODUCTION

....

FAR from the rugged climate of the remote, high-desert Hopi villages in northeastern Arizona, where I do my repatriation work, I had the chance to interview a prominent scholar-archivist in her elegantly furnished, temperature- and humidity-controlled office situated among the university's carefully guarded special collections. I was just beginning an effort to reclaim a collection of Hopi ceremonial song recordings from Columbia University on behalf of my people, but was still feeling unsettled about how to do the project. Hoping to draw from her decades of experience, I asked the archivist about her approach to working with tribes to repatriate culturally affiliated materials. Knowing, as we both did, that Native American tribal governments rarely have the resources, financial or political, to make repatriating archived materials a priority, I was interested to know whether she ever conducted repatriation work at the grass-roots level, placing Indigenous archival materials directly into the hands of tribal members.[1] I was surprised by her response. Balking at my question, she explained that while repatriation was clearly an important part of contemporary archival practice after the passage of the Native American Graves Protection and Repatriation Act (NAGPRA) in 1990, "We do our best to stay out of community politics. . . . We will go and participate in a community conversation, but we don't lead it because that wouldn't be appropriate, and not terribly bright . . . we're talking about a sovereign nation. We have to respect whatever rules are in place there."

Those of us who do work on tribal lands are all too familiar with the tragic history of research conducted on Indigenous peoples (Tuhiwai-Smith 1999; Smith 2005), and the resulting expansion of tribal and federal laws put in place to protect tribal members from further exploitation.[2] Indeed, there is a sense of general unease among archivists over the topic of Native American archival materials, as they collectively not only represent research paradigms that have fallen out of favor but also give a vivid picture of the social sciences' colonialist past with all of that past's current political (and potentially legal) liabilities (Brady 1999; Sterne 2003; First Archivists Circle 2007; Coombe 2009; Ishii 2010). Efforts to repatriate archival materials generated from past research on Native Americans have often been framed as social justice, placing illegitimately or unfairly taken property back into the hands of present-day community members.[3]

In this chapter, I reconsider the concept of repatriation and its deployment as a reconciliatory property transaction between sovereigns. Certainly, some Indigenous peoples have no difficulty treating their ancestors' songs and ceremonies as property, fully transferable to a modern, federally recognized government. And yet, others might question the very logics underlying such transactions. They might wonder why current repatriation practice relies so heavily on logics of exclusion and difference to effectuate a reclamation and reincorporation of Indigenous materials from institutional archives. They might point out that treating voices of one's ancestors as "property"—a bundle of exclusive rights first defined under the philosophies of Enlightenment Europe[4]—potentially limits the possibilities of what repatriation can accomplish for Indigenous peoples and, at worst, may cause substantial harm to them.[5] In this chapter I ask, is repatriation best conceived through an appeal to property principles, or are there other principles of ownership and circulation on which repatriation might be more effectively based? And, if Indigenous principles should be the basis for the ownership and circulation of the archived Indigenous voice, to what extent should repatriating institutions be engaged in Indigenous "community politics" as part of their repatriation efforts?

REPATRIATION AS (RE)POSSESSION?

What is repatriation supposed to do—what is the purpose that gives rise to its methods, the ends for which the means are justified? In the next few sections, I explore the different narratives surrounding repatriation that give it meaning. To do this, I draw from my own experiences in a specific repatriation context—the Hopi Music Repatriation Project (HMRP)—to shed light on what repatriation might do for Indigenous peoples. This example is particularly salient, as the Hopi Tribe has been among the most aggressive in its efforts to reclaim culturally sensitive materials (Brown 2003; Riley and Carpenter 2016). In this ethnographic exploration of repatriation, I pay close attention to the narratives that arise as various stakeholders are asked to conceptualize repatriation from their particular points of view, doing what I consider to be acts of generative translation, incorporating Indigenous concepts and values into more actionable discourses of Indigenous sovereignty and cultural property.

In December 2010, I nervously arrived at my first meeting of the Hopi Cultural Preservation Office to bring home a number of Laura Boulton's[6] 1933 and 1940 field recordings. Early in her career, Boulton had visited Hopi lands on a collecting expedition to the Native Southwest, which she hoped would boost her career as an exotic music specialist on the public lecture circuit. She had also just released a widely acclaimed recording of African music on the RCA Victor label, garnering the attention of scholars and government officials, and she hoped to have the same success with domestic Indigenous musics now that World War II was imminent, and her prospects for international travel were sharply curtailed. The ceremonial singers she recorded at Hopi—David Monongye, Thomas Bahnaqya, and Dan Qötshongva, among others—likely had their own, possibly politically motivated reasons for performing songs for Boulton.[7] But what becomes clear from a search of Boulton's papers and her course of dealing with her informants generally is that she never considered how her informants valued the music she collected. While she was clearly adept at negotiating intellectual property instruments with agents and record labels to secure her rights, she never once executed a written agreement with her Indigenous informants (Fox 2017). Seventy-five years later, with the recordings of these prominent Hopi individuals in hand, I was tasked with developing a community-partnered methodology to repatriate them successfully back to the Hopi community, including any existing intellectual property rights (see Fox and Sakakibara 2009).

I knew from my own experiences at Hopi and my interactions with Hopi singers and performers that owning, transferring, and reproducing Hopi songs was not a new or foreign concept at the time early fieldworkers like Boulton arrived to record our ancestors. Prior to the use of recording devices at Hopi (which are now ubiquitous for the purposes of preservation and ceremonial preparation), individual and collective memories did the work of recording, circulating, and preserving Hopi songs. Because recordation and preservation were contained within Hopi bodies, the circulation of Hopi song was subject to local protocols rooted in people's relationships with one another. As Erika Brady recounts, no one was surprised or shocked when recording devices were first brought to Walpi, a remote Hopi village, in the 1890s. Instead, early American recording devices were burlesqued by Hopi clowns as the ridiculous fascination of overly curious, and often intrusive visitors (Brady 1999, 31; Fewkes 1899, 87n1; see also Ishii 2010).

Before Boulton, visitors like Natalie Curtis-Burlin (1907) and Jesse Walter Fewkes (with assistance of Benjamin Ives-Gilman) (1908) had used the phonograph to help them produce transcriptions of the abstract "musicality" of Hopi songs, meant primarily for artistic or scientific exploration and experimentation. The recordings themselves were preserved in archives, but all but forgotten until recently (see List 1994; Sekaquaptewa, Washburn, and Hill 2015). In contrast, Boulton's recordings of Hopi singers in 1940 using her Fairchild disc recorder accomplished something quite different from early collectors. Her collaboration with Monongye, Bahnaqya, and others had created a reproducible rendering of Hopi ceremonial voices that did not rely on Hopi performers, relationships of reciprocity, or specialized musical skills to perform them. The greatly increased quality and stability of Boulton's recordings not only made the melodies and lyrics available for future generations but also captured a sampling of human and nonhuman beings—beings that had been experienced and remembered for generations—on easily reproducible media. Unlike her predecessors, her goal was not to understand Hopi society and its musicality, but rather to exploit Hopis and their spirituality directly for their exoticness, which she had overtly sought to render audible for an audience of non-Indigenous settlers.[8]

Additionally, as Hopi tribal lands were, as of 1937, recognized as land held in trust by the federal government, which claimed ultimate jurisdiction over activities happening thereon, Boulton and her Hopi informants had, through the act of recording these ceremonial songs, produced a right of ownership under non-Hopi intellectual property frameworks that would govern the circulation of these recordings (Reed 2017). The right had no attachment to the particular ways Hopi ceremonial composers, performers, and their villages had managed ceremonial songs to that point. Instead, this new rendering of Hopi songs acquired a social-legal life outside the sets of relations within which the songs were generated. They became—as Boulton presumed—her possession and property, with rights she could (and did) exercise though assignment and licensing to various institutions and distributors, including Columbia University and what is now Smithsonian Folkways Recordings.

Given the breadth and sensitivity of the materials contained in Boulton's recordings, Hopi Cultural Preservation Office Director Leigh Kuwanwisiwma strongly supported the repatriation of Boulton's recordings, but also knew of the project's potential for harm should the songs be improperly circulated.[9] Kuwanwisiwma believed that the best group to provide advice on the project was the Cultural Resources Advisory Task Team (CRATT). A group of twenty to thirty village and religious society leaders (almost exclusively elders) from across Hopi lands, the CRATT regularly advised the tribe on matters of cultural significance. Each member of the CRATT held a unique perspective on Hopi culture—especially their villages' ceremonial practices—in addition to knowledge gained through a lifetime of listening, remembering, and importantly (as I discuss in the following sections), farming on Hopi lands.[10] Kuwanwisiwma set up a meeting for me to present the recordings to the CRATT members for their guidance.

I came into the meeting with the assumption that CRATT, acting under what I believed to be a sovereign delegation of authority from both their home villages and the tribe, would specify exactly what terms should govern the repatriation transaction between the archives holding the recordings and the Hopi community. That, as I explain later, never happened. Instead, a particular moment in my presentation to CRATT allowed me to begin to understand what repatriation really meant for these Hopi leaders, and the problems it would pose for me as mediator.

We began the meeting with the story of Laura Boulton's visit to Hopi, followed by me playing a couple of lighthearted *povoltawi* (butterfly dance songs) and *mosayrutawi* (buffalo dance songs) from the collection, songs that several CRATT members recognized from their youth. I then decided to play a particular ceremonial song recorded by Boulton that had been released commercially by Folkways in 1957. Looking down at my presentation notes as the song played, in my peripheral vision I began to notice gestures of recollection in the elders' bodies as the song progressed through its *kuyngwa* (the initial stylized tag that introduces the audience to the voices of the beings depicted in the song) and into the main part of the *atkyaqw* (the first in the five-verse form). As the song progressed, I gradually heard the grainy, monophonic sound of the recording transform, increasing in depth and weight. The verses, which I later learned had been composed for the purpose of bringing the performers, audience, clouds, crops, and other living things into productive relation, were bringing members of CRATT—each from distinct village cultures—together. By the third verse, the sound had completely enveloped the room. I realized that everyone in the room was articulately retracing the contour and content of this seventy-year-old song with his voice in a kind of seamless, hopeful unison I cannot adequately describe. The replaying of the song—one still sung in its ceremonial context today—performed a kind of meaningful connecting that acquired affective power through the revoicing of the past into the present.

At the time, I did not realize the significance of what I had just witnessed. Instead, I continued my presentation by plainly asking the CRATT members who the rightful owner or owners of the recordings should be. In doing so I was fishing for a unanimous, "tradition"-based directive that would "express the sovereign will of the autochthonous Hopi sociopolitical organization" (Richland 2011, 223)—an unrealistic and, as I now know, a somewhat un-Hopi request. What I actually witnessed was a contentious debate that juxtaposed cultural property discourses and traditional principles of Hopi knowledge circulation. Some of the elders reasoned that the Hopi Tribal Council, as representative of the sovereign Hopi people, should control access to this kind of "cultural property."[11] Others objected, arguing that the tribal council was not a body of village ceremonial leaders and held no obligation to manage Hopi ritual songs respectfully. Finally, at one point in the meeting the suggestion was made that some of the recordings might be useful for traditional composers in the creation of new songs, but several elders found this problematic: they recalled how some Hopi musicians—while acting in "legal" ways—had mishandled their knowledge of the Hopi voice by selling their performances to record labels or fusing ceremonial songs with popular vocal techniques, rhythms, and timbres.[12] What would prevent this from happening again with these songs, already existing in highly transportable formats?

The dialogue on ownership was never resolved. And yet, it was interwoven with important narratives that attempted to relate concepts of property and sovereignty into larger discourses of collective ownership, village-based circulation protocols, and reciprocity. As each of these narratives represents a vital contribution to contemporary Hopi concepts of repatriation that informed action-based research projects we later developed, I explain each in greater detail.

Narrative 1: Framing Our Claims to Archival Materials in Terms of Cultural Property Rights Reinforces Tribal Sovereignty.

By taking the position that the tribe should control recordings of ceremonial songs as its "cultural property," several elders were asserting a mode of circulation and ownership altogether distinct from traditional practice, one that exerts clear power in the non-Hopi world. The Hopi Tribe, a limited government created under the procedures set out by the US Congress in the Indian Reorganization Act, has always had a tenuous relationship to the Hopi polity (Richland 2011) and is by no means regarded as an authority for Hopis on cultural matters. However, when acting on behalf of Hopi constituents on matters of culture importance, it wields considerable authority.[13] In 1994, for example, the Hopi Tribal Council, acting as the representative of the sovereign Hopi villages, passed resolution H-70-94, which declared "archival records . . . which describe and depict esoteric ritual, ceremonial and religious knowledge" to be the "cultural property of the Hopi [Tribe]." Thereafter, all archival materials subject to the tribe's jurisdiction that reproduced ritual or ceremonial performances not only became legal possessions of the Hopi Tribe—an entity that had never before owned ceremonial expressions—but also became property, legally transferrable even without the consent of ceremonial practitioners.

From some analytical perspectives, the tribe's move to define rituals as its own property could be seen as following other marginalized groups in converting a lived culture into a marketable natural resource, akin to coal, wood, or wildlife. In the era of globalization, there is a strong impulse for culture to become what George Yudice (2004) has called an "expedient," a resource in need of management, development, and conversion into property so that its owner has the exclusive ability to perform its uniquenesses in ways that legitimize the group under the terms of the nation-state or the international capital economy. Yudice argues that as growing world economies increasingly turn to the production of easily circulating, immaterial goods like digital music, movies, or software, minority groups are leveraging their "cultural resources" in like manner as they fight for greater political autonomy. Negotiations over cultural "rights" between Indigenous groups and settler-states (and now, archives) create economic, political, and social fields of force, which act to secure and traditionalize culture while at the same time restricting or privileging certain forms of its circulation for the sake of meeting these groups' political demands.

For Native American tribes, the use of cultural-property-as-resource to assert or reinforce political sovereignty has both positive and negative implications. When tribes assert "restitutionist" claims to what they deem cultural property (Handler 1991), they are redeploying the settler-state's logic of "rights" to justify "more equitable divisions of cultural property" (70–71). As political moves, these claims work to reverse the tide of colonial power in a language power understands (70–71). However, at the same time, as Handler has argued and as I argue later, the metaphor of cultural property is "epistemologically bankrupt" and dependence on property logics to guide repatriation frameworks may reinforce the legitimacy of the settler-state (70). As Michael Brown (2003) has suggested, property-based claims to the ownership of Native culture also espouse "capitalism's commodifying logic" in the name of cultural protection, which may contradict Indigenous economic principles (Brown 2003, 287).

Narrative 2: Limiting the Circulation of Archival Materials to Those under Appropriate Ceremonial Authority Will Prevent Misappropriation While Promoting Cultural Continuity.

Alternatively, some CRATT members understood repatriation as a tool for exclusion—specifically, a way of preventing those who would reuse recorded Hopi ceremonial songs in nontraditional ways from having access. In the contemporary American ethos catalyzed by the copyleft, such a restriction amounts to "silencing and surveillance" of culture in the name of cultural continuity (Brown 2003, 8; Lessig 2004)—essentially a legally enforceable form of censorship. The American public, for example, presumptively finds restrictions on the circulation of culture an unnecessary limitation on our "vision of human expressive possibility" (Coombe 1998, 226). This is because our individual attachments to culture can often be the very thing that "gives meaning to our lives" (226). Moreover, when access to those properties that constitute who we are, are placed off limits, such restraints may cause considerable individual harm (Radin 1982). For example, they may "obscure people's historical agency and transformations, their internal differences, the productivity of intercultural contact, and the ability of peoples to culturally express their position in a wider world" (Coombe 1999, 226).

Some might argue that, in advocating for the use of property laws to limit innovation, these Hopi elders are simply nostalgic for the past. But no member of the CRATT team would argue that Hopi ceremonial song practices should be static; for many Hopi ceremonies, songs are generated anew each time the ceremony is performed. Moreover, as I explore later, Hopi composers consciously incorporate new elements into their songs through various modes of appropriation and cross-cultural exchange. Instead of nostalgia, I believe these elders' desire to prevent the use of old sound recordings to foster innovation may not actually be aimed at limiting cultural expression in a wider world—it may actually reflect a desire to increase Hopi composers' expressive capabilities through reliance on contemporary Hopi creative practices (rather than simply reworking existing Hopi songs into new forms), and a desire to maintain ongoing relationships of reciprocity with Hopi social and environmental networks (rather than an individual art form meant to produce personal gain).

Narrative 3: Access to and Ownership of Repatriated Materials Should Depend on Indigenous Protocols Inherent in the Material.

A third point raised by CRATT members was that tribal ownership of the songs was inappropriate because the governing body of the tribe, the Hopi Tribal Council, while holding jurisdiction over the cultural property of the tribe, lacked sufficient obligations to appropriately govern uses of the contents of the repatriated materials. Tribal councils are typically elected bodies, recognized by settler governments as being capable of bestowing, receiving, and enforcing property rights. However, does a tribal government's recognition of ceremonial knowledge as property necessarily mean it rightly controls the flow of that knowledge? As I explore in the following section, Hopi ceremonial songs seem to exceed the epistemological limits of Euro-American property in substantial ways, leaving such knowledge underprotected.[14] Thus, while governments elected by Indigenous peoples possess the authority to secure and defend property, they may lack the modes of relation and access to networks necessary for the appropriate recirculation of these materials.

Effecting the repatriation of our ancestors' voices strictly through the lens of property, I argue, grossly underestimates the ways Indigenous peoples value and experience these materials. While empowering for Indigenous communities as they seek to reinforce Indigenous sovereignty in the geopolitical arena, dependence on such an Enlightenment-colored framework may perpetuate a "conceptual colonialism" over these groups (Leach 2007, 99), displacing Indigenous modes of ownership and networks of sonic exchange.

Is there an alternative to the logics of property in contemporary repatriation practice? In the next section, I explore the development of the HMRP. Very much a work in progress today, HMRP is a long-term effort to bring the voices of our ancestors back home. Our goal has evolved from simply determining and carrying out the most ethically and legally sound intellectual property transaction possible, toward one that seeks to identify and embrace ancestral Hopi voices' existing and potential networks of relations within the Hopi community and the contemporary world, and then acts to emplace these voices within those networks in meaningful ways.

Exploring actual and potential networks for these recordings, rather than asking who owns the property rights to them, has required starting at the most fundamental level of inquiry: the level of ontology. We have had to ask, What is the nature of Hopi song? What are the obligations through which Hopi song is created and circulated? What do the relationships surrounding those obligations tell us about the world Hopi song operates in and how those songs are "owned"? After addressing these questions, I present two case studies involving experimental repatriation activities that have helped expand our views of what repatriation might accomplish.

What Is Hopi Song?

Marilyn Strathern suggests that rather than trying to understand the ownership of "intangible" resources like Indigenous songs in terms of individuals' rights to them, it may "make more sense to start with relations and the way in which resources of various kinds are embodied in social relationships" (2004, 7). Unlike limited tangible resources (e.g., water or coal) where the management of their exploitation often necessitates exclusionary claims, intangible assets like songs "only acquire the properties of 'things' (they can be owned and transacted) in the course of communication" (7).

Hopi ceremonial songs, or *taatawi* (the plural of *tawi*), are composed and performed as a means of connecting living things to the rest of the universe. As Lee Wayne Lomayestewa, a Hopi ceremonial leader from the village of Songoopavi, explains, "When the priest does the ceremony . . . when he sings, its not just for us Hopis. It's for all the little insects that crawl the earth, the animals, the plants, the birds, the butterflies, all the people that live on the earth . . . even the stars, the galaxies" (personal interview, February 5, 2011). The knowledge and skill required to bring cosmological entities into meaningful relation not only requires significant discipline but also requires entering into musical relations with human and nonhuman collaborators, including the generations of more experienced men and women within the *kiva*, or ceremonial society, and perhaps more importantly, with the environment, including certain local plants, which many Hopi farmers call their "children." Because taatawi have an impact on more than just human lives, there is a politics surrounding their management and control that necessarily exceeds discourses of intellectual property.

In the following excerpt from a 2009 interview, Hopi composer Leigh Kuwanwisiwma describes through his own experience of becoming a composer the kinds of relations that undergird Hopi compositional practice. The story begins with Kuwanwisiwma's father, a respected ceremonial drummer, praising him for his first attempts at composing ritual songs by rearranging those he had heard from other members of his kiva. As his father pointed out, there was something missing in his song:

> My dad was sitting there listening like this [arms folded], and I was intimidated, and I was stuttering, trying not to lose memory and all of that, so I was singing my song staggering through it. Finally I got my song together, and then he started tapping his feet. He looked at me, straining the eyes, and said:
> "Is Alí! Good song! But," he said, "no feeling."
> So I said, "What?"
> "I'll tell you what. You composed your song here [pointing to his head]. . . . You didn't compose it here [pointing to the heart], the spiritual part of you. . . . You need to know that if you really want to get that feeling, you've got to get it yourself, too, not just the others [meaning other members of the kiva]. And the way that the old folks do it, to get it in here, so that your kiva group can feel it too, you've got to do it like the old folks."

And, as a thirty-year-old, I was slowly shrinking. . . . So he said, "You've got to do it like the old folks. You've got to get up early in the morning, every morning. Greet the sun, son. Ask for your spiritual well being, physical well being, a good day . . . that's one—that's the discipline. Second, if you really want to have these [ceremonial] songs really mean something, you've got to go sleep in the corn field, be there with your children. Be there and witness . . . the horizon as it comes up in the morning. Figure out which birds are the first to chirp, look at the dew on the corn plants, and sing down there, and witness once you start singing and composing these songs, then these corn plants will start dancing to you."

(L. Kuwanwisiwma, personal interview, September 2, 2009)

From this and several other interviews with Hopi composers, it became apparent to me that creating the right "feeling" in a Hopi tawi was more than an aesthetic trope. Hopi songs are not simply a reworking of other people's creative work or a result of building from an established musical genre. Songs have real implications for living things like plants and birds, which can hear and respond to sound; therefore, a composer can only get the appropriate "feeling" of a ceremonial song through relations of exchange with those entities.[15]

But how do Hopi taatawi influence rocks, plants, spirit beings, and animals when they are presumably a human art form? Tania Stolze Lima suggests that we look beyond the notion of "metaphor," directly examining purported interspecies interactions from the perspectives of the actors themselves, giving space to what some might believe to be the "underlying logic of apparently irrational propositions" (116).[16] As the Hopi linguist Emory Sekaquaptewa conceptualizes them, Hopi taatawi are *condensations* (literally, making perceptible that which exists in the ether) of lived, culturally attuned beliefs (Sekaquaptewa and Washburn 2004). In other words, the evocative language used in Hopi ceremonial songs appears to be more than just artful poetics. While taatawi draw from a cultural sensibility or "ethos" based on poetic devices like rain metaphors and on-omatopoeic environmental sounds (cf. Feld 1990), there are key cosmological relations that become activated in the production of Hopi song. While song may be performed by humans, its resonance need not be confined solely to the human ear. As Kuwanwisiwma and others suggest, Hopi taatawi affect multiple kinds of entities at once by speaking/singing to their unique auditory perspectives. Power in taatawi is manifest through the collective and individual transformations that occur during ceremonial performances as humans, animals, plants, spirit beings, weather patterns, and so forth, are brought into meaningful relation.

Stewart B. Koyiyumptewa and Clark Tenakhongva, both respected Hopi intellectuals, explained to me that well-composed taatawi hold significant power because they fuse *lavayi* (speech)—the human mode of bringing people into relation—to *tawvö* (melody or music)—the mode of relation among nonhuman entities in the world. In other words, the prosodies of the singing voice—the timbre and pitch selected for singing, as well as a careful poetics that invokes archaic Hopi and non-Hopi words—have real implications for what a song does for different beings in the cosmos, beings who listen for patterns of sonic elements in the voice to motivate them to act. As Kuwanwisiwma explained, composers acquire compositional power by learning the aesthetics for each taawi form, observing and feeding their corn plants with song as a Hopi father would watch over his children and feed them with the corn from his field. Corn plants, wet with dew, will dance when taatawi become saturated with profound meanings (*tu'awi'ytangwu*). And, these same taatawi, when sung with a collective-oriented, "good heart" (*lolma'unangwa*) in context of ceremonial dance, will encourage rain clouds, birds, butterflies, humans, and others into productive collaboration, encouraging one another as they provide life to the crops, which will in turn feed all who live in the village, and potentially, the world.

Taatawi, then, can never be composed or fully experienced through a single perceptive frame, and for that matter, cannot be "owned" within the subjective domain of an individual entity. This understanding of the ontological status of Hopi song has implications for how these songs should circulate (or in the context of repatriation, recirculate). According to Lomayestewa and the Hopi elder Wilton Kooyahoema, rather than a property right, the circulation of taatawi usually operates under the principle of *nasimokyaata*, or owner-obligated borrowing, which allows for the revoicing of taatawi in another time, place, or form, even without the consent of the composer (personal interview, August 2011). However, nasimokyaata is not to be confused with the "free culture" of the "public domain" or "commons" to which Indigenous songs are often relegated in intellectual property discourses (Howes 1995). Just as one borrows money, a book, or a piece of ceremonial regalia, *nasimoktaatawi* (borrowed songs) implicitly carry an obligation of reciprocity coinciding with the song's original purposes: either to be returned with a reciprocal gift or to be remembered and performed for the good of the world. Nasimokyaata, the Hopi concept of borrowing, can be instructively contrasted with another Hopi term, *sokopta*, or "to steal with intent to take advantage of," a term whose most salient definitions include the clandestine taking of Hopi sacred ceremony for selfish purposes, adultery, and rape (Hopi Dictionary 1998, 517).

In this way, ownership of Hopi songs is not based on a logic of exclusion like that of copyright, in which uses of copyrighted songs are reserved to the copyright holder so as to accumulate benefit to the individual. Rather, it operates by a logic of inclusion, where songs are protected against "selfish" uses, to accumulate benefits to entire networks of exchange. Consequently, while intellectual property laws, like copyright, could be crafted to enjoin those misappropriations of Hopi song that do not respect Hopi logics of ownership—assuming the Hopi Tribe is the exclusive owner of the copyright and the songs meet copyright's minimum requirements (authorship, fixation in a "tangible" medium, and minimal creativity, for example)—property-based law can do little justice by itself to restore taatawi to those networks of relationships where they most powerfully affect living beings.

The Hopi Music Repatriation
Project: Two Case Studies

From the foregoing discussion of the nature of Hopi song, it becomes clear that Indigenous repatriation methodologies should be expanded beyond the transactionalism of property, toward models that reflect the actual networks of exchange in which these materials flow. But how does that play out on the ground? In the Hopi context, if nasimokyaata exceeds the potential of "property" to effect the most beneficial circulation of Hopi song, how might we then use this Indigenous principle to alter the way we do archival repatriations, particularly those involving Hopi ceremonial voices? Through the following case studies, I argue that repatriation of archived Indigenous voices might be done most effectively by seeking out and/or developing social networks that can recirculate them again in meaningful ways. These social networks ideally would be able to generate new possibilities for archived materials and also help to creatively bridge or at least reframe, the seemingly irreconcilable gaps between property regimes and Indigenous modes of exchange such as nasimokyaata.

Case 1: Obtaining Youth Perspectives on Repatriation

One of the first suggestions I received for repatriating Boulton's Hopi recordings involved using them to generate a music curriculum that would complement the Hopi language and culture curricula being taught at the tribe's junior/senior high school (HJSHS).[17] This academic use of the recordings seemed like a natural fit. As Sheilah Nicholas (2009) explains, "Western education is highly valued [at Hopi]; its acceptance and integration into the Hopi way of life is premised on an understanding that the benefits of an education will enhance the lifeway of the individual as well as the collective" (323). Hopi parents do not overtly resist or resent Western education in the same ways that some of our grandparents once did; perhaps this is because compulsory education no longer poses the same kind of threat to the Hopi community's way of life as when Navajo military officers forced Hopi children to attend *pahaana* or white boarding schools at the turn of the twentieth century (Udall 1969; James 1974). For one, HJSHS and several other Hopi schools fall under the jurisdiction of the Hopi Tribe, and are currently managed by local, community-elected school boards, which oversee their policies and selection of personnel. With local management comes an understanding that the Hopi community can determine, to a large extent, the future of its children's education.[18] As many Hopi youth eventually leave the reservation for a time to pursue college or job opportunities, the education provided by local schools provides a necessary basis for success in negotiating "mainstream society" (Nicholas 2009, 324).

At the same time, while many Hopis still believe cultural training should take place either at home or in the village, Hopi-language acquisition, and more recently, traditional agricultural training, have become vital parts of both primary and secondary education at Hopi schools (see Natwani Coalition 2012). Hopi parents are generally okay with the teaching of language and culture in the schools as there is a general feeling among Hopis that Hopi language is gradually eroding, and as a result, cultural understanding and self-fulfillment may diminish because songs and ceremonies are not being entirely understood (Nicholas 2009, 321–323).

As one of our initial goals for the HMRP was to find culturally salient uses for the Hopi songs Laura Boulton recorded in 1933 and 1940, I met with Hopi language and culture instructor Anita Poleahla[19] to discuss the possibilities for using the recordings in HJSHS classrooms. She in turn extended an invitation for me to present a few of the Boulton recordings to her five Hopi language and culture classes. This case study explores the feedback we received from those sessions with Hopi secondary students, and how it helped to expand the model of Hopi song ownership and exchange described above.

Our purpose for consulting with the students was twofold. First, Poleahla and I had the goal of helping the students become more familiar with the components of Hopi taatawi by teasing out melodic, linguistic, and contextual features from a small sample of song recordings in the collection. Second, we wanted students to develop critical perspectives on what they thought should be the future of the archival recordings, and to be able to express those views both verbally and in writing. We decided to use the same songs from Boulton's 1933 and 1940 field recordings that had been used with the Hopi elders during the CRATT meeting discussed earlier. We also created a graphic organizer for each student. This allowed them a personal space to write down what they knew about each song, as well as a space on the back of the sheet to privately leave us their thoughts on what we should do with the songs.[20]

Following the presentation of each song, we held a discussion about the content and context of the songs. Students had a variety of initial responses to the songs, often in the form of personal experiences with either the kinds of beings depicted or other events happening in their lives at the time they first heard the songs.[21] Nearly every student knew the lullaby, and many were noticeably calmed by having experienced it as children. And many knew the final song, a povoltawi (butterfly dance song) from the 1940s, because they had danced to it during a ceremony only a week before. (The song is instantly recognizable because it borrows Spanish words—what one elder explained were Hopi imitations of seventeenth-century Spanish utterances—in the introduction.) Many of the students were fascinated by the recording because it was virtually identical to the version sung during the ceremony, despite the song having remained unpublished and presumably inaccessible to the Hopi community (except through oral transmission) for the previous seventy-five years.

After playing the songs, we briefly asked the students to write down and discuss what they would do with the recordings if they were brought home to Hopi lands. These responses provided a rich opportunity to see how Hopi youth perceive archival materials, the kinds of stakes they envision themselves having in them, and what possibilities they imagine for repatriated recordings if they alone could determine their

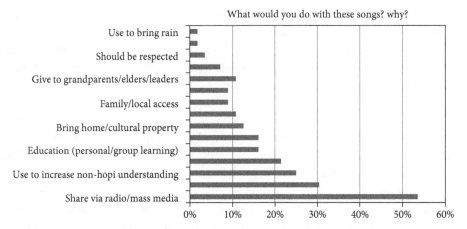

FIGURE 34.1 Hopi language and culture class students' responses to the question: "What would you do with these songs? Why?"

future.[22] Figure 34.1 shows their responses to the questions: "What would you do with these songs? Why?"

The students identified a number of uses for the recordings, many of which we had not anticipated.

- *Broadcast/Social Media (54%).* The majority of students believed the Boulton recordings should be made available to KUYI (the local radio station), to other radio stations for public broadcast, or through other media outlets. Many students also felt the recordings could be broadcast globally. One student explained, "We need to get them out, or they will be lost for good." Another wrote, "I think everyone should hear this kind of music."
- *Perpetuate/Preserve Culture (30%).* Slightly less than one-third of the students felt the songs could help in preserving or perpetuating Hopi culture. Said one student in Poleahla's beginning Hopilavayi class, "Sing them to your kids so the tradition can live on to the following generation of people."
- *Increase Non-Hopi Understanding of Hopi Lives (25%).* One-quarter of the students felt the repatriated songs could effectively be used to help non-Hopis understand Hopi culture. "They should be shared and not kept somewhere where no one listens to them. They should be known and admired," commented one student. Another wrote, "I think you should put the [songs] on YouTube or just like try to tell people to listen to them so that people can hear what types of songs we listen to out here on the reservation in Arizona."
- *Release the Recordings for Sale (21%).* "They should make them into CDs and sell them all over the world," commented one student. However, the scale of public release differed greatly from student to student. Several advocated for only a local release, while others saw a large-scale release of Hopi songs as a potential way

of garnering recognition for Hopi culture or income to support charitable work at Hopi.

- *Cultural Education and Personal/Group Learning (16%)*. For some students, these songs are valuable teaching tools for Hopi youth: "I think the songs should come back here so that the kids could learn from them." Other students thought they could be successfully integrated into educational curricula or used as a reference: "You should play these songs in a history class . . . and learn what the song means . . . and put it in different libraries in different places."

- *Use in Ceremony and Other Performances (16%)*. For many students, the recordings provided a valuable cultural text that could be successfully recontextualized in the present. One student thought of the songs as being valuable for older generations of Hopis: "I will sing it to my So'o [grandmother]. She wants to listen to old songs." However, others considered the songs to have broader appeal. One student wrote, "You should get some men and women to perform around the US." Other students wrote about why the performance of the songs was so important: "I think these songs should be used because the things that are sung are for all mankind."

- *Bring Home—Cultural Property (13%)*. Other students were more interested in simply having the songs located closer to home and under the control of Hopis rather than a university. As one student succinctly explained, "I think you should bring them back to Hopi because they belong to us, they were made by Hopis, and it is a part of who we are."

- *Do Something Enjoyable (11%)*. One overarching principle that emerged several times was the directive to do something "enjoyable"; something that would bring happiness to people either by directly listening to the songs or through the benefits that would come with the kinds of relationships the songs enact. Said one student, "Let people listen because anybody could listen to them to bring rain."

While the aggregated results show the general trends in the responses of seventh to twelfth grade students in all of Poleahla's Hopi language classes, the responses from her advanced Hopilavayi class—students who were both older and more fluent in the language, and presumably more experienced with Hopi culture—differed in significant ways from those of the younger, beginning students. Half of the advanced students considered cultural perpetuity and preservation to be important in deciding the future of the recordings. Approximately one third used cultural property logics to support their position that the songs should be returned to the tribe. A handful of students also noted that some of the songs should not be listened to or shared by other cultures or races that could not use them appropriately. Many of the advanced students emphasized the usefulness of the recordings for showing members of their communities the continuity of Hopi song practices from the past into the present and future. Far fewer students in the advanced class expressed a desire to use the recordings to help non-Hopis understand Hopi life, and only one mentioned public broadcast. For the advanced class, then, it seemed that the narratives surrounding cultural property had overshadowed students' interests in generating goodwill beyond the borders of the tribe.

On the whole, many of the students' responses complemented the opinions of the Hopi CRATT team discussed earlier, while others added new concerns and dimensions. Like those elders advocating for tribal control over the songs to prevent individual artists' misuse of them, one student argued for collective control over the songs "because they are sacred and have powerful meanings to them . . . not [to be] abused for one person's needs or wants." As just mentioned, cultural property discourse played a significant role in CRATT members' and students' responses, particularly for the more advanced students. And students' desires to perform the songs in ways that connect themselves to their grandparents, future children, and the environment evidenced similar desires to those of the CRATT team that the recordings should be returned to those who could maintain the important obligations embodied in them.

But in contrast, younger Hopi students expressed a desire to allow the songs to inhabit intercultural spaces that did not appear in the CRATT responses. These included off-reservation radio broadcasts, YouTube, and public performances—sites of exchange that could connect Hopi and non-Hopi publics. The commodification of the recordings as purchasable music, something viewed as harmful by the elders, was for the younger students a means whereby the Hopi community could achieve notoriety and respect through the ears of non-Hopis. For most of these students, exercising their rights to determine the future of the recordings did not automatically mean restricting them to what one might think of as traditional Hopi networks of exchange. "Put it on the radio in New York," suggested one student; "elevator music," suggested another. One advanced student was even comfortable allowing me, as a representative of Columbia, to decide the recordings' future circulations, with one caveat—"I think in traditional ways they say not to be selling Hopi stuff, but if you're not going to be selling them around, yeah, why not." Another student said simply: "Give it to a kiva chief. Sing it to the people. Put them on your iPod."

Finally, some students expressed a desire to keep the songs in the Columbia archive rather than return them to the tribe. This was later elaborated upon to me as a response to their anxieties over how these powerful cultural resources might become divisive within an already fracturing community often divided by local politics. While this opinion was in the minority, it raised important questions still needing to be addressed about the potentially negative impacts of old voices from another time inhabiting the politics of the present.

Remarkably, while several students noted that the songs might complement their current classes, the development of a formal, in-school Hopi music curriculum never came up.

One of the key takeaways from this case study was a recognition that engaging youth allows us to expand repatriation discourses beyond fundamental principles and into the lived realities of song circulation in which Indigenous youth, as key stakeholders in Indigenous social networks, already play an active role. Such efforts may also complement, or even contradict the perspectives of elders who may have greater knowledge about the contents and contexts of the materials. Of course, as was apparent in this case study, elders' voices may already be embedded in the responses of Indigenous youth, who often interpret and apply them to the increasingly interconnected, global realities they face. These types of interactive and intergenerational dialogue over archival materials—already marked as "theirs" through discourses of cultural property—allows Indigenous peoples to personally and collectively determine their own affinity to them and to propose the forms that affinity will take into the future.

Case 2: Reanimating Hopi-Zuni Sonic Exchange

Thinking archival repatriation from Indigenous perspectives rather than property-centric discourses also helps us to rethink notions of "cultural affiliation," which have taken a central role in repatriation practice (see NAGPRA, 17 USC § 3001). In this respect, community-partnered research is critical in the repatriation process, because it has the potential to elucidate modes of circulation that exceed the valences of any single stakeholder (Fox and Sakakibara 2009; Reed 2010). One example of this arose in our first intensive listening session with Lee Wayne Lomayestewa, a ceremonial leader from the Hopi village of Songoopavi, in July 2010. As we sat side by side for hours at a time, attempting to corroborate Boulton's recordings with what were often very scattered fieldnotes, Lomayestewa would periodically turn to me and say, "Those are Zuni words" or "That's a Supai song." At first, I figured the tracks were just mislabeled like many of the others in the collection; but as we replayed them and compared the voices to the other Hopi tracks we had heard, we confirmed they were, in fact, Hopis singing Zuni (the commonly used name for A:shiwi people) songs. When I asked what Hopis were doing by singing like "Zunis," Lomayestewa turned to me, and said, matter-of-factly, "Let's go up to Zuni." Zuni Pueblo, a five-hour drive via indirect roads connecting Navajo settlements and former Mormon frontier towns, seemed to me as distant from Hopi as New York City, both culturally and geographically.

After two years of work to secure an initial meeting, Stewart B. Koyiyumptewa, Hopi tribal archivist, and I planned and carried out two trips to Zuni Pueblo to meet with the Zuni Cultural Resources Advisory Team (ZCRAT) to return repatriated songs one step further to the community that had created them. Along with the Hopi tracks Lomayestewa determined contained Zuni words, we also brought with us several recordings Boulton had made at or near Zuni Pueblo just prior to her visit to Hopi lands in 1940 that had likewise been housed at Columbia University. Perhaps most importantly, under the advice of Hopi CRATT members and our own relatives, Stewart and I also brought melons and other staples to share with our Zuni collaborators. Unbeknownst to me, we were actually retracing a path and a mode of relation that had historically connected our communities.

After eighteen months of collaborative work with ZCRAT, our work reached an important milestone. Early in the morning on September 17, 2013, the Hopi elder and radio DJ Bruce Talawyma introduced KUYI Hopi Radio's rush-hour audiences to two Zuni elders from the ZCRAT—Octavius Seowtewa and Ronnie Cachini. The 1.5-hour public reunion of Hopi and Zuni cultures made possible by these elders' visit to Hopi was not without precedent, but it had been quite some time—likely more than a century—since the last public cultural exchange between the two tribes. Sitting in the control room, there was considerable anxiety—no one was quite sure what to expect and how the Hopi and Zuni publics would react.

As has been the case throughout the HMRP, the songs themselves generated most of the discussion and camaraderie we had been hoping for. The recordings acted as key sites of memory out of which the rich details of the Hopi-Zuni alliance could be rearticulated (Nora 1989). While most Hopis and Zuni are taught at some point about the two tribes' shared involvement in the Pueblo Revolt of 1680, in which their strategic collaboration contributed to the expulsion of Spanish colonists and missionaries from the Southwest and the preservation of Pueblo Indigenous cultures, most did not know the more substantive and enduring aspects of the alliance. As Seowtewa explained to KUYI listeners, groups from both tribes regularly traversed the 150-mile Hopi-Zuni road to visit their respective "aunts" and "uncles"—clan relations who share genealogies, histories, and responsibilities of care. In a way similar to how clan relatives are honored today in each tribe, Hopis would journey to the borders of Zuni Pueblo with their wagons laden with the fruits from their fields. The Hopi visitors would then build a massive fire to signal their arrival, and the Zuni hosts would prepare their homes to receive their Hopi guests. Once the Hopis were welcomed into the village by Zuni, *koko/katsinam* would fill the plaza, alternating the singing of ceremonial songs in Hopi and Zuni languages. Recounting the experience of this elaborate cultural exchange told to him by his great-grandfather, Seowtewa explained, "Some of these dances would probably go on for days, and if the people liked the dances, then they would ask them to dance and dance. . . . [Then] some of the Zuni people would bring some of their dances here to the Hopi mesas." The purpose of these lengthy travels and visits was, as Seowtewa put it, "to exchange culture, to exchange our way of life," and this often led to the cross-cultural borrowing of songs and ceremonies, the gifting of salt and other necessary goods, and in a number of cases, intermarriage between members of Hopi and Zuni villages.

As the elders pointed out, Laura Boulton had somewhat ironically captured the sonic aspects of this historic Hopi-Zuni relationship on her field recordings. In her autobiography, Boulton reveals her intense desire to collect songs over which American Indigenous tribes had become increasingly stingy, secretive, and possessive (an understandable reaction to nearly a century of missionary, government, and scholarly scrutiny of Indigenous lives).[23] When Boulton recorded David Monongye (Hopi), Jimmy A:washu (Zuni), and the Hoya Maidens (a Zuni women's singing group created by Mu:Daisy, a Hopi woman), along with several other Hopi and Zuni singers in the summer and fall of 1940, she was no doubt hoping to capture traditional songs that authentically represented the distinctive sounds of "Hopiness" and "Zuniness."[24] And yet, many of the singers she recorded chose nasimoktawi—Hopi songs borrowed and adapted by Zuni, or Zuni songs borrowed and adapted by Hopis—to perform into her recorder.

On one hand, this "bait and switch" tactic could be ascribed to tricksterism—a way of defying Boulton's totalizing and objectivizing ethnological gaze (Vizenor 1989). But on the other hand, the performance of Zuni songs by Hopi performers may say something more profound about how important Zuni presence had been and continues to be, in the Hopi sonic world (and vice versa). As Hopi composers have explained to me in interviews, Zuni ceremonial song words are considered by many Hopis to be imbued with significant power—they speak to the world through a unique voice integrally connected to their particular place and history in relation to Hopis. In this way, Zuni presence in Hopi ceremonial songs works to generate relationships that are important for Hopis' understandings of their own position in the world. As for Zuni singers' similar usage of Hopi sonic references in their ceremonial songs, Seowtewa explained, "These songs were borrowed from the Hopi itself, and there's always this trade—of cultural exchange—that we've been identifying: *all these different traditions and culture that we have—was comprised of borrowing from each other*" (emphasis added). Sonic-based cultural exchanges not only perpetuated an alliance between the two groups through periodic joint performances but also appear to have worked to constitute each group's identity. As we came to realize, such an understanding of Indigenous song—not as derivative of an Indigenous sovereign, but as a constitutive force that generates multiple group identities—deeply disturbs the very notion of repatriation as a matter of property.

In addition to providing a forum for the elders to talk about the history of Hopi-Zuni cultural exchange, the elders also decided to use their time to publicly discuss issues affecting both of their communities and to share potential solutions. One challenge both Hopis and Zunis identified was language loss and its effect on ceremonial participation and youth identity. When asked about change in language fluency and its effects on song-learning at Zuni Pueblo, Seowtewa responded:

> Well, I think it's pretty much like everywhere else. We're having our young children speaking not in Zuni and . . . it really makes it hard I guess for our people to make our younger generation realize that these songs are who we are, these songs are identified not only to the Zuni Tribe, but also the Hopis.

Cachini, speaking from his perspective as a Zuni ceremonial leader, followed by adding that profound and impactful songs are generated not only through language, but also through performances (and remembrances) of traditional practices and obligations:

> It's very, very important to keep up with traditions so songs like these won't disappear, and the songs' makers, so they won't all disappear. We have it in our hearts you know; we can't change a person, who we are. . . . I just want to say to my Hopi brothers and sisters, never let your language die out, keep on your traditions, just keep talking to your kids in your language and it will never disappear.

During their time on the air, the elders also suggested that perpetuating the Hopi-Zuni alliance through the exchange of culture had the potential to strengthen both tribes. As Seowtewa explained, relationships of cultural exchange are "what makes us very unique in the Puebloan lifestyle that we have . . . things are done in a way that unifies the people, brings people together, and so we have this tradition that the younger generation are not abiding to. . . . But events like this really bring back what we need to do to keep our people strong, our tradition alive."

The journey to repatriate Hopi voices back one step further—to the Zuni people whose ancestors had provided the sounds our Hopi ancestors had borrowed—proved to be much more than a simple return of twice-borrowed goods. The Hopi-Zuni songs discussed here, which existed as a constitutive force between the two groups, could never function as cultural property, because they were not derived from a particular culture. Indeed, if the songs were simply broken down into what are assumed to be their culturally authored component parts for the sake of repatriating them to the Indigenous group with the closest cultural affiliation, then an increasing portion of the "thing" being repatriated—the centuries-old relationship of exchange embedded in and generated from shared sound—would have been left entirely unaccounted for. In our work to return what might be perceived as Hopi appropriations of Zuni sonic property back to their rightful Zuni owners, we came to understand that what made these hybrid songs meaningful and powerful was not only their particular Hopi or Zuni "properties," but the relationships of exchange and histories embodied through their performance and circulations that are vital to the future of both Indigenous groups. In this way, repatriation may be a way of not only recognizing ownership stakes but also reanimating an important alliance between deeply connected peoples.

Conclusion: Repatriation as "Indigenous Cosmopolitics"

If repatriated materials have the potential to circulate productively within Indigenous networks of exchange in ways that exceed the epistemological and ontological limits of property, how might we be "more imaginative" (Leach 2007, 113) in our efforts to reclaim the Indigenous voice? One strategy involves engaging Indigenous publics over questions of ownership of the Indigenous voice and its future, even if those publics disagree as to the future of the materials. Another strategy involves rethinking our notions of repatriation as grounded in a sovereign, bounded concept of culture to which expressions—like ceremonial songs—necessarily attach, looking instead to how archival materials bring individuals and groups into relation as our basis for recirculating these materials. As discussed in the case studies, such an engagement necessarily involves "getting involved in community politics" because the contents of Indigenous archives have the potential to play an active role in constituting Indigenous communities in the present and beyond.

Allowing Indigenous conceptual frameworks like nasimokyaata to supplement or even supplant property principles as the basis for reclamation and recirculation of ancestral voices is, in the words of Marisol de la Cadena, to do an Indigenous "cosmopolitics"—to thrust Indigenous philosophies into colonized intellectual spaces "with the possibility of becoming legitimate adversaries not only within nation-states but also across the world" (de la Cadena 2010, 361). I do not assert here that Hopis or other Indigenous peoples are by nature adversarial to the purposes and practices of institutional archives or even to the researchers that originally produced them. Rather, I want to suggest that when repatriation practitioners insist that Indigenous archival materials be repatriated in ways based not on logics of property but on real-life obligations between actors in Indigenous sonic networks, Indigenous worldviews (and modes of relation and the cosmological entities that constitute them) can enter the national and global political realm on their own terms—as legitimate adversaries with those of settler-states. Archives, and ultimately the settler state, must then deal with Indigenous claims on their own terms rather than sidestepping them by means of reference to the Enlightenment-derived notions of ownership and circulation embedded in property law.

In this way, repatriation becomes an intervention into both archival practice and Indigenous rights discourses, one that not only critiques settler hegemony and power but also makes Indigenous propositions that advance Native sovereignty beyond the logics of exclusion imposed by the settler state. Repatriation need not be only a mode of remedying the misappropriation of culturally affiliated properties, but may be a way of enabling the voices of the past to become present again within Indigenous communities. Musical repatriation, then, can be just as much about reclaiming our ancestors' voices as it is about learning to hear, recognize, grapple with, and reassert those very modes of relation that have played an active role in constituting who we are.

NOTES

1. For many tribes, including my own, the council-style tribal government imposed on our people following the 1934 Indian Reorganization Act is not necessarily the primary authority on issues of cultural importance.
2. Tribes may even exercise jurisdiction over both member and nonmember archivists in matters involving Indigenous materials when those archivists engage in a consensual relationship with the tribe, or when their conduct threatens or has some direct effect on the economic security, health, or welfare of the tribe. See *Montana v. United States*, 450 US 544 (1981); Sarah Krakoff, "Tribal Civil Judicial Jurisdiction over Nonmembers: A Practical Guide for Judges," *University of Colorado Law Review* 81 (2010): 1187–1244.
3. Rosemary Coombe's (2009) recent review of cultural property literature in anthropology provides a substantial overview of changes in attitude toward archived Indigenous culture. See the evolving dialogue over rights to materials collected from Indigenous peoples in Vine Deloria (1969), Anthony Seeger (1996), Linda Tuhiwai-Smith (1999), Michael Brown (2003), and the drafters of the United Nations Declaration on the Rights of Indigenous Peoples (2007), in particular as expressed in §11 and §32.
4. As Jane Anderson (2013) explains, the rise of the "author" as the creator of "works" in Enlightenment legal discourse led to the formation of intellectual property law as we know it today. The innovation of "authorship," however, encoded a certain racialized, colonialist privilege into intellectual property frameworks, for only certain categories of humans

could be considered authors. As Anderson explains, "The relationship between the rise of modern authorship and colonization is not just a coincidence. The 'author' was also a figure of dispossession, working to legally and socially reduce and exclude other cultural forms of articulation, expression and association with cultural knowledge products" (Anderson 2013, 7). The fact that most forms of Indigenous creativity were not considered worthy of legal protection until they were captured and/or interpreted by social scientists is clear in anthropological practice through the early 1990s (Tuhiwai-Smith 1999; Seeger 2000). As a result, "the capacity for Indigenous people to account for their own histories and practices" was greatly reduced (Anderson 2013, 7).

5. The forced transformation of Indigenous ontologies into property structures is not new. The Dawes Act of 1887 (General Allotment Act) allowed for the conversion of Indigenous territories into individually owned parcels of land with their respective property rights. The law had the effect of undermining the political power of tribal governments and allowed tribal lands to be alienated to nonmembers. The subsequent Indian Reorganization Act of 1934, while repudiating the logic of allotment, permitted tribes to organize politically as long as the structure was consistent with federally recognized republican principles, thereby allowing tribes to reclaim a diminished portion of control over their now fragmented territories without fully restoring traditional ownership forms or tribal modes of community governance.

6. For a more comprehensive discussion on Laura Boulton's collecting activities and her archive's institutionalization, see Fox (2013).

7. Not long after their recording session with Boulton, these men would become leaders locally, nationally, and internationally, widely proclaiming Hopi prophecy and ritual knowledge to influential orgaganizations so as to demonstrate the value of Hopi culture and to secure equal human rights for Indigenous peoples (Clemmer 1995).

8. Boulton was by profession a public intellectual who toured the CBS lecture circuit during the 1930s. The primary content of her lectures included elaborate travelogues of her adventures among Indigenous peoples, complemented by audio clips of their traditional musics. The lectures were titled, among other things, "Rhythm in Jungle" and "Music of the Red Man." Boulton regularly praised the Indigenous peoples she recorded, but that praise was often couched in a colonialist framework. In her album *Indian Music of the Southwest*, for example, she writes, "The Indian has kept what many more 'progressive' civilizations have lost and are stringing to recover: a rich, intimate and natural use of music and art in their ordinary lives." But her notes go on to describe only the exotic features of her interlocutors' ceremonial practices rather than their individual, contemporary agency as composers, authors, and performers. In trying to explain Hopi ceremonial practices that include both human and nonhuman entities, for example, she writes, "The Hopis, *like most primitive people*, ascribe human qualities to animals, plants, mountains, clouds, practically everything."

9. Many Hopi ceremonial songs contain sensitive knowledge and are "owned" by a particular individual, clan, or ceremonial society, and therefore they are not ordinarily shared or performed beyond those boundaries. The return of one of these songs to the wrong ceremonial society had the potential of causing division and disempowering the affected group. Because many of the songs contained in Boulton's collection were particularly sensitive, the possibility for harm was great.

10. As I got to know several of these Hopi elders, I found them to be "anthropologists" in their own right (Wagner 1981, 2–4): skilled in the apprehension of other clans', other villages',

other societies'—and even other species'—dynamic worlds in order to interpret and understand them for the many Hopi social contexts in which they played a vital part. The CRATT was no doubt the only body on Hopi that could positively identify the contents of each recording.

11. The Hopi Tribe has been recognized as one of the most aggressive in its protection of cultural properties. In 1994, the tribe passed H-70-94, a tribal resolution claiming exclusive right to all Hopi "esoteric" and ritual knowledge. As Brown recounts, the tribe then sent out letters to museums and archives holding Hopi materials demanding that the archives recognize Hopi ownership in them (Brown 2003, 23).

12. In discussing popular vocal techniques, rhythms, and timbres, I refer to comments made by Hopi elders and ceremonial composers who have been offended by certain forms of nontraditional ceremonial song performance. One female artist—who uses open-throated, non-nasal singing and invokes climactic glides in the higher registers of songs—was pointed out to me as a deviation from traditional practice, where women typically sing in more nasal timbres with pitch-sliding functioning as a melodic rather than climactic component. Likewise, the elders criticized two other Hopi singers for their adaptations of Hopi *katsina* and butterfly songs into country music idioms.

13. A recent example of the leadership role the Hopi Tribe has played in matters of cultural importance included the legal action and protests surrounding the auction of Hopi ceremonial items being sold at a Paris auction house, and the ongoing actions to prevent the desecration of the San Francisco Peaks (near Flagstaff, Arizona).

14. Property, in general, is a non-Indigenous ownership category that may or may not parallel, or be embraced by, Indigenous ownership systems. As a sociolegal construction, property traditionally describes to what extent a particular "bundle" of exclusivities pertaining to an object becomes the right of its owners (see Locke 1689, §27). That which is not made exclusive to an individual either due to noncompliance with positive laws that generate property rights or by the absence of his or her "labor" in the object's creation or development, is typically considered "common property" or "public domain" in this mode of ownership. Because property regimes determine which forms of human creativity become private or public, they "play a constitutive role in the creation of contemporary cultures and in the social life of interpretive practice" (Coombe 1998, 6).

    Property, particularly intellectual property, is saturated with Enlightenment notions of the self and the worldview that philosophical basis provides. Modern subjects rely on intellectual property's logics to distinguish naturally occurring thoughts and ideas and their externalizable (and commodifiable) "expressions" (Leach 2007). Intellectual property provides a useful logic—creative labor—through which those thoughts and expressions can become attached to us as our own (Leach 2007). But this sort of logic relies on a philosophical separation of the (human) subject from the rest of the (natural) world that Indigenous peoples, including Hopis, may not share (Leach 2007): Whereas intellectual property logics would view creativity as an act of human extractive labor that takes "things" *out* of an inanimate or unconscious world and binds them to us, many Indigenous worldviews might see creativity as the enactment of relationships *with* and obligations *to* a world which is just as alive and thoughtful as we are.

15. It is important to note that descriptions of the practice of Hopi composition outlined here are more or less consistent throughout all of my interviews with Hopi composers.

16. In parsing through her ethnographic material surrounding the peccary hunt, Stolze Lima (1999) finds that the Juruna people of the Amazon always insert linguistic markers

denoting perspective (e.g., to the peccary he was X; to me, the peccary was a Y), implying that "the world only exists for someone . . . there is no reality independent of the subject" (117). In this way, the Juruna conceptualize the world in such a way that humans are not the only ones with a subjective "point of view"—human speech (and, as I argue for the Hopi context, song) "is a part of the various realities for others" including some, but not all, species of animals, plants, and other cosmological entities. The fact that Juruna think and exist within the perspectives of other subjects whose temporalities and conceptions of space are distinct from their own means that their own understanding of self is dispersed and decentered across multiple realities (127).

17. Hopi Junior/Senior High School (HJSHS) is a large concrete complex located on the far east side of the Hopi Reservation, occupying the same terrain as the tribal prison complex and the local radio station. Built in 1986, the school significantly changed the environment for Hopi education, in effect replacing the handful of distant urban public schools and boarding schools that had educated Hopi children and kept them from regularly returning home to their families and villages (see Clemmer 1995; Sakiestewa-Gilbert 2010). With the advent of HJSHS, seventh- through twelfth-grade Hopi youth—for perhaps the first time—made up the majority of their high school student body. Walking into Hopi High School in 2011, one could inevitably see a sea of blue jeans with black T-shirts (and the occasional Bruins sports uniform) and hear the constant sounds of laughter, teasing, trickster antics, and coquetry one might find at any high school.

18. This was made particularly clear during the 2013 Hopi Tribal Council elections, as the trajectory and non-Hopi leadership at HJSHS were raised as important issues for candidates seeking election to the chairman's office.

19. Anita Poleahla, the head of the HJSHS humanities department and a Hopi language and culture teacher, became one of the HMRP's first collaborators. Poleahla has always been an active participant in her village's ceremonial culture and an enthusiastic scholar/ activist, studying a combination of tribal government administration and linguistics as a graduate student before coming to HJSHS. Poleahla has dedicated much of her life to developing Hopi-language curricula in consultation with Hopi elders and Hopi-language scholars. Poleahla has innovatively used recorded media to teach Hopi language and cultural concepts to Hopi youth, particularly through the use of Hopi and non-Hopi traditional songs. Importantly, Poleahla's efforts are not meant to replace the work that many Hopi families that have done to teach the language "in their homes in the way it ought to taught." Those Hopi families that remain culturally connected to Hopi ceremonies and traditional ways of life are to be thanked for preserving the Hopi language for the benefit of those around them. For more information on Poleahla's work, visit http://www. mesamedia.org.

    Poleahla is by no means alone in this effort, as Hopi-language acquisition is seen as critical for the perpetuation of Hopi culture. Scholars including Emory Sekaquaptewa and Sheila Nicholas have done significant work on language issues in the Hopi context. The Hopi Cultural Preservation Office, KUYI Hopi Radio, the Hopi Foundation, and many other community and village organizations have also played an active role in teaching Hopi-language concepts, as have local community performing artists who actively promote Hopi-language use.

20. The specific prompt on the back of the sheet said, "What should we do with these songs? Why? Be creative." While telling students to "be creative" may have skewed the results away from typical, standard, or traditional uses of the recordings (assuming such

categories actually exist), the emphasis on creativity was important for us, as it encouraged the students to think as broadly as possible.

21. A handful of students from each village recognized the *kooyemsi* song from their experiences attending the winter katsina dances; and as the lyrics of the song associated basic words like colors and cardinal directions, many of the students were also able to ascertain the meaning of the song from the training they receive in Poleahla's class. The third song, a *mosayotawi* (buffalo song) to which couples would typically dance, was more complex; it told a narrative of a man at his wits' end over his relationship with his *wuuti* (wife or girlfriend). Most students (with the exception of a few advanced ones) were not able to catch the nuances of the song until we discussed it with them, but many could identify the song's type based on the rapid drumbeat and the introductory tag, which typically precedes these songs.

22. Several caveats need to accompany these results. First, this event was meant specifically as an educational exercise rather than an in-depth research study on Hopi youth opinions on Hopi songs. These descriptions are not necessarily representative of either the students themselves or of Hopi youth broadly, but they show the range of ideas that can be generated by engaging Indigenous students in classroom dialogue over an often charged topic like repatriation. Second, this exercise was only conducted with students in Poleahla's Hopi-language classroom on the Hopi Reservation and has not yet been repeated in other Hopi youth contexts on or off Hopi lands. Factors such as Poleahla's teaching methods, the content and style of my presentation, and the social environment of the classroom may have had an effect on the kinds of ideas generated in the session.

23. In one example from her autobiography, Boulton seems to take great pride in capturing the proprietary musics Hopis had seemingly been unwilling to give up to previous fieldworkers (Boulton 1968, 428–429).

24. For more on Boulton's overarching purpose, see her autobiography, *The Music Hunter* (Boulton 1968, 1).

References

Anderson, Jane. 2013. "Anxieties of Authorship in the Colonial Archive." In *Media Authorship*, edited by C. Chris and D. Gerstener, 1–17. New York: Routledge.

Boulton, Laura. 1968. *The Music Hunter: An Autobiography of a Career*. New York: Doubleday.

Brady, Erika. 1999. *A Spiral Way: How the Phonograph Changed Ethnography*. Jackson: University Press of Mississippi.

Brown, Michael F. 2003. *Who Owns Native Culture?* Cambridge, MA: Harvard University Press.

Cadena, Marisol de la. 2010. "Indigenous Cosmopolitics in the Andes: Conceptual Reflections beyond 'Politics.'" *Cultural Anthropology* 25 (2): 334–370.

Clemmer, Richard O. 1995. *Roads in the Sky: The Hopi Indians in a Century of Change*. Boulder: Westview Press.

Coombe, Rosemary J. 1998. *The Cultural Life of Intellectual Properties: Authorship, Appropriation, and the Law*. Durham, NC: Duke University Press.

Coombe, Rosemary J. 2009. "The Expanding Purviews of Cultural Properties and Their Politics." *Annual Review of Law and Social Science* 5: 393–412.

Deloria, Vine. 1969. *Custer Died for Your Sins: An Indian Manifesto*. Norman: University of Oklahoma Press.

Feld, Steven. 1990. *Sound and Sentiment: Birds, Weeping, Poetics, and Song in Kaluli Expression.* 2nd ed. Philadelphia: University of Pennsylvania Press.

Fewkes, J. Walter. 1899. "Hopi Basket Dances." *Journal of American Folklore* 12 (45): 81–96.

First Archivists Circle. 2007. "Protocols for Native American Archival Materials." http://www2.nau.edu/libnap-p/protocols.html (accessed November 26, 2012).

Fox, Aaron A. 2013. "Repatriation as Animation." In *Cambridge History of World Music*, edited by P. Bohlman, 522–554. Cambridge: Cambridge University Press.

Fox, Aaron A. 2017. "The Archive of the Archive: The Secret History of the Laura Boulton Collection." In *The Routledge Companion to Cultural Property*, edited by Jane Anderson and Haidy Geismar, 194–212. New York: Routledge.

Fox, Aaron A., and Chie Sakakibara. 2009. "Community-Partnered Repatriation." National Science Foundation Grant Proposal.

Handler, Richard. 1991. "Who Owns the Past? History, Cultural Property and the Logic of Possessive Individualism." In *The Politics of Culture*, edited by B. Williams, 63–74. Washington, DC: Smithsonian Institution Press.

Hopi Dictionary Project, University of Arizona. 1998. *Hopi Dictionary: Hopikwa Lavaytutuveni: A Hopi-English Dictionary of the Third Mesa Dialect with an English-Hopi Finder List and a Sketch of Hopi Grammar.* Tucson: University of Arizona Press.

Howes, David. 1995. "Combating Cultural Appropriation in the American Southwest: Lessons from the Hopi Experience Concerning the Uses of Law." *Canadian Journal of Law and Society* 10: 129–154.

Ishii, Lomayumptewa C. 2010. "Western Science Comes to the Hopis: Critically Deconstructing the Origins of an Imperialist Canon." *Wicazo Sa Review* 25 (2): 65–88.

James, Harry C. 1974. *Pages from Hopi History.* Tucson: University of Arizona Press.

Leach, James. 2007. "Creativity, Subjectivity and the Dynamic of Possessive Individualism." In *Creativity and Cultural Improvisation*, edited by T. Ingold and E. Hallam, 99–116. ASA Monograph 43. Oxford: Berg.

Lessig, Lawrence. 2004. *Free Culture: How Big Media Uses Technology and the Law to Lock Down Culture and Control Creativity.* New York: Penguin Press.

List, George. 1994. *Stability and Variation in Hopi Song.* Philadelphia: American Philosophical Society.

Locke, John. 1689. "Property" In *Second Treatise of Government*. http://www.earlymoderntexts.com/assets/pdfs/locke1689a.pdf (accessed February 9, 2017).

Natwani Coalition. 2012. Natwani Coalition website. http://www.hopifoundation.org/programs/natwani (accessed April 11, 2018).

Nicholas, Sheila. 2009. "'I Live Hopi, I Just Don't Speak It'—The Critical Intersection of Language, Culture, and Identity in the Lives of Contemporary Hopi Youth." *Journal of Language, Identity & Education* 8 (5): 321–334.

Nora, Pierre. 1989. "Between Memory and History: Les Lieux de Memoire." *Representations* 26 (Spring): 7–25.

Radin, Margaret Jane. 1982. "Property and Personhood." *Stanford Law Review* 34 (5): 957–1015.

Reed, Trevor G. 2010. "Returning Hopi Voices: Toward a Model for Community-Partnered Repatriation of Archived Traditional Music." MA thesis, Teachers College, Columbia University.

Reed, Trevor G. 2017. "Who Owns Our Ancestors' Voices? Tribal Claims to Pre-1972 Sound Recordings." *Columbia Journal of Law and the Arts* 40 (2): 275–310.

Richland, Justin B. 2011. "Hopi Tradition as Jurisdiction: On the Potentializing Limits of Hopi Sovereignty." *Law and Social Inquiry* 36 (1): 201–234.

Riley, Angela R., and Carpenter, Kristen A. 2016. "Owning Red: A Theory of Indian (Cultural) Appropriation." *Texas Law Review* 94: 859–931.

Sakiestewa-Gilbert, Matthew. 2010. *Education beyond the Mesas: Hopi Students and Sherman Institute, 1902–1929*. Lincoln: University of Nebraska Press.

Seeger, Anthony. 1996. "Ethnomusicologists, Archives, Professional Organizations and the Shifting Ethics of Intellectual Property." *Yearbook for Traditional Music* 28: 87–105.

Seeger, Anthony. 2000. "Folk Heritage in Crisis: Intellectual Property and Audiovisual Archives and Collections." Keynote given at the American Folklife Center. Washington, DC: Library of Congress. https://www.loc.gov/folklife/fhcc/propertykey.html.

Sekaquaptewa, Emory, and Dorothy Washburn. 2004. "They Go Along Singing: Reconstructing the Hopi Past from Ritual Metaphors in Song and Image." *American Antiquity* 69 (3): 457–486.

Sekaquaptewa, Emory, Dorothy Washburn, and Kenneth C. Hill. 2015. *Hopi Katsina Songs*. Lincoln: University of Nebraska Press.

Smith, Andrea. 2005. *Conquest: Sexual Violence and American Indian Genocide*. Cambridge, MA: South End Press.

Smith, Linda Tuhiwai. 1999. *Decolonizing Methodologies: Research and Indigenous Peoples*. London: Zed Books.

Strathern, Marilyn. 2004. "Introduction: Rationales of Ownership." In *Rationales of Ownership: Ethnographic Studies of Transactions and Claims to Ownership in Contemporary Papua New Guinea*, edited by Lawrence Kalinoe and James Leach, 1–12. Herefordshire, UK: Sean Kingston.

Sterne, Jonathan. 2003. *The Audible Past: Cultural Origins of Sound Reproduction*. Durham, NC: Duke University Press.

Stolze Lima, Tania. 1999. "The Two and Its Many: Reflections on Perspectivism in a Tupi Cosmology." *Ethnos* 64 (1): 107–131.

Udall, Louise. 1969. *Me and Mine: The Life Story of Helen Sekaquaptewa*. Tucson: University of Arizona Press.

Vizenor, Gerald. 1989. *Narrative Chance: Postmodern Discourse on Native American Indian Literatures*. Albuquerque: University of New Mexico Press.

Wagner, Roy. 1981. *The Invention of Culture*. Chicago: University of Chicago Press.

Yúdice, George. 2004. *The Expediency of Culture: Uses of Culture in the Global Era*. Durham, NC: Duke University Press.

....

CHAPTER 35

YOLNGU MUSIC, INDIGENOUS "KNOWLEDGE CENTERS" AND THE EMERGENCE OF ARCHIVES AS CONTACT ZONES

....

PETER G. TONER

INTRODUCTION

....

IN early 1997, as I was tying up the loose ends of my doctoral research on music and so-ciality in the Yolngu community of Gapuwiyak, in the Northern Territory of Australia, a Yolngu friend approached me with a request. He wanted me to track down a recording of his deceased father and other men of his father's generation, a recording of a musical performance made in the 1960s or 1970s by some unidentified academic who had been conducting some unspecified research project. The exact details were unclear, but my friend knew the recording existed, because a cassette copy had once been in circulation within the community. My friend would have been a child at the time of the recording, and he had a recollection of the recording being made, but could provide no further details. Although I had some hunches, I was never able to identify the recordist or lo-cate the recording. But my friend's request made me think long and hard about what happens to ethnographic field recordings when they leave their communities of origin, and end up, I presumed, on some dusty shelf in someone's study.[1]

Although that specific recording remained a mystery, the general question of the af-terlife of field recordings stayed with me. Between 2002 and 2004 I conducted a post-doctoral research project[2] that involved the digitization of almost four hundred hours of archival sound recordings made of Yolngu singers and musicians in northeast Arnhem Land, northern Australia, between the mid-1920s and late-1970s. Made primarily by anthropologists and ethnomusicologists, these recordings documented something of the richness of Yolngu musical life, and either constituted a primary research object in themselves, or else were an adjunct to a larger research project. Once these were digitized, I undertook a process of repatriating the digital copies to their Yolngu communities of origin. I rapidly learned not only that the social meaning of ethnographic field recordings is different for those recorded compared to those making the recording, but also that there can be profound intergenerational changes between those recorded compared to their descendants.

This chapter examines different systems of knowledge management, sometimes complementary, sometimes competing. On the one hand we have archives—usually state-run, often with a specific mandate, sometimes with a specific constituency, but all dedicated to certain globally accepted forms and standards of knowledge management. On the other hand we have Indigenous "knowledge centers," "keeping places," or "tribal museums"—usually run by local Indigenous communities, often with a specific mandate, always with a specific constituency, and usually dedicated to certain locally accepted forms and standards of knowledge management. To the extent that these two kinds of institutions collaborate with or compete over the same archival collections, we can usefully consider them to be examples of "contact zones."

The chapter has three parts. First, I briefly outline some of the main issues surrounding Indigenous cultural materials as they are conceptualized and managed in archives. Archives adhere to certain internationally accepted standards of knowledge management, and are substantially geared around a cluster of interrelated concepts: "intangible cultural heritage," "traditional cultural expressions," "cultural property," and "intellectual property." Second, I examine specifically Yolngu cultural materials[3] as they are conceptualized and managed in Yolngu cultural contexts, which involve specifically Yolngu concepts that bear a family resemblance to, but are perhaps incommensurable with, Western notions of "heritage" and "property." Finally, I explore these issues of incommensurability through the prism of the notion of "contact zones," with particular reference to the audiovisual archives of the Australian Institute of Aboriginal and Torres Strait Islander Studies (AIATSIS) and a number of Yolngu "knowledge centers," institutions established in part to manage the same materials. I argue that the archival and the Yolngu systems of knowledge management represent competing and perhaps incommensurable epistemologies, and that Yolngu recourse to archival principles of knowledge management may eventually lead to an erosion of their own.

ARCHIVES AND ARCHIVAL
KNOWLEDGE MANAGEMENT

Far from being neutral repositories of documents, archives have long been recognized by archival scholars as "centres of interpretation" (Osborne 1999, 52) that serve particular interests, particularly those of the state, and that there have been significant shifts in the forms of power associated with archives. Early archives were associated with sovereign forms of power; they were nonpublic and in some cases were "centralized expressions of enlightened despotism" (55). This stands in contrast to the liberal forms of power associated with the modern archive, which exhibited a "transition from secrecy to publicity: the opening-up of the archive to become a public possession" (Shentalinsky 1995, cited in Osborne 1999, 56), represented in France by the opening of archives to the public in 1794, and the creation of the Public Record Office in England in 1838 (55). In either case, there is no archive without a politics of the archive (55), and all archives serve as instruments of power (56). This shift from sovereign to liberal forms of power, supported by archival practices, is relevant to the role of archives in supporting the neoliberal forms of power today.

The archive is also a political expression of the nation-state. There was a close relationship between the national and the social in England through the nineteenth century, understandable in terms of a liberal governmentality and the fact that archives and libraries served as instruments of liberalism (Joyce 1999, 36). Liberalism took a democratic form in the nineteenth century, and archives and libraries played a role in that process, such as the creation of "public" archives and libraries and the constitution of new meanings for the "public" (38). Patrick Joyce writes that the library "involved the formation of a political subject in whose name liberal rule could go forward, and an object of that rule, something to be known and operated upon" (38). Politicians and public intellectuals in mid-nineteenth-century England advocated for the social benefits of the library, in particular the free library, which in turn generated new meanings of "the public." Libraries became publicly funded and thereby were not attached to certain groups, and were explicitly aimed at opening up to all socioeconomic classes in a project of civilizing the working class (39). The archive and the library helped to create the liberal citizen through fostering self-help and voluntary action, and through the idea that knowing one's society led to knowing oneself and future cultural improvement (39). This in turn led to the notion of amassing information on the condition of "the people" and that the library should represent a sense of community (40). For Joyce, these developments in England were a form of "anthropologizing" the metropolitan, which paralleled anthropologizing the colonial archive (40).

The politics of archival memory have been recognized for some time among scholars interested in archival theory and practice: the recognition that "those in power decided who was allowed to speak and who was forced into silence, both in public life and in archival records" (Cook 1997, 18). A useful place to begin examining exactly how modern archival theory and practice developed is with the 1898 publication in the Netherlands of the *Manual for the Arrangement and Description of Archives*. This influential text contained one hundred rules or principles concerning "the nature and treatment of archives" (21), two of the most important of which are the concepts of provenance and original order, "the twin pillars of classic archival theory" (21). Provenance refers to the fact that archives by one creator "are not be mixed with those of other creators, or placed into artificial arrangements based on chronology, geography, or subject" (21). Original

order refers to the principle that the arrangement of archives "must be based on the original organization of the administrative body that produced it" (21). Archivists now note
that the emphasis in the *Manual* was based on the management of government and corporate records and is inadequate for private and personal archives (21); it is also not up
to the task of the changing administrative structures of the twentieth century (22).

The second very influential publication on archival theory and practice was Hilary
Jenkinson's *A Manual of Archive Administration*, first published in 1922. Jenkinson's archival principles were based on the idea of the archivist as the impartial guardian of
evidence:

> The Archivist's career is one of service. He exists in order to make other people's work
> possible. . . . His Creed, the Sanctity of Evidence; his Task, the Conservation of every
> scrap of Evidence attaching to the Documents committed to his charge; his aim to
> provide, without prejudice or afterthought, for all who wish to know the Means of
> Knowledge. . . . The good Archivist is perhaps the most selfless devotee of Truth the
> modern world produces . . .
>
> (cited in Cook 1997, 23)

The capitalization of the words "archivist," "sanctity," "evidence," "documents," "knowledge," and "truth" reflects Jenkinson's positivist belief that evidence could be maintained
impartially and objectively, and that the archivist's role was to keep rather than select
archives (Cook 1997, 23). However, the selection or appraisal of archival records soon
developed as a key principle of archival management. Earlier principles of archival
management were based on closed series of records, whereas the rapid accumulation
of modern records from ongoing organizations required entirely new approaches to archival management: most fundamentally, the shift from the preservation of records to
the selection of records for preservation or appraisal (26–27). It is here in the act of appraisal that we can clearly see the influence of the archivist. In exercising the appraisal
function, it is the archivist who decides "who gets invited into the archival 'houses of
memory' and who does not" (27). In the process, archival practices came to reflect prevailing regimes of power in the form of "New Deal statism, with its emphasis on the
benefits of a management technocracy and of efficiency" (Craig 1990, 139, cited in Cook
1997, 28).

More recent approaches in archival theory advocate the appraisal and selection of
records as a reflection of the society that creates them and that society's values, rather
than one based on the state's ideological values (Cook 1997, 30). Society's values are to
be determined by considering the functions and activities of the records creators themselves, on the assumption that those records creators indirectly represent "the collective functioning of society" (31). In this theoretical framework, context is of the essence,
and provenance is more conceptual and functional than physical and structural; "but
it is provenance nonetheless, whereby the contextual circumstances of record creation
are again made the center of the archivist's universe of activities" (31). We are moving
toward what is referred to as a "postcustodial paradigm": a shift away from physical

records under the custody of the archive, toward a focus on "the context, purpose, intent, interrelationships, functionality, and accountability of the record, its creator, and its creation process" (48). With a postcustodial conception of provenance, archivists will be an integral part of "a dynamic relationship between all connected functions, creators, and 'records'" (48). This new archival orientation seems to point to potential intercultural dialogue over records and to potential points of incommensurability, issues I explore later in this chapter.

Another important issue related to archival theory and practice, and to relatively recent and cosmopolitan developments in Indigenous cultures, is the idea of "heritage." The heritage movement emerged in European "architectural revivals and preservation crusades" as a means of affirming "moral and aesthetic standards believed to be threatened by the last stages of a ruthless industrial revolution" (Taylor 1982, 119). The acceptance of archives as heritage took longer, emerging especially after World War II (120).

There has been a connection between the concept of "heritage" and non-Western cultures since the late nineteenth century, and the collection of materials from such cultures for ethnological collections has been linked to a shifting conceptualization of the concept of "man" (Dominguez 1986, 548). Virginia Dominguez notes that the collecting impulse was connected to a belief that collecting had to be done "before it is too late." This particular kind of historical consciousness makes possible a "double displacement": first, objects are collected not for their intrinsic value but as metonyms for the people who produced them; and second, the people who produced them are objects of examination not because of their intrinsic value but because of what they reveal about our own historical trajectory (548). Dominguez identifies what she calls the three paradoxes of ethnological collecting:

> that in intending to depict other cultures it is seeking to complete a depiction of our own, that it rests on a strong historical consciousness but concentrates its work on peoples perceived to be without history . . . , and that it continually depicts "man" as subject—objectifier, creator, producer—but transforms him into an object and vehicle of knowledge.
>
> (Dominguez 1986, 548)

Extending these insights to a consideration of Hobsbawm and Ranger's *The Invention of Tradition* (1983), Dominguez views ethnological collecting as the invention of heritage: the interest in collecting came from Americans and Europeans, the objects had ethnological significance and formed part of ethnological displays rather than Indigenous self-representation, and so therefore "heritage" must be seen as a concept of Euro-American origin, invented by societies "intent on finding legitimacy through history" (Dominguez 1986, 550).

The past twenty-five years have seen a remarkable extension and universalization of the concept of "heritage," with a profound impact on cultural life and public policy (Hartog 2005, 10). François Hartog notes, "Memory, heritage, history, identity, and nation are united in the polished style of the legislator . . . heritage comes to define less that which one possesses, what one *has*, than circumscribing what one *is*" (10). This is also true on the international stage, with international nongovernmental organizations (NGOs) becoming involved in the management of heritage. Among the best known, of course, is UNESCO's 2003 *Convention for the Safeguarding of the Intangible Cultural Heritage*. In this document, adopted in 2006, "intangible cultural heritage" is defined as "the practices, representations, expressions, knowledge, skills—as well as the instruments, objects, artefacts and cultural spaces associated therewith—that communities, groups and, in some cases, individuals recognize as part of their cultural heritage" (UNESCO 2003, 2). It is also relevant to provide the convention's definition of "safeguarding," which means "measures aimed at ensuring the viability of intangible cultural heritage, including the identification, documentation, research, preservation, protection, promotion, enhancement, transmission, particularly through formal and non-formal education, as well as the revitalization of the various aspects of such heritage" (3). It is clear that the notion of "safeguarding heritage" is compatible with the archival knowledge management practices described above. Similarly, other related concepts including "intellectual property" and "copyright," together with the legal and institutional frameworks that operationalize them, create a complex technological and ideological landscape in which Indigenous cultural practices and values may be inadequately served, if not marginalized altogether (Feld 1996; Mills 1996; WIPO 2004).

Michael Brown has written astutely about these issues from the perspective of anthropology, noting that the rise of the "Information Society," together with its attendant global flows of culture, has led to "a moral panic about intellectual property and its impact on the political, cultural, and economic life of societies everywhere" (Brown 2005, 44). UNESCO's *Convention for the Safeguarding of the Intangible Cultural Heritage* is designed to combat such global flows and protect Indigenous communities but, ironically, "its language and administrative strategies are patterned on the very Information Society practices they are ostensibly trying to counter" (48). In particular, the *Convention* adopts a legalistic perspective in which "heritage" cannot be protected until it is thoroughly documented, a move Brown notes is reminiscent of early salvage anthropology; at any rate, many Indigenous communities are suspicious of the documentation of intangible cultural heritage because it may facilitate its exploitation (48).

Beyond these general orienting concepts, the modern archive operates according to particular standards and practices of knowledge management that are linked to international organizations. State-level archives like the one at AIATSIS may take their lead, in part, from international bodies like UNESCO, which has published its own "Philosophy and Principles" of audiovisual archiving. Among the most general principles are these:

> Audiovisual archivists have, amongst other responsibilities, the task of maintaining the authenticity, and guaranteeing the integrity, of the material in their care. It needs

to be protected from damage, censorship or intentional alteration. Its selection, protection and accessibility in the public interest should be governed by objective policies, not by political, economic, sociological or ideological pressures such as current perceptions of political correctness. The past is fixed. It cannot be changed.

(Edmondson 2004, 8)

Archivists seek to achieve a balance between ownership and copyright, on the one hand, and "a universal right of access to the public memory" (Edmondson 2004, 8), on the other. A fundamental principle of archival practice is that archival materials are organized according to context—"the linkage to its creator, activity, or other related records are the prime considerations and collections are developed, managed and accessed accordingly" (34).

Archivists also work at the interstices of two fundamental principles: preservation and access. Preservation is defined as "the totality of things necessary to ensure the permanent accessibility—forever—of an audiovisual document with the maximum integrity" (Edmondson 2004, 20) and may include technical processes including conservation, restoration, copying, storage, and editing. Access is defined as "any form of use of an archive's collection, services, or knowledge, including playback in real time of sound and moving image holdings and reference to sources of information about sound and moving image holdings and the subject areas they represent" (20). These two principles, in turn, lead to a whole range of more specific management issues undertaken by audiovisual archivists, including the use of technology and technical expertise (37); copying to new audiovisual formats (40); decay, obsolescence, migration between formats (45); and processes of collection development (selection, acquisition, deselection, and disposal) (53). Careful documenting of collections, including the observation of global standards of metadata and respecting the intellectual property legalities, are important facets of archival practice.

Taken together, these principles and practices pertaining to archival modes of knowledge management point to the fact that they are inseparable from the very particular social, cultural, and historical contexts—that is, Western European nation-states from the eighteenth to the twentieth centuries—from which they have sprung. The challenges of archival modes of knowledge management are substantial enough when dealing with cultural materials springing from Western European contexts themselves. When managing Indigenous cultural materials from very different cultural contexts, however, the challenges are inevitably multiplied as possibly incommensurable epistemologies are brought together. This was the case when I repatriated digital copies of archival field recordings of Yolngu music back to their communities of origin, where they came under the management of a number of local institutions sometimes referred to as "knowledge centers." It was here, in these archival "contact zones," where the challenges of cross-cultural repatriation and knowledge management became clear.

YOLNGU KNOWLEDGE MANAGEMENT

For Yolngu people, digitized and repatriated field recordings of music can be thought of as a form of *maḏayin*, a term that encompasses all expressive forms related to the ancestral beings that gave the world its form during the *wangarr* era, sometimes translated into English as "Dreamtime." *Maḏayin*, then, are the artifacts of religious belief and practice, and typically include songs (*manikay*), dances (*bunggul*), painted designs (*miny'tji*), and sacred objects (*rangga*), but can be extended to audio, filmic, or photographic versions of these. Therefore, when objects are returned to Yolngu communities, their management in local "knowledge centers" must conform, at least to some extent, with the ways the original forms are managed.

Yolngu religious knowledge is a system of restricted access and, sometimes, secrecy. Some ceremonies, and the songs, dances, and paintings that make them up, are public or *garma*, and men, women, and children may be actively involved. Other kinds of ceremonies, together with their songs, dances, and paintings, are secret or *dhuyu*, and include secret portions, which are off limits to women and uninitiated men, in addition to public portions.

However, the line between public and secret can be blurry. Public ceremonies may include restricted segments from which women and children are formally excluded—although occasionally very senior women will, in fact, be present. The most sacred and restricted Yolngu ceremony is the Ngärra or Maḏayin, which pertains to the production and maintenance of secret sacred objects and the indoctrination of young men into religious secrets. During the Ngärra the men spend most of their time in a secluded area that is off-limits to the uninitiated, but every evening there is a public performance of songs and dances, during which the men wear normally restricted painted designs on their chests (see Keen 1990). Occasionally a painting that is considered very sacred is produced on an initiate's chest, but it is intentionally smudged before the initiate goes out in public, indicating a Yolngu emphasis on the process of producing *maḏayin* as much as the products themselves. So it would be incorrect to state simplistically that Yolngu religion contains two entirely separate domains, one public and one secret. In fact, as Howard Morphy has pointed out, it is misleading to suggest that Yolngu religious knowledge is powerful merely because it is restricted and some people are denied access to it; rather, we must consider that such knowledge is powerful because of the ways in which it is thought with and used, because it is internally coherent, logically consistent, and powerful in an explanatory way (Morphy 1991, 77).

Perhaps more useful is the Yolngu distinction between two categories of knowledge: "inside" (*djinawa*) and "outside" (*warrangul*). These terms represent a continuum of more restricted to less restricted knowledge of *wangarr* ancestral beings or their manifestations in *maḏayin*, and what is "inside" and what is "outside" must be understood to be relative. An aspect of religious knowledge may be considered inside until one is told a second interpretation that is *more* inside; after which the former is then considered to be outside relative to the latter. Inside interpretations are not necessarily secret, although secret knowledge does certainly belong to a level of inside knowledge restricted to adult initiated men (Morphy 1991, 78). Furthermore, in the Yolngu context, we must distinguish between *having* knowledge and *demonstrating* that one has knowledge. Senior rights-holders demonstrate their understanding of religious matters frequently, whereas others, even those who may, in fact, be very knowledgeable, defer to those senior rights-holders and do not demonstrate their knowledge publicly (88–89). Women, in particular, will publicly deny knowledge about religious matters, even when men insist that they know a great deal.

According to Ian Keen, Yolngu control over religious knowledge is based on the twin modalities of (1) control of space or physical access and (2) the encoding of information in ambiguous forms (Keen 1994, 251). Secret rituals are conducted in places that are physically off-limits to the uninitiated, and even during public rituals, there may be performances of "secret" dances and songs from which women and children are temporarily excluded. The ambiguity of religious forms means that a song may be heard, or a design may be seen in public, which concerns restricted knowledge; but because it is not interpretable by the uninitiated, then religious knowledge is still controlled. The same painted design, for example, may have an "outside" or public meaning as well as several layers of increasingly "inside" or restricted meanings, and each person looking at the design will interpret it according to the level of religious knowledge to which he or she has access.

The politics of Yolngu religious knowledge, then, is a politics of assertion and denial. To claim rights over tangible property—most prominently, rights to land—requires a person to claim rights over the intangible—like the songs and painted designs that function as "title deeds" to land, the knowledge of which is essential to any credible claim over land.

Although there are Yolngu concepts that are clearly analogous to "ownership," they are not identical to Western concepts and so they must be qualified. Yolngu believe that tracts of land, and their associated *madayin*, were bestowed by the ancestral beings upon the first groups of people associated with those places, and people often refer to those groups as the "owners" of those estates and the *madayin* that goes along with them. The range of rights associated with this "ownership" include the right to use, the right to be consulted by others prior to their use, and the right to knowledge about land and *madayin* (see Williams 1986).

There are two major qualifications to a straightforward extension of Western understandings of ownership. First, other individuals and groups possess their own distinctive rights over the land and *madayin* of any group. Individuals have rights over the land and *madayin* of their mother's group (in which case they are referred to as "managers"), and of their mother's mother's group, although these rights are not identical with those of the "owners." Additionally, groups whose own land and *madayin* are linked to another group's because they are connected mythologically by ancestral journeys also have certain rights. So, even though a group of people may be acknowledged as "owners," other groups and individuals have certain rights to be consulted by, to receive royalties from, and to veto decisions by those "owners."

The second major qualification has to do with the notion of "ownership" itself. Yolngu discourse about rights to *ma*d*ayin* is very often phrased in terms of custodianship rather than ownership. Writing of paintings, one key aspect of *ma*d*ayin*, Howard Morphy states that "[t]hey are not so much owned as integral to the very existence of the clan" (Morphy 1991, 57). Yolngu languages use the suffix *-wa*t*angu*, or "-holders," to articulate this notion: those primarily responsible for land (*wänga*) are known as *wänga-wa*t*angu* or "land-holders" (rather than landowners); those with primary rights over a set of songs (*manikay*) might be referred to as the *manikay-wa*t*angu*. Therefore, although Yolngu people clearly hold and exercise rights over property, both tangible and intangible, Yolngu concepts of "ownership" are not identical with our own.

ARCHIVES AS "CONTACT ZONES"

Mary Louise Pratt writes that "contact zones" are "social spaces where disparate cultures meet, clash, and grapple with each other, often in highly asymmetrical relations of domination and subordination—like colonialism, slavery, or their aftermaths as they are lived out across the globe today" (Pratt 1992, 4). In Pratt's usage:

> "contact zone" is an attempt to invoke the spatial and temporal copresence of subjects previously separated by geographic and historical disjunctures, and whose trajectories now intersect. By using the term "contact," I aim to foreground the interactive, improvisational dimensions of colonial encounters so easily ignored or suppressed by diffusionist accounts of conquest and domination. A "contact" perspective emphasizes how subjects are constituted in and by their relations to each other. It treats the relations among colonizers and colonized, or travelers and "travelees," not in terms of separateness or apartheid, but in terms of copresence, interaction, interlocking understandings and practices, often within radically asymmetrical relations of power.
>
> (Pratt 1992, 7)

A key concept related to the notion of the contact zone is "transculturation," describing "how subordinated or marginal groups select and invent from materials transmitted to them by a dominant or metropolitan culture" (Pratt 1992, 6). Pratt notes, "While subjugated peoples cannot readily control what emanates from the dominant culture, they do determine to varying extents what they absorb into their own, and what they use it for" (6). This is an apt description of the Indigenous engagement with archival materials today. For the most part, archival collections were created by non-Indigenous scholars, missionaries, or officials, and so Indigenous peoples are not in control of what emanates from archives. Through the unique position of Indigenous "knowledge centers," however, they do develop control over how these materials are reabsorbed and used within their communities.

James Clifford extends Pratt's ideas to consider the idea of museums as "contact zones." In part, he was trying to account for his experiences in 1989 as a consultant for the Portland Museum of Art, when the museum invited Tlingit elders to discuss its Northwest Coast Indian collection. The objects themselves, the focus of the museum, were left at the margins of discussions, acting as "aides-mémoires" for a series of performances among those gathered (Clifford 1997, 188–189). Clifford uses the term "contact zone" in relation to museums to point to a movement away from the organizing structure of the collection toward "an ongoing historical, political, and moral relationship" (192), in which the museum was called on "to be accountable in a way that went beyond mere preservation" (193). Clifford notes that the objects in the care of the museum "could never be entirely possessed by the museum. They were sites of a historical negotiation, occasions for an ongoing contact" (194).

A new dynamic is clearly at play, and the transcultural tensions inherent in "contact zones" can help us to understand it. Clifford notes that collections and the contact histories that they represent are caught in a dichotomous relationship between community "experience" and curatorial "authority," and are subject to contingent and political processes of power, negotiation, and representation (Clifford 1997, 208). This contact work is made even more complex by the emergence of "tribal museums" that overlap with and diverge from conventional museum practices, as these new institutions "are differently centered, expressing partial histories and locally inflected aesthetic, cultural contexts" and necessitate "active collaboration and a sharing of authority" (210). Co-curation and repatriation are placed on the table as part of the process of transculturating the museum by the tribal world (212). Clifford states that museums "increasingly work the borderlands between different worlds, histories, and cosmologies" (212). The same holds true for archives.

I turn now to an examination of archives as an extension of Pratt's and Clifford's ideas, as examples of "contact zones." Although I suspect that the ideas I present will have resonances across a range of institutions, I have in mind a specific set. On the more conventional side is the audiovisual archive of AIATSIS. Although AIATSIS is specifically mandated to document and preserve Australian Aboriginal culture, its archives function according to principles of knowledge management followed by state archives worldwide. The AIATSIS audiovisual archive contains over 650,000 photographic images and over 45,000 hours of sound recordings, a small set of which I digitized and repatriated. On the other side are a range of Yolngu "keeping places" which have taken on the task of managing such archival materials upon their return to Yolngu communities: two art and cultural centers, one school library and literature production center, and one newly established "knowledge center." Although the mandates of each of these differ, the methods of knowledge management are all very similar.

CASE STUDY, PART 1: DAVID BIERNOFF'S RECORDINGS AND PHOTOGRAPHS OF DHALWANGU MUSICIANS

To illustrate some of these ideas, I present a brief case study representing a relatively unproblematic set of archival materials: a set of photographs and field recordings made by the anthropologist David Biernoff in Numbulwar, Northern Territory, in 1972. The occasion was a *dhapi* circumcision ceremony for a boy named Gudawuma, and the relevant materials include three hours of sound recordings of music and roughly three dozen photographs.

These materials generated a great deal of interest in the community of Gapuwiyak, where I conducted much of my fieldwork. Biernoff did not conduct fieldwork himself in Gapuwiyak, but a number of men and women who had lived in Numbulwar during the middle of the twentieth century moved to Gapuwiyak when it was established in the late 1960s, and so there is a strong social (and cosmological) connection between the two communities. Biernoff's photographs and recordings contain the images and voices of many of the fathers, grandfathers, mothers, and grandmothers of the current generation of adults in Gapuwiyak, especially those of the Dhalwangu patrifilial group. Particularly noteworthy are three Dhalwangu men: Gandalal, Walumarri, and Rruyilnga, whose descendants represent much of the political and ritual leadership of the Dhalwangu at Gapuwiyak. Rruyilnga, who was venerated as a great singer and ritual leader and was also the initiate Gudawuma's father, died less than a year after the recordings were made, during another of his sons' *dhapi* circumcision ceremony. That boy, Bangana, grew up to be a formidable singer, and was my own main research collaborator before he died at the age of thirty-seven in 2002.

The AIATSIS catalog entry pertaining to Biernoff's field recordings displays at a glance that some of the main principles of archival knowledge management are present in the form of metadata fields (Figure 35.1). Many of these fields, and the metadata contained within them, are obviously of primary use to non-Indigenous archivists. The listing under Biernoff's name acknowledges his intellectual property rights over the physical recordings themselves as the recordist. Anyone wishing to make use of the recording, including the singers themselves and their descendants, must get the permission of the recordist for that purpose. In my experience, most recordists were all too happy for their field recordings to be digitized and repatriated back to their communities of origin. However, there are a number of individuals who refuse for a variety of reasons, and so any use of their materials by the Yolngu community would constitute a breach of copyright law. Copyright over the creative content (rather than the physical recording) could in principle be granted to the Yolngu singers on the recording, but Western copyright law is typically unreliable in protecting Indigenous interests because the authorship and originality requirements of copyright law are ill-suited to collectively owned,

Call Number: BIERNOFF_D01
Accession no : 002712 - 002721
Title: Ceremonial songs and stories from Numbulwar, NT
Creator.: Biernoff, D. C.
Publication Information: 1971-1972
Physical Description: 19 audiocassettes (approximately 60 min. each)
Series: BIERNOFF_D01
General Note: Auditioned
Digital copies are available
Duration: 19 hours 47 minutes
Abstract: Circumcision corroborees, men's song cycle, Dhambul
corroboree; Dreaming stories, discussion of country, Mara sites, law,
traditions, skin groups and traditional medical practices from Numbulwar
area
Access: Restricted - ceremonial and gender specific material
Date/Place: Recorded at Numbulwar, N.T., 1971-1972, by David Biernoff.
Place: Numbulwar / Rose River (East Arnhem Land SD53-11)
Collection: Sound Collection
Source of acquisition: Biernoff, David C.; deposited on 21 December
1972
Performer: Laibich; Larranggana; Tommy Reuben; Wurramarbi; Galiliwa;
Rimili; Nambadj; Mongoana; Peter Yarrawu; Rex; Tommy; Homer; Wiyulwi;
Don; Rruyilnga; Djima; Gumuk; Dunggi; Waguti Marawilli; Ken; Bob; Mac
Riley; Lindsay Joshua; Alex
Language/group: Alawa people (N92) (NT SD53-10)
Dhalwangu people (N143.1) (NT SD53-03)
Dhiyakuy language (N149) (NT SD53-03)
Mara / Marra people (N112) (NT SD53-11)
Nunggubuyu people (N128) (NT SD53-11)
Unclassified languages
Duration: 194700
Sound characteristics: analogue
Subject Term : Music - Traditional - Ceremonial
Sites
Indigenous knowledge - Health and medicine
Electronic Access: Click here to view PDF finding aid
The recordings in this collection are not accessible on-line. To make an
appointment to listen to this material please contact the Audiovisual Access
Unit.

FIGURE 35.1 Screen capture of catalog entry for David Biernoff, "Ceremonial songs and stories from Numbulwar, NT," Mura online catalog, Australian Institute of Aboriginal and Torres Strait Islander Studies.

orally transmitted musical traditions (see Feld 1996, 2000; Mills 1996; Seeger 1996). This certainly represents a potential site of incommensurability between the knowledge systems intersecting in the archival contact zone. For Yolngu, rights over music are based on a person's own patrifilial group identity, as well as on matrilateral connections to mother's and mother's mother's groups, and access is potentially restricted based on age and gender. Although AIATSIS does take these kinds of cultural factors into consideration in allowing access, they are still bound by depositors' conditions, and Yolngu are sometimes perplexed when they are unable to obtain existing recordings of their fathers, for example, because a depositor's intellectual property rights trump their own Yolngu intellectual property rights. At the other end of the spectrum, some archival recordings of Yolngu music are lodged at AIATSIS by depositors who have indicated a desire for them to be made as widely available as possible, which obviously raises the prospect of copies of the recordings being disseminated far too broadly.

Other metadata fields, based on Dublin Core metadata principles, are clearly designed with archival knowledge management in mind. The series "BIERNOFF_Do1" represents the entire deposit of materials at a particular moment in time (in this case, December 21, 1972), and subsequent deposits by the same depositor are given sequential series numbers. This illustrates the archival principle of *respect des fonds*, whereby items in a collection are linked to other items to form an organic whole that has documentary precedence over the individual items within it. Archive numbers, creation dates, and topical, place of origin, and language/group identifiers allow the entire AIATSIS collection to be organized and cross-referenced. Metadata fields indicating that the material has been auditioned or digitized assist archivists in managing the collection. These metadata fields, in general, do not reflect Yolngu concerns. It is not uncommon for a Yolngu person to be aware that some non-Aboriginal researcher, exact identity unknown, some years previously had recorded a particular, named Yolngu individual. The archival principle of provenance prioritizes creators of fonds and manages collections around them, but in my experience of repatriating digital copies of such recordings back to Yolngu communities, people almost always requested recordings by particular singers, with no concern whatsoever with recordists' identities.

The physical description of "19 audiocassettes (approximately 60 min. each)," together with the indication that the recordings have been digitized, glosses over a massive area of archival management of sound recordings, pertaining to preserving original media and making preservation copies. An earlier version of the AIATSIS catalog provided additional information on the Biernoff recordings that indicated five different sets of copies from the original cassettes: two sets of reel-to-reel recordings (one on 7-inch reels and one on 10.5-inch); twenty 24-bit, 48 kHz WAV sound files; twenty 128 kb/sec. MP3 files; and two CD-Rs containing 16-bit, 48 kHz WAV files. There is a general philosophical discussion to be had about the status of the copies vis-à-vis the original recording, and the status of the recording vis-à-vis the original performance. More practically, in archival circles the main point is that a digital copy represents a unique object in and of itself—so every digital transfer from one format to another requires a new archival record with its own metadata. Multiple copies in different formats serve other archival purposes: reel-to-reel tape is still valued as an archival preservation medium and is used because of its stability and known shelf life, whereas the less well-known shelf life of digital media is mitigated in part by multiple copies allowing for a certain digital attrition rate. During my 2002–2004 research, 24-bit, 48 kHz resolution was considered to be a minimal archival standard, but medium-quality MP3 files were considered to be ideal for public access. So it seems that copying for a variety of purposes serves practical functions for archival management.

The infinite availability of copies, however, creates certain problems for a system of knowledge management like that found among the Yolngu, based as it is on the restriction rather than the provision of access. In the case of recordings made in public ceremonial contexts, like the initiation ceremony recorded by Biernoff, the potential problems are fewer, as women and uninitiated men would have access to those contexts anyway— although there is still a question of whether the traditional owners of those songs desire for an unlimited number of copies to be available. Recordings made in more restricted contexts, however, present a different set of problems. Access to these contexts is carefully controlled, and even once inside them, a person's exposure to more restricted materials may be partial. The availability of multiple copies of such recordings, therefore, creates challenges for traditional owners of the songs in regard to their ability to exercise some control over access.

Preservation, too, may be thought of differently among the Yolngu. My collaborators indicated their approval for my field recordings on the grounds that they would preserve their music for future generations, and indeed Yolngu are quite active in making their own recordings of music. Traditionally, however, music was entirely ephemeral, not surviving longer than the moment of its performance. Once recordings are made, they may be taken to provide a definitive and authoritative rendition of a set of songs, something which is simply not possible in oral transmission. Moreover, what exactly is "the song" or "the performance" that is to be recorded anyway? In my fieldwork, I took to recording entire sessions without pausing between songs, largely because the musicians I was recording almost never gave me advance warning that they were about to begin singing again; so pausing would result in a failure to record the very beginnings of songs. I noticed that Yolngu recordists were rather indifferent to these opening sections, and to the sometimes quite elaborate a cappella vocal codas at the ends of songs, opting only to record the more substantial, accompanied, middle section. Regarding entire recording sessions, the question of when to begin raised similar issues about the ontological status of the musical work. A Yolngu musical performance is clearly underway when one or more men sing a sequence of songs, accompanied by one singer's clapsticks and a single didjeridu player. But when does the performance begin? There may be an initial period of up to thirty minutes during which a singer hums to himself, or sings lightly with minimal vocal articulation, barely audible clapsticks, and no didjeridu accompaniment (often because the singer is waiting for him to arrive). If musical performances lack definitive beginnings, and Yolngu themselves are indifferent to recording segments of individual songs that ethnomusicologists recognize, then this raises the prospect that the musical work is ontologically different in Western and Yolngu contexts. If this is the case, then it is possible that everything following from that, including the recording, documentation, and preservation of such performances, may also have a different and even incommensurable status.[4]

An examination of the field tape audition sheets for the Biernoff recordings, produced by the AIATSIS archives, reveals some of the same archival documentation discussed earlier, as well as some additional information. Being broken down by each separate field tape, the metadata is more specific and, therefore, more useful. Six men are listed under "performer/speaker," although not all of them would have been singers—Rex and Wiyulwi [sic] were men of the Dhuwa moiety, and therefore would not sing Yirritja moiety songs. The subject keywords narrow the context, but they are still standardized categories. The "language/people" field is interesting in that it lists "Nargala," a term of reference referring to the Dhalwangu group that is no longer in widespread use. The "places" field specifies "Numbulwar/Rose River" (the latter being the name of the former mission station), together with a standardized geographical reference used for cross-referencing. "Recording quality," listed as "fair to good," is of course a subjective judgment on the part of the sound archivist, focusing on surface features rather than the content of a recording. The same "restricted, men only" warning is listed under "notes," but in fact, the content is of the public *manikay* genre and is open to all listeners. The "archive item number" again references the fonds and the accession number. The "timing point" indicates the beginning and end of the recording—in this case, it is a single event, but in principle, a single sound recording could capture a number of discrete musical events but be treated as a single archival object. The "description," "date," and "place" provide information on the event itself.

One interesting feature of documentation at the AIATSIS audiovisual archives is seen in the particularities of field tape audition sheets. When sound archivists audition a field recording as part of the documentation process, they identify the sounds on the recording and note the time that they begin and their duration. In this case, Biernoff's field recording is reduced to a notation of "m" for male voices, in addition to the notations "calls, dj, sts," meaning vocal calls by performers, plus accompaniment by didjeridu and hardwood clapsticks, and each song item is given a length in seconds. Other notes include "calling out," "speech," "coughing," and vocables like "Aaah!" understood to occur in between song items. In the absence of any knowledge of Yolngu languages or musical traditions, archivists must revert in their documentation to the most superficial surface features of the content, with a focus on the alternation of musical sounds and silences.

These metadata categories indicate a focus on particular styles of documentation that conform to globally accepted principles of archival knowledge management. For archivists, to know an item of intangible cultural heritage is to quantify its contents, to make use of established metadata fields, and to apply certain predetermined categories. Performers' names and general context are certainly noted, but dates, places, recordists' names, field tape numbers, archival reference numbers, and analog and digital audio formats are the predominant concerns. Having participated in this kind of work myself, and having the greatest respect for sound archivists, it is nonetheless easy for the rich and culturally specific content of sound recordings to be reduced to documentation like this, focusing on detailed knowledge of who made them and how to find them within the archive. Documentation, preservation, and access are the keys to archival knowledge management.

In contrast, Yolngu auditioning of archival recordings of music focuses almost exclusively on the specific content of the recordings, not as alternating sounds and silences with a time-code, but as distinct musical utterances conveying specific cultural meanings. Listeners note poetic phrasing, vocal quality and timbre, and didjeridu style. Listeners also spend a great deal of time identifying as accurately as possible the singers on a recording and listen with great amusement to the conversations between songs. A Yolngu audition sheet of a recording, in other words, would concern itself with very different metadata fields, ones that are largely ignored in archival practices.

CASE STUDY, PART 2: THE RECEPTION
OF BIERNOFF'S RECORDINGS AND
PHOTOGRAPHS IN GAPUWIYAK

How, then, are such materials managed by Yolngu people themselves when they have been repatriated in digital form? How can we understand this "second life" of intangible cultural heritage? A return to the archival principles of preservation and access is instructive. The field recordings made by David Biernoff are categorized by Yolngu as *garma* or public, which removes some of the thornier issues in managing secret materials. Nevertheless, even with public musical genres, there is a strong sense of rights in who should speak for those collections. Listening to public musical genres never presented a problem, in the sense that anyone was permitted to listen, although it was frequently the case that direct descendants of the singers on the recordings should be prioritized in regard to playing the recordings for them and making copies for them. In discussing the content of the recordings, people were slightly more circumspect—even if a listener was knowledgeable about the content, her or his comments were usually of the most general kind (identifying a song subject), deferring to the most senior male of the group in question who lived in the community for more detailed information.

Some Yolngu communities had developed ideas of how access to repatriated cultural heritage materials should be managed, representing an interesting amalgam of Yolngu and Western archival notions. A brochure for the Galiwin'ku Indigenous Knowledge Centre provided a painted depiction of the physical and philosophical space that the center would take, and makes it clear that issues of access and the restriction of access are important. A Yolngu painting representing the knowledge cente shows separate computers for Yolngu and non-Yolngu, separate computers for public and secret information, and separate storage for "top secret information and objects." It is also notable that this conceptualization of knowledge management was presented explicitly in the form of a map, with symbolic depictions of the land and the seas surrounding the island community. This relates directly to the foundation of all Yolngu *maḏayin* in the land and sea and the exploits of the creative ancestral beings. In Gapuwiyak, the "knowledge center" concept has been developed more recently, and in a different direction, based primarily within the context of an art and craft center, with a multimedia component for producing Yolngu films and other media. The field recordings that I repatriated back to Gapuwiyak were stored on the Gapuwiyak Culture and Arts Centre computer, where they can be incorporated into a variety of creative projects.

In a Yolngu sense, the preservation of intangible *maḏayin* is achieved through continued performance—so, a knowledge of songs and their meanings is preserved through musical performance, whereby knowledgeable older singers sit together with younger singers, the latter learning through repeated exposure. For one to become knowledgeable about religious doctrine, one must attend a great many ceremonies and participate as a singer. In the case of archival field recordings of Yolngu music that have been repatriated back to the community, it is possible to extend musical and religious knowledge by participating "virtually" in ceremonies held generations ago. Listening to archival recordings in Yolngu communities results in a great deal of "memory work": listeners comment on the superior musical and poetic abilities of their fathers and grandfathers, discuss musical change, and reminisce about the ceremonies of the past, especially if listeners were present at the events on the recording. They also listen closely to the words of the songs to improve their own poetic techniques.

The main singer on the Biernoff recordings, as mentioned earlier, was Rruyilnga, the father of my main research collaborator, the late Bangana Wunungmurra. Playing the Biernoff recordings elicited a large outpouring of Rruyilnga memorialization, especially on the part of my friend Micky Wunungmurra. Micky's and Bangana's grandfathers were classificatory brothers who had both been married to the same woman (meaning that they were connected through both patrilateral and matrilateral links). Micky told me that Rruyilnga had taught him to sing, especially certain distinctive features of phrasing and poetics, which he pointed out to me as we listened to the recording. Micky said that he then passed along this style to Rruyilnga's own sons, who had been relatively young when he died, so that his style would "stay in the family." It also became apparent to me that Micky had been studying the recording closely over the previous several days, as he sang along verbatim to many different passages.

People in Gapuwiyak put the repatriated archival materials into circulation within the community in some interesting ways. My visit in 2010 happened to coincide with the National Aboriginal and Islander Day of Celebration (NAIDOC). For this event, people involved with the Gapuwiyak Culture and Arts Centre wanted to put together computerized slideshows, making use of both archival images and archival sound recordings, to be played in the community center. This became a major preoccupation as I worked with a variety of different people, listening to archival recordings of their groups, making appropriate selections, selecting photographs, and editing them all together with synchronized timings (see Figure 35.2). For the Dhalwangu group, Biernoff's recordings of Rruyilnga were unquestionably of the most interest. I was asked to use audio editing software to reduce the rather overpowering didjeridu drone on the original recording to enable the words to be heard more clearly, underscoring the Yolngu aesthetic that the words of a song are its most important attribute. The Dhalwangu elder Paul Gurrumuruwuy had very specific ideas of which songs on the Biernoff recordings should be used in the soundtrack, many corresponding to dances depicted in some of Biernoff's photographs of the ceremony, such as *marandjalk* (stingray) and *calico* (cloth or flag).

In the end, the slideshow representing the Dhalwangu comprised 198 photographs and thirty-three minutes of accompanying audio. Twenty-eight photographs from Biernoff's collection were used together with selections from his field recordings, followed by 134 photographs taken in the 1970s and 1980s by a researcher and a pilot, accompanied by archival field recordings from the 1970s made by the Yolngu elder Daymbalipu Mununggurr (on a grant from AIATSIS). Finally, three dozen photographs

FIGURE 35.2 Micky Wunungmurra and Paul Gurrumuruwuy Wunungmurra listen to recordings from the David Biernoff Collection, Gapuwiyak, July 2010.

Photograph courtesy of the author.

provided by me and the anthropologist Jennifer Deger were accompanied by selections from my field recordings. The slideshow attracted well over one hundred people, who enthusiastically cheered as the different photographs emerged.

Conclusion

I would like to return to the notion of archives as "contact zones," and to Pratt's emphasis on the spatial and temporal copresence of subjects in a postcolonial context, in particular, interactive and improvisational situations within asymmetrical relations of power (Pratt 1992, 4). Her related notion of "transculturation" describes how subordinated groups select from and reinvent materials transmitted to them from the dominant culture (6). Both ideas seem to me to be very productive in scrutinizing the relationship between the archives of the state, like AIATSIS, and Indigenous "knowledge centers."

Most archival collections were created under the conditions of colonialism and its aftermath by agents of the settler state. The relations of power were such that Yolngu musicians had relatively little control over the fact that recordings were made by anthropologists and ethnomusicologists, and practically no knowledge of what happened to these recordings after the initial schizophonic act. With the advent of Aboriginal autonomy, beginning in the 1970s, Yolngu people would have had more control over research activities; but field recordings still disappeared into archives that most people knew little or nothing about.

As an institution, AIATSIS was established to document and preserve Australian Aboriginal culture, and it has always had a very high degree of Aboriginal involvement. Aboriginal cultural values permeate AIATSIS archival policies, and many Aboriginal people work in the archives, so it would be incorrect to state that AIATSIS is paternalistic (although it may have been when it was first established). However, even with a strong dose of Aboriginal values, the institution nonetheless is committed to globally recognized archival standards and practices.

As a result, there is a virtual space between state archives and Indigenous "knowledge centers," mediated by digitized and repatriated archival collections, which might well be characterized as a contact zone. The two kinds of archives and their agents are copresent in the sense that they agree to manage certain archival materials jointly. However, there is a clear power differential, in the sense that it is the AIATSIS archive that controls the release of those collections, subject to the state of documentation, deposit conditions, and intellectual property considerations. The archival principle of access is upheld, but only under conditions set by the archive and its functioning as an artifact of neoliberal governance.

For their part, Yolngu "knowledge centers" themselves walk a fine line. On the one hand, they facilitate the transcultural reinvention of these archival materials that had been collected under one set of colonial and postcolonial conditions and returned under another. Given their moribund conditions in the archive, the only social life these things have is a second life in a transgenerational Yolngu context. On the other hand, it is also clear to me that, in order to protect their culture, Yolngu are increasingly being called on to adopt the language and practices of the archive—namely, "intangible cultural heritage," "intellectual property," and everything that goes with them, and these differ in many key respects from the language and practices of *madayin*. This raises the prospect of the erosion of Yolngu knowledge management practices, as identified by George Yúdice:

> In accepting Western forms of law in order to protect their technologies . . . and cultural practices . . . , non-Western peoples may undergo even more rapid transformation. If a particular technology or ritual is not currently included as a form of protectable property, the recourse to Western law to ensure that others do not make profits therefrom almost certainly entails the acceptance of the property principle. What will it mean when non-Western forms of knowledge, technology, and cultural practices are incorporated into intellectual property and copyright law?
>
> (Yúdice 2003, 2)

The challenge for both kinds of institutions is to recognize the epistemological hurdles inherent in managing knowledge in the contact zone. There are some indications that the ontological status of musical works themselves, as well as of archival objects resulting from musical performances, may be somewhat different and possibly incommensurable in Western and Yolngu contexts. If this is the case, then both archivists and traditional owners must be cognizant of these differences. Through a robust intercultural dialogue, it may be possible for archivists to learn more about how music and their resulting recordings are constituted in Yolngu discourse (cf. Keen 1995; 2011, 115), creating the possibility for archival practices to be expanded to make room for Yolngu knowledge management practices (Toner 2003). If this can be accomplished, then not only will archival recordings of Yolngu music be documented and preserved into the future but also they will continue to live a "second life" in Yolngu communities, where they maintain their status as forms of *madayin*, with all that entails.

NOTES

1. The ideas in this chapter were first formulated in presentations at the 2005 annual meeting of the Society for Ethnomusicology in Atlanta, at the 2007 annual meeting of the Canadian Anthropology Society in Toronto, and at the 2011 annual meeting of the Canadian Anthropology Society in Fredericton. I thank the chairs and copresenters in those sessions, and members of those audiences for insightful commentary.
2. This postdoctoral project was carried out at the Centre for Cross-Cultural Research at the Australian National University and was funded by the Australian Research Council. I am grateful to both institutions for their support.
3. As an anthropologist whose focus is on music in its social and ritual contexts, I have conducted research since 1995 among the Yolngu people of northeast Arnhem Land in northern Australia. In addition to making over ninety hours of field recordings of Yolngu music, during my postdoctoral work I digitized and repatriated nearly four hundred hours of archival field recordings back to their Yolngu communities of origin.
4. Other representations of *madayin*, like paintings, take hours to painstakingly produce, but may be either smudged before being seen in public (Morphy 1991, 194), or else may be covered up entirely and never seen in public (1). These practices also suggest that Yolngu value works of art not only in their finished form, but perhaps more in terms of the processes of their production.

REFERENCES

Brown, Michael F. 2005. "Heritage Trouble: Recent Work on the Protection of Intangible Cultural Property." *International Journal of Cultural Property* 12: 40–61.

Clifford, James. 1997. *Routes: Travel and Translation in the Late Twentieth Century*. Cambridge, MA: Harvard University Press.

Cook, Terry. 1997. "What Is Past Is Prologue: A History of Archival Ideas since 1898, and the Future Paradigm Shift." *Archivaria* 43: 17–63.

Craig, Barbara L. 1990. "What Are the Clients? Who Are the Products? The Future of Archival Public Services in Perspective." *Archivaria* 31: 135–141.

Dominguez, Virginia R. 1986. "The Marketing of Heritage." *American Ethnologist* 13 (3): 546–555.

Edmondson, Ray. 2004. *Audiovisual Archiving: Philosophy and Principles*. Paris: UNESCO.

Feld, Steven. 1996. "pygmy POP: A Genealogy of Schizophonic Mimesis." *Yearbook for Traditional Music* 28: 1–35.

Feld, Steven. 2000. "A Sweet Lullaby for World Music." *Public Culture* 12 (1): 145–171.

Hartog, François. 2005. "Time and Heritage." *Museum International* 57 (3): 7–18.

Hobsbawm, Eric, and Terence Ranger. 1983. *The Invention of Tradition*. Cambridge: Cambridge University Press.

Joyce, Patrick. 1999. "The Politics of the Liberal Archive." *History of the Human Sciences* 12 (2): 35–49.

Keen, Ian. 1990. "Images of Reproduction in the Yolngu Madayin Ceremony." *Australian Journal of Anthropology* 1 (2/3): 192–207.

Keen, Ian. 1994. *Knowledge and Secrecy in an Aboriginal Religion*. Oxford: Clarendon Press.

Keen, Ian. 1995. "Metaphor and the Metalanguage: 'Groups' in Northeast Arnhem Land." *American Ethnologist* 22 (3): 502–527.

Keen, Ian. 2011. "The Language of Property: Analyses of Yolngu Relations to Country." In *Ethnography and the Production of Anthropological Knowledge: Essays in Honour of Nicolas Peterson*, edited by Yasmine Musharbash and Marcus Barber, 101–119. Canberra: ANU E Press.

Mills, Sherylle. 1996. "Indigenous Music and the Law: An Analysis of National and International Legislation." *Yearbook for Traditional Music* 28: 57–86.

Morphy, Howard. 1991. *Ancestral Connections: Art and an Aboriginal System of Knowledge*. Chicago: University of Chicago Press.

Osborne, Thomas. 1999. "The Ordinariness of the Archive." *History of the Human Sciences* 12 (2): 51–64.

Pratt, Mary Louise. 1992. *Imperial Eyes: Travel and Transculturation*. New York: Routledge.

Seeger, Anthony. 1996. "Ethnomusicologists, Archives, Professional Organizations, and the Shifting Ethics of Intellectual Property." *Yearbook for Traditional Music* 28: 87–105.

Shentalinsky, V. 1995. *The KGB's Literary Archive*. London: Harvill.

Taylor, Hugh. 1982. "The Collective Memory: Archives and Libraries as Heritage." *Archivaria* 15: 118–130.

Toner, Peter G. 2003. "History, Memory and Music: The Repatriation of Digital Audio to Yolngu Communities, or, Memory as Metadata." In *Researchers, Communities, Institutions, Sound Recordings*, edited by Linda Barwick, Allan Marett, Jane Simpson, and Amanda Harris, separately paginated PDF. Sydney: University of Sydney.

UNESCO. 2003. *Convention for the Safeguarding of the Intangible Cultural Heritage*. Paris: UNESCO.

Williams, Nancy M. 1986. *The Yolngu and Their Land: A System of Land Tenure and the Fight for Its Recognition*. Canberra: Australian Institute of Aboriginal Studies.

WIPO. 2004. *WIPO Intellectual Property Handbook: Policy, Law and Use*. Geneva: World Intellectual Property Organization.

Yúdice, George. 2003. *The Expediency of Culture: Uses of Culture in the Global Era*. Durham, NC: Duke University Press.

CHAPTER 36

TRADITIONAL RE-APPROPRIATION

Modes of Access and Digitization in Irish Traditional Music

BRET WOODS

In an appropriately dialectical notion of history, the very loss of something creates the lost dimension.

—Slavoj Žižek[1]

OPENING

ARCHIVES (particularly sound recordings comprising audiovisual media) function in their pure form as an incredibly apt model of Mikhail Bakhtin's concept of hetero-glossia,[2] in that they can be potentially (and abstractly) explored in infinite spacetime. In other words, archives can represent expressions by way of encapsulating them, to be explored ad nauseam in multiple and unforeseeable contexts, making them at once authoritatively representative and dynamically unbound to any one authoritative representation. In a fundamental and dialogical sense, archives only exist to manifest socially constructed subjects.[3] Subjects, however, mediate their interactions in various frameworks. This is why—regardless of the issues and logistics involved in archival repatriation projects—repatriation ethics ultimately defer not to the essence of the archives themselves, but to establishing contextually relevant rights and privileges over the materials contained within archives (and typically over their study and representative use). In his often-quoted work on the subject, Jacques Derrida reminds us, "there is no political power without control of the archive, if not memory. Effective democratization can always be measured by this essential criterion: the participation in and access to the archive, its constitution, and its interpretation" (Derrida 1995, 4).

Repatriation is a modern phenomenon; inasmuch as it is connected to Indigeneity it is inextricably linked to colonialism, nationalism, and formalist hierarchies. Beyond its overt goals and ethical concerns, it must be remembered that repatriation only exists because collections exist, and abstractly generalized both are the product of historicization and capitalism as discursive modes of social legitimacy (cf. Foucault 1972, 127–128). Repatriation, as an act, is often seen as a restorative measure, a systematic (and in many cases, necessary) answer to cultural appropriation.[4] But as I explore in this chapter, repatriation—even beyond its active complications—is an intersection of subjects much more conceptually varied than can be articulated through simply negotiating the relocation of archival materials from one place to another. From a Bakhtinian standpoint, it is a reductive position to mediate archival interactions in systematic ways (methodologically or legally). Cultural collections are complexes, clusters, and "congealed events"[5] of data too impossibly complex to fathom all at once—or ever completely experience. This is likely why Derrida's lasting Freudianism is to abstract generically our fascination with archives as "nostalgia for the return to the most archaic place of commencement" (1995, 91).

On the surface, the modern hegemonic pretension about archives (especially collections of recorded expressions) claims that they are historically and pragmatically created "to preserve"[6] traditions—to safeguard "heritage,"[7] and by extension, to safeguard the tradition-bearers themselves. As the literal body of knowledge—the text—from which we draw our study and understanding of cultures, we tend to fetishize archives and their role in society. Thus, in a literal sense, archives regularly become the representations of expressions that are socially considered at risk of being forgotten. As we stare into the void and question "Are we here?" the archive calls back, often tentatively: "Yes?" This can be enough, at least, to quell our anxiety and legitimize our reality. Dominick LaCapra articulated this Freudianism, noting:

> For Freud, a fetish is a substitute for a lost object, and it is related to the quest for full identity and narcissistic unity. The archive as fetish is a literal substitute for the "reality" of the past which is "always already" lost. . . . When it is fetishized, the archive is more than the repository of traces of the past which may be used in its inferential reconstruction. It is the stand-in for the past that brings the mystified experience of the thing itself.

(LaCapra 1984, 310)

We can never ask these questions from the void, though, and the archive technically does not exist there. So, even though it is a poetic frame, it is more accurate to suggest that we *imagine* a void into which we *project* our recordings, where they become *representations* of us in the void. These imaginings can only function dialogically—that is, in their dialogue with the always fluid socioeconomic contexts and conditions into which they are projected (in our case, those typically associated with colonization and cultural assimilation). Moreover, archives are (historically) assembled and curated by people with specialized resources and the privilege to historicize and fetishize elements of culture, establishing and mediating their reality from their specialized position and then claiming ownership of that reality. In short, archives are never just the record of the reality of life; they are also the models we use to create our generic realities. It is in this sense of self-actualization and agency that I discuss current Irish traditional music archives, the appropriation of cultural ideology (through Bakhtin's sense of hetero-glossia), and (returning to Derrida) the ideology embedded in modes of access.

HISTORICAL APPROPRIATION
AND RE-APPROPRIATION

In the truly Western sense of a "fatherland,"[8] to which cultural expressions are imagined to "belong," Irish traditional music provides an interesting case study for analyzing how archives can function actively in various interdependent public spheres. Colonial distribution of resources has established the model for the curated development of traditional music in Ireland into the present day. While music has remained an oral tradition in many communities around Ireland, the first "official" archival collections of melodies that created a legitimized historical record were typically gathered by music collectors from Britain and continental Europe.[9] Between the eighteenth and nineteenth centuries,[10] collectors were usually not musicians in the traditionalist sense; they were curators with far more resources than the musicians who lived the oral traditions they recorded. Song and tune[11] collectors appropriated (often to their own lucrative success) collections of traditional melodies, recording the music in Western notation (though usually without adequate detail in transcription regarding ornamentation and rhythmic emphasis). Collections were also typically lacking in contextual and social history. Even after the advent of the Edison wax cylinder, Western notation was the primary mode of recording traditional songs and tunes well into the 1930s, when preserving language and music became of national concern under Éamon de Valera (prime minister, 1932–1973) as Ireland became a republic (see Brown 1981, 147, 211–212). From then on, collecting recordings of language, music, and dance was imagined as an imperative to the preservation of Irishness,[12] even as much as the archives themselves were used to create a brand new national identity.

As such, the authoritative hierarchy that had been established in appropriating and collecting cultural materials from the countryside of Ireland in the form of language, songs, and tunes became the source and model of nationalist archiving. As the only visible representation of marginalized rural communities, archives of language and music became reimagined in the new valence of nationalist necessity, and the communities who had once upon a time "created" these traditions were newly embraced as the idyllic "folk."[13] In the modern tension between progress and authenticity, re-appropriating archival collections became a nationalist enterprise. As Terence Brown observed, "The challenge [was] to construct a new culture in a new context, a culture that will at once be new and relevant in that context and at the same time preserve the best of the old . . . a culture that will be considerably industrial yet without losing what is of lasting value in our rural social fabric" (1981, 229). This structural model is incidentally the same one that perpetuates the authority of safeguarding, espousing that preservation is a legitimate activity and should be undertaken by those with the capability, means, and expertise to consider the ethics and logistics of safeguarding (and, by extension, of discarding). Such a structure makes those archival authorities the de facto or explicit owners of the traditions in question. Even among those Indigenous communities where tradition bearers oversee the trajectory of traditional expression, people likewise capitalize on this framework.

Thus, in terms of its national identity, Ireland depended both on the re-appropriation of cultural materials originally collected by outside parties (ostensibly only since the eighteenth century, as the measure of politics and technology would suggest), and on re-appropriating the identity of the people who still carried on traditional (rural) practices within a volatile economy. This Indigenous imagination was a captivating one (and perhaps, in many ways it still is), evocatively articulated in Daniel Corkery's *Hidden Ireland* (1967) and championed by folk musicians and artists during the folk revival of the 1950s, 1960s, and 1970s—particularly Séamus Ennis, through *Raidió Teilifís Éireann* (RTÉ), and Seán Ó Riada with RTÉ and with his group Ceoltóirí Chualann (among others).[14] Their varied work was influential in creating a new public tradition of Irish music (especially nationally) in the mid-twentieth century, one that has become globally embraced among the broader "trad"[15] scene as the exemplary, original aesthetic of "Irish traditional music."

Archives were at the forefront of this "authentic"[16] representation of tradition, but more than just the preservation of musical performances was at stake here. Central to this negotiation were *modes of access*—specifically, who had access to music archives and which contexts facilitated traditional representation. Since, in a national context, re-appropriated collections also needed to be distributed as a mainstream ideology, the frequency of dissemination was also a factor in creating a national style of Irish traditional music. These facets fell under the purview of RTÉ. Appropriating culture (even in the best of scenarios) has long served colonial interests of assimilation. It is a somewhat staggering realization for those who discover for the first time that Irish culture is not a quintessentially British folk or rural genre; even those acutely aware of the longstanding tension between Irish and English culture—born out of colonial abuses since before the sixteenth century—fail to notice a cultural difference between Irish and English identity apart from their historically political separateness. This is a testament to how colonial assimilation left a legacy over Irish culture well into the twentieth century.[17] In developing a mainstream identity, RTÉ relied on re-appropriating this model—to re-assimilate, essentially, Ireland proper under the example of the idyllic "folk." The example of this "folk" was found in the Gaeltacht,[18] and Seán Ó Riada wholly embraced it in his work.

It helps to keep in mind that during the twentieth century, while this nationalist cultural identity was taking shape in the mainstream, communities in the Gaeltacht were largely ignored economically, technologically, and otherwise, apart from how their "folkiness" exemplified the popular essentialization of authenticity and distinct Irishness. Rural communities continued to serve as their own tradition bearers, without (necessarily) a pressing need to preserve their traditions by way of extensive archiving—they simply continued living as they had done.[19] Modern ideology granted special attention to figures like Ó Riada and to industry giants like RTÉ (as an extension of their role in establishing polity-wide communications—first through radio broadcasts and then through television beginning in 1960). Ó Riada's legitimacy was based on his authority in music (trained in the European classical tradition) as a serialist composer. And the work that Ó Riada did in the form of many audiovisual recordings during his exploration and "reclamation" of his Irishness became the content of many broadcasted archives via RTÉ, where he served as director beginning in 1954. By 1970, RTÉ boasted "one of the finest folk music archives in Europe," tracing "its origin back to 1936" (McGettrick, 1994).

Ó Riada actively contributed to RTÉ, but even while serving as the station's director, and for the whole of his life, RTÉ telecommunications legalities controlled to a large degree how Ireland (and the world) interacted with his music (and with the other recordings and musicians he chose to share). The limited access to his music successfully realized an authoritative model of Irish traditional music style; but it was the company's perpetuation of the Western (colonial) hierarchy of authority—in that the framework of Ó Riada's "expertise" played a role in articulating "authenticity"—that cast a shadow further marginalizing the subjects who performed their traditions as lived expressions instead of as fetishized curiosities or as material for nationalistic campaigns.

It is in this intersection of disparate voices and subjects that I want to return briefly to the concept of heteroglossia, because I think it articulates well the dynamic nature of interacting with traditions, particularly traditional expressions. For Bakhtin, heteroglossia is "the situation of a subject surrounded by the myriad responses he or she might make at any particular point, but any one of which must be framed in a specific discourse selected from the teeming thousands available" (Holquist 1990, 69). This is a dialogical exchange, one that tends to be navigated by generic forms—organizations of utterances that Bakhtin et al. calls "speech genres" (1986, 78). "Even in the most [pure], the most unconstrained conversation, we cast our speech in definite generic forms, sometimes rigid and trite ones, sometimes more flexible, plastic, and creative ones (everyday communication also has creative genres at its disposal)" (78, parentheses in original). Heteroglossia governs the operation of meaning in any discourse; in other words, our very reality (language) is always heteroglossia. We mediate our reality through utterances organized by generic forms (and combinations of forms).

The utility of this model is that it helps us navigate discourse in less systematic and more dynamic ways. Put in the framework of our current discussion, when we acknowledge the presence of heteroglossia it reveals the extremely multifaceted intersection of subjects inherent in Irish traditional music practices (in and beyond history) and thus problematizes the systematic hierarchy and "expertise" of *controlling* those certain subjects (which challenges presumed authority). This helps when navigating the complex groups of interactive subjects in their organized, generic, repeatable forms (such as the multi-instrumentalist model of performance first introduced by Ó Riada and Ceoltóirí Chualann that has been copied in numerous variations ever since); it gives way to a more fluid understanding.[20]

A telling dialogical example of this interpretive concept can be found in an interview Ó Riada did in 1970, shortly before his untimely death at the age of forty. The interview is recorded as having been taken for "Danish Television," though it is notable that the only accessible archival footage, which is cited in several academic papers and Internet articles, is currently only found on YouTube.[21] As transcribed here, an em-dash at the end of an utterance by either speaker marks a point in which Ó Riada and the interviewer interject into each other's speech during the dialogue. Here we see heteroglossia through speech genres at work:

> **Interviewer:** Now there isn't, or there doesn't seem to be—if you come from outside Ireland—a classical music tradition in this country; it's entirely a folk music tradition that you find here—
>
> **Seán Ó Riada:** Well no, I would differentiate between a "folk" and "classical." When you say classical you mean "European classical." There is not a European classical music tradition in this country. There is, on the other hand, a highly developed traditional music, which, because it's orally transmitted must not be considered essentially as folk music. For example, in the Orient, you have music which is orally transmitted but is still highly developed. You have the court music of Japan, for example, and the Korean novices music, that kind of thing. Here we also have a highly developed traditional music—very complex, very sophisticated—but it's more Oriental than Western.
>
> **Interviewer:** And it's still alive?
>
> **Ó Riada:** Oh it's—very much so—
>
> **Interviewer:** And it's transmitted in an oral tradition?
>
> **Ó Riada:** Oh yes, absolutely. The main part of it is vocal—the songs in Irish. The Big Songs, many of which can be traced back, you know, four centuries, five centuries in their origins. It involves a very highly complex linear ornamentation, so that people hearing it for the first time think that it sounds like Arabic music, or Persian music.
>
> **Interviewer:** Now this music that has been orally transmitted, it hasn't been written down somehow, later on?
>
> **Ó Riada:** It has been collected, but you need a very different method of notation to write it down correctly from the ordinary European notation. And so far, this kind of notation has not been used by collectors, it's just beginning to be used.
>
> **Interviewer:** Now when you write your music—your own music—that would be in the Irish tradition also?
>
> **Ó Riada:** Well, no I wear two hats, so to speak, as a composer. I wear a hat as a traditional musician in the Irish tradition, but also, because I've been trained in the European background, I compose European music, twelve-note music, serial music.
>
> **Interviewer:** Oh yes.
>
> **Ó Riada:** And naturally enough, that's written as you would write serial music.
>
> **Interviewer:** Yes.

Ó Riada: The Irish music, well. . . . You don't write it as such. You—it—this has to
   be—it's spontaneous—
Interviewer: It's very much improvised. . . .
Ó Riada: Improvised. . . . Yes. Just the same as Indian rāgs.

Ó Riada, for his part, does the best he can to represent the Gaeltacht, Irish musicians, and himself as he negotiates for the interviewer—and by extension for presumed national and international audiences—his distinctive sense of what Irish traditional music "is" against the backdrop of the growing global interests within the Folk revival. If we analyze Ó Riada's words here as those of an authority on the subject—an authoritative systematic analysis—it calls into question the interpretation of the musical systems he describes in a way that eventually proves impossible to defend, due to dynamic and unforeseen contexts and outcomes. Ignoring his contemporary use of the term "Orient" (in current vernacular that term would not be used), it would be difficult enough for Ó Riada to frame a historical precedent for his comparisons in mid-twentieth century music. These frames would have to be interpreted in a similarly systematic fashion, taken at face value as either right (useful) or wrong (irrelevant). But not only is the systematic comparison a conventional approach here, its ideology is also suggested in the qualifying language that both conversants use, such as: "very complex," "differentiate between 'folk' and 'classical' music," "like Arabic music," "highly developed," and so on. Historically, similar language is used to negotiate the role that archives play in national identity and for cultural "heritage." A framework that incorporates more voices (heteroglossia) provides more opportunity to realize the lasting worth of the archive.

   For example, the United Nations Educational, Scientific, and Cultural Organization (UNESCO) states in a similar fashion its authoritative stance on "intangible cultural heritage"[22] as a primary goal:

> The importance of intangible cultural heritage is not the cultural manifestation itself but rather the *wealth of knowledge* and *skills* that is transmitted through it *from one generation to the next*. The social and economic *value* of this transmission of knowledge is *relevant for minority groups* and for mainstream social groups *within a State*, and is as important for developing States as for developed ones.
>
>   (UNESCO n.d., italics added)

The language here has an authoritative framework, not just by way of convention, but out of the complex power relationships embedded in the institution itself. Such a reality cannot disguise that intangible cultural heritage and its imaginings are localized to a few authoritative voices. Negotiating whose voices those are—or should be—rests at the center of identifying the difficult (and often strained) identity politics inherent in archives. To limit broad agency, under the mantle of safeguarding (UNESCO also states an intent to "safeguard without freezing," a task whose goal seems implicit), and to fetishize in a way not serving (or even apparent to) Indigenous sensibilities, has the effect of extending the colonial hand, so to speak. In such contexts, power is not challenged systematically—it is perpetuated. And this further marginalizes subjects who regularly perform their traditions as lived expressions instead of as the specialized, "valued" heritage as articulated by an (authoritative) "other's" lens.[23]

Archives (especially audiovisual archives) of Irish traditional music (like any reality) comprise generic expressions that "provide a horizon of expectation to a knowledgeable audience that cannot be derived from the semantic content of the discourse alone" (Tonkin 1992, 2). For Tonkin, "genres are the level of discourse through which any interpretation is organized" (2). The more dynamically we imagine and interpret archival realities, and the more multiple voices are allowed into the polyphony of interpretation, the more lasting its utility will be for practitioners and interested parties alike. The framework of heteroglossia suggests the potentially unpopular but sincerely held possibility that perhaps the only "importance of intangible cultural heritage" *is* "the cultural manifestation itself."

THE IRISH TRADITIONAL MUSIC ARCHIVE AND NEW MODES OF ACCESS

The Irish Traditional Music Archive (ITMA) began in 1987, at first in a humble way as a proposal made by Harry Bradshaw and Nicholas Carolan to the Arts Council in Dublin to preserve several recordings held by RTÉ—the focus of which was a program that was broadcast on the RTÉ Radio series titled "The Irish Phonograph."[24] Bradshaw coproduced the program and had worked as a sound engineer with RTÉ since 1968 (he was promoted to radio producer in 1979). It was an expectant proposal in that the Arts Council of Dublin had been in negotiations with several Dublin-based musicians and engineers, including a developing committee chaired by Breandán Breathnach,[25] about building an archive with the intent "to preserve historic sound recordings of Irish traditional music" (ITMA n.d.). However, that committee stalled after Breathnach's unfortunate death in 1985. When their proposal passed two years later, Nicholas Carolan signed on as the director of the ITMA, a position in which he served until he retired in September 2015. The ITMA has changed locations twice before settling in its current facility at 73 Merrion Square in Dublin.

Over the past few decades, the scope of the ITMA has changed somewhat, as seen in their mission statement. Certainly, their holdings have grown since 1987, and they now boast "the largest collection of Irish traditional music in existence, and the largest collection of information on this tradition" (ITMA 2016). Of interest to our discussion, though, are the "definitions" they outline as their approach to archiving. "The Archive understands 'Irish traditional music' as a broad term which encompasses oral-tradition song, instrumental music, and dance of many kinds and periods. It interprets the term in the widest possible sense, and always tries to include rather than exclude material" (ibid.). They also make distinctive notes about their broad scope: "Items are collected if they could be considered traditional in any way—in origin, or in idiom, or in transmission or style of performance, etc.—or if they are relevant to an understanding of traditional music and its contexts" (ibid.). After pointing out some of the specific aspects of their holdings, the ITMA introduces an epitome of the *archive* in its pure form, and of Bakhtin's concept of heteroglossia, in allowing the archives to exist (and thus, to manifest realities) in a less systematically mediated form:

> Traditional music is regarded by the Archive as being simultaneously a vigorous element of contemporary Irish culture, one which enjoys widespread popularity even outside Ireland, and a valuable part of historic Irish culture. It therefore emphasizes the on-going collection of modern publications in Irish traditional music—in audio, printed and visual forms—and live field-collection, as well as assembling classic and little-known historical documents of the music.
>
> (ibid.)

The focus here is less on qualifying language (though they do, at least, point out that traditional music is "a valuable part of historic Irish culture") and more on pointing out the myriad ways by which the archive always and already takes shape—a continuation of their goal to "include rather than exclude." In short, their scope envisions the archive as being closer to its pure, heteroglot form.

During his ITMA retirement speech in 2015, Carolan noted:

> This is a collection of the materials of Irish traditional music and of information on Irish traditional music, but it is not Irish traditional music. Irish traditional music is a living thing, created nightly, daily, not just in Ireland north and south, not just among the Irish diaspora, but in very many parts of the world. The Archive exists to support and enrich that living tradition—to connect it with its past—but we really value traditional music as a contemporary Irish art form, a living art, as important as Irish literature, visual art, theatrical arts, or any other art form—and that has been a guiding principal for me over the last 28 years.
>
> (JOM Staff 2015)

Carolan's distinction here is seemingly obvious, yet profound: collections are distinct from the things they collect, but they simultaneously support (even create) the reality of the concepts that allowed them to be created. The ITMA's (by way of Carolan's) guiding principle has been to equalize the generic hierarchies that have historically segmented elements of archival collections, to recognize that traditions themselves exist (though never statically) both inside and outside the collection, and to extend privileges of the archival space to anyone who cares to look and study. The ITMA also continues an ambitious digitization project[26] intent on making the whole of its collections available online, ostensibly allowing unmediated digital replication of any component of the archive, in many cases without restriction.[27]

It is the policy, scope, and open nature of *access* that allows the ITMA to hold their archive in a purer sense; but, since the archive staff oversees voluminous collections, that puts them in a very real position of power (and thus of scrutiny), exercised through the ways they mediate modes of access to their archive. For their part, as noted here, archive employees do maintain facilities that are "open, free of charge, to anyone with an interest in the contemporary and historical artforms of Irish traditional music"—in other words, ITMA considers its archives to be *open access* (ITMA 2016). The reality of this position, much like the archive itself, is not monolithic; the collection is located and curated in Dublin and follows standard business hours, so the physical reality of the collection's point in spacetime must first be accessible before the archive can be. In this strangely obvious distinction,[28] we can explore the agency that various modes of access govern.

In *Archive Fever*, Derrida elaborates on what he calls his "retrospective science fiction" regarding how the archive of psychoanalysis would be vastly different—not just in terms of its position in spacetime, but overall—if "Freud, his contemporaries, collaborators and immediate disciples, instead of writing thousands of letters by hand, had had access to MCI or ATT telephonic credit cards, portable tape recorders, computers, printers, faxes, televisions, teleconferences, and above all E-mail" (1995, 17). He turns this fiction around to propose a revealing hypothesis:

> This is another way of saying that the archive . . . is not only the place for stocking and for conserving an archivable content of the past, which would exist in any case, such as, without the archive, one still believes it was or will have been. No, the technical structure of the archiving archive also determines the structure of the archivable content even in its very coming into existence and in its relationship to the future. The archivization produces as much as it records the event. This is also our political experience of the so-called news media. (17)
>
> (Derrida 1995, 17)

Inasmuch as Derrida's assertion is telling, my suggestion here may be a radical one: that the Freudian dialectic Derrida proposes—where archives produce as much as they record—is a systematic false equivalence. Rather, as it comes into focus, the archive is a complex that is always already collecting and creating by way of our mediated interactions with it, our understandings of its technological possibilities, and our subsequent socially driven actions regarding it. This suggests, more than anything, that archives always tell us how to imagine what is collected within them, and by extension how to imagine "collection" and ourselves. In other words, it is this technological reality of the archive that places power in the realm of "the participation in and access to the archive, its constitution, and its interpretation" (Derrida 1995, 4). As technology allows people more direct access to one another and to the archive, the archaic and systematic hierarchies that govern how we continue to standardize our interactions in and around it are thought to erode; but it is only the idea of these distinctions that are masked by the shifting frames of the institutions who control the technological mediation itself. Technological limitations are simply an extension of the physical limitations of socially constructed subjects in and around archives. Our modes of access are what govern our closer or more distant proximities to the archive as heteroglossia, and our ability to imagine, ultimately, our complex role in socially constituted spacetime.

ACCESS AND PERFORMANCE AGENCY:
THESESSION.ORG

Most trad players and contemporaneous Irish musicians alike are familiar with the *seisiún* ("session")—an informal gathering where people exchange their favorite tunes (typically by way of performing them on a variety of instruments), share songs and stories, and even learn new melodies. Sessions are another type of archive, echoing the historical practice of the house *céili* (or "gathering" in this context) where musicians play traditional music together (from memory). Nowadays, sessions are typically held in public spaces such as pubs, bars, coffee shops, and restaurants, where the dissemination of music often follows the generic Western framework of "performer" and "audience" expectations, and thus the informal nature of music transmission operates as only visible to the performers themselves and other informed parties. However, sessions also take place in more informed public spaces (especially longstanding session venues, and locales in the Gaeltacht), as well as homes and schools all over the world.

Sessions continue the oral and aural practice of creating and preserving Irish traditional music. An interesting facet of this practice in twenty-first-century sessions, however, is that performers in most sessions—especially outside of the Gaeltacht, and internationally overall—tend to play music in ways inspired by recent popular recordings. Learning new tunes is more than just an oral tradition, it is actively pursued as a sort of archival research by musicians in the trad scene. Depending on a performer's level of interest and engagement in Irish traditional music, archives like the ITMA are less accessible than the latest album floating around the trad scene. Sessions still operate ostensibly as oral transmission, but the modes of access to Irish traditional music for most players via popular recordings homogenizes the sound expectations and performance practices throughout the tradition.[29]

The ease of access to the music of popular Irish trad musicians (both in the proliferation of their recordings and in their live show presence) directs the trajectory of other trad performers—many of whom will never "tour" or play on stage, but who regularly play communally and inspire other locals to carry on traditions in much the same way. Players adopt and adapt to stylistic tendencies that transcend oral and aural transmission in local communities, reflecting the influence that this mode of accessibility has over tradition itself. The oral component of the Irish tradition at present, in the global sense, is almost exclusively governed by this phenomenon.

While players can learn exclusively from these recordings (and some musicians who cannot "read music" do),[30] most musicians learning trad tunes explore other archival sources. One such source is the openly accessible database of Irish traditional music frequently used by trad players: a popular website called "thesession.org" (hereafter "TS"). Since ITMA—even though it is ostensibly the most comprehensive and authoritative source—contains a lot of materials that are either obscure or localized in Dublin, or out of style, many musicians have gravitated toward the more established model of accessing published and notated collections of tunes. TS is one such collection, though it functions differently than a published book of tunes, in that accessing TS is not a "transactional exchange" in the psychoanalytical sense (cf. Berne 1964; Steiner 1990).

TS functions as a folksonomy; it is a user-driven database where anyone can contribute tune settings, metadata, links to recordings, and discussions about Irish music traditions. Users can construct their own "tunebooks" and maintain a profile identified by their chosen username. The site is completely open to anyone with Internet access; there is no requirement to register with the site to access its database. Tunes are searchable primarily by keyword or title, which due to the nature of tune titles[31] in Irish traditional music can make it tricky at times to find the tune one seeks. That alone reduces its accessibility for participants who are not already well informed in the tradition. Accessibility to traditional music via TS is not without its difficulties and limitations, many of which are explored elsewhere;[32] but even though it has technological pitfalls as a framework, TS makes no overt attempt to position itself as a specific type of archival authority. There is active potential for agency in this framework, even though its technological structure by association necessitates, in some ways, a perpetuation of authority.

TS was created and is maintained by Jeremy Keith, a web developer and programmer from Ireland who now lives in the UK. In an interview (Keith 2016), we spoke about his approach to access and to the archive. Jeremy first built TS in the late 1990s as a space where he uploaded one tune each week in the style of a blog, adding the tunes in ABC format (a letter-based notation system that has existed in the folk music arena since the 1980s), as well as sheet music in GIF images, and later as MIDI files. Soon he began including notes about his personal experiences with the tunes, as well as a space for comments. Over the course of 1999 to 2000, users continued showing interest in the site, leaving a wealth of comments and suggesting alternative variations of certain tunes and contextual information. As interest grew, Jeremy shifted his vision toward a user-generated site where "as long as somebody out there is playing the tune at a session," they can post it to TS. He explained how the archive developed:

> Jeremy Keith: [Around 2001] was when [TS] changed to having a membership idea and you could submit a tune yourself in ABC. But it was still this bottleneck where you'd submit the tune in ABC, and it was on the site in ABC, but I still had to do the conversion to sheet music and the conversion to midi; that all happened manually at my end. And I added the discussion section, and then over time I added, you know, the ability to add sessions, the ability to add events, recordings, track listings. And yeah, bit by bit it grew, you know, beyond my wildest expectations. I remember the moment that it went over 1,001 tunes and I realized there were more tunes on the session than were in O'Neill's, that really blew my mind. I couldn't believe that. And now there's ten times that many, which is really crazy. But for a long time it stagnated as well. Because it was going fine, it was working okay, but, you know: I was a bottleneck with the sheet music. The location stuff I didn't really do anything with it, I had all these sessions and events. So the site got a big overhaul about three or four years ago, into its current form . . . a lot more clever stuff under the hood, I guess.

Bret Woods: I remember that change pretty well, too. From the user's side of things, it felt like all of a sudden we had so much more power and control to contribute tunes, and so on. And it felt more like an actual session. . . .

JK: Yeah, I think mentally I was kind of putting it more into the category of something like Wikipedia, and opening up the privileges for the user—what the user could do, any user. It used to be, if you added a session to the site, *you* could edit the session but nobody else could edit that session. Now anyone can edit any session, anyone can edit any event, any recording, and so on. So yeah, I was kind of trying to make it more Wikipedia-like. I don't know if that came across, but it seems to be working out pretty well. So yeah, that's how it got to be in its current form that it's in now. And the big change then, if you remember, was that one tune could now have many settings. That kind of grew out of the way things happened anyway—that people would post stuff in the comments to the tune. So, instead of there being—instead of a first-come, first-serve attitude with what you would see when you went to the page, it needed to be more egalitarian.

BW: I do want to ask about settings, too, because I'm curious about your take on multiple settings per tune and how there are a bunch of different names. How does the site decide—or who gets to decide—what the primary, authoritative name of that tune is, is that egalitarian as well?

JK: So, as it is now, anybody can do that. Anybody can go in and edit this tune and change the primary name. And you can also add aliases. But then if someone else disagrees with that, they can go in and change it.

BW: Nice.

JK: So, it's kind of just down to, you know, what the crowd decides, really. It is tough, though, that there isn't this one-to-one correlation between a tune and a name. As you know, one tune can have many names, and one name can be applied to many tunes. It makes it particularly difficult because now I'm trying to work together with some other sites out there. There's tunepal.org, and there's the comhaltas archive[33] of stuff, and we all kind of want to work together and have content flowing between the sites. So it would be really nice if, on comhaltas, they could link to a tune underneath a video—somebody playing that tune could link to the tune on TS. Or from TS I could link to that tune on comhaltas. But first you'd have to establish that it is *that* tune, and you can't just [automatically] do that from the name. So there isn't a canonical identifier like you kind of get with books, with ISBN numbers, you know. With other media there's databases for this stuff— nothing like that really exists for traditional music.

In his push toward a more "egalitarian" approach, Jeremy is distancing himself from the authoritative conventions of collecting or curating archives, which gives agency to users who actively contribute their time and ideas to TS. We noticed in TS statistics, too, that users arrange collections of tunes in ways that make sense to them. "Yeah, you know there's definitely the 'fat head and the long tail' of submissions. I think most of the tunes come from the minority of users. Then there's other people who contribute a lot in terms of, say, comments and discussion, but might never have submitted a single tune in, like, ten to fifteen years on the site" (ibid.). Those users who spend their time contributing to TS add tunes, discussions of tunes, multiple settings, and other content found in comments, recordings, and contextual information that situates traditional music, broadly imagined, within a multitude of voices which in their chorus manifest socially constructed subjects.

Jeremy's pragmatic lament regarding the difficulty of organizing information on TS reflects not just a facet of the tradition, but one that he (and other users on the site) actively complicate by way of participating in that tradition. He noted later in the interview, "Something that I'm actively trying to encourage, is that submitting multiple settings of the same tunes is actually a good thing—in trying to capture some of those variations." The fluidity of voices that increases agency regarding tunes and performance practice (and thus the tradition itself) arises when users hear tunes on popular recordings, then turn around and add the variations heard on those recordings as additional settings to tunes. While the credit is usually attributed to the recording, this practice dynamically challenges standard frameworks of intellectual property and ownership. Many trad musicians regularly perform each other's variations or even self-composed tunes without any sense of violating "ownership."[34] Irish traditional music represents an inclusive practice geared toward open and active participation in the tradition as the foundation of what manifests that tradition in any real sense. Enabled by media compression and streaming technologies, these online platforms for musical transmission have further challenged the core concept of ownership, and have deeply changed the functional role and understanding of the collection.

CLOSING

A tendency in archival research and repatriation studies is to perpetuate the Freudianism that conceptualizes cultural materials (and the cultural categories to which they "belong") as existing abstractly—as "things"—outside of the social dimension and the dialogical realm. The case of Irish traditional music gives us a model for how archives of cultural heritage exist literally to manifest socially constructed subjects, and how modes of access to these archives navigate the predominant ideology surrounding the dynamically intersecting, ongoing definitions of the tradition. Modern collections are imbued with a colonial property framework that—even in the transfer of ownership—remains after repatriation. This is evident in how many explorations of archives (and subsequent repatriation projects) call for decolonization and the institutional relinquishing of rights over archives, only to perpetuate that same framework (essentially not extending privilege, but appropriating it). But who gets to "own" tradition, or even manage the rights to participate in it? Expanding the conventional framework to become more inclusive and less specialized—and encouraging multiple modes of access—chips away at the established control over cultural collections and is the only way the archive can truly begin to function in a purer state. This reality should not be ignored, especially under the very modernist guise of inscribing "intangible" value in cultural expressions thought at risk of being eradicated (which all but explicitly shows that colonialism is still the predominant social framework assumed to have an unchallenged power for navigating its future and that of the archives it oversees).

Memory and expression are by their nature ephemeral, so the process of "preservation" is ultimately a violent[35] one (at best a deeply discerning sort of mediation), and typically of late it is (still) used as an acquisition of social and cultural capital. As intersections with Indigenous cultures reveal, whenever social expressions encourage their own typical memetic[36] qualities through their polyphonic use, there is no internal artificial need to prevent those traditions from being "lost." Safeguarding is an activity that cannot disguise the fact that the very processes that create the resource and privilege to "ensure careful safeguarding of heritage" are the same ones creating the specific need for cultural expressions (as imagined through the colonial lens) to need safeguarding. It is this paradox that reveals the fetishized nature of archives in general.

Once we move past the romanticized, Freudian story of differences and expectations between colonizer and the colonized and navigate the postmodern minefield of nihilism, we are confronted with actual (tangible) media (the archive) that articulates (and sometimes reinforces) the power dynamic of varied, arbitrary realities—ones that create and reinforce socially constructed subjects. Thus, depending on who has control over access to that media, the subject's stories will take a certain shape based on social expectation and interaction. Archival tendencies toward deconstructing modern hierarchical assumptions (such as those embedded in global capital, or intellectual property) regarding cultural traditions, and more resources expanding access and restoring power to broadly imagined cultural manifestations, will encourage more inclusivity and reinvigorate tradition.

Archives (especially audiovisual recordings) are like fractured bits of culture—they are complex recordings of congealed events. In some cases, collections may need to "belong," to be mediated under specific modes of access, but only insomuch as they reinforce contiguous modes of cultural power. Apart from the direct deconstruction of colonialism, perhaps it is inappropriate, in many cases, to continue fetishizing in an intellectual sense the intrinsic value in cultural expressions (which essentially perpetuates the problematic social relationships born out of colonialism but with no real intention to do anything about them). Perhaps, instead, a re-appropriation of archives, one that becomes resourceful for anyone who cares to engage with them, would be a more lasting course to take.

NOTES

1. Quoted from Žižek (2013).
2. Heteroglossia, or разноречие (*raznorechie*), literally "differing-speech-ness," refers to the philosophical concept of multiple voices participating dynamically, in irreducible valences, in varied modes of discourse. Mikhail Bakhtin's (1895–1975) concept of heteroglossia can first be found in his 1934 work "Discourse in the Novel" (Bakhtin 1981[1934]) Bakhtin spent much of his career developing this idea and building on its definition in an appropriately

dynamic way. The core concepts behind Bakhtinian heteroglossia and "polyphony" were the inspired philosophy behind his dialogical approach that sought never to reduce the complex interrelationships and expressions of humanity into static, systematic, or archetypical forms. Additionally, my use of the words "pure" and "purity" here and throughout simply invokes its conceptual frame, as in that which is ontologically functioning without additional (often oppressive) forces working to corrupt or manipulate it.

3. Socially constructed subjects are meaningful subjects who exist completely in the realm of language interaction, but not merely as an abstraction. In other words, those subjects with whom you are not currently in physical proximity—but who are held to some thought or purpose in your life in a meaningful way—are socially constructed subjects. Since all reality is literally social (or mediated as such), these subjects are also how and with whom we negotiate most of our interactions, and are still in their pure, unmediated forms, complex subjects who have agency and autonomy.

4. I use "appropriation" (adopting for a specific purpose) and "re-appropriation" (adopting again for a different, but still specific purpose) in this chapter both literally and by way of their colonial connotations. As I explore throughout the chapter, the complexity of intersecting subjects captured in and represented by archives is often obscured through valuative, systematic ideology.

5. Not to essentialize them as "systems," Bakhtin imagined genres as единство (*edinstvo*), which translates as "unity." This term served (in a not-so-definitive sense) as Bakhtin's sense of singular simultaneity of the self, not a recognizable fusion of parts or a systematic whole, but a coming together of the complex interrelationships and combinations that are often overtheorized and reduced as such. See Bakhtin (1993).

6. I am often consumed with the question of preservation, since it never seems at face value (or as the hegemonic pretension dictates) to function adequately as a mechanism of social record. Do traditions *want* to be preserved? Or do *all* traditions want to be preserved? In the spirit of Bakhtinian simultaneity, there is always a hidden level beneath the impetus to "preserve" a tradition (especially when thought to be at risk of being "forgotten"), a level that reveals we cannot capture a tradition, we can only decontextualize a specter of it. In other words, we cannot "preserve" traditions a priori without destroying the fundamental event of existence that comes into being whenever traditions are expressed and exchanged. There is far more that should be unpacked, but for the purposes of this chapter, "preservation" should be considered at its most surface level in creating texts used to represent traditional modes of expression.

7. There is an incredibly diverse international and interdisciplinary debate regarding the social, cultural, political, and economic realms of "heritage"; I put it in quotes to recognize that it is in too much conceptual flux to unpack here.

8. Repatriation—literally, "returning to the fatherland"—is a term couched in patriarchal gendered assumptions about power and authority (and, subsequently, ownership). It is astonishing how deeply embedded this authoritative model is in most literature, and in society, globally imagined. For an interesting article about how the legal framework of repatriation is typically cast in the same definitional mode, see Werner and Barcus (2015).

9. The primary representative collections are so numerous it would be ridiculous to list them all here. Many Irish tune collectors, especially from the twentieth century, have contributed to the cataloging of traditional music, but some of the most famous tomes were collected from non-Irish parties in both Ireland and Scotland during the late eighteenth and early nineteenth centuries. Probably the most influential collections that helped

establish a corpus of contemporary Irish tunes were the Captain Francis Ó Neill collections (1903), particularly the one called the "Ó Neill 1850" (due to the number of tunes collected in total). Nicholas Carolan, the director emeritus of the Irish Traditional Music Archive, wrote the definitive biography on Ó Neill, titled, *A Harvest Saved: Francis O'Neill and Irish Music in Chicago* (1997).

10. The European Enlightenment was seen for some as the "beginning of the end" of Irish traditional music as it was known then, and for our discussion we might mark this as the start of the alarmist notions of folklore and music "preservation" activities. By 1792, the year of the "Belfast Harpers' Assembly," commerce had already brought a shifting socio-economic climate to what was perceived by many as a tightly woven community. Several dignitaries decided to hold a harp convention, only shortly after civil war had erupted in France, primarily to gather the "brightest musicians" in the Irish tradition of the day. The twentieth-century collector Breandán Breathnach noted that local Edward Bunting was commissioned to collect the music that the harpers played, paid by "patriotic gentlemen ... who hoped to preserve the music, poetry, and oral traditions of Ireland from extinction before the last of the old race of harpers had passed away" (1977, 104).

11. Songs in this case particularly refer to *Óran Mór*, the Great Songs or Big Songs often relegated to the *sean-nós* tradition. These often inform but operate somewhat differently than tunes, which are melodies that exist in the Irish tradition, and whether still directly connected to songs or divorced as instrumental pieces are distinguishable as a part of the instrumental performance of Irish traditional dance music that has proliferated throughout the twentieth century to the present day.

12. The intersections of Irish politics, nationalism, and culture have been well documented (see Armstrong 1982; Gellner 1983; Hobsbawm and Ranger 1983; Smith 1986).

13. Note that during this re-appropriation the distribution of resources did not change; what changed was the idea of what the "folk" represented in the minds of curators and nationalists. This sensibility of the "folk" being purer, simpler, more organic, and more authentic does not challenge the essentialist facets of appropriation, but reinforces them, distancing the cultural subject from those who fetishize their culture. See Ian McKay's thoughtful breakdown of this concept (1994), *The Quest of the Folk: Antimodernism and Cultural Selection in Twentieth-Century Nova Scotia*.

14. Seán Ó Riada was born as John Reidy, but later in his career he re-appropriated his Irishness by adopting the Gaeilge form of his name, and later when he was appointed as a lecturer at University College, Cork, he and his family relocated to the Gaeltacht in Ballyvourney, Muskerry. Ó Riada was a primary figure in the negotiation of an Irish national aesthetic; others included Seán Potts, Paddy Moloney, Willie Clancy, Proinsias Ó Conluain, Seán Mac Reamoinn, Ciaran Mac Mathuna, Nuala O'Connor, Philip King, and Aindreas Ó Gallchoir, followed by Frankie Gavin, Liam Ó Floinn, Johnny Moynihan, Andy Irvine, Paul Brady, Dónal Lunny, Christy Moore, and several others. They established—in some cases through completely new experimentations with instrumentation, recording collaborations, and diaspora inspiration—a central aesthetic that has become the global representation of Irish traditional music to date.

15. "Trad" is the frequently used abbreviation for "traditional" among folk music and traditional music communities. This is exemplified in a recent social media site called "tradconnect" (http://tradconnect.com/), geared toward connecting and networking musicians in the scene.

16. This is not meant to be a flippant use of the word, but rather to question the authoritative assumptions often accompanying the concept of authenticity. Like any process of meaning, this concept tends to shift rapidly in spacetime.

17. I am glossing over quite a bit of historical and political contextualization here, but my main point is that assimilation is a powerful force that, even when it does not eradicate cultural traditions outright, typically still replaces Indigenous modes of interaction that govern how those cultural traditions are remembered, preserved, and collected at the macro level, and thus how they are subsequently interpreted. For more on this theoretical logic, see Fishman, Gertner, Lowy, and Milán (1980), Freedman (2002), and Comaroff and Comaroff (2009), among others.

18. In Irish this simply refers to an area where Irish (Gaeilge) is spoken as a primary language. In the mid-twentieth century during the music/culture revival, influential radio and television broadcasters looked toward the Gaeltacht, particularly places like west Donegal, and in places like Ballyvourney in Muskerry, Cork, where Seán Ó Riada settled with his family (and where they still live today), as representations of the idyllic "folk."

19. This is not in any way to suggest a wholly disparate existence for people among the Gaeltacht, or to essentialize some imagined simplistic, purely authentic, or otherwise one-dimensional sort of Indigeneity. And, of course, this subjective (socioeconomic) relationship has continued to change, especially lately in the age of YouTube, when more individual voices can create and use their own audiovisual recordings to mediate and articulate their traditions.

20. By necessity, we only see and interact with generic forms (genres). When taken at face value, generic forms have historically become organized systematically, thus reducing into symbols or functions the complexity of the intersecting voices that contribute to ongoing meaning or tradition in the first place. Put simply, tradition is always already more complex than just one "thing" to fetishize, with one linear developing meaning—it is a complex.

21. There are a few instances of this interview on YouTube, but the most popular one is located at https://www.youtube.com/watch?v=bSno7vfWwKM (accessed January 2, 2017). A segment of the interview is also featured in the documentary film *Aisling Gheal Uí Riada*, 2006 (RTÉ TG4). In December 2016, an ethnomusicologist named Patrick Egan, studying at the University College Cork, asked openly in the comments section if anyone "who would be familiar with Danish TV" recognized the "voice of this interviewer," but as of this writing there have been no responses.

22. UNESCO adopted the phrase "intangible cultural heritage" in 2001 after its Washington conference (though the phrase of course existed in folklore studies before that year); while engaged in continued negotiations toward convention the organization concluded the term "folklore" was no longer appropriate. There was a vote, and then the subsequent adoption of the new phrase.

23. It may seem excessive or exhaustive to analyze the minutia of linguistic meaning in this case, but I think ethnographers would do well to consider a more heteroglossia-oriented approach when engaging in field and archival research, to steer away from conventional models that disguise time-honored colonial trends with appropriately considerate or colloquially engaging language. While these models may have served nationalistic campaigns in the wake of the modern era, there is little lasting utility in conventional "wisdom," in dutifully succumbing to authority, and in the perpetuation of archetypal tropes when it comes to systematically mediating archives. Furthermore, there is no lasting efficacy in postmodern irony or antagonism (for a telling example of this systematic frame, read

Joseph Heller's *Catch-22* [1961], which displays a similar archetypal framework). Thus, considering the sweeping implications for archives and contemporary scholarship (as in, archives make scholarship possible in a very literal sense), it seems like how and why we continue to mediate them is worth deep, sincere, critical thought. Heteroglossia is a helpful, dynamic framework that digs beneath the surface of systematic symbols and reveals how meaning (and by extension, reality) is produced in discourse through a "social diversity of speech types" (Bakhtin 1981 [1934], 32).

24. *The Irish Phonograph* (1983–1986) was an LP sound-recording set that collected many various performances of tune types, dances, varied instrumentations, and ornamentations from the 1930s, 1940s, and 1970s and released in 1986 as volume 1 of an ongoing series. Bradshaw mastered the recordings. The ITMA entry can be found here: http://www.itmacatalogues.ie//Default/en-GB/RecordView/Index/26336 (accessed January 1, 2017).

25. Breandán Breathnach (1912–1985) was a Dublin-based Irish traditional music collector, curator, and uilleann piper known for a recording a prolific amount of tunes in his life, comprising the majority of his magnum opus, *Ceol Rince na hÉireann*, vols. 1–5 (1963–1985), and *Folk Music and Dances of Ireland* (1977), amounting to more than a reported seven thousand tunes in total. The five volumes of *Ceol Rince na hÉireann* can be found, with their original Irish notes translated into English by Paul de Grae, located in this online database: http://www.nigelgatherer.com/books/CRE/index.html (accessed January 1, 2017).

26. The ITMA's online collections (http://www.itma.ie/digitallibrary) represent currently a small portion of their overall holdings, and their search algorithm is fraught with issues, making access challenging. For example, it is difficult to find a single tune by name, given how their catalog is organized, which encourages many users (myself included) to find more utility in pressing the "shuffle" symbol to be directed to a "random selection," and then follow the endless hypertextual trail of "discover more" related links. Their actual archive "proper" catalog is part of a different database, and has far more extensive metadata.

27. Mediated as he was by modern social tensions, Walter Benjamin wrote inspired essays about the changing generic realities of *The Work of Art in the Age of Mechanical Reproduction* (1969 [1935]): "Even the most perfect reproduction of a work of art is lacking in one element: its presence in time and space. . . . The presence of the original is the prerequisite to the concept of authenticity." A later, telling passage can situate our current contemplations of digital archives and modes of access, which reflect the core assumptions we tend to hold regarding the ethics of digital materials (often without understanding why we mediate our experiences as such), and the subjects they constitute. Benjamin wrote,

> The nineteenth-century dispute as to the artistic value of painting versus photography today seems devious and confused. This does not diminish its importance, however; if anything, it underlines it. The dispute was in fact the symptom of a historical transformation the universal impact of which was not realized by either of the rivals. When the age of mechanical reproduction separated art from its basis in cult, the semblance of its autonomy disappeared forever. The resulting change in the function of art transcended the perspective of the century; for a long time, it even escaped that of the twentieth century, which experienced the development of the film. Earlier much futile thought had been devoted to the question of whether photography is an art. The primary question—whether the very invention of photography had not transformed the entire nature of art—was not raised. (1969 [1935], II, VII)

In this (very Derridaian) sense of the power modes of access hold in our current conversation, Benjamin's words are thought-provoking and suggestive.

28. Of course, there are real and definite physical qualities of any archive—even of any memory. I state the obvious here to remind the reader that I am not intending to suggest that people who manage archives should fix the incongruities of the world, but rather to consider (to understand) that privilege over archives is a dynamic intersection of socially constructed subjects who should never be essentialized as monolithic systems.

29. While outside the scope of this chapter, "the homogenization effect," as I am calling it, is viewed by many as a sort of assimilation of Irish traditions into current Western expectations. This multifaceted topic is explored brilliantly in the 2007 documentary produced by RTÉ titled *Canúintí Ceoil* ["Musical Accents"]—*Regional Styles in Traditional Irish Music*, distributed as a six-part series from October to November 2007 on RTÉ TG4. The underlying message of the film champions the prevailing notion among the Gaeltacht that regional styles deserve more attention and performance. Perhaps thematically related to modes of access, in part one of the series, the fiddler Caoimhín Ó Raghallaigh notes,

> "We can't pass on music orally—really—anymore, because there's too many external influences [*sic*]. So, what you need is to raise your level of understanding and be aware of all the influences that can influence you, and your reaction to them. And then you just approach the music from a greater understanding, but you do limit yourself—like, let's say you want to play traditional music, you're going to limit yourself to a certain set of rules within which you operate.... Music is always about excluding things, because rather than constructing something from scratch, if you start with the idea that anything is possible, any music is an imposition of a set of filters on that vast field of possibilities."

Essentially, he's recognizing that traditional music (or any music) is mediated in generic forms. Sometimes those generic forms are homogenized under more dominant or authoritative forms that become prevalent or popular social expectations. Other influences even in Ireland contribute to some homogenization of style and practice, such as increased Internet access, regional and national competitions, institutionalized study of music at a University, and subscription-based study, such as through the Online Academy of Irish Music (OAIM).

30. Being able to "read music" is an interesting sphere of access in and of itself, one that might be too difficult to unpack here. I will add nuance to this concept, though, by pointing out that many players who cannot read Western staff notation well—or at all—can read ABC notation (a text-based musical notation system regularly exchanged in the folk music scene). Since the 1990s, ABC notation proliferated on the Internet, and there are now computer programs that can convert ABC notation directly to standard notation; this has increased the "literacy" and the discursive interactions between ABC and Western recordings of traditional tunes.

31. Like other folk music traditions, Irish tunes typically go by a multitude of names, reflecting the fluid and dialogical nature of oral transmission. For example, if you search TS for the title of one my favorite jigs, as I learned it, you would type "The Cuil Aodha" (named for the town near Muskerry, Cork, in Ireland) into the search bar (https://thesession.org/search?where=&q=Cuil+Aodha). Immediately there is a discrepancy, as the search returns three tunes with that name, one a "slide," one a "jig," and one a "polka." This requires at least the basic knowledge that the tune in question is a jig. But then on the

jig page, you can notice this jig also goes by many other names (some of which do not link to this jig page), and you notice there are six settings. While the melody is similar in each setting of the tune—which is displayed in ABC and staff notation—there are variations in contour and key. Incidentally, none of these settings is the one that I learned. Below the six settings, there is quite a bit of discussion (and some disagreements) regarding the tune overall, as well as links to recordings of it. While this may seem strangely limiting and counterproductive, I argue that this is rife with agency—archive heteroglossia.

32. Lynnsey Weissenberger explores modes of access and limitations on TS in her article on music information retrieval (MIR) systems, "When 'Everything' Is Information: Irish Traditional Music and Information Retrieval" (2014). Particularly in a section called "Limitations of the Physical Paradigm," she notes, "Having one authoritative version of the tune for retrieval purposes denies the individuality, uniqueness, and personalization that is a part of Irish traditional music. Group consensus as to the correct setting of a particular tune is impossible, as practitioners often disagree about large and small elements of their shared culture, making the perspective of one practitioner potentially equal to the perspective of another" (498–499). The ongoing dialogue embedded within the Irish tradition is a hallmark of oral transmission, an archival feature often overshadowed by more conventionally established (colonial) collection formats and mediations that conform to popular generic trends. Weissenberger is implicitly revealing that the very technologies developed to provide access to Irish traditional music typically ignore information vital to the tradition itself, because the conventional MIR modes of access treat information outside of the markers of a standard notated melody as irrelevant. The archival "lack of evidence" causes a rift among practitioners that perpetuates authoritative assumptions about the tradition a priori with respect to the archive proper. The rift is then invoked by users who use the same authoritative social framework in their own assertions about how to interpret the tradition "correctly," a concern that would not exist without the archive itself.

33. Comhaltas Ceoltóirí Éireann (the Association of Musicians of Ireland) is a nonprofit cultural movement whose headquarters (like ITMA) is also based in Dublin, but is known to have hundreds of local branches around the world. Since 1951, Comhaltas has worked toward promoting and performing Irish music and culture in Ireland and abroad, and for the past several decades (particularly since the late 1990s), Comhaltas has amassed a large collection of recordings of performances and festivals. Their website makes all their collections—especially audio and video recordings—available to all users (https://comhaltas.ie/, accessed January 29, 2017).

34. Of course, this is complicated by how popular recordings are instantly recognizable to most practicing musicians in the tradition. Even when noticing specific variations as inspired by popular recordings, people tend to attribute those variations to the performers on the recording, or the regional style they exemplify, in a very communal sense. Sometimes popular recordings become a new point of reference, but they are already enmeshed with several other exchanges inside and outside of various collections or institutional archives. This coupled with the proliferation of numerous names for many older tunes makes it difficult to know in some cases when the tune first transitioned from the oral tradition to the archive.

35. I use "violent" in the theoretical sense here (cf. Derrida 1976, 1978 [1967]; Žižek 2008). In this sense preservation—and any act that makes permanent the ephemeral modes of subjective expression—can be seen as a symbolically violent process.

36. See Kate Distin's 2005 book, *The Selfish Meme: A Critical Reassessment.*

REFERENCES

Armstrong, John. 1982. *Nations before Nationalism*. Chapel Hill, NC: University of North Carolina Press.

Bakhtin, Mikhail. 1981 [1934]. "Discourse in the Novel." In *The Dialogic Imagination: Four Essays*, by Mikhail Mikhailovich Bakhtin and Michael Holquist, 259–422. Austin: University of Texas Press.

Bakhtin, Mikhail. 1993. *Toward a Philosophy of the Act*. Translation and notes by Vadim Liapunov, edited by Vadim Liapunov and Michael Holquist. Austin: University of Texas Press.

Bakhtin, Mikhail, Michael Holquist, and Carl Emerson. 1986. *Speech Genres and Other Late Essays*. Austin: University of Texas Press.

Benjamin, Walter. 1969 [1935]. *The Work of Art in the Age of Mechanical Reproduction*. Translated by Harry Zohn, edited by Hannah Arendt. New York: Schocken Books.

Berne, Eric. 1964. *Games People Play: The Basic Handbook of Transactional Analysis*. New York: Ballantine Books.

Breathnach, Brendan. 1977. *Folk Music and Dances of Ireland*. Cork: Ossian Press.

Brown, Terence. 1981. *Ireland: A Social and Cultural History 1922 to the Present*. Ithaca, NY: Cornell University Press.

Carolan, Nicholas. 1997. *A Harvest Saved: Francis O'Neill and Irish Music in Chicago*. Loudon, NH: Ossian Publications.

Comaroff, John L., and Jean Comaroff. 2009. *Ethnicity, Inc*. Chicago: University of Chicago Press.

Corkery, Daniel. 1967. *Hidden Ireland: A Study of Gaelic Munster in the Eighteenth Century*. Dublin: Gil and MacMillan.

Derrida, Jacques. 1976. *Of Grammatology*. Translated by Gayatri Chakravorty Spivak. Baltimore: John Hopkins University Press.

Derrida, Jacques. 1978 [1967]. "Violence and Metaphysics: An Essay on the Thought of Emmanuel Levinas." In *Writing and Difference*, translated by Alan Bass, 79–174. London: Routledge.

Derrida, Jacques. 1995. *Archive Fever: A Freudian Impression*. Translated by Eric Prenowitz. Chicago: University of Chicago Press.

Distin, Kate. 2005. *The Selfish Meme: A Critical Reassessment*. New York: Cambridge University Press.

Fishman, Joshua A., Michael H. Gertner, Esther G. Lowy, and William G. Milán. 1980. *The Rise and Fall of the Ethnic Revival: Perspectives on Language and Ethnicity*. Berlin: Mouton Publishers.

Foucault, Michel. 1972. *The Archeology of Knowledge and the Discourse on Language*. Translated by A. M. Sheridan Smith. New York: Pantheon Books.

Freedman, Jonathan. 2002. *The Temple of Culture: Assimilation and Anti-Semitism in Literary Anglo-America*. New York: Oxford University Press.

Gellner, Ernest. 1983. *Nations and Nationalism*. Oxford: Basil Blackwell.

Heller, Joseph. 1961. *Catch-22*. New York: Simon and Schuster.

Hobsbawm, Eric and Terence Ranger (eds.). 1983. *The Invention of Tradition*. Cambridge: Cambridge University Press.

Holquist, Michael, 1990. *Dialogism: Bakhtin and His World*. London: Routledge.

ITMA. n.d. "About the ITMA." itma.ie. http://www.itma.ie/about/about-the-itma (accessed December 31, 2016).

JOM Staff. 2015. "Nicholas Carolan's Retirement Marked by ITMA." *Journal of Music Online.* September 2015. University of Limerick. http://journalofmusic.com/news/nicholas-carolans-retirement-marked-itma (accessed January 1, 2017).

Keith, Jeremy. 2016. Personal interview with author. May 11, 2016.

McGettrick, Paul. 1994. "Press Release Announcing the RTE/Irish Traditional Music Archive Re-Mastering Project." https://listserv.heanet.ie/cgi-bin/wa?A3=ind9403&L=IRTRAD-L&E=0&P=167274&B=--&T=text%2Fplain (accessed January 1, 2017).

McKay, Ian. 1994. *The Quest of the Folk: Antimodernism and Cultural Selection in Twentieth-Century Nova Scotia.* Montreal: McGill-Queens University Press.

RTÉ. 2007. *Canúintí Ceoil—Regional Styles in Traditional Irish Music.* Dublin: RTÉ TG4.

Smith, Anthony D. 1986. *The Ethnic Origins of Nations.* Oxford: Blackwell.

Steiner, Claude. 1990. *Scripts People Live: Transactional Analysis of Life Scripts.* New York: Grove Press.

Tonkin, Elizabeth. 1992. *Narrating Our Pasts: The Social Construction of Oral History.* New York: Cambridge University Press.

UNESCO. n.d. "What Is Intangible Cultural Heritage?" http://www.unesco.org/culture/ich/en/safeguarding-003 (accessed January 1, 2017).

Weissenberger, L. K. 2014. "When 'Everything' Is Information: Irish Traditional Music and Information Retrieval." In *iConference 2014 Proceedings.* https://www.ideals.illinois.edu/bitstream/handle/2142/47317/131_ready.pdf (accessed January 1, 2017).

Werner, Cynthia, and Holly Barcus. 2015. "The Unequal Burdens of Repatriation: A Gendered View of the Transnational Migration of Mongolia's Kazakh Population." *American Anthropologist* 117 (2): 257–271.

Žižek, Slavoj. 2008. *Violence: Six Sideways Reflections.* New York: Picador Press.

Žižek, Slavoj. 2013. "Love as a Political Category." *Cinema Europa, 6th Subversive Festival.* Moderator: Srećko Horvat. https://www.youtube.com/watch?v=b44IhiCuNw4 (accessed January 1, 2017).

CHAPTER 37

....

CLAIMING KA MATE

Māori Cultural Property and the Nation's Stake

....

LAUREN E. SWEETMAN AND KIRSTEN ZEMKE

INTRODUCTION
....

IN this chapter, we unpack the wide-ranging cultural, economic, and legal issues surrounding the Ka Mate *haka*. Composed by the Māori chief Te Rauparaha of the southern North Island's Ngāti Toa Rangatira *iwi* (tribe),[1] this *ngeri* or short haka (dance/chant) tells the story of the chief's cunning escape from the enemy tribe Ngāti Maniapoto in the 1820s. Over the past two centuries, Ka Mate's use in rugby and other contexts has led it to become perceived as "New Zealand's national war cry" (Sportal.co.nz 2006) both at home and abroad, an icon of the country's culture, prowess, and virility. Ironically, Ka Mate as a work can also have anticolonial resonances. Sullivan (2005) asserts that performances can represent the "refusal to be subsumed by an empire" and demonstrate the "vigour of Māori culture" (8). Yet, the famous haka has been widely used by the state in Aotearoa/New Zealand—in advertising, tourism, sport, and formal events, as well as in commercial industries—as a symbolic display of biculturalism, a national ritual, and an institutional strategy for the creation of a national imaginary. As such, Ka Mate occupies an ambiguous and conflicting status, at once the most beloved, exploited, misunderstood, and "world famous" New Zealand composition ever written (Sullivan 2005). In this chapter, we explore some of Ka Mate's history and meanings, looking especially at the work in relation to issues of cultural and intellectual property. Ka Mate is emblematic both its cultural currency and in its status as the first piece of cultural property to be legislated through the Haka Ka Mate Act of 2014—two intersecting spheres constituting the crux of our discussion.

More specifically, we first reprise the original significance and usages of the work to ensure that its continued circulation in global discourse does not become detached from its core heritage. We then present a brief history of Ka Mate's legal history with the Intellectual Property Office of New Zealand (IPONZ), the Waitangi Tribunal, and the New Zealand legislature, discussing Ngāti Toa's extensive and ultimately successful battle for tribal ownership and rights—albeit limited—over Ka Mate. Subsequently, to unpack Ka Mate's wider notions of proprietorship and its role in representing "the nation" of New Zealand itself—what we view as potential factors in Ngāti Toa's limited rights—we review Ka Mate's use in World Wars I and II, and in the national sport, rugby, both of which reify overassociations of the haka with war and masculinity. We then link Ka Mate to the larger iconization of Māori cultural performance seen in the Māori performing arts genre *kapa haka*, linking Ka Mate to the contemporary Māori cultural revival and the global interests in and of Māori tourism. We conclude by discussing the role of the media in the circulation and (mis)perception of Ka Mate, providing examples of the range of misappropriations and racist misunderstandings that continue to plague its usage within New Zealand and internationally.

Overall, in this chapter we aim to explore the many struggles and dialogues emerging from Ka Mate's complex location at the intersection of Indigenous cultural property, the public imagination, the Western nation-state, and spheres of global circulation. This type of discourse can be even more complex when applied to nonmaterial artifacts often referred to as "intangible cultural heritage," such as music and dance. Here, we highlight the issues surrounding the repatriation of an "intangible" *taonga*, or treasure, underscoring the very tangible impacts that the circulation of such cultural material has for multiple stakeholders. We conceive of repatriation more generally throughout this chapter as the returning of rights to key stakeholders—a repatriation of history and *mana* (integrity/power) and acknowledgment of colonial injustice. Such a view moves beyond the question of how to give back a set of objects (i.e., recording, archive, etc.) to think through the complications of returning something that has become too large and too publically engaged to be "returned" to one people or community. In truth, Ka Mate cannot be given back to Ngāti Toa per se—as we show, it is an integral part of the national imagination in New Zealand that circulates internationally. So what, then, in this context does "repatriation" mean?

The ultimate goal for the haka is that respect, honor, context, and other key Māori values always accompany its use and performance. However, while seeking permission for its performance would acknowledge the historical colonial process and power imbalances in the work's legacy and creation, this is not always straightforward in the current global and technological exchanges of culture. As such, while understanding this endeavor is never complete, we offer a platform to consider Ka Mate's uses and misuses, specificities, meanings, and intertextual associations as a case study of the fraught location of Indigenous cultural property in our (post)colonial, globalized era. This discussion may resonate with other Indigenous communities who continue to face similar issues within the contexts of settler-colonialism. This haka, born in conflict, continues to serve as a metaphor for the Māori struggle and New Zealand's contested bicultural national identity, as well as the broader experience of Indigenous peoples operating within Western regimes of knowledge and power.

MEANINGS AND SIGNIFICANCE

Part of the reason that the global circulation and decontextualization of Ka Mate is problematic is that in performance, the haka is often removed from its original and significant meanings. In this section, we reiterate some of the power and detail of the "poetic performance" (Sullivan 2005) that is Ka Mate. While the text tells a specific story of a particular event, there are complex and profound allegories transmitted about life and death as well as strength, resilience, and success. Contemporary performances present a link to historical genealogies and offer a transformative moment for audiences and performers. The wartime setting of the poem and its assertion of *te reo Māori* (the Māori language) into modern life mark every performance of Ka Mate as an emblem of colonization, race, loss, and triumph.

The word "haka" is a generic word for dance in te reo Māori; however, "the haka" is widely used to refer to one particular performative dance/poetry/music genre, where performers vocalize a loud chant accompanied by a range of athletic and percussive physical movements. Governed by the male god of war, Tūmatauenga, this genre has, until recently, commonly been viewed as a male domain where men perform either alone or, where women are involved in such performance, in front of the women who "lend vocal support" at the back (Kāretu 1993, 24). However, as performance of the haka varies according to the *tikanga* and *kawa* (cultural values and protocols) of different iwi and *hapū* (subtribe), as well as the reason for performance, the role of women also varies. In contemporary performance, both men and women do haka, though their vocal and physical attributes and actions continue to vary by gender (women, for example, do not stick out their tongues).

The original term for these short haka was "ngeri," whose purpose was "to stiffen the sinews, to summon up the blood" (Karetu 1993, 41). In addition to its ceremonial functions and use as a mode of physical conditioning, haka also provided a means for cultural transmission, leading Armstrong (1964) to view the haka as "the ultimate vehicle for delivery of a message" (as cited in Matthews 2004, 12). The texts incorporate proverbs, genealogy, archaic language, metaphor, simile, allegory, pun, and ambiguity (Milroy 1996, as cited in Matthews 2004). In Māori performing arts, the words and message are primary (Matthews 2004), and the body is an "instrument of delivery," there to emphasize the words (9). As such, the body is used expressively, with rhythmic stamping movements accompanied by *wiri* (hand-shaking) and *pūkana* (facial grimaces, bulging eyes). Movement also includes jumping, kicking the legs up, and pounding the hands on the thighs and chest. An important aesthetic of the performance is to communicate *ihi*, an individual's authority, psychic power, and charisma. The performance should also inspire *wehi* (fear, awe, respect) from the audience, and create an aura of *wana* (thrill, fear, excitement) for all present (Matthews 2004). Understanding these aesthetics is important so as not to misread Ka Mate simplistically as an act of aggression or violence (Gardiner 2007). Rather, Ka Mate is a performance of vigor, history, triumph, and celebration; hence the haka's suitability at ceremonial events including *pōwhiri* (welcome ceremonies), *tangi* (funerals), graduations, sports events, or any event of high importance. The misperception of the haka as an aggressive or violent act is continued by its common popular definition as a "war chant"—a reduction that encompasses only one aspect of the haka's varied usage and meanings.

The narrative of the Ka Mate text tells the story of how Te Rauparaha, the leader of Ngāti Toa, escaped from his enemies by hiding in a pit underneath the wife of an ally. The text was written to commemorate and celebrate his innovative and lucky escape, and to express exhilaration at facing his fear (Hartigan, 2011). Tengan (2002) calls the piece "an artful slice of oral history" that enunciates "ethnic and personal resonances" of death and life. Gardiner (2007) asserts that performing Ka Mate in the present "tears open a space in time," reenacting the "bloody legacy" of the colonial history between Māori and the New Zealand Crown (and between Māori iwi as well). The chant, each time it is performed, reiterates a "historical moment," which activates and enacts history in the present (Hartigan 2011, 39), and is subject to many interpretations. The text describes the hero emerging from the hiding place, safe from capture; Matthews (2004) sees this as a symbol of moving from darkness into light. This "knife edge" of contrast is reaffirmed by the part of the chant, which says, "I live, I live, I die, I die." This recalls the constant presence of death in life, "to live and die in an instant." Sullivan (2005) sees the imagery of upward progression as an allegory of the god Tāne's journey to heaven to collect baskets of knowledge[2]—the enlightenment Te Rauparaha received from being so close to death. Turetsky (2002) further reiterates how the concepts of time and space are evoked in every performance. He argues that the haka exceeds mere past and present; it is a "synthesis of the future" producing new assemblages from the previously "individuated bodies of the dancers" (134). Te Rauparaha's narrative is thus viewed as a "dynamic virtual multiplicity," which is "continuously becoming the actual, becoming present" (129).

While Ka Mate's relationship to war, sport, and masculinity is discussed later, it is important to note here that the haka also has sexual and feminist aspects to it (Jackson and Hokowhitu 2002). Te Rauparaha hid in a kumara pit, the entrance of which was concealed by the chief's wife. In doing so, she revealed her genitals to him ("the hairy man" in the text), which could be considered lewd for such a widely performed piece of art. Te Rauparaha's enemies could not locate him there, for to be in such a position blocked the spiritual power of the *tohunga* (seer) searching for him. In the story, he is thus saved both by a female and by the protection and strength embodied in the female body. Jackson and Hokowhitu (2002) argue that this meaning is often overlooked or denied because it does not conform to notions of white male power, especially when the chant is used in the context of a contemporary sporting identity.

The haka is one of the foundational genres of kapa haka, a broader genre of Māori music and dance that, since the 1970s, has come to represent Indigenous nationalism and Māori identity. As Biddle (2012) argues, kapa haka provides a "lived experience" for Māori, and a means to keep their stories, authors, language, iwi, and history alive. Kapa haka thus serves as tangible evidence of the aspects of Māori culture that are of value (both for Māori and non-Māori), and transform and create what it means to be Māori. The performance of the haka (and of kapa haka) continues historic trends that have used Māori art and iconography as a means to establish New Zealand's "national visual culture" in the early twentieth century (Thomas 2001). The use of such images in art, architecture, fashion, advertising, tourism, and other industries have been adeptly detailed by scholars (e.g., Thomas 1995, 1997, 2001; Shand 2002; Pound 2009; Werry 2011; Geismar 2013b), all of whom assert that, in Thomas's (2001) words, the route to "national distinctiveness has been reference to, or appropriation of, elements of the Indigenous art traditions" (139). The government's use of Indigenous art can be explained, in part, as an attempt to assert what Mullin (1995) calls, in her examination of early-twentieth-century primitive art in the United States, a "utopian affirmation of cultural differences," whereby new colonial power comes to grips with multiculturalism within the liberal empire (166). In the United States, Indigenous culture became the means to root settler culture in a particular native history at a time when the broader public was undergoing "the 'discovery' of the concept of culture" (Mullin 1995, 167). In New Zealand, a similar process occurred. This discovery can be seen in the emergence of nationalist painting and the birth of early kapa haka as a tourist- and government-funded form of "traditional" Indigenous performance in the early twentieth century. Such tourism—deeply rooted in Māori imagery—was a foundational aspect of the New Zealand state, and as Werry (2011) argues, "a component of sovereignty, enabling the young state to consolidate and symbolize its territory, as well as to open it to intervention, circulation, and inhabitation" (5). As we show, this inextricable relationship between Māori culture and the New Zealand imaginary continues to persist and has a significant impact on the consumption of Māori culture on a global scale.

CULTURAL AND INTELLECTUAL PROPERTY

Like its historical story, Ka Mate's legal story highlights the ongoing dissonance between Māori culture and the colonial nation-state. As evidenced in the recent claims of the Waitangi Tribunal[3] and the new guidelines from Wai 262,[4] the notion of intellectual property rights over traditional knowledge, cultural ideas, language, and taonga has been brought to the fore in contemporary New Zealand. Indeed, Ka Mate's problematic location within the realm of intellectual and cultural property has been thoroughly documented in recent literature (Scherer and Jackson 2008, 2013; Dawson 2009; Gray and Scott 2013; Scherer 2013; Frankel 2014; Lai 2014). While the historical case of Ka Mate and its use extends back over a century, its legal cases stem from the late 1990s. Ngāti Toa negotiated various attempts to retain the composition's rights of ownership and acknowledgment within the Western intellectual property system while maintaining its *wairua* (spirit), *whakapapa* (genealogy), and communal properties. This fight was manifested in two main cases: the eight-year case of the Raukawa Trust Board versus the IPONZ and the Ngāti Toa claim brought to the Waitangi Tribunal settled in February 2009. Ultimately successful,

Ngāti Toa have been awarded official attribution as *kaitiaki* (guardians) of Ka Mate following the recommendation of the tribunal, which was ratified in New Zealand legislation
through the Haka Ka Mate Act of 2014. However, while named *kaitiaki* in the legislation,
Ngāti Toa cannot control the haka's performance, and therefore cannot prevent offensive
misuse or misinterpretation, or claim any financial remuneration from its performance.
This happens in spite of the extensive use of the haka in commercial enterprises such as
the New Zealand All Blacks' significant revenue from Ka Mate recordings or the tourism
industry's range of Ka Mate merchandise; not to mention the many commercials and
advertisements that make use of it. Such limitations raise important questions concerning
what it means to hold "rights" to the haka (or any piece of Indigenous cultural property),
and why something clearly "attributed" to a particular community (i.e., Ngāti Toa) cannot
be truly "owned" by—and therefore repatriated to—that community.

The IPONZ Claim

In the first case, spanning 1998–2006, the Raukawa Trust Board, acting on behalf of
Ngāti Toa, attempted to trademark Ka Mate through IPONZ. After a series of widely
publicized debates concerning the commercial use of Ka Mate, sparked largely by a
NZ$120 million Adidas sponsorship of the All Blacks and several national and inter-
national advertising campaigns, Ngāti Toa tried to assert what they viewed as their genealogical right to ownership over Ka Mate as intellectual property. Though Ngāti Toa
did not object to the use of Ka Mate in performance (and they have never tried to stop
its use by the All Blacks or any individual or community group), they sought rights to
the economic profits resulting from its use. However, they lost in 2006 when IPONZ
turned their claim down on the grounds that Ka Mate had achieved wide recognition
or "common use" in Aotearoa/New Zealand and abroad as a representation of New
Zealand national culture. As such, it was not "distinctive" enough to be trademarked,
nor had it remained under Ngāti Toa's control. At the time of the loss, Ngāti Toa intended to appeal the decision; however, representatives noted that the cost of intellectual
property lawyers to continue pursuing the case exceeded their financial resources, and
they were not optimistic about a favorable resolution in the future (Crewdson 2006).
This highlights what Jiang (2008) calls "a paradox for the poor," where the enforcement
of rights designed to protect against exploitation is too costly for the very people being
exploited (31).

The Waitangi Tribunal Claim

On February 11, 2009, Ngāti Toa won a controversial, decade-long battle, winning the
first Indigenous intellectual property rights claim in New Zealand history through the
Waitangi Tribunal. Specifically regarding Ka Mate, Ngāti Toa petitioned the tribunal to
fulfill its "moral obligation" and attribute Ngāti Toa historical authorship of the haka

as the genealogical descendants of Te Rauparaha. In a related matter, they also sought acknowledgment of human rights violations committed by the Crown for the un-lawful eighteen-month imprisonment of Te Rauparaha, during which the Crown sold much of the tribe's land. This consequently framed the issue as one of cultural as op-posed to economic reparation (Dawson 2009). As part of the larger multitribal land claims settlement, they were awarded $73.35 million NZD in redress, $46.5 million NZD of accumulated rentals on Crown forest land and emissions credits, and an important intellectual/cultural property right to Ka Mate: attribution.

This settlement followed the Letter of Offer to Ngāti Toa drafted on December 12, 2008, by the Ngāti Toa Rangatira Committee on behalf of the Waitangi Tribunal proposing the terms of settlement. In this offer, they agreed to "record the significance of the Ka Mate haka to Ngāti Toa," and to develop an approach to address issues of Ka Mate's regulation and use in accordance with two government initiatives: Wai 262 and the Government's Traditional Knowledge Work Programme (Articles 39 and 40). Among the itemized principles of this approach were a commitment "to respect and give effect" to Ngāti Toa's rights, while also preserving "legitimate third party interests and the interests of the general public," and striking a "balance between the rights and interests of Ngāti Toa, users, and the broader public." This follows a longstanding trend articulated by Orange (1987) in her history of the Treaty of Waitangi: "the sat-isfaction of Māori claims depends, as it always has, upon whether or not Māori and Pākehā [New Zealand European] interests coincide" (250). In addition, two other distinctions were made: rights were attributed to the Ngāti Toa as a group rather than to any individual, and it was recognized that "special protection" fell *outside* existing conventional intellectual property protection, and therefore was accountable to those systems (Article 40, Items A–E). This settlement thus denied any rights for Ngāti Toa to royalties or other economic benefits stemming from its performance, or to control over its use (Article 41). Yet, according to the letter, "It is the expectation of Ngāti Toa that the primary objective of this redress is to prevent the misappropriation and cul-turally inappropriate use or performance of the haka 'Ka Mate'" (Article 42). Again, such language raises a few questions: How can the misuse of Ka Mate be prevented if Ngāti Toa cannot control its performance? What consequences does the right Ngāti Toa was given over the attribution of authorship have socially, economically, or politi-cally? Do the limitations of Ngāti Toa's right to Ka Mate undermine the precedent this case sets?

The Haka Ka Mate Attribution Act of 2014

Following the recommendations and settlement of the 2009 tribunal claim, the precedent-setting Haka Ka Mate Attribution Act (Public Law 2014 No. 18) was adopted by the New Zealand legislature on April 22, 2014. The law states the "right of attribution" of Ka Mate to Ngāti Toa, specifying "anything to which the right of attribution applies must include a statement that Te Rauparaha was the composer of Ka Mate and a chief of

Ngāti Toa Rangatira" (Section 9, Article 3). Such attribution must be "clear and reasonably prominent" and "likely to bring Te Rauparaha's identity, as the composer of Ka Mate and a chief of Ngāti Toa, to the attention of a viewer or listener" (Section 9, Article 4) unless so waived or agreed by a rights representative. The right applies to "any publication of Ka Mate for commercial purposes," "any communication of Ka Mate to the public," and "any film that includes Ka Mate and is shown in public or issued in public" (Section 10, Articles 1). However, it does not apply to "any performance of Ka Mate, including by a kapa haka group," "any use for educational purposes of anything that includes Ka Mate," "anything made for the purpose of criticism, review, or reporting current events," or "any communication to the public of anything described by paragraph (a) or (c) for a purpose that is not commercial" (Section 10, Article 2). If the act is violated, the court may "award costs" if a declaratory judgment or order is obtained against a person who breaches the act by a rights representative. In other words, according to the act, as long as a product or performance—whatever that may be—correctly attributes the haka to Te Rauparaha and Ngāti Toa, it can legally continue to use, profit from, and otherwise appropriate Ka Mate for any purpose (Gray and Scott 2013). To facilitate correct attribution, a guide is available from the Ministry of Business, Innovation, and Employment (n.d.) that details the haka's *whakapapa* and further implications of the act. It is our assertion that such legislation, while an important and much-needed sign of progress in terms of Māori cultural acknowledgment within New Zealand, may not be sufficient to uphold the full meaning of *kaitiakitanga* (guardianship, stewardship). The same question then arises: how can Ngāti Toa act as guardians of Ka Mate when they cannot control its use?

The Limits of Western Intellectual Property

Several scholars have pointed out the problematic differences between Indigenous versus Western conceptions of authorship (e.g., Boyle 1996; Brown 1998, 2004; Dutfield 2001; Shand 2002; Hafstein 2007; Geismar 2013b). Among the biggest discrepancies between the way creativity is conceived is that of individual versus collaborative creation, a fundamental tenet of Western intellectual philosophy and international law (Holder and Corntassel 2002). According to Brown (1998) and Hafstein (2007), the rights of the author are predicated on notions of individual genius, invention, and imagination tied to the rise of capitalism in the eighteenth and nineteenth centuries. As publishing began to grow as a lucrative industry, copyright became a means to capitalize on the market system. This system, then, simply cannot account for the ways Indigenous communities envision creativity. According to some epistemologies, cultural material is not invented per se, but rather channeled, dreamed, or inspired. Authorship and, consequently, ownership ultimately belongs to a spiritual deity (Blakeney 2002).

In arguing for Western intellectual property protection, Indigenous communities who view creation in this way may be forced to divorce their spirituality from their creativity in an unfair separation of church and state. Western intellectual property regulation does not consider the spiritual significance or consequence cultural material can have for Indigenous communities, as it innately denies the spiritual power of intangible heritage. Incorporating Indigenous cosmology into structures of governance can cause anxiety for some public officials. Within Māori contexts, the idea of whakapapa is an important concept. Ngāti Toa's claim to Ka Mate was grounded in their genealogical claim to intellectual ownership over the haka. Genealogy here is a kind of active presence, not merely a historical tie to cultural material but rather a living embodiment of it that transcends boundaries of past and present (Kapchan 2014). Legally, this could suggest what Capell (1949) identified early on as "indirect ownership" (170). However, though the legal system is beginning to acknowledge communal heritage as an indicator of ownership, in the case of Ka Mate, we argue it is in large part its ability to fall within aspects of Western intellectual property discourse that has resulted in Ngāti Toa's success.

Many view Western intellectual property law as an imposition forcing Indigenous communities into compliance by simply saying, "You don't have tangible rights to your material," or rather, "We *all* have rights to your material." According to a statement written by the Tulalip Tribe (2003), "the concept of public domain is not accepted by many Indigenous peoples for their knowledge" for these very reasons (1). This positions intellectual property as a kind of intellectual colonialism. We refer here to Kirshenblatt-Gimblett's (2007) assertion: some heritage is more equal than others (23). In the case of Ka Mate, in the IPONZ claim, for example, Ngāti Toa could not be awarded a trademark because, among other reasons, they could not meet the burden of proof of the Western intellectual property system that "the claimants [have] maintained control over its use and because 'Ka Mate' 'may now simply belong to everyone' " (Scherer 2013, 52). Indeed, Scherer (2013) argues that the failure of Ngāti Toa's IPONZ claim signaled that Ka Mate "no longer represented a particular iwi but all of New Zealand" (52). As Lai (2014) argues, Ka Mate thus offers "as a good example of the integration of aspects of Māori culture into general national culture and how this can make it difficult to draw the line of what should be or should not be protected as being 'Māori,' if such protection or rights are to be recognised" (25). Further supporting Scherer's assertion is the utter outrage and fury sparked in the New Zealand public during the IPONZ and Waitangi proceedings at the thought Ngāti Toa may restrict or receive financial gains for the haka. For example, on the day the letter of agreement between Ngāti Toa and the Crown was signed marking the landmark Ka Mate settlement (February 11, 2009), a political cartoon was published on the front page of the *New Zealand Herald* by Rod Emmerson depicting an obese Māori in skimpy traditional dress in a haka stance shouting, "Ka mate Kate mate Dollar Dollar." So contentious was this issue that the cartoon was discussed in parliament by Minister for Treaty Negotiations Chris Finlayson, who hurriedly reassured the House that it was "puerile and inaccurate," a position later echoed by Prime Minister John Key. Why did the public react as it did? Why has Ka Mate come to hold such a sacred place in the New Zealand public imaginary? In the following sections, we turn to a detailed discussion of Ka Mate's role in New Zealand nationalism to address these questions.

FOSTERING NATIONAL UNITY
THROUGH MĀORI PERFORMANCE

As previously stated, the dance/chant/poetry form known as the haka is an important component of the broader Māori performing arts genre kapa haka, which includes five main subgenres of music/dance: haka, *waiata tira* (choral group singing), *waiata-ā-ringa* (action songs), *mōteatea* (traditional chants), and *waiata poi* (women's dance with poi, covered foam balls attached to a length of cord). Kapa haka as a genre can be traced to the 1920s (though its elements are arguably much older), when the dissemination of blended choral and chant styles through figures such as Sir Āpirana Ngata laid the foundation for its modern form. In keeping with the wider Māori cultural revival since the 1970s, kapa haka has seen a resurgence in popularity over the last forty years and has become a mainstay in both local public institutions and the global representation of New Zealand. As such, as a contemporary postcolonial art, movement, and competitive performance genre, kapa haka is often used as a display of an unproblematic biculturalism, apparent through its use on a global stage in such events as the opening of the Rugby World Cup in Auckland in 2011.

The relationship of kapa haka to the political realm can be viewed in multiple ways. As illustrated in Sweetman's doctoral research (2017), the Māori cultural revival (including kapa haka) and its institutionalization can be viewed as a success of Māori self-determination, proof that the goals of Māori education and cultural preservation are indeed working. However, considered in another light, the national kapa haka festival can be presented as, in Kaiwai and Zemke-White's (2004) words, a "culture-making" state-funded institution that serves as a "symbolic display" and "public expression" of New Zealand biculturalism. Such expressions aim to promote unity and a sense of nationalism that may be misleading. For example, according to Papeschi (2006), the creation of the amalgamated kapa haka genre has "heralded the advent of pan-tribalism in haka" and "may have encouraged the shift from iwi to 'nation' where Māori are seen as an 'uber-group'" (33). Papeschi (2006) contests this paradigm shift, stating that this presentation of kapa haka creates a false national ideal, which fails to acknowledge the geographical, cultural, and musical differences between iwi. Ka Mate itself is an example of this, as it tells the story of one tribe's victory over another, and therefore may not be suitable to represent all Māori despite its usage as a national symbol.

Thus, Ka Mate's layers of complexity, metaphor, and historical intertextualities paradoxically challenge notions of national unity, even while being used as a symbol of a harmonious New Zealand. In this way, the narrative of Ka Mate and its poetic extrapolations confront the "disjunctures and liminalities" of New Zealand's postcolonial society (Gardiner 2007). The text is a storehouse of Māori learning, which retains and reworks memories, debates, and individuals, thus keeping them "alive in the tribal memory" (Gardiner 2007, 14). Ka Mate reinserts Māori stories, ideologies, and language into popular culture and contemporary contexts, despite the colonial government's best efforts at assimilation. Kāretu (2008) explores the importance of Ka Mate's role as emissary of the Māori language. Te reo Māori, he argues, is an "essential feature of the landscape of Aotearoa" (90) and it is what makes New Zealand "unique in the world" (90). Ka Mate's ability to maintain its popularity despite being in te reo is a constant reminder of the significant decline of Māori language speakers and colonizers' vehement attempts to eradicate it. Kāretu (2008) warns that many may learn the dance component of a haka, but that equal time must be devoted to pronunciation and maintaining the correct lyrics, because, as stated earlier, the "message" is the key feature of the genre. As such, like kapa haka more broadly, Ka Mate can be used for "nation-making" and "citizen-making" (Thomas 1997, 215) because it entails the social performance of heritage. Ka Mate thus acts as what Smith (2006) would call a "national ritual" that frames the public exchange of meaning and memory essential to nation-building: "The engagement of emotion and the sharing of this emotive experience or performance, together with sharing acts of remembering and memory making, are vital elements of the glue that creates and binds collective identities" (70). This point is further elucidated in explorations of Ka Mate's relationship to twentieth-century war and rugby.

The Māori Battalions: World Wars I and II

In addition to Ka Mate's text, legend, and early history, its reputation as a war dance is amplified by its use by Māori within the context of twentieth-century war. Such use is also embroiled in the haka's connection to Māori masculinity (despite the previous discussion about the acknowledgment of female power in the story), and no doubt features in its contemporary expression. Both World Wars I and II "lionized Māori Battalions" (Tengan 2002, 247). Gardiner (1992, as cited in Tengan 2002) argues that various cultural notions such as the accruement of personal mana (integrity/power) and the mana of the tribe through battle, leadership development, and the exacting of *utu* (revenge) figured prominently in Māori participation in the wars. Gardiner (1992) argues that in World War I, the formation of the first Pioneer Battalion was a part of a broader social movement among Māori to achieve equal status (as men) to that of Pākehā (as cited in Tengan 2002). Tengan (2002) further argued that the experiences of Māori soldiers were situated in gendered and racist structures in relation to the different points of privilege and subordination they were subject to: "By proving that their courage and fighting capabilities were equal to, if not superior to, their white counterparts that they were serving with, Indigenous men could repudiate the colonizers' superiority and validate their own masculinities" (247). Tengan (2002) also cites this participation in the world wars as Māori being complicit with the "maintenance of a Euro-American hegemonic institution" which "naturalizes colonial rule" (247).

During World War II, over 3,300 Māori enlisted in the New Zealand armed forces. Over half of these men particularly opted to join the 28th Battalion, commonly known as the Māori Battalion. The 28th Māori Battalion was an integral part of the second New Zealand Expeditionary Force (2 NZEF), fighting in Greece, Crete, Egypt, Libya, Tunisia, and Italy. They were involved in some of the heaviest fighting throughout the war, suffering a high toll of death, wounding, and prisoners of war. The 28th Battalion became renown for the haka, in particular Ka Mate and their courageous efforts to conquer the Germans (Beatson 1996). Sullivan (2005) recounts how the 28th (Māori) Battalion would leap to their feet with Ka Mate during World War II to inspire themselves and their comrades, and the famous ngeri was performed after their victory at Tebaga Gap in Tunisia. Similarly, a news commentator from the 1940s (Wiremu Parker) describes a haka used to welcome Māori soldiers home:

> For the Māori here present this is a day of sorrow and grief, but it is grief mingled with pride and gratitude for they are proud of their sons, noble sons of Māori land. Proud to welcome home those remnants of that famous galaxy of youth, whose blood has been freely shed on the altars shrine of democracy, they're proud of their boys, who have by their mortal deeds extolled their fame on high.
>
> (Beatson 1996, 77)

This narration highlights the understanding of the haka's complex use as welcome, pride, commemoration, sorrow, and "identity of the race" (Armstrong, as cited in Kāretu 1993, 25). It also solidifies the use of haka as a part of modern warfare.

According to Papuni (2004), Māori veterans experienced a violation of their mana (dignity, authority, power) and *tapu* (purity, blessings, spiritual connection) during the war that left them in a state of *noa* (contamination, ordinary). War also tested their faith and relationship with *Atua* (God). Potentially, the addition of haka to Western war rituals for Māori soldiers can help restore some of the loss of mana and tapu (Papuni 2004).

This (re)iteration of Ka Mate and war—or "the haka" and war—articulates "specifically Indigenous forms of masculinity through their involvement in the military" (Tengan 2002), and perpetuates the connection between the haka and Māori masculinity. It also reproduces the notion of a Māori warrior masculinity upheld through its modern association with rugby and sport. Here, however, it was not in relation to the violence, intensity, or supposed anger of the dance movements and actions, but rather a masculinity based on entering the military to fulfill obligations to the community, to increase the mana of one's family or tribe, to improve one's socioeconomic status, and to put food on the table. As Tengan (2002) states, "actively working to promote the survival and growth of their people" in a "racist colonial society with very few employment options available" (248) offered a means to achieve a masculinity based on notions of family, leadership, and providing in the face of a history of dehumanizing, demasculinizing, colonizing processes (Ihimaera 2000, as cited in Tengan 2002). Ka Mate's links with masculinity and conflict are further exacerbated by its association with rugby and New Zealand's highly respected, globally dominating team, the All Blacks.

The All Blacks and Rugby Nationalism

New Zealand's national rugby team, the All Blacks, originally the New Zealand Natives, have since their inception used a haka to begin their matches. The earliest documented instance of this was the first New Zealand rugby tour to New South Wales, Australia, in 1884. The first specific use of the Ka Mate haka was documented in matches against Scotland and Wales in 1905, around the same time the team's name became the All Blacks, and the mutually defining relationship between the two was formed. Though some, most notably George Nepia in 1924, have attempted to use other haka chants more centered on rugby themes, Ka Mate has become the standard All Black haka and a well-known figure of New Zealand nationalism (Chandler and Nauright 1999, xvi). Indeed, new haka, such as the late former All Black and *kaumatua* (elder) Whetu Tipiwai's haka Timatanga, have been written in recent years for the All Blacks, though none have achieved the widespread familiarity or popularity of Ka Mate.

The link between rugby, nationalism, and colonialism/postcolonialism has been well established in the literature (Chandler and Nauright, 1996, 1999; Richards, 1999; Cashman, O'Hara, and Honey, 2001; Hokowhitu and Jackson, 2002; Hokowhitu 2003, 2004; Ryan, 2005). As Tomlinson and Young (2006) argue, "Sports events celebrating the body and physical culture have long been driven by political and ideological motives" (1). These motives embed in colonial sport specific power structures that are continually refigured to correspond with the emergent political structures of the nation, and the politics of inclusion and exclusion in sport are often contingent on serving a specific national interest. In the case of New Zealand, rugby carries this weight. Positioned as an appeal to a Māori sense of community and mana, rugby—and by extension Ka Mate—has since the late nineteenth century provided a forum for both Māori and Pākehā to participate locally and globally as New Zealand nationals. Rugby has come to represent, in the historic words of All Blacks manager George Dixon, "the manhood and virility of the colony" (1902, as cited in Philips 1996, 88) and the unity of the nation, providing "important points of connection to celebrate the nation's bicultural identity" (Scherer 2013, 43). As Hokowhitu and Jackson avow (2002), "It is during these key periods that a large segment of the population focuses its attention on 15 men who, before entering the battlefield of sport, demonstrate a unity of passion, commitment, and assertiveness that, although explicitly masculine and uniquely New Zealand, is expressed in Māori terms" (127). This process is significantly helped along by the All Black's unprecedented success in rugby, a continual point of pride for most New Zealanders.

Despite its utility as a nation-building tool, the use of Ka Mate in this rugby context is problematic for several reasons. Notably, the popularization of this one essentializing image of indigeneity exoticizes and stereotypes Māori as the "primitive savage warrior, the immoral sexual predator, the naïve comical simpleton, the spiritual/irrational environmentally-aware tribesperson" (Wall 1997, 41) on an international stage. This is especially problematic when, as MacLean (1999) suggests, Ka Mate is not *the* haka, but rather *a* haka, one of many performed (3). Yet, it is probably the only haka most Pākehā know and is most certainly so for audiences abroad. Moreover, as mentioned earlier, the use of Ka Mate is "heartily maligned" by some Māori tribes—especially those on the South Island—due to its use in contexts of war, particularly during the devastating historical invasion of tribes from the North in the mid-nineteenth century. This contestation was evident in protests at an All Blacks versus Wallabies test match in Dunedin in 1994, which erupted after it was publically proposed that the crowd perform the haka en masse (Nauright and Chandler 1999, xvi). Regardless of such objections, so intrinsic is the relationship between Ka Mate and its use in rugby that Barlow (1996) poses the question as not whether a test match would be the same without the haka, but whether the haka would be the same without the All Blacks (as cited in MacLean 1999, 17).

RACISM, THE MEDIA, AND APPROPRIATION

Despite its popularity and ubiquity, Ka Mate, other haka, and Māori performance art in general are still subject to grave misunderstandings, disrespectful appropriations, and outright racism. Moon (as cited in Milne 2013) asserts that the haka has become too detached from its original motives and meanings, and has become an "entertainment spectacle." He argues that it has been corrupted, lacks authenticity, and its "felt tip *mokos*" (tattoos done temporarily with markers for performing) are degrading to those with real *moko* (tattoos; a skin art that depicts and contains ancestral meanings and affiliations specific to the wearer). Moon is against the performance of haka in sport, entertainment, and big business (ibid.), as are many who view the haka as becoming distorted by its stereotypes. Indeed, a grievance noted by participants in Sweetman's research (2017) was the misperception that the haka was all aggression, all the time—an inaccuracy that can restrict how and when haka can be performed within mainstream institutions.

This misperception is consistently upheld in the media. Hartigan (2011), for example, cites articles from the British newspaper the *Guardian* about the All Blacks haka, which is referred to as a "charmless eye rolling tongue squirming dance," a "prenative rumba," a "politically correct lunacy" which "should be greeted with adult disdain," and a "troubling pre-colonial relic that embarrassingly refuses to disappear" (n.p.). A reference to another haka the All Blacks have performed (Kapa O Pango), which featured a throat-slitting gesture, has been called "just short of an exhortation to murder" (Hartigan 2011, n.p.). This haka has also sparked controversy in Australia: the *Sydney Morning Herald* columnist Paul Sheehan (Stuff 2011) wrote, "The violence suggested by throat-slitting gestures has no place in sport or sportsmanship, especially in the national colours" (n.p.). The article reports that a review by the New Zealand Rugby Union claimed that according to Māori consulted, the gesture instead means "the drawing of the breath of life into the heart and lungs" (Stuff 2011, n.p.). The movement was officially withdrawn in 2007 but can be seen to have crept back into some performances of Kapa O Pango.

Continuing this trend in media coverage, take, for example, the following recent episodes—but a few of many: In 2013, a right-wing Danish politician, Marie Krarup, was welcomed onto the navy's Te Taua Moana Marae with a haka. On her personal blog she noted that the haka was "uncivilised" and "grotesque." She said she was greeted by a "half-naked man in grass skirt, shouting and screaming in Māori" (Stuff, 2013, n.p.). Unfortunately, this view was publicly supported by New Zealand Conservative Party leader Colin Craig, who added, not all visitors are impressed by "a bare bottomed native making threatening gestures" (Newshub 2013, n.p.). In 2014, the respected CNN reporter Jeanne Moos was urged by the public to apologize for an "insensitive" report, where she derided the pōwhiri performed at Wellington's Government House on April 7 to honor and welcome Prince William and the Duchess of Cambridge, Kate Middleton, during their official visit to New Zealand. Moos derided the "decorated exposed buns" as no way to "welcome a future king and queen" (Lowery 2014, n.p.). In another part of the CNN segment, Moos showed archival footage of former First Lady Laura Bush, who was offered a haka by New Zealand army officers serving in Afghanistan, saying that the "slapping and thrusting" looked like "a cross between a Chippendale's lap dance and the mating dance of an emu" (Selby 2014, n.p.). A petition for a public apology from CNN was posted to Change.org and reached its goal of twenty-five thousand signatures, and Moos did apologize (Indian Country Today Media Network, 2014).

In a more positive story, the global pop sensation Beyoncé was presented with a haka backstage at her concert by the Māori singer Stan Walker (her support act) in 2013 (Glucina 2013; Jackson 2013; Kenny 2013; Hyland 2015). Phone videos taken on the night show that she responded enthusiastically to the performance and responded in kind with stamping and *pūkana* (a facial expression that often accompanies a haka). Stan called her "awesome" and declared her an "undercover wahine" (Māori woman). Hyland (2015) suggests that Beyoncé was an honored outsider who could reciprocate and understand "the intensity of a vigorously performed haka," which "reinforced the potency of haka as a mode that electrifies and activates its audience" (81). In 2015, at Oprah's well-publicized visit to Orakei marae in Auckland as part of her New Zealand tour, performers were told, "show Oprah your pūkana eyes—she wants to see your pūkana eyes"; Oprah subsequently called her pōwhiri "truly a spiritual experience" (*New Zealand Herald* 2015, n.p.).

Besides ignorant and racist reactions and misinterpretations, there are other examples of peculiar haka appropriations occurring largely in advertising that utilize the haka inappropriately, such as having it performed by lip-syncing Italian women (New Zealand Herald, 2006) or by cartoon gingerbread men (BIANZ, 2007). These appropriations are not limited to commercials. As apparent in any gift store in New Zealand, Ka Mate and the haka more generally have yielded a whole repertoire of odd and often-offensive merchandise ranging from printed Ka Mate boxer shorts; to tea towels and shot glasses; to a stuffed kiwi bird toy in an All Blacks' jersey that, when squeezed, plays a muffled recording of the Ka Mate haka; to coasters, aprons, magnets, oven mitts, notebooks, puzzles, dolls, T-shirts, sweatshirts, stickers, toys, key chains, artwork, and an array of postcards all donning some Ka Mate or haka-related imagery or text. Part of the problem of such appropriations is that they not only occur without penalty or consequence in terms of cultural accreditation, responsibility, or sensitivity but they also fuel an economy of commercialism and commodification that is profiting off cultural property *that has a designated guardian.* This returns us to one of the central questions of this chapter: What are the limits of Indigenous cultural property within Western systems of knowledge and power? In the case of Ka Mate and Ngāti Toa, what does attribution (or kaitiakitanga) give Ngāti Toa in the face of the widespread abuse of Ka Mate? What are the implications of this issue for Māori and Indigenous cultural property in other contexts?

CONCLUSION

Intellectual and cultural property have emerged as powerful imaginaries that are used by communities . . . to develop ideas about Indigenous sovereignty and alternative economies.

—Haidy Geismar, *Treasured Possessions: Indigenous Interventions into Cultural and Intellectual Property*

The Ka Mate haka has profound and significant connections to Māori history, war, culture, and identity; the chant straddles metaphors of life, death, gender duality, and the movement of darkness into light. Every performance brings the past into the present, seeing the continued power and resonance of the story accompanied by intertextual resonances of sovereignty, indigeneity, and colonization. Its misuse and misappropriations are affronting not due to copyright-related financial loss—though this, of course, affects Ngāti Toa—but rather because its misplacements and misunderstandings reiterate and reenact colonizing histories. Ka Mate has become an essentializing image of indigeneity appropriated by sport, commerce, and the New Zealand government as a symbol of a harmonious nation. Ignorant misinterpretations of the piece as solely aggressive and primitive highlight how its circulation outside appropriate contexts and permissions suppresses Māori requirements and rights, allowing racist views of Indigenous masculinities to fester.

The chant itself is only one example of a distinctive Māori genre (haka), which is primarily used for formal activities—funerals, welcomes, inaugurations, graduations, and celebrations. The Ka Mate text may stem from an incident of war and conflict, but it also depicts ingenuity, sacrifice, female power, enlightenment, and survival. Ka Mate's links to war in the twentieth century persisted through its use by Māori military, but this was not about violence or anger; rather it articulated a contemporary Indigenous masculinity based on fulfilling obligations to community, family, and tribe. The falsely ascribed "war dance" was used in World War II by Māori troops for identity, mourning, unity, patriotism, and homesickness. Ka Mate's appropriation by New Zealand's rugby team has become a symbol of winning, masculinity, and New

Zealand, giving the work global spread and recognition. While for the most part a welcome association, this has seen the haka become subject to use for commercial corporate interests.

This examination explored the complexities of protecting Ka Mate's ownership and mana within modern intellectual property systems while retaining Indigenous notions of taonga. Repatriation is not always clear-cut or even possible when it comes to "intangible" manifestation of culture and identity that have circulated into the global marketplace, such as music, chant, and dance. The idea of whakapapa is an important concept in the assertion of Māori heritage. Ngāti Toa's claim to Ka Mate is grounded in their genealogical claim to cultural ownership over this haka, which has led to their official designation as its guardians. While the importance of cultural attribution should not be ignored—indeed it is a necessary first step in increasing Indigenous agency over cultural property—this attribution has limitations. Ngāti Toa cannot restrict or prevent the use of the haka, nor claim any financial stake in its continued commercialization. This raises important questions about the limits of Indigenous cultural property within Western regimes of knowledge and power that have yet to be fully excavated.

This unique and phenomenal haka is rightfully appreciated and beloved by many. Its narrative and sentiments contain both specific and universal elements, and it has remained widely performed and popular over centuries. However, its usages and exploitations highlight rifts between competing notions of what it means to own, repatriate, or have a stake in cultural property. Misappropriations of Ka Mate collude in modern cultural recolonizations that tend to hijack and homogenize the integration of a unique and complex Māori identity into New Zealand nationalism. For these reasons, Ka Mate's contemporary circulation, multiple meanings, and complex layers of "ownership" may resonate with other examples of Indigenous cultural appropriations. There seems to be support and goodwill from the tribal guardians of Ka Mate, proud of the chant's global popularity and national adoration. However, many continue to express reservations around Ka Mate's loss of meaning, disrespectful misuse, and the lack of acknowledgment toward its guardians and status as taonga. This exploration of one chant thus underscores the colonial residues that still permeate art and life in New Zealand, leading us to reconsider what it means to engage with Māori culture in a meaningful way.

NOTES

1. This chapter is based on historical information and is not intended to represent the views of Ngāti Toa Rangatira. Our commentary on the social, cultural, and political implications of the circumstances surrounding Ka Mate, while it may resonate with Ngāti Toa readers, belongs to us alone.

2. In Māori mythology, the god Tāne ascended to twelfth heaven (the highest realm), overcoming a series of obstacles, and retrieved three baskets of knowledge (*te kete aronui, te*

kete tuauri, and *te kete tuatea*) and two stones to bring back to mankind that held all esoteric knowledge and wisdom.

3. The Waitangi Tribunal is a claims court created in 1976 to process alleged breaches to the Treaty of Waitangi, the founding colonial document between the British and a group of Māori chiefs signed in 1840. The treaty provided the alleged basis for Crown ownership and control of the country, though it is debated to what extent (if at all) Māori intended to relinquish sovereignty. The treaty is commonly cited in contemporary culture as the precedent for biculturalism and crown responsiveness to Māori—namely, through its three main tenets of partnership, participation, and protection—though its interpretation and impacts in contemporary government policy continue to be contested, reinterpreted, and redefined. Through legal hearings, the tribunal makes recommendations for government action on claims brought forward by Māori, after which the Crown and claimants consider how they wish to respond. The tribunal cannot enforce its recommendations, though it may assist in settlement negotiations.

4. Wai 262, known as the "flora and fauna claim," was a claim brought to the Waitangi Tribunal in 1991 concerning the recognition of Māori knowledge and ownership over the natural environment. The lengthy report, issued in 2011, offers guidelines for the protection of Māori intellectual and cultural knowledge in a range of areas including natural medicine (*rongoā*), language (te reo Māori), and arts and culture. For a more detailed discussion of its implications within the settler-colonial state, see Geismar (2013a) and Lai (2014).

References

Barlow, Cleve. 1996. *Tikanga Whakaaro: Key Concepts in Māori Culture*. Auckland: Oxford University Press.

Beatson, Donna. 1996. "A Genealogy of Maori Broadcasting: The Development of Maori Radio." *Continuum* 10 (1): 76–93.

BIANZ (Baking Industry Association of New Zealand). 2007. "Gingerbread Haka." Television advertisement. Archived at http://theinspirationroom.com/daily/2007/gingerbread-haka/.

Biddle, Teurikore. 2012. "The Mediation of Tikanga in Haka Competition." *Te Kaharoa* 5: 64–78.

Blakeney, Michael. 2002. "The Protection of Traditional Knowledge under Intellectual Property Law." *European Intellectual Property Review* 22: 251–261.

Boyle, James. 1996. *Shamans, Software, and Spleens: Law and the Construction of the Information Society*. Cambridge, MA: Harvard University Press.

Brown, Michael Fobes. 1998. "Can Culture Be Copyrighted?" *Current Anthropology* 39 (2): 193–222.

Brown, Michael Fobes. 2004. *Who Owns Native Culture?* Cambridge, MA: Harvard University Press.

Capell, A. 1949. "The Concept of Ownership in the Languages of Australia and the Pacific." *Southwestern Journal of Anthropology* 5 (3): 169–189.

Cashman, Richard, John O'Hara, and Andrew Honey, eds. 2001. *Sport, Federation, Nation*. Sydney: Walla Walla Press.

Chandler, Timothy, and John Nauright. 1996. *Making Men: Rugby and Masculine Identity*. London: Frank Cass.

Chandler, Timothy, and John Nauright, eds. 1999. *Making the Rugby World: Race, Gender, Commerce*. London: Frank Cass.

Crewdson, Patrick. 2006, July 2. "Iwi Claim to All Black Haka Turned Down." *New Zealand Herald*. http://www.nzherald.co.nz/nz/news/article.cfm?c_id=1&objectid=10389347.

Dawson, Rachel. 2009, March 9. "The Ka Mate Haka: Generic IP Law versus Indigenous Rights." *Asialaw*. http://www.alphk.com/Article/2121743/Channel/16962/The-Ka-Mate-HakaGeneric-IP-Law-v-Indigenous-Rights.html.

Dutfield, Graham. 2001. TRIPS-Related Aspects of Traditional Knowledge. *Case Western Reserve Journal of International Law* 33 (2): 233–275.

Frankel, Susy. 2014. "'Ka Mate Ka Mate' and the Protection of Traditional Knowledge." In *Intellectual Property at the Edge: The Contested Contours of IP*, edited by Rochelle Cooper Dreyfuss and Jane C. Ginsburg, 193–214. Cambridge: Cambridge University Press.

Gardiner, Wira. 1992. *Te Mura O Te Ahi: The Story of the Maori Battalio*. Auckland: Reed Books.

Gardiner, Wira. 2007. *Haka: A Living Tradition*. Auckland: Hodder Moa.

Geismar, Haidy. 2013a. "Resisting Settler-Colonial Property Relations? The WAI 262 Claim and Report in Aotearoa New Zealand." *Settler Colonial Studies* 3 (2): 230–243.

Geismar, Haidy. 2013b. *Treasured Possessions: Indigenous Interventions into Cultural and Intellectual Property*. Durham, NC: Duke University Press.

Glucina, Rachael. 2013. "The Diary: Gifts and Farewell Haka Move Beyoncé to Tears." *New Zealand Herald*, October 23, 2013. http://www.nzherald.co.nz/entertainment/news/article.cfm?c_id=1501119&objectid=11144453.

Gray, Earl, and Raymond Scott. 2013. "Rights of Attribution for Ka Mate Haka." *Journal of Intellectual Property Law and Practice* 8 (3): 200–202.

Hafstein, Victor. 2007. "Claiming Culture: Intangible Heritage Inc., Folklore, Traditional Knowledge TM." In *Prädikat "Heritage": Wertschöpfungen aus kulturellen Ressourcen*, edited by Dorothee Hemme, Markus Taushek, and Regina Bendix, 75–100. Berlin: Lit Verlag.

Hartigan, Ryan. 2011. "Embarrassing Time, Performing Disunity Rugby, the Haka, and Aotearoa New Zealand in the United Kingdom." *Performance Research* 16 (2): 37–43.

Hokowhitu, Brendan. 2003. "'Physical Beings': Stereotypes, Sport, and the 'Physical Education' of New Zealand Māori." *Culture, Sport, Society: Cultures, Commerce, Media, Politics* 6 (2/3): 192–218.

Hokowhitu, Brendan. 2004. "Tackling Māori Masculinity: A Colonial Genealogy of Savagery and Sport." *Contemporary Pacific* 16 (2): 259–284.

Hokowhitu, Brendan, and Stephen J. Jackson. 2002. "Sport, Tribes, and Technology: The New Zealand All Blacks Haka and the Politics of Identity." *Journal of Sport and Social Issues* 26: 125–139.

Holder, Cindy L., and Jeff J. Corntassel. 2002. "Indigenous Peoples and Multicultural Citizenship: Bridging Collective and Individual Rights." *Human Rights Quarterly* 24: 126–151.

Hyland, Nicola. 2015. "Beyoncé's Response (eh?): Feeling the Ihi of Spontaneous Haka Performance in Aotearoa/New Zealand." *Drama Review* 59 (1): 67–82.

Ihimaera, Witi. 2000. "Masculinity and Desire: Rewriting the Polynesian Body." Lecture delivered April 18, 2000, University of Hawai'i.

Indian Country Today Media Network. 2014. "Did CNN Need to Apologize for This Racist Segment? 25,000 Said Yes." April 15, 2014. http://indiancountrytodaymedianetwork.com/2014/04/15/did-cnn-need-apologize-racist-segment-25000-said-yes-154458.

Jackson, Steven J., and Brendan Hokowhitu. 2002. "Sport, Tribes, and Technology: The New Zealand All Blacks Haka and the Politics of Identity". *Journal of Sport and Social Issues*. 26 (2): 125–139.

Jackson, Willie. 2013. "Rihanna's Ink and Beyoncé's Haka." *Stuff*, October 31, 2013. http://www.stuff.co.nz/auckland/local-news/local-blogs/willie-jackson/9347078/Rihannas-ink-and-Beyonces-haka.

Jiang, F. 2008. "The Problem with Patents: Traditional Knowledge and International IP Law." *Harvard International Review* 30 (3): 30–33.

Kaiwai, Hector, and Kirsten Zemke-White. 2004. "Kapa Haka as a 'Web of Cultural Meanings.' " In *Cultural Studies in Aotearoa New Zealand: Identity, Space and Place*, edited by Claudia Bell and Steve Matthewman, 139–160. Victoria: Oxford University Press.

Kapchan, Deborah, ed. 2014. *Cultural Heritage in Transit: Intangible Rights as Human Rights*. Philadelphia: University of Pennsylvania Press.

Kāretu, Timoti S. 1993. *Haka: The Dance of a Noble People*. Auckland: Reed.

Kāretu, Timoti S. 2008. "Te Kete Tuawha, Te Kete Aroiti: The Fourth Basket." *Te Kaharoa* 1:87–98.

Kenny, Katie. 2013. "Beyoncé and the Haka" *Stuff*, October 25, 2013. http://www.stuff.co.nz/entertainment/celebrities/9326953/Beyonce-and-the-haka.

Kirshenblatt-Gimblett, Barbara. 2007. "World Heritage and Cultural Economics." In *Museum Frictions: Public Cultures/Global Transformations*, edited by Ivan Karp, Corinne A. Kratz, Lynn Szwaja, and Thomas Ybarra-Frausto, 161–202. Durham, NC: Duke University Press.

Lai, Jessica Christine. 2014. *Indigenous Cultural Heritage and Intellectual Property Rights: Learning from the New Zealand Experience?* New York: Springer.

Lowery, Sophie. 2014. "CNN Reporter Apologises for Tone of 'Royal Bummer.' " *Newshub*, April 12, 2014. http://www.newshub.co.nz/nznews/cnn-reporter-apologises-for-tone-of-royal-bummer-2014041217#axzz4GoLEmnal.

MacLean, Malcolm. 1999. "Of Warriors and Blokes: The Problem of Māori Rugby for Pākehā Masculinity in New Zealand." In *Making the Rugby World: Race, Gender, Commerce*, edited by Timothy Chandler and John Nauright, 1–28. London: Frank Cass.

Matthews, Nathan. 2004. "The Physicality of Māori Message Transmission: Ko Te Tinana, He Waka Tuku Kōrero." *Junctures* 3: 9–17.

Milne, Jonathan. 2013. "Haka, Pōwhiri 'Cringing' Spectacles, Says Historian." *New Zealand Herald*, July 28, 2013. http://www.nzherald.co.nz/nz/news/article.cfm?c_id=1&objectid=10904344.

Ministry of Business, Innovation, and Employment. n.d. "Haka Ka Mate Attribution Act 2014 Guidelines." http://docplayer.net/60037641-Haka-ka-mate-attribution-act-2014-guidelines.html.

Mullin, Molly H. 1995. "The Patronage of Difference: Making Indian Art 'Art, Not Ethnology.' " In *The Traffic in Culture: Refiguring Art and Anthropology*, edited by George E. Marcus and Fred R. Myers, 166–198. Berkeley: University of California Press.

New Zealand Herald. 2015, December 15. "Oprah Welcomed onto Orakei Marae." https://www.nzherald.co.nz/entertainment/news/article.cfm?c_id=1501119&objectid=11561448.

New Zealand Herald. 2006, July 4. "Italians Drive ahead with Car Mate Haka." http://www.nzherald.co.nz/nz/news/article.cfm?c_id=1&objectid=10389619.

Newshub. 2013, April 8. "Bare Bottom Welcomes 'Should Be Optional.' " http://www.newshub.co.nz/politics/bare-bottom-welcomes-should-be-optional-2013040814#axzz4GoLEmnal.

Orange, Claudia. 1987. *The Treaty of Waitangi*. Wellington: Allen and Unwin.

Papeschi, Te Rita. 2006. "Kapa Haka." *State of the Māori Nation: Twenty-First-Century Issues in Aotearoa*, edited by Malcolm Mulholland, 33–40. Auckland: Reed.

Papuni, Jack Rangi Matenga. 2004. "'We Answer the Call to Arms'": War Experience and Its Toll on the Spirituality of the Māori Soldier Post-WWII." PhD diss., University of Auckland.

Philips, Jock. 1996. "The Hard Man: Rugby and the Formation of Male Identity in New Zealand." In *Making Men: Rugby and Masculine Identity*, edited by Timothy Chandler and John Nauright, 50–69. London: Frank Cass.

Pound, Francis. 2009. *The Invention of New Zealand: Art and National Identity, 1930–1970*. Auckland: Auckland University Press.

Richards, Trevor. 1999. *Dancing on Our Bones: New Zealand, South Africa, Rugby and Racism*. Wellington: Bridget Williams.

Ryan, Greg, ed. 2005. *Tackling Rugby Myths: Rugby and New Zealand Society 1854–2004*. Dunedin, NZ: University of Otago Press.

Scherer, Jay. 2013. "Promotion of Culture and Indigenous Identity: Trading the Other." In *The Fourth Eye: Māori Media in Aotearoa*, edited by Brendan Hokowhitu and Vijay Devadas, 42–59. Minneapolis: University of Minnesota Press.

Scherer, Jay, and Steven J. Jackson. 2008. "Cultural Studies and the Circuit of Culture: Advertising, Promotional Culture and the New Zealand All Blacks." *Cultural Studies—Critical Methodologies* 8 (4): 507–526.

Scherer, Jay, and Steven J. Jackson. 2013. *Contested Terrain of the New Zealand All Blacks: Rugby, Commerce, and Cultural Politics in the Age of Globalization*. Oxford: Peter Lang.

Selby, Jenn. 2014. "CNN Reporter Forced to Apologise for 'Insensitive' and 'Racist' Coverage of the Royal Visit to New Zealand." *Independent*, April 2014. http://www.independent.co.uk/news/people/cnn-reporter-forced-to-apologise-for-insensitive-and-racist-coverage-of-the-royal-visit-to-new-zealand-9262465.html.

Shand, Peter. 2002. "Scenes from the Colonial Catwalk: Cultural Appropriation, Intellectual Property Rights, and Fashion." *Cultural Analysis* 3:47–88.

Smith, Laurajane. 2006. *Uses of Heritage*. New York: Routledge.

Sportal.co.nz. 2006. "Haka Inspired Aussie Dave Brockhoff." *allblacks.com*, October 24, 2006. http://allblacks.com/News/4998/haka-inspired-aussie-dave-brockhoff.

Stuff. 2011. "Australian: Throat-Slitting Haka Has No Place." October 20, 2011. http://www.stuff.co.nz/sport/rugby/5818998/Australian-Throat-slitting-haka-has-no-place.

Stuff. 2013. "Danish Politician Slams Māori Welcome." April 6, 2013. http://www.stuff.co.nz/national/8517466/Danish-politician-slams-Maori-welcome.

Sullivan, Robert. 2005. "Ka Mate, Ka Ora: I Die, I Live." *Ka Mate Ka Ora* 1: 1–9.

Sweetman, Lauren E. 2017. "Ngā Waiata O Tāne Whakapiripiri: Māori Cultural Expression, Transformation, and Healing in a Māori Forensic Psychiatric Unit." PhD diss., New York University.

Tengan, Ty Kāwika. 2002. "(En)Gendering Colonialism: Masculinities in Hawai'i and Aotearoa." *Cultural Values* 6 (2): 239–256.

Thomas, Nicholas. 1995. "Kiss the Baby Goodbye: 'Kowhaiwhai' and Aesthetics in Aotearoa New Zealand." *Critical Inquiry* 22 (1): 90–121.

Thomas, Nicholas. 1997. "Nations' Endings: From Citizenship to Shopping?" In *Narratives of Nation in the South Pacific*, edited by Ton Otto and Nicholas Thomas, 211–220. Amsterdam: Overseas Publishers Association.

Thomas, Nicholas. 2001. "Appropriation/Appreciation: Settler Modernism in Australia and New Zealand." In *The Empire of Things: Regimes of Value and Material Culture*, edited by Fred R. Myers, 139–163. Sante Fe, NM: School of American Research Press.

Tomlinson, Alan, and Christopher Young, eds. 2006. *National Identity and Global Sports Events: Culture, Politics, and Spectacle in the Olympics and the Football World Cup.* New York: SUNY Press.

Tulalip. 2003, July 9. "Statement by the Tulalip Tribes of Washington on Folklore, Indigenous Knowledge, and the Public Domain." Intergovernmental Committee on Intellectual Property and Genetic Resources, Traditional Knowledge and Folklore, Geneva, Washington.

Turetzky, Philip. 2002. "Rhythm: Assemblage and Event." *Strategies* 15 (1): 121–138.

Wall, Melanie. 1997. "Stereotypical Constructions of the Māori 'Race' in the Media." *New Zealand Geographer* 53 (2): 40–45.

Werry, Margaret. 2011. *The Tourist State: Performing Leisure, Liberalism, and Race in New Zealand.* Minneapolis: University of Minnesota Press.

CHAPTER 38

REPATRIATION AND DECOLONIZATION

Thoughts on Ownership, Access, and Control

ROBIN R. R. GRAY

INTRODUCTION: KEEPING AN EYE OUT FOR OUR SONGS

REPATRIATION means to return something or someone to their place of origin. The politics of Indigenous repatriation—whether it involves human remains, objects, or songs—requires that it be restorative so that the source community can find a sense of resolution from historical injustices. For example, Ts'msyen from Lax Kw'alaams, British Columbia experienced a form of hyperdispossession from settler colonial contact that is quite remarkable in terms of time and space. In our small coastal village, which became the political home of the Nine Allied Tribes, we had to contend with missionization (1857–1948), the Hudson Bay Company (1834–1856), and Indian residential schools (1879–1948) like other Indigenous communities in Canada, but we also experienced a targeted attack on our particular ways of knowing, being, and doing from the Potlatch Ban (1884–1951).[1]

In the same period, anthropological thought promulgated the notion that modernity would overtake indigeneity as if the two concepts were mutually exclusive. Anthropologists were particularly fond of northwest coast cultural aesthetics and curious about our complex forms of social organization, so Ts'msyen became early recipients of the anthropological gaze and burden bearers of the salvage era, when capturing Ts'msyen cultural heritage was part and parcel of the overall project of Indigenous dispossession. It therefore took a series of concurrent and overlapping settler colonial processes to create the conditions for the mass expropriation of our cultural heritage by a range of individuals interested in salvaging what was thought and hoped to be the remnants of a "vanishing Indian" culture. What is most telling about settler greed of this period is that while our culture was being suppressed, and while our heritage was being captured, various individuals and institutions were giving new value and meaning to our objects, bodies, and knowledges through processes of objectification, appropriation, and commoditization. Consequently, there is an incredible amount of Ts'msyen cultural material located in universities, museums, archives, and personal collections around the world, but Ts'msyen are not considered the owners by default of Western property frameworks. For repatriation purposes, how do we deal with issues of ownership, access, and control in a manner that contributes to a decolonial future? For consideration, I discuss the potential repatriation of a collection of songs to the Ts'msyen community of Lax Kw'alaams.

I have been a member of the Lax Kxeen Ts'msyen Dance Group based in Vancouver, British Columbia, for nearly twenty years. Lax Kxeen represents an intergenerational community of families who primarily trace their lineage to the Ts'msyen village of Lax Kw'alaams. Over the years, conversations about the role of song and dance and the importance of cultural reclamation have increased among members, leading to a request of me by the leader of our dance group. She asked, "Can you keep an eye out for our songs while you're out there doing your studies?" As a graduate student in anthropology and Indigenous studies at the time, I was both compelled to respond to the unique needs, priorities, and values of my community and intrigued by questions of property, ownership, access, and control where it concerned captured forms of Indigenous cultural heritage. As I thought through the possibility of reclaiming songs that our group leader knew were "out there somewhere," and as I thought about how repatriation could take form in various contexts, I was informed by a student colleague in my department about a collection of Ts'msyen songs located at Columbia University. The detection of our songs not only presented an opportunity for repatriation, but it would also allow me to test the application of a decolonial ethic to an actual case study. With consultation and guidance from Ts'msyen people, I began to implement a comprehensive, community-based Indigenous research paradigm to explore the motivations, possibilities, and obstacles associated with repatriating Ts'msyen songs from archives. Since 2012 I have engaged nearly three hundred Ts'msyen from infants to elders in a multisited, ethnographic research project: (1) in Lax Kw'alaams, the contemporary village for nine of the fourteen tribes of the Ts'msyen nation; (2) in Prince Rupert, a Ts'msyen place and the main urban locale; and (3) in Vancouver, where there is a large population of the Ts'msyen diaspora. The entirety of the research process was approached as much as possible per the ethics and protocols of our people—*Ayaawxsm Ts'msyen*—to reflect a distinctive Indigenous research paradigm based on the precedent of Ts'msyen laws, and our ways of knowing, being, and doing. While the case study is ongoing, and we have yet to find resolution, the research contributes to contemporary discussions about ownership, access, and control of Indigenous cultural heritage.

THE CASE STUDY

The repatriation case study began with knowledge about a collection of Ts'msyen songs that became caught up in the Laura Boulton Collection of Traditional and Liturgical Music, located in the Center for Ethnomusicology at Columbia University. While this was the initial detection and point of entry for a potential repatriation, the preliminary research revealed that answers to questions about provenance were not as straightforward as one might think. In consultation with the former and current director of the center, Aaron Fox, and largely due to his knowledge of the center's lineage and research about Boulton's activities leading up to the acquisition of her music collection by Columbia, I immediately discovered that there were complicated webs of meaning and ownership associated with the Laura Boulton Collection, and thus the Ts'msyen content therein. Boulton was originally funded by the National Film Board of Canada (NFB) to document the traditions of ethnic communities for the Peoples of Canada project, which she did in the years 1941 and 1942. The primary point of the project was to use her documentary resources, including photographs, film footage, and sound recordings, for inclusion in a series of films for the NFB. This endeavor resulted in her accumulation of documented musical traditions from mostly ethnic white minority communities, but she also recorded songs and oral histories of three northwest coast Indigenous peoples: Gitxsan, Haida, and Ts'msyen. Her encounter with Ts'msyen was brief, taking place in June of 1942 with two men in their eighties: Matthew Johnson in Lax Kw'alaams and someone named "Pearce" in Prince Rupert.

In 1962, Boulton arranged to both sell the music that she recorded between 1933 and 1962 to Columbia University and curate her collection in the newly founded archives of what would become the Center for Ethnomusicology. She included the Peoples of Canada recordings in this sale. Dated June 14, 1962, the contract between the Trustees of Columbia University and Laura Boulton regarding what was originally named the Laura Boulton Collection of Traditional and Exotic Music stipulated that, beginning January 21, 1964, the collection, notes, rights, title, and interest would be transferred to the university. The contract specifies that Boulton would be paid $5,000 on February 15 and August 15 of each year during her lifetime—she passed in 1980. Boulton thus made $170,000 over a seventeen-year period from the sale of this collection (in which the Ts'msyen content is caught up), while the university placed value in having rights to the recorded material in perpetuity. In June of 1973, Columbia entered into a contractual agreement with the Library of Congress to deposit the original master recordings of the Boulton Collection on "permanent loan." Meanwhile, Columbia would retain the rights to the collection, including the authority to determine who can transcribe, analyze, or publish the speech and music contained therein. By accepting the masters, the Library of Congress agreed to produce three sets of listening copies on reel-to-reel tapes. Two sets went to Columbia, and one set went to Boulton for her personal files. After her death in 1980, her personal files, including an endowment and royalty rights to her commercial publications, were left in trust to Indiana University Bloomington by way of the Laura Boulton Foundation. And since a tape copy of the collection that she sold to Columbia was in her personal files (which included the Peoples of Canada recordings), Indiana, Columbia, and the Library of Congress represent default stakeholders with various assemblages of rights, managing access to and control of Ts'msyen cultural heritage. Indeed, complicated webs of meaning and ownership are demonstrated in the fact that an additional 1982 final agreement about access and control clarified that Indiana and the Library of Congress might be in the position to provide public access to our songs for scholarly interests, but Columbia maintains ownership, and decisions about who can duplicate or transcribe the collection rests with the director of the Center for Ethnomusicology (Fox 2013). It is also worth noting here that the Columbia center has digitized the Boulton collection for permanent retention, raising additional concerns about the potential for remote access and future use.

Yet, for all of the transactions that took place leading to the documentation, commoditization, preservation, duplication, and circulation of the Ts'msyen content caught up in the Boulton collection, there was not one instance in which either of the actors or institutions have acknowledged the legal, cultural, or moral rights of Ts'msyen, nor the rights of any other Indigenous community, whose knowledge, history, ceremonies, and creative expressions were captured by Boulton (see Fox 2013). In all instances, Ts'msyen songs and oral histories were given new meaning and value ex situ—divorced from the appropriate sociocultural context, without consultation from the community, and without due consideration of the laws and protocols of the people whom the performers represented. The primary reason why these transactions could proceed without due consideration of Ayaawxsm Ts'msyen is that copyright ascribes protection over products of knowledge rather than to knowledge itself. In the Western property view, Ts'msyen never owned the copyright to the knowledge product, the tangible recording. Laura Boulton, the researcher, claimed ownership of it, then sold it and bequeathed it, and now multiple institutions control the means of access to our songs by default of them being recorded, duplicated, and homogenized into a self-named collection for their archives. This signals one of the colonizing properties of Western property frameworks, especially in a settler colonial context where Indigenous societies are hyper-researched, and where Indigenous knowledge is hyper-represented in the archive even though the people are not. Through intellectual property laws like copyright, a researcher arbitrarily gains ownership of knowledge when it becomes documented and transformed into a knowledge product in the form of a manuscript, a film, a photograph, or in this case an audio recording and its metadata. Even though Ts'msyen are the original creators of their knowledge expressions and have unique laws and protocols that govern their relationship to cultural heritage, in most countries around the world copyright laws have not allowed, and do not provide space, for the incorporation of Indigenous customary laws, systems of property, or notions of property ownership (Torsen and Anderson 2010). As Rebecca Tsosie (1997, 5) notes, "The clash between indigenous peoples and European colonial nations has largely concerned property rights." Indigenous dispossession in settler colonies has resulted from the appropriation of Indigenous cultural heritage—lands, resources, knowledge, objects—into the property of a settler entity such as a researcher, an institution, the state, or the commons. And in this case, since "it is copyright which historically and contemporarily makes, maintains and distributes the figure of the 'author' and correspondingly the 'work,' both of which are folded into the classificatory frameworks of the archive" (Anderson 2013, 229), the Boulton collection, in all of its iterations, becomes an important locus for studying the coloniality of power, knowledge as property, and Indigenous dispossession (Anderson 2009a, 2009b, 2013). Beyond theory, however, there is praxis, so for the purpose of repatriating Ts'msyen songs from these archives, it raises the question: how ethical, or even practical, is it to use the same legal frameworks for restitution that were leveraged to dispossess us of our heritage and rights in the first place? Ayaawxsm Ts'msyen predates and persists alongside the existence of settler states in North America even if the understanding of our laws have been shrouded by colonial geopolitics, and embodiment of our laws have been restricted by the ban. Furthermore, from a strictly educational or scientific perspective, how ethical, or even responsible, is it to make our cultural heritage accessible to the public when the original collector and the aforementioned gatekeepers do not even know what it is they hold, or the significance of what they have assumed control over? The scientific argument for Indigenous repatriation is just as important as the legal or moral one.

AURAL RESUSCITATIONS: BREATHING LIFE INTO OUR SONGS

In September 2012—exactly seventy years after our songs were recorded, and fifty years after they ended up at Columbia—I visited the Center for Ethnomusicology to confirm the Ts'msyen content in the Boulton collection with Aaron Fox. To both of our knowledge, it was the first time a Ts'msyen had accessed the Ts'msyen recordings, and it was the first time that the Peoples of Canada files, in this collection, had been given any attention. Because there were accumulated inaccuracies and noncorrespondences between their metadata and audio files, Aaron wanted to be sure that I was accessing the correct content, and so this visit was not only meant for me to gain access to our songs but also to clarify that they indeed had Ts'msyen songs, and to determine whether their collection was actually complete. Unfamiliar with northwest coast Indigenous cultural sensibilities, Aaron was uncertain how to distinguish between the northwest coast audio files labeled Haida, Ts'msyen, and Gitxsan, and so he needed my ear to help make the distinctions. Even though I did not have linguistic fluency in Sm'algyax, I knew enough words, sounds, and tones, and I also had my instincts as a Ts'msyen, to at least give it a try. We began by listening to all the northwest coast audio files so that I could try to isolate the Ts'msyen content. When I felt confident that I had the Ts'msyen content isolated, we then sought to determine whether the track numbers aligned with the notes in the metadata.

The Columbia metadata listed forty-one individual files labeled "Tsimsyan Indian."
Out of these, thirty-two were attributed to "Matthew Johnson (Age 87)" and nine to
"Pearce." However, through that initial listening process, I was certain that only half
of the metadata had a corresponding audio file; I was sure that at least twenty were
missing. I was not able to confirm which exact files were missing on the spot because
I did not have the linguistic expertise to translate them. I did suspect, however, that the
missing files were associated with Matthew Johnson because, among the Ts'msyen content, I heard two distinct voices. Here the metadata was useful—because Boulton associated nine individual files with "Pearce," and because I heard nine continuous sound
recordings that contained one of those distinct Ts'msyen voices, I deduced that they
could be associated with "Pearce," and that the missing files could be associated with
Matthew Johnson. I was already overloaded with information, confused by the matrix
of property transfers that occurred with the Boulton collection, when I realized that if
Columbia did not have a complete collection, to boot, this was not going to be a straightforward repatriation case at all. Indeed, after my first visit to Columbia, Aaron provided
me with digital access to the entire Peoples of Canada collection so that I could investigate whether perhaps the missing Ts'msyen files were cataloged incorrectly and could
be found somewhere else among the collection. After listening to the approximately one
thousand recordings on my own time, I could not locate the missing songs anywhere.

Although the Ts'msyen files that I did get to hear seemed to match up with the metadata, there were some serious shortcomings that illuminated the politics of representation with Indigenous cultural heritage (Smallacombe 2000). The metadata was
inadequate, with curious titles like "Indian Song" and scant descriptions like "Folk
Song." Instinctively I knew that our songs had suffered the same fate as most forms
of captured Indigenous cultural heritage: they were collected, copyrighted, poorly
documented, disseminated, and archived, "in a 'vacuum' apart from the proper cultural setting" (Gii-dahl-guud-sliiaay 1995, 194), and as a result they lacked sociocultural
context including translations, statements of history, lineage, and hereditary rights to
ownership. The notes that Laura Boulton made can be described as overly simplistic
labels for classification given by someone who did not understand the content. In fact,
it was not until 1962 when she negotiated the terms of her sale that Boulton collated and
cataloged the metadata for her collection—twenty years after the moment of capture.
This is haphazard, even by the standards of the time, and can be owed to the curious
life of Boulton. She was not so much a researcher as she was a typical amateur collector
of her era, albeit one who adamantly sought professional and academic legitimacy for
most of her life (McMillan 1991; Fox 2013).

I also consulted Boulton's book, *The Music Hunter: The Autobiography of a Career*
(1969), to see whether there was additional information or context to consider beyond
the pithy descriptions that she does provide in her notes. I found that she made fleeting
references to Ts'msyen, oddly in chapter 25, which is arbitrarily titled, "The Queen
Charlotte Islands and the Northwest Coast Indians" (Boulton 1969, 393–410). There
were two things that I found from this book—something about "Pearce" but nothing
about Matthew Johnson. She writes, "William Pierce was my best informant with the

Tsimshian at Prince Rupert, an important coast village of British Columbia. He belonged to the Eagle clan by birth and the Blackfish clan by adoption. When he sang these clan songs for me he was eighty-four years old but still knew very many songs, which he sang well" (Boulton 1969, 409). Boulton went on to conclude the chapter with a transcription of William Pierce sharing an *Ayaawx* (oral history) in English about how the halibut became dark on one side. I was able to corroborate that there were two files with this title that were attributed to "Pearce" in the metadata—one recounted in Sm'algyax and the other in English. The book turned out to be useful with regard to figuring out the last name and age of "Pearce," but it too proved to be inadequate for many reasons—namely, that there were no other references to William Pierce, nor a single reference to Matthew Johnson throughout her book. Even the assertion that William Pierce was "Eagle clan by birth" but "Blackfish clan by adoption," and that he sang "clan" songs raises the questions: Which clan songs was he singing? Were they Laxsgiik (Eagle) songs or were they Gisbutwada (Blackfish) songs? Could they even be described as clan songs at all?

Given all of the confusion associated with this particular collection of Ts'msyen songs—ex situ meaning and value, various assemblages of rights, an incomplete archive, limitations in the metadata, and a short-lived reference to a Ts'msyen encounter in her book—it was clear that repatriating Ts'msyen songs would require a great deal of community-based participatory action research with, by, and for Ts'msyen. Community-based research would be necessary to "breathe life" into our songs, to re-transform static heritage into activated and then active heritage once more. Our songs remained static, confined to archives for so long, but they became activated through our collective research, and will be active once more when Ts'msyen themselves determine rights to ownership based on our Ayaawx, and the appropriate people or entity are singing/dancing their songs again in ways suited to time, place, and protocol. Regarding the ownership concept, it should not be thought of solely in the Western legal sense. "What is sacred and what is law is entirely bounded by culture" (Bell and Napoleon 2008, 5). In the Ts'msyen worldview, ownership is more synonymous with responsibility than it is with possession. In a general sense, tangible and intangible forms of Ts'msyen cultural heritage are collectively owned, with rights to crests, names, masks, hereditary titles, and songs, for example—possessing intra- and interdependent levels of individual, family, house, tribe, clan, community, and nation-based ownership and responsibilities. Ts'msyen trace lineage through our mother's line to determine our clan, house, and tribal identities within the Ts'msyen sovereignty structure. We all belong to the clan of our mother, first and foremost. The clans are represented as multiple house groups that are organized among the fourteen tribes of the Ts'msyen nation based on a complex system of matrilineal descent and inheritance. Therefore, aural resuscitation of the Ts'msyen songs in the Boulton collection is only possible through collective inquiry, in the appropriate cultural contexts and based on the laws and protocols of the people. Repatriating Ts'msyen songs is about giving meaning and value in situ *again*. With these guiding sensibilities, derived from consultation with Ts'msyen, I employed interrelated research methodologies that set forth a decolonial path for studying the wholistic reclamation of Ts'msyen songs. Since October 2012, Ts'msyen in three locations have come together *sagayt k'uluum goot* (of one heart) in a series of seven listening gatherings, six translation workshops, and four talking circles to breathe life into the songs again. As a complementary case study, I also facilitated an accompanying research project on embodied heritage with Lax Kxeen, which demonstrates how Ts'msyen laws are enacted whenever we sing and dance (see Gray 2015).

The listening gathering format was important because it helped to address accessibility issues for Ts'msyen. It was important for Ts'msyen to gain access to the old songs, not as individuals but as collectives, in a manner that would facilitate the co-creation of knowledge in the appropriate cultural contexts. Furthermore, the Sm'algyax word *amuks'm*, which means to listen and pay attention, is a core sensibility in the Ts'msyen worldview, relevant to the act of witnessing that is so critical to the Ts'msyen oral tradition and to concomitant feasting protocols, for example. While there was space for interpretation in the listening gatherings, the complexity of our language, and the varying levels of linguistic fluency among Ts'msyen, required a more focused attempt to breathe life into the songs with hereditary leaders and Sm'algyax experts in Lax Kw'alaams. The focused translation workshops, importantly, were place-based in consideration of the linguistic nuances (primarily pitch and intonation) that range among Ts'msyen village communities. And finally, the talking circles created the necessary space for community members to confront the issue of control with more precision. Sure, it was nice to have access to our songs through the listening gatherings, and extremely powerful to be able to listen to them together—but how would we apply our Ayaawx to a repatriation case if the goal is control? Many were already aware of repatriation cases that have occurred for neighboring nations, like Haida, Haisla, and Kwakwaka'wakw, but were astutely cognizant of the fact that what worked for our neighbors might not work for us. Ts'msyen were clear that we need a process for repatriation that accounted for Ts'msyen sensibilities, considerate of our unique history, and based on our Ayaawx. As Łuum (Smooygit, Ganhada, Waap Łuum, Gitgiis) noted in one of the talking circles, there will inevitably be "problems whenever you're trying to apply the white man's law instead of going by our own law." This was affirmed by a Haisla elder who was present with her husband at the very first listening gathering in Lax Kw'alaams:

> Robin, just a suggestion . . . one of the things that we had to do at the very beginning of our repatriation process—and people call it the largest repatriated article in history [the G'psgolox totem pole from Sweden]. But one of the tasks that we had to do at the very beginning was to hash out the word ownership. Our ownership, and the museum's ownership or whatever organization calls ownership, are two very different things. And ownership with the songs . . . you don't know yet who they belong to, which tribe, which community. Make sure there's the ownership idea that it belongs to a specific family, or a specific clan or a specific tribe. And just because the lady tape-recorded these songs, doesn't mean she's the owner of those songs. And just because she sold and willed it to the universities, doesn't mean that it's theirs. That's their law. But you need to help educate them on your Ayaawx.
>
> (Louisa Smith, Kitamaat, Haisla Nation, Eagle Clan,
> G'psgolox House, Nli'skusa Tribe)

Based on our Ayaawx, in/tangible forms of Ts'msyen cultural heritage are collectively owned in a general sense—rights encompass intra- and interdependent levels of individual, family, house, tribe, clan, community and nation-based ownership and responsibility. There are many ways that we can describe Ayaawxsm Ts'msyen; it is not easily defined, but it absolutely defines us as Ts'msyen. It governs our relationship to everything and everyone. It is our precedent, law, policy, and ethic, and it shapes our ways of knowing, being, and doing. Ayaawxsm Ts'msyen is the reason for our in/tangible cultural heritage. Ayaawx is not prone to generalizations, however—we apply Ayaawxsm Ts'msyen to various contexts. In the case of song repatriation, Ts'msyen are the only people who have the collective authority and expertise to give value and meaning to the songs, and to affirm ownership and responsibility. Furthermore, from a humanist perspective, "what could be more reasonable than a desire to ensure that you are the custodian of your own cultural heritage? And what could be more unreasonable than holding another people's cultural heritage, of ongoing significance to them, in your hands?" (Asch 2009, 394).

Ayaawxsm Ts'msyen informs our sensibilities, and therefore the creative expressions that connect us to people, places, and processes of the past and present. Ts'msyen songs cannot be fit into a neat category of intangibility—let us just think about how they became transformed into a knowledge product, or how the intangible is made tangible, from utterance to record. Beyond that, however, from a Ts'msyen perspective, songs are always connected to something else like a process (mourning, feasting, teachings) or a cultural object (masks, drums, regalia), and they are enacted through embodiment (dancing, ritual, protocol), for example. That is Ayaawx in motion:

> That's why these songs are so important; because it connects the art, to the piece, to the dance, to the story. Because that's what our dances are—they're a reflection of who we are. When you see it on the dance floor, at a feast, or in a big house, that's what that is. It's, "this is who I am, this is a dance and a song that comes from my [tribal] house in my territory and this is what it's all about." Like when you're feasting, you're telling your oral history to people, so that's a reflection of who you actually are. And that's the legal part; that is ours. That is our tribal system, and we own it. It doesn't belong to anybody except the people who own those songs, and the people that own the art, the people that own the mask that goes with that certain song, etcetera. And some songs are so sacred they're only brought out once every five, ten years, depending on the situation, right? So there are levels of spirituality within all of our stuff. Spirituality is part of who we are. Like our Nax Nox songs, those are so sacred, it just hurts me to know that it's just sitting somewhere and I can't get access to that because somebody said, "Well, we got a law about that." Well, what about our law that says you had no right to take it in the first place? (people agreeing). Who gave you the right to take my song from us and what gave you that right to do that? And they made a law that says I can't get it back unless I talk to you first, or I have to negotiate with you? That's just wrong. Because it's not theirs, it's ours.
>
> (Mosgm Gyaax, Sigyidmhana'a, Ganhada, Waap Lugiisgagyoo, Gitwilgyoots)

Even with the assertion that they are "ours" and that they belong to Ts'msyen, my research partners remained aware and cautious to respect the various intra- and interdependent levels of rights and responsibilities that anchor the Ts'msyen sovereignty structure. We might know that they are Ts'msyen songs that trace to the one of the Nine Allied Tribes, but "you have to be careful about who actually owns the songs before you say, 'I'm gonna sing a song'" (Aldm łxah, Smooygit, Ganhada, Waap Aldm łxah, Gitwilgyoots). Uncritically ascribing legal ownership over the songs to any given social entity within our sovereignty structure before doing the appropriate research-based Ayaawxsm Ts'msyen would be a serious breach of protocol. But settler colonialism has had devastating effects on our community and an enormous amount of Ts'msyen cultural heritage has been extracted from the Nine Allied Tribes in Lax Kw'alaams, so I have been advised that it is appropriate to consider the songs as part of the collective history and cultural heritage of the people of Lax Kw'alaams, especially since the men recorded indeed belonged to one of the Nine Allied Tribes and were also recorded within our tribal territories. "Our songs belong somewhere. Some tribe, house or family. And even though we don't know it now—where they all belong—we do know that they belong here" (Wii Haughtkm Skiik, Laxsgiik, Waap Laax, Gitando). Ts'msyen continued to assert that issues of ownership within our community must be dealt with by our community.

Establishing ownership over Ts'msyen cultural heritage based on Western property systems, and establishing ownership based on Ayaawxsm Ts'msyen, will inevitably result in two different approaches and outcomes. For example, if following the Western system one will likely be concerned with tracing ownership based on the collector and their descendants, or the institution where the collector deposited the recorded material. Even if beginning with an acceptance of the agency of performers from the Boulton collection, one is still likely to privilege an inquiry based on lineal descent—who were Matthew Johnson and William Pierce's direct descendants? This is certainly a question that Ts'msyen would ask, but it would not be the only question to determine ownership and, importantly, responsibility. By following our Ayaawx, we begin with a different set of questions: Where did these two men stand within the Ts'msyen sovereignty structure; did they hold any hereditary leadership titles; have they feasted; what Ts'msyen names have they worn; what types of songs were they singing, or what kinds of stories were they telling; and what ceremonies or processes did they connect to? And the list goes on. But because the songs were at a university, Ts'msyen had additional questions to ask. At every listening gathering, for example, I was met with the same questions: Who recorded the songs? Were they ever copyrighted? Did the recorder ever have a relationship with Ts'msyen? Did the recorder note which tribe or house or family the songs belonged to? Whenever I played the songs for people I would be sure to read the metadata before each recording to see if they reflected the titles and descriptions, but folks weren't only interested in clarifying Boulton's notes. They wanted to know where the songs fit within our sovereignty structure, for our own accountability.

At a listening gathering in Prince Rupert with Sm'algyax experts, I was asked about a song that had just finished playing, "What do her notes say, again?" And I responded, "The title says Death Song for Chief and the description says Funeral Song." She reacted, "Is that it?!" "Yup, that's all she wrote," I replied, and the room erupted with disappointed giggles: "Wow!" They knew it was another inadequate recording of the song, not only because of its suspect title and description, but because there were no additional notes related to statements of lineage, history, and rights. This was extremely disappointing to Ts'msyen because our Ayaawx was never considered, but also because Boulton's pithy notes were misleading—which also cast a light on the politics of misrepresentation about Ts'msyen lived social realities. At another listening gathering in Prince Rupert with Ts'msyen elders and hereditary leaders, the issue of misrepresentation was tackled when I attempted to play the first song. I explained that it was titled "A'alos (Chief's Song)" and was described as a "Canoe Song, Sung When Going to Buy Skins." Before even hearing the song, Xbinhoon (Smooygit, Ganhada, Waap Xbinhoon, Gitzaxłał) interrogated the description of the song in relation to our sociocultural history in Lax Kw'alaams:

> Sung when going to buy skins? I know Hudson Bay [Company] used to be in Port Simpson [Lax Kw'alaams] there. But they [our people] sell skins when they go there after their trapping. They come back from trapping, they sell. They don't go there to buy skins! I hear my grandfather's story, that Hudson Bay made it a total rip-off for the First Nation people, the trappers; especially the trappers. He said the gun was so high, and they used to stand it up on the wall, and they'd say, "This is how much skins you have to pile up to get that gun." That's what my grandfather said. So, it took him a long, long, time to get his skins on account of the way they worked. "If you want that gun," they said, "this is how much furs you got to pile up, right to the end." And those guns there were this big—a musket. And, you know, they were pretty long. And that's how many skins—it must've taken about one hundred skins to get one gun. So imagine how much they made out of that one gun, eh, for all the skins they got. My grandfather said it took him all winter.

In this instance, Boulton did not only provide a pithy description of a song; she provided an inaccurate description of our sociocultural reality in Lax Kw'alaams. "Buying" skins versus "selling" skins did not account for the unequal power dynamics between Ts'msyen and the company that set up a trading post in our community to exploit our labor and resources. Whether or not it is actually a canoe song related to trapping, the note was written as evidence, created as metadata, transformed into property, and now the public can access it—with permission, of course, but not from Ts'msyen. In this case, the colonizing properties of property, the socioeconomic power afforded to authors, and the force of objectified knowledge in the archive work to reduce Ts'msyen as exotic, knowable, exploitable, and ultimately, invisible.

Throughout our community-based research process, Ts'msyen worked together to breathe life into the songs from the Boulton collection. Although there are more questions than answers, we found that the songs and oral histories said a lot about Ts'msyen peoples, places, and processes. They gave us clues about Matthew Johnson and William Pierce's lives, they contained teachings about significant places in Ts'msyen territory, and they represented aspects of significant cultural processes such as mourning through song. Furthermore, Ts'msyen challenged the classificatory logic and representational status of the metadata, and thus the archive, by clarifying the titles and descriptions, and providing important sociocultural context that could not have come from anywhere else other than from Ts'msyen. The research shows that, even if there were an argument for gatekeepers to make about the need for public access to our songs and their metadata for the advancement of knowledge, it is clearly a public disservice to make the Ts'msyen songs in the Boulton collection available when it would only perpetuate decontextualized, misleading, and incorrect information about Ts'msyen culture, society, and people.

Concluding Thoughts: Repatriation as Decolonization

Indigenous repatriation is an opportunity to right historical wrongs, to remedy settler colonial violations, and to build new nation-to-nation relationships with Indigenous peoples. With each case of repatriation—whether it involves human remains, objects, or audio recordings such as songs and oral histories—it is necessary to historicize the situation and give sociocultural context to contemporary claims for access and control. For example, when Matthew Johnson and William Pierce were recorded in 1942: (1) the Potlatch Ban was still in effect, making it illegal to practice our culture, (2) our children were still being mandated to attend Indian residential schools for assimilation, (3) Indigenous people did not yet have citizen rights in Canada, and (4) universal standards of human rights and human subjects research were not yet institutionalized. Therefore, there were no real means of protection against the unethical and illegal collecting of Ts'msyen cultural heritage, nor from the commoditization of our knowledge into property. In this case study, we had to confront the fact that the right of ownership to our songs was never vested with Ts'msyen by settler entities. Ts'msyen laws were not considered in the transactions that transformed our knowledge and heritage into the intellectual property of the researcher and then, by her claiming alienable wealth, the property of Columbia, and so forth. Ts'msyen gained access to the songs through a community-based research process—which has been a powerful act of healing and reclamation—but the fact remains that the issue of ownership and control has not yet been addressed for restitution. Therefore, I have described this case as a *potential* repatriation.

Western property frameworks present ongoing obstacles for repatriation as decolonization. Repatriation refers to a process of returning to a place of origin, and decolonization refers to a process aimed at changing the larger social structure. However, there exists a core tension within these aims—Western property frameworks remain largely unchanged, and settler societies continue to overwhelmingly favor, indeed rely on, Western sensibilities about property and ownership. As a result, the repatriation of Indigenous cultural heritage has taken many forms in settler colonial contexts such as Canada and the United States. Where there are laws it has been legally enforced, and where there are not it has taken form through negotiation. In many cases, an institution will debate the terms of access and control, and this can result in the digital return of songs, borrowing arrangements for masks and regalia, or replica transfers of totem poles, for example. For some Indigenous communities, access is enough to find resolution. For Ts'msyen, however, reclaiming control over our captured cultural heritage is integral to a successful repatriation, as it would allow the community to appropriately reset the terms of ownership, access, and control based on Ts'msyen laws, ethics and protocols, and without settler interference. If an Indigenous community wants to pursue custodial arrangements with museums, libraries, and archives, then that is their prerogative. But an institution or a gatekeeper of Indigenous cultural heritage should not assume that access is enough for every community. Institutions that hold Indigenous material must not only be open to potential repatriation cases; they must also be prepared to give up control of Indigenous cultural heritage if that is what the source community wishes.

In this case study, three primary decolonial sensibilities have framed the discussions about ownership, access, and control. First, Ayaawxsm Ts'msyen is a precedent for access and control of Ts'msyen cultural heritage, and the power to determine legality rests with Ts'msyen who make up the sovereignty structure. This means that political authority is located in our hereditary leaders and the people, not necessarily in the band council or in some other settler colonial-approved system of governance. Second, it is necessary to distinguish that access to Ts'msyen cultural heritage is not the same as control over Ts'msyen cultural heritage. Accessing Ts'msyen songs in digital format is not a successful repatriation because the rights to ownership, and the power to control access, is maintained by the institutions. In this scenario, paradigms of colonial control and Indigenous dispossession remain intact. And finally, we do not need to argue for copyright or even for the incorporation of Ayaawxsm Ts'msyen into Western property frameworks to make the claim for repatriation. Western laws have proven to be inadequate for protection, and there remain incorrigible tensions between the two legal traditions. Therefore, where it concerns decisions about Ts'msyen cultural heritage, Ayaawxsm Ts'msyen should prevail. In fact, the most important finding from this repatriation case study is that the Ts'msyen songs caught up in the Boulton collection should not be in circulation, should not be accessible to the public, and should not be considered research material for non-Ts'msyen interests. Thus, in consideration of a decolonial future, the institutions in question must be willing to surrender rights and title for Ts'msyen to find resolution from historical injustices. Only then will it be a successful repatriation.

NOTE

1. In 1884, the Canadian government amended the Indian Act (1876) to include a Potlatch Ban, outlawing the feasting and potlatching activities of northwest coast Indigenous people by 1885. Motivated by particularly Christian, racist, and capitalist ideals, missionaries and Indian agents insisted that the potlatch system was an impediment to cultural assimilation in the area. In 1951, the Potlatch Ban was finally lifted. For further reading on the Potlatch Ban and perspectives on the potlatch system vis-à-vis Aboriginal rights see: *An Iron Hand upon the People: The Law against the Potlatch on the Northwest Coast* (Cole and Chaikin 1990); *The Potlatch Papers: A Colonial Case History* (Bracken 1997); *The Reunification of the Kwakwaka'wakw Mask with Its Cultural Soul* (Sanborn 2009); and *Feasting Judicial Convergence: Reconciling Legal Perspectives through the Potlatch Complex* (Ebert 2013).

REFERENCES

Anderson, Jane. 2009a. "(Colonial) Archives and (Copyright) Law." *Nomorepotlucks Art Journal* 4 (July). http://nomorepotlucks.org/site/colonial-archives-and-copyright-law/.

Anderson, Jane. 2009b. *Law, Knowledge, Culture: The Production of Indigenous Knowledge in Intellectual Property Law*. Cheltenham, UK: Edward Elgar.

Anderson, Jane. 2013. "Anxieties of Authorship in the Colonial Archive." In *Media Authorship*, edited by Cynthia Chris and David A. Gerstner, 229–246. New York: Routledge.

Asch, Michael. 2009. "Concluding Thoughts and Fundamental Questions." In *Protection of First Nations Cultural Heritage: Laws, Policy, and Reform*, edited by Catherine Bell and Robert K. Paterson, 394–411. Vancouver: UBC Press.

Bell, Catherine, and Val Napoleon. 2008. "Introduction, Methodology, and Thematic Overview." In *First Nations Cultural Heritage and Law*, edited by Catherine Bell and Val Napoleon, 1–30. Vancouver: UBC Press.

Boulton, Laura. 1969. *The Music Hunter: The Autobiography of a Career*. New York: Doubleday.

Bracken, Christopher. 1997. *The Potlatch Papers: A Colonial Case History*. Chicago: University of Chicago Press.

Cole, Douglas, and Ira Chaikin. 1990. *An Iron Hand upon the People: The Law against the Potlatch on the Northwest Coast*. Vancouver, BC: Douglas and McIntyre.

Ebert, Mark. 2013. "Feasting Judicial Convergence: Reconciling Legal Perspectives through the Potlatch Complex." *Appeal* 18: 21–35.

Fox, Aaron. 2013. "Repatriation as Reanimation through Reciprocity." In *Cambridge History of World Music*, edited by Philip V. Bohlman, 522–554. Cambridge: Cambridge University Press.

Gii-dahl-guud-sliiaay (Terri-Lynn Williams). 1995. "Cultural Perpetuation: Repatriation of First Nations Cultural Heritage." *UBC Law Review*, Special Edition: 183–201. http://www.whiteravenlaw.ca/pdf/Cultural-Perpetuation%2c-Repatriation-of-First-Nations-Cultural-Heritage.pdf.

Gray, Robin. 2015. "Ts'msyen Revolution: The Poetics and Politics of Reclaiming." PhD diss., University of Massachusetts, Amherst.

McMillan, Robert. 1991. "Ethnology and the NFB: The Laura Boulton Mysteries." *Canadian Journal of Film Studies* 1 (2): 67–82.

Sanborn, Andrea. 2009. "The Reunification of the Kwakwaka'wakw Mask with its Cultural Soul." *Museum International* 61 (1–2): 81–86.

Smallacombe, Sonia. 2000. "On Display for Its Aesthetic Beauty: How Western Institutions Fabricate Knowledge about Aboriginal Cultural Heritage." In *Political Theory and the Rights of Indigenous Peoples*, edited by Duncan Ivison, Paul Patton, and Will Sanders, 152–162. Cambridge: Cambridge University Press.

Torsen, Molly, and Jane Anderson. 2010. *Intellectual Property and the Safeguarding of Traditional Cultures: Legal Issues and Practical Options for Museums, Libraries and Archives*. Geneva: World Intellectual Property Organization.

Tsosie, Rebecca. 1997. "Indigenous Peoples' Claims to Cultural Property: A Legal Perspective." *Museum Anthropology* 21 (3): 5–11.

INDEX

BATS
of Britain, Europe and Northwest Africa

BATS

of Britain, Europe and Northwest Africa

Dietz · Helversen · Nill

A&C Black

Contents

This book is dedicated to DAGMAR VON HELVERSEN

Dagmar von Helversen, who died much too early on 20 July 2003, was an unusually creative scientist, whose clear thinking was an example to others, who could pass on her enthusiasm to others, and who was a modest, intelligent, affectionate woman, open to all other people.

In memoriam for
PROFESSOR OTTO VON HELVERSEN

On 2 March 2009 Otto von Helversen died at the age of 65. A focus of his research was the ecology and behaviour of bats, particularly of neotropical flower bats. Other main topics were the evolution of grasshopper song and the taxonomy of spiders. He was, however, interested in all aspects of zoology and ecology. With Otto we lost a widely interested behavioural biologist, ecologist, evolutionary biologist and physiologist. We mourn the loss of a good friend and a paternal teacher, who imparted his enormous knowledge and ideas readily, and fired our scientific curiosity. Otto von Helversen loved life, nature and science. With his intensity, his ability to spread knowledge and his creativity he remains for us a great model.

Preface

When first leafing through this book one immediately notices that here are three authors who have come together and who follow bats with commitment and passion. Firstly Christian Dietz, a talented, communicative field researcher and critical observer, who is outstanding at the beginning of his scientific career. Then Otto von Helversen, a successful university professor with a long professional experience, who over decades has investigated bats and organised and led many exciting projects in the field and in the laboratory. And thirdly Dietmar Nill, one of the best animal photographers, whose contribution, we can be certain, has produced not only a competent, but also an aesthetically beautiful work, as an important tool for the promotion of research and the protection of bats. Our night fliers are not easy to see, especially not at all closely. The numerous amazing, often unique picture images in this book can only suggest how much expenditure and trouble must have been required for their presentation here.

If Martin Eisentraut, the great pioneer of German bat research, were still alive, then I would gladly have looked into this magnificent book with him. Before he moved to Bonn, I became acquainted with him in 1957 as an apprentice in the museum of natural history in Stuttgart. I stuffed bats that he had collected in Cameroon. Already in 1932 Eisentraut began to mark individual bats with aluminium clips. In the following decades exciting recoveries were obtained with this method, which showed not only long-distance migrations, but also different movements in species, yes, even in the sexes. Valuable views of the structure of populations were compiled. It became confusing, however, when it became apparent that there were twin species, of which one had not been recognised for a long time, and which are differentiated only with extreme difficulty from external characters. In recent years, genetic investigations contributed towards clarifying many such uncertainties but also to discovering numerous further cryptic species. Now in this book the new methods and most current results are clearly described. It is shown that successful field research is substantially supplemented today by laboratory research. With molecular-genetic analyses it is now possible to make statements about origin, relationship or rearrangements of populations. But, certainly in the future some classical research methods, even such as individual marking, remain indispensable.

Thus, much has changed in recent years in the knowledge of this group of animals. Also experienced specialists have again and again doubted whether they have interpreted their data and observations correctly. This book helps for a re-orientation. Since the work does not only wish to address specialists, but equally amateurs and friends of wildlife, it is valuable in including useful basic information on the biology and protection of bats, while specialist topics such as echolocation are also dealt with in detail here.

I wish this book a wide distribution and that it may sensitise and win many interested readers to the protection of our fascinating bats.

Dr H.C. Jürgen Gebhard
Basel

Foreword

With this book we wanted to fulfil a long-cherished dream and write a book that introduces the biology, distribution and threats of the bats of Europe and northwest Africa and to combine the up-to-date knowledge of all the species occurring in the working area of this book. Bats enjoy increasing popularity and many people are interested in their biology. Since research progresses rapidly and numerous species have been discovered in recent years, it is often difficult to maintain an overview. With this book we want to help and to offer current information. The discovery of new species in Europe, after a century of intensive investigations in this region, shows how little we actually know about bats and how far we still are from a comprehensive understanding of the ecology, behaviour, biology and biogeography.

The importance of a comprehensive knowledge of bats is shown by the threats to many species. Often it is barely possible to make even general statements about the possible threats and to make firm proposals for conservation measures. In the closely watched area of an increasing number of species, through the discovery of additional bat species, and increasing threats from habitat loss and fragmentation of suitable habitats by development, increased traffic and intensive agriculture, it is all the more necessary to pull together the existing knowledge and prioritise planned work on outstanding questions that could help to protect bats.

We tried to address and inspire a wide readership on the one hand, and on the other hand to provide results of the most current research and unpublished data, and an exciting book also for specialists. Due to our own research work in Bulgaria and Greece and the energetic support of colleagues who researched for many years on the Balkan Peninsula, the species accounts in particular may appear too focussed on the Balkans. We hope, however, that this also makes our book more interesting for specialists, since we cover a region of Europe that has been neglected in many other works. For us it was also a major request to discuss parts of North Africa, a region in which research on bats is only at its beginning, and that allows exciting comparisons with different habitats.

We are conscious that our book, with so much of the data on the ecology and distribution of species that may be of the moment, will become outdated in a few years. There are still many outstanding questions and we hope that at least some can be answered in the forthcoming years towards a comprehensive understanding of the bat fauna in Europe and northwest Africa.

English language edition

For this English language edition, a number of corrections and updates have been incorporated, many of these at the request of the original authors.

Additional comment and references have been added, particularly with reference to the UK fauna and its study and conservation. This includes more specific comment within species accounts for the species that occur in the UK.

A table has been incorporated to reflect the latest IUCN conservation status assessments for species, and this includes five extra species that occur in the wider Europe recognised by the Bern Convention, Eurobats and others. These five species are discussed briefly in the species accounts. But for the most part we hope that the text is a fair reflection of the original.

▸ Acknowledgements

The book would never have been finished without the huge support of numerous friends and colleagues, and we cordially thank all who encouraged us again and again. We particularly would like to thank I. Dietz/Horb (D) and C. Koch-von Helversen/

Erlangen (D) for their support and the incorporation of their bat knowledge. We thank all members of the chair of Animal Physiology of the University of Tubingen and of the chair of Zoology II of the University of Erlangen for their assistance and that they spared us from other tasks and activities.

We cordially thank R. Roesler/London (GB) for the wonderful illustrations of bats and for good co-operation. Our thanks are due also to R Britz/London (GB) for support with the production of the illustrations. For the graphic illustrations, the production of the sonograms and various further assistance we thank M. Bauer/Erlangen (D). We also thank the photographers D. Cordes/Erlangen (D), B. Fenton/Ontario (Canada), A. Kiefer/Mainz (D), E. Levin/Tel Aviv (Israel), T. Pröhl/Schmölln (D), J. Sachteleben/Munich (D), B. Siemers/Gilching (D), D. Trujillo/Los Realejos (ES) and I. Wolz/Neunkirchen (D) for the supply of their photographs. The paragraph about prey spectrum and hunting strategy was provided by I. Wolz/Neunkirchen (D).

The general chapters were reviewed by C. Koch-von Helversen and F. Mayer/Erlangen (D) and the species accounts by K. Koselj/Tuebingen (D), I. Dietz/Horb (D) and L. Dietz/Horb (D) with the utmost care; they provided countless notes and substantial technical and stylistic improvements, for which we would like to thank them cordially.

For intensive discussions, for their constant readiness to provide updates of bat systematics, and for analysing countless DNA samples from bats, we cordially thank F. Mayer/Erlangen (D) and A. Kiefer/Mainz (D). For critical examination of parts of the manuscript, intensive discussions about individual species and their biology, and for providing unpublished data, we thank M. Biedermann/Schweina (D), T. Blohm/Prenzlau (D), R. Brinkmann/Gundelfingen (D), A. Demetropoulos/Nicosia (Cyprus), P. Estok/Eger (HU), J. Fahr/Ulm (D), G. Heise/Prenzlau (D), I. Kaipf/Tuebingen (D), I. Karst/Erfurt (D), A. Kiefer/Mainz (D), Y. le Bris/Glénac (F), C. Harrje/Kiel (D), A. le Houédec/Saint Aubin du Comier (F), E. Levin/Tel Aviv (Israel), F. Mayer/Erlangen (D), M. Mucedda/Sassari (I), H. Nicolaou/Nicosia (Cyprus), I. Niermann/Hanover (D), B. Ohlendorf/Stolberg (D), E. Papadatou/Athens (GR), B. Petrov/Sofia (BG), H. Pieper/Kiel (D), K. Piksa/Cracow (PL), P. Presetnik/Ljubljana (SLO), G. Reiter/Alkoven (A), S. Roué/ Besançon (F), K. Safi/Zurich (CH), K. Sachanowicz/Toruń (PL), W. Schorcht/Walldorf (D) and A. Tsoar/Jerusalem (Israel).

During our field excursions and research visits many persons were helpful to us and we would like to thank cordially those who have spent the night with us, accompanied us into various underground sites or supported us in other ways, in particular O. Behr/Erlangen (D), A. Boonman/Marseille (F), K. Christov/Burgas (BG) K. Echle/Freiburg (D), H. Geiger/Erfurt (D), R. Güttinger/Wattwil (CH), U. Häussler/Hohenstein (D), U. Hofmeister/Berlin (D), M. Holderied/Leeds (GB), T. Ivanova/Rousse (BG), M. Jerabek/Elsbethen (A), I. Kaipf/Tuebingen (D), E. Kalko/Ulm (D), V. Kati/Joannina (GR), U. Marckmann/Erlangen (D), F. Matt/Erlangen (D), K. Meakin/Leeds (GB), D. Merdschanova/Sofia (BG), S. Merdschanov/Sofia (BG), A. Nagel/Münsingen (D), R. Nagel/Stuttgart (D), L. Oussouilh/Agadir (Morocco), E. Papadatou/Athens (GR), A. Petrinjak/Ljubljana (SLO), B. Petrov/Sofia (BG), W. Pflästerer/Tuebingen (D), K. Pröhl/Schmölln (D), T. Pröhl/Schmölln (D), V.Runkel/Erlangen (D), A. Schaub/Tuebingen (D), H.-U. Schnitzler/Tuebingen (D), P. Schuhmacher/Oberkessach (D), B. Siemers/Gilching (D), N. Simov/Sofia (BG), D. von Staden/Tuebingen (D), D. Teixeira/Funchal (ES), S. Teixeira/Funchal (ES) and M. Zagmajster/Ljubljana (SLO).

For permission to print diagrams and illustrations, we thank M. Braun/Bruchsal (D), R. Hutterer/Bonn (D), E. Kalko/Ulm (D), G. Neuweiler/Munich (D), H.-U. Schnitzler/Tuebingen (D) and B. Siemers/Gilching (D).

We address special thanks to T. Baethmann, R. Gerstle and S. Tommes of Kosmos Publishing House for their competence and patience with us in supporting the production of the book.

Christian Dietz, Otto von Helversen and Dietmar Nill

Life history of bats

Bats are mammals and consequently show all the characteristics typical of mammals: they are homoeothermic, have fur and external ears and bear live young and suckle them. They possess a typical mammalian dentition and the mandibular articulation resembles that of other mammals.

Bats possess, however, some unusual adaptations, which distinguish them from all other mammals.

Active flight
Bats are the only group of mammals to have developed the ability of true flight. Flying squirrels (Sciuridae) and possums (Petauridae and Acrobatidae), like the strange colugos (Dermoptera) from South-east Asia, are only capable of jumping from a tree and then gliding long distances in the air with their parachute-like flight membranes stretched between arms and legs, but they cannot actively gain height with wingbeats. That is restricted to bats, in which the fingers are incorporated into the flight membranes. For this reason the order of bats has acquired the name *Chiroptera* – 'hand wing'.

Old age
Bats can achieve an extremely great age for their size. They can live approximately 10 times as long as a mouse or a shrew of equal size. This longevity they owe ultimately to the conquest of an ecological niche with extremely low predator risk and a low mortality rate: their night activity and flight ability make it possible for them to escape from most enemies. Whilst there are many predators of mice and shrews, from fox, marten or wildcat to birds of prey and owls, there are only very few predators specialised on bats.

Fig.1. Bats are capable of active flight and can fly through narrow gaps effortlessly. Here an Alpine Long-eared Bat (*Plecotus macrobullaris*). Photo: D. Nill.

Long viability of the sperm cells
While sperm cells survive only a few days in other mammals, bats have developed mechanisms that make it possible for the sperm cells to remain fertile over many months. This allows the males, before they begin copulation, to store sperm in the epididymis for a long time. Further, this characteristic allows mating by bats in temperate latitudes in the summer or early autumn, while ovulation and fertilisation of the egg cell only take place in the next spring. The sperm cells remain alive in the uterus of the female during the winter and so are immediately available for ovulation after emergence from hibernation. The embryonic development can thereby begin in the very short period immediately at the end of the hibernation and before vegetation has developed, without time delay in searching for a mate.

Echolocation
Bats have developed and improved, uniquely within land animals, a new system of orientation, the ultrasonic echolocation, which made them independent of sight and thus of the daylight. We humans – visual animals that we are – can only imagine with difficulty how it is possible for bats to orient themselves only with the help of the echoes of their emitted calls reflected by the environment. They are thereby not only able to avoid small obstacles in fast flight but also to detect, recognise, locate and capture flying insects at the same time. Even motionless objects, such as flowers, can be recognised on the basis of their spatial shape, despite the many other echoes which are reflected in the dense vegetation of tropical rainforests.

Diversity of different ecological niches
Finally, none of the other mammal orders conquered such a diversity of different ecological niches. Among the bats of the tropics there are not only insect hunters, but also flesh, fruit and leaf consumers, even some species that have become specialised in fishing or as highly adapted 'bloodsuckers', better to say blood-lickers,

which are able to create small wounds in other warm-blooded animals at night and lick the blood that runs from the wound. Other tropical bats can be designated as the 'hummingbirds of the night': they nourish themselves with nectar and pollen, which they take in hovering flight from nocturnally opening flowers. They are the most important pollinators of numerous tropical plants, which have become adapted to be pollinated by bats through a long co-evolution.

These five characteristics of bats, which distinguish them from all other mammals, will be the central features of the following general chapters.

Body structure of bats

Many bats are lightweight, which is expressed particularly in a relatively small body size. The wingspan gives the appearance, however, of a substantially larger animal and most people are surprised by the small size of a bat in the hand. The largest bats in the world are the Old World fruit bats of the genus *Pteropus*, which

reach a weight of 1.5kg with a wingspan of approximately 1.7m. The majority of bat species are, however, very much smaller; the smallest mammal in the world is a bat: the Bumblebee Bat (*Craseonycteris thonglongyai*), with a weight of barely 3g, occurring in South-east Asia. The lower limit of physiological possibility is probably reached in such a small size; smaller mammals can probably not exist, because with their relative large surface area the loss of energy would become too great. The greatest possible body weight is probably limited by the ability to undertake active flight. Very large birds, such as vultures, pelicans or storks, can undertake active flight, but they use thereby enormous amounts of energy. With their size, only with the ability to soar long distances is flight energetically still possible. For an insect hunter or a fruit eater living in tree tops soaring flight is, however, not an option, particularly since the thermals required by large fliers are absent at night. The wings are the most remarkable characteristic of bats and the characteristics connected with flight are described in a separate chapter (see p. 28). The flight membranes of bats are stretched between the body, the extremities and the tail (Fig. 2 and 3). In particular the metacarpals and phalanges are greatly extended, but the basic five-digit structure of the mammalian limb (pentadactyl mammalian limb) is clearly recognisable. As with other mammals, the body of bats is densely haired in order to improve the active thermoregulation. Some desert bats have very short fur and an increased area of naked skin. The species occurring in temperate latitudes conversely have more dense fur. The flight membranes, parts of the face and the ears are relatively hairless or only covered with fine hairs. Moult takes place once in the year in adult bats, usually beginning in the late summer. The regenerating fur areas are often darker than the mostly faded older fur. Most bats can walk – even run. The ability of bats to walk or climb is aided by a striking modification, in that the upper leg bone of the hind leg (the femur) is rotated through 180° from the normal

Fig. 2. In flight the broad flight membranes stretched between the wing extremities and the tail are good features of Bechstein's Bat (*Myotis bechsteinii*). Photo: D. Nill.

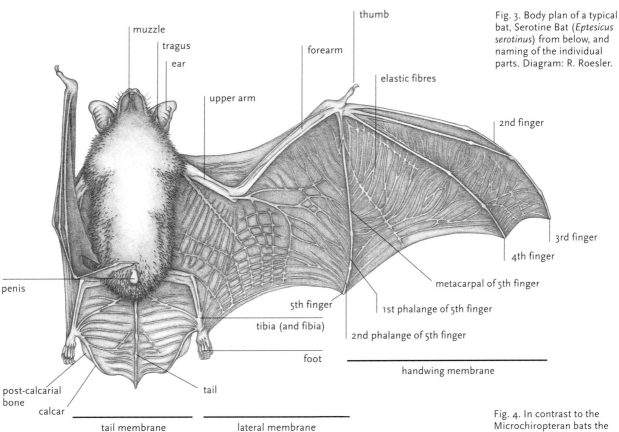

muzzle
tragus
ear
upper arm
thumb
forearm
elastic fibres
penis
5th finger
tibia (and fibia)
post-calcarial bone
calcar
tail
foot
2nd finger
3rd finger
4th finger
metacarpal of 5th finger
1st phalange of 5th finger
2nd phalange of 5th finger
handwing membrane
tail membrane
lateral membrane

Fig. 3. Body plan of a typical bat, Serotine Bat (*Eptesicus serotinus*) from below, and naming of the individual parts. Diagram: R. Roesler.

position in most terrestrial mammals. Thus the knee is directed backwards, or upwards, in bats. But the leg bones are long and slender and the hind limbs are no longer able to carry the weight of the animal. Thus bats are very active 'crawlers' and climbers, and their legs also provide an attachment for the wing and tail membranes, important in the coordinated control of these flight membranes.

Head and skull of bats

From the obvious characteristics of the head two main groups of bats can be immediately distinguished: the flying foxes or fruit bats (Megachiroptera) with large eyes and small ears and the generally small-eyed and large-eared bats (Microchiroptera). These differences are so obvious that they have been used since the beginning of zoological systematics for the distinction of these two main groups. It remained for the

modern systematics, based on genetic characteristics, to clarify this as an error [gen. lit. 141]. The pronounced differences in the structure of the ears and the size of the eyes

Fig. 4. In contrast to the Microchiropteran bats the fruit bats orientate mainly by sight, for that they have large eyes, while the ears are simple, as in this Egyptian Fruit Bat (*Rousettus aegyptiacus*). Photo: C. Dietz.

Fig. 5. In this portrait of a bat the large ears are particularly noticeable compared with the relatively small eyes; here a Maghrebian Mouse-eared Bat (*Myotis punicus*). Photo: C. Dietz.

are adaptations to the method of spacial orientation of the species and are only conditional on clarifying the underlying relationship.

The large eyes of the fruit bats (Fig. 4) quickly show that they orient themselves mainly by sight and also seek their food, usually fruits, by sight. Only some species of the genus *Rousettus* have developed a simple form of echolocation based on tongue clicks. This makes it possible for them to use roosts in deep caves, which are not accessible to the other fruit bats purely orienting by sight. In the Microchiropteran bats, conversely, the ears (Fig. 5) are particularly obvious on the head, and many species also have nose appendages. In connection with the development of a

specialised echolocation system (see p. 32), a high selection pressure existed on the development of the best-adapted receiver for the echolocation detection system, and the ear structure is accordingly diverse. In most bat species the ears are very mobile, depending upon condition of alertness of the animal, and they can be fully erect or slightly curled. In only a few species they can be folded fully, particularly in the long-eared bats of the genus *Plecotus*.

Under the fur and skin of the head are massive muscle packages set on the outside of the skull (Fig. 6). Besides a strong neck musculature, which supports the head during flight and holds it straight, the mandibular muscles are particularly pronounced. They make possible strong chewing movements, including the lateral shifting of the jaw for cutting and breaking up food items and for seizing and holding prey that may be able to defend itself.

Under the muscle tissue lies the skull (Fig. 7), which shows specialised dentition typical for a mammal, Depending upon the means of nourishing the bats species, features of the teeth and jaws can be completely differently emphasised. The teeth of frugivorous species, such as many fruit bats, have only flat cusps. Flower-visiting and nectar-feeding bats have reduced their dentition to a large extent and the jaws are slenderly built. In insectivorous or carnivorous species the dentition resembles that of a predator, with numerous cusps, cutting edges and strong canines. All European bat

▶ Fig. 6. On the skinned head of a Maghrebian Mouse-eared Bat (*Myotis punicus*) the large larynx and the strong musculature from the lower jaw to the upper skull are noticeable. Photo: C. Dietz.

▶▶ Fig. 7. The strong dentition of Maghrebian Mouse-eared Bat (*Myotis punicus*) with long canines and the molars and premolars provided with many cutting edges indicate an adaptation to insect food. Photo: C. Dietz.

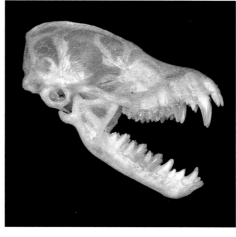

species are insectivorous, although with at least two of them, the Greater Noctule (*Nyctalus lasiopterus*) and the Long-fingered Bat (*Myotis capaccinii*), vertebrate animals are also known to be additional food items. In the first case it is birds, in the second small fish. The differences in diet within the insectivorous bats are expressed by the structure of the skull and in the kind of dentition (Fig. 8). Bats have a common blueprint for the dentition with the following dental formula:

$$\frac{2-1-3-3}{3-1-3-3} = 38 \text{ teeth}$$

This dentition can be found in the native *Myotis* species. The upper series of numbers represents the upper jaw, the lower for the lower jaw. The first column indicates the number of incisors, the second the canines, third the premolars and the fourth the molars. However, in most species the number of teeth is reduced, which is often accompanied by a shortening of the tooth row or a reduction of the premaxilla. The teeth frame of opposite teeth interlink so precisely that various cutting edges are formed, which makes the dividing of hard insects possible. As an adaptation to the diet the teeth are exposed to a high selection pressure, and in the course of evolution various characteristics have developed (Fig. 8). Closely related and externally very similar bat species can, despite all external similar features, be distinguished by characteristics of dentition. As characteristic features, the length of the tooth row, the relative height of individual teeth, or the profile of cusps of individual teeth are used.

Further characteristics of the body plan

As is the case for all organisms, so in bats all areas of the body are adapted in their structure to their respective function in the way of life. Thus a relatively large stomach, in which much prey can be stored, represents an

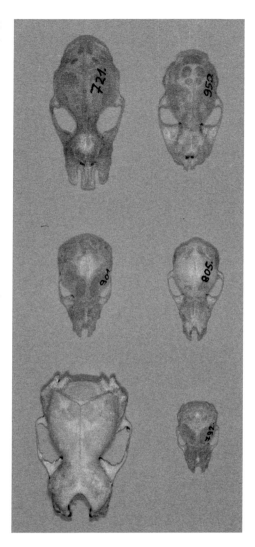

Fig. 8. Six bat skulls for comparison; from top left to bottom right: Greater Horseshoe Bat (*Rhinolophus ferrumequinum*), Lesser Mouse-tailed Bat (*Rhinopoma hardwickii*), Gaisler's Long-eared Bat (*Plecotus gaisleri*), Geoffroy's Bat (*Myotis emarginatus*), Greater Noctule (*Nyctalus lasiopterus*) and Soprano Pipistrelle (*Pipistrellus pygmaeus*). Photo: C. Dietz.

adaptation to the short period of high availability of prey in the night. Conversely, the short intestine permits a rapid digestion and hence a low flight weight.

Common in bats is the way of hanging – with the head downward. This requires adaptations in the blood circulation system but also of the skeleton and structure of muscles. The effortless hanging is obtained by means of a refined mechanism on the foot: a special locking mechanism allows the claws to grip whether the muscles are relaxed or not, whereby during long periods, such as even in hibernation, no extra muscle power is needed.

Evolution of bats

Fossil history

Bats had obviously already separated from the other mammals towards the end of the Cretaceous period, approximately 70 million years ago. While birds already controlled the air space in daytime, the bats succeeded in conquering the night, which is anyway a more appropriate niche for mammals. The oldest complete fossils of bats originate from the early Eocene of North America and Europe and are about 50 million years old. In particular the fossils from the oil shale pit at Messel near Darmstadt (Germany) became world famous (Fig. 10). The Eocene bats were already insect hunters, like our current native species. The fossils are sometimes so well preserved that the contents of their stomachs, particularly moth scales, could even be detected. The research team of the Senkenberg Museum (Frankfurt) also managed to show by precise measurements of the internal ear that the fossil bats of the Messel pit must have already oriented themselves with ultrasound. Interestingly enough some of the Eocene insectivorous bats (both *Icaronycteris* from Wyoming in the USA, and *Archaeonycteris* from Messel) still show another primitive characteristic, which occurs today only in the Old World fruit bats: not only the thumb but also 'the index finger' bears a claw. This characteristic perhaps helped the early bats to climb in trees or in rock crevices.

The Eocene, about 56 to 36 million years ago, was a time of rapid evolution of mammals. At that time many groups developed that correspond to the contemporary families of the mammals. Similarly for the bats, the Eocene was the 'big bang' for their evolution, because in this comparatively short time its adaptive radiation (species separation and adaptation to habitats) took place to occupy the most diverse ecological niches. At the end of the Eocene most families and different lifestyles of bats had essentially been developed (Fig. 11). With modern molecular-genetic methods one can examine not only the relationship of the species and thus their family tree, but also calculate the number of mutation steps, and how long ago the separation occurred. Figure 11 shows a family tree of all contemporary bat families, based on molecular-genetic findings. Also this family tree indicates impressively the rapid division of the bats in the beginning of the Eocene into all currently existing larger groups.

Family tree of bats

At present over 1,100 bats species are recognised worldwide [gen. lit. 126]. With that, bats are the second largest order of mammals on our planet after rodents. It is quite probable that in reality there are still clearly more bat species, some of which look morphologically so similar to each

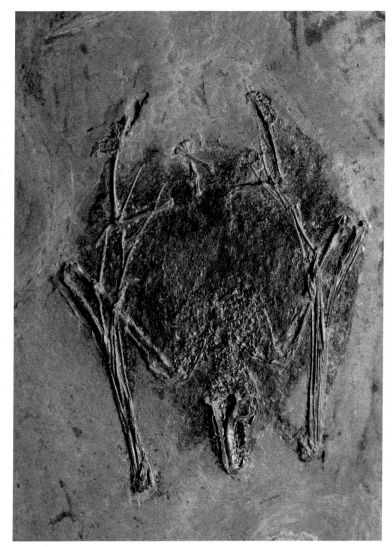

Fig. 10. *Palaeochiropteryx tupaiodon*, an Eocene bat from the Messel quarry, Germany, which lived about 50 million years ago. Photo: D. Nill.

Fig. 9. Part of a colony of Bechstein's Bat (*Myotis bechsteinii*). Photo: D. Nill.

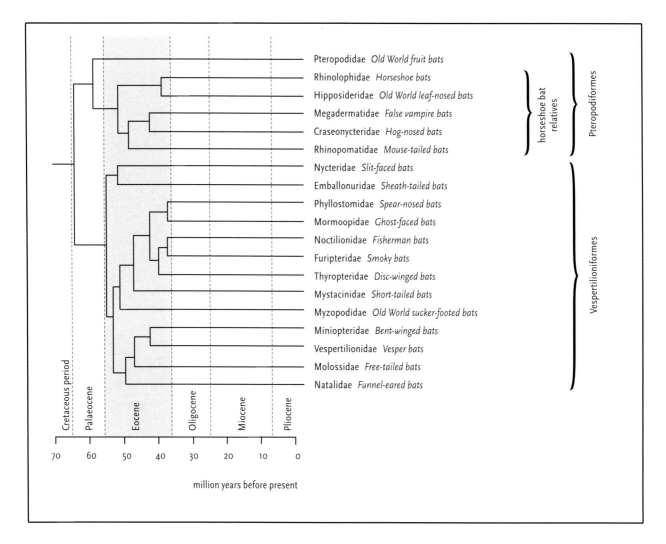

Pteropodidae *Old World fruit bats*
Rhinolophidae *Horseshoe bats*
Hipposideridae *Old World leaf-nosed bats*
Megadermatidae *False vampire bats*
Craseonycteridae *Hog-nosed bats*
Rhinopomatidae *Mouse-tailed bats*
Nycteridae *Slit-faced bats*
Emballonuridae *Sheath-tailed bats*
Phyllostomidae *Spear-nosed bats*
Mormoopidae *Ghost-faced bats*
Noctilionidae *Fisherman bats*
Furipteridae *Smoky bats*
Thyropteridae *Disc-winged bats*
Mystacinidae *Short-tailed bats*
Myzopodidae *Old World sucker-footed bats*
Miniopteridae *Bent-winged bats*
Vespertilionidae *Vesper bats*
Molossidae *Free-tailed bats*
Natalidae *Funnel-eared bats*

horseshoe bat relatives

Pteropodiformes

Vespertilioniformes

Cretaceous period | Palaeocene | Eocene | Oligocene | Miocene | Pliocene

70   60   50   40   30   20   10   0

million years before present

Fig. 11. A family tree of the bats following the most recent results of molecular-genetic investigations. The two main groups of the Chiroptera, the Pteropodiformes with the fruit bats and horseshoe bats and their relatives, and the Vespertilioniformes, which includes most small echolocating bats, were probably already separated towards the end of the Cretaceous period. The main splitting to all currently recognised families took place in the Eocene. Modified after gen. lit. 127. Diagram: M. Bauer.

other that they have, as yet, not been recognised as separate species. Thorough morphological, ecological and particularly molecular-genetic research reveal again and again that previously unrecognised 'cryptic' forms are in reality different species, which have their own gene pool. Just in Europe, seven previously unrecognised species have been newly discovered in the last 10 years. Following the current valid systematic classification, there are over 1,100 species within the order of Chiroptera [gen. lit. 54, 126, 127], divided into 19 families. For two families there is still controversy as to whether they should actually be regarded as independent (Miniopteridae and Hipposideridae). Figure 11 illustrates a family tree in which all these

families and their scientific names are given. Only three of these families, the vesper bats (Vespertilionidae), the free-tailed bats (Molossidae) and the Old World sheath-tailed bats (Emballonuridae) occur in both the Old and New Worlds. The Old World families of horseshoe bats (Rhinolophidae) and Old World leaf-nosed bats (Hipposideridae), the South American spear-nosed bats (Phyllostomidae), the vesper bats (Vespertilionidae) and the free-tailed bats (Molossidae) are large and species-rich families, and they comprise the majority of all bat species. On the other hand, there is one family with only one species, the South-east Asian Craseonycteridae. The Mystacinidae from New Zealand, Malagasy Myzopodidae and the

three South American families Thyropteridae, Furipteridae and Noctilionidae comprise only two species in each case and
another South American family, the Natalidae, only four species.

Only in recent years could the family
relationships between the bat families be
examined by extensive molecular-genetic
comparisons [gen. lit. 127, 141]. While for a
long time it was believed that the fruit bats,
orienting by sight, and the other bats, orienting with ultrasound, were the two large
'sister groups' of the Chiroptera, new molecular-genetic studies revealed surprising
results: the horseshoe bats and their relatives (including the Megadermatidae, the
Rhinopomatidae and *Craseonycteris* as well
as the two *Mystacina* species from New
Zealand) are more closely related to the Old
World fruit bats than to the other echolocating bats. These two groups together, the Old
World fruit bats and horseshoe bat relatives, which can be grouped as 'Pteropodiformes', are the sister group of the
'Vespertilioniformes', with most of the
echolocating bats. That has the interesting
consequence that the echo-orientation of
bats must have evolved independently
twice, once in the horseshoe bats and once
in the Vespertilionid bats and their relatives, or that echolocation was lost later in
the evolution of the Old World fruit bats.
This currently provides hot discussion for
scientists. There is much to suggest that the
truth lies somewhere between the two:
probably at the time of the division echolocation was not yet developed to the level that
it could to be used for recognising stationary objects close to backgrounds, such as
fruits and flowers amongst tree branches,
twigs and leafs. An insect in the open air
space is much easier to detect with the help
of echolocation, because the echo is not
overlain with clutter. Probably the fruit
bats, with their specialisation on fruit food,
lost the as yet imperfectly developed echo-
orientation, while the insectivorous groups
perfected their echolocation. In the frugivorous spear-nosed bats of South America the
echo-orientation was already so well developed that it could be used for recognising
and locating stationary objects.

Taxonomy

Different bat species can be very similar
and are often not easy to differentiate externally or even from the skull and other skeleton features. This is reflected in the
changing history of species differentiation
in bats: some authors, even in just one publication, described several different variants
of the same species as new species and
introduced thereby new names, which were
later not recognised by other authors and
were placed in synonymy. The first large
revision of the Palaearctic bat species in
1951 [gen. lit. 33] listed 19 different names
just for the Common Pipistrelle, which
were all included in a list of synonyms. In
principle, the first valid name after Linnaeus 1758 assigned in the first description
of a species has priority. Sometimes it is,
however, not easy to determine which is the
correct name, and occasionally scientists
cannot agree which name must be used.
Particularly if the type specimen (the original specimen), which should be deposited
in a museum for each new species, was lost
and the description does not contain clear
characteristics, an agreement can be difficult. In such cases the International Commission on Zoological Nomenclature can
make a decision. Thus opinions were
agreed once and for all for the Parti-
coloured Bat to be *Vespertilio murinus*
instead of *Vespertilio discolor*, or for
Soprano Pipistrelle to be *Pipistrellus pygmaeus* instead of *Pipistrellus mediterra-
neus*. If an earlier revision of a species had
resulted in a long list of synonymous
names, it sometimes turned out later that
included in the species placed in the list of
synonyms were nevertheless different valid
species. Thus around 1960 the Grey Long-
eared Bat (*Plecotus austriacus*) was only
recognised again by precise comparison of
the morphology and way of life with the
Brown Long-eared Bat (*Plecotus auritus*)
[gen. lit. 7]. Also Whiskered Bat (*Myotis
mystacinus*) and Brandt's Bat (*Myotis
brandtii*) were separated again as different
species only a little later [gen. lit. 37]. In
both cases the species had been confused

Box 1

Molecular taxonomy and the 'minimum spanning tree'

The genetic information is laid down as a sequence of four possible bases on the DNA of the chromosomes, as in a pearl necklace. In most cases one gene codes for the amino acid sequence of one protein.

The sequencing of genes became possible, particularly following the discovery of a method to selectively multiply a certain section of DNA in the laboratory. This method, PCR (polymerase chain reaction), also opened the gate for the molecular-genetic investigation of phylogenetic and taxonomic questions.

If one examines the base sequence in a section of a gene in many individuals of a population, then one often finds differences in the pairs of bases at certain positions, which one therefore designates as 'informative positions' or markers. One calls the different base sequences 'haplotypes'. Different haplotypes differ in at least one base position, often in several or many.

A clear description of the haplotypes of a population gives a 'haplotype network', the 'minimum spanning tree' (see Fig. 12), in which the distances of different haplotypes are registered as the number of individual point mutations (= base substitutions) that would, at the least, be necessary in order to transfer one haplotype into the others.

In the case of the comparison of closely related species such as the Common Pipistrelle (*Pipistrellus pipistrellus*) and Soprano Pipistrelle (*Pipistrellus pygmaeus*), one can see that the distances between all haplotypes of the two species is far greater than the distances between the haplotypes of the individuals within either species.

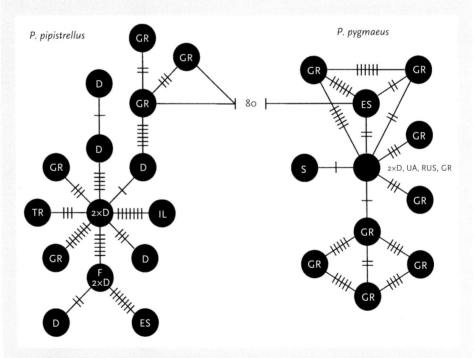

Fig. 12. A 'minimum spanning tree' of the Common and Soprano Pipistrelle. These two species were only differentiated about 13 years ago. The circles mean sequence types (haplotypes); the lines represent the exchange of individual bases; the abbreviations in the circles indicate the countries of origin of the examined individuals. The mitochondrial gene ND1 was examined. Very many larger differences exist between the two species than between the haplotypes within a species. After gen. lit. 78. Diagram: F. Mayer.

for many decades and the 'new' species was raised from synonymy.

Molecular genetics

Only in the last 10 years has the application of molecular-genetic procedures permitted the development of a substantially more exact and reliable picture of the number of species and the relationship between the different species and this process is still being developed. For such molecular-genetic studies, firstly genes must be selected which one can extract relatively easily, including replication with the help of PCR (see Box 1). In a great many investigations mitochondrial genes were selected (genes from a DNA strand of the mitochondria). The sequence differences between the 'haplotypes' (see Box 1) of such genes result in specific characteristics, which supplement the morphological species characteristics. In relation to morphological characteristics, they have the advantage that many more specific distinguishing characteristics are available. Certainly it also creates more effort to analyse this much information. While one can sometimes recognise morphological characteristics with a single glance, a molecular-genetic distinction requires a laboratory. For the molecular investigation one needs tissue samples of the bat. But a tiny piece from the flight membrane is sufficient. Since bats frequently damage their flight membranes on obstacles, they have in their evolution developed a very rapid regeneration capability for small holes in their flight membranes, and the small holes caused by taking the tissue samples recover in a very short time.

In recent years the number of bat species recognised in Europe increased significantly due to these more exact analysis methods. Thus the Soprano Pipistrelle (*Pipistrellus pygmaeus*) was separated from Common Pipistrelle (*P. pipistrellus*), Alcathoe Whiskered Bat (*Myotis alcathoe*) from Whiskered Bat (*M. mystacinus*), Maghrebian Mouse-eared Bat (*Myotis punicus*) from Lesser Mouse-eared Bat (*M. oxygnathus*) and in the genus of long-eared bats (*Plecotus*) the equivalent of three new species were discovered, Alpine Long-eared Bat (*Plecotus macrobullaris*), Balkan Long-eared Bat (*Plecotus kolombatovici*) and Sardinian Long-eared Bat (*Plecotus sardus*). These species are discussed in the species section, and the identification key gives assistance as to how these molecular-genetically separated species can be recognised. It is to be expected that some further bat species, not recognised so far, occur in Europe. In all likelihood this is true for the Anatolian and North African fauna. During the printing procedure of the German edition of this book between December 2006 and March 2007 indications of six new bat species in Europe were reported (*Myotis* cf. *escalerai*, *Myotis* spp. from the *M. nattereri* lineage, *Eptesicus isabellinus*, *Pipistrellus lepidus*, *Hypsugo caucasicus*, *Plecotus begognae*), as well as five further species in adjacent regions [gen. lit. 77, 167]. This shows, however, that increasingly the often closely related sibling species can be separated genetically with some certainty, but which could be finally proven through strict reproductive isolation only within areas of sympatric (common or shared) occurrence. Many currently still outstanding questions of systematic classification are closely linked to the species concept used in each case, and discussions over this currently occupy numerous scientists.

Species richness of bats

The species diversity in the tropics is incomparably much higher in many animal and plant groups to that in the temperate latitudes. That is also true for bats: their core distribution area is clearly in the tropics. While, for example, 130 species can occur sympatrically (together) in an area of 500 by 500 kilometres in Costa Rica, there are far fewer in Canada or Argentina (Fig. 13). This reduction of the species diversity from equatorial regions to the poles is also true for Europe. The 51 species described in this book are comparatively few when compared with the total number of about 1,100 bat species. But even within Europe there are diversity gradients from north to south (Fig. 14). The much smaller number of ecological niches that are occupied by the European bats, compared, for example, with the South American tropics, is even more notable. In Europe there are, with respect to food niches, essentially only insectivorous bats. For the Greater Noctule (*Nyctalus lasiopterus*) it is now known, however, that it also catches birds as well as insects, and the Long-fingered Bat (*Myotis capaccinii*) is also able to capture small fish. And on Cyprus the Egyptian Fruit Bat (*Rousettus aegyptiacus*) occurs, which is a purely frugivorous species. All other European bat species nourish themselves with insects and other arthropods. Nevertheless, how can so many insectivorous bat species occur together in Europe without having too much competition for their food? The 'niching' of these species greatly relates to their prey spectrum, which differs from species to species due to the different 'design' of their echolocation calls, and their hunting strategies: the prey spectrum is affected by the size of the bat species, by the manoeuvrability during flight, by the specifically used habitats, by the relative size of the ears and the frequency and design of the echolocation signals.

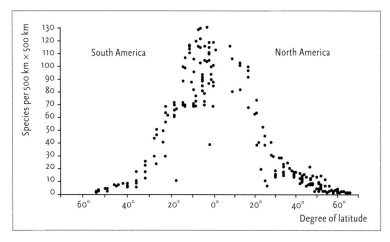

Fig. 13. The number of bat species within 500 x 500 km grid squares according to the geographical latitude in the New World. The clear increase of the species numbers towards the tropics is obvious. Modified after gen. lit. 146. Diagram: R. M. Willig.

Fig. 14. The number of families, genera and species of bats also increases in Europe from north to south. As examples, four countries with approximately the same surface area were selected, the countries being separated by an average of 10 degrees of latitude. Graph: M. Bauer.

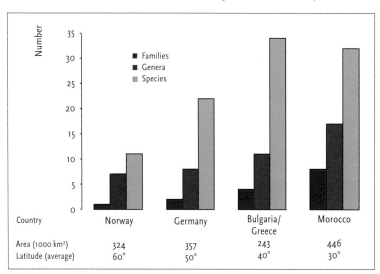

The global diversity gradient

Why is the species variety and niches in the tropics so much greater? What is the basis for this 'global diversity gradient'? Is the species diversity so much higher because the actual range of existing ecological opportunities is larger? Or is a certain array of parameters, specified by physical limits, used more intensively? It could be used more intensively, firstly because of the availability of narrowly defined niches, whereby more specialised niches of individual species would fit into the same array of large-scale niches. On the other hand, in the tropics a greater tolerance regarding the overlap of niches might exist. If the niches of several species could overlap, then more species might occur together in the same habitats.

Already a relatively superficial view shows that the parameter range that marks the ecological niches of the bats must be greater in the tropics than in the temperate zones of the earth: the weight range between the smallest tropical bat at only 3g weight, the Bumblebee Bat, and the largest tropical bats, the fruit bats, with up to 1,500g weight, or the South American False Vampire (*Vampyrum spectrum*) is substantially greater than in Europe, where the size class range is only from approximately 5g (Common Pipistrelle) to approximately 50g (Greater Noctule). Symbiosis, such as between flower-feeding bats and bat-pollinated flowers, would a priori exist with difficulty at temperate latitudes. Also, in the tropics flower-visiting bats can only occur where there are flowers which offer sufficient nectar and pollen all year round – and conversely bat-pollinated plants can only exist where there are also flower-visiting bats at least at the appropriate flowering time of the plant species. The enormous diversity of the tropical biocenoses reinforces itself in a certain way: where there are already many differently niched species, new and still more complex life possibilities always develop.

These phenomena also appear within the broad food niches of the bats. When one considers echolocation and flight ability as the two most important niche parameters of insectivorous bats, then one can try to construct simple parameters for their description. Thus a comparison of the relative size of the ears (as a measure of the sensitivity of the hearing system) with the ratio of the length of third and fifth fingers (as a measure of the width of the wings and thus for manoeuvrability in flight) of bats from different areas will result in the density and the overlap of niches hardly differing. On the other hand there are distinct regional differences in the overall possible parameter covered by insectivorous bats (Fig. 15).

These examples show very clearly which mechanisms enabled the enormous species diversity in the tropics – and perhaps also, how we Europeans, inhabitants of the temperate and northern latitudes, should be very concerned for the protection of this enormous diversity of the tropics – the rainforests

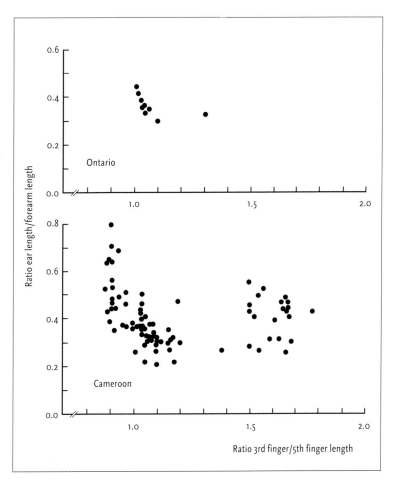

Fig. 15. Comparison of the two most important niche dimensions of bats (hearing and manoeuvrability in flight: relative size of the ears and relative width of the wings) for one country in temperate latitudes (Ontario in Canada) and Cameroon in tropical West Africa. After gen. lit. 35. Graph: M. B. Fenton.

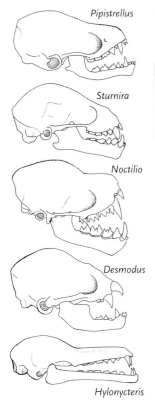

Pipistrellus

Sturnira

Noctilio

Desmodus

Hylonycteris

Fig. 16. From top to bottom: an insectivorous bat (the Common Pipistrelle, *Pipistrellus pipistrellus*), a frugivore (spear-nosed bat, *Sturnira*), a piscivore (Fisherman Bat, *Noctilio leporinus*), a sanguinivore (Common Vampire Bat, *Desmodus rotundus*) and a flower-feeding bat (*Hylonycteris underwoodi*). Diagram: O. von Helversen.

Fig. 17. *Peropteryx macrotis*, a representative of the sheath-tailed bats (Emballonuridae) from Venezuela. Photo: O. von Helversen.

and likewise the tropical savannahs and mountain forests.

▶ Variety of forms and species

Bats could appear to a large extent to be a uniform group of small mammals with dense fur and with wings. However, no other order of the mammals has actually utilised so great an abundance of ecological niches as the bats. This is particularly obvious in the tropics, where this variety is hardly surpassed.

In the tropics many bat species nourish themselves essentially with insects. Among them the sheath-tailed bats (Emballonuridae), which can be regarded from their echolocation and morphology as relatively primitive bats (Fig. 17). Some species of this family have peculiar, scented glandular sacs in the flight membranes. In these glands they store a secretion with a strong musky odour, which plays an important role in the display of the males. Their hunting method resembles that of our native insectivorous bats. The Old World leaf-nosed bats (Hipposideridae) are a family of highly specialised insect hunters (Fig. 18). Thanks to their similarity to horseshoe bats in echolocation calls they can detect wing flapping of insects, or even merely the wings vibrating, even when the insects sit near to or in the vegetation.

For other bat families insects also form the main food, as in some species of the False Vampires (Megadermatidae), which have a distant relationship to the horseshoe bats (Fig. 19). However, the large Greater False Vampire (*Megaderma lyra*) not only hunts insects, but supplements its diet with amphibians, reptiles and small mammals and so is not purely insectivorous. The frugivorous bats are the largest group of bats after the insect hunters. Here belong almost all the Old World Megachiropteran fruit bats (in the geographical scope of this book, only the Egyptian Fruit Bat). In the New World this niche is particularly well occupied by spear-nosed bats (Phyllostomidae) (Fig. 21).

The fruit eaters can utilise a diversity of different fruits as food and can change the food according to the availability through the course of the year. In fruit-poor times it has been observed that some species also feed on fresh young leaves of some trees.

Probably from an origin of powerful insect hunters, a whole suite of bats has also specialised in the hunting of reptiles, amphibians, and sometimes even of birds. An example is the Fringe-lipped Bat (*Trachops cirrhosus*), a highly specialised frog hunter (Fig. 24). This species particularly frequently captures male frogs, which betray themselves by their croaking. Probably the bats learn the song of the different frog species in their habitat, and learn to avoid the bad-tasting or poisonous species, while they experience others as edible.

More amazing is that some bats that turned from insect catching to the hunting of small vertebrate animals, specialise in fishing. The Greater Bulldog or Fisherman Bat (*Noctilio leporinus*) from South America became a specialist fish hunter and uses its enormous feet in hunting for fish at the water surface (Fig. 25). It probably recognises schools of fish from the surface rippling when they come close to the water surface at night when their

Fig. 18. An insect eater from South-east Asia, the Diadem Leaf-nosed Bat (*Hipposideros diadema*), a representative of the Old World leaf-nosed bats (Hipposideridae). Photo: D. Nill.

Fig. 19. The 'Lesser False Vampire' (*Megaderma spasma*) from South-east Asia is an insectivorous species from the family of the false vampire bats (Megadermatidae). Photo: O. von Helversen.

principal enemies, terns and kingfishers, are sleeping. The large Greater Bulldog Bat can even sometimes be observed in moonlight circling with leisurely wingbeats over quiet sea bays.

The specialisation of the true vampire bats of South America is just as fascinating. The most common species is the Common Vampire Bat (*Desmodus rotundus*) (Fig. 26). With its razor-sharp teeth it makes a small wound in the skin of sleeping large animals, usually horses or cattle, often in the neck region. Since the saliva contains anticoagulant substances, the blood can flow as a tiny runlet from the wound and, unnoticed by the victim, be licked up carefully. The

Fig. 20. A group of neotropical spear-nosed bats, *Uroderma bilobatum*, a 'tent'-making bat which constructs tents by biting through the ribs of large leaves of bananas or some palms. The leaf blades then fold downwards, similar to a tent, and the bats have a rain-free refuge. Photo: D. Nill

Fig. 21. The Common Fruit Bat (*Artibeus jamaicensis*), a spear-nosed bat, is a lover of many different fruits, especially various fig species. Photo: D. Nill.

▶ Fig. 22. The noseleaf is characteristic for most species of spear-nosed bats (Phyllostomidae) and is useful for recognition in this frugivorous Big-eyed Bat of the genus *Chiroderma*. Photo: O. von Helversen.

▶▶ Fig. 23. Noseleaf of the Sword-nosed Bat (*Lonchorhina aurita*), an insectivorous spear-nosed bat. Photo: O. von Helversen.

▶▶▶ Fig. 24. The Frog-eating Bat (*Trachops cirrhosus*) similarly belongs to the spear-nosed bats, but is a highly specialised frog hunter, which recognises prey by its croaking and can even use it to differentiate poisonous and tasty frog species. Photo: D. Nill.

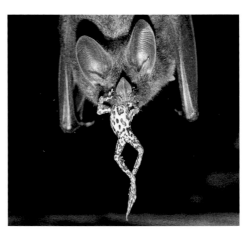

teeth of the Common Vampire Bat are as sharp as razor-blades (Fig. 27), because they sharpen each other as with a whetstone. In that way the victim does not feel the bite at all. The loss of blood is usually slight so that it has probably no great impact. However, the transmission of diseases from prey animal to prey animal, particularly rabies, can be dangerous.

Particularly fascinating bats are the small, hovering flower-feeding bats of South and Central America, which nourish

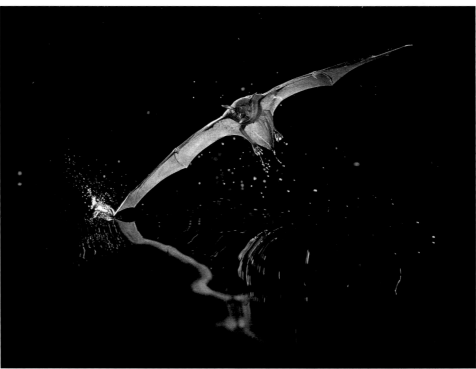

Fig. 25. With its large feet the Fisherman Bat (*Noctilio leporinus*) from South America is adapted to touch and catch prey that is swimming close to the water surface. Photo: D. Nill.

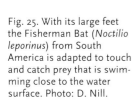

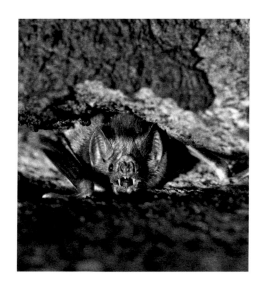

themselves with nectar. Some highly specialised species exclusively nourish themselves with nectar and pollen of the flowers visited by them – and their whole way of life is fine-tuned to flower visiting (Fig. 28). As the 'hummingbirds of the night', they are able to hover in front of flowers while lapping up the nectar. With their visits to

different plants they transfer pollen in their fur from the stamens of one plant to the pistil of other flowers. Many tropical plants have in the process of their evolution become specialised for visits by bats and have become 'bat flowers', which are now dependent on this group of animals for pollination.

Most bats are fairly plainly coloured – perhaps not surprisingly, being night creatures. Nevertheless, some are strikingly coloured or patterned, particularly those that roost in trees, such as many of the Old World flying foxes, or some of the foliage-roosting New World tropical fruit-eating bats, the hoary bat (Fig. 439), and a number of striking black and white or orange and black bats. Such colouring may help with camouflage. In the Neotropics, there are two white species and a range of species with stripes on their faces or down their back: one stripe in the spear-nosed bats and two in some sheath-tailed bats that roost exposed on tree trunks. A number of other bats have coloured spots or patches, usually for display.

Fig. 26. The Common Vampire Bat (*Desmodus rotundus*) is specialised in digesting blood as food. With the sharp incisors it makes small wounds in its victim and laps up the exuding blood. Photo: D. Nill.

Fig. 27. The dentition of the Common Vampire Bat (*Desmodus rotundus*) shows razor-sharp teeth, which sharpen each other. Blood remains from the last meal are still recognisable in the corner of the mouth after the animal was caught while foraging. Photo: O. von Helversen.

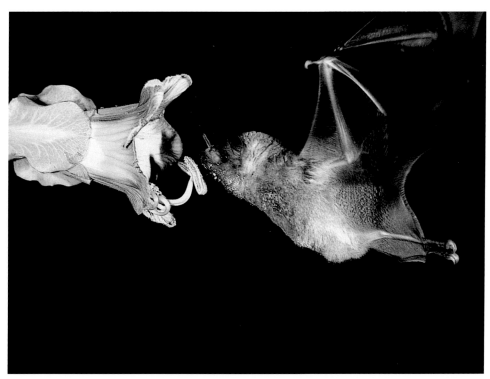

Fig. 28. The Common Long-tongued Bat (*Glossophaga soricina*) during the approach to a flower of the Mexican Cup and Saucer Vine (*Cobaea scandens*). There is pollen visible on throat and belly, which can now be transferred to the stamens of other flowers. Photo: O. von Helversen.

The flight of bats

Fig. 29. Comparison of the wings of a flying saurian, a bird and a bat. Modified after gen. lit. 87. Diagram: W. Lang.

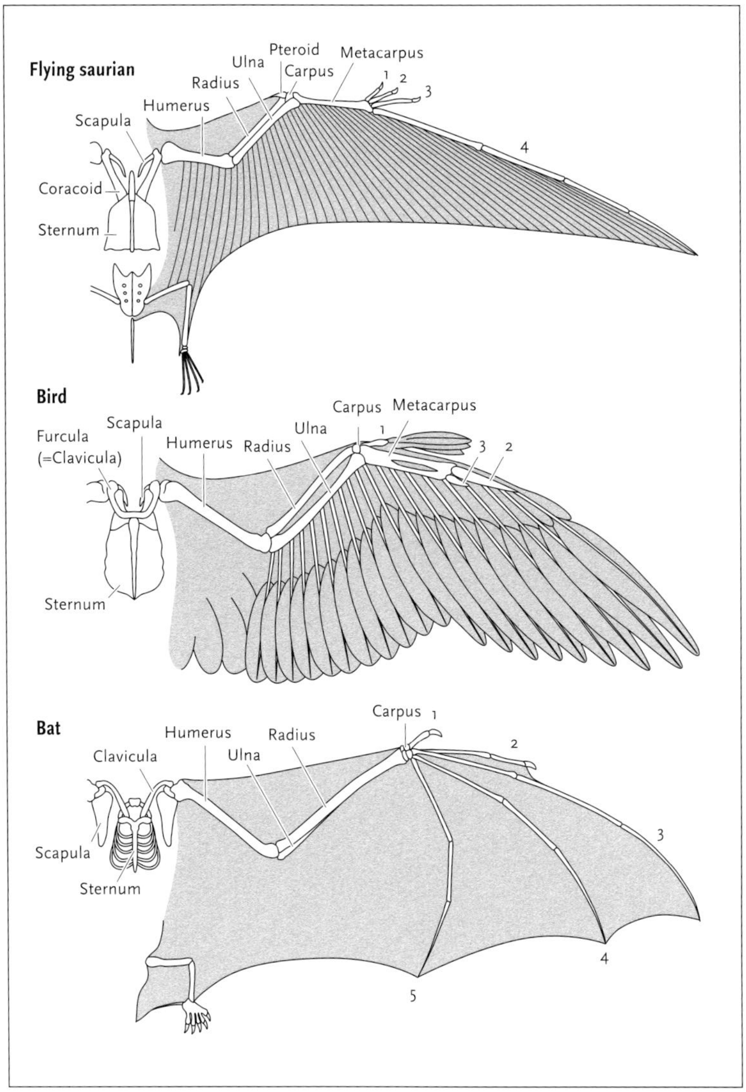

Nearly all characteristics of bats are connected in one way or another with their ability to fly – either because they are adaptations for flying or because they were only made possible by the ability to fly – or in reverse, because they are not possible from the limitations imposed by flying. Bats are

the only mammals which are capable of 'active flight'; they can gain height not only by soaring or gliding, but also in active flight.

What advantages does active flight offer, despite the fact that it is an energy-expensive means of locomotion? In order to evolve this way of locomotion, it had to offer advantages right from the beginning. It was probably not even possible for the first true flying mammals in the Palaeocene to open up a new food niche of the capture of flying insects by the newly acquired ability of flight. This is because the first phases of the evolution of flight must have been made by gliding flight, and this is not suitable for the capture of insects in flight.

Some time ago it became ever more clear to scientists that flight is the most energy-costly form of locomotion **per unit of time**, but the most economical form of locomotion **per distance covered**, and that was the primary selection advantage. A fruit eater, for example an ape, must climb a tree, then descend again, search for a new tree, climb this, etc., and in between it might perhaps cover a long distance on the ground. From its day roost a fruit bat can easily reach a fruit tree that is one or more kilometres distant, and within a few minutes it can check many different possible fruit trees as to whether they have fruits, and if they have none, it can visit just as quickly the next tree full of fruits. The evolution of flight was first of all also an evolution in the direction of an energetically economical means of locomotion. This is particularly important for animals which must cover long distances to and from their permanent roost, e.g. a cave, for their foraging flights ('central place foraging').

Among vertebrate animals active flight was independently 'invented' three times: in the flying saurians, in the birds, and in the bats. All use their forelimbs as wings (see Fig. 29), which are consequently developed from common homologous elements (corresponding to each other), the elements of the 'pentadactyl limb' of vertebrate animals. However, different elements were used in a completely different way. Thus, in the flying saurians the flight membrane was attached to the fourth finger; in birds the phalanges and metacarpals were substantially reduced – and feathers appeared in their place; in the bats the flight membranes are stretched between the four fingers (only the thumb remained free), the hind legs and the tail. The wings of a flying saurian, bird and bat are homologous to each other as far as they correspond to the fore-limb of the vertebrate animal blueprint, but they were completely independently and convergently developed with respect to their function as a wing.

The flight of bats sometimes seems more awkward and less elegant in comparison with birds – and indeed bats cannot soar like a Common Buzzard or reach the speeds of a Peregrine Falcon. However, the flight of bats is, due to the large flight membrane, markedly agile, and it can slow down or change flight direction within the shortest time (Fig. 32). With regard to their manoeuvrability, they are clearly superior to birds. Interestingly enough, it turned out that bats, compared with birds and insects, even with respect to the efficiency of energy use, work out particularly well [gen. lit. 144, 148]. Fig. 30 shows the flight costs for several bats of different weight in comparison with birds. It appears that bats can fly overall 'more cheaply', and thus more energy-efficiently, than birds. This is particularly noticeable during flight on the spot, that is, when hovering. Fig. 31 shows the energy expenditure of different flower-visiting animals of different weights, and which are particularly adapted to hovering flight. As well as the hawk-moths (Sphingidae), hummingbirds and flower-feeding bats can stand hovering in the air in front of flowers, while they suck or lap the nectar. This figure shows on the one hand that the costs of the hovering flight naturally rise with increased body weight – and that is true for all three groups. Additionally, it shows that the bats have the most energetically efficient flight: the same output for hovering flight (1.1 Watt) is needed of a 3g hawk-moth, a more than 4g hummingbird and a 6.5g, clearly heavier, bat.

U. Norberg, who was involved in many studies on the flight biophysics of bats, says with good reason: 'aerodynamics is still no accurate science, it depends too much on assumptions, simplifications and estimated values' [gen. lit. 87]. Many questions of bat flight are so far not quantitatively answerable. Why is there no stalling during a bat's hovering flight, although the approach angle is very high? Obviously the movement is just fast enough that it prevents such falling.

If aerodynamics and energetics of bat flight in individual cases still do not allow quantitative computation, then the general concepts nevertheless suggest many interesting adaptations. Fig. 33 shows the connection between the travel costs and the airspeed. The aerodynamic output needed for flight consists of three components: one the output generated by the flapping of wings, the upstroke and thrust produced (pi); furthermore the so-called 'parasitic' output Ppar, which is the output needed to overcome the friction resistance of the body; and finally Ppro, the so-called profile

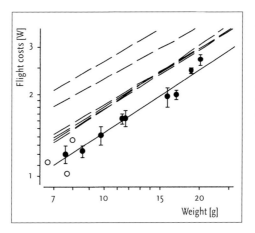

Fig. 30. Flight costs (in Watts) as a function of the body weight in birds (interrupted lines from different models) and for bats (measured values particularly for flower-feeding bats). Bat flight is apparently 'cheaper' than birds. After gen. lit. 148. Graph: Y. Winter.

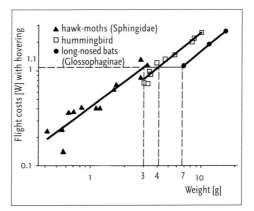

Fig. 31. Flight costs (in Watts) of hovering in front of a flower, as a function of the body weight, in hawk-moths, hummingbirds and flower-feeding bats. The flower-feeding bats hover most efficiently. After gen. lit. 144.

Fig. 32. Parti-coloured Bat
(*Vespertilio murinus*) in
flight. Photo D. Nill.

Fig. 32. Parti-coloured Bat (*Vespertilio murinus*) in flight. Photo D. Nill.

output, which describes the friction resistance of the wings. While Ppro and Ppar increase with increased speed, pi is greatest at low speed. Altogether a total output as a function of the airspeed results in an approximately U-shaped curve. Which airspeed is a bat to select for its hunting flight? It could fly Vmp with that speed which costs least energy ('minimum power'). However, if it wishes to arrive with as little energy expenditure as possible from its roost to a hunting ground, then it should select a different, clearly higher speed, the Vmr ('maximum range'). The speed at which it can fly the longest distance with minimal possible expenditure results from the point at a tangent from the zero point of the curve in Figure 33.

The estimates so far show, however, that bats mostly fly even faster than corresponds to this consideration, thus even faster than Vmr. Perhaps saving of energy is not so important when the increased energy consumption is counterbalanced by a larger profit, some increased probability to catch prey, or having a lower risk of being taken by a predator. For most small bat species the airspeeds lie between 5 and 8 m/s, corresponding to about 18 to 29 km/h. Fast-flying species, such as the European Free-tailed Bat (*Tadarida teniotis*) or Noctule (*Nyctalus noctula*), achieve distinctly higher speeds of at least 50km/h [gen. lit. 21]. If a Noctule, having discovered a large insect below it, wheels over and

dives towards the ground, it will certainly reach even higher speeds.

In regard to manoeuvrability and airspeed bats can have completely different niches, depending upon their hunting habitat and their hunting strategy. Apart from the variety of wing shapes there are also remarkable differences in the size of the tail membrane and in some species there is on the calcar, which supports the tail membrane, yet another small skin flap, the post-calcarial lobe (Fig. 34). This lobe is supported by a small T-piece of cartilage as muscle attachment, which enables a fast stretching of the tail membrane with the outward movement of the calcar. The adaptations of the wing shape are noticeable and

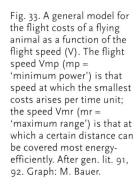

Fig. 33. A general model for the flight costs of a flying animal as a function of the flight speed (V). The flight speed Vmp (mp = 'minimum power') is that speed at which the smallest costs arises per time unit; the speed Vmr (mr = 'maximum range') is that at which a certain distance can be covered most energy-efficiently. After gen. lit. 91, 92. Graph: M. Bauer.

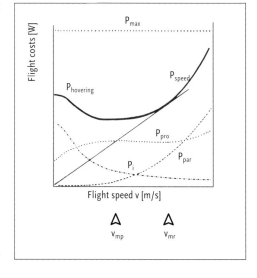

also easily related to the flight style: for a manoeuvrable flight broad wings and a low wing-loading are needed, for a fast and energy-saving flight particularly narrow, long wings are used.

Fig. 35 shows that in this respect the majority of the European species have selected a compromise: a dense cloud of dots can be found in the area of average wing widths and average wing-loading. Only a few species are at the right edge, far outside this aggregation: these are the fast and high-flying three European *Nyctalus* species, and the North African Lesser Mouse-tailed Bat (*Rhinopoma hardwickii*). Also Schreibers' Bent-winged Bat (*Miniopterus schreibersii*) belongs here, although for other reasons. Schreibers' Bent-winged Bats can also fly high and fast, but it usually hunts with a pigeon-like, rather slow flight, whereby probably the large tail membrane and the long wing-tip, completely differently formed from that of the Vespertilionids, enable a special flight style.

The Lesser Horseshoe Bat (*Rhinolophus hipposideros*) has an extremely manoeuvrable flight style (far to the left in Fig. 35). With its extremely broad wings and the small body weight this species can dive through the smallest gaps in vegetation with ease and pick insects off the ground or leaves in hovering flight.

At the other extreme is the European Free-tailed Bat, which, with its long, narrow wings and tail membrane, is much less manoeuvrable, needs a greater clear space below the roost exit point to get up air speed and must maintain a higher flight speed, and so tends to stay out in open spaces and avoid cluttered environments. It is members of this family that have been found at the highest altitudes, with feeding at 400–500m above ground level and even up to c. 900m above ground level. There are many more detailed accounts of the flight of bats, including UK gen. lit. 151 and a lot of earlier papers by Norberg and Rayner.

Fig. 34. The post-calcarial lobe of many bat species is a small flap of skin attached to the calcar, the spur from the heel, as in this Leisler's Bat (*Nyctalus leisleri*). The post-calcarial lobe offers a root for a muscle which unfolds the tail membrane. It is particularly pronounced in fast-flying species, which can nevertheless brake fast. Photo: C. Dietz.

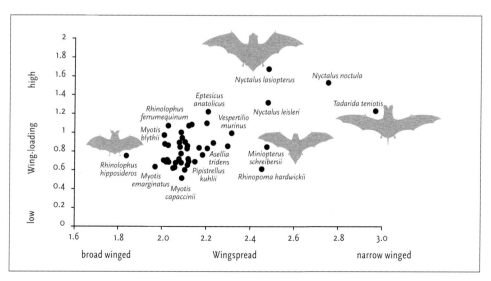

Fig. 35. The diagram shows the relationship of wing-loading (weight to wing area) and aspect ratio (ratio of wing length to wing width) for European bats. A majority of the species lie close together. The noctules (*Nyctalus* spp.) and the European Free-tailed Bat (*Tadarida teniotis*) are extremely long-winged and Lesser Horseshoe Bat (*Rhinolophus hipposideros*) is particularly broad-winged. Graph: M. Bauer.

Echolocation

Discovery of echolocation

More than 200 years ago L. Spallanzani, an Italian scientist and a bishop in Pavia, used an ingenious experiment to demonstrate the fact that in absolute darkness, and thus independently of their vision, bats could avoid obstacles without difficulty and could orient themselves quickly and with confidence in an unknown environment. He stretched thin wires in a darkened room and provided them with small bells. While owls released into the area flew into the wires and made the bells ring on every test flight as soon as it was completely dark, bats were able to avoid the wires, even under these conditions. When he blinded the bats, this did not reduce their sense of orientation, but when he glued the ears or the muzzle together, then they flew against the wires, as if they could not 'see' any more. Spallanzani even glued small tubes into the ears of the bats: when he left the tubes open, the animals showed a perfect sense of orientation; however, when he blocked them with small plugs, the bats were disoriented and flew against the wires.

Interestingly enough, Spallanzani was not, however, courageous enough to draw the conclusion from these results that bats orient themselves with the information from the echoes from calls inaudible to us humans. In the year 1794 he terminated his experiments with a correct, but rather unfortunate, diary entry: '... so blinded bats can use their ears when they catch insects at night... This discovery is unbelievable' [gen. lit. 87]. He assumed, however, that bats could orient themselves rather by a kind of 'sense of remote touch' on their sensitive flight membranes. He obviously took this hypothesis from G. Cuvier, the most important and most influential zoologist of his time, who had not carried out any experiments at all, but whose opinion it was not allowed to contradict around 1790. This false conclusion is also remarkable, because blind humans, who can detect close large objects (such as, for example, walls) with the echoes of loud noises, believe, if one asks them for an explanation, that they have sensitive feelings in the skin of the face.

Thus it was left to D. Griffin, nearly 150 years later, to discover the ultrasonic echolocation of bats. Only in the time shortly before the Second World War was the technology sufficiently advanced as to be able to recognise acoustic waves whose frequencies are above the audible range of the human ear. In 1938, Griffin, still as a student, introduced bats to a microphone built by the physicist G.W. Pierce and showed that bats emit short clicking calls that are inaudible for us but that, in fact, possess an enormous sound pressure level. Actually it is amazing that only the development of ultrasonic microphones made the discovery of echolocation possible, because with some bats, such as Noctule Bats (*Nyctalus noctula*) or European Free-tailed Bats (*Tadarida teniotis*) in the Mediterranean area, for young people, particularly for children and for younger women, the calls are quite audible. Probably the scientists who worked with the orientation of bats were too old for that – the human hearing loses its ability to register the high frequencies at increasing age. An exception seems to have been the Dutch zoologist S. Dijkgraaf: in 1943 he published a note that he had heard a quiet ticking in a small *Myotis* species, and in 1946 he resumed the experiments of Spallanzani. Dijkgraaf's acceptance that the animal from which he had heard the sounds was a Geoffroy's Bat is, however, rather improbable; since this species emits echolocation calls with a high terminal frequency, it is more likely to have been the very similar Natterer's Bat (*Myotis nattereri*), which emits echolocations calls that particularly extend well into the range of human hearing. With his attempts, Dijkgraaf stated that when he prevented the bat

Fig. 36. Young animal of the Lesser Horseshoe Bat (*Rhinolophus hipposideros*) at night roost. Young animals must learn the use of echolocation quickly, in order to be able to hunt independently; this animal is yawning, the horseshoe bats emit the echolocation sounds through the nose. Photo: D. Nill.

from calling by pasting tape over the muzzle, the bat hardly wanted to fly off and, as in Spallanzani´s experiments, lost the ability to avoid obstacles during flight.

The 'unbelievable' ability of bats to orient themselves through the reception of the self-generated echolocation calls is then really only known since the middle of the last century and has subsequently been intensively investigated.

The term echolocation describes only a small part of the abilities that the bats obtain with this system of an active acoustic image reception. 'Location' describes much too little: bats cannot only detect and locate objects, their entire orientation in the world, not only for the hunting of prey, has been based on their ability to process and evaluate, through the central nervous system, the returning echoes from their calls. 'Echo sound picture' would perhaps be an adequate expression for this achievement. Because bats also differentiate forms and surface textures, they can use them to 'recognise' interesting objects in their environment – such as fruit-feeding bats to recognise the trees and fruits on which they live, or tropical flower-feeding bats that visit and pollinate different flowers that are specially adapted to bats.

The principles of acoustic echolocation

Echolocation is, at least in theory, rather simple; it resembles radar, except that acoustic (sound) waves are used instead of electromagnetic radiation, which is why in this technology the expression 'sonar' is used. A transmitter/receiver combination produces short sound pulses, which can be radiated from the transmitter and be registered by the receiver as returning echoes. The sound pulses must be short, since the receiver is overridden during the transmission time and during this time cannot pick up the substantially quieter echoes. The running time (time delay) of the echo indicates the distance of the object reflecting the sound. The more precisely the time delay can be measured, the more exactly the distance is known. The most exact possible measurement of a running time is achieved by the information-theory procedure of cross-correlation (see Box 2). Some approximation methods produce nearly equivalent achievements, so that one can quite imagine that in the brain of a bat neural arithmetic operations are accomplished that correspond to a cross-correlation.

While the distance of an echo-giving structure can thus be measured very exactly, the determination of the direction from which the echo returns is substantially more difficult. In principle, there are several possibilities of determining the direction. Either one uses a closely concentrated beam, with which the environment can be scanned, so that echoes can return only from the direction to which the sound

beam was directed, or one needs several receivers in order to compute the direction from the run-time differences between them. If one uses 'wide-band' signals (signals that cover a larger frequency range) and inserts different frequency directional filters, one can use also the 'tone quality' of the echo for determination of direction. As explained in more detail in the following, different bats selected different combinations of these three possibilities.

The basic problem, from which direction an echo returns, remains substantially more difficult and substantially more inaccurate to determine than measuring the distance of the reflecting object. When one compares the 'visual world' of we humans or, for example, a bird with the 'hearing world' of a bat, then there are crucial differences. Our eyes receive the 'visual world' over the two-dimensional retina, and a very exact analysis of all directions can be made but only a relatively inaccurate estimation of the distances, and this is reversed with the 'hearing world' of the bats. Bats live, to a certain extent, in the centre of an 'onion-skinned world', in which the distances are very exactly known but the directions of the objects can only be determined with great difficulty and inaccurately. When one compares the rapid and confident flight of a bat in an obstacle-rich world, such as the dense vegetation of a tropical rainforest, with the ability of birds to manoeuvre in the same environment, then one will find barely any difference in precision and certainty. The brain of bats is obviously able to construct, from the data obtained with the help of echolocation, just as complete and precise a picture of the spatial structure of the environment as humans and many other vertebrate animals can do with the help of their eyes. How that is possible is still an incomprehensible information-theoretical and physiological mystery.

Some information – theoretical terms

Cross-correlation: F(τ) of two time functions g(t) and f(t)

$$F(\tau) = \int g(t) \times f(t+\tau) \times dt$$

Cross-correlation can be used to measure time difference Δt = τ by analysis of similarity between two waveforms. When f(t) describes the waveform of the emitted calls and g(t) the waveform of the echoes, then a sharply distinct maximum of F(τ) characterizes the time difference (and hence range) Δt which results in maximum similarity (overlap) of call and echo. This time difference is the travel time between emitting the call and receiving the echo, and indicates target range.

Impulse function of the echo: the echo of a short (theoretically infinitely short) click.

Spectrum: frequency composition of a sound. The spectrum of an echo can be calculated by a Fourier analysis of the impulse function of the echo. Subjectively, the spectrum of a sound is observed as tone quality ('pitch composition'). Different tone qualities ('colour') develop if, in the inner ear, different areas of the basilar membrane are stimulated.

Echolocation calls of bats

The echolocation calls of bats are not produced differently from the sounds of other mammals, as air with high pressure is pushed over the vocal cords and these are thereby moved in oscillations. The vocal cords of bats are small and tautly strained and can produce very high frequencies. These oscillations are strengthened and frequency filtered in resonance chambers in the nose and throat area. The echolocation calls are nearly always frequency-modulated sinus tones, which can possess a few harmonic overtones. Which harmonic is the loudest radiated is decided with the frequency filtering in the resonance chambers. The calls can show enormous volumes. In free flight, sound volumes (intensity) of more than 130dB SPL were measured, recorded from a distance of 10cm in front of the muzzle. By way of comparison, the pain threshold in humans for their audible range lies at about this value, at approximately 130dB SPL; such volumes radiated in the hearing range of humans can cause permanent damage to the hearing ability, and bats may not be able to call even louder for the same reason.

Most vesper bats (Vespertilionidae) stress the fundamental mode – often so much so that almost only this constitutes the echolocation calls. The horseshoe bats (Rhinolophidae) and many tropical species of other families stress the first harmonic (the second harmonious wave) and suppress the fundamental. Some species, such as the long-eared bats (Genus *Plecotus*), use several harmonics. Fig. 37 shows the most important types of echolocation calls in European bats. Horseshoe bats (Rhinolophidae) emit constant-frequency (CF) calls that only show a sharp frequency rise and fall, respectively, at the beginning and at the end, corresponding to stretching and slackening of the vocal cords (Fig. 37, centre). These sounds can be very long, often longer than 50ms.

Vesper bats (Vespertilionidae), in principle, use frequency-modulated (FM) calls, which begin with a high frequency and end with lower frequencies. These calls can be very steeply modulated in their frequency, as in the species of the genus *Myotis*, or they can become increasingly flatter at the end, as, for example, in Leisler's Bat (*Nyctalus leisleri*) and Soprano Pipistrelle (*Pipistrellus pygmaeus*) (Fig. 37). When these species fly high in the air in obstacle-free environments (in the 'search flight' or in 'commuting flight'), they often reduce the steepness of the frequency-modulation

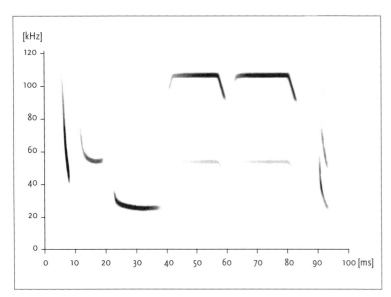

[kHz]

Fig. 37. Spectrogram of the echolocation calls of some bat species. The frequency is shown against time. From left to right: Alcathoe Whiskered Bat (*Myotis alcathoe*), Soprano Pipistrelle (*Pipistrellus pygmaeus*), Leisler's Bat (*Nyctalus leisleri*), Mediterranean Horseshoe Bat (*Rhinolophus euryale*) and Brown Long-eared Bat (*Plecotus auritus*). Graph: M. Bauer.

part, until the calls become more or less completely flat modulated or almost constant-frequency calls. Hence such calls have been termed 'quasi-constant frequency' (qCF). Apart from the call duration and the frequency of the echolocation calls, the bandwidth, i.e. the frequency range of the call is a particularly important parameter. Wide-band calls develop either when the fundamental mode extends over a very broad frequency range, as, for example, with the Alcathoe Whiskered Bat (*Myotis alcathoe*) (Fig. 37, far left), or when several overlapping harmonics cover a broad frequency range, as in the Brown Long-eared Bat (*Plecotus auritus*) (Fig. 37, far right).

A fundamental problem of this active acoustic orientation system is the low intensity of the echoes. Medium-sized insects can have a 'target strength' ('reflecting strength') of approximately –30dB, i.e. the reflected echo is quieter by around 30dB than the sound meeting the object, and this is without the consideration of the absorption (or attenuation) of the sound on its way from the bat to the prey animal. Thus the call should have as great a volume (intensity) as possible. But that has the consequence of the bat 'blasting' its own ears during calling, such that it cannot register an echo returning at the same time. The overlap of call and echo thus leads to a 'blind window' in front of the bat. A small

calculation (Fig. 38) results in the following: if the call of a bat is 5ms long, a typical value for many small bat species, with the speed of sound being 340m/s (thus also mm/ms), in this time the sound runs back and forth a total of 1,700mm. The bat can detect prey animals removed up to 850mm distance. But yet another acoustic–physiological effect occurs, which one calls 'forward masking'. Loud hearing events mask subsequently arriving hearing events as they increase the auditory threshold, with which the 'blind window' becomes even more increased.

The problem of the overlap of call and echo with detecting obstacles and prey animals can be solved in two ways. The most frequently used is a shortening of the call duration, whereby, however, the returning sound energy is considerably reduced. However, since the object is already relatively close, this does not play a very significant role, because the absorption of the sound is only small. With a shortening of the call to 1ms, the 'blind window' would still amount to about 170mm distance in front of the mouth. Some bats can shorten their calls down to approximately 0.3ms in the final phase before the catch, which corresponds to a 'blind window' of only approximately 50–60mm. Then they seize the prey with the mouth, tail membrane or wing membrane in the following milliseconds. As they approach a prey animal closer and closer, they shorten the call duration step by step and thereby, almost up to the last moment, avoid an overlap of call and echo, as shown by E. Kalko (Fig. 39). A second, completely different solution to this problem is used by the horseshoe bats (see page 38).

The overlap of call and echo is not the only problem, because there is also the danger that the quiet echoes of insects are overshadowed by the many louder echoes, for example of a wall or a tree, and thus become unrecognizable (Fig. 38). Here the same considerations are valid: an object which can be discriminated and which produces only a quiet echo must not be too close in front of a structure that is producing a very loud echo. With a call duration of

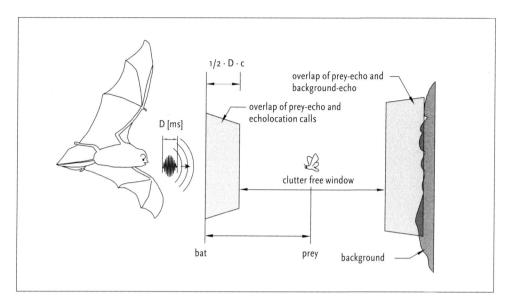

Fig. 38. In front of every echolocating bat extends a 'blind window', since the returning echo arrives while the bat is still calling. A similar area, within which the bat can barely detect faint echoes, is associated with any reflecting background. Only between them lies an 'interference-free window' (clutter-free window), in which the bat can detect the faint echoes of small insects.

5ms, the overlap range of these disturbance echoes (so-called 'clutter') will again amount to approximately 850mm. Also here comes another acoustic–physiological effect, 'backward masking', which is aggravating because the hearing of a quiet event is also masked when it occurs directly in front of a following very loud hearing event. For the bat only a limited disturbance-free window remains between the area disturbed by the overlap of the echo with its own call and by the overlap with areas disturbed by loud background echoes, the so-called 'clutter-free window'.

Apart from the problems of disturbance, the distance of an echo-reflecting object can nevertheless be very exactly determined from the run-time, by cross-correlation or similar methods. As different experiments have shown, this accuracy lies within the range of a few millimetres.

The determination of the direction from which an echo returns is very much more difficult and more inaccurate. The distance between the ears, which is much smaller than in humans, is unsuitable as a basis for the measurement of the time difference between arriving echoes. When one considers an ear distance of 8mm, then there is an exact time difference Δt between the right or the left ear of the arriving sound of approximately 24μs, which the bat could probably still detect if one assumes that

their acoustic system has a similar resolution to our human hearing. But even for a rough 'sound picture', it would have to differentiate angle differences of a few degrees, at least, for instance, 5° or 10° between two objects. With 10° (sin (10°) = 0.17), the time difference would amount to around only approximately 4μs, which is probably below the limit of physiological perception. Perhaps, therefore, the measurement of run-time differences between the ears can supply a certain contribution to directional hearing but cannot alone make exact direction determination possible. A neural evaluation of the phase differences is likewise not possible with the high ultrasonic frequencies.

Since a bat in flight needs exact information about obstacles not only in the direction of flight but also from the side

Fig. 39. As a Common Pipistrelle (*Pipistrellus pipistrellus*) approaches a prey, it continually shortens its calls, in order to avoid an overlap of call and echo. After gen. lit. 62. Graph: W. Lang.

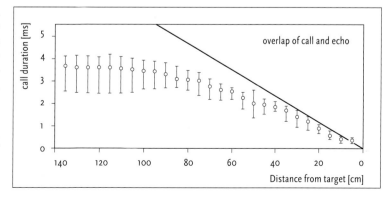

areas, as well as from above and below, the sound cone of most bats, with the exception of the horseshoe bats, is relatively broad. The complex form of the auricles permits the deduction, from the tone quality of the echoes, via a ' direction-specific, frequency filter', of the direction from which an echo returns to the bats. The auricles are built in such a way that the sound arriving takes different possible routes to the eardrum causing interference and modulating a direction-specific frequency spectrum onto the echo. In this way, some frequencies are strengthened or decreased in their amplitude. The tragus plays a particularly important role here. Its form, like that of the complete form of the ears, is remarkably species-specific; obviously it is accurately adapted in each bat species to the neural analysis of the hearing signals in the brain. However, it is only possible for those bat species that have echolocation calls of a sufficiently wide band to use this method.

A specialist: the echolocation of the horseshoe bats

The complicated structure on the nose,

Fig. 40. Greater Horseshoe Bat (*Rhinolophus ferrumequinum*) approaching a prey. The narrow field of echolocation calls is then exactly directed towards the prey. Photo: D. Nill.

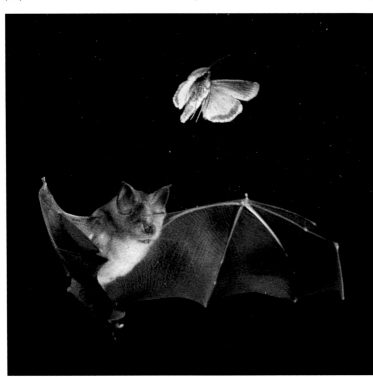

which has given the horseshoe bats (Rhinolophidae) their name, already indicates that these bats emit their echolocation calls through the nostrils and not through the mouth. Although the horseshoe bats represent their own evolution lineage, related to the Megachiroptera, and from that some of their characteristics perhaps become more understandable, they have the emission of the calls through the nose in common with many other bat families, for example the tropical Old World leaf-nosed bats and the European long-eared bats (Genus *Plecotus*). The selection pressure to emit precise echolocation calls while, 'with a full mouth', consuming a larger prey animal is not without some sense for this convergent development.

Emitting the calls from the pair of nostrils within an acoustic funnel formed by the horseshoe results in focussing and makes possible a substantially more precise directionality of the sound beams. Since the echolocation calls have a constant, precisely maintained frequency, the wavelength λ of the acoustic waves remain constant over the whole call. If the nostrils, from which two coherent acoustic waves are emitted, are separated by the distance $\lambda/2$, the acoustic waves emitted in both lateral directions are completely cancelled out by interference and the entire sound energy is focussed forward. Together with the horseshoe-shaped acoustic funnel, the horseshoe bats can thus produce a rather closely bunched sound beam (Fig. 41). A further highly directional selectivity comes from the agile ears, with which the bats can scan their environment very rapidly. In order to be able to appreciate the change of the echo during an ear movement, its calls must persist much longer and repeat as fast as possible. Hence, the so-called 'duty cycle', the ratio of call to call interval, must be high.

The long duration of the calls and the high duty cycle presuppose that horseshoe bats can hear the echoes of their environment even during calling. For that they have developed unusual adaptations.

Fig. 42 shows the auditory threshold curve of a Greater Horseshoe Bat. One can recognise a very low threshold passage in the range of about 82kHz. At this frequency, the hearing shows an extremely high sensitivity. In the neighbouring frequency ranges, the threshold is comparatively high and the sensitivity low. When a horseshoe bat flies, the Doppler effect results in the fact that the echoes return with a clearly higher frequency than that with which the calls were emitted. Greater Horseshoe Bats can now, depending upon flight speed, call with a frequency of 77–81kHz, despite the fact that they do not hear much since they are relatively insensitive to this frequency. But the returning echoes have a higher frequency due to the Doppler effect and hence now fall in the most sensitive acoustic range.

When a horseshoe bat is hanging calmly at rest, it does not have the possibility of using the Doppler effect, and it must then call with that frequency for which its hearing system is most sensitive. Fig. 43 shows the course of the call frequencies of a Greater Horseshoe Bat during flight from one hanging place to another. During the flight, the call frequency is lowered by approximately 2–3kHz. Experiments have shown that the frequency emitted by the bat is adjusted accurately in each case in such a way that the returning echo falls exactly into the range of its highest acoustic sensitivity.

Adaptations of the inner ear in horseshoe bats

Apart from these special auditory adaptations, the horseshoe bats show a particularly important morphological adaptation of the inner ear. The cochlea of the inner ear in most mammals is firmly fused together with the petrosal bone within the bulla tympani. In bats, particularly the horseshoe bats, however, the bulla tympani is only attached to the skull with soft connective tissue, in such a way that as small as possible sound transfer can be made via the bones (Fig. 44).

The purely soft suspension of the cochlea has a further consequence, in that with the skulls of horseshoe bats, which one can find, for example, on the floor of a cave roost, the bullae tympani are usually missing, because of the decomposition of

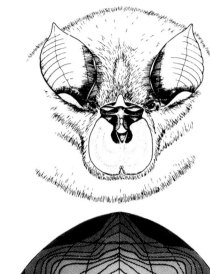

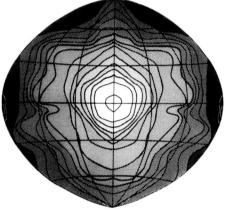

Fig. 41. Sound cone of a Greater Horseshoe Bat (*Rhinolophus ferrumequinum*) seen from the front – the paler the grey tone, the higher the intensity of the call. Above, the face of a horseshoe bat – one can recognise the acoustic funnel, which focuses forward calls emitted from both nostrils. Graph: G. Neuweiler.

Fig. 42. Auditory threshold of a Greater Horseshoe Bat (*Rhinolophus ferrumequinum*). The volume of sound perceived is presented as a function of the sonic frequency. One recognises a narrow band of extreme sensitivity at *c.* 82–83kHz and directly below it a band of particularly low sensitivity, hence a higher threshold. After gen. lit. 87.

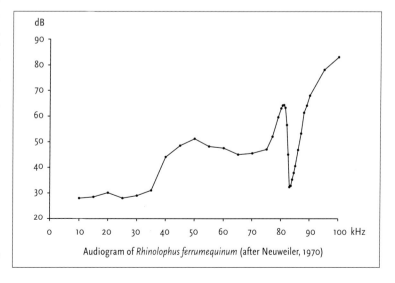

Audiogram of *Rhinolophus ferrumequinum* (after Neuweiler, 1970)

Box 3
The Doppler effect

The Doppler effect (Doppler shift) occurs when a sender and a receiver move relative to each other. For example, if a receiver moves against an acoustic wave, towards the sender, then it meets each wave faster in turn on the wave crest, whereby the observed frequency increases.

With a moving receiver then the following applies:
$$f \text{ (near the observer)} = f_{emitted} + df$$
$$df = f_{emitted} \times v/c$$

whereby df means the frequency change, v the speed of motion of the receiver, and c the speed of sound.

With a moving acoustic source then the following applies:
$$f \text{ (near the observer)} = f_{emitted} + df$$
$$df = f_{emitted} \times 1\,(1 - v/c)$$

With a calling bat (moving sender) that, in addition, flies towards the echo, which is reflected from an object (moving receiver), approximately valid is:

$$df = 2 \times f \times v/c$$

With an airspeed of approximately 5 m/s, which is quite typical for bats, the frequency change amounts to approximately 3%, which, for example, results in 3kHz with a call frequency of 100kHz.

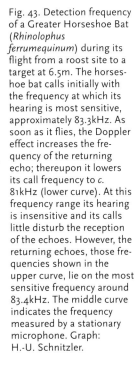

Fig. 43. Detection frequency of a Greater Horseshoe Bat (*Rhinolophus ferrumequinum*) during its flight from a roost site to a target at 6.5m. The horseshoe bat calls initially with the frequency at which its hearing is most sensitive, approximately 83.3kHz. As soon as it flies, the Doppler effect increases the frequency of the returning echo; thereupon it lowers its call frequency to *c.* 81kHz (lower curve). At this frequency range its hearing is insensitive and its calls little disturb the reception of the echoes. However, the returning echoes, those frequencies shown in the upper curve, lie on the most sensitive frequency around 83.4kHz. The middle curve indicates the frequency measured by a stationary microphone. Graph: H.-U. Schnitzler.

the connective tissue. The bullae tympani can thus be found separately, and as the name 'cochlea' (which equals 'snail') already tells us, they resemble small snails'

shells (Fig. 44). This resulted in a particularly good example of a mistake in the history of zoology (Fig. 45). In 1962 the famous snail researcher C. Boettger described a new species of worm snail from a cave on Crete [gen. lit. 13]. Therein he noticed that in the two type specimens one showed clockwise rotation and the other was wound anticlockwise, which is very unusual in snails, but without him having any suspicions. A little later, however, he was himself compelled to print, in the same magazine, a sheepish correction [gen. lit. 14]: C. Boettger had erroneously described the bullae tympani of a Greater Horseshoe Bat as a new species of snail!

Call 'design' and ecological adaptation for habitat and hunting method

Why do different bat species call so differently and not all in the same way? One would think that there would be an optimal solution for the basis of the physical and information-theoretical problem of echolocation. An answer to this question can at least be partly understood if one examines the physical limiting conditions of echolocation (see also Box 4).

Variable 1: The frequency of echolocation calls
The frequency of an acoustic wave determines the possible resolution of structures, since sound is bent around obstacles and is not reflected if these are within the dimension of the wavelength or smaller than this. Just as the electron microscope is far

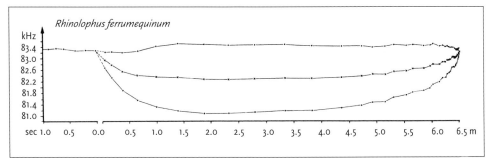

superior in the resolution of an object than the optical microscope because the wavelengths used are much smaller than that of light, an Old World leaf-nosed bat (Hipposideridae) calling with a frequency of 200kHz can resolve structures more than 10 times smaller than, for instance, can the European Free-tailed Bat (*Tadarida teniotis*), which calls at approximately 13kHz.

The fact that not all bats call with very high frequencies is because with increased frequency there is drastically increasing atmospheric absorption during sound dispersion in the air (see Box 4). High frequencies have only very small ranges and can only be used where this plays no role, for example because the species always hunts in more enclosed vegetation.

Variable 2: The bandwidth of echolocation calls

A further crucial parameter is the bandwidth of the echolocation signal. Collecting all the energy into a narrow frequency band has the advantage that the acoustic sensory cells of only one group of frequencies in the inner ear are then stimulated, and these impulses can be summed up, which makes a higher sensitivity possible. The consistent use of the same narrow frequency band also opens up new possibilities for the evolution of the specialisation of the acoustic system on this frequency band.

A wide-band signal, however, stimulates many groups of frequencies in the inner ear. Thus the time difference between call and echo, and between different echoes, can be based, to a certain extent, on different parallel places on the basilar membrane, so that a cross-correlation comparable accuracy can be obtained. Wide-band signals have yet another further crucial advantage: they permit a spectrographic analysis within the frequency range of the spectrum generated by the signal. Notches in the spectrum are an indicator of multiple superimposed reflections within the echo. These notches are either due to different surface textures from which echoes were produced and thus can contain important information about the structure of an object, or they can be produced by the morphology of the pinna of

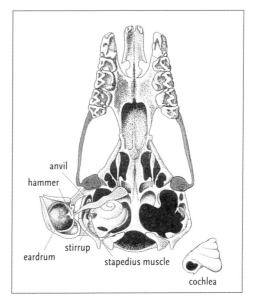

Fig. 44. Head of a Greater Horseshoe Bat (*Rhinolophus ferrumequinum*) from below. A tympanic bulla with the cochlea is already separated from the weathering skull, since it is not connected by bony substance, as in other mammals, but only by connective tissue. After gen. lit. 87.

Fig. 45. Title page of a publication by the famous malacologist Caesar Boettger, in which he described a new worm snail from a cave on Crete. Unfortunately it was based upon a mistake: he had actually found the two cochleae of a Greater Horseshoe Bat. After gen. lit. 13.

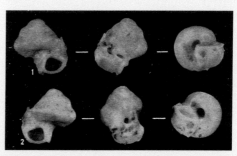

Arch. Moll. | Band 91 | Nummer 1/3 | Seite 57—59 | Frankfurt am Main, 30. 6. 1962

Schalen juveniler Wurmschnecken (Fam. Vermetidae) in einer Höhle der Insel Kreta.

Von

CAESAR R. BOETTGER, Braunschweig.

Mit 2 Abbildungen.

Im Jahre 1955 durchforschte Herr Dr. K. LINDBERG aus Lund in Schweden eine Reihe von Höhlen auf der Insel Kreta zur Untersuchung ihrer Fauna. Dabei fanden sich im östlichen Teil der Insel in der 460 m über dem Meeresspiegel befindlichen Höhle Megalo Katofyngui, etwa 30 Minuten Fußmarsch von dem 12 km südwestlich von Sitia gelegenen Dorf Turtuli, neben vielerlei Land- und Süßwasser-Arthropoden, Oligochaeten sowie Fledermaus-Schädeln und Guano (K. LINDBERG, 1955, pag. 173) zwei einzelne Molluskenschalen. Diese beiden Exemplare haben verschiedenen Bearbeitern vorgelegen, ohne daß diese zu einer Identifizierung kamen, offenbar weil man Landschnecken in der Höhle vermutete, wie sie 50 m südöstlich der Höhle Megalo Katofyngui in der kleineren Höhle Micro Katofyngui auch tatsächlich angetroffen wurden (pag. 174).

Abb. 1-2. *Tenagodus* sp. juv., 5/1. Höhle Megalo Katofyngui, Kreta. — 1) von vorn, hinten und unten (Nat. Hist. Mus. Lund). 2) von vorn, hinten und unten (SMF 164364).

57

Fig. 46. Muzzle of Schreibers' Bent-winged Bat (*Miniopterus schreibersii*). Photo: C. Dietz.

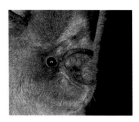

Fig. 47. Muzzle of Sundevall's Leaf-nosed Bat (*Hipposideros caffer*). Photo: C. Dietz.

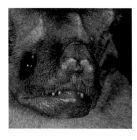

Fig. 48. Muzzle of Lesser Mouse-tailed Bat (*Rhinopoma hardwickii*). Photo: C. Dietz.

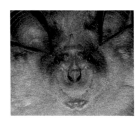

Fig. 49. Muzzle of Mehely's Horseshoe Bat (*Rhinolophus mehelyi*). Photo: C. Dietz.

Box 4
What is sound?

By sound one understands pressure fluctuations that reproduce themselves as a longitudinal wave in the air (or another medium), with a constant speed, c. By a tone one understands an acoustic wave with a single oscillating frequency, which one measures in cycles per second (Hertz = number of oscillations per second). For frequency f and wavelength λ the oscillation depends upon the equation $c = \lambda \times f$. Sounds are generally sound events that are compounded from different frequencies.

The speed of sound in air depends on temperature and humidity; at 25°C and 50% RH (= relative humidity) it is 340m/s (thus also 340mm/ms). An acoustic wave of 10,000Hz (= 10kHz) thus has a wavelength of 34mm, and an acoustic wave of 100kHz has a wavelength of 3.4mm.

The energy of an acoustic wave is proportional to the square of the sound pressure amplitude. One usually indicates the volume as a logarithm of the energy in decibels (dB). 1dB = 10 logs (sound energy) = 20 logs (sound pressure), relative to a sound pressure of $2 \times 10^{-5} N/m^2$, which corresponds approximately to the auditory threshold of humans. In order to mark this reference to the auditory threshold of humans, one speaks of volumes as dB SPL (sound pressure level).

If an acoustic wave spreads, its energy distributes itself on an ever larger surface. Through that the sound energy decreases with the square of the distance. Therefore the sound pressure amplitude decreases with the linear distance, thus by 6dB for each doubling of the distance.

Apart from this so-called 'geometrical weakening' the sound pressure amplitude also becomes gradually lower with its extension, because it loses energy to air ('atmospheric absorption'). The atmospheric absorption (or attenuation) of an acoustic wave depends strongly on the frequency, but beyond that also on temperature and humidity. High frequencies are much more strongly absorbed than low frequencies (which is why thunder 'rumbles', although at the location of lightning striking rather clear crashing is to be heard).

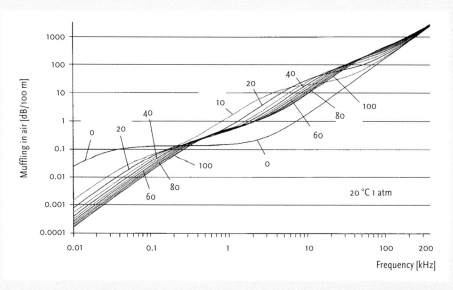

Fig. 50. Dependence of the atmospheric decrease on the frequency between 10Hz and 200kHz with a logarithmic application of the absorption on both axes. A temperature of 20°C and an air pressure of 1 atmosphere are adopted as constant, the curves for different relative air humidity are given. The absorption – even in a logarithmic scale as measured dB/100m – the attenuation within the given frequency range increases by the power of seven! After gen.lit. 34.

the ear and thus permit conclusions on the direction from which the echo arrives.

Variable 3: The call duration

Finally, bats can vary the duration of the emitted calls. Long calls increase the probability of detecting an interesting echo signal by improving the signal-to-noise ratio. For insect hunters in particular, it can be important to discover the periodic volume peaks ('glints'), which occur once per wingbeat with flying prey insects, from a direct reflection of the echo of the wings. A disadvantage of long calls, however, is the danger of swamping returning echoes when calling.

The 'design' of echolocation sounds

From these considerations it follows that it is very probably understandable that the ecological separation (or niching) of bats led to very different types of echolocation calls. A bat that predominantly hunts in open spaces high over the vegetation and, flying with high speed, needs particularly to locate far-distance obstacles and relatively large prey animals should use long calls of narrow bandwidth with a rather low frequency. A bat that mostly hunts in relatively more dense vegetation and which must particularly find insects against the background of this vegetation should use high-frequency calls with a large bandwidth.

It is also understandable that, generally, larger bats have calls with a lower frequency, because they are more interested in larger prey animals. Smaller bat species must detect and recognise rather smaller insects, for which they need higher frequencies and do not need a large range to seek their prey (see also Fig. 187, page 125). Naturally, the allometric relationship between the body size and the laryngeal size, which additionally results in longer vocal cords, also plays a role. But there are quite distinct exceptions to this rule: thus Mehely's Horseshoe Bat (*Rhinolophus*

mehelyi), despite being the second largest of the European horseshoe bats, has a very high call frequency, at around 110kHz, and overlaps with the calls of the smallest and lightest of our species, the Lesser Horseshoe Bat (*Rhinolophus hipposideros*). Similarly, Schreibers' Bent-winged Bat (*Miniopterus schreibersii*) has a surprisingly high call frequency, which seems to be connected with the high repetition rate of its echolocation calls.

The echolocation calls of the bats are not only specifically different, but each species adapts its calls to the respective flight habitat and hunting situation. A characteristic example is given in Fig. 57 on the basis of a series of echolocation calls of the Soprano Pipistrelle (*Pipistrellus pygmaeus*). When it flies from its roost far from the vegetation to a hunting ground ('commuting flight') or is still searching for a suitable hunting ground and has not yet discovered a prey animal ('search flight'), it calls with relatively long, nearly constant frequency qCF calls, usually at *c.* 52–56kHz (Fig. 57). If it is passing closer to obstacles, such as a house wall or trees, it uses calls with a larger bandwidth, which can begin well above 70kHz but still end with a flatter frequency-modulated part at about 52–56kHz. If it detects a possible prey insect, the 'approach phase' begins: the calls get steeper and shorter, the bandwidth is further enlarged, and the calls are emitted several times per wingbeat. Finally, with the direct catch attempt, a series of successive, extremely shortened calls are emitted very rapidly. One calls this final series of calls the 'terminal buzz'. After that, a brief call break usually follows – the bat has either caught the insect or missed it at the last moment – and then a new series of echolocation calls begins, which usually resemble in their rhythm and frequency those that are characteristic of the approach phase.

Wingbeat and call detection

Most bats have adapted the repetition rate of their calls to the rhythm of their wingbeats and call, at least in the search phase, once per flap of the wings. The echolocation call is normally emitted during the downward wingbeat; the contraction of the large

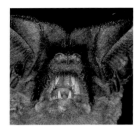

Fig. 51. Muzzle of European Free-tailed Bat (*Tadarida teniotis*). Photo: C. Dietz.

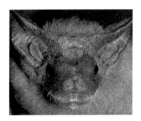

Fig. 52. Muzzle of Greater Mouse-tailed Bat (*Rhinopoma microphyllum*). Photo: C. Dietz.

Fig. 53. Muzzle of Egyptian Pipistrelle (*Pipistrellus deserti*). Photo: C. Dietz.

Fig. 54. Muzzle of Christie's Long-eared Bat (*Plecotus christiei*). Photo: C. Dietz.

Fig. 55. Ear of Mediterranean Horseshoe Bat (*Rhinolophus euryale*). Photo: C. Dietz.

Fig. 56. Typical call series of a high flying Noctule (*Nyctalus noctula*). It alternates a somewhat low frequency call (sounding through the detector as 'plop') and a somewhat higher frequency and more strongly modulated call (sounding more like 'plip'). In this way the later returning echoes are identifiable by their frequency and can be assigned to the correct call. Graph: M. Bauer.

flight muscles probably eases the expelling of air from the lungs and additional energy for the call is thus not needed. Only when in the approach or terminal phase is successive information more frequently needed about an object, and then several calls may follow during one wingbeat cycle.

In bat species that use calls which have a particularly long range (generally relatively long, constant-frequency and low-frequency calls), there is a further problem. What happens if the echo of an object, especially a large obstacle, such as a wall or the edge of a forest, which may be far distant but its size produces a very loud echo, arrives only after one wingbeat cycle, and hence after a new call has been emitted? Such an echo may be quite quiet, because of the large distance, but will possibly arrive very soon after the end of the second call. In this event, there exists, for the bat, a danger of confusion with a similar echo which might be received from a small, but nearby, obstacle, perhaps a branch or thorn, so that, in this case, the bat must brake or swerve immediately in order to prevent a collision.

In order to avoid such unpleasant situations, some fast-flying species have two different strategies available: either they emit the echolocation call in such a situation with each second wingbeat or they mark the echoes of their calls by the fact that they use another frequency with every second call, so that they can recognise immediately, by their frequency, echoes that still originate from the preceding call cycle. This is the reason for the well-known 'plip–plop' of Noctule Bats, which, in a hunting situation

in the search flight, always alternate a somewhat lower frequency echolocation call with a somewhat higher frequency call (see Fig. 56).

Evolution of echolocation

How can a so tremendously complex and nevertheless precise detection system have developed through evolution? For such a question one can look for an answer only from comparative observation. On a search the following observation stands out: two unrelated bird species have developed echolocation, although far more primitive than that of the bats. These are, first, the Oilbird (*Steatornis caripensis*), which was discovered by A. von Humboldt in some large caves in Venezuela. These large birds, related to nightjars, nest deep inside large caves and nourish themselves particularly with palm fruits, from which even the young become so fat that the Indians take them in their hundreds to collect their fat above small fires and to use the fat for lamps. In order to find their way in the darkness of the large caves, in which they build their nests in cavities in the walls, they constantly emit loud cries and orient themselves with the help of the echoes. A second group of birds that have developed a system of echolocation are the cave swiftlets of Southeast Asia, which likewise live in large dark caves, where they stick their nests, made from their own saliva, to the walls. These are the 'swift nests', which are a special delicacy of the Chinese markets for 'birds' nest soup'. These cave swiftlets (Genus *Collocallia* – the species that echolocate are sometimes considered to form a separate genus, *Aerodramus*) have developed an echolocation system using sounds for orientation in the darkness of caves, but these sounds also lie in the range audible for humans.

The only other land mammals that have developed echolocation independently from the other bats are the fruit bats of the genus *Rousettus*, which likewise live in

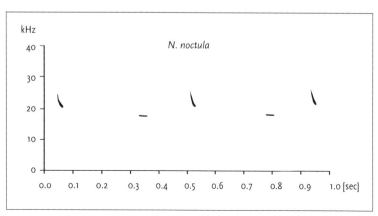

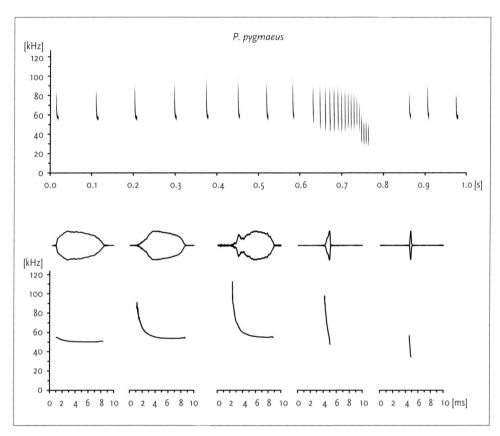

P. pygmaeus

Fig. 57. Approach and prey-catch by a Soprano Pipistrelle (*Pipistrellus pygmaeus*). The echolocation calls in the approach phase are always steeper and with a wider bandwidth and their repetition rate increases. Then follows a 'final group', the terminal buzz, with two extremely short call types differing in their frequency. In the lower line is one detection call each from the search phase, the early and the somewhat later approach phase and representation of the two parts of the terminal buzz. Graph: M. Bauer.

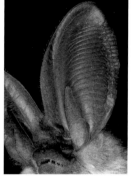

Fig. 58. Ear of Balkan Long-eared Bat (*Plecotus kolombatovici*). Photo: C. Dietz.

Box 5

Physical parameters that determine the 'design' of echolocation calls

		Advantages	Disadvantages
Call duration	long	high signal-to-noise ratio of the echo, since much energy is integral	overlap of echoes of close objects with the call – 'blind window' very large
	short	'blind window' small, more accurate measurement of runtime & distance	smaller signal-to-noise ratio
Frequency	high	high resolution of structures	strong absorption in air limits range
	low	large range, because the atmospheric absorption is smaller	poor resolution of structures
Bandwidth	large	frequency spectrum of the echoes analysable (direction, structure), cross-correlation of call and echo more precise	no specialisation of the hearing on certain frequencies possible, less energy in a group of frequencies
	small	hearing can be particularly sensitive for the call frequency, Doppler effect usable	spectrum of the echo does not contain information about the direction, distance & object structure

Fig. 59. Ear of Greater Mouse-eared Bat (*Myotis myotis*). Photo: C. Dietz.

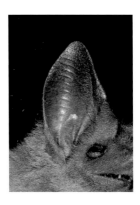

Fig. 60. Ear of Lesser Mouse-tailed Bat (*Rhinopoma hardwickii*). Photo: C. Dietz.

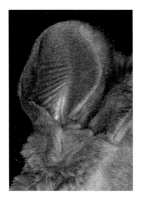

Fig. 61. Ear of European Free-tailed Bat (*Tadarida teniotis*). Photo: C. Dietz.

Fig. 62. Ear of Northern Bat (*Eptesicus nilssonii*). Photo: C. Dietz.

caves. They produce sounds by tongue clicking. This thus speaks much for the idea that the crucial selection pressure for the development of an echolocation system proceeded from the necessity to orient in dark caves. In addition, the extensive cave walls, well adapted for sound reflection, and the silence that usually prevails in caves might have facilitated the evolution of an acoustic orientation by echoes.

The question is undecided as to whether the Megachiroptera later lost an acoustic detection system, even if only the possible beginning of such a system, which is probably the most economical explanation, or whether the horseshoe bat relatives have redeveloped their echolocation in convergence with the Vespertilioniformes. Considering the structure and size of their ear capsules, the Eocene bats (*Icaronycteris* and the Eocene bats of the Messel pit in Germany) already had a system for ultrasonic echo-orientation.

A conception of how echolocation could have been developed within the bats is outlined in Fig. 65. If one assumes that the common ancestors of the Pteropodiformes and the Vespertilioniformes perhaps already had an, as yet simple, echolocation system, then it is noticeable that, examining the echolocation calls of both, they are relatively similar, especially in the original families of the two basal branches of the family tree, the Hipposiderids and the Emballonurids respectively. Their calls are not too long, more or less constant frequency, calls often with several harmonics available and with a short rise of frequency at the beginning of the call and a short, falling-frequency part at the end of the call. One would also expect calls of this structure if a mammal wants to produce a loud call and with that harnesses its vocal cords tightly for a short time. Also the endemic bat species of New Zealand, *Mystacina*, has similar calls.

Calls of this type could have been, on the one hand, developed further in the direction of the horseshoe bats (Rhinolophidae), by using the constant frequency for a Doppler effect compensation, with all its advantages already described, and which

would then have led particularly to an extension of the echolocation calls, a high 'duty cycle' and the restriction to only one harmonic, exactly as is the case in the horseshoe bats. Both today's Emballonurids and the Rhinolophids use the first harmonic for their echolocation calls and suppress the fundamental frequency.

For those bats that did not, in their evolution, hit upon the 'ingenious idea' of the horseshoe bats, the original call type has the disadvantage that it, even with the use of many harmonics, does not become truly wide-banded. Yet, if such calls modulate their frequency, then as soon as the harmonics overlap such calls completely cover a broad frequency band. That is exactly the case in the beginning with the Rhinopomatids, *Mystacina* and Craseonycteris. In the Megadermatids, and in many Vespertilioniformes, this was developed further, obviously in parallel, to perfection. Some vesper bats (Vespertilionidae) have maintained this type of call, e.g. the long-eared bats (Genus *Plecotus*), likewise most of the spear-nosed bats of the New World (Phyllostomidae). In contrast, most vesper bats have themselves specialised in emitting the fundamental frequency (and thus filtering out the upper harmonics) and have developed completely different, steeply modulated calls. Their echolocation calls range from narrow-banded, flat modulated calls up to extremely wide-banded, steeply modulated calls. Also some spear-nosed bats, e.g. the species of the genus *Phyllonycteris*, use such calls, whose fundamental frequency is stressed. Some other relatives of the spear-nosed bats have developed rather horseshoe-bat-like calls from the basic type, such as the Fisherman Bat (Genus *Noctilio*) or secondarily also Parnell's Moustached Bat (*Pteronotus parnellii*).

An overview

There was, then, a long gap between the early experiments on bat orientation by Spallanzani and Jurine in the 1790s and the demonstration of ultrasound and its use by bats in the late 1930s. Even then things moved slowly, and it was not until the early 1960s that portable field equipment for the study of bat echolocation calls became available. But in the following 45 years there were huge advances in this fascinating and complex field of bat biology. These advances have developed in many directions: in the basic understanding of echolocation and how it works; the evidence that it may have been developed more than once, possibly several times, in bats; the way it has diversified to meet the requirements of different bat species (or, perhaps, that it has rather offered the opportunities for bats to diversify to the extent that they have); in the information it gives us about the general behaviour of bats; and the opportunities for the study of bats and their behaviour in the field.

Perhaps it is the latter area – the study of bats in the field – that will be the main contributor to bat study and conservation. The traditional study of bats at their roosts is considerably boosted by the development of field equipment to study, survey and monitor bats in the field. Protecting the roosts is important but of limited value without a good knowledge of the wider habitats needed for foraging. We may never be able to identify every bat that passes by, but the opportunities to collect information and, if needed, to verify information from subsequent on-site or laboratory analysis have developed enormously in recent years and will continue to develop and to become more accessible to both amateurs and professionals (see under Bat detectors, p. 124).

Fig. 63. Ear of Natterer's Bat (*Myotis nattereri*). Photo: C. Dietz.

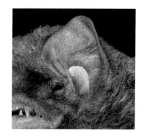

Fig. 64. Ear of Schreibers' Bent-winged Bat (*Miniopterus schreibersii*). Photo: C. Dietz.

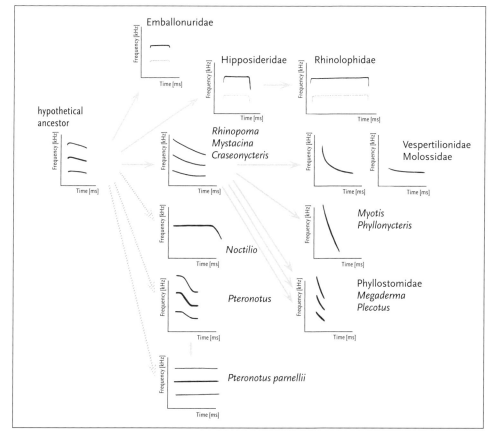

Fig. 65. A hypothesis for the evolution of echolocation calls. The original form might have been a weak frequency-modulated call with several harmonics, as is still found in *Rhinopoma*, *Mystacina* and *Craseonycteris*. The Emballonurids and the Hipposiderids also have similar calls. From here the special echolocation calls of the Rhinolophids developed. But this type of call also led to the development of the calls of the Vespertilionids and Molossids, which use only one harmonic, and also convergently the repeatedly developed multi-harmonic echolocation calls of *Plecotus*, most Phyllostomids and the Megadermatids. An independent development leads to the Noctilionids and the Mormoopids. Graph: M. Bauer.

Foraging and feeding behaviour

Bats hunt mostly during the night and so use the great sensitivity of their hearing in order to hear the noises of prey animals, for instance the humming of a fly or the rustling of a ground beetle in leaves, or to receive the echoes of the ultrasonic sounds that the bats have emitted. They need no light for orientation, but are by no means blind. Probably they can, even on dark nights, identify the horizon outline of forests and mountains and perhaps use these, and also the moon, as landmarks for remote orientation.

There are a few observations that bats also use their eyes for hunting: thus long-eared bats preferred feeding saucers of mealworms that were a little illuminated in preference to those in complete darkness [gen. lit. 31]. Northern Bats were observed to have the ability to recognise optically and hunt in the dusk the remarkably white males of the Ghost Swift Moth (*Hepialus humuli*), which often swarm in tall grass [gen. lit. 32, 108].

Normally bats hunt with the help of their sense of hearing. If one observes swallows and bats hunting insects together, which is possible sometimes at dusk, then it is particularly noticeable that swallows nearly always capture individual insects in horizontal flight or flying slightly upward. Bats, however, make a nose dive from above on larger prey insects. That is probably connected with the fact that swallows detect prey animals with the eyes – they see the insects best against the bright sky above the line of the horizon. For an echolocating bat, it is, however, unimportant whether an object is above or below the horizon. However, it is important that it is in a clutter-free window. If the insect flies underneath the bat, it is even easier to capture it, because the bat can achieve higher speeds in a dive.

Why are bats almost exclusively active at night? Only rarely can one see bats hunting in the daytime, for example when they emerge very early through hunger to hunt after a long period of bad weather, or in the autumn when Noctules begin to hunt high in the sky in the late afternoon, in order to further increase their fat reserves for the winter. But, generally speaking, there are no day-active bat species, despite the large number of bat species world-wide. Several explanations have been discussed, such as the pressure of predation by birds of prey, competition for food with day-active birds and the danger of overheating from sunlight, since the large surface area of bats' flight membranes can absorb a lot of heat [gen. lit. 132].

Bats are rather helpless against birds of prey. When one observes in Europe a Peregrine Falcon (*Falco peregrinus*), which hunts Noctule Bats, in South America a specialist bat predator in the Bat Falcon (*Falco rufigularis*), or a Bat Hawk (*Machaeramphus alcinus*) at a cave in Borneo, then one has the impression that it is child's play for the birds of prey to capture bat after bat in flight. It looks as if the bats simply cannot detect at all a falcon attacking from the rear. Probably the echolocation is unsuitable for this. The fact that bats are easy prey seems to be known to birds of prey, because if a bat is forced to leave its roost in daytime and it flies off without quickly finding a hiding place, then it will usually be attacked immediately, if a falcon or a sparrowhawk is nearby.

One also often sees song birds, e.g. swallows, chasing day-flying bats. Crag Martins (*Ptyonoprogne rupestris*) once attacked a Greater Noctule (*Nyctalus lasiopterus*) so violently that it had to make dives to safety [own observation].

If the predator pressure from birds of prey is the principal reason for the nocturnal life of bats, in areas where there are no birds of prey they should be at least partly day-active. Such a bird of prey-free area is the Azores Islands. Here there are no bat-hunting falcons or other such enemies. And actually one can observe the Azorean Noctule Bat (*Nyctalus azoreum*) much more often in day time than its closest relative on the European mainland, Leisler's Bat (*Nyctalus leisleri*). Nevertheless, detailed studies have shown that the main hunting period of the Azorean Noctule Bat is still in the night [gen. lit. 59]. But why then do bats prefer to fly in the night?

Perhaps it is because of the fact that bats simply find much more prey at night, because the competition with birds is avoided. A further factor, which was particularly raised into discussion by J.R. Speakman, is the possibility of overheating of the bat's body by the absorption of sunlight through the large wings, which are not protected by fur and represent a very large surface area [gen. lit. 132]. Radiation measurements show that the wings actually show a very high light absorption and an associated heat uptake; this heat is released by the passage of air running over the wing. But that can probably be interpreted rather as a secondary, just an additional, adaptation to the night activity, which was forced in the evolution of the bats primarily by the selection factors of danger from birds of prey and food competition with birds.

Even if bats orient themselves essentially with 'active acoustics' and use the help of the echo's 'sound picture' as a means to seek out their prey, there are also many bats that locate their prey animals by 'passive listening'. Many insects produce sounds and the excellent hearing of bats can naturally detect these noises. Thus, particularly threatened are those insects which use intraspecific acoustic communication, particularly bush crickets and crickets. Singing bush cricket males go silent if they hear the echolocation sounds of bats. The bats are very good at it, because they can hear the bush cricket singing at least as well as the bush cricket females.

But many other insects similarly produce noises without 'wanting' to use these as communication signals. Mosquitoes and other Diptera hum when they fly, because the beating of the wings produces rhythmic pressure fluctuations of air. Who

Fig. 66. Long-eared bats are very agile fliers and can capture their prey, usually moths, even close to the vegetation. Photo: D. Nill.

has not been driven mad by the high whine of a mosquito flying in the bedroom at night? Beetles also hum in flight and are just as audible. In particular bats are immediately attentive when they hear rustling sounds. Even we can actually hear the sound of mealworms creeping around in a small plastic bowl, and can be astonished as to how clearly one hears it. Ground beetles hunting in the dry leaves of a beech forest are much louder. In dry leaves one can even hear a running spider. It is clear that many bats utilise these unintended sounds.

The hunting methods of bats are at least as varied as those of birds. Besides the hunters in open spaces ('aerial hawking bats'), there are also perch hunters, which like the flycatchers among the birds watch the surroundings from a hanging place (perch) and only fly off if they discover a prey animal. Other species hunt close amongst the vegetation ('gleaning bats'); with them also belong the ground foragers, which fly with slow flight low over the forest floor and then drop onto prey insects whose rustlings they have heard.

Hunting in the open

The detection of prey animals is easiest in open spaces, since there are no or only a few faint confusing background echoes. Most insectivorous bats in Europe, such as the Common Pipistrelle (*Pipistrellus pipistrellus*) (Fig. 69) or the Noctule (*Nyctalus noctula*) are aerial hawkers. While many *Myotis* species or the Common Pipistrelle mostly hunt close to trees, above clearings or above forest trails and use for their echolocation the 'clutter-free window', other bats such as Noctule, European Free-tailed Bat (*Tadarida teniotis*), or the North African tomb bats (*Taphozous* spp.) fly high and

Fig. 67. To drink, bats fly close above the water surface. Usually they prefer the calmest water areas. Photo: D. Nill.

Fig. 68. Long-eared bats usually transport large prey like this tiger moth (Arctiidae) to a special feeding site in order to consume it in peace. Photo: D. Nill.

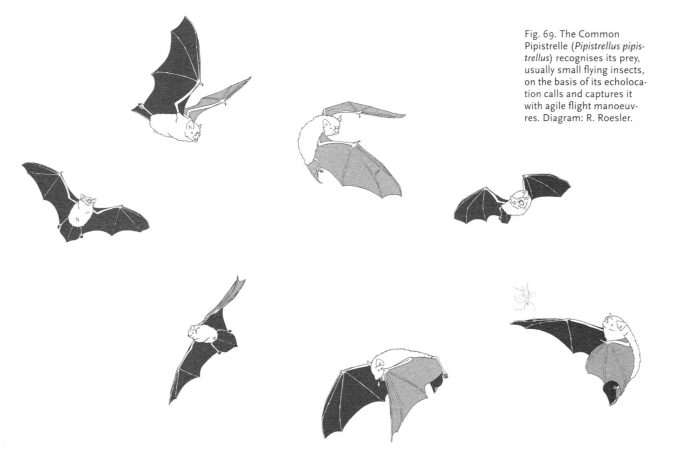

Fig. 69. The Common Pipistrelle (*Pipistrellus pipistrellus*) recognises its prey, usually small flying insects, on the basis of its echolocation calls and captures it with agile flight manoeuvres. Diagram: R. Roesler.

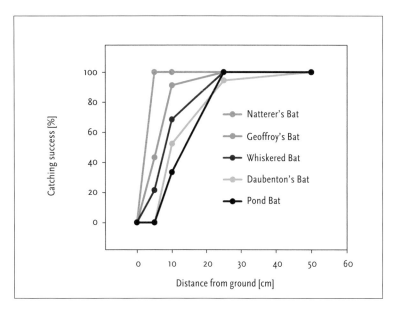

Fig. 70. Catch success as a function of the distance of prey from an echo-producing background. Björn Siemers hung mealworms on fine threads at different distances from a solid background (abscissa), and recorded in what percent of all observations a bat had taken the mealworm within 5 minutes. It showed that with the different *Myotis* species, species with a wider-bandwidth echolocation call did this task the better. Natterer's Bat (*Myotis nattereri*) was the best, catching all mealworms even with a wall distance of only 5 centimetres. From gen. lit. 125. Graph: B. Siemers.

Fig. 71. Geoffroy's Bat (*Myotis emarginatus*) is a regular specialist in capturing spiders. Photo: D. Nill.

fast in the sky, often far above the tree canopy or over mountain meadows. If a Noctule discovers a prey animal below it (or if one throws a small stone, which it mistakenly identifies as a prey animal), it can dive very fast by rolling itself over its shoulder, flying momentarily on its back and then rushing perpendicularly downward. Other species fly more slowly, but are, however, much more manoeuvrable.

Hunting near vegetation

The overlap of the prey animal's echoes with echoes arriving at the same time from vegetation behind or around it, or from a tree trunk or a rock on which the prey animal rests, represents the largest problem for the echo sound picture of bats. Through evolution two solutions have been developed in principle to cope with even this niche. Horseshoe bats with their long echolocation calls detect the wing fluttering of an insect, even if this flies directly in front of the vegetation, or possibly sits on a tree trunk buzzing with its wings. They detect the flapping of the wings, because the echo volume (because of the effect of the reflection of the sound from certain wing positions) and audio frequency (because of the Doppler effect) change with the frequency of the flapping of the wings.

The vesper bats solved this problem

differently. The small species of the genus *Myotis* improve the resolution of the distance to the background by using extremely short calls and in addition increasing the bandwidth. In experiments, B. Siemers offered a mealworm hanging on a thread at different distances from a wall, and he showed how well in the Central European *Myotis* species the detection ability at different background distances correlates with the call design and with the ecological niche (Fig. 70); the wider the bandwidth and the shorter the echolocation calls of a species are, the better it can recognize prey insects when they fly relatively close to an echoing background.

Hunting on the ground

The Greater Mouse-eared Bat (*Myotis myotis*) (Figs 73–75) and also Bechstein's Bat (*Myotis bechsteinii*) sometimes hunt for flying insects, but at other times their prey spectrum contains numerous flightless arthropods, particularly beetles and bush crickets with the Greater Mouse-eared Bat, with Bechstein's Bat insects such as small ground beetles and earwigs, caterpillars, ground spiders, harvestmen and even centipedes. These prey animals are in particular passively located. The Greater Mouse-eared Bat often flies as low as less

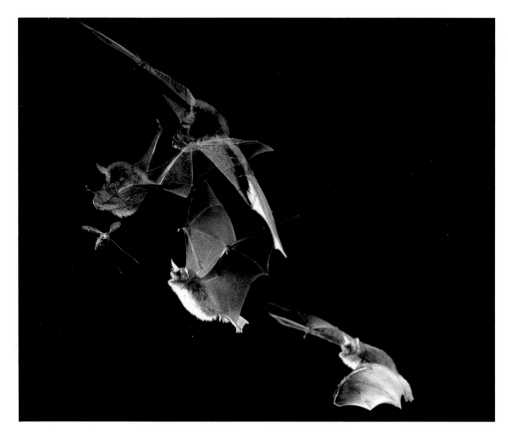

Fig. 72. Hunting sequence of a Natterer's Bat (*Myotis nattereri*) chasing a crane-fly, using stroboscope exposure. Photo: D. Nill.

than half a metre above the forest floor or over a meadow [gen. lit. 4, 5] and lands if it hears a rustling insect. If it does not have immediate success in capturing the prey, it tries to pursue the insect on foot and seize the insect with its mouth.

Perch hunting

The flycatcher technology is particularly used by horseshoe bats. Horseshoe bats can hang on a branch for many minutes, often a regular perch that they visit again and again, and from there scan the surroundings (Figs 76 and 77). Hanging by their long hind legs they twist the body around its longitudinal axis and thus watch the entire surroundings for 180°. If they detect an insect, they fly off and try to catch it, then often return straight to their perch. Greater Mouse-eared Bats readily interrupt their low hunting flight for a short rest on a tree trunk in the forest, from which they then listen attentively to all noises of crawling insects in the surroundings.

Hunting over water

Several indigenous bats species hunt preferentially over water surfaces and pick up insects that have fallen onto the water surface and are swimming there. They may take the prey with their feet, in order to then pass it to their mouth. These species include Daubenton's Bat (*Myotis daubentonii*), Pond Bat (*Myotis dasycneme*) and particularly Long-fingered Bat (*Myotis capaccinii*), but also Balkan Whiskered Bat (*Myotis mystacinus bulgaricus*). One recognises these species morphologically by their large hind feet with very long toes, and by the fact that the hind feet are free from the flight membrane. This is most noticeable in the Long-fingered Bat, in which the lateral flight membrane is set above the heel on the tibia. In the moonlight it can be seen that Daubenton's and Long-fingered Bats often draw a small silvery furrow through the water surface as they trawl with their feet and tail tip for an insect on the water surface.

Fig. 73. The Greater Mouse-eared Bat (*Myotis myotis*) uses the scuffling sound produced by the preferred prey, usually ground-living insects, to locate it. On the ground or in the vegetation this prey cannot be recognised by echolocation signals. Diagram: R. Roesler.

Objects on a calm water surface are particularly good to detect by an echolocating bat, since the water surface essentially reflects the echo itself away from the bat during the diagonal approach, but the body of a swimming insect on the water surface sends an echo back to the bat (Fig. 78). In this way a prey is very noticeable and the signal-to-noise ratio is almost as good as in open spaces – with the additional large advantage that prey animals that swim on the water surface cannot escape so fast.

Fig. 74. Shortly before grabbing the prey the Greater Mouse-eared Bat (*Myotis myotis*) locates the scuffling sound directly below it. Photo: D. Nill.

Fig. 75. Take-off of a Greater Mouse-eared Bat (*Myotis myotis*) after taking prey from the ground. Photo: D. Nill.

Flexibility of the hunting strategy

Bats can be very flexible when they use alternative available hunting strategies to catch different prey animals, as they often do. Thus it has been observed that Long-fingered Bats (*Myotis capaccinii*) regularly feed on small fish, as soon as these swim in shoals close to the water surface [gen. lit. 2]. Also the Greater Noctule (*Nyctalus lasiopterus*) probably became a bird hunter in much the same way. A migrating Wren does perhaps not differ too much in its echo image from a large grasshopper. However, it is surely not so easy for an insectivorous animal to eat meat, because then the ballast material of the chitinous wing cases, etc. are absent. That is why a Greater Noctule, if one gives it a dead bird, first eats many

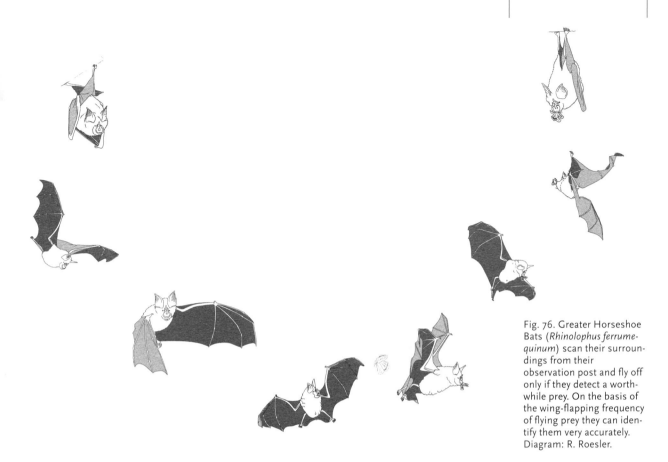

Fig. 76. Greater Horseshoe Bats (*Rhinolophus ferrumequinum*) scan their surroundings from their observation post and fly off only if they detect a worthwhile prey. On the basis of the wing-flapping frequency of flying prey they can identify them very accurately. Diagram: R. Roesler.

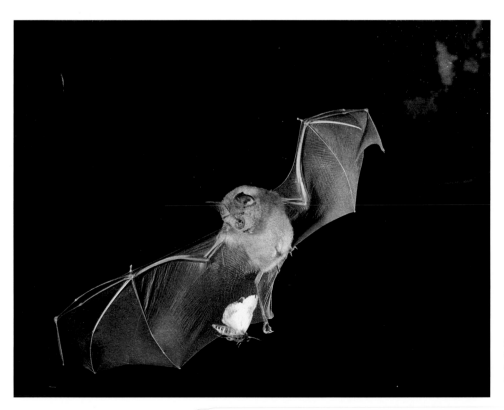

Fig. 77. The Greater Horseshoe Bat (*Rhinolophus ferrumequinum*) usually captures an insect with the wing and passes it to the mouth. Photo: D. Nill.

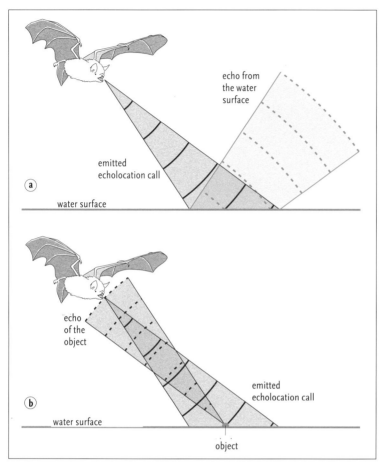

feathers before it begins the consumption of the meat or entrails [own data]. Probably they need the feathers to aid their digestion. Similarly, one knows from Great Crested Grebes that the chicks, when they are still very small, are fed by the parent not only with fresh, small fish but also with downy feathers plucked from itself.

Prey spectra

The prey spectra of the different bat species, which can be constructed, for example, from droppings analysis (see page 58), differ clearly from species to species. Only in this way it is possible that so many insectivorous bat species can occur together in Europe, without excluding each other by mutual competition. They all have occupied different food niches in their evolution – even if these food niches often overlap to a great extent. In an oak forest, if the Green Oak Moth (*Tortrix viridana*) flies, then almost all bats eat Green Oak Moths. When sexually active ants of different species swarm in the pine–dune forests of the Mediterranean region, then nearly all bats eat ants on this night.

Fig. 78. Hunting over a smooth water surface gives the advantage that sound hitting the surface is mostly reflected away from the bat (a), and it only gets an echo back if an object, e.g. a prey animal, is on the water surface (b). Diagram: R. Roesler.

Fig. 79. Daubenton's Bats (*Myotis daubentonii*) hunt close above the water surface and grab swimming prey with their feet. At least in the laboratory they also readily accept small fish as prey. Photo: D. Nill.

Prey range

Do bats hunt 'opportunistically' or do they hunt 'selectively'? This question actually sounds at first like an alternative, but it is not. A bat will consume first any prey animal that it can discover and capture with its catching strategy, as long as it is not distasteful and is not dangerous, e.g. stings. Why should it not take it? In the event of a choice it will prefer that prey animal that has the most favourable cost/use ratio – thus with the smallest expenditure of time and effort provides the most calories. The selectivity of the hunt is that different bat species visit different habitats for hunting, e.g. because their flight technology is adapted to different degrees for the level of clutter, because different species discover particularly quickly different prey animals through specialisation of their hearing and their echolocation calls, and because they can capture different insect species with less expenditure with their respective foraging technology.

Thus bats hunt selectively, but are thereby opportunistic.

An understanding of the foraging habitats and feeding behaviour of bats has become increasingly recognised as crucial for the conservation of many species. Thus the earlier concentration on conservation of roost sites is now complemented with studies of their habitat preferences and feeding activity. This is largely due to a range of technological advances that have been made in recent years, in particular the development in the ability to deploy ultrasonic receivers (bat detectors) in the field, either hand operated or as remote automatic recording devices, and the use of transmitters to give detailed information about the habitat use of individual bats. Other techniques are available and may be more or less intrusive, but may be more or less restricted in their application and the costs involved can vary greatly.

For the study of bats in the field, see UK gen. lit. 158.

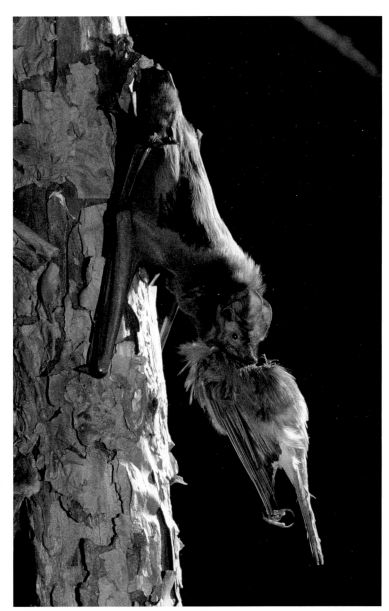

Fig. 80. The Greater Noctule (*Nyctalus lasiopterus*) has been shown to include small birds in its diet. Whether they consume these in flight or, as here, in a hanging position is not yet clarified. Photo: D. Nill.

Food of bats

The European bat species feed almost exclusively on insects and other arthropods, including spiders, harvestmen and centipedes. These prey animals possess an external skeleton made of chitin, which will be chewed into small pieces by the bats during eating. In the digestive tract the chitin is not decomposed, and so it is possible to determine the prey species with the help of the analysis of the fragments in the faecal pellets.

Faecal analysis

For analysis the faecal pellets (droppings) are soaked in water or alcohol and then teased apart under a binocular microscope, whereafter the prey remains are determined, as far as is possible. Usually a specialist with experience in this practice recognises the arthropod orders associated with included prey items (e.g. moths, Hymenoptera, beetles, harvestmen) relatively quickly – often by small, but characteristic features of the tiny fragments. The prey remains can be divided firstly into these rough categories. Also characteristic bits specific to a family of the prey items frequently survive passage through the gut of the bat intact. An example is that moths (Noctuidae) may be recognised by a conspicuous distinctive spur on the tarsal claws, the large scarabeid and chafer beetles (Scarabaeidae) by the typically formed antennae, the ground beetles (Carabidae) by a deep notch on the tibia of the first leg, or the family Hydropsychidae of the caddis flies (Trichoptera) recognised by a dark diagonal line on the basal part of the antenna.

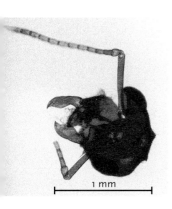

Fig. 81. Ant head from the faeces of a Serotine Bat (*Eptesicus serotinus*). Photo: I. Wolz.

Identification of prey animals

Characteristic parts for genus or species identification are comparatively rarely found in the fragmented material, but have a special value: if these fragments come from prey animals that occur in particular habitats, e.g. with many spiders, then this allows the possibility of obtaining an insight into the hunting behaviour of the bats from the prey. For example, the finding of the funnel-web spider, *Coelotes terrestris*, (species-typical characteristic: pedipalp of the males) shows that Bechstein's Bat (*Myotis bechsteinii*) can take its prey directly from the ground [gen. lit. 149, 150]. Another species-specific characteristic for such interesting ecological references is the coxal pores of the 15th pair of legs of the Brown Centipede (*Lithobius forficatus*), which can also only be captured by bats from the ground. Yet another example of an ecological statement deriving from the ability to determine prey remains precisely are the cerci of the large crane fly (*Tipula scripta*), a Diptera species, which occurs particularly in May and at the beginning of June in coniferous forests.

From a quantitative collection of the prey spectrum it is possible to estimate the percentage by volume of different prey animal groups in the total amount of existing material (percentage by volume), or the frequency of appearance of a prey item in the number of faecal pellets of a sample examined (proportional frequency). It should be noted that due to heavy chewing of the prey animals a number of possible errors with the analysis can occur. Hard, strongly chitinised and multicoloured arthropods, such as beetles or bugs, are recorded more easily in the fragmented material than soft-bodied prey animals (lacewings, mayflies or small midges). This can lead to an overestimation of individual groups of prey in the diet spectrum. Also, moth scales in the pellets can be misleading. After a meal with many moths one can still find scales in the bat excrement for days afterwards, even if the animal has eaten no more moths. That can suggest an overestimation of the moths in the diet spectrum.

Prey range and hunting strategy

In the prey spectrum the niching of a species with regard to its hunting strategy will be apparent. Leisler's Bat (*Nyctalus leisleri*) hunts its prey in flight, with moths, Diptera, caddis flies and other airborne insects (left area in Fig. 92) forming its main prey. Plant remains in the droppings are always a reference to the bats failing to catch prey close to vegetation or to gleaning prey from plants or from leaves on the ground.

Bat species such as the Brown Long-eared Bat (*Plecotus auritus*), Bechstein's Bat (*Myotis bechsteinii*) or Natterer's Bat (*Myotis nattereri*) are able to pick their prey directly from leaves, branches and bark, but also hunt in flight, or can land on the ground to catch arthropods. Their prey spectrum typically contains both flying prey and non-flying animals, such as bugs, earwigs or bush-crickets (middle area in Fig. 93) or completely non-flying prey such as spiders, harvestmen and various larvae (right area in Fig. 93). The prey spectrum of the Brown long-eared Bat shows this particularly clearly: besides moths and bugs, many non-flying animals (earwigs, spiders, lepidopteran caterpillars) form a large part of the prey at some seasons. But many plant remains in the faecal samples indicate the frequent contact of the hunting bat with vegetation or the ground.

Greater Mouse-eared Bat as a food specialist

Beetles have a privileged position as prey animals of bats. With approximately 380,000 species worldwide they form the most species-rich order of animals and are found in all hunting habitats of bats. There are both flying and completely flightless beetle species. Thus almost all bat species

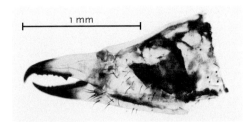

Fig. 82. Mouth parts of a harvestman from the faeces of a Brown Long-eared Bat (*Plecotus auritus*). Photo: I. Wolz.

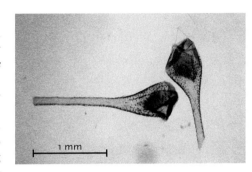

Fig. 83. Two halteres of a common crane-fly from the faeces of an Alpine Long-eared Bat (*Plecotus macrobullaris*). Photo: I. Wolz.

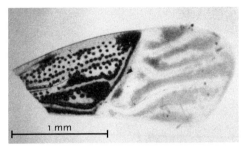

Fig. 84. Wing fragment of a heteropteran bug from the faeces of a Serotine Bat (*Eptesicus serotinus*). Photo: I. Wolz.

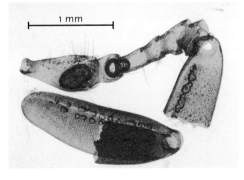

Fig. 85. Fragment of the antenna of a beetle of the family Scarabaeoidea from the faeces of a Greater Noctule (*Nyctalus lasiopterus*). Photo: I. Wolz.

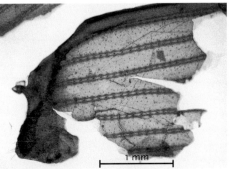

Fig. 86. Portion of a beetle elytron from the faeces of a Greater Mouse-eared Bat (*Myotis myotis*). Photo: I. Wolz.

Fig. 87. Antenna of a heteropteran bug from the faeces of an Alcathoe Whiskered Bat (*Myotis alcathoe*). Photo: I. Wolz.

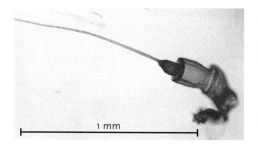

►► Fig. 88. Tarsomere of a large cockchafer (Scarabaeidae) from the faeces of a Greater Noctule (*Nyctalus lasiopterus*). Photo: I. Wolz.

► Fig. 89. Gizzard fragment of a large bush cricket from the faeces of a Greater Noctule (*Nyctalus lasiopterus*). Photo: I. Wolz.

►► Fig. 90. Portion of a moth antenna from the faeces of a Bechstein's Bat (*Myotis bechsteinii*). Photo: I. Wolz.

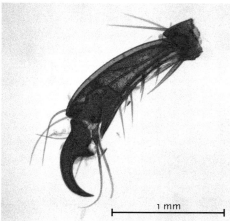

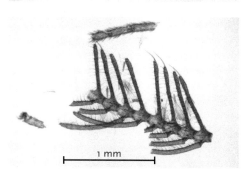

can be said to include beetles in their prey spectrum. For the Greater Mouse-eared Bat (*Myotis myotis*) it is known that it feeds mainly on ground-dwelling large beetles, particularly ground beetles, which are recognised by the rustling sounds of the beetles on the forest floor. In their hunt for food the Greater Mouse-eared Bats then land on the ground and search for their preferred food. If one catches them during their foraging period, they often smell intensively of the pungent odour that large ground beetles (*Carabus* species) exude as a defence secretion. The prey spectrum of Greater Mouse-eared Bats is characterised

Fig. 91. Depending upon the body size of the bat and kind of food, the faeces of different bat species can look very different. At the top: the ruler shows divisions of 1 mm. Upper row from left to right: Greater Mouse-eared Bat (*Myotis myotis*), Bechstein's Bat (*Myotis bechsteinii*), Whiskered Bat (*Myotis mystacinus*). Lower row from left to right: Leisler's Bat (*Nyctalus leisleri*), Brown Long-eared Bat (*Plecotus auritus*) and Common Pipistrelle (*Pipistrellus pipistrellus*). Photo: C. Dietz.

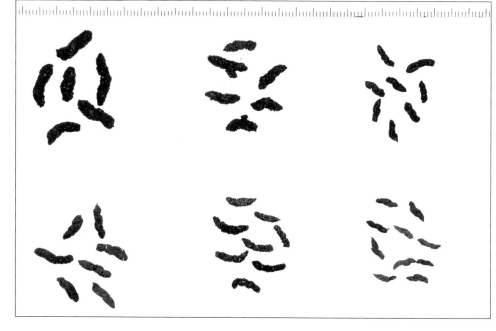

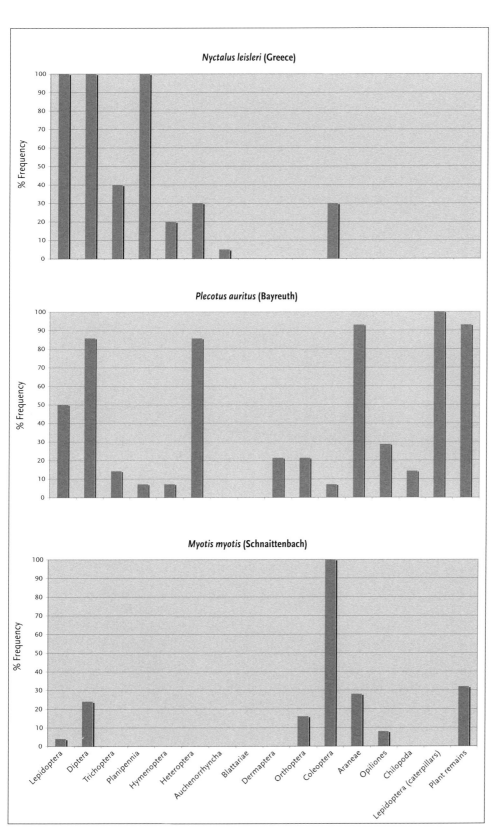

Fig. 92. Prey spectrum of Leisler's Bat (*Nyctalus leisleri*) from Greece. Data: I. Wolz.

Fig. 93. Prey spectrum of Brown Long-eared Bat (*Plecotus auritus*) from Bayreuth (Germany). Data: I. Wolz.

Fig. 94. Prey spectrum of the Greater Mouse-eared Bat (*Myotis myotis*) in the Schnaittenbacher forest (Germany). Data: I. Wolz.

by a small number of flying prey, ground-dwelling beetles usually forming the main food item, followed by flightless arthropods, such as spiders, harvestmen, centipedes and various larvae. Also plant remains, such as bits of leaf and moss fragments, are regularly found in their droppings.

Prey preferences

Many variations of the typical prey spectra are possible. Bats forage to a great extent 'opportunistically' since they take such prey animals that can be acquired frequently and easily during a night's foraging, and so may include prey not typical of the usual prey spectrum of the particular bat species. Thus the prey spectrum of the mouse-eared bats can, at times, be dominated by moths or large flies of the family Tipulidae, if these are common in the hunting period and represent an easy prey.

Investigations at a netting location in Greece showed that for seven of ten trapped bat species (from small species such as Common Pipistrelle (*Pipistrellus pipistrellus*), up to the Greater Noctule (*Nyctalus lasiopterus*)), ants provided the main prey caught when these were swarming during the foraging period. Under such conditions the differences between the prey spectra are reduced, as all foraging animals concentrate on catching great quantities of flying prey that can be acquired easily. Techniques for the study of prey remains in bat faecal pellets can be found in UK gen. lit. 162 and a summary of results of such studies for bat species occurring in Britain in UK gen. lit. 163.

Species identification from their droppings

When checking bat boxes, roof spaces or crevice roosts in building facades, one is more likely to find evidence, usually droppings, of the seasonal presence of bats, rather than seeing the bats themselves, particularly since the droppings keep many years under good conditions.

Once one excludes other animals as a source – bat droppings have a coarse surface, have no white uric acid cap, consist almost exclusively of chitinous remains of arthropods and are crumbly – the details of the situation and the known roost preferences of bats are a first indicator to the species.

When droppings are found in large roof spaces in Central Europe, usually Greater Mouse-eared Bats (*Myotis myotis*), Serotine (*Eptesicus serotinus*), long-eared bats (Genus *Plecotus*) or, due to their scarcity, occasionally also Geoffroy's Bats (*Myotis emarginatus*), Pond Bats (*M. dasycneme*) or horseshoe bats (Genus *Rhinolophus*) are the source.

A more precise species allocation is possible from the form and size of the droppings (Fig. 91). Since similar-sized bats produce comparable-sized droppings, very different species, such as long-eared bats and mouse-eared bats, can be differentiated with some certainty [gen. lit. 129]. From droppings contents analysis a further identification can be made: almost identical-looking droppings of some species can be readily separated. Mouse-eared bats eat ground beetles to a large extent, Serotines bugs and Diptera, Greater Horseshoe Bats dung beetles and moths. The best method of species identification is certainly by hairs in the droppings. These hairs, which are swallowed by the bats when grooming, particularly their tips, are often species-specific from the cuticular structure, and enable a reliable species identification from comparison with hair samples of known origin. Ectoparasites in droppings may make identification possible due to their high host specificity. The safest, but the most expensive method, is species identification by sequencing of DNA fragments of the cells of the stomach and intestinal mucosa isolated from the droppings.

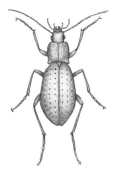

Fig. 95. Large carabids (*Carabus* species) constitute a substantial portion of the prey of the Greater Mouse-eared Bat (*Myotis myotis*). Diagram: R. Roesler.

Fig. 96. Chafers (*Melolontha* species) are a desired prey of numerous bat species, which can nourish them to a large extent during the short flight time of the beetles. Diagram: R. Roesler.

Fig. 97. Bugs (Heteroptera) appear particularly in autumn in the food of Serotines (*Eptesicus serotinus*) and Noctules (*Nyctalus noctula*). Diagram: R. Roesler.

Fig. 98. Crane-flies (Tipulidae) are a desired prey of many different bat species. Diagram: R. Roesler.

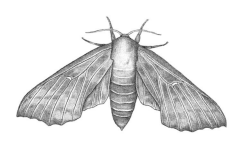

Fig. 99. Hawk moths (Sphingidae) are large to very large prey animals, which are readily caught during their flying time by Greater Horseshoe Bats (*Rhinolophus ferrumequinum*) and Mehely's Horseshoe Bats (*Rhinolophus mehelyi*). Diagram: R. Roesler.

Fig. 100. Noctuid moths (Noctuidae) sometimes represent the main prey of long-eared bats (*Plecotus* spp) and horseshoe bats (*Rhinolophus* spp.). Diagram: R. Roesler.

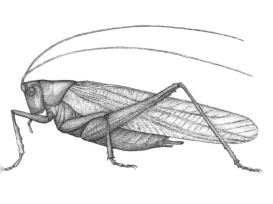

Fig. 101. Bush crickets (Tettigoniidae) appear particularly in the food of the Greater Mouse-eared Bat (*Myotis myotis*) and the Greater Noctule (*Nyctalus lasiopterus*), but also of the long-eared bats (*Plecotus* spp.). Diagram: R. Roesler.

Fig. 102. Earwigs (Dermaptera) are particularly eaten by long-eared bats (*Plecotus* spp.) and Bechstein's Bat (*Myotis bechsteinii*). Diagram: R. Roesler.

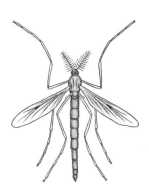

Fig. 103. Non-biting midges (Chironomidae) represent the main prey of numerous bat species that forage over water, such as Daubenton's Bat (*Myotis daubentonii*) or the Common Pipistrelle (*Pipistrellus pipistrellus*). Diagram: R. Roesler.

Annual cycle of bats

The major food resource for bats is insects and other arthropods, which are subject to strong fluctuations in their availability through the course of the year. For any animal it is important to have reproduction at the time of year in which sufficient food is available, and to be able to withstand the food-free period, for which they may move away or close down their energy consumption drastically. It is therefore understandable why the course of the year in Central European bats, with births in summer and hibernation in winter, is relatively uniform. Fig. 104 gives an overview of the annual cycle of a Central European bat.

If one begins with the reproduction time, starting approximately from May, the females are gathering into reproduction colonies, the so-called nursery (or maternity) colonies. Here they bear, often amazingly synchronously, their young. This synchrony is probably caused by the warming up in spring similarly affecting all females at the same time and stimulating ovulation and the ensuing fertilisation with sperm cells stored over the winter. If one finds an injured female bat in the autumn, feeds it over the winter and keeps it warm so that it does not hibernate, it will often have its young as early as January or February. The synchronisation of the births perhaps also has a special ecological advantage: in larger colonies it reduces the predation risk; since there are helpless young as prey only once in the year for a short time, predators, such as owls and martens, cannot 'invest' in this prey over a longer period.

For most Central European species the time of births is in June. In the Mediterranean area it can, however, be different: Long-fingered Bats (*Myotis capaccinii*), which are common in the warm coastal regions of the Mediterranean, often have their young in the beginning of May on the Balkan Peninsula and in Spain, and the young may be weaned at the beginning of June.

In most species there are no or only very occasional adult males in the nursery colonies. In the Greater Mouse-eared Bat (*Myotis myotis*), Noctule (*Nyctalus noctula*) or Nathusius's Pipistrelle (*Pipistrellus nathusii*) only very exceptionally does one find a male in the nursery roost, and even then in Greater Mouse-eared Bat it is mostly in another corner of the loft separated from the females. However, in long-eared bats (Genus *Plecotus*) and horseshoe bats (Genus *Rhinolophus*) there are frequently adult males in the summer colonies. The males of other species spend the summer either individually or form male groups in which the animals associate with each other. At least in Lesser Mouse-eared Bat (*Myotis oxygnathus*) males already occupy their display arenas in cave entrances in May, and they defend their territories, often in small ceiling indentations, against any intruder.

In July and August the young animals begin to fly, but are still nourished with milk by the mother. They gradually become independent, starting to hunt, but are not yet very efficient. This is a sensitive period for the population: now there must be food-rich hunting grounds in the nearby environment of the colony.

The rearing of the young is hardly over when the mating period starts. The long-distance migrants among the female bats often find mating roosts of the males on the migration route or in the winter roost. For hibernating species this phase in the year is characterised by swarming at caves or other sites. In this period, species that are relatively sedentary throughout the year, move at night to different potential winter roosts and meet other animals of the same species, probably also to find mating partners. It is particularly important that these more sedentary species avoid in-breeding. In the migratory species the genetic mixing takes place automatically.

The time before hibernation, in September and October, is also equally important for the bats as they must now build up fat for hibernation. Figures 105 and 106 show the development of the body weight in Daubenton's Bat (*Myotis daubentonii*) in the course of the year. Males of Daubenton's Bats have a weight of between 7 and 8g in summer. Flying costs much energy and each gram counts: the lighter the body, the more energy-efficient is the flight. It is, therefore, not economic to become fat. In

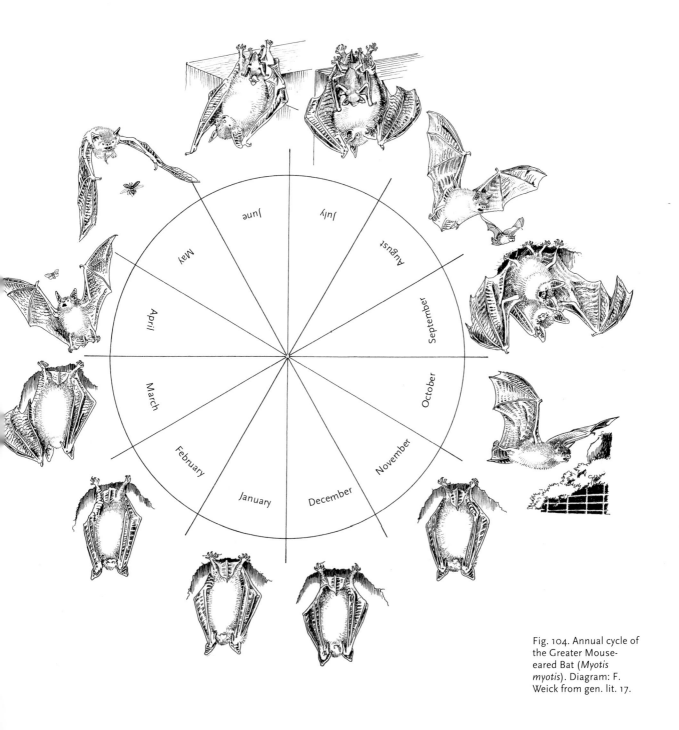

Fig. 104. Annual cycle of the Greater Mouse-eared Bat (*Myotis myotis*). Diagram: F. Weick from gen. lit. 17.

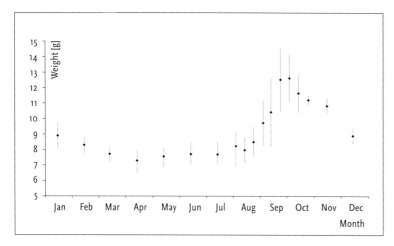

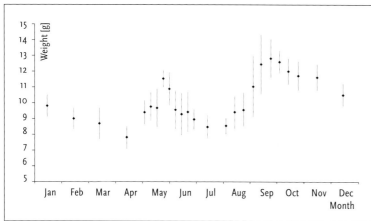

Fig. 105. Weight changes of adult males of Daubenton's Bat (*Myotis daubentonii*). The increase of body weight in September when the animals deposit fat for hibernation is remarkable. Graph: M. Bauer after data of C. Harrje, H. Geiger *et al.*

Fig. 106. Weight changes of adult females of Daubenton's Bat (*Myotis daubentonii*). At the end of May/ beginning of June the increase of body weight is clearly due to pregnancy. Graph: M. Bauer.

September and October the body weight of the males then rises steeply and reaches 12–13g, in some animals even more. During hibernation 4–5g, more than one-third of the body weight, is lost. In the females there is, understandably, an additional peak in weight in June, toward the end of the pregnancy – before the females give birth, when they loose about one-third of their body weight, returning during the lactation period to their 'energetic optimal weight' of *c.* 8g, similar to the males.

Depending upon the weather, bats move in October or November to their winter roosts. The typical cave hibernators arouse during hibernation only a few times and remain with a distinctly lowered metabolism until the spring (Fig. 107). Other species will emerge to hunt on relatively warmer winter evenings or may change their winter roost – depending upon the ambient temperature. Bat species that migrate into the Mediterranean area, such as Nathusius's Pipistrelles (*Pipistrellus nathusii*) and Leisler's Bats (*Nyctalus leisleri*), often still hunt each night – as long as insects fly and it does not become too cold.

In the spring, when it becomes warmer again, often even in March, the deeply hibernating species start to leave their winter roosts and begin to hunt in the warmer evenings. This time, at the end of March and April, is probably a very sensitive time for most bat populations with respect to the food availability. Now it comes down to either whether the energy reserves of the bats are still sufficient, or whether there are already sufficient insects available in the proximity of the winter roosts to supplement the reserves again. At this time of the year the body weights (Figs 105 and 106) are at their lowest. In Daubenton's Bat the weight then can be around 7g, in some animals 6g.

After hibernation, the females move, often via other warm, favourable transition roosts, to their summer roosts. At this time ovulation and fertilisation take place and pregnancy begins. In indigenous species the duration of pregnancy is *c.* 6–8 weeks, until the time when the births take place – with which we have completed the annual cycle.

Fig. 107. The availability of food is a crucial influence on the course of the year for bats in Europe. Only by succeeding to survive the food-free time of winter can bats occur with us. In the case of hibernation, the fat reserves must be sufficient to last until spring, in this Greater Mouse-eared Bat (*Myotis myotis*) it has already been mostly used up. Photo: C. Dietz.

Movements

Not only birds but also many mammals migrate seasonally over long distances, such as the reindeer and caribou of the northern polar areas, or the large animal herds of Africa. However, in the mammals, migrants comparable to the migratory birds, with movements of more than 1,000km, are only found in whales and bats.

As with birds, which can be separated into sedentary, regional migrant and long-range migratory species, there are bat species that are more or less sedentary (with seasonal migration of usually less than 50 or 100km), species that regularly change their locations by more than 100km and up to some hundreds of kilometres, and long-distance migrants with annual migrations over thousands of kilometres.

Sedentary species

Typical of our sedentary species are the horseshoe bats (Genus *Rhinolophus*), long-eared bats (Genus *Plecotus*), Common Pipistrelle (*Pipistrellus pipistrellus*), Bechstein's Bat (*Myotis bechsteinii*) and probably most of the other small *Myotis* species. In these species movement is essentially determined by the distance between suitable summer habitats, where the nursery roosts are situated, and possible winter roosts.

Species adapted to migration

This is also valid for most species of the second group, which corresponds rather to the 'locally migrant birds'. Migration of more than some hundreds of kilometres occurs particularly in species that need frost-free underground roosts for hibernation, such as caves, but in summer find more food in areas where underground sites are poorly represented. The Pond Bat (*Myotis dasycneme*), for example, has nursery roosts in water-rich areas of the Netherlands, northern Germany, through the Baltic countries into the western part of Russia. In these lowland areas there are few suitable sites for winter hibernation. Therefore the animals migrate in autumn in a southerly direction to caves and mines in low mountain ranges, and other kinds of underground sites, such as bunker systems. The plentiful populations in the Netherlands migrate up to 300km to the south and southeast into areas rich in underground sites around Maastricht (the Netherlands) and in Germany into the Eifel, Sauerland or the Teutoburg Forest [gen. lit. 131]. In this case the availability of the nearest underground winter sites determines the migration direction. In contrast, the Danish Jutland Pond Bats are relatively sedentary, since there are local subterranean limestone quarries suitable for hibernation and hence the short migrations can be in any direction [gen. lit. 30].

The Greater Mouse-eared Bat (*Myotis myotis*) behaves similarly, regularly accomplishing migrations of up to 100km or more, and with no apparent preferred direction. Rather the migration directions of marked animals from both the summer and the winter roosts radiate to more or less all points of the compass.

In many species the migration is not primarily directed to the winter roost but initially to a swarming and mating site. The purpose of migration is believed to be, on the one hand, to obtain knowledge of potential winter roosts, on the other hand it seems to be important for the genetic mixing of populations.

The exceptional Schreibers' Bent-winged Bat

Schreibers' Bent-winged Bat (*Miniopterus schreibersii*), a typical cave-dwelling bat of the entire Mediterranean area, accomplishes seasonal migration in several regions. These migrations are directed from numerous summer roosts towards a few mass winter roosts. The populations of different winter roosts seem thereby to remain separated to a large extent from each other also in summer. Also, the former winter colony of Schreibers' Bent-winged Bat in Kaiserstuhl (Germany) was occupied by animals whose nursery roosts occurred up until the 1960s in Burgundy (France) [gen. lit. 116]. Schreibers' Bent-winged Bats were also active in the winter in warmer weather, when they fed particularly on winter moth, a species which occurred frequently in the Kaiserstuhl area, particularly in the soft fruit plantations. The disappearance of Schreibers' Bent-winged Bats from Kaiserstuhl occurred at the same time as large-scale control of winter moth by aerial insecticide spraying. Nowadays, this bat species is considered to be extinct in Germany. In some areas of southern Europe, Schreibers' Bent-winged Bat also occurs all year round in some large populations that, at least there, seem to be more or less sedentary.

▶ Long-distance migration

The achievements of long-distance migrants among the bats are amazing. Comparable with birds, such seasonal long-distance migrant bat species occur particularly in the temperate latitudes of Europe and North America. The evolution of migratory birds – and the long-distance migrants among bats – apparently coincided with the post-ice-age resettlement of Europe (and also North America). The spread northward was, for some species, only possible if they could spend the winters back in warmer and food-rich areas. A possibility was the evolution of a highly specialised hibernation, which permits wintering for several months of the cold season in protected roosts. The other possibility was seasonal migration. The option to maintain winter activity, like many of our sedentary bird species in Central and northern Europe, is not possible for insectivorous bats.

In particular the Noctule (*Nyctalus noctula*), Leisler's Bat (*N. leisleri*), Nathusius's Pipistrelle (*Pipistrellus nathusii*), the Parti-coloured Bat (*Vespertilio murinus*) and probably also the Greater Noctule (*N. lasiopterus*) cross large areas of Europe as long-distance migrants in spring and autumn. Bat ringing (or banding), which was introduced in Germany by Martin Eisentraut as long ago as 1932, made it possible to record the hundreds of recoveries of some species between wintering and summer areas (Figs 108 and 109). The maximum proven distances, to a certain extent 'the records', are 1,546km for the Noctule (*Nyctalus noctula*), 1,567km for Leisler's Bat (*Nyctalus leisleri*), 1,780km for the Parti-coloured Bat (*Vespertilio murinus*) and even 1,905km for Nathusius's Pipistrelle (*Pipistrellus nathusii*) [gen. lit. 57]. These distances are enormous and also demand enormous physiological achievements.

Migration direction

Through the majority of Europe the migration direction is, as seen from the summer to the winter roosts, toward the southwest. In Russia there are also populations of Noctule, Nathusius's Pipistrelles and Greater Noctule that sometimes migrate less to the west, but more strictly to the south and even slightly to southeast to

Fig. 108. Migration pattern of Noctule (*Nyctalus noctula*) in Europe as obtained by ringing. In western Europe the preferred migration direction is southwest in autumn. From gen. lit. 57. Map: R. Hutterer.

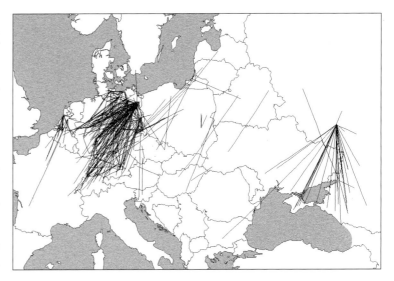

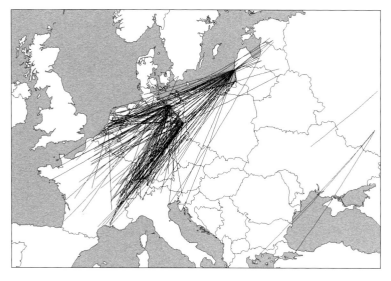

Fig. 109. Migration pattern of Nathusius's Pipistrelle (*Pipistrellus nathusii*) in Europe as obtained by ringing. From gen. lit. 57. Map: R. Hutterer.

reach the coasts of the Black Sea, from where some animals probably migrate on into the Caucasus or to Anatolia. Other records in Russia confirm a more southwest migration to the Bosphorus and Greece, which was demonstrated by two ringing recoveries of Nathusius's Pipistrelles.

Similar long-distance migrations are achieved in North American bat species. A particular migration-driven species is the Hoary Bat (*Lasiurus cinereus*), whose migration may even take it out over the Atlantic and it has been recorded somehow reaching Iceland and the Faroe Islands.

Adaptations to migration

The long-distance migrants are characteristically fast-flying narrow-winged species, which hunt on insects in the open air ('aerial hawking bats') and are usually species that do not hibernate in underground roosts but in tree holes or rock crevices, which are far more exposed to the elements and consequently to cold weather. A further common feature is that all of them are species that have a high reproductive rate and can usually produce two young. The Hoary Bat and its relatives in North America (Genus *Lasiurus*) are even more extreme in this respect. They can have up to three or four young and do not even need tree holes as roosts, during the day time they hang freely from branches.

The fact that the average mortality of the migratory species is substantially higher than the mortality of the sedentary species that hibernate in underground sites strongly suggests that migration has additional dangers and risks.

Migration speed

The daily (strictly nightly!) migration distances in bats are not as long as in birds, but apparently mostly lie within the range of 30–50km per night (in Noctule and Nathusius's Pipistrelle). Some animals, however, achieve distinctly greater distances, such as a Parti-coloured Bat that apparently

Fig. 110. Phenology of the migration of Nathusius's Pipistrelle (*Pipistrellus nathusii*) in Central Europe. In summer the females and newborn animals occur in the nursery roost area, e.g. in Brandenburg (red). In August males and females collect in the mating roosts (pink). The departure in Poland takes place toward the end of August (blue), while it reaches its maximum just at the end of September at the Bodensee (Germany), and is observed in the next spring as early as the end of March/ beginning of April (green). Graph: M. Bauer.

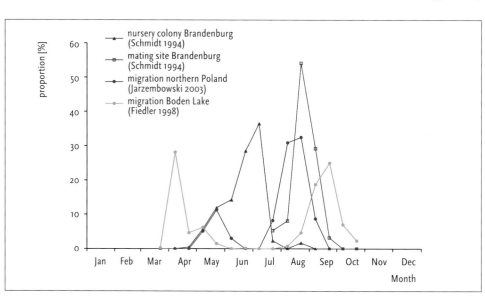

migrated 180km per night [gen. lit. 140].

Since bats migrate relatively slowly compared with birds, the peaks of the passage times in Europe are clearly extended (Fig. 110): while the peak of the passage of Nathusius's Pipistrelle (*Pipistrellus nathusii*) at the Bodensee (Germany) in spring can be observed at the beginning of April and in autumn at the end of September/beginning of October, the passage in northern Poland takes place only at the end of May and the autumn migration is already in full swing in August. The nursery roosts in Brandenburg are occupied in the course of June, with the maximum number of females reproducing there being in June. The maximum accumulations of animals in mating roosts can be observed in Brandenburg toward the end of August/beginning of September.

Separation of the sexes

A further interesting common feature of migrating bat species is the fact that the males, at least the males of some populations, do not return to the reproduction areas but remain in more southern regions, to which the females return only in the autumn and winter. Some of the males establish mating roosts in the passage area of the females, others within the region of the winter roosts. Each spring the females migrate northward into the food-rich summer areas in order to give birth and rear their young there. Males of Noctule and Nathusius's Pipistrelle are almost absent in the most northern parts of the reproduction area [for example see gen. lit. 140]. From the other point of view, in Greece, for instance, there are numerous Leisler's Bats and Greater Noctules for the whole summer, but exclusively males. The females of both species return from their reproduction areas to Greece only in September, where they often remain active and hunting insects at night during the winter – if it is not too cold. Also in the Crimea, where the south Russian Noctules hibernate, in summer there are almost exclusively males [gen. lit. 1, 140]. In northern Bulgaria there is a very large summer colony of Noctule Bat (*Nyctalus noctula*) with up to 2,000 males in the crevices of a

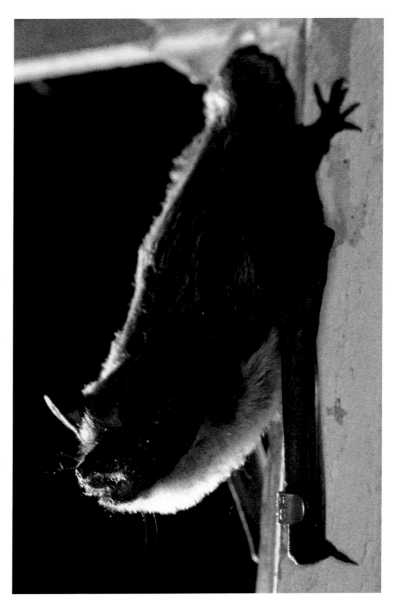

cave ceiling, but only very few females [own data]. This spatial separation of the sexes on one hand saves the males from the probable perils of migration, but on the other hand reduces the intraspecific competition in the summer habitat.

Migratory routes

In contrast to birds, for which detailed studies are known for almost all species about migration routes, migration behaviour and orientation mechanisms, knowledge in these areas for bats is still extremely

Fig. 111. For the individual marking of bats light metal alloy manufactured rings are used, which are numbered consecutively. Here a ringed Parti-coloured Bat (*Vespertilio murinus*), one of the long-distance migrants among the European bats. Photo: D. Nill.

limited and central questions are still unexplored. It is unclear whether bats prefer to migrate along corridors such as river valleys, or migrate over a broad front. As far as possible, Nathusius's Pipistrelles (*Pipistrellus nathusii*) avoid migrating across the Baltic Sea and follow the coastline, in particular the Curonian Spit (Lithuania/Kaliningrad) and along the Vistula Lagoon (Kaliningrad/Poland). With migration on the main continental block, it seems that most animals follow large river valleys, such as the Rhine valley. It is not clear whether they indeed use these river valleys as guidelines, or whether the valleys are chosen because they provide suitable hunting habitats during migration. However, Parti-coloured Bats (*Vespertilio murinus*) have been observed flying straight out to sea, or they have been seen on ships on the open sea.

Some bats migrate singly. Noctules (*Nyctalus noctula*) seem to migrate in groups, sometimes in large flocks; at least on autumn days one can see Noctules flying in such a way early in the evening. Sometimes large numbers of animals arrive in day roosts during one night – this also suggests group migration. On the basis of ringed animals it has been shown from time to time that apparently associated animals turn up again and again together and more or less at the same time in the same roost.

Orientation mechanisms

The orientation mechanisms of migration are almost unknown. Echolocation can be excluded for distance orientation, due to its small operational range. Whether bats possibly orientate using a magnetic field, as with many birds, has only recently been more intensively studied. Also considered is orientation by the perception of infrasound, which comes from air currents over mountains or from sea surf. So far, however, there is no scientifically confirmed evidence for the hearing of infrasound

Conversely, it was recently shown that

North American Big Brown Bats (*Eptesicus fuscus*) may use magnetic cues for homing. Bats were taken from their roost during the daytime and were kept for three-quarters of an hour before and after sunset in chambers with an artificially shifted magnetic field. Control animals returned directly to their roosts, but the others headed in the wrong direction, corresponding to the deviations imposed in their captive conditions [gen. lit. 166]. This is the first direct evidence for the influence of magnetic perception on the orientation behaviour of bats. Our own attempts with a Northern Bat (*Eptesicus nilssonii*) during migration time indicated that the animal was able to align itself exactly to southwest under different site conditions. We found this all the more astonishing since the Northern Bat is not ranked among the migratory bat species.

From the most recent knowledge [gen. lit. 166] it is quite probable that orientation by the earth's magnetic field can give the migration direction relatively accurately and detailed orientation is effected on the basis of landmarks. From the above experiment the calibration of the magnetic compass seems to take place with each journey and can be corrected later, as happens with pigeons. It is still unclear how bats can monitor the magnetic field, possibly the magnetic molecules in the retina are responsible.

Homing ability

The homing ability of bats has been confirmed in earlier studies by displacement experiments [reviewed in gen. lit. 23]. Individuals of the North American Big Brown Bat (*Eptesicus fuscus*), a species related to the European Serotine, returned from up to 720km to the site of capture. Similar to our Daubenton's Bat, the North American Little Brown Bat (*Myotis lucifugus*) found its way back to its roosts over a distance of up to 430km. With translocation experiments with Common Pipistrelles (*Pipistrellus pipistrellus*) in Germany homing distances of up to 143km were recorded, with the first animals already returned to the catching site after a few days [gen. lit. 101].

How these achievements are possible is probably one of the most interesting questions of the physiological senses of bats. Bats are animals whose eyes are so bad that they can hardly use the starry skies for their orientation, and their echolocation, like the ability of a car driver in the densest fog, cannot gain information about objects more than 20 or 30m away.

Site memory and genetic fixation

And we still have absolutely no understanding as to how bats generally not only determine their migration direction and the migration distance, but can return to their exact roost of birth after a migration of 1,000 or 2,000 kilometres. Maybe genetic determination of the migration direction, as well as imprinting enabling the establishment of traditions, play important roles. The different preferential directions of different populations of Nathusius's Pipistrelle (*Pipistrellus nathusii*) do assume a genetic programming [gen. lit. 115]. But with which parameters is a young female Noctule (*Nyctalus noctula*) in Uckermark (Germany) imprinted, such that it returns to the exact tree hole in which it first saw the light of the world after a migration of 1,000km to its winter quarters and the same back?

It is to be assumed that there is a very high selective pressure on different genetic variants of migration behaviour – including the migration direction and the strength of the migration instinct. On the one hand migration is risky – particularly in the fact that a migrating bat has no knowledge of roost-availability at the end of a night's flight. This latter factor is used by the displaying males along the migration routes, whose loud display calls in the morning hours can lure females into their mating roost.

Selection pressure determines migration

In the north, when some winters are mild, there are probably advantages to those animals which did not migrate or not far. Conversely, occasional cold winters can be sufficient to decimate or exterminate whole non-migratory subpopulations of bats hibernating in tree holes and rock crevices: such winters can be the cause of mass mortality. This was, for example, reported for the cold winters of 1928/29 and 1962/63, in which Noctule Bats died in large numbers from exposure in cold weather.

With their relatively high reproduction rates, Noctules and Nathusius's Pipistrelles probably have the ability to recover quickly from such losses – at least faster than species with only one young/year, which tend to hibernate in comparatively well-protected underground roosts.

Probably the migration behaviour of bats is also influenced by a constant but accurate and fast-operating selection due to the influences of climate, as has been described so impressively by P. Berthold for birds, especially for the Blackcap (*Sylvia atricapilla*).

'Autumn swarming' and 'swarming sites'

As the end of the summer period of rearing young approaches and the young become independent, many bats begin to migrate to distant areas that are beyond their normal hunting grounds. In this period, which can last to the onset of hibernation, some species fly in and out of certain caves during the night, sometimes they circle around in front of a cave entrance while calling, or they may fly rapidly through gaps between rocks. They can do this in large numbers at several caves – or at other roosts which are suitable for hibernation, such as the famous Spandau Citadel (Berlin). Often one can observe short pursuits when two or a few animals follow each other. This behaviour is called 'autumn swarming'. It marks the most remarkable activity for many bat species in the months between the weaning of the young and hibernation.

The behaviour and the main activity time of swarming are different from species to species. Figure 112 shows the occurrence of some species based on more than 20 years of observations at a cave in the Franconian Alb. The Northern Bat (*Eptesicus nilssonii*) is, at least in south Germany, the first species; its main activity period starts as early as July. Some species, particularly Brown Long-eared Bat (*Plecotus auritus*), already have an activity peak in early spring after waking up from hibernation, which coincides with the spring display. Other species, such as Daubenton's Bat (*Myotis daubentonii*), appear in August at the caves; Natterer's Bat (*Myotis nattereri*) arrives particularly late. Sometimes one recognises clearly different activity peaks.

In all species, except Greater Mouse-eared Bat (*Myotis myotis*), the males are far in the majority. The Esper cave in the Franconian Alb is used by Greater Mouse-eared Bat females from neighbouring nursery colonies throughout the summer as a night roost for a short rest during foraging. Starting from August a few males visit the site as a display roost, whereby they hang separately in small cavities in the ceiling, and finally, in the autumn, many animals, particularly further males, appear for swarming. At other caves the sex ratio of Whiskered Bat (*Myotis mystacinus*) is almost equal.

The real reason for this very characteristic behaviour of bats has not been completely understood for a long time. The following hypotheses are discussed; they are in no way mutually exclusive, but highlight different aspects which could have different levels of importance for different species.

1. Swarming sites could be **meeting places** for **display** and **mating**. A high proportion of males is notable in nearly all species. Swarming mostly coincides with the time of maximally filled epididymis and thus the time in which males have the largest sperm supply (the testes have usually achieved their largest volume earlier). The loud social calls and pursuit flights could be important aspects of the display. Genetic analyses show that males of different metapopulations meet at the swarming sites, which could be important for the genetic mixing of the populations. However, one relatively rarely sees mating in the swarming time.

2. Swarming allows the **exploration of winter roosts**. Since survival particularly depends on finding a safe winter roost in all bats of temperate latitudes, it could be crucially important for all bats to make sure that the winter roost still exists and if necessary alternate roosts are available in the neighbourhood. However, preferred swarming sites are not by any means always also the most popular winter roosts. Besides, one would then have to expect a more balanced sex ratio and a higher portion of young animals.

3. Swarming could particularly **help** the still **inexperienced young animals to become acquainted with suitable winter roosts**. All species seem to swarm primarily at places

with the characteristics of the winter roosts of the species. Thus Common Pipistrelles (*Pipistrellus pipistrellus*) in Central Europe swarm at large old buildings, such as the Marburg Landgrave Castle, the Freiburg Cathedral or the Bartholomaeus Church in Demmin (Germany), Noctules (*Nyctalus noctula*) at rock crevices in Switzerland or in Bulgaria, and cave-hibernating bats, such as long-eared bats (Genus *Plecotus*), *Myotis* species or Northern Bats (*Eptesicus nilssonii*), at cave entrances. The location is imprinted in the memory by the frequent approach to and flying into the roost, and enables later finding in an emergency.

4. The most important function of swarming could be a general **social information transfer** about suitable winter roosts, in which all adult animals also participate. Swarming sites could be, to a certain extent, **fixed points on a bat's map**, sites remembered year after year by a visit, even if the bat has no intention to stay here for hibernation. At the Esper cave in the Franconian Alb swarming Greater Mouse-eared Bats (*Myotis myotis*) were sometimes found in winter roosts 60–80km away. The nursery roosts from which swarming females at the Esper cave originated were even distributed over some hundreds of kilometres, from throughout north Bavaria to Hessen and Bohemia. Comparable results were found with studies by A. Nagel in Greater Mouse-eared Bat in the Swabian Alb. In England a swarming sites' catchment area of up to 4,100 km² was found for Daubenton's and Natterer's Bats (*M. daubentonii* and *M nattereri*).

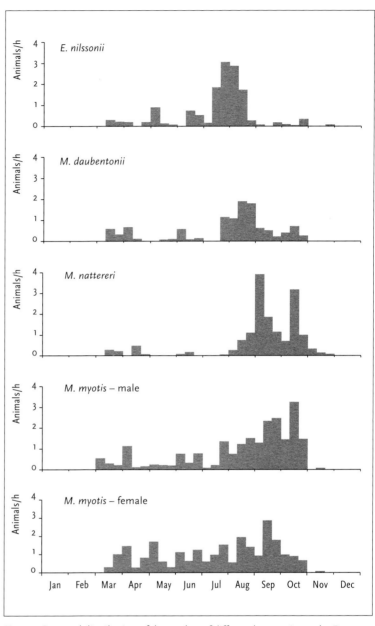

Fig. 112. Seasonal distribution of the catches of different bat species at the Esper cave in the Franconian Alb (Germany) between 1985 and 2004. The average catch frequency is given per hour for each 10-day period of the year. In all species, except the Greater Mouse-eared Bat (*Myotis myotis*), the number of males caught exceeded by far that of females. Northern Bats (*Eptesicus nilssonii*) swarm earliest in the year, even in July; last is Natterer's Bats (*Myotis nattereri*).

Torpor and hibernation

Bats have developed one ability obviously repeated independently within the mammals: they can lower their body temperature deliberately, in order to decrease the energetic expenditure for heat production. Their homoeothermy is by no means turned off, but the automatic temperature control system allows the adjustment of the desired level of body temperature to between the normal 37°C and the ambient temperature. That is an active process. The desired value can be raised, for example due to external stimuli, or at any time danger threatens.

When the animal, as a consequence of a disturbance, wants to produce warmth as fast as possible in order to wake up, it can turn on the heat production very effectively. The entire utilised energy is not, as is usual, first directed into the production of high-energy molecules such as ATP, but directly and completely into heat production. Fat serves as energy storage, because its utilisation (burning off) results in the largest quantity of energy per unit of weight. A particularly important store of energy in bats is the so-called 'brown fat tissue', which with bats prepared for the winter sleep covers large parts of the back below the skin and over the scapulae.

The advantage of lowering the body temperature is an enormous saving of energy. The homoeothermy of mammals was an expensive acquisition, if one looks at it from the energetic side. But a decrease of body temperature of around 10°C can save 50–70 % of the energy used per time unit. This saving is to a certain extent doubled: on the one hand the energy necessary for keeping warm is avoided, on the other hand all metabolic processes slow down due to the lower body temperature and hence the need for less energy.

The disadvantage of the temperature reduction is naturally the decrease in the response rate of the central nervous system. In particular the reaction rate is decreased, and if the body temperature is markedly lowered, as with hibernation, the central nervous system must be warmed up at once, before any coordinated motor reaction is possible. The temperature reduction in torpor is always a compromise between energy saving and an assessment of the risk of predation – or for reactivity for intraspecific disputes, such as display or the defence of a territory.

Bats must, as it were, be constantly asking themselves the question: how safe do I feel in this roost, in this situation? Does not the risk of becoming prey to a predator exist because of decreased reactivity? How important it is to defend my roost or my territory against competitive animals of the same species? And this in company with the question: how quickly will I be able to replenish my fat reserves again on the following night? For pregnant females the additional question arises as to whether a faster development of the embryo through a higher body temperature is more important than energy saving. With bad weather bats must be more prepared to take risks, while they can remain very much awake in periods of large insect availability, ready for escape, defence and attack.

Fig. 113. Lesser Horseshoe Bats (*Rhinolophus hipposideros*) hang free in hibernation and usually wrap themselves completely within their wing membranes. Photo: D. Nill.

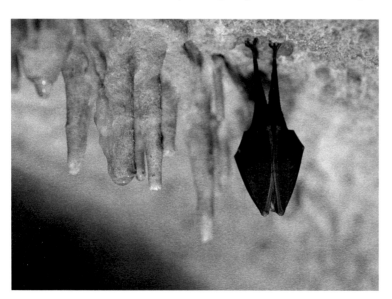

These questions arise, at least in the summer period, each day and again each evening and probably explains why the requirements for roosts by bats in summer are often not well understood. Sometimes warmer, sometimes cooler roosts are preferred. In cooler roosts a bat can lower the body temperature and go into torpor and save a lot of energy; in warmer roosts the body uses more energy, but the growth of a baby can be accelerated by the higher milk production of the mother.

G. Kerth showed in field experiments on Bechstein's Bat (*Myotis bechsteinii*) how much the choice of day roost can depend on the respective season and weather conditions. In a simple, but ingenious experiment he offered a choice of two boxes to the bats, in each case one black painted, which was markedly warmed up in sunshine, and one white painted one, which remained cooler [gen. lit. 65]. In addition he offered bat boxes in sunny places to compare with boxes in shady places. Particularly in the autumn Bechstein's Bats clearly preferred the warmer boxes, thus the black-painted ones, and particularly those that hung on sun-exposed tree trunks.

C. Willis in Canada has succeeded in comparing continuously the ambient temperature and the skin temperature in free-flying bats with the help of telemetric monitoring [gen. lit. 147]. The experimental

animals were lactating females of Hoary Bat (*Lasiurus cinereus*). This species rests during the daytime not in tree holes or in rock crevices, but hangs freely amongst vegetation, between branches or the leaves of a tree. It was shown that the females sometimes went only into a superficial torpor, sometimes, particularly in the early hours of the morning when it was bitterly cold, into a deep torpor and lowered their body temperature to below 10°C (Fig. 118). This was, however, not the case in all nights; sometimes they maintained warmth and went hunting. At noon, when the air temperature reached nearly 30°C, the animals remained warm, with a high body temperature between 34 and 37°C.

Bats must also question whether to lower their body temperature, constantly settling the conflict between energy saving and being awake – not only by selecting the best suitable roost but also a position within the roost.

More drastic than lowering the body temperature for the condition of torpor in the day roost is the hibernation of bats in temperate latitudes. In north and Central Europe, bats can only survive in winter by withdrawing into protected places, in which

Fig. 114. Hibernating Lesser Horseshoe Bats (*Rhinolophus hipposideros*) do not form clusters but usually hang separated by an individual distance. Photo: D. Nill.

Fig. 115. In complete contrast to the Lesser Horseshoe Bats, Schreibers' Bent-winged Bats (*Miniopterus schreibersii*) form regular 'wall carpets' of thousands of densely clustered individuals in winter. Photo: D. Nill.

▶ Fig. 116. Hibernating bats, such as this Whiskered Bat (*Myotis mystacinus*), are often densely covered with condensation. Photo: C. Dietz.

▶▶ Fig. 117. A hibernating Bechstein's Bat (*Myotis bechsteinii*) is easy to recognise by its long ears. Photo: O. von Helversen.

Fig. 118. Skin temperature (open circles) and ambient temperature (filled circles) on some successive summer days in a free-flying, lactating female of the Hoary Bat (*Lasiurus cinereus*) in Canada. On different days the animal used its possibility of going into torpor completely differently: on the morning of 6 July it dropped its temperature to 10°C and fell into deep torpor, two days later it remained active the whole morning. After gen. lit. 147. Graph: C.K.R. Willis.

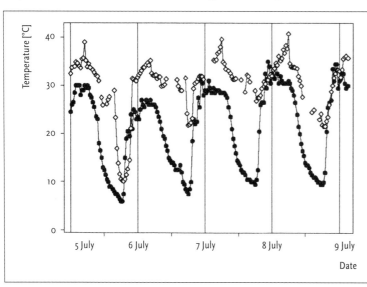

on the one hand they find low, but nevertheless frost-free temperatures and on the other hand are not at the mercy of predators. Most bat species hibernate in caves, in natural rock openings such as in the karst caves in limestone hills, but also in man-made underground sites, such as mines, tunnels or cellars. Some species also hibernate in rock crevices or even, as with some populations of Noctule Bat (*Nyctalus noctula*), in tree holes, mostly then in thick trunks that do not readily cool down. Noctules then form dense, compact clusters with their bodies and can jointly regulate the temperature. It is advantageous if the roost itself has as good as possible insulation. The temperature should not normally drop below 0°C or not lower than -4°C.

Since one finds far fewer individuals of most bat species in caves in the winter as are known to be around in summer, it is assumed that many bats are hibernating in roosts which are inaccessible to humans. Besides tree holes these are probably also wood piles, rock crevices, rubble and scree, possibly also holes in the ground, such as mammal burrows or between roots of trees.

Energy saving has absolute priority during hibernation. This will be achieved by deep-seated physiological changes. Apart from lowering the body temperature the heart and respiration rate are also lowered by hormonal regulating mechanisms. While the heartbeat frequency of a Greater Mouse-eared Bat (*Myotis myotis*) in flight reaches up to 880 beats per minute and at rest is between 250 and 450, the rate in deep hibernation is only 18–80. Then too the interval between two breaths is up to 90 minutes, in active condition only six seconds [gen. lit 73]. Through winter bats often use more than one-third of their body weight, in order to actually utilise the tiny quantity of energy that they need for their daily metabolism at such low temperatures. Fig. 119 shows the weight decrease of Daubenton's Bats (*Myotis daubentonii*) in a winter roost in Kiel. C. Harrje caught the individually marked animals when they awoke and flew around in the winter roost – which they do regularly – and he weighed them at this time [gen. lit. 47]. One recognizes the fact that from day to day each animal loses only about 0.2 % of its weight but over the months of the hibernation period this adds up to 30–40 % of the initial weight.

In spring the bat can then go on surviving; if the bats have not yet used up their fat supply in years with a cold spring, then they have to attack the remaining body resources. Sometimes one can find extremely emaciated animals in winter roosts in spring (Fig. 107). Thus, in the proximity of the winter roost in spring, warm weather is equally important to a good supply of prey being available.

One could thus actually expect that the phase of the hibernation toward its end would be accompanied by a particularly high mortality of the bat populations. Interestingly enough this has never been

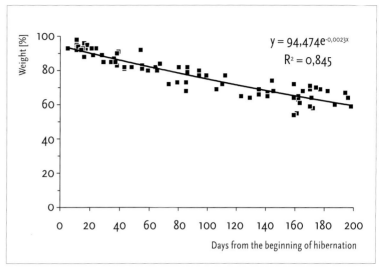

quantitatively proved. For the Common Pipistrelle (*Pipistrellus pipistrellus*) T. Sendor and M. Simon even found that in a large winter roost in Marburg the mortality was distinctly lower over the winter than the mortality rate in the summer period [gen. lit. 120]. However, perhaps these findings are true only for certain years, and will be dependent on the weather conditions and also on the hibernation behaviour of different bat species. Common Pipistelles are often active at amazingly low temperatures in the winter, and go out foraging.

In the south, in the Mediterranean region, many bats interrupt their hibernation as soon as the temperatures are high enough that the offer of huntable insects is to be expected. So, in Greece even in January, Nathusius's Pipistrelle (*Pipistrellus nathusii*) and Grey Long-eared Bats (*Plecotus austriacus*) emerge to forage if the weather is reasonably favourable.

Fig. 119. Weight decrease in individually marked hibernating Daubenton's Bats (*Myotis daubentonii*) in a tunnel in the city of Kiel, Germany. Their weight was set at 100 % with the first catch in the autumn and registered with all following catches (n = 76 recaptures of 44 animals). The average weight decrease over six months amounted to 37 % of the initial weight, a daily weight loss of an average of 0.23 %. Graph: M. Bauer after gen. lit. 47.

Behaviour of bats

Social behaviour

Bats are, in various respects, distinctly social animals. Not only do the females gather in groups during the time of giving birth and rearing of their young in nursery (or maternity) colonies, but also the males of many species spend the day together in groups. Only during the mating time, are the males of most species territorial and so live alone – or at least as long as they fail to succeed in luring females into their mating roost. The size of the nursery colonies depends very considerably on the ecological requirements of the species. Sometimes, as with Alcathoe Whiskered Bat (*Myotis alcathoe*), only a few females group together when they colonise, for example, a finger-thick gap in a damaged tree trunk. In other species the nursery colonies comprise

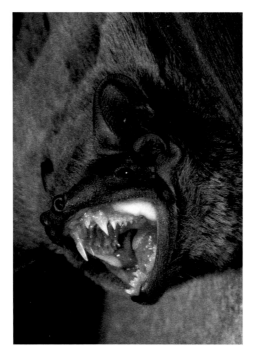

Fig. 120. As threatening display Leisler's Bats (*Nyctalus leisleri*) open their mouth very widely and show their buccal glands, which exude an intense smell. Photo: D. Nill.

more, around 20–50, females, while others, e.g. Greater Mouse-eared Bat (*Myotis myotis*), can amount to well over 1000 animals. In cave-dwelling species, the aggregations can be even larger and amount to many thousands of animals, or as with some tropical species, hundreds of thousands of animals. Worldwide the largest density of mammalian individuals at a specific site is achieved by colonies of Mexican Free-tailed Bat (*Tadarida brasiliensis*), which have comprised up to 20 million animals in just one cave.

Due to their social way of life bats have close bodily contact. But, even when aggressive sounding chirping is always apparent in large groups of bats, for example when an animal moves through the group, bats are generally peaceful to each other.

If one holds bats carefully in a warm hand, they behave similarly to animals in a group of the same species. Either they become calm, or – if they feel threatened – they nip the finger, often with a short, loud cry, but without really biting fiercely. It is as if they wanted to say to an animal of the same species 'that's enough!'. They behave completely differently when one tries to take by hand a more aggressive species such as a Noctule (*Nyctalus noctula*) that is crawling on the ground. Then it identifies the hand as a predator and bites as strongly as it can. With large species such as Greater Noctule (*Nyctalus lasiopterus*), that can be quite painful.

A group of bats always produces a strong attraction for single animals. If a group of Common Pipistelles (*Pipistrellus pipistrellus*) in the autumn, still half-awake in the winter roost, hears the echolocation calls of a passing individual of the same species, they answer with a quiet whispering and lure it into their roost. Also with 'invasions' of Common Pipistrelle it has been observed that sometimes numerous animals collect together into a trap. When an individual animal has fallen inadvertently into a smooth open vase or a bucket from which it is unable to escape, it will begin to chirp loudly. This has the effect that further bats fall into the same trap. For ringing studies of bats one can create such traps intentionally; but one must monitor it regularly, in order to be able to release the animals again after marking.

Advantages of group life

What is the advantage of this grouping, which is so characteristic of almost all bats? The group life also has, of course, costs: predators are more easily attracted; parasites and diseases are much more easily transferred. Probably there are two main advantages of the grouping in bats, which outweigh these disadvantages. Bats can go into torpor: they can lower their body temperature and by that save energy. One major advantage is that, as a group, they can mutually warm each other during cool weather and so share the costs of heat regulation. A second important advantage is the information transfer between the group members. They show each other, even if they have no special signals, the location of important roosts. During the joint emergence from the roost inexperienced animals probably receive information about the location of favourable hunting grounds, which they would not find so easily alone. And which is a favourable hunting ground can depend very much on the current weather conditions and season. Experienced animals make such associations; they probably even remember them from earlier years.

Signals

Bats have developed echolocation through their sensitive hearing and their world is therefore what they 'see' acoustically in front of them. Most of their social signals consist of a complex of different calls. At least for some species smell also seems to have almost as important a role in the social behaviour. Thus territorial males mark their roost with secretions from their buccal glands. These glands are in the corners of the mouth, and they swell enormously during the mating season (Figs 120, 121, 122). Further glands on the upper lip also deliver their secretions, particularly during the mating period, and the males daub the surroundings of their roost site with such

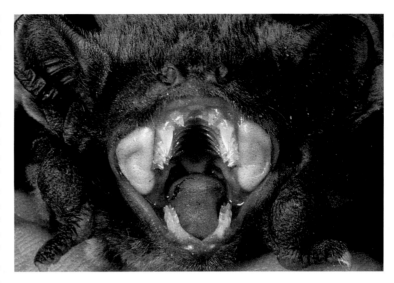

secretions. Often such roosts can be recognised for years from the brown staining from these secretions that were spread as a marker by the owner. In addition the scent of the whole body is transferred to the roost. Some bat species have an intense species-specific scent. The intensity of this scent – as far as it is perceptible for we humans – can also be very different in closely related species. Males of the Common Pipistrelle (*Pipistrellus pipistrellus*) do not have a particularly noticeable scent for our human nose, but Soprano Pipistrelles (*Pipistrellus pygmaeus*) secrete an intense Noctule-like scent of musk. The European Free-tailed Bat (*Tadarida teniotis*) has a typical pungent odour, a scent that is reminiscent

Fig. 121. In the courtship time in autumn, males of *Nyctalus* species develop large glands (buccal glands) in the corners of the mouth, seen here with a threatening Leisler's Bat (*Nyctalus leisleri*). With the secretion of these glands they mark the entrance to their mating roosts. Photo: O. von Helversen.

Fig. 122. The buccal glands of a male Kuhl's Pipistrelle (*Pipistrellus kuhlii*) in frontal view. Photo: O. von Helversen.

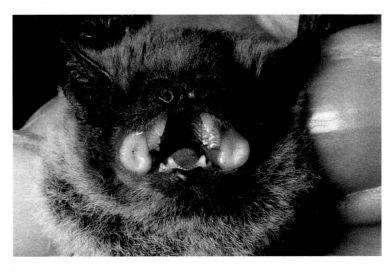

Fig. 123. Bats of the genus *Pipistrellus* will feign death in the case of danger; this is called akinesis. Photo: D. Nill.

of vegetable spices such as lovage.

Also tactile signals are not unimportant. In their colonies bats are accustomed to close bodily contact. If a female bat returns from its foraging flight and wants to land again in the already more or less crowded colony of closely wedged females, then it often flies somewhere into the centre, grasps with its legs into the group, whereby it might hang quite briefly on the ears of another female, and then quickly with-

draws into the group.

Within their social communication bats also use many vibrating signals during their bodily contact. Repetitive violent jerking of the body, for example, is the signal for a young animal to release from the nipple of the mother, so that the mother can go out to hunt. These jerks can be repeated for several minutes if – as is often the case – the young actually does not readily release. Before mating, males of Parti-coloured Bat (*Vespertilio murinus*) hop rhythmically on the roost like a wind-up metal frog. Many species show a species-specific, soft rhythmic vibrating of the whole body in situations in which they are unfamiliar with either the context or function, when one can even detect a quiet humming or purring sound (Fig. 124).

▶ Courtship

How males and females find each other and where mating takes place is still to a large extent unknown for many bat species. There are more precise observations for only a few species. For the Soprano

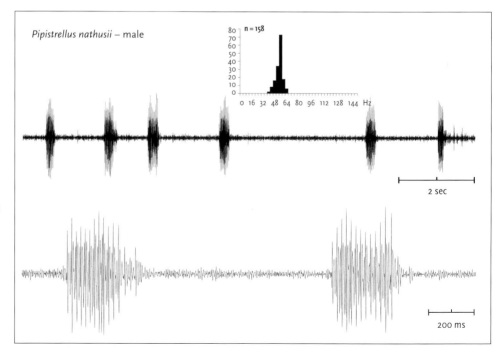

Fig. 124. Rhythmic body vibrations of a male Nathusius's Pipistrelle (*Pipistrellus nathusii*). The animal was gently held with a miniature acceleration adaptor pressed to its body in a warm hand and it began then to vibrate with rhythmic pulses to about 300–400ms long, with the frequency of the vibration (small graph) of *c.* 50Hz. Graph: M. Bauer.

Pipistrelle (*Pipistrellus pygmaeus*), Nathusius's Pipistrelle (*Pipistrellus nathusii*), Noctule (*Nyctalus noctula*) and some other species we know that individual males occupy mating roosts in areas in which females are to be expected. With these three species, these are tree holes or, as an alternative, also bat boxes. The males defend such display roosts against other males, foraging only briefly during the night, and try to lure females into their roosts with special calls. For much of the night the males of Soprano Pipistrelle fly around in the surroundings of their roost and emit loud display calls [gen lit. 40]. If they notice a female, they pursue her and try to lure her into the roost.

The Common Pipistrelle has a similar display call, which the males keep repeating at intervals of a few seconds. They thereby fly for hours on fixed routes within their display territory. The display roosts of these males are established especially in the vicinity of the winter roosts, where in the late summer the females are visiting to check the winter roosts.

The males of the Noctule Bat normally sit at the entrance to their display roost and call loudly. From time to time they fly around, briefly calling to drive away another male or to display for a female. J. Gebhard has, with his comprehensive studies on this species, observed that the male immediately welcomes an arriving female, encouraging it into his roost, and returns to the roost entrance and waits there until further females arrive [gen. lit. 39]. In this case mating takes place during the daytime.

The Parti-coloured Bat (*Vespertilio murinus*) has the most distinctive display for us humans. Their display songs are easy to locate, because the frequency of their calls is approximately 15kHz, well within the audible range for humans (Fig. 125). The display behaviour of the Parti-coloured Bat can be observed amazingly late in the year. Particularly in October and November nights the males fly for many hours on regular flight paths, which can cover an area with a diameter of several hundred metres, along cliffs or – as a common alternative – high buildings. During these display flights one can see that two animals pursue each other – perhaps this is the calling male trying to lure a female into his mating roost. Nathusius's Pipistrelles and Noctule Bats establish their display roosts along the southerly migration routes of the females, or around the winter roost. This is probably true for all migrating species, including for the Parti-coloured Bat. With Leisler's Bat (*Nyctalus leisleri*) in Greece it was observed that males do not directly display from their tree hole, but hang in exposed sites at the edge of forest, always at a particular freely visible spot on a tree trunk, and from there they emit their characteristic display calls. Probably the male attempts, when a female shows interest, to lead her onward into his day roost.

With the Lesser Mouse-eared Bat (*Myotis oxygnathus*) one can observe the fact that many males have their display roost relatively close together in indentations on the ceiling of a cave entrance, or, as a

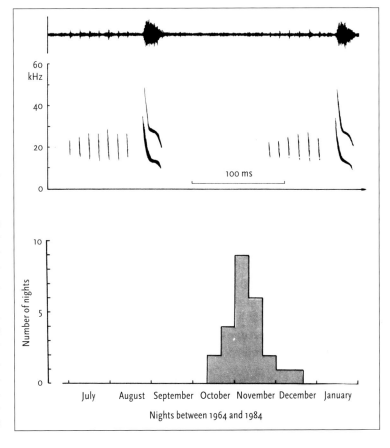

Fig. 125. Spectrogram of the display song of a male Parti-coloured Bat (*Vespertilio murinus*). The shown element is continuously repeated, sometimes for several hours, while the male tirelessly circles in a display area which can have a diameter of several hundred metres. Near Freiburg cathedral (Germany) one can particularly observe this behaviour on misty, sometimes rainy, November nights. From gen. lit. 51.

Fig. 126. A male Greater Mouse-eared Bat (*Myotis myotis*) looks from its display roost, a small hollow in the ceiling of a cave. With the secretion of its upper lip glands it has coloured the edges of its roost brown. Here it waits at night for females ready for mating. Photo: O. von Helversen.

Fig. 127. The individually colour-marked male Lesser Mouse-eared (*Myotis oxygnathus*) has lured a female into its mating roost in a water drain of a bridge and has mated with it. Photo: O. von Helversen.

substitute, use the joints or holes under road bridges. The males fight energetically for the possession of their roost site. A male can attempt to approach the owner of a roost site with a wide open mouth, but the owner also opens his mouth widely to defend his roost. Only if one of the two succeeds to be faster than the other, and is able to bite over the closed muzzle of its opponent, can it then pull the other out from the ceiling roost site and throw it to the ground. With these fights the Lesser Mouse-eared Bat can often accrue substantial injuries; sometimes one find males with damaged or scarred ears. That must be particularly disturbing for a bat, since its entire orientation system might be affected.

With Mehely's Horseshoe Bat (*Rhinolophus mehelyi*) large groups of both sexes gather in September, the males hanging to display with excited wingbeats. From the group, individual females approach the male that attracts it, and mating will follow. We found indications that the heaviest and most robust males have the greatest mating success. To what extent this affects the actual reproduction is completely unknown.

Such accumulations of closely grouped displaying males resemble the lek behaviour of some birds. Such display sites allow the females to select mating partners from amongst different males particularly effectively. Straight after hibernation the males of Lesser Mouse-eared Bat visit their display roosts and defend them against other males from spring right through the whole summer, until finally in August and September the actual display time begins and the females begin to be interested in their advertisement. The females then select a male along with its day roost, sometimes staying for several nights with the same male, often each night a different male. With Mehely's Horseshoe Bat it seems that the weight of the males is the main criterion by which the females judge the males.

Mating

With the actual mating the male embraces the female from behind with its forearms and in many species, but not in all, bites firmly into the neck fur of the female. The fur of the female is often distinctively covered with saliva, so that one can recognise, even hours later, which females have copulated. With the Lesser Mouse-eared Bat the male embraces and protects its female, often all day long, by putting its half-opened wings around it – probably in order to keep other males from this female, a behaviour that one calls 'mate guarding' (Fig. 128).

In some species, particularly Daubenton's Bat (*Myotis daubentonii*) and Natterer's Bat (*Myotis nattereri*), one can regularly also observe mating in the winter roost. Then one can see a male actively flying around in, for example, a cave in the middle of the winter. It tries again and again to land on other bats and examines them – often resulting in protest screaming. When it has found a female, the male tries to wake her up and mate with her.

Mating strategies

Obviously the males of several species can use different mating strategies. In the Noctule (*Nyctalus noctula*), a species which has been very well studied by J. Gebhard, he observed the following different strategies. During the late summer and in the autumn males vigorously occupy and defend a tree hole and use this as a mating roost. From the entrance of the hole, they call loudly to lure females. On each morning the female can decide which of the males it wants to visit in his mating roost. They do not always return to the same male. In the course of the autumn they may mate with a whole series of different males. Molecular-genetic investigations of the sperm cells stored in the uterus over the winter has shown that several males, on average about four males, have often contributed to the sperm supply [gen lit. 80, Mayer pers. com.]. When the females of Noctule Bats bear twins, these often originate from different fathers. What role any possible sperm cell competition plays and whether the females have any post-copulation mechanisms for sperm cell selection is to a large extent unknown. It is, however, easily conceivable that, during what is often a period of many months in which sperm cells of different males come together and are stored in the receptaculum seminis of the female, further factors operate that could affect in one way or another the paternity of the future young.

As J. Gebhard observed, it can also happen that another male sneaks inconspicuously, perhaps 'camouflaged' as a female, into a display roost of a resident territorial male. Such 'satellite males' can then mate during the day with the females that were attracted by the roost owner. It is still unclear whether the owner of the roost tolerates such 'satellite males' – perhaps if

they are related to it – or whether it simply does not recognise them as males.

Apart from strategies that essentially leave the choice of male to the females, there also seem to be other strategies. In the environment of larger winter roosts, particularly on the Balkan Peninsula, in the autumn a real 'mass display' can appear. Males and females can be in a condition of considerable excitement for some days, swarming extensively at night and calling loudly during the day – and mating. Perhaps this behaviour occurs par-

Fig. 128. In a cave with no hollows in the ceiling, when the male Lesser Mouse-eared Bat (*Myotis oxygnathus*) has attracted a female and mated with it, it guards this female until the next day and protects it from harassment by other males – a behaviour called 'mate guarding'. Photo: J. Sachteleben.

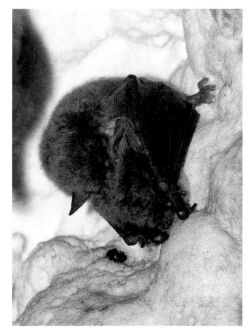

Fig. 129. Long-fingered Bat (*Myotis cappaccinii*) mating in a cave on Sardinia. The male wraps his wings round the female and firmly bites the fur on the nape. Photo: D. Nill.

Fig. 130. In the reproduction cycle of the males the testes begin to swell in summer with the production of the sperm cells, which are stored in the epididymis, where they stay viable for more than half a year. In this Long-fingered Bat (*Myotis capaccinii*) the tightly filled epididymides either side of the tail base are easy to recognise. Photo: C. Dietz.

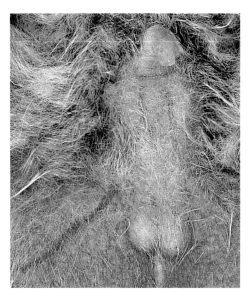

Fig. 131. A female Noctule (*Nyctalus noctula*) with its largely hidden young. The young often have feet as large as a mature animal soon after birth . On the right the foot of the one-day-old neonate can be compared with the foot of its mother (left). Photo: O. von Helversen.

ticularly when as yet unmated females arrive at the winter roost in a larger group.

As a fourth possible mating strategy there is also the phenomenon with the Noctule that healthy males awake in the middle of the winter and begin to wake individual females in their hibernation group and mate with them. J. Gebhard has repeatedly observed this in one of his hibernation groups. That is particularly amazing, because one knows that with the Noctules the females form a vaginal plug at the end of the mating period. In this way they can keep the sperm cells in the uterus as in a tightly filled pouch over the winter, without any danger of it running out again or that any germs penetrate into the receptaculum seminis. If there is such a vaginal plug, then it is not easy to understand what purpose mating has during hibernation. Probably the vaginal plug is at least not yet complete in some of the females.

Mother and infant

Nursery roost

The birth of the young takes place in nursery (or maternity) roosts in colonies, which usually comprise only females. 'Nursery roost' is therefore a beautiful and suitable expression for the place at which

the females meet in summer, give birth to and rear their young. In the vesper bats, to which most of the European species belong, the birth normally takes place in such a way that the female, when contractions have started, crawls a little away from the group of other females. Then it takes either a horizontal position, whereby it holds with both the feet and the thumb claws to the ceiling of the roost, or holds itself firmly upright against a perpendicular wall, with the head upward, and anchored to the wall with thumb claws and hind feet. In this position the young can be caught within the tail membrane as soon as the umbilical cord does not retain them any longer.

Birth

The birth probably rarely takes place with the head first, but usually as a breech birth with the body end first. As soon as the membrane of the amniotic sac opens, one sees the strong feet of the young, which anchor themselves immediately to the fur of the mother. Sometimes one has the impression that the neonate almost actively climbs onto the mother. Young bats have enormous feet for their size – their feet, and in some species also the thumbs, are already nearly as large at birth as in adult bats (Fig. 131). The mother licks the young and cleans it; the young tries, as soon as it can, to attach itself to the nipple of the mother. The afterbirth is eaten by the mother (Fig. 132). The umbilical cord, however, dries and is bitten off by the mother after a short time and dropped. On the large heaps of droppings under a Greater Mouse-eared Bat colony one can therefore find the umbilical cords of many young animals after the birth period. As soon as the young is licked clean and dry, it is tucked firmly within the flight membranes and the female goes back to the other females and looks for their bodily contact. Then one usually sees the young only as a bulge under the mother's flight membrane.

In the horseshoe bats (but also in the tropical Old World leaf-nosed bats and the sheath-tailed bats) birth takes place somewhat differently, in as much as the mother hangs, as usual, head downwards. The mother immediately catches the young with its wings, if necessary holds it with them, licks it and leads it to the false nipple (Fig. 133). The babies of horseshoe bats have the privilege to be allowed to sleep for some time like a normal mammal with the head upward.

Raising the young

For the first days the young cling to the mother's body and the mother may carry it even in flight. However, the mothers usually try not to go hunting in the first days but live on their reserves. The nutrition of the young bats is exclusively milk. Feeding with insects has only been observed in tropical bats. The flower-feeding bats feed their young additionally with nectar and the vampire bats with blood – however, our indigenous species cannot do that. There is probably hardly any other mammal in which the young are nourished exclusively with mother's milk until they reach almost their adult weight. Since the young bats can only hunt once they are so well grown that they can fly, a premature weaning is not possible.

The young normally get milk to drink before and after the mother's nightly foraging flight; only some mothers return again in the middle of the night to suckle their young, probably when the foraging conditions are particularly favourable. Of Greater Mouse-eared Bats (*Myotis myotis*) we know that the mothers can spend a whole day away in the hunting ground during bad weather conditions, when the hunting is not very successful, so their young must starve during this time.

When the mother returns, she greets her young by sniffing it. The mothers know both the scent of their children and their 'isolation calls'. When the young is hungry, and a bat comes into its proximity, it emits these 'isolation calls' or 'abandonment calls'; calls that are mostly still very simply structured in small young animals (Fig. 134 above). They are individually so different that the mother can recognise its own young by the isolation calls. M. Knörnschild discovered that twins of the Noctule Bat

have isolation calls that are much more similar than the calls of non-related young animals. Perhaps the characteristic signature of each call has a genetic basis, the mother reacts perhaps to certain calls particularly strongly and coupled with that a certain type of call which the young learns.

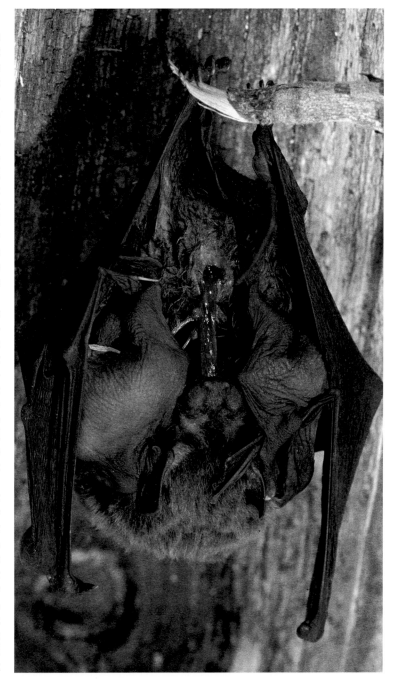

Fig. 132. The female of Leisler's Bat (*Nyctalus leisleri*) eats the afterbirth straight after the birth of its twins. Photo: D. Nill.

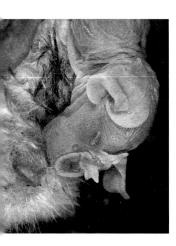

Fig. 133. A neonate Mehely's Horseshoe Bat (*Rhinolophus mehelyi*) about three hours after birth. After the young animal has sucked first from the mammary gland, it has clung to one of the false nipples located near the genital opening. The eyes of the young are still closed. Photo: C. Dietz.

As the young become older, their vocalisations become more varied and more complex; on the one hand the isolation calls develop in the direction of echolocation calls, on the other hand they can continuously develop different complex social calls (Fig. 134 below).

If the mother wants to go out foraging in the evening, it must get its young to release the nipple, to move it away and let it hang alone. The signal it gives to tell the young is rhythmic jerks with the whole body. However, some young may not release the nipple of its mother at all readily, and so the jerking can be a longer ritual each evening. Particularly in horseshoe bats the young have good possibilities to hang on at both the milk and the false nipples and it can take a mother a long time to get rid of its young. Perhaps in order to facilitate the young in releasing, the horseshoe bats form proper 'creches' of closely packed young animals within a protected area of the roost (Fig. 135).

When the mother returns, the young hastens to it and often first licks at its muzzle – a behaviour that one finds in many mammals. Fig. 140 shows this behaviour in a young Natterer's Bat (*Myotis nattereri*). Perhaps with this licking at the lips of the mother important symbiotic germs for the intestinal flora are transferred. Often the mother leads the young immediately to its nipples and holds it within its wings. When the young are getting older,

however, they often become rather annoying to their mothers. G. Heise has observed that females of Noctules often feed the larger young in the morning, and then generally fly off to another roost where they are not constantly begged and bothered by the young.

Many tropical bats carry their young from the roost when emerging for the night's flight, but hang their young individually in a hiding places that only they know, and then go off to forage. This is probably a precautionary measure, because the accumulation of young in the nursery roost could be a large, welcome meal for some predators during the night. An individual young animal, hidden somewhere amongst the lichen on a tree trunk or behind loose bark, will be discovered by a predator only with great difficulty. In the morning the mother then takes the young and carries it back to the common nursery roost.

Normally bats only suckle their own young. But J. Gebhard has observed occasional instances of 'milk theft' in the Noctule (*Nyctalus noctula*). This can happen when a young has lost its mother and in desperation tries to feed from another female. However, the females will mostly roughly reject a strange youngster. J. Gebhard observed only once that a mother also accepted the child of its own mother [gen. lit. 39]. Perhaps there is an altruistic behaviour between close relatives in

Fig. 134. Isolation calls of a neonate Noctule (*Nyctalus noctula*). These calls in one-day-old young animals are already so individual that a mother can recognise her own young. The isolation calls develop on the one hand towards more complex social calls, and on the other hand to the echolocation calls.

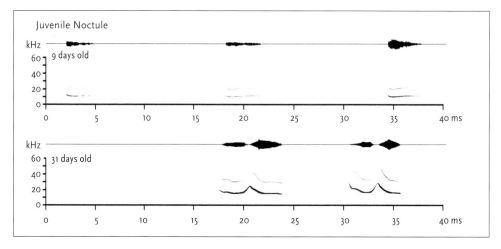

indigenous bats, as is assumed for some tropical species, such as the vampire bat and some free-tailed bats.

Becoming independent

When the young gradually starts to fly, it stretches its wings repeatedly and runs to the entrance of the roost, where it sniffs the outside air. In the Noctule, one of the few bat species that has been studied more carefully in this respect, J. Gebhard was able to state that the young normally go on their first solo flight while their mothers are out hunting. They try to note the exact situation of the roost entrance and after the first flight return again to the roost in relatively short time. Often they are only to be found together again when the returning adults approach the roost entrance. Probably the colony members also help them with their continuously emitted twittering sounds. With the first flights from complicated roost entrances there can be high losses among the young animals, as was observed several times with the Common Pipistelle (*Pipistrellus pipistrellus*), when they could not find their way back to their roost behind metal cladding and ended up in a fireplace.

In some other species, such as Whiskered Bat (*Myotis mystacinus*), Natterer's Bat (*Myotis nattereri*) and Geoffroy's Bat (*Myotis emarginatus*), it has been observed that the mothers accompany their young on their first flight attempts. If the young has lost its way back to the roost entrance, one can, on the next day, sometimes find a mother in the proximity of the roost covering its flying, grown-up young with its body. Probably in the next evening the mother will try to give enough milk to the young that it can make the return flight into the colony.

Young Noctules must learn completely alone how to go out hunting. We have weighed young Noctules before their flight and after returning to the roost in the first days of their hunting activity and in this way examined whether they caught prey independently. Fig. 139 shows the result: on average the young animals return after the first three nights lighter than they flew off,

and thus have probably still not caught any prey. But on the fourth or fifth night they return 2g heavier than on departure, and thus obviously are now able to forage effectively.

Thus the degree to which mothers teach their young the important feeding and roosting sites and other essentials of life may vary from species to species, but it is, in general, probably less than has been traditionally thought. It is undoubtedly an important area worthy of further study. As stated above, it is clear that juvenile Noctule Bats get little or no help from their parents, and there was one instance where the offspring of one captive and flightless mother Noctule Bat left its mother in the autumn. In the spring it returned to the same site and eventually established its own thriving maternity colony in the artificial site within which it had been reared. In many species, such as Serotine Bat, the adults leave the maternity roost as soon as their young can fly, possibly to reduce the foraging competition. When mother and juvenile pairs of Greater Horseshoe Bat were radio-tagged, they were observed to spend almost no time together outside the roost. At many autumn swarming sites at caves or other places, the number of juveniles can greatly outnumber the adult females. Even where parental care of juveniles on their first flights has been observed (as with the *Myotis* species mentioned above), this care may be rather short-lived.

Fig. 135. Greater Horseshoe Bats (*Rhinolophus ferrumequinum*) leave their young at night in regular 'creches', in which they can hang in dense clusters, often in inaccessible and safe parts of a roost. Photo: C. Dietz.

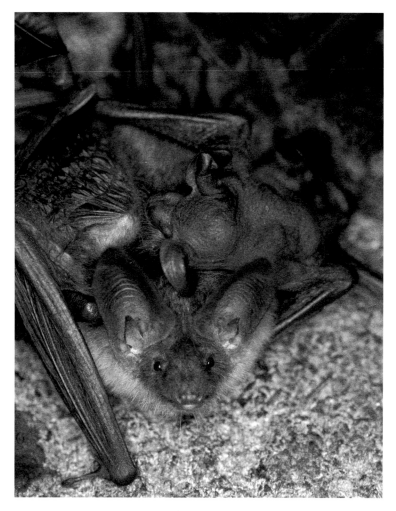

of birth is obviously optimised by the different species. One factor supporting this is the generally high synchronisation of the births in a colony, which certainly also has yet other advantages. The time of birth is often clearly different in different populations of the same species living in different habitats. The birth in Long-fingered Bats (*Myotis capaccinii*) on the Greek coast takes place as early as the beginning of May, but in the mountains only much later.

While there has been a great deal of research on the maternity colony behaviour, there has been relatively little study of the summer groups of males of species such as Daubenton's Bat, and the mating strategies of many species are still quite unknown. Other questions on group behaviour relate to the function of autumn swarming, which does not always appear to be associated with mating, and the smaller peak of swarming in late spring is not. Similarly the lek-like display behaviour of some species has a curious distribution within the diversity of bats and is worth further investigation.

Fig. 136. Whenever possible young animals keep close bodily contact with their mothers, as with this juvenile Bechstein's Bat (*Myotis bechsteinii*). Photo: D. Nill.

Fig. 137. A juvenile Natterer's Bat (*Myotis nattereri*) tries to crawl under the wing of the mother in order to get to the nipple. Photo: D. Nill.

Birth period

In this phase of the year, in which the young gradually start to fly, it is particularly important that a good supply of prey exists close to the roost. The young should not yet fly too far from the maternal roost. An interesting question, but one which cannot easily be answered experimentally, is whether bats plan the time of birth such that the time of weaning of the young coincides with the optimum food availability that can be expected in the year. Possibly it could also be that the mothers rather use the optimum food availability for their own advantage, by using this period for the time of pregnancy and milk production, since they then need a great deal of energy. This question is not yet answered with certainty for the European bats. In any case, the time

Fig. 138. As with most bat species, Alpine Long-eared Bats (*Plecotus macrobullaris*) can transport their young in flight. Photo: D. Nill.

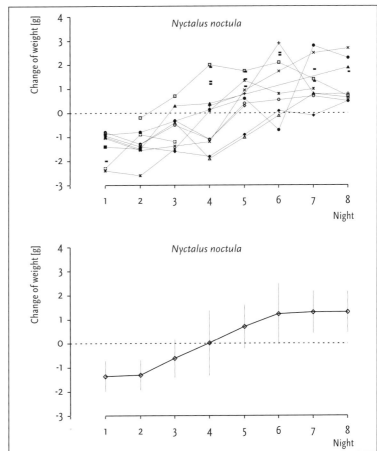

Fig. 139. Young Noctule Bats (*Nyctalus noctula*) learn to go foraging alone. In the first nights they return after some hours independently, without assistance from their mother, to the roost, having noted where the entrance is. The illustration shows the weight change between emergence and return (upper for 10 different young animals, lower for the average value) in the first eight flight nights: in the first three nights all animals returned around 1–3g lighter; they evidently had not fed. They climbed immediately to their mothers and took milk. On average, after four days the young maintain or increase their weight, an indication that they are now hunting successfully.

Fig. 140. A mother Natterer's Bat (*Myotis nattereri*) returning from a foraging flight welcomes her young. Characteristically, as for many mammals, not only for bats, the young is licking the muzzle of the mother, thereby probably transferring important organisms of the intestinal flora. Photo: D. Nill.

Bat roosts

The adoption of caves as daytime roosts was probably one of the key innovations in the evolution of the bats, and thereby led to the fundamental adaptation to nightly activity and echolocation. Indeed, even today caves are the preferred daytime roosts for many bat species. Caves have the great advantage for an animal with a night-oriented lifestyle to offer a safe place of refuge for the day: in the darkness of the caves, predators that orient themselves by sight, have difficulties. Only a few bat predators, such as some snake species, hunt bats within caves. These are especially constrictor snakes, with their infrared sensitive sensory organs, which help them to seek prey in the darkness of the cave.

In Central and Northern Europe caves are usually too cold to serve as summer roosts. Here, caves are particularly used as safe winter roost. But in the Mediterranean area there is a whole series of bat species that lives during the day particularly in caves: all five horseshoe bat species (Genus *Rhinolophus*), with Lesser Horseshoe Bat (*Rhinolophus hipposideros*) less tied to caves, since it can also establish nursery colonies in large hollow trees, such as rotten plane trees. Also Schreibers' Bent-winged Bat (*Miniopterus schreibersii*), the three large species of mouse-eared bats (*Myotis myotis*, *M. oxygnathus* and *M. punicus*) and the Long-fingered Bat (*Myotis capaccinii*) are typical cave bats. Following the last ice age some of these species were able to expand their distribution to Central Europe, since they could colonise large

Fig. 141. Blasius's Horseshoe Bats (*Rhinolophus blasii*) emerging from a cave roost in the evening. Some caves can be occupied by more than 10 species together. Photo: D. Nill.

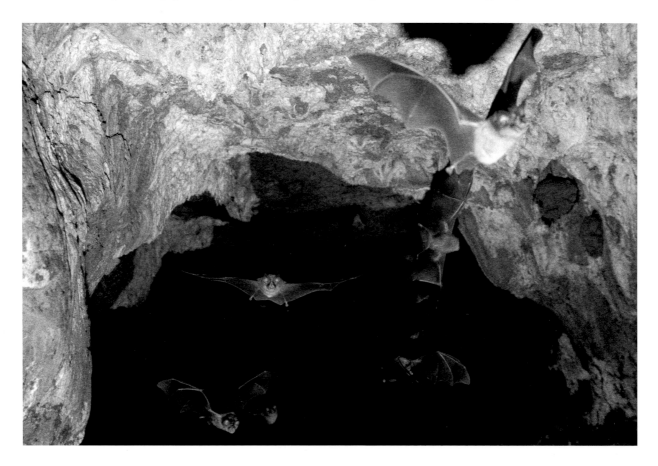

Fig. 143. The formation of dense clusters, here of Geoffroy's Bat (*Myotis emarginatus*), serves social thermoregulation. Photo: D. Nill.

different roosts. Therefore many bat species use tree holes as day roost. Tree holes are particularly often the result of the activity of hole–creating woodpeckers, or of holes rotted when dampness penetrates into the trunk through a broken branch.

Yet other bats use narrow crevices, either in rock (and as a substitute in buildings), or in cracks of trees, sometimes simply behind raised bark of large trees. These species prefer spaces where they can have back and belly contact with the roost walls, and wedge themselves into the most narrow cracks.

Bats may select not only rock crevices for their day roost, but if necessary also under stones in the rubble of streams or in heaps of boulders in mountain scree. Sometimes they are amazingly flexible and use also apparently exotic cavities, such as abandoned nests of Red-rumped Swallow (*Hirundo daurica*).

The adaptation to tree holes is particularly noticeable in the migratory bat species. Noctule (*Nyctalus noctula*), Leisler's Bat (*N. leisleri*), Nathusius's Pipistrelle (*Pipistrellus nathusii*) and, to a lesser extent also Parti-coloured Bat (*Vespertilio murinus*), rarely use large underground roosts and few hibernate in caves: they prefer tree holes or rock crevices. This remarkable correlation may be connected with the fact that large caves are relatively rare and particularly difficult to find. Hence, possibly, the long-distance migratory species cannot rely on finding another such roost in the morning after the night's flight.

The Barbastelle (*Barbastella barbastellus*) is more or less a specialist in roosting under raised bark of trees in summer, or, as an alternative roost, under timber cladding of buildings. In winter, however, it visits deep caves. Nevertheless, it is often a species that only moves into larger winter roosts during heavy frost. Then, it will even hang against icicles.

man-made cavities, such as roof spaces, in lieu of spacious caves. So, today, roof spaces are the typical nursery colony site in Central Europe for Greater Mouse-eared Bat (*Myotis myotis*), whereas in the Mediterranean area mostly caves are occupied.

Many areas of our planet are poor in rock caves and, here, bats had to search for

Roost change

It is known that particularly tree-dwelling bats very frequently change their roost in summer. I. Wolz and G. Kerth found that often a small part of a large association of Bechstein's Bat (*Myotis bechsteinii*) moves first, and only in the next morning the larger part of the nursery colony follows. Different hypotheses have been discussed regarding the reasons for these remarkably frequent roost changes. Since the temperature conditions are different in each roost, as a function of the weather conditions, it could be that different roosts supply particularly favourable conditions at different times. In their constant essential compromise between energy saving and staying awake, when the bats are searching for particularly favourable conditions, they must change their roosts accordingly. Another possibility is that roost changes serve to 'lose' ectoparasites. Most ectoparasites must leave the bat on which they live from time to time, and then a hasty escape could help to lose these parasites. Particularly frequent moves are mostly observed when the young are beginning to fly. At least in this time it may be particularly important to show the still inexperienced young animals as much as possible of the available roosts in the area of the nursery roost.

How do bats find roosts?

When locating roosts the excellent local memory of the bats certainly plays an important role. But sometime bats must also find new roosts. When one releases a bat in an unknown area, one can often be astonished by how quickly the animal finds a small crack in a wall or some other possible hiding place. Bats probably pay constant attention to potential cracks and cavities that could serve as a roost.

Obviously they can compile specific search images from experience. One observes for months, or even years, in areas where new bat boxes were installed, that they may be occupied only occasionally. Then, suddenly the boxes are found and

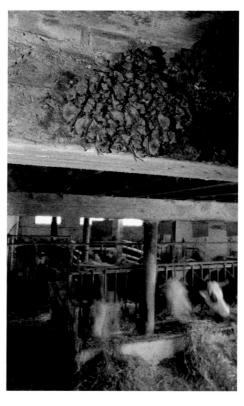

Fig. 144. Geoffroy's Bat (*Myotis emarginatus*) visits unusually well-lit roosts, as here in a stable ceiling. Photo: D. Nill.

increasingly occupied. Probably, in many cases the local population developed a search image that an unusual 'bump' on a trunk could be a usable roost. The increase in population is thus only apparent; the truth is that local population increasingly switched to bat boxes as roosts.

Obviously some bat species, such as Noctule (*Nyctalus noctula*), which, as a fast flier, cannot so easily find tree holes when they are hidden by branches and leaves, use the social calls of other species. Around Munich F. Kronwitter discovered that Noctules also use Great Spotted Woodpecker holes amongst dense growth of spruces as day roosts [gen. lit. 71]. It is assumed that these Noctules follow other bats, e.g. Daubenton's Bats (*Myotis daubentonii*). Daubenton's Bats can discover such hidden holes much more easily with their manoeuvrable flight. J. Gebhard assumes that also Greater Mouse-eared Bats (*Myotis myotis*) often find their roosts by following smaller species, such as Brown Long-eared Bats (*Plecotus auritus*), which are more skilful in finding new roosting opportunities.

The long-distance migratory species have, of course, special difficulties, since they have to find a roost at dawn in an area which they do not know. J. Gebhard pointed out that the display calls of the males in their mating roost have a special attracting effect, sometimes not only for mating-compliant females. This was particularly observed in Noctules (*Nyctalus noctula*) and Nathusius's Pipistrelles (*Pipistrellus nathusii*).

Roost defence

In some species, such as Lesser Mouse-eared Bat (*Myotis oxygnathus*), males defend their mating roosts at great expense against other males throughout the whole summer. But there are often different prospective customers for the day roosts: e.g. dormice, many hollow-tree-dwelling bird species or insects, such as bees and hornets. Fat Dormice (*Glis glis*) and Garden Dormice (*Eliomys quercinus*) apparently usually win over the bats. With bees, it was observed that swarms looking for a new roost, drove the bats out. A. Kiefer observed once that such a bee swarm not only drove out Noctules from their roost, but even stung to death a large proportion of the animals, which probably would not vacate their roost fast enough.

Some bats, particularly single males of Greater Mouse-eared Bat (*Myotis myotis*), which have selected a bat box as a display roost, exhibit a further behaviour with which they can probably deter intruders such as dormice or song birds: if one disturbs them a little, they begin a loud 'wasp-like humming', which sounds just as if a swarm of wasps or hornets are occupying the bat box. Figure 149 shows a recording of this sound. The bat produces a compact series of extraordinarily short sounds, which in principle have the spectrum of an echolocation call, but with a frequency that for our ears – and probably also for the ears of dormice and Great Tits – results in a distinct humming, approximating to the buzzing of a hornet. It is very probably that bats can thereby prevent enemies from entering the hole; something that breeding Great Tits do with a noise like that of a hissing snake.

Roosts and colony size

Large caves in the tropics provide accommodation for not only thousands, but for millions of bats. It is a magnificent spectacle when these bats leave the cave entrance at dusk and ascend in spiralling swarms, which look almost like a cloud of smoke, and then move off to their hunting grounds.

But even in Central Europe nursery roosts can reach amazing numbers of bats. In the Greater Mouse-eared Bat (*Myotis myotis*) nursery colonies are known which comprise several thousand females with their young. Such colonies need, of course, large roosts, such as the spacious lofts of churches or other buildings, and in which disturbance of the colony should be limited. Since the bat females normally return each morning to their colony to suckle their young or to keep contact with the other females, it is necessary to fly many kilometres to hunting grounds. Telemetric studies revealed that Greater Mouse-eared Bats hunting grounds are often 8–15km from their roost. Individual females can have several preferred hunting grounds that are visited night after night, and these individual hunting grounds can then have a relatively small area of only several hectares.

An interesting, but still not clarified question is: how is the allocation of the individual hunting grounds regulated? One should firstly assume that each animal would like to hunt as close as possible to the roost, because it would then save the not inconsiderable costs of the long commuting flights. It is not well known to what extent individual bats defend their foraging territories against others of the same species. In relatively many species one can readily hear aggression calls when two animals meet while hunting and can see short pursuits. J. Sachteleben studied this in more detail in e.g. the Common Pipistrelle (*Pipistrellus pipistrellus*) in Bayreuth (Germany). The call heard in the spring with aggressive meeting of different animals, also serves in the autumn – emitted at short and regular intervals – as a display call.

It would nevertheless be conceivable that the distribution of the hunting grounds is essentially a statistical phenomenon: if good hunting grounds in the proximity of the roosts are over-used because too many animals are hunting in the same area, some individuals leave to search less-used areas, which could be more favourable even if the flight path is now longer. In this way they can find perhaps the most favourable

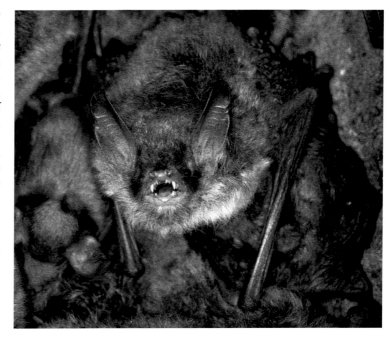

Fig. 148. Cluster of Natterer's Bats (*Myotis nattereri*) in a bat box. Photo: D. Nill.

uncontested allocation. On the other hand each individual animal has a large advantage if it knows precisely its nearest hunting grounds, places in which it already knows it can quickly find prey depending upon weather conditions and season. Therefore it will probably be reluctant to change its hunting ground.

It can be seen that with increasing size of the colony, the more rare is a particular and suitable type of roost in the surrounding area. The colonies of species dependent on caves in Europe, such as Long-fingered Bat (*Myotis capaccinii*) and Scheiber's Bentwinged Bat (*Miniopterus schreibersii*), reach way over 10,000 animals, while the colonies of species roosting in rock crevices comprise barely more than two dozen animals. An infomative example is a comparison of the similarly-sized Long-fingered Bat (*Myotis capaccinii*) and Daubenton's Bat (*Myotis daubentonii*), with their comparable wing morphology. The small colonies of Daubenton's Bat with up to 200 animals practically never hunt more than 15km from their roost, usually within 5km. The members of colonies of Long-fingered Bat, which may comprise up to 5,000 or more animals, must, conversely, regularly fly 20km or more to their hunting grounds.

In the same way, it is also quite conceivable that the increasing colony size of Greater Mouse-eared Bat (*Myotis myotis*) in some regions of southern Germany is indicating that sufficient roosting opportunities are not available to allow the increasing numbers to establish new colonies.

Some other roost sites

Around the tropics we can find a range of roost sites not demonstrated by our temperate bats. Perhaps the most famous are the tent-making bats of Central and South America. These are fruit-feeding species of spear-nosed bats (Phyllostomidae) that modify the leaves of different plant species in different ways, such that parts of the leaf collapse to form a tent (see Fig. 20). Here they can live in small groups for up to six weeks, when the leaf is sufficiently deterio-

rated that they must move on. There are also fruit bats in southern Asia that modify plants to provide a covered roost. A few species (particularly sucker-footed bats of South America and Madagascar) have adhesive pads on their wrists (and, in Madagascar, also the feet) and roost stuck to the inside of the still furled leaves of certain plants; once the leaf opens, they too must move on. The flat-headed Bamboo Bats (*Tylonycteris* species) live inside older, large bamboo canes, entering and leaving via holes left when a beetle had previously emerged. The fish-eating bat, *Myotis vivesi*, can roost under rocks on the beach of Baja California, while African woolly bats, *Kerivoula* species, will roost in old weaverbird nests, even sometimes lurking behind an active wasps' nest occupying the same disused bird's nest.

Fig. 149. The wasp-like humming noise of a Greater Mouse-eared Bat (*Myotis myotis*) is probably intended for protection from enemies. The small graph above left indicates the relative frequency of the sound pulses, the small graph above right the frequency division of individual pulses, the large graph shows the spectrogram of the sound. Graph: M. Bauer.

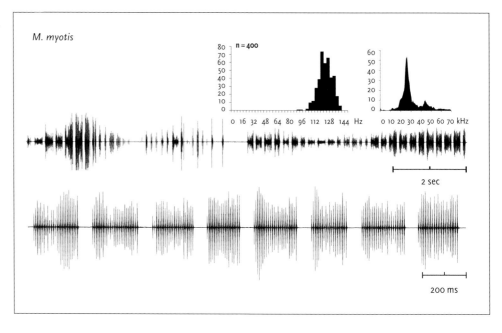

Foraging habitats of bats

Bats are found almost everywhere in the world – except in the Arctic and Antarctic regions. In Europe the Northern Bat (*Eptesicus nilssonii*) is a particularly cold-resistant species occurring far above the Arctic Circle. The enormous species diversity in the tropics comprises bat species communities occurring in desert and steppe biotopes as well as those occurring in lowland rain forests or in the damp forests of high mountains. In Central Europe many bat species have a clear affiliation with forest. Some species could occupy Central and Northern Europe following the end of the ice age, probably only following the regeneration of forest. These could probably be followed by other species only when humans made their buildings making additional suitable roosts available. While Greater Mouse-eared Bat (*Myotis myotis*) hunts predominantly in forest, its nursery roosts mostly lie in buildings in the areas of human settlement, but other species, such as Bechstein's Bat (*Myotis bechsteinii*), spend their entire life in the forest and are thus dependent on suitable tree holes for their day roost. Other species, such as the Grey Long-eared Bat (*Plecotus austriacus*) and the Lesser Mouse-eared Bat (*Myotis oxygnathus*) in Central Europe use buildings as roost and hunt particularly in the open countryside.

For bats hunting in forests the spatial structure of this habitat type is an important factor for the resource partitioning of different species. Dense vegetation is avoided by many species, which, particularly for commuting flight from roost to hunting ground, prefer to use forest edges, forest tracks and rides. Often tree lines, forest edges or hedges are used as guidance structures for the flight from roost to hunting ground – but also for hunting, since such structures accumulate many flying insects in the evening. On the other hand some species, such as the Lesser Horseshoe Bat (*Rhinolophus hipposideros*), Whiskered and Brandt's Bat (*Myotis mystacinus* and *M. brandtii*) or also long-eared bat (genus *Plecotus*), have adapted their flight style to fly through the smallest gaps in the vegetation. With their type of

echolocation calls these species are particularly effectively able to detect prey insects close to vegetation and to catch them in extremely slow or hovering flight. The combination of different characteristics makes it possible for different species to use different features of habitat types, without competing too much for prey.

Water surfaces, from ponds and lakes to smaller streams or pools in forests, provide a particularly rich supply of insects. Many flying insects develop in water and, when the adults hatch, offer a rich food supply. When mayflies or caddis flies fly over water, then not only the usual Daubenton's Bats (*Myotis daubentonii*) come to take advantage of this resource, but at the waterside also long-eared bats, all small *Myotis* species, Common Pipistrelle (*Pipistrellus pipistrellus*) and Nathusius's Pipistrelle (*P. nathusii*) and, high above, the *Nyctalus* species.

While the Lesser Horseshoe Bats (*Rhinolophus hipposideros*) usually visit very small hunting grounds close to their nursery roosts and rarely go more than 5 kilometres from the roosts in one night, Greater Mouse-eared Bats (*Myotis myotis*) often hunt at distances of 8–15 kilometres from their nursery roosts, but once arrived in the hunting ground, use only a comparatively small area of a few hectares. This core hunting ground is usually visited by an individual each night, whereby it acquires an exact knowledge of the area. Other species, such as Greater Horseshoe Bat (*Rhinolophus ferrumequinum*) or Mediterranean Horseshoe Bat (*Rhinolophus euryale*) visit each night up to 10 separate hunting grounds, approaching some only for a few minutes, possibly to examine the current prey availability, spending hours in other areas. It is assumed that a horseshoe bat, which can live for over 20 years, in the course of its life develops an extremely detailed knowledge about which sub-areas of its total habitat are most favoured at different times of year. Some bat species visit the same hunting grounds over years and, depending upon the species, can be territorial and aggressively drive out animals of the same species, or even members of their own nursery colony. In other species the density of hunting animals seems to be regulated by the prey density without intraspecific aggression.

Some of the fast flying bats hunt completely differently, the European Free-tailed Bat (*Tadarida teniotis*) may travel far greater distances of up to 100km from its roost. In this way they can visit the most favourable foraging areas, in spring the coasts of the Mediterranean, in autumn the pastures of high mountains. Consequently they usually have, like *Nyctalus* species, no defined hunting grounds that are visited each night, but wander more widely.

It is common in all species that they can hunt flexibly within certain limits, despite a frequently high specialisation on a certain habitat type. Thus, it is not unusual for an individual Daubenton's Bat (*Myotis daubentonii*), usually hunting over water, to hunt in forest or over an orchard meadow for several hours, habitats in which Natterer's Bat (*Myotis nattereri*) would be much more expected.

Fig. 150. Stroboscope record of a Natterer's Bat (*Myotis nattereri*) hunting in an orchard. A negative black and white shot is shown with 24 very short flashes within an exposure time of 2 seconds.
Photo: B. Siemers.

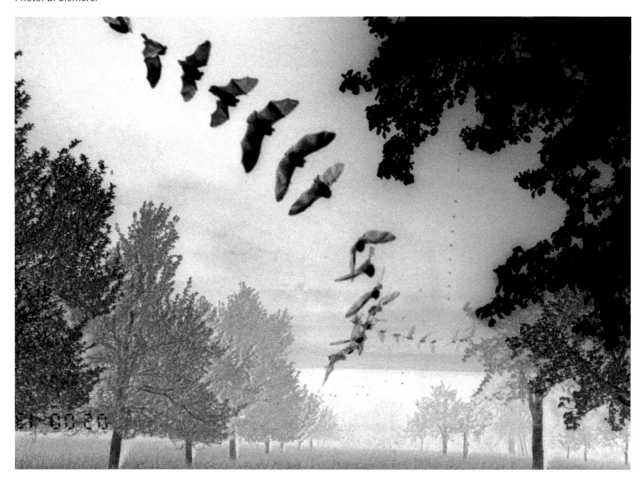

Population biology

Structure of bat populations

All organisms are members of populations. Smaller associations, e.g. nursery colonies in bats, belong to larger group systems, these form a network with neighbouring colonies, which again form larger common subpopulations. In this way more or less hierarchical populations are divided at different levels, up to the highest level: all individuals of the species. Within 'population structure' one understands the way these different levels are organized. How related are the different individuals and subpopulations to each other? How much exchange is there between the groups?

In some bats, e.g. Bechstein's Bat (*Myotis bechsteinii*), the groups of females one may find at a particular time in a tree hole belong to a larger nursery colony association, which is called a 'nursery colony network' (a fission-fusion society). Within such a network the individual groups exchange their members, they may come together in such a way in completely different smaller or larger groups over few days. The nursery colony networks of some species can, however, be very strongly isolated from each other. In Bechstein's Bats intruders from other colonies are repelled immediately and driven away. A young female generally remains in the colony of its mother.

Isolation of colonies can be observed in principle, but less pronouncedly, in other species e.g. in Greater Mouse-eared Bat (*Myotis myotis*) or Common Pipistrelle (*Pipistrellus pipistrellus*). While the nursery colony associations of Bechstein's Bat or Brown Long-eared Bat (*Plecotus auritus*) are confined to some parts of a forest, the populations of, e.g. Common Pipistrelle, are much larger and seem to be organised around large winter roosts. Ringing studies of Common Pipistrelle have shown that the individuals which, for instance, use the Freiburg Cathedral for swarming and later for hibernation, or in the Bartholomaeus Church in Demmin (eastern Germany), or in Marburg Castle, almost all accumulate from nursery roosts that occur up to 50km around these large winter roosts.

Females of the Greater Mouse-eared Bat remain faithful to their nursery colonies, but there are many observations of the exchange of individual females between such colonies, over distances of up to 100km or more.

The populations of migratory species are differently organised. In the Noctule (*Nyctalus noctula*) and Nathusius's Pipistrelle (*Pipistrellus nathusii*) the young females are extraordinarily faithful to their place of birth. Their first return from the hibernation area in spring is almost always exactly to the nursery roost in which they were born. The fact that such fidelity to the place of birth does not lead to in-breeding is because of the males. The males of the migratory species rarely establish their mating roosts in the nursery roost area, mostly somewhere on the migration route or in the hibernation area. Therefore the population is constantly mixed genetically. However, the males can also become faithful to a certain place once they have selected a mating roost. In Nathusius's Pipistrelle it has been observed that males that have selected a mating roost along the migration route will use this roost repeatedly year after year.

In some species a majority of the males remain in the wintering area and wait there in the late summer and autumn for the arriving females. In Greece in summer, almost exclusively males of Leisler's Bat (*Nyctalus leisleri*), Greater Noctule (*Nyctalus lasiopterus*) and Nathusius's Pipistrelle are found. Only at the beginning of the migration period in September do females arrive, and mate there with the displaying males. Apart from the avoidance of in-breeding it has the advantage for the whole population that during the summer, when the females rear their young in the northern distribution areas, there is no competition with the males for food. In the comparatively short time of pregnancy, birth and raising the young the females have, to a certain extent, all resources to themselves.

Genetic population structure

With the progress that molecular genetics has made in the last decades, a picture of the behaviour (with respect to local fidelity, migration and population exchange) can be acquired, to a certain extent, from the level of the genetic variability of populations. For this two very different and hence informative examples are given by the Noctule and Bechstein's Bats, which were examined in detail by F. Mayer and G. Kerth [gen. lit. 63, 64, 80].

Firstly for an investigation of the population structure, one selects genetic 'markers' that are sequence sections of the DNA which are variable within a species. Due to this variability different individuals of a population would possess different alleles

(or 'haplotypes', see Box 1). When one selects on the one hand genes from the mitochondria of the cells and on the other hand sequence sections from the cell nucleus, one has yet another possibility for comparison: the mitochondria are (almost) exclusively transferred by the egg cells to the next generation, inheriting in each case the maternal lineage (= matrocliny). The genes of the cell nucleus come half from the father, and half from the mother.

Figures 151 and 152 show how differently the genetic structure of the population of two bat species, Noctule and Bechstein's Bat, can be. In both species the nursery colonies comprise of females that were even born in this nursery roost, together with daughters, mothers, grandmothers, aunts, and so on. Fig. 152 shows that the exchange between the nursery colonies of Bechstein's Bat is so small that nearly all females have the same genotype. Similarly in the Noctule Bat, almost all daughters return to their maternal nursery colony, but the associations are clearly wider and also a little more 'loose'. Therefore more different haplotypes occur in a nursery colony and the spectrum overlaps more strongly with that of the neighbouring colonies (Fig. 151).

A different picture is shown when one examines the genetic structure on the basis of nuclear sequences. Then one finds a nearly complete genetic mixing within the nursery colonies. This is because the females of both species do not mate with males born in the same colony. The females of Noctule Bat mate during migration or in the winter roost, the females of Bechstein's Bat mate during the autumn swarming at caves, often similarly far from the summer site. In this way the nuclear genes in the entire population are mixed over a large geographical distance.

Age structure of bat populations

Why do bats become so old?

Bats become unbelievably old in comparison with other mammals of the same size.

Fig. 151. Genetic diversity of three neighbouring nursery colonies of Noctule Bat (*Nyctalus noctula*) in Uckermark, eastern Germany. Each nursery colony is symbolized by a circle, with the haplotypes of mitochondrial (purely matrilineal relationship) marker genes represented by a colour. The width of the sector corresponds to the frequency of the haplotypes within the respective nursery colony. With the relatively individual-strong nursery colony of the Noctule the small occasional exchange of females between the colonies is sufficient to produce a high genetic diversity (symbolised by the many colours), i.e. only some of the females are particularly closely related to each other. Data after F. Mayer and G. Heise.

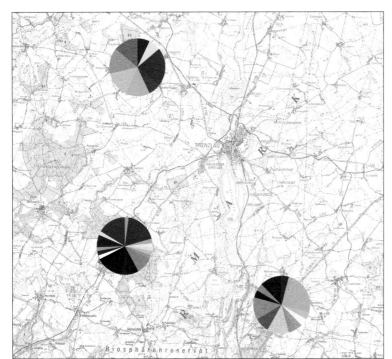

A ringed Brandt's Bat reached at least 41 years old and holds the present age record [gen. lit. 66, 95]. This record originates from southern Siberia, where bats should, however, have an unusually long hibernation from September to May, but find a plentiful insect supply in the summer. This unusual case is surely an exception, but ringing in Central Europe of different bat species yielded age records of between 25 and over 30 years.

Why do bats become so old? Firstly, one can consider that probably there could not be bats at all if they did not become so old: in most species a female bat can bear and rear only one young per year in temperate latitudes. Only some populations of species such as the Noctule and Nathusius's Pipistrelle can regularly bear twins. The weight that can be carried by a flying mammal during pregnancy and that hunts at the same time, is obviously limited. Above all, the weight of the embryos limits the possible birth rate of bats.

That can be, however, only half the answer to the question of the high potential age of bats. An individual that lives longer (and is reproductive up to its death, as in bats), must produce more descendants for the next generation and with that is contributing to selection! Thus there must be a natural selection pressure on 'getting old'. A body to 'grow', and which is 'very long-lasting', is, however 'expensive' – it is worthwhile only when the mortality due to other causes – e.g. being eaten by a predator

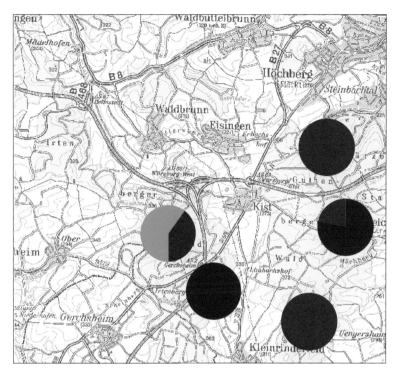

– is not a main limitation on survival. The life-span of an animal like a bat, living in the wild, is rarely limited by death from old age, but normally by any 'accident': caught by a cat, trapped on burdock or barbed wire, caught by an owl, frozen during hibernation – or nowadays perhaps more frequently ending as victims of traffic, or from the blades of a wind turbine.

Our bats have no real predators which are specialised on them. In the tropics, however, there are specialised hunters of bats, such as the Bat Falcon (*Falco rufigularis*). But these are not soley dependent on bats as prey. Other birds of prey sometimes capture a careless bat, but all these predators capture only a tiny percentage of the existing bats as prey. In a certain sense nearly each death of a bat is 'an accidental death', which is only statistically predictable, but from which the individual cannot escape, and is, to a large extent, independent of its age.

Survival rates

The survival curves of bat populations have one thing in common: from year to year a certain percentage of the population dies,

Fig. 152. Genetic diversity of five nursery colonies of Bechstein's Bat (*Myotis bechsteinii*) in the vicinity of Wuerzburg (Germany). Each nursery colony association is symbolized by a circle, with the haplotypes of separate mitochondrial (purely matrilineal relationship) marker genes indicated by colour. The width of the sector corresponds with the frequency of the haplotypes in the respective nursery colony. In Bechstein's Bat there is hardly any exchange between the nursery colonies, therefore only a few different haplotypes appear in each colony, all the animals are maternally closely related. Data after G. Kerth.

Fig. 153. A Bat Hawk (*Machaeramphus alcinus*) attacks emerging molossids in front of the entrance to a cave in Borneo. Photo: D. Nill.

▶ Fig. 154. Peregrine Falcon (*Falco peregrinus*) and Hobby (*F. subbuteo*) capture bats flying in day time or hunt them at dusk. Photo: D. Nill.

▶▶ Fig. 155. Wing remains of Noctule Bats (*Nyctalus noctula*) under a feeding site of Levant Sparrowhawk (*Accipiter brevipes*) near a roost crevice of the bats in North Bulgaria. Photo: C. Dietz.

Fig. 156. Barn-Owls (*Tyto alba*) can seek out and capture bats in their attic roost. Photo: D. Nill.

almost independent of the age of the individuals involved. One recognises this in Fig. 161 from the example of three particularly well-examined species. The annual mortality rate amounts, at least in the closer-examined species in Central Europe, between 20 and nearly 50 per cent of all animals. The question must read thus in reverse: because bats have only a few unspecialised enemies, they remain alive for a comparatively long time. The small predator pressure and the impossibility to rear more than one or two young per year complement each other. Only both characteristics together make 'bat lifestyle' possible. If there were as many bat predators as mouse hunters (and if a bat would let itself be caught as easily as a mouse – and were it not so difficult to catch with its agile flight), then this type of lifestyle would have no chance to exist in this world. The 'conditioned design' of bats does not allow it to have as many young as a mouse or a shrew in a so short a reproduction time, which

makes it possible for the latter to have several generations in only one year.

Age structure

An important characteristic of a population is its age structure, which is expressed in 'the age pyramid' (see Box 6). The age pyramid of many animal species (e.g. the present British human population) can take

▶ Fig. 157. Some Eagle-owls (*Bubo bubo*) can regularly specialize in bats and acquire a substantial part of their food in the proximity of large roosts. Photo: D. Nill.

▶▶ Fig. 158. Pellets of an Eagle-owl (*Bubo bubo*) from a North Bulgarian cave which consist, to a large extent, of skeletal remains of Noctule Bats (*Nyctalus noctula*). Photo: C. Dietz.

◄ Fig. 159. Large colonies attract enemies, here at least 17 Blasius's Horseshoe Bats (*Rhinolophus blasii*) were captured in one night by a cat at a small cave entrance in the Bulgarian Rhodopians. Photo: C. Dietz.

◄◄ Fig. 160. Under a large colony of Schreibers' Bent-winged Bats (*Miniopterus schreibersii*) lies an animal completely skeletonised by a freshwater shrimp (*Gammarus*). Photo: D. Nill.

complicated forms – some age classes are strongly represented, others hardly, and events such as 'the pill effect' left their traces for long time. The age pyramids of bat populations are substantially simpler (they correspond with Fig. 161). Over almost the entire possible lifetime the mortality is constant. Only the newly flying young animals in some species seem to pay for their inexperience in the first year of life with a somewhat higher mortality rate. But very old animals, which are near the possible maximum age, have similarly a somewhat increased mortality compared to the total population.

Whether the increased juvenile mortality actually applies generally to bats is not easy to say. All population studies on free-living bat populations were and are carried out with ringing. With such studies emigration cannot be differentiated in principle from mortality. Perhaps young animals of some species are on average simply not yet completely faithful to their locality in their first year of life, as occurs in older age groups. The result would be an overestimated value for the mortality of the young animals in their first year of life.

The extremely old animals with their apparent slightly increased rate of mortality are on the other hand hardly important, because there are only a very few individuals they hardly affect the statistics.

Bat populations approximate thus to a very obviously model population, which is excellent through the possession of a constant mortality – independent of the age of the individuals. In this case there are relatively simple mathematical formulae, with which one can compute many important parameters of the population (see Box 6). If in addition the population is in equilibrium, thus as many animals die in each year as new young are recruited, then at a particular time the derived age pyramid reflects the survival rate of an age cohort, an age group.

Population development in Nathusius's Pipistrelle

As can be seen in Figure 162, the observed birth rate is not always identical with the birth rate required for the maintenance of the population in nature. When Nathusius's Pipistrelles colonised bat boxes

Fig. 161. Average survival rates of three bat species with different reproduction strategies: Noctule (*Nyctalus noctula*) – low survival rate, high birth rate (green, after gen. lit. 48); Greater Mouse-eared Bat (*Myotis myotis*) with a smaller number of deaths per year (blue, after gen. lit. 44); Whiskered Bat (*Myotis mystacinus*) with high annual survival rate and a very low reproduction rate (red, after gen. lit. 130). Graph: M. Bauer.

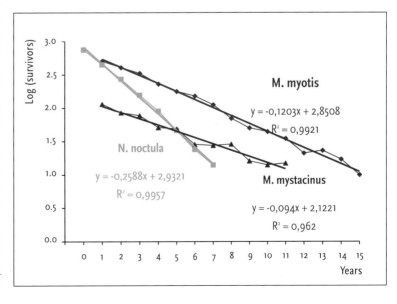

Box 6

The age (or population) pyramid

If one follows a certain age group of a population, a 'cohort', then one can determine the survival rate from year to year. The **survival rate**, **p**, is the counterpart to the mortality rate (mortality = **m**), thus **p = 1−m**. In most populations, the survival rate from year to year depends on the age. Very often young animals have a higher mortality rate, adults over a longer period of life a more or less constant, relatively lower, mortality rate, and old animals again a higher mortality.

For some purposes simple population models are very close to nature – or draw attention to deviations from nature contrary to the basis of the models. The following model is particularly clear: (1) the mortality from year to year remains approximately constant, independent of the age of the individuals, (2) the birth rate for males and females is on average the same, and (3) if the population is additionally still in equilibrium, thus the births replace the deaths, a stable age pyramid arises. In this case the chronological sequence of the survival of a cohort is illustrated as 1:1 from the parallel co-existence of animals of different ages in a population, in the so-called 'age (or population) pyramid'.

Since bats form close to ideal populations (see Fig. 161) one can simply calculate: if one indicates the population size before the birth of the young as N (1) and t is the age, then:
N (t) = N (1) x (1−m)$^{t−1}$, whereby also (1−m) = p indicates the probability of survival from year to year.

Under these conditions some relatively simple formulae result:

(1) The age pyramid, considered in the summer before the birth of the young, remains constant. When N (t) is the number of animals of the age t in the population, then:

$$N\,(t) = N\,(1) \times (1-m)^{t-1} \quad t = 1, 2, 3 \dots \text{ years}$$

This corresponds to the probability of survival of a cohort of one year old animals over the following years.

(2) The total size of the population (before the birth of the young) is:

$$N = \frac{N\,(1)}{m}$$

(3) The average life expectancy of an animal from its birth is:

$$E_0 = -\frac{1}{\ln\,(1-m)}$$

The average life expectancy of the one-year-old animals, shortly before the birth of the young is:
$$E_1 = m \times \Sigma\ N(1) \times t \times (1-m)^{t-1}$$

(4) The proven maximum age (longevity, **L**) of a certain species depends of course on many factors, both in regard to the survival risk of the individual animal, and also with regard to the probability of it being retrapped or recovered. One can measure, however, the age that, on average, 1% of all animals will reach, which is:

$$L\,1\% = 1 - \frac{2}{\log\,(1-m)}$$

With large number of ringed animals, it can also be interesting to estimate the age which 1/1000 of all animals would reach:

$$L\,1\text{‰} = 1 - \frac{3}{\log\,(1-m)}$$

(5) A further very important estimated value, in comparison with the observed rate, is the birth rate **n** that is required to maintain a constant population level: :

$$n = \frac{2\,m}{1-m}$$

In this case it is worthwhile also to look at the case in which the general mortality in all age groups is constantly equal to **m**, but the mortality of the young animals from weaning to the next summer, m_1, is higher than the average mortality rate, **m**. Then

$$n = \frac{2\,m}{1-m_1}$$

In this formula the mortality rate, **m**, is of crucial importance.

installed by A. Schmidt around 1980 in the Brandenburg pinewoods (eastern Germany), the birth rate was about 1.8 young per female, while a birth rate of, for example, one young per female for the observed mortality of 31% per year would have maintained the balance. This population of Nathusius's Pipistrelle could therefore increase rapidly in the study area [gen. lit. 113, 114, 115].

In other cases, particularly in the 'DDT period' of Central Europe, the mortality very strongly outweighed the birth rate and the consequence was local extinction of whole populations. Such an example is the Lesser Horseshoe Bat (*Rhinolophus hipposideros*) in the years after 1950 (see species account and Fig. 174); many bat populations have not yet recovered from this decline.

Prime example: Noctule Bat

A particularly well-examined example of a balanced bat populations is the study of the Noctule (*Nyctalus noctula*) in northern Brandenburg by G. Heise and T. Blohm [gen. lit. 48]. Figure 161 shows the progress of the survival curve of a population, in which over several years 747 young females were ringed, after they had become fully weaned. Further studies on the population had to be limited to the females, because only they are faithful to their place of birth and return the following year to the bat boxes where they were born. (The males, however, settle after migration in a different winter area, only a few ever return to their birth forests.) Between 1996 and 2002 the nursery colonies showed the following age pyramid when one considers only the Noctules ringed as a young animal: 412 first year females had been ringed in the year before as weaned young, 260 were two years old, 137 females three years old and so on, as represented in fig. 161 (with logarithmic measure on the coordinate). When one interprets this age pyramid of the model appropriately as a survival curve of a cohort (age group), it gives an annual mortality of 44%. To compensate for the mortality rate of adult animals in a stable population, which corresponds for instance with the

supporting capacity of the habitat, each female would have to rear about 1.5 young per year (see formula in Box 7). The observations showed that in the studied colony a total of 1056 females reared 1519 young in the course of the years, which corresponds with a birth rate of 1.44 young per female per year. In the context of the accuracy that such studies can reach in the field, it is a very good agreement. Alternatively, these findings confirm the hypothesis that the Noctule population in the studied forest area was in equilibrium and one can assume therefore that the age pyramid corresponds to the number of deaths in an age class.

Further population parameters in the Noctule

From these data one can derive a whole further series of interesting details of the studied Noctule population (see Fig. 162): the average age of the females (just before giving birth) was *c.* 2.3 years. The average life expectancy of a post-weaned young Noctule was, however, only 1.74 years. One per cent of all Noctules could become 8.5 to 9 years old, one out of thousand 13 years old. The maximum age of the Noctule observed so far is actually 12 years.

For a bat, Noctules have a relatively high reproduction rate. Many females, particularly the older ones, regularly bear twins. Due to the majority of females in the nursery colony being one year old animals, which have only one young per year, the reproduction rate is overall only *c.* 1.5 per year.

Comparison of reproduction rates

An even higher reproductive rate in Central Europe was observed so far only in Nathusius's Pipistrelle: 1.8 young per female per year – but in a phase of strong population growth. A similar picture applies to Common Pipistrelle with mortality rates between 30 and 37%. Since the mortality in Common Pipistrelle and Nathusius's Pipistrelle, is, from earlier investigations, lower than in the Noctule, a lower reproduction rate would be sufficient for the maintenance of the populations: between

Fig. 162. Different population parameters for five
selected Central European
bat species. See text for
explanations.

	Noctule	Common Pipistrelle	Nathusius's Pipistrelle	Greater Mouse-eared	Whiskered
Mortality as adult animal m [per year]	0.44	0.31–0.37	0.32–0.34	0.21–0.24	0.19
Expected average lifespan (as from birth) E_0 [years]	1.7	2.1–2.6	2.4–2.7	3.6–4.2	4.6
Expected average lifespan of animals reaching at least one year E_1 [years]	2.2	3.2	2.9–3.2	4.0–4.5	4.8
Observed average age of animals reached at least one year [years]	2.2–2.3	2.7–2.9	2.6–2.9	3.9–4.0	4.5
Max. age L1% [years] (see box 6)	8.5–9	11–23	11–13	18–20	22
Max. age L1‰ [years] (see box 6)	12.5–13	16–19	17–19	26–30	33
Observed maximum age [years]	12	16	14	25	23
Required birth rate for maintenance of the population n [per year]	1.5–1.6	0.9–1.2	0.9–1.05	0.54–0.64	0.48
Observed birth rate [per year]	1.4–1.5	–	1.8	0.68	–

0. 9 and 1.2 young per year per female.

The picture is completely different when we turn to the *Myotis* species. The mortality rate found for the Greater Mouse-eared Bat is between 0.21 and 0.24, that means that 76 % to 79 % of all animals survive to the following year. The average age of the populations observed so far is 4 to 4.5 years. For the maintenance of a population the reproduction rate should be only c. 0.6 young per female per year. Whether this value is actually valid in the wild population, is, however, not easily measurable in the Greater Mouse-eared Bat: of the one-year-old females only some are in the nursery roosts in the summer, and also only some of the one-year-old animals produces a young. When one estimates the rate of the one-year-old females present in the nursery colony at c. 70–80 per cent, and the low reproduction rate of the one-year-old females (only 20 per cent) , then it becomes clear that the total Greater Mouse-eared Bat population could have on average a reproduction rate of c. 0.68 young per female per

year. That is a value that only allows for a slow growth of the Greater Mouse-eared Bat populations at present.

When one considers Fig. 162 more closely, one can recognise amazing differences between the species. The Noctule must survive with a mortality/year more than twice as high as that for the Greater Mouse-eared Bat or whiskered bat (*Myotis mystacinus/brandtii*). Consequently more young must be produced per year and become independent animals.

Why the Noctule can do that (and the Whiskered Bat not) and why – on the other hand – its mortality is so much higher, so far no ecologist and particularly no physiologist can answer. One can make only assumptions. Such basic questions of ecology, science can hardly address so far, so deep seems their answer and we are still far from a sufficiently detailed understanding. Ecology is one of the most advanced systems that nature offers, a biological systems theory of the interactions of organisms is still in its infancy, the details a long

Box 7

Population growth

Populations change size because, on the one hand, young are born, with the **birth rate n** ('new generation rate' or 'natality'), and, on the other hand, members of the population die, with the **mortality rate m** ('mortality'). If n is larger than m, the population grows with the **growth rate r = n – m**. If r is less than 0, also m > n, the population size is reduced, perhaps leading to extinction. When r remains constantly > 0 for a period, the population grows exponentially, as with the global human population, which reached 6 billion at the end of 1999, and at present increases annually by about 80 million (r= 0.013), which corresponds to a doubling time of *c.* 50 years. (If it continues in this way, in 2100 the world will have not 6 billion humans, but the even more inconceivably total population of 20 billion humans).

No natural population can grow indefinitely, because all organisms use natural resources, which are limited. If the **population size N** grows, resources (e.g. food, roosts, or areas with few enemies or parasites) become scarce. Then the mortality m rises and the birth rate n falls. The simplest model, i.e. a linear increase of the mortality and a linear reduction of the birth rate of the population density, will result in a now famous equation, the so-called 'logistic growth function'

$dN/dt = r \times N \times (K-N)/K$. This means that there is a certain population size, K, below this the population grows and above this it falls, so that a natural population always fluctuates around this 'N more or less equals K' value. This quantity K therefore refers to the 'carrying capacity of the habitat'.

It was important for some animal and plant species in their evolution (i.e. a selection advantage) to be able to increase fast – e.g. as new occupants of frequent, but unforeseen, newly developing habitats. Such species have a high reproduction rate r, but they leave their descendants poorly equipped with reserves and do not invest much in their future. Therefore one calls such species '**r-strategists**'. Other animal species nearly always live in populations that are close to carrying capacity K. For such species a rapid increase is relatively unimportant. It is much more important to equip their offspring – of which on average only two per pair of parents will in any event survive – with the best possible reserves and protection for a long time to make them fit for competition with animals of the same species. Accordingly one calls these species '**K-strategists**'. Most animal species naturally lie somewhere between these two extremes.

way from a comprehensive solution.

Some obvious explanations do not seem to apply, or rather may not be the main factor: the migration to the winter roosts of Noctule and Nathusius's Pipistrelle is certainly dangerous, the Common Pipistrelle, closely related to Nathusius's Pipistrelle and having almost the same mortality and birth rate, does not migrate and hibernates in the reproduction area. Also the common conception that the weakening from utilisation of remaining fat supplies toward the end of the winter represents the most important cause of mortality for the bats of temperate latitudes, does at least not seem to apply generally: studies of Common Pip-

istrelle in a large hibernation association in Marburg castle resulted conversely in only a small number of deaths between the beginning of hibernation and leaving the winter roost in spring [gen. lit. 120].

Although one calls all bats 'K-strategists (see Box 7) – as without any doubt they all are when one compares them with mice or shrews, or even with song birds or most amphibians – species comparison nevertheless shows that also they arrange themselves in the 'r – K continuum': Noctules and Nathusius's Pipistrelles are much more r-strategists than, for example, *Myotis* or *Rhinolophus* species, which belong to the most extreme K-strategists within the mammals; such that, for example, the support of weaned young animals is more pronounced in Whiskered Bat than in the Noctule.

Population densities in bats

The density of bat populations is more difficult to estimate than for instance the population density of birds: one cannot count, as with many song birds, the number of territorial singing males in spring. Bats often hunt far from their nursery roosts and collect at areas with particular promise related to the ambient weather conditions and season. So, they can hunt in an Oak forest for a few days when the European Oak-leaf Roller (*Tortrix viridana*) flies there, and a week later over water where perhaps caddis flies hatch. The density of observed foraging bats is difficult to relate to the population density of a species.

Population density in the Greater Mouse-eared Bat

In theory one has the possibility either to catch all the bats in a sufficiently large area, or one can use the 'capture/mark/recapture' method. Only in some species is it possible to trace all – or nearly all – nursery colonies in a large area. This was successful to a large extent in recent decades with Greater Mouse-eared Bat (*Myotis myotis*) in Bavaria [gen. lit. 102]. One can, of course, never be absolutely sure of having found all colonies but Greater Mouse-eared Bat is so strongly tied to buildings in Central Europe that one can contemplate the attempt. The number of animals found in the nursery colonies cannot correspond to the total population density, because the adult males are absent from the nursery roosts. There are other reasons why the animals counted in nursery colonies can only indicate a minimum value for the population density. Some adult females, depending on the weather, even in summer, sometimes roost in tree holes in the foraging area or in other hidden daytime roosts. The most reliable assessment of the size of nursery colonies can be obtained when the young are recently born, but not yet weaned, because at this time most adult females are in the colonies.

In order to gain an estimated value of the real population density, one can proceed with the Greater Mouse-eared Bat using the following simplifying assumptions: that the mortality is *c.* 20 % per year, and that *c.* 70 % of all females in a colony have one young (see Fig. 162). The one-year-old females are an additional problem, because, in their first year, many of them do not return to the colony in which they will later bear their young. Newer estimates suggest that only *c.* 70 – 80 % of the one-year-old females are present in the colony in the first summer, and of these only *c.* 20 % give birth in their first year of life.

If one uses these values, one can calculate as follows: 100 females have about 70 young; thus one counts *c.* 170 animals at the end of raising the young in July. Of the young animals, however, only half is female, therefore the population counted includes 135 females. Therein are missing, however, 20 – 30 % of the one-year-old females, that might account for 6 – 10 missing animals in our numerical example, therefore the studied population includes *c.* 143 females. When one considers – which is confirmed by all previous observations – that the sex ratio is 1 : 1, and if one sets the same mortality for the males as for the females, then there must be twice as many, i.e. *c.* 290, Greater Mouse-eared Bats in total in the study area. In order to find an estimated value for the total population at the end of July, the number of counted nursery colony individuals (170) is to be multiplied by a factor 1.7. The number of adult females remaining next May will presumably amount on average to *c.* 110 animals, thus still about 38 % of the total.

With the help of such estimations we can say that in some nature areas of South Germany, the Swabian and the Franconian Alb, five to seven individuals of Greater Mouse-eared Bat are present per km² [gen. lit. 102]. In the Franconian Alb e.g. at least

29,455 nursery colony individuals (females with young in July/August) were counted directly in 7,400km² (the value of 5–7 individuals/km² indicates the population density in August, following the rearing of the young, according to the above formula). The population density of the adult females in spring was accordingly 1.9–2.6 females per km². In other natural areas, e.g. in the Alps or in the area of the Main-Franconian Plains, the population density is substantially smaller, e.g. 0.2 to 2 individuals/km². If one calculates the total population of Bavaria (70,776km²), then one achieves an average population density of at least 2 individuals/km². Of course, not all Greater Mouse-eared Bat colonies of Bavaria were sampled. This value is thus a minimum value, by how much the real population densities differ is so far unknown.

Only for few other bat species are there comparable data available. The broad, including all habitats, density of Common Pipistrelle in northern England in an area of 2,500km² was estimated at 3.9 females per km² [gen. lit. 61], similar values were also found for Scotland, where probably the Common and Soprano Pipistrelle were combined [gen. lit. 133]. The minimum population density of the Noctule in a *c.* 800km² area in Brandenburg was *c.* 2.4 adult females per km² [Blohm pers. com.]; the Noctule population there almost exclusively uses bat boxes as daytime roost and therefore allows relatively reliable counts. The population density at the end of July amounts then to about 5.8 individuals per km².

Capture/mark/recapture method

Another feasible possibility is to determine the population densities of individual species by the capture/mark/recapture method, but only for small areas. The basic idea of this method is simple: as a first step one catches as many animals as possible, marks them and releases them again. The number of animals marked is Nm. Later, in a second step under as similar conditions as possible, one catches again and determines now the ratio between the marked and the unmarked animals. If the second session is substantially later than the first, one must bring in another estimation value for the mortality of the marked animals. From the ratio R = marked recaptured/unmarked and the known (or estimated) survivor numbers of the marked animals one can now simply conclude the population size: N = Nm (1 + 1/R). The main problem with this method is the area reference: to what area can one refer this number of individuals? In order to be able to measure this, one must examine a sufficiently large area, so that the exchange with neighbouring populations no longer plays a role. A study of Daubenton's Bat in an area with ponds favourable for this species in the Central Franconian Aischgrund, north of Nuremberg (25km²), resulted in an overall population density of *c.* 51 individuals/km², which remained quite constant over four consecutive years. The 51 individuals/km² consisted of 33 females/km² and 18 males/km² together [own data, Geiger & von Helversen unpubl.]. Such high densities are, of course, only reached locally and are not generalised over large areas.

Comparison of the population density between birds and bats

A comparison with the population density of birds is interesting. With birds completely different values are obtained, depending on whether one considers a relatively small (< 10km²) area, with habitat characteristics favourable for a species, or larger areas. In Fig. 163 comparative data for some bird species for large areas (in total usually 20,000–30,000km², averaged) are given [gen. lit. 11] and compared with the values for bats.

In studies on birds the density of territories (or breeding pairs) is normally determined. At the end of the breeding season there are, however, as with the bats, far more animals/km² than these values indicate. The densities of bird species can best be compared with the densities of female bats before the beginning of the reproductive phase in the summer.

However, one should also consider in this comparison that the estimated values for bats are minimum values, because an

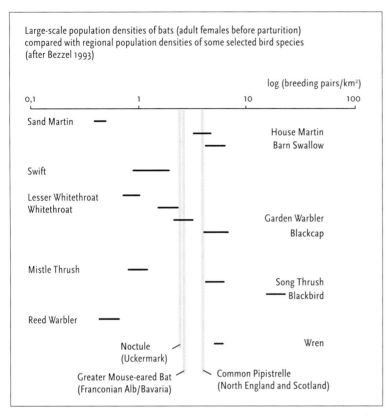

Large-scale population densities of bats (adult females before parturition) compared with regional population densities of some selected bird species (after Bezzel 1993)

log (breeding pairs/km²)

0,1   1   10   100

Sand Martin
House Martin
Barn Swallow
Swift
Lesser Whitethroat
Whitethroat
Garden Warbler
Blackcap
Mistle Thrush
Song Thrush
Blackbird
Reed Warbler
Noctule (Uckermark)
Wren
Greater Mouse-eared Bat (Franconian Alb/Bavaria)
Common Pipistrelle (North England and Scotland)

Fig. 163. Comparison of the large-scale population densities of three relatively common bat species in Central Europe with the population density of some selected bird species. See the text for data, population densities of birds after gen. lit. 11.

unknown proportion of the population might nevertheless have escaped observation in the broadscale investigations. But the conclusion can be drawn that the population density of the Noctule, Greater Mouse-eared Bat and Common Pipistrelle, which are among the most common species in Central Europe, rank approximately in the lower middle zone of comparably sized song birds.

Population monitoring

The need to monitor populations for conservation purposes is increasingly being recognised. Many European countries have very long-term data on populations in caves

and other underground sites, but the data has not always been collected in a systematic way and for many countries the data is still not collated. Eurobats has compiled guidelines on the monitoring of bats in Europe, including recommended techniques for each of the European species. Good reliable data on population trends is an essential these days in convincing authorities of the needs of conservation. In the UK, a National Bat Monitoring Programme was initiated through the Bat Conservation Trust in 1996, with government funding. This programme has a selection of target species and a range of monitoring techniques (basically monitoring of hibernation sites, emergence from maternity colonies, and bat detector transects), and aims to collect statistically robust data that is representative of the UK bat fauna, roost types, foraging habitats and methods [UK gen. lit. 164]. In principle, it should be aiming to be able to relate population changes to environmental changes. The programme is also able to contribute to a much wider project on biological indicators of environmental change, be such changes natural or through human-induced changes (which may be negative, as with increased intensive agriculture, or positive, such as a result of encouragement for replacement of lost hedgerows and woodland), or wider changes brought about by such factors as climate change.

Many countries have also tried to make population estimates for each species. Such estimates can be found in national reports to Eurobats or in other national publications. These estimates will probably always be fraught with doubts as to their accuracy, but they can give a useful indication of relative status, while the rates of change from monitoring data may be more important.

Ectoparasites

Bats have an array of unusual ectoparasites. The large bat-flies (Nycteribiidae) are particularly noticeable, especially if one holds a bat in the hand and a large, long-legged, brightly coloured, wingless insect runs through the fur of the bat. These parasites look rather like spiders, but belong to the true flies (Diptera). Their wings are absent, probably to reduce the risk of being blown away.

The ectoparasites of bats have millions of years of long co-evolution with their hosts and have adapted themselves in such a way that they do not excessively damage their hosts, although many nourish themselves with their blood. All these parasites are harmless to humans. Often bat parasites are not only specific to bats, but are restricted to only one bat species. During the evolutionary separation of the host species such parasites can similarly develop new species. The co-evolution of hosts and parasites led, therefore, in many cases to the fact that from the relationship of the parasites one can nowadays also draw conclusions about the relationship of the hosts. A parasite species that has adapted to a certain host must take its chances with the losses and gains of the evolution of its host. However, since the environment of the parasites is generally only slightly changed, compared to the changes in the environment of the host, the parasites have in their evolution diverged less from each other than have the bat species and hence their relationship is generally very much easier to recognize.

Parasites that have a long history of adaptation to a certain host species, normally hardly affecting the host. Detailed investigations of the metabolic conversion of bats have, however, shown that bat individuals carrying many parasites show a higher metabolic rate, and thus use more energy than parasite-free animals of the same species. Sometimes one finds weakened bats, particularly young animals, which are suffering an excessive parasite load, usually mites. In such a case it is, of course, difficult to determine what is cause and effect. Are sick, weakened animals unable to control their ectoparasites and therefore heavily infested with parasites? Or is it the many parasites that caused the weakening of the bat? Nearly all ectoparsites that one finds on bats belong to one of four groups of parasites: bat-flies, bat-bugs, fleas or mites.

Bat-flies

The bat-flies belong to two different families, the Nycteribiidae and the Streblidae, which both occur exclusively on bats. The Nycteribiidae have no wings and therefore look rather like a 'six-legged spider'; most Streblidae have kept their wings and in Europe occur only on horseshoe bats. Both families belong to the 'Pupipara', a group of flies that do not follow the usual insect pattern of laying eggs, from which larvae hatch, which then grow and shed their skin several times until they pupate. In the bat-flies the whole development from egg to prepupa takes place within the body of the mother. The mother then attaches the prepupa to the wall of the roost and it immediately pupates. One finds such pupae frequently in bat or bird boxes inhabited, e.g., by Bechstein's Bats (*Myotis bechsteinii*). When the bat colony - possibly only a year later – revisits the box, the flies within their pupae are aware and immediately emerge, crawl onto a bat and live thereafter in its fur.

One finds most bat-flies on cave-dwelling bats. With some tree-dwelling bats colonies may be completely free from bat-flies, since the bats apparently avoid them by frequent roost changes. Of course, the danger always exists that they reinfest themselves from an unknown roost and then pass the parasites back to the nursery roost and the whole colony. Perhaps the frequent roost changes of many tree-dwelling bats is an essential strategy to get rid of the bat-flies and other parasites.

Fig. 164. *Penicillidia dufourii* is a wingless parasite belonging to the bat-fly family Nycteribiidae Photo: C. Dietz.

Fig. 165 The parasitic flies of the family Nycteribiidae often occur in pairs, here *Penicillidia dufourii*. Photo: D. Nill.

Fig. 166. The family Streblidae also belongs to the true flies, unlike the Nycteribiidae many species are still volant. Just one species occurs in Europe: *Brachytarsina flavipennis*. Photo: C. Dietz.

Fig. 167. Bats spend several hours daily on care of their body condition, they try to remove parasites from the fur with the muzzle and by combing with the feet. Here a grooming Lesser Horseshoe Bat (*Rhinolophus hipposideros*). Photo: D. Nill.

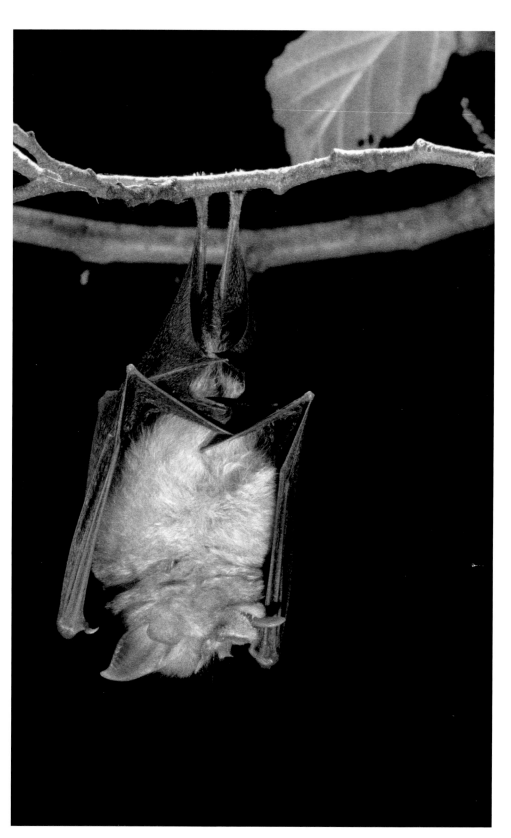

Bugs

A whole series of species of the genus *Cimex*, related to the bed-bug, have specialised on bats. While most parasites of humans represent an old phylogenetic 'inheritance' from our relationship with the anthropoids, this is not true of the bed-bugs: we inherited these from bats when we still lived in the entrance zones of caves. The bed-bug, *Cimex lectularius*, is clearly related to bat-bugs. We share other human parasites, such as body and head lice, with chimpanzee and gorilla, respectively adopted through a common evolutionary lineage.

Fleas

A number of different flea genera (all from one family) live on bats, particularly *Ischnopsyllus* and *Nycteridopsylla*. They are not so closely tied to individual bat species as e.g. wing mites or many bat-fly species. With dense bristles on the body they can firmly hook into the fur of the bats and are thus protected against being combed out easily by the bats during grooming, or protected against falling from a flying bat. The larvae of the fleas mostly develop on the ground of the roost, usually in the faeces of the bats.

Mites

Most noticeable are the wing mites of the Spinturnicidae, which one finds on almost every bat, and are particularly common on mouse-eared bats and Daubenton's Bats. These mites can hold onto the membranes against the enormous wind forces that develop with the flapping of the bat wings. They reproduce at the same time as the bats have their offspring, and can transfer to the young animals before they become volant. Besides the wing mites there are further mites that live in the fur of the bats, and which may infest particularly weakened animals in tremendous mass populations. Bats also have specific itch-mites, which burrow under the skin, and also ticks of the genera *Argas* and *Ixodes*.

In fact, the variety of mites is extensive, including labidocarpid mites that live on the large bristles on the noseleaf of horseshoe bats, sarcoptid mites in sacs on the wings or in little plasma tubes on the feet of Daubenton's bat, trombiculid mites on the ears of Barbastelle Bat (Fig. 441), or demodicid mites inside the nose.

Despite the diversity of parasites on bats (including some groups restricted to tropical bats), it is interesting to note the absence of lice, which occur widely on other mammals. A review of the parasites of European bats can be found in UK gen. lit. 159. For the UK, bat mites are listed in UK gen. lit. 152, bat-flies discussed in UK gen. lit. 156 and fleas in UK gen. lit. 165.

Fig. 168. The tick on the belly of this Schreibers' Bent-winged Bat (*Miniopterus schreibersii*) is embedded in such a way that the bat had scratched bare the whole belly in attempts to remove it. Photo: D. Nill.

Fig. 169. The mites of the genus *Spinturnix* live particularly on the wing membrane of bats. Photo: C. Dietz.

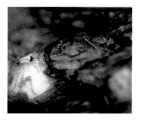

Fig. 170. Itch mites of the family Sarcoptidae on the wing membrane of a Daubenton's Bat (*Myotis daubentonii*). Photo: D. Cordes.

◄◄ Fig. 171. There are several species of bed bug on bats, here *Cimex dissimilis* on a Noctule (*Nyctalus noctula*) in North Greece. Photo: C. Dietz.

◄ Fig. 172. Ticks are often found in bat colonies in the Mediterranean area, here in the ear of a Mediterranean Horseshoe Bat (*Rhinolophus euryale*). Photo: O. von Helversen.

Conservation status of European bats

▶ Historical Development

Threats in Central Europe

Since the middle of the 20th Century some European bat populations, particularly in Central Europe, have undergone dramatic declines. In the horseshoe bats the collapse of the Central European populations began in the 1960s, followed by the Greater Mouse-eared Bat and other species in the 1970s. Winter roosts in caves that were previously used by hundreds of bats were abandoned, the populations declining at some sites from several thousands of bats to a few individuals (Fig. 173). While there have certainly always been population fluctuations and changes in the species composition, including a suite of bat species benefiting from the landscape changes in Central Europe, the decline of bat populations at that time was so rapid that a complete extinction of several bat species had been feared (Fig. 174).

For a long time the causes were a puzzle. Changes in the economic structure of agriculture with increasing mechanisation, grassland loss and an increasing urban sprawl affecting habitat changes of the landscape, without doubt encouraged the threatened extinction of many species. These factors were, however, certainly not the only causes. The building-dwelling species experienced an enormous decimation by direct roost loss, but even more serious was the use of highly toxic wood preservatives based on DDT, PCP and lindane. Bats absorbed the toxic substances from the treated timberwork through the skin, and this accumulated in the animals and finally led to the complete poisoning of many colonies [gen. lit. 72]. There are numerous reports of thousands of poisoned bats from church lofts and other public buildings. The first victims were Greater and Lesser Horseshoe Bat, Greater Mouse-eared Bat, Grey Long-eared and Pond Bat [gen. lit. 76]. Particularly in large winter roosts it quickly became clear that not only these building-dwellers were dramatically declining, but also species such as Barbastelle Bat, which only occasionally uses building roosts. Here the use of similarly highly toxic pesticides, in particular insecticides, might have affected them on their hunting grounds. As the last link in the food chain, bats readily accumulate the fat-soluble toxins such as DDT and their derivatives, and in times of high energy consumption they are released and lead to the death of the bats (Fig. 175). In some caves known as mass winter roosts the disturbance by cave tourism as well as the ringing of hibernating bats were believed to be causes of decline, factors which probably accelerated the effects of pesticides.

The rapid population decline was nevertheless surprising, since large and robust populations should be able to compensate for even heavy losses at least over a long period. The declines seem to be caused by mutual reinforcement of numerous individual factors, with a development in the changes in agriculture that probably go back to the 1930s. The establishment of ever larger farms and the wide intensification of agriculture, together with the clearing of the landscape by removing of field boundary ridges and hedges, the drastic

Fig. 173. The decline of bat populations in Central Europe in the second half of the 20th Century cannot readily be assessed from the absence of sufficient data. The counts of winter population of Greater Mouse-eared Bat (*Myotis myotis*) in the Bismarck cave in the Franconian Alp indicate a dramatic decrease and then a clear increasing recovery in the last two decades. Graph: M. Bauer after data from gen. lit. 102].

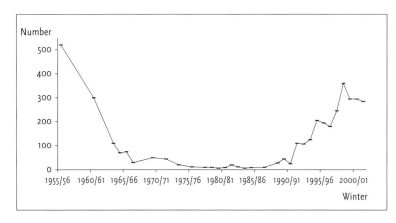

reduction of free-ranging grazing livestock and the widespread radical change of grass-land to arable land are here mentioned only as examples. Similar, although usually not such serious changes, affected the forests in Central Europe, from the widespread losses of locally-adapted natural hardwood forests, the afforestation with coniferous trees and the reduced turn-over time, with an associated reduction of old and dead wood, affected both the roost and food availability.

Threats in the Mediterranean area

The knowledge about the bat populations in the Mediterranean region is incomplete. It appears, however, clearly that the bat populations in intensively agriculturally used areas (e.g. Po-plain, parts of Spain) declined drastically. The decline was first recorded in France [gen. lit. 20], particularly in the horseshoe bats, which spread subsequently to other species and regions. Unfortunately it is hardly possible to calculate the real population changes. By comparison of extensively managed and intensively used agricultural areas, local population declines can, however, be estimated at 70 – 100 %.

▶ Current threats

Threats in Central Europe

The decades-long efforts towards bat protection and the withdrawal of highly toxic substances, such as lindane and DDT, were effective in Central Europe. Individual roosts are still victims of repair work. But,

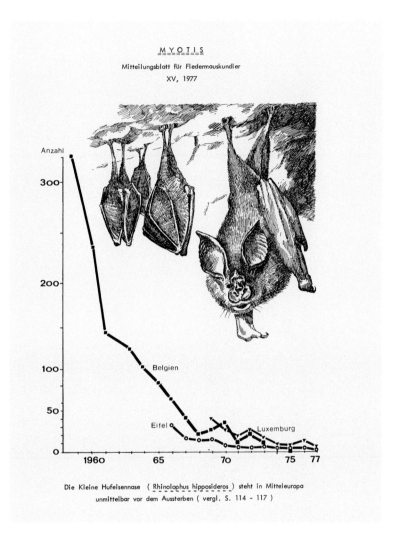

MYOTIS

Mitteilungsblatt für Fledermauskundler
XV, 1977

Die Kleine Hufeisennase (*Rhinolophus hipposideros*) steht in Mitteleuropa
unmittelbar vor dem Aussterben (vergl. S. 114 - 117)

in general, it seems that the populations of most species are stabilising, and species such as the Greater Mouse-eared Bat are clearly increasing again in Germany (Fig. 173). But in this species the population increase is rarely associated with the establishment of new nursery colonies, possibly an indication of severe limitation of the roost availability. At present, increasing habitat fragmentation seems to be a main threat, from the construction of new motorways and increasing urban sprawl with the simultaneous decline of village structure. In addition, at least locally, high mortality rate for some species by, e.g., traffic (Fig. 176) [gen. lit. 43, 67, 82, 97, 112] and at wind-power plants (Fig. 177) [gen. lit. 19, 29, 56] may play a significant role. It is still

Fig. 174. From the middle of the 1970s the population decline of many bat species became so clear that their extinction was feared. The illustration on the cover of volume 15 of the Chiropterological journal *Myotis* showed the predicted extinction of the Lesser Horseshoe Bat (*Rhinolophus hipposideros*).

Fig. 175. The use of highly toxic chemicals, such as DDT and lindane, as wood preservatives in roof spaces, particularly in the 1960s-1970s, poisoned whole colonies (here with Greater Mouse-eared Bat (*Myotis myotis*). Photo: C. Dietz.

Fig. 176. Low flying bats like this Brown Long-eared Bat (*Plecotus auritus*) can especially easily become traffic victims when crossing roads. The losses are difficult to quantify. Photo: C. Dietz.

difficult to estimate how new developments will affect bat populations on a long-term basis e.g. in forestry (utilisation of all remaining wood for power production, and pesticide use) or in agriculture (widespread cultivation of bio-energy plants); concerns are, however, quite justified.

Threat in the Mediterranean area

As previously mentioned, most mass roosts of bats, particularly in the eastern Mediterranean region, on the Balkan Peninsula and in North Africa are not yet effectively protected. Through increasing disturbance by

tourism, or the use for, e.g., mushroom growing, many colonies in large caves are threatened (Fig. 178). Some roost caves are threatened by quarrying or the construction of dams (Fig. 179) [gen. lit. 103]. For all species equally the progressive changes in agriculture represent a substantial threat. The loss of steppe-like meadow associated with extensive pasturing, the radical changes of meadow into arable land or afforestation threaten particularly the Lesser Mouse-eared Bat and Mehely's Horseshoe Bat. The clearing of extensively used Holm and Cork Oak forests, of mixed oak woodlands and semi-natural olive groves, and their replacement with fast growing timber plantations threaten among other things the local horseshoe bats, as well as the migratory bats from Central and Eastern Europe, such as Leisler's Bat, which spends the winter here. The increasing use of pesticides (Fig. 180) and with that a reduction of the food resources for bats, will in the future represent a critical factor in the survival of bat populations. The current available data do not permit firm predictions, but they give numerous indications of a creeping decline of a range of bat species.

Fig. 177. Wind-power plants, as here near Tariffa in Spain, represent a substantial threat to bats. Particularly at important junctions with migration routes many bats can die. Photo: C. Dietz.

The threats to bats, including European bats, was discussed in a review in UK gen. lit. 157. While measures are available in

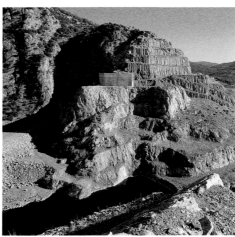

◄◄ Fig. 178. Disturbance at the roosts can have strong impact on bats. Here, through a campfire in a Bulgarian cave, a mixed colony of about 500 Long-fingered Bats and 50 Mehely's Horseshoe Bats was driven away. Numerous animals, particularly still dependent young, died. Photo: C. Dietz.

◄ Fig. 179. In the Mediterranean area the loss of large roost caves represents a serious problem. Through the building of a dam near Havran in western Turkey a cave with up to 20,000 bats is now flooded [see gen. lit. 103]. Photo: C. Dietz.

most states of Europe for the conservation of bat roosts, the way these are implemented varies from country to country and there is no doubt that loss continues in all states. However, probably more important is the general erosion of habitat and landscape features needed by bats. The full impact of infrastructure development, especially roads, is still not clear, but there are mechanisms to compensate for that (even if they often need considerable improvement both in design and in implementation). The new threats of, for example, wind turbines still prove difficult to address, both in terms of assessing their impact and in developing appropriate mitigation measures [UK gen. lit. 161]. Another 'new' threat of uncertain impact is climate change, although at present it is considered that most bat species may not suffer too badly from the impacts of the climate change scenarios so far proposed [UK gen. lit. 160].

Fig. 180. With the artificial irrigation of agricultural areas, here in eastern Greece, large quantities of pesticides are added to irrigation systems (e.g. sprinklers), which can sometimes be returned via surplus water directly into waterbodies and affect directly or indirectly the bat species hunting there. Photo: C. Dietz.

Conservation of European bats

▶ **Basic legal statutes**

International legislations

The Convention on the Conservation of European Wildlife and Natural Habitats, the so-called Bern Convention, regulates internationally the protection of natural habitats and species. All European bat species, with the exception of the Common Pipistrelle, are listed in Appendix II of the **Bern Convention** as strictly protected, the Common Pipistrelle is listed in Appendix III and has a lower level of protection. The legal aspects of the Bern Convention have meanwhile to a large extent been superseded by the EU Habitats Directive (Council Directive 92/43/EEC of 21 May 1992 on the conservation of natural habitats and of wild fauna and flora).

The Convention on the Conservation of Migratory Species of Wild Animals (CMS), the so-called **Bonn Convention**, regulates the world-wide protection and conservation of migratory animal species. Appendix II of the Bonn Convention includes species that are not threatened with extinction, but which would benefit from internationally co-ordinated conservation measures; this includes all European bat species.

Numerous European states have become a Party to the Agreement on the Conservation of Populations of European Bats (**EUROBATS**). This Agreement has the goal to protect all bat species occurring in Europe through international and national legislation, public relations, and conservation measures. A basis for monitoring procedures has been developed.

The Habitats Directive of the European Union has the conservation of natural habitats as well as the wild living plants and animals as a goal. A priority here is the creation of a Europe-wide protected areas system, **Natura 2000**. Each Member State is obliged to implement the Directive in national legislation and should designate protected areas for all habitat types and species listed in its appendices. Beyond that the Directive demands regular reporting and population monitoring as well as evidence of preventative measures taken and of the achievement of conservation targets. Impacts on Natura 2000 sites must be examined for compatibility with strict consideration of the importance for the species concerned. The priority animal species are listed in Appendix II of the Directive for which protected areas must be designated. These include the Egyptian Fruit Bat, all five European horseshoe bats, Greater and Lesser Mouse-eared Bat, Long-fingered, Pond, Geoffroy's, Bechstein's, Barbastelle and Schreibers' Bent-winged Bat. Appendix IV comprises species of community interest that are to be strictly protected, and includes all European bat species.

UK National legislation

The UK had offered protection to two bat species in 1976, but in 1981 introduced the Wildlife and Countryside Act, which protected all bats and, in particular, offered special measures for the conservation of roosts, even where they are in private dwellings (where there is a requirement to seek advice if householders wish to remove bats or carry out building works that may affect bats). This act was the UK's response to the Bern Convention and has undergone several amendments since [gen. lit. 85]. The other main legislation is the Conservation (Natural Habitats, etc.) Regulations 1994, which has also undergone some amendment, and is designed to meet the UK's obligations under the EU Habitats and Species Directive. This gives further protection to roosts and identifies further requirements for ensuring the maintenance of a favourable conservation status for bat species. Eurobats also agrees conservation actions that are legally binding to parties, including the UK.

Practical conservation measures

Data collection and management

All conservation measures should be based on available data. Only with extensive data can decisions be made on how and where conservation measures can be applied effectively and meaningfully. Due to personnel and financial constraints conservation measures should be seized where they are most urgent and where they can possibly achieve the greatest effect. In some cases it can be difficult to decide, but, as a guideline the threatened status of individual species, the importance of a habitat element in the ecological network of the respective species, and the number of individuals concerned should be considered. Summer colonies, nursery colonies and large winter roosts usually have the highest priority. It would be logical that for conservation measures the entire habitat network of the species concerned is considered in each case. The high mobility of bats requires the inclusion of daytime roosts, flight paths, hunting grounds, swarming sites, mating roosts, transit areas and winter roosts. In practice it is rarely possible to consider all these aspects, but with the consistent conservation of nursery and winter roosts and large-scale suitable hunting habitats a whole series of further subhabitats are protected, not only for bats.

Biotope protection

The serious population declines in bats relate, for a substantial part, to the large-scale loss of suitable hunting habitats or to the drastic reduction of food availability in the hunting grounds. Examples are the extinction of Schreibers' Bent-winged Bat along its northern border and the dramatic decline of Barbastelle in Central Europe after large-scale pesticide use in forests used as hunting grounds (see the respective species accounts). The substantial social changes in Central Europe and current transfer to the Mediterranean area led and lead to large-scale changes in the economic structure and agricultural and forestry economic production and hence to a pro-

gressive loss of suitable habitats for many bat species. For the conservation of the existing bat populations and to improve their population status some core conservation measures are essential:

– Protection of large-scale natural forest areas with locally adapted and naturally occurring tree species as well as their re-establishment and connectivity. In particular consistent protection of damp, lowland and riparian woodland as well as cork and holm oak forests and natural mountain forests. Halting the transformation of natural hardwood forest to

Fig. 181. During the redevelopment of buildings in which bat roosts occur, intuition and experience is necessary to maintain the roosts and to avoid disturbance. Photo: C. Dietz.

Fig. 182. With inappropriate redevelopment of natural stone bridges the cracks in the arch can be sealed and bats present can be killed. Supervision of the redevelopment by a bat expert can help the long-term preservation of such roost sites. Photo: C. Dietz.

Fig. 183. An example of protection of a winter roost: the grilling of the bunker entrance makes undisturbed hibernation for the bats possible. Photo: C. Dietz.

eucalyptus and coniferous forests. Increase of the proportion of old and dead wood in forests for the improvement of the natural roost and food availability. Abandon the complete utilisation of remaining wood in forests.
– Protection of extensively used grassland, extensive management of species-rich meadow associations, maintaining extensive pasturing of livestock in open land and large-scale pasturing in steppe-like meadowland. Abandon the large-scale cultivation of (genetically modified) bio-energy plants.
– Preservation and creation of fruit tree meadows, hedgerows and semi-natural associations of forest edges as hunting habitats and corridor structures between separate habitats.
– Preservation of large unfragmented landscape elements and their communities.
– Abandon large-scale pesticide use, complete abandonment of pesticides in forests.

Roost protection
Bats are dependent on safe roosts, which must be free from disturbance during the hibernation and particularly during the raising of young. Due to the spatial and climatic requirements suitable roosts are

naturally very limited. The rarer a certain type of roost is, the more susceptibly a species is to disturbance of such roosts. In several caves, particularly on the Balkan Peninsula, up to 100,000 bats concentrate in the winter, with up to 16 species (see species accounts for Long-fingered Bat, Common Pipistrelle and Schreiber´s Bent-winged Bat). It is assumed that these roosts are traditionally used and, due to their particular spatial and climatic conditions, are used by bats from an enormous area. How seriously disturbances could affect such concentrations is hard to contemplate. It is, therefore, understandable that those species that are dependent on such special roosts of limited availability are particularly threatened: such as cave-dwelling bats (e.g. horseshoe bats) or species that need large, undisturbed roof spaces (mouse-eared bats, horseshoe bats). In such species, which often form very large colonies, the loss of only one such roost can have a serious effect. Forest bats can also be affected by the loss of roosts, e.g. by widespread thinning of a substantial proportion of hollow trees. Important roost preservation measures are:
– Consistent protection of all known colony sites in and at buildings (Figs 181 and 182), in underground systems (caves, mines, tunnels, see Fig. 183) and in forests.
– Strict protection with strict access control of roosts used by large concentrations of bats, protection of the surrounding landscape areas and prevention of fragmentation, which can disconnect roosts from the surrounding countryside.
– Re-establishment of a high roost availability for building-dwelling bats by the provision of access possibilities into unused roof spaces.
– Selective felling in forests and maintenance and encouragement of a high proportion of old and dead wood. Designation of large-scale protected forest areas.

Construction of new roosts
The construction of new roosts should be considered, particularly as supplementary measures during the application of protective measures. The construction of access possibilities to unused roof spaces or underground

corridor systems, the construction of crevice roosts in house facades and the installation of bat boxes in forests (Fig. 184) can substantially improve the sometimes scarce roost availability for bats. But, the construction of new roosts cannot serve as a general replacement for the loss of existing roosts.

Prevention of accident risks

In some buildings pipes and chimneys blocked off inside or spaces with basket-type entrances (e.g. open cantilever windows) can operate as bat traps. By emitting calls individual bats which have fallen into such traps can attract many other animals of the same species, such death traps with over 1,000 dead Common Pipistrelle (see species account) are known. Wherever possible, such traps should be avoided. The prevention of risk of accident at roads or at wind-power plants is substantially more difficult. Investigations show that the mortality on some road sections or at some wind-power plants can be alarmingly high [gen. lit. 19, 29, 43, 56, 67, 82, 97, 112]. Only by consistent monitoring of the mortality rate can countermeasures be taken. Therefore it is all the more important to keep semi-natural. large-scale suitable bat habitats free from potential sources of danger, such as roads and wind-power plants.

Rehabilitation centres

The care of bats found injured or weakened or the hand-rearing of young animals is unlikely to contribute significantly to the preservation of populations, but is a substantial component of public awareness. Only if people have the possibility to deliver grounded bats to a trusted rehabilitation centre can a broad understanding of the interests of bat protection be established.

Public awareness

Public awareness is a substantial component of lobbying for bat protection. Only through widely available information it is possible that bats, usually living unnoticed but nevertheless very close to humans, can be given the necessary protection against decline. Too often roosts are lost through unawareness or ignorance: the number of roosts lost annually and animals killed by sealing houses or cementing joints is difficult to realise. Only by a widespread consciousness and knowledge about bats and competent support with repair works through bat specialists can such unnecessary losses be avoided [gen. lit. 25, 98].

General

Recommendations for the conservation of bats in Europe are given in UK gen. lit. 157. Throughout Europe there is a growing development of national (and local) NGOs that undertake a lot of the practical activities. Currently a partnership of national NGOs, a 'BatLife Europe', is being established. Through international collaboration the NGOs should have a stronger voice on key conservation issues. The EU Habitats Directive has significant influence on the national policy of member countries, and Eurobats considers particular conservation issues as part of its rolling Conservation and Management Plan.

Eurobats also has a publications series including general guidance on key issues of bat conservation, currently available or in preparation on such matters as underground sites, overground roosts, wind turbines and population monitoring. The activities of a number of working groups also result in the adoption of legally binding resolutions on a range of issues. An annual European bat night has done much to highlight the conservation of bats to the general public, but 2011 has been designated International Year of the Bat.

Fig. 184. The installation of bat boxes can substantially improve the roost availability for tree hole-living bat species and is a clear aid to recording bats. Photo: C. Dietz.

Fig. 185. Through public awareness and opportunities for close contact with permanently disabled bats which cannot be released, it is possible to inspire many people to support bat conservation. Photo: C. Dietz.

Bat detectors: species identification from echolocation calls

Each species of bat has a certain range of echolocation calls, which are adapted to its respective foraging situations. Some bat species allow clear identification on the basis of their echolocation calls, while between many other species the characteristics of the calls overlap considerably, depending on their respective flight situations, so much so that one cannot separate individual species with certainty. Echolocation calls do not have the same role as bird song, which is used for communication and to mark territories; they are signals to show immediately, to other animals of the same species, to which species the active singer belongs. The echolocation calls of bats are adapted to the requirements of orientation and thus to the respective ecological niches. Nevertheless, when they are species-specific, then it is because their function in the ecological niche of the species requires it. However, with some specific ecological niches, due to factors other than those that are reflected in the 'design' of the echolocation calls, then completely different species cannot be differentiated on the basis of their calls.

The identification of different bat species from their echolocation calls has attracted considerable attention in the last two decades; where one can differentiate a species on the basis of its echolocation calls, then one can investigate much more easily its hunting behaviour, its use of habitats, the preference for certain structural habitat components and many other factors, without having to catch the animals for species identification. Also the distribution of bat species would be much easier to determine in this way and one could gain important information for nature and species protection.

How can one make the inaudible ultrasonic sounds audible for humans? For that electronic devices have been built, which are called bat detectors. The function of bat detectors follows different technical principles, which have varying advantages and disadvantages, but also have specific physical limitations and, in particular, different technical complexity and thus can be markedly different prices.

The simplest basic principle is the frequency division system on the basis of a zero crossing analysis; somewhat more difficult is the so-called heterodyne principle, and, by far the most expensive method, by direct recording of the ultrasonic waves with facilities for slowing down the playback (time expansion).

With all three different procedures the initial, very small voltage, which is supplied by an ultrasound-sensitive microphone, must be amplified. From that an approximately sinusoidal voltage function is generated, which electronically reflects the sound pressure function of the echolocation call.

Frequency division detectors

Beginning with frequency division, the zero crossings of the sinusoidal voltage are determined. In the simplest case, for every 10 zero crossings that are counted a single pulse is generated, resulting in a tenth of the output frequency being produced. Either this can be made directly audible, or by sampling and copying the input envelope, the original wave form can be regenerated. The advantage of such frequency division is that bat calls in the entire frequency range that the microphone receives are made audible. The most important disadvantage is that all harmonic waves and many other important characteristics of the call that aid species identification are lost.

Heterodyne detectors

With heterodyne detectors the voltage function produced by the microphone is mixed with an internal variable frequency oscillator. Then the difference between the recorded and the oscillator frequency results in a beat

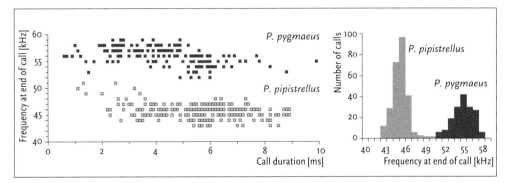

Fig. 186. The end frequencies of the echolocation calls of the two very closely related *Pipistrellus* species: Soprano Pipistelle (*Pipistrellus pygmaeus*) and Common Pipistrelle (*Pipistrellus pipistrellus*). The two species clearly differ and the distribution of their frequency hardly overlaps, particularly when only longer, over 5ms, calls are considered. Graph: M. Bauer.

frequency. When the beat frequency, i.e. the difference between the bat call frequency and oscillator frequency, lies within the human audio range (usually within a range of ± 5kHz) it can be made audible over a loudspeaker. A sound is thereby produced within the range of human hearing, irrespective of whether the frequency difference is positive or negative, i.e. whether the bat call is above or below the oscillator frequency. A disadvantage of this procedure is that one hears only bats whose echolocation frequency lies in a comparatively narrow band around the adjusted mixed frequency. A further disadvantage is that a detailed reconstruction of the output signal is not possible, because the mixed frequency cannot normally be registered in recordings for analysis.

Time expansion detectors

The only procedure which permits a complete reconstruction of the echolocation calls is a direct recording of the signal supplied through the ultrasonic microphone. In principle this is possible with the help of high-speed tape recorders; today, however, digital devices are nearly always used. The signal from the ultrasonic microphone is scanned with a high sampling rate, and, after being converted to a digital signal, is written to an electronic memory. The sound recording process retains the whole waveform, with the full call range being preserved. This waveform can be made graphically directly visible (as an oscillogram) and can be stored for further analysis. After data processing, e.g. to a Fourier transformation, a diagram can be produced, which is termed a spectrogram or alternatively a sonogram. In addition,

one can play the recording slowed down and can measure different components of the call, such as decibels (denoted by a different colour). On the following pages some characteristic calls of selected European species are shown in this form (Fig. 188).

Species identification

For many of the species hunting in open spaces with qCF (quasi-constant frequency) calls, the final frequency of the echolocation call is the most important parameter for species identification. Because these calls end at almost constant frequency, the terminal or 'end' frequency is usually also the loudest frequency represented in the call. Fig. 188 shows the distribution of the end frequencies for the Common and Soprano Pipistrelle – one can differentiate these two species on the basis of sufficient recordings of the end frequency of the calls. Fig. 187 shows the range of the end frequencies for a number of European bat species that use such qCF calls.

Fig. 187. Distribution of the end frequencies in European bat species which use echolocation calls of the qCF type. The situation dependence and the individual variation lead, however, to considerable band ranges and so to overlaps. The overlap of the frequencies often allows no simple identification based solely on this parameter. After gen. lit. 145. Graph: M. Bauer.

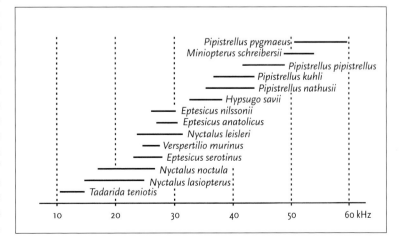

Limits to the species identification

Since the echolocation calls of the different species are extraordinarily variable and dependent upon the situation, the call repertoires of different species often overlap to a considerable extent. Therefore the correct species allocation from echolocation sounds to the respective bat species presupposes a high degree of experience and particularly knowledge about the potential and limitations of the method used in each case. Sometimes, one finds the conception that with expensive equipment species identification is almost automatically possible on the basis of the echolocation calls. Only too often one forgets how many confusing possibilities there are. Particularly in the field of applied nature and environmental protection, sometimes accuracy of the data acquisition and interpretation is claimed but which does not correspond to reality.

Working with the echolocation calls of bats and with the possibilities of species identification is an exciting occupation and can contribute much to our understanding of the biology, ecology and distribution of species, as long as they are applied critically

Pages 126/127:
Fig. 188. Frequency characteristics of selected, typical echolocation calls of 12 European bat species. The echolocation calls (only search and approach phase) originate in each case from hunting situations relatively close to vegetation (further left) and further away from obstacles (further right). The illustration is also to give an idea of how variable the calls of individual species can be. Graphs: M. Bauer.

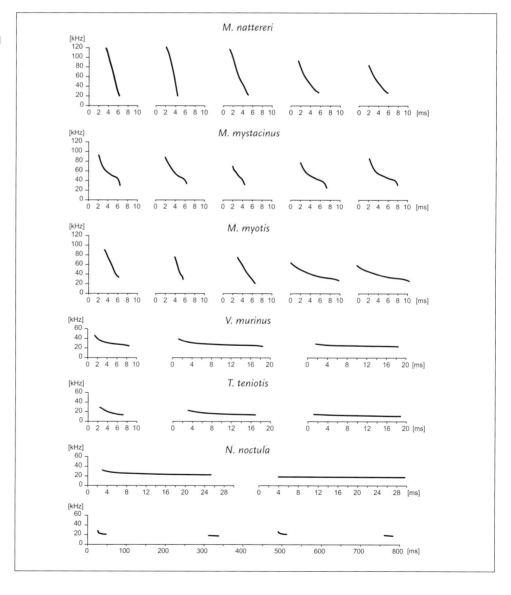

enough. For detailed training in sound analysis we recommend the two detailed standard works by Skiba [gen.lit. 128] and for social calls by Pfalzer [gen. lit. 93]. See also UK gen. lit. 154.

In the meantime, different working groups have developed systems for an automatic computer-assisted species analysis with the help of complex statistical processes (through so-called 'neural networks'

and/or different procedures of discriminant analysis, which are programmed with the help of large sets of confirmed reference data). Therefore, the calls must be recorded with high-quality devices and stored digitally. The large advantage of such devices and programs is that they can receive statistically confirmed data, for which confidence and error rate can be indicated precisely.

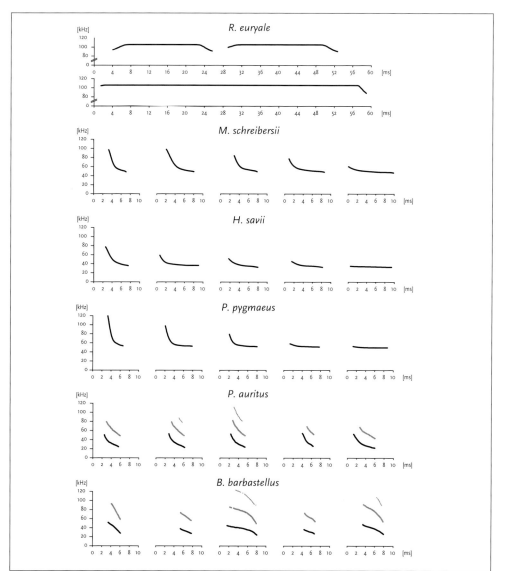

Pages 128/129 (overleaf):
Fig. 189. Natterer's Bat (*Myotis nattereri*) shortly before catching a crane-fly. Head and ears are exactly aligned to the prey, which will be 'netted' with the tail membrane a little later. Photo: D. Nill.

The Species

Introduction to the species descriptions

In the species accounts all 51 species recorded up to the end of 2006 for Europe, the northern part of northwest Africa, the Atlantic islands and the western part of Asia Minor are described. During the printing process of the manuscript of this book at least four further previously unrecognised species were proposed in Europe [gen. lit. 77, 167]: two cryptic sister species of Natterer's Bat (*Myotis nattereri*): *Myotis* cf. *escalerai* and a so far unnamed species; a sister species to the Brown Long-eared Bat (*Plecotus auritus*): *Plecotus begognae*; and a relative of Kuhl's Pipistrelle (*Pipistrellus kuhlii*): *Pipistrellus lepidus*. Unfortunately, at present no published data are available of their characteristics, distribution or ecology; therefore these possible additional species are here discussed within their long-known sibling species.

Identification keys

Many characteristics used in the identification keys can only be examined with the animal in the hand and some species are even then only to be differentiated with much practice. The inclusion of rare Mediterranean species in the identification keys makes this significantly more complicated. For Central and northern Europe we recommend, therefore, a rough pre-identification with the 'picture book method', with a follow-up identification based on the species accounts and the three sub-keys. With some experience, with a few exceptions, all bat species occurring in Central Europe can be identified from a good view in their roost site. Due to the risks to many species, capture and other disturbing activities are usually only possible with special permission from the relevant nature conservation agency. In order to gain experience in handling and identifying bats it is recommended to contact local bat specialists.

Identification

We have limited ourselves to the most important external characteristics, and only added dentition characteristics where necessary. Some of the recently discovered species can only be identified so far at best from the skull, since handy criteria that can be used with living animals are not available. The description of the fur colouring is made more difficult by the intraspecific variation, particularly variation with age, where there is additional reference to the figures. Descriptions of anomalies of colouring such as partial or complete albinism is deliberately avoided, since this occurs in practically all species, but is biologically unimportant. The given measurements are based on our own measurement of over 30,000 animals in the wild and many museum specimens. For measurements of length we give the extreme measurements (Fig. 190). For body weight we indicate the mass of non-reproducing animals in the summer and omit extreme values (Fig. 191).

Echolocation calls

The very short descriptions are based on our own records and for the European species on the compilations by Skiba [gen. lit. 128] and Russo & Jones [gen. lit. 105].

Distribution and distribution maps

The distribution maps are based on *The Atlas of European Mammals* [gen. lit. 84], supplemented with new literature data and our own unpublished records.

Systematics, subspecies and geographical variation

For the nomenclature and data on sub-

Fig. 190. Range of the forearm lengths of adult female Greater Horseshoe Bats (*Rhinolophus ferrumequinum*) from Bulgaria. The wingspan ranges are given in the species accounts. Graph: C. Dietz.

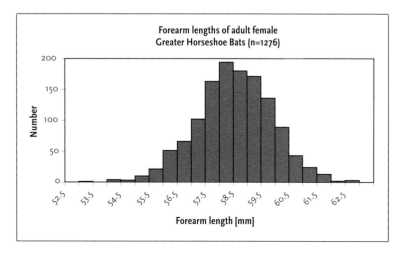

Forearm lengths of adult female Greater Horseshoe Bats (n=1276)

species we rely on Horáček *et al.* [gen. lit. 55] and in particular follow Simmons [gen. lit. 126], but deviate with newly described species or following new genetic findings [gen. lit. 77, 167]. Many data on outstanding taxonomic questions were evaluated by F. Mayer, A. Kiefer and J. Fahr, who are greatly acknowledged.

Habitat, ecology, behaviour and reproduction

In some species data on the ecology are barely available, in others an incomprehensible abundance of details are known, so only a rough summary could be given. It must be recognised that within certain limits many bats are very flexible in their ecological requirements and the data given here are relatively widely applicable. Many data on Mediterranean species originate from unpublished studies by I. Dietz, K. Koselj, E. Papadatou and P. Presetnik.

Food

The data on the diet of bats rely on the comprehensive work by A. Beck [gen. lit. 8] and other work quoted in each case. I. Dietz analysed samples from southeast Europe and North Africa for almost all species and supplemented the data on the food.

Maximum age

While there are relatively many data on maximum recorded age of bats, reliable figures are rare for average life expectancy. It is to be assumed that single animals of all non-migratory bat species can reach a maximum age of at least 30 years.

Migration

The data on migrations in bats are based as far as possible on the comprehensive summary by Hutterer *et al.* [gen. lit. 57].

Threats and conservation measures

There are few reliable Europe-wide population data. As reference points we have mentioned the classification of the Red List of IUCN [gen. lit. 171] and of the European Union [gen. lit. 172, 170]. Additionally, we have formulated our personal assessments of important conservation goals.

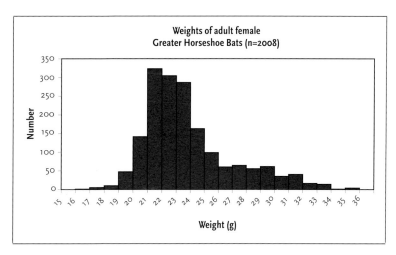

References

In very well-studied species a large number of original works are deliberately quoted and there is also reference to review works, such as Schober & Grimmberger [gen. lit. 119] and the *Handbuch der Säugetiere Europas* [gen. lit. 69, 70].

The English language edition

Under 'Threats' in the species accounts, some comments about the UK status and activity are included, together with additional references to UK publications, and with general reference to the 2008 edition of the *Handbook of British Mammals* [UK gen. lit. 155].

The results of the recent IUCN Red List assessments have been incorporated into a table on pages 382–384, which includes further explanatory text. Note that the IUCN 2008 Red List website includes updated distribution maps for each species.

Where appropriate, very brief accounts have been added for five additional species; these are species that occur in the wider Europe used for the purposes of the Bern Convention, Eurobats, etc. These have also been included in the table.

Omitted here are a series of 'unanswered questions' that were included under each species account in the original German edition. It is hoped, however, that for most of these questions, they can be extracted from elsewhere in the species accounts, where they are given (explicitly or implicitly).

Fig. 191. Range of the weight of adult female Greater Horseshoe Bats (*Rhinolophus ferrumequinum*) from Bulgaria from April to October. In the species descriptions only the weight ranges in non-pregnant animals between May and August before foraging are given. Graph: C. Dietz.

Measurements and characteristics

In order to be able to compare measurements, they must be taken in a standardised form. Therefore callipers or a steel ruler, such as used by ornithologists, is necessary. A further condition is that the measured values come from full-grown animals. For age estimates the degree of ossification of the phalanges can be used into the autumn (Fig. 192). In juvenile animals the finger bones grow near the joint, against bright light the growth zones can be recognised as translucent bands (Fig. 192, **1**), and the measured values, depending upon age, are far below those of adult animals. At the end of the growth phase these growth zones are ossified, the bands are no longer translucent, and the adult measurement has been reached. However, after the end of the growth the finger joints remain longitudinally expanded (swollen) for some weeks (Fig. 192, **2**) and only in the late autumn become knobbly as in the full-grown animals (Fig. 192, **3**). Further characteristics such as fur colouring (young animals are usually greyer) and in some *Myotis* species also the face and particularly the lower lip colouring, together with the development of the genital organs or the nipples, represent good features for age estimation, but require considerable experience and comparison between many individuals of a species.

In order to take wing measurements, it is recommended that right-handed people take the bat loosely in the left hand. With larger species one should wear soft gloves or hold the bat in a light cotton cloth. The measurements can be taken with the right hand, with the callipers supported with the fingers of the left hand. The forearm length is measured with a closed wing from the elbow to the wrist (Fig. 193); in older works the forearm length is sometimes given without the wrist. During the measurement it must be ensured that the callipers lie parallel to the forearm and are tight against the joints. The lengths of the fifth and third finger are best taken with a fully opened

wing, while the bat is held on its back (Fig. 194). The wrist is not measured, the callipers being set inside the wrist. The thumb length is based on the fully stretched thumb without the claw (Fig. 195), the foot length from the beginning of the calcar to the toes without the claws (Fig. 196). For measurement of the ear width a ruler is preferable and the measurement is at the height of the tragus tip, pressing the ear lightly against the ruler to reduce the curvature (Fig. 197). The tragus width is measured similarly (Fig. 198). The tragus length is measured without the basal fold (Fig. 198). In particular with measuring the upper tooth row length (only necessary in mouse-eared bats) and for the separation of Balkan Long-eared Bat and Anatolian Serotine Bat from their more common sibling species) the highest care and concentration is required, in order not to injure the animals, and should only be carried out by experienced specialists. The callipers are set against the rear edge of the rear upper molar to the front of the base of the canine.

Fig. 192. Degree of ossification of the finger joints of the wing during the growth of young animals. **1**. Juvenile animal before the end of longitudinal growth, the epiphysis joints are visible as pale bands. **2**. Young animal post longitudinal growth, the joint is still elongated. **3**. Full-grown animal with knobbly joints. a. metacarpal, b. joint gap, c. phalanx, d. epiphysis joints (= growth zones). Diagram: R. Roesler.

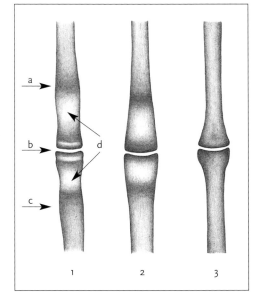

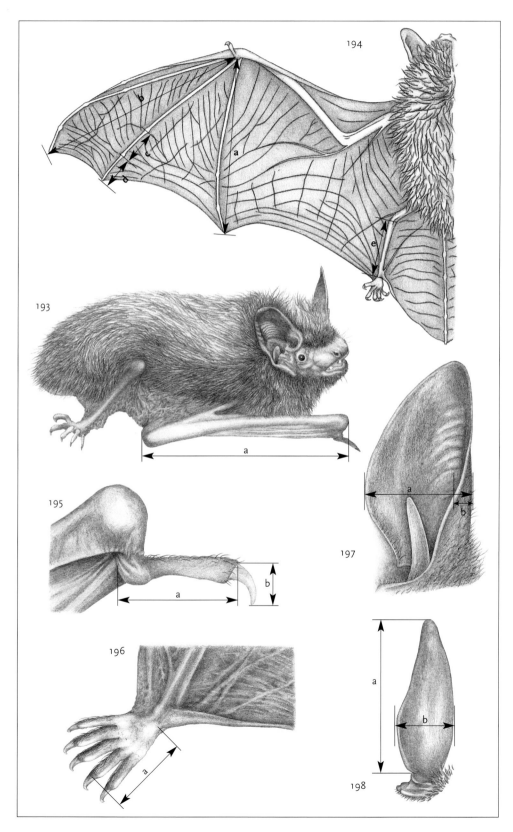

Fig. 193. Measuring the forearm length (a) of a bat with closed wing, for example a Northern Bat (*Eptesicus nilssonii*). Diagram: R. Roesler.

Fig. 194. Further measuring of a bat, for example a Whiskered Bat (*Myotis mystacinus*): a. length of fifth finger, b. length of third finger, c. length of first phalanx of fourth finger, d. length of second phalanx of fourth finger, e. length of tibia. Diagram: R. Roesler.

Fig. 195. Measuring the thumb of a bat: a. thumb length. b. thumb claw length. Diagram: R. Roesler.

Fig. 196. Measuring the foot of a bat: a. foot length. Diagram: R. Roesler.

Fig. 197. The ear width measurement of a bat is taken at the height of the tragus tip by adding the length of 'a' and 'b'. Diagram: R. Roesler.

Fig. 198. Measuring sections of the tragus of a bat: a. tragus length, b. tragus width. Diagram: R. Roesler.

Identification key to bat families

1a Very large bats, forearm length >80mm. Ear simple, without tragus or antitragus. Thumb and second digit (1st finger) each with a claw.
Megachiropteran fruit bats (Pteropodidae). Only one species in the scope of this book: **Egyptian Fruit Bat** (*Rousettus aegyptiacus*) p. 150

1b Smaller bats, forearm length <80mm. Ear more complex, with tragus or antitragus. Second digit (1st finger) without claw.   . .   **2**

2a Muzzle with complicated appendages (Fig. 199). Ear without tragus, but with distinct antitragus. Tail equal to or shorter than length of legs. **3**

2b Muzzle without complicated appendages (Fig. 200). Ear usually with tragus. Tail completely within tail membrane and longer than legs or the tail projects well beyond edge of narrow membrane. **4**

3a Horseshoe-shaped noseleaf with a perpendicular lancet above (Fig. 199).
Horseshoe bats (Rhinolophidae). – See species identification key 1 p. 136

Fig. 199. The horseshoe bats (Rhinolophidae, here *Rhinolophus ferrumequinum*) and some other families have characteristic skin appendages. Photo: C. Dietz.

Fig. 200. The vesper bats (Vespertilionidae, here *Eptesicus serotinus*) and some other families lack skin appendages or other skin bulges. Photo: C. Dietz.

3b Horseshoe-shaped noseleaf, above which either three perpendicular projections (Fig. 214) or no perpendicular projections (Fig. 213).
Old World leaf-nosed bats (Hipposideridae). – See species identification key 2 p. 137

4a Tail completely included in a broad tail membrane, at most two tail vertebrae project a few millimetres beyond edge of tail membrane. **5**

4b Tail extends far beyond narrow tail membrane, emerging from either the end or the centre of the tail membrane. **7**

5a Muzzle with a deep longitudinal central groove partly covered laterally by a fold of skin (Fig. 203). Last tail vertebra T-shaped.
Slit-faced bats (Nycteridae). Only one species in the scope of this book: **Egyptian Slit-faced Bat** (*Nycteris thebaica*) p. 159

5b Muzzle simple and smooth, without deep groove. Last tail vertebra simple, without lateral projections. **6**

6a Wing-tips not folded at rest and second phalanx of third digit at most twice as long as first (Fig. 204). Ears usually projecting above fur of head (Fig. 200).
Vesper bats (Vespertilionidae). – See species identification key 3 p. 138

6b Wing-tips folded at rest and second phalanx of third finger about three times length of first (Fig. 202). Ears do not project above fur on head (Fig. 201).
Bent-winged bats (Miniopteridae) Only one species in the scope of this book: **Schreibers' Bent-winged Bat** (*Miniopterus schreibersii*) p. 369

7a Narrow tail membrane, with less than a third of the slim tail included, appearing mouse-like and more or less equal to forearm length. Ear with distinct tragus.
> **Mouse-tailed bats** (Rhinopomatidae)
> Only one species in the scope of this book:
> **Lesser Mouse-tailed Bat**
> (*Rhinopoma hardwickii*) p. 155

7b Narrow tail membrane, but including up to half the strong tail, which is much shorter than forearm. Ear without tragus, but with antitragus.
> **Free-tailed bats** (Molossidae).
> Only one species in the scope of this book:
> **European Free-tailed Bat**
> (*Tadarida teniotis*) p. 375

◄ Fig. 201. The ear of Schreibers' Bent-winged Bat (Miniopteridae, *Miniopterus schreibersii*) does not project above the top of the head. Photo: C. Dietz.

▼ Fig. 202. The wing-tip of Schreibers' Bent-winged Bat (Miniopteridae, *Miniopterus schreibersii*) is folded at rest, the second phalanx of the third finger is about three times as long as the first. Photo: C. Dietz.

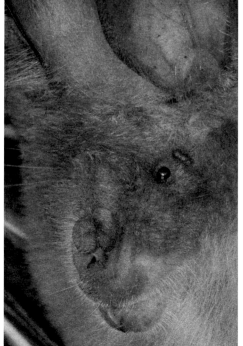

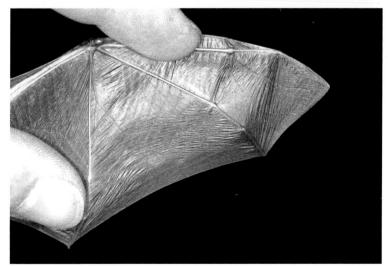

◄ Fig. 203. Slit-faced bats (Nycteridae, *Nycteris thebaica*) have a deep longitudinal furrow which flows laterally into skin folds. Photo: C. Dietz.

▲ Fig. 204. The wing-tips of a vesper bat (Vespertilionidae) are not folded at rest, and the second phalanx of the third finger is about twice as long as the first. Photo: C. Dietz.

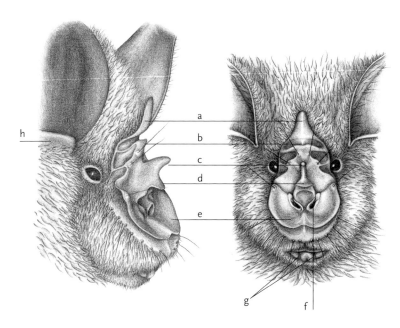

Fig. 205. The construction of the noseleaf and further characteristics of the head of the horseshoe bats, for example of the Mediterranean Horseshoe Bat (*Rhinolophus euryale*). *a*. lancet, *b*. horizontal fold under the lancet, *c*. connecting process. *d*. sella, *e*. horseshoe, *f*. nostril, *g*. groove in lower lip ('mental' groove), *h*. antitragus. Diagram: R. Roesler.

Species identification key 1: Horseshoe bats (Rhinolophidae)

1a Connecting process broad, rounded and short (Fig. 206). One or three small 'mental' grooves on lower lip. Forearm length <43mm or >53mm. **2**

1b Connecting process clearly extends beyond sella (Fig. 207). Two small 'mental' grooves on lower lip. Forearm length 43–54mm. . **3**

2a Largest of the horseshoe bats, forearm >54mm (rarely 53mm).
Greater Horseshoe Bat
(*Rhinolophus ferrumequinum*) p. 176

2b Smallest of the horseshoe bats, forearm <43mm
Lesser Horseshoe Bat
(*Rhinolophus hipposideros*) p. 168

3a Second (outer) phalanx of the fourth digit less than twice as long as first (Fig. 212). Sella narrow, rounded when viewed from front, viewed from below narrowed with shouldered sides towards the tip. Horizontal fold below lancet slightly indented in centre (Fig. 208).
Blasius's Horseshoe Bat
(*Rhinolophus blasii*) p. 195

3b The second (outer) phalanx of the fourth digit more than twice as long as first (Fig. 211). Sella broad and rounded when seen from front, and parallel-sided from below. Horizontal fold under lancet only rarely indented in centre (Figs. 209 and 210). **4**

4a Lancet tapers more or less evenly towards tip (Fig. 210). In profile, connecting process pointed and bent slightly downwards. Forearm length 45–51 mm, usually <50mm.
Mediterranean Horseshoe Bat
(*Rhinolophus euryale*) p. 184

4b Lancet narrows sharply in its upper half and tapers to a slender point (Fig. 209). In profile connecting process slightly rounded and not bent downwards. Forearm length 48–55mm, usually >49mm.
Mehely's Horseshoe Bat
(*Rhinolophus mehelyi*) p. 190

▶ Fig. 206. The connecting process in the Greater and Lesser Horseshoe Bat is broadly rounded and short (here *Rhinolophus ferrumequinum*). Photo: C. Dietz.

▶▶ Fig. 207. The connecting process in the three medium-sized horseshoe bats clearly extends beyond the lower sella (here *Rhinolophus blasii*). Photo: C. Dietz.

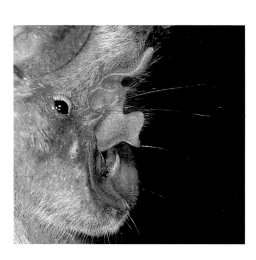

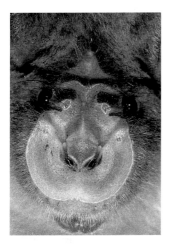  

◄◄◄ Fig. 208. The horizontal fold under the lancet is distinctly indented in Blasius's Horseshoe Bat (*Rhinolophus blasii*). Photo: C. Dietz.

◄◄ Fig. 209. The lancet in Mehely's Horseshoe Bat (*Rhinolophus mehelyi*) narrows sharply. Photo: C. Dietz.

◄ Fig. 210. In the Mediterranean Horseshoe Bat (*Rhinolophus euryale*) the lancet tapers gradually and evenly to the tip. Photo: C. Dietz.

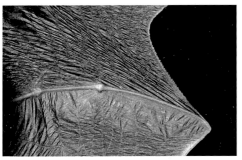 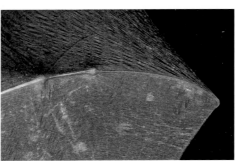

◄ Fig. 211. The second (outer) phalanx of the fourth finger in the Mediterranean and Mehely's Horseshoe Bat (*Rhinolophus euryale & mehelyi*) is more than twice as long as the first. Photo: C. Dietz.

◄◄ Fig. 212. The second (outer) phalanx of the fourth finger in Blasius's Horseshoe Bat (*Rhinolophus blasii*) is less than twice as long as the first. Photo: C. Dietz.

Species identification key 2: Old World leaf-nosed bats (Hipposideridae)

1a Without upright perpendicular projections above noseleaf (Fig. 213).
                    Sundevall's Leaf-nosed Bat
                    (*Hipposideros caffer*) p. 162

1b With three perpendicular projections above noseleaf (Fig. 214).
                    Trident Leaf-nosed Bat
                    (*Asellia tridens*) p. 165

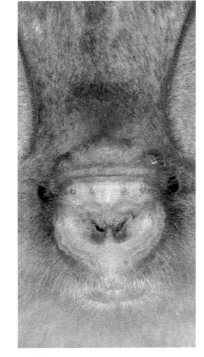 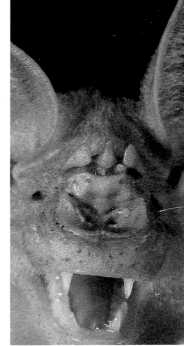

▶ Fig. 213. The upper edge of the noseleaf of Sundevall's Leaf-nosed Bat (*Hipposideros caffer*) does not have vertical projections. Photo: C. Dietz.

▶▶ Fig. 214. The upper edge of the noseleaf of Trident Leaf-nosed Bat (*Asellia tridens*) carries three vertical projections. Photo: B. Fenton.

Fig. 215. The ears of the long-eared bats (Plecotini, here *Plecotus kolombatovici*) are joined together at the base by a fold of skin. Photo: C. Dietz.

Species identification key 3: Vesper bats (Vespertilionidae)

1a One pair of incisors in upper jaw (only in *Lasiurus*, North American vagrant to Iceland and the Orkney Islands, and in Hemprich's Long-eared Bat *Otonycteris* of North Africa). **24**

1b Two pairs of incisors in upper jaw (all species from Europe and Middle East and, except *Otonycteris*, also all from northwest Africa). **2**

2a Ears connected at base by a fold of skin (Fig. 215) and touch each other when erected. Nostrils open upwards. **3**

2b Ears separated and not connected at their base by a fold of skin. Nostrils open forwards. **4**

3a Ears shorter than 20mm and with 5–6 transverse folds. Ears not folded at rest. Post-calcarial lobe with a T-piece cartilage.
Western Barbastelle
(*Barbastella barbastellus*) p. 337

3b Ears longer than 30mm and with many transverse folds, folded when at rest. Calcar without post-calcarial lobe.
Long-eared bats (genus *Plecotus*). –
See separate sub-key 3 p. 148

4a Tragus short, curved forward and with round tip or widened into mushroom shape (Fig. 216). Usually a distinct post-calcarial lobe (Figs 226–228). Only one or two premolars in the upper and lower jaw. **14**

4b The tragus is long and perpendicular (Figs 217–222). No post-calcarial lobe (only 'whiskered' bats and Bechstein's Bat sometimes have a very narrow post-calcarial lobe, but in these tragus distinctly perpendicular and without broadly rounded tip). Three premolars in the upper and lower jaw. . . **5**

5a Large bats, forearm >50mm. **12**

5b Small to medium-sized bats, forearm <50mm. **6**

6a Very long ear, more than 20mm long; when bent forward projecting beyond tip of nose by about half. 9–11 ear folds (Fig. 218). Wing membrane attached to base of toe.
Bechstein's Bat
(*Myotis bechsteinii*) p. 247

6b Ear shorter than 20mm; when bent forward projecting less than half its length beyond tip of nose. Less than 9 ear folds. **7**

Fig. 216. The tragus of Serotine Bat (*Eptesicus serotinus*) and related species is short, bent forward and broadly rounded. Photo: C. Dietz.

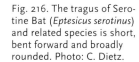

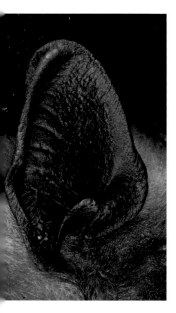

7a Calcar long and S-shaped. The free edge of the tail membrane wrinkled and densely beset with strong curved bristles. Tragus long and lancet shaped.
Natterer's Bat
(*Myotis nattereri*) p. 236

7b Calcar straight or slightly bent but never S-shaped. Edge of tail membrane at most with sparse soft hairs. **8**

8a Very large feet more than half length of tibia. Wing membrane attached to heel or to middle of foot. Outer edge of ear without a distinct notch. **10**

8b Feet at most half tibia length. Wing membrane attached at base of toe. Outer edge of ear with distinct notch. **9**

9a Notch at outer edge of ear almost right-angled. Tragus not reaching notch (Fig. 219). Forearm usually >37mm, only a few individuals with 36mm.
Geoffroy's Bat
(*Myotis emarginatus*) p. 242

9b Notch at outer edge of ear not right-angled. Tragus projects in most species above the notch (only one species has a shorter tragus, then a forearm <35mm). Forearm length usually <37mm, only a few individuals reach 38.2mm.
'Whiskered' bats. –
See separate sub-key 1 p. 142.

10a Forearm >42 mm (usually >43mm). Tragus less than half ear length. Wing membrane attached at ankle.
Pond bat
(*Myotis dasycneme*) p. 208

10b Forearm <42 mm. Tragus usually more than half ear length. Wing membrane attached at tibia or foot, but not at the ankle. **11**

11a Wing membrane attached at tibia (above ankle). Feet very large. Long tragus, slightly S-shaped (Fig. 220). Tibia and tail

 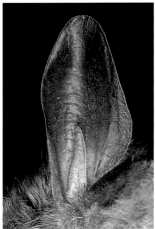  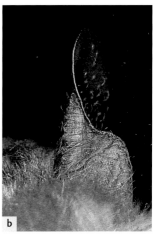

membrane covered with dense downy hairs.

Long-fingered Bat
(*Myotis capaccinii*) p. 212

11b Wing membrane attached at middle of foot. Feet large. Tragus reaches half ear length and is bent forward, but not S-shaped (Fig. 221). Tibia and tail membrane without hairs.

Daubenton's Bat
(*Myotis daubentonii*) p. 200

12a Ear length 26–29mm with no small black spot on the tip of the tragus. No firm separation from the two other large species of mouse-eared bats is possible on the basis of external characters. Occurs on Sardinia, Corsica, Malta and in northwest Africa.

Maghrebian Mouse-eared Bat
(*Myotis punicus*) p. 264

12b Ear length either shorter than 25mm or tragus tip with small black spot. No firm

separation from Maghrebian Mouse-eared Bat is possible on the basis of external characters. Occcurs in Europe or Asia Minor, but not on Corsica, Sardinia and Malta or in northwest Africa. **13**

13a Large bat, forearm 55–67mm. Ears broad (>16mm) and long (>24.5mm) often with 7–8 transverse folds. Upper tooth row >9.4mm. Almost always a small black spot at the tip of the tragus (Fig. 222). No whitish hair on the forehead.

Greater Mouse-eared Bat
(*Myotis myotis*) p. 252

13b A little smaller, forearm 50–62mm. Ears narrower (<16mm) and shorter (<24.5mm) often only with 5–6 transverse folds. Upper tooth row <9.5mm. Usually no black spot at tip of tragus. In Central Europe usually with whitish hairs on forehead.

Lesser Mouse-eared Bat
(*Myotis oxygnathus*) p. 260

◄◄◄ Fig. 217. The tragus of Lesser Mouse-eared Bat (*Myotis oxygnathus*) is, like most species of the genus, upright and not broadly rounded. Photo: C. Dietz.

◄◄ Fig. 218. The ear of Bechstein's Bat (*Myotis bechsteinii*) is over 20mm long and usually has 9–11 transverse folds. Photo: C. Dietz.

◄ Fig. 219 a+b. The ear of Geoffroy's Bat (*Myotis emarginatus*) is almost perpendicularly notched on the outer edge, the tragus does not reach the notch. Photo: C. Dietz.

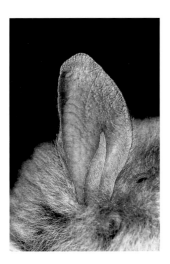  

◄◄◄ Fig. 220. The tragus of Long-Fingered Bat (*Myotis capaccinii*) is relatively long and has a slightly S-shaped curve. Photo: C. Dietz.

◄◄ Fig. 221. The tragus of Daubenton's Bat (*Myotis daubentonii*) reaches to half the ear length and is bent forward, but not S-shaped. Photo: C. Dietz.

◄ Fig. 222. The tragus of Greater Mouse-eared Bat (*Myotis myotis*) usually shows a small black spot at the tip. Photo: C. Dietz.

Fig. 223. The skin fold from the ear of the Isabelline Serotine (*Eptesicus isabellinus*) ends before the corner of the mouth. Photo: C. Dietz.

Fig. 224. The skin fold from the ear of Leisler's Bat (*Nyctalus leisleri*) reaches the corner of the mouth. Photo: C. Dietz.

Fig. 225. The penis of Savi's Pipistrelle (*Hypsugo savii*) is bent at a right-angle at the base. Photo: C. Dietz.

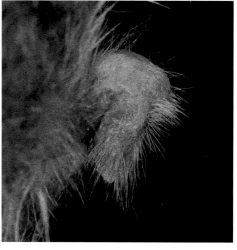

14a Smaller species: forearm length <38mm.   **23**

14b Larger species: forearm length >38mm.   . **15**

15a Outer edge of ear with a fold of skin running towards the corner of the mouth, but not reaching it (Fig. 223). Tragus clearly longer than broad. Post-calcarial lobe usually narrow and usually without a visible T-piece cartilage (Fig. 226). **20**

15b Outer edge of ear with a fold of skin reaching to the corner of the mouth (Fig. 224). Tragus widened towards apex. Post-calcarial lobe broad with a clearly visible T-piece cartilage (Fig. 228). **16**

16a Tragus short and widened towards apex, but not mushroom-shaped. Underwing with only fine grey hairs along the forearm. Dark brown-black dorsal fur with silver-white tips. Ventral side whitish grey or white, distinctly contrasting with the dorsal fur.
Parti-coloured Bat
(*Vespertilio murinus*) p. 315

16b Tragus widened towards tip to mushroom shape. Wings densely brown-haired on the lower side along forearm and body. Dorsal fur brown to red-brown, ventral fur only slightly paler than dorsal fur. **17**

17a Occurs only on the Azores. Forearm <40.7mm.   **Azorean Noctule Bat**
(*Nyctalus azoreum*) p. 282

17b Not on the Azores, but occurs in all remaining areas covered by this book. Forearm >38mm. **18**

18a Very large species, forearm 61–68mm. Long neck fur giving lion-like mane.
Greater Noctule Bat
(*Nyctalus lasiopterus*) p. 273

18b Forearm length <59mm. Neck fur not remarkably longer. **19**

19a Forearm length 48–59mm. Ear base not pale.
Noctule Bat
(*Nyctalus noctula*) p. 267

19b Forearm length <47mm. Ear base and base of outer edge of ear pale.
Leisler's Bat
(*Nyctalus leisleri*) p. 277

20a Upper tooth row (CM³) usually 7.0–7.4mm long. Face and ears brownish, not brown-black or black. Occurring in northwest Africa (Morocco, Algeria, Tunisia, Libya) Canary Islands and in southern part of Iberian Peninsula.
Isabelline Serotine Bat
(*Eptesicus isabellinus*) p. 332

20b Upper tooth row (CM³) usually >7.4mm or <7.0mm. Face and ears black-brown to deep black. Occuring in remaining scope of this book (Europe, Middle East), not known in northwest Africa. **21**

21a Large species, forearm length >48mm, length of the fifth finger >60mm. Penis widens towards apex and has no roof-shaped transverse fold. Upper tooth row length >7.2mm.
Serotine Bat
(*Eptesicus serotinus*) p. 320

21b Smaller species, forearm length <50mm, length of fifth finger <60mm. Penis widens distinctly towards apex and has a roof-shaped fold or is broadly egg-shaped. Upper tooth row length < 7.0mm. **22**

22a North European species, which reaches its southern border of distribution in the Balkan Peninsula and in the Caucasus. Does not occur in the Mediterranean area.
Northern Bat
(*Eptesicus nilssonii*) p. 326

22b Small Asian species, which occurs only along the Anatolian coast and on its off-shore islands (Rhodes).
Anatolian Serotine Bat
(*Eptesicus anatolicus*) p. 334.

23a Last two tail vertebrae project 4–5mm beyond edge of tail membrane. Post-calcarial lobe absent or narrow and without a T-piece cartilage (Fig. 229). Face and ears lacquer-black. Dorsal fur usually with golden yellowish tips, ventral fur usually pale beige to white. The short tragus widens somewhat towards tip. Penis with characteristic right-angled bend at base (Fig. 225).
Savi's Pipistrelle Bat
(*Hypsugo savii*) p. 310

23b Last tail vertebra projects at most 1–2mm beyond tail membrane. Post-calcarial lobe broad with distinct T-piece cartilage (Fig. 227) (post-calcarial lobe absent only in *P. rueppellii*, which occurs only in North Africa, and has very high-contrast pattern of snow-white ventral fur, grey-brown dorsal fur). Face and ears dark, but not lacquer-black. The dorsal fur brownish, sometimes with blond tips, but not with a gold-blond tinge. Tragus not widened towards tip. Penis not bent at right-angles.
Pipistrelle bats (Genus *Pipistrellus*). –
See separate sub-key 2 p.144

24a A very large desert bat with long ears (>35mm), white underside and pale-grey dorsal colouring.
Hemprich's Long-eared Bat
(*Otonycteris hemprichii*) p. 342

24b A large species with short ears (<25mm), ears haired inside. Very contrasting fur pattern, hair tips, particularly of the dorsal fur, with a silver touch. Vagrant from North America recorded on Iceland and the Orkney Islands.
Hoary Bat
(*Lasiurus cinereus*) p. 336

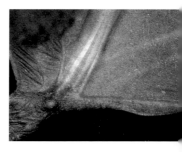

▲ Fig. 226. The post-calcarial lobe of the Serotine Bat (*Eptesicus serotinus*) is narrow, as in other species of the genus, and without a visible T-piece. Photo: C. Dietz.

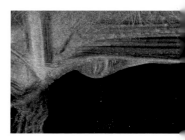

▲ Fig. 227. The post-calcarial lobe of the Common Pipistrelle (*Pipistrellus pipistrellus*) is broad, as in most other species of the genus, and has a clearly visible T-piece. Photo: C. Dietz.

◄ Fig. 228. The post-calcarial lobe of the Greater Noctule (*Nyctalus lasiopterus*) shows, as in other species of the genus, a clearly visible T-piece. Photo: C. Dietz.

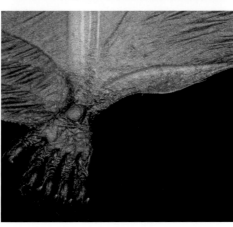

Fig. 229. The post-calcarial lobe of Savi's Pipistrelle (*Hypsugo savii*) is narrow and without a T-piece or is absent. Photo: C. Dietz.

▲Fig. 230. The ear of Alcathoe Whiskered Bat (*Myotis
alcathoe*) is short and the
short tragus usually does
not project above the notch
in the outer edge. Photo:
C. Dietz.

▲▶ Fig. 231. The ear of the
Whiskered Bat (*Myotis mystacinus*) is usually not strongly narrowed at the tip
Photo: C. Dietz.

▲▶▶ Fig. 232. The ear of the
Steppe Whiskered Bat
(*Myotis aurascens*) is clearly
narrowed at the tip. Photo:
C. Dietz.

Fig. 233. In side view the characteristically short
muzzle and smooth rounding of the head in the
Alcathoe Whiskered Bat (*Myotis alcathoe*) is visible.
Photo: C. Dietz.

Sub-key 1: 'Whiskered' bats

The 'whiskered' bats are relatively difficult to identify. Due to a large intraspecific variation and age-
related colour differences, the species can only be
differentiated reliably with much experience. The
characteristic variation of the Steppe Whiskered Bat
(*Myotis aurascens*) is still very poorly known, and a
reliable field identification and distinction from
Whiskered Bat (*Myotis mystacinus*) is at present
barely possible.

1a Very small bat, forearm usually <32.8mm
(only a few individuals up to 34.8mm) with
appearance of Daubenton's Bat and similar
colouring, but with very delicate feet. Short
ears with short tragus, which does not extend beyond the notch of the outer edge of
ear (Fig. 230). Short muzzle, so that fur on
the head reaches nearly to nose tip (Fig.
233). Short thumb (<4.5mm, rarely up to
5.0mm), short tibia (<14.5mm, rarely up to
15.9mm), short feet (<5.6mm, rarely up to
5.8mm). Dentition strongly resembles
Brandt's Bat, with a clearly recognisable
protocone on third upper premolar (P4),
usually extending above height of tip of second premolar (P3), (Fig. 236), and usually
distinct protoconules on upper molars (see
Fig. 234). It thus differs distinctly from
Whiskered and Steppe Whiskered Bat. Nostrils usually heart-shaped, as in Brandt's Bat.
Alcathoe Whiskered Bat
(*Myotis alcathoe*) p. 230

1b Small bat, forearm usually >33mm (rarely
32.0 mm). Predominantly dark brown often
with yellowish-blond fur tips and longer
ears, hence quite dissimilar to Daubenton's
Bats. Tragus nearly always extends above
notch in outer edge of overall longer ear.

▶ Fig. 234. Dentition of
Brandt's Bat (*Myotis brandtii*). In frontal view the
protoconules (cusps on the
upper molars (M¹⁻³)) are
usually clearly visible, and
also the high protocone
(cusp of the third upper
premolar (P4)) is clearly
recognisable. Diagram:
R. Roesler.

▶▶ Fig. 235. Dentition of the
Whiskered Bat (*Myotis mystacinus*). In frontal view the
protoconules (cusps on the
upper molars (M¹⁻³), and
the protocone (cusp on the
third upper molar (P4)) are
usually absent. Diagram:
R. Roesler.

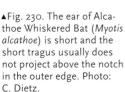

protocone

protoconule

p4

M¹

M²

M³

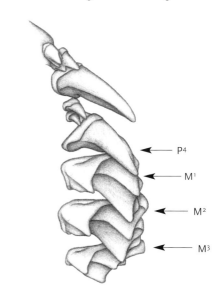

P4

M¹

M²

M³

Longer muzzle, which is clearly separated from the forehead hair. Longer thumb (>4.6mm, rarely only 4.3mm), longer tibia (>14.6mm), larger feet (>5.8mm). **2**

2a Large 'whiskered' bat, second upper premolar (P^3) in the tooth row and reaching to two-thirds height of first upper premolar (P^2) (Fig. 237). Similarly in lower jaw, second lower premolar (P_3) almost as large as first lower premolar (P_2) (Fig. 237). Protocone of third upper premolar (P^4) well developed and usually projects above tip of second premolar (P^3) (Fig. 237). Protoconules on upper molars usually visible (Fig. 234). Penis swollen and obviously club-shaped at tip (Fig. 240). Juvenile males already have the swollen penis, which differs distinctly from the evenly thin penis of Whiskered and Steppe Whiskered Bat. Nostrils are usually heart-shaped.

Brandt's Bat
(*Myotis brandtii*) p. 217.

2b Medium-sized to large 'whiskered' bats. Second upper premolar (P^3) often set inside the tooth row and reaching only half height of first upper premolar (P^2) (Fig. 238). Similarly in the lower jaw, second lower premolar (P_3) is distinctly smaller than first lower premolar (P_2) (Fig. 238). Protocone of third upper premolar (P^4) only weakly developed or absent and almost always lower than tip of second premolar (P^3) (Fig. 238). Protoconules on upper molars only rarely developed (Fig. 235). Penis evenly narrow for whole length (Fig. 239). Nostrils are usually comma-shaped, with rear part narrow and elongated. **3**

3a Very variable species, southeast European animals differing clearly from Central European individuals and range of variation so large that it may include several cryptic species. Ears broader at tip than in Steppe Whiskered Bat (Fig. 231). A relatively common species throughout Europe
Whiskered Bat
(*Myotis mystacinus*) p. 221

3b Little-known species from southeast Europe. Many of the individuals identified as this species in recent years actually belong to Whiskered Bat (*Myotis mystacinus*); at present there are only four confirmed individuals, known from north Bulgaria. Distinction from Whiskered Bat with a living animal is hardly possible. Ears somewhat narrower, with front edge somewhat more strongly convex and particularly ear tip clearly narrower than in Whiskered Bat (Fig. 232). A firm species identification at present is only possible with genetic methods.
Steppe Whiskered Bat
(*Myotis aurascens*) p. 227

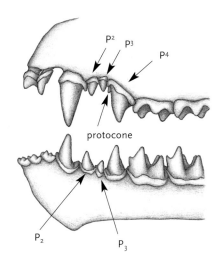

Fig. 236. In the dentition of the Alcathoe Whiskered Bat (*Myotis alcathoe*) the protocone of the third upper premolar (P^4) is clearly pronounced and usually projects above the tip of the second premolar (P^3). Diagram: R. Roesler.

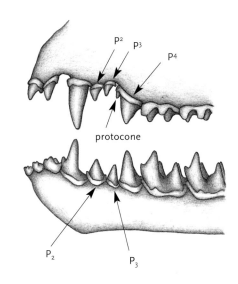

Fig. 237. In the dentition of Brandt's Bat (*Myotis brandtii*) the second upper premolar (P^3) is in the tooth row and reaches to two-thirds of the height of the first upper premolar (P^2). The protocone of the third upper premolar (P^4) usually projects above the tip of the second premolar (P^3). In the lower jaw the second lower premolar (P_3) is almost as large as the first lower premolar (P_2). Diagram: R. Roesler.

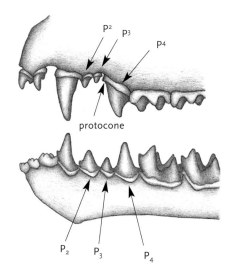

Fig. 238. Dentition of the Whiskered Bat (*Myotis mystacinus*). The second upper premolar (P^3) is often set inside the tooth row and reached only half the height of the first upper premolar (P^2). The protocone of the third upper premolar (P^4) is only weakly developed or absent. In the lower jaw the second lower premolar (P_3) is distinctly smaller than the first lower premolar (P_2). Diagram: R. Roesler.

Fig. 239. The penis of
the Whiskered Bat (*Myotis
mystacinus*) is evenly narrow
for the whole length. Photo:
C. Dietz.

Fig. 240. The penis of
Brandt's Bat (*Myotis
brandtii*) is distinctly broadened towards the end and is
club-shaped at the end.
Photo: C. Dietz.

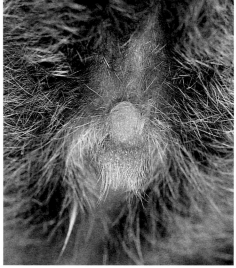

Sub-key 2: Pipistrelle bats (Genus *Pipistrellus*)

1a First upper incisor (I²) with two points (Figs 243 and 244). Between upper canine (C¹) and large upper premolar (P⁴) another small premolar (P³) is visible from outside (Figs 243 and 244). **3**

1b First upper incisor (I²) has one point (Fig. 242). Upper canine (C¹) and large upper premolar (P⁴) close together or in direct contact, from outside view no small premolar (P³) visible (Fig. 242). **2**

2a Occurs on Canary Islands, Madeira and perhaps on the Azores. Dorsal and ventral side uniformly dark-brown, red to orange-brown or chocolate-brown. Basal three-quarters of length of dorsal hairs black-brown. End frequency of echolocation calls >42kHz.
Madeiran Pipistrelle Bat
(*Pipistrellus maderensis*) p. 306

2b Occurs in the remaining distribution area and on the Canary Islands, not on Madeira and the Azores. Ventral side paler than dorsal side, which is brown, often with paler tips. Basal two-thirds of dorsal hairs black-brown. End frequency

of the echolocation calls usually <42kHz.
Kuhl's Pipistrelle Bat
(*Pipistrellus kuhlii*) p. 301

3a Tail membrane without post-calcarial lobe. Very highly contrasted pattern of grey-brown dorsal colouring sharply delineated from white ventral side. Skin areas black. Desert regions of North Africa.
Rüppell's Pipistrelle Bat
(*Pipistrellus rueppellii*) p. 308

3b Tail membrane with broad post-calcarial lobe. Weakly contrasted colouring, no white ventral side, skin areas dark, but not black. . **4**

4a Fifth finger >43mm. First upper premolar (P³) in tooth row and clearly visible from outside (Fig. 243). Tip of second upper incisor (I³) projects beyond short cusp of first incisor (I²) (Fig. 243). Usually a clear gap between second and third lower incisors (I₂ and I₃). The wing cell between fifth finger and elbow usually divided by a distinct bar (Fig. 245). Densely and long haired on lower surface of tail membrane along the tibia and on upper surface of tail membrane. Dorsal fur dark-brown to grey-brown.
Nathusius's Pipistrelle Bat
(*Pipistrellus nathusii*) p. 296

4b Fifth finger < 43mm. First upper premolar (P³) inside tooth row, only the tip usually visible (Fig. 244). Tip of second upper incisor (I³) is shorter than small cusp of first upper incisor (I²), the three points form a steady gradation (Fig. 244). Usually no gap between second and third lower incisors (I_2 and I_3). The wing cell between the fifth finger and the elbow is usually not divided (Figs 246 and 247). With only sparse and short hairs on lower surface of tail membrane along tibia and on upper surface of tail membrane. **5**

5a On average a larger species, forearm

length 28.0–34.5mm. No perpendicular skin bulge present between nostrils (Fig. 248). Muzzle tapers evenly. Buccal glands white or grey-white. Inner edge of ear 8–9mm long. Dorsal fur brown, ears and face dark-brown to brown. Only paler skin areas of face contrast with fur colouring. Penis grey-brown with distinctive pale median band (Fig. 250). In females skin around vagina brownish, not yellow-orange. Cell between fifth finger and elbow not divided by a bar, but the cell above is divided (Fig. 246). Upper side of tail membrane not densely haired. Without strong musk scent. Echolocation

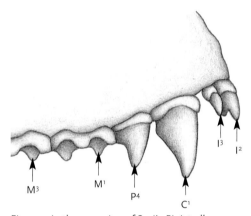

Fig. 241. In the upper jaw of Savi's Pipistrelle (*Hypsugo savii*) the canine (C¹) and the large premolar (P⁴) touch each other, the small premolar (P³) between them is not visible from outside. Diagram: R. Roesler.

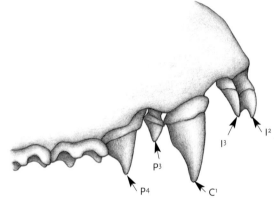

Fig. 243. In the upper jaw of Nathusius's Pipistrelle (*Pipistrellus nathusii*) the first premolar (P³) lies in the tooth row and is well visible from the outside. The point of the second (outer) incisor (I³) projects above the short point of the first incisor (I²). Diagram: R. Roesler.

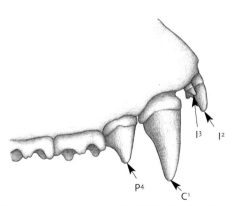

Fig. 242. In the upper jaw of Kuhl's Pipistrelle (*Pipistrellus kuhlii*) the first (inner) incisor (I²) has one point, or, as with the illustrated skull, with a second small point often almost covered by the gums. The second incisor (I³) is very small. The canine (C¹) and the large premolar (P⁴) are close together or in direct contact, from side view the small premolar (P³) is not visible between them. Diagram: R. Roesler.

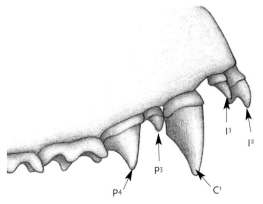

Fig. 244. In the upper jaw of Common and Soprano Pipistrelle Bats (*Pipistrellus pipistrellus* and *pygmaeus*) the first premolar (P³) is set inside the tooth row, only the point is usually visible. The point of the second (outer) upper incisor (I³) is lower than the small point of the first upper incisor (I²), the three points form a steady gradation Diagram: R. Roesler.

Fig. 245. Wing of Nathusius's Pipistrelle (*Pipistrellus nathusii*) seen from below; the cell that runs from the elbow to the fifth finger (grey shaded) is divided by a distinct bar. Diagram: R. Roesler.

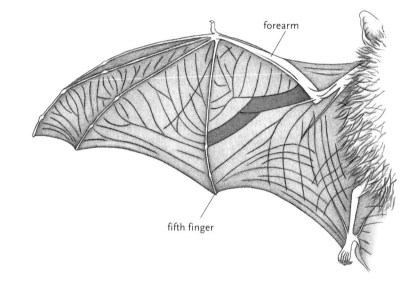

Fig. 246. Wing of the Common Pipistelle (*Pipistrellus pipistrellus*) seen from below (and is the same in Kuhl's Pipistrelle, *P. kuhlii*); the cell between the fifth finger and the elbow (grey shaded) is not divided by a bar, the field lying over it (light grey) is, on the other hand, divided. Diagram: R. Roesler.

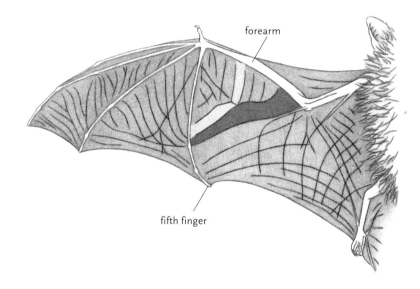

Fig. 247. Wing of the Soprano Pipistrelle (*Pipistrellus pygmaeus*) seen from below; the cell between the fifth finger and the elbow (grey shaded) as well as the cell lying over it are not divided by a bar. Diagram: R. Roessler.

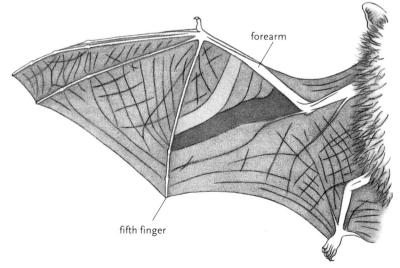

calls in the open with end frequencies of 44–49kHz, rarely to 52kHz.

Common Pipistrelle Bat
(*Pipistrellus pipistrellus*) p. 284

5b On average a smaller species, forearm length 27.7–32.2mm. Usually a distinct perpendicular skin bulge present between nostrils (Fig. 249). Short muzzle parallel-sided for approximately two-thirds of its length, then suddenly tapers. Buccal glands yellowish-white or orange-yellowish. Inner edge of ear only 7–8mm. Dorsal fur sandy to reddish-brown, in winter also olive-brown, ventral surface yellowish-grey. Ears and face light brown. Distinctly paler skin areas in face, particularly between eyes and ears. Bare skin areas contrast only a little with fur colouring. Penis yellowish-grey and without a pale median band. In sexually active animals the lateral folds of penis can be yellow to bright orange (Fig. 251). In females, skin around vagina, at least in the reproduction time, yellowish-orange. Cell between fifth finger and elbow, as well as cell above, is not divided by a bar (Fig. 247). Upper surface of tail membrane relatively densely haired. At mating time smell intensively of a musk scent. Echolocation calls in the open with end frequencies of 52–58kHz, only rarely to 50kHz.

Soprano Pipistrelle Bat
(*Pipistrellus pygmaeus*) p. 290

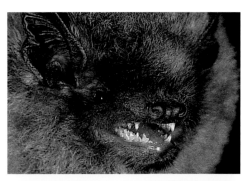

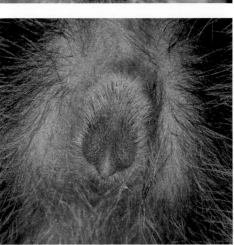

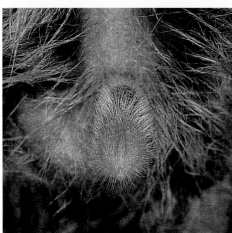

◄◄ Fig. 248. In the Common Pipistrelle (*Pipistrellus pipistrellus*) there is no perpendicular skin bulge present between the nostrils. Photo: C. Dietz.

◄ Fig. 249. In the Soprano Pipistrelle (*Pipistrellus pygmaeus*) a clear perpendicular skin bulge is usually present between the nostrils. Photo: C. Dietz.

◄◄ Fig. 250. The penis of the Common Pipistrelle (*Pipistrellus pipistrellus*) is grey-brown with a pale median stripe. Photo: C. Dietz.

◄ Fig. 251. The penis of the Soprano Pipistrelle (*Pipistrellus pygmaeus*) is yellowish white and without a bright median stripe, often with orange lateral folds of the preputium. Photo: C. Dietz.

Sub-key 3: Long-eared bats (Genus *Plecotus*)

1a Occurs on the Canary Islands (only Tenerife, La Palma, El Hierro). Relatively large with dark grey dorsal fur and pale ventral fur.
Canary Long-eared Bat
(*Plecotus teneriffae*) p. 365

1b Occurs in the remaining scope of this book, not on the Canary Islands. **2**

2a Occurs in northwest Africa (Morocco, Algeria, Tunisia). Pale brownish.
Gaisler's Long-eared Bat
(*Plecotus gaisleri*) p. 367

2b Occurs in Europe, Middle East, on the Mediterranean islands and Madeira, not in North Africa. **3**

3a Occurs on Sardinia. Long tragus (>18mm). Thumb medium-long (6.0–6.5mm). Foot medium-sized (6.7–7.7mm). Penis parallel-sided and tapering only at tip (Fig. 252).
Sardinian Long-eared Bat
(*Plecotus sardus*) p. 356

3b Europe, Middle East and Mediterranean islands, not known on Sardinia, or if occurring on Sardinia then with shorter tragus (<16mm) and penis conical or broadly egg-shaped. **4**

4a Thumbs short (<6.5mm), short thumb claw (<2mm), short foot (<8mm). Hairs on the toes short and decumbent. Penis broadly egg-shaped (Fig. 253). Glands above eye small. **6**

4b Thumbs long (>6.5mm), thumb claw long and strongly bent (>2 mm), hind foot larger (>8mm long). Hair on the toes long and erect. Penis either parallel-sided and tapering only at tip (Fig. 252), or evenly conical tapering to tip (Fig. 254). Glands above eyes large. **5**

5a Upper edge of lower lip with a narrow smooth shining skin area, lower edge rounded, in the broadest sense banana-shaped and usually unpigmented (Fig. 255). The whole foot very densely haired. Tragus short (usually <15.5mm, rarely up to 16.7mm), fifth finger short (<55mm), third finger short (<67mm). Dorsal fur brown or red-brown. Ventral fur lighter, usually yellowish brown. Penis conical, tapering evenly to tip (Fig. 254).
Brown Long-eared Bat
(*Plecotus auritus*) p. 345

5b Upper edge of lower lip with a smooth triangular area (Fig. 256). In many individuals this area darkly pigmented. Foot hardly haired, long bristles only on toes. Tragus usually longer than 16mm. Fifth finger long (>51mm), third likewise (>63mm). Fur long and loose, dorsal fur grey-brown and ventral fur almost pure white, only sometimes grey-white. Penis parallel-sided and only tapering close to the tip (Fig. 252).
Alpine Long-eared Bat
(*Plecotus macrobullaris*) p. 353

6a Small species, forearm length in males <38mm, in females <39 mm (only rarely up to 41.0mm). Third finger short (<65mm), fifth finger short (<52mm), tibia short (<18mm, rarely up to 18.3mm). Tragus

► Fig. 252. The penis of the Alpine and Sardinian Long-eared Bat (*Plecotus macrobullaris* & *sardus*) is evenly broad and tapered only at the tip. Diagram: R. Roesler.

►► Fig. 253. The penis of the Grey, the Balkan, Canary and Gaisler's Long-eared Bat (*Plecotus austriacus*, *kolombatovici*, *teneriffae* and *gaisleri*) is broadly egg-shaped. Diagram: R. Roesler.

►►► Fig. 254. The penis of the Brown Long-eared Bat (*Plecotus auritus*) tapers as an even triangle to the tip. Diagram: R. Roesler.

short (<14mm) and narrow (<5.2mm). Upper tooth row length <5.7mm. Occurs along the Adriatic coast, in Greece and in Turkey.

Balkan Long-eared Bat
(*Plecotus kolombatovici*) p. 362

6b Larger species, forearm length in males usually >38mm, in females usually >39mm.

Third finger long (>64mm), fifth finger long (>51mm, rarely only 48mm), tibia long (>18mm), tragus medium long (14–16mm) and broad (>5.4mm). Upper tooth row length >5.7mm. Large parts of Europe, also on the Adriatic coast and in Greece.

Grey Long-eared Bat
(*Plecotus austriacus*) p. 358

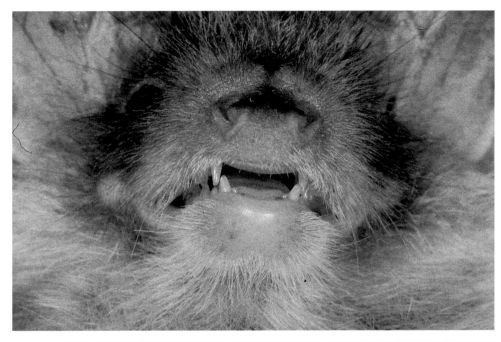

Fig. 255. The skin spot on the lower lip of the Brown Long-eared Bat (*Plecotus auritus*) is rounded and usually not pigmented. Photo: C. Dietz.

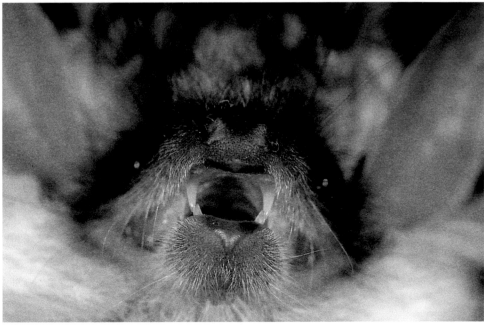

Fig. 256. The hard leather-like triangular spot on the lower lip of the Alpine Long-eared Bat (*Plecotus macrobullaris*) is often darkly pigmented. Photo: C. Dietz.

Fruit Bats or Flying Foxes
Pteropodidae

Large to very large bats of the suborder Megachiroptera. Head often of a fox-like appearance, simple ears without a tragus. Large eyes. As well as the thumb, the second finger also has a claw. The tail is short or not visible externally and the tail membrane is very narrow or absent. A sturdy snout, in many species the teeth are flat crowned and so adapted to a diet of principally fruit, and nectar and pollen of flowers. The body size ranges from very large species with a wingspan of over 170cm and weight of 1500g to small species with a 24cm wingspan and 11g weight. The flying foxes orient themselves visually as well as with the sense of smell. Only the cave-dwelling fruit bats of the genus *Rousettus* have an echolocation system, using tongue clicks, an independent development convergent with the bats of the suborder Microchiroptera. The family covers 42 genera with 186 species in the tropics and subtropics of the Old World [16]. In the geographical scope of this book only one species: *Rousettus aegyptiacus* on Cyprus and on the south coast of Turkey. Nine further species of the genus occur from Africa to Indonesia.

Egyptian Fruit Bat
Rousettus aegyptiacus
(Geoffroy, 1810)

NAMES
D: Nilflughund
F: Rousette d'Egypt
E: Murciélago egipcio
I: Pipistrello della frutta
NL: Nijlrousette
S: Egyptisk flyghund, nilflyghund
PL: Rudawka nilowa

Measurement

Forearm	83.0–99.0mm
Fifth finger	100–112mm
Third finger	135–154mm
Normal weight	108–140g
CBL	39.6–43.3mm
CM²	15.6–16.2mm

IDENTIFICATION
Large robust animals with very strong feet and thumbs. Typical fox-like fruit bat head with large eyes and simple ears. The fur is short; dorsal and ventral sides are uniformly grey or brownish coloured, belly and throat in some animals yellowish. Young animals grey and more sparsely haired than the adults.

Similar species
Unmistakable within the region covered by this book due to the size.

ECHOLOCATION CALLS
As echolocation calls, short paired clicks are emitted between 12 and 70kHz [3], on the Sinai Peninsula between 7 and 60kHz, and 0.3–0.6ms long. The clicks are produced with the tongue. The double clicks are caused by tongue beats to the right and left side. As long as the light is sufficient orientation takes place by sight.

DISTRIBUTION
Distributed through the whole of Africa south of the Sahara, Egypt, Cyprus, the south coast of Turkey, the Near East and the boundary regions of the Arabian Peninsula to Pakistan and northwest India. Since

Fig. 257. Portrait of an Egyptian Fruit Bat. The eyes are very large compared with the eyes of the Microchiropteran bats and the ears are simple. The second finger of most Old World fruit bats carries a small claw. Photo: C. Dietz.

2000 there are two introduced populations on Tenerife (Canary Islands), descended from escaped captive animals [12].

Subspecies and geographical variation

The subspecies *R. a. aegyptiacus* occurs within the geographical scope of this book. At least five further subspecies recognised, with *R .a. arabicus* on the Arabian Peninsula.

HABITAT

Subtropical Mediterranean cultivated land with fruit trees, oases, also cities with fruit trees and gardens.

Roosts

Cave-dwelling fruit bat, which is usually found in the highest parts of caves and in other spacious underground corridors. By the ability to echolocate with tongue clicks, the Egyptian Fruit Bat is able to use deep dark caves as roosts, while other fruit bats, which orient only by sight, cannot do this. On Cyprus exclusively in caves in the winter, in the summer also roosts in buildings or hanging freely in trees [2]. In Egypt sometimes large summer colonies in trees, even in the middle of large cities such as Cairo.

BEHAVIOUR

Colonies usually comprise 50–500 animals, in some caves several thousand. In the winter both sexes hang together; in the summer the females form nursery colonies and the males smaller separate groups [5, 7]. The species can occur with other cave-dwelling bats. Does not hibernate, cool and wet periods are spent in the roost with reduced activity. Foraging sites are visited up to 24km from the roost [7, 8], on the Sinai Peninsula probably even further.

Fig. 258. Echolocation with clicking sounds makes it possible for the Egyptian Fruit Bat to use caves as roosts while most other Old World fruit bats orientate exclusively by sight. Photo: T. Pröhl.

REPRODUCTION

In North Africa, on Cyprus and in Asia Minor the period of high food availability is too short to breed twice a year, as occurs in the tropics. Consequently, females undertake only one reproductive phase per year, with one young or rarely with twins. Mating takes place either in the winter or in the spring, after which females are pregnant for four months. Depending upon the time of mating, birth takes place from March to April or from August to September [9, 13]. Females can occasionally carry two differently sized embryos and thus participate in both reproduction phases [13]. Neonates have a forearm length of approximately 38mm and begin to fly at the age of seven weeks; they are weaned at 12 weeks [8, 10]. In the roost dependent young animals are carried by the mothers against the body and are completely wrapped within the wings. The sexual maturity is reached at 9–12 months.

FORAGING

The food is located by sight or with the very well-developed sense of smell and ripe fruits are selected. The fruits are picked from a hanging position and sometimes carried for up to 400m to feeding sites for consumption. Hard-skinned fruits are peeled, using wings, feet and thumb claws to hold the fruit. Food plants are spread by the transport of seeds. Egyptian Fruit Bats consume 50–150% of their body weight in fruits per night [4]. Indigestible parts and large seeds, e.g. of dates, are spat out; small seeds pass through the digestive tract. Egyptian Fruit Bats can climb well and rapidly and use the claws of thumbs and second fingers for support. Flying animals can also hover briefly at fruits.

FOOD

Fruit bats eat various fruits, particularly those cultivated by humans: figs, apricots, peaches, apples, citrus fruits, bananas, as well as mulberries and dates. In times of food shortage, particularly in the winter, the leaves of carob and fig trees are eaten, as well as shoots of carob trees. Pollen probably plays a minor role. At plantations over-ripe or damaged fruit is often eaten; hence there is limited damage for fruit growers, who usually harvest unripe fruits for export [8]. Egyptian Fruit Bats play an important role in seed dispersal of their food plants.

MAXIMUM AGE

In captivity 25 years [10], data from the wild are not available.

MOBILITY AND MIGRATION

Long-distance migrations are not known, but local migrations between summer and winter areas occur on Cyprus and in the Near East. On the Sinai Peninsula the animals seem to cross large desert areas in order to find food in oases.

THREATS

Red list of the IUCN 2006: LC (Least Concern), EU Habitats Directive, Annex II & IV. Even into the 1970s colonies with over 800 animals occurred on Cyprus [13]; after eradication efforts the colonies went down to less than 20 animals [2]; nowadays there are again about a dozen caves with several hundred individuals [Demetropoulos pers. com., 15]. In Israel, despite major eradication campaigns in the 1950s [8], nowadays common again, particularly in the coastal plains. Meanwhile, other cave-dwelling bats (mouse-eared and horseshoe bats) were

Fig. 259. In the wingbeat during flight, Egyptian Fruit Bats roll the wing tips inward. Photo: T. Pröhl.

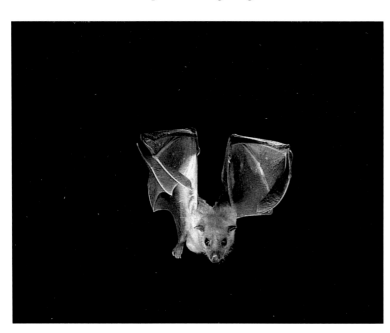

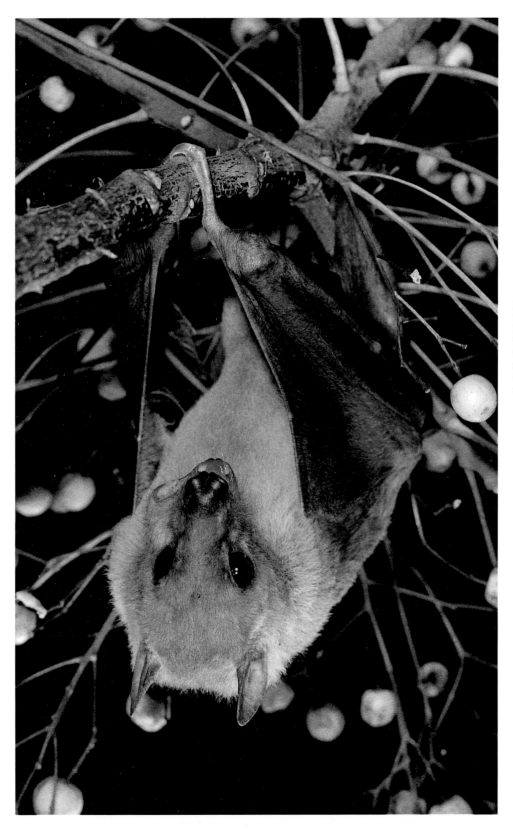

Fig. 260. Egyptian Fruit Bats are pure vegetarians. Here an animal consumes the fruits of the white cedar tree (*Melia azedarach*), which serves as food on Cyprus, particularly in the winter. Photo: T. Pröhl.

almost exterminated by these poisonings. The species seems to recover relatively quickly from control programmes with sufficient food availability and undisturbed roosts. In Israel it is regarded as a pest and its killing is still permitted. The relative flexibility and a high reproductive potential of the introduced populations on Tenerife have resulted in damage to endemic plants, as well as negative impacts on two highly endangered endemic pigeon species by food competition [12].

CONSERVATION MEASURES

On Cyprus and in Asia Minor the colony caves should be protected from disturbance, in the Near East also from extermination campaigns. For the fruit growers damage can be reduced by the protection of fruit plantations with nets. On Tenerife measures for the removal of the introduced populations are under discussion.

REFERENCES

1. Bergmans, W. (1994): Taxonomy and biogeography of African fruit bats (Mammalia, Megachiroptera). 4. The genus *Rousettus* Gray, 1821. *Beaufortia* 44: 79–126.
2. Boye, P., B. Pott-Dörfer, K. Dörfer & A. Demetropoulos (1990): New records of bats from Cyprus and notes to their biology. *Myotis* 28: 93–100.
3. Holland, R.A., D.A. Waters & J.M.V. Rayner (2004): Echolocation signal structure in the megachiropteran bat *Rousettus aegyptiacus*. *J. Exp. Biol.* 207: 4361–4369.
4. Izhaki, I., C. Korine & Z. Arad (1995): The effect of bat (*Rousettus aegyptiacus*) dispersal on seed germination in eastern Mediterranean habitats. *Oecologia* 101: 335–342.
5. Karataç, A., N. Yi it, E. Çolak & T. Kankiliç (2003): Contribution to *Rousettus aegyptiacus* (Mammalia: Chiroptera) from Turkey. *Folia Zool.* 52: 137–142.
6. Korine, C., I. Izhaki & D. Makin (1994): Population structure and emergence order in the fruit-bat (*Rousettus aegyptiacus*). *J. Zool.* 232: 163–174.
7. Korine, C. & Z. Arad (1999): Changes in milk composition of the Egyptian fruit bat, *Rousettus aegyptiacus* during lactation. *J. Mammal.* 80: 53–59.
8. Korine, C., I. Izhaki & Z. Arad (1999): Is the Egyptian fruit-bat *Rousettus aegyptiacus* a pest in Israel? An analysis of the bat's diet and implications for its conservation. *Biol. Conserv.* 88: 301–306.
9. Korine, C., J. Speakman & Z. Arad (2004): Reproductive energetics of captive and free-ranging Egyptian fruit bats (*Rousettus aegyptiacus*). *Ecology* 85: 220–230.
10. Kulzer, E. (1979): Physiological ecology and geographical range in the fruit-eating cave bat *Rousettus* – a review. *Bonn. Zool. Beitr.* 30: 233–275.
11. Kwiecinski, G.G. & T.A. Griffiths (1999): *Rousettus aegyptiacus*. *Mammalian Species* 611: 1–9.
12. Nogales, M., J.L. Rodriguez-Luengo & P. Marrero (2006): Ecological effects and distribution of invasive non-native mammals on the Canary Islands. *Mammal Rev.* 36: 49–65.
13. Spitzenberger, F. (1979): Die Säugetierfauna Zyperns Teil II: Chiroptera, Lagomorpha, Carnivora und Artiodactyla. *Ann. Nat. Hist. Mus. Wien* 82: 439–465.
14. Waters, D. A. & C. Vollrath (2003): Echolocation performance and call structure in the megachiropteran fruit-bat *Rousettus aegyptiacus*. *Acta Chiropterologica* 5: 209–219.

ADDITIONAL REFERENCES

15. Hadjisterkotis, E. (2006): The destruction and conservation of the Egyptian Fruit bat *Rousettus aegyptiacus* in Cyprus: a historic review. *Eur. J. Wildl. Res.* 52: 282–287.

Sheath-tailed bats
Emballonuridae

Members of the family of sheath-tailed bats are characterised by having a simple face without adornments and the tail emerging from part way down the tail membrane when the bat is at rest. A worldwide tropical and subtropical family of just over 50 species in 13 genera.

The species are insectivorous, and although most form fairly small colonies or groups in a variety of situations, some species of *Taphozous* can form large colonies in underground sites, such as caves or rock crevices.

A single species, the Naked-rumped Tomb Bat (*Taphozous nudiventris* Cretzschmar 1830), is recorded from Gaziantep, eastern Turkey [1] and is widely distributed further south [gen. lit. 46]. It is a large species (forearm length *c.* 74mm), foraging high in the open air and roosting in rock crevices in cliffs, caves and buildings. It may migrate north into Turkey to breed.

REFERENCES

1. Sachanowicz, K., W. Bogdanowicz and S. Michalak (1999): First record of *Taphozous nudiventris* Cretzschmar 1830 (Chiroptera: Emballonuridae) in Turkey. *Mammalia* 63: 105–107.

Mouse-tailed Bats
Rhinopomatidae

Medium-sized insectivorous bats with a long tail, which extends far beyond the narrow tail membrane. The narrow wings allow a very fast flight, and the strong ears are stabilised with skin folds. On the nose a small erect triangular skin leaf stands directly above the nostrils. As with the horseshoe and leaf-nosed bats the females have, in addition to the mammary glands, a pair of false nipples in the pelvic region. Only one genus: *Rhinopoma*, with four species which occur in the tropics of the Old World: two species in Africa and eastwards, another one distributed from the Arabian Peninsula to Asia, and one species restricted to Africa. In the geographical scope of this book only one species, *Rhinopoma hardwickii* at the northern edge of the Sahara, which is regarded by some authors as a separate species, *R. cystops*.

Fig. 261. The Lesser Mouse-tailed Bat is narrow-winged and a fast flier and usually hunts in the open air space. Photo: T. Pröhl.

Lesser Mouse-tailed Bat
Rhinopoma hardwickii
GRAY, 1831

NAMES
D: Kleine Mausschwanzfledermaus
F: Petit rhinopome
NL: Kleine klapneusvleermuis

IDENTIFICATION
Slightly built bat with a very long and thin tail, which is longer than the forearm and extends for three-quarters of its length beyond the narrow tail membrane. Slender long legs and feet. Distinct triangular skin leaf on the snout. The snout and the nose ridge are densely beset with sebaceous and sweat glands and are sparsely haired. Large strong ears and curved tragus. Short silky fur, chin and belly hardly haired. The hairs are evenly pale grey or grey-brown for their whole length, on the ventral side whitish grey.

Similar species
Unmistakable within the region covered by this book, the more southerly-occurring Greater Mouse-tailed Bat (*R. microphyllum*) is larger and more sturdily built, its tail shorter than the forearm length.

ECHOLOCATION CALLS
In the open air 10–50ms long, almost

constant-frequency calls with three to four harmonics [9]. The second harmonic between 30 and 36kHz contains the most energy and is best detected at 32kHz. The calls of *R. microphyllum* (second harmonic with the most energy on average at 28kHz) and *T. teniotis* (the best frequency 10–14kHz) are lower; in *Taphozous* species the harmonics have about equal energy.

DISTRIBUTION
Distributed around the Sahara and in its

Measurements	
Forearm	54.0–62.2mm
Fifth finger	51–60mm
Third finger	59–97mm
Normal weight	8–11g
CBL	14.8–17.2mm
CM³	5.0–6.2mm

boundary regions. In the northwest up to the high Atlas in Morocco and to the Sahara Atlas in Algeria and Tunisia. In the south into Sudan and Kenya; over the whole Arabian Peninsula, northward to Syria and Israel. In Asia eastward to India, Thailand and the Sunda archipelago.

Subspecies and geographical variation

Many subspecies are described [10]; they are, however, difficult to define. The substantial intraspecific variation can be interpreted as local adaptation to food availability. The Lesser Mouse-tailed Bats of North Africa are regarded by some authors [12] as a separate full species *R. cystops*,

Fig. 262. Portrait of Lesser Mouse-tailed Bat: a small erect triangular skin leaf stands directly above the nostrils and the muzzle and nose ridge are beset with sebaceous and sweat glands. Photo: C. Dietz.

with *R. c. cystops* in North Africa, *R. c. arabium* in the Near East and on the Arabian Peninsula, and *R. hardwickii* as a separate species eastwards from Iran [12]

HABITAT
In particular semi-deserts and deserts, in which suitable roosts in cliffs of wadies, in rocks and caves are preferred.

Roosts
A cave-dwelling bat which can also be found in other underground passages, cellars and ruins as well as in rock crevices and in scree.

BEHAVIOUR
In the autumn extensive fat reserves can be built up in the pelvic region at belly and back. There is no hibernation, but with unfavourable weather the animals remain in the roost, reduce their activity (260–340 heart beats per minute, instead of 540–620 during activity [6]) and slightly lower the body temperature. In the roosts the animals often hang on the walls, more rarely on the ceiling. They cling by the feet and thumbs on the walls, with the tail bent forward antenna-like. When disturbed the head is bent far back and the environment is scanned with rapid head movements. In cracks animals crawl rapidly backwards using the tail as a probe, similar to *Tadarida* [own data]. Usually colonies from a few dozen to several hundred animals. In Morocco in April, mixed colonies of both sexes [own data], but pure male groups were also found. In Egypt, often mixed with the Greater Mouse-tailed Bat and Tomb Bats (*Taphozous perforatus*), but also with horseshoe bats, leaf-nosed bats or fruit bats. In April in Morocco a behaviour similar to late summer swarming of bats in Central Europe was observed: over 100 *R. hardwickii* and *R. microphyllum* circled for hours in front of a cave entrance and the surrounding cliffs [own data]. During agitation (e.g. with capture) sweat drops are excreted on the face. The nostrils are closed after each breath, probably in order to minimise the respiratory loss of water (by breath).

REPRODUCTION

To a large extent unknown; in Egypt and on the Arabian Peninsula one young per female is nursed to August [7, gen. lit. 46].

FORAGING

The food is captured in a rapid swallow-like flight, gliding flight alternating with rapid wingbeats. In particular the characteristic undulating flight pattern punctuated by long glides differentiates *Rhinopoma* readily from other bats in open areas. In flight very agile, when pursuing insects the Lesser Mouse-tailed Bat dives down to close to the ground. They can also use updraughts, hovering calmly in the air to catch insects drifting past. Mouse-tailed bats often hunt in groups [3].

FOOD

Depending upon season the food consists particularly of flying beetles and swarming ants [11] or of moths. In India beetles and crickets play a major role during the dry season; during the rainy season termites, ants and moths dominate [1]. Mouse-tailed bats meet their water demand as far as possible from their food.

MOBILITY AND MIGRATION

The species accomplishes seasonal migrations, which are so far, however, hardly investigated in the Near East. The brief occurrence of large to very large colonies in areas in which the species is not found in other seasons is noticeable.

THREATS

To a large extent unknown. Red list of the IUCN 2006: LC (Least Concern). Records in the geographical scope of this book are relatively rare, which might be due to insufficient fieldwork and difficulties in the recording of high-flying species.

Fig. 263. Lesser Mouse-tailed Bats usually hang on the wall of their roost; they can also crawl backwards into narrow cracks, using the long tail as a probe. Photo: C. Dietz.

REFERENCES

1. Advani, R. (1983): Seasonal fluctuations in the diet composition of *Rhinopoma hardwickei* in the Rajasthan Desert. *Nyctalus* (N.F.) 1: 544–548.
2. Feldman, R., J.O. Whitaker & Y. Yom-Tov (2000): Dietary composition and habitat use in a desert insectivorous bat community in Israel. *Acta Chiropterologica* 2: 15–22.
3. Habersetzer, J. (1981): Adaptive echolocation sounds in the bat *Rhinopoma hardwickii. J. Comp. Physiol.* 144: 559–566.
4. Kowalski, K. & B. Rzebik-Kowalska (1991): *Mammals of Algeria.* Polish Academy of Sciences.
5. Kulzer, E. (1966): Thermoregulation bei Wüstenfledermäusen. *Natur und Museum* 96: 242–253.
6. Kulzer, E., I. Helmy & G. Necker (1985): Untersuchungen über die Drüsen der Gesichtsregion der ägyptischen Mausschwanz-Fledermaus *Rhinopoma hardwickei cystops. Z. Säugetierk.* 50: 57–68.

Fig. 264. Lesser Mouse-tailed Bat inhabits caves and roomy rock crevices in semi-desert areas, such as here in the Moroccan anti-Atlas. Photo: C. Dietz.

7. Qumsiyeh, M.B. & J.J. Knox (1986): *Rhinopoma hardwickii* and *Rhinopoma muscatellum*. *Mammalian Species* 263: 1–5.
8. Schmidt, U. & G. Joermann (1983): Untersuchungen zur Echoortung im Gruppenflug bei Mausschwanzfledermäusen (*Rhinopoma microphyllum*). *Z. Säugetierk.* 48: 201–210.
9. Simmons, J.A., S.A. Kick & B.D. Lawrence (1984): Echolocation and hearing in the mouse-tailed bat, *Rhinopoma hardwickei*: acoustic evolution of echolocation in bats. *J. Comp. Physiol.* A 154: 347–356.
10. van Cakenberghe, V. & F. de Vree (1994): A revision of the Rhinopomatidae, with description of a new subspecies. *Senckenb. Biol.* 73: 1–24.
11. Whitaker, J.O. & Y. Yom-Tov (2002): The diet of some insectivorous bats from northern Israel. *Mamm. Biol.* 67: 378–380.

ADDITIONAL REFERENCES

12. Hulva, P., I. Horáček, & P. Benda (2007): Molecules, morphometric and new fossils provide an integrated view of the evolutionary history of Rhinopomatidae (Mammalia: Chiroptera). *BMC Evolutionary Biology* 7: 165. 28 pp.

Slit-faced Bats or Hollow-faced Bats
Nycteridae

Small to medium-sized insectivorous and carnivorous bats. The muzzle has a characteristic deep longitudinal groove, through which the echolocation calls are emitted. The ears are remarkably long and rounded. The entire tail is included in the tail membrane, and the last tail vertebra has a characteristic T-shape. Only one genus: *Nycteris*, with 16 species and a palaeotropic distribution. Fourteen species in Africa including one in the Arabian Peninsula, two species in the Far East. In the geographical scope of this book only *Nycteris thebaica* occurs on the Moroccan Atlantic coast.

Egyptian Slit-faced Bat
Nycteris thebaica
GEOFFROY, 1818

NAMES
D: Ägyptische Slitznasenfledermaus
F: Nyctère de la Thébaide
E: Murciélago egipcio
I: Nitteride di Tebe
NL: Thebaanse spleetneusvleermuis
S: Egyptisk klyvsvans

IDENTIFICATION
Medium-sized bat with long fluffy fur. Dorsal fur brownish or yellowish-grey, the ventral side paler. The complicated muzzle has a deep longitudinal furrow which flows laterally into skin folds. The remarkable ears are more than half as long as the body, separated at the base and bluntly rounded at the end. The wings are broad and the entire tail is included in the tail membrane. The last tail vertebra ends with a T-shaped bar which supports the margin of the tail membrane.

Similar species
Unmistakable within the region.

ECHOLOCATION CALLS
Quiet frequency-modulated calls of two or more harmonics which drop in less than 2ms from 100 to 65kHz. Not confusable with the echolocation calls of any other species in North Africa.

Fig. 265. Mixed colony of the Egyptian Slit-faced Bat and Sundevall's Leaf-nosed Bat in a sewer pipe in southern Morocco. Photo: T. Pröhl.

DISTRIBUTION
Distributed in the whole of Africa up to the central ranges of the Sahara and the tropical forests, on the Arabian Peninsula to Israel. The alleged records from Corfu and Sicily relate to mislabelled specimens. In the geographical scope of this book, limited to a patchy occurrence in Morocco.

Subspecies and geographical variation
Many subspecies are described, at present seven to nine are recognised by the authors. A genetic revision is, however, pending. The Egyptian Slit-faced Bat possibly has several cryptic species. *N. t. thebaica* is found in Morocco.

Measurements	
Forearm	41–49mm
Fifth finger	58–62mm
Third finger	76–81mm
Normalweight	8–12g
CBL	16.6–17.8mm
CM³	6.1–7.1mm

HABITAT

A typical bat of savannah, as well as riverine forest and in oases, and semi-deserts can also be occupied. In Morocco occurs along the Atlantic coast in semi-arid areas. A colony occurs in the national park Oued Massa [2] and is surrounded by dense riparian vegetation (reed and willow scrub).

Roosts

As daytime roosts caves, buildings, ruins, mines and wellheads are used, often within limited arid areas. As night roosts buildings and rooms are used, and can be visited for years by the same individuals [11].

BEHAVIOUR

The broad wings and large tail membrane give a low wing-loading and wingspan. Accordingly, a very manoeuvrable and slow-flying species. In the roost usually hangs free. Probably active all the year round. Colonies comprise a few up to 100, in southern Africa also several thousand animals. Slit-faced bats can roost with horseshoe bats, Old World leaf-nosed bats and mouse-tailed bats.

REPRODUCTION

On the Arabian Peninsula a single young per female is born in spring. Females sometimes carry their dependent young on foraging flights, possibly an adaptation to the use of low roosts easily accessible to predators. In Namibia display and mating apparently occur in flight [9].

FORAGING

The food is captured by 'flycatching', i.e. forays from a resting site, in agile and slow flight in the air, or is picked off the ground. Slit-faced bats frequently use perches or rocks and scan the vicinity with rapid head and ear movements. With the large ears the prey can be located passively by rustling sounds [6]. They can also flutter, almost noiselessly, low over the ground. Large prey is consumed at feeding sites [6].

FOOD

The food comprises grasshoppers, crickets and beetles, and a multiplicity of other flightless invertebrates: cockroaches, scorpions [5], spiders [3] and moth caterpillars. In Zambia adult moths are of little importance, while caterpillars constitute up to half of the prey, particularly in winter [13].

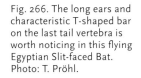

Fig. 266. The long ears and characteristic T-shaped bar on the last tail vertebra is worth noticing in this flying Egyptian Slit-faced Bat. Photo: T. Pröhl.

MAXIMUM AGE

The maximum age is at least 10 years [11].

MOBILITY AND MIGRATION

From South Africa a distance of over 107 km is recorded [10].

THREATS

To a large extent unknown. Red list of the IUCN 2006: LC (Least Concern).

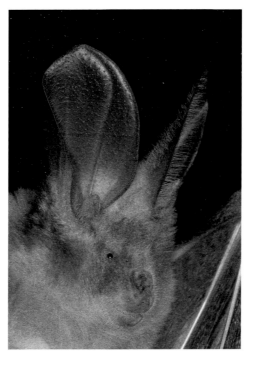

Fig. 267. The longitudinal furrow on the nose of the Egyptian Slit-faced Bat is partly covered by lateral skin folds and by fur. Photo: C. Dietz.

REFERENCES

1. Aldridge, H.D.J.N., M.K. Obrist, H.G. Merriam & M.B. Fenton (1990): Roosting, vocalizations, and foraging behaviour by the African bat, *Nycteris thebaica*. *J. Mammal.* 71: 242–246.

2. Arlettaz, R. & S. Aulagnier (1988): Statut de trois espèces de chiroptères rares au Maroc: *Nycteris thebaica, Hipposideros caffer* et *Pipistrellus rueppelli*. *Z. Säugetierk.* 53: 321–324.

3. Bowie, R.C.K., D.S. Jacobs & P.J. Taylor (1999): Resource use by two morphologically similar insectivorous bats (*Nycteris thebaica* and *Hipposideros caffer*). *S. Afr. J. Zool.* 34: 27–33.

4. Feldman, R., J.O. Whitaker & Y. Yom-Tov (2000): Dietary composition and habitat use in a desert insectivorous bat community in Israel. *Acta Chiropterologica* 2: 15–22.

5. Felten, H. (1956): Fledermäuse fressen Skorpione. *Natur & Volk* 86: 53–57.

6. Fenton, M.B., C.L. Gaudet & M.L. Leonard (1983): Feeding behaviour of the bats *Nycteris grandis* and *Nycteris thebaica* (Nycteridae) in captivity. *J. Zool.* 200: 347–354.

7. Gray, P.A., M.B. Fenton & V. van Cakenberghe (1999): *Nycteris thebaica. Mammalian Species* 612: 1–8.

8. LaVal, R.K. & M.L. LaVal (1980): Prey selection by the large slit-faced bat *Nycteris thebaica* (Chiroptera: Nycteridae) in Natal, South Africa. *Biotropica* 12: 241–246.

9. Lindeque, M. (1987): Observation on mating behaviour in the common slit-faced bat *Nycteris thebaica. Madoqua* 15: 183–185.

10. Monadjem, A. (2006): Longevity and movement of the common slit-faced bat *Nycteris thebaica. African Bat Conservation News* 9: 7.

11. Roer, H. (1992): Jagdbiotop-Quartiertreue und Lebenserwartung der Großohr-Hohlnase (*Nycteris thebaica*) (Mammalia: Chiroptera) in der Namibwüste. In: I. Horáček & V. Hanák (eds): *Prague Studies in Mammalogy:* 143–147; Charles University Press.

12. van Cakenberghe, V. & F. de Vree (1998): Systematics of African Nycteris (Mammalia: Chiroptera) Part III. The *Nycteris thebaica* group. *Bonn. Zool. Beitr.* 48: 123–166.

13. Whitaker, J.O. & H. Black (1976): Food habits of cave bats from Zambia, Africa. *J. Mammal.* 57: 199–204.

Old World Leaf-nosed Bats
Hipposideridae

Mostly small insectivorous bats which are closely related to the horseshoe bats and are included by some authors as a subfamily. The upper nose is formed of a horseshoe-shaped noseleaf and further complex skin bulges, but without the sella and the lancet found in horseshoe bats. The echolocation calls are emitted through the nostrils. The ears have no tragus, but an anti-tragus, and are usually tapered. The tail is completely included in the tail membrane or free for up to half of its length. Besides the two mammary glands in the pectoral region, females have two so-called false nipples in the pelvic region, to which the young can cling. The family comprises 9 genera with 81 species which have a palaeotropic distribution. Within our region only two genera, each with one species occurring marginally: *Hipposideros caffer* in savannah-like habitats at the Moroccan Atlantic coast and *Asellia tridens* in deserts and semi-deserts of North Africa.

Sundevall's Leaf-nosed Bat
Hipposideros caffer
(SUNDEVALL, 1846)

NAMES
  D: Kleine Rundblattnase
  F: Rhinolophe de Cafrerie
  NL: Gewone rondbladneus
  S: Liten bladnäsa

Measurements

Forearm	44.6–47.8mm
Fifth finger	48–52mm
Third finger	57–62mm
Normal weight	7–10g
CBL	14.1–14.4mm
CM³	5.1–5.3mm

IDENTIFICATION
A delicate leaf-nosed bat with a relatively simple round noseleaf. The fur is dense and fluffy; the Moroccan animals are grey-brown on the dorsal side and paler on the ventral side. The relatively large ears are tapered.

Similar species
In the geographical scope of this book only confusable with the Trident Leaf-nosed Bat, which is larger and the upper edge of the noseleaf carries three vertical projections.

ECHOLOCATION CALLS
In Morocco constant-frequency calls with a zero-crossing frequency around 135kHz (133–137kHz) with a weak frequency-modulated end part to the call [own data].

From the frequency not confusable with any other species in North Africa.

DISTRIBUTION
Nearly the whole of Africa south from Sahara. Also in the south of the Arabian Peninsula (Yemen and Saudi Arabia). In Morocco a patchy occurrence on the Atlantic coast with records to Tangier.

Subspecies and geographical variation
At least three subspecies, in Morocco *H. c. tephrus* which is regarded by some authors

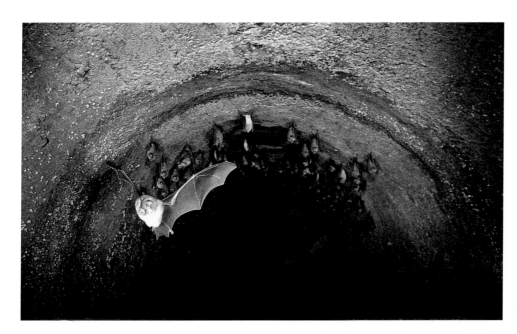

Fig. 268. Sundevall's Leaf-nosed Bat has similar flight manoeuvrability to the Lesser Horseshoe Bat, here in a sewer pipe in Morocco used as roost. Photo: T. Pröhl.

Fig. 269. Like the horseshoe bats Sundevall's Leaf-nosed Bat folds the tail onto the back when at rest. Photo: T. Pröhl.

as a full species [9]. Within the *H. caffer* group there are considerable taxonomic problems; there are probably several cryptic species.

HABITAT

In northwest Africa a typical bat of savannahs, gallery forests and oases. Semi-arid areas and semi-deserts are only marginally occupied. In Morocco along the Atlantic coast in overgrown shrub or in savannah-like open areas with Persian iron wood trees. A large colony occurs in the national park Oued Massa [1, gen. lit. 10] and is surrounded by dense riparian vegetation (reed belts and willow scrub), which changes on the slopes through *Euphorbia* lands into semi-desert.

Roosts

As daytime roosts, uses caves and other underground passages, as well as human constructions such as wells and cellars. In Morocco a colony with over 250 individuals occurs in a low sewer pipe. South of the Sahara colonies in caves with over 1,000 animals. On the Arabian Peninsula single animals were found in trees [gen. lit. 46]. As night roost sites, spaces in buildings are also used.

BEHAVIOUR

In a colony in Morocco adult males and

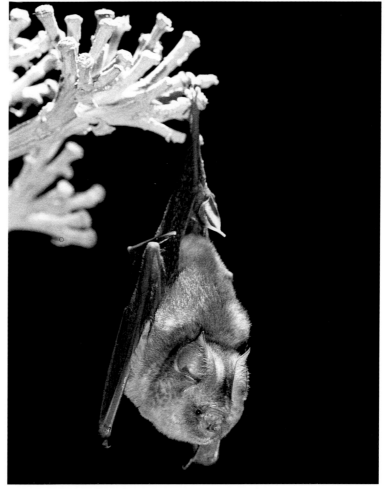

Fig. 270. Portrait of Sundevall's Leaf-nosed Bat. Photo: C. Dietz.

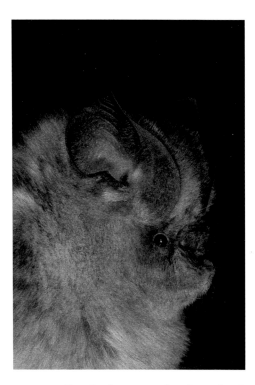

pregnant females hung together [own data]. Similarly, in southern Africa mixed colonies from a few dozen to many hundreds [4]. Roosts are shared with horseshoe bats, other leaf-nosed bats and slit-faced bats. Probably active all year round.

REPRODUCTION
To a large extent unknown. In Morocco, females were visibly pregnant in the middle of April and weighed 1.5g more than males [own data].

FORAGING
Sundevall's Leaf-nosed Bat has similar flight behaviour to the Lesser Horseshoe Bat: the short broad wings with a low wing-loading make very manoeuvrable flight possible. The long constant-frequency calls allow detection of flying prey from acoustic glints of the echoes. The insect food is captured in flight close to the ground or at vegetation; larger prey is eaten at feeding sites [3].

FOOD
In Zambia, Zimbabwe and South Africa moths comprise the main part of the prey (> 80%) followed by beetles [2, 3, 5, 8]. Other insects have lesser importance as food.

THREATS
To a large extent unknown. Red list of the IUCN 2006: LC (Least Concern). For the Moroccan populations no reliable data are available.

REFERENCES
1. Arlettaz, R. & S. Aulagnier (1988): Statut de trois espèces de chiroptères rares au Maroc: *Nycteris thebaica, Hipposideros caffer* et *Pipistrellus rueppelli. Z. Säugetierk.* 53: 321–324.
2. Bowie, R.C.K., D.S. Jacobs & P.J. Taylor (1999): Resource use by two morphologically similar insectivorous bats (*Nycteris thebaica* and *Hipposideros caffer*). *S. Afr. J. Zool.* 34: 27–33.
3. Dunning, D.C. & M. Krüger (1996): Predation upon moths by free-foraging *Hipposideros caffer. J. Mammal.* 77: 708–715.
4. Eisentraut, M. (1956): Beitrag zur Ökologie Kameruner Chiropteren. *Mitt. Zool. Mus. Berlin* 25: 245–274.
5. Fenton, M.B., N.G.H. Boyle, T.M. Harrison & D.J. Oxley (1977): Activity patterns, habitat use, and prey selection by some African insectivorous bats. *Biotropica* 9: 73–85.
6. Hill, J.E. (1963): A revision of the genus *Hipposideros. Bull. Br. Mus. (Nat. Hist.) Zool.* 11: 1–129.
7. Jones, G., M. Morton, P.M. Hughes & R.M. Budden (1993): Echolocation, flight morphology and foraging strategies of some West African hipposiderid bats. *J. Zool.* 230: 385–400.
8. Whitaker, J.O. & H. Black (1976): Food habits of cave bats from Zambia, Africa. *J. Mammal.* 57: 199–204.

ADDITIONAL REFERENCES
9. Vallo, P., A. Guillén-Servent, P. Benda, D.B. Pires & P. Koubek (2008): Variation of mitochondrial DNA in the *Hipposideros caffer* complex (Chiroptera: Hipposideridae) and its taxonomic implications. *Acta Chiropterologica* 10(2): 193–206.

Trident Leaf-nosed Bat
Asellia tridens
(GEOFFROY, 1813)

NAMES
  D: Dreizack-Blattnase
  F: Trident
  NL: Drietandbladneusvleermuis

IDENTIFICATION
Medium-sized leaf-nosed bat with complicated noseleaf, which has three perpendicular projections at its upper edge. The middle projection is pointed, the lateral two blunt-tipped. The ears are large. The short fur is brownish grey on the dorsal side and on the ventral side cream or reddish brown to bright orange coloured. In Morocco a yellowish-brown fur colouring prevails; the ventral side is paler cream. The tail tip protrudes at rest 3–5mm, and in flight substantially well beyond the margin of the tail membrane.

In this species males seem to be larger than the females.

Similar species
Unmistakable from the three perpendicular projections at the upper edge of the nose-leaf.

ECHOLOCATION CALLS
Long constant-frequency calls between 117 and 124kHz with an obvious distinct frequency-modulated final part [own data, Tsoar pers. com.]. Due to the frequency, not confusable with other species in North Africa.

DISTRIBUTION
In Africa, distributed particularly in the Sahara, including in its central areas. Occurs in northwest Africa south of the High Atlas [gen. lit. 10] and the Saharan Atlas. In Tunisia, Libya and Egypt the distribution ranges to the Mediterranean Sea, south of the Sahara to the Gambia and Somalia. In Asia throughout the Arabian

Measurements	
Forearm	46.0–54.1mm
Fifth finger	46–52mm
Third finger	59–66mm
Normal weight	ca. 10g
CBL	15.8–18.4mm
CM³	6.3–7.7mm

Fig. 271. Colony of Trident Leaf-nosed Bat in a cellar in Israel. The brightly coloured juveniles are easily differentiated from the brown adult animals. Photo: E. Levin.

Peninsula, north to Israel and Syria, eastward to Pakistan [gen. lit. 46].

Subspecies and geographical variation

In northwest Africa *A. t. diluta* occurs, which is usually synonymised with *A. t. tridens* occurring in Egypt and Yemen. Genetic analysis is necessary to confirm the status of *A. t. diluta* in Algeria, as well as of *A. t. murraiana*, which probably occurs in the north of the Arabian Peninsula and in the Near East. *A. t. italosomalica* south of

the Sahara. The subspecies are poorly differentiated, the size differences possibly reflecting adaptation to different food availability and climates.

HABITAT
A typical desert and semi-desert bat which occurs in large parts of the Sahara. Oases provide roosts and food.

Roosts
Cave-dwelling species which can be found in underground galleries, ruins and wells. In Morocco colonies in underground irrigation channels of oases (khettara) and caves, sometimes roosting low over the water.

BEHAVIOUR
The females can accumulate colonies of several hundreds [2], on the Arabian Peninsula up to 5,000 animals [gen. lit. 46]. Apart from such reproductive colonies there are also male groups with up to 50 individuals [1]. Trident Leaf-nosed Bats are active all year round. In the roost the species can occur with other bat species.

REPRODUCTION
One young is born in the late spring.

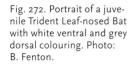

Fig. 272. Portrait of a juvenile Trident Leaf-nosed Bat with white ventral and grey dorsal colouring. Photo: B. Fenton.

Fig. 273. Portrait of a Trident Leaf-nosed Bat more than one year old with a largely uniform orange-brown colouring. Photo: B. Fenton.

FORAGING

The Trident Leaf-nosed Bat has longer wings and a higher wing-loading than the otherwise very similar small noseleafed bats [4]. This may be an adaptation for a faster and less agile flight in open hunting habitats such as deserts and semi-deserts. Nevertheless foraging animals can also be found within oases, hunting around palm trees and houses. Probably almost exclusively foraging on flying prey.

FOOD

The food consists mainly of beetles (35–80%), followed by moths, Diptera and Orthoptera [3, 4, 7]. Very large moths and grasshoppers are sometimes captured, and are eaten at feeding sites [6].

THREATS

To a large extent unknown. Red list of the IUCN 2006: LC (Least Concern).

REFERENCES

1. Brosset, A. (1955): Observations sur la biologie des chiroptères du Maroc oriental. *Bulletin de la Société des Sciences Naturelles et Physiques du Maroc* 35: 295–306.
2. Brosset, A. & B. Caubère (1960): La colonie d'Asellia tridens de l'oasis de Figuig (Chiroptères). *Mammalia* 24: 222–227.
3. Feldman, R., J.O. Whitaker & Y. Yom-Tov (2000): Dietary composition and habitat use in a desert insectivorous bat community in Israel. *Acta Chiropterologica* 2: 15–22.
4. Jones, G., M. Morton, P.M. Hughes & R.M. Budden (1993): Echolocation, flight morphology and foraging strategies of some West African hipposiderid bats. *J. Zool.* 230: 385–400.
5. Owen, R.D. & M.B. Qumsiyeh (1987): The subspecies problem in the Trident leaf-nosed bat, *Asellia tridens*: homomorphism in widely separated populations. *Z. Säugetierk.* 52: 329–337.
6. Whitaker, J.O., B. Shalmon & T.H. Kunz (1994): Food and feeding habits of insectivorous bats from Israel. *Z. Säugetierk.* 59: 74–81.
7. Whitaker, J.O. & Y. Yom-Tov (2002): The diet of some insectivorous bats from northern Israel. *Mamm. Biol.* 67: 378–380.

ADDITIONAL REFERENCES

8. Aulagnier, S. & R. Destre (1985): Introduction à l'étude des Chiroptères de Tafilalt (sud-est marocain. *Mammalia* 49 : 329–337.

Horseshoe Bats
Rhinolophidae

Fig. 274. Portrait of a Lesser Horseshoe Bat from Sardinia showing the nose structure typical for the genus. Photo: C. Dietz.

Small to medium-sized predominantly insectivorous bats with a complex nose structure: a horseshoe-shaped skin fold on the nose, above which is a protruding saddle (or 'sella') and a 'lancet', which are connected by further skin formations (the 'connecting process'). The nose structure represents an adaptation to the highly specialised echolocation: the long constant-frequency signals are emitted through the nose and arranged and focused by the skin formations. Fluttering prey can be recognised and classified on the basis of the pattern of frequency and amplitude changes from the echoes (acoustic glints). In order to be able to evaluate returning echoes, the horseshoe bats have a highly specialised hearing system with acoustic fovea (see chapter about echolocation). The calls are long and constant-frequency, with short frequency-modulated sections at the beginning and end. The ears have no tragus and move rapidly and synchronously with the direction of emissions of the signals. Besides the two mammary glands in the pectoral region, females have a further pair of so-called false nipples in the pelvic region, to which the young can cling during the first days after birth. At rest the horseshoe bats fold the tail onto the back. In hibernation some species wrap themselves completely within the flight membranes. The premaxilla is reduced and not fused with the palate and only has rudimentary incisors.

The horseshoe bats are closely related to the leaf-nosed bats, indeed they were often combined into one family. The latter are distributed in the tropics of the Old World from Africa to Australia, with a few species reaching temperate latitudes. The horseshoe bats comprise only one genus, *Rhinolophus*, with at least 77 Old World species, which are identifiable on the basis of the structure of the noseleafs [gen. lit. 22]. Five species occur in Europe, of which two reach Central Europe; the other three are to a large extent limited to the Mediterranean region and Balkan Peninsula.

Lesser Horseshoe Bat
Rhinolophus hipposideros
(Bechstein, 1800)

Measurements

Forearm	36.1–39.6mm
Fifth finger	47–53mm
First phalanx of fourth finger	5.7–7.5mm
Second phalanx of fourth finger	12.0–14.2mm
Normal weight	4–7g
CCL	13.2–14.1mm
CM³	5.0–5.5mm

NAMES
D: Kleine Hufeisennase
F: Petit rhinolophe
E: Murciélago pequeño de herradura
I: Ferro di cavallo minore
NL: Kleine hoefijzerneus
S: Dvärghästskonäsa
PL: Podkowiec maly

IDENTIFICATION
The smallest European horseshoe bat. On this delicate animal the horseshoe and particularly the lancet appear very large. The connecting process is short and rounded, the sella tip distinctly longer and pointed in profile. The fluffy dorsal fur is brownish to yellowish-brown, on the ventral side paler grey-white. Young animals are generally grey. Flight membranes and ears are brown. The wings are very broad, short and rounded. In hibernation the Lesser Horseshoe Bat wraps itself completely within the flight membranes. The feet are small. The lower lip shows only one small groove.

Similar species
Unmistakable from the small size (forearm length <43mm) and the short rounded connecting process.

ECHOLOCATION CALLS
The long (up to 60ms) constant-frequency parts of the calls are at 108–114kHz. The frequency range overlaps with those of

Mediterranean and Mehely's Horseshoe Bats. A species identification in the Mediterranean region should be confirmed at least with a good view.

DISTRIBUTION

The horseshoe bat with the northernmost distribution. It reaches west Ireland and southwestern Great Britain. Originally the distribution extended to the southern Netherlands and southern edge of the northern German lowland along 51–52°N across Germany, Poland and Ukraine. Following a catastrophic decline in the 1960s Lesser Horseshoe Bats are nowadays absent from the majority of Germany, parts of west France, Poland and Switzerland, and became extinct in the Netherlands and Luxembourg. In the Mediterranean area the species is still widely distributed, it occurs in North Africa and on all larger islands to Asia Minor and around the Black Sea. Outside the geographical scope of this book, distributed in Asia to Kashmir, the Near East, Iran, Iraq, Arabian Peninsula and parts of East Africa.

Subspecies and geographical variation

The Lesser Horseshoe Bat is quite variable in size, colouring and appearance, and animals from different parts of the distribution can differ markedly. Consequently many subspecies have been described, of which at present six are recognised, but not

undisputed: the nominate form *R. h. hipposideros* occurs in large parts of Europe, *R. h minutus* in the British Isles, *R. h. escalerae* in northwest Africa, *R. h. majori* on Corsica and Sardinia *R. h. midas* in East Turkey, the Near East and on Cyprus, and *R. h. minimus* in Eritrea. Some subspecies may be cryptic species.

HABITAT

Found in warmer regions in foothills but also highlands, occurring to altitudes of 2,000m in climatically favourable areas. Habitats of the Lesser Horseshoe Bat are characterised by high structure richness. Hunting grounds in Switzerland, Germany, Austria, and in Britain are almost exclusively in forests, although no preference for a particular type of forest is identified [4, 5, 16]. Only the proximity to water seems to be important. In southeast Europe a broader habitat spectrum of tall herbaceous vegetation, hedge areas, forest-like biotopes, to ditches and riparian forests are used for foraging. Radio-tracked animals in Bulgaria spent up to more than 80% of their foraging time visiting villages [I. Dietz unpublished]. Within the villages bats visited vegetation-rich garden areas with fruit trees and hedges and pasturelands used during the day by cattle. In North Africa, in semi-desert areas populated by *R. h. escalerae* and *R. h. midas*, sparsely overgrown plains, gardens and oases serve as hunting grounds.

Roosts

In the north of the distribution nursery roosts are often in draught-free roof spaces of churches, castles and other larger buildings but also in closets, boiler rooms or in mines [18]. Often the whole of complex buildings are used, with the roosting sites changed depending upon temperature. In Thuringia a nursery roost is known in a southern exposed karst cave in the Kyffhäuser (a hill ridge in the lower Harz area, Germany) [11]. In the south, nursery roosts occur more often in caves, more rarely in tunnels and mines. In Slovenia a small nursery roost was found under a bridge [gen. lit. 96]; in Bulgaria and Greece very small roosts such as holes in plane

Fig. 275. Portrait of a Lesser Horseshoe Bat from the Sinai. Photo: C. Dietz.

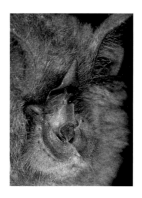

Fig. 276. Portrait of a Lesser Horseshoe Bat from Bulgaria. Photo: C. Dietz.

Fig. 277. Portrait of a Lesser Horseshoe Bat from west Turkey. Photo: C. Dietz.

Fig. 278. With cool weather Lesser Horseshoe Bats, which otherwise usually hang separately, form dense clusters. Photo: D. Nill.

trees, ventilation pipes or crevices in bridge abutments are used as colony roost sites. Males use a broad spectrum of caves, tunnels, roof spaces and larger rock crevices as summer roosts; in the north of the distribution area they can also use caves and mines all year round [11]. In winter in karst caves and mines or in large mountain cellars. A very broad spectrum of night roosts is used.

BEHAVIOUR

The nursery colonies comprise 10–200 females; there are also some colonies with up to 800 females. In Bulgaria often mini nursery colonies with only 1–2 reproducing females. In the nursery roost the proportion of males can amount to a fifth of the animals [12] but often the groups are exclusively of females. The animals of a nursery colony hang separated in the roof space, only with low ambient temperatures and in the last stages of pregnancy do they hang in dense clusters. The Lesser Horseshoe Bat shows strongly developed social behaviour. Between mothers and young extensive greeting scenes take place following the return from foraging. Young animals some-

times carry out flight training while hanging on the mother. In nursery roosts often associated with mouse-eared bats, Geoffroy's Bats and long-eared bats, but usually spatially separated. In the winter roosts the animals hang separately with an individual distance of 20–30cm. There are only a few winter roosts with over 100 animals; the largest cave roost in Slovenia accommodates up to 1,000 animals [gen. lit. 96].

REPRODUCTION

The proportion of reproducing females in a nursery colony (50–70%) is relatively small because not all adult females give birth each year and only a small proportion of the young females (about 15%) reproduce in the first year. The single young is born in the middle of June to the middle of July, with a forearm length of 17–18mm and a weight of 2g [17]. At three weeks the young animal trains for its first flights, leaves the roost for the first time at four weeks and is weaned and independent at six weeks. Males and most females reach sexual maturity only in the second autumn. After some preliminary chasing, the very short mating takes place free hanging in the autumn in underground roosts, or in the winter roost.

FORAGING

The food is exclusively captured in flight; whether the Lesser Horseshoe Bat carries out perch hunting from a resting place in the last days of the pregnancy is, as yet, unclear. The very agile and butterfly-like, often fluttering, flight makes foraging possible very close to the vegetation, sometimes in dense foliage. When circling closely around shrubs and trees small insects are startled and then captured. Prey can also be picked directly from surfaces. Hunts in the forest, particularly in the shrub layer at levels up to 10m, often also within the crown area of trees or close to the ground. Lesser Horseshoe Bats fly very manoeuvrably over tall herbaceous vegetation between the tops of high thistles and shrubs. On bare surfaces of semi-deserts *R. h. midas* hunts at 5–20cm height above the ground [own data].

FOOD

The food consists particularly of small Diptera (crane-flies), Hymenoptera, lacewings and small moths [2, 6, 15]. The Lesser Horseshoe Bat seems to hunt opportunistically within its preferential prey size-class, the prey composition corresponding with the availability [4]. Among the Diptera, apart from crane-flies and non-biting midges, at least locally mosquitoes play a major role as prey [13]. Other than the main prey animals, caddis flies, small beetles, aphids and spiders are also found in droppings [2, 6, 15]. In the semi-deserts, at least seasonally, the food of *R. h midas* consists almost exclusively of flying ants [own data].

MAXIMUM AGE

The oldest known animal was recovered 21 years after ringing [9]; the average age of the animals in nursery roost systems is substantially lower at 4–5 years [12].

MOBILITY AND MIGRATION

A particularly sedentary species whose

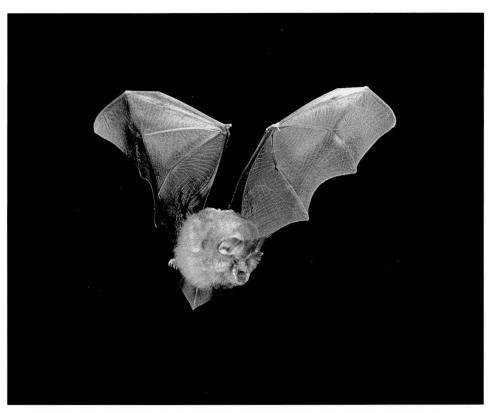

Fig. 279. Up to the age of more than one year juvenile Lesser Horseshoe Bats are substantially greyer than the adults. Photo: D. Nill.

Fig. 280. Juvenile Lesser Horseshoe Bats begin to train their flight muscles at the age of two and a half weeks. At first they hang on the shoulders of the mother, always ready to cling again onto the protecting belly. Photo: C. Dietz.

radius around the roost, the furthest distances being about 4–6.4km [4, 5, 20]. The size of the individual hunting grounds reaches 150–400ha [3, 5], within which up to seven separate hunting grounds are used, with an average area of 3–50ha [5, 10]. On commuting flights Lesser Horseshoe Bats normally follow linear structures such as hedges, ditches and edges of forest; single animals can cross open land, such as arable fields and meadows, and even fly as far as 1.5km over water [20].

THREATS

Red list of the IUCN 2006: LC (Least Concern), Red list of the European Union: VU (Vulnerable), EU Habitats Directive, Annex II & IV. In Germany and adjacent areas a dramatic population decline began in the 1950s. The Lesser Horseshoe Bat, until then one of the most common bat species, became extinct or reduced to minimum populations by the end of the 1970s. In Saxony, Saxony-Anhalt, Thuringia and Bavaria some nursery colonies were maintained. In the neighbouring countries to Germany similar dramatic population declines took place, sometimes leaving less than 1% of the original population [14]. In Luxembourg and the Netherlands the species became extinct. New research results confirm what had been

radius of activity extends less than 20km [12]. Some distances of up to 50km have been recorded among more than 20,000 marked animals, the five furthest distances reaching 112–153km. Due to the dramatic decline and the fact that the Lesser Horseshoe Bat can be very sensitive to bat rings, marking was largely abandoned in the 1970s.

Habitat use

In Switzerland, Germany and England the hunting grounds are usually within a 2.5km

Fig. 281. At higher temperatures in the roost Lesser Horseshoe Bats hang with an individual distance of approximately 20cm from each other. Photo: D. Nill.

assumed for a long time: competition with other bat species [1] or climatic change were not responsible for the collapse of the populations, rather the application of highly toxic pesticides such as DDT and lindane, both in agriculture and as wood preservatives in buildings [4]. Since the 1990s the number of Lesser Horseshoe Bats has been increasing in many roosts [4], but the previous densities will probably never be reached. Population growth and re-colonisation seem to take place very slowly. In south Europe the species is still common, but large and stable populations are only found in Slovenia, Slovakia, Hungary, Romania, Bulgaria and probably also in other Balkan states. The occurrence of this, the most common species of the Mediterranean region in the 1970s, is greatly reduced by changes in landscape, habitat loss, habitat fragmentation and the negative effects of applications of pesticides in agriculture and forestry. Although the highly toxic pesticides like DDT and lindane are no longer used, most threats are still acute.

Restricted in UK to southwest Britain and southwest Ireland [UK gen. lit. 153, 155]. Populations thought to be recovering at present, but still a rare species and subject to a wide range of concerted conservation measures, including for the design of or improvement

to roost sites, maintenance of commuting and foraging routes and feeding habitat [see, for example, 21]. A target species of the UK National Bat Monitoring Programme, with protocols for monitoring of hibernation sites and maternity colonies. Included as a Priority Species in the UK's Biodiversity Action Plan.

Fig. 282. Two juvenile Lesser Horseshoe Bats about 14 days old in the nursery roost. Photo: D. Nill.

POPULATION SIZE

The Lesser Horseshoe Bat is one of the few species for which reliable numbers from some countries are available. The estimates are: Great Britain: 18,000 [gen. lit. 6], Germany: 2,000, Switzerland: 4,200 [4], Austria: 8,000 [gen. lit. 136].

CONSERVATION MEASURES

In Central Europe sustainable protection of all known roosts and suitable landscape management in the catchment area of the colonies. Good connections via flight paths between roosts with wooded areas used as hunting grounds, prevention of fragmentation effects by traffic and bright lighting. In the Mediterranean area, protection of the large winter roosts in caves, of nursery colony roost sites in buildings, particularly with redevelopments, and conservation of wider semi-natural landscape areas.

Fig. 283. During hibernation Lesser Horseshoe Bats wrap themselves almost completely within the wing membranes. Photo: D. Nill.

REFERENCES

1. Arlettaz, R., S. Godat & H. Meyer (1994): Competition for food by expanding pipistrelle bat populations (*Pipistrellus pipistrellus*) might contribute to the decline of lesser horseshoe bats (*Rhinolophus hipposideros*). *Biol. Conserv.* 93: 55–60.

2. Beck, A., H.-P.B. Stutz & V. Ziswiler (1989): Das Beutespektrum der Kleinen Hufeisennase *Rhinolophus hipposideros*. *Rev. Suisse Zool.* 96: 643–650.

3. Biedermann, M., I. Karst & W. Schorcht (2005): *Erfassung von Wochenstubenvorkommen der Kleinen Hufeisennase (*Rhinolophus hipposideros*) in Thüringen im Rahmen der Umsetzung des Artenhilfsprogrammes für die Art 2005*. Studie im Auftrag der Koordinationsstelle für Fledermausschutz in Thüringen und der Thüringer Landesanstalt für Umwelt und Geologie, Jena, 27 pp.

4. Bontadina, F., T. Hotz & K. Märki (2006): *Die Kleine Hufeisennase im Aufwind*; 79 pp; Haupt Verlag.

5. Bontadina, F., H. Schofield & B. Naef-Daenzer (2002): Radio-tracking reveals that lesser horseshoe bats (*Rhinolophus hipposideros*) forage in woodland. *J. Zool.* 258: 281–290.

6. Feldman, R., J.O. Whitaker & Y. Yom-Tov (2000): Dietary composition and habitat use in a desert insectivorous bat community in Israel. *Acta Chiropterologica* 2: 15–22.

7. Gaisler, J. (1960): Ökologische Beobachtungen in einer Kolonie der Kleinen Hufeisennase (*Rhinolophus hipposideros*). *Acta Musei Reginaehradecensis Ser.A., Scientiae Naturales* 2: 83–99.

8. Gaisler, J. (1966): Reproduction in the lesser horseshoe bat (*Rhinolophus hipposideros hipposideros*). *Bijdragen tot de Dierkunde* 36: 45–64.

9. Harmata, W. (1982): Wiederfund einer Kleinen Hufeisennase (*Rhinolophus hipposideros*) nach 21 Jahren. *Myotis* 20: 74.

10. Holzhaider, J., E. Kriner, B.-U. Rudolph & A. Zahn (2002): Radio-tracking a lesser horseshoe bat (*Rhinolophus hipposideros*) in Bavaria: an experiment to locate roosts and foraging sites. *Myotis* 40: 47–54.

11. Interessengemeinschaft Fledermausschutz und –forschung Thüringen e.V. (2002): *Erfassung von unterirdischen Sommerquartieren der Kleinen Hufeisennase (*Rhinolophus hipposideros*) in Thüringen im Rahmen der Umsetzung des Artenhilfsprogrammes.* Studie im Auftrag der Thüringer Landesanstalt für Umwelt und Geologie, Jena, 61 pp.

12. Issel, W. (1951): Ökologische Untersuchungen an der Kleinen Hufeisennase (*Rhinolophus hipposideros*) im mittleren Rheinland und unterem Altmühltal. *Zoologische Jahrbücher (Systematik, Ökologie und Geographie)* 79: 71–86.

13. Kayikçio lu, A.A. & A. Zahn (2005): Zur Bedeutung von Mücken (Culiciden und Chironomiden) als Nahrung für die Kleinhufeisennase (*Rhinolophus hipposideros*). *Nyctalus* (N.F.) 10: 71–75.

14. Kokurewicz, T. (1990): The decrease in abundance of the lesser horseshoe bat *Rhinolophus hipposideros* in winter quarters in Poland. *Myotis* 28: 109–118.

15. McAney, C.M. & J.S. Fairley (1989): Analysis of the diet of the lesser horseshoe bat *Rhinolophus hipposideros* in the West of Ireland. *J. Zool.* 217: 491–498.

16. Reiter, G. (2004): The importance of woodland for lesser horseshoe bats *Rhinolophus hipposideros* in Austria. *Mammalia* 68: 403–410.

17. Reiter, G. (2004): Postnatal growth and reproductive biology of *Rhinolophus hipposideros* (Chiroptera: Rhinolophidae). *J. Zool.* 262: 231–241.

Fig. 284. Lesser Horseshoe Bat in the nursery roost with a young on its belly. Photo: D. Nill.

Fig. 285. In Bulgaria Lesser Horseshoe Bats often hunt within villages, often around small-scale cattle and poultry sheds. The semi-natural residential areas offer good food resources. Photo: C. Dietz.

18. Reiter, G., U. Hüttmeir & M. Jerabek (2004): Quartiereigenschaften von Wochenstuben-quartieren Kleiner Hufeisennasen (*Rhinolophus hipposideros*) in Österreich. *Ber. nat.-med. Ver. Salzburg* 14: 143–159.

19. Roer, H. & W. Schober (2001): *Rhinolophus hipposideros*, Kleine Hufeisennase. In: F. Krapp (ed.): *Handbuch der Säugetiere Europas* 4–I: 39–58; Aula Verlag.

20. Zahn, A. & P. Weiner (2004): Kleine Hufeisennase, *Rhinolophus hipposideros*. In: A. Meschede & B.-U. Rudolph (eds): *Fledermäuse in Bayern*: 111–126; Ulmer Verlag.

ADDITIONAL REFERENCES

21. Schofield, H.W. (2008): *The Lesser Horseshoe Bat: Conservation Handbook*. Vincent Wildlife Trust, London. 78pp.

Greater Horseshoe Bat
Rhinolophus ferrumequinum
(SCHREBER, 1774)

NAMES

- D: Große Hufeisennase
- F: Grand rhinolophe
- E: Murciélago grande de herradura
- I: Ferro di cavallo maggiore
- NL: Grote hoefijzerneus
- S: Stor hästskonäsa
- PL: Podkowiec duży

IDENTIFICATION

The largest European horseshoe bat has brown to grey-brown dorsal fur, often with a yellowish or reddish tinge. The ventral side is only a slightly demarcated paler grey-white to yellowish-white. Young animals are mostly grey; the adult colour is reached at about two years, when the hairs of the face finally change from grey to brown. The connecting process is broadly rounded and short. In deep hibernation animals hang separately and wrap themselves almost completely within the flight membranes; in warmer caves of the Mediterranean area the body is, however, usually only partly covered. The dentition is very strong; the lower lip has three small grooves ('mental' grooves).

Similar species

Unmistakable due to the size (forearm usually >54.0mm) and by the broadly

Measurements	
Forearm	53.0–62.4mm
Fifth finger	63–77mm
Third finger	79–94mm
First phalanx of fourth finger	9.5–13.4mm
Second phalanx of fourth finger	16.0–22.5mm
Normal weight	18–24g
CCL	19.5–21.8mm
CM³	8.3–9.1mm

rounded and short connecting process.

ECHOLOCATION CALLS

The long constant-frequency part of the calls is between 79 and 84kHz, varying slightly within the distribution area. Since there is no overlap with the call frequencies of the other horseshoe bats the species can be confidently determined.

DISTRIBUTION

The distribution extends from northwest Africa through the whole European Mediterranean region, including all larger islands, to Central Europe. In western UK the species reaches its northernmost occurrence in South Wales. The former distribution on the continent extended to the southern parts of the Netherlands, Germany, Poland and Ukraine. Particularly in Central Europe the distribution border shifted far to the south with a catastrophic decline. In Germany the species is extinct apart from a very small isolated nursery colony in Upper Palatinate and isolated hibernating animals from summer occurrence in neighbouring countries (Luxembourg, Switzerland). Eastwards the distribution extends into the Near East and through the southern Caucasus states to China, Korea and Japan.

Subspecies and geographical variation

The nominate form, *R. f. ferrumequinum*, occurs in Europe, North Africa and Asia Minor. For Crete, *R. f. creticum* was described, but it is doubtful that a subspecies status is justified. The forms *obscurus* (Iberia) and *martinoi* (Macedonia) only represent the ends of a gradual increase in size from west to east [4]. There are five recognised subspecies outside the region, with at least *R. f. nippon* from eastern Asia possibly being a separate subspecies, even possibly a full species.

HABITAT

The species has its core distribution in Europe in the Mediterranean region and occurs in Central Europe only in richly structured and climatically favourable

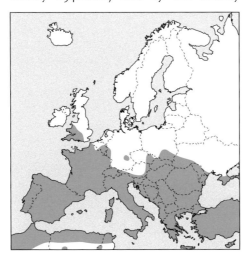

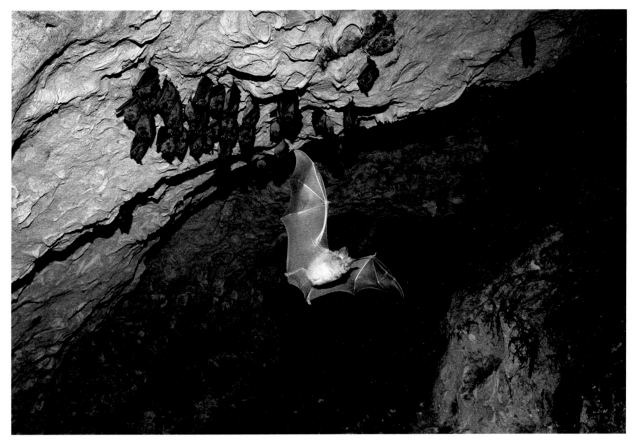

Fig. 286. Take off of a Greater Horseshoe Bat in a cave roost. In the Mediterranean region caves are mostly occupied in summer, in Central Europe mostly in roof spaces and buildings. Photo: D. Nill.

situations. Usually the warm low altitudes are occupied, in the Mediterranean area also in mountains to over 1,500m. A diverse structure with a habitat mosaic including hardwood forest, pastures, hedges, tree lines and orchard meadows seems to be suitable for colonisation [8]. Pasture animal husbandry contributes considerably to the creation of adequate food sources with dung beetles. Riparian and hardwood forests are major foraging habitats in cooler weather and with mass emergence of chafers, but are probably not adequate foraging habitats on their own. Only richly structured landscapes can carry populations of the Greater Horseshoe Bat on a long-term basis. In North Africa and the Middle East deserts and semi-deserts are not occupied; the species occurs only within areas influenced by the Mediterranean.

Roosts

In the north of the distribution almost exclusively in roof spaces or other warm roosts. In the southern part of the distribution mainly in caves and mines, where there are also nursery roosts in buildings and cellars, particularly outside karst areas. The winter roosts are in caves and mines, usually at temperatures of over 7°C.

BEHAVIOUR

Nursery colonies usually comprise 20–200 in the northern parts of its distribution, in the south up to 1,000 animals. In nursery roosts of the Mediterranean region the proportion of males is less than 1% [own data], in Great Britain up to 25%. Usually dense clusters are formed, but the animals spread out in high temperatures. At night the young are sometimes separated in a 'creche'. The Greater Horseshoe Bat usually occurs in the south with the medium-sized horseshoe bats, Natterer's, Schreibers' Bent-winged and Long-winged Bats. In winter, clusters of 30–500 animals are formed, often mixed with other species. Some animals hibernate individually.

Fig. 287. Detail of the nose-leaf structure of Greater Horseshoe Bat. Photo: D. Nill.

REPRODUCTION

The birth of the single young takes place between the end of June and the end of July [10, 14], in the Mediterranean region and in Bulgaria usually in the first three weeks of June [7]. At birth the neonate has an average forearm length of 24mm and a weight of 5–6g. The growth of the young animals is considerably affected by the climate; both the roost climate and the ambient temperature have a distinct effect, since the prey density is lower at low temperatures [7, 14]. In Great Britain the females reach sexual maturity at the age of 3–4 years and the first young is usually born at an average age of 5.7 years [14, 15]. In Bavaria the onset of sexual maturity was demonstrated at three years [10]. In Bulgaria almost all young females give birth to their first young at the age of two years, with the false nipples being developed during the first pregnancy

[own data]. The false nipples provide a very good criterion for the classification of the females into nulliparous (females that have not yet given birth), primiparous (first pregnancy/raising of young) and multiparous [own data]. From late summer males occupy fixed mating roosts in roof spaces, caves and mines, in which they are visited by the females. Mating can also be observed in spring. Females visit the same males for years for mating and share the same partner with their daughters, but without mating with their own father [20].

FORAGING

The flight is slow and often low above the ground, or close to the vegetation, or is adapted to the predominant prey: usually closely over the blossoms in thistle fields since the density of moths is particularly large here, or at a height of 4–6m over pasture for the preferred height of prey dung beetles [I Dietz unpublished]. For at least half of the time the Greater Horseshoe Bat hunts from a roost site: it scans the environment from an exposed place on a branch or from a cliff and flies when a worthwhile prey is detected. Such perch hunting occurs predominantly with lower insect density and in the second half of the night, concentrating on large prey animals. Large insects are consumed at a regular feeding site. The catch usually takes place using the wing as a collecting net.

FOOD

The food consists mainly of beetles (chafers and dung beetles) and moths (noctuids, hawk-moths) [1, 8]. Very large prey to the size of Emperor moths can be taken. As is the case for all bats the food changes distinctly through the course of the year; besides the beetles and moths, seasonally other prey animals, such as Diptera, Hymenoptera and also caddis flies and spiders, play a role [1, 8, I Dietz pers. com.]. With very high prey densities they probably hunt opportunistically, i.e. prey is taken in proportion to its availability. With low prey density or high body weight (during pregnancy, in the late autumn or in the second half of the night) hunting may be more

Fig. 288. A mother Greater Horseshoe Bat at least five years old shows the typical brown colouring of adult animals, which differs clearly from the young animal scarcely two months old. Photo: C. Dietz.

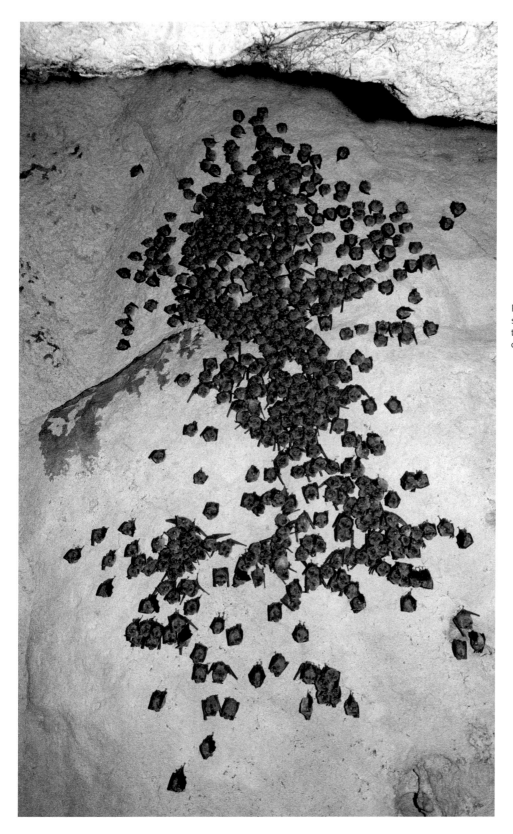

Fig. 289. Greater Horse-
shoe Bats usually hang in
their nursery roosts in loose
clusters. Photo: D. Nill.

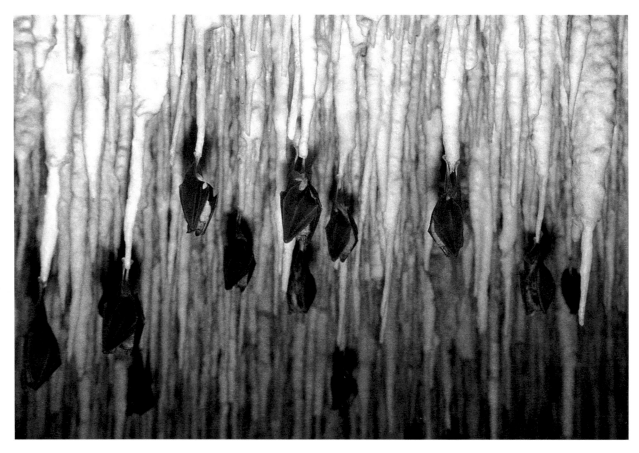

Fig. 290. In hibernation Greater Horseshoe Bats often form loose groups and wrap themselves partly within the wing membranes. Photo: D. Nill.

selective [I Dietz pers. com.]. How quickly Greater Horseshoe Bats can react to changing prey density is shown by the impressive results of prey choice studies in the laboratory: if large prey is offered above a certain density then it is strictly selected, if the environment is poor in larger prey, anything available is eaten [K. Koselje pers. com.].

MAXIMUM AGE

The maximum age amounts 30.5 years [3]. Animals over 15 years can constitute a substantial part of the population.

MOBILITY AND MIGRATION

The Greater Horseshoe Bat is sedentary [10], with only occasional migrations of over 100km. The longest distances are 180km in Spain, 320km in Hungary and 500km in France. While in eastern France the winter roosts are usually only a few kilometres from the summer roosts, in England they can be at distances of up to 30km. In northern Bulgaria the summer populations of the Danube plain hibernate up to 90km away in caves of the Balkan mountains, with an average distance between summer and winter roosts of 57km [5].

Habitat use

In Great Britain and Central Europe Greater Horseshoe Bats usually forage within a 5km radius of the roost, on average 2.1km distance [2, 8, 12, 13]. In Bulgaria almost all animals are found at substantially greater distances of up to 10 km, the average distance to the hunting grounds being 5km, with up to eight partial hunting grounds visited each night [I Dietz unpublished]. Here, some animals cross the Danube, up to 2.5km wide, to hunt in Romania and return in the middle of the night to suckle their young in the roost; in one night a distance of over 45km may be covered [own data]. In Bulgaria adult females were observed to change nursery roosts over distances of up to 45km [5]. As guidance for seasonal roost changes river valleys seem particularly to be used [5]. On commuting routes the animals fly along hedge features, only rarely crossing large open areas, such as fields.

THREATS

Red list of the IUCN 2006: LC (Least Concern), Red list of the European Union: VU (Vulnerable), EU Habitats Directive, Annex II & IV. From the 1950s the populations in the north underwent a dramatic decline, in many parts to less than 1% of the original population. In Germany the species became almost extinct. The main reasons might have been, as with the Lesser Horseshoe Bat, the use of highly toxic pesticides (particularly lindane and DDT) in agriculture and forestry and as timber preservative in the roosts. With the decline of the food source by habitat loss and poisoning, and the accumulation of poison in the animals, the population declined within two decades. The largest populations were maintained on the Iberian and Balkan Peninsulas. At present habitat loss and fragmentation, and the reduction of food availability through pesticides are the main causes of threat. Additionally, disturbance in the roosts through human use, redevelopment and tourism contribute to the loss of building and cave roosts. In Great Britain the use of anti-parasitic drugs for livestock reduces the availability of dung-feeding insects, so that this widespread food source declines.

One of the rarest bat species in the UK and restricted to southwest England and south Wales, following major declines in distribution and populations in the 1950s–1970s [UK gen. lit. 153, 155]. Subject to major measures for the conservation of the remaining maternity colonies (*c.* 14) and hibernation sites, management of habitat around summer colonies and wider habitat advice. Roger Ransome has been studying the species for over 50 years, including research on some particular sites for all that period [see, for example, 14]. He is author or co-author of a wide range of papers, including the results of detailed studies of population

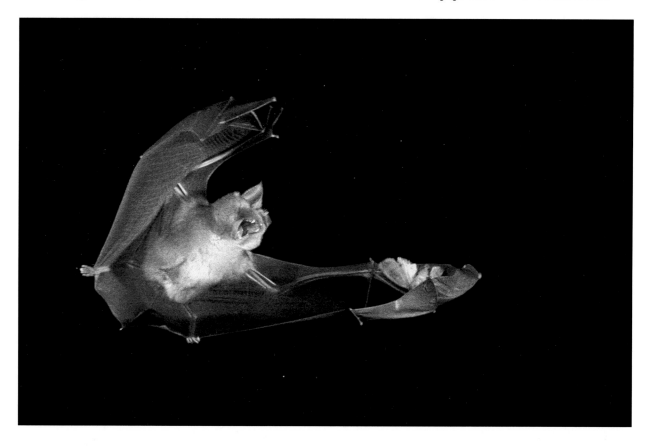

Fig. 291. Greater Horseshoe Bats usually catch their prey with the wing and then seize them with the mouth within fractions of a second. Photo: D. Nill.

Fig. 292. At night Greater Horseshoe Bats leave their young in the roost, sometimes, as in this Bulgarian cave, in chambers far from the entrance; here a dense cluster of juveniles is formed. Photo: C. Dietz.

structure from ringing and DNA analysis. However, there is still little evidence of the recovery of the populations, in either distribution or numbers; certainly any increase in population numbers is very slow, but there is some evidence of possible expansion of range towards other formerly occupied areas in the south of England. A target species of the National Bat Monitoring Programme from winter hibernation sites and summer maternity colonies, and a Priority Species under the UK's Biodiversity Action Plan.

POPULATION SIZE

Estimated values for the population sizes amount to: Great Britain: 6,600 [gen. lit. 6], Belgium: 200–500 [18], France: 26,000 [18], Germany: 50–70 [13], Switzerland: < 500 [18], Austria: 200 [gen. lit. 136], Slovenia: 5,000 [gen. lit. 96], Bulgaria: 15,000–30,000 [18, own data], Spain: < 25,000 [18]. Total population in the European Union countries might be under 100,000 animals.

CONSERVATION MEASURES

For the preservation of the species European-wide efforts are necessary, since apart from the relict populations in Central Europe, in particular all the still large and connected populations on the Balkan and the Iberian Peninsula should be preserved. Due to the eastern enlargement of the European Union a drastic reduction of interconnected woodlands and extensive pastures, together with the loss of large-scale foraging habitats, is expected, especially on the Balkan Peninsula. The transformation of holm and cork oak forests to arable land or plantations on the Iberian Peninsula similarly represents a major threat. All larger roost caves should be placed effectively under protection. The separate habitats should not be isolated from each other; fragmentation effects by new human settlements, industrial areas and road constructions should be avoided. In Central Europe the remaining populations can be preserved only by a sustainable landscape management with management contracts geared to the species.

REFERENCES

1. Beck, A., S. Gloor, M. Zahner, F. Bontadina, T. Hotz, M. Lutz & E. Mühlethaler (1997): Zur Ernährungsbiologie der Großen Hufeisennase in einem Alpental der Schweiz; Arbeitskreis Fledermäuse Sachsen-Anhalt e.V.: 15–18.

2. Bontadina, F., T. Hotz, S. Gloor, A. Beck, M. Lutz & E. Mühlethaler (1997): Schutz von Jagdgebieten der Großen Hufeisennase. Umsetzung der Ergebnisse einer Telemetrie-Studie in einem Alpental der Schweiz; Arbeitskreis Fledermäuse Sachsen-Anhalt e.V.: 33–40.

3. Caubère, B., P. Gaucher & J.F. Julien (1984): Un record mondial de longévité in natura pour un chiroptère insectivore? *Rev. Ecol.* (Terre Vie) 39: 351–353.

4. de Paz, O. (1995): Geographic variation of the greater horseshoe bat (*Rhinolophus ferrumequinum*) in the west-half of the Palearctic region. *Myotis* 32/33: 33–44.

5. Dietz, C., I. Dietz, T. Ivanova & B.M. Siemers (2009): Seasonal and regional movements of horseshoe bats (*Rhinolophus*, Chiroptera: Rhinolophidae) in Northern Bulgaria. *Nyctalus* (NF) 14(1–2): 52–64.

6. Dietz, C., I. Dietz & B.M. Siemers (2006): Wing measurement variations in the five European horseshoe bat species (Chiroptera: Rhinolophidae). *J. Mammal.* 87: 1241–1251.

7. Dietz, C., I. Dietz & B.M. Siemers (2007): Growth of horseshoe bats (Chiroptera: Rhinolophidae) in temperate continental conditions and the influence of climate. *Mamm. Biol.* 72 (3): 129–144.

8. Duvergé, P.L. & G. Jones (1994): Greater horseshoe bats – activity, foraging behaviour and habitat use. *British Wildlife* 6: 69–77.

9. Gaisler, J. (2001): *Rhinolophus ferrumequinum*, Große Hufeisennase. In: F. Krapp (ed.): *Handbuch der Säugetiere Europas* 4–I: 15–37; Aula Verlag.

10. Issel, B. & W. Issel (1960): Beringungsergebnisse an der Großen Hufeisennase (*Rhinolophus ferrumequinum*) in Bayern. *Bonn. Zool. Beitr.*, Sonderheft 11/ 1960: 124–142.

11. Jones, G. (1990): Prey selection by the greater horseshoe bat (*Rhinolophus ferrumequinum*): optimal foraging by echolocation? *J. Anim. Ecol.* 59: 587–602.

12. Jones, G., P.L. Duvergé & R.D. Ransome (1995): Conservation biology of an endangered species: field studies of greater horseshoe bats. *Symp. Zool. Soc. Lond.* 67: 309–324.

13. Liegl, A. (2004): Große Hufeisennase, R*hinolophus ferrumequinum*. In: A. Meschede & B.-U. Rudolph (eds): *Fledermäuse in Bayern*: 102–110; Ulmer Verlag.

14. Ransome, R.D. (1990): *The natural history of hibernating bats*, 235 pp.; Christopher Helm, London.

15. Ransome, R.D. (1995): Earlier breeding shortens life in female greater horseshoe bats. *Phil. Trans. Soc. Lond.* B 350: 153–161.

16. Ransome, R.D. (1996): The management of feeding areas for greater horseshoe bats. *English Nature Research Reports* 174: 1–74.

17. Ransome, R.D. (1998): The impact of maternity roost conditions on populations of greater horseshoe bats. *English Nature Research Reports* 292: 1–80.

18. Ransome, R.D. & A.M. Hutson (2000): Action plan for the conservation of the greater horseshoe bat in Europe (*Rhinolophus ferrumequinum*). *Nature and Environment* 109: 56 pp.

19. Rossiter, S.J., G. Jones, R.D. Ransome & E.M. Barratt (2002): Relatedness structure and kin-biased foraging in the greater horseshoe bat (*Rhinolophus ferrumequinum*). *Behav. Ecol. Sociobiol.* 51: 510–518.

20. Rossiter, S.J., R.D. Ransome, C.G. Faulkes, S.C. Le Comber & G. Jones (2005): Mate fidelity and intra-lineage polygyny in greater horseshoe bats. *Nature* 437: 408–411.

Mediterranean Horseshoe Bat
Rhinolophus euryale
BLASIUS, 1853

NAMES

D: Mittelmeer-Hufeisennase
F: Rhinolophe euryale
E: Murciélago mediterráneo de herradura
I: Ferro di cavallo euriale
NL: Paarse hoefijzerneus
S: Mellanhästskonäsa
PL: Podkowiec śródziemnomorski

Measurements

Forearm	45.0–51.0mm
Fifth finger	53–62mm
Third finger	63–76mm
First phalanx of fourth finger	5.7–8.2mm
Second phalanx of fourth finger	16.4–20.1mm
Normal weight	9–14g
CCL	16.0–17.1mm
CM³	6.1–6.7mm

IDENTIFICATION

One of the medium-sized horseshoe bats with relatively uniform colouring, the grey-brown to red-brown dorsal fur contrasts little with the grey or grey-white ventral side. Young animals are uniformly grey. The connecting process tapers to a pointed tip which is slightly curved downwards; the profile of the connecting process above the sella is half-moon shaped. The sella looks broadly rounded at the end from below and has parallel sides. The lancet tapers evenly towards the tip. The lower lip has two small grooves. In the wing, the second phalanx of the fourth finger is more than twice as long as the first one.

Similar species

In Mehely's Horseshoe Bat the lancet narrows abruptly and tapers to a fine tip and the connecting process is more rounded and not curved downward. Blasius's Horseshoe Bat has a distinct indentation in the horizontal skin fold below the lancet, and the second phalanx of the fourth finger is less than twice as long as the first.

ECHOLOCATION CALLS

At rest the long constant-frequency call has a frequency of 104–109kHz. In Italy the frequency is 104kHz [gen. lit. 106], lower than in Bulgaria at 105–106kHz [17]. The calls of the Lesser Horseshoe Bat and Mehely's Horseshoe Bat are usually higher, but the range can overlap by several kHz with the Mediterranean Horseshoe Bat.

DISTRIBUTION

Distributed in the Mediterranean area from northwest Africa over most Mediterranean islands (not on the Balearics or Crete), throughout the Iberian Peninsula, southern France, Italy, the entire Balkan Peninsula, Slovakia, Hungary, Romania and the western parts of Asia Minor. The Slovakian–Hungarian population is distinctly isolated from the remaining distribution area. Outside of the geographical scope of this book, the species occurs in the Near East, in Iran, Iraq and the Caucasus area to Turkmenistan.

Subspecies and geographical variation

Only the nominate form occurs in this region. *R. e. judaicus* occurs in the Middle East, a subspecies seemingly isolated from *R. e. euryale* by a gap in Asia Minor.

HABITAT

By a clear preference for caves as summer roosts limited to a large extent to karst areas. Nursery roosts are usually in climatically favourable areas below 800m. As hunting grounds all deciduous forests (oak, holm oak and mixed woodlands) and riparian forests and scrub lands are visited, also olive groves and eucalyptus plantations, but open land and coniferous forest are strictly avoided [1, 7, 14, 15, own data]. The largest known nursery roosts in Bulgaria are in hardwood forest-rich areas. From a nursery

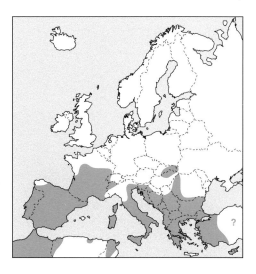

Fig. 293. The Mediterranean Horseshoe Bat usually flies close to vegetation and also hunts in dense bushes. Photo: D. Nill.

roost of over 10,000 individuals the animals hunt exclusively in oak or riparian woodland (hornbeam, elm and lime tree forests) [own data]. Smaller colonies can forage in deforested areas, remnants of riparian woodland (also poplar plantations) and scrublands [own data].

Roosts

Summer roosts and nursery roosts are mainly in caves, outside karst areas, and in the northern part of the distribution in roof spaces [6, 18], or cellars and other shelters. Winter roosts mainly in caves, more rarely in mines.

BEHAVIOUR

Nursery colonies in buildings comprise 20–300, in caves up to 1,000 animals. Larger nursery colonies are rare. In south Bulgaria a colony of over 10,000 Mediterranean Horseshoe Bats was formed in some years in the cellar spaces of an abandoned hotel complex [own data]. In the summer dense clusters are formed and the animals hang together with the other middle-sized and large horseshoe bats, often also with Natterer's, Long-fingered, Schreibers' Bent-wing Bats and mouse-eared bats. Frequently in the winter very dense clusters of 100–2,000 medium-sized and Greater Horseshoe Bats are formed, in which the Mediterranean Horseshoe Bats often dominates. In the roost the species is very sensitive to disturbance; the dense clusters dissolve immediately upon disturbance and the animals fly around the roost. In Bulgaria nightly foraging trips cover very large distances, with females being so far away from the roost that they only return in the morning to suckle.

REPRODUCTION

The birth of the single young usually occurs from mid-June, with some females giving birth only in July [13, own data]. Neonates have a forearm length of 18–20mm. At night the young are left in a 'creche' and form dense clusters; females can also be observed carrying their young outside the cave. At the age of four weeks the young become independent. Young females give birth first at the age of 2–3 years [6, own data]. Mating takes place in the autumn in caves, but is also recorded in the winter in large roosts [18].

FORAGING

The Mediterranean Horseshoe Bat can use

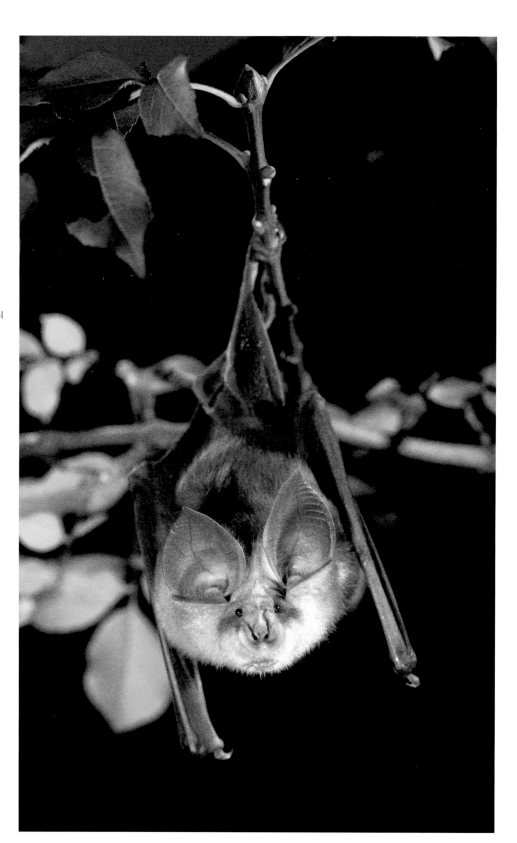

Fig. 294. Particularly in cool weather or in the second half of the night Mediterranean Horseshoe Bats hunt from a perch. Photo: D. Nill.

very agile flight manoeuvres to hunt in almost impenetrable bushes, and radio-tracked animals were found hunting in dense vegetation [own data]. The species mostly feeds in flight, only with very low prey density (rain, low temperatures) and with pregnant females or young animals is more perch hunting carried out [own data]. Foraging flights take place in dense vegetation, in open forests close to the ground, around edge features or in the crowns of tree to heights of over 20m. Dense vegetation can be approached very closely from outside or the animals hunt within the crown between branches and twigs [12, own data].

FOOD

The food consists mainly of small moths, Diptera (crane-flies) and small beetles [8]. Usually moths constitute up to 90% of the food, additionally lacewings, cockroaches and crane-flies and other occasional prey form a further 10–15% [12, I.Dietz pers. com.]. The average length of moth wings gathered at feeding places is 15–20mm [12, I.Dietz pers. com.] and of all prey 14.8mm [12]; the calculated size of prey items from droppings analysis is 5–11mm [8].

MAXIMUM AGE

The maximum age proven so far is at least 13 years [2].

MOBILITY AND MIGRATION

The Mediterranean Horseshoe Bat is little studied; roost changes are usually to distances of less than 50km [5]. The furthest distances are 83km [5] and 134km [11]. In Bulgaria distances of up to 60km were recorded several times, with individual reproductive females reaching separate caves up to 43km away [3].

Habitat use

Telemetric studies in Spain resulted in average distances between the hunting grounds and the roosts of 1.4–5.3km [7, 9, 14], in Italy of 2.2km [15] and in Bulgaria of 9.3km [16]. Maximum distances in Spain were 4.2–10km [1, 8, 9, 14], in Italy 5km [15] and in Bulgaria 24km [16]. Foraging area of individual animals in Italy included (MCP)

up to 1,300ha [15], in Spain up to 200ha (with very few location points per animal) [1, 9] or 1,200ha [7] and in Bulgaria up to 10,000ha with an average of 2,800ha [16].

THREATS

Red list of the IUCN 2006: VU (Vulnerable), Red list of the European Union: VU (Vulnerable), EU Habitats Directive, Annex II & IV. In France a strong population decrease since the 1950s [gen. lit. 20] with now only a small percentage of the original population [10, 13]. Also, in parts of north Slovakia the species seems to have already disappeared [18]. In contrast to Mehely's Horseshoe Bat, the loss of foraging habitats may play a lesser role in the declines than the negative effects of disturbance of the colonies in caves (cave tourism, also in former times from ringing activities [gen. lit. 20]), and possibly by pesticide use in forests, riparian forests (crane-fly control) and orchards. Mediterranean Horseshoe Bats are very sensitive to disturbance in their roosts and disappear immediately from caves used for tourism or other purposes. The largest populations occur in the Iberian Peninsula, in northern Bulgaria and possibly in Serbia, Albania and Macedonia. Blasius's Horseshoe Bat dominates in south Bulgaria, Greece and Turkey.

Together with the Long-fingered Bat (*Myotis capaccinii*) and Schreibers' Bent-winged Bat (*Miniopterus schreibersii*), the

Fig. 295. A cluster of juvenile Mediterranean Horseshoe Bats in a Bulgarian cave, with a few adults and nearly volant Long-fingered Bats also present. Photo: C. Dietz.

European Horseshoe Bat is under investigation by a working group of Eurobats, to assess the information available and research requirements for these Mediterranean species, which have been designated under the Agreement as Priority Species for ecological research. It is considered that further understanding of key aspects of the ecology of these vulnerable species will help in their conservation. In particular, the general areas of roost choice, foraging habitat and diet, and population structure and dispersal are considered important areas of study. While it is not intended that the Agreement itself should undertake such research, it is hoped that in highlighting relevant questions, it will help to encourage the availability of resources for the work to be carried out. Nevertheless, the Agreement does also have a fund for the support of research and conservation projects.

CONSERVATION MEASURES

Protection of the colony caves and strict access control, with no permits for commercial tourism in roost caves. Preservation of corridors of hedges and tree lines between roosts and forest habitats.

Fig. 296. Mediterranean Horseshoe Bats can transport their young well in flight, as with all horseshoe bats the young grip onto the false nipple in the pelvic region and cling with their feet firmly at the shoulders. Photo: C. Dietz.

Prevention of fragmentation effects between separate habitats. Preservation of semi-natural hardwood forests in the vicinity of the roosts. Prevention of a significant reduction of prey density by prohibition of pesticide use in forests and riparian woodland and prevention of attracting effect of lighting.

REFERENCES

1. Aihartza, J.R., I. Garin, U. Goiti, J. Zabala & I. Zuberogoita (2003): Spring habitat selection by the Mediterranean horseshoe bat (*Rhinolophus euryale*) in the Urdaibai Biosphere Reserve (Basque Country). *Mammalia* 67: 25–32.
2. Crucitti, P. (1976): Interessanti ricatture di rhinolofidi nella grotta la Pila 71 La (Lazio). *Doriana* 5: 1–5.
3. Dietz, C., I. Dietz, T. Ivanova & B.M. Siemers (2009): Seasonal and regional movements of horseshoe bats (*Rhinolophus*, Chiroptera: Rhinolophidae) in Northern Bulgaria. *Nyctalus* (NF) 14(1–2): 52–64.
4. Dietz, C., I. Dietz & B.M. Siemers (2006): Wing measurement variations in the five European horseshoe bat species (Chiroptera: Rhinolophidae). *J. Mammal.* 87: 1241–1251.
5. Dinale, G. (1967): Studii sui chirotteri italiani: VIII. Spostamenti di *Rhinolophus euryale inanellati* in Liguria. *Atti della Società Italiana di Science Naturali e del Museo Civico di Storia Naturale in Milano* 106: 275–282.
6. Gaisler, J. (2001): *Rhinolophus euryale*, Mittelmeerhufeisennase. In: F. Krapp (ed.): *Handbuch der Säugetiere Europas* 4-I: 59–74; Aula Verlag.
7. Goiti, U., J.R. Aihartza, D. Almenar, E. Salsamendi & I. Garin (2006): Seasonal foraging by *Rhinolophus euryale* (Rhinolophidae) in an Atlantic rural landscape in northern Iberian Peninsula. *Acta Chiropterologica* 8: 141–155.
8. Goiti, U., J.R. Aihartza & I. Garin (2004): Diet and prey selection in the Mediterranean horseshoe bat *Rhinolophus euryale* (Chiroptera, Rhinolophidae) during the pre-breeding season. *Mammalia* 68: 397–402.
9. Goiti, U., J.R. Aihartza, I. Garin & J. Zabala (2003): Influence of habitat on the foraging behaviour of the Mediterranean horseshoe bat, *Rhinolophus euryale*. *Acta Chiropterologica* 5: 75–84.
10. Hamond, B. & Y. Gerard (1995): Répartition et éléments d'écologie du rhinolophe euryale (*Rhinolophus euryale*) en Franche-Comté. *Annales Scientifiques de l'Universitée de Franche-Comté Besançon, Biologie-Écologie* 3: 51–61.
11. Heymer, A. (1964): Résultats du baguage de chauves-souris dans les Pyrénées-orientales de 1945 à 1959. *Vie et Milieu* A 15: 765–799.
12. Koselj, K. (2002): *Diet and ecology of Mediterranean horseshoe bat (*Rhinolophus euryale; Mammalia: Chiroptera) in south-eastern*

Slovenia. Masters thesis, University of Ljubljana, 126 pp.

13. Masson, D. (1999): Histoire naturelle d'une colonie de parturition de Rhinolophe euryale, *Rhinolophus euryale*, (Chiroptera) du sud-ouest de la France. *Arvicola* 11: 41–50.

14. Russo, D., D. Almenar, J. Aihartza, U. Goiti, E. Salsamendi & I. Garin (2005): Habitat selection in sympatric *Rhinolophus mehelyi* and *R. euryale* (Mammalia: Chiroptera). *J. Zool.* 266: 327–332.

15. Russo, D., G. Jones & A. Migliozzi (2002): Habitat selection by the Mediterranean horseshoe bat, *Rhinolophus euryale* (Chiroptera: Rhinolophidae) in a rural area of southern Italy and implications for conservation. *Biol. Conserv.* 107: 71–81.

16. Schunger, I., C. Dietz, T. Ivanova & B.M. Siemers (2004): *Habitat selection and home ranges of four sympatric species of European horseshoe bats.* Abstracts of the 13th International Bat Research Conference; Warsaw.

17. Siemers, B.M., K. Beedholm, C. Dietz, I. Dietz & T. Ivanova (2005): Is species identity, sex, age or individual quality conveyed by echolocation call frequency in European horseshoe bats? *Acta Chiropterologica* 7: 259–274.

18. Uhrin, M., S. Danko, J. Obuch, I. Horáček, S. Pačenovsky, P. Pjenčák & M. Fulín (1996): Distributional patterns of bats (Mammalia: Chiroptera) in Slovakia. Part 1, horseshoe bats (Rhinolophidae). *Acta Soc. Zool. Bohem.* 60: 247–279.

Fig. 297. Mediterranean Horseshoe Bats usually form very dense clusters, in which they are often mixed with other bat species, here with Lesser Mouse-eared and Long-fingered Bats. Photo: C. Dietz.

Mehely's Horseshoe Bat
Rhinolophus mehelyi
MATSCHIE, 1901

NAMES
D: Mehely-Hufeisennase
F: Rhinolophe de Mehely
E: Murciélago mediano de herradura
I: Ferro di cavallo di Mehely
NL: Mehely's hoefijzerneus
S: Mehelys hästskonäsa
PL: Podkowiec średni

Measurements

Forearm	48.3–54.8mm
Fifth finger	57–67mm
Third finger	71–83mm
First phalanx of fourth finger	6.5–9.3mm
Second phalanx of fourth finger	17.4–21.5mm
Normal weight	12–17g
CCL	16.7–17.8mm
CM³	6.6–7.2mm

IDENTIFICATION
The largest of the three medium-sized horseshoe bats is highly contrastingly coloured: the pale, often almost white ventral side is sharply delineated from the grey-brown dorsal fur. On Sardinia, animals with an intense red-brown colouring are relatively common, in other parts of Europe very rare. The fur is relatively dense. In most older animals dark 'spectacles' of grey-brown hairs around the eyes, but this can also occur in other species. The connecting process is usually bluntly rounded and extending beyond the tip of the sella. Seen from the front the sella is wide at the tip and seen from below parallel sided. The lancet narrows sharply in its upper half and tapers to a slender point. The lower lip has two small grooves. The wings are broad and shortly rounded. The second phalanx of the fourth finger is more than twice as long as the first phalanx.

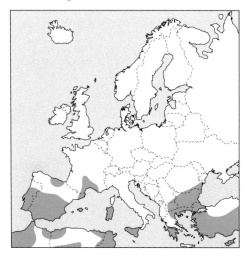

Similar species
In the Mediterranean Horseshoe Bat the lancet tapers gradually and evenly to the tip. The connecting process is pointed and slightly curved downwards. Blasius's Horseshoe Bat has a distinct indentation in the horizontal skin fold under the lancet and the second phalanx of the fourth finger is less than twice as long as the first.

ECHOLOCATION CALLS
The long constant-frequency part of the call is between 104 and 111kHz. This frequency range overlaps with those of the Mediterranean and Lesser Horseshoe Bat. The latter can be mostly differentiated by sight on the basis of its small size. Frequencies of over 108kHz will almost certainly exclude the Mediterranean Horseshoe Bat [14].

DISTRIBUTION
Distributed in a narrow band around the Mediterranean Sea from northwest Africa across Portugal, Spain, the Balearics, southern France, Sardinia, Sicily and the Balkan Peninsula to Asia Minor and Cyprus. Former occurrences on the Croatian and Adriatic coasts have not been confirmed for a long time; the species has probably already disappeared there. The distribution on the Balkan Peninsula is poorly known. Outside the geographical scope of this book only a patchy and limited occurrence from records from the southern edge of the Caucasus across Iran, Iraq and Afghanistan, also south into the Middle East and Egypt.

Subspecies and geographical variation
Usually regarded as monotypic, but some authors recognize *R. m. tuneti* as a subspecies from northwest Africa.

HABITAT
Mehely's Horseshoe Bat usually occurs at low altitudes of below 700m and is dependent on cave-rich karst areas. Foraging territories include steppes, semi-steppes, meadows, pastures, arable land and savannah-like biotopes, as well as light cork and holm oak forests and olive groves [4, 10]. In Spain dense forest habitats are also

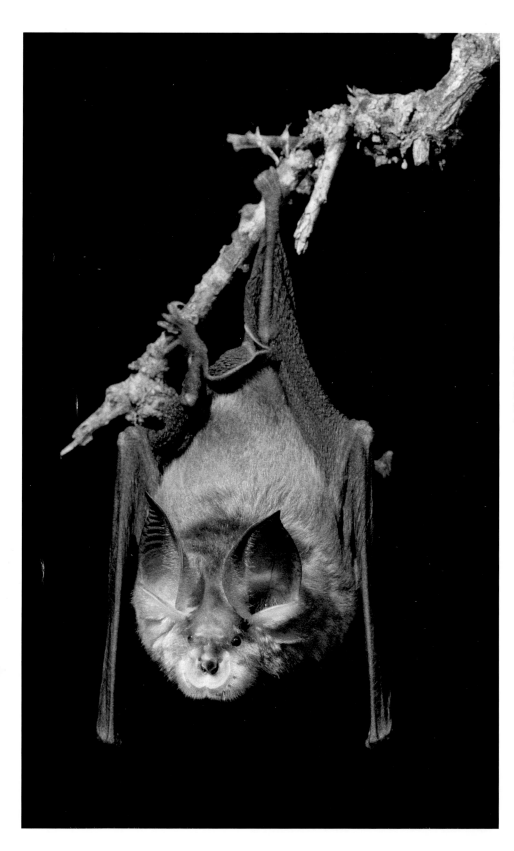

Fig. 298. Mehely's Horse-
shoe Bats use isolated
shrubs for perch hunting
and from there often carry
out flycatcher-like hunting
flights of only half a minute;
the prey is then consumed
at the perch. Photo: D. Nill.

Fig. 299. Loose hibernation cluster of Mehely's Horseshoe Bat in a cave on Sardinia. Towards the left a reddish-yellow individual is noticeable. Photo: D. Nill.

Fig. 300. Mehely's Horseshoe Bat hunts particularly in open, steppe-like landscapes; its broad wings with rounded tips make agile flight possible. Photo: D. Nill.

used [10]; in northern Bulgaria the species hunts almost exclusively over meadows, extensively used pasture lands, fallow fields and sunflower fields, with evidence of a clear preference for open land biotopes [4].

Roosts
Summer and winter roosts exclusively in caves, sometimes also in mines; very rarely single animals spend the daytime in buildings or cellars.

BEHAVIOUR
Nursery colonies comprise 20–200, rarely up to 500 animals. In northern Bulgaria, a nursery roost with up to 5,000 adult animals was present in 2000–2004, but in 2006 there were only a few non-reproducing animals [own data]. Nursery colonies are not exclusively female groups; males can constitute up to a third of the animals [own data]. In the roost often with Mediterranean Horseshoe Bats and other cave species, with which they can even hang intermixed. In Bulgaria mixed hibernation groups with up to 4,500 medium-sized horseshoe bats [Petrov & Ivanova pers. com.].

REPRODUCTION
Only one young is born; the forearm length is about 18–19mm [own data]. The birth time can be relatively widely spread; in Bulgaria births occur in some years in the first days of June, in other years only at the beginning of July [3]. The first young animals fly within the roost at three weeks after the first births and can be captured one week later outside of the caves [own data]. The high proportion of non-reproducing females indicates that sexual maturity is reached only in the second year [3]. In Azerbaijan females may become sexually mature only in the third year [9]. In Bulgaria mating takes place from the end of September. At this time dense clusters of up to 300 animals are formed in some caves; copulations take place at short distances from such clusters. Before copulation the males hang and display with fluttering wings, and are visited by a female that crawls from the main cluster [own data]. The heaviest males pair often, light males only rarely [own data].

FORAGING
The manoeuvrable flight is usually very low over grass, often between grass stems, or along bush edges at up to 6m height [4]. Perch hunting ('flycatching') is carried out in the second half of the night, or during the whole night by pregnant animals. For this, animals hang on individual higher plants (Common Mulleins, high sunflowers, bushes) and scan the environment. Prey flights usually last less than 30 seconds [4].

FOOD
Exclusively moths were found in stomach

analysis from Romania [15]. With extensive diet analyses in Bulgaria, moths comprise over 90% of the prey animals [4], but seasonally crane-flies and beetles (June beetles) play a significant role, rarely lacewings [4]. Among the food remains under feeding sites, many large moths, with an average wing length of 31mm, were found [4]. In Iran, moths were the main prey animals, followed by beetles, and regionally also dragonflies, homopterans, caddis flies and Diptera were found [12, 13].

MAXIMUM AGE
From Europe no records, in Azerbaijan the maximum estimated age by tooth wear was 12 years [9].

MOBILITY AND MIGRATION
So far, only few data from ringing studies are available, distances of up to 90km in Portugal and up to 94km in Bulgaria are recorded [1]. One of the greatest long-range flights refers to a pregnant female in Bulgaria, which was found 94km away in another colony 19 days after marking and attaching a radio transmitter [1]. Since it appeared that Mehely's Horseshoe Bats show a high injury rate with forearm bat rings the ringing activities in Bulgaria have ceased [gen. lit. 26].

Habitat use
Mehely's Horseshoe Bat hunts at distances of up to 10km from the roost; the average distance between hunting grounds and the roosts was 3.3km in Spain [10] and 5.3km in Bulgaria [4]. The foraging areas in Spain averaged 4.5km² [10], substantially smaller than in Bulgaria, with an average of 10.5km² and an extreme of up to 30km² [4].

THREATS
Red list of the IUCN 2006: VU (Vulnerable), Red list of the European Union: VU (Vulnerable), EU Habitats Directive II & IV. The rarest of the medium-sized horseshoe bats, a remnant population in France is almost extinct. No data are available for the current occurrence on Sicily. The Bulgarian population might comprise about 15,000 individuals with an optimistic estimate; the

Fig. 301. The abrupt narrowing of the lancet is characteristic of Mehely's Horseshoe Bat. Photo: C. Dietz.

Fig. 302. Particularly on Sardinia Mehely's Horseshoe Bats sometimes have areas of reddish-yellow fur. Photo: C. Dietz.

numbers of animals in Greece and European Turkey may be much smaller [own data]. The total European population is probably *c*. 50,000 animals, which are concentrated into a few core populations. The species can probably only be maintained on the Balkan Peninsula by a comprehensive transboundary conservation plan. Outside Europe hardly anything is known about the population situation. In Israel the species is almost extinct [Tsoar pers. com.]

CONSERVATION MEASURES
Protection of all colony caves, in particular the central main colonies, from disturbance, e.g. through cave tourism. Providing a management plan for the preservation of extensively used open land in the vicinity of colony caves. Prevention of habitat degradation by extensive grazing or by fragmentation.

REFERENCES
1. Dietz, C., I. Dietz, T. Ivanova & B.M. Siemers (in press): Movements of horseshoe bats (*Rhinolophus*, Chiroptera: Rhinolophidae) in Northern Bulgaria. *Nyctalus*.
2. Dietz, C., I. Dietz & B.M. Siemers (2006): Wing measurement variations in the five European horseshoe bat species (Chiroptera: Rhinolophidae). *J. Mammal.* 87: 1241–1251.
3. Dietz, C., I. Dietz & B.M. Siemers (2007): Growth

Fig. 303. The colonies of Mehely's Horseshoe Bats usually comprise only up to a few hundred animals, but the animals flying in this cave in north Bulgaria belong to a colony of up to 5,000 adult Mehely's Horseshoe Bats. Photo: C. Dietz.

of horseshoe bats (Chiroptera: Rhinolophidae) in temperate continental conditions and the influence of climate. *Mamm. Biol.* 72 (3): 129–144.

4. Dietz, I. (2001–2006): *Bislang unveröffentlichte Daten zur Raumnutzung, Nahrungs- und Jagdökologie der Mehely-Hufeisennase in Bulgarien.*

5. Gaisler, J. (2001): *Rhinolophus mehelyi*, Mehely-Hufeisennase. In: F. Krapp (ed.): *Handbuch der Säugetiere Europas* 4–I: 91–104; Aula Verlag.

6. Masson, D. & J.-P. Besson (1988): *Rhinolophus mehelyi* dans le sud-ouest de la France. *Mammalia* 52: 275–278.

7. Mucedda, M. (1994): Note su *Rhinolophus mehelyi* (Chiroptera, Rhinolophidae) della Sardegna. *Bollettino del Gruppo Speleologico Sassarese* 15: 43–46.

8. Paunović, M., A. Paunović & M. Ivovič (1998): Mehely's horseshoe bat *Rhinolophus mehelyi* new to the Yugoslavian bat fauna. *Myotis* 36: 115–119.

9. Rakhmatulina, I.K. (1992): *Major demographic characteristics of populations of certain bats from Azerbaijan.* Prague Studies in Mammalogy: 127–141, Prague.

10. Russo, D., D. Almenar, J. Aihartza, U. Goiti, E. Salsamendi & I. Garin (2005): Habitat selection in sympatric *Rhinolophus mehelyi* and *R. euryale* (Mammalia: Chiroptera). *J. Zool.* 266: 327–332.

11. Sharifi, M. (2004): Postnatal growth and age estimation in the Mehely's horseshoe bat (*Rhinolophus mehelyi*). *Acta Chiropterologica* 6: 155–161.

12. Sharifi, M. & Z. Hemmati (2001): Food of Mehely's horseshoe bat *Rhinolophus mehelyi* in a maternity colony in western Iran. *Myotis* 39: 17–20.

13. Sharifi, M. & Z. Hemmati (2004): Variation in the diet of Mehely's horseshoe bat, *Rhinolophus mehelyi*, in three contrasting environments in western Iran. *Zoology in the Middle East* 33: 65–72.

14. Siemers, B.M., K. Beedholm, C. Dietz, I. Dietz & T. Ivanova (2005): Is species identity, sex, age or individual quality conveyed by echolocation call frequency in European horseshoe bats? *Acta Chiropterologica* 7: 259–274.

15. Valenciuc, N. (1971): Données concernant la nourriture et la maniere de se la procurer chez quelques espèces de la faune de Romanie. *Studii si Comunicari* 1971: 353–357.

Blasius's Horseshoe Bat
Rhinolophus blasii
PETERS, 1866

NAMES

D: Blasius Hufeisennase
F: Rhinolophe de Blasius
E: Murciélago dálmata de herradura
I: Ferro di cavallo di Blasius
NL: Blasius' hoefijzerneus
S: Blasius hästskonäsa
PL: Podkowiec Blasiusa

IDENTIFICATION

A medium-sized horseshoe bat with fluffy fur which is tinged pale brown to sand or yellowish. Where the fur separates the whitish base to the hairs is particularly visible in adult animals, a regular feature of Blasius's Horseshoe Bat. The ventral fur is only a little paler than the dorsal fur, with a gradual colour transition at the sides. The connecting process is pointed and straight, not curved downwards. The sella tip is narrowed and rounded when seen from the front. Seen from below the sella is narrowed with shouldered sides towards the tip. The horizontal fold below the lancet is slightly indented in the middle. The first phalanx of the fourth finger is more than half the length of the second phalanx. The lower lip has two small grooves.

Similar species

The other two medium-sized horseshoe bats are very similar. Mehely's and the Mediterranean Horseshoe Bats rarely have a small indentation in the upper edge of the transverse fold below the lancet; in both species the sella tip is broader when seen from the front, and from below the sella is parallel-sided. In both species the first phalanx of the fourth finger is less than half as long as the second phalanx.

ECHOLOCATION CALLS

The long constant-frequency calls are at 92–98kHz in roosting animals [13]. There is no overlap with the frequency in the other European horseshoe bats, hence a confident species identification is possible.

DISTRIBUTION

In the geographical scope of this book, limited to southeast Europe, some east Mediterranean islands (Crete, Cyprus), Asia Minor and North Africa [1]. Large parts of the recorded distribution are only known from historical records, where the correct species identification is often questionable. Alleged records from Spain, Central Italy and Sicily are surely misidentifications. The (historical) European distribution includes the entire eastern Adriatic coast [7] to Trieste, parts of Serbia and Montenegro [11], Romania within the southern Carpathian basin [8, 10], the whole of Bulgaria [4], Greece and western Turkey. The species is, however, probably extinct in Italy and Slovenia [gen. lit. 96] and there is only one recent record from the northern Adriatic area on

Measurements

Forearm	42.6–50.1mm
Fifth finger	53–61mm
Third finger	63–74mm
First phalanx of fourth finger	7.6–9.2mm
Second phalanx of fourth finger	13.3–17.4mm
Normal weight	10–14g
CCL	16.3–17.5mm
CM³	6.5–6.9mm

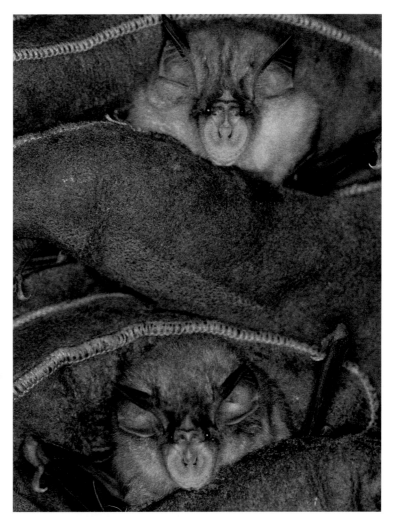

Fig. 304. Adult Blasius's Horseshoe Bats have brown dorsal fur (upper); young animals are uniformly grey coloured (lower). Photo: D. Nill.

Pakistan, in the Near East, the Arabian Peninsula, and in Iran and Iraq. Occurs south of the Sahara to South Africa in savannah landscapes.

Subspecies and geographical variation

In our region only the nominate form in the remaining distribution area three further subspecies: *R. b. meyeroehmi* (Afghanistan), *R. b. andreinii* (Ethiopia) and *R. b. empusa* (southern Africa). Whether the animals from Africa and Asia are actually Blasius's Horseshoe Bats or related cryptic species needs further investigation.

HABITAT

A typical bat of Mediterranean landscapes with a small-scale mosaic of open habitats and shrub lands. It usually occurs at lower altitudes and hunts particularly in scrub, in low-growing hornbeam and oak forests and along hedges in a highly structured landscape. From a preliminary habitat analysis

Fig. 305. Blasius's Horseshoe Bats flying from a roost cave in the Rhodopians. Photo: D. Nill.

the Croatian island of Čres [Tschapka pers. com.]. In Romania the species seems likewise to be extinct [10, Nagy pers. com.]. In Bulgaria the distribution border has withdrawn to the south of the Balkan mountains [own data, 4]. In the east distributed through Asia Minor along the Caucasus to

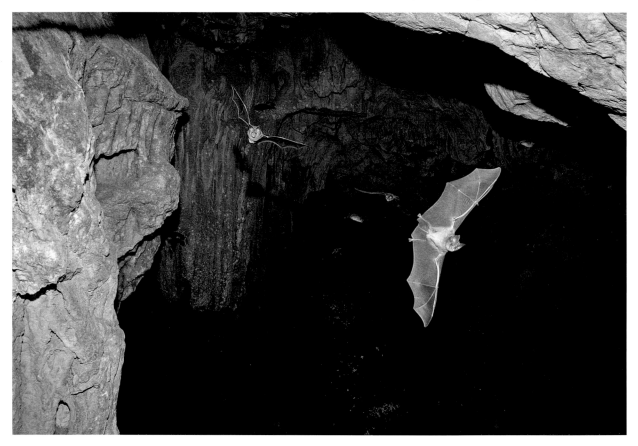

from Bulgaria, there is a preference for broadly savannah-like habitats with open wooded vegetation and closely connected open areas with scrub and forest [I. Dietz unpublished].

Roost

Almost exclusively karst caves are inhabited all the year round. Single animals can be found in mines and other underground roosts. In Romania there are earlier records of roost sites and a nursery roost in buildings [2, 3]; nowadays no building roosts are known. Often different caves are visited in winter from in summer; hibernation temperatures are usually 13.8–17°C [7].

BEHAVIOUR

Blasius's Horseshoe Bat forms nursery colonies of 30–500 animals, in a South Bulgarian cave in some years up to 3,000 animals [4]. Numerous adult males occur in nursery roosts, and they hang in dense clusters. Before the birth time males and non-reproducing females can constitute up to one-third of the animals in the nursery roost [own data]. Blasius's Horseshoe Bat forms dense clusters through the whole summer, only with disturbances, before emergence, and sometimes in winter the animals hang separated from each other [own data]. In the roost, usually occur with, and often in mixed clusters with, the Mediterranean, Mehely's and Greater Horseshoe Bats, Greater and Lesser Mouse-eared Bats, and Schreibers' Bent-winged and Long-fingered Bats; there are also single-species colonies.

REPRODUCTION

In south Bulgaria, birth takes place in late June, only one young per female, with a forearm length of 17–19mm and a weight of nearly 3g [own data]. In the middle of September some lactating females can still be captured in the Rhodopians, indicating a very late birth date in some animals. The high portion of nulliparous females, i.e. animals that have not yet given birth to young, suggests that sexual maturity is reached in the second year at the earliest [own data]. Mating takes place at least partly in September: in caves males hang in front of

a female and display with flapping wings and court her before mating occurs [own data].

FORAGING

Two radio-tracked animals hunted only in flight, circling around shrubs and hedges at 0.5–5m height and searching systematically [own data]. Blasius's Horseshoe Bats are extremely agile, can flutter and readily catch prey close to vegetation. In flight-tent experiments, Blasius's Horseshoe Bat could pick prey from the ground [12].

FOOD

In the Bulgarian and Greek Rhodopians

Fig. 306. Blasius's Horseshoe Bat hunts mostly in flight and only hangs during a break; perch hunting is hardly carried out. Photo: D. Nill.

Blasius's Horseshoe Bats fed on moths almost exclusively throughout the summer period: in more than 400 faecal samples examined remains of moths usually comprised 95–100% of the components [I. Dietz unpublished].

MOBILITY AND MIGRATION

To a large extent sedentary, with summer and winter roosts usually in different but close neighbouring caves. Local movements have been recorded within 10km around the ringing site, which is less than the distance between the hunting grounds and the roost shown by telemetry [own data]. As with the two other medium-sized species, Blasius's Horseshoe Bat can probably cover seasonal movements of up to 100km. Since the medium-sized horseshoe bats can suffer a high injury rate with bat rings, the ringing of these animals was abandoned [gen. lit. 26].

THREATS

Red list of the IUCN 2006: NT (Near Threatened), Red list of the European Union: VU (Vulnerable), EU Habitats Directive, Annex II & IV. Within this region's limits of southeast Europe, Asia Minor and North Africa, the European populations in particular are heavily threatened. Occurrence at the recorded northern edge of the distribution in Romania and in north Bulgaria is probably finished, and the distribution border is pushed 250–300km to the south. With the

winter monitoring in Romania, no Blasius's Horseshoe Bats have been observed in recent years [10] in areas in which they were regularly still recorded into the 1960s–70s [2, 3, 5, 8] , and no Blasius's Horseshoe Bats were among more than 5,000 trapped horseshoe bats in northern Bulgaria [own data]. A similar picture is evident along the Adriatic coast, particularly in Dalmatia [7], where there are only very isolated current observations, such as on Čres [Tschapka pers. com.]. The historical occurrence in Trieste and in Slovenia has not be confirmed for decades [gen. lit. 96]. In southeast Bulgaria and in Greece there are still stable populations. A transboundary conservation programme is urgently needed in order to preserve the European populations. In Israel the species is almost completely exterminated by eradication campaigns with cave fumigation against the Egyptian Fruit Bat [Levin & Tsoar pers. com.].

CONSERVATION MEASURES

Protection of the colony caves in summer and winter. Preservation of semi-open landscapes and abandonment of pesticide use in agriculture. The preservation of more spacious extensively used landscape areas with a cultural landscape mosaic around the known occurrence is urgently needed. In the case of possible conversion of small-scale rural agriculture to wide intensive cultures the preservation of at least extensively managed peripheral areas, a high structural richness and limited pesticide use should be taken into account.

Fig. 307. Portrait of Blasius's Horseshoe Bat, in side view the typical forward pointing connecting process is characteristic. Photo: C. Dietz.

REFERENCES

1. Aellen, V. (1955): *Rhinolophus blasii*, chauve-souris nouvelle pour l'Afrique du Nord. *Mammalia* 19: 361–366.
2. Barbu, P. & E. Bazilescu (1977): Nouvelles données concernant l'espèce *Myotis emarginatus* en Roumanie. *Anal. Univ. Bucuresti Biologie* 26: 93–94.
3. Bazilescu, E. (1971): Des donées concernant la colonie de chauves-souris de Runcu-Gorj. *Studii si Comunicari* 1971: 359–363.
4. Benda, P., T. Ivanova, I. Horáček, V. Hanák, J. Červený, J. Gaisler, A. Gueorguieva, B. Petrov & V. Vohralík (2003): Bats (Mammalia: Chiroptera) of the Eastern Mediterranean. Part 3. Review of bat distribution in Bulgaria. *Acta Soc. Zool. Bohem.* 67: 245–357.

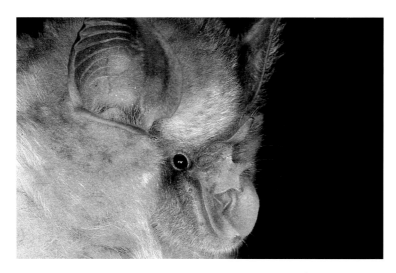

5. Beron, P. (1963): Le baguage des chauves-souris en Bulgarie de 1940 à 1961. *Acta Theriol.* 7: 33–49.
6. Dietz, C., I. Dietz & B.M. Siemers (2006): Wing measurement variations in the five European horseshoe bat species (Chiroptera: Rhinolophidae). *J. Mammal.* 87: 1241–1251.
7. Ðulič B. (1961): Contribution a l'étude de la répartition et de l'écologie de quelques chauves-souris cavernicoles de Dalmatie. *Mammalia* 25: 287–313.
8. Dumitrescu, M., J. Tanasachi & T. Orghidan (1963): Raspindirea chiropterelor in R. P. Romina. *Lucrarile Institutului Speleologie "Emil Racovita"* 1–2: 509–575.
9. Gaisler, J. (2001): *Rhinolophus blasii*, Blasius' Hufeisennase. In: F. Krapp (ed.): *Handbuch der Säugetiere Europas* 4-I: 75–90; Aula Verlag.
10. Nagy, Z.L., L. Barti, A. Doczy, C. Jere, T. Postawa, L. Szanto, A. Szodoray-Paradi & F. Szodoray-Paradi (2005): Survey of Romania's underground bat habitats. Status and distribution of cave-dwelling bats. *Report for BP Conservation Programme.* 44 pp.
11. Paunović, M. & S. Stamenković (1998): A revision of the distribution and status of *Rhinolophus euryale* and *Rhinolophus blasii* in Yugoslavia, based on the discrimination properties of distinctive morphological characters. *Myotis* 36: 7–23.
12. Siemers, B.M. & T. Ivanova (2004): Ground gleaning in horseshoe bats: comparative evidence from *Rhinolophus blasii*, *R. euryale* and *R. mehelyi. Behav. Ecol. Sociobiol.* 56: 464–471.
13. Siemers, B.M., K. Beedholm, C. Dietz, I. Dietz & T. Ivanova (2005): Is species identity, sex, age or individual quality conveyed by echolocation call frequency in European horseshoe bats? *Acta Chiropterologica* 7: 259–274.

Fig. 308. Blasius's Horseshoe Bat has a characteristic indentation in the horizontal skin fold under the lancet. Photo: C. Dietz.

Vesper or Plain-nosed Bats
Vespertilionidae

Small to medium-sized, predominantly insect-eating bats. Nose plain, without appendages ('noseleafs'). All species possess a long tail, which is completely within the tail membrane, except for the last two or three tailbones in some species. The ear length varies greatly; all vesper bats have a tragus, which is often species specific. The majority of the species use frequency-modulated calls as echolocation calls, which can span a broad frequency range. Modifications in the structure of the calls occur as an adaptation to special hunting behaviour. When at rest the wings are folded and held laterally along the body. The tail is folded onto the belly when at rest.

The vesper bats are the largest family of the order Chiroptera, with 48 genera and at least 410 species. The family is distributed on all continents except Antarctica. The family is very varied through adaptation to a wide range of climate zones, diverse habitats and prey. Within some genera, however, very similar appearance makes identification often quite difficult. Eight genera with 30 species of vesper bats occur in Europe, and in addition seven species in adjacent areas. One species of the genus *Lasiurus* can occur as an exceptional vagrant from North America. In North Africa another genus (*Otonycteris*) with one species extends to within the geographical scope of this book.

Daubenton's Bat
Myotis daubentonii
(KUHL, 1817)

NAMES

> D: Wasserfledermaus
> F: Murin de Daubenton
> E: Murciélago de ribera
> I: Vespertilio di Daubenton
> NL: Watervleermuis
> S: Vattenfladdermus
> PL: Nocek rudy

Measurements

Forearm	33.1–42.0mm
Fifth finger	39–52mm
Third finger	53–65mm
Normal weight	6–10g
CBL	12.8–14.5mm
CM³	5.0–5.5mm

IDENTIFICATION

A small bat with relative short ears for a *Myotis* species. The woolly and shining dorsal fur is usually brown, brown-grey, darkly bronze or coloured with a slightly reddish tinge. The light-grey to whitish-grey ventral side is usually clearly delineated from the dorsal side. The face of older animals is reddish brown. Young animals have a darker face and up to an age of over one year a sharply delineated black-blue mark on the lower lip. With increasing age this mark gets increasingly more vague and has usually disappeared completely at 4–5 years [7]. The ears are brown, with their inside usually distinctly paler. The short pale tragus is slightly blunt-tipped and curved slightly forward. The large feet are about half as long as the tibia and covered with long stiff bristles.

Similar species

The similar large-footed Pond Bat is substantially larger; the Long-fingered Bat has a slightly bent S-shaped tragus and a dense downy growth of hair on the thighs and tail membrane. Natterer's Bat has much longer ears, a paler and longer narrow-pointed tragus, a more pointed snout and an S-shaped calcar. Geoffrey's bat has a distinct right-angled notch at the outer edge of the ear and strikingly reddish-brown fur. The Iberian Daubenton's Bats, which were

Fig. 309. Daubenton's Bat with an unpigmented chin typical for an animal more than one year old. Photo: D. Nill.

described as *M. nathalinae*, look at first sight very similar to Whiskered and Brandt's Bat. The Whiskered and Brandt's Bat have, however, a longer and rather pointed tragus and distinctly smaller feet. In harbours and large cities, especially in Great Britain, the very similar North American Little Brown Bat (*Myotis lucifugus*) is occasionally found. Its ears are, however, longer (14–18mm) than those of Daubenton's Bat (10–14mm).

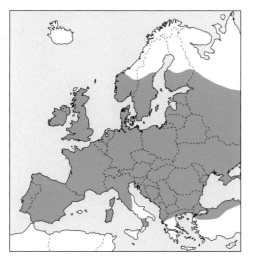

ECHOLOCATION CALLS

The 3–7ms long frequency-modulated calls begin quite variably between 55 and 95kHz, and usually end at *c.* 30kHz, within a range of 40–25kHz. Daubenton's Bats are identified best on the basis of their typical hunting behaviour over water surfaces, but there is possible confusion with Long-fingered and Pond Bat.

DISTRIBUTION

Nearly all of Europe to 63°N, but the distribution seems to be relatively fragmented in the Mediterranean region, where the occurrence is often limited to hilly and mountainous areas. The species is absent on some islands such as Sicily or the Balearics. Outside of the geographical scope of this book it occurs into Asia.

Subspecies and geographical variation

Only the nominate form occurs within our region. In the Iberian Peninsula, *M. nathalinae* was described as a species occurring sympatrically with the nominate form, [22] and later placed as a subspecies of Daubenton's Bat. After several revisions

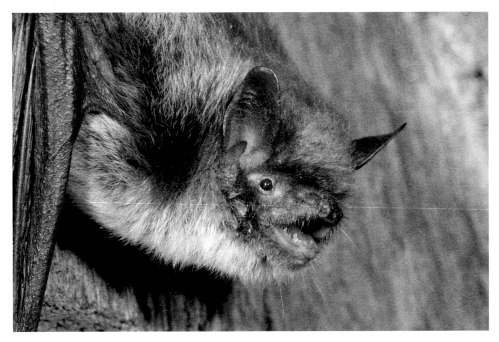

nathalinae was synonymised with the nominate form; there are, however, clear morphological differences present compared with the Central European Daubenton's Bats. In Europe, there is a size increase in the skull from south to north [3]. In the Asiatic distribution several subspecies are recognised; the easternmost is now regarded as a separate species: *M. petax*.

HABITAT

A flexible bat, for which habitat requirements can be restricted only in the broadest sense to forest and water. In addition, the majority of the animals hunt over water or in the vicinity of water, while individual animals can hunt in forests, parks, or meadows with fruit trees. The roost areas can be found in riparian woodlands, streamside trees, or in remote forest and urban areas. In the Mediterranean region Daubenton's Bat occurs sympatrically with the Long-fingered Bat here, sometimes at least, it is found more at the upper reaches of streams and over smaller, still waterbodies, while the Long-fingered Bat occupies the larger sections of standing or slowly flowing waters.

Roosts

Nursery colonies are formed in the summer, particularly in tree holes and bat boxes but also in cracks in bridges and more rarely in buildings. The original roosts are probably tree holes and in the south also rock crevices. Nursery roosts in underground sites are rare, as in a cave in Bavaria [23] and in the entrance area of a Bulgarian cave [own data]. Tree roosts can be in narrow trunk cracks, rot holes, or in woodpecker holes. Trees near fire breaks, wide forest trails and edges of woods are preferred [1]. Male roosts are frequently found in cracks of bridges and in tree holes, but also in underground channels. Hibernating animals are in particular found in caves, mines, bunker systems and cellars; a majority of the animals might, however, hibernate in tree holes and rock crevices.

BEHAVIOUR

Nursery colonies usually comprise 20–50 females, in building roosts exceptionally up to 600 animals. The summer roosts in tree holes are changed every 2–5 days. Nursery roosts in bridges and buildings are used continuously during substantially longer periods. Males form their own colonies of up to 20 animals, while clusters of up to 200 males are rarely found. In summer males usually occur at higher altitudes, while females dominate in the temperature-favoured and usually more prey-abundant waters of lower altitudes [5, 14, 17, 18]. Traditional flight paths occur between roosts and hunting grounds, along which several hundred animals may fly within a short time, particularly in the evening. Flight paths usually follow linear landscape elements such as ditches, hedges, forest edges, and forest trails. In Scandinavia in summer the animals hunt especially in forest during brighter light conditions, and change to water surfaces only with lower light intensities [15]. In Central and Northern Europe Daubenton's Bat is one of the most common species during autumn swarming at caves entrances, starting in August. In a few North European hibernation sites, particularly in the lowlands, there are enormous winter aggregations. Similarly, 20,000 Daubenton's Bats hibernate in the former bunker system of Nietoperek in Poland, and up to 5,000 animals in the Spandau citadel in Berlin [10], in the limestone quarry of Bad Segeberg (Schleswig-Holstein, Germany) and in the limestone quarries in the Danish Jutland. In such mass roosts, clusters of up to 140 animals are formed. Daubenton's Bats rarely hang free; they are frequently hidden in crevices or also in ground rubble.

REPRODUCTION

Usually one young is born from the second half of June, which at birth has an average forearm length of *c.* 14.9mm and a weight of 2.3g [13]. Within three weeks the young begin to fly, with a forearm length of 32.7mm and a weight of 5.5g. At the age of approximately four weeks the young animals leave the nursery to hunt independently; two weeks later the nurseries are usually abandoned. Young animals of both sexes can become sexual mature in the first autumn [11]; a relatively high portion of non-reproducing young females suggests, however, that only a small proportion successfully gives birth and raises a young.

Fig. 311. Daubenton's Bats hunt close to the surface of calm water and catch insects gliding or floating on water. Photo: D. Nill.

Fig. 312. Daubenton's Bats often use tree holes as roosts. Photo: D. Nill.

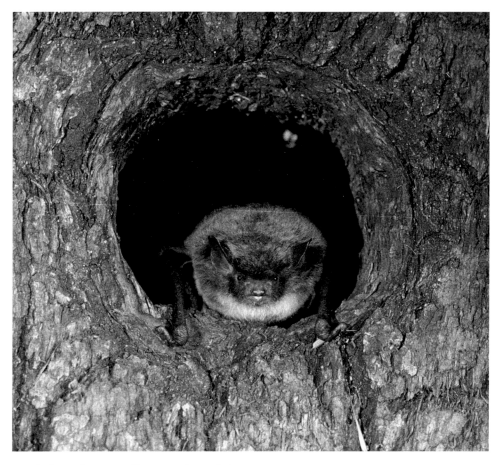

Similarly, only a small proportion of the young males show clearly filled epididymides in the first year of life. In August and the beginning of September Daubenton's Bats swarm at caves, mines and large bunker systems [10], the animals coming together from large areas [16]. Some mating occurs during the swarming period; further mating can take place through the whole winter, but with a clear peak in October and November. In the winter roosts, males search purposefully through the bats present for possible partners and mate even with torpid females. Through the ability to store sperm, the females have a whole set of post-copulation possibilities for sperm cell selection, i.e. they can possibly determine which of the stored sperm cells will fertilise the egg. It seems likely that those males which settle close to nurseries in the summer have the highest reproduction success [18].

FORAGING

The fast and agile hunting flight is usually at 5–40cm height over water. Insects are usually captured directly from the water surface; Daubenton's Bats are typical 'trawling bats'. If a swimming prey is discovered in the search flight, it is approached, and the feet and tail are lowered only shortly before the attack. Directly before the catch the bat straightens up almost perpendicularly; during the contact of the prey with the tail membrane the feet strike together and sweep up the prey. The bat rolls forward to take the food from the tail membrane or claws in flight. In this way Daubenton's Bats are also able to capture larger moths and even small fish like the Motherless Minnow (*Leucaspius delineatus*) [gen. lit. 122]. On calm water, floating prey or newly emerged aquatic insects can be very easily recognised acoustically by the bats [19], as long as they are not masked by floating leaves or plant material. Therefore vegetation-free calm water areas are sought for foraging [4]. Water surfaces agitated by wind or flow make prey detection substantially more difficult. Individual animals regularly spend a relatively high proportion of foraging time in forest or over damp meadows.

FOOD

Daubenton's Bats hunt partially opportunistically over waters, i.e. within certain limits insects of a preferred prey size of approximately 7.2mm [20] are captured according to their availability. Non-biting midges constitute the majority of the food; other Diptera (crane-flies, mosquitoes), aphids, mayflies, lacewings, Hymenoptera, moths and caddis flies are also seasonally captured [6, 20]. In laboratory tests Daubenton's Bats readily captured dead small fish when these broke the water surface [gen. lit. 122]. This behaviour has not yet been confirmed in the wild.

MAXIMUM AGE

The maximum age proven so far is 30 years [8], but the average life expectancy, at 4.5 years, is clearly lower [2].

MOBILITY AND MIGRATION

This mobile species usually covers distances of less than 150km between summer and winter roosts. The most distant recoveries were 257, 261 and 304km from the ringing site [21, gen. lit. 139]. Lowland populations migrate longer distances between seasonal habitats than the short-distance migrating animals of the mountain regions [21]. Swarming sites are visited from within 30km [16].

Habitat use

Through regular roost changing a nursery colony can utilise up to 40 tree holes during the year, which are distributed up to 2.6km from each other in an area of up to 5.3km² [8]. Females use hunting grounds in a 6–10km radius around the roost [1], on average within 2.3km [5]. Conversely, males hunt on average up to 3.7km from the roost [5], and a single animal can cover a distance of over 15km in its hunting ground. The size of the hunting ground varies greatly,

usually consisting of 2–8 separate hunting grounds from 0.1ha to 7.5ha [1].

THREATS

Red list of the IUCN 2006: LC (Least Concern), EU Habitats Directive, Annex IV. Daubenton's Bat increased markedly in large parts of its Central European range in the 1950s [12, gen. lit. 51] and is not threatened anywhere. The main reason for the increase might have been the eutrophication of waters together with an increase of the food supply: the larvae of some common non-biting midge species thrive in eutrophic waters.

Widespread and relatively common throughout the UK and Ireland [UK gen. ref. 153, 155]. Through long-term detailed passive surveillance and active survey, a high proportion (eight of *c.* 25) of the records of the rabies-related virus EBLV2 have been isolated in the UK [24, 25, 26]. The species is a target species under the UK National Bat Monitoring Programme, with evidence of a slow population increase. One of the most numerous species in hibernation sites, widely recorded on waterbodies, but limited number of summer maternity colonies known.

Fig. 313. Hibernating Daubenton's Bat in a bunker system. Photo: C. Dietz.

CONSERVATION MEASURES
Protection of colony and swarming sites, and particularly all large hibernacula.

REFERENCES
1. Arnold, A., M. Braun, N. Becker & V. Storch (1998): Beitrag zur Ökologie der Wasserfledermaus (*Myotis daubentoni*) in Nordbaden. *Carolinea* 56: 103–110.
2. Bezem, J.J., J.W. Sluiter & P.F. van Heerdt (1960): Population statistics of five species of the bat genus *Myotis* and one of the genus *Rhinolophus*, hibernating in the caves of S. Limburg. *Archives Néerlandaises de Zoologie* 13: 511–539.
3. Bogdanowicz, W. (1994): *Myotis daubentonii*. *Mammalian Species* 475: 1–9.
4. Boonman, A.M., M. Boonman, F. Breitschneider & W.A. van de Grind (1998): Prey detection in trawling insectivorous bats: duckweed affects hunting behaviour in Daubenton's bat, *Myotis*

daubentonii. *Behav. Ecol. Sociobiol.* 44: 99–107.
5. Encarnação, J.A., U. Kierdorf, D. Holweg, U. Jasnoch & V. Wolters (2005): Sex-related differences in roost-site selection by Daubenton's bats *Myotis daubentonii* during the nursery period *Mammal. Rev.* 35: 285–294.
6. Flavin, D.A., S.S. Biggane, C.B. Shiel, P. Smiddy & J.S. Fairley (2001): Analysis of the diet of Daubenton's bat *Myotis daubentonii* in Ireland. *Acta Theriol.* 46: 43–52.
7. Geiger, H., M. Lehnert & C. Kallasch (1996): Zur Alterseinstufung von Wasserfledermäusen (*Myotis daubentoni*) mit Hilfe des Unterlippenflecks ('chin-spot'). *Nyctalus* (N.F.) 6: 23–28.
8. Geiger, H. & B.-U. Rudolph (2004): Wasserfledermaus, *Myotis daubentonii*. In: A. Meschede & B.-U. Rudolph (eds.): *Fledermäuse in Bayern*: 127–138; Ulmer Verlag.
9. Grimmberger, E., H. Hackethal & Z. Urbanczyk (1987): Beitrag zum Paarungsverhalten der Wasserfledermaus, *Myotis daubentoni*, im Winterquartier. *Z. Säugetierk.* 52: 133–140.
10. Kallasch, C. & M. Lehnert (1995): Zur Populationsökologie von Wasser- und Fransenfledermäusen (*Myotis daubentoni* und *M. nattereri*) in der Spandauer Zitadelle. *Sitzungsber. Ges. Naturforschende Freunde Berlin, N.F.* 34: 69–91.
11. Kokurewicz, T. & J. Bartmanska (1992): Early sexual maturity in male Daubenton's bats (*Myotis daubentoni*); field observations and histological studies on the genitalia. *Myotis* 30: 95–108.
12. Kokurewicz, T. (1995): Increased populations of Daubenton´s Bat (*Myotis daubentoni*) in Poland. *Myotis* 32/33: 155–161.
13. Kratky, J. (1981): Postnatale Entwicklung der Wasserfledermaus, *Myotis daubentonii* und bisherige Kenntnis dieser Problematik im Rahmen der Unterordnung Microchiroptera (Mammalia: Chiroptera). *Folia Musei Rerum Naturalium Bohemiae Occidentalis* 16: 1–34.
14. Leuzinger, Y. & C. Brossard (1994): Répartition de *Myotis daubentoni* en fonction du sexe et de la période de l´année dans le Jura bernois. Résultats préliminaires. *Mitt. natf. Ges. Schaffhausen* 39: 135–143.
15. Nyholm, E.S. (1965): Zur Ökologie von *Myotis mystacinus* und *Myotis daubentoni*. *Ann. Zool. Fenn.* 2: 77–123.
16. Parsons, K.N. & G. Jones (2003): Dispersion and habitat use by *Myotis daubentonii* and *Myotis nattereri* during the swarming season: implications for conservation. *Anim. Conserv.* 6: 283–290.
17. Russo, D. (2002): Elevation affects the distribution of the two sexes in Daubenton's bats *Myotis daubentonii* (Chiroptera: Vespertilionidae) from Italy. *Mammalia* 66: 543–551.
18. Senior, P., R.K. Butlin & J.D. Altringham (2005): Sex and segregation in temperate bats. *Proc. R. Soc. Lond.* B 272: 2467–2473.
19. Siemers, B.M., P. Stilz & H.-U. Schnitzler (2001): The acoustic advantage of hunting at low

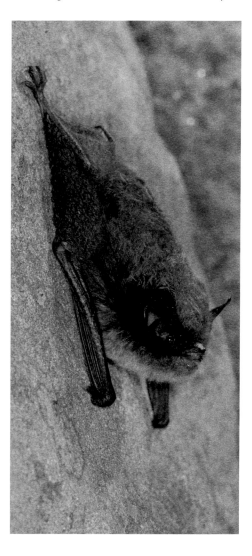

Fig. 314. The small and dark-coloured Daubenton's Bats from central Spain were described as a separate species (*Myotis nathalinae*), but are nowadays considered to be small-sized Daubenton's Bats (*Myotis daubentonii*). Photo: C. Dietz.

heights above water: behavioural experiments on the European 'trawling' bats *Myotis capaccinii, M. dasycneme* and *M. daubentonii. J. Exp. Biol.* 204: 3843–3854.

20. Taake, K.-H. (1992): Strategien der Ressourcennutzung an Waldgewässern jagender Fledermäuse. *Myotis* 30: 7–74.

21. Tress, J., C. Tress, W. Schorcht, M. Biedermann, R. Koch & D. Iffert (2004): Mitteilungen zum Wanderverhalten von Wasserfledermäusen (*Myotis daubentonii*) und Rauhhautfledermäusen (*Pipistrellus nathusii*) aus Mecklenburg. *Nyctalus* (N.F.) 9: 236–248.

22. Tupinier, Y. (1977): Description d'une chauvesouris nouvelle: *Myotis nathalinae* nov. sp. *Mammalia* 41: 327–340.

23. Zahn, A. & I. Hager (2005): A cave-dwelling colony of *Myotis daubentonii* in Bavaria, Germany. *Mamm. Biol.* 70: 250–254.

ADDITIONAL REFERENCES

24. Fooks, A.R., A.R. Brookes, N. Johnson, L.M. McElhinney & A.M. Hutson (2003): European bat lyssavirus: an emerging zoonosis. *Epidemiological Infection* 131: 1029–1039.

25. Harris, S.L., S.M. Brookes, G. Jones, A.M. Hutson & A.R. Fooks (2006): Passive surveillance (1987 to 2004) of United Kingdom bats for European bat lyssaviruses. *Veterinary Record* 159: 439–446.

26. Harris, S.L., S.M. Brookes, G. Jones, A.M. Hutson, P.A. Racey, J. Aegerter, G.S. Smith, L.M. McElhinney & A.R. Fooks (2006). European bat lyssa viruses: distribution, prevalence and implications for conservation. *Biological Conservation* 131: 193–210.

Fig. 315. Males of Daubenton's Bat can form pure 'bachelor' groups, which can include up to 200 animals. Photo: C. Dietz.

Pond Bat
Myotis dasycneme
(Boie, 1825)

NAMES
- D: Teichfledermaus
- F: Murin des marais
- E: Murciélago lagunero
- I: Vespertilio dasicneme
- NL: Meervleermuis
- S: Dammfladdermus
- PL: Nocekłydkowłosy

Measurements

Forearm	43.0–49.0mm
Fifth finger	51–61mm
Third finger	72–77mm
Normal weight	13–18g
CBL	16.2–17.1mm
CM³	5.9–6.5mm

IDENTIFICATION

A medium-sized bat with dense pale grey-brown or brownish-coloured dorsal fur, sharply demarcated from the white or light-greyish ventral fur. Face colour of adults reddish light brown, of juveniles darker. Ears and other skin parts are grey-brown. As in Daubenton's Bat, young animals have a sharply delineated black-blue mark on the lower lip up to the age of over one year. The tragus is unusually short for a *Myotis* species and slightly bent inwards; the tip is rounded. The feet are very large with long bristles.

Similar species

The only *Myotis* species with a forearm length exceeding 43mm and with large feet (the foot length greater than half the length of the tibia). Only the smaller Long-fingered Bat has similar large feet but its wing membrane originates from the tibia, while the wing membrane of the Pond Bat starts from the heel.

ECHOLOCATION CALLS

The 4–8ms-long frequency-modulated signals start at 65–85kHz and end at 25–35kHz, mostly lower than 30kHz. The calls are very similar of those of Daubenton's Bat, but the Pond Bat has a characteristic social call (a quail-like call), lasting 15–25ms at 30–40kHz.

DISTRIBUTION

In northern Europe a patchy distribution from northern France through Belgium and the Netherlands, Denmark, southern Sweden and the Baltic states to Russia. The southern border runs through northern France, Rhineland-Palatinate, Hessen, Thuringia and Saxony. In eastern Central Europe the southern distribution reaches northern Croatia and Romania. From the Ukraine and Belarus the continuous distribution extends between 48°N and approx. 60°N, through Russia to Kazakhstan and to the River Yesiney in central

Fig. 316. Pond Bat in flight. Photo: D. Nill.

Siberia. Thus far, one record in England, possibly by assisted passage. One record of a single animal from the south coast of Finland (13)

Subspecies and geographical variation

Monotypic species, which does not show pronounced variation.

HABITAT

Occurs in areas rich in slow-flowing broad rivers, canals, lakes and ponds, almost exclusively in lowlands in the summer period. Winter roosts often in low mountain ranges.

Roosts

Summer roosts in roof spaces of churches and church towers, in cavity walls, behind cladding or under roof covering [12], also in flat-roofed houses [4]. Possibly nursery roosts are also in tree holes. Single animals also roost in tree holes and bat boxes on buildings. Winter roosts in caves, mines, bunkers and cellars.

BEHAVIOUR

Nursery colonies usually consist almost exclusively of adult females with their young and comprise 20–300 animals. Males may form small separate colonies of up to 40 animals [3]. Nursery roost sites are regularly changed and can be shared with Natterer's Bats and Common Pipistrelles [4]. From the middle of August to the

beginning of September Pond Bats usually visit swarming sites that are also used by several other species [8]. Large accumulations are rare in winter roosts, but roosts with up to 700 animals are known from Russia [11].

REPRODUCTION

The young are born from mid-June [11]. The females probably reach sexual maturity only in the second year. Males occupy mating roosts in buildings, tree holes and bat boxes [5], which are sought out by females. Mating takes place from the second half of August in the male roosts or in the winter roosts, probably also at swarming sites.

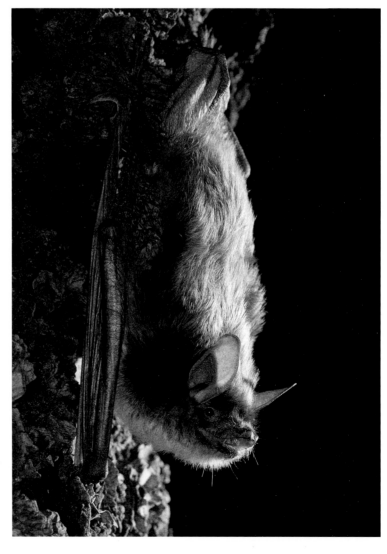

Fig. 317. Pond Bats have the largest feet of European bats; they use these to catch prey from water. Photo: D. Nill.

FORAGING

Usually over calm water surfaces, clear of vegetation such as duck weed [Boonman pers. com.]. Faster, more straight and somewhat higher flying than Daubenton's Bat [7]. Large reedbeds, meadows and forest edges are also used as hunting grounds.

FOOD

The food consists almost exclusively of aquatic insects such as gnats, mosquitoes and caddis flies [2, 14], which are captured directly from the water surface. Pond Bat, like Daubenton's and Long-fingered Bat, takes prey with its long hind feet or tail membrane from the water surface. Moths and beetles are captured over meadows and along woodland edges. Remains of spiders can also be found in the faeces.

MAXIMUM AGE

The maximum age proven so far is 20.5 years [11].

MOBILITY AND MIGRATION

The Pond Bat is a medium-range migrant. The lowland populations (northern German lowland, the Netherlands) hibernate in the adjacent low mountain ranges at distance of up to 300km from the summer roosts. In Russia migration similarly takes place from the lowland areas into the low mountain ranges [11]. The longest distance thus far recorded is 350km in Belgium. If suitable winter roosts are present in the environment of the summer habitats, the populations remain partly sedentary [gen. lit. 30]. Females seem to migrate over longer distances than males. The latter tend to be more or less sedentary.

THREATS

Red list of the IUCN 2006: VU (Vulnerable), Red list of the European Union: VU (Vulnerable), EU Habitats Directive, Annex II & IV. In the middle of the last century there were serious population declines due to obstructing roosts or the use of toxic timber treatment chemicals. At present the use of pesticides represents an increasing cause of poisoned food [10]. The Pond Bat is a highly endangered species due to its fragmented occurrence and relatively low population density.

CONSERVATION MEASURES

Protection of summer and winter roosts. Connection of roosts with water bodies by linear landscape elements such as hedges and tree rows, avoidance of habitat fragmentation.

Fig. 318. In this portrait the very short and forwardly curved tragus of Pond Bat is notable. Photo: D. Nill.

Fig. 319. Habitat of Pond Bat. Hunting animals prefer larger water surfaces free of vegetation. Photo: D. Nill.

REFERENCES

1. Boonman, A., H.J.G.A. Limpens & B. Verboom (1995): The influence of landscape elements on the echolocation of the pond bat, *Myotis dasycneme*. *Le Rhinolophe* 11: 39–40.
2. Britton, A.R.C., G. Jones, J.M.V. Rayner, A.M. Boonman & B. Verboom (1997): Flight performance, echolocation and foraging behaviour in pond bats, *Myotis dasycneme*. *J. Zool.* 241: 503–522.
3. Dense, C., K.-H. Taake & G. Mäscher (1996): Sommer- und Wintervorkommen von Teichfledermäusen (*Myotis dasycneme*) in Nordwestdeutschland. *Myotis* 34: 71–79.
4. Dolch, D., A. Hagenguth & U. Hoffmeister (2001): Erster Nachweis einer Wochenstube der Teichfledermaus, *Myotis dasycneme*, in Brandenburg. *Nyctalus* (N.F.) 7: 617–618.
5. Grimmberger, E. (2002): Paarungsquartier der Teichfledermaus (*Myotis dasycneme*) in Ostvorpommern. *Nyctalus* (N.F.) 8: 394.
6. Limpens, H.J.G.A. & R. Schulte (2000): Biologie und Schutz gefährdeter wandernder mitteleuropäischer Fledermausarten am Beispiel von Rauhhautfledermäusen (*Pipistrellus nathusii*) und Teichfledermäusen (*Myotis dasycneme*). *Nyctalus* (N.F.) 7: 317–327.
7. Limpens, H.J.G.A. (2001): Assessing the European distribution of the pond bat (*Myotis dasycneme*) using bat detectors and other survey methods. *Nietoperze* 2: 169–178.
8. Ohlendorf, B. (2004): Zum Status der Teichfledermaus (*Myotis dasycneme*) in Sachsen-Anhalt. *Nyctalus* (N.F.) 9: 336–342.
9. Řehák Z., J. Zukal & J. Gaisler (1996): Contribution to the knowledge of distribution of *Myotis dasycneme* (Mammalia: Chiroptera) in the Czech Republic. *Acta Soc. Zool. Bohem.* 60: 199–205.
10. Reinhold, J.O., A.J. Hendriks, L.K. Slager & M. Ohm (1999): Transfer of microcontaminants from sediment to chironomids, and the risk for the pond bat *Myotis dasycneme* (Chiroptera) preying on them. *Aquatic Ecology* 33: 363–376.
11. Roer, H. (2001): *Myotis dasycneme*, Teichfledermaus. In: F. Krapp (ed.): *Handbuch der Säugetiere Europas* 4–I: 303–319; Aula Verlag.
12. Schikore, T. & M. Zimmermann (2000): Von der Flugstraße über den Wochenstubennachweis zum Quartier der Teichfledermaus (*Myotis dasycneme*) in der Wesermarsch – erster Fortpflanzungsnachweis dieser Art in Niedersachsen. *Nyctalus* (N.F.) 7: 383–395.
13. Siivonen, Y. & T. Wermundsen (2003): First records of *Myotis dasycneme* and *Pipistrellus pipistrellus* in Finland. *Vespertilio* 7: 177–179.
14. Sommer R. & S. Sommer (1997): Ergebnisse zur Kotanalyse bei Teichfledermäusen, *Myotis dasycneme*. *Myotis* 35: 103–107.
15. Van de Sijpe, M., B. Vandendriessche, P. Voet, J. Vandeberghe, J. Duyck, E. Naeyaert, M. Manhaeve & E. Martens (2004): Summer distribution of the Pond bat *Myotis dasycneme* (Chiroptera, Vespertilionidae) in the west of Flanders (Belgium) with regard to water quality. *Mammalia* 68: 377–386.
16. Verboom, B., A.M. Boonman & H.J.G.A. Limpens (1999): Acoustic perception of landscape elements by the pond bat (*Myotis dasycneme*). *J. Zool.* 248: 59–66.

Long-fingered Bat
Myotis capaccinii
(Bonaparte, 1837)

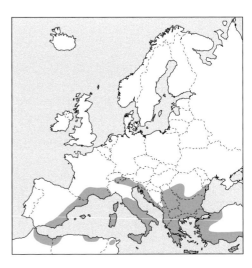

NAMES

D:	Langfußfledermaus
F:	Vespertilion de Capaccini
E:	Murciélago patudo
I:	Vespertilio di Capaccini
NL:	Capaccini's vleermuis
S:	Capaccinis fladdermus
PL:	Nocek długopalcy

Measurements

Forearm	38.4–44.0mm
Fifth finger	48–56mm
Third finger	64–71mm
Normal weight	7–10g
CBL	14.2–15.0mm
CM³	5.2–5.8mm

Fig. 320. At night the young of Long-fingered Bats are left in the roost; even when all animals are absent the roost sites are easily identified by the urine discolorations. Photo: C. Dietz.

IDENTIFICATION

A medium-sized *Myotis* species with grey to grey-brown dorsal fur and grey-white ventral fur. Young animals are inconspicuously grey coloured. The ears and flight membranes are grey-brown. The tragus is slightly S-shaped. The nostrils markedly protrude forwards. Noticeably large and strong feet with long bristles. Downy hairs extend onto the tail membrane along the whole tibia. The wing membrane starts at the tibia.

Similar species

Only the Long-fingered Bat has such heavily haired legs and protruding nostrils. It is the only European bat species in which the wing membrane starts at the tibia and not at the foot.

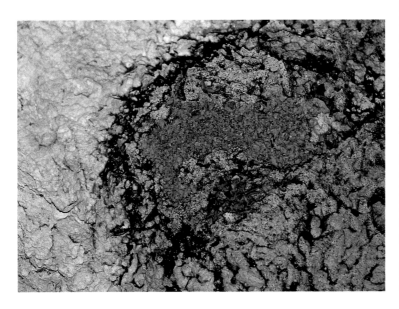

ECHOLOCATION CALLS

The 3–7ms-long frequency-modulated signals drop from 70–90kHz usually down to 35–39kHz, rarely reaching 30kHz. The signals are very similar to those of Daubenton's Bat and the range of the end frequencies overlap, but the end frequency of the Long-fingered Bat is usually higher [gen. lit. 105].

DISTRIBUTION

Occurs in the Mediterranean area of northwest Africa (Morocco, Algeria, Tunisia) and many islands, as well as within the European Mediterranean region along the coast to 46°N. In the western Mediterranean area the distribution is fragmented and limited to a few coastal areas. Only on the Balkan Peninsula does distribution extend far into continental area. In the eastern Mediterranean area also distributed from eastern Turkey across Syria and Lebanon to Israel. Further occurrence in Iran, Iraq and Uzbekistan. Occurrence on Cyprus and Malta is doubtful since the historical records are uncertain [2]

Subspecies and geographical variation

Monotypic species, the animals of the Balkans have been described as the subspecies *M. c. bureschi*, but do not differ from the nominate form.

HABITAT

Mediterranean and mild continental

habitats in cave-rich karst limestone areas with large waterbodies. In the basin of large lowland rivers such as the Rhône, Ebro, Po, Danube and Maritza/Evros and their tributaries with significant riparian woodland, or at large lakes, and over smaller karst limestone rivers with partial underground streams [gen. lit. 96]. Almost exclusively in karst limestone areas. Areas with other geological strata are only populated if underground roosts (mines) are available and are available in the proximity to limestone caves. Hunting grounds particularly over standing or slowly flowing waters and standing water areas of smaller waterways [1]. At the coast often hunts over lagoons, sometimes also over open sea.

Roosts

All year round in caves or mines; there are only a few building roosts known. Single animals can be found in a variety of other roost types such as cracks in bridges, buildings, cellars or larger rock crevices.

BEHAVIOUR

The species forms all year round colonies with dense clusters of 30–500 animals and very often occurs mixed with other cave-dwelling bat species, usually with the Bent-winged Bat. The Long-fingered Bat probably benefits with regards to thermo-regulation from the Schreibers' Bent-winged Bat. In some caves close to optimal hunting habitats (large riparian grasslands, lakes) very large colonies of 5,000–10,000 Long-fingered Bats can be formed; such huge colonies are well known from three Bulgarian caves and from one cave in Albania. Males usually constitute only a small proportion, but occasionally up to a third, of the individuals in large nursery colonies. Males can also form separate clusters of up to several hundred animals [5, own data]. In the winter individually hanging animals occur, but most hibernate in dense clusters. The winter groups can get very large, with concentrations in some winters of 20,000–50,000 animals in the three central Bulgarian winter roosts [Ivanova & Petrov pers. com.].

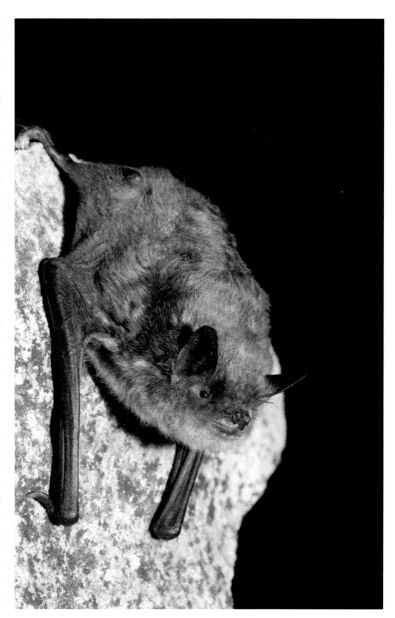

Fig. 321. Long-fingered Bats are mostly grey coloured. Photo: D. Nill.

REPRODUCTION

In Bulgaria births take place from the beginning to the end of May; neonates have a forearm length of 15.5–16mm [own data]. On the Iberian Peninsula the birth period is later [6]. Already at 18 days old, young animals fly in the cave and leave the roost a little later [own data]. The first young animals forage independently by the first 10 days of June, when most other species only begin giving birth [own data]. Thus far, only a few matings were

FOOD

The food consists to a large extent of flies (non-biting midges) and caddis flies. In Spain, fish scales were found in the faeces of four animals, probably from Tooth Carp (Cyprindontidae) and Mosquito Fish (*Gambusia affinis*) [gen. lit. 2]. In Israel, scales and bones of Mosquito Fish were found in 12% of almost 2,000 analysed droppings [3], which indicates regular capture of these fish. Besides the above, mainly non-biting midges but also water boatmen were found, plus small proportions of moths and Hymenoptera [3].

MOBILITY AND MIGRATION

The Long-fingered Bat is a short- to middle-range migrant, but data are exclusively known from the Balkan Peninsula. Animals from widely distributed summer colonies in Bulgaria and northern Greece aggregate in a few (so far three known) large winter colonies of far over 20,000 animals in each. The recorded distances so far are mainly around 100km, the longest distance about 150km [5, own data, Petrov & Ivanova pers. com.]; however, the range of two large winter colonies in the Bulgarian Rhodopian mountains probably extends far into northern Greece and the Bulgarian Maritza plain [5, Petrov pers. com.]. The Long-fingered Bats of the Danube plain hibernate particularly in a cave in the northern Balkan foothills [own data, Petrov & Ivanova *in litt.*].

observed, in Bulgaria at the end of September and early October in caves which are used as winter roosts. The mating system and mechanisms to avoid in-breeding are not well understood; possibly mating takes place particularly in the winter roosts, where animals from numerous summer colonies mix. Up to 70% of the young females give birth in their first year [5, own data]. Males become sexual mature in their second autumn at the age of 1.5 years [5, own data]. Both females and males return at least partly to their nursery area [own data].

FORAGING

Similar to Daubenton's Bat, usually in large circles above water at 10–25cm height. The Long-fingered Bat flies more steadily and in wider circuits than Daubenton's Bat. A located prey is taken from the water surface with the long feet or the end of the tail membrane [9]. The diet also suggests that a substantial portion of the prey is formed of animals swimming immediately below the water surface (fish, water boatmen) [3]. Such prey animals are probably detected if they break through the water surface (for respiration or in flight with water boatmen, air-snatching and/or prey-catching by the Mosquito Fish) [7] and then pulled from the water with the large hind feet. Often up to four, sometimes up to 10, animals hunt over water in the same closely limited area. Apart from the main use of calm water bodies [1, 5], some radio-tracked animals spent part of their hunting time in forests or bushes away from the river [5], capturing food in flight.

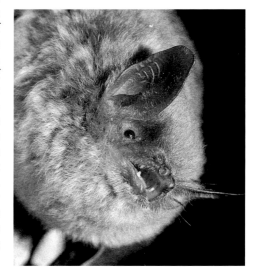

Habitat use

In Spain, hunting grounds lie up to 10km from the roost [1], in Greece sometimes at substantially greater distances of at least 26km (average 13.6km) [5]. Separate hunting grounds have sizes of up to 11ha[1]; up to five of such individual hunting grounds are visited each night [5]. In Greece the species seems to be very mobile; roost changes over distances of up to 39km take place in the summer period [5]. In northern Bulgaria closely neighbouring caves are often used by related groups [own data].

THREATS

Red list of the IUCN 2006: VU (Vulnerable), Red list of the European Union: VU (Vulnerable), EU Habitats Directive, Annex II & IV. Major decline at the northern limits of the range [2, 4, 8], extinct in southern Switzerland and parts of northern Italy [9]. Only a few reproductive colonies left in France and Spain [2, 4, 6]. In Bulgaria there are still large populations, but following crane-fly control and pesticide use with spray planes in agricultural areas, in recent years some traditional roost caves at the northern limit of the distribution were deserted; at present it cannot be determined whether this is a general trend or only a local and/or short-term incident [own data]. In northern Greece, there is a serious pollution impact on hunting grounds of the species, since pesticides are mixed with irrigation sprinkler water and hence directly end up in water bodies [Papadatou pers. com.].

CONSERVATION MEASURES

Abandonment of crane-fly control in damp areas and riparian pastures, restriction of pesticide use in agricultural areas and prevention of aerial drifting of pesticides in damp areas and riparian grasslands (no high-flying spray planes). Protection of colony caves from disturbances and tourist use.

REFERENCES

1. Almenar, D., J. Aihartza, U. Goiti, E. Salsamendi & I. Garin (2006): Habitat selection and spatial use by the trawling bat *Myotis capaccinii. Acta Chiropterologica* 8: 157–167.

2. Cosson, E. (2001): Les Chiroptères de la directive habitats: le murin de Capaccini, *Myotis capaccinii. Arvicola* 13: 31–35.

3. Levin, E., A. Barnea, Y. Yovel & Y. Yom-Tov (2006): Have introduced fish initiated piscivory among the long-fingered bat? *Mamm. Bio.* 71: 139–143.

4. Médard, P. & E. Guibert (1990): Disparition d'un milieu et raréfaction d'une espèce en France: le murin de Capaccini, *Myotis capaccinii. Mammalia* 54: 297–300.

5. Papadatou, E. (2006): *Ecology and conservation of the long-fingered bat* Myotis capaccinii *in the National Park of Dadia-Lefkimi-Soufli, Greece.* PhD-thesis at the University of Leeds.

6. Serra-Cobo, J. (1992): Contribution to the

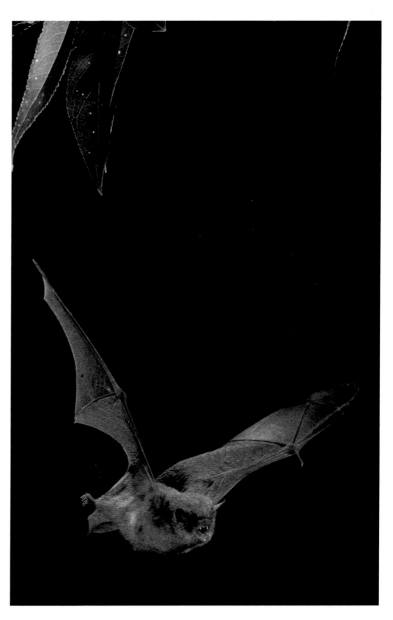

Fig. 324. Long-fingered Bat in flight. The species shows a similar hunting behaviour to Daubenton's Bat; prey is seized with the large feet from the water surface. Photo: D. Nill.

Fig. 325. The Long-fingered Bat forms large colonies in caves and usually hangs mixed with other species, here with Lesser Mouse-eared Bats. Photo: C. Dietz.

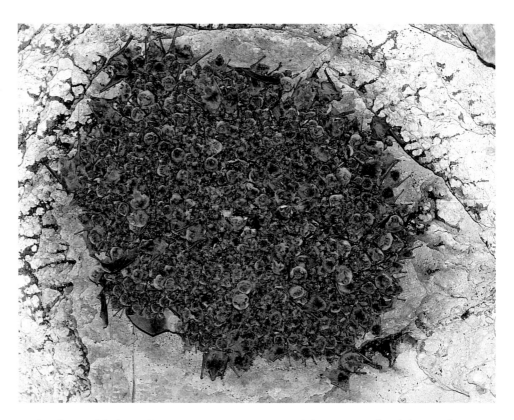

chorology and biology of *Myotis capaccinii* in Spain. *Prague Studies in Mammalogy*: 183–188.

7. Siemers, B.M., P. Stilz & H.-U. Schnitzler (2001): The acoustic advantage of hunting at low heights above water: behavioural experiments on the European 'trawling' bats *Myotis capaccinii*, *M. dasycneme* and *M. daubentonii*. *J. Exp. Biol.* 204: 3843–3854.

8. Spitzenberger, F. & A. Mayer (1988): Aktueller Stand der Kenntnis der Fledermausfauna Osttirols und Kärntens; zugleich Mammalia austriaca 14 (*Myotis capaccinii, Pipistrellus kuhli* und *Pipistrellus savii*). *Ann. Nat. Hist. Mus. Wien* 90 B: 69–91.

9. Spitzenberger, F. & O. von Helversen (2001): *Myotis capaccinii*, Langfußfledermaus. In: F. Krapp (ed.): *Handbuch der Säugetiere Europas*, 4–I: 281–302; Aula Verlag.

Brandt's Bat
Myotis brandtii
(Eversmann, 1845)

NAMES

D:	Brandtfledermaus
F:	Vespertilio de Brandt
E:	Murciélago de Brandt
I:	Vespertilio di Brandt
NL:	Brandts vleermuis
S:	Brandts fladdermus
PL:	Nocek Brandta

IDENTIFICATION

A small bat with long ears. The relatively long fur in older animals is light brown, mostly with gold-shining tips; the ventral side is not clearly demarcated from the dorsal side and is light grey coloured, with a slightly yellowish tinge. The bare skin areas are brownish. The 'typical' appearance of Brandt's Bats is only reached at the age of approximately seven years: from the almost black '*mystacinus*-like' young animals, from year to year they become increasingly brighter; older animals finally showing light-golden hair tips and pale skin parts [6]. The lower part of the tragus and the ear, particularly inside the auricle near the base, is paler. The nostrils of Brandt's Bat are usually wide heart-shaped; in the Whiskered Bat the rear end is usually very narrow. The penis of adult males is obviously club-shaped at the end; in juvenile males it is already thicker than in the Whiskered Bat. A reliable identification is possible on the basis of tooth characteristics: the large upper premolar (P4) has a clear cingulum cusp (protocone), which often reaches the height of the smaller premolar (P3). The two small upper premolars (P2+3) are almost equal in size. Of the two small lower premolars (P2+3) the second one reaches at least two-thirds of the height of the first one. The upper molars (M1−3) have small but clearly visible cusps (protoconules) until the dentition gets worn.

Similar species

The Alcathoe Whiskered, Whiskered and Steppe Whiskered Bat can be clearly distinguished from Brandt's Bat by the thin penis. The tooth characteristics exclude Whiskered and the Steppe Whiskered Bat, which have a tall protocone only in the rarest cases. The protoconules are almost absent in the Whiskered and Steppe Whiskered Bat or are small and inconspicuous [11]. The second small premolars (P3 and P3) in the Whiskered and Steppe Whiskered Bat are clearly smaller than the first ones, often slightly displaced inwards from the tooth row. The Alcathoe Whiskered Bat has similar tooth characteristics to Brandt's Bat, but is smaller. Daubenton's Bat has very large feet and a shorter tragus; Geoffroy's Bat has an almost perpendicular notch at the outer edge of the ear.

ECHOLOCATION CALLS

Mostly 4–7ms-long frequency-modulated calls, which drop from about 100kHz to 26kHz. Some calls end above 30kHz. The calls of the Whiskered Bat are very similar.

DISTRIBUTION

Particularly in Central and northern Europe, in Scandinavia and Russia to 65°N

Measurements	
Forearm	33.0–38.2mm
Fifth finger	40–49mm
Third finger	48–61mm
Normal weight	5–7g
CBL	12.8–14.2mm
CM3	5.0–5.7mm

Fig. 326. This subadult male Brandt's Bat shows the typical juvenile fur with dark face and dark ears. Photo: C. Dietz.

Fig. 327. The base of the ear of older Brandt's Bats is usually clearly lighter. Photo: C. Dietz.

and therefore further north than the Whiskered Bat [3]. Not recorded thus far from wide areas of western Europe (western France) and the Mediterranean area. Several records known from Ireland. In the Balkans distributed very discontinuously and limited to the mountains (the Balkans, Rhodopians, Carpathians). The distribution in south and southeast Europe is, in general, insufficiently known. The main distribution extends in a wide area of Russia up to the Urals and further eastward. The eastern distribution border is unclear, possibly through confusion with *M. gracilis*. Isolated occurrence in the Caucasus.

Subspecies and geographical variation
In the geographical scope of this book only the nominate form occurs, the variation within *M. b. brandtii* is extremely small. The eastern forms *gracilis* and *fujiensis* are separate species.

HABITAT
The most important habitat elements of Brandt's Bat are forests and waters. The species is much more strongly linked to forests than Whiskered Bat [9]. It seems mainly to occur in woodland, moorland and in other damp areas, but also in damp ravines and mountain forests to high altitudes of over 1,500m. Apart from forest biotopes (deciduous, mixed and coniferous forests) tree lines and hedges play an

important role as hunting grounds. In southeast Europe the species seems to occur almost only in mountain to high mountain forests up to the tree line but rarely in riparian forests; in northern Europe a broader habitat range is used.

Roosts
Summer roosts in tree holes, trunk cracks and behind peeling bark as well as in bat boxes. Also in crevices of wooden building cladding and in crevices in roof spaces, here often under roof boarding, between timbers, or in spaces between adjacent beams and rafters [5]. Building roosts are usually situated very close to forest edges [8] or in structure-rich areas within direct reach of linear woodland elements and forests. They switch between neighbouring tree roosts [2]. Winter roosts in caves and mines, rarely in mountain cellars.

BEHAVIOUR
Nursery colonies usually comprise 20–60 females. However, a number of roosts with over 200 animals are known [5]. In bat boxes usually colonies of approximately 20 females, and mixed colonies with Nathusius's and Soprano Pipistrelles are possible [7]. In winter roosts usually single animals hang free or in crevices; larger groups of Brandt's Bats are not known outside central Siberia [gen. lit. 66].

REPRODUCTION
The birth of the single young takes place from the beginning to the end of June in Central Europe; neonates have a forearm length of approximately 13mm. At the age of three weeks the first flights take place, with independent foraging flights at four weeks. Soon afterwards the young become independent, so at the end of July the nursery colonies disperse. The young females become sexual mature only in the second year [6]. From the beginning of August mainly males are present at swarming sites; mating probably takes place here and in the winter roosts.

FORAGING
Very agile flight in light riparian or beech

and oak tree forests, over water or along associated vegetation. The wing morphology and the associated flight abilities hardly differ from those of Whiskered Bat [4]. The flight altitude varies, often close to the ground vegetation, up to the crown of trees. Like Geoffroy's Bat it frequently shows an undulating flight. Brandt's Bat hunts over water, similar to Daubenton's Bat, but normally higher above the water surface.

FOOD

The majority of the food consists of moths, spiders, Diptera (crane-flies, non-biting midges and other flies) [10]. With an average prey size of 7.3mm, the prey size of the Whiskered Bat (7.5mm) cannot be differentiated [10]. At least locally and seasonally, non-flying prey such as spiders, harvestmen and earwigs can constitute the main part of the diet [2].

MAXIMUM AGE

The maximum age of ringed animals in Europe is 25.5 and 28.5 years [5]. In Central Siberia in the 1960s–1970s over 1,500 Brandt's bats were ringed. Recently, recoveries became known from animals ringed at that time, and ringed males had reached the record age of 38 and 41 years [gen. lit. 66, 95].

MOBILITY AND MIGRATION

Brandt's Bat is to a large extent sedentary and the seasonal migration distance is usually below 40km. At least five recoveries of over 100km are known [1, 5], the two longest being 308km in eastern Germany [gen. lit. 139] and 618km from Lithuania to the Czech Republic.

Habitat use

Up to 13 hunting grounds of 1–4ha are used within up to 10km from the roost [2], in this way a colony can use an area of over 100km² [2]. In open landscape, the flight paths follow guiding linear structures such as windbreaks or stream courses.

THREATS

Red list of the IUCN 2006: LC (Least Concern), Red list of the European Union:

Fig. 328. Habitat of Brandt's Bat. The species especially hunts in damp areas and beech forests. Photo: D. Nill.

VU (Vulnerable), EU Habitats Directive, Annex IV. Within wide areas clearly rarer than the Whiskered Bat (*c.* 9:1). In the past, habitat destruction, particularly such activities as large-scale destruction of riparian and mountain forests, had a negative impact. Beside this, there are, nowadays, direct threats, such as the destruction of roosts through redevelopment works or by forestry. Isolation of foraging units could be a further serious threat.

Distributed throughout England and Wales and just reaching southern Scotland; recently first recorded from Ireland but subsequently a few further records. Widely recorded in small numbers in hibernation sites (where difficult to separate from Whiskered Bat without disturbance); rarely possible to identify specifically in the field

Fig. 329. Brandt's Bat usually hunts close to the vegetation. Photo: D. Nill.

with a bat detector and relatively few summer maternity colonies known [UK gen. lit. 153, 155]. Subject of a recent comparison with Whiskered Bat by L. Berge, looking at foraging habitat and behaviour, diet [see UK gen. lit. 155], roost characteristics, and morphological and DNA discrimination of species. Most results not yet published. Included in hibernation site data collected by the National Bat Monitoring Programme, where usually recorded as Whiskered/Brandt's. Also found during autumn swarming at underground sites but usually in small numbers.

CONSERVATION MEASURES
Maintenance of damp areas and semi-natural forests and their connection by windbreaks and hedges. Avoidance of habitat fragmentation e.g. by roads. Re-establishment of linkages between habitat units. Protection of colony sites.

REFERENCES
1. Blohm, T. & G. Heise (2003): Zweiter Fernfund einer im Sommer in der Uckermark beringten Großen Bartfledermaus (*Myotis brandtii*). *Nyctalus* (N.F.) 9: 85.
2. Dense, C. & U. Rahmel (2002): Untersuchungen zur Habitatnutzung der Großen Bartfledermaus (*Myotis brandtii*) im nordwestlichen Niedersachsen). *Schriftenreihe für Landschaftspflege und Naturschutz* 71: 51–68.
3. Gerell, R. (1987): Distribution of *Myotis mystacinus* and *Myotis brandtii* in Sweden. *Z. Säugetierk.* 52: 338–341.
4. Jones, G. (1991): Hibernal ecology of whiskered bats (*Myotis mystacinus*) and Brandt's bats (*Myotis brandti*) sharing the same roost site. *Myotis* 29: 121–128.
5. Kraus, M. (2004): Große Bartfledermaus, *Myotis brandtii*. In: A. Meschede & B.-U. Rudolph (eds): *Fledermäuse in Bayern*: 144–154; Ulmer Verlag.
6. Ohlendorf, B., B. Hecht & J. Haensel (2001): Zur Einstufung des Alters der Großen Bartfledermaus (*Myotis brandtii*) in Sachsen-Anhalt. *Nyctalus* (N.F.) 7: 504–516.
7. Ohlendorf, L., B. Ohlendorf & B. Hecht (2002): Beobachtungen zur Ökologie der Großen Bartfledermaus (*Myotis brandtii*) in Sachsen-Anhalt. *Schriftenreihe für Landschaftspflege und Naturschutz* 71: 69–80.
8. Sachanowicz, K. & I. Ruczynski (2001): Summer roost sites of *Myotis brandtii* (Chiroptera, Vespertilionidae) in Eastern Poland. *Mammalia* 65: 531–535.
9. Taake, K.-H. (1984): Strukturelle Unterschiede zwischen den Sommerhabitaten von Kleiner und Großer Bartfledermaus (*Myotis mystacinus* und *M. brandti*) in Westfalen. *Nyctalus* (N.F.) 2: 16–32.
10. Taake, K.-H. (1992): Strategien der Ressourcennutzung an Waldgewässern jagender Fledermäuse. *Myotis* 30: 7–74.
11. Taake, K.-H. (1997): Artbestimmung weiblicher Bartfledermäuse (*Myotis mystacinus/brandti*). *Nyctalus* (N.F.) 6: 318.
12. Tupinier, Y. (2001): *Myotis brandtii*, Große Bartfledermaus (Brandtfledermaus). In: F. Krapp (ed.): *Handbuch der Säugetiere Europas* 4–I: 345–368; Aula Verlag.

Fig. 330. At several years old, Brandt's Bats have a pale face and ears and resemble Daubenton's Bat. Photo: D. Nill.

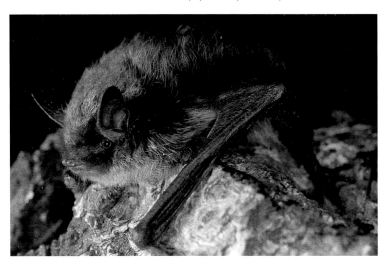

Whiskered Bat
Myotis mystacinus
(KUHL, 1817)

NAMES
D: Bartfledermaus
F: Murin à mustaches
E: Murciélago bigotudo
I: Vespertilio mustacchino
NL: Baardvleermuis
S: Mustaschfladdermus
PL: Nocek waşatek

GENERAL INFORMATION
The name 'whiskered' bat has been applied for decades to a very difficult group, which is characterised by a high variation between different populations and pronounced differences between adult fur colouring. The wide variation in measurements and other characteristics make not only the identification but also the systematic classification more difficult. Benda & Tsytsulina carried out a comprehensive revision in 2000 [gen. lit. 9]. The new description of the Alcathoe Whiskered Bat [gen. lit. 52] revealed that the Balkan Whiskered Bats belong with considerable certainty to the Whiskered Bat [gen. lit. 79], while the discovery of the true Steppe Whiskered Bats in Bulgaria [own data, gen. lit. 77] showed that a comprehensive taxonomic understanding of the 'whiskered' bats has not yet been achieved. One should, therefore, note that probably further more extensive changes can be expected.

IDENTIFICATION
A small and very lively bat with dark, often black face and ears, and with a long tragus. The frizzy fur on the back is dark-brown or nut-brown coloured, with some animals showing bright, reddish or golden hair tips. The ventral side varies markedly in different shades of grey. Young animals can have a dark brown-black or dark grey-brown dorsal fur. The penis is evenly narrow for the whole length. The Balkan Whiskered Bat (*M. m. bulgaricus*) is altogether somewhat larger, often with higher-contrasted colouring and the skin parts are often paler. The feet are clearly larger than those in the nominate form (up to 8.7mm); these animals look similar to Brandt's Bat. The Iberian Whiskered Bat (*M. m. occidentalis*) is likewise larger than the nominate form and more brightly coloured.

Similar species
Very similar to the Steppe Whiskered, Alcathoe Whiskered, and Brandt's Bat. The Steppe Whiskered Bat is so far known only from Bulgaria, probably also in Romania, Moldova and the Ukraine, but confirmed identification from external characteristics is not yet possible. The Alcathoe Whiskered Bat is smaller; in particular the tragus, tibia, foot and thumb are shorter. The males of Brandt's Bat have a clearly bulbous penis. Females can be clearly differentiated from the dentition: Brandt's Bats have a high protocone on the large upper premolar (P^4) and small protoconules on the molars (M^{1-3}), which are almost always missing in the Whiskered Bat.

ECHOLOCATION CALLS
The 3–6ms-long frequency-modulated calls start at 75–120kHz and end mostly

Measurements	
Forearm	32.0–36.5mm
Fifth finger	38–46mm
Third finger	48–58mm
Thumb	4.3–5.9mm
Tibia	14.6–16.8mm
Foot	5.8–7.4mm
Normal weight	4–7g
CBL	12.2–13.3mm
CM³	4.7–5.3mm

In *M. m. bulgaricus* and *M. m. occidentalis* all the measurements can be a little larger.

Fig. 331. A one-year-old female Whiskered Bat with dark face and ear colouring typical of many Central European animals. Photo: C. Dietz.

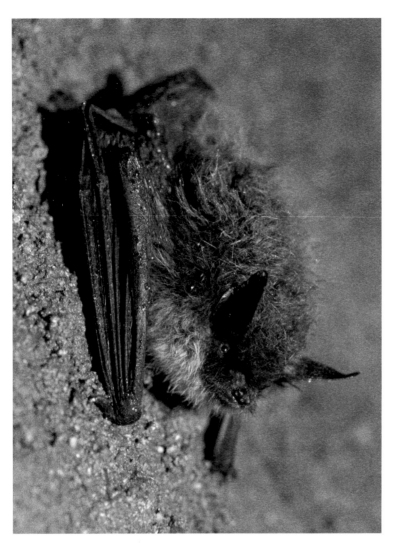

Fig. 332. Whiskered Bats have relatively long fur that often looks tousled in hibernation. Photo: D. Nill.

Subspecies and geographical variation

The subspecies *M. m. occidentalis* occurs on the Iberian Peninsula and in Morocco, and is larger than the nominate form [gen. lit. 9, but see 8 here]. *M. m. mystacinus* is distributed in Central and northern Europe up to the Balkan Peninsula. On the Balkan Peninsula and in Asia Minor the Balkan Whiskered Bat *M. m. bulgaricus* (sometimes confused with the Steppe Whiskered Bat [gen. lit. 9]) occurs, but it belongs genetically to the Whiskered Bat [gen. lit. 77]. *M. m. caucasicus* occurs in the Caucasus region [gen. lit. 9]. The large variation in colour and size characteristics makes a practical separation of subspecies more difficult. With a direct comparison between the Iberian, Central European and Bulgarian/Greek animals the former subspecies classification is convincing anyway; however, in Central Europe, beside the typical *mystacinus* animals that have a strong resemblance (also genetically) to *occidentalis* also occur, and in the Balkans *bulgaricus* and *mystacinus* occur, together with the Steppe Whiskered Bat, Brandt's Bat and Alcathoe Whiskered Bat [own data]. Without a comprehensive analysis of the group with genetic, morphologic and ecological data from a large sample across a geographical axis over the whole of Europe no clarification will be possible. Other as yet not clearly classified species/subspecies occur in Asia.

slightly above 30kHz, on rare occasions they drop to 28kHz. The calls are very similar to those of Brandt's Bat and the Steppe Whiskered Bat.

DISTRIBUTION

From Morocco throughout Europe to 64°N and so into southern Scotland and southern Scandinavia. No records from southern Italy and Sicily. In Denmark only on Bornholm. Widely distributed on the Balkan Peninsula. The eastern distribution border is largely unknown due to confusion with the Steppe Whiskered Bat. There are confirmed records from the Caucasus, the Turkish west coast and Israel [gen. lit. 77, Mayer pers. com.].

HABITAT

In Central Europe a bat of open and semi-open landscapes with isolated patches of woodland and hedges. Frequently in villages and their surroundings (meadows with fruit trees, gardens) as well as in damp areas and in richly structured small-scale landscapes. Forests are also used as hunting grounds, often along stream courses and other waterbodies. Forests play a significant role, particularly in southern Europe. Occurs from plains into mountains, in urbanised sites and on mountain meadows up to the tree line. The Balkan Whiskered Bat occurs particularly in riparian woods and at waterbodies at all altitudes.

Roosts

Summer roosts often in spaces in houses, such as window shutters, cladding or other cracks and gaps, also in other situations such as behind peeling bark or in hunting towers. In the Balkans nursery roosts also in bridges. Roosts in tree holes or in rock crevices are rarely observed. Isolated animals have a wide range of roosts: in winter in caves, mines and mountain cellars, rarely in rock crevices.

BEHAVIOUR

Nursery colonies comprise 20–60, rarely to several hundred, females, males usually spending the summer individually. In southeast Europe the nursery colonies of the Balkan Whiskered Bat are usually smaller (2–10 females) and mixed with males. The roost site is changed frequently, every 10–14 days, and in longer-occupied roosts there is a pronounced exchange of individuals. Window shutter roosts are also changed during the day, in order to ensure optimal temperatures. Nursery colonies often mixed with pipistrelle bats and single animals of other species. From the beginning of August one of the numerous swarming species at caves. While in most bat species adult males dominate clearly in swarms, the sex ratio in Whiskered Bats is almost balanced, but the number of young animals is high. In the winter roosts mostly individuals, just a few roosts known with over 100 animals. Often

Fig. 333. The Whiskered Bat, here a juvenile, is the smallest bat species in Central Europe. Photo: D. Nill.

hangs free during hibernation, but also in narrow crevices or ground rubble.

REPRODUCTION

Females can give birth in their first year. The birth of one, in rare cases of two, young takes place from the middle to the end of June. In the Balkan Whiskered Bat no females with twins were observed so far

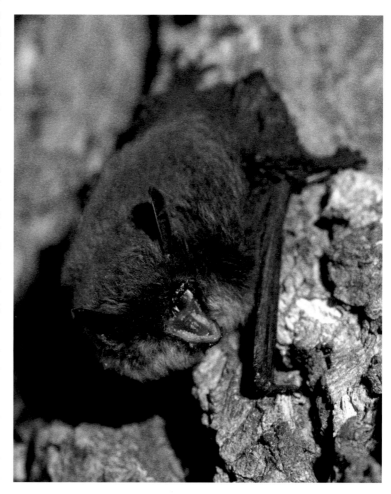

Fig. 334. Whiskered Bats have a lively temper and threaten with loud screaming at the slightest disturbance. Photo: D. Nill.

[own data]. At birth the forearm length is approximately 13mm and weight 2g. The nursery colonies disperse at the latest in August. Mating occurs in the male roosts, at swarming sites, or in the winter roosts into the early spring.

FORAGING

Hunting takes place in very manoeuvrable flight along vegetation edges such as hedges or forest edges. Also in areas with open stands of trees such as orchards in meadows. Often at heights of 1–6m, also into the crown area of trees. Over water, calm water areas are preferred. While the Central European Whiskered Bats hunt particularly over very small waterbodies, the Balkan Whiskered Bat seems to be more strongly associated with larger calm waterbodies, over which it can hunt for hours in wide circuits. Foraging on flying prey is the general rule, but prey can also be collected close to vegetation or taken from surfaces.

FOOD

The diet is markedly broad, but in particular includes flying insects such as Diptera (crane-flies, window-flies, mosquitoes, non-biting midges, black-flies), moths, Hymenoptera and lacewings [5]. In addition, numerous other groups of insects have been identified, which locally can constitute a larger proportion of the prey: e.g. beetles [5, 6] and non-flying arthropods such as spiders or caterpillars. The average prey size is about 7.5mm [6].

MAXIMUM AGE

The maximum age is over 23 years [7]; the average age of 3.5–5 years is substantially lower. The mortality rate of young animals is six times higher than that of adults [gen. lit. 130].

MOBILITY

Due to possible confusion with Brandt's Bat many former ringing results are not absolutely reliable as to which species was actually ringed. The Whiskered Bat seems, however, with considerable certainty to be sedentary or only a short-range (<50–100km) migrant. There are only four

Fig. 335. Whiskered Bat in flight. Photo: D. Nill.

Fig. 336. On the Balkan Peninsula the Whiskered Bats are larger and more brightly coloured than in Central Europe and have larger feet; their systematic position is still under discussion. Probably they represent their own subspecies, the Balkan Whiskered Bat. Photo: C. Dietz.

records of flights over 150km, of which the longest was in France, with 625km [3].

Habitat use

Uses up to 12 separate hunting territories at distances of up to 2.8 km from the roost [1].

THREATS

Red list of the IUCN 2006: LC (Least Concern), EU Habitats Directive, Annex IV.

The populations in Germany and Great Britain seem to be stable. Locally a significant decline through the loss of village roost structures by renovation of buildings and through new housing development in areas with open orchards in meadows.

Distributed throughout England and Wales and southern Scotland; widely but sparsely recorded from Ireland. Widely recorded in small numbers in hibernation

Fig. 337. A female Whiskered Bat more than one year old from Central Europe: the base of the ear and tragus are usually a little pale. Photo: C. Dietz.

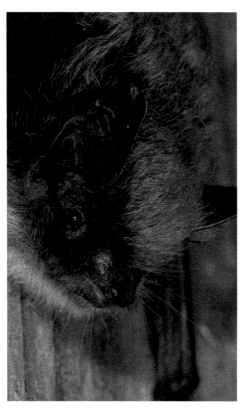

REFERENCES

1. Cordes, B. (2004): Kleine Bartfledermaus – *Myotis mystacinus*. In: A. Meschede & B.-U. Rudolph (eds): *Fledermäuse in Bayern*: 155–165; Ulmer Verlag.
2. Häussler, U. (2003): Kleine Bartfledermaus, *Myotis mystacinus*. In: M. Braun & F. Dieterlen (eds.): *Die Säugetiere Baden-Württembergs, Band 1: Allgemeiner Teil, Fledermäuse (Chiroptera)*: 406–421; Ulmer Verlag.
3. Heymer, A. (1964): Résultats du baguage de chauves-souris dans les Pyrénées-orientales de 1945 à 1959. *Vie et Milieu* A 15: 765–799.
4. Hübner, G. (2001): Phänologische Beobachtungen an einem Wochenstubenstandort der Kleinen Bartfledermaus (*Myotis mystacinus*). *Nyctalus* (N.F.) 7: 603–610.
5. Rindle, U. & A. Zahn (1997): Untersuchungen zum Nahrungsspektrum der Kleinen Bartfledermaus (*Myotis mystacinus*). *Nyctalus* (N.F.) 6: 304–308.
6. Taake, K.-H. (1992): Strategien der Ressourcennutzung an Waldgewässern jagender Fledermäuse. *Myotis* 30: 7–74.
7. Tupinier, Y. & V. Aellen (2001): *Myotis mystacinus*, Kleine Bartfledermaus (Bartfledermaus). In: F. Krapp (ed.): *Handbuch der Säugetiere Europas* 4–I: 321–344; Aula Verlag.

ADDITIONAL REFERENCES

8. Garcia-Mudarra, J.L., C. Ibanez & J. Juste (2009): The Straits of Gibraltar: barrier or bridge to Ibero-Moroccan bat diversity. *Biological Journal of the Linnaean Society* 96: 434–450.

sites (where difficult to separate from Brandt's Bat without disturbance); rarely possible to identify specifically in the field with a bat detector and relatively few summer maternity colonies known [UK gen. lit. 153, 155]. Subject of a recent comparison with Brandt's Bat by L. Berge (see under that species). Included in hibernation site data collected by the National Bat Monitoring Programme, where usually recorded as Whiskered/Brandt's. Also found during autumn swarming at underground sites but usually in small numbers.

CONSERVATION MEASURES

Maintenance of colony sites. Maintenance of structure-rich connections of urban sites with the surrounding countryside by wind breaks, encouragement and maintenance of small-scale and extensive agriculture with grassland, hedges and meadows with open stands of fruit trees and maintenance of damp areas.

Asiatic Whiskered Bat
Myotis nipalensis
(DOBSON, 1871)

Myotis nipalensis was recognised as a species by Benda & Tsytsulina [gen. lit. 9] and is widely distributed in Asia, west to the Caucasus (Azerbaijan, Georgia) and northwest Turkey. It is a medium-sized, rather pale-coloured member of the *M. mystacinus* group but really only separable on features of the skull and dentition, penis and baculum. Almost nothing is known of its behaviour or requirements.

Steppe Whiskered Bat
Myotis aurascens
Kuzjakin, 1935

NAMES
  D: Steppen-Bartfledermaus
  F: Murin doré
  NL: Steppebaardvleermuis

GENERAL INFORMATION

In 2000, Benda & Tsytsulina published a comprehensive revision of the 'whiskered' bats of the western Palaearctic region [gen. lit. 9]. They concluded that a subspecies of the Whiskered Bat occurring in the Caucasus is morphologically so different that it should have the status of a separate species: *Myotis aurascens*. Due to the prevailing habitat choice in Asia it was named Steppe Whiskered Bat [gen. lit. 9]. Unfortunately they also ascribed the 'whiskered' bats occurring in southeast Europe to the Steppe Whiskered Bat, which would thereby be distributed over the entire Balkan Peninsula and along the Adriatic coast into north Italy [1, 2, gen. lit. 9]. Genetic analyses could not show specific differences between Central European whiskered bats and the alleged Steppe Whiskered Bats in the Balkans [gen. lit. 79]. Only with extensive DNA analyses [general lit. 77] did it become clear that the true Steppe Whiskered Bat of the Caucasus differs from the Balkan Whiskered Bats, which are a subspecies of the Whiskered Bat: *Myotis mystacinus bulgaricus*. This means that animals which were previously named as *Myotis aurascens* in Europe are, with considerable certainty, Balkan Whiskered Bats *Myotis mystacinus bulgaricus*. Thus it was the more surprising that extensive genetic analyses [gen. lit. 77] revealed that there are, nevertheless, genuine Steppe Whiskered Bats in northern Bulgaria, for which DNA sequences agree with those of the Caucasian *Myotis aurascens*. The actual distribution of the Steppe Whiskered Bat in Europe is unknown and is, thus far, limited to an area approximately 20km^2 in the Bulgarian Danube plain [own data].

INDENTIFICATION

In order to avoid confusion with the distinctly similar Balkan Whiskered Bat, the measurements of four individuals, clearly identified and supported with genetic methods, are given below. These do not cover a reliable full range of variation in the species, and all data must, therefore, be regarded as provisional. One of the bats was ringed as a young animal and recovered in the same summer and again three years later. The Steppe Whiskered Bat looks very

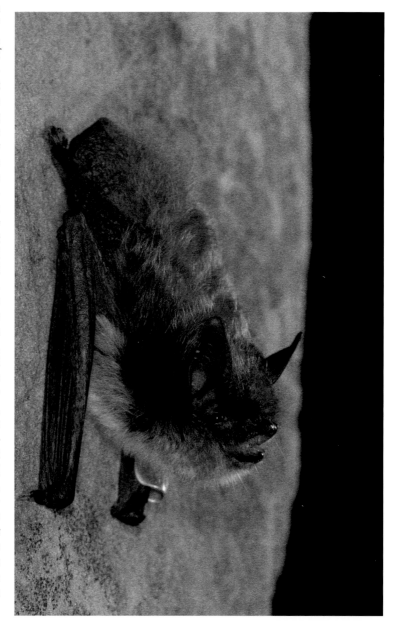

Fig. 338. The Steppe Whiskered Bat looks similar to the sympatrically occurring Balkan Whiskered Bats, and for the time being reliable identification is only possible with genetic methods. Photo: C. Dietz.

Measurements

Gender	♂	♂	♀	♀
Age	adult	adult	adult	adult
Reproduction	o	o	pregnant	pregnant
Forearm (mm)	35.0	36.9	36.3	37.5
Fifth finger (mm)	45.2	46.9	47.7	48.2
Third finger (mm)	55.7	57.4	57.8	57.2
Thumb (mm)	5.7	5.8	5.8	5.5
Tibia (mm)	17.3	17.8	17.9	18.1
Foot (mm)	7.4	7.6	7.2	8.1
Weight (g)	6.2	6.0	7.7	8.9

similar to the southeast European subspecies of the Whiskered Bat (*M. mystacinus bulgaricus* = Balkan Whiskered Bat). It similarly exhibits relatively large feet and a 'mixed' skin colouring. The snout of the Steppe Whiskered Bat is shorter and the ears, particularly at the tip, are narrower than those of the Whiskered Bat, the outer edge of the ear seems also to be more strongly convexly curved. At present clear separation from the Whiskered Bat is only possible by genetic methods and perhaps also from provisional comparisons of the skull.

SIMILAR SPECIES
Very similar to Whiskered Bat, reliably distinguished from Brandt's and Alcathoe Whiskered Bat on the basis of the above characteristics.

ECHOLOCATION CALLS
In a spacious flight area a genetically identified animal was observed with approximately 3ms-long frequency-modulated calls starting between 105 and 112kHz and ending between 37 and 43kHz.

DISTRIBUTION
In the geographical scope of this book, the Steppe Whiskered Bat is so far only known from an area of about 20km² in the Bulgarian Danube plain. The species probably occurs from north Bulgaria through eastern Romania and the Ukraine up to the Caucasus. How far the species is distributed to the south and the west cannot be assessed at present. Over 100 analysed tissue samples did not provide evidence for further occurrence in Bulgaria, Greece, Croatia and Hungary. The known range outside our region is limited to the Caucasus region and adjacent ranges of east Turkey and Iran [Tsytsulina *in litt.*].

HABITAT AND ROOSTS
Two nursery roosts are known in Bulgaria in construction joints of bridges at 8–35m height. One animal was captured at its

Fig. 339. The same individual of the Steppe Whiskered Bat as in Fig. 340 at the age of three years. The ear tips are clearly tapered in this species Photo: C. Dietz.

Fig. 340. A juvenile Steppe Whiskered Bat about two months old from northern Bulgaria. Photo: C. Dietz

foraging ground, in open landscape near a river. The site is surrounded by secondary scrub in an extensively pastured area [own data].

BEHAVIOUR, REPRODUCTION AND FOOD

The Steppe Whiskered Bat forms mixed nursery colonies with the Balkan Whiskered Bat, which formed by far the majority. In addition, the roost was shared with Nathusius's Pipistrelles. Captured animals were extraordinarily lively. In the beginning of June the females are clearly visibly pregnant. The food is captured in flight, and the few droppings of the genetically identified animals contained small moths and Diptera (in particular Brachycera, only a few Nematocera) [I. Dietz pers.com.].

THREATS AND CONSERVATION MEASURES

Not yet included in the Red list of the IUCN. No threats are observed for the present known occurrence, except possible redevelopment works at the roost sites. The existing roosts should be protected. The Steppe Whiskered Bat is substantially rarer than the Balkan Whiskered Bat. Among the 21 genetically identified animals from both known nursery colonies three were Steppe Whiskered Bats and 18 Balkan Whiskered Bats.

REFERENCES

1. Benda, P. (2004): *Myotis aurascens* – Steppen-Bartfledermaus. In: F. Krapp (ed.): *Handbuch der Säugetiere Europas*, 4–II: 1149–1158; Aula Verlag.
2. Benda, P. & A. Karataç (2005): On some Mediterranean populations of bats of the M*yotis mystacinus* morpho-group (Chiroptera: Vespertilionidae). *Lynx* n.s. 36: 9–38.
3. Kuzjakin, A.P. (1935): Neue Angaben über Systematik und geographische Verbreitung der Fledermäuse (Chiroptera) der U.d.S.S.R. *Bulletin de la Société des Naturalistes de Moscou, section Biologique*, 44: 428–438.

Armenian Whiskered Bat
Myotis hajastanicus
ARGYROPOULO, 1939

This large member of the *M. mystacinus* group was recognised by Benda & Tsytsulina [gen. lit. 9] and is restricted to the area of Lake Sevan, Armenia. One larger aggregation was recorded in a cave; more recently it has only been found in small numbers (ones and twos) in caves in the vicinity of Lake Sevan. Forearm length 35–37mm, fur colouring quite pale, main identification features are in the skull and dentition.

Alcathoe Whiskered Bat
Myotis alcathoe
HELVERSEN & HELLER, 2001

Measurements

Forearm	30.8–34.6mm
Fifth finger	37–44mm
Third finger	49–56mm
Thumb	3.8–5.0mm
Tibia	13.5–15.9mm
Foot	5.1–5.8mm
Normal weight	3.5–5.5g
CBL	11.7–12.6mm

NAMES
D: Nymphenfledermaus
F: Murin d'Alcathoe
NL: Nimfvleermuis

GENERAL INFORMATION
From the late 1970s remarkable small 'whiskered' bats that differed from the sympatric Balkan Whiskered Bats were found in shady valleys of forest-rich areas in Greece [gen. lit. 50]. The morphological differences from the Central European whiskered bats were, however, so small that only with the application of genetic methods could it be confirmed that they actually represent a separate species. It was described in 2001 as the Alcathoe Whiskered Bat, *Myotis alcathoe*, with records from Greece and Hungary [gen. lit. 52]. Since then the species has also been found in some other European countries, for example in 2005 it was identified as a new mammal species for Germany [Brinkmann, Niermann, Mayer pers. com.].

IDENTIFICATION
The smallest European *Myotis* species. At first sight it resembles the colouring of a Daubenton's Bat but is, however, clearly smaller. The brown dorsal fur shows a reddish glow in older animals; the ventral side is only a little lighter brown-grey. Younger animals can also be totally grey-brown. In comparison with the Whiskered Bat the feet are noticeable small, the thumbs short and the ears shorter and paler. The short tragus does not reach the notch on the edge of the ear or only scarcely (in the Whiskered, Steppe Whiskered and Brandt's Bat the tragus usually reaches above the notch). The nostrils are usually broad heart shaped, comparable with those of Brandt's Bat. The skin areas are less pigmented in older animals. The edge of the tail membrane near the calcar is often pale. The penis is uniformly narrow or only

Fig. 341. In flight the pale post-calcarial lobe is noticeable in Alcathoe Whiskered Bat. Photo: O. von Helversen.

insignificantly thickened at the end. The large upper premolar (P4) has a distinct protocone, which is often taller than the small premolar (P3) before it. The upper molars (M1–3) have small protoconules in unworn dentition. The large lower premolar (P4) is short in basal cross-section and is rectangular to almost square, and at its interior edge is not emarginated.

Similar species
Very similar to the Whiskered and Brandt's Bat. With the exception of a few large-sized animals from Greece all animals examined so far could be separated on the basis of measurements from Brandt's, Whiskered and Steppe Whiskered Bats: forearm <32.8mm, fifth finger <44mm, third finger <56mm, thumb <4.7mm, tibia <14.8mm, foot <5.6mm. These measurements, in combination with a short pale snout, evenly rounded transition from the skull to the snout, the short tragus and the pale-coloured face and ear, are characteristic of the species. Some Alcathoe Whiskered Bats from Greece with large biometric measurements were as large (within the same array of measurements) as Whiskered Bats from Central Europe, but were smaller than Whiskered Bats occuring sympatrically. Apart from this they showed the full specific characteristics. Clear species identification is possible with genetic characterisation [5, gen. lit. 52, 77].

ECHOLOCATION CALLS
Up to 4ms-long calls which drop on average from 120kHz to 46–43kHz. The high starting frequency and, in particular, the unusually high end frequency seem to be characteristic.

DISTRIBUTION
Originally described on the basis of animals from Greece, and by DNA sequences also found in Hungary [gen. lit. 52], the species is subsequently recorded from other countries: Spain [1], France [3, 4, 7, 8], Switzerland [11], Germany [Brinkmann, Niermann, Schorcht, Sauerbeer, Biedermann, Mayer pers. com.], Poland [Piksa, Bogdanowicz *in litt.*], Slovakia [2], Hungary [gen. lit. 52,

Fig. 342. Two colour varieties of Alcathoe Whiskered Bat: most animals are brown to reddish brown on the back; the greyer animals are probably yearlings. Photo: O. von Helversen.

Estok pers. com.], Bulgaria [9, own data, Petrov pers. com.], Greece [gen. lit. 52, own data], Romania [6], Austria [10], Slovenia [P. Presetnik, C. Dietz & F. Mayer pers. com.], Italy [Russo pers. com] and Albania [Sachanowicz, Ciechanowski, Rachwald *in litt.*]. From most countries only observations of single animals are available so far; the widest distribution and the highest numbers of individuals are recorded in France, northern Hungary and northern Greece. From older literature, data of very small 'whiskered' bats (sometimes identified as *Myotis ikonnikovi*) suggests further occurrence probably exists in Romania, Moldova and the Ukraine. The distribution probably extends through the entire

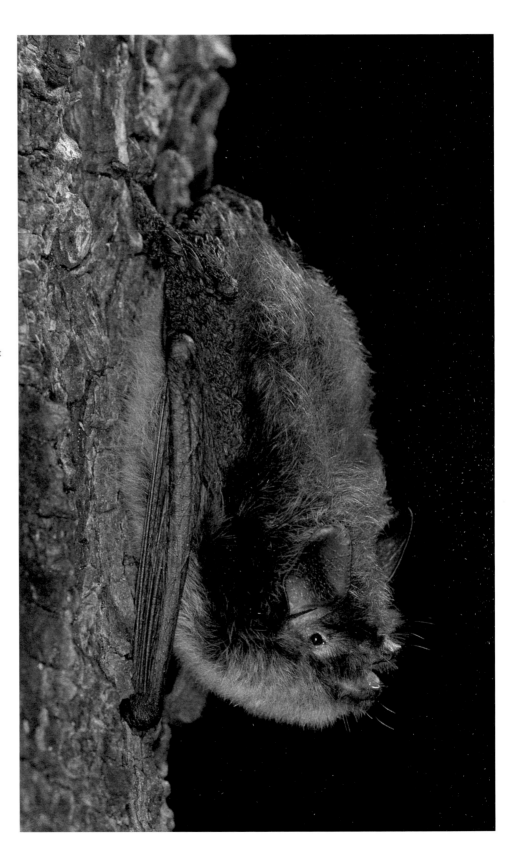

Fig. 343. Alcathoe
Whiskered Bat is reminis-
cent of Daubenton's Bat
with its short pale ears,
short face and the dorsal
colouring; however, the feet
are much smaller. Photo:
C. Dietz.

Mediterranean region, to Central Europe and into the Caucasus region where, however, it may be limited to a few island-like areas. Investigation of hundreds of museum specimens showed that the Alcathoe Whiskered Bat must be rare, since it is almost absent from collections [own data]. While the first record for Germany in 2005 followed the well-known French occurrence nearby in the Rhine Valley [Brinkmann, Niermann, Mayer pers. com.], findings in 2006, well away from this occurrence, in the Kyffhäuser area in Thuringia (Germany) by the Thuringian Working Group for Bat Protection and Research [Schorcht, Sauerbeer, Biedermann, Mayer pers. com.] and in the Tatra Mountains in Poland [Piksa *in litt.*] demonstrate that further attention should be paid to potential occurrence in Central Europe.

HABITAT

Stream courses with dense deciduous woodland areas (alders, planes), riparian hardwood areas (oaks, hornbeams) and mountain forests are characteristic for the species. The animals hunt in more dense vegetation, along richly structured edges and over water, here usually under overhanging branches. Most of the previous-finding sites are in areas that are not much affected by forestry, such as ravines, steep mountain slopes or areas which have been protected for a long time. There is reason to assume that its occurrence is restricted to forest areas unaffected by forestry for centuries.

Roosts

Thus far, only a few roosts of the species are known. Summer roosts are found in cracks in trees; the only nursery colony found so far was in a crack 8m high in a plane tree [5]. Four roosts found by telemetry in the French Jura were in oaks, three of them behind peeling bark of trunks and branches, another in a narrow crack in the trunk [Roué *in litt.*]. All roosts found so far were less than 100m from waterbodies [own data, Roué *in litt.*]. Caves are visited during swarming; all three Bulgarian swarming caves are at altitudes of over

1,400m [9, Petrov *in litt.*]. From France, a winter roost in a cave was described [7] and three other unpublished winter records were noted.

BEHAVIOUR

The species arrives at caves for swarming from early to mid-August, and can be caught here with other *Myotis* species and long-eared bat species. Three of the five known localities in Bulgaria [9] and the only data so far for Switzerland [11] and Slovakia

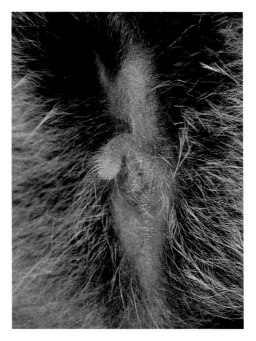

Fig. 344. In this portrait the short pale muzzle with the heart-shaped nostril and short pale ears of Alcathoe Whiskered Bat are visible. Photo: C. Dietz.

Fig. 345. The penis of Alcathoe Whiskered Bat is more or less equally broad for its whole length and thereby differs markedly from the club-shaped penis of Brandt's Bat. Photo: C. Dietz.

[2] were recorded in this way. On the foraging grounds and at swarming sites it usually occurs together with the morphologically similar Whiskered Bat.

REPRODUCTION

So far pregnant females were caught in the second half of June [5, own data], but in a nursery roost in Greece small young animals were found on 17 June [gen. lit. 52]. Mating probably takes place at the swarming sites.

FORAGING AND FOOD

The food is probably caught in flight and from a few analysed droppings consists of Diptera [own data]. Foraging grounds so far identified are banks and still water areas of small streams and mountain brooks, dense riparian vegetation and the lower crown areas of deciduous trees. A radio-tracked animal in the French Jura hunted within 800m of the roost in a riparian forest and along streams and their associated vegetation [Roué pers. com.].

THREATS

Thus far, not yet in the Red list of the IUCN and the European Union as well as in the Natura 2000 appendixes (except in the overall listing in Annex IV). The species can be classified as strongly endangered because of its restricted ecological requirements and its specialisation on old forests, in particular on natural riparian hardwood forests and mountain forests. The Alcathoe Whiskered Bat has little opportunity to settle in new areas due to a very small population density and isolated occurrence. Forest history could be an explanation for the substantially higher population density in France compared with Germany: through historical development many forests were completely cleared in the Middle Ages, and with that major destruction of the habitat of the Alcathoe Whiskered Bat. Only a few riparian and mountain forests remained intact, from which resettlement into modern expanded forests could occur with difficulty. On the other hand, due to the manorial structures in France many forests had sustainable timber use for a long time. Now, in south-east Europe threat exists from timber extraction in mountain forests and habitat fragmentation (forming island habitats). Two of the discovery sites in Greece were destroyed by the construction of dams. The only museum specimen from France so far was a traffic victim on a busy motorway through an extensive deciduous forest area [3].

Fig. 346. The hunting grounds of Alcathoe Whiskered Bat are usually in damp deciduous forests, often over small water bodies with dense overhanging vegetation. Photo: C. Dietz.

CONSERVATION MEASURES

Protection of virgin riparian hardwood forests and other hardwood forests in damp locations with a high proportion of mature timber and dead wood. Protection of old mountain forests with a high proportion of mature timber and dead wood and of richly structured edge habitats. Old forests should be managed by selective felling without clearing. Protection of swarming caves.

REFERENCES

1. Agirre-Mendi, P.T., J.L. Garicia-Mudarra, J. Juste & C. Ibáñez (2004): Presence of *Myotis alcathoe* Helversen & Heller, 2001 (Chiroptera: Vespertilionidae) in the Iberian Peninsula. *Acta Chiropterologica* 6: 49–57.
2. Benda, P., M. Ruedi & M. Uhrin (2003): First record of *Myotis alcathoe* (Chiroptera: Vespertilionidae) in Slovakia. *Folia Zool.* 52: 359–365.
3. Dietz, C. (2004): On a record of *Myotis alcathoe* in the region of Puy-de-Dôme, France. *Le Rhinolophe* 17: 7–10.
4. Groupe Chiroptères Bretagne Vivante (2006): Les chauves-souris de Bretagne. Bretagne Vivante SEPNB, Penn ar Bed 197–198, 68 pp. http://www.bretagne-vivante.asso.fr.
5. Helversen, O. von (2004): *Myotis alcathoe* – Nymphenfledermaus. In: F. Krapp (ed.): *Handbuch der Säugetiere Europas*, 4–II: 1159–1167; Aula Verlag.
6. Jére, C. & A. Dóczy (2007): First record of bat species *Myotis alcathoe* Helversen & Heller, 2001 (Chiroptera, Vespertilionidae) from Romania. *Acta Siculica* 2007: 179–183.
7. Maillard, W. & D. Montfort (2005): Premier signalement du Murin d'Alcathoe, *Myotis alcathoe* en Loire-Atlantiqe (France), et nouvelles observations du Minioptère de Schreibers, *Miniopterus schreibersii*. *Bull. Soc. Nat. Ouest de la France* n.s. 27: 196–198.
8. Ruedi, M., P. Jourde, P. Giosa, M. Barataud & S.Y. Roué (2002): DNA reveals the existence of *Myotis alcathoe* in France (Chiroptera: Vespertilionidae). *Rev. Suisse Zool.* 109: 643–652.
9. Schunger, I., C. Dietz, D. Merdschanova, S. Merdschanov, K. Christov, I. Borissov, S. Staneva & B. Petrov (2004): Swarming of bats (Chiroptera, Mammalia) in the Vodnite Dupki cave (Central Balkan National Park, Bulgaria). *Acta Zoologica Bulgarica* 56: 323–330.
10. Spitzenberger, F., I. Pavlini & M. Podnar (2008): On the occurence of *Myotis alcathoe* von Helversen and Heller, 2001 in Austria. *Hystrix It. J. Mamm.* (n.s.) 19 (1): 3–12.
11. Stadelmann, B., D.S. Jacobs, C. Schoeman & M. Ruedi (2004): Phylogeny of African *Myotis* bats (Chiroptera, Vespertilionidae) inferred from cytochrome b sequences. *Acta Chiropterologica* 6: 177–192.

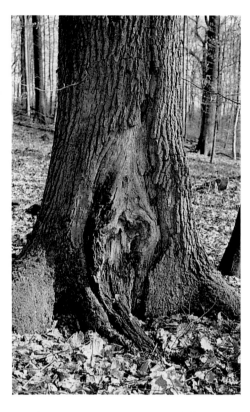

Fig. 347. A roost of up to six Alcathoe Whiskered Bats is behind loose bark and in a finger-wide gap in the lower trunk of an oak. Photo: C. Dietz.

Natterer's Bat
Myotis nattereri
(KUHL, 1817)

NAMES

- D: Fransenfledermaus
- F: Murin de Natterer
- E: Murciélago de Natterer
- I: Vespertilio di Natterer
- NL: Franjestaart
- S: Fransfladdermus
- PL: Nocek Natterera

Measurements

Forearm	34.4–44.0mm
Fifth finger	48–58mm
Third finger	65–74mm
Normal weight	7–10g
CBL	14.0–15.2mm
CM³	5.6–6.3mm

IDENTIFICATION

A medium-sized bat with long ears and a narrow snout. The white to grey-white ventral side is sharply demarcated from the brown-grey dorsal side. The face is usually bare and remarkably brightly pink coloured. The tragus is slightly bent and longer than half the ear length, the ear usually shows 5–6 transverse folds at its outer edge. The tail membrane is supported by a long and S-shaped curved calcar. The wrinkled edge of the tail membrane is densely covered with two rows of short curved bristles.

Similar species

Bechstein's Bat has obviously longer ears, with 9–11 transverse folds, which project more than half beyond the tip of the nose when bent forward, and has a straight calcar. Daubenton's Bat has shorter ears that do not or hardly project beyond the tip of the nose when bent forward, a substantially shorter tragus and a shorter face. Geoffroy's Bat has a distinct, almost perpendicular notch at the outer edge of the ear. No other bat species described so far in the region covered by this book has an S-shaped calcar (see, however, under subspecies).

ECHOLOCATION CALLS

Usually 2–5ms-long frequency-modulated calls, which can start very high (100–150kHz) and drop to approximately 20kHz. With this they reach the audible range of humans and it is possible to hear a very close-flying Natterer's Bat with the naked ear. The extremely broad frequency range usually makes species identification possible.

DISTRIBUTION

Large parts of Europe from 60°N and thus all of Great Britain and southern Scandinavia in the north to the entire Mediterranean area with all large islands (thus far no records from Malta) and northwest Africa (Morocco, Tunisia, Algeria). In the Near East in Israel, Lebanon and Jordan, into Iraq, Iran and Turkmenistan.

Subspecies and geographical variation

In our region only the nominate form. However, the North African and south Iberian populations ascribed so far to Natterer's Bat probably represent an ecologically, morphologically and genetically clearly distinguishable, but not yet formally described, species, for which the name *M. escalerai* has been suggested [gen. lit. 55, 167]. *M. escalerai* is also described from France. In the Southern Alps (Kärnten and South Tyrol) and in the mountains of the Iberian Peninsula a further cryptic sibling species of Natterer's Bat possibly occurs, of which so far, however, only a few DNA sequences but no diagnostic characters are available [25, gen. lit. 77, 167]. The populations of the Near East (*M. n. hoveli*) and east of the Caucasus (*M. n. tschuliensis*) may also possibly represent separate species. In East Turkey and the southern Caucasus region the related *M. schaubi* occurs.

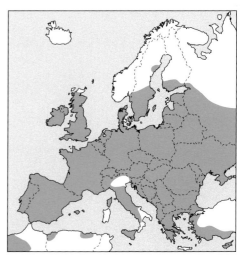

HABITAT

A bat with a very variable habitat use, in Central and northern Europe predominantly in forests and open woodland such as parks and open orchards and along vegetated watersides. Almost all forest types are used, from beech and oak forests up to pure spruce, fir or pine forests. The species occurs from low altitudes to the tree line. Open areas are rarely used, but it can hunt in the vicinity of orchards and forests, and especially over freshly mowed meadows [1, 5]. In the Mediterranean area, forest-like biotopes in the broadest sense, such as olive groves or pasture with trees, are populated.

Roosts

Summer roosts in Central Europe particularly in tree holes and bat boxes, also enters buildings; more frequently, however, in hollow bricks of non-plastered buildings (sheds, silos, garages) [20]. In the Mediterranean area particularly in rock crevices and wall cracks, in southern Spain free hanging clusters on cave ceilings (*escalerai*). Single animals can be found in the entire distribution area in and at trees, cliffs, buildings and in cracks under bridges. Winter roosts in rock crevices, caves, mountain cellars and other underground corridors, also in ground rubble.

BEHAVIOUR

Nursery colonies comprise 20–50 in Central Europe, in building colonies also over 120 animals [5]. The populations of the southern Iberian Peninsula, ascribed to *M. escalerai*, form colonies of several hundred animals in caves [gen. lit. 167]. In Bulgaria the nursery colonies in rock crevices are usually small with 4–10 females [own data]. Mostly, single males are found in the nursery roosts, but they can also form their own colonies of up to 25 animals [21]. The roosting sites are changed every 2–5 days and the size of some colonies varies constantly. Probably it relates, as with Bechstein's Bat, to fission–fusion communities, i.e. a colony divides itself into constantly changing satellite or subcolonies. In buildings and rock roosts the bats often remain

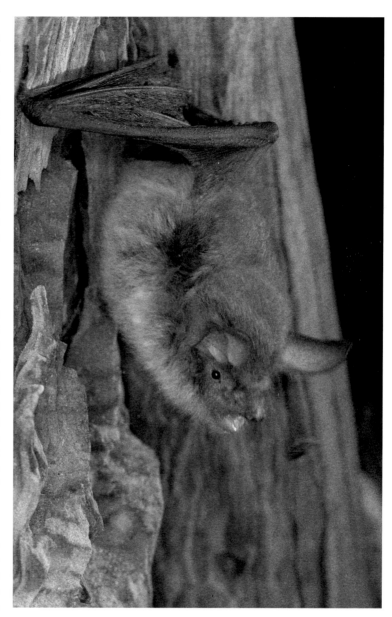

longer within the building or the cliff, but change the actual roost site regularly. Swarming in front of the roosts takes place in the morning, particularly pronouncedly before or after roost changes. Natterer's Bats swarm particularly in September and October at caves [9, 12, 13, 14]; next to Daubenton's Bat and Greater Mouse-eared Bat it is the most frequently captured species during swarming in Central Europe. Natterer's Bats arrive from a very large area of up to 4,100km² [12] to large

Fig. 348. Males of Natterer's Bat usually hang individually in nest boxes, tree holes or in buildings, often hidden in the timberwork. Photo: D. Nill.

Fig. 349. Natterer's Bat can locate and catch prey at a distance of only a few centimetres from the background. Photo: D. Nill.

Fig. 350. Part of a colony of Natterer's Bat. Photo: D. Nill.

caves; males overwhelmingly outnumber females. The largest winter roost (the Spandau citadel in Berlin and the subterranean limestone quarry in Bad Segeberg, Schleswig-Holstein, Germany) includes up to 8,000 animals [4, 10]; however, the estimated numbers from capture and recapture attempts are probably distinctly too high [9]. In mountain cellars and caves usually single animals, in larger caves up to 100 animals.

REPRODUCTION

One young is born between the beginning of June and the beginning of July. Neonates have an average forearm length of scarcely 17mm and a weight of 3.4g [22]. Within approximately 20 days the first flights take place within four weeks the young animals are independent [22] and the nursery colonies then quickly disperse. Females are already sexual mature in the first autumn [3]. Mating takes place both at the swarming sites [13, 14] and in the winter roost [8]. In particular the mating at the swarming sites provides a high genetic mixing of the widely distributed colonies [13, 14].

FORAGING

A very manoeuvrable species, which can fly very slowly and also hover close to ground level. Usually it flies close to vegetation. The prey is often picked off leaves with the tail membrane but can also be caught in flight. It can also land beside located prey and capture this by walking to it [1, 23]. Natterer's Bats also hunt regularly over water. However, feeding takes place mainly by gleaning, including from the ground [23]. Echolocation may help the location of prey if they stand out far enough from the substrate (spiders in the web, harvestmen and crane-flies with their long legs raising them

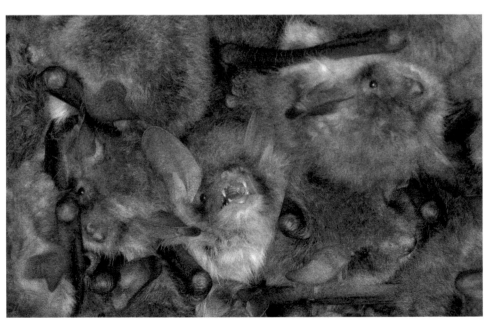

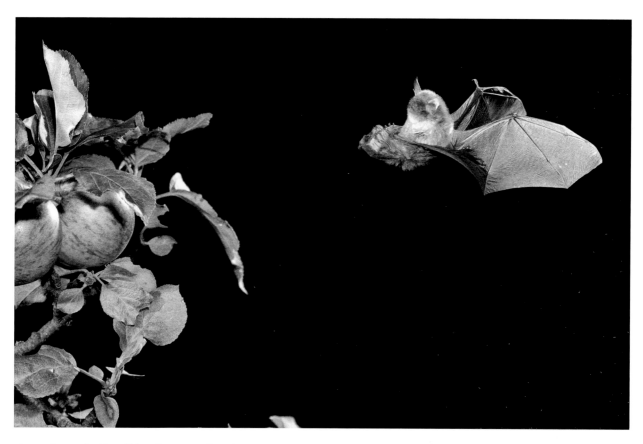

above leaves). Possibly the prey is also caught by trial and error at estimated and/or known places [18]. Day-active flies are caught when the bats approach their nocturnal resting places. Since at least a part of the prey is caught with the tail membrane and from surfaces [1], the suspicion exists that the bristles at the margin of the tail membrane function as sensory organs. As with Geoffroy's Bat, Natterer's Bat also visits cowsheds to hunt for flies. From a comparison of five examined *Myotis* species, Natterer's Bat, with only a 5cm prey–background-distance discrimination, was the species which could locate insects closest to their substrate [17, 19, gen. lit. 125].

FOOD
The food consists, for a considerable part, of non-flying prey such as spiders, harvestmen and flies. Beetles and moths increase seasonally. Some animals have larger portions of centipedes, wood lice, or aquatic insects, such as caddis and stone flies, in their droppings [2, 6, 7, 15, 19].

MAXIMUM AGE
Over 21.5 years [11, gen. lit. 139], with two further marked animals of at least 17.5 years [11, 24].

MOBILITY AND MIGRATION
Usually a sedentary species, but at least some animals accomplish shorter migrations. Distances of over 40km are rare between different separate habitats such as summer, swarming and winter roosts [9]. However, there are also some longer distances of 266–327km known. Swarming sites are visited at distances of 20–60km [12, 14].

Habitat use
In the course of a summer, a nursery colony can use a complex of roost sites in an area of up to 2km² [16, 20]. Hunting grounds cover 170–580ha [5, 16], on average 215ha [5]. Within this area up to six partial foraging grounds of 2–10ha are hunted more intensively. Hunting grounds are up to 4km from the roost [5, 16].

Fig. 351. Natterer's Bat often catches its prey with the tail membrane from the air or from the substrate and can roll completely over in the air. Photo: D. Nill.

Fig. 352. Nursery colony of Natterer's Bat in a bat box. Photo: D. Nill.

internationally important populations of the species. Reported in low numbers in the field from bat detector surveys (probably related to their quiet style of echolocation); relatively few summer colonies known and rate of loss, for example from barn conversions, a cause of concern. Very common at underground autumn swarming sites, usually outnumbering all other species, especially later in the season. A habitat management guidance note published [23]. A recent study by N.M. Rivers has added to the knowledge, especially of seasonal changes in population structure, movements and swarming behaviour; some results already published.

CONSERVATION MEASURES

Protection of colony sites and large swarming roosts as mating sites for maintaining a good genetic mixing. Protection and reconstruction of hedges, wood banks and meadows with fruit trees as connecting elements in fragmented habitats. Protection of structure-rich forest areas. Prevention of fragmentation. Abandon use of pesticide in the wider countryside.

THREATS

Red list of the IUCN 2006: LC (Least Concern), EU Habitats Directive, Annex IV. The Central European population seems to be stable. Due to their feeding habits, apart from Brown Long-eared Bats, Natterer's Bats are the species most frequently found stuck on sticky flypapers.

Widespread in England, Wales and Scotland to a little north of the Great Glen, and in Ireland [UK gen. lit. 153, 155]. Relatively common in underground sites of all types in winter; some sites with large numbers, suggesting that the UK may support

REFERENCES

1. Arlettaz, R. (1996): Foraging behaviour of the gleaning bat *Myotis nattereri* in the Swiss Alps. *Mammalia* 60: 181–186.
2. Beck, A. (1991): Nahrungsuntersuchungen bei der Fransenfledermaus, *Myotis nattereri*. *Myotis* 29: 67–70.
3. Dolch, D. (2003): Langjährige Untersuchungen an einer Wochenstubengesellschaft der Fransenfledermaus, *Myotis nattereri*, in einem Kastenrevier im Norden Brandenburgs. *Nyctalus* (N.F.) 9: 14–19.
4. Eichstädt, H. (1997): Untersuchung zur Ökologie von Wasser- und Fransenfledermäusen (*Myotis daubentoni* und *M. nattereri*) im Bereich der Kalkberghöhlen von Bad-Segeberg. *Nyctalus* (N.F.) 6: 214–228.
5. Fiedler, W., A. Illi & H. Alder-Eggli (2004): Raumnutzung, Aktivität und Jagdhabitatwahl von Fransenfledermäusen (*Myotis nattereri*) im Hegau (Südwestdeutschland) und angrenzendem Schweizer Gebiet. *Nyctalus* (N.F.) 9: 215–235.
6. Geisler, H. & M. Dietz (1999): Zur Nahrungsökologie einer Wochenstubenkolonie der Fransenfledermaus (*Myotis nattereri*) in Mittelhessen. *Nyctalus* (N.F.) 7: 87–101.
7. Gregor, F. & Z. Bauerová (1987): The role of Diptera in the diet of Natterer's bat, *Myotis nattereri*. *Folia Zool.* 36: 13–19.

8. Grimmberger, E. (2002): Zur Paarung der Fransenfledermaus, *Myotis nattereri*, im Winterquartier. *Nyctalus* (N.F.) 8: 396–398.

9. Haensel, J. (2004): Zum saisonbedingten Ortswechsel der Fransenfledermaus (*Myotis nattereri*) im Raum Berlin/Brandenburg unter besonderer Berücksichtigung des Schwärmverhaltens. *Nyctalus* (N.F.) 9: 305–327.

10. Kallasch, C. & M. Lehnert (1995): Zur Populationsökologie von Wasser- und Fransen-fledermäusen (*Myotis daubentoni* und *M. nattereri*) in der Spandauer Zitadelle. *Sitzungsber. Ges. Naturforschende Freunde Berlin, N.F.* 34: 69–91.

11. Ohlendorf, B. (2002): Höchstalter einer Fransenfledermaus (*Myotis nattereri*) im Harz (Sachsen-Anhalt). *Nyctalus* (N.F.) 8: 395–396.

12. Parsons, K.N. & G. Jones (2003): Dispersion and habitat use by *Myotis daubentonii* and *Myotis nattereri* during the swarming season: implications for conservation. *Anim. Conserv.* 6: 283–290.

13. Rivers, N.M., R.K. Butlin & J.D. Altringham (2005): Genetic population structure of Natterer's bats explained by mating at swarming sites and philopatry. *Mol. Ecol.* 14: 4299–4312.

14. Rivers, N.M., R.K. Butlin & J.D. Altringham (2006): Autumn swarming behaviour of Natterer's bats in the UK: population size, catchment area and dispersal. *Biol. Conserv.* 127: 215–226.

15. Shiel, C.B., C.M. McAney & J.S. Fairley (1991): Analysis of the diet of Natterer's bat *Myotis nattereri* and the common long-eared bat *Plecotus auritus* in the West of Ireland. *J. Zool.* 223: 299–305.

16. Siemers, B.M., I. Kaipf & H.-U. Schnitzler (1999): The use of day roosts and foraging grounds by Natterer's bats (*Myotis nattereri*) from a colony in southern Germany. *Z. Säugetierk.* 64: 241–245.

17. Siemers, B.M. & H.-U. Schnitzler (2000): Natterer's bat (*Myotis nattereri*) hawks for prey close to vegetation using echolocation signals of very broad bandwidth. *Behav. Ecol. Sociobiol.* 47: 400–412.

18. Siemers, B.M. (2001): Finding prey by associative learning in gleaning bats: experiments with a Natterer's bat *Myotis nattereri*. *Acta Chiropterologica* 3: 211–215.

19. Siemers, B.M. & S.M. Swift (2006): Differences in sensory ecology contribute to resource partitioning in the bats *Myotis bechsteinii* and *Myotis nattereri* (Chiroptera: Vespertilionidae). *Behav. Ecol. Sociobiol.* 59: 373–380.

20. Smith, P.G. & P.A. Racey (2005): The itinerant Natterer: physical and thermal characteristics of summer roosts of *Myotis nattereri* (Mammalia: Chiroptera). *J. Zool.* 266: 171–180.

21. Swift, S.M. (1997): Roosting and foraging behaviour of Natterer's bats (*Myotis nattereri*) close to the northern border of their distribution. *J. Zool.* 242: 375–384.

22. Swift, S.M. (2001): Growth rate and development in infant Natterer's bats (*Myotis nattereri*) reared in a flight room. *Acta Chiropterologica* 3: 217–223.

23. Swift, S.M. & P.A. Racey (2002): Gleaning as a foraging strategy in Natterers's bat *Myotis nattereri*. *Behav. Ecol. Sociobiol.* 52: 408–416.

24. Topál, G. (2001): *Myotis nattereri*, Fransenfledermaus. In: F. Krapp (ed.): *Handbuch der Säugetiere Europas* 4-I: 405–442; Aula Verlag.

ADDITIONAL REFERENCES

25. Garcia-Mudarra, J.L., C. Ibanez & J. Juste (2009): The Straits of Gibraltar: barrier or bridge to Ibero-Moroccan bat diversity. *Biological Journal of the Linnaean Society* 96: 434–450.

26. Smith, P.G. & P.A. Racey (2002): Habitat Management for Natterer's Bat (*Myotis nattereri*). Mammals Trust UK/ PTES, London. 14pp.

Schaub's Bat
Myotis schaubi
KORMOS, 1934

Originally described from fossil material from Hungary and later recognised as an extant species by Horáček & Hanák [1, see also gen. lit. 55]. It is only known from Armenia and northwest Iran and is very rarely recorded, from very few localities and with no recent records. This is a large relative of Natterer's Bat (*M. nattereri*), with pale fur and wing membranes, and some differences in the skull and dentition. There is no information on its ecology and requirements. The extant form is recognised as a separate subspecies, *M. s. araxenus* (Dahl, 1947).

REFERENCES

1. Horáček, I. and V. Hanák (1984): Comments on the systematics and phylogeny of *Myotis nattereri* (Kuhl, 1817). *Myotis* 21–22: 20–29.

Fig. 353. Natterer's Bat is easily identified from other European bats by the S-shaped curved calcar and the stiff and curved bristles at the free edge of the tail membrane. Photo: C. Dietz.

Geoffroy's Bat
Myotis emarginatus
(GEOFFROY, 1806)

NAMES

- D: Wimperfledermaus
- F: Murin à oreilles échancrées
- E: Murciélago orejirroto
- I: Vespertilio smarginato
- NL: Ingekorven vleermuis
- S: Geoffroys fladdermus
- PL: Nocek orzęsiony

Measurements

Forearm	36.1–44.7mm
Fifth finger	49–58mm
Third finger	59–71mm
Normal weight	6–9g
CBL	14.1–15.2mm
CM³	6.0–6.8mm

IDENTIFICATION

Medium-sized bat with long woolly fur, which is rust-brown to remarkably fox-red coloured on the dorsal side. Ventral side is a poorly delineated pale yellowish brown. Young animals are more grey coloured. The face is light brown, darker in younger animals. The brown ears have a remarkable almost right-angled notch at the outer edge and on the auricle many scattered wart-like growths. The tip of the tragus does not reach the notch on the edge of the ear. The wings are relatively broad and brown coloured. The edge of the tail membrane is supported by a straight calcar and a part has

short, straight soft hairs, which are, however, much thinner and shorter in comparison with Natterer's Bat.

Similar species

At first sight relatively similar to Natterer's Bat. This has, however, a brown-grey dorsal fur, a substantially paler belly, a longer tragus, no perpendicular notch at the outer edge of the ear and an S-shaped calcar.

ECHOLOCATION CALLS

The mostly 1.5–4ms frequency-modulated calls often begin at over 140kHz and end at approximately 38kHz, sometimes at 48kHz, rarely under 30kHz. On the basis of good sound recordings the species can often be clearly identified by the high start and end frequencies.

DISTRIBUTION

Distributed through the entire Mediterranean area including many islands (Sardinia, Corsica, Crete, Cyprus) to Belgium, southern Netherlands and southern Poland. In Germany it occurs only within warm, favourable areas (Rhine Valley, Rosenheimer basin); there exists a remarkable distribution gap between the occurrence in Luxembourg and Poland. From the

Fig. 354. Colonies of Geoffroy's Bat are often in well-lit and little-protected places, such as this cattle shed in the Rhine Valley. Photo: D. Nill.

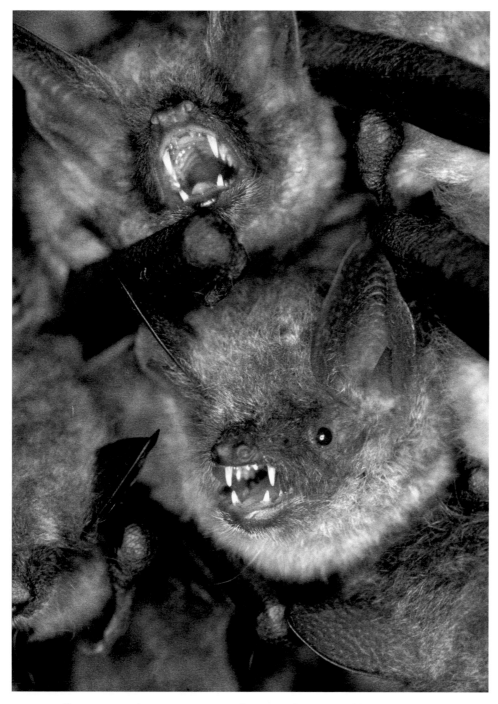

Fig. 355. Geoffroy's Bats can be recognised by the relatively pale face, a distinctive, almost perpendicular, notch in the outer edge of the ear and woolly reddish dorsal fur. Photo: D. Nill.

entire Balkan Peninsula to Romania and parts of the Ukraine (Crimea). In addition in northwest Africa (Morocco, Algeria, Tunisia) and distributed at least on the west and south coast of Asia Minor. Occurs outside the region in the Caucasus, the Near East, the Arabian Peninsula and in Central Asia to Afghanistan.

Subspecies and geographical variation

Within the geographical scope of this book only the nominate form. However, animals from Sardinia are remarkably dark grey

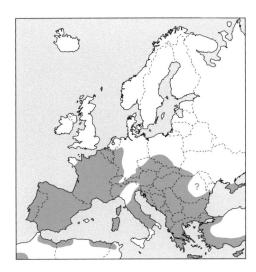

coloured; they lack the otherwise typical red tones in the fur. In the Near East *M. e. desertorum* occurs, and in Central Asia *M. e. saturatus* (= *M. e. turcomanicus?*).

HABITAT

The distribution assumes a certain connection with climatically favourable hardwood forest-rich areas. As hunting grounds hardwood forests, meadows with fruit trees, parks, and wilder gardens are visited [2, 5, 7]. Cattle sheds seem also to be a strong component of hunting grounds in Central Europe and are particularly used during nursing of the young to hunt for flies [2, 7]. With telemetric studies in the Rhine Valley eight of ten animals spent over half of the feeding time in cow sheds [2]. Such records are also known from the Netherlands. In Bulgaria, Geoffroy's Bats can be regularly observed hunting in and around sheep pens [own data]. In general, an high structure richness with many shrubs and deciduous trees seems to be important; coniferous forests are avoided.

Roosts

In the summer in buildings in the north of the distribution area, usually in roofs of churches, private houses and cattle sheds [8]. Relatively bright and cool roofs are occupied [3, 12]. In the south particularly in caves, but some nursery roosts in buildings. Sometimes also small rock niches and rock overhangs are used. Single animals can use

a multiplicity of roosts in roof spaces, outside on buildings [gen. lit. 96], entrances to caves and also in tree holes [7]. In winter in underground roosts, often at relatively high temperatures of 6–12°C.

BEHAVIOUR

In roosts, particularly in the Mediterranean area, frequently together with horseshoe, mouse-eared, Long-fingered and Schreibers' Bent-winged Bats, often in communal clusters. In homogeneous groups relatively tolerant of short-term disturbances. With changes affecting mixed colonies, when the very disturbance-sensitive middle-sized horseshoe bats change their roost site, Geoffroy's Bats will follow them after a few days [own data]. Nursery roosts are occupied over decades and colonies comprise 20–500 females and some adult males. In individual cases, for example in the Bulgarian–Greek border area, nursery colonies of over 7,000 females appear, but do not have a long existence and disperse quickly. Dense clusters are formed in the roosts, in which the animals sometimes hang one on another, as in a bee swarm. In August and September Geoffroy's Bats swarm like other *Myotis* species at caves, with males dominating. In the winter roost mostly free-hanging within the innermost ranges of caves and mines with constant temperature. The hibernation of Geoffroy's Bat can last for an unusually long time, in south Germany to the middle of April, some animals staying in their winter roosts to the middle of May.

Fig. 356. Geoffroy's Bats can pick flies off the ceiling of a stable and thus utilise a small-scale hunting ground with very high prey density. Photo: D. Nill.

REPRODUCTION

Births take place in the middle of June to the middle of July. Neonates have a forearm length of 14.1–14.6mm [own data]. Some of the young females mate in the first autumn [11], but in Bulgaria, the majority of the first year females do not take part in reproduction [own data].

FORAGING

Dependent on structure-rich forests, forest edges and meadows with fruit trees. Geoffroy's Bats hunt here close to the vegetation, also within the canopy, and collect insects from leaves (foliage gleaning). In cattle sheds flies are picked off the ceiling; the animals show a remarkable pendulum flight, 0.5–1m below the ceiling (surface gleaning) [9]. Open areas are avoided; the animals usually follow wooded banks and stream courses.

FOOD

Geoffroy's Bat is a food specialist; its prey consists, to a large part, of spiders and harvestmen, followed by lacewings, moths and Diptera. Besides these, beetles and Hymenoptera form a smaller proportion [1]. Day-active flies (*Musca*) dominate in the droppings of animals which use stables as hunting grounds [2].

MAXIMUM AGE

The maximum age proven so far is 18 years [11].

MOBILITY AND MIGRATION

Geoffroy's Bat is to a large extent a sedentary species with distances between summer and winter roost usually less than 40km. Only a few recoveries at greater distances are known. The longest distance proven so far, 105km, is of an animal that was ringed as a young male in north Bulgaria and which was recaptured in the following year at a swarming roost [10].

Habitat use

Hunting grounds lie up to 12.5km from the roost [5] and have a size of 50–70ha [7]. Within the hunting ground up to six core hunting grounds are intensively visited per

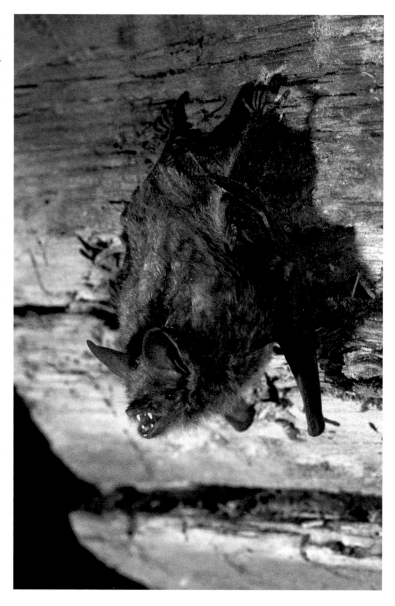

Fig. 357. Geoffroy's Bat echolocating before take o
Photo: D. Nill.

night [2]. Such partial hunting grounds cover usually only a few hectares [2] and can, as in the case of cow sheds, be very small. Roosts are frequently used in a group, so the numbers in nursery colonies can vary greatly [gen. lit. 136].

THREATS

Red list of the IUCN 2006: VU (Vulnerable), Red list of the European Union: VU (Vulnerable), EU Habitats Directive, Annex II & IV. Since the 1950s the populations at the northern edge of the distribution

Fig. 358. In winter Geoffroy's Bats usually hang free on the walls of underground passages. Photo: C. Dietz.

declined very strongly due to the loss of hunting grounds and probably also through the use of pesticides, in Poland by approximately 90% [6]. At present the populations are stable in Germany; in the Netherlands the population is improving. Increasing fragmentation of different habitat elements by roads should, however, be regarded as a very significant problem.

CONSERVATION MEASURES

Protection of nursery roosts in buildings and caves. Protection of feeding habitats in hardwood forests and richly structured cultural landscape, prevention of fragmentation effects between separated habitats.

REFERENCES

1. Bauerová, Z. (1986): Contribution to the trophic bionomics of *Myotis emarginatus*. *Folia Zool.* 35: 305–310.

2. Brinkmann, R., E. Hensle & C. Steck (2001): Artenschutzprojekt Wimperfledermaus. – Gutachten im Auftrag der Landesanstalt für Umweltschutz, 50 pp; Freiburg.

3. Gaisler, J. (1971): Zur Ökologie von *Myotis emarginatus* in Mitteleuropa. *Decheniana-Beihefte* 18: 71–82.

4. Heller, K.-G., M. Volleth & R. Achmann (2001): First record of *Myotis emarginatus* (Chiroptera: Vespertilionidae) from Cyprus. *Myotis* 39: 123.

5. Huet, R., M. Lemaire, L. Arthur & N. Del Guidice (2002): First results in radio-tracking Geoffroy's bats *Myotis emarginatus* in Centre region, France. *Abstracts, IXth European Bat Research Symposium, Le Havre* 2002: 25.

6. Kokurewicz, T. (1990): *Myotis emarginatus* in Poland; the past, the present status and the perspectives. *Myotis* 28: 73–82.

7. Krull, D., A. Schumm, W. Metzner & G. Neuweiler (1991): Foraging areas and foraging behavior in the notch-eared bat, *Myotis emarginatus*. *Behav. Ecol. Sociobiol.* 28: 247–253.

8. Richarz, K., D. Krull & A. Schumm (1989): Quartieransprüche und Quartierverhalten einer mitteleuropäischen Wochenstubenkolonie von *Myotis emarginatus* im Rosenheimer Becken, Oberbayern, mit Hinweisen zu den derzeit bekannten Wochenstubenquartieren dieser Art in der BRD. *Myotis* 27: 111–130.

9. Richarz, K. (1997): Biotopschutzplanung für Fledermäuse. Entwurf eines kurzen Leitfadens zum Schutz der Lebensräume im Sinne des Abkommens zur Erhaltung der Fledermäuse in Europa. *Nyctalus* (N.F.) 6: 289–303.

10. Schunger, I., C. Dietz, D. Merdschanova, S. Merdschanov, K. Christov, I. Borissov, S. Staneva & B. Petrov (2004): Swarming of bats (Chiroptera, Mammalia) in the Vodnite Dupki cave (Central Balkan National Park, Bulgaria). *Acta Zoologica Bulgarica* 56: 323–330.

11. Topál, G. (2001): *Myotis emarginatus*, Wimperfledermaus. In: F. Krapp (ed.): *Handbuch der Säugetiere Europas* 4–I: 369–404; Aula Verlag.

12. Zahn, A. & B. Henatsch (1998): Bevorzugt *Myotis emarginatus* kühlere Wochenstubenquartiere als *Myotis myotis*? *Z. Säugetierk.* 63: 21–31.

Bechstein's Bat
Myotis bechsteinii
(KUHL, 1817)

NAMES

D: Bechsteinfledermaus
F: Murin de Bechstein
E: Murciélago de Bechstein
I: Vespertilio di Bechstein
NL: Bechsteins vleermuis
S: Bechsteins fladdermus
PL: Nocek Bechsteina

IDENTIFICATION

A medium-sized bat with remarkably long ears. The dorsal fur is brown to reddish-brown and is clearly demarcated from the bright beige or grey ventral side. The face is reddish brown; the other skin parts are pale brown. The very long ears (21–26mm) have 9–11 transverse folds and are well separated from each other. The long tragus reaches about half the length of the ear. The wings are broad.

Similar species

By the long ears, the small body size and the much slimmer face compared with the mouse-eared bats, unmistakable. In the long-eared bats the ears are connected by a fold of skin.

ECHOLOCATION CALLS

The usually 2.5–5ms-long calls descend from *c.* 100kHz to *c.* 35kHz. Distinction from other *Myotis* species is only possible on the basis of sound recordings or in combination with good visual observation (size, ear length, flight style). The calls of Natterer's Bats, similar in size and flight style, cover a substantially broader frequency spectrum.

DISTRIBUTION

Bechstein's Bat is common within the temperate beech forest zone throughout west, Central and eastern Europe. In the

Measurements	
Forearm	39.0–47.1mm
Fifth finger	50–57mm
Third finger	61–69mm
Normal weight	7–10g
CBL	15.8–16.6mm
CM³	6.6–7.0mm

Fig. 359. During hunting breaks Bechstein's Bats hang in trees and rest. Photo: D. Nill.

Fig. 360. For suckling their young the females of Bechstein's Bat often withdraw to the edge of the colony. Photo: D. Nill.

Subspecies and geographical variation

No subspecies recognised; however, animals in Turkey differ morphologically, but not genetically, from European animals [own data; Kerth pers. com.].

HABITAT

A typical bat of the temperate beech forest zone [2], in deciduous and mixed woodlands, occurring from lowland plain up to high mountain ranges. In southern Europe usually in mountains or in riparian forests. The highest population densities, with up to 20 animals per 100ha, are found in beech or oak forests with a high proportion of old trees, in south Germany also in meadows with fruit trees near forest edge [10]. It also occurs, however, in pine and fir forests, only occasionally in pure spruce forests, but only if they are structure-rich and have a pronounced species-rich scrub layer [1, 12]. Pure coniferous forests are usually only populated when adjacent to optimal habitats, and the population densities are lower.

Roosts

Roosts in tree holes, trunk crevices and, as an alternative, frequently in bird and bat boxes. In south Germany tree roosts are used in spring and autumn, in summer mainly boxes [4]. Natural tree roosts can be close above the ground to a height of over 10m, but mainly at 1–5m height. There are only a few roosts known in buildings. In winter single animals are found in tree holes or in all kinds of underground roosts; the majority of the animals probably hibernate in tree holes.

BEHAVIOUR

Nursery colonies comprise 10–50, in rare cases up to 80, females. Bechstein's Bats mostly occur alone, but can live together with Natterer's and Daubenton's Bats. The nursery colonies subdivide frequently, recombine and subdivide again (fission–fusion societies). Roosts are changed every 2–3 days; only with a complete lack of roosts will individual colonies stay for weeks in just one bird or bat box. As soon as the number of roosts is increased,

south, records from the Iberian Peninsula and in Italy [13] are very scarce; on the Balkan Peninsula the density is locally higher. Throughout southern Europe, in general, it has an island-like distribution. In the north the distribution extends through southern England, the southern point of Sweden and across central Poland southeastwards across Ukraine to the Black Sea. Outside of Europe Bechstein's Bat occurs locally in Anatolia and northern Iran as well as in the Caucasus.

e.g. by bat boxes, they subdivide to the new roosts and change these regularly [own data]. The males live solitarily in summer. Young females usually join their colony of birth, which consists of closely related animals [gen. lit. 63, 64]. Young males move away from their area of birth and settle somewhere in the surrounding area. The face glands of Bechstein's Bat produce individually recognisable secretions, from which the members of a colony and different colonies can recognise each other [9].

REPRODUCTION

The nursery colonies are formed from the beginning of April and consist of closely related animals (grandmothers, mothers and daughters) [gen. lit. 63, 64]. The birth of the young takes place from the beginning of June to the beginning of July. From the end of August the nursery colonies disperse and Bechstein's Bats swarm, like many other *Myotis* species, at underground sites. Mating also takes place here. At the swarming sites many bats of the same species from a wide area meet, consequently the population present forms a high genetic diversity. Mating in this way leads to a substantial gene–flow between different nursery roost communities, and avoids danger of in-breeding [7, 8].

FORAGING

Hunting flight takes place at levels of 1–5m very close to vegetation, also at ground level in old vegetation-free forests, or in the canopy of trees. The manoeuvrable animals can fly very slowly and hover; they frequently collect prey from the substrate, e.g. from leaves (foliage gleaner). Prey detection is based on the scuffling sounds of the prey, which are detected with the large ears [11].

FOOD

The food of Bechstein's Bat consists particularly of forest-inhabiting arthropods and with a high proportion of non-flying insects [14, gen. lit. 149, 150]. In the course of the summer the dominant prey changes due to the changing availability at the hunting habitat. In contrast to Natterer's Bat, Bechstein's Bat has a higher proportion of

insects that allow themselves to be located by scuffling sounds [11]. The food consists to a large extent of moths, beetles, Diptera (crane-flies), lacewings and spiders. Additionally, harvestmen, earwigs, caterpillars, bush-crickets, bugs and ground-beetles also play a role seasonally or locally. Hymenoptera, centipedes, bugs, caddis flies and aphids are sometimes also captured [14, general lit. 149, 150].

MAXIMUM AGE

The maximum age recorded, so far, is 21 years [2].

MOBILITY AND MIGRATION

Bechstein's Bat is a very sedentary species; summer and winter roosts lie usually only a few kilometres from each other. The longest recorded movements are, so far, 48–73km in Germany [gen. lit. 139] and 53.5 km in Belgium.

Habitat use

A nursery colony of about 20 animals uses an area of approximately 250ha as summer habitat. Hunting grounds usually lie within 1km of the roost, rarely at distances of up to 2.5km [12]. Males usually hunt closer to their roosts than females do, sometimes only a few hundred metres from the roost tree. The hunting areas of the females are substantially larger (on average 17–61ha) than those of the males (on average 11–17ha) [6]. Foraging areas are substantially smaller in structure-rich and old hardwood forests than in coniferous forests; single animals can hunt here in large areas of up to 700ha [12]. Within the foraging area 3–9 small core hunting sites are intensively used. Hunting sites are visited very faithfully in different seasons and also over years by the same individuals [5]. Females change their roosts frequently; in the course of one summer up to 50 roosts are visited in an area of approximately 40ha. Males have a high fidelity to their roosts, but they can change roosts at distances of up to 2.5km [12].

THREATS

Red list of the IUCN 2006: VU (Vulnerable), Red list of the European Union: VU

(Vulnerable), EU Habitats Directive, Annex II & IV. Bechstein's Bats are adapted to long-term stable habitats in old hardwood forests. Before human interferences in forest ecological systems the populations were probably substantially larger. Bechstein's Bats cross open spaces, including roads, very low and thereby meet substantial dangers. Underpasses are readily accepted, therefore crossing passages in particular should be included with road constructions.

Very rare and sparsely recorded in southern England and borders of Wales. Until quite recently no breeding colonies were known, and records were based on occasional occurrence in underground hibernation sites and casual finds of individuals [UK gen. lit. 153, 155]. Currently the subject of a detailed distribution survey (including the use of a lure) and research with colonies in bat boxes and tree holes (mainly in oak). Some preliminary guidance on woodland management for the species has been published [15]. Included in data collected from hibernation sites for the National Bat Monitoring Programme. Records and some biological data also collected through autumn swarming studies. A priority species under the UK's Biodiversity Action Plan.

CONSERVATION MEASURES

Small-scale mosaic forest management, only felling of single trees, advancement of the hardwood forest proportion, protection and advancement of old and dead wood populations. Abandonment of pesticide use in forests. Prevention of habitat fragmentation by roads and other interruptions. Protection of swarming roosts as mating sites in order to maintain a high gene flow.

REFERENCES

1. Albrecht, K., M. Hammer & J. Holzhaider (2002): Telemetrische Untersuchungen zum Nahrungshabitatanspruch der Bechsteinfledermaus (*Myotis bechsteinii*) in Nadelwäldern bei Amberg in der Oberpfalz. *Schriftenreihe für Landschaftspflege und Naturschutz* 71: 109–130.
2. Baagøe, H.J. (2001): *Myotis bechsteinii*, Bechsteinfledermaus. In: F. Krapp (ed.): *Handbuch der Säugetiere Europas* 4–I: 443–471; Aula Verlag.
3. Kerth, G. & B. König (1999): Fission, fusion and nonrandom associations in female Bechstein's bats (*Myotis bechsteinii*). *Behaviour* 136: 1187–1202.
4. Kerth, G., K. Weissmann & B. König (2001): Day roost selection in female Bechstein's bats (*Myotis bechsteinii*): a field experiment to determine the influence of roost temperature. *Oecologia* 126: 1–9.
5. Kerth, G., M. Wagner & B. König (2001): Roosting together, foraging apart: information

Fig. 361. The strikingly long ears are obvious in this flying Bechstein's Bat. Photo: D. Nill.

Fig. 362. Bechstein's Bat taking off from a bird box used as roost. Photo: D. Nill.

transfer about food is unlikely to explain sociality in female Bechstein's bats (*Myotis bechsteinii*). *Behav. Ecol. Sociobiol.* 50: 283–291.

6. Kerth, G., M. Wagner, K. Weissmann & B. König (2002): Habitat- und Quartiernutzung bei der Bechsteinfledermaus: Hinweise für den Artenschutz. *Schriftenreihe für Landschaftspflege und Naturschutz* 71: 99–108.

7. Kerth, G., A. Kiefer, C. Trappmann & M. Weishaar (2003): High gene diversity at swarming sites suggest hot spots for gene flow in the endangered Bechstein's bat. *Conservation Genetics* 4: 491–499.

8. Kerth, G. & L. Morf (2004): Behavioural and genetic data suggest that Bechstein's bats predominantly mate outside the breeding habitat. *Ethology* 110: 987–999.

9. Safi, K. & G. Kerth (2003): Secretions of the interaural gland contain information about individuality and colony membership in the Bechstein's bat. *Anim. Behav.* 65: 363–369.

10. Schlapp, G. (1990): Populationsdichte und Habitatansprüche der Bechstein-Fledermaus *Myotis bechsteini* im Steigerwald (Forstamt Ebrach). *Myotis* 28: 39–58.

11. Siemers, B.M. & S.M. Swift (2006): Differences in sensory ecology contribute to resource partitioning in the bats *Myotis bechsteinii* and *Myotis nattereri* (Chiroptera: Vespertilionidae). *Behav. Ecol. Sociobiol.* 59: 373–380.

12. Steinhauser, D. (2002): Untersuchungen zur Ökologie der Mopsfledermaus, *Barbastella barbastellus* und der Bechsteinfledermaus, *Myotis bechsteinii* im Süden des Landes Brandenburg. *Schriftenreihe für Landschaftspflege und Naturschutz* 71: 81–98.

13. Vergari, S., G. Dondini & A. Ruggieri (1998): On the distribution of *Myotis bechsteinii* in Italy (Chiroptera: Vespertilionidae). *Hystrix* (n.s.) 10: 49–56.

14. Wolz, I. (2002): Beutespektren der Bechsteinfledermaus (*Myotis bechsteinii*) und des Großen Mausohrs (*Myotis myotis*) aus dem Schnaittenbacher Forst in Nordbayern. *Schriftenreihe für Landschaftspflege und Naturschutz* 71: 213–224

ADDITIONAL REFERENCES

15. Greenaway, F.R. & D. Hill (2005): *Woodland Management Advice for Bechstein's Bat and Barbastelle Bat*. English Nature, Research Reports no 658, Peterborough. 29pp.

Greater Mouse-eared Bat
Myotis myotis
(BORKHAUSEN, 1797)

NAMES
D: Mausohr
F: Grand murin
E: Murciélago ratonero grande
I: Vespertilio maggiore
NL: Vale vleermuis
S: Större musöra
PL: Nocek duży

Measurements

Forearm	55.0–66.9mm
Fifth finger	67–84mm
Third finger	89–107mm
Ear length	24.4–27.8mm
Ear width	16.2–19.3mm
Normal weight	20–27g
CBL	21.5–23.3mm
CM³	9.2–10.6mm

IDENTIFICATION
A large bat with a long broad snout and long broad ears. The dorsal fur is brown to reddish-brown coloured, the ventral side dirty white or beige, often with yellowish colouring at the throat and sides of the neck. Young animals are darker and smokey-grey, the hairs, particularly on the back, shorter and dense. The face in adult animals is light brown, darker in young animals. The ears are longer and broader than in the Lesser Mouse-eared Bat; in most animals the tragus shows a small black tip.

The membranes of the broad wings are brownish.

Similar species
Very similar to Lesser Mouse-eared Bat, but this usually has shorter (<26mm) and narrower (<16mm) ears with often only 5–6 transverse folds (often 7–8 in Greater Mouse-eared Bat), a shorter upper tooth row (<9.5mm) and, at least in southern Central Europe, often a whitish spot on the forehead and never a black tragus tip. In the Greater Mouse-eared Bat the upper tooth row length is usually >9.8mm, in exceptional small-sized animals it reaches only 9.4mm.

ECHOLOCATION CALLS
Up to 10ms-long, usually substantially shorter, frequency-modulated calls. The frequency falls from approximately 70–120kHz to 26–29kHz [gen. lit. 15].

DISTRIBUTION
Occurs from the European Mediterranean coast throughout Europe to the southern Netherlands, Schleswig-Holstein in Germany and northern Poland. The eastern border in Europe runs through western

Fig. 363. Nursery colony of Greater Mouse-eared Bat with still clearly grey-coloured, but almost full-grown, young animals, compared to the brown adults. Photo: D. Nill.

Ukraine to the Black Sea. Occurs in Asia Minor up to the Caucasus and the Middle East (Syria, Lebanon, Israel). A single animal was found in southern Sweden [11]. Until the 1980s there were also a few animals in Great Britain; in 1990 the species was considered to be extinct; since 2002 a single animal hibernates in a winter roost. Completely isolated from the main distribution area, the skeletons of three animals were found on the Azores [16]. The Greater Mouse-eared Bat is absent from North Africa, Corsica, and Malta, where the Maghrebian Mouse-eared Bat occurs.

Subspecies and geographical variation

The nominate form occurs in our region. From west to east the size increases; the largest animals are found in Turkey; they show similarity to the even larger subspecies *M. m. macrocephalicus* from eastern Turkey and the Middle East (Lebanon, Syria, Israel) [1, 21].

HABITAT

The Greater Mouse-eared Bat occurs typically at altitudes below 800m, higher in warm situations. Colonies usually in areas with a high proportion of forest. The hunting grounds are characterised by free access to the ground and to ground-dwelling arthropods. Of the different forest types deciduous and mixed woodlands with small quantities of ground cover are usually preferred [25]. They also hunt in coniferous forests, usually medium–old timber without ground vegetation [24]. They hunt over meadows, pastures and fields that are freshly mown, grazed or harvested. The population density correlates closely with the amount of hardwood forest, respectively the proportion of deciduous and mixed woodlands of the total forest area [25, gen. lit. 102]. Foraging animals spend up to 98% of their time in forests [gen. lit. 102].

Fig. 364. Greater Mouse-eared Bat in flight. Photo: D. Nill.

Fig. 365. Through lack of pigment there are rare cases of albino or partial albino animals in almost all bat species, as in this Greater Mouse-eared Bat in an Austrian nursery roost. Photo: D. Nill.

Roosts

In Central Europe, the reproductive colonies dwell, with few exceptions, in larger roof spaces [11, gen. lit. 102]. In cases where colonies are in cellars or underground corridors, they are only there after the original attic roosts were lost. Other Central European nursery roosts occur in abutments of large bridges. In the Mediterranean area caves are mostly used as maternity sites. Summer roosts of individual males are in roof spaces and towers, behind window shutters and in fissures of bridges, in tree holes and bat boxes, additionally in mines and caves. Winter roosts are usually in caves, mines, bunkers and mountain cellars. Single animals are regularly found in rock crevice; probably far more animals hibernate in this type of roost than is so far shown.

BEHAVIOUR

Large clusters are formed in the summer roost, in the Mediterranean area often with other species such as horseshoe bats and Lesser Mouse-eared, Geoffroy's, Long-fingered and Schreibers' Bent-winged Bats. Only a few males stay in the nursery roosts [22]. The colony sites are occupied from the last days of March to the beginning of May

and vacated after the young are weaned, starting from the end of August. During this time the hanging places in the roost are regularly changed according to the microclimate and the parasite density [15]. Central European nursery colonies comprise 50–1,000 females, in exceptional cases up to 5,000 females [11]. In Bavaria the size of the nursery colonies is between 3 and 2,183 animals, with an average of 311 animals [gen. lit. 102]. In the Mediterranean area nursery colonies frequently include around 1,000, rarely up to 8,000 animals [11]. Females are extremely faithful to their place of birth, over 90% return to their birth roost. The permanent exchange of adult animals between colonies is very small, although short-term visits take place in larger numbers [23]. Males roost alone during the summer, with regular hanging places visited over years. In particular in the vicinity of nursery roosts and in large caves, males roost a small distance (sometimes only a few meters) from each other. The males mark their roost sites with secretions from face glands; their roosts are easy to recognise by dark discolorations on cave ceilings or on beams [22]. In the winter, larger clusters of several hundred animals are rarely formed; single animals or small groups usually hang free from the ceiling or are deeply hidden in crevices. In winter in Central Europe sites with constant damp and relatively warm temperatures (up to 12°C) are used, in caves and mines often in the rear parts. Only at the end of the winter are sites closer to the entrance visited.

REPRODUCTION

From the middle of August Greater Mouse-eared Bats swarm at caves [gen. lit. 102]; sporadically they also come here to mate. A larger number of matings can, however, be observed at male roosts in the proximity of roost sites of maternity colonies or at other roosts in tree holes, bat boxes, bridges or buildings [22]. The male lures usually one to five females to its roost site and encloses them with the wings. During the average four-day stay of the females in the male roost there can be repeated mating. A female gives birth to only one young; there are, so far, only two exceptions known: one female found dead in Switzerland [2] and an animal in Bulgaria [own data], dying during birth, carried twins. In Central Europe birth takes place sometimes as early as the end of May, usually, however, only in June; in the Mediterranean area births start from the beginning of April [15, 20]. The birth period in a colony can last 3–5 weeks; individual animals can become completely dissociated from the normal rhythm and can even give birth in the winter [14]. In a Bulgarian cave, when the animals did not go out during a night with thunderstorms, hundreds of births took place almost simultaneously in a colony numbering several thousand animals [own data]. Neonates weigh 4–6.5g with a forearm length of 17–23.7mm [6, 11]; the lower end of the range mostly relates to premature births, which were collected dead under maternity colony sites. The first practice flights are accomplished at the age of 3–4 weeks in the roost; the first fledging takes place at five weeks [6]. In Germany about 40% of young females mate successfully in the first autumn and give birth in the subsequent year [gen. lit. 44], in Portugal approximately

Fig. 366. Hibernating *Myotis* species often hang together, here Greater Mouse-eared Bats with the smaller Natterer's Bats. Photo: D. Nill.

95% [20]. In Germany, 95% of the females between four and 14 years of life are involved in reproduction, older animals no longer give birth annually [gen. lit. 44].

FORAGING

The Greater Mouse-eared Bat often searches with rapid and moderately agile flight, usually at low height (1–2m) and with head and ears facing the ground [3, 11]. If prey is located on the basis of a rustling sound, the bat approaches the place, hovers, and swoops down on the prey. The insect is partly covered with the wings and then seized with the mouth [3]. Large prey is eaten by hanging at a temporary perch, small prey in flight at 5–10m height. During close orientation (e.g. to find the prey below the wings) the well-developed sense of smell probably plays a large role. Since the prey is usually directly on the substrate, it cannot be detected with echolocation calls; Greater Mouse-eared Bats are, therefore, dependent on the rustling sounds of the prey. So the apparent preference for some groups of prey could be mostly explained as the loudest-rustling species [gen. lit. 123]. Chafers and other large insects can also be pursued and taken in flight.

FOOD

For the Greater Mouse-eared Bat, with its readily accessible roosts and additionally quite large prey remains in the droppings, the prey preferences are very comprehensively examined [3, 7, 10, 19, gen. lit. 4, 123]. Greater Mouse-eared Bats capture mostly ground-dwelling crawling animals over 10mm long. The most common prey are ground-dwelling beetles, of which a very high proportion are large ground-beetles (*Carabus*), followed by other ground-dwelling arthropods such as chilopods, spiders and beetle larvae. Only sporadically or seasonally other beetles (chafers and dung beetles), mole crickets [7], crane-flies or grasshoppers play a larger role as prey. In the Mediterranean area spiders can form a very high proportion in the food, particularly in the summer, when other prey is limited [19]. Meanwhile, the record of a lower jaw of a shrew appears quite remarkable [17].

MAXIMUM AGE

The average age of nursery colony animals varies, depending upon the colony, with 2.7–4.9 years. The maximum age of a single animal proven so far was 25 years [gen. lit. 139]. The mortality rate in young animals in the nursery roosts amounts to

Fig. 367. Before the emergence from the roost Greater Mouse-eared Bats groom their wings and carry out stretching exercises. Photo: D. Nill.

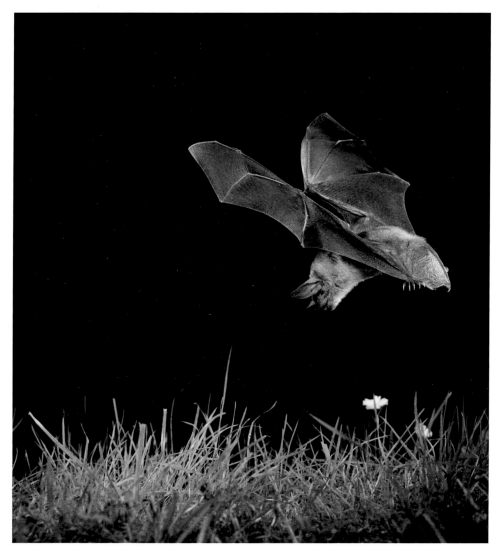

Fig. 368. Greater Mouse-eared Bats capture the majority of their food on the ground. Photo: D. Nill.

5–15%; in extremely cool and wet years it can, however, reach 90% [15, gen. lit. 102]. Altogether the mortality rate for young animals in the first year is 46–60%; for older animals it is annually about 18–21%.

MOBILITY AND MIGRATION

The first ringing studies in Europe were carried out with Greater Mouse-eared Bats in Germany, with the relatively rapidly obtained impressive results being the stimulus for comprehensive, nowadays continuous, studies on the migration behaviour of bats [9]. The Greater Mouse-eared Bat is a regionally migrating species with movements between summer, swarming and winter sites of distances of usually 50–100km. Large winter roosts with several hundred animals often form the centre of a star-shaped migration pattern. Movements average 27.5km for males and 51.3km for females. The longest movements found so far are 368km northeast from the swarming site Esper cave in Bavaria to northeast of Berlin [12], 390km in Spain [6] and 436km from the Netherlands to Germany.

Habitat use

The hunting grounds lie usually in a 5–15km periphery around the roost, but can be up to 26km [5, 8, 10, gen. lit. 102]. The estimation of the foraging area is difficult; it is at least

Fig. 369. Habitat of Greater Mouse-eared Bat. In Central Europe the species prefers beech forests without bushes; on vegetation-free surfaces the Greater Mouse-eared Bat has ready access to its main food, ground beetles. Photo: D. Nill.

100ha, but can also be 500–1,000ha. Within these areas one to five core hunting grounds of 1–10ha are visited. Changes of roosts can take place up to a distance of 34km [23]. Females search for mating roosts at distances of up to 12km from the nursery roosts [22]; swarming sites may be over 100km distant [gen. lit. 102, Nagel pers. com.].

THREATS

Red list of the IUCN 2006: LC (Least Concern), EU Habitats Directive, Annex II and IV. In this species the population declines are well documented. Until the 1970s the population in Germany decreased to only 10% of the numbers existing before World War II. Both the number of nursery roosts, and the number of animals in the remaining colonies and in the winter roosts declined. Initially roost destruction, pesticide use in agriculture and in forestry (DDT), the utilisation of highly toxic timber preservatives in the roost (lindane), and the loss of extensively managed hunting habitats were responsible. Since the 1980s existing nursery colony populations have partly recovered. The summer population in Bavaria at that time was estimated at 140,000 [gen. lit. 102]; so far, however, only in very rare cases has there been re-establishment of lost colonies. The species is still endangered by

building renovation and increasing habitat fragmentation, by road construction and the use of environmental poisons [18]. In many south European countries there is, so far, no considerable decline observed, but increasing cave tourism and increasing pesticide use are serious factors of risk.

The rarest bat in Britain; currently known only from a single male found hibernating as a youngster in 2002 and seen in the same site every winter since [UK gen. lit. 155]. The species has never been well established in the UK, with two known hibernation areas (Dorset and Sussex). The few in Dorset were first located in 1956 and died out in the 1970s. A larger group in Sussex was found in the late 1960s, but few females returned in the winter of 1974 and it is assumed that some catastrophe had occurred while they were together at a maternity site [26]. By 1980 two males remained, and from 1985 to 1989 only a single male, which then disappeared at 18 years of age. The current male uses the same hibernation site as the earlier Sussex population. On the discovery of this individual, efforts were made to identify likely summer roost and foraging sites, but survey did not produce any further records. Records from hibernation are incorporated into the National Bat Monitoring Programme database. The species was included in the UK's Biodiversity Action Plan, but has recently been delisted.

CONSERVATION MEASURES
Protection of the colonies and winter roosts, promotion of locally suitable and native hardwood forest populations, abandonment of pesticides in agriculture and forestry, conservation of large non-fragmented habitats.

REFERENCES
1. Albayrak, I. & N. Aşan (1998): Geographic variations and taxonomic status of *Myotis myotis* in Turkey (Chiroptera: Vespertilionidae). *Tr. J. Zool.* 22: 267–275.
2. Arlettaz, R. (1993): Une femelle de Grand Murin *Myotis myotis* porteuse de deux embryons. *Mammalia* 57: 148–149.
3. Arlettaz, R. (1995): Myotis myotis *and* Myotis blythii, *ecology of the sibling mouse-eared bats*, 206 pp.; Horus Publishers Martigny, Switzerland.
4. Arlettaz, R. (1999): Habitat selection as a major resource partitioning mechanism between the two sympatric sibling bat species *Myotis myotis* and *Myotis blythii. J. Anim. Ecol.* 68: 460–471.
5. Audet, D. (1990): Foraging behaviour and habitat use by a gleaning bat, *Myotis myotis. J. Mammal.* 71: 420–427.
6. de Paz, O. (1986): Age estimation and postnatal growth of the greater mouse-eared bat *Myotis myotis* in Guadalajara, Spain. *Mammalia* 50: 243–251.
7. Drescher, C. (2000): Woodsmen or farmers? The diet of the greater mouse-eared bat (*Myotis myotis*) in an intensively used agricultural landscape. In: B.W. Woloszyn (ed.): *Proceedings of the VIIIth European Bat Research Symposium* 1: 243–251.
8. Drescher, C. (2004): Radiotracking of *Myotis myotis* (Chiroptera, Vespertilionidae) in South Tyrol and implications for its conservation. *Mammalia* 68: 387–395.
9. Eisentraut, M. (1947): Die mit Hilfe der Beringungsmethode erzielten Ergebnisse über Lebensdauer und jährliche Verlustziffern bei *Myotis myotis. Experientia* 3: 157–158.
10. Güttinger, R. (1997): Jagdhabitate des Großen Mausohrs (*Myotis myotis*) in der modernen Kulturlandschaft. *Schriftenreihe Umwelt* 288: 1–138.
11. Güttinger, R., A. Zahn, F. Krapp & W. Schober (2001): *Myotis myotis*, Großes Mausohr, Großmausohr. In: F. Krapp (ed.): *Handbuch der Säugetiere Europas* 4–I: 123–207; Aula Verlag.

12. Haensel, J. (2004): Fernfund eines Mausohrs (*Myotis myotis*) aus Bayern über 368 km im Land Brandenburg. *Nyctalus* (N.F.) 9: 327–328.
13. Horáček, I. (1985): Population ecology of *Myotis myotis* in central Bohemia. *Acta Univ. Carol., Biol.* 1981: 161–267.
14. Ibáñez, C. (1997): Winter reproduction in the greater mouse-eared bat (*Myotis myotis*) in South Iberia. *J. Zool.* 243: 836–840.
15. Kulzer, E. (2003): Großes Mausohr *Myotis myotis*. In: M. Braun & F. Dieterlen (eds): *Die Säugetiere Baden-Württembergs* 1: 357–377; Ulmer-Verlag.
16. Palmeirim, J.M. (1979): First record of *Myotis myotis* on the Azores Islands (Chiroptera: Vespertilionidae). *Arquivos do Museu Bocage* 7, notas e suplementos 46: 1–2.
17. Pont, B. & J. Moulin (1986): Un cas de consommation d'une musaraigne par le grand murin (*Myotis myotis*). *Mammalia* 50: 398–401.
18. Rackow, W. (1991): Nachweise von Blei und Cadmium im Kot des Mausohrs (*Myotis myotis*). *Nyctalus* (N.F.) 4: 140–144.
19. Ramos Pereira, M.J., H. Rebelo, A. Rainho & J.M. Palmeirim (2002): Prey selection by *Myotis myotis* (Vespertilionidae) in a Mediterranean region. *Acta Chiropterologica* 4: 183–193.
20. Rodrigues, L., A. Zahn, A. Rainho & J.M. Palmeirim (2003): Contrasting the roosting behaviour and phenology of an insectivorous bat (*Myotis myotis*) in its southern and northern distribution ranges. *Mammalia* 67: 321–335.
21. Spitzenberger, F. (1996): Distribution and subspecific variation of *Myotis blythi* and *Myotis myotis* in Turkey. *Ann. Nat. Hist. Mus. Wien* 98 B Suppl.: 9–23.
22. Zahn, A. & B. Dippel (1997): Male roosting habits and mating behaviour of *Myotis myotis. J. Zool.* 243: 659–674.
23. Zahn, A. (1998): Individual migration between colonies of greater mouse-eared bats (*Myotis myotis*) in Upper Bavaria. *Z. Säugetierk.* 63: 321–328.
24. Zahn, A., H. Haselbach & R. Güttinger (2005): Foraging activity of central European *Myotis myotis* in a landscape dominated by spruce monocultures. *Mamm. Biol.* 70: 265–270.
25. Zahn, A., A. Rottenwallner & R. Güttinger (2006): Population density of the greater mouse-eared bat (*Myotis myotis*), local diet composition and availability of foraging habitats. *J. Zool.* 269: 486–493.

ADDITIONAL REFERENCES
26. Stebbings, R.E. (1992): Mouse-eared bat – extinct in Britain? *Bat News* 26: 2–3.

Lesser Mouse-eared Bat
Myotis oxygnathus
MONTICELLI, 1885

NAMES
D: Kleines Mausohr
F: Petit murin
E: Murciélago ratonero mediano
I: Vespertilio minore
NL: Kleine vale vleermuis
S: Mindre musöra
PL: Nocek ostrouszny

GENERAL INFORMATION
The Lesser Mouse-eared Bat from Europe has been considered as the subspecies *oxygnathus* of *Myotis blythii* from India. Due to clear differences in DNA sequences between the Asian and the European subspecies they are, however, now often regarded as separate species [gen. lit. 104, 126]; the European Lesser Mouse-eared Bat has again, as in some earlier literature, the scientific name *Myotis oxygnathus*.

IDENTIFICATION

Measurements

Forearm	50.5–62.1mm
Fifth finger	63–81mm
Third finger	85–103mm
Ear length	21.0–24.3mm
Ear width	12.7–15.9mm
Normal weight	19–26g
CBL	19.2–21.7mm
CM³	8.1–9.5mm

A large bat, very similar to the Greater Mouse-eared Bat. The dorsal side is grey with a brownish tinge, the ventral side pale grey-white, usually somewhat paler than in the Greater Mouse-eared bat. Animals in Switzerland and adjacent countries often have a pale forehead spot between the ears, which is, however, often missing in southeast Europe. The face is somewhat shorter than in the Greater Mouse-eared Bat, the ears somewhat narrower and shorter, the front edge of the ears somewhat less convex. The tragus is pale coloured to the tip, without a dark spot at the end.

Similar species
Very similar to the Greater Mouse-eared and Maghrebian Mouse-eared Bat. The ears of the Lesser Mouse-eared Bat are shorter than in the Maghrebian Mouse-eared Bat (<24.3mm) and in comparison with the Greater Mouse-eared Bat narrower (<16mm). At usually less than 9.4mm the upper tooth row length is shorter than in the Greater Mouse-eared Bat; only in the southeast part of our region do the Lesser Mouse-eared Bats occasionally reach 9.8mm, where the sympatric-occurring Greater Mouse-eared Bats are also larger, with an upper tooth row >9.8mm. Single individuals can be very difficult to identify since they may show characteristics of both species. The Lesser Mouse-eared Bat is the only species to frequently show a pale forehead spot. In roosts the whitish ventral side of Lesser Mouse-eared Bats looks brighter.

ECHOLOCATION CALLS
Resembles strongly the calls of the Greater Mouse-eared Bat, see under that species.

DISTRIBUTION
In Europe distributed throughout the Mediterranean area, northwards to central France, Switzerland (to close to the German border), Czech Republic, Slovakia and Ukraine. Absent on Sardinia, Corsica and Malta as well as in North Africa (where the Maghrebian Mouse-eared Bat occurs). Widely distributed in Asia Minor, also on Cyprus and Crete. Eastwards in the Caucasus, the Near East and to Central Asia.

Subspecies and geographical variation
Beside the nominate form *M. o. oxygnathus*, occurs in the majority of the geographical scope of this book, a further recognised subspecies, *M. o. omari*, occurs on Crete, Cyprus and the south coast of Asia

Minor into the Near East and is very slightly larger and particularly paler coloured than the nominate form. Possibly it represents a separate species comparable to the Maghrebian Mouse-eared Bat. On the other hand, it is controversial whether *M. o. lesviacus*, which occurs only on the Greek island of Lesbos, qualifies for the status of a subspecies. The Asian forms belong at least partly to *M. blythii*.

HABITAT

Warm open landscape, extensively used meadowlands, damp meadows, pastures, karst areas, steppe landscapes and extensively agriculturally used areas. Avoids to a large extent large closed forest areas, in which the Greater Mouse-eared Bat dominates.

Roosts

Summer and nursery roosts in the northern distribution area (Switzerland, Austria) in attics, in the Mediterranean area almost exclusively in large caves and other underground sites. Males occupy caves and bunkers all year round, in summer also fissures in bridges or buildings. Winter roosts in caves or other underground sites.

BEHAVIOUR

Roosts in caves are nearly always used together with other bat species: with Greater Mouse-eared, Long-fingered, Schreibers' Bent-winged and Geoffroy's Bats and horseshoe bats, with mixed clusters often formed [12]. An almost pure cluster of Lesser Mouse-eared Bats in a Bulgarian cave comprised approximately 8,000 animals [own data]; however, the colonies are usually substantially smaller, with 50–500 females. No males occur in the nursery clusters but during the maternity period they are quite often found in the vicinity of the roost. Captures at cave entrances sometimes contain a relatively high number of males. Clusters of several hundred animals are possible in winter.

REPRODUCTION

Mating takes place from August; before that the males occupy their display roosts,

Fig. 370. The ears of Lesser Mouse-eared Bat are shorter and narrower than those of the closely related Greater Mouse-eared Bat. Photo: D. Nill.

usually small holes in cave ceilings [6], also in cracks in bridges. These roosts are vehemently defended against rivals, which can include violent biting. In some caves the male roosts are spaced at less than 1m apart. With loud display calls two to three and sometimes up to six females are lured together as a mating group. In Bulgaria a male with a double broken forearm after a bite incident was mating for over two weeks in its display roost and was consequently thoroughly emaciated [own data]. Births usually take place in May, in Bulgaria usually in the second half of the month.

FORAGING

The steady hunting flight is made at 1–2m height above the ground. The Lesser Mouse-eared Bat reacts very agilely having discovered prey and can pick it in flight from grass-stalks [1, 4, general lit. 4]. Sometimes prey on the ground is located by scuffling and overwhelmed by a nose dive [gen. lit. 5]. In Switzerland unmown meadows with bush-crickets are preferred; mown meadows are only visited just after the mowing [5]. Edges of forest are also

scoured, usually in order to catch larger insects such as chafers.

FOOD
The food consists of a large portion of bush-crickets, but also of crane-flies, chafers, grasshoppers, carabids and mole crickets, particularly in the Mediterranean area also of preying mantises and lepidopteran caterpillars [1, 5, 9, 12, gen. lit. 4].

MAXIMUM AGE
The highest proven age is 33 years, far above the average maximum age of 14–16 years [3].

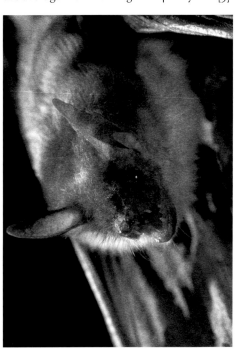

MOBILITY AND MIGRATION
To a large extent a sedentary species, summer and winter roosts are usually just 15km apart from each other, rarely more. Apart from a few distances of 100–150km an unusually long-distance recovery is known of 488km from the ringing site in Spain (often wrongly quoted as 600km) [12, gen. lit. 57].

Habitat use
The average distance between the hunting grounds and the roosts reaches 4–7km [1, 2, 8,10], the longest distances to some hunting grounds being 9–25km [5, 8, 10].

THREATS
Red list of the IUCN 2006: LC (Least Concern), EU Habitats Directive, Annex II & IV. Loss of habitat in the 1950s–1970s by radical ploughing of meadows and reclamation of steppe areas in Hungary [12], Romania and northeast Bulgaria as well as the abandonment of the use of extensive hay meadows since the middle of the last century caused population collapse. As before, open land habitats and extensively used green land areas are among the most strongly declining areas in southern Europe. In Switzerland the availability of suitable extensively managed open land biotopes is the limiting factor for the occurrence of the species [5, 9]. Increasing disturbance of large colony caves by tourism. The Lesser Mouse-eared Bat must be, therefore, classified as strongly endangered.

CONSERVATION MEASURES
Protection of the colony caves, and in the northern distribution area of the colony sites in buildings. Conservation of extensively used open and grassland habitats with late mowing times [5]. Re-establishment of steppe and extensive cultural steppe areas and connecting the remaining steppe habitats. Prevention of fragmentation effects by roads between separate foraging habitats. Appropriate conservation measures for the Lesser Mouse-eared Bat are also beneficial for the rare Mehely's Horseshoe Bat, since both have similar habitat requirements.

REFERENCES

1. Arlettaz, R. (1995): Myotis myotis *and* Myotis blythii, *ecology of the sibling mouse-eared bats,* 206 pp; Horus Publishers Martigny, Switzerland.

2. Arlettaz, R. (1999): Habitat selection as a major resource partitioning mechanism between the two sympatric sibling bat species *Myotis myotis* and *Myotis blythii. J. Anim. Ecol.* 68: 460–471.

3. Arlettaz, R., P. Christe & M. Desfayes (2002): 33 years, a new longevity record for a European bat. *Mammalia* 66: 441–442.

4. Güttinger, R., J. Lustenberger, A. Beck & U. Weber (1998): Traditionally cultivated wetland meadows as foraging habitats of the grass-gleaning lesser mouse-eared bat (*Myotis blythii*). *Myotis* 36: 41–49.

5. Güttinger, R., M. Lutz & E. Mühlethaler (2006): Förderung potenzieller Jagdhabitate für das Kleine Mausohr (*Myotis blythii*). Interreg IIIB-Projekt Lebensraumvernetzung; 76 pp; www.livingspacenetwork.bayern.de.

6. Horáček, I. & J. Gaisler (1986): The mating system of *Myotis blythii. Myotis* 23/24: 125–130.

7. Iliopoulou-Georgudaki, J.G. (1984): Intraspecific and interpopulation morphologic variation in the sharp-eared bat, *Myotis blythii* (Chiroptera: Vespertilionidae), from Greece. *Bonn. Zool. Beitr.* 35: 15–24.

8. Rey, E. (2004): *How modern agriculture reduces the overall ecological space: comparison of mouse-eared bats' niche breadth in intensively vs. extensively cultivated areas.* Masters thesis Zoological Institute, University of Bern. 59 pp.

9. Roesli, M., F. Bontadina, T. Maddalena, K. Märki, T. Hotz, A.-S. Genini, D. Torrioni, R. Güttinger & M. Moretti (2005): Ambienti di caccia e regime alimentare del Vespertilio maggiore (*Myotis myotis*) e del Vespertilio minore (*Myotis blythi*) (Chiroptera: Vespertilionidae) nel Cantone Ticino. *Boll. Soc. tic. Sci. Nat.* 93: 63–75.

10. Roesli, M., F. Bontadina, T. Maddalena & M. Moretti (2004): *Studio sulla colonia di riproduzione di* Myotis myotis *e* Myotis blythii *delle Collegiata Sant'Antonio a Locarno.* Dipartimento del territorio Cantone Ticino. 44 pp.

11. Spitzenberger, F. (1996): Distribution and subspecific variation of *Myotis blythi* and *Myotis myotis* in Turkey. *Ann. Nat. Hist. Mus. Wien* 98 B Suppl.: 9–23.

12. Topál, G. & M. Ruedi (2001): *Myotis blythii,* Kleines Mausohr. In: F. Krapp (ed.): *Handbuch der Säugetiere Europas* 4–I: 209–255; Aula Verlag.

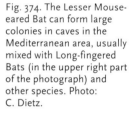

Fig. 373. Before the morning return into the roost Lesser Mouse-eared Bats, like many other bat species, swarm for up to half an hour outside the roost entrance. Photo: C. Dietz.

Fig. 374. The Lesser Mouse-eared Bat can form large colonies in caves in the Mediterranean area, usually mixed with Long-fingered Bats (in the upper right part of the photograph) and other species. Photo: C. Dietz.

Maghrebian Mouse-eared Bat

Myotis punicus
FELTEN, 1977

NAMES

D: Punisches Mausohr
NL: Fenicische vale vleermuis

GENERAL INFORMATION

The classification of the mouse-eared bats of Sardinia, Corsica and North Africa in relation to the species known in the 1990s, the Greater Mouse-eared or the Lesser Mouse-eared Bat, was causing difficulties for a long time. In 1977 Felten *et al.* described a subspecies of the Lesser Mouse-eared Bat and named it *Myotis blythii punicus* [6]. Only following investigations into the degree of gene exchange between mouse-eared bat populations across the Strait of Gibraltar was it shown that the mouse-eared bats of North Africa differ more from the two European species than the latter do from each other [5]. Hence, Felten's *punicus* is considered as a separate species [gen. lit. 77, 126].

Measurements

Forearm	54.0–63.9mm
Fifth finger	71–79mm
Third finger	92–102mm
Ear length	26.1–29.0mm
Ear width	14.7–17.9mm
Normal weight	19–25g
CBL	20.1–22.5mm
CM³	8.7–10.0mm

IDENTIFICATION

A large bat with light brown dorsal fur sharply demarcated from the whitish-grey ventral side. Remarkably long ears, the front edge of which is distinctly convex. Outer edge of the tragus very evenly bent, tragus tip without black spot.

Similar species

Hard to distinguish from the Greater Mouse-eared and Lesser Mouse-eared Bat with external characters. The ears of the Lesser Mouse-eared Bat are shorter (<24.5mm) and the upper tooth row is usually similarly shorter, although an overlap exists. The face form and size is rather reminiscent of Lesser Mouse-eared Bat and also the tragus tip does not show the black colouration that is typical for many Greater Mouse-eared Bats. So far there is no evidence of sympatry of the Maghrebian Mouse-eared Bat with either the Greater Mouse-eared or Lesser Mouse-eared Bat, so field identification is not necessary at present. Genetically clearly separable.

DISTRIBUTION

Limited to the islands of Sardinia, Corsica,

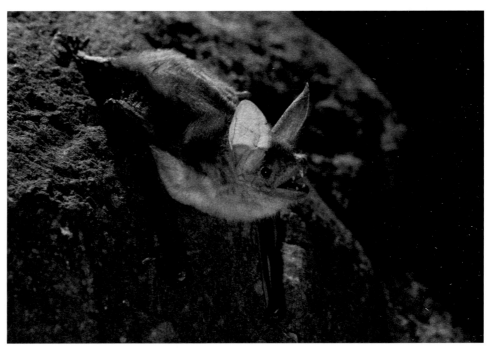

Fig. 375. The Maghrebian Mouse-eared Bat has the longest ears in relation to the body size of all three species of the large mouse-eared bats. Photo: D. Nill.

Malta and Gozo and the northwest African countries Morocco, Algeria, Tunisia and Libya. Occurs in Morocco in the entire area north of the High Atlas, in Algeria from available data only in a 100–200km broad strip along the Mediterranean coast, and in Libya only found in the northwest of the country [8, 9].

Subspecies and geographical variation

So far no subspecies are described and the genetic differences between populations are small [gen. lit. 77]. However, the animals from North Africa and Malta are larger than those from Sardinia and Corsica [6].

HABITAT, ROOSTS AND BEHAVIOUR

Hunting grounds in open landscape (pastures, meadows) or in large vegetation-free areas and only rarely at edges of forest [3]. In North Africa also in semi-desert regions. The so far known nursery roosts were exclusively in caves [4, 7–10] and can comprise up to 1,000 females, usually together with other cave-dwelling species such as horse-shoe bats, Schreibers' Bent-winged Bats and Long-fingered Bats [7, 8, 10]. Single animals can be found in a variety of roosts in underground tunnels, ruins, roofs and cracks in bridges.

REPRODUCTION

Mating especially from August, as with Lesser Mouse-eared Bat the males defend individual crevices and holes in the cave ceilings, sometimes at distances of less than a metre from each other, and lure up to four females [8, 9]. In Algeria the births take place between the end of March and the end of April [8, 9]; in Morocco the young were not yet born in the first days of May [own data].

FORAGING AND FOOD

Usually areas of low vegetation or strongly grazed areas are searched in low flight (<2m); prey is picked from the ground or captured in flight [3, 4]. The food consists mostly of grasshoppers, bush-crickets, crickets, beetles (ground-beetles, chafers) and moths (hawk-moths, noctuids) [1, 2, 3,

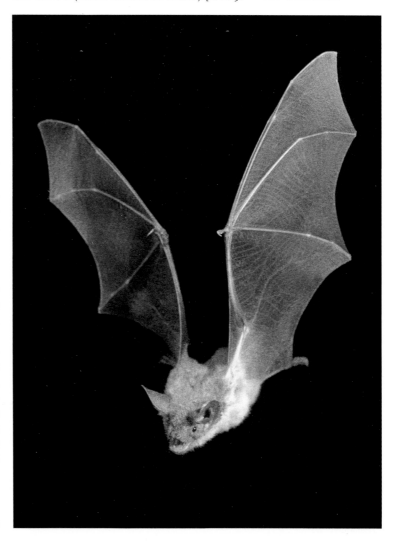

Fig. 376. Hunting flight of a Maghrebian Mouse-eared Bat. Photo: D. Nill.

Fig. 377. Habitat of Maghrebian Mouse-eared Bat on Sardinia. Foraging animals can be found particularly over sparsely overgrown surfaces and in light cork oak stands. Photo: D. Nill.

4]. Seasonally, bugs, cicadas and spiders can also be of great importance [1, 2].

MOBILITY AND MIGRATION
Probably sedentary to a large extent. A male ringed on Malta was found in a mating roost on Gozo at 22km distance [4].

THREATS AND CONSERVATION MEASURES
Red list of the IUCN 2006: DD (Deficient Data), EU Habitats Directive, Annex IV. The population on Malta declined very strongly since the 1960s and includes at present only 250–300 animals [4]. Colony caves should be protected against disturbance and foraging habitats should be preserved.

REFERENCES
1. Arlettaz, R. (1995): Myotis myotis *and* Myotis blythii, *ecology of the sibling mouse-eared bats*, 206 pp. Horus Publishers Martigny, Switzerland.
2. Arlettaz, R., N. Perrin & J. Hausser (1997): Trophic resource partitioning and competition between the two sibling bat (Vespertilionidae) in Corsica. *J. Anim. Ecol.* 66: 897–911.
3. Beuneux, G. (2004): Morphometrics and ecology of Myotis cf. punicus (Chiroptera,
Vespertilionidae) in Corsica. *Mammalia* 68: 269–273.
4. Borg, J.J. (1998): The lesser mouse-eared bat *Myotis blythi punicus* in Malta. Notes on status, morphometrics, movements, and diet (Chiroptera: Vespertilionidae). *Il Naturalista Siciliano* 22: 365–374.
5. Castella, V., M. Ruedi, L. Excoffier, C. Ibáñez, R. Arlettaz & J. Hausser (2000): Is the Gibraltar Strait a barrier to gene flow for the bat *Myotis myotis*? *Mol. Ecol.* 9: 1761–1772.
6. Felten, H., F. Spitzenberger & G. Storch (1977): Zur Kleinsäugerfauna West-Anatoliens, Teil IIIa. *Senckenb. Biol.* 58: 1–44.
7. Frick, H. & H. Felten (1952): Ökologische Beobachtungen an sardischen Fledermäusen. *Zoologische Jahrbücher* (Systematik) 81: 175–189.
8. Kowalski, K., J. Gaisler, H. Bessam, C. Issaad & H. Ksantini (1986): Annual life cycle of cave bats in northern Algeria. *Acta Theriol.* 13: 185–206.
9. Kowalski, K. & B. Rzebik-Kowalska (1991): *Mammals of Algeria*, 370 pp; Polish Academy of Sciences.
10. Mucedda, M., G. Murittu, A. Oppes & E. Pidinchedda (1995): Osservazioni sui Chirotteri troglofili della Sardegna. *Bollettino della Societa Sarda di Scienza Natural* 30: 97–129.
11. Mucedda, M. & M.T. Nuvoli (2000): Indagine biometrica sul "grande *Myotis*" (Chiroptera, Vespertilionidae) della Grotta Sa Rocca Ulari (Borutta) e di altre località della Sardegna. *Sardegna Speleologica* 17: 46–51.

Noctule Bat
Nyctalus noctula
(SCHREBER, 1774)

NAMES
D: Abendsegler
F: Noctule commune
E: Murciélago nóctulo común
I: Nottola comune
NL: Rosse vleermuis
S: Stor fladdermus
PL: Borowiec wielki

IDENTIFICATION
A large bat with broad rounded ears. The short flat-lying dorsal fur shines rufous-brown; the ventral side is a little lighter and duller. In winter the dorsal colour is dark-brown, sometimes with paler tips. The bare parts are black-brown. Long, and particularly towards the tip, narrow wings.

Similar species
No size overlap with the other two European mainland *Nyctalus* species. The Serotine has relatively longer and narrower ears, differently formed tragus and is usually darker coloured.

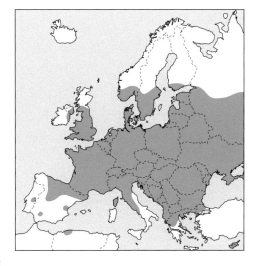

ECHOLOCATION CALLS
Often two alternately emitted sounds, which are, as follows, designated after the sounds heard with a heterodyne detector: the higher 'plip' (or 'chip') sounds are long and frequency-modulated, up to 13ms from 30–60kHz down to 22–28kHz; the 'plop' (or 'chop') sounds are up to 28ms long and almost constant-frequency, usually between 19 and 22kHz, rarely dropping to 16kHz. For humans with good hearing, audible in hunting flight with the naked ear. Possibilities for confusion exist particularly with the

Measurements	
Forearm	47.3–58.9mm
Fifth finger	47–58mm
Third finger	85–98mm
Normal weight	21–30g
CBL	17.6–19.6mm
CM^3	7.0–8.3mm

Fig. 378. In the flight photograph the narrow wings and the dense hairing along the forearm of the Noctule Bat are visible. Photo: D. Nill.

on the Mediterranean islands, in southern Greece very rarely. Only recently could the earlier doubtful records on Cyprus be confirmed (Nicolaou pers. com.). In the north a few records from southern Scotland. In Scandinavia and Russia up to the transition of the hardwood forest zone to the boreal coniferous forests at 60–61°N.

Subspecies and geographical variation
In the scope of this book only the nominate form. As can be expected in migratory species, there are no subspecific geographical differences; the European populations are also genetically not much structured [gen. lit. 80]. How the isolated population on Cyprus is to be classified taxonomically is still unclear. In the Middle East (Syria, Lebanon, Israel, Oman) *N. n. lebanoticus* is recognised. Several Asian subspecies, in particular *velutinus* and *furvus*, probably represent separate species.

HABITAT
A bat that occurred originally in hardwood forests and during the maternity period rarely over 550m. Besides the original biotope types: riparian forests, temperate beech forests and their transitions to the Mediterranean oak forests, nowadays a large spectrum of habitats, including cities, are used, as long as they have sufficient tree populations or a high density of high-flying insects. As hunting grounds almost all landscape types are used, although coniferous forest areas are less visited, and water bodies and riparian forests favoured relative to their availability.

Roosts
As summer roosts woodpecker holes are heavily favoured, otherwise a substantially smaller proportion use other tree holes, usually at heights of 4–12m, but also much higher [5]. Beeches are particularly frequently used, conversely coniferous trees rarely. Tree holes are visited preferentially near forest edges or along roads [2]. Noctule Bats readily use bat boxes. In the southern distribution nursery roosts frequently in buildings, behind house exterior panelling

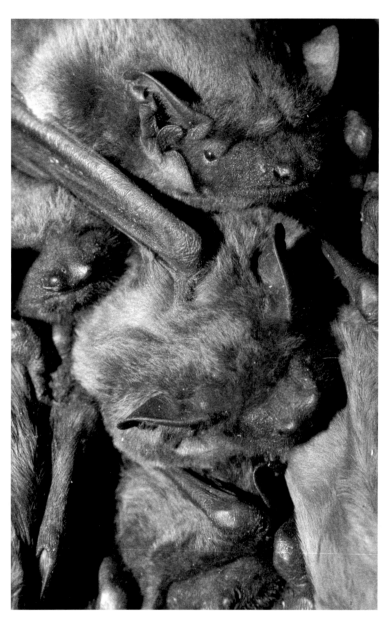

Fig. 379. In hibernation Noctules form dense clusters in tree holes. Photo: D. Nill.

Greater Noctule. Leisler's Bat calls are usually higher.

DISTRIBUTION
Large parts of Europe, also in North Africa(?), Asia Minor and the Near East. Eastward to central Russia and across the Urals and Caucasus and central Asia to Siberia, China, Japan, Nepal, India, Taiwan and Malaysia. On the Iberian Peninsula only isolated populations, particularly in the north. Apart from Corsica, not recorded

or in roll-down shutter boxes [gen. lit. 96]. In a north Bulgarian cave in a number of years a small nursery colony occurred in crevices of the roof [own data]. Males can likewise form groups in summer, these in tree holes, in rock crevices or in roof crevices of larger caves as well as in buildings. Winter roosts can be found in thick-walled tree holes, in crevices in buildings and bridges, rock crevices and in roof crevices of caves.

BEHAVIOUR

Nursery roosts comprise 20–60 females. Male groups are usually smaller with up to 20 animals. The animals of a colony are very active at higher temperatures and can be located from the clearly audible social calls. In a north Bulgarian cave over summer up to 2,000 male Noctules collect in high ceiling crevices; in the autumn a kind of mass display takes place with the influx of the females [own data]. Hundreds of swarming Noctules, assuming a mass display, were also observed in northern Greece in narrow rock ravines and in front of high cliffs [own data]. Winter roosts in trees can include 100–200 animals, a maximum of 420 animals was found [3], in buildings up to 500 animals. At cliffs and caves in southeast Europe several thousand Noctules hibernate in crevices, up to 5,000 animals in the joints of the high-level bridge over the Kiel canal near Levensau

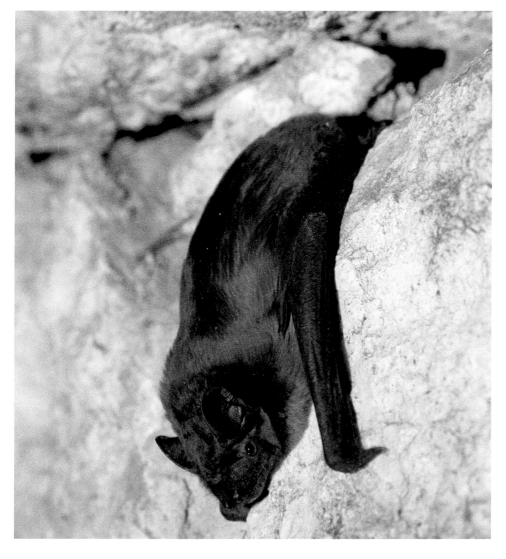

Fig. 380. While hanging, Noctules are easy to recognise by the compact body and the colouring. Photo: D. Nill.

(Germany) [10]. Very close clustering protects against low temperatures. From time to time shares roosts with Daubenton's and Nathusius's Pipistrelle Bats, in Russia and Ukraine also with the Greater Noctule.

REPRODUCTION

A proportion of the young females give birth in the year after birth. The young males are probably mature only after one year. Birth takes place from mid-June; from the end of July the adult females begin to leave the nursery roost. The 1–3-year-old females form the majority of the nursery colony animals in Central Europe (83%); some individual animals reproduce up to an age of nine years. A female gives birth to 1–2 young, in Great Britain usually one young, in Central Europe usually two; triple births occur very rarely [3, 13]. Twins often come from different fathers [gen. lit. 80]. Neonates have an average forearm length of 19mm and a weight of 5g; after 10 days they reach 33mm and 12g, and after 22 days a forearm length of 49mm and a weight of 21g. After four weeks they leave the roost for their first flights [6]. From the beginning of August the males occupy mating roosts in tree holes, which they defend vigorously against other sexually mature males. By singing from the roost entrance, more rarely by song flights, they attract usually 4–5, but also up to 20 females, who spend 1–2 days there. Only older, experienced males are believed to be able to occupy and defend attractive display roosts [3, gen. lit. 39]. The roost entrance is marked with secretions from the face and buccal glands [gen. lit. 39]. In southeast Europe there can be a mass display at prominent cliffs, ravines or large caves, where the animals show a kind of swarming behaviour. Mating groups are then formed in nearby rock crevices [own data]. In the autumn and winter active males making loud twittering can search large clusters of lethargic animals very energetically for females; then sometimes individual lethargic animals fall from ceiling crevices and become easy prey for predators.

FORAGING

Very fast (to over 50km/h) and direct flight, often at heights of 10–50m, partly, however, also at several hundred metres. Rapid dives for seizing prey. Forage over waterbodies, meadows and at streetlamps, and can also hunt at a few metres height, but usually maintain a distance of several metres from dense vegetation. In the autumn and winter also frequently hunt during the day, in winter particularly in warm spells, in cities also at temperatures around freezing point.

FOOD

The food consists particularly of Diptera, bugs, caddis flies, beetles and moths. Hunts readily on mass emergences of chafers or dung beetles. Hunting grounds and prey are used opportunistically, depending upon prey availability, the predominant prey item being hunted, hence dietary studies give variable results [3, 4]. Small to medium-sized flying insects represent the main prey [3]. In the autumn hunting flights frequently occur during the day, often in the late afternoon in sunshine, when mainly shield bugs and hover flies are captured [3]. In winter the food consists particularly of moths, Diptera and beetles [8].

MAXIMUM AGE

The maximum proven age is 12 years [3, gen. lit. 48]; the average age might, however, usually be distinctly lower; the age of adult females in nursery colonies averages 2.2 years [gen.lit. 48].

MOBILITY AND MIGRATION

A typical migratory bat, which migrates from the beginning of September into the late autumn, principally to the southwest, and returns to northeast from the middle of March to the middle of April [14]. These migrations take place, at least partly, during the day. Noctules can then be observed with swallows, in the south also with swifts. For the investigation of the migration pattern in Europe over 55,000 animals have been marked. The recorded distances are usually less than 1,000km; the longest distance recorded is 1,546km (often wrongly quoted as 2,347km!). The reproduction areas are predominating in northeast and northern Central Europe, with an emphasis on

Russia [3, 7], the winter and mating areas in the south and southern Central Europe. The populations at the northern limit of the distribution in the British Islands and in Sweden seem to be sedentary. The suspicion of sedentary populations exists also in northern Italy [3] and in northern Spain [12]. The presence all year of very many males in southeast Europe suggests that they are likewise sedentary and await the respective passage or influx of females. In Bulgaria and Greece, Noctules breed only in small numbers in Bulgaria a small maternity colony (up to 60 females) forms annually in proximity to a huge male roost area, and in north Greece only recently individual late-pregnant females have been found [own data].

Habitat use

Tree roosts, in particular the nursery roost, are changed frequently, within an area of up to 200ha. Roost shifts have been demonstrated to distances up to 12km. Hunting flights can extend to areas up to 2.5km distant [9], but some animals forage up to 26km from the roost [3]. With high insect density relatively small areas can be visited regularly, but often there are no well-defined hunting grounds, and the animals seem to roam more or less freely.

THREATS

Red list of the IUCN 2006: LC (Least Concern), EU Habitats Directive, Annex IV. Roosts are lost with building renovations and with intensive forestry. Pesticide use in forests and the destruction of natural riparian habitats can limit the food availability. Wind-turbines present a considerable danger during seasonal migration.

Widespread in England and Wales to southern Scotland, absent Ireland [UK gen. lit. 153, 155]. There is increasing concern about a marked decline in the population, and so the species was recently added to the list of Priority Species under the UK's Biodiversity Action Plan. A major decline had already been suggested as early as the 1960s and 1970s but without any supporting data. However, analysis for population trends from the data accumulated in recent

years by bat detector surveys for the National Bat Monitoring Programme so far does not show any significant trend. Being a fairly obvious species (emerges early, flies in the open with loud echolocation calls, often noisy in roost) may give a false impression of a relatively common and widespread species. At present there is no hard evidence of migration to or from the UK, but one or two records from North Sea oil installations and some anecdotal evidence suggest migration is possible. [If so,

Fig. 381. Hibernating group of Noctule Bats in a tree hole. Photo: D. Nill.

Fig. 382. In the ceiling cracks of the enormous Devetaška Peštera cave in north Bulgaria up to 2,000 Noctules summer. Photo: D. Nill.

it may be necessary to look wider than within the UK for reasons for decline.]

CONSERVATION MEASURES
Conservation of migration routes and keeping these free of sources of danger such as wind-turbines. Nature-friendly forestry and conservation of mature timber stands, especially of natural riparian woodland. Avoidance of the use of pesticides in forest. Protection of mass roosts during renovations.

REFERENCES

1. Blohm, T. (2003): Ansiedlungsverhalten, Quartier- und Raumnutzung des Abendseglers, *Nyctalus noctula*, in der Uckermark. *Nyctalus* 9: 123–157.
2. Boonman, M. (2000): Roost selection by noctules (*Nyctalus noctula*) and Daubenton's bats (*Myotis daubentonii*). *J. Zool.* 251: 385–389.
3. Gebhard, J. & W. Bogdanowicz (2004): *Nyctalus noctula* – Großer Abendsegler. In: F. Krapp (ed.): *Handbuch der Säugetiere Europas* 4–II: 607–694; Aula Verlag.
4. Gloor, S., H.-P. Stutz & V. Ziswiler (1995): Nutritional habits of the Noctule Bat *Nyctalus noctula* in Switzerland. *Myotis* 32/33: 231–242.
5. Heise, G. (1985): Zu Vorkommen, Phänologie, Ökologie und Altersstruktur des Abendseglers (*Nyctalus noctula*) in der Umgebung von Prenzlau/Uckermark. *Nyctalus* (N.F.) 2: 133–146.
6. Heise, G. (1993): Zur postnatalen Entwicklung des Abendseglers, *Nyctalus noctula*, in freier Natur. *Nyctalus* (N.F.) 4: 651–665.
7. Kaňuch, P. & M. Cel'uch (2004): On the southern border of the nursing area of the noctule in Central Europe. *Myotis* 41/42: 125–127.
8. Kaňuch, P., K. Janećková & A. Krištín (2005): Winter diet of the noctule bat *Nyctalus noctula*. *Folia Zool.* 54: 53–60.
9. Kronwitter, F. (1988): Population structure, habitat use and activity patterns of the noctule bat, *Nyctalus noctula*, revealed by radio-tracking. *Myotis* 26: 23–85.
10. Kugelschafter, K. & C. Harrje (1996): Die Levensauer Brücke bei Kiel als Massenüberwinterungsstätte für Große Abendsegler (*Nyctalus noctula*). *Z. Säugetierk.*, Sonderheft zu Band 61: 33–34.
11. Ruczyński, I. & W. Bogdanowicz (2005): Roost cavity selection by *Nyctalus noctula* and *N. leisleri* (Vespertilionidae, Chiroptera) in Białowieża Primeval Forest, Eastern Poland. *J. Mammal.* 86: 921–930.
12. Ruedi, M., Y. Tupinier & O. de Paz (1998): First breeding record for the noctule bat (*Nyctalus noctula*) in the Iberian Peninsula. *Mammalia* 62: 301–304.
13. Vedder, A. (1999): Drillingsgeburt beim Abendsegler (*Nyctalus noctula*). *Nyctalus* (N.F.) 7: 229–230.
14. Weid, R. (2002): Untersuchungen zum Wanderverhalten des Abendseglers (*Nyctalus noctula*) in Deutschland. *Schriftenreihe für Landschaftspflege und Naturschutz* 71: 233–257.

Greater Noctule Bat
Nyctalus lasiopterus
(SCHREBER, 1780)

NAMES
D: Riesenabendsegler
F: Grande noctule
E: Murciélago nóctulo grande
I: Nottola gigante
NL: Grote rosse vleermuis
S: Jättefladdermus
PL: Borowiec olbrzymi

IDENTIFICATION
The largest European bat. Very robust and massive appearance, with a broad snout, strong head and broad ears. Dense, relatively long and unicoloured fur, the dorsal side is reddish-brown or dark-brown, the ventral side only a little lighter. Particularly in males the hairs in the neck are long, up to 17mm and can be erected mane-like when agitated, whereby the head looks even more massive. The skin areas are dark-brown. The wings are very long with narrow tips, underwing quite broadly hairy even for a *Nyctalus* species between the body and the fifth finger and up to the elbow.

Similar species
Unmistakable due to the size.

ECHOLOCATION CALLS
Up to 28ms-long, almost constant-frequency and very loud calls between 14 and 23kHz. In open areas the long sounds usually lie between 17 and 20kHz. Clearly audible with the naked ear. Distinguishable from the Noctule in open areas by the very long calls, but the frequency range of both species strongly overlaps.

DISTRIBUTION
Little is known about the distribution, since from most areas only single records are available. In principle throughout northwest Africa [11], Asia Minor and Europe to about 50°N and into the Netherlands [14], northern France [10], southern Germany [9] and southern Poland. In the west the main distribution area is, however, very patchy and limited to the Mediterranean area [4]. The few regular occurrences are in Spain [4], southern France [3, 4], Tuscany [15] and Greece [8], but also in Hungary. The continuous main distribution area extends from Belarus, across Ukraine to Russia [gen. lit. 1]; here the occurrence reaches to about 60°N. Beyond the scope of this book to the

Measurements	
Forearm	61–70mm
Fifth finger	69–74mm
Third finger	108–116mm
Normal weight	35–53g
CBL	21.0–23.7mm
CM³	8.6–9.3mm

Fig. 383. The Greater Noctule is the largest bat species in Europe. Here an adult animal with the reddish-brown summer fur. Photo: O. von Helversen.

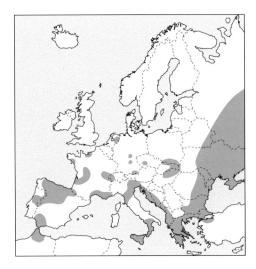

Urals, Caucasus, Iran and Kazakhstan. In Germany three records: 19th century – monastery Banz, Bavaria; 1827 – Renthendorf, Thuringia; 05.10.2001 – Tegern lake, Bavaria [7, 9]. In Switzerland several animals were captured at the Col de Bretolet and the Col de Jaman; a new record followed in the canton Aargau in May 2000 [9]; no records from Austria so far.

Fig. 384. Like the other species of the genus the tragus of Greater Noctule is short and mushroomshaped. Photo: D. Nill.

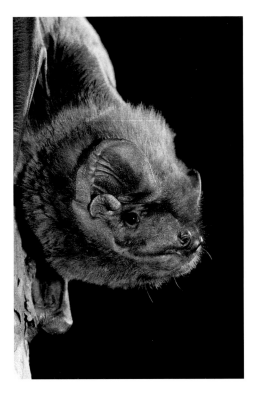

Subspecies and geographical variation

Only the nominate form. *N. aviator* from Japan, Korea and China, previously regarded as an eastern subspecies, is now considered a separate species.

HABITAT

Most localities lie in deciduous or mixed woodlands, in mountains in old fir tree woods. In the Mediterranean area also parks with plane trees are used. In the main distribution area in Russia and Ukraine the species occurs in beech and hornbeam forests [4, gen. lit. 1]. Particularly strong standard timber, and thus old trees, seem to be important.

Roosts

The few known roosts are found in tree holes of deciduous trees and firs [gen. lit. 1]; the roosts in Seville are in plane trees at 4–10m height [4]. Some animals also use bat boxes [2], roof spaces or crevices in larger caves.

BEHAVIOUR

In Spain nursery colonies with up to 80 animals [5], which consist only of females. In Ukraine and Russia the nursery roosts comprise often only 2–10 animals, shared with Noctule, Leisler's, Nathusius's Pipistrelle or Common Pipistrelle Bats [gen. lit. 1]. In summer males stay separate or in smalls groups [3]. In Greece almost exclusively males are found in summer, only in the autumn the females arrive [own data]. Supposedly they come from more northerly reproduction areas [8].

REPRODUCTION

Females of the Greater Noctule can become pregnant in the first autumn. It is unclear whether twins are exceptional or normal. Birth takes place at the beginning of June; the neonates have an average forearm length of 26–27mm and a weight of 9–10g [4].

FORAGING

Very fast and direct flight, sometimes at great heights; observations at twilight allow estimations of several hundred metres above the ground [own data]. If prey is detected, they make a very fast dive and then return to the original flight altitude. Drinking places are sometimes similarly approached.

FOOD

The food consists of large insects such as moths, dragonflies and beetles, which are captured in open areas [2]. Only in recent years in Italy [2], Spain [5] and Greece [own data] the presence of bird remains in faeces samples has been shown. Amongst more than 14,000 analysed faecal samples collected during bird migration in Spain from March to May and from August to November bird remains were found in up to 70%. In June and July no birds as prey were demonstrated [5]. At drinking places some trapped animals had blood on the snout or feathers at the claws. Two of the bird species identified by feathers (Robin and Wood Warbler) were probably captured in flight, conversely Blue Tits could be captured better at the night roost [2]. How the overwhelming of birds weighing 7–22g in flight takes place is unclear. It is easily conceivable that Greater Noctules seize and kill songbirds in a dive; however, whether they are able to cope with the additional weight and to consume the prey in flight is controversional [1]. The wings are very broad; however, a Robin would constitute an additional load of up to 50% of the bat's body weight. There are several conceivable scenarios: catching at the roost of the migratory birds [2], capturing in the air and dropping down to the ground or into the crowns of trees, or capturing at high altitude (some hundred metres) and thus when descending having enough time to stabilise the flight and to dismember the bird. Taking in flight seems the most likely by the absence of feathers in the faeces outside the migration time, the absence of resting places of migratory birds in the Spanish research area and findings of torn-off bird wings [5, 6].

MOBILITY AND MIGRATION

Single animals seem to migrate very far

Fig. 385. Only a few years ago faecal analyses demonstrated that Greater Noctules also eat birds. It is still unclear how the birds are captured in the field; in captivity they accept song birds readily as food. Photo: D. Nill.

and thus may reach northern France, the Netherlands [14], South Germany [9] and Poland [4]. The seasonal absence of females in the summer in Greece [8] and of animals of both sexes in the winter in northern areas [gen. lit.1] indicate seasonal migration.

Habitat use

So far data are scarce. Radio-tagged animals were located 12–25km from their roost [4], some animals covering more than 50km [12]. They appear to have no defined hunting ground, but fly around a wide area [4].

THREATS

Red list of the IUCN 2006: LC (Least Concern), EU Habitats Ditective, Annex IV. The main cause of threat might be forestry exploitation of old mountain forests.

Fig. 386. When agitated, particularly the males of Greater Noctule can erect the neck hairs like a mane and threaten with their strong teeth. Photo: C. Dietz.

Particularly in southeast Europe clearing of old towering mountain forests may form a serious threat.

CONSERVATION MEASURES

Preservation of old mountain forests with a high proportion of mature trees, large-scale protection of mountain forest areas in southeast Europe against legal and illegal logging. Preservation of large-scale holm and cork oak populations and of old trees in riverine habitats.

REFERENCES

1. Bontadina, F. & R. Arlettaz (2003): A heap of feathers does not make a bat's diet. *Func. Ecol.* 17: 141–142.
2. Dondini, G. & S. Vergari (2000): Carnivory in the greater noctule bat (*Nyctalus lasiopterus*) in Italy. *J. Zool.* 251: 233–236.
3. Haquart, A., P. Bayle, E. Cosson & D. Rombaut (1997): Chiroptères observés dans les départements des Bouches-du-Rhône et du Var. *Faune de Provence* 18: 13–32.
4. Ibáñez, C., A. Guillén & W. Bogdanowicz (2004): *Nyctalus lasiopterus* – Riesenabendsegler In: F. Krapp (ed.): *Handbuch der Säugetiere Europas*, 4–II: 695–716; Aula Verlag.
5. Ibáñez, C., J. Juste, J.L. Garcia-Mudarra & P.T. Agirre-Mendi (2001): Bat predation on nocturnally migrating birds. *PNAS* 98: 9700–9702.
6. Ibáñez, C., J. Juste, J.L. Garcia-Mudarra & P.T. Agirre-Mendi (2003): Feathers as indicators of a bat's diet: a reply to Bontadina & Arlettaz. *Func. Ecol.* 17: 141–142.
7. Helversen, O. von & W. Issel (1989): Über Jäckels Nachweis des Riesenabendseglers *Nyctalus lasiopterus* in Franken. *Myotis* 27: 151–155.
8. Helversen, O. von & R. Weid (1990): Die Verbreitung einiger Fledermausarten in Griechenland. *Bonn. Zool. Beitr.* 41: 9–22.
9. Meschede, A. & O. von Helversen (2004): Riesenabendsegler, *Nyctalus lasiopterus*. In: A. Meschede & B.-U. Rudolph (eds): *Fledermäuse in Bayern*: 262; Ulmer Verlag.
10. Nicolas, N. (1988): Une Grande noctule (*Nyctalus lasiopterus*) en Bretagne. *Mammalia* 52: 599–600.
11. Palmeirim, J.M. (1982): On the presence of *Nyctalus lasiopterus* in North Africa. *Mammalia* 46: 401–403.
12. Popa-Lisseanu, A.G., C. Ibáñez, O. Mora & C. Ruiz (2004): *Roost utilization of an urban park by the greater noctule*, Nyctalus lasiopterus, *in Spain*. Abstracts of the 13th International Bat Research Conference in Poland: 100; Museum and Institute of Zoology PAS, Warsaw.
13. Uhrin, M., P. Kaňuch, P. Benda, E. Hapl, H.D.J. Verbeek, A. Krištín, J. Krištufík, P. Mašán & J. Andreas (2006): On the Greater noctule (*Nyctalus lasiopterus*) in central Slovakia. *Vespertilio* 9–10: 183–192.
14. Verbeek, J. (1994): First record of the greater noctule, *Nyctalus lasiopterus* in the Netherlands. *Bat Research News* 35: 74.
15. Vergari, S., G. Dondini & P. Agnelli (1997): Supplementary records of greater noctule (*Nyctalus lasiopterus*) in Italy. *Myotis* 35: 111–112.

Leisler's Bat
Nyctalus leisleri
(KUHL, 1817)

NAMES
- D: Kleinabendsegler
- F: Noctule de Leisler
- E: Murciélago nóctulo pequeño
- I: Nottola di Leisler
- NL: Bosvleermuis
- S: Leislers fladdermus
- PL: Borowiaczek

IDENTIFICATION
Medium-sized dark-brown bat with powerful rounded ears and snout. The dorsal fur relatively short and flat-lying, particularly in males the neck fur can be longer and is erected when agitated. The base of the hair is dark black-brown, the tips red-brown; depending upon the situation the hairs give a dark glossy impression. Often darker

colouring in the autumn after the moult than in the summer. The ventral side is little delineated, at the throat more brightly yellow-brown. The skin areas are black-brown. The ear base and the base of the outer ear edge are usually distinctly lighter. Long and narrow wings, underfur extends thickly onto wing membrane and along forearm.

Similar species
In comparison with the two other mainland European *Nyctalus* species, clearly differentiated by the smaller size and the darker bicoloured fur.

ECHOLOCATION CALLS
Up to 20ms-long, almost constant-frequency calls with an end frequency of 21–26kHz, mostly around 24kHz. Partial frequency-modulated initial part, particularly with short calls. Noctule calls usually lower, the Northern Bat higher. Serotine normally has stronger frequency-modulated sounds in the initial part. Calls of the Parti-coloured Bat can be confused, here additional visual information can be helpful.

DISTRIBUTION
Throughout Europe to nearly 57°N, where large differences in the record density make general statements more difficult. The apparent absence within parts of the Mediterranean area, such as in eastern Spain [1], southern Italy and Sicily, might be due to observation gaps. Also from North Africa there are only a few single records (Morocco, Algeria, Libya). Occurs on the Balkan Peninsula [10], in large parts of Greece up to the Peloponnesus and along the west coast of the Black Sea. In the north the species reaches southern Scotland, conversely observations are lacking from Denmark and Scandinavia, with the exception of two detector records in south Sweden. The distribution border goes through Latvia and at almost about 57°N through Russia up to the Urals. Beyond the Caucasus [6] distributed to central China and India. Isolated populations on the Canary Islands (Las Palmas, Tenerife) and Madeira. Individual vagrant animals were found on the Färöe and Shetland Islands [3].

Measurements	
Forearm	38.0–47.1mm
Fifth finger	43–51mm
Third finger	70–78mm
Normal weight	13–18g
CBL	14.7–15.9mm
CM^3	5.3–6.1mm

Fig. 387. This young Leisler's Bat about two months old shows the grey-brown juvenile fur and characteristic light outer edge to the ear. Photo: C. Dietz.

Subspecies and geographical variation

Two subspecies: *N. l. verrucosus* on Madeira is smaller than *N. l. leisleri* from throughout the remaining distribution area.

HABITAT

A typical woodland bat, in particular in hardwood forests, more rarely in orchards and parks. Distributed from coasts and lowland riparian areas into mountain regions. On the Canary Islands and Madeira in subtropical laurel forests, in the Mediterranean area in oak, in Central Europe mainly in mixed beech woodlands. There is a clear preference for forests with high mature timber populations. As hunting grounds forests and their edge structures are likewise preferred, also cattle pasture particularly in the British Isles.

Roosts

In the majority of the distribution area a typical tree-dwelling bat, which occupies woodpecker holes, wood rot holes, overgrown crevices from lightening, rotted cavities in knot holes or branch holes [2]. Leisler's Bats prefer naturally developed tree holes to woodpecker holes [13], which are mainly occupied by Noctules. As an alternative bat boxes are readily accepted. In tree holes and bat boxes the animals prefer to hang close to the top [11]. Roosts often occur in beeches or oaks and can be found at all heights up to the crown. In the Białowieża Primeval Forest (eastern Poland) an average height of 18–19m was found [13]. Particularly in Ireland [3, 9, 15, 16, 17], on the Canary Islands and Madeira and at some localities in Germany roosts are found in roof spaces of buildings. Winter roosts likewise in tree holes, but also at buildings. Leisler's Bats are only rarely found in rock crevices.

BEHAVIOUR

Nursery colonies comprise usually 20–50 females; in buildings in Ireland a nursery roost with up to 1,000 animals has been recorded [3]. Males can form small colonies of up to 12 animals in tree holes and bat and

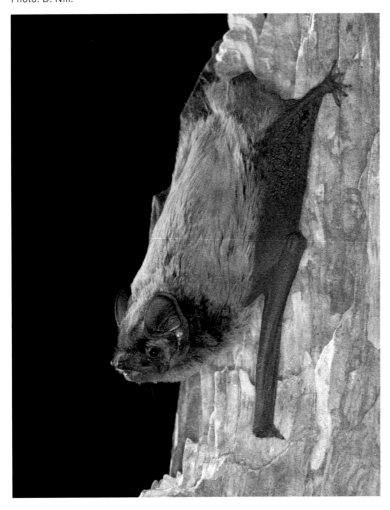

Fig. 388. Leisler's Bats mostly use tree roosts. Photo: D. Nill.

bird boxes. In late autumn hunting animals can also be observed in the late afternoon; Leisler's Bats are also active in winter on the Canary Islands and Madeira. In the roost they can live with a number of other tree-dwelling bats, such as the Noctule, Nathusius's Pipistrelle, Daubenton's, Natterer's and Bechstein's Bats.

REPRODUCTION

Mating takes place from the end of July to September in mating groups, into which the male lures up to 10 females, particularly with a song flight, or more rarely from the roost entrance [7, 11]. Between the beginning and end of June 1–2 young are born (in Great Britain and Ireland one young, but elsewhere usually two). A proportion of the young animals reach sexual maturity in their first autumn.

FORAGING

Very fast and usually direct flight just above or also below the canopy of trees and along forest trails and fire breaks but also over larger waterbodies and around streetlamps. The dense and flat-lying fur is, like the strong and short ears, an adaptation to prey capture in open areas and the fast flight, which can reach a hunting speed of over 40km/h.

FOOD

The food consists mainly of moths, but in addition also Diptera and caddis flies [8, 19]. In Irish and British animals, which hunt over pastureland, the Yellow Dung Fly (Scathophaga) as well as beetles comprise up to the half of the food [16]. In animals hunting along waterbodies non-biting midges, window-flies, mosquitoes and caddis flies dominate [16]. May and June bugs (melolonthids) are captured in large numbers with mass emergences, so large densities of profitable prey are probably selectively hunted. Overall, Leisler's Bats can be considered as opportunistic consumers of flying insects [3].

MAXIMUM AGE

The highest proven age is 11 years [gen. lit. 139].

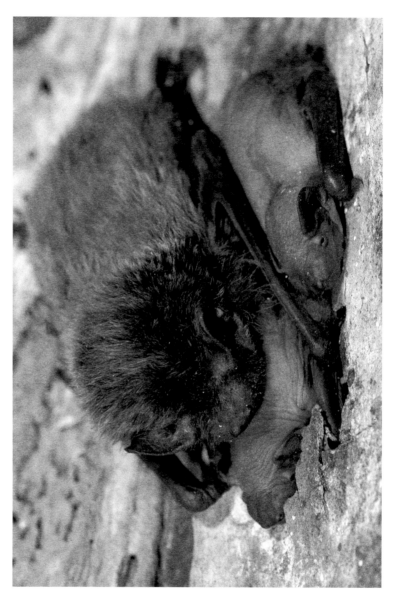

Fig. 389. Females Leisler's Bat usually bring twins into the world. Photo: D. Nill.

MOBILITY AND MIGRATION

One of the migratory bat species that seasonally covers long distances [3, 4]. At present six records of flights over 1,000km, with three over 1,500km. The record holder is, so far, a female that was recovered in a one-way straight-line distance of 1,567km in a site in northern Spain in the autumn after being ringed in Saxon-Anhalt (Germany) and was found again one and a half years later at the original ringing site [12]. Most of the, so far, 36 recorded recoveries of long distance flights lie in a southwest to northeast direction, but an animal

Fig. 390. This flight picture of Leisler's Bat shows the hairing on the body sides, which extends far onto the wing membrane along the forearm. Photo: D. Nill.

ringed in Russia flew to the south to the Turkish north coast. Possibly, however, some Leisler's Bats, like the populations in Great Britain and Ireland, in the northern Iberian Pennisula [1], on the Canary Islands [1], and in the Balkans are sedentary. Males remain, at least partly, in the transit and winter areas [7].

Habitat use

Roost changes take place sometimes daily and on small-scale distances of up to 1.7km [5]. A Leisler's Bat colony can use a large area in the course of one summer – up to 50 roosts in 300ha [14]. Hunting grounds are visited at distances of 4.2km from the roost [20] and can cover 7.4–18.4km². There are no individual hunting grounds; suitable habitats are visited on a broad scale [14]; only very profitable hunting grounds, such as street-lamps and waterbodies, may also be visited on a smallscale. Single animals can hunt up to 17km away from the roost [14, 17].

THREATS

Red list of the IUCN 2006: LC (Least Concern), EU Habitats Directive, Annex IV. Threatened by logging in summer, loss of roosts by the clearing of old mature trees or improvement to buildings (particularly in Ireland). Wind-farms are recently recognised as a substantial threat during migration. Habitat loss in the hibernation areas (Spanish cork and holm oak forests) could similarly have serious effects.

Widespread England and Wales to southern Scotland, but scarce in much of that range [UK gen. lit. 153, 155]. Widespread and common in Ireland and Isle of Man, which may form a stronghold of world population. Irish population considered stable. Little studied in Great Britain, but several studies in Ireland (Eire and Northern Ireland), where maternity colonies more frequently found in buildings. Although a scarce and possibly vulnerable species [21], there is currently no priority national initiative to establish details of status and conservation requirements in Great Britain. This is probably partly from difficulties due to limited summer roost data currently available, almost no hibernation site data, and concerns about ability for positive identification of bat detector records.

CONSERVATION MEASURES
Protection of large non-fragmented and semi-natural managed woodlands and preservation of large-scale holm and cork oak populations in the Mediterranean area. Protection of old mature trees and hole-rich standing dead timber. Preservation of safe migration routes.

REFERENCES
1. Agirre-Mendi, P.T. (2005): Distribucion y estado del conocimiento sobre el Noctulo pequeno *Nyctalus leisleri*, en Espana. *Nyctalus* (N.F.) 10: 233–241.
2. Beck, A. & W. Schorcht (2005): Baumhöhlenquartiere des Kleinabendseglers (*Nyctalus leisleri*) in Südthüringen und der Nordschweiz. *Nyctalus* (N.F.) 10: 250–254.
3. Bogdanowicz, W. & A.L. Ruprecht (2004): *Nyctalus leisleri* – Kleinabendsegler. In: F. Krapp (ed.): *Handbuch der Säugetiere Europas*, 4-II: 717–756; Aula Verlag.
4. Fischer, J.A. (1999): Zu Vorkommen und Ökologie des Kleinabendseglers, *Nyctalus leisleri*, in Thüringen, unter besonderer Berücksichtigung seines Migrationsverhaltens im mittleren Europa. *Nyctalus* (N.F.) 7: 155–174.
5. Fuhrmann, M., C. Schreiber & J. Tauchert (2002): Telemetrische Untersuchungen an Bechsteinfledermäusen (*Myotis bechsteinii*) und Kleinen Abendseglern (*Nyctalus leisleri*) im Oberurseler Stadtwald und Umgebung (Hochtaunuskreis). *Schriftenreihe für Landschaftspflege und Naturschutz* 71: 131–140.
6. Gazaryan, S.V. & A.K. Bukhnikashvili (2005): Preliminary data on the status of Leisler's bat (*Nyctalus leisleri*) in the Caucasus. *Nyctalus* (N.F.) 10: 261–266.
7. Helversen, O. von & D. von Helversen (1994): The 'advertisement song' of the lesser noctule bat (*Nyctalus leisleri*). *Folia Zool.* 43: 331–338.
8. Kaňuch, P., A. Kristín & J. Kristofík (2005): Phenology, diet, and ectoparasites of Leisler's bat (*Nyctalus leisleri*) in the Western Carpathians (Slovakia). *Acta Chiropterologica* 7: 249–257.
9. McAney, C. & J. Fairley (1990): Activity of Leisler's bat *Nyctalus leisleri* at a summer roost in Ireland. *Myotis* 28: 83–92.
10. Mirić, D. & M. Paunovi (1997): New data on the Leisler's bat *Nyctalus leisleri* from the Balkan Peninsula, with a review of the Balkan range. *Myotis* 35: 67–75.
11. Ohlendorf, B. & L. Ohlendorf (1998): Zur Wahl der Paarungsquartiere und zur Struktur der Haremsgesellschaften des Kleinabendseglers (*Nyctalus leisleri*) in Sachsen-Anhalt. *Nyctalus* (N.F.) 6: 476–491.
12. Ohlendorf, B., B. Hecht, D. Strassburg, A. Theiler & P.T. Agirre-Mendi (2001): Bedeutende Migrationsleistung eines markierten Kleinabendseglers (*Nyctalus leisleri*): Deutschland-Spanien-Deutschland. *Nyctalus* (N.F.) 8: 60–64.
13. Ruczyński, I. & W. Bogdanowicz (2005): Roost cavity selection by *Nyctalus noctula* and *N. leisleri* (Vespertilionidae, Chiroptera) in Białowieża Primeval Forest, Eastern Poland. *J. Mammal.* 86: 921–930.
14. Schorcht, W. (2002): Zum nächtlichen Verhalten von *Nyctalus leisleri*. *Schriftenreihe für Landschaftspflege und Naturschutz* 71: 141–161.
15. Shiel, C.B. & J.S. Fairley (1998): Activity of Leisler's bat *Nyctalus leisleri* in the field in southeast county Wexford, as revealed by a bat detector. *Proc. R. Irish Acad.* 98 B: 105–112.
16. Shiel, C.B., P.L. Duvergé, P. Smiddy & J.S. Fairley (1998): Analysis of the diet of Leisler's bat (*Nyctalus leisleri*) in Ireland with some comparative analyses from England and Germany. *J. Zool.* 246: 417–425.
17. Shiel, C.B. & J.S. Fairley (1999): Evening emergence of two nursery colonies of Leisler's bat (*Nyctalus leisleri*) in Ireland. *J. Zool.* 247: 439–447.
18. Shiel, C.B. & J.S. Fairley (2000): Observations at two nursery roosts of Leisler's bats *Nyctalus leisleri* in Ireland. *Myotis* 37: 41–53.
19. Sullivan, C.M., C.B. Shiel, C.M. McAney & J.S. Fairley (1993): Analysis of the diets of Leisler's *Nyctalus leisleri*, Daubenton's *Myotis daubentoni* and pipistrelle *Pipistrellus pipistrellus* bats in Ireland. *J. Zool.* 231: 656–663.
20. Waters, D., G. Jones & M. Furlong (1999): Foraging ecology of Leisler's bat (*Nyctalus leisleri*) at two sites in southern Britain. *J. Zool.* 249: 173–180.

ADDITIONAL REFERENCES
21. Hutson, A.M. 1993. *Action Plan for the Conservation of Bats in the United Kingdom.* The Bat Conservation Trust, London. 49pp.

Azorean Noctule Bat
Nyctalus azoreum
(THOMAS 1901)

NAMES
D: Azoren-Abendsegler
F: Noctule des Açores
E: Murciélago nóctulo de Azores
I: Nottola delle Azzorre
NL: Azoren rosse vleermuis
PL: Borowiec azorski

Measurements

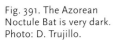

Forearm	37.8–40.7mm
Fifth finger	29–32mm
Third finger	?
Normal weight	6–13g
CBL	13.4–14.2mm
CM³	5.0–5.4mm

IDENTIFICATION
Similar to the Leisler's Bat, however, on average smaller and usually darker coloured, in particular face and ears almost black, without pale areas.

Similar species
On the Azores unmistakable. No paler skin on the ears.

ECHOLOCATION CALLS
In open areas the main energy of the almost constant-frequency sounds lies between 28 and 32kHz and thus clearly higher than in Leisler's Bat; the pulse length can extend to 16ms. Uses frequency-modulated sounds near obstacles [gen. lit. 128].

DISTRIBUTION
Endemic species of the Azores, recorded from all islands except Flores and Corvo [3, 4].

Subspecies and geographical variation
Often considered as a subspecies of Leisler's Bat, however, morphologically clearly different [2, 7]. Genetic studies show only slight genetic differences with Leisler's Bat and demonstrate the descent from the European Leisler's Bat [6]. Between populations of the Azorean Noctule Bats from two different islands there is a relatively large genetic diversity in fast-evolving gene sections, indicating a limited gene exchange [5, 6]. In Ireland two genotypes are found, of which one is very closely related to the Azorean Noctule Bat [Boston pers. com]

HABITAT
Hunting occurs in open areas over almost all available habitat elements [1], frequently at edges of forest and parks, also hunts

Fig. 391. The Azorean Noctule Bat is very dark. Photo: D. Trujillo.

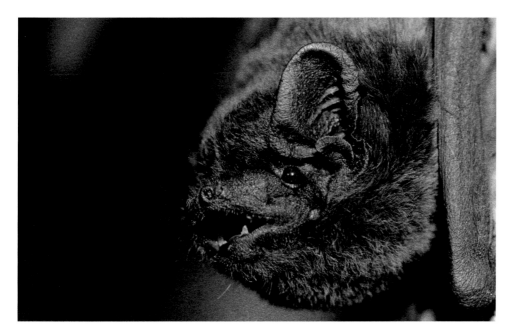

Fig. 392. In contrast to Leisler's Bat the ear of Azorean Noctule Bat is not pale inside. Photo: D. Trujillo.

readily around streetlamps in villages and hamlets. During the day usually hunts inland, at night particularly at the coast [3, 7].

Roosts
So far, roosts are only known in cracks and cavities in or on buildings [gen. lit. 59].

BEHAVIOUR
Frequently active at daytime, particularly hunting in the afternoon [1]; however, the main activity is in the night [7]. The frequently observed diurnal flights may be caused by the absence of day-active predators such as birds of prey, a higher food availability in daytime or less competition with insectivorous birds [1].

FORAGING
Fast hunting flight similar to Leisler's Bat, up to 25m height, often around streetlamps, but also close to the ground.

THREATS AND CONSERVATION MEASURES
Red list of the IUCN 2006: VU (Vulnerable), Red List of the European Union: VU (Vulnerable), EU Habitats Directive, Annex IV. On the Azores relatively common with a high population density (10 individuals per km²) [7]. Protection of the roosts in and on

buildings. The intended or inadvertent import of possible food competitors or predators must be prevented.

REFERENCES
1. Moore, N.W. (1975): The diurnal flight of the Azorean bat (*Nyctalus azoreum*) and the avifauna of the Azores. *J. Zool.* 177: 483–506.
2. Palmeirim, J.M. (1991): A morphometric assessment of systematic position of the *Nyctalus* from Azores and Madeira. *Mammalia* 55: 381–388.
3. Rainho, A., J.T. Marques & J.M. Palmeirim (2002): Arquipélago dos Açores. Pp. 8–28 In: *Os morcegos dos arquipélagos dos Açores e da Madeira: Um contributo para a sua conservação.* Technical Report. Centro de Biologia Ambiental / Instituto da Conservação da Natureza, Lisboa, 49 pp.
4. Rainho, A., T.J. Marques, P. Salgueiro & J.M. Palmeirim (2004): *Bats of the Atlantic archipelagos of Azores and Madeira: status and habitat use.* Abstracts of the 13th International Bat Research Conference: 50; Warsaw.
5. Salgueiro, P., M.M. Coelho, J.M. Palmeirim & M. Ruedi (2004): Mitochondrial DNA variation and population structure of the island endemic Azorean bat (*Nyctalus azoreum*). *Mol. Ecol.* 13: 3357–3366.
6. Salgueiro, P., M. Ruedi, M.M. Coelho & J.M. Palmeirim (2007): Genetic divergence and phylogeography in the genus *Nyctalus* (Mammalia, Chiroptera): implications for population history of the insular bat *Nyctalus azoreum*. *Genetica* 130: 169–181.
7. Speakman, J.R. & P.I. Webb (1993): Taxonomy, status and distribution of the Azorean bat (*Nyctalus azoreum*). *J. Zool.* 231: 27–38.

Common Pipistrelle Bat
Pipistrellus pipistrellus
(SCHREBER, 1774)

NAMES
D: Zwergfledermaus
F: Pipistrelle commune
E: Murciélago enano
I: Pipistrello nano
NL: Gewone dwergvleermuis
S: Dvärgfladdermus
PL: Karlik malutki

GENERAL INFORMATION
The Common and Soprano Pipistrelle Bats were recognised as separate species only a few years ago and the distribution of both sibling species overlaps to a large extent. In many previous studies the full species cannot be identified with certainty or many contain mixed data. Here only publications that refer clearly to the Common Pipistrelle are quoted.

IDENTIFICATION
A small brown-coloured bat with triangular ears. Dorsal side dark-brown, sometimes red-brown, in the south more brightly coloured. Ventral side a little paler yellow-brown, sometimes grey-brown. The bare skin areas are black-brown; the skin around the eyes and inside the ear is not significantly paler. No perpendicular skin bulge between the nostrils. The free edge of the wing membrane between the fifth finger and the foot ocasionally with a narrow, vaguely delineated pale border. The tail membrane is only furred near the body. The penis is grey-brown and shows a distinctive pale median band. The first upper incisor (I^2) is strong and has two cusps; the cusp of the second upper incisor (I^3) is shorter than the short (outer) point of the first – the three tooth tips thus form a steady gradation. Between the canine (C^1) and the large premolar (P^4) a small premolar (P^3) is visible from outside but sometimes shifted inwards and only the tip is visible.

Similar species
Very similar to the other *Pipistrellus*

species, however, differentiated from most by the graduated appearance of the three tips of the upper incisors and the penis morphology. Nathusius's Pipistrelle has a longer fifth finger (> 42mm) and a haired upper side of the tail membrane. For separation from Soprano Pipistrelle see under that species.

ECHOLOCATION CALLS
Up to 10ms long, frequency-modulated in the initial part and in the final part almost constant-frequency calls with an end frequency of 42–51kHz, usually of 44–47kHz. Social calls are usually four- to five-part trills [3].

DISTRIBUTION
Large parts of Europe up to 56°N. The northern border of distribution is not yet clear, since many of the previous records are based on the occurrence of Soprano Pipistrelle. The northernmost confirmed records originate from southern Finland near 60°N [17]. Recently also found in Norway. Occurs also on Cyprus [18]. Outside of Europe there are occurrences in northwest Africa, Asia Minor, and from the Middle East eastward to Iran and Afghanistan [4, 10]. The population on Crete belongs to *P. hanaki* [19].

Subspecies and geographical variation
In this region only the nominate form. The northwest African Common Pipistrelle

Measurements	
Forearm	28.0–34.5mm
Fifth finger	37–41mm
Third finger	50–56mm
Normal weight	3–7g
CBL	10.4–11.9mm
CM^3	3.8–4.4mm

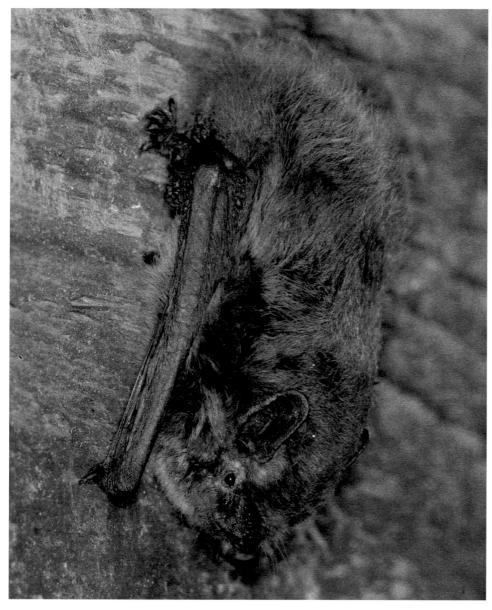

Fig. 393. The Common Pipistrelle belongs to the most common bat species in Central Europe, where it occurs throughout the area. Photo: C. Dietz.

possibly represents a subspecies [4]. In eastern Turkey, the Middle East and in the Caucasus region the somewhat smaller and paler *P. p. aladdin* occurs. The Libyan pipistrelles are meanwhile described as a full species (*P. hanaki*) and are closely related to the Soprano Pipistrelle [4]. The great variation within the *P. pipistrellus* group does not allow, so far, a full classification of the Mediterranean populations. In eastern Greece and in Turkey there are very small, pale-coloured animals with penis morphology very reminiscent of Soprano Pipistrelle.

Within the Moroccan Common Pipistrelles there are both animals with a typical *P. pipistrellus* penis and animals which actually show typical penis colouring for *P. pygmaeus* but there is no significant genetical difference [own data].

HABITAT
A very flexible species regarding its habitat requirements [12], occuring from city centres to rural human settlements and in almost all habitats. Where available, however, forests and waters are preferred.

Fig. 394. The Common Pipistrelle has little contrast in colouring between the dorsal and ventral side. Photo: D. Nill.

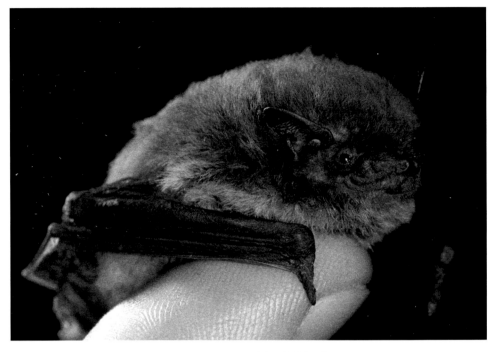

Roosts

An extensively synanthrophic species: summer and nursery colonies roost in a wide spectrum of crevice-like spaces in buildings, usually behind board cladding and under roof covering. Single animals can also be found in rock crevices and occasionally also behind tree bark. A diversity of isolated finds suggest that winter roosts are probably in buildings. Larger groups of hibernating animals are also found in rock crevices and some mass winter roosts in caves [11].

BEHAVIOUR

Nursery colonies usually comprise 50–100 animals, rarely up to 250 females. Earlier data of 1,000 animals and more may refer to Soprano Pipistrelle. Roost buildings are often marked with faeces, which are deposited in flight on walls and windows. The females are less loyal to roosts than other building-dwelling species; individual females and also whole nursery colonies move on average every 12 days [7]. Winter roosts in buildings are used by single animals or in suitable rock crevices several hundred individuals. Some dry cellars of castle complexes are visited by up to 5,000 Common Pipistrelles [14, gen. lit. 120]. In Slovakia and particularly in Romania there are mass winter roosts in caves. In the 1960s a cave in the Romanian Carpathians was discovered with over 60,000 Common Pipistrelles [6], a colony that nowadays amounts to 34,000 animals [11]. Such enormous winter aggregations seem to be typical for the Carpathian basin, but they are not found in the Mediterranean area, nor in other regions of Europe [9]. At large winter roosts Common Pipistrelles swarm from May to September, with the peak in August [14]. Invasions into unoccupied

Fig. 395. With incidents of mass invasion of Common Pipistrelle into buildings in the late summer numerous animals can die, as here in a fireplace. Photo: C. Dietz.

Fig. 396. Common Pipistrelle emerging from the roost. The entrance to the roost of this species is usually obvious from the droppings sticking to the wall. Photo: D. Nill.

buildings and into spaces being unsuitable as a roost are regularly observed [8]. In some cases, hundreds of Common Pipistrelles, particularly young animals, are trapped in houses by cantilever windows. Double-glazed windows, lamp casings, chimneys or pipes can also be traps, in which more than 1,000 animals can die [13]. In some buildings, usually in large cities, such invasions take place in several consecutive years. The dominance of young animals (90–99%) and the neighbourhood to winter roosts might indicate passing inexperienced animals in exploratory searches (exploring new roosting possibilities) or on migration. Once some bats are caught by such a trap they attract others of the same species by their social calls. A mass accumulation invasion site was observed near a mass winter roost in Marburg (Germany) [15].

REPRODUCTION

The majority of young animals reach sexual maturity in the first autumn. Adult males establish mating roosts, into which they lure females with song flights, and so mating groups of up to 10 females develop. Nursery colonies are occupied from May; the birth of 1–2 young occurs in the middle of June, sometimes only at the beginning of July. Neonates have a forearm length of 11–12mm and a weight of 1–1.4g, in 10 days grow to 19mm and 3.3g, in 20 days to 27mm and 4.1g. They are independent at four weeks at the latest the nursery colony then rapidly disperses.

FORAGING

The flight is agile and erratic. Usually patrolling along linear structures on fixed flight paths they capture prey in rapid manoeuvres and dives. Individual animals can hunt in small areas for hours, e.g. around streetlamps.

FOOD

The Common Pipistrelle is a generalist feeder, with Diptera always forming the majority of the food [2], with numerous other small flying insects occuring in the diet. Depending upon the foraging habitat non-biting midges or other flies dominate; with very good food availability selective preying on a few species of insect is assumed.

MAXIMUM AGE

The maximum age is over 16 years, although the average life expectancy is only

Fig. 397. In Common Pip-
istrelles of west Turkey the
face and ears are much
paler than in wide parts of
Europe; the animals resemble Soprano Pipistrelle.
Photo: C. Dietz.

2.2 years. The annual survival rate of juvenile Common Pipistrelles in Marburg castle
was estimated to average 53%, the more
adult animals up to 80% [gen. lit. 120].

MOBILITY AND MIGRATION

A sedentary species with seasonal flights
between summer and winter roosts of less
than 20km. A few long-distance migrations
are published. Some are based on errors for
Nathusius's Pipistrelles, with others there
is now the suspicion that they could refer to
Soprano Pipistrelles. The longest distance
of 1,123km relates to an animal from
Ukraine which was found dead in Bulgaria
and was incorporated into the collection of
the natural history museum in Sofia. The
animal is clearly a Common Pipistrelle, but
it is assumed that the ring used for exhibition purposes had been taken from another
specimen [Ivanova, Petrov pers. com.].

Habitat use

Nursery roosts are changed by some individuals to 15km distance and by the entire
nursery colony up to 1.3km [7]. Swarming
roosts are visited at up to 22.5km [7]. Conversely, the hunting grounds are normally
substantially closer to the nursery roosts; in
England the average distance to the hunting
grounds is 1.5km and the average area 92ha
[5].

THREATS

Red list of the IUCN 2006: LC (Least
Concern), EU Habitats Directive, Annex IV.
In large areas of Europe common, some
populations still growing after decades of
increase [1]. Nevertheless, locally threatened by roost disturbance and pesticide
use. In particular the mass winter roosts in
the Carpathian basin are threatened by cave
tourism.

Widespread and by far the most common species throughout the UK and Ireland [UK gen. lit. 153, 155]. Considered to have suffered major declines into the 1980s, but more recent data for the National Bat Monitoring Programme shows a conflict of trends between field surveys and maternity colony counts, the former suggesting a small increase, the latter a significant continuing decrease. Initially included as a Priority Species in the UK's Biodiversity Action Plan before the separation of this species and Soprano Pipistrelle; currently only the latter is included in the UK BAP, but both species are covered by many local BAPs. Together the two species comprise about 65–70% of the bats in Britain. Most summer colonies are in buildings, where they are widely accepted but equally the most frequent source of requests for advice over concerns about their presence.

CONSERVATION MEASURES

Protection from disturbance of the colony sites and in particular the mass winter roosts in caves.

REFERENCES

1. Arlettaz, R., G. Berthoud & M. Desfayes (1998): Tendances démographiques opposées chez deux espèces sympatriques de chauves-souris, *Rhinolophus hipposideros* et *Pipistrellus pipistrellus*: un possible lien de cause à effet? *Le Rhinolophe* 13: 35–41.
2. Arnold, A., U. Häussler & M. Braun (2003): Zur Nahrungswahl von Zwerg- und Mückenfledermaus (*Pipistrellus pipistrellus* und *P. pygmaeus*) im Heidelberger Stadtwald. *Carolinea* 61: 177–183.
3. Barlow, K.E. & G. Jones (1997): Differences in songflight calls and social calls between two phonic types of the vespertilionid bat *Pipistrellus pipistrellus*. *J. Zool.* 241: 315–324.
4. Benda, P., P. Hulva & J. Gaisler (2004): Systematic status of African populations of *Pipistrellus pipistrellus* complex (Chiroptera: Vespertilionidae), with a description of a new species from Cyrenaica, Libya. *Acta Chiropterologica* 6: 193–217.
5. Davidson-Watts, I. & G. Jones (2006): Differences in foraging behaviour between *Pipistrellus pipistrellus* and *Pipistrellus pygmaeus*. *J. Zool.* 268: 55–62.
6. Dumitresco, M. & T. Orghidan (1963): Contribution a la connaissance de la biologie de *Pipistrellus pipistrellus*. *Annales de Spéléologie* 18: 511–517.
7. Feyerabend, F. & M. Simon (2000): Use of roosts and roost switching in a summer colony of 45kHz phonic type pipistrelle bats (*Pipistrellus pipistrellus*). *Myotis* 38: 51–59.
8. Godmann, O. & W. Rackow (1997): Invasionen der Zwergfledermaus (*Pipistrellus pipistrellus*) in verschiedenen Gebieten Deutschlands. *Nyctalus* (N.F.) 5: 395–408.
9. Horáček. I. & H. Jahelková (2005): History of *Pipistrellus pipistrellus* group in Central Europe in light of its fossil record. *Acta Chiropterologica* 7: 189–204.
10. Hulva, P., I. Horáček, P.P. Strelkov & P. Benda (2004): Molecular architecture of *Pipistrellus pipistrellus/Pipistrellus pygmaeus* complex (Chiroptera: Vespertilionidae): further cryptic species and Mediterranean origin of the divergence. *Mol. Phyl. Evol.* 32: 1023–1035.
11. Nagy, L.Z. & L. Szanto (2003): The occurrence of hibernating *Pipistrellus pipistrellus* in caves of the Carpathian basin. *Acta Chiropterologica* 5: 155–160.
12. Oakeley, S.F. & G. Jones (1998): Habitat around maternity roosts of the 55kHz phonic type of pipistrelle bats (*Pipistrellus pipistrellus*). *J. Zool.* 245: 222–228.
13. Roer, H. (1981): Zur Heimkehrfähigkeit der Zwergfledermaus (*Pipistrellus pipistrellus*). *Bonn. Zool. Beitr.* 32: 13–30.
14. Sendor, T., K. Kugelschafter & M. Simon (2000): Seasonal variation of activity patterns at a pipistrelle (*Pipistrellus pipistrellus*) hibernaculum. *Myotis* 38: 91–109.
15. Smit-Viergutz, J. & M. Simon (2000): Eine vergleichende Analyse des sommerlichen Schwärmverhaltens der Zwergfledermaus (45kHz Ruftyp, *Pipistrellus pipistrellus*) an Invasionsorten und im Winterquartier. *Myotis* 38: 69–89.
16. Taake, K.-H. & H. Vierhaus (2004): *Pipistrellus pipistrellus* – Zwergfledermaus. In: F. Krapp (ed.): *Handbuch der Säugetiere Europas* 4–II: 761–814; Aula Verlag.
17. Wermundsen, T. & Y. Siivonen (2004): Distribution of *Pipistrellus* species in Finland. *Myotis* 41/42: 93–98.

ADDITIONAL REFERENCES

18. Benda, P., V. Hanák, I. Horáček, P. Hulva, R. Lučan & M. Ruedi (2007): Bats (Mammalia: Chiroptera) of the Eastern Mediterranean. Part 5. Bat fauna of Cyprus: review of records with confirmation of six species new for the island and description of new subspecies. *Acta Soc. Zool. Bohem.* 71: 71–130.
19. Hulva, P., P. Benda, V. Hanák, A. Evin & I. Horáček (2007): New mitochondrial lineages within the *Pipistrellus pipistrellus* complex from Mediterranean Europe. *Folia Zoologica* 56 (4): 378–388.

Fig. 398. The pale skin areas between eye and ear and the pale ear base are typical of Soprano Pipistrelle. Photo: D. Nill.

Soprano Pipistrelle Bat
Pipistrellus pygmaeus
(LEACH, 1825)

NAMES
D: Mückenfledermaus
F: Pipistrelle pygmée, Pipistrelle soprane
E: Murciélago pigmeo
I: Pipistrello pigmeo
NL: Kleine dwergvleermuis
S: Dvärgfladdermus
PL: Karlik drobny

GENERAL INFORMATION
Since the 1980s it became known in various parts of Europe that there are two call types in the 'Common Pipistrelle', which differ clearly in their frequency range, with a peak at around 45kHz and around 55kHz respectively. In England, the two call types were found to be sympatric and it was shown that they form separate colonies [21, 23], thus suspicion arose that there could be two species. This was confirmed shortly afterwards with genetic analysis [5, gen. lit. 78]. With the description of distinct features for identification, separating the newly discovered Soprano Pipistrelle by its echolocation calls and morphological features in the hand [15, 17], there was the possibility to examine the full extent of its distribution. New records are available from almost the whole of Europe. Because of the absence of the Common Pipistrelle in Scandinavia older Swedish work could be assigned to the Soprano Pipistrelle [13, 14, gen. lit. 40].

IDENTIFICATION
A very small bat with a noticeably short pale snout, strongly curved forehead and short pale ears. The very dense fur is only slightly paler on the ventral side than the rather pale dorsal side, which is typically sand- or reddish brown. Overall, it therefore often appears more multicoloured than the Common Pipistrelle. All skin areas in the Soprano Pipistrelles are paler brown than in the Common Pipistrelle; the inside of the auricle and the weakly haired region

Measurements
Forearm	27.7–32.3mm
Fifth finger	33–40mm
Third finger	46–55mm
Normal weight	4–7g
CBL	10.7–11.4mm
CM³	3.7 –4.4mm

around the eye in particular are very pale. A small raised bulge between the nostrils is present almost exclusively in the Soprano Pipistrelle. In contrast to the pale to whitish glands in the corners of the mouth in the Common Pipistrelle, this has yellowish-brown to orange buccal glands. The hair cover on the tail membrane is similar to that of Nathusius's Pipistrelle and extends substantially further than in the Common Pipistrelle. A very reliable feature is the colouring of the penis, which in the Soprano Pipistrelle is yellowish-white often with orange lateral folds of the preputium, while the penis of the Common Pipistrelle is grey-brown with a pale median stripe on the upper side of the glans penis between the lateral folds of the preputium. In the females of Soprano Pipistrelle the skin around the vagina is, at least in the reproduction time, likewise yellowish-orange coloured. Adults of Soprano Pipistrelle, in particular the males, often have a strong musk scent. The hind margin of the wing is often edged pale to whitish. A feature of the wingtip earlier considered to be diagnostic [15, 16] is not reliable for species identification. The cells in the wing, formed of elastic fibres, are nevertheless, a very useful feature: above the cell running uninterruptedly between the fifth finger and the elbow in the Soprano Pipistrelle there is also a second undivided cell that goes from the forearm to the fifth finger (see Fig. 247, page 146). The dentition features resemble those of the Common Pipistrelle.

Similar species
Easy to confuse with the Common Pipistrelle (see identification). Smaller than Nathusius's and Kuhl's Pipistrelle, in which the fifth finger is longer than 40mm.

ECHOLOCATION CALLS
Very similar calls to the Common Pipistrelle, up to 10ms-long calls with an end frequency of 50–60kHz, usually around 54–55kHz. Possible confusion exists in an overlap range of 50–52kHz with the normally lower frequency of the Common Pipistrelle and with the end frequency of the calls of Schreibers' Bent-winged Bat, lying

between 49 and 53kHz. The triple pulse display and social calls are, on the other hand, characteristic and clearly different from the Common Pipistrelle [4, gen. lit. 40].

DISTRIBUTION
Occurs throughout south and Central Europe, where sympatric with the Common Pipistrelle [gen. lit. 78], but details of the distribution are still insufficiently known. From the present knowledge using confirmed records, a distrubution can be assumed of the entire European Mediterranean area including western Asia Minor and Cyprus to about 63°N in Norway, eastwards to the Caucasus and further to Siberia. So far no records from North Africa or the Middle East [7, 20]. Based upon the published records distribution ranges from the Iberian Peninsula to Ireland, Scandinavia, the European Mediterranean area and the whole of the Balkan Peninsula to Turkey and Cyprus, in Moldova, Georgia, Ukraine, Azerbaijan and Russia [6, 8, 10, 11, 15, 16, 24, 25, 26, 28, gen. lit. 78, Kapfer, Limpens, Sachanowicz *in litt.*, own data].

Subspecies and geographical variation
Monotypic species, genetic investigations reveal a great uniformity of the sequences from across the distribution area [20, gen. lit. 78]. The closely related larger *P. hanaki* occurs in Libya and in Crete. A newly described subspecies, *P. p. cyprus*, occurs in Cyprus [29].

Fig. 399. View into a nursery roost of Soprano Pipistrelle, in the animal to the right the species-characteristic bulge between the nostrils can be seen. Photo: D. Nill.

HABITAT

Substantially more strongly dependent on riparian (hard- and softwood) forests, lowlands and waters of any size, in particular still waters, than the Common Pipistrelle, which uses a broader habitat spectrum. Particularly during pregnancy and the period of raising the young, water and its surrounding areas are used as the main hunting grounds; following weaning of the young a wider spectrum is used, e.g. also along vegetation edges [6]. In the Mediterranean area and on the Black Sea coast the species can often be found hunting over the sea in shallow bays and over lagoons [own data]. Agricultural areas and grassland are avoided throughout the distribution area.

Roosts

Nursery roosts are located in wall claddings of houses, under flat roof coverings, between underboarding and tiled roofs and in cavity walls [4, 9, 11, 15, 16], in hunting towers [16] or in tree holes and in bat boxes [8]. In the mating period exposed tree holes, bat boxes and buildings, as well as observation towers, are occupied [11, 23]. Winter records are, so far, scarce and usually originate from buildings [15, 24] and tree roosts [18], but also from bat boxes [8]. Probably the majority of the animals hibernate in tree roosts.

BEHAVIOUR

Nursery colonies of Soprano Pipistrelle are usually substantially larger than those of Common Pipistrelle: in England they can comprise at least 800 females [4, 9], the largest colonies in Germany included up to 300 [16], in Bulgaria 120 animals [11]. There are, however, also quite small nursery colonies of 15–20 females. In bat boxes it was found sharing with Brandt's Bat [8, Ohlendorf pers. com.].

REPRODUCTION

The juveniles reach sexual maturity in the first autumn [14, gen. lit. 40, own data]. In Bulgaria birth (usually twins) occurs from the second half of June [own data], in Uckermark (Germany) in the first days of June [8]. Adult males occupy display and mating roosts from June, into which, from the end of July, they use song flights to lure up to 12 females [13]. Such mating roosts are revisited over years [13]. The territorial male will accept sexually immature males into the roost, but not sexually mature males [11]. Mating takes place in August and September, also October [8, gen. lit. 40, own data], and copulation has been observed in March [19].

FORAGING

The Soprano Pipistrelle is extremely agile and hunts in a limited area and is more strongly associated with vegetation than Common Pipistrelle [1, 9]. Often hunts under branches overhanging water, in small glades in forests or over small waterbodies. Single shrubs or trees are patrolled more intensively than by the more wide-ranging patrolling Common Pipistrelle. However, hunting often occurs together with the Common Pipistrelle [24].

FOOD

The food is not fundamentally different from that of the Common Pipistrelle and comprises Diptera, Hymenoptera, mayflies and lacewings, only a very small proportion of other flying insects [1]. Due to the difference in habitat choice from the Common Pipistrelle, however, insects of river valleys such as non-biting midges, biting midges and mayflies dominate in the Soprano Pipistrelle [3].

MAXIMUM AGE
The proven longest age of Swedish animals is over eight years, but the average life expectancy is at least 1.2–1.6 years [14].

MOBILITY AND MIGRATION
Few available records. Some of the long-distance flights so far assigned to the Common Pipistrelle could relate to Soprano Pipistrelle. The occurrence of displaying animals and of mating groups in areas in which the species was not found in summer suggests at least some short-range migration. Two animals marked in Saxony-Anhalt were recovered over longer distances. An animal marked in a nursery roost was found about one year later at the Croatian Adriatic coast, a distance of 775km [Ohlendorf *in litt.*]. Another recovery in Germany covered at least 178km [Ohlendorf *in litt.*].

Habitat use
The Soprano Pipistrelle uses hunting grounds that are more distant from the nursery roost than those of Common Pipistrelle, with an average of 1.7km from the roost. Further, the total area of the foraging grounds is larger, although the individual hunting territories are smaller than those of Common Pipistrelle [9]. Overall, Soprano Pipistrelle seems to have more specific hunting requirements and uses smaller areas than Common Pipistrelle, but within a larger total foraging area [9].

THREATS
Red list of the IUCN 2006: so far not considered, EU Habitats Directive, Annex IV. No reliable population information available, local but not rare. Rarer than Common Pipistrelle within wide parts of the distribution. Quantitative data available so far only from Switzerland, where it is estimated that the Common Pipistrelle is 30 times more frequent [27]. In contrast, the Soprano Pipistrelle is the more common species in Greece [own data]. The preference for near-natural riparian forests and the large colonies present in buildings makes the species susceptible to damage from forestry and renovation works in human settlements.

Widespread and common throughout the UK and Ireland (slightly less widespread than Common Pipistrelle, particularly around northern Scotland and its islands) [UK gen. lit. 153, 155]. With fewer, but larger, colonies it appears to be as common as Common Pipistrelle in parts of its distribution, but may be significantly rarer in others, perhaps partly due to more restricted habitat requirements. The National Bat Monitoring Programme suggests a significant decline in this species since it was separated from Common Pipistrelle. It has recently been incorporated

Fig. 400. Foraging Soprano Pipistrelle in its typical habitat. Photo: D. Nill.

into the list of Priority Species for the UK's Biodiversity Action Plan and so is the subject of a dedicated conservation programme.

CONSERVATION MEASURES

Near-natural forestry with a high proportion of mature timber and preservation of natural riparian woodlands. Preservation of natural river courses and spacious inundation areas. Protection of colonies, in particular with building renovation.

REFERENCES

1. Arnold, A., U. Häussler & M. Braun (2003): Zur Nahrungswahl von Zwerg- und Mückenfledermaus (*Pipistrellus pipistrellus* und *P. pygmaeus*) im Heidelberger Stadtwald. *Carolinea* 61: 177–183.
2. Barlow, K.E., G. Jones & E.M. Barratt (1997): Can skull morphology be used to predict ecological relationships between bat species? A test using two cryptic species of pipistrelle. *Proc. R. Soc. Lond.* B 264: 1695–1700.
3. Barlow, K.E. (1997): The diets of two phonic types of the bat *Pipistrellus pipistrellus* in Britain. *J. Zool.* 243: 597–609.
4. Barlow, K.E. & G. Jones (1999): Roosts, echolocation calls and wing morphology of two phonic types of *Pipistrellus pipistrellus*. *Z. Säugetierk.* 64: 257–268.
5. Barratt, E.M., R. Deaville, T.M. Burland, M.W. Bruford, G. Jones, P.A. Racey & R.K. Wayne (1997): DNA answers the call of pipistrelle bat species. *Nature* 387: 138–139.
6. Bartonička, T. & Z. Řehák (2004): Flight activity and habitat use of *Pipistrellus pygmaeus* in a floodplain forest. *Mammalia* 68: 365–375.
7. Benda, P., P. Hulva, M. Andreas & M. Uhrin (2003): Notes in the distribution of *Pipistrellus pipistrellus* complex in the Eastern Mediterranean: First records of *P. pipistrellus* for Syria and *P. pygmaeus* for Turkey. *Vespertilio* 7: 87–95.
8. Blohm, T. & G. Heise (2005): Erste Ergebnisse zu Phänologie, Biometrie, Artkennzeichen, Ökologie und Vorkommen der Mückenfledermaus, *Pipistrellus pygmaeus*, in der Uckermark. *Nyctalus* (N.F.) 9: 544–552.
9. Davidson-Watts, I. & G. Jones (2006): Differences in foraging behaviour between *Pipistrellus pipistrellus* and *Pipistrellus pygmaeus*. *J. Zool.* 268: 55–62.
10. Dietz, C., I. Schunger, D. Nill, B.M. Siemers & T. Ivanova (2002): First record of *Pipistrellus pygmaeus* (Leach, 1825) (Chiroptera: Vespertilionidae) for Bulgaria. *Historia Naturalis Bulgarica* 14: 117–121.
11. Dietz, C., I. Schunger, Ö. Keşapli-Didrickson, A. Karataş & F. Mayer (2005): First record of *Pipistrellus pygmaeus* (Chiroptera: Vespertilionidae) in Anatolia. *Zoology in the Middle East* 34: 5–10.
12. Downs, N.C., V. Beaton, J. Guest, J. Polanski & S.L. Robinson (2003): The effects of illuminating the roost entrance on the emergence behaviour of *Pipistrellus pygmaeus*. *Biol. Conserv.* 111: 247–252.

Fig. 401. Soprano Pipistrelles hunt particularly in damp areas and riparian woodland. Photo: D. Nill.

13. Gerell, R. & K. Lundberg (1985): Social organization in the bat *Pipistrellus pipistrellus*. *Behav. Ecol. Sociobiol.* 16: 177–184.

14. Gerell, R. & K. Lundberg (1990): Sexual differences in survival rates of adult pipistrelle bats (*Pipistrellus pipistrellus*) in south Sweden. *Oecologia* 83: 401–404.

15. Häussler, U., A. Nagel, M. Braun & A. Arnold (1999): External characters discriminating sibling species of European pipistrelles, *Pipistrellus pipistrellus* and *P. pygmaeus*. *Myotis* 37: 27–40.

16. Häussler, U. & M. Braun (2003): Mückenfledermaus *Pipistrellus pygmaeus*. In: M. Braun & F. Dieterlen (eds): *Die Säugetiere Baden-Württembergs, Band 1: Allgemeiner Teil, Fledermäuse (Chiroptera)*: 544–568; Ulmer Verlag.

17. Helversen, O. von & M. Holderied (2003): Zur Unterscheidung von Zwergfledermaus (*Pipistrellus pipistrellus*) und Mückenfledermaus (*Pipistrellus mediterraneus/pygmaeus*) im Feld. *Nyctalus* (N.F.) 8: 420–426.

18. Helversen, O. von & C. Koch (2004): Mückenfledermaus, *Pipistrellus pygmaeus*. In: A. Meschede & B.-U. Rudolph (eds): *Fledermäuse in Bayern*: 276–279; Ulmer Verlag.

19. Horn, J. (2006): Paarung der Mückenfledermaus (*Pipistrellus pygmaeus*) im März. *Nyctalus* (N.F.) 11: 95–98.

20. Hulva, P., I. Horáček, P. P. Strelkov & P. Benda (2004): Molecular architecture of *Pipistrellus pipistrellus/Pipistrellus pygmaeus* complex (Chiroptera: Vespertilionidae): further cryptic species and Mediterranean origin of the divergence. *Mol. Phyl. Evol.* 32: 1023–1035.

21. Jones, G. & S.M. van Parijs (1993): Bimodal echolocation in pipistrelle bats: are cryptic species present? *Proc. R. Soc. Lond.* B 251: 119–125.

22. Oakeley, S.F. & G. Jones (1998): Habitat around maternity roosts of the 55kHz phonic type of pipistrelle bats (*Pipistrellus pipistrellus*). *J. Zool.* 245: 222–228.

23. Park, K.J., J.D. Altringham & G. Jones (1996): Assortative roosting in the two phonic types of *Pipistrellus pipistrellus* during the mating season. *Proc. R. Soc. Lond.* B 263: 1495–1499.

24. Presetnik, P., K. Koselj & M. Zagmajster (2001): First records of *Pipistrellus pygmaeus* (Leach, 1825) in Slovenia. *Myotis* 39: 31–34.

25. Rakhmatulina, I.K. & N.A. Hassanov (2002): *Pipistrellus pygmaeus* in Azerbaijan. *Plecotus et al. pars spec.* 2002: 98–99.

26. Russo, D. & G. Jones (2000): The two cryptic species of *Pipistrellus pipistrellus* occur in Italy: evidence from echolocation and social calls. *Mammalia* 64: 187–197.

27. Sattler, T. (2003): *Ecological factors affecting the distribution of the sibling species* Pipistrellus pygmaeus *and* Pipistrellus pipistrellus *in Switzerland*. – Diplomarbeit am Zoologischen Institut der Universität Bern.

28. Stadelmann, B., D.S. Jacobs, C. Schoeman & M. Ruedi (2004): Phylogeny of African *Myotis* bats (Chiroptera, Vespertilionidae) inferred from cytochrome b sequences. *Acta Chiropterologica* 6: 177–192.

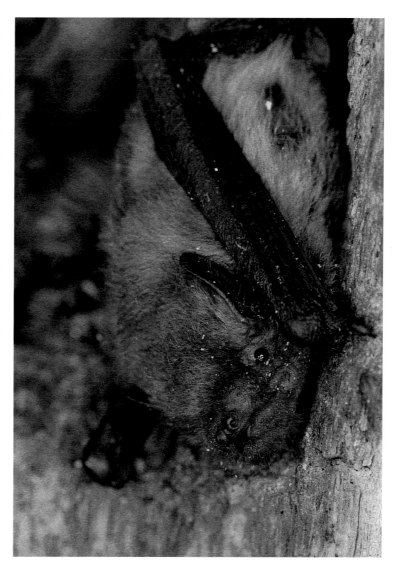

Fig. 402. Typical adult colouring of the Soprano Pipistrelle. Photo: D. Nill.

ADDITIONAL REFERENCES

29. Benda, P. V. Hanák, I. Horáček, P. Hulva, R. Lučan & M. Ruedi (2007): Bats (Mammalia: Chiroptera) of the Eastern Mediterranean. Part 5. Bat fauna of Cyprus: review of records with confirmation of six species new for the island and description of new subspecies. *Acta Soc. Zool. Bohem.* 71: 71–130.

Nathusius's Pipistrelle Bat
Pipistrellus nathusii
(Keyserling & Blasius, 1839)

NAMES
- D: Rauhhautfledermaus
- F: Pipistrelle de Nathusius
- E: Murciélago de Nathusius
- I: Pipistrello di Nathusius
- NL: Ruige dwergvleermuis
- S: Trollfladdermus
- PL: Karlik większy

Measurements

Forearm	32.2–37.1mm
Fifth finger	41–48mm
Third finger	57–62mm
Normal weight	6–10g
CBL	12.5–13.3mm
CM³	4.5–4.8mm

IDENTIFICATION
Small, relatively unicoloured brown bat, the dorsal fur is reddish-brown in summer, after the moult dark-brown, from the end of July with grey tips. The ventral side is scarcely delineated, somewhat more paler yellowish brown. The tail membrane is furred on the upper side to about half the length. The skin areas are dark-brown, the wings relatively long and often with a vaguely paler border at the lateral edge. In the lateral membrane of the wing (plagiopatagium) the cell that runs from the elbow to the fifth finger is divided by a distinct bar (see Fig. 245, page 146). The first (inner) upper incisor (I^2) is strong and has two cusps; the second upper incisor (I^3) is long and extends above the short (outer) tip of the first. From outside a small premolar (P^3) in the upper jaw is clearly visible between the canine (C^1) and the large premolar (P^4). Males have a characteristic egg-shaped penis.

Similar species
Very similar to the other pipistrelle species, however the fifth finger is usually longer than 43mm (very rarely only 41mm long) and thus longer than in Common and Soprano Pipistrelles. Kuhl's Pipistrelle has a single cusp on the first upper incisor (I^2) and the smaller upper premolar (P^3) is set inside the tooth row and barely or not visible from outside. Between the second and third lower incisor (I_2 and I_3) Nathusius's Pipistrelle usually has a distinct gap; in Kuhl's and the Common Pipistrelle the tooth row is closed.

ECHOLOCATION CALLS
Up to 12ms-long calls with an initial frequency-modulated part and the final part with almost constant frequency at 37–41kHz. A reliable distinction from Kuhl's Pipistrelle is only possible on the basis of the social calls.

DISTRIBUTION
Large parts of Europe, northernmost record nearly 60°N in Scotland, Sweden, Finland and Russia. In the west in eastern Ireland, France and northern Spain. In the east the distribution reaches the Urals and the Caucasus. Due to its long-distance seasonal migration the species can also occur in the south and reaches Corsica, Sardinia, Sicily, the Peloponnes peninsula and western Turkey. Two records from Iceland are regarded as ship-assisted animals [7]. The reproduction areas are particularly in the northeast of the distribution, while the hibernation areas are situated more southwest. In Germany, however, an apparent expansion of the reproduction area was observed from the first record of a nursery colony in Mecklenburg-Western Pomerania in 1965, followed by settlement in the Uckermark, Brandenburg, Schleswig-Holstein and Saxony-Anhalt, and then records in Bavaria [10, 14]. The species seems also to have become established in the Netherlands, Great Britain and

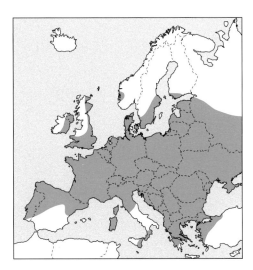

northern Italy, where nursery colonies have only been recorded in recent decades [6, 9, 12]. In the Balkan Peninsula only in Greece and Bulgaria are there many observations [own data] but these are mainly scattered individuals. However, there are summering males in north Bulgaria and mating roosts in suitable areas in northwest Turkey, so that permanent occurrence here, comparable with the new finds in the northeast of the Iberian Peninsula [5], and possibly the establishment of small nursery colonies can be expected [own data, 4].

Subspecies and geographical variation

Only the nominate form. There is possibly a size gradient from west to east, with larger forearm lengths in the east.

HABITAT

Mostly natural richly structured forest habitat: deciduous mixed woodlands, damp lowland forests, riparian forests, but also coniferous forests and park landscapes. Often near waterbodies. Hunting grounds are in forests and forest edges, often also over water [2]. Hunting animals can also be found, particularly during migration, in built-up areas. Nursery roosts in lowlands, the highest recorded observation is below 500m.

ROOSTS

Roost sites are primarily crevices in bark, tree holes, and the species readily adopts bat and bird boxes. Records of nursery colonies are also known from timber claddings of barns, houses and wooden churches. Some animals can be found in quite different roosts: besides tree roosts also in expansion joints and construction fissures of bridges and in rock crevices. Mating roosts are frequently in exposed places: tree avenues, detached buildings, bridges and observation towers. Winter roosts particularly in tree holes and wood piles but also in crevices of buildings and cliffs.

BEHAVIOUR

Nursery roosts comprise 20, but also up to 200 females, depending upon the available

space in the roost [14] and are occupied from the beginning of May. Roost often shared with Common Pipistrelles, Brandt's or Pond Bats.

Fig. 403. Nathusius's Pipistrelle is inconspicuously coloured with brown tones. Photo: D. Nill.

REPRODUCTION

The young, mostly twins, rarely also triplets [13], are born at the end of May/beginning of June. The nursery roosts are already abandoned by the end of July. Mating takes place near the nursery roost (at the end of August/beginning of September) or during

Fig. 404. Nathusius's Pipistrelle in flight. Photo: D. Nill.

migration until the beginning of November, when even the 3–4–month-old young females successfully participate. Mostly 1–3-year-old females are effectively reproductive and constitute 75% of the nursery colony [gen. lit. 114]. Males occupy their mating roosts in autumn near the nursery roosts, as well as along migration routes and near the winter roosts. With display calls they attract passing animals and in this way also provide roosts to animals unaquainted with the local area. Mating groups comprise 3–10 animals; young males are also accepted in the roost and are not seen as rivals [3]. In Bulgarian and Turkish mating roosts it was noticeable that the local resident males still had the typical red-brown summer fur, while the arriving females aready had the grey tint of winter fur [own data].

FORAGING

Hunting takes place in a rapid and direct flight, often along linear structures such as forest trails, fire breaks and edges of forest but also along and over waterways, sometimes also around streetlamps. Not so manoeuvrable as Common Pipistrelle. Flight height usually at 3–20m, sometimes lower over water.

FOOD

The food consists exclusively of flying insects, usually of waterborne Diptera (particularly non-biting midges, but also mosquitoes and black-flies), to a lesser extent also caddis flies, aphids, lacewings and other small insects [1, 12].

MAXIMUM AGE

The proven maximum age is over 12 years (females) and over 14 years (male) [10]. The average age of the females of a nursery colony is 2.7–3.0 years, that of the males 2.5 years. 56% of the young females survive their first year of life, thereafter the annual survival rate for adult females is 70.8%, for adult males at least 60.7%. The average life expectancy of females amounts to 1.95 years [gen. lit. 113].

MOBILITY AND MIGRATION

A seasonal long-distance migrant, whose migration behaviour has been intensively studied for several decades. European-wide over 60,000 animals have been marked; the longest distance recorded so far is 1,905km [8]. In the autumn the animals migrate mainly in a southwest direction, along coastlines and river valleys they also migrate over mountains such as the Alps or Pyrenees. The hibernation areas of northeast German and Baltic populations lie 1,000–2,000km away, particularly in the Netherlands, France, south Germany, Switzerland, north Italy and the northwest of the Balkan Peninsula. Animals from the Russian Voronesch area were recovered up to 1,600km distance in Bulgaria, Greece and Turkey [12]. In August, the females migrate first from the reproduction areas; the males follow, with the last leaving in October (in the north until September). Passage migrants can be seen in southern Germany at the beginning of November [gen. lit. 36] and in Slovenia until the end of November [gen. lit. 96]. The migration capacity is 29–48km per night, rarely some animals reach 80km per night. The date of the first and last observation in a bat box area in northern Brandenburg is shifting increasingly to earlier and later dates respectively, a development that may be connected with climate change [10].

Habitat use

Hunting grounds lie up to 6.5km from the roost and can extend over 20km², within which hunting is in 4–11 substantially smaller areas of a few hectares [2, 11].

THREATS

Red list of the IUCN 2006: LC (Least Concern), EU Habitats Directive, Annex IV. In northern Germany clear increase of occurence and spreading to the west and south. Threats result from insect control measures and, during migration, from wind-farms and roads. Forestry has a large influence on the availability of natural roosts.

Formerly regarded as a vagrant to the UK, Nathusius's Pipistrelle is now regarded as a regular migrant and with some resident population (probably mostly males) and a few recorded maternity colonies

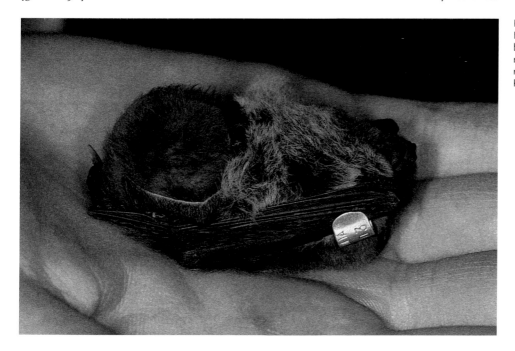

Fig. 405. The migrations of Nathusius's Pipistrelle have been studied for decades by marking with individually numbered aluminium rings. Photo: C. Dietz.

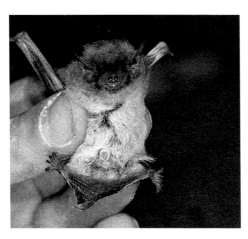

Fig. 406. Nathusius's Pipistrelle has a mating system in which both sexes mate with numerous partners. Consequently the epididymis at the tail root of the males is very large, in order to make a large supply of sperm cells possible. Photo: C. Dietz.

(although none may be currently known) [UK gen. lit. 153, 155]. First recorded in 1969, with a hugely increasing number of records in recent years [9], which may be more a product of observer effort and capacity to separate the species than to any wider change in status or range.

CONSERVATION MEASURES

Preservation of riparian forests and protection of mature trees in forests. Abandonment of pesticide use in forests. Preservation of non-fragmented corridor areas and prevention of increased mortality during migration e.g. by wind turbines or roads.

REFERENCES

1. Arnold, A., M. Braun, N. Becker & V. Storch (2000): Zur Nahrungsökologie von Wasser- und Rauhhautfledermaus in den nordbadischen Rheinauen. *Carolinea* 58: 257–263.
2. Arnold, A. & M. Braun (2002): Telemetrische Untersuchungen an Rauhhautfledermäusen (*Pipistrellus nathusii*) in den nordbadischen Rheinauen. *Schriftenreihe für Landschaftspflege und Naturschutz* 71: 177–189.
3. Ciechanowski, M. & T. Jarzembowski (2004): The size and number of harems in the polygynous bat *Pipistrellus nathusii* (Chiroptera: Vespertilionidae). *Mamm. Biol.* 69: 277–280.
4. Dietz, C., I. Schunger, Ö. Keşapli-Didrickson, A. Karataş & F. Mayer (2005): First record of (Chiroptera: Vespertilionidae) in Anatolia. *Zoology in the Middle East* 34: 5–10.
5. Flaquer, C., R. Ruiz-Jarillo, I. Torre & A. Arrizabalaga (2005): First resident population of *Pipistrellus nathusii* in the Iberian Peninsula. *Acta Chiropterologica* 7: 183–188.
6. Martinioli, A., D.G. Preatoni & G. Tosi (2002): Does Nathusius' pipistrelle *Pipistrellus nathusii* breed in northern Italy? *J. Zool.* 250: 217–220.
7. Petersen, A. (1994): The occurrence of bats (Order Chiroptera) in Iceland. *Natturufraedingurinn* 64: 3–12.
8. Petersons, G. (2004): Seasonal migrations of north-eastern populations of Nathusius' bat *Pipistrellus nathusii* (Chiroptera). *Myotis* 41/42: 29–56.
9. Russ, J.M., A.M. Hutson, W.I. Montgomery, P.A. Racey & J.R. Speakman (2001): The status of Nathusius' pipistrelle (*Pipistrellus nathusii*) in the British Isles. *J. Zool.* 254: 91–100.
10. Schmidt, A. (2000): 30–jährige Untersuchungen in Fledermauskastengebieten Ostbrandenburgs unter besonderer Berücksichtigung von Rauhhautfledermaus (*Pipistrellus nathusii*) und Abendsegler (*Nyctalus noctula*). *Nyctalus* (N.F.) 7: 396–422.
11. Schorcht, W., C. Tress, M. Biedermann, R. Koch & J. Tress (2002): Zur Ressourcennutzung von Rauhhautfledermäusen (*Pipistrellus nathusii*) in Mecklenburg. *Schriftenreihe für Landschaftspflege und Naturschutz* 71: 191–212.
12. Vierhaus, H. (2004): *Pipistrellus nathusii* – Rauhhautfledermaus. In: F. Krapp (ed.): *Handbuch der Säugetiere Europas* 4–II: 825–873; Aula Verlag.
13. Wohlgemuth, R. (1997): Erstnachweis einer Drillingsgeburt bei der Rauhhautfledermaus (*Pipistrellus nathusii*). *Nyctalus* (N.F.) 6: 393–396.
14. Zahn, A., B. Hartl, B. Henatsch, A. Keil & S. Marka (2002): Erstnachweis einer Wochenstube der Rauhhautfledermaus (*Pipistrellus nathusii*) in Bayern. *Nyctalus* (N.F.) 8: 187–190.

Kuhl's Pipistrelle Bat
Pipistrellus kuhlii
(KUHL, 1817)

NAMES
- D: Weißrandfledermaus
- F: Pipistrelle de Kuhl
- E: Murciélago de borde claro
- I: Pipistrello albolimbato
- NL: Kuhls dwergvleermuis
- S: Kuhls fladdermus
- PL: Karlik Kuhla

IDENTIFICATION
A small bat with a variable colouring, the brown dorsal fur often pale, beige or ochre tones. The ventral side is a poorly delineated pale beige, whitish or pale yellowish colour. Ears and face in adult animals reddish-brown, in younger animals dark-brown. At the free edge of the flight membrane, particularly between the fifth finger and the foot, extends a usually sharply defined wide white border of 1–2mm. In rare cases it is absent, but in North Africa the edge is often even broader. The pattern of the wing area in the lateral membrane (plagiopatagium) resembles that of the Common Pipistrelle; the open field from the elbow to the fifth finger is, except in very large animals, not divided (see Fig. 246, page 146). The dentition gives the best possibility for species identification: the first upper incisor (I²) is long and has only one cusp; the second (outer) upper incisor (I³) is very small. Between the canine (C¹) and the large premolar (P⁴), which are more or less in contact in the upper jaw, the very small premolar (P³) is set behind the tooth row and is hardly or not at all visible. Males have a characteristic spear-shaped penis.

Similar species
Very similar to the other European pipistrelle species, but easy to distingish by the unicusped first (inner) upper incisior (I²) (two cusps in all other pipistrelle species). Usually paler coloured than Common

Measurements	
Forearm	30.3–37.4mm
Fifth finger	40–45mm
Third finger	54–61mm
Normal weight	5–8g
CBL	12.2–13.1mm
CM³	4.7–5.1mm

Fig. 407. Kuhl's Pipistrelle is the most common bat species in human settlements in the Mediterranean coastal ranges. Photo: D. Nill.

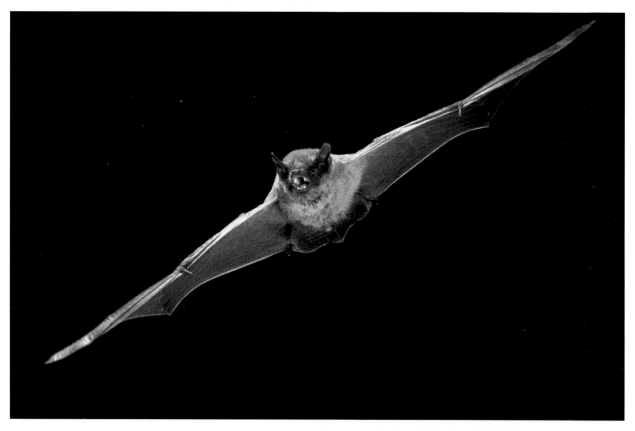

Pipistrelle, and like Soprano Pipistrelle shows an undivided wing field between the elbow and the fifth finger. For discrimination from Madeiran Pipistrelle see under that species. The Egyptian Pipistrelle (*P. deserti*) of North Africa is smaller (especially the upper tooth row <4.5mm). In Savi's Pipistrelle the tragus is shorter and wider in the upper part, the tail protrudes 3–5mm beyond the tail membrane and the first upper incisor (I²) has two cusps.

ECHOLOCATION CALLS

Calls up to 12ms long, frequency-modulated in the initial part and in the end part almost constant-frequency with an end frequency of 36–40kHz. Certain distinction from Nathusius's Pipistrelle is only possible on the basis of the social calls [13]. In both Madeiran Pipistrelle and Egyptian Pipistrelle calls are higher (end frequency >42kHz).

DISTRIBUTION

Distributed throughout the Mediterranean area. The present northern limit of the distribution extends in the west substantially further northward than in the east: to northwest France (Normandy), the southernmost areas of Germany (Konstanz, Augsburg, Munich), Austria, Hungary, southern Bulgaria and Ukraine, where the distribution extends northwards along the Dnieper. Along the entire northern border expansion has been reported since the 1980s. Thus only a few years ago the species reached

southern Germany [5, 11] and Poland [gen. lit. 111], a little earlier Austria [6] and Bulgaria [8]. Some of the records from England [3, 16] were attributed to transported animals, but in view of continual northwards spreading others could easily represent the pioneers of a colonisation. The single record in the Netherlands, so far, was via transport of a container with machine parts from northern Italy. Occurs on all large Mediterranean islands, on the Canary Islands (Gran Canaria, Fuerteventura, Lanzarote), in all of North Africa north of the desert areas, in all of Asia Minor and in the Near East, over the whole Arabian Peninsula to Afghanistan, Turkmenistan and Kazakhstan. South of the Sahara, Kuhl's Pipistrelles are nowadays regarded as a separate species, the Dusky Pipistrelle (*P. hesperidus*) [10].

Subspecies and geographical variation

In the geographical scope of this book only the nominate form is usually recognised, with a high probability that eastwards from Ukraine animals belong to the form *lepidus* and form a separate species. In the southern and eastern Mediterranean area the present taxonomic classification of the *kuhlii* group is, however, very unsatisfactory; a comprehensive revision with genetical and morphological methods, and if possible including the echolocation calls, is urgently required. Genetical investigations [12, gen. lit. 77] revealed that *P. kuhlii* in the North African desert area [gen. lit. 10, 126], usually regarded as a separate species *P. deserti*, *P. maderensis* of the Atlantic islands, Kuhl's Pipistrelles of the Canary Islands, and African *P. hesperidus* as classified by Simmons [gen. lit. 77], are very similar. The genetic differences cannot be reconciled with the morphologically justified species classification. Conversely, the east Mediterranean and Pontic forms (cf. *lepidus*) show very strong genetic deviations from the actual *kuhlii–deserti–maderensis*-group [gen. lit. 77]. In the future, extensive changes to the species allocation and nomenclature within the *kuhlii*-group should be taken into account.

HABITAT

A strongly synanthropic species which is very common in cities and settlements. Usually at lower altitudes below 1,000m. The hunting grounds are also often within residential areas, frequently at streetlamps, in gardens and parks or at waterbodies. Kuhl's Pipistrelle survives well in anthropogenic over-developed landscapes, agricultural areas and cleared forest areas and thus finds suitable living conditions in the entire Mediterranean area and spreading through built-up areas into Central Europe. Rarely found in larger continuous forest areas.

Roosts

Nursery colonies are usually found at cliffs or in gaps of buildings: wall cladding, roll-down shutter boxes, window blinds, wall fissures, roof under-boarding and roofing tiles. Exotic roosts are reported in hollow concrete poles, in a Booted Eagle's nest [9] or in nests of Swallows and Sand Martins. Locally also in tree holes (in North Africa between the scales of the date palm) or in bat boxes. Winter roosts often in outer wall cavities of buildings and in expansion joints, but also in rock crevices.

BEHAVIOUR

Nursery colonies comprise usually about 20, rarely up to 100 animals, adult males remaining in the colony only exceptionally [3]. Although the species forms mixed nursery colonies with Savi's and the Common Pipistrelle, it seems a stronger species that outcompetes at least the Common Pipistrelle from the developed city areas, and in the Mediterranean area the latter is, therefore, rather found in rural or forest areas. From Italy invasions of up to 400 Kuhl's Pipistrelles are known [15]; at some buildings a kind of swarming behaviour occurs at the end of August and in the autumn, including especially young animals, which also fly into buildings and sometimes die. In the Mediterranean area the species is also active on mild winter days, and hibernation is regularly interrupted.

REPRODUCTION

Young animals can become sexual mature

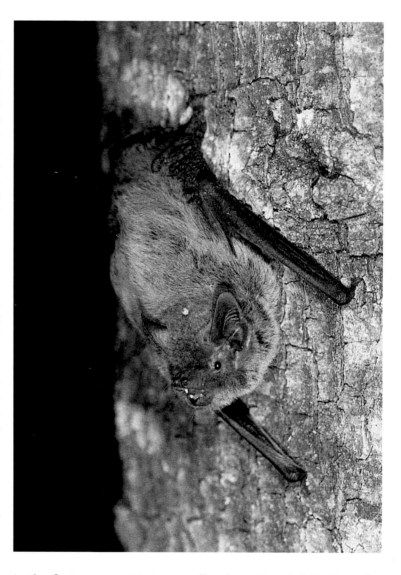

Fig. 408. Kuhl's Pipistrelle with typical fur colouring. Photo: O. von Helversen.

in the first autumn. Mating usually takes place in August and September either at swarming sites [15] or the females are attracted by flight display to individual males [2]. The males perform their flight display into November. At the end of May or the beginning of June 1–2 young are born with a forearm length of 10.7mm and a weight of 1.2–1.6g [3].

FORAGING

The flight style is very similar to that of Common Pipistrelle: agile, rapid and highly manoeuverable in small spaces. Often circles around streetlamps or patrols along long stretches of flight corridors. Groups of jointly hunting Kuhl's Pipistrelles can be regularly observed [1]. The flight height is between 2 and 10m; however, particularly in the early evening, insect swarms can be hunted at a height of several hundred metres. Kuhl's Pipistrelles can be regularly observed hunting before sunset. They drink frequently at water tanks, disused ponds or other small waterbodies.

FOOD

The food is captured opportunistically in flight and within urban areas and at water-bodies and consists largely of Hymenoptera (ants) and Diptera (non-biting midges, mosquitoes) and a diversity of other flying insects: especially moths, but also bugs, mayflies and caddis flies [3, 4, 7]. Seasonally small beetles (*Rhizotrogus*) and crane-flies dominate [7].

MAXIMUM AGE

In the eastern distribution area eight years, from Europe no details [3].

Fig. 409. Some individuals of Kuhl's Pipistrelle are dull brown coloured, like this animal from Greece. Photo: C. Dietz.

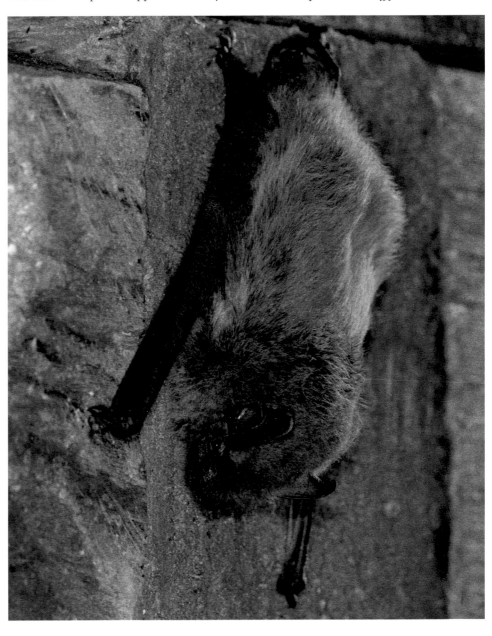

MOBILITY AND MIGRATION

Sedentary, at least in areas in which it is established. The shift of the northern distribution border can also be explained by relatively small-scale dispersion movements.

THREATS

Red list of the IUCN 2006: LC (Least Concern), EU Habitats Directive, Annex IV. Very common in human settlements in the Mediterranean area. Colonies and single animals are sometime threatened by re-developments.

First recorded in the UK in 1991 [UK gen. lit. 155]; now known from about 15 records. Some clearly imported bats, but mostly natural occurrence on the south coast of Britain and from the Channel Islands, where it breeds. Although breeding in Normandy in recent years, following a major spread northwards, there is no evidence of breeding in the UK yet.

Fig. 410. In many older Kuhl's Pipistrelles of the Mediterranean area the hair tips are very pale, and they often have highly contrasted fur colour. Photo: C. Dietz.

REFERENCES

1. Barak, Y. & Y. Yom-Tov (1989): The advantage of group hunting in Kuhl's bat *Pipistrellus kuhli*. *J. Zool.* 219: 670–675.
2. Barak, Y. & Y. Yom-Tov (1991): The mating system of *Pipistrellus kuhli* in Israel. *Mammalia* 55: 285–292.
3. Bogdanowicz, W. (2004): *Pipistrellus kuhlii* – Weißrandfledermaus. In: F. Krapp (ed.): *Handbuch der Säugetiere Europas*, 4-II: 875–908; Aula Verlag.
4. Feldman, R., J.O. Whitaker & Y. Yom-Tov (2000): Dietary composition and habitat use in a desert insectivorous bat community in Israel. *Acta Chiropterologica* 2: 15–22.
5. Fiedler, W., H. Alder & P. Wohland (1999): Zwei neue Nachweise der Weißrandfledermaus (*Pipistrellus kuhlii*) für Deutschland. *Z. Säugetierk.* 64: 107–109.
6. Freitag, B. (1996): *Pipistrellus kuhli*, Erste Fortpflanzungsnachweise für die Steiermark. *Mitt. naturwiss. Ver. Steiermark* 125: 235–236.
7. Goiti, U., P. Vecin, I. Garin, M. Salona & J.R. Aihartza (2003): Diet and prey selection in Kuhl's pipistrelle *Pipistrellus kuhlii* (Chiroptera: Vespertilionidae) in south-western Europe. *Acta Theriol.* 48: 457–468.
8. Ivanova, T.J. & V.V. Popov (1994): First record of *Pipistrellus kuhli* from Bulgaria. *Acta Zoologica Bulgarica* 47: 79–80.
9. Jones, A.M. & M. Manez (1989): Kuhl's pipistrelle *Pipistrellus kuhli* roosting in the nest of a booted eagle *Hieraaetus pennatus*. *J. Zool.* 219: 684–685.
10. Kock, D. (2001): Identity of the African *Vespertilio hesperida* Temminck 1840. *Senckenb. Biol.* 81: 277–283.
11. Liegl, C. & F. Seidler (2005): Erstnachweis einer Wochenstube der Weißrandfledermaus, *Pipistrellus kuhlii*, in Deutschland mit phänologischen Angaben. *Nyctalus* (N.F.) 10: 5–8.
12. Pestano, J., R.P. Brown, N.M. Suarez & S. Fajardo (2003): Phylogeography of pipistrelle-like bats within the Canary Islands, based on mtDNA sequences. *Mol. Phyl. Evol.* 26: 56–63.
13. Russo, D. & G. Jones (1999): The social calls of Kuhl's pipistrelles *Pipistrellus kuhlii*: structure and variation *J. Zool.* 249: 476–481.
14. Schnitzler, H.U., E. Kalko, L. Miller & A. Surlykke (1987): The echolocation and hunting behaviour of the bat *Pipistrellus kuhli*. *J. Comp. Physiol.* A 161: 267–274.
15. Vernier, E. (1995): Seasonal movements of *Pipistrellus kuhli*: 18 years of observations on a single colony in Padova (N.E. Italy) *Myotis* 32/33: 209–214.

ADDITIONAL REFERENCES

16. Hutson, A.M. (2008). Kuhl's pipistrelle *Pipistrellus kuhlii*: 355. In: S. Harris & D.W. Yalden (eds) *Mammals of the British Isles: Handbook, 4th edition*. The Mammal Society, Southampton. 799 pp.

Madeiran Pipistrelle Bat
Pipistrellus maderensis
(DOBSON, 1878)

NAMES

D: Madeira-Fledermaus
F: Pipistrelle de Madère
E: Murciélago de Madeira
I: Pipistrello di Madeira
NL: Madeira dwergvleermuis
PL: Karlik maderski

Measurements

Forearm	31.0–34.7mm
Fifth finger	39–41mm
Third finger	53–56mm
Normal weight	4–7g
CBL	11.4–12.2mm
CM³	4.3–4.8mm

GENERAL INFORMATION

A geographically isolated form, which is mostly regarded as a separate species. However, Kuhl's Pipistrelles of the Canary Islands are more closely related to the Madeiran Pipistrelle than are both to the European Kuhl's Pipistrelles [3], a result that contradicts the traditional systematic classification of the *kuhlii* group.

IDENTIFICATION

Small pipistrelle with remarkably chocolate-brown coloured fur, in some animals orange-brown. The ventral side is not or hardly paler than the dorsal side. The base of the hair is black-brown; young animals give the impression of being generally darker than the adults due to absence of pale hair tips. Face, ears and flight membranes are black; the edge of the wing in many animals is paler, similar to that of Kuhl's Pipistrelle. Dentition as in Kuhl's Pipistrelle with a single cusp on the first incisor (I²).

Fig. 411. The pale edge of the lateral wing membrane of Madeiran Pipistrelle is distinctive. Photo: D. Trujillo.

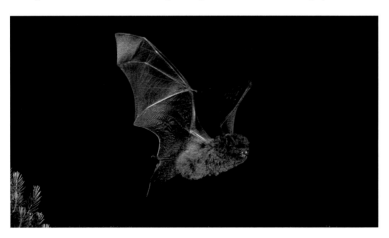

Similar species

Distinguishable on the basis of the dentition from all *Pipistrellus* species with the exception of Kuhl's Pipistrelle. The latter is very similar, also in the penis morphology; however, the white edge of the wing membrane is more strongly pronounced in Kuhl's Pipistrelles, the colouring usually paler and the ventral side usually paler coloured than the dorsal side. On the back, the basal three-quarters of the hair in the Madeiran Pipistrelle is black-brown, in Kuhl's Pipistrelle only to two-thirds [gen. lit. 143]. The best distinction criterion is, however, the echolocation calls, which are higher in Kuhl's Pipistrelle [own data].

ECHOLOCATION CALLS

The echolocation calls loosely resemble those of the Common Pipistrelle. In open areas long almost constant-frequency calls are emitted and end at 42–47kHz [own data, Kaipf pers. com.].

DISTRIBUTION

Endemic species on Madeira [1] and the Canary Islands: La Palma, La Gomera, El Hierro, Tenerife and Gran Canaria [2, 6, gen. lit. 143]. Perhaps also on the Azores [4, 5, 7].

Subspecies and geographical variation

No subspecies.

HABITAT

Can be found hunting in all habitats on Madeira, in settlements, parks, gardens, agricultural areas, equally in eucalyptus and pine afforestations and in natural laurel forests. The species can be found from the coast up to high altitudes in the mountains; the density of hunting animals is, however, highest at lower altitudes and along the coast.

ROOSTS

Nursery colonies in crevices at buildings, behind window shutters, panelling and roof boardings but also in brick cavities. Single animals in rock crevices, fissures in bridges and walls, cracks of trees and in bird and bat boxes [2, gen. lit. 143].

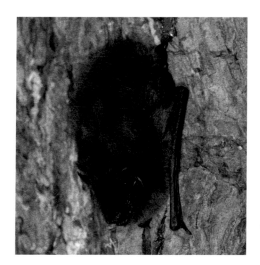

BEHAVIOUR

Nursery colonies on Madeira can comprise over 100 individuals, on the Canary Islands over 30 animals [2, 6, gen. lit. 143]. In suitable weather active all year.

REPRODUCTION

One or two young are born at the end of May to the beginning of June. The mating period is in September/October

FORAGING AND FOOD

Flight style and hunting behaviour resemble that of the Common and Kuhl's Pipistrelle. The species can hunt both in open areas and around streetlamps, inside open forests and along forest trails. On the Canary Islands Diptera are captured, but also moths and beetles. For drinking, disused ponds and irrigation ditches are visited. A large pond on Madeira was visited in the twilight by 50–100 Madeiran Pipistrelles [own data].

MOBILITY AND MIGRATION

Sedentary, of 366 animals ringed on the Canary Islands the most distant recovery was at 2km from the ringing site [2]. Genetic analyses suggest that the populations of the individual islands are isolated from each other [3].

THREATS

Red list of the IUCN 2006: VU (Vulnerable), Red list of the European Union: VU (Vulnerable), EU Habitats Directive, Annex IV. On Madeira and the Canary Islands widely distributed and common, on Porto Santo and the Azores rare. The intensive use of pesticides may possibly affect the occurrence.

REFERENCES

1. Da Luz Mathias, M. (1988): An annotated list of the mammals recorded from the Madeira Islands. *Bol. Mus. Mun. Funchal* 40: 111–137.
2. Fajardo, S. & J. Benzal (2002): Datos sobre la distribución de quirópteros en Canarias (Mammalia: Chiroptera). *Vieracea* 30: 213–230.
3. Pestano, J., R.P. Brown, N.M. Suarez & S. Fajardo (2003): Phylogeography of pipistrelle-like bats within the Canary Islands, based on mtDNA sequences. *Mol. Phyl. Evol.* 26: 56–63.
4. Rainho, A., T.J. Marques, P. Salgueiro & J.M. Palmeirim (2004): *Bats of the Atlantic archipelagos of Azores and Madeira: status and habitat use.* Abstracts of the 13th International Bat Research Conference: 50; Warsaw.
5. Skiba, R. (1996): Nachweis einer Zwergfledermaus, *Pipistrellus pipistrellus*, auf der Azoreninsel Flores (Portugal). *Myotis* 34: 81–84.
6. Trujillo, D. & R. Barone (1991): La Fauna de Quiropteros del Archipielago Canario. In: Benzal & de Paz (eds): *Los Murciélagos de España y Portugal*: 95–111.

ADDITIONAL REFERENCES

7. Rainho, A. & J.M. Palmerim (2002): Arquipelago da Madeira. Pp 30–49 In: *Centro de Biologia Ambiental, & Instituto da Conservacao da Natureza* (publ) Os Morcegos dos Arquipelagos dos Acores e da Madeira: Um contributo para a sua conservacao.

Fig. 412. The colouring of the dorsal fur of Madeiran Pipistrelle varies from dark-brown to orange-brown. Photo: C. Dietz.

Fig. 413. Portrait of Madeiran Pipistrelle. Photo: C. Dietz.

Rüppell's Pipistrelle Bat
Pipistrellus rueppellii
(FISCHER, 1829)

NAMES
D: Rüppells Zwergfledermaus
F: Pipistrelle de Rüppell
NL: Rüppelsdwergvleermuis

Measurements

Forearm	30.7–34.4mm
Fifth finger	42–45mm
Third finger	57–62mm
Normal weight	4–7g
CBL	12.7–13.3mm
CM³	4.6–4.9mm

IDENTIFICATION
Small, very highly contrastingly coloured bat with black-brown face and ears, a fine dense fur which is pale grey-brown above and snow-white below. In contrast to other pipistrelle species with no post-calcarial lobe.

Similar species
Unmistakable within the geographical scope of this book.

ECHOLOCTION CALLS
Typical pipistrelle calls, which are almost constant-frequency in open areas, end frequency in Morocco 54–57kHz [own data], in Israel 49–53kHz [Schnitzler, Denzinger, Tsoar pers. com.], in Kenya 33–35kHz [7] and in Zimbabwe 40kHz [4].

DISTRIBUTION
Afrotropical distribution around the Sahara up to Sudan and Senegal; in the south to Angola and Botswana. Recorded in the Middle East and on the Arabian Peninsula.

In northwest Africa particularly south of the Atlas mountains, but also further northwards in northeast Morocco [gen. lit. 10]. Observations of the species are limited almost everywhere to single individuals.

Subspecies and geographical variation
Several subspecies: in North Africa and Israel *P. r. rueppellii*, in Iraq *P. r. coxi*. The northwest African population is sometimes classified as *P. r. senegalensis* [2]. The large differences in the echolocation calls could be adaptation to prey, in reaction to other sympatrically occurring species, or due to several cryptic species being confused. Genetic analyses suggest that the species should possibly be placed into a separate genus, *Vansonia* [gen. lit. 77].

HABITAT
Rüppell's Pipistrelle avoids the central Sahara and occurs in semi-desert-like regions as well as in wadies and oases.

Roosts
There are few records of roosts; usually they relate to single animals in buildings [gen. lit. 46]. Only in Sudan groups of a dozen or more animals have been found in roofs of thatched houses. Rock crevices are probably the natural roosts.

FORAGING AND FOOD
The prey is captured in flight and

Fig. 414. In profile the large eyes of Rüppell's Pipistrelle are noticeable. Photo: C. Dietz.

comprises small flying insects, usually moths [8, 9], but also caddis flies, Diptera and beetles [3]. For drinking, it visits wells, ponds and stream courses, where most observations of the species are recorded.

THREATS
To a large extent unknown. Red list of the IUCN 2006: LC (Least Concern).

REFERENCES

1. Arlettaz, R. & S. Aulagnier (1988): Statut de trois espèces de chiroptères rares au Maroc: *Nycteris thebaica, Hipposideros caffer* et *Pipistrellus rueppelli. Z. Säugetierk.* 53: 321–324.
2. Benda, P., V. Hanák, M. Andreas, A. Reitter & M. Uhrin (2004): Two new species of bats (Chiroptera) for the fauna of Libya: *Rhinopoma hardwickii* and *Pipistrellus rueppellii. Myotis* 41/42: 109–124.
3. Feldman, R., J.O. Whitaker & Y. Yom-Tov (2000): Dietary composition and habitat use in a desert insectivorous bat community in Israel. *Acta Chiropterologica* 2: 15–22.
4. Fenton, M.B. & G.P. Bell (1981): Recognition of species of insectivorous bats by their echolocation calls. *J. Mammal.* 62: 233–243.
5. Padial, J.M. & C. Ibáñez (2005): New records and comments for the Mauritanian mammal fauna. *Mammalia* 69: 239–243.
6. Qumsiyeh, M.B. & D.A. Schlitter (1981): Bat records from Mauritania, Africa (Mammalia: Chiroptera). *Ann. Carn. Mus.* 50: 345–351.
7. Taylor, P.J., C. Geiselman, P. Kabochi, B. Agwnda & S. Turner (2005): Intraspecific variation in the calls of some African bats (Order Chiroptera). *Durban Mus. Novit.* 30: 24–37.
8. Van Cakenberghe, V., A. Herrel & L.F. Aguire (2002): Evolutionary relationships between cranial shape and diet in bats (Mammalia: Chiroptera). In: P. Aerts, K. D'Aout, A. Herrel & R. Van Damme (eds) *Topics in Functional and Ecological Vertebrate Morphology:* 205–236.
9. Whitaker, J.O., B. Shalmon & T.H. Kunz (1994): Food and feeding habits of insectivorous bats from Israel. *Z. Säugetierk.* 59: 74–81.

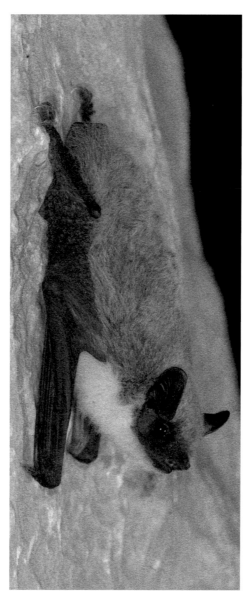

Fig. 415. Rüppell's Pipistrelle has remarkably contrasting fur colour. Photo: C. Dietz.

Fig. 416. Typical habitat of Rüppell's Pipistrelle in Morocco. The animals hunt particularly in semi-deserts and in wadies; for drinking they visit various kinds of waterbodies. Photo: C. Dietz.

Savi's Pipistrelle Bat
Hypsugo savii
(Bonaparte, 1837)

NAMES

D: Alpenfledermaus
F: Vespère de Savi
E: Murciélago montañero
I: Pipistrello di Savi
NL: Savi's dwergvleermuis
S: Alpfladdermus
PL: Karlik Saviego

Measurements

Forearm	31.4–37.9mm
Fifth finger	38–47mm
Third finger	52–63mm
Normal weight	5–9g
CBL	12.2–13.4mm
CM3	4.4–4.9mm

IDENTIFICATION

A small and remarkably varicoloured bat. In most individuals the long dark-brown dorsal fur exhibits intense golden or yellowish hair tips, and the ventral side is contrasting delineated white or yellowish-white. Uniformly brown to brown-grey animals usually have a dirty grey-white vental side. The ears are short, broad and mostly shiny black. The tragus widens somewhat in the upper part and is distinctly broader than in Common Pipistrelle or in *Eptesicus* species. Face and flight membranes dark brown. Very variable post-calcarial lobe from almost missing to broad, but without a cartilage bar. The penis is characteristic, bent at right-angles toward the tail in its central section and with long dark hairs. In the upper tooth row the canine (C^1) and the large premolar (P^4) are in contact so that the small upper premolar (P^3) is not visible from the outside, being displaced to inside the tooth row or it is missing.

Similar species

Only confusable with the larger Northern Bat (forearm >37mm) and the *Pipistrellus* species (check dentition and penis).

ECHOLOCATION CALLS

Up to 16ms long, frequency-modulated in the initial part, and in the final part almost constant-frequency calls with an end frequency of 32–37kHz. Calls higher than in the Northern Bat and lower than in all *Pipistrellus* species, making a clear identification usually possible. However, there is a small overlap in the frequency range with Kuhl's and Nathusius's Pipistrelle.

DISTRIBUTION

From the Iberian Peninsula distributed throughout the European Mediterranean area and the Balkans to Asia Minor and the Middle East. On all Mediterranean islands including Cyprus. In the north up to the French Central Massif, in southern Switzerland and the Bavarian alps [8], Austria, Hungary, the whole of Bulgaria and in the Crimea. Occurs through the Caucasus to Kazakhstan, Turkmenistan, Uzbekistan, Kyrgyzstan, Tadzhikistan, Afghanistan, northern India and Myanmar. In North Africa in Morocco, Algeria and Tunisia. On the Canary Islands (Tenerife, La Gomera, El Hierro, Gran Canaria) and Cape Verde. In Europe there are single finds far north of the actual distribution border, in England, Scotland, Jersey and northern Germany [3, 6, 10]. Mostly, these probably relate to shipped animals. However, the animal found dead in the summer of 1947 in Franconian Switzerland, district Bayreuth (Germany) [7], and a dead female found under a wind-power plant on 14 September 2006 near Domnitz, district Saalkreis (Germany) [Lehmann, Ohlendorf pers. com.] are more certainly animals which arrived under their own power, which clearly shows long-range wandering by individual animals.

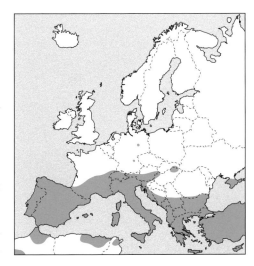

Fig. 417. Portrait of a brown-coloured Savi's Pipistrelle. Probably this colour variant is related to younger animals, but this is not yet clearly demonstrated. Photo: C. Dietz.

Subspecies and geographical variation

Traditionally Savi's Pipistrelle Bat was placed in the genus *Pipistrellus*. Numerous morphological features, particularly the penis morphology, but also biochemical, caryological and recently also genetic findings, confirm its position in the separate genus *Hypsugo* [4, 13, gen. lit. 77]. In the geographical scope of this book three recognised subspecies: *H. s. ochromixtus* on the Iberian Peninsula, *H.s. savii* in the Mediterranean area and Asia Minor, *H. s. caucasicus* on the Crimea and eastwards. *H. s. ochromixtus* is described as larger than *H. s. savii* [6], but agrees extensively in size with our Greek material. Genetic studies show that animals from Morocco and from the Canary Islands are so strongly different that full species status might be attributed to them [12, gen. lit. 77, see also 18 here]. A possible name for this new species could be *darwini* since Tomes, 1859, designated the Savi's Pipistrelle of the Canary Islands as *Scotophilus darwini*. Moreover, in Israel, apart from *H. ariel* (synonymous with *H.*

bodenheimeri) and *H. savii*, there is another, as yet, unnamed species [own data]. *H. alaschanicus* was earlier separated as a full species [gen. lit. 55, 77] and was similarly confirmed by genetic studies. *H. s. caucasicus* is not yet genetically examined. A majority of the Asian forms east of the Caucasus might likewise belong to forms other than the nominate form [6].

HABITAT

Mediterranean habitats from the coast to high mountains of 3,300m [6], usually in karst areas with an extensive cultivated landscape mosaic and a high portion of Mediterranean scrub forms such as macquis or garrigue. Relatively rare in large dense forest areas, in Greece similarly in open pine forests. Regularly over water and riparian land, in Switzerland and Austria hunting over meadows, mountain pastures and around human settlements, everywhere common in rocky areas and along cliffs. In Italy and in the coastal regions of the Balkan Peninsula the species seems to have adapted well to urban areas and hunts

Fig. 418. A grey-brown-coloured Savi's Pipistrelle. Photo: D. Nill.

mountains but also in semi-desert and around oases in desert areas.

Roosts

Rock or wall crevices are almost exclusively used. Nursery roosts have been found in Bulgaria close to the northern border of the distribution behind horizontal rock crevices and in vertical cracks, in the Rhodopians also in wall crevices of buildings at 2m above the ground [own data]. Cracks in the entrance area of caves are also used. In Italy and on the Dalmatian coast nursery colonies are often found under roof tiles or in wall joints of buildings [6, 16] and also in expansion joints of tower block houses. Single animals can be found in bridges or arches. In North Africa behind bark or in rock crevices

BEHAVIOUR

Bulgarian nursery colonies in rock crevices and wall cracks comprise often only few, up to 15, females [own data]; the largest colonies in Croatia and Italy comprise 40–70 animals [1]. They emerge quite early in the high summer, sometimes before sunset. Sometimes, they even hunt in the afternoon.

REPRODUCTION

A wide range of birth dates recorded, from the beginning of June to the end of July [1, 6], in northern Greece and Bulgaria most of the young are born between the beginning and middle of June [own data]; usually two young [6, 16].

FORAGING

Prey is exclusively caught in flight; Savi's Pipistrelles hunt alone or with 2–5 animals, along cliffs, above tree crowns or over more sparsely overgrown areas or around and above streetlamps, only rarely low above the ground. Savi's Pipistrelles can be observed at heights of over 100m above karst valleys, forests and shrub land. Hunting animals fly higher, faster and more directly than *Pipistrellus* species, with less abrupt changes of direction. When hunting at streetlamps, usually longer circuits than *Pipistrellus* species. In particular in karst areas in the

within large cities, such that in Florence [16] and Sofia [own data] it is one of the most common bat species. The ability to settle in cities is probably also the reason for a northward spread in recent decades [14]. In North Africa mostly in the evening Savi's Pipistrelles come in large numbers to drinking places at streams, water basins and fire water ponds.

FOOD

The food consists of small swarming insects dominated by, depending upon prey availability, moths, bugs, cicadellids, Hymenoptera, aphids or Diptera. So, swarming cicadellids and other bugs can constitute a high proportion of the food early in the night above meadows [6]. In Dalmatia numerous Savi's Pipistrelles were observed in the late afternoon in September hunting for swarming insects at heights up to 100m; faeces samples of animals captured close to a drinking place contained exclusively remains of ants [own data]. Also two Savi's Pipistrelle Bats were observed at night, circling at 2–3m above an anthill and directly catching rising flying ants [own data].

MAXIMUM AGE, MOBILITY AND MIGRATION

No results of ringing studies from Europe are available. An often-quoted distance of

250km cannot be attributed to an original source.

THREATS

Red list of the IUCN 2006: LC (Least Concern), EU Habitats Directive, Annex IV. In the Mediterranean area no direct threat is recognised. Building renovations and the use of pesticides, which may get into water in large quantities, represent possible threats

REFERENCES

1. Đulić, B. (1958): Über die Ökologie der Alpenfledermaus, *Pipistrellus savii*, auf der Insel Mljet (Meleda) in Süddalmatien. *Säugetierk. Mitt.* 6: 10–11.
2. Đulić, B. & M. Mrakovčič (1984): Morphological characteristics of a population of *Pipistrellus savii* from some Adriatic islands. *Myotis* 21/22: 37–40.
3. Fisher, C. (1998): Savi's pipistrelle *Pipistrellus savii* in Britain. *Myotis* 36: 77–81.
4. Horáček, I. & V. Hanák (1986): Generic status of *Pipistrellus savii* and comments on classification of the genus *Pipistrellus*. *Myotis* 23/24: 9–16.
5. Horáček, I. (2004): Hypsugo. In: F. Krapp (ed.): *Handbuch der Säugetiere Europas*, 4–II: 909–910; Aula Verlag.

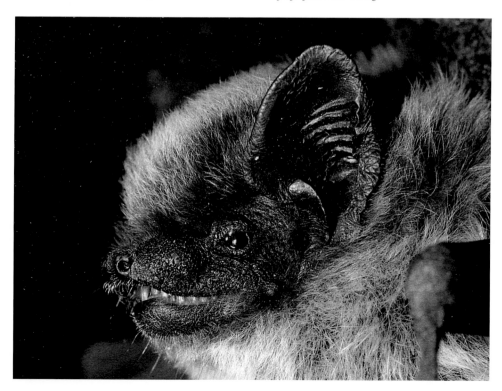

Fig. 419. Portrait of a 'multi-coloured' Savi's Pipistrelle. This colour variant dominates in most populations, probably it relates to older animals of more than one year. Photo: C. Dietz.

Fig. 420. Savi's Pipistrelles from southern Morocco. Animals of North Africa differ genetically so clearly from the European animals that they probably represent a separate species. Photo: C. Dietz.

9. Katzenstein, H. (2000): Nachweis einer Alpenfledermaus (*Hypsugo savii*) in Ostholstein. *Nyctalus* (N.F.) 7: 453–454.
10. Ohlendorf, B., H. Vierhaus, M. Heddergott & F. Bodino (2000): Korrektur: Fund einer Nordfledermaus (*Eptesicus nilssonii*) in Hamburg (Nyctalus (N.F.) 5: 220) betraf eine Alpenfledermaus (*Hypsugo savii*). *Nyctalus* (N.F.) 7: 454.
11. Panouse, J.B. (1955): Contribution à l'étude des chauves-souris du Maroc: *Pipistrellus savii* et *Barbastella barbastellus*. *Bulletin de la Société des Sciences Naturelles et Physiques du Maroc* 35: 259–263.
12. Pestano, J., R.P. Brown, N.M. Suarez & S. Fajardo (2003): Phylogeography of pipistrelle-like bats within the Canary Islands, based on mtDNA sequences. *Mol. Phyl. Evol.* 26: 56–63.
13. Ruedi, M. & R. Arlettaz (1991): Biochemical systematics of the Savi's bat (*Hypsugo savii*) (Chiroptera: Vespertilionidae). *Z. Zool. Syst. Evol.* 29: 115–122.
14. Spitzenberger, F. (1997): Distribution and range expansion of Savi's bat (*Hypsugo savii*) in Austria. *Z. Säugetierk.* 62: 179–181.
15. Vergari, S. & G. Dondini (1997): The influence of body weight on the quantity of food ingested in *Pipistrellus kuhlii* and *Pipistrellus savii*. *Z. Säugetierk.* 62: 203–208.
16. Vergari, S. & G. Dondini (1998): Causes of death in two species of bats (*Pipistrellus kuhli* and *Hypsugo savii*) in urban areas of north-central Italy. *Myotis* 36: 159–166.
17. Zingg, P.E. (1988): Search calls of echolocating *Nyctalus leisleri* and *Pipistrellus savii* recorded in Switzerland. *Z. Säugetierk.* 53: 281–293.

ADDITIONAL REFERENCES
18. Garcia-Mudarra, J.L., C. Ibanez & J.Juste (2009): The Straits of Gibraltar: barrier or bridge to Ibero-Moroccan bat diversity. *Biological Journal of the Linnaean Society* 96: 434–450.

6. Horáček, I. (2004): *Hypsugo savii* – Alpenfledermaus. In: F. Krapp (ed.): *Handbuch der Säugetiere Europas*, 4–II: 911–941; Aula Verlag.
7. Issel, B., W. Issel & M. Mastaller (1977): Zur Verbreitung und Lebensweise der Fledermäuse in Bayern. *Myotis* 15: 19–97.
8. Kahmann, H. (1958): Die Alpenfledermaus *Pipistrellus savii* in den Bayrischen Alpen, und biometrische Mitteilungen über die Art. *Zool. Anz.* 160: 87–94.

Parti-coloured Bat
Vespertilio murinus
Linnaeus, 1758

NAMES
D: Zweifarbfledermaus
F: Sérotine bicolore
E: Murciélago bicolor
I: Serotino bicolore
NL: Tweekleurige vleermuis
S: Gråskimlig fladdermus
PL: Mroczek posrebrzany

IDENTIFICATION
A medium-sized, robust and strong bat with long dorsal fur, black-brown with striking silver-whitish 'frosted' tips. The ventral side is variable [1] whitish or uniformly brownish-yellowish, but usually clearly and sharply delineated from the dorsal colouring. Often some yellowish skin around the ears. The short strong ears extend with a wide fold to below the line of the corner of the mouth and then curve back up. Tragus broad short. Face blackish-brown, the flight membranes grey, the wings narrow and pointed. The penis is thin and long; female has four nipples, which otherwise only occurs in Hemprich's Long-eared Bat, the North American *Lasiurus*, and exceptionally also in the Serotine Bat [15, 24].

Similar species
Unmistakable due to the characteristic colouring. The Serotine is larger; the Northern Bat has golden tipped hair but not on the forehead; Savi's Pipistrelle is smaller.

ECHOLOCATION CALLS
Up to 20ms long, beginning with a frequency-modulated part and ending with an almost constant-frequency part with an end frequency between 22 and 25kHz [19]. Can be confused with Leisler's Bat, the Serotine (shorter pulse interval) and the Northern Bat (higher end frequency). Certain identification only possible by analysis of sound recordings or in combination with good visual observations.

DISTRIBUTION
In Europe distributed northwards from eastern France and the Alpine region as well as at low density across the Balkan Peninsula. In the north the distribution border runs through the Netherlands, Denmark, along 60°N through southern Scandinavia, across Russia to Siberia. Occurs eastwards over the Caucasus and Iran into Mongolia, northeast China, Korea, Afghanistan and northern Pakistan. The distribution in Central and southeast Europe is complicated by the seasonal occurrence of migrating animals and local occurrence of nursery colonies. Nursery colonies and large male colonies are found only locally in the west and the south of the distribution, such as in Switzerland, Bavaria and Austria [3, 5, 20, 21]. Vagrant

Measurements	
Forearm	40.8–50.3mm
Fifth finger	48–54mm
Third finger	69–76mm
Normal weight	10–15g
CBL	14.1–15.6mm
CM³	5.8–6.4mm

Fig. 421. Parti-coloured Bat. Photo: D. Nill.

atics [1]; this confusion still occurs from time to time [7]. In the older literature the scientific designation *Vespertilio discolor* is often used.

HABITAT

Hunting grounds over water, open agricultural areas, meadows, riparian zones and around human settlements [1, 18]. In Switzerland radio-tracked female Parti-coloured Bats hunted particularly over water and human settlements [9, 18] while males hunted particularly over open countryside and forests [18]. In southeast Europe many records originate from mountains [14, own data].

Roosts

Nursery roosts and roosts of single animals are found in cracks, roll-down window shutter boxes and roof cavities of low-rise houses, barns and mountain refuges [6, 24], but also found in high buildings and in rock crevices [1]. Records from tree holes and bat boxes originate particularly from the east of the distribution area [1, 12]. For hibernation likewise buildings, usually preferring tower blocks and other high buildings such as church towers, and cliffs. With

and migrating animals can reach Finland, Norway, Belgium, Great Britain, on oil rigs in the North Sea and the Shetland Islands.

Subspecies and geographical variation

In the geographical scope of this book only one subspecies, *V. m. murinus*. In Siberia, northern China and Korea *V. m. ussuriensis*. The naming and classification of the species described by Linnaeus led to a unique chaos in vertebrate animal system-

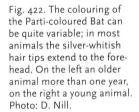

Fig. 422. The colouring of the Parti-coloured Bat can be quite variable; in most animals the silver-whitish hair tips extend to the forehead. On the left an older animal more than one year, on the right a young animal. Photo: D. Nill.

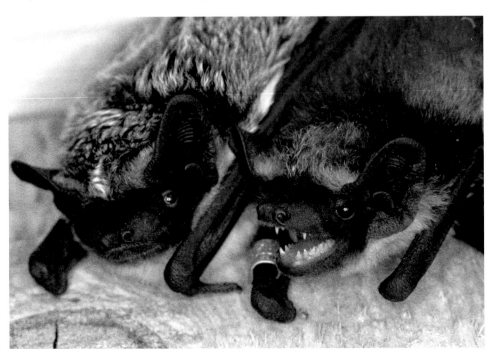

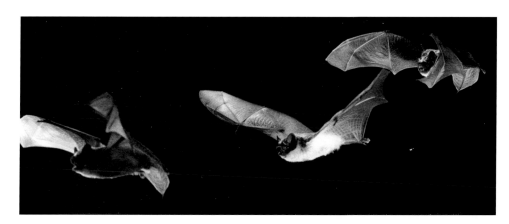

Fig. 423. Stroboscope record of a flying Parti-coloured Bat. Photo: D. Nill.

a strong temperature drop in roosts in cracks the animals may retreat to inside the buildings and are then often found.

BEHAVIOUR
Nursery roosts are occupied from May to August and usually comprise 20–60, but also up to 200, females. At this time males form colonies of up to 300 or more animals, sometimes far away from the nursery roosts [1, 24]. Males use a network of up to seven roosts [18], consequently numbers fluctuate widely. In the late autumn (October and November) the males display very obviously and are audible with the naked ear around high buildings (cathedrals, tower blocks), at quarries and cliffs. In the absence cliffs extended display flights can also take place over forest areas [22, 23].

REPRODUCTION
Mating takes place during the late autumn display time. The young are born mainly from the end of May, but the birth period extends from the end of April to the middle of June. Most often twins, and exceptionally three young are born, rarely only one. The neonates have a weight of about 2–2.5g and a forearm length of about 14.9mm, after seven days around 23.3mm, after 14 days around 35.0mm, after 21 days around 41mm, and after 28 days around 42.2mm [11].

FORAGING
The food is captured in a very rapid and direct flight, similar to *Nyctalus* species, at a height of 10–40m. The patrolled sites are usually open spaces above waterbodies and open land, more rarely over forest. In particular in the autumn streetlamps are visited with relatively close flight paths. Rest periods during the night can be spent hanging on trees [10]. The hunting grounds of individual animals overlap markedly [18].

FOOD
Small Diptera (non-biting midges) and aphids constitute the majority of the food [2, 4, 16]; also caddis flies and moths play a role [4, 16]. Insect swarms are often exploited, which explains a certain preference for water surfaces [8, 9].

MAXIMUM AGE
The proven maximum age is 12 years [1]. This is relatively short and thus, as in the Noctule, is typical for a migratory species whose females usually raise two young per year.

MOBILITY AND MIGRATION
While some European populations, such as in Denmark and in the Bohemian forest, seem to be sedentary, to a great extent the East European populations migrate. The longest migration distances recorded so far are 1,440km from Estonia to Austria [13] and 1,787km from Rybachy (Russia) to France [12]. Migration takes place in the autumn mainly to the southwest, also to southeast from Belarus and Russia.

Habitat use
The habitat use seems to differ markedly between the sexes [18]. Hunting grounds of the males average 87km², substantially larger than the average size of that of

Fig. 424. Parti-coloured Bats can use relatively narrow crevices as roosts, here a nursery colony behind timber cladding. Photo: D. Nill.

females at 16km² [8, 18]. Similarly the hunting grounds of the males are on average 5.7km and up to 20.5km from the roost, while those of the females are significantly closer, with an average of 2.4km and up to 6.2km [18].

THREATS

Red list of the IUCN 2006: LC (Least Concern), EU Habitats Directive, Annex IV. The distribution in Europe is very patchy. While the species is notably common in Denmark [1], particularly in western and southern Europe known reproductive colonies are very thinly spread and there require special protection. Particularly in the renovation of the facade of buildings roosts can be lost. During migration windfarms and roads can be serious threats.

Currently 25–30 records from the UK, mainly from eastern coastal parts of Britain, from the Shetland Islands to the Isle of Wight [UK gen. lit. 155]. Almost certainly a regular migrant to the UK, probably from Scandinavia and presumably capable of crossing the North Sea at almost any point. Although it has been recorded in most months of the year, most records are from the migration periods and there is no evidence of breeding or of their characteristic autumn display 'song flight' in the UK.

CONSERVATION MEASURES

Preservation of the colonies, in particular in renovation works. Preservation of migration routes.

REFERENCES

1. Baagøe, H.J. (2001): *Vespertilio murinus*, 'Zweifarbfledermaus. In: F. Krapp (ed.): *Handbuch der Säugetiere Europas* 4–I: 473–514; Aula Verlag.
2. Bauerová, Z. & A.L. Ruprecht (1989): Contribution to the knowledge of the trophic ecology of the parti-coloured bat, *Vespertilio murinus*. *Folia Zool.* 38: 227–232.
3. Blant, J.D. & C. Jaberg (1995): Confirmation of the reproduction of *Vespertilio murinus* in Switzerland. *Myotis* 32/33: 203–208.
4. Burger, F. (1999): Zum Nahrungsspektrum der Zweifarbfledermaus (*Vespertilio murinus*) im Land Brandenburg. *Nyctalus* (N.F.) 7: 17–28.
5. Freitag, B. (1993): Erster Fortpflanzungsnachweis der Zweifarbfledermaus *Vespertilio murinus* in Österreich und neue Funde in der Steiermark. *Mitt. Naturwiss. Ver. Steiermark* 123: 219–221.
6. Hermanns, U., H. Pommeranz & H. Schütt (2001): Erste Ergebnisse einer systematischen Erfassung der Zweifarbfledermaus, *Vespertilio murinus*, in Mecklenburg-Vorpommern im Vergleich zu Untersuchungen in Ostpolen. *Nyctalus* (N.F.) 7: 532–554.
7. Hinkel, A. (2003): Ein Beitrag über die wissenschaftliche Umbenennung der Zweifarbfledermaus. *Nyctalus* (N.F.) 9: 51–56.
8. Jaberg, C. (1998): Influence de la distribution des ressources alimentaires sur le comportement de chasse et la sélection de l'habitat d'une chauve-souris insectivore aérienne, *Vespertilio murinus*. *Le Rhinolophe* 13: 1–15.

9. Jaberg, C., C. Leuthold & J.-D. Blant (1998): Foraging habitats and feeding strategy of the parti-coloured bat *Vespertilio murinus* in western Switzerland. *Myotis* 36: 51–61.

10. Jaberg, C. & J.-D. Blant (2003): Spatio-temporal utilisation of roosts by the parti-coloured bat *Vespertilio murinus* in Switzerland. *Mamm. Biol.* 68: 341–350.

11. Kozhurina, E.I. (1999): Early postnatal ontogeny and main periods of the development in parti-coloured bats *Vespertilio murinus*. *Folia Zool.* 48: 33–48.

12. Markovets, M.J., N.P. Zelenova & A.P. Shapoval (2004): Beringung von Fledermäusen in der Biologischen Station Rybachy, 1957–2001. *Nyctalus* (N.F.) 9: 259–268.

13. Masing, M. (1989): A long-distance flight of *Vespertilio murinus* from Estonia. *Myotis* 27: 147–150.

14. Pavlinić, I. & N. Tvrtkovi (2003): The presence of *Eptesicus nilssonii* and *Vespertilio murinus* in the Croatian bat fauna confirmed. *Nat. Croat.* 12: 55–62.

15. Ruprecht, A.L. (2005): Über das Auftreten zusätzlicher Saugwarzen bei einer Breitflügelfledermaus, *Eptesicus serotinus*, aus Polen. *Nyctalus* (N.F.) 9: 577–580.

16. Rydell, J. (1992): The diet of the parti-coloured bat *Vespertilio murinus* in Sweden. *Ecography* 15: 195–198.

17. Rydell, J. & H.J. Baagøe (1994): *Vespertilio murinus. Mammalian Species* 467: 1–6.

18. Safi, K. (2006): *Die Zweifarbfledermaus in der Schweiz. Status und Grundlagen für den Schutz*, 100 pp.; Haupt Verlag.

19. Schaub, A. & H.-U. Schnitzler (2006): Echolocation behavior of the bat *Vespertilio murinus* reveals the border between the habitat types 'edge' and 'open space'. *Behav. Ecol. Sociobiol.* DOI 10.1007/s00265-006-0279-9.

20. Spitzenberger, F. (1984): Die Zweifarbfledermaus (*Vespertilio murinus*) in Österreich, Mammalia austriaca 7. *Die Höhle* 35: 263–276.

21. Stutz, H.-P. & M. Haffner (1984): Summer colonies of *Vespertilio murinus* in Switzerland. *Myotis* 21/22: 109–112.

22. Weid, R. (1988): Occurrence of the particoloured bat *Vespertilio murinus* in Greece and some observations on its display behaviour. *Myotis* 26: 117–128.

23. Zagmajster, M. (2003): Display song of parti-coloured bat *Vespertilio murinus* (Chiroptera, Mammalia) in southern Slowenia and preliminary study of its variability. *Natura Sloveniae* 5: 27–41.

24. Zöllick, H., E. Grimmberger & A. Hinkel (1989): Erstnachweis einer Wochenstube der Zweifarbfledermaus, *Vespertilio murinus*, in der DDR und Betrachtungen zur Fortpflanzungsbiologie. *Nyctalus* (N.F.) 2: 485–492.

Fig. 425. Portrait of Parti-coloured Bat. Photo: C. Dietz.

Serotine Bat
Eptesicus serotinus
(SCHREBER, 1774)

NAMES
D: Breitflügelfledermaus
F: Sérotine commune
E: Murciélago de huerta
I: Serotino comune
NL: Laatvlieger
S: Sydfladdermus
PL: Mroczek późny

Measurements

Forearm	48.0–58.0mm
Fifth finger	59–69mm
Third finger	84–92mm
Normal weight	18–25g
CBL	18.4–21.8mm
CM³	7.2–7.9mm

GENERAL – BAT RABIES
A rabies-related virus was discovered in 1985 and designated as European Bat Lyssavirus 1 (EBLV1). This virus occurs in Europe, almost exclusively in the Serotine and 95% of the rabies records are allocated to this species [11, gen lit. 86], while in other species only isolated infections are recorded [22]. Most records of EBLV1 are concentrated in the coastal regions of northern Germany, Denmark, the Netherlands and Poland. Individual cases have, however, also been found widely in Europe to Turkey. In Denmark in the 1980s, 160 of 663 Serotines examined were rabies positive, and in adjacent populations up to 20% of the animals were infected [1]. Most Serotines recover from an infection but probably continue to carry the virus [16, 22]. Heavily diseased bats are weak and unable to fly. They usually behave abnormally, screeching with the slightest disturbance, showing spasms, moving slowly and uncoordinatedly, and are partly paralysed, refusing food and water. A increased tendency to bite is only rarely recorded [2, 11]. There is certainly no reason for excessive concern or panic. Transmission can only take place via bites or licking of damaged skin; simple precautionary measures such as using proper gloves when handling the animals are sufficient. Humans who frequently come into contact with bats should get appropriate rabies vaccination, which reliably protects against infection [gen. lit. 86]. For occupants of buildings with Serotine colonies no risk exists as long as bats are not handled.

IDENTIFICATION
A large robust bat with a broad snout. The long fur has a variable colouring, usually medium to dark-brown, particularly in the eastern Mediterranean region with yellow-golden tips. There are also black-brown, grey-brown and red-brown animals. The ventral side is a poorly delineated paler brown to yellowish brown. The face is usually black-brown coloured, the ears medium long, thick skinned and rounded at the tip. The wings appear broad compared with *Nyctalus* species.

Similar species
The sympatrically occurring Northern Bat in Central and northern Europe is clearly smaller than the Serotine. In the southern Mediterranean area confusion is possible with the Isabelline Serotine and Anatolian Serotine. Sympatric occurrence with the generally smaller and paler Isabelline Serotine in North Africa is, so far, not recorded and the Anatolian Serotine has a shorter fifth finger (<60mm) and a shorter upper tooth row (<7.0mm).

ECHOLOCATION CALLS
Up to 23ms-long frequency-modulated calls with an almost constant-frequency end part at 23–27kHz.

DISTRIBUTION
Throughout Europe, in the north to 55°N to include south England, the southernmost parts of Sweden and Latvia. It is absent from Ireland, Norway, Finland and Estonia. There are indications that the species may be spreading slowly northward [1]. Widely distributed in the Mediterranean region, but no records from the Canary Islands and North Africa (earlier data probably refer to Isabelline Serotine). Outside Europe occurs in Turkey, across the Middle East and the Caucasus to Central Asia, China, Taiwan and into the northern Indomalayan region. Far Eastern populations could represent a separate species.

Subspecies and geographical variation
In Europe only the nominate form *E. s.*

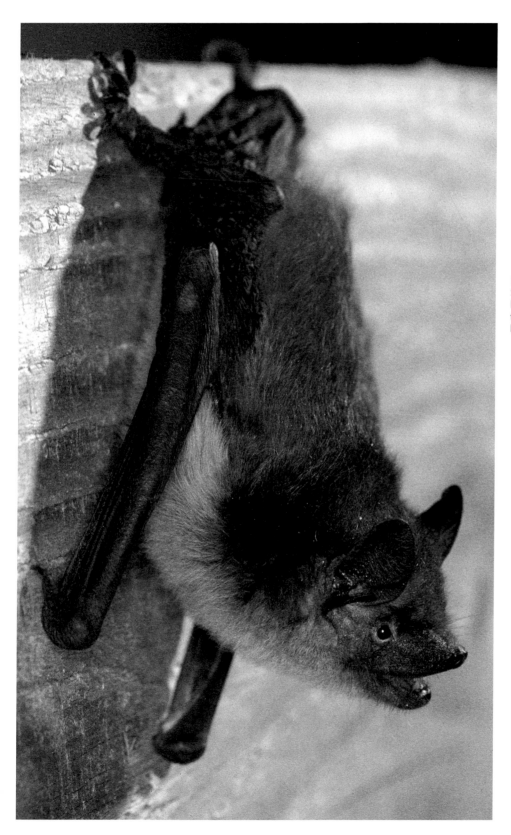

Fig. 426. In Central Europe Serotine Bats are usually brown or grey-brown above; the lower surface is only a little paler. Photo: D. Nill.

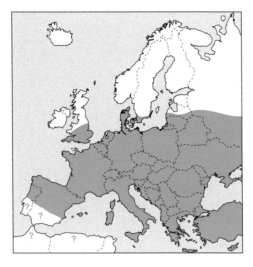

roosts rarely occur over 800m, although single animals and males regularly occur at higher altitudes. The abundance is very much greater in the northern German lowlands and neighbouring areas than in southern Central Europe.

Roosts

Nursery roosts in Central Europe are almost exclusively in buildings. Single animals can occupy tree holes and bat boxes, as well as a diversity of roosts at buildings: behind under-boarding, cladding and gutters or in wall cracks and drillholes. Nursery roosts are usually found in cracks in unused roof structures or in large spaces behind claddings, under roof ridges, in larger ventilation shafts, cavity walls and in expansion joints of large block houses. In the Mediterranean region, besides buildings and bridges, crevices in cliffs and entrance zones of large caves are also occupied. In winter a majority of the animals probably remain in roof spaces [7] and cavity walls of buildings [1] as well as in rock crevices. In caves individual animals and rarely small groups are found in dry and cold places in cracks and in ground rubble.

BEHAVIOUR

Nursery colonies comprise 10–60 adult females, in some cases up to 300 animals. The colonies are formed from the beginning of May, then normally maintained the whole summer through and dispersed again in August. In the roost some males are accompanied by a range of other species; nursery colonies may also sometimes occur in the same building as other bat species, but are usually separated from them. Males can form groups of up to 20 animals.

REPRODUCTION

Mating takes place in September and October; the birth of a single young occurs in Central Europe at about the middle of June; twins are rare. There are, however, also late births, even in August [1]. Also, in the Mediterranean area individual pregnant females can still be captured in August. The relatively high proportion of non-reproducing but full-grown females in

serotinus. E. s. boscai (Iberian Peninsula) and *E. s. meridionalis* (Italy) cannot be differentiated from the nominate form and are usually not recognised. The North African subspecies regarded for a long time as *E. s. isabellinus* is now considered a full species [gen. lit. 77]; it could be the same with the subspecies *shirazensis* (Iran), *turcomanus* (Central Asia), *pallens* (Korea, China) and other forms. On the other hand *E. sodalis*, described as a full species, is only a small-sized form of the Serotine [21]. Genetic data clearly shows that the European Serotine is not, as sometimes assumed, synonymous with the North American *E. fuscus* [Mayer pers. com.]. With genetic markers so far examined a distinction between *E. serotinus* and *E. nilssonii* is not possible [gen. lit. 79].

HABITAT

Occurs in the whole spectrum of Central European and Mediterranean habitats and is little dependent on forest. As hunting grounds, cleared agricultural areas, structurally rich edges of human settlement, parks, meadows with fruit trees, pastures, forest edges, waterbodies, but also in the centre of villages, towns and large cities. In forests usually only firebreaks and forest trails are used. The highest density of foraging animals can be observed over pasture, meadows with fruit trees, parks with isolated trees and at water edges. Open vegetation with deciduous trees seems to be important. In Central Europe nursery

some nursery colonies, and with data from mistnet catches, suggests the reaching of sexual maturity in the second year of life. Young animals are born with a forearm length of approximately 22mm and a weight of 5.8g; they open their eyes after 5–7 days, and are fully haired at the end of the first week. At 14 days they reach 13g. Starting from approximately the 17th day the juveniles start to stretch their wings and, in Central Europe, start to fly at the end of the third week. The dispersion from the roosts occurs at 4–5 weeks, with young weaned a little later [1, 14].

FORAGING

The prey is captured with agile and rapid flight along vegetation edges, while circling around individual trees, or in open areas. Often individual streetlamps are patrolled for longer periods. Search flights are made with long steady circuits, which are interrupted when prey is discovered. Picking prey directly from the ground (freshly mown meadows) or from the canopy of trees (cockchafers) also occurs [11]. Large prey such as chafers are consumed in flight, the bats usually flying regular circuits in open spaces. At some places up to 20 Serotines can be found concentrated in a small area. In such cases insect swarms are probably being exploited [11, 20].

FOOD

Serotines react flexibly to the availability of prey. In the respective flying periods, dung beetle and chafer species form the main prey [11, 17]. Additionally, moths and a range of other insects, particularly ichneumons [1, 4, 5, 11, 17] and bugs are captured. In the spring Diptera play a large role. The prey greatly differs locally and is not limited to flying insects. With mass occurrences of mole crickets or emerging cockchafers, prey can also be picked from the ground [1, 18].

MAXIMUM AGE

The proven maximum age is approaching 24 years [20, gen. lit. 139].

MOBILITY AND MIGRATION

Serotines are usually sedentary and the distances between summer and winter roosts are small. The majority of the winter records lie within 50km radius of the summer roosts. Some long-distance flights, up to 330km [13], probably refer to distance colonists and dispersal movements.

Habitat use

During the nursery period individual females can move up to 10km to an alternative roost for one night [5]. Females usually hunt within 4.5km of the roost, occasionally up to 12km [5, 11, 18]. Up to 10 separate hunting grounds are visited, which are usually connected by linear structures such as hedges, waterways and roads [11, 17]. Commuting flights are fast and take place at 10–15m height. Individuals forage in a hunting area averaging 4.6km² and at the most up to 48km² [11, 15, 17, 18].

THREATS

Red list of the IUCN 2006: LC (Least Concern), EU Habitats Directive, Annex IV. The population seems to be stable. Local threats from building renovations or pesticide use. In the long term, particularly the loss of pasture and extensively used grassland and managed grasslands with fruit trees near the roost can destroy food resources.

Distributed in southern England to Norfolk and the Severn Estuary and just

Fig. 427. Serotine in flight. Photo: D. Nill.

into southeast Wales [UK gen. lit. 153, 155]. The Serotine Bat is another species for which there are concerns about a significant decline in the southeast, but there may equally have been some recent expansion into the southwest. Analysis of trends from data submitted over recent years to the National Bat Monitoring Programme suggests no significant trend from maternity colony counts or from bat detector field survey. Nevertheless, apparent roost loss over a longer period is significant, but does not allow for possible relocation of colonies (although colonies in most areas show a very high site fidelity). Despite routine passive surveillance over the last 20 years and recent active survey, there is no evidence that the rabies-related virus EBLV1 is established in the UK [23, 24, 25].

CONSERVATION MEASURES

Preservation of species-rich meadows and permanent grasslands, extensively managed pastures, managed grassland with fruit trees and structurally rich edges to human settlement. Abandonment of pesticide use.

REFERENCES

1. Baagøe, H.J. (2001): *Eptesicus serotinus*, Breit-flügelfledermaus. In: F. Krapp (ed.): *Handbuch der Säugetiere Europas* 4–I: 519–559; Aula Verlag.
2. Becker, U. & K.-H. Becker (1991): Beobachtungen an einer an Tollwut erkrankten Breit-flügelfledermaus *Eptesicus serotinus*. *Naturschutz und Landschaftspflege in Niedersachsen* 26: 159.
3. Catto, C., A.M. Hutson & P.A. Racey (1994): The diet of *Eptesicus serotinus* in southern England. *Folia Zool.* 43: 307–314.
4. Catto, C.M.C., P.A. Racey & P.J. Stephenson (1995): Activity patterns of the serotine bat (*Eptesicus serotinus*) at a roost in southern England. *J. Zool.* 235: 635–644.
5. Catto, C.M.C., A.M. Hutson, P.A. Racey & P.J. Stephenson (1996): Foraging behaviour and habitat use of the serotine bat (*Eptesicus serotinus*) in southern England. *J. Zool.* 238: 623–633.
6. Degn, H.J. (1983): Field activity of a colony of serotine bats (*Eptesicus serotinus*). *Nyctalus* (N.F.) 1: 521–530.
7. Dinger, G. (1991): Winternachweise von Breit-flügelfledermäusen (*Eptesicus serotinus*) in Kirchen. *Nyctalus* (N.F.) 7: 614–616.
8. Gajdošik, M. & J. Gaisler (2004): Diet of two *Eptesicus* bat species in Moravia (Czech Republic). *Folia Zool.* 53: 7–16.
9. Gerber, E., M. Haffner & V. Ziswiler (1996): Vergleichende Nahrungsanalyse bei der Breit-flügelfledermaus *Eptesicus serotinus* in ver-

Fig. 428. Portrait of Serotine. Photo: D. Nill.

schiedenen Regionen der Schweiz. *Myotis* 34: 35–43.

10. Haensel, J. (1994): Zum Eintritt der Geschlecht-sreife bei der Breitflügelfledermaus (*Eptesicus serotinus*) und zum Aufenthalt adulter Män-nchen in ihren Wochenstubengesellschaften. *Nyctalus* (N.F.) 5: 181–184.

11. Harbusch, C. (2003): *Aspects of the ecology of Serotine bats (*Eptesicus serotinus*) in contrast-ing landscapes in southwest Germany and Lux-embourg.* PhD-thesis, University of Aberdeen, 217 pp.

12. Harbusch, C. & P.A. Racey (2006): The sessile serotine: the influence of roost temperature on philopatry and reproductive phenology of *Eptesi-cus serotinus* (Mammalia: Chiroptera). *Acta Chiropterologica* 8: 213–229.

13. Havekost, H. (1960): Die Beringung der Breit-flügelfledermaus (*Eptesicus serotinus*) im Old-enburger Land. *Bonn. Zool. Beitr., Sonderheft* 11: 222–233.

14. Kleiman, D.G. (1969): Maternal care, growth rate, and development in the noctule (*Nyctalus noctula*), pipistrelle (*Pipistrellus pipistrellus*), and serotine (*Eptesicus serotinus*) bats. *J. Zool.* 157: 187–211.

15. Pérez, J.L. & C. Ibáñez (1991): Preliminary results on activity rhythms and space use optained by radio-tracking a colony of *Eptesicus serotinus*. *Myotis* 29: 61–66.

16. Pérez, J.L., J.R. Boyero & C. Ibáñez (1991): Epi-demiologia de la Rabia en Quiropteros In: Benzal & de Paz (eds): *Los Murcielagos de España y Portugal*: 237–252.

17. Robinson, M.F. & R.E. Stebbings (1993): Food of the serotine bat, *Eptesicus serotinus* – is fecal analysis a valid qualitative and quantitaive tech-nique? *J. Zool.* 231: 239–248.

18. Robinson, M.F. & R.E. Stebbings (1997): Home-range and habitat use by the serotine bat, *Eptesi-cus serotinus*, in England. *J. Zool.* 243: 117–136.

19. Rosenau, S. (2001): *Untersuchungen zur Quartiernutzung und Habitatnutzung der Breit-flügel-fledermaus* Eptesicus serotinus *im Berliner Stadtgebiet (Bezirk Spandau).* Diplo-marbeit an der Freien Universität Berlin.

20. Rudolph, B.-U. (2004): Breitflügelfledermaus, *Eptesicus serotinus*. In: A. Meschede & B.-U. Rudolph (eds): *Fledermäuse in Bayern* 305–313. Ulmer Verlag.

21. Ruprecht, A.L. (1990): Zur Variabilität der Breit-flügelfledermäuse und zum Problem um *Eptesi-cus sodalis* in Polen. *Nyctalus* (N.F.) 3: 129–143.

22. Serra-Cobo, J., B. Amengual, C. Abellan & H. Bourhy (2002): European bat Lyssavirus infec-tion in Spanish bat populations. *Emerging Infectious Diseases* 8: 413–420.

ADDITIONAL REFERENCES

23. Fooks, A.R., A.R. Brookes, N. Johnson, L.M. McElhinney, and A.M. Hutson (2003): European bat lyssavirus: an emerging zoonosis. *Epidemio-logical Infection* 131: 1029–1039.

24. Harris, S.L., S.M. Brookes, G. Jones, A.M. Hutson & A.R. Fooks (2006): Passive surveil-lance (1987 to 2004) of United Kingdom bats for European bat lyssaviruses. *Veterinary Record* 159: 439–446.

25. Harris, S.L., S.M. Brookes, G. Jones, A.M. Hutson, P.A. Racey, J. Aegerter, G.S. Smith, L.M. McElhinney, & A.R. Fooks (2006): European bat lyssa viruses: distribution, prevalence and impli-cations for conservation. *Biological Conserva-tion* 131: 193–210.

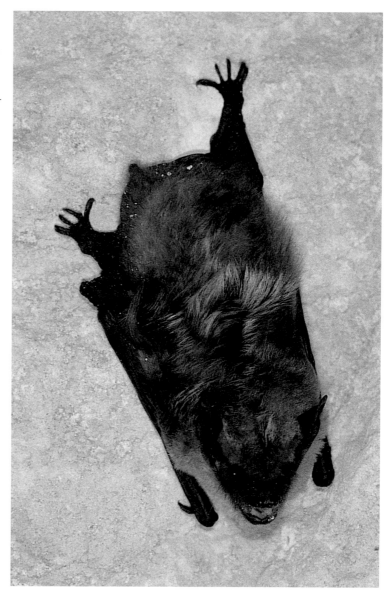

Fig. 429. In the Mediter-ranean area Serotines fre-quently have gold-blond coloured tips to the dorsal fur. Photo: C. Dietz.

Northern Bat
Eptesicus nilssonii
(KEYSERLING & BLASIUS, 1839)

NAMES
D: Nordfledermaus
F: Sérotine de Nilsson
E: Murciélago de huerta norteño
I: Serotino di Nilsson
NL: Noordse vleermuis
S: Nordisk fladdermus
PL: Mroczek pozłicisty

Measurements

Forearm	37.1–44.2mm
Fifth finger	45–56mm
Third finger	62–68mm
Normal weight	9–13g
CBL	14.5–15.4mm
CM³	5.1–5.8mm

IDENTIFICATION
A medium-sized bat with long dark brown to brown-black fur on the dorsal side, and gold-yellow tips on the back and neck. The skin at the inner edge of the ears exhibits typically dense yellowish hair tufts. The ventral side is yellowish brown or beige coloured, more sharply delineated at the neck from the dorsal side compared with other species of the genus. The ears are broadly rounded and as with all skin areas dark-brown coloured. The last tail vertebra is free for up to 4mm.

Similar species
Only confusable with the distinctly larger Serotine (forearm length 48–58mm) as well as with the Parti-coloured Bat and Savi's Pipistrelle. The Parti-coloured Bat shows silvery hair tips which extend up to the forehead, has a broad post-calcarial lobe, females with two pairs of nipples and males a narrow penis (contrary to the broadly oval penis of the Northern Bat). Savi's Pipistrelle is usually smaller (forearm length <37.9mm), has a white ventral side and the tragus widens somewhat in the upper part.

ECHOLOCATION CALLS
Up to 20ms-long frequency-modulated calls with an almost constant-frequency end part between 26 and 29kHz [3]. The Serotine calls in the same location are 2–4kHz lower and the call intervals are longer. Thus the 15ms-long calls have an end frequency of 27kHz in the Northern Bat, with those of Serotine at 23kHz [3].

DISTRIBUTION
Central and Eastern Europe, in the west to eastern France [2] and Switzerland, in the south to northern Italy. The only bat species

Fig. 430. The Northern Bat is adapted to a life at high latitudes by dense and long fur and a stocky build. Photo: C. Dietz.

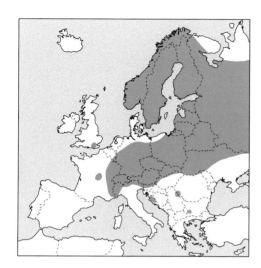

with a distribution border to 70°N, north of the Arctic Circle [6, 17]. In the east to northern Ukraine and the Caucasus. Outside of the more or less continuous distribution area, single records from England [7], the Faroe Islands, the Netherlands, in the Romanian Carpathians [14], and in the Bulgarian Rila mountains [8]. To what extent populations occur in the mountains of the Balkans, suggested by new finds in Croatia [13], is so far unclear. Inventories in Bulgaria have so far produced no evidence of permanent occurrence. Occurs outside Europe in Siberia, Mongolia, northwest China, Iraq, Iran, Korea, Japan and on the Sachalin Peninsula.

Subspecies and geographical variation

In Europe only the nominate form *E. n. nilssonii*. The many Asian subspecies are badly defined from each other and some could represent full species. The species requires a thorough revision.

HABITAT

A typical bat of boreal and montain forest areas. Consequently, it occurs in northern Europe in the lowlands, while it occurs in southern Central Europe and southeast Europe almost exclusively from foothills into the high mountains at over 2,000m. Usually wet coniferous and hardwood forests dominate the surroundings of the nursery roosts. Foraging grounds often lie close to lakes and streams but also over high moorland, meadows, along edges of forests, in forests and around human settlements.

Roosts

The majority of nursery roosts are in roofs covered with slates or sheet metal and in wall linings of houses [6], exceptionally also in tree holes [10]. In the north of the distribution often by sources of heat such as chimneys or behind claddings which are heated rapidly by the sun. Single animals can be found in a multiplicity of roosts such as bridges, tree holes, but also in scree [22]. In the winter usually single or in small groups in distinctly cool mines, bunkers and caves. Either in the entrance zone with temperatures scarcely above freezing point or in downward sloping roosts in which cool air pools accumulate. At low temperatures wedged in crevices, also in ground rubble. In the northern Black Forest (Germany) single animals were found several times in firewood piles. Northern Bats probably hibernate particularly in roosts above ground in buildings, in rock crevices and scree. This explains why the highest numbers are found in mines during the lowest outside temperatures (<−20°C) or during temporary winter gales [own data].

BEHAVIOUR

Nursery colonies usually comprise 20–50, in individual cases up to 150, females [11, 18] and are already occupied in April, at the latest in May. The nursery colonies disperse early in the year (at the end of July) but can stay in the roost to the end of August. Roosts are sometimes switched within a limited area. In southwest Germany, often found with other species such as Serotine, Whiskered and Common Pipistrelle Bats. Strongly territorial in the hunting grounds, even females of the same nursery colony are chased away [16]. The small hunting grounds are regularly visited [16, 18]. A special adaptation of this, the only bat species reproducing north of the Arctic Circle [17], is the ability to go into torpor with bad weather in the summer and thereby to delay the birth date by up to one month. Males spend the summer solitarily but

Fig. 431. The hibernating Northern Bat is easy to recognise by the yellowish hair tufts behind the ears. Photo: C. Dietz.

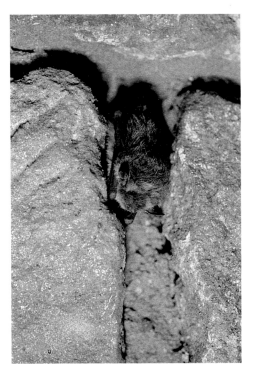

appear at swarming sites at caves and mines from the middle of July into the late autumn.

REPRODUCTION

One to two young per female are born with a forearm length of 12.5–14mm. Births take place, depending upon geographical latitude and altitude above sea level, in the middle of June (south Germany) to the end of July (northern Europe) [18]. The neonates grow very fast and already have their first independent hunting flights at three weeks [18]. The juvenile males leave the nursery roost area in the autumn; the juvenile females return to their nursery roosts of birth. Mating probably takes place from the late summer, at swarming sites and in winter roosts.

FORAGING

The food is usually captured with rapid and agile flight along vegetation edges, but also in open areas at 50m height, and at street-lamps [6, 15]. Larger insect swarms are encircled and the insects are captured in a dive. At streetlamps the Northern Bat uses rapid dives to close above the ground to pursue tympanate moths, which drop when they hear the echolocation calls. During the

courtship of Ghost Swift Moths (*Hepialus*) their males are preferentially hunted and captured in low flight over meadows. Since the Ghost Swift Moths are usually within the grass tips and thus in the echoclutter the prey can be detected with difficulty using echolocation calls; recent investigations show that Northern Bats can visually recognise large and brightly coloured prey [gen. lit. 32, 108].

FOOD

The food comprises up to half small Diptera, usually Nematocera; the other half are beetles, moths like the Ghost Swift Moth, locally also bugs [5, 15, 17]. Mostly flying insects are captured, usually species that occur in swarms. Summer chafers and Ghost Swift Moths are preferred during their flight time.

MAXIMUM AGE

The proven maximum age is 21 years and 9 months [11, gen. lit. 139].

MOBILITY AND MIGRATION

Usually a sedentary species from the few ring recoveries. But four distances of over 100km to 450km are recorded [21]. Several records on oil rigs in the North Sea and on the Faroe Islands similarly indicate at least occasional migratory behaviour. Whether these finds relate to fixed migration movements or to more or less random dispersal is unclear. However, an animal held in captivity in the northern Black Forest in the late autumn had an amazing ability to align itself clearly to southwest in orientation experiments [own data], which can only be explained by aligning with the earth's magnetic field and for orientation for migration.

Habitat use

Depending upon the season, the individual foraging areas of approximately 20ha are relatively small, but can become distinctly larger in the autumn at up to 66km² [4]. In a colony in Lower Saxony, they foraged over an average of 524ha and maximum of 732ha [9]. During the maternity period the hunting grounds lie approximately 800m from the nursery roosts [6], but they may also lie up to 10km distant [20] and even further [9]. After the nursing period adult animals cover a distance of up to 30km [4]. This explains why only following the dispersal of the nursery colonies large numbers of Northern Bats turn up in unpopulated high altitudes of the northern Black Forest [own data]. Up to eight separate hunting grounds are used [20], often very small areas covering only a few hundred square meters, sometimes even a single streetlamp. If the density of available insects drops, the hunting ground is changed.

THREATS
Red list of the IUCN 2006: LC (Least Concern), EU Habitats Directive, Annex IV. In northern Europe the most common and widely distributed species [6]. Apart from building renovations, it does not seem to be suffering from direct threats.

There arc only four UK records of Northern Bat and two of those are clearly of imported individuals [UK gen. lit. 155]. One of the other two is from a North Sea oil platform and one was an individual found hibernating in Surrey. While there are occasionally such stray records from elsewhere in Europe, the species is still regarded as essentially sedentary and can only be regarded as a vagrant to countries like the UK.

REFERENCES
1. Arlettaz, R. & F. Catzeflis (1990): Reprise in natura d'une Sérotine boréale, *Eptesicus nilssoni*, agée d'au moins quinze ans. *Le Rhinolophe* 7: 37.
2. Barataud, M., C. Joulot & D. Demontoux (1998): Synthèse des données sur la répartition en France d'*Eptesicus nilssoni* et de *Vespertilio murinus*. *Le Rhinolophe* 13: 23–28.
3. Baumann, S. (2006): *Inter- und Intraspezifischer Vergleich des Echoortungsverhaltens der Breitflügel- (*Eptesicus serotinus*) und Nordfled-*

Fig. 432. Northern Bats often visit coniferous forests for hunting. Photo: D. Nill.

*ermaus (*Eptesicus nilssonii*).* Diplomarbeit der Fakultät für Biologie, Universität Tübingen.

4. De Jong, J. (1994): Habitat use, home-range and activity pattern of the northern bat, *Eptesicus nilssoni*, in a hemiboreal coniferous forest. *Mammalia* 58: 535–548.

5. Gajdosik, M. & J. Gaisler (2004): Diet of two *Eptesicus* bat species in Moravia (Czech Republic). *Folia Zool.* 53: 7–16.

6. Gerell, R. & J. Rydell (2001): *Eptesicus nilssonii*, Nordfledermaus. In: F. Krapp (ed.): *Handbuch der Säugetiere Europas* 4–I: 519–559; Aula Verlag.

7. Greenaway, F. & J.E. Hill (1988): First British record of the northern bat (*Eptesicus nilssonii*). *J. Zool.* 215: 357–388.

8. Hanák, V. & I. Horáček (1986): Zur Südgrenze des Areals von *Eptesicus nilssoni*. *Ann. Nat. Hist. Mus. Wien* 88/89 B: 377–388.

9. Haupt, M., S. Menzler & S. Schmidt (2006): Flexibility of habitat use in *Eptesicus nilssonii*: Does the species profit from anthropogenically altered habitats? *J. Mammal.* 87: 351–361.

10. Markovets, M.J., N.P. Zelenova & A.P. Shapoval (2004): Beringung von Fledermäusen in der Biologischen Station Rybachy, 1957–2001. *Nyctalus* (N.F.) 9: 259–268.

11. Morgenroth, S. (2004): Nordfledermaus, *Eptesicus nilssonii*. In: A. Meschede & B.-U. Rudolph (eds.): *Fledermäuse in Bayern*: 314–321; Ulmer Verlag.

12. Ohlendorf, B. (2001): Quartiere der Nordfledermaus *Eptesicus nilssonii* im Harz. *Abh. Ber. Mus. Heineaneum* 5: 125–133.

13. Pavlinić, I. & N. Tvrtkovi (2003): The presence of *Eptesicus nilssonii* and *Vespertilio murinus* in the Croatian bat fauna confirmed. *Nat. Croat.* 12: 55–62.

14. Rauschert, K. (1963): Zur Säugetierfauna der rumänischen Karpaten *Säugetierk. Mitt.* 11: 97–101.

15. Rydell, J. (1986): Foraging and diet of the

Fig. 433. Habitat of Northern Bat. It is the only species to reach the Arctic Circle. Photo: D. Nill.

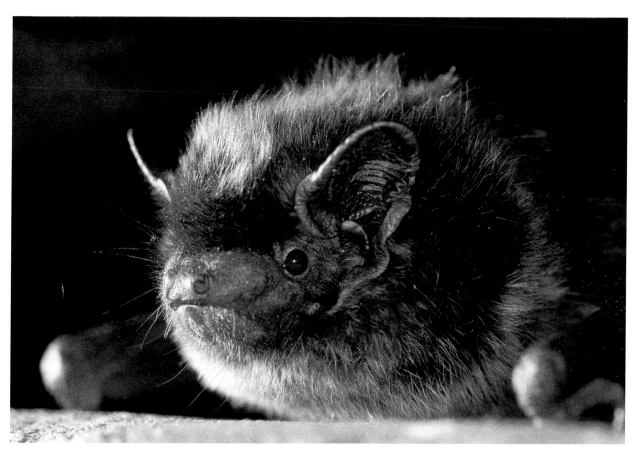

Fig. 434. Portrait of Northern Bat. Photo: D. Nill.

northern bat *Eptesicus nilssoni* in Sweden. *Holarctic Ecology* 9: 272–276.

16. Rydell, J. (1986): Feeding territoriality in female northern bats, *Eptesicus nilssoni*. *Ethology* 72: 329–337.

17. Rydell, J. (1989): Occurence of bats in northernmost Sweden (65°N) and their feeding ecology in summer. *J. Zool.* 227: 517–529.

18. Rydell, J. (1993): *Eptesicus nilssonii*. *Mammalian Species* No. 430: 1–7.

19. Skiba, R. (1989): Die Verbreitung der Nordfledermaus, *Eptesicus nilssoni*, in der Bundesrepublik Deutschland und der Deutschen Demokratischen Republik. *Myotis* 27: 81–98.

20. Steinhauser, D. (1999): Erstnachweis einer Wochenstube der Nordfledermaus (*Eptesicus nilssonii*) im Land Brandenburg mit Hinweisen zur Ökologie dieser Fledermausart. *Nyctalus* (N.F.) 7: 208–211.

21. Tress, C. (1994): Zum Wanderverhalten der Nordfledermaus (*Eptesicus nilssoni*). *Naturschutzreport* 7: 367–372.

22. Van der Kooij, J. (1999): Northern bat *Eptesicus nilssonii* found in a scree. *Fauna* 52: 208–211.

Isabelline Serotine Bat
Eptesicus isabellinus
(TEMMINCK, 1840)

NAMES
  D: Isabelfledermaus
  F: Sérotine isabelle
  N: Isabelvleermuis

GENERAL INFORMATION
Originally described as a full species from Libya and regarded as such by numerous authors [3, 7], but was classified by Harrison (1963) as a subspecies of the Serotine Bat, *E. serotinus* [5]. This classification was accepted to a large extent [gen. lit. 126]. Benda *et al.* (2004) reclassified the Isabelline Serotine again as a full species [gen. lit. 10]. Genetic comparisons with other *Eptesicus* forms of Europe and the Middle East confirmed the separation of the species [gen. lit. 77]. From the most recent results the species also occurs in the south of the Iberian Peninsula [gen. lit. 167].

IDENTIFICATION
Very similar to the European Serotine, but smaller and paler coloured. The dorsal fur is pale sandy to gold-blond coloured, the ventral side light cream to yellowish. Face and ears are brownish, in contrast to the black colouring in *E. serotinus*. The upper tooth row (CM³) is usually shorter than 7.4mm, in *E. serotinus* usually longer. As in other sibling species, differences in penis morphology may be good characters.

DISTRIBUTION
In northwest Africa limited to the north of the Sahara, occuring from Morocco to Libya. The southernmost records lie in the Atlas mountains. Also found on the Canary Islands (Lanzarote) [gen. lit. 143]. Only

Measurements

Forearm	44.2–50.8mm
Fifth finger	53–63mm
Third finger	75–89mm
Normal weight	13–16g
CBL	17.6–19.5mm
CM³	6.9–7.6mm

Fig. 435. The Isabelline Serotine prefers to hunt in oases or wadies. Photo: T. Pröhl.

recently it has been shown that populations from the southern Iberian Peninsula also belong to the Isabelline Serotine [gen. lit. 167], with details still unavailable.

HABITAT

The habitat includes open cultural landscape and forests from Mediterranean regions of the southern Iberian Peninsula and the North African coast, and also all transitions to the borders of the Sahara. In semi-desert areas closely associated with waterbodies and oases with more dense vegetation.

Roosts

Suspected to be a rock crevice dweller. So far few roosts have been found, mostly single animals in buildings [1], rock crevices, caves or in cracks of ruins and Roman aqueducts. A nursery of at least 30 animals was found in Algeria in a hollow date palm [6].

BEHAVIOUR, REPRODUCTION AND FOOD BIOLOGY

Very little is known about the species, most records refer to mistnet catches in foraging habitats and at drinking places. Pregnant females were captured in Algeria in the middle of June and mostly carried two embryos [6]. Foraging flight manouevrable around trees and rocks [2].

THREATS

So far not evaluated as a full species. In Morocco and north Algeria widely distributed, but nowhere common.

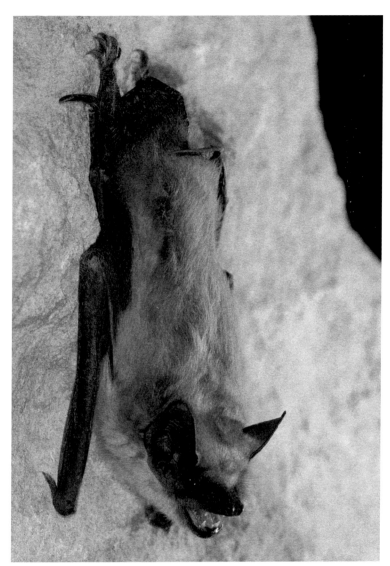

Fig. 436. The Isabelline Serotine resembles the Serotine, but is substantially paler. Photo: C. Dietz.

REFERENCES

1. Aulagnier, S. & M. Thevenot (1986): Catalogue des mammifères sauvages du Maroc. *Travaux de l'Institut Scientifique, Série Zoologie* 41: 1–163.
2. Brosset, A. (1955): Observations sur la biologie des chiroptères du Maroc oriental. *Bulletin de la Société des Sciences Naturelles et Physiques du Maroc* 35: 295–306.
3. Dorst, J. & J.B. Panouse (1957): Note sur la distribution d'*Eptesicus isabellinus* au Maroc. *Comptes Rendus Mensuels des Séances de la Société des Sciences Naturelles et Physiques du Maroc* 23: 68–69.
4. Hanák, V. & A. Elgadi (1984): On the bat fauna (Chiroptera) of Libya. *Vestnik Ceskoslovenske Spolecnosti Zoologicke* 48: 165–184.
5. Harrison, D.L. (1963): Observations on the North African serotine bat, *Eptesicus serotinus isabellinus* (Mammalia: Chiroptera). *Zoologische Mededelingen, Rijksmuseum van Natuurlijke Historie te Leiden* 38: 207–212.
6. Kowalski, K. & B. Rzebik-Kowalska (1991): *Mammals of Algeria*, 370 pp; Polish Academy of Sciences.
7. Panouse, J.B. (1951): Les chauves-souris du Maroc. *Travaux de l'Institut Scientifique Chérifien* 1: 1–120.

Anatolian Serotine Bat
Eptesicus anatolicus
FELTEN, 1971

NAMES
D: Küstenfledermaus
F: Sérotine d'Anatolie
E: Murciélago de huerta turco
NL: Anatolische laatvlieger

GENERAL INFORMATION
Felten described a new species, *Eptesicus anatolicus*, in 1971 on the basis of individuals from Turkey [4]. This was subsequently classified as a subspecies of Botta's Serotine (*E. bottae*). Apart from considerations as to whether a relationship could exist with the Isabelline Serotine [6] the large differences from the desert forms of Botta's Serotine, *E. b. hingstoni* and *E. b. taftanimontis*, led Hanák *et al.* in 2001 to suggest that the Anatolian Serotine might again be regarded as a full species [5]. Genetic comparisons with the Isabelline Serotine and the subspecies *E. b. innesi* of Botta's Serotine supported the opinion that the Anatolian Serotine may actually be a full species [gen. lit. 77].

Measurements

Forearm	43.3–52.1mm
Fifth finger	54–58mm
Third finger	72–80mm
Normal weight	14–21g
CBL	17.0–18.3mm
CM³	6.1–7.0mm

IDENTIFICATION
Very similar to the southeast European Serotine Bats but smaller, short snout and narrow tragus. Face, ears and flight membranes are deep black and contrast with the paler sand to blond-coloured dorsal fur and the whitish-grey ventral side. The hairs of the dorsal side are bicoloured with a brown base and honey to blond-coloured tips. Young animals are darker with more grey shades and have a less strongly contrasting ventral side. The dorsal fur is shorter than in the Serotine and appears more dense and silkier.

Similar species
In the region covered by this book only confusable with the Serotine Bat, differing by the length of the forearm and particularly of the fifth finger. The penis is also clearly different from all other *Eptesicus* species of Europe, North Africa and the Middle East: it is distinctly broader at the tip and carries a characteristic roof-shaped transversal fold, which is absent in all other species [6].

ECHOLOCATION CALLS
In open areas almost constant-frequency calls with a reduced frequency-modulated initial part and an end frequency of 28kHz and a call duration of about 14ms. The call structure is very similar to that of Northern Bat [6].

DISTRIBUTION
In Anatolian Turkey in a coastal strip from the middle of the Aegean coast along the whole south coast [7] to Syria [1]. The eastern distribution border is unclear. In

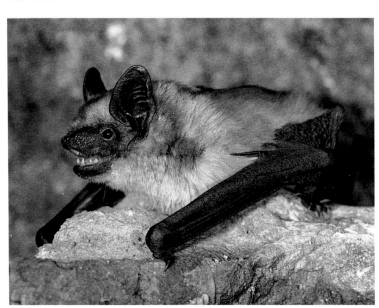

Fig. 437. The Anatolian Serotine is smaller than the Serotine and paler coloured. Photo: O. von Helversen.

Europe only recorded on the islands of Rhodes [6] and Cyprus [2]. Possibly also on other islands near the coast such as Samos.

Subspecies and geographical variation

So far only the nominate form is known. The relationship with the numerous forms attributed to Botta's Serotine, including *E. b. taftanimontis*, *E. b. ognevi* and the nominate form *E. b. bottae* is not yet sufficiently clarified.

HABITAT

On Rhodes the hunting grounds are in coastal zones, barely vegetated or with overgrown Mediterranean scrub, on karst slopes and dry stream courses. On the other hand, the species is absent in forest areas and in the mountain zones of the island [6]. Similarly established in a narrow strip in Turkey along the coast at low altitudes and to 50km inland [7]. In Syria likewise within coastal ranges [1].

Roosts

Records of roosts in wall cracks of ancient ruins or under bridges. Probably originally a rock crevice dweller.

BEHAVIOUR

Nursery colonies with volant juveniles in Turkey comprise individual females with their young or small groups of up to 11 animals [7].

FORAGING

In open areas but also around streetlamps and in the semi-open area along cliffs and vegetation. The wings are somewhat narrower than in the Serotine and the flight accordingly more rapid and more similar to that of *Nyctalus* species [5].

FOOD

No data are available about the diet. Probably similar to Botta's Serotine, taking ants, ichneumon wasps, moths, beetles and other flying insects [3].

THREATS

As full species so far not identified. EU

Fig. 438. The Anatolian Serotine occurs particularly in cultural landscape in the Mediterranean coastal range and often seeks its roosts in ruins. Photo: C. Dietz.

Habitats Directive, Annex IV. Threats cannot be derived from the few available data. It is a relatively common species on Rhodes. The status on Cyprus is as yet unclear. Some roosts are possibly threatened by restoration of ancient ruins.

REFERENCES

1. Benda, P., M. Andreas, D. Kock, R. Lucan, P. Munclinger, P. Nova, J. Obuch, K. Ochman, A. Reiter, M. Uhrin & D. Weinfurtova (1999): Bats (Mammalia: Chiroptera) of the Eastern Mediterranean. Part 4. Bat fauna of Syria: distribution, systematics, ecology. *Acta Soc. Zool. Bohem.* 70: 1–329
2. Benda, P., V. Hanák, I. Horáček, P. Hulva, R. Lučan & M. Ruedi (2007). Bats (Mammalia: Chiroptera) of the Eastern Mediterranean. Part 5. Bat fauna of Cyprus: review of records with confirmation of six species new for the island and description of new subspecies. *Acta Soc. Zool. Bohem.* 71: 71–130
3. Feldman, R., J.O. Whitaker & Y. Yom-Tov (2000): Dietary composition and habitat use in a desert insectivorous bat community in Israel. *Acta Chiropterologica* 2: 15–22.
4. Felten, H. (1971): Eine neue Art der Fledermaus-Gattung *Eptesicus* aus Kleinasien. *Senckenb. Biol.* 52: 371–376.
5. Hanák, V., P. Benda, M. Ruedi, I. Horáček & T.S. Sofianidou (2001): Bats (Mammalia: Chiroptera) of the Eastern Mediterranean, Part 2. New records and review of distribution of bats in Greece. *Acta Soc. Zool. Bohem.* 65: 279–346.
6. Helversen, O. von (1998): *Eptesicus bottae* (Mammalia, Chiroptera) auf der Insel Rhodos. *Bonn. Zool. Beitr.* 48: 113–121.
7. Spitzenberger, F. (1994): The genus *Eptesicus* (Mammalia, Chiroptera) in southern Anatolia. *Folia Zool.* 43: 437–454.

Hoary Bat
Lasiurus cinereus
(PALISOT DE BEAUVOIS, 1796)

NAMES
D: Eisgraue Fledermaus
F: Chauve-souris cendrée
E: Murciélago escarchado
I: Pipistrello cenerino
NL: Grijze vleermuis
S: Grå fladdermus

Measurements
Forearm 50.7–56.8mm
(L. c. cinereus)
Weight 20–38g

Fig. 439. The Hoary Bat is an exceptional vagrant from North America to Iceland and the Orkney Islands. Photo: B. Fenton.

IDENTIFICATION
A large strong bat, with a short snout and short rounded ears. The dorsal fur is light brown, with pale silver-grey tips on the back giving a 'frosted' appearance. Yellowish-brown with a light orange tint on the throat, on the snout and around the ears. The ears are furred contrasting dense beige inside and towards the bare hind margin. The chest has a silver-grey sheen, the belly light-grey. Long narrow wings are heavily pale furred along the forearm and the fifth finger, particularly on the lower surface. The tail membrane is strongly furred on the upper surface. Only one pair of lower incisors. Females have four nipples. Occurs from the southern half of Canada over the entire United States to Central Argentina, also on Hawaii and the Galapagos islands. In North America L. c. cinereus. One record from the Orkney Islands (South Ronaldsay) in September 1847 [1], four records from the southwest coast of Iceland in October 1943, October and December 1957 and October 1964 [3]. Pennant had earlier listed the Hoary Bat for Iceland in 1784 [2], but no specimen from this time is available. As with numerous North American migratory birds single Hoary Bats appear to be blown by the strong westerly winds to Iceland and the Orkneys in September/October. Another animal was found dead in August 1981 in the port of Reykjavik, on board a ship originating from North America [3]. Hoary Bats are very good and rapid fliers and are seasonally long-distance migrants. They can fly at very high altitudes; a collision with a military aircraft at 2,438m above the ground was recorded [4]. Suitable habitats are deciduous and coniferous forests, individual animals hanging freely in the trees or amongst foliage. In June two young are born. Flying insects (moths) are the main prey [5].

REFERENCES
1. Hill, J.E. & D.W. Yalden (1990): The status of the hoary bat, Lasiurus cinereus, as a British species. J. Zool. 222: 694–697.
2. Pennant, T. (1784): Arctic Zoology; Vol. 1; London.
3. Petersen, A. (1994): The occurrence of bats (Order Chiroptera) in Iceland. Natturufraedingurinn 64: 3–12.
4. Peurach, S.C. (2003): High-altitude collision between an airplane and a hoary bat, Lasiurus cinereus. Bat Research News 44: 2–3.
5. Shump, K.A. & A.U. Shump (1982): Lasiurus cinereus. Mammalian Species 185: 1–5.

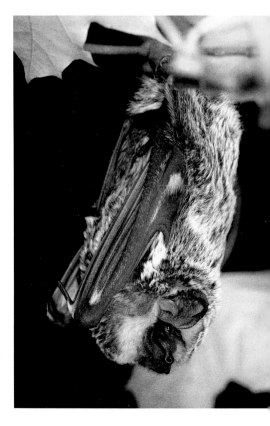

Western Barbastelle Bat
Barbastella barbastellus
(SCHREBER, 1774)

NAMES
D: Mopsfledermaus
F: Barbastelle d'Europe
E: Murciélago de bosque
I: Barbastello
NL: Mopsvleermuis
S: Barbastelle
PL: Mopek

IDENTIFICATION
Medium-sized bat with a short blunt snout. The fur is dense, long and silky, dark black-brown, particularly on the back the hairs have whitish tips, giving a 'frosted' appearance. The skin areas are dark black-brown. The broad, trapezium-shaped ears project forward, with the inner edges joined together over the top of the head; in most animals the middle of the outer edge has a distinctive knob-like flap of skin. The tragus tapers very abruptly at half its length and has a long rounded tip. Small mouth and weak dentition.

Similar species
Only confusable with *B. darjelingensis* from eastwards of the Caucasus, and *B. leucomelas* in the Middle East, neither of which is known to occur within the geographical scope of this book. Morphological differences are not known.

ECHOLOCATION CALLS
Two call types are emitted alternately [2]. Type 1 has a low intensity, lasts 3–6ms, is frequency-modulated and drops from *c.* 45kHz to 30–35kHz. Type 2 is a 2–3ms-long frequency-modulated call, which drops from *c.* 36 to *c.* 28kHz. The sonogram of type 2 is flat convex curved. Denzinger *et al.* assume that type 2 is oriented downwards while the weaker type 1 is emitted horizontally forwards, using rapid head movements between the calls [2]. Conversely our own investigations on the European and the Sinai Barbastelle reveal that the type 1 calls are emitted from the nostrils and type 2

calls from the mouth [own data from emergence investigations]. The 'switching' is probably caused either by a shift of the larynx or by the soft palate. In dense vegetation and at emergence very short calls of type 1 are exclusively emitted with the mouth closed [own data].

DISTRIBUTION
Throughout Europe to 58°–60°N, thus the northern distribution border runs across England and Sweden. Only a single record from Norway [22]. Occurs also on the Balearics, Corsica, Sardinia, the Canary Islands (Tenerife, La Gomera) [7, 19], and in Morocco (Middle Atlas) [4]. The species has, so far, not been observed in southern central Spain, on Crete and Cyprus, as well as in some parts of Turkey. The eastern border of the distribution lies in eastern Turkey in the Pontic region and in the Caucasus. Contrary to the given distribution map the species does not occur in Sicily or in the south of the Appennine Peninsula.

Measurements	
Forearm	36.5–43.5mm
Fifth finger	47–54mm
Third finger	63–71mm
Normal weight	7–10g
CBL	12,0–14,8mm
CM³	4.5–4.8mm

Fig. 440. Western Barbastelles often hunt just below or above the tree crowns. Photo: D. Nill.

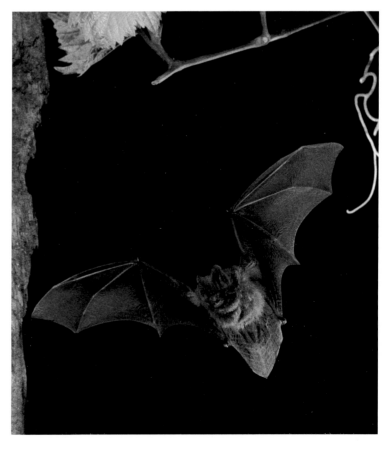

Subspecies and geographical variation

Only the nominate form *B. b. barbastellus*, and on the Canary Islands a more brownish-coloured subspecies without silvery hair tips: *B. b. guanchae* [19]. The forms *leucomelas* (Sinai Peninsula) and *darjelingensis* (Asia), sometimes regarded as subspecies, represent full species [gen. lit. 77, own data]. The proportion of animals with the small skin flap on the outer edge of the ear varies in different populations. Particularly in eastern Central Europe (Czech Republic) partial albinism is relatively frequent (1.2% of the animals [12]).

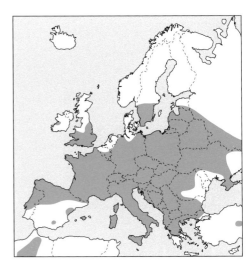

HABITAT

To a large extent limited to a wide range of forests but also in gardens near forests and areas with hedges. In the north of the distribution area also in lowlands, and occurs in the southern Mediterranean region and in Morocco in foothills to high mountainous forests up to over 2,000m. In Switzerland in richly structured productive forests [16]. The tree species composition seems to have little significance, but a high structural abundance with different age groups and edge structures is important.

Roosts

Summer roosts in forests behind loose bark, in tree cracks and in bat boxes (flat boxes) [10, 18]. In buildings behind window shutters and timber claddings. In southern Europe in rock crevices in summer. Winter roosts likewise behind bark but also in caves, mines, disused railway tunnels, rubble heaps, rock crevices and ruins. As a cold-resistant species often in the entrance zone of underground roosts within cold areas. Single animals usually wedged in

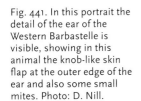

Fig. 441. In this portrait the detail of the ear of the Western Barbastelle is visible, showing in this animal the knob-like skin flap at the outer edge of the ear and also some small mites. Photo: D. Nill.

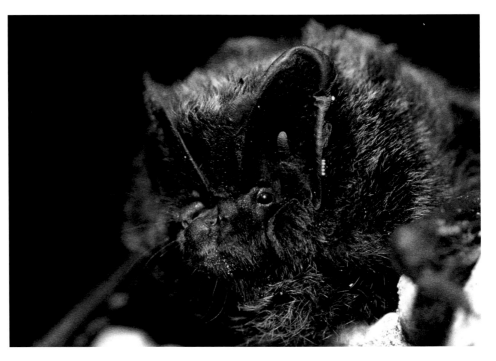

narrow cracks; groups form free-hanging clusters, which can comprise up to 1,000 animals in northern Central Europe [20].

BEHAVIOUR

Building roosts can comprise up to 100 or more females, in tree roosts 10–20 females. Tree roosts are frequently changed, often daily, while building roosts are occupied over the whole summer [10, 18]. Mass winter roosts in Slovakia and in Poland can comprise up to 8,000 animals [20]. In former times there were also large winter accumulations in Baden-Württemberg (Sontheimer cave) and Bavaria (silver mine, Bodenmais) with up to 3,000 animals; the populations collapsed in the 1970s and have not recovered in the Sontheimer cave and only slightly in Bavaria [5, 9]. Often with other species in winter roosts, even in the same clusters, in summer roosts usually the only species. The body weight decreases during hibernation by about 29–37%. In the late summer Western Barbastelles visit caves for swarming; in the Frankish Alps marked animals were recovered in subsequent years at the same swarming site [9].

REPRODUCTION

Reach sexual maturity in the first year, mating takes place in the late summer in mating roosts, when swarming and in the winter roosts. Mating groups can be formed of one male with up to four females [18]. Starting from the middle of June, 1–2 young are born and suckled for up to six weeks.

FORAGING

Emerging early in the dusk and entering nearby vegetation, frequently hunting closely above the tree crowns, but also under the canopy, or along vegetation edges [14, 16, 18]. Very agile flight, usually fast and close to vegetation. Rapid dives close to branches are observed in animals hunting above the tree canopy [16].

FOOD

The food consists almost exclusively of small moths such as pyralids and arctiid moths, plus a small proportion of Diptera, small beetles and other flying insects [11, 14, 15, 16].

MAXIMUM AGE

The average life expectancy lies between 5.5 and 10 years, the proven maximum age at almost 22 years [1].

MOBILITY AND MIGRATION

To a large extent a sedentary species, summer and winter roosts lie close together, usually less than 40km distance [5]. Among more than 15,000 ringed animals long-distance flights have been demonstrated relatively rarely, with only four recoveries over 100km, the furthest being 290km.

Habitat use

The hunting grounds are usually near the nursery colonies at a distance of up to 4.5km, young animals and males hunt on average closer to their roost than do adult females [18]. The foraging area is about 8.8ha [16]. Single animals hunt each night in up to 10 separate hunting grounds [18]. A nursery colony association can have a complex of roosts in an area of at least 64ha [18].

Fig. 442. Western Barbastelles, in contrast to most other vesper bats, fly with the muzzle closed, since they can emit the ultrasonic calls for orientation through the nose. Photo: C. Dietz.

THREATS

Red list of the IUCN 2006: VU (Vulnerable), Red list of the European Union: VU (Vulnerable), EU Habitats Directive, Annex II & IV. Enormous population decrease in 1950s–1970s in the former mass hibernation sites. These decreases, from which even today the species has recovered only slightly, were probably caused by substantial pesticide use in forests and with that the collapse of the food resources for this highly specialised species. It is all the more worrying that nowadays increasing use of insecticides in forest ecological systems is again being applied. Intensive forest management with little old and dead wood likewise represents a threat.

Widespread in England and Wales, but rarely recorded [UK gen. lit. 153, 155]. Rare in hibernation sites, and few summer colonies known. Subject of current detailed study in the south. A Priority Species under the UK's Biodiversity Action Plan.

CONSERVATION MEASURES

Abandonment of insect control in forests, semi-natural forest management in forests with a high proportion of old and dead wood. Protection of the mass winter roosts and building roosts. Preservation and re-establishment of large coherent and unfragmented forest biotopes.

REFERENCES

1. Abel, G. (1970): Zum Höchstalter der Mopsfledermaus (*Barbastella barbastellus*). *Myotis* 8: 38.
2. Denzinger, A., B.M. Siemers, A. Schaub & H.-U. Schnitzler (2001): Echolocation by the barbastelle bat, *Barbastella barbastellus*. *J. Comp. Physiol.* A 187: 521–528.
3. Dolch, D. & D. Arnold (1989): Beobachtungen an einer Wochenstube von *Barbastella barbastellus*. In: D. Heidecke & M. Stubbe (eds): *Populationsökologie von Fledermausarten; Martin-Luther-Universität Halle-Wittenberg*: 115–118.
4. Fonderflick, J., M. Grosselet & P. Pade (1998): Capture méridionale de la barbastelle d'Europe (*Barbastella barbastellus*) et de la pipistrelle commune (*Pipistrellus pipistrellus*) au Maroc. *Mammalia* 62: 610–611.
5. Frank, H. (1960): Beobachtungen an Fledermäusen in Höhlen der Schwäbischen Alb unter besonderer Berücksichtigung der Mopsfledermaus (*Barbastella barbastellus*). *Bonn. Zool. Beitr., Sonderheft* 11/1960: 143–149.
6. Gombkötö, P. (2003): Die Sommerlebensräume der Mopsfledermaus (*Barbastella barbastellus*) im Bükkgebirge (Nordungarn). *Nyctalus* (N.F.) 8: 544–547.
7. Juste, J., C. Ibáñez, D. Trujillo, J. Munoz & M. Ruedi (2003): Phylogeography of barbastelle bats (*Barbastella barbastellus*) in the Western Mediterranean and the Canary Islands. *Acta Chiropterologica* 5: 165–175.
8. Paunović, M., R. Pandurska, T. Ivanova & B. Karapan a (2003): Present knowledge of distribution and status of *Barbastella barbastellus* on the Balkan Peninsula. *Nyctalus* (N.F.) 8: 633–638.
9. Rudolph, B.-U., M. Hammer & A. Zahn (2003): Die Mopsfledermaus (*Barbastella barbastellus*) in Bayern. *Nyctalus* (N.F.) 8: 564–580.

Fig. 443. Colony roost sites of Western Barbastelle are usually in crevices behind bark or window shutters, or as here in a flat bat box. Photo: T. Pröhl.

Fig. 444. Hunting ground of the Western Barbastelle over the crowns of a coniferous forest. Photo: D. Nill.

10. Russo, D., L. Cistrone, G. Jones & S. Mazzoleni (2004): Roost selection by barbastelle bats (*Barbastella barbastellus*) in beech woodlands of central Italy: consequences for conservation. *Biol. Conserv.* 117: 73–81.

11. Rydell, J., G. Natuschke, A. Theiler & P.E. Zingg (1996): Food habits of the barbastelle bat (*Barbastella barbastellus*). *Ecography* 19: 62–66.

12. Rydell, J. & W. Bogdanowicz (1997): *Barbastella barbastellus. Mammalian Species* 557: 1–8.

13. Schober, W. (2004): *Barbastella barbastellus* – Mopsfledermaus. In: F. Krapp (ed.): *Handbuch der Säugetiere Europas* 4-II: 1071–1091; Aula Verlag.

14. Sierro, A. & R. Arlettaz (1997): Barbastelle bats (*Barbastella* spp.) specialize in the predation of moths: implications for foraging tactics and conservation. *Acta Oecologica* 18: 91–106.

15. Sierro, A. (1999): Habitat selection by barbastelle bats (*Barbastella barbastellus*) in the Swiss Alps (Valais). *J. Zool.* 248: 429–432.

16. Sierro, A. (2003): Habitat use, diet and food availability in a population of *Barbastella barbastellus* in a Swiss alpine valley. *Nyctalus* (N.F.) 8: 670–673.

17. Spitzenberger, F. (1993): Die Mopsfledermaus (*Barbastella barbastellus*) in Österreich, Mammalia Austriaca 20. *Myotis* 31: 111–153.

18. Steinhauser, D. (2002): Untersuchungen zur Ökologie der Mopsfledermaus, *Barbastella barbastellus* und der Bechsteinfledermaus, *Myotis bechsteinii* im Süden des Landes Brandenburg. *Schriftenreihe für Landschaftspflege und Naturschutz* 71: 81–98.

19. Trujillo, D., C. Ibáñez & J. Juste (2002): A new subspecies of *Barbastella barbastellus* (Mammalia: Chiroptera: Vespertilionidae) from the Canary Islands. *Rev. Suisse Zool.* 109: 543–550.

20. Uhrin, M. (1995): The finding of a mass winter colony of *Barbastella barbastellus* and *Pipistrellus pipistrellus* in Slovakia. *Myotis* 32/33: 131–133.

21. Urbanczyk, Z. (1991): Hibernation of *Myotis daubentoni* and *Barbastella barbastellus* in Nietoperek Bat Reserve. *Myotis* 29: 115–120.

ADDITIONAL REFERENCES

22. Flåten, M. & T. Røed (2007): Bredøreflaggermusa *Barbastella barbastellus* ikke utdødd likevel! *Fauna* 60 (3–4): 142–144.

23. Greenaway, F.R. & D. Hill (2005): *Woodland Management Advice for Bechstein's Bat and Barbastelle Bat.* English Nature, Research Reports no 658, Peterborough. 29pp.

Eastern Barbastelle Bat
Barbastella darjelingensis
Hodgson, 1855

A species occurring in the Caucasus, where sympatric with *B. barbastellus*, and eastwards south of the Russian Federation to Japan and south to the Middle East. It averages slightly larger, is often somewhat paler, and it lacks the small lobe on the outer edge of the ear, which is usually present in *B. barbastellus*. Its ecology in the arid-zone habitat parts of its range may be quite different from that in the temperate woodland favoured by Western Barbastelle.

Hemprich's Long-eared Bat
Otonycteris hemprichii
PETERS, 1859

NAMES
D: Wüsten-Großohr
F: Oreillard d'Hemprich
NL: Woestijngrootoorvleermuis

Measurements

Forearm	55.1–66.4mm
Fifth finger	64–79mm
Third finger	83–109mm
Normal weight	19–24g
CBL	21.9–26.9mm
CM³	7.4–9.4mm

IDENTIFICATION
The largest long-eared bat within our region. The fluffy fur is light-grey to brownish on the dorsal side, on the ventral side white. The tragus is long and straight and, in contrast to *Plecotus* species, the nostrils are simple. The flight membranes are thick and sturdy. The females have two pairs of nipples; the penis of the male is unusual and complicated with a bifurcated and curved glans penis.

Similar species
Unmistakable by size and pale skin colouring. In contrast to *Plecotus* species, the ears are not joined together by a fold of skin.

ECHOLOCATION CALLS
Frequency-modulated calls with two harmonics, the lower drops from approximately 40kHz to approximately 18kHz, with maximum energy around 30–32kHz [4].

DISTRIBUTION
A typical bat of deserts and semi-deserts, distributed throughout North Africa along the Sahara, in the south to central Niger and southern Sudan, across the Arabian Peninsula to Pakistan, Kashmir and Tadzhikistan.

Subspecies and geographical variation
Several barely distinguishable subspecies have been described. The nominate form *O. h. hemprichii* occurs in North Africa.

HABITAT
Hemprich's Long-eared Bat is adapted by an ability to acquire its water requirements from its food of a wide spectrum of ground-living prey in arid areas such as deserts and semi-deserts [6]. It inhabits wadies and mountain regions with cliffs. The meagre habitats are unsuitable for large colonies and explains the low population density of the species

Roosts
Crevices in cliffs and occasionally cracks at buildings are recorded as roosts [3, 4].

BEHAVIOUR
The nursery colonies are small and comprise 3–18 females [4, 5]. Outside of the lactation period the roosts are changed at least every 1–2 days [3]. The evening emergence takes place late; hunting grounds and watering sites are close to the roosts [3]. Captured animals are very tame and do not bite; held in the hand they vibrate strongly and emit a bumblebee-like humming.

REPRODUCTION
Little is known about the reproduction; according to the few available data two young are born in June.

FORAGING
A typical ground-gleaner which has a *Plecotus*-like flight close to the ground or along cliffs. Sparsely overgrown areas are continuously patrolled with a slow flight in wide circuits [5]. The prey can be located in hovering flight and picked up from the ground. Hemprich's Long-eared Bat probably

Fig. 445. Hemprich's Long-eared Bat is a very large and pale-coloured bat species. Photo: C. Dietz.

locates the prey partly or to a large extent by rustling sounds. Captive animals react immediately to rustling sounds and dive onto the prey. Flycatcher-like hunting from a perch does not seem to occur in this species [3]. The flight morphology is very similar to the partially carnivorous North American species *Antrozous pallidus*, which suggest the potential ability to prey on small reptiles and mammals [7]. Waterbodies, wells and cattle watering places are visited for drinking.

FOOD
A broad spectrum of large ground-living animals is captured, depending upon region and season, including scarabeid beetles and chafers, grasshoppers, bugs or even scorpions, centipedes, spiders and whip scorpions [3, 4, 5, 8]. Flying prey such as moths plays a minor role. In captivity, vertebrate animals such as geckos are also eaten [4], but that has not yet been confirmed in the wild.

THREATS
To a large extent unknown. Red list of the IUCN 2006: LC (Least Concern). The species is nowhere common, but this can be an adaptation to the poor habitat.

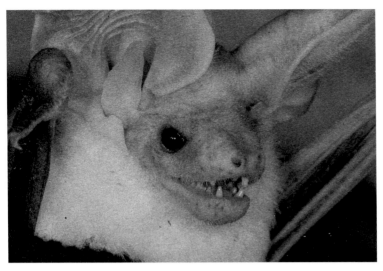

5. Horáček, I. (1991): Enigma of *Otonycteris*: ecology, relationship, classification. *Myotis* 29: 17–30.
6. Marom, S., C. Korine, M.S. Woiciechowski, C.R. Tracy & B. Pinshow (2006): Energy metabolism and evaporative water loss in the European free-tailed bat and Hemprich's long-eared bat (Microchiroptera): species sympatric in the Negev desert. *Phys. Biochem. Zool.* 79: 944–956.
7. Norberg, U.M. & M.B. Fenton (1988): Carnivorous bats? *Biol. J. Linn. Soc.* 33: 383–394.
8. Whitaker, J.O., B. Shalmon & T.H. Kunz (1994): Food and feeding habits of insectivorous bats from Israel. *Z. Säugetierk.* 59: 74–81.

Fig. 446. In Hemprich's Long-eared Bat the ears are not connected at the base by a skin fold and the strong muzzle is more reminiscent of mouse-eared bats than the closely related long-eared bats. Photo: C. Dietz.

REFERENCES

1. Arlettaz, R., G. Dändliker, E. Kasybekov, J.-M. Pillet, S. Rybin & J. Zima (1995): Feeding habits of the long-eared desert bat, *Otonycteris hemprichii*. *J. Mammal.* 76: 873–876.
2. Aulagnier, S. & P. Mein (1985): Note sur la présence d'*Otonycteris hemprichi* au Maroc. *Mammalia* 49: 582–584.
3. Fenton, M.B., B. Shalmon & D. Makin (1999): Roost switching, foraging behavior, and diet of the vespertilionid bat, *Otonycteris hemprichii*. *Israel J. Zool.* 45: 501–506.
4. Gharaibeh, B.M. & M.B. Qumsiyeh (1995): *Otonycteris hemprichii*. *Mammalian Species* 514: 1–4.

Fig. 447. Hemprich's Long-eared Bat occurs in semi-desert and desert areas of North Africa. Photo: C. Dietz.

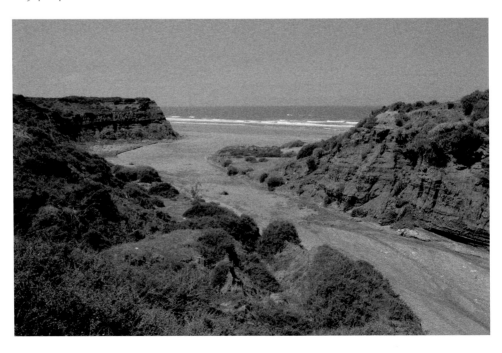

Brown Long-eared Bat
Plecotus auritus
(LINNAEUS, 1758)

NAMES

- D: Braunes Langohr
- F: Oreillard roux
- E: Murciélago orejudo dorado
- I: Orecchione comune
- NL: Gewone grootoorvleermuis
- S: Långörad fladdermus
- PL: Gacek brunatny

IDENTIFICATION

Medium-sized bat with very long delicate ears, which are, as in the other species of the genus, folded and tucked under the wings when torpid or hibernating. The long lancet-shaped tragus projects forward even when the ear is folded. The long and fluffy dorsal fur is brown, often with a reddish tinge and blends gradually into the cream to yellowish-grey coloured ventral fur. The face is usually light brown, appearing short with a pair of glands at the rear of the muzzle. The ears and the tragus are little pigmented. The eyes are remarkably large.

Thumbs, thumb claws and feet are large and the toes have strong bristle-like hairs. The penis tapers evenly to the end. The wings are broad with short broad hand-wing membranes (dactylopatagia).

Similar species

Very similar to the Grey Long-eared Bat but slimmer and usually smaller. Distinguishable from all other *Plecotus* species by a long thumb (usually over 6.5mm), a long thumb claw (> 2mm), large feet (> 8mm) with long distinct hairs, a semi-circular to banana-shaped chin spot (not triangular as in the Alpine Long-eared Bat), and a conical penis narrowing to the tip.

ECHOLOCATION CALLS

The frequency-modulated calls consist of two harmonics. The lower drops from *c.* 55 to 25–20kHz, the upper from over 80 to 40kHz. Thus the harmonics overlap each other in frequency, which is usually not the case in the Grey Long-eared Bat. The calls are very quiet and are particularly used for spacial orientation; the food is, at least partly, located by rustling sounds of the prey. The echolocation calls can be emitted by the mouth or by the nose [gen. lit. 68].

Measurements

Forearm	35.5–42.8mm
Fifth finger	47–54mm
Third finger	63–67mm
Thumb	6.2–8.2mm
Tibia	19.5–21.8mm
Foot	8.2–9.7mm
Tragus length	14.0–16.7mm
Tragus width	4.4–5.5mm
Normal weight	6–9g
CBL	14.3–15.6mm
CM^3	5.0–5.8mm

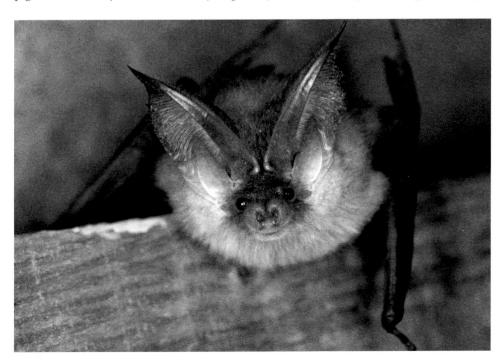

Fig. 448. Portrait of a Brown Long-eared Bat. The tragus is little pigmented towards the base. Photo: D. Nill.

DISTRIBUTION

Through the whole of Europe, northward to 63–64°N. In the southern parts, distribution patchy, usually in wooded mountain regions. In the Mediterranean area there are, so far, no records in the southeast of the Iberian Peninsula, in southern Greece, North Africa, the Near East and on most islands [15], occurs definitely only on Sardinia. The Brown Long-eared Bat is, from the most recent knowledge, a genuine West Palearctic faunal element with an eastern distribution border in the Urals and Caucasus. All the formerly recognised forms from Asia to the Sachalin Peninsula, Korea, Japan, North China, India and Nepal represent full species [gen. lit. 138].

Subspecies and geographical variation

On the Iberian Peninsula *P. a. begognae* [6], *P. a. auritus* in the remaining geographical scope of this book. The Iberian subspecies is on average larger (forearm length: 38.3–43.5mm, thumb length: 5.9–7.7mm, foot length: 7.7–9.6mm,

tragus length: 12.6–17.1mm, tragus width: to 4.4–5.8mm) and genetically clearly different from the nominate form and probably has the status of a full species [6, 11, gen. lit, 77, 167]. For clarification a detailed study would be necessary in the Pyrenees area in order to find possible sympatric occurrence of both forms. Within *P. a. auritus* there are two lineages, an eastern and a western, which probably relate to respective glacial refuges [gen. lit. 137, 138]. The Asian forms, formerly classified as subspecies, such as *P. a. homochrous*, *P. a. sacrimontis* or *P. a. uenoi*, represent full species [gen. lit. 138].

HABITAT

A typical species of forest. Hunting grounds, according to telemeteric studies in Germany and Scotland [7, 12], are in forests but also at individual trees in parks and gardens. A broad spectrum of forest types is inhabited from boreal mixed coniferous woodlands, spruce forests, to beech stocks. On the other hand, it seems to be rather rare in lowland pine forests [7]. Occurs in northern Europe from lowlands into the mountains, in Central Europe from 200m to over 2,000m. In south Europe in mountain forests, a majority of the Greek and Bulgarian localities lie over 1,000m.

Roosts

There are two predominant summer roost types in Europe: tree and building roosts. In the winter in diverse underground roosts

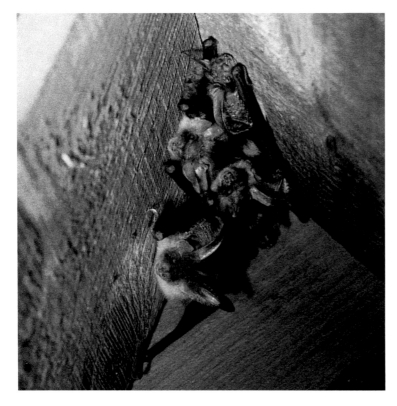

Fig. 449. The roosting sites of Brown Long-eared Bat in buildings are usually concealed in gaps between beams. Photo: A. Kiefer.

Fig. 450. The Brown Long-eared Bat also readily adopts bat boxes as roost sites, as an alternative to tree holes. Photo: T. Pröhl.

from caves to rock crevices but also in tree holes. It seems that the western Brown Long-eared Bats prefer building roosts in the summer and underground roosts in the winter (western Europe to Central Europe), while the eastern ones particularly use trees as roosts in the summer as well as in winter (Central Europe up to the Russian lowlands). The synanthropic degree is highest in the British Isles (it almost exclusively dwells in buildings), while in Eastern Europe and Russia tree roosts clearly dominate [8, 15]. Possibly these two different behaviours in roost selection correspond with two genetic lineages [Kiefer pers. com., 23, gen. lit. 138]. In trees, all kind of spaces are used, from loose bark to rot holes and woodpecker holes [13]. The tree population takes readily to bird and bat boxes. In roof spaces the animals roost usually between tiles, battens and timberwork but also in mortices or behind claddings. In the transition period in the spring and autumn the species can be found in any conceivable (and inconceivable) roosts, from organ pipes to toilet paper holders and wheel houses. In underground winter roosts chooses temperatures of between 3 and 7°C. In caves and mines the animals occur solitarily and males dominate. Strong fluctua-

tions in the numbers, single finds in rubble, scree, wood piles and even in a badger's sett, point to alternative hibernation places: probably tree holes play a central role [15]. In Central Europe the Brown Long-eared Bat is the species most frequently found in small roosts, such as small mountain cellars, small caves and well pits.

BEHAVIOUR

Nursery colonies comprise 5–50 females, at the northern edge of the distribution to over 80 females, and roosts are occupied from April into September. Nursery roosts in buildings are often stable over the whole summer six months (but frequently moving within the roof space), while tree and box roosts are switched regularly every 1–5 days within a periphery of a few hundred metres [12]. During the morning return flight to the roost the colony members swarm for up to a half hour in front of the roost entrance. The males live solitarily in summer, although individual males also stay in nursery roosts [9, 23]. The first mating groups are formed from the beginning of August. At this time and into October distinct swarming occurs at the entrance to and in caves; a weaker second swarming

Fig. 451. Brown Long-eared Bat during the approach to a moth, the large ears are aligned to the prey. Photo: D. Nill.

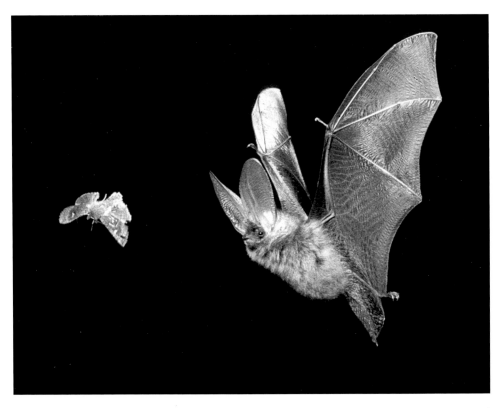

period occurs in the spring (February until April). As with *Myotis* species, males dominate in the swarming populations. In the winter Brown Long-eared Bats usually hang separately, rarely in small groups of up to five individuals and rarely together with other species. Frequently barely observable fissures are occupied. The nursery colonies comprise closely related females [2, 23], which can inhabit a small territory of approximately 1km² over decades [14, 15]. The members of a nursery colony association probably recognise each other by smell, as in Bechstein's Bat. While the young females remain faithful to the nursery roost of their birth and even reproduce there, at least some of the young males leave the territory of the colony, the remaining males settling close to or even in the nursery roost [2, 10]. As with other species perhaps swarming at caves plays a major role in the mating and providing genetic mixing – with mating in the proximity of the nursery roost the risk of in-breeding would clearly be higher [2, 3, 23]. Close to the roosting sites in the nursery roost there

can be socialising with the Grey Long-eared Bat. The Serotine, Greater Mouse-eared Bat, Lesser Horseshoe Bat or Natterer's Bat can also occur in the same attic.

REPRODUCTION

Sexual maturity begins, at least in some young animals (5–10%), as early as the first autumn, in most only in the second year [9, 20]. The first mating can be observed in swarming roosts in August, the last in the winter roost in April; the main mating time lies probably in the late autumn. The gestation period is about 60–70 days; the juveniles are suckled for 40–50 days [15]. Usually only one young is born, in the north and in older females, however, also twins. Depending upon the area, birth takes place in the last three weeks of June (Central Europe) or in the first three weeks of July (Moscow region) [15]. Neonates are born with a forearm length of 14.5–16mm and a weight of approximately 2.5g [5]. The initial weight doubles within the first 10 days to approximately 5g. The forearm grows in this time to 25–30mm; the eyes open within 5–6 days and the fur begins to grow. In the second week of life the body is covered with dense down; at 15 days the weight is over 6g and the forearm approximately 35mm. The ears attain their full mobility only in the fourth to fifth week of life and can then, typically of long-eared bats, be tucked under the wings. From the fourth week the juveniles start to stretch and regularly train their flight muscles and make their first flight attempts. At the age of approximately six weeks the young animals are fully volant [5, 19]. The energy consumption of the females during pregnancy and rearing of young was investigated in detail [16–19, 21]. The energy consumption of a reproducing female is highest at the end of pregnancy and at the end of the lactation period. This is partially accommodated by the body's own reserves or by changes in the behaviour (torpor). In particular, late pregnant females have an enormously increased energy requirement, coupled with decreasing manoeuvrability [19].

FORAGING

The emergence usually takes place only with complete darkness. Two main prey capture strategies can be observed: the catching of flying insects in the air (with the help of the wings or the tail as a scoop) and picking prey off surfaces, usually from the vegetation (foliage gleaning). The prey is searched for with a slow fluttering flight close to the vegetation, located by rustling sounds [1] or visually [gen. lit. 31] and picked off with hovering flight. Prey sitting on the ground can only be noticed when it moves, i.e. produces noise [1], or when the light intensity is over 4 lux [gen. lit. 31]. As an adaptation to prey detection by rustling sounds the highest sensitivity of the hearing is unusually low for bats, at 8–18kHz [4]. Adaptation for slow flight and hovering are the broad wings with short broad hand-wing membranes (dactylopatagia). Prey capture occurs from the ground to into the crown areas of high trees. Larger prey is carried to feeding perches.

FOOD

Moths dominate in the prey remains collected under feeding perches; additionally Diptera, grasshoppers and bugs, also many non-flying invertebrates, such as spiders, harvestmen, earwigs and caterpillars are included in the prey spectrum, particularly in the spring and autumn [22]. Contrary to the opinion that Brown Long-eared Bats hunt opportunistically, large moths, Diptera and beetles are over-proportionally found in the food compared with the local prey availability (determined with light traps). Within the moths, medium-sized noctuids and Ghost Swift Moths are preferred, whereas tiger moths and geometers are avoided. In the Brown Long-eared Bat, dehydration through the flight membranes and ears is very high,

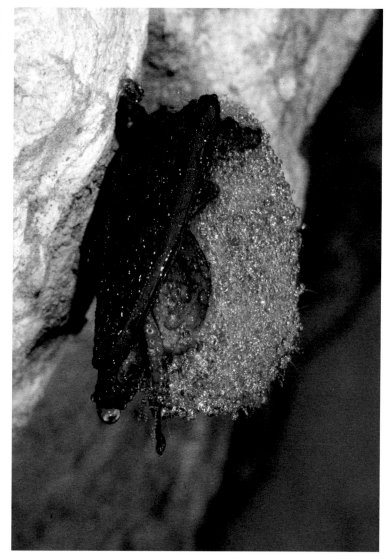

Fig. 452. Like the other species of the genus the Brown Long-eared Bat folds its ears and tucks them under the wings when torpid or hibernating. Photo: D. Nill.

hence 2–5g of water is taken per day [24, 25], water is usually taken in flight directly from the water surface.

MAXIMUM AGE

The annual survival rate is 50–78% and the average life expectancy 4.0 years. The proven maximum age of a female was over 30 years [15].

MOBILITY AND MIGRATION

Very sedentary species; with over 30,000 animals marked in Europe, migration over 30km was rarely observed, and usually relates to dispersing young males. The 'record holder' is a female from Germany at 90km [gen. lit 139]. Usually small-scale area used, with flights under 10km.

Habitat use

Typical small colonies with usually only 20 females use hunting grounds near the nursery roosts [8]. The population density can be very high locally, and lies between 0.2 individuals/ha in Scotland, 0.4 individuals/ha in Central European hardwood forests and 1 individual/ha in areas rich in bat box roosts in Central European forests [15]. Summer foraging grounds lie within a

few hundred meters or up to 2.2km from the roost, in the autumn also up to 3.3km away [12, 22]. The animals spend most of the time, however, within a periphery of 500m around the roost [7, 12, 22]. Hunting grounds are predominantly up to 4ha, rarely to 11ha, with the core hunting grounds usually smaller than 1ha, in some cases hunting is restricted to some individual groups of trees.

THREATS

Red list of the IUCN 2006: LC (Least Concern), EU Habitats Directive, Annex IV. The species is particularly common in Central and northern Europe. Damage is by intensive forestry, removal of mature timber, renovations of roof spaces and netting them (e.g. against pigeons). Also traffic is a threat: by their low slow flight *Plecotus* species are the most frequent traffic victims among bats.

Common and widespread species throughout the UK and Ireland [UK gen. lit. 153, 155]. Most known colonies in buildings (houses, barns, etc.) and so probably threatened there by building works and development. With very low numbers in hibernation sites, late and erratic emergence behaviour,

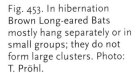

Fig. 453. In hibernation Brown Long-eared Bats mostly hang separately or in small groups; they do not form large clusters. Photo: T. Pröhl.

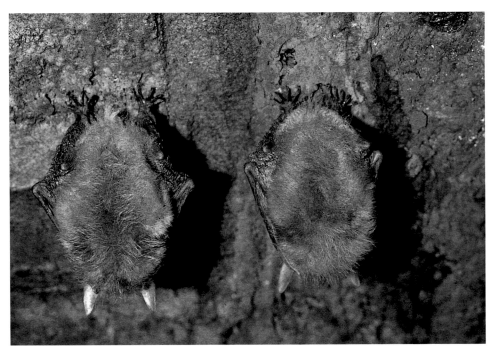

and quiet echolocation calls of foraging bats, the species is difficult to monitor, and early data from hibernation counts and emergence counts of maternity colonies give no significant trend. Nevertheless, there is sufficient concern that the species has recently been adopted as a Priority Species under the UK's Biodiversity Action Plan.

CONSERVATION MEASURES

Almost natural forestry with maintainance of high old and dead wood compartments and preservation of large-scale coherent habitats without fragmentation by roads. Abandonment of pesticide use in forests. Preservation of the status quo of nursery and winter roosts; in particular vegetation-rich edges and orchards (which are often lost in new housing development) are important hunting grounds for near building roosts and should be preserved.

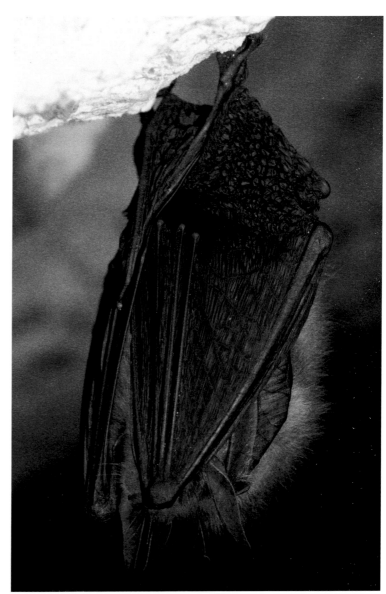

Fig. 454. In hibernation Brown Long-eared Bats sometimes wrap themselves completely into the wing membranes. Photo: D. Nill.

REFERENCES

1. Anderson, M.E. & P.A. Racey (1993): Discrimination between fluttering and non-fluttering moths by brown long-eared bats, *Plecotus auritus*. *Anim. Behav.* 46: 1151–1155.

2. Burland, T.M., E.M. Barratt, M.A. Beaumont & P.A. Racey (1999): Population genetic structure and gene flow in a gleaning bat, *Plecotus auritus*. *Proc. R. Soc. Lond.* B 266: 975–980.

3. Burland, T.M., E.M. Barratt, R.A. Nichols & P.A. Racey (2001): Mating patterns, relatedness and the basis of natal philopatry in the brown long-eared bat, *Plecotus auritus. Mol. Ecol.* 10: 1309–1321.

4. Cole, R.B., A. Guppy, M.E. Anderson & P. Schlegel (1989): Frequency sensitivity and directional hearing in the gleanig bat, *Plecotus auritus. J. Comp. Physiol.* A 165: 269–280.

5. de Fanis E. & G. Jones (1995): Post-natal growth, mother-infant interactions and development of vocalizations in the vespertilionid bat *Plecotus auritus. J. Zool.* 235: 85–97.

6. de Paz, O. (1994): Systematic position of *Plecotus* from the Iberian Peninsula. *Mammalia* 58: 423–432.

7. Entwistle, A.C., P.A. Racey & J.R. Speakman (1996): Habitat exploitation by a gleaning bat, *Plecotus auritus. Phil. Trans. R. Soc. Lond.* B 351: 921–931.

8. Entwistle, A.C., P.A. Racey & J.R. Speakman (1997): Roost selection by the brown long-eared bat *Plecotus auritus. J. Appl. Ecol.* 34: 399–408.

9. Entwistle, A.C., P.A. Racey & J.R. Speakman (1998): The reproductive cycle and determination of sexual maturity in male brown long-eared bats (*Plecotus auritus*). *J. Zool.* 244: 63–70.

10. Entwistle, A.C., P.A. Racey & J.R. Speakman (2000): Social and population structure of a gleaning bat, *Plecotus auritus. J. Zool.* 252: 11–17.

11. Felten, H. & G. Storch (1970): Kleinsäuger von den italienischen Mittelmeer-Inseln Pantelleria und Lampedusa. *Senckenb. Biol.* 51: 159–173.

12. Fuhrmann, M. & A. Seitz (1992): Nocturnal activity of the brown long-eared bat (*Plecotus auritus*): data from radio-tracking in the Lenneberg forest near Mainz (Germany). In: I.G. Priede & S.M. Swift (eds): *Wildlife Telemetry: Remote Monitoring and Tracking of Animals*: 538–548.

13. Fuhrmann, M. & O. Godmann (1994): Baumhöhlenquartiere vom Braunen Langohr und von der Bechsteinfledermaus. Ergebnisse einer

Fig. 455. Stroboscope record of a Brown Long-eared Bat emerging from a bat box roost. Photo: D. Nill.

telemetrischen Untersuchung. In: AGFH (ed.): *Die Fledermäuse Hessens:* 181–186; Manfred Hennecke Verlag.

14. Heise, G. & A. Schmidt (1988): Beiträge zur sozialen Organisation und Ökologie des Braunen Langohrs (*Plecotus auritus*). *Nyctalus* (N.F.) 2: 445–465.

15. Horáček, I. & B. Đulić (2004): *Plecotus auritus* – Braunes Langohr. In: F. Krapp (ed.): *Handbuch der Säugetiere Europas* 4–II: 953–999; Aula Verlag.

16. McLean, J.A. & J.R. Speakman (1996): Suckling behaviour in the brown long-eared bat (*Plecotus auritus*). *J. Zool.* 239: 411–416.

17. McLean, J.A. & J.R. Speakman (1997): Non-nutritional maternal support in the brown long-eared bat. *Anim. Behav.* 54: 1193–1204.

18. McLean, J.A. & J.R. Speakman (1999): Energy budgets of lactating and non-reproductive brown long-eared bats (*Plecotus auritus*) suggest females use compensation in lactation. *Funct. Ecol.* 13: 360–372.

19. McLean, J.A. & J.R. Speakman (2000): Morphological changes during postnatal growth and reproduction in the brown long-eared bat *Plecotus auritus*: implications for wing loading and predicted flight performance. *J. Nat. Hist.* 34: 773–791.

20. Speakman, J.R. & P.A. Racey (1986): The influence of body condition on sexual development of male brown long-eared bats (*Plecotus auritus*) in the wild. *J. Zool.* 210: 515–525.

21. Speakman, J.R. & P.A. Racey (1987): The energetics of pregnancy and lactation in the brown long-eared bat, *Plecotus auritus*. In: M.B. Fenton, P. Racey & J.M.V. Rayner (eds): *Recent advances in the study of bats*: 367–393; Cambridge University Press.

22. Swift, S.M. (1998): *Long-eared bats*, 182 pp.; Poyser Ltd, London.

23. Veith, M., N. Beer, A. Kiefer, J. Johnnesen & A. Seitz (2004): The role of swarming sites for maintaining gene flow in the brown long-eared bat (*Plecotus auritus*). *Heredity* 93: 342–349.

24. Webb, P.I., J.R. Speakman & P.A. Racey (1993): Defecation, apparent absorption efficiency, and the importance of water obtained in the food for water balance in captive brown long-eared (*Plecotus auritus*) and Daubenton's (*Myotis daubentoni*) bats. *J. Zool.* 230: 619–628.

25. Webb, P.I., J.R. Speakman & P.A. Racey (1995): Evaporative water loss in two sympatric species of vespertilionid bat, *Plecotus auritus* and *Myotis daubentoni*: relation to foraging mode and implications for roost site selection. *J. Zool.* 235: 269–278

Alpine Long-eared Bat
Plecotus macrobullaris
KUZJAKIN, 1965

NAMES
D: Alpen-Langohr
F: Oreillard des Alpes
I: Orecchione alpino
NL: Alpengrootoorvleermuis

GENERAL INFORMATION
Since the separation of the Brown and Grey Long-eared Bats there had been difficulties in clearly assigning some long-eared bats of the Alpine region [4, 11]. Only genetic investigations demonstrated another species, which was decribed almost at the same time in 2002 by Kiefer *et al.* as *P. alpinus* and by Spitzenberger *et al.* as *P. microdontus* [7, 13]. Due to the earlier publication date the name *P. alpinus* got priority [10]. However, Spitzenberger *et al.* then pointed out that the Alpine Long-eared Bat agrees morphologically and genetically with *P. macrobullaris*, described by Kuzjakin in 1965 from the Caucasus as a subspecies of the Brown Long-eared Bat. The scientific name *P. macrobullaris* has been accepted since then for the Alpine Long-eared Bat [14]. However, some European populations of the Alpine Long-eared Bat (one western and one eastern) differ genetically so distinctly [14, gen. lit. 138] that they possibly relate to two further cryptic species [gen. lit. 77].

IDENTIFICATION
Medium-sized to large long-eared bat. The dorsal fur is dense and long. The dorsum is mostly pale grey tones, differentiated from the pale, often almost pure white, ventral side. The face in older animals is little pigmented and pale. On the lower lip is a hard leather-like triangular spot, which is darkly pigmented, at least in younger animals. Thumb, thumb claw and foot are medium long, the tragus is long. The toes have long protuding bristles. The penis is for almost its entire length evenly broad (parallel sided) and tapers only at the tip.

Similar species
Very similar to the other *Plecotus* species, occurring together with the Brown and Grey, and in the south also with the Balkan Long-eared Bat. The characteristic triangular chin spot and penis shape in the males, together with a combination of measurements, makes species identification possible.

ECHOLOCATION CALLS
Typical frequency-modulated long-eared bat calls with two harmonics; with short calls of up to 4 ms length the two harmonics do not overlap each other, with longer calls they do [3]. With short calls the first harmonic begins at approximately 46kHz and ends at approximately 23kHz; longer calls begin at 42kHz and end at 15kHz [3].

DISTRIBUTION
The distribution is poorly known. Recorded from the Pyrenees [5, 6, 9], Corsica [9], the entire Alpine massif from France, Switzerland, Liechtenstein, Italy and Austria to Slovenia [9, 13, 15]. Also in the Dinaric mountains in Croatia, Bosnia-Herzegovina and Albania [12, 13, 16], in Greece in the Pindus mountains [9], and on Crete [6]. Probably also on Cyprus. In Turkey in the middle Taurus mountains [gen. lit. 138], the distribution continuing eastward through the Caucasus (Georgia, Armenia, Azerbaijan, the northern Caucasus republics) [gen. lit. 138] and the Near East (Iran and Syria)

Measurements

Forearm	37.3–46.0mm
Fifth finger	49–55mm
Third finger	63–69mm
Thumb	6.5–8.2mm
Tibia	19.5–22.9mm
Foot	8.1–9.2mm
Tragus length	16–19mm
Tragus width	5–6mm
Normal weight	6–10g
CBL	15.2–16.9mm
CM^3	5.3–5.9mm

Fig. 456. The Alpine Long-eared Bat is the only European long-eared bat species with a smooth triangular spot on the chin, which is darkly pigmented in younger animals. Photo: C. Dietz.

Fig. 457. Mother Alpine Long-eared Bat with young. Even from a distance the dark chin spot is obvious and makes it possible to identify the species. Photo: D. Nill.

[6, 9, gen. lit. 138]. Perhaps also in Israel [Tsoar pers. com.]. In Europe the assumed occurrence in the Balkan mountains and in the Carpathian massif is, so far, not proven.

Subspecies and geographical variation

Two possible subspecies: *P. m. alpinus* in the west (Pyrenees, Corsica, Alps) and *P. m. macrobullaris* in the east. In Europe the eastern subspecies is, so far, recorded in Greece and Italy (Udine, Friaul). Both forms differ genetically so clearly [9, 14, gen. lit. 77, 138] that they may relate to two recently separated species. Studies in the area of sympatric distribution of both forms could furnish clarification.

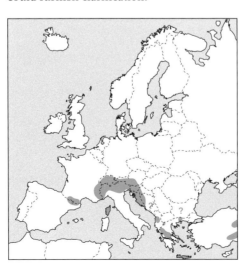

HABITAT

Most records originate from montane and alpine habitats above 800m [9]. However, in Slovenia and Istria, nursery colonies are usually at lower altitudes [16], the six Slovenian nursery roosts being between 300 and 660m [gen. lit. 96] in the middle of a sub-Mediterranean mosaic of managed cultural landscape (wine growing, fruit growing and forests). In the Tyrol 16 nursery roosts recorded at altitudes of 500–1,400m [17]. Mist-net catches in the Pyrenees were made on mountain meadows and thinly overgrown rocky areas at altitudes of over 2,800m [5].

Roosts

All known summer roosts, both nursery and male roosts, occur in slate-, stone-, clapboard or metal-covered attics, often of churches [9, 17]. Some winter records in caves [gen lit. 96].

BEHAVIOUR, FOOD AND REPRODUCTION

The ecology of the species is, so far, very little known. In Austria the young are born in June in nursery colonies of up to 30 females. The average size of nursery colonies in the Tyrol amounts to 13 animals. In contrast to the Brown Long-eared Bat, adult males are rarely found in these colonies [17].

THREATS

So far not identified, however, at least included in the EU Habitats Directive, Annex IV. At present threats are difficult to estimate; a threat of loss of roosts in buildings through renovation is probable.

REFERENCES

1. Benda, P. & T. Ivanova (2003): Long-eared bats, genus *Plecotus* (Mammalia: Chiroptera), in Bulgaria: a revision of systematic and distributional status. *J. Nat. Mus., Nat. Hist. Ser.* 172: 157–172.
2. Benda, P., A. Kiefer, V. Hanák & M. Veith (2004): Systematic status of African populations of long-eared bats, Genus *Plecotus* (Mammalia: Chiroptera). *Folia Zool.* 53, Monograph 1: 1–47.
3. Dietrich, S., D.P. Szameitat, A. Kiefer, H.-U. Schnitzler & A. Denzinger (2006): Echolocation signals of the plecotine bat, *Plecotus macrobullaris* Kuzyakin, 1965. *Acta Chiropterologica* 8: 465–475.

4. Đulić, B. (1980): Morphological characteristics and distribution of *Plecotus auritus* and *Plecotus austriacus* in some regions of Yugoslavia. In: D.E. Wilson & A.L. Gardner (eds): *Proceedings Fifth International Bat Research Conference*: 151–161; Texas Tech Press.

5. Garin, I., J.L. Garcia-Mudarra, J.R. Aihartza, U. Goiti & J. Juste (2003): Presence of *Plecotus macrobullaris* (Chiroptera: Vespertilionidae) in the Pyrenees. *Acta Chiropterologica* 5: 243–250.

6. Juste, J., C. Ibáñez, J. Munoz, D. Trujillo, P. Benda, A. Karata & M. Ruedi (2004): Mitochondrial phylogeography of the long-eared bats (*Plecotus*) in the Mediterranean Palearctic and the Atlantic Islands. *Mol. Phyl. Evol.* 31: 1114–1126.

7. Kiefer, A. & M. Veith (2002): A new species of long-eared bat from Europe (Chiroptera: Vespertilionidae). *Myotis* 39: 5–16.

8. Kiefer, A., F. Mayer, J. Kosuch, O. von Helversen & M. Veith (2002): Conflicting molecular phylogenies of European long-eared bats (*Plecotus*) can be explained by cryptic diversity. *Mol. Phyl. Evol.* 25: 557–566.

9. Kiefer, A. & O. von Helversen (2004): *Plecotus macrobullaris* – Alpenlangohr. In: F. Krapp (ed.): *Handbuch der Säugetiere Europas*, 4–II: 1051–1058; Aula Verlag.

10. Kock, D. (2002): The publication dates of *Plecotus alpinus* Kiefer and Veith, 2002 and of *Plecotus microdontus* Spitzenberger, 2002. *Acta Chiropterologica* 4: 219–220.

11. Martino, V. & E. Martino (1949): Preliminary notes on five new mammals from Yugoslavia. *Ann. Mag. Nat. Hist.* 5: 493–498.

12. Sachanowicz, K. & M. Ciechanowski (2006): *Plecotus macrobullaris* Kuzyakin, 1965 (Chiroptera: Vespertilionidae) – new for Albanian bat fauna. *Lynx* (n.s.) 37: 241–246.

13. Spitzenberger, F., E. Haring & N. Tvrtkovi (2002): *Plecotus microdontus* (Mammalia, Vespertilionidae), a new bat species from Austria. *Nat. Croat.* 11: 1–18.

14. Spitzenberger, F., P. Strelkov & E. Haring (2003): Morphology and mitochondrial DNA sequences show that *Plecotus alpinus* Kiefer & Veith, 2002 and *Plecotus microdontus* Spitzenberger, 2002 are synonyms of *Plecotus macrobullaris Kuzjakin*, 1965. *Nat. Croat.* 12: 39–53.

15. Trizio, I., E. Patriarca, P. Debernardi, D. Preatoni, G. Tosi & A. Martinoli (2003): The Alpine long-eared bat (*Plecotus alpinus*) is present also in Piedmont region: first record revealed by DNA analysis. *Hystrix* (n.s.) 14: 113–115.

16. Tvrtković, N., I. Pavlinić & E. Haring (2005): Four species of long-eared bats (*Plecotus*; Mammalia, Vespertilionidae) in Croatia: field identification and distribution. *Folia Zool.* 54: 75–88.

17. Wohlfahrt, S. (2003): *Morphologie und Verbreitung der Schwesternarten Braunes Langohr*, Plecotus auritus *und Alpenlangohr*, Plecotus alpinus *(Chiroptera, Vespertilionidae) in Tirol.* Diplomarbeit an der Universität Innsbruck, 71 pp.

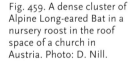

Fig. 458. In flight the markedly pale ventral side of the Alpine Long-eared Bat is apparent. Photo: D. Nill.

Fig. 459. A dense cluster of Alpine Long-eared Bat in a nursery roost in the roof space of a church in Austria. Photo: D. Nill.

Sardinian Long-eared Bat
Plecotus sardus
MUCEDDA, KIEFER, PIDINCHEDDA & VEITH, 2002

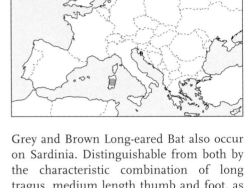

NAMES
D: Sardischer Langohr
F: Oreillard de Sardaigne
I: Orecchione sardo
NL: Sardijnse grootoorvleermuis

GENERAL INFORMATION
Described by Mucedda *et al.* only in 2002 after a morphological and genetical examination of the long-eared bats of Sardinia [2].

INDENTIFICATION
Medium-sized long-eared bat species with brownish-grey dorsal fur and sharply delineated, paler cream-coloured underside. Older animals with a slightly pigmented face.

Similar species
Similar to the other long-eared bats, the Grey and Brown Long-eared Bat also occur on Sardinia. Distinguishable from both by the characteristic combination of long tragus, medium length thumb and foot, as well as by the parallel-sided penis (the penis in the Grey Long-eared Bat is egg-shaped, in the Brown Long-eared Bat conical tapered).

DISTRIBUTION
Endemic species on Sardinia, so far only found in three closely limited areas in central Sardinia [1, 2].

Measurements

Forearm	40.9 42.3mm
Fifth finger	54–56mm
Third finger	67–72mm
Thumb	6.0–6.5mm
Tibia	> 20mm
Foot	6.7–7.7mm
Tragus width	6.0–6.5mm
Tragus length	18.0–19.8mm
Normal weight in autumn:	7–8g
CBL	~ 15.9mm
CM³	~ 5.7mm

Fig. 460. Sardinian Long-eared Bat in flight. Photo: D. Nill

Fig. 461. Colony of Sardinian Long-eared Bats in the flat roof of a building. Photo: A. Kiefer.

HABITAT

Olive groves and holm and cork oak forests dominate in the environment of roosts.

Roosts

The roosts recorded so far are situated in attics as well as in karst caves, viaducts, tunnels and inside dams. A nursery colony in an attic comprises about a dozen animals, another one about 200 animals [Kiefer, Mucedda *in litt.*].

BEHAVIOUR, REPRODUCTION AND FOOD

So far no knowledge is available about the ecology of the species.

THREATS

So far not recognised, but the species is included in the EU Habitats Directive, Annex IV. At present any threats can hardly be identified, but it appears to be threatened by its restricted occurrence.

REFERENCES

1. Kiefer, A. & M. Mucedda (2004): *Plecotus sardus* – Sardisches Langohr. In: F. Krapp (ed.): *Handbuch der Säugetiere Europas* 4–II: 1067–1070; Aula Verlag.
2. Mucedda, M., A. Kiefer, E. Pidinchedda & M. Veith (2002): A new species of long-eared bat (Chiroptera, Vespertilionidae) from Sardinia (Italy). *Acta Chiropterologica* 4: 121–135.

Fig. 462. The Sardinian Long-eared Bat has the longest tragus of all species of the genus. Photo: D. Nill.

Grey Long-eared Bat
Plecotus austriacus
(FISCHER, 1829)

NAMES

D: Graues Langohr
F: Oreillard gris
E: Murciélago orejudo gris
I: Orecchione meridionale
NL: Grijze grootoorvleermuis
S: Grå långörad fladdermus
PL: Gacek szary

Measurements

Forearm	36.5–43.5mm
Fifth finger	48–55mm
Third finger	64–71mm
Thumb	5.0–6.4mm
Tibia	18.3–21.0mm
Foot	7.0–8.8mm
Tragus length	14.0–17.8mm
Tragus width	5.2–6.6mm
Normal weight	6–10g
CBL	15.2–17.1mm
CM³	5.4–6.5mm

IDENTIFICATION

Medium-sized bat with long ears. The muzzle, in contrast to that of the Brown Long-eared Bat, is somewhat longer and usually dark grey. The long dorsal fur is grey, at most a slight brownish tint (particularly in the eastern Mediterranean area). The ventral side is sharply delineated light-grey to whitish. The relatively broad tragus is almost entirely darkly pigmented. Short thumbs, thumb claws and feet, the latter only weakly haired. The club-shaped penis widens towards the tip.

Similar species

Very similar to the other *Plecotus* species. Distinguishable from the Brown and Alpine Long-eared Bat by the generally broader tragus (in Central Europe > 5.5mm, narrower in southeast Europe), shorter thumbs (< 6.5mm), shorter thumb claws (< 2.5mm) and feet (usually < 8.5mm). Upper tooth row longer (CM³ usually > 5.5mm) and tragus longer (TL > 14mm) than in the smaller Balkan Long-eared Bat.

ECHOLOCATION CALLS

The frequency-modulated echolocation calls consist of two harmonics, which are differently stressed depending on whether the calls are emitted by mouth or nose. The first harmonic drops on average from 35 to 20kHz, the second from 70 to 38kHz. Thus the two harmonics do not usually overlap in frequency.

DISTRIBUTION

Occurs throughout the Mediterranean area and on the Balearics, Sardinia, Corsica and Sicily (the latter not indicated on the map); however, no records from North Africa, Malta, Pantelleria, Crete, Cyprus and the Near East. The record on Madeira possibly relates to animals shipped by humans. In the north the species reaches nearly 53°N and thus reaches south England, but not the Baltic Sea coast. Extralimital records in the north from Skåne (Sweden). Probably all Asian forms represent other species [gen. lit. 138], thus the uncertain eastern border of the distribution lies in Ukraine and Turkey (see subspecies).

Subspecies and geographical variation

Two subspecies described for Europe, *P. a. meridionalis* (Slovenia) and *P. a. hispanicus* (Iberian Peninsula), are synonymous with the nominate form, and this is a very uniform taxon throughout Europe. All other previously described subspecies: *teneriffae* (Canary Islands), *kolombatovici* (Adriatic range), *christiei* (North Africa and the Near East), *macrobullaris* (Caucasus), *wardi* (India, Pakistan, Nepal), *turkmenicus* (Turkmenistan, Kazakhstan) and probably

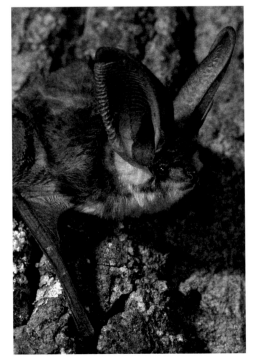

Fig. 463. In Grey Long-eared Bat the tragus is usually pigmented for the whole length. Photo: D. Nill.

also *ariel* (China) have been regarded as full species [gen. lit. 138].

HABITAT

In Central Europe a typical village bat, otherwise a species of the Mediterranean managed cultural mosaic landscape [8]. In Central Europe, hunting grounds lie consequently in warm valleys and in human settlements, gardens and extensively managed agricultural areas. The species is rarely found in larger forest areas; establishment seems only to occur with open landscape. This is also reflected in the altitudinal distribution: although there are records of over 1,000m, most nursery roosts in Central Europe are situated below 550m. In southern Europe much less tied to human settlement, here it also occurs within a range of suitable rocky situations and a complex of succession phases of the open landscape.

Roosts

Summer roosts are in buildings in the northern part of the distribution, often in roof spaces. In the Mediterranean area nursery roosts are, conversely, often found in rock crevices or in cracks in the entrance zone of caves. Summer roosts are regularly changed. Males can be found in a range of roost sites, including in expansion joints of bridges, only exceptionally in bird or bat boxes. Very cold tolerant, in the winter roosting in caves, cellars and rock crevices, often close to the entrance. Hibernating animals are regularly found in roof spaces that are also occupied in summer [8].

BEHAVIOUR

Nursery colonies usually comprise only 10–30 [8], in Bulgaria often only around five females [own data]. In buildings, exceptionally also colonies of over 100 animals. At high temperatures the colonies break up within the roost and hang in small groups scattered away from each other. Susceptible to disturbance in the roosts. Contrary to the Brown Long-eared Bat the Grey Long-eared Bat in Central Europe is only observed at a few caves when swarming, and usually only single animals are captured. On the other hand, on the Balkan Peninsula the species can be found regularly at caves during the swarming time [own data].

REPRODUCTION

Usually one young is born between the middle and the end of June. Neonates have a forearm length of approximately 15mm and a weight of about over 2g [8]. Mating may take place as early as July; in contrast to the Brown Long-eared Bat mating in spring is not known [8].

FORAGING

The proportion of flying insects is far higher than in the Brown Long-eared Bat, but it can also pick prey from leaves. Insects

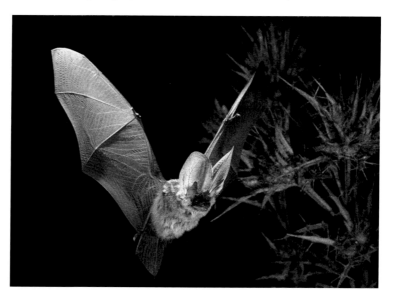

Fig. 464. Grey Long-eared Bats usually hunt in open country. Photo: D. Nill.

Geometrid moths dominate in the food remains. With mass occurrence scarabaeoid beetles up to the size of cockchafers are also eaten. In the autumn crane-flies and other Diptera are also captured. In contrast to the Brown Long-eared Bat evidence of non-volant prey animals is almost absent.

MAXIMUM AGE
The life expectancy is between five and nine years; the maximum age is over 25 years [8].

MOBILITY AND MIGRATION
A very sedentary species, recoveries usually only a few kilometres from the marking site. The longest proven migration distance is 62km.

Fig. 465. Grey Long-eared Bats can use a multiplicity of roosts, often they are in unfinished walls. Photo: D. Nill.

are caught in slow flight close to vegetation from close to the ground to heights of over 10m (usually 2–5m). As probable in all long-eared bats, the echolocation calls can be emitted by either mouth or nose.

FOOD
The proportion of moths in the prey is higher than in the Brown Long-eared Bat, comprising 70–100% of the prey [2, 8, 12].

Habitat use
Just as confined as in the Brown Long-eared Bat; hunting grounds can, however, be found at up to 5.5km distance from the roosts, and can be very large areas of up to 75ha [9]. Within the hunting area, however, small feeding sites can be frequently visited (over 10 changes per night possible) [9]. Also the roosts can be moved by distances of up to 4km [8].

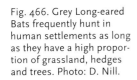

Fig. 466. Grey Long-eared Bats frequently hunt in human settlements as long as they have a high proportion of grassland, hedges and trees. Photo: D. Nill.

THREATS

Red list of the IUCN 2006: LC (Least Concern), EU Habitats Directive, Annex IV. Since in the north of the distribution area nursery colonies occur almost only in roof spaces, the species is particularly affected by renovations (also remedial timber treatments). Pesticide use in horticulture and agriculture probably impacts more strongly on this species than on the Brown Long-eared Bat.

Well established in the Channel Islands, where more common than Brown Long-eared Bat, but scarce on the mainland of UK, where more or less restricted to coastal areas from Sussex to Devon and into Somerset [UK gen. lit. 153, 155]. Little data on its behaviour and ecological requirements from the UK yet available. Currently the scarcity of information and the fact that it often shares roosts with Brown Long-eared, on top of the reasons given for Brown Long-eared, make monitoring impossible at present. There is currently no concerted action specifically for the conservation of this species in the UK.

CONSERVATION MEASURES

Protection of the colonies, application of bat-friendly wood preservatives, preservation of access possibilities in buildings, abandonment of pesticide use, preservation of fruit tree belts and extensively used grassland such as species-rich hayfields.

REFERENCES

1. Barataud, M. (1990): Eléments sur le comportement alimentaire des Oreillards brun et gris *Plecotus auritus* et *Plecotus austriacus*. *Le Rhinolophe* 7: 3–10.
2. Bauerová, Z. (1982): Contribution to the trophic ecology of the grey long-eared bat, *Plecotus austriacus*. *Folia Zool.* 31: 113–122.
3. Benda, P. & T. Ivanova (2003): Long-eared bats, genus *Plecotus* (Mammalia: Chiroptera), in Bulgaria: a revision of systematic and distributional status. *J. Nat. Mus., Nat. Hist. Ser.* 172: 157–172.
4. Benda, P., A. Kiefer, V. Hanák & M. Veith (2004): Systematic status of African populations of long-eared bats, Genus *Plecotus* (Mammalia: Chiroptera). *Folia Zool.* 53, Monograph 1: 1–47.
5. Berg, J. (1989): Beobachtungen zur Ökologie und Quartierverhalten des Grauen Langohrs *Plecotus austriacus* außerhalb der Wochen-

Fig. 467. In the eastern Mediterranean region Grey Long-eared Bats sometimes have brown dorsal fur. Photo: C. Dietz.

stube. In: D. Heidecke & M. Stubbe (eds): *Populationsökologie von Fledermausarten*; Martin-Luther-Universität Halle-Wittenberg 1989/20: 223–232.
6. Flückiger, P.F. & A. Beck (1995): Observations on the habitat use for hunting by *Plecotus austriacus*. *Myotis* 32/33: 121–122.
7. Haensel, J. (1998): Hohes Alter eines in den Rüdersdorfer Kalkstollen überwinternden Grauen Langohrs (*Plecotus austriacus*). *Nyctalus* (N.F.) 6: 638.
8. Horáček, I., W. Bogdanowicz & B. Ðulić (2004): *Plecotus austriacus* – Graues Langohr. In: F. Krapp (ed.): *Handbuch der Säugetiere Europas* 4–II: 1001–1049; Aula Verlag.
9. Kiefer, A. & M. Veith (1998): Untersuchungen zum Raumbedarf und Interaktion von Populationen des Grauen Langohrs, *Plecotus austriacus*, im Nahegebiet. *Nyctalus* (N.F.) 6: 531.
10. Ševčík, M. (2003): Does wing morphology reflect different foraging strategies in sibling bat species *Plecotus auritus* and *P. austriacus*? *Folia Zool.* 52: 121–126.
11. Stebbings, R.E. (1970): A comparative study of *Plecotus auritus* and *P. austriacus* inhabiting one roost. *Bijdragen tot de Dierkunde* 40: 91–94.
12. Swift, S.M. (1998): *Long-eared bats*, 182 pp; Poyser Ltd, London.
13. Tvrtković, N., I. Pavlinić & E. Haring (2005): Four species of long-eared bats (*Plecotus*; Mammalia, Vespertilionidae) in Croatia: field identification and distribution. *Folia Zool.* 54: 75–88.

Balkan Long-eared Bat
Plecotus kolombatovici
Đulić, 1980

NAMES
D: Balkan-Langohr
F: Oreillard des Balkans
NL: Balkangrootoorvleermuis

GENERAL INFORMATION
The Balkan Long-eared Bat was described by Đulić in 1980 as a subspecies of the Grey Long-eared Bat from the Adriatic islands and the Croatian coast. Only recent genetic investigations have shown that it is a full species [6, gen. lit. 79], within which the Alpine and the Balkan Long-eared Bat were erroneously combined [gen. lit. 137]. The relationship with Gaisler's and the Canarian Long-eared Bats is not yet clarified with certainty [2, gen. lit. 138]. Based upon the interpretation of new morphological and genetic data, the Balkan Long-eared Bat, as with Gaisler's Long-eared Bat, was classified as a subspecies of the Canarian Long-eared Bat [2] or regarded as a full species including Gaisler's Long-eared Bat [gen. lit. 138]. Until a final clarification of the taxonomic questions, the populations of the Balkan Long-eared Bat occurring in Europe and Asia Minor are regarded here as a full species [see also gen. lit. 77].

IDENTIFICATION
The Balkan Long-eared Bat is the smallest *Plecotus* species in Europe. Very similar to the Grey Long-eared Bat in most characteristics, the penis is also distinctly club-shaped at the end. But can be quite well separated by the smaller average measurements of the forearm, thumb, tibia and foot. The dorsal fur is brown-grey coloured. Can be differentiated from all other *Plecotus* species by the short tragus (usually < 14mm), contrasting with the long ears. Sparsely haired toes with very short hairs.

Similar species
Very similar to the other *Plecotus* species, in Europe most easy to confuse with the Grey Long-eared Bat but differentiated by the usually short tragus, tibia and upper tooth row (CM³). The brownish dorsal colour can lead to confusion with the Brown Long-eared Bat without measurements.

ECHOLOCATION CALLS
The echolocation calls are not well known, similar to the Grey Long-eared Bat from a few recordings [own data]. Usually no overlap of the two harmonics (final frequency of the second harmonic lies above the initial frequency of the first harmonic).

DISTRIBUTION
Occurs from Istria over the Adriatic Islands (type locality on the island of Korčula) and along a narrow coastal strip along the

Fig. 468. The Balkan Long-eared Bat is very similar to the Grey Long-eared Bat, but distinctly smaller in most measurements. Photo: C. Dietz.

Measurements

Forearm	36.1–39.3mm
Fifth finger	46–51mm
Third finger	61–66mm
Thumb	5.4–6.4mm
Tibia	15.2–18.3mm
Foot	<7.0mm
Tragus width	<5.2mm
Tragus length	Usually <14.0mm
Normal weight	6–9g
CBL	14.1–15.4mm
CM³	5.1–5.6mm

Adriatic Sea, a wider area near the Greek coast, on some islands in the Aegaean Sea and along the west and south coast of Turkey to near the Syrian border. Also on Crete, Rhodes and possibly on Cyprus. Perhaps a part of the populations on the islands of Pantelleria and Malta similarly belong to the Balkan Long-eared Bat. If this is the case, attention should be paid to possible occurrence in the Italian coastal regions. The distribution is altogether only partially known.

HABITAT
Dry, from current records, almost exclusively near Mediterranean coastal karst areas of the (eastern) Mediterranean region, usually at low altitudes [4, 7, 8]. Often on islands, near the coast or in river valleys, highest record at a swarming site in Greece at 1,300m. Hunting grounds in holm oak forests with boulders or olive groves [3], over shrubland and in clearings [8], in Greece over slopes overgrown with maquis [7].

Roosts
Single animals in rock crevices, wall cracks, arches (e.g. under bridges) and caves. Nursery roosts were found, so far, in a church tower on the island of Hvar [3, Koselj *in litt.*], in a church roof in Istria [8] and in a former railway tunnel on Peloponnisos [7].

BEHAVIOUR AND REPRODUCTION
Nursery colonies comprise 15–20 [3] and up to 90 animals [7]. Birth probably occurs at the end of June [7]. Mixed with Alpine Long-eared Bats in a nursery roost in Istria [8]. In the late summer the males swarm at cave entrances [7].

FORAGING AND FOOD
Like the other long-eared bat species, partly in dense vegetation but also flying along vegetation edges. In captivity flight manoeuvres in very confined spaces and immediately catches moths. In 10 faecal pellets from the island of Hvar remains of moths exclusively were found [own data]. Visits ponds, wells and cisterns for drinking.

THREATS
So far not identified, included in the EU Habitats Directive, Annex IV. Relatively common on the island of Hvar; however, no conclusions on the conservation situation can be drawn from that.

REFERENCES
1. Benda, P. & T. Ivanova (2003): Long-eared bats, genus *Plecotus* (Mammalia: Chiroptera), in Bulgaria: a revision of systematic and distributional status. *J. Nat. Mus., Nat. Hist. Ser.* 172: 157–172.
2. Benda, P., A. Kiefer, V. Hanák & M. Veith (2004): Systematic status of African populations of long-eared bats, Genus *Plecotus* (Mammalia:

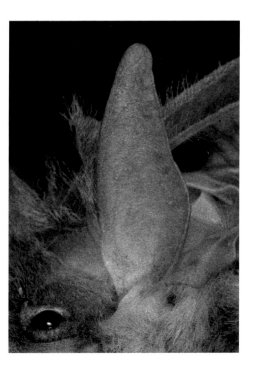

Fig. 469. The Balkan Long-eared Bat has the shortest tragus among all European long-eared bat species. Photo: C. Dietz.

Fig. 470. Colony of Balkan Long-eared Bats in a former railway tunnel in southern Greece. Photo: A. Kiefer.

Chiroptera). *Folia Zool.* 53, Monograph 1: 1–47.

3. Đulić, B. & N. Tvrtkovi (1970): The distribution of bats on the Adriatic islands. *Bijdragen tot de Dierkunde* 40: 17–20.

4. Đulić, B. & N. Tvrtkovi (1979): On some mammals from the Central Adriatic and South Adriatic Islands. *Acta Biologica* 43: 15–35.

5. Đulić, B. (1980): Morphological characteristics and distribution of *Plecotus auritus* and *Plecotus austriacus* in some regions of Yugoslavia. In: D.E. Wilson & A.L. Gardner (eds): *Proceedings Fifth International Bat Research Conference*: 151–161; Texas Tech Press.

6. Kiefer, A., F. Mayer, J. Kosuch, O. von Helversen & M. Veith (2002): Conflicting molecular phylogenies of European long-eared bats (*Plecotus*) can be explained by cryptic diversity. *Mol. Phyl. Evol.* 25: 557–566.

7. Kiefer, A. & O. von Helversen (2004): *Plecotus kolombatovici* – Balkanlangohr. In: F. Krapp, (ed.): *Handbuch der Säugetiere Europas* 4–II: 1059–1066; Aula Verlag.

8. Tvrtković, N., I. Pavlinić & E. Haring (2005): Four species of long-eared bats (*Plecotus*; Mammalia, Vespertilionidae) in Croatia: field identification and distribution. *Folia Zool.* 54: 75–88.

Canary Long-eared Bat
Plecotus teneriffae
BARRETT-HAMILTON, 1907

NAMES

D:	Kanaren-Langohr
F:	Oreillard de Tenerife
E:	Murciélago orejudo canario
I:	Orecchione di Tenerife
NL:	Canarische grootoorvleermuis
PL:	Gacek kanaryjski

GENERAL INFORMATION

Initially considered as a subspecies of the Grey Long-eared Bat, elevated to species status by Ibáñez & Fernández 1985 [2]. The Balkan Long-eared Bat of the Adriatic region and Gaisler's Long-eared Bat of northwest Africa have been considered as subspecies of the Canary Long-eared Bat due to their genetic similarity [1, 3] or as a separate group [gen. lit. 138]. For convenience we consider here the Canary, Gaisler's and the Balkan Long-eared Bats as separate species, but would stress that this is not well confirmed by the available data.

IDENTIFICATION

A large long-eared bat with very dark grey-brown dorsal fur, which contrasts distinctly with the pale whitish-grey ventral fur. Ears and tragus are evenly grey for their entire length to the base.

Similar species

The only known long-eared bat species on the Canary Islands. Unmistakable due to the size and dark dorsal colouring in strong contrast with the belly colouring.

DISTRIBUTION

Endemic to the Canary Islands. So far observed on Tenerife, La Palma and El Hierro [4, 5, gen. lit. 143]

Subspecies and geographical variation

Within the small distribution area no morphological differences exist. However, differences in sequences of the mitochon-drial DNA point to very limited exchange between the three island populations [4].

HABITAT

A wide habitat spectrum is used, from laurel forests, through pine forests to dwarf bush heaths. Occurs at all altitudes up to 2,300m [gen. lit. 143].

Roosts

The few roosts found so far were in volcanic caves and rock crevices, but also in buildings [gen. lit. 143].

BEHAVIOUR AND REPRODUCTION

So far only small nursery colonies with up to 37 females in volcanic caves on La Palma and Tenerife [gen. lit.143] are recorded. Young are probably born in June. In a studied nursery roost only about two-thirds of the females had (one) young. The males are in mating condition from September [gen. lit. 143].

FORAGING AND FOOD

The prey is captured, as typical for long-eared bats, in flight or picked off vegetation. Noctuids, as well as other moths and exceptionally long-horned beetles, are captured [gen. lit. 143].

Measurements	
Forearm	40.1–46.0mm
Fifth finger	?
Third finger	?
Thumb length	5.3–7.0mm
Weight	?
CBL	16.0–16.9mm
CM^3	5.8–6.2mm

Fig. 471. In the Canary Long-eared Bat the ventral side is clearly delineated from the dark dorsal side. Photo: D. Trujillo.

Fig. 472. Canary Long-eared
Bat in flight. Photo:
D. Trujillo.

THREATS

To a large extent unknown. Red list of the
IUCN 2006: DD (Data Deficient), Red list
of the European Union: VU (Vulnerable),
EU Habitats Directive, Annex IV. Possibly
threatened by habitat loss and disturbance
in the roosts.

CONSERVATION MEASURES

Protection of roost caves from disturbance.
Prevention of introduction of other bat
species on the Canary Islands

REFERENCES

1. Benda, P., A. Kiefer, V. Hanák & M. Veith
   (2004): Systematic status of African populations
   of long-eared bats, Genus *Plecotus* (Mammalia:
   Chiroptera). *Folia Zool.* 53, Monograph 1: 1–47.
2. Ibáñez, C. & R. Fernández (1985): Systematic
   status of the long-eared bat *Plecotus teneriffae*.
   Säugetierk. Mitt. 32: 143–149.
3. Juste, J., C. Ibáñez, J. Munoz, D. Trujillo, P.
   Benda, A. Karata & M. Ruedi (2004): Mitochondrial phylogeography of the long-eared bats
   (*Plecotus*) in the mediterranean Palearctic and
   the Atlantic Islands. *Mol. Phyl. Evol.* 31:
   1114–1126.
4. Pestano, J., R.P. Brown, N.M. Suarez, J. Benzal
   & S. Fajardo (2003): Intraspecific evolution of
   Canary Island plecotine bats, based on mtDNA
   sequences. *Heredity* 90: 302–307.
5. Trujillo, D. & R. Barone (1991): La Fauna de
   Quiropteros del Archipielago Canario. In: J.
   Benzal & O. de Paz (eds): *Los Murciélagos de
   España y Portugal*: 95–111.

Gaisler's Long-eared Bat
Plecotus gaisleri
BENDA, KIEFER, HANÁK & VEITH, 2004

NAMES
D: Lybisches Langohr
NL: Gaislers grootoorvleermuis

GENERAL INFORMATION
For a long time the North African long-eared bats were regarded as belonging to the Grey Long-eared Bat (*P. austriacus*). Studies revealed that two species differing from the Grey Long-eared Bat occur in North Africa: *P. christii* in northeast Africa from the western Libyan desert across Egypt into the Middle East and another species in northwest Africa. Due to genetic similarity this form was described as a subspecies of the Canary Long-eared Bat: *Plecotus teneriffae gaisleri* [1]. Shortly afterwards the Canary Long-eared Bat was again regarded as a full species and Gaisler's Long-eared Bat was aligned with the Balkan Long-eared Bat [gen. lit. 138]. Further genetic analysis and the geographically isolated occurrence pointed, however, to a separate entity for the northwest African long-eared bats [gen. lit. 77]. Also within the northwest African distribu-tion separate lines can be identified in the Maghreb (Morocco, Algeria, Tunisia) and in Libya. Probably this is the result of a rela-tively recent separation, which will make it almost impossible without comprehensive studies to agree upon a clear species alloca-tion. We regard the northwest African lines provisionally as full species, certainly knowing that the basis for that is far from conclusive.

IDENTIFICATION
Gaisler's Long-eared Bat is pale brownish, with a bright yellowish-brown ventral side. The skin areas are pale brownish. Animals from the Mediterranean region in the north of the distribution are darker coloured than the very pale animals of the northern edge of the Sahara [1]. The penis is club-shaped at the end, as in the Grey Long-eared or Balkan Long-eared Bats.

Similar species
At present, a clear distinction from the Balkan and Canary Long-eared Bats is only possible on the basis of genetic compar-isons or from the skull. However, Gaisler's Long-eared Bat is, so far, only sympatric with *P. christiei*, a much paler animal, in Libya. Gaisler's Long-eared Bat possibly occurs with the Balkan Long-eared Bat on Pantelleria Island. Distinctly smaller,

Measurements
Forearm	36.9–42.4mm
Fifth finger	49–53mm
Third finger	64–70mm
Thumb	5.2–6.8mm
Tibia	14.7–18.2mm
Foot	6.5–7.0mm
Tragus width	5.3 – 5.4mm
Tragus length	14.6–15.6mm
Normal weight (April):	5–6g
CBL	15.2–16.5mm
CM^3	5.5–6.0mm

Fig. 473. Portrait of Gaisler's Long-eared Bat. Photo: C. Dietz.

Fig. 474. Gaisler's Long-eared Bat is particularly pale coloured in desert areas. Photo: C. Dietz.

FOOD
In Morocco, in April, remains of large moths (noctuids) were found at a night roost [own data].

THREATS
So far not known.

REFERENCES
1. Benda, P., A. Kiefer, V. Hanák & M. Veith (2004): Systematic status of African populations of long-eared bats, Genus *Plecotus* (Mammalia: Chiroptera). *Folia Zool.* 53, Monograph 1: 1–47.
2. Juste, J., C. Ibáñez, J. Muńoz, D. Trujillo, P. Benda, A. Karataş & M. Ruedi (2004): Mitochondrial phylogeography of the long-eared bats (*Plecotus*) in the Mediterranean Palaearctic and Atlantic Islands. *Mol. Phyl. Evol.* 31: 1114–1126.
3. Kowalski, K. & B. Rzebik-Kowalska (1991): *Mammals of Algeria*, 370 pp; Polish Academy of Sciences.

browner dorsal fur and with paler skin areas than the Canary Long-eared Bat.

DISTRIBUTION
Entire northwest Africa from Morocco to northeast Libya. From the northern edge of the Sahara (Anti-Atlas and Sahara Atlas) to the Atlantic and Mediterranean coast. Possibly also on Pantelleria and Malta.

HABITAT
Particularly within the North African range that is influenced by the Mediterranean region, and along watercourses and oases, also semi-deserts and desert areas. Recorded up to 2,600m in the High Atlas.

Roosts
Single animals in rock crevices, caves, cellars, ruins and in arch fissures. So far only one small nursery colony with a dozen animals was found in a cave entrance. In winter similarly in caves [3].

BEHAVIOUR AND FORAGING
As with other long-eared bats the ears are tucked under the wings at rest. The hunting flight resembles that of other long-eared bats and occurs close to vegetation or low above the ground. In the mating period males form mating groups in caves [gen. lit. 10].

Bent-winged Bats
Miniopteridae

Traditionally regarded as a subfamily of the vesper or plain-nosed bats (Vespertilionidae). However, characteristics of morphology and reproductive biology exhibit many differences between these groups [10], and the genetic findings of recent years show that the bent-winged bats represent their own well-defined family [2, gen. lit. 54]. Bent-winged bats are medium-sized insectivorous bats of the Old World, which are morphologically relatively uniform. They have short, widely separated ears, which do not project above the top of the head, and long wings narrowing at the tip, which is bent inwards at rest. Long tail and wide tail membrane. The head is highly domed and forms a steep forehead. A baculum is missing. All species are cave dwellers and can form enormous colonies. The egg is fertilised immediately after the mating, but, in contrast to the vesper bats, in temperate latitudes the implantation of the egg is delayed until spring. Only one genus *Miniopterus*, with at least 19 species in Africa, southern Europe, Asia to Australia. The single European species, *M. schreibersii*, includes forms that probably represent further cryptic species [2, gen. lit. 54] and so the actual number of species may be higher.

Schreibers' Bent-winged Bat
Miniopterus schreibersii
(KUHL, 1817)

NAMES
- D: Langflügelfledermaus
- F: Minioptère de Schreibers
- E: Murciélago troglodita
- I: Miniottero
- NL: Schreibers' vleermuis
- S: Schreibers fladdermus
- PL: Podkasaniec Schreibersa

IDENTIFICATION
Medium-sized slender bat with a short snout and short triangular ears, which are widely separated and do not project above the top of the head. Short curved tragus. Due to the short upright fur on the domed forehead the transition between the fur on the back and on the nose is quite flat. Second phalanx of the third finger three times as long as the first phalanx. At rest the wing-tip is folded back on itself between the first and second phalanx of the third and fourth finger. Grey-brown to dark grey dorsal colouring, ventral side paler. Adult animals in Bulgaria and Romania have a distinctly defined yellow- to cinnamon-brown throat patch in summer. Flight membranes variable grey-brown.

SIMILAR SPECIES
Within our region easy to recognise on the basis of the short and characteristically formed ears, the short snout, domed forehead and the way the wing-tips are folded.

ECHOLOCATION CALLS
Up to 15ms-long calls begin with a frequency-modulated part and end with an

Measurements	
Forearm	42.4–48.0mm
Fifth finger	48–56mm
Third finger	78–89mm
Normal weight	10–14g
CBL	14.2–15.5mm
CM³	5.3–6.2mm

Fig. 475. Portrait of Schreibers' Bent-winged Bat: the short ears do not project above the crown. Photo: C. Dietz.

Fig. 476. Small cluster of hibernating Schreibers' Bent-winged Bats. Photo: D. Nill.

almost constant-frequency section. The main energy is at 49–53kHz. The start frequency is situation-dependent at 75–55kHz and ends at *c.* 52kHz. In search-phase flight the pulse intervals vary between 65 and 140ms.

DISTRIBUTION

In Europe throughout the Mediterranean region including all larger Mediterranean islands; the northern distribution border-runs across central France, south-west Germany (Kaiserstuhl, where extinct), the western part of Switzerland, north Italy, Slovenia, southeast Austria (small population size), Slovakia, Romania and Ukraine. In North Africa only in the west (Morocco,

Algeria, Tunisia and northwest Libya) down to the northern edge of the Sahara. In the Middle East and in the west of the Arabian Peninsula. Beyond the Mediterranean region, from a traditional view, the species is distributed through the Caucasus and Iran to China, Japan, the Philippines, Solomon Islands, the Bismarck Archipelago to Australia, as well as through sub-Saharan Africa. *M. schreibersii* would be limited to the Mediterranean region if most subspecies actually relate to full species.

Subspecies and geographical variation

All European and northwest African populations belong to the morphologically and genetically uniform *M. s. schreibersii.* Romanian and Bulgarian animals sometimes have a yellow- to cinnamon-brown throat patch and are described as *M. s. inexpectatus.* However, this characteristic relates rather to a moulting phenomenon and might not justify a separate subspecies status. In the eastern Mediterranean area and in the Middle East the pale-coloured *M. s. pallidus* occurs, which is genetically so clearly separate from *M. s. schreibersii* that it might get the status of a full species [1, 5]. Many of at least 15 further described subspecies, particularly in southern Africa and Asia, are probably also full species [2]; extensive taxonomic studies are necessary for clarification.

HABITAT

Habitats cover the whole spectrum of the Mediterranean landscapes, but overall there seems to be a preference for hardwood forest-rich areas. Nursery roosts to over 1,200m, with some individuals and groups of non-reproducing animals also substantially higher.

Roosts

Mainly in karst caves, which are occupied all year round, but also in mines, cellars and other underground sites. Often roosts in the largest chambers, in winter also in smaller side-corridors. Small groups or single animals can be found in numerous other roost types such as expansion joints of bridges, dome crevices and attics. At the northern border of the distribution in Slovenia [gen. lit. 96], Austria [15] and Hungary [6] single nursery colonies are known in roof spaces. The northernmost roost in Europe is in an uncompleted railway tunnel in the Muráň plateau in Slovakia [16].

BEHAVIOUR

Nursery colonies comprise usually only reproductive females and their young. Non-reproductive females and males form separate colonies in the same cave or in neighbouring caves. Nursery colonies can comprise some hundreds to many thousands of animals. The largest nursery colonies are known from Portugal with approximately 20,000 animals [7] and from Bulgaria. In north Bulgaria several summer roosts lie along the River Osam and are connected to each other to comprise jointly at least 30,000 animals, in some years in one of the caves even up to 60,000 individuals, whereas in other years only a few hundred animals are present [4, own data]. This contradicts the findings from Portugal, where in particular the females return each year to their roost of birth and are thus strictly philopatric [8]. Some large caves are used all year round as roosts [4, gen. lit. 96], others only seasonally. In the winter large accumulations are also possible between November and March: in north Bulgaria in some years colonies of respectively 52,000 and 65,000 animals are found in two caves, in which in other years 'only' a few thousand animals hibernate [4]. A similar picture is exhibited in a cave of the western Rhodopians with 12,000–41,000 animals [4]. In the Pyrenees winter colonies can

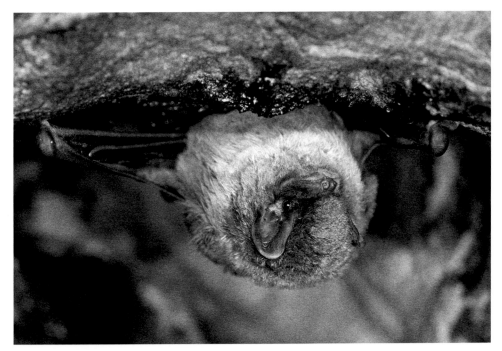

Fig. 477. Schreibers' Bent-winged Bats have very short ears and a domed forehead. Photo: D. Nill.

reach 70,000 animals [13]. The winter roosts have a large catchment area and seem, at least in Bulgaria, not to be visited each year. In the roosts Schreibers' Bent-winged bats usually hang free and form dense clusters reminiscent of wall carpets in summer and in winter. They are hardly ever found alone, being frequently mixed with the entire spectrum of other free-hanging cave bats. Flight paths to the hunting ground frequently follow roads or fire breaks, with the animals sometimes flying within 1–2m of the ground and about 2m from the vegetation.

REPRODUCTION

After mating in the autumn the egg is immediately fertilised; however, the blastocyst is implanted only after hibernation. Birth takes place from the middle of June to the beginning of July. The young are left behind in the roost at night and then form spectacular clusters. Also during the day in large undisturbed caves the young can form large clusters separate from the mothers. The high proportion of non-reproducing females in the population indicates that

they become sexual mature only in the second year of life or later.

FORAGING

Schreibers' Bent-winged Bats can hunt manoeuvrably around streetlamps or below the canopy of hardwood forests, over streams and other waterbodies, as well as close to vegetation [own data, 9]. The broad tail membrane makes an unusually manoeuvrable flight possible despite the narrow wings. Dense vegetation is avoided.

FOOD

With the delicate dentition, the short tooth row and the skull morphology, the prey spectrum is likely to be mainly small insects. In Slovenia the food consists particularly of moths (79%), followed by Neuroptera (green lacewings – *Chrysopa*) and Diptera [9]. Other insects play a minor role.

MAXIMUM AGE

At least 16 years [15].

MOBILITY AND MIGRATION

The species undertakes regular seasonal

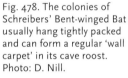

Fig. 478. The colonies of Schreibers' Bent-winged Bat usually hang tightly packed and can form a regular 'wall carpet' in its cave roost. Photo: D. Nill.

Fig. 479. Schreibers' Bent-wing Bats use caves as roosts almost exclusively. Photo: D. Nill.

migrations between summer and winter roosts with distances of on average 40–100km. The longest recorded movements were 422km, 524km and 833km in France and Spain. Thus part of the winter group that could be observed at the Kaiserstuhl in the 1960s travelled to the southwest up to 200 km to a nursery colony in the French Jura [gen. lit. 116]. In the Balkans a movement of 225km took place in only four days [11].

Habitat use

The occurrence of enormous summer and winter colonies suggests that with limited availability of food very long distances must be travelled to the foraging grounds. So far, however, no telemetry studies have been published.

THREATS

Red list of the IUCN 2006: LC (Least Concern), Red list of the European Union: VU (Vulnerable), EU Habitats Directive, Annex II & IV. European populations threatened by habitat loss, pesticide use and loss of roosts. In particular in the northern parts of the distribution a major decrease of the species has been recorded, in south Germany (extinct), Switzerland, France, Austria, Hungary and Romania [15, gen. lit. 136]. Apart from disturbance in the roosts, mass ringing [gen. lit. 116] and unsuitable protection measures of roosts, the substantial use of insecticides (including DDT) for controlling winter moths (Winter Moth and Mottled Umber) in the upper Rhine area [6, gen. lit. 51], poisoning of oak forests in Slovakia [15] and the control of crane-flies in the 1950s–1960s are also responsible for this decrease.

CONSERVATION MEASURES

Protection of the colony caves from disturbances, but grilling is difficult since this species is reluctant to fly through normal bat grilles. Preservation of hardwood forest areas and abandonment of large-scale pesticide use. Preservation of migration routes.

REFERENCES

1. Albayrak, I. & S. Coşkun (2000): Geographic variations and taxonomic status of *Miniopterus schreibersii* (Kuhl, 1819) in Turkey (Chiroptera: Vespertilionidae). *Turkish J. Zool.* 24: 125–133.
2. Appleton, B.R., J.A. McKenzie & L. Christidis (2004): Molecular systematics and biogeography of the bent-wing bat complex *Miniopterus schreibersii* (Chiroptera: Vespertilionidae). *Mol. Phyl. Evol.* 31: 431–439.
3. Balcells, E. (1964): Ergebnisse der Fledermaus-Beringung in Nordspanien. *Bonn. Zool. Beitr.* 15: 36–44.
4. Benda, P., T. Ivanova, I. Horáček, V. Hanák, J. Červený, J. Gaisler, A. Gueorguieva, B. Petrov &

Fig. 480. Within the enormous nursery colonies of Schreibers' Bent-winged Bat the young animals often hang separately from their mothers. Photo: C. Dietz.

gal. In: V. Hanák, I. Horáček & J. Gaisler (eds): *European Bat Research* 1987: 373–379; Charles Univ. Press Prague.

8. Palmeirim, J.M. & L. Rodrigues (1995): Dispersal and philopatry in colonial animals: the case of *Miniopterus schreibersii. Symp. Zool. Soc. Lond.* 67: 219–231.

9. Presetnik, P. (2002): Diet and biology of Schreibers' bat (*Miniopterus schreibersii*) at castle Grad na Goričkem (NE Slovenia). *Diplomarbeit, Universität Ljubljana*, 56 pp.

10. Mein, P. & Y. Tupinier (1977): Formule dentaire et position systématique du Minioptère. *Mammalia* 41: 207–211.

11. Mirić, D. (1960): Die Fledermäuse (Chiroptera) der unterirdischen Gänge der Festung Petrovaradin. *Bull. Mus. Hist. Nat. Belgrad* 16: 163–175.

12. Serra-Cobo, J. (1989): Primary results of the study on *Miniopterus schreibersi* growth. In: V. Hanák, I. Horáček & J. Gaisler (eds): *European Bat Research* 1987: 169–173; Charles Univ. Press Prague.

13. Serra-Cobo, J., V. Sanz-Trullén & J.P. Martínez-Rica (1998): Migratory movements of *Miniopterus schreibersii* in the north-east of Spain. *Acta Theriol.* 43: 271–283.

14. Serra-Cobo, J., M. Lopez-Roig, T. Marques-Bonet & E. Lahuerta (2000): Rivers as possible landmarks in the orientation flight of *Miniopterus schreibersii. Acta Theriol.* 45: 347–352.

15. Spitzenberger, F. (1981): Die Langflügelfledermaus (*Miniopterus schreibersi*) in Österreich. Mammalia austriaca 5. *Mitt. Abt. Zool. Landesmus.* Joanneu 10: 139–156.

16. Uhrin, M. (1994): Further occurrence of the longwinged bat, *Miniopterus schreibersii* (Mammalia, Chiroptera) in the Muráň plateau. *Biologia Bratislava* 49: 287–288.

V. Vohralík (2003): Bats (Mammalia: Chiroptera) of the Eastern Mediterranean. Part 3. Review of bat distribution in Bulgaria. *Acta Soc. Zool. Bohem.* 67: 245–357.

5. Bilgin, R., A. Karataş, E. Çoraman, I. Pandurski, E. Papadatou & J.C. Morales (2006): Molecular taxonomy and phylogeography of *Miniopterus schreibersii* (Chiroptera: Vespertilionidae), in the Eurasian transition. *Biol. J. Linn. Soc.* 87: 577–582.

6. Boye, P. (2004): *Miniopterus schreibersii* – Langflügelfledermaus. In: F. Krapp (ed.): *Handbuch der Säugetiere Europas* 4–II: 1093–1122; Aula Verlag.

7. Palmeirim, J.M. (1989): Status of bats in Portu-

Free-tailed Bats
Molossidae

Small to large insectivorous bats. The very long narrow wings and the tail, with the greater part extending beyond the tail membrane, are characteristic. The feet are covered with long bristle-like hairs. The lips are folded and can be very flexible. Most species forage in open areas. The head morphology reflects the predominant food: species which capture large hard-shelled beetles have a solid head musculature; hunters of softer moths have substantially slender-built heads. In some species the ears project forwards, which possibly facilitates crawling in narrow crevice roosts, or may be to provide additional lift in flight for the relatively heavy head [16]. Worldwide family of 16 genera with 100 species in the tropics and subtropics of the Old and New World. In our region only one species *Tadarida teniotis*. Nine further species of the genus *Tadarida* occur in Africa, Asia, Australia, and North and South America.

European Free-tailed Bat
Tadarida teniotis
(RAFINESQUE, 1814)

NAMES

D:	Europäische Bulldoggfledermaus
F:	Molosse de Cestoni
E:	Muricélago rabudo
I:	Molosso del Cestoni
NL:	Europese bulvleermuis
S:	Veckläppad fladdermus
PL:	Molos europejski

IDENTIFICATION

A large and robust bat with large ears and very long wings. The fur is short with soft hairs, very dense and mole-like, without a sheen. The fur colouring is black-grey, brightly silver-grey or grey-brown; the ventral side is slightly paler. Contrary to earlier opinions warmly brown-coloured as well as grey animals, typical of the Middle East and North Africa, occur in Europe. Ears, nose and wing membranes grey-brown. The large rounded ears are joined at the base and project beyond the snout. Active animals hold the ears almost perpendicularly; when crawling in crevices they are held forward horizontally. The eyes are large and the upper lip usually has five folds and is very flexible. The tail extends for about half its length beyond the narrow tail membrane and is provided with many bristles at the tip. This fulfills a sensory function when creeping backwards into crevices. Typical smell of lovage or fennel.

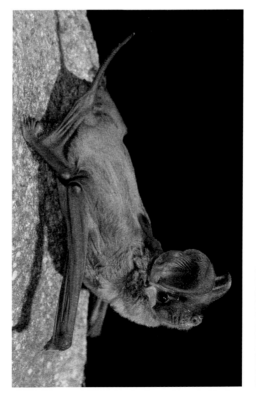

Fig. 481. By the folds of the lips, the large egg-shaped ears and the free tail, the European Free-tailed Bat clearly differs from all other European bat species. Photo: D. Nill.

Measurements

Forearm	54.7–69.9mm
Fifth finger	55–60mm
Third finger	102–115mm
Normal weight	20–30g
CBL	21.9–23.6mm
CM³	8.3–8.8mm

Similar species

Unmistakable within the geographical scope of this book. The smaller *T. aegyptiaca* occurs at the northern edge of the Sahara, and has a forearm length usually <55mm and only two lower incisors (three in *T. teniotis*).

ECHOLOCATION CALL

Up to 27ms long, in the open almost constant-frequency calls. The main energy is at 10–14kHz and thus in the audible range of humans. Two call types with different end frequencies of respectively 9–11kHz and 13–15kHz [8, 15]. The pulse interval is usually between 450 and 550ms, but up to 900ms.

DISTRIBUTION

Distributed from the Canary Islands (Las Palmas, La Gomera, Tenerife and El Hierro) [6] and Madeira through the whole Mediterranean area, Asia Minor, the Caucasus and the Middle East to India, southern China and Indonesia. In Europe in north to southern France, southern Switzerland, Croatia, Bosnia-Herzegovina, Serbia and Bulgaria. Single animals also further north into northern Switzerland, south Germany (a record in Stuttgart in 1992) and on the Channel Islands (Jersey) and England. In North Africa to the northern edge of the Sahara; absent in the south of the Arabian

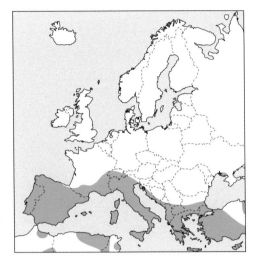

Peninsula. Far Eastern records may refer to separate species.

Subspecies and geographical variation

The European populations are assigned to *T. t. teniotis*, those of North Africa and the Middle East to *T. t. rueppellii*, a subspecies that is barely distinguishable from *teniotis* and is probably synonymous [11, gen.lit. 55]. Meanwhile several eastern subspecies are regarded as full species, such as *T. insignis* and *T. latouchei*.

HABITAT

In Mediterranean areas at all altitudes from sea level to well above 2,000m. Usually in mountainous landscapes or at coasts which offer suitable roosts. Hunting grounds particularly over forest, plantations or olive groves [13], but also over water, cities and cultivated landscape. In semi-deserts often along water courses and over oases.

Roosts

A typical dweller of rock crevices. Usually in high inaccessible cliffs in mountains, ravines or in narrow cracks just over the width of a thumb at 20–40m and which allow an uninterrupted take-off. Often in vertical crevices. Also in crevices of high cave ceilings, expansion joints of high bridges and cracks in the façade of high buildings (water towers, churches, tower blocks). Occasionally in cracks of isolated tall trees.

Fig. 482. Roosts of European Free-tailed Bats are in narrow crevices of high cliffs. In the roost the ears are projected horizontally sideways. Photo: D. Nill.

BEHAVIOUR

Nursery colonies comprise 5–50 animals, occasionally up to 400 animals [8]. Outside the nursery period mixed colonies, during the nursery period males usually roost separately. Usually clusters are not formed, the animals hang separately or next to each other in cracks. At the northern border of the distribution in Switzerland hibernation phases last only a few, up to eight, days, with the body temperature lowered to a minimum of 7–5°C. If the ambient temperature drops below 7–5°C the animals arouse. European Free-tailed Bats also fly at low temperatures [4]. In the morning and evening dusk the animals can orient themselves visually without echolocation [2].

REPRODUCTION

Females are sexual mature after one year, only one young per birth, which is suckled for 6–7 weeks. The main birth period is from the end of June to the beginning of July, but births even occur at the end of August. Consequently, lactating females can still be caught in October. Display and mating take place in the autumn and in April; it is unclear whether delayed fertilisation, as in most other European species, or delayed implantation takes place. Mating groups with one male and up to nine females have been observed; the male 'sings' characteristically, particularly in the evening hours, and during the mating period behaves aggressively towards other males.

FORAGING

The emergence from the roost takes place in the late dusk. A very strong and fast flier that can reach at least 65km/h and, in open spaces, hunts in direct flight at heights of 10–300m over a very broad habitat spectrum. Apart from near-natural areas, large cities are visited, where foraging can take place around tower blocks and isolated streetlamps. With high insect densities up to 25 animals can hunt in the same place. When several animals hunt together they use one of the two possible call types. Whether this acts as an individual identification to avoid echo overlaps [15] is unclear.

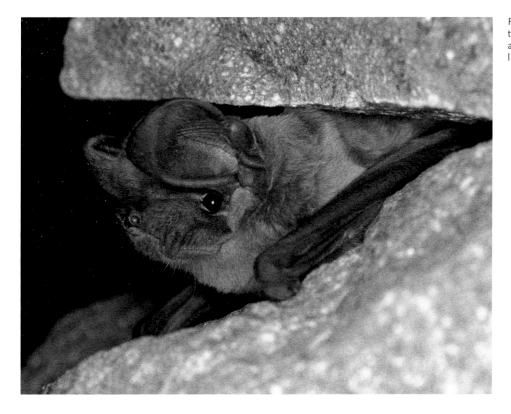

Fig. 483. European Free-tailed Bats have large eyes and a flexible folded upper lip. Photo: D. Nill.

Fig. 484. European Free-tailed Bats are the fastest fliers among the European bats. Photo: D. Nill.

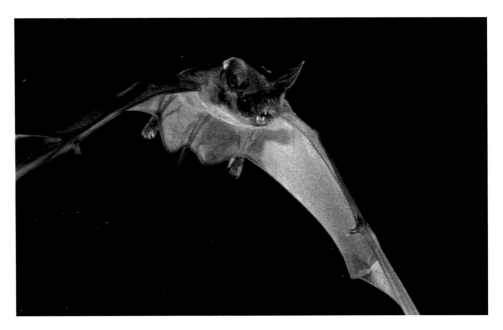

Probably the low echolocation frequencies are an adaptation to the habitat (low-frequency calls carry further) and to the available prey (frequencies are below the hearing range of the tympanic organs of moths and lacewings) [14]. With the long-range echolocation and the high flight speed a very large airspace can be searched for prey.

FOOD
The food consists almost exclusively of flying insects; 65–90% of the prey are moths [14], and very large moths, including hawk moths, are included. Seasonally Diptera play a role as prey; other groups of prey are beetles, lacewings and Hymenoptera.

MAXIMUM AGE
At least 13 years [7].

MOBILITY AND MIGRATION
Contrary to older data, faithful to roosts and stationary, marked animals in Spain and Switzerland were found all year in the roost [8].

Habitat use
Roosts are changed at distances of over 30km [4]. Individual hunting grounds are about 100ha and usually within 30km of the roost [13]. Hunting grounds in the summer can be up to 100km from the roost, in the winter to 20km distance [2].

THREATS
Red list of the IUCN 2006: LC (Least Concern), EU Habitats Directive, Annex IV. In some Mediterranean countries locally common. Only a few records from Madeira.

CONSERVATION MEASURES
Prevention of widespread open agriculture and limitation of pesticide use. Protection of colony cliffs from destruction by quarrying, conservation of building roosts.

REFERENCES
1. Aellen, V. (1966): Notes sur *Tadarida teniotis* (Mammalia, Chiroptera) – I. Systématique, paléontologie et peuplement, répartition géographique. *Rev. Suisse Zool.* 73: 119–159.
2. Arlettaz, R. (1990): Contribution à l'éco-éthologie du Molosse de Cestoni, *Tadarida teniotis*, dans les Alpes valaisannes (sud-ouest de la Suisse). *Z. Säugetierk.* 55: 28–42.
3. Arlettaz, R. (1993): *Tadarida teniotis* tail. *Myotis* 31: 155–162.
4. Arlettaz, R., C. Ruchet, J. Aeschimann, E. Brun, M. Genoud & P. Vogel (2000): Physiological traits affecting the distribution and wintering strategy of the bat *Tadarida teniotis*. *Ecology* 81: 1004–1014.
5. Červený, J. & B. Kryštufek (1988): A contribution to the knowledge of the bats of Central an

Southern Dalmatia, Yugoslavia (Chiroptera, Mammalia). *Biol. Vestn.* 36: 17–30.

6. Hutterer, R. (1989): Distribution of *Tadarida teniotis* in the Canary Islands. *Myotis* 27: 157–160.

7. Ibáñez, C. & J.L. Perez-Jorda (1998): Longevity in the European free-tailed bat (*Tadarida teniotis*). *J. Zool.* 245: 213–214.

8. Ibáñez, C. & J.L. Perez-Jorda (2004): *Tadarida teniotis* – Europäische Bulldoggfledermaus. In: F. Krapp (ed.): *Handbuch der Säugetiere Europas* 4–II: 1125–1143; Aula Verlag.

9. Kalpakis, S., E. Papadatou & O. von Helversen (2005): Balcony of an urban building: an unintended trap for free-tailed bats (*Tadarida teniotis*) in the city of Thessaloniki. *Nyctalus* (N.F.) 10: 79–81.

10. Kock, D. (1977): Körper-Vibrissen bei Bulldogg-Fledermäusen, eine Anpassung an das Tagesquartier. *Natur und Museum* 107: 274–279.

11. Kock, D. (1987): *Tadarida teniotis*: Zweiter Nachweis für Marokko, w-paläarktische Arealgrenzen und taxonomische Anmerkung (Chiroptera: Molossidae). *Z. Säugetierk.* 52: 194–196.

12. Paolillo, G. (1992): A colony of European free-tailed bat (*Tadarida teniotis*) discovered in Calabria. *Hystrix* (n.s) 4: 73–74.

13. Rainho, A., T. Marques, M. Carapuco, P. Oliveira & J.M. Palmeirim (2002): Foraging patterns of the European free-tailed bat *Tadarida teniotis* studied by radio-tracking. *Bat Research News* 43: 104.

14. Rydell, J. & R. Arlettaz (1994): Low-frequency echolocation enables the bat *Tadarida teniotis* to feed on tympanate insects. *Proc. R. Soc. Lond.* B 257: 175–178.

15. Ulanovsky, N., M.B. Fenton, A. Tsoar & C. Korine (2004): Dynamics of jamming avoidance in echolocating bats. *Proc. R. Soc. Lond.* B 271: 1467–1475.

16. Vaughan, T.A. (1966): Morphology and flight characteristics of molossid bats. *J. Mammal.* 47: 249–260.

17. Zbinden, K. & P.E. Zingg (1986): Search and hunting signals of echolocating European free-tailed bats, *Tadarida teniotis*, in southern Switzerland. *Mammalia* 50: 9–25.

Fig. 485. The European Free-tailed Bat has, like many other species of the family Molossidae, strong bristles on the feet, which serve as combs for grooming. Photo: C. Dietz.

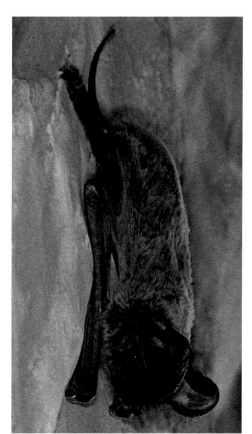

Fig. 486. A brown European Free-tailed Bat from Morocco. Photo: C. Dietz.

Conservation status of European bats

The conservation status of bats has recently been assessed by IUCN, the International Union for Conservation of Nature, through a European Mammals Assessment (EMA) and a Global Mammal Assessment. The status for each species identified by these programmes is given in the following table.

Details of the information used to give these assessments for Europe can be found in Temple, H.J. & Terry, A. (Compilers) 2007. *The Status and Distribution of European Mammals.* Luxembourg: Office for Official Publications of the European Communities. 48pp. [Printed summary; species details available at http://ec.europa.eu/environment /nature/conservation/species/ema/]

The results of the Global Mammals Assessment were incorporated into The IUCN Red List of Threatened Species 2008, available only on the web at http://www. iucnredlist.org/.

In Europe bats are protected by a range of international treaties which are incorporated into national legislation, as is the protection afforded through the European Union.

Under the European Union's Habitats and Species Directive, the Council Directive 92/43/EEC of 21 May 1992 on the conservation of natural habitats and of wild fauna and flora (OJ L 206, 22 July 1992, p. 7), all bat species are included in Annex IV. In addition, 14 species are included in Annex II and these are identified in the table below. These Annexes expect a high level of protection and monitoring of damage to the species and their habitats. Further details can be found at http://eur-lex.europa.eu/en/index.htm.

There are currently 32 Parties to the UNEP/CMS Agreement on the Conservation of Populations of European Bats (EURO-BATS). Under Article III of this Agreement the first Fundamental Obligation is for Parties to provide protective legislation for their bats. Parties also agree to develop a range of other protective measures and to adopt resolutions and other policies that should assist in the protection of bats. Some of these policies are expressed in issues of the recently initiated Eurobats Publications Series. See www.eurobats.org/.

The Berne Convention, or Convention on the Conservation of European Wildlife and Natural Habitats (1982), includes some states that are not yet party to either of the above. It includes an Appendix II, which gives strict protection to all species of bat except *Pipistrellus pipistrellus*. All bat species are included in Appendix III, which offers protection and regulation of exploitation.

The definition of 'Europe' is not always the same. For the purposes of Eurobats and the Bern Convention, Europe includes the whole of Turkey and the Caucasus states, and the Russian Federation to 50°E, and south to include the main Mediterranean islands. EMA did not include the Caucasus states or Turkey.

The table covers all those species included in this book, including species occurring within the wider Europe defined by Eurobats and the Berne Convention. Where appropriate species have been marked as Not Evaluated (NE) or Not Applicable (N/A), because the species was not recognised at the time, does not occur in the region defined, or the regional populations were considered insignificant in the overall distribution.

Red List categories:
CR: Critically Endangered
EN: Endangered
VU: Vulnerable
NT: Near Threatened
LC: Least Concern
DD: Data Deficient
NE Not Evaluated

COMMON NAME	SCIENTIFIC NAME	RED LIST EUROPE	RED LIST GLOBAL	EU HABITATS DIR APP II
Egyptian Fruit Bat	*Rousettus aegyptiacus*	NE, N/A	LC	Yes
Naked-rumped Tomb Bat	*Taphozous nudiventris*	NE	LC	N/A
Lesser Mouse-tailed Bat	*Rhinopoma hardwickii*	N/A	LC	N/A
Egyptian Slit-faced Bat	*Nycteris thebaica*	N/A	LC	N/A
Sundevall's Leaf-nosed Bat	*Hipposideros caffer*	N/A	LC	N/A
Trident Leaf-nosed Bat	*Asellia tridens*	N/A	LC	N/A
Lesser Horseshoe Bat	*Rhinolophus hipposideros*	NT	LC	Yes
Greater Horseshoe Bat	*Rhinolophus ferrumequinum*	NT	LC	Yes
Mediterranean Horseshoe Bat	*Rhinolophus euryale*	VU	NT	Yes
Mehely's Horseshoe Bat	*Rhinolophus mehelyi*	VU	VU	Yes
Blasius's Horseshoe Bat	*Rhinolophus blasii*	VU	LC	Yes
Daubenton's Bat	*Myotis daubentonii*	LC	LC	No
Pond Bat	*Myotis dasycneme*	NT	NT	Yes
Long-fingered Bat	*Myotis capaccinii*	VU	VU	Yes
Brandt's Bat	*Myotis brandtii*	LC	LC	No
Whiskered Bat	*Myotis mystacinus*	LC	LC	No
Steppe Whiskered Bat	*Myotis aurascens*	LC	LC	No
Alcathoe Whiskered Bat	*Myotis alcathoe*	DD	DD	No
Asiatic Whiskered Bat	*Myotis nipalensis*	NE	LC	No
Armenian Whiskered Bat	*Myotis hajastanicus*	NE	CR	N/A
Natterer's Bat	*Myotis nattereri*	LC	LC	No
Schaub's Bat	*Myotis schaubi*	NE	DD	N/A
Geoffroy's Bat	*Myotis emarginatus*	LC	LC	Yes
Bechstein's Bat	*Myotis bechsteinii*	VU	NT	Yes
Greater Mouse-eared Bat	*Myotis myotis*	LC	LC	Yes
Lesser Mouse-eared Bat	*Myotis oxygnathus*	NT	(LC)	Yes
Maghrebian Mouse-eared Bat	*Myotis punicus*	NT	NT	No
Noctule Bat	*Nyctalus noctula*	LC	LC	No

COMMON NAME	SCIENTIFIC NAME	RED LIST EUROPE	RED LIST GLOBAL	EU HABITATS DIR APP II
Greater Noctule Bat	*Nyctalus lasiopterus*	DD	NT	No
Leisler's Bat	*Nyctalus leisleri*	LC	LC	No
Azorean Noctule Bat	*Nyctalus azoreum*	EN	EN	No
Common Pipistrelle Bat	*Pipistrellus pipistrellus*	LC	LC	No
Soprano Pipistrelle Bat	*Pipistrellus pygmaeus*	LC	LC	No
Nathusius's Pipistrelle Bat	*Pipistrellus nathusii*	LC	LC	No
Kuhl's Pipistrelle Bat	*Pipistrellus kuhlii*	LC	LC	No
Madeiran Pipistrelle Bat	*Pipistrellus maderensis*	EN	EN	No
Rüppell's Pipistrelle Bat	*Pipistrellus rueppellii*	N/A	LC	N/A
Savi's Pipistrelle Bat	*Hypsugo savii*	LC	LC	No
Parti-coloured Bat	*Vespertilio murinus*	LC	LC	No
Serotine Bat	*Eptesicus serotinus*	LC	LC	No
Northern Bat	*Eptesicus nilssonii*	LC	LC	No
Isabelline Serotine Bat	*Eptesicus isabellinus*	NE	NE	No
Anatolian Serotine Bat	*Eptesicus anatolicus*	NE, N/A	(LC)	No
Hoary Bat	*Lasiurus cinereus*	N/A	LC	N/A
Western Barbastelle Bat	*Barbastella barbastellus*	VU	NT	Yes
Eastern Barbastelle Bat	*Barbastella leucomelas*	NE	LC	N/A
Hemprich's Long-eared Bat	*Otonycteris hemprichii*	NE	LC	N/A
Brown Long-eared Bat	*Plecotus auritus*	LC	LC	No
Alpine Long-eared Bat	*Plecotus macrobullaris*	NT	LC	No
Sardinian Long-eared Bat	*Plecotus sardus*	VU	VU	No
Grey Long-eared Bat	*Plecotus austriacus*	LC	LC	No
Balkan Long-eared Bat	*Plecotus kolombatovici*	NT	LC	No
Canary Long-eared Bat	*Plecotus teneriffae*	EN	EN	No
Gaisler's Long-eared Bat	*Plecotus gaisleri*	N/A	NE	N/A
Schreibers' Bent-winged Bat	*Miniopterus schreibersii*	NT	NT	Yes
European Free-tailed Bat	*Tadarida teniotis*	LC	LC	No

Glossary

Acoustic fovea: An area of the hearing system with an exceptional sensitivity to a specific frequency range, which is arranged as the preferentially used frequency for echolocation. Horseshoe bats are able to analyse even the smallest frequency changes (glints).

Allopatric distribution: The occurrence of two or more (related) species in areas of geographical distribution that do not overlap, i.e. they do not occur together anywhere.

Annex II of the EU Habitats Directive: see Eu Habitats Directive.

Annex IV of the EU Habitats Directive: see Eu Habitats Directive.

Antitragus: Skin fold at the lower edge of the ear in bats.

Aspect ratio: A derived value for a description of the wing shape, which results from the squared wingspan divided by the wing area.

Baculum: Small bone in the penis of bats (the *Os penis*).

Buccal gland: Well-developed glandular pad inside the cheeks in the corners of the mouth of bats.

Bat detector: Device for making ultrasonic sounds audible to humans.

Calcar: A long and thin cartilaginous spur from the foot of a bat, supporting the trailing edge of the tail membrane.

Canine (C): see Tooth (or dental) formula.

Carnivorous: Flesh-eating.

Caryology: Study of the cell nucleus and its chromosomes (often 'karyology').

CBL = condylobasal length: Length of the skull from the front edge of the skull (the premaxilla) to the back of the occipital condyles.

CCL = condylocanine length: Length of the skull from the front edge of the canine to the back of the occipital condyles.

CF: Abbreviation for constant frequency: See Constant frequency.

Cingulum: Ring of tooth material at the base of the emergent tooth, which can appear as a shelf.

Cline: Gradual transition.

Cluster: Close aggregation of bats in a roost.

Clutter: See Echo-clutter.

CM³: Upper tooth row length. Length from the front edge of the upper canine (C^1) to the rear edge of the last upper molar (M^3).

Cochlea: Snail-shaped structure in the inner ear of mammals, which is specialised in sound recognition and the distinction of different frequencies.

Constant frequency: A typical sound structure in which the frequency of the emitted sound remains largely constant, i.e. pure tones are emitted.

Cryptic species = twin or 'sister' species: A pair of species that so closely resemble each other morphologically that they were not recognised as separate species for a long time.

Data Deficient (DD): Conservation category of IUCN: insufficient data known for the assessment of a category of threat.

Doppler shift: A shift in the sonic frequency due to the movement of the acoustic source in relation to the sound receiver.

Duty cycle: That portion of time that is used for sending sound signals.

Echolocation: Orientation and navigation in the environment and detection of prey by interpretation of echoes of previously emitted sounds.

Echo-clutter: Multiplicity of echoes from the background (e.g. from leaves, the ground or other surfaces), which can mask the echo of a prey animal.

Endemic: A species or subspecies that occurs naturally only in a certain and limited area.

Feeding buzz: Increase of the emission rate of echolocation calls during the final approach to the prey. So-called after the characteristic audible 'buzz' on the bat detector.

EU Habitats Directive: Has the provisions of a European protected area system (Natura-2000) as a goal and contains lists of selected habitats and species that are to be protected. Appendix II lists Europe-wide strongly threatened animal and plant species, for which they and their habitats are to be protected. In Appendix IV, species of community interest are listed and which should be strictly protected.

Frequency: The number of waves per second in air created by a sound, measured in cycles per second (Hertz).

Frequency-modulated (fm): A typical sound structure used for echolocation, in which the frequency changes during the emission of the calls. Usually the sound begins with a high frequency and drops rapidly and continuously to a low frequency.

Frugivorous: Fruit-eating.

Fundamental frequency: The lowest natural frequency part of a sound.

Gleaning: Term for the catching of stationary prey animals from the ground, leaves or other surfaces.

Glint: Interference sample, which results from the amplitude modulation of the echo if the emitted sound meets rhythmically moving surfaces, e.g. the flapping wing of an insect. Glints can be used by horseshoe bats for the distinction of different flying prey animals.

Habitat: Natural home of an organism.

Harmonic: One of the secondary tones produced by the vibration of a sound-producing body.

Incisor (I): See Tooth (or dental) formula.

Insectivorous: Insect-eating.

IUCN: International Union for the Conservation of Nature. The global assembly of government and non-government bodies for the conservation of nature and natural resources.

kHz: Unit of frequency of 1,000 cycles per second (1 kilohertz).

Lactation: The milk production and the suckling of a young animal.

Lancet: Triangular vertical skin projection at upper edge of the noseleaf of horseshoe bats.

Least Concern (LC): Conservation category of IUCN: usually a common and widely distributed species not currently threatened with extinction.

MCP: Minimum convex polygon. Convex area including all points, e.g. roost sites, of a radio-tracked animal.

Molar (M): See Tooth (or dental) formula.

Near Threatened (NT): Conservation category of IUCN: a species that is expected to fall into a threatened category in the near future.

Nominate form: the first-named form of a taxonomic unit.

Nursery colony: An aggregation of females collected together to give birth to young.

Nursery roost: Place where female bats collect together to give birth and raise their young.

Protocone: Small cusp at anterior inner corner of large upper premolar (P4).

Protoconule: Small ancillary cusp on the anterior edge of the molars in some bat species.

Philopatry: Having fidelity to an area or location, usually the place of birth.

Post-calcarial lobe: A small skin flap projected beyond the calcar of some bat species.

Premolar (P): See Tooth (or dental) formula.

Sella (saddle): Forward-projecting skin lobe above the nostrils of horseshoe bats.

Sonogram: Diagram of sounds by plotting the frequency and intensity against time.

Sympatric distribution: Where the distribution of two or more species overlaps geographically, i.e. they occur together.

Synanthrophy: Living in or around human settlement.

Syntopic occurrence: Occurrence of two or more species that are not only sympatrically distributed but also occur in the same habitat.

Swarming: 1. Night-time aggregation of a large number of bats in the late summer and autumn at the entrance area of (underground) winter roosts. 2. Prolonged circling around a roost or its entrance with the morning return flight after foraging.

Taxon: Group of organisms defined as a unit within biological systematics.

Telemetry: Tracking an animal by mounting a (radio) transmitter on it, used to study the behaviour.

Tooth (or dental) formula: The numbers and the respective position of the four kinds of teeth in the dentition: I (incisor), C (canine), P (premolar) and M (molar). Numbers in superscript mean teeth in the upper jaw, numbers in subscript mean teeth in the lower jaw.

Torpor: Physiological process of induced lethargy in which energy is saved by reduction of the body temperature.

Tragus: Membranous projection by the ear opening of many bat species.

Tympanal organ: Hearing organ of insects. Insects with a hearing organ are said to be tympanate.

Ultrasonic: High frequencies above 20kHz and thus above the range of human hearing.

Vulnerable (VU): Conservation category of the IUCN: a species facing a high risk of extinction in the wild.

Wing-loading: The ratio between the body weight and the wing surface. This has a large influence on the flight behaviour and flight performance.

Addresses

Organisations for bat studies and conservation

International
Eurobats. www.eurobats.org

Bat Conservation International. www.batcon.org

Austria
Koordinationsstelle für Fledermausschutz und –forschung in Österreich, Bäckerstraße 2a/4, 4072 Alkoven. www.fledermausschutz.at

Belgium
Plecotus. www.chauves.souris.be

Natuurpunt. www.natuurpunt.be

Croatia
Croatian Natural History Museum Bat Group, Demetrova 1, 10000 Zagreb, Croatia.

Czech Republic
Czech Bat Conservation Trust. www.ochranaprirody.cz

Estonia
Eptesicus. www.hot.ee/eptesicus

Finland
Chiropterological Society of Finland (CSF). www.lepakko.org

France
Muséum d'Histoire Naturelle à Bourges. www.museumbourges.net

Le Groupe Chiroptères de la SFEPM. www.sfepm.org/groupeChiropteres.htm

Germany
Naturschutzbund Deutschland (NABU). www.nabu.de/fledermausschutz/adressenliste.pdf

Hungary
Bats and Bat Conservation in Hungary. www.hunbat.hu

Ireland
Bat Conservation Ireland. www.batconservationireland.org

Italy
The Italian Chiroptera Research Group. www.pipistrelli.org

Center for the Study and Protection of Bats in Sardinia. www.pipistrellisardegna.org

Lithuania
The Society for Bat Conservation in Lithuania, Naftininku 16–36, 89121 Mazeikiai. www.chiroptera.lt

Bat Workers Group of the Theriological Society of Lithuania, Erdves Street 15, 46265 Kaunas.

Luxembourg
Association Transfrontaliere de Protection des Chauves-Souris. http://aptcs.ciril.fr

Netherlands
Dutch Bat Working Group. www.vleermuis.net

Norway
Bat Group of the Norwegian Zoological Society. www.zoologi.no/flmus

Poland
Bat Conservation Group, PTPP 'Pro Natura', Podwale 75, 50–449 Wroclaw.

Russia
The Russian Bat Research Group. http://zmmu.msu.ru/bats

Slovak Republic
Slovak Bat Conservation Group. www.netopiere.sk

Slovenia
SDPVN-Slovenian Association for Bat Research and Conservation. www.sdpvn-drustvo.si

Spain
Speleological Group at the University of Cadiz. www2.uca.es/huesped/giex/murciesp.htm

Sweden
Bat protector homepage. www.bat-protector.se

Switzerland
SSF-Stiftung zum Schutze unserer Fledermäuse in der Schweiz. www.fledermausschutz.ch

Centre de coordination ouest pour l'étude et la protection des chauves-souris en Suisse. www.ville-ge.ch/mhngh/cco

Verein 'Pro Chiroptera'. www.fledermaus.ch

Ukraine
Ukrainian Centre for Bat Protection. www.kazhan.org.ua

United Kingdom
The Bat Conservation Trust. www.bats.org.uk

General literature

1. Abelencev, W.I., I.G. Pidoplitschko & B.M. Popov (1956): *Fauna Ucraini (Mammalia, Insectivora – Chiroptera).* Kiev.

2. Aihartza, J.R., U. Goiti, D. Almenar & I. Garin (2003): Evidences of piscivory by *Myotis capaccinii* in Southern Iberian Peninsula. *Acta Chiropterologica* 5: 193–198.

3. Altringham, J. (2003): *British Bats.* The New Naturalist, HarperCollins Publishers, London.

4. Arlettaz, R. (1996): Feeding behaviour and foraging strategy of free-living *Myotis myotis* and *Myotis blythii. Anim. Behav.* 51: 1–11.

5. Arlettaz, R., G. Jones & P.A. Racey (2001): Effect of acoustic clutter on prey detection by bats. *Nature* 414: 742–745.

6. Battersby, J. (2005): *UK mammals: species status and population trends.* First report by the Tracking Mammals Partnership; Peterborough.

7. Bauer, K. (1960): Die Säugetiere des Neusiedlersee-Gebietes (Österreich). *Bonn. Zool. Beitr.* 7: 296–319.

8. Beck, A. (1995): Fecal analyses of European bat species. *Myotis* 32–33: 109–119.

9. Benda, P. & K.A. Tsytsulina (2000): Taxonomic revision of *Myotis mystacinus* group in the western Palearctic. *Acta Soc. Zool. Bohem.* 64: 331–398.

10. Benda, P., M. Ruedi & S. Aulagnier (2004): New data on the distribution of bats (Chiroptera) in Morocco. *Vespertilio* 8: 13–44.

11. Bezzel, E. (1993): *Kompendium der Vögel Mitteleuropas: Passeres – Singvögel.* Aula Verlag, Wiesbaden.

12. Berthold, P. (1990): *Vogelzug. Eine kurze aktuelle Gesamtübersicht.* Wissenschaftliche Buchgesellschaft, Darmstadt.

13. Boettger, C.R. (1962): Schalen juveniler Wurmschnecken (Fam. Vermetidae) in einer Höhle der Insel Kreta. *Arch. Moll.* 91: 57–59.

14. Boettger, C.R. (1963): Die als Schalen juveniler Wurmschnecken (Fam. Vermetidae) angesprochenen Funde aus einer Höhle der Insel Kreta. *Arch. Moll.* 92: 77–78.

15. Boonman, A. & H.-U. Schnitzler (2005): Frequency modulation patterns in the echolocation signals of two vespertilionid bats. *J. Comp. Physiol.* A 191: 13–21.

16. Braun, M. & F. Dieterlen (eds) (2003): *Die Säugetiere Baden-Württembergs, Band 1: Allgemeiner Teil, Fledermäuse (Chiroptera)*; Ulmer Verlag.

17. Braun, M. & F. Weick (1994): *Fledermäuse brauchen Freunde.* Führer zu Ausstellungen, 12. Museum am Friedrichsplatz Karlsruhe.

18. Brinkmann, R. (2005): Positionspapier: Querungshilfen für Fledermäuse – Schadensbegrenzung bei der Lebensraumzerschneidung durch Verkehrsprojekte. *Nyctalus* (N.F.) 10: 76–78.

19. Brinkmann, R., H. Schauer-Weisshahn & F. Bontadina (2006): Untersuchungen zu möglichen betriebsbedingten Auswirkungen von Windkraftanlagen auf Fledermäuse im Regierungspräsidium Freiburg. *Der Flattermann* 18: 12–14.

20. Brosset, A., L. Barbe, J.-C. Beaucournu, C. Faugier, H. Salvayre & Y. Tupinier (1985): La raréfaction du rhinolophe euryale (*Rhinolophus euryale*) en France. Recherche d´une explication. *Mammalia* 52: 101–122.

21. Bruderer, B. & A.G. Popa-Lisseanu (2005): Radar data on wing-beat frequencies and flight speeds of two bat species. *Acta Chiropterologica* 7: 73–82.

22. Csorba, G., P. Ujhelyi & N. Thomas (2003): *Horseshoe bats of the world (Chiroptera: Rhinolophidae).* Alana Books.

23. Davis, R. (1966): Homing performance and homing ability in bats. *Ecological Monographs* 36: 201–237.

24. Dietz, C. (2005): *Identification key to the bats of Egypt.* Electronic publication, version 1.0, 36 pp.; Tübingen. www.uni-tuebingen.de/tierphys/Kontakt/mitarbeiter_seiten/dietz.htm.

25. Dietz, C. (2005): *Fledermäuse schützen. Berücksichtigung des Fledermausschutzes bei der Sanierung von Natursteinbrücken und Wasserdurchlässen.* Erfahrungsbericht aus der Straßenbauverwaltung; Innenministerium Baden-Württemberg.

26. Dietz, C., I. Dietz, T. Ivanova & B.M. Siemers (2006): Effects of forearm bands on horseshoe bats (Chiroptera: Rhinolophidae). *Acta Chiropterologica* 8: 523–535.

27. Dietz, C. & O. von Helversen (2004): *Identification key to the bats of Europe.* Electronic publication, version 1.0; Tübingen & Erlangen. www.uni-tuebingen.de/tierphys/Kontakt/mitarbeiter_seiten/dietz.htm.

28. Dobat, K. (1985): *Blüten und fledermäuse.* Kramer Verlag, Frankfurt.

29. Dürr, T. (2002): Fledermäuse als Opfer von Windkraftanlagen in Deutschland. *Nyctalus* (N.F.) 8: 115–118.

30. Egsbaek, W., K. Kirk & H. Roer (1971): Beringungsergebnisse der Wasserfledermaus (*Myotis daubentoni*) und der Teichfledermaus (*Myotis dasycneme*) in Jütland. *Decheniana-Beihefte* 18: 51–55.

31. Eklöf, J. & G. Jones (2003): Use of vision in prey detection by brown long-eared bats, *Plecotus auritus. Animal Behaviour* 66: 949–953.

32. Eklöf, J., A.M. Svensson & J. Rydell (2002): Northern bats, *Eptesicus nilssonii*, use vision but not flutter-detection when searching for prey in clutter. *Oikos* 99: 347–351.

33. Ellerman, J.R. & T.C.S. Morrison-Scott (1951): *Checklist of Palaearctic and Indian mammals 1758 to 1946.* Trustees of the British Museum (Natural History), London.

34. Evans, L.B., H.E. Bass & L.C. Sutherland (1972): Atmospheric absorption of sound: Theoretical predictions. *J. Acoust. Soc. Am.* 51: 1565–1575.

35. Fenton, M.B. (1972): The structure of aerial-feeding bat faunas as indicated by ears and wing elements. *Can. J. Zool.* 50: 287–296.

36. Fiedler, W. (1998): Paaren – Pennen – Pendelzug: Die Rauhhautfledermaus (*Pipistrellus nathusii*) am Bodensee. *Nyctalus* (N.F.) 6: 517–523.

37. Gauckler, A. & M. Kraus (1970): Kennzeichen und Verbreitung von *Myotis brandti. Z. Säugetierk.* 35: 113–124.

38. Gebhard, J. (1983): Die Fledermäuse in der Region Basel (Mammalia: Chiroptera). *Verhandlungen der Naturforschenden Gesellschaft in Basel* 94: 1–41.

39. Gebhard, J. (1997): *Fledermäuse.* Birkhäuser-Verlag, Basel.

40. Gerell-Lundberg, K. & R. Gerell (1994): The mating behaviour of the pipistrelle and the Nathusius' pipistrelle (Chiroptera), a comparison. *Folia Zool.* 43: 315–324.

41. Gleich, A. (2002): Großräumige Analysen mittels GIS zum Vorkommen von Wald und Fledermäusen in Bayern. *Schriftenreihe für Landschaftspflege und Naturschutz* 71: 7–18.

42. Gruppo Italiano Ricerca Chirotteri (2004): The Italian bat roost project: a preliminary inventory of sites and conservation perspectives. *Hystrix* (n.s.) 15: 55–68.

43. Haensel, J. & W. Rackow (1996): Fledermäuse als Verkehrsopfer – ein neuer Report. *Nyctalus* (N.F.) 6: 29–47.

44. Haensel, J. (2003): Zur Reproduktions-Lebensleistung von Mausohren (*Myotis myotis*). *Nyctalus* (N.F.) 8: 456–464.

45. Harbusch, C., E. Engel, & J.B. Pir (2002): Die Fledermäuse Luxemburgs. *Ferrantia, Travaux Scientifiques du Musée National d'Histoire Naturelle Luxembourg* 33: 7–149.

46. Harrison, D.L. & P.J.J. Bates (1991): *The mammals of Arabia,* 2nd edition; Harrison Zoological Museum Publication.

47. Harrje, C. (1999): Etho-ökologische Untersuchungen an winterschlafenden Wasserfledermäusen (*Myotis daubentoni*). *Nyctalus* (N.F.) 7: 78–86.

48. Heise, G. & T. Blohm (2003): Zur Altersstruktur weiblicher Abendsegler (*Nyctalus noctula*) in der Uckermark. *Nyctalus* (N.F.) 9: 3–13.

49. Heller, K.-G. & O. von Helversen (1989): Resource partitioning of sonar frequency bands in rhinolophid bats. *Oecologia* 80: 178–186.

50. Helversen, O. von (1989): Bestimmungsschlüssel für die europäischen Fledermäuse nach äußeren Merkmalen. *Myotis* 27: 41–60.

51. Helversen, O. von, M. Esche, F. Kretzschmar & M. Boschert (1987): Die Fledermäuse Südbadens. *Mitt. bad. Landesver. Naturkunde u. Naturschutz* 14: 409–475; Freiburg.

52. Helversen, O. von, K.-G. Heller, F. Mayer, A. Nemeth, M. Volleth & P. Gombkötö (2001): Cryptic mammalian species: a new species of whiskered bat (*Myotis alcathoe* n.sp.) in Europe. *Naturwissenschaften* 88: 217–223.

53. Hoch, S. (1997): Die Fledermäuse im Fürstentum Liechtenstein. *Bergheimat, Jahresschrift des Liechtensteiner Alpenvereins* 1997: 27–62.

54. Hoofer, S.R. & R.A. Van den Bussche (2003): Molecular phylogenetics of the chiropteran family Vespertilionidae. *Acta Chiropterologica* 5, Supplement: 1–63.

55. Horáček, I., V. Hanák & J. Gaisler (2000): Bats of the Palearctic region: a taxonomic and biogeographic review. – In: B.W. Woloszyn (ed.): *Proceedings of the VIIIth EBRS* 1: 11–157; Krakow.

56. Hötker, H., K.-M. Thomsen & H. Jeromin (2006): *Impacts on biodiversity of exploitation of renewable energy sources: the example of birds and bats.* Books on Demand, Norderstedt.

57. Hutterer, R., T. Ivanova, C. Meyer-Cords & L. Rodrigues (2005): Bat migrations in Europe, a review of banding data and literature. *Naturschutz und Biologische Vielfalt* 28: 1–162.

58. Hůrka, L. (1988): Die Zwergfledermaus (*Pipistrellus pipistrellus*) (Mammalia: Chiroptera) in Westböhmen. *Folia Musei Rerum Naturalium Bohemiae Occidentalis* 27: 1–31.

59. Irwin, N.R. & J.R. Speakman (2003): Azorean bats *Nyctalus azoreum,* cluster as they emerge from roosts, despite the lack of avian predators. *Acta Chiropterologica* 5: 185–192.

60. Jarzembowski, T. (2003): Migration of the Nathusius' pipistrelle *Pipistrellus nathusii* (Vespertilionidae) along the Vistula Split. *Acta Theriologica* 48: 301–308.

61. Jones, K.E., J.D. Altringham & R. Deaton (1991): Distribution and population densities of seven species of bats in northern England. *J. Zool. Lond.* 240: 788–798.

62. Kalko, E. & H.-U. Schnitzler (1993): Plasticity in echolocation signals of European pipistrelle bats in search flight: implications for habitat use and prey detection. *Behav. Ecol. Sociobiol* 33: 415–428.

63. Kerth, G., F. Mayer & B. König (2000): Mitochondrial DNA (mtDNA) reveals that female Bechstein's bats live in closed societies. *Molecular Ecology* 9: 793–800.

64. Kerth, G., F. Mayer & E. Petit (2002): Extreme sex-biased dispersal in the communally breeding, nonmigratory Bechstein's bat (*Myotis bechsteinii*). *Mol. Ecol.* 11: 1491–1498.

65. Kerth, G., K. Weissmann & B. König (2001): Day roost selection in female Bechstein's bats (*Myotis bechsteinii*): a field experiment to determine the influence of roost temperature. *Oecologia* 126: 1–9.

66. Khritankov, A.M. & N.D. Ovodov (2001): Longevity of Brandt's bats (*Myotis brandtii*) in Central Sibiria. *Plecotus et al.* 4: 20–24.

67. Kiefer, A., H. Merz, W. Rackow, H. Roer & D. Schlegel (1995): Bats as traffic casualties in Germany. *Myotis* 32/33: 215–220.

68. Kolb, A. (1965): Über die Orientierung einheimischer Fledermäuse während des Fressens. *Zeitschrift für vergleichende Physiologie* 49: 412–419.

69. Krapp, F. (ed.) (2001): *Handbuch der Säugetiere Europas, Band 4: Fledertiere I*. 602 pp.; Aula Verlag.

70. Krapp, F. (ed.) (2004): *Handbuch der Säugetiere Europas, Fledertiere II*. Aula Verlag.

71. Kronwitter, F. (1988): Population structure, habitat use and activity patterns of the noctule bat, *Nyctalus noctula*, revealed by radio-tracking. *Myotis* 26: 23–85.

72. Kulzer, E. (1994): Methoden zur Prüfung von Holzschutzmitteln auf Verträglichkeit bei Fledermäusen. *Nyctalus* (N.F.) 5: 149–168.

73. Kulzer, E. (2005): *Chiroptera, Vol. 3: Biologie. – Handbuch der Zoologie VIII (Mammalia)*. de Gruyter, Berlin.

74. Kunz, T.H. & M.B. Fenton (eds) (2003): *Bat ecology*. The University of Chicago Press.

75. Lancaster, W.C., S.C. Thomson & J.R. Speakman (1997): Wing temperature in flying bats measured by infrared thermography. *J. Therm. Biol.* 22: 109–116.

76. Leeuwangh, P. & A.M. Voûte (1985): Bats and woodpreservatives. Pesticide residues in the Dutch pond bat (*Myotis dasycneme*) and its implications. *Mammalia* 49: 517–524.

77. Mayer, F., C. Dietz & A. Kiefer (2007): Molecular species identification boosts bat diversity. *Frontiers in Zoology* 4: 4.

78. Mayer, F. & O. von Helversen (2001): Sympatric distribution of two cryptic bat species across Europe. *Biol. J. Linn. Soc.* 74: 365–374.

79. Mayer, F. & O. von Helversen (2001): Cryptic diversity in European bats. *Proc. R. Soc. Lond.* B 268: 1825–1832.

80. Mayer, F., E. Petit & O. von Helversen (2002): Genetische Strukturierung von Populationen des Abendseglers (*Nyctalus noctula*) in Europa. *Schriftenreihe für Landschaftspflege und Naturschutz* 71: 267–278.

81. Menu, H. & J.-B. Popelard (1987): Utilisation de caractères dentaires pour la détermination des Vespertilionines de l'Ouest Europeen. *Le Rhinolophe* 4: 1–88.

82. Merz, H. (1993): Fledermäuse als Opfer des Straßenverkehrs in Baden-Württemberg. *Beih. Verö Naturschutz Landschaftspflege Bad.-Württ.* 75: 151–157; Karlsruhe.

83. Meschede, A. & B.-U. Rudolph (eds) (2004): *Fledermäuse in Bayern*. Eugen Ulmer.

84. Mitchell-Jones, A.J., G. Amori, W. Bogdanowicz, B. Kryštufek, P.J.H. Reijnders, F. Spitzenberger, M. Stubbe, J.B.M. Thissen, V. Vohralik & J. Zima (1999): *The atlas of European mammals*. Poyser Natural History.

85. Mitchell-Jones, A.J. & A.P. McLeish (2004): *Bat workers' manual, 3rd edition*. Joint Nature Conservation Committee.

86. Müller, T. & C. Freuling (2006): Zu Fragen der Fledermaustollwut. *Nyctalus* (N.F.) 11: 190–197.

87. Neuweiler, G. (1993): *Biologie der fledermäuse*. Thieme-Verlag, Stuttgart.

88. Norberg, U.M. (1987): Wing form and flight mode in bats. In: M.B. Fenton, P. Racey & J.M.V. Rayner (eds) *Recent advances in the study of bats*: Cambridge University Press.

89. Norberg, U.M. & J.M.V. Rayner (1987): Ecological morphology and flight in bats: wing adaptations, flight performance, foraging strategy and echolocation. *Phil. Trans. R. Soc. Lond.* B 316: 335–427.

90. Norberg, U.M. & M.B. Fenton (1988): Carnivorous bats? *Biol. J. Linn. Soc.* 33: 383–394.

91. Pennycuick, C.J. (1968): Power requirements for horizontal flight in the pigeon *Columba livia*. *J. Exp. Biol.* 49: 527–555.

92. Pennycuick, C.J. (1972): Animal flight. *Studies in Biology* 33. Arnold, London.

93. Pfalzer, G. (2002): *Inter- und intraspezifische Variabilität der Soziallaute heimischer Fledermausarten (Chiroptera: Vespertilionidae)*. PhD Thesis of the University of Kaiserslautern, Mensch und Buch Verlag, Berlin.

94. Pfalzer, G. & J. Kusch (2003): Structure and variability of bat social calls: implications for specifity and individual recognition. *J. Zool.* 261: 21–33.

95. Podlutsky, A.J., A.M. Khritankov, N.D. Ovodov & S.N. Austad (2005): A new field record for bat longevity. *J. Gerontol. A Biol. Sci. Med. Sci.* 60: 1366–1368.

96. Presetnik, P., K. Koselj, M. Zagmajster, N. Aupič Zupančič, K. Jazbec, U. Žibrat, A. Petrinjak & A. Hudolkin (in press): *Atlas of bats (Chiroptera) of Slovenia*. Atlas faunae et florae Sloveniae 2; Centre for Catrography of Fauna and Flora; Ljubljana.

97. Rackow, W. & D. Schlegel (1994): Fledermäuse (Chiroptera) als Verkehrsopfer in Niedersachsen. *Nyctalus* (N.F.) 5: 11–18.

98. Reiter, G. & A. Zahn (2006): *Leitfaden zur Sanierung von Fledermausquartieren im Alpenraum*. Interreg IIIB-Projekt Lebensraumvernetzung; www.livingspacentework. bayern.de.

99. Richarz, K. (2004): *Fledermäuse beobachten, erkennen und schützen*. Franckh-Kosmos.

100. Richarz, K. & A. Limbrunner (1992): *Fledermäuse: fliegende Kobolde der Nacht*. Frankh-Kosmos.

101. Roer, H. (1988): Field experiments about the homing behaviour of the common pipistrelle (*Pipistrellus pipistrellus*). In: Hanák, V., I. Horáček & J. Gaisler (eds). *European Bat Research* 1987: 551–558; Charles Univ. Press, Prague.

102. Rudolph, B.-U., A. Zahn & A. Liegl (2004): Mausohr – *Myotis myotis*. In: A. Meschede & B.-U. Rudolph (eds) *Fledermäuse in Bayern*: 203–231; Ulmer Verlag.

103. Rudolph, B.-U., A. Liegl & A. Karataş (2005): The bat fauna of the caves near Havran in Western Turkey and their importance for bat conservation. *Zoology in the Middle East* 36: 11–20.

104. Ruedi, M. & F. Mayer (2001): Molecular systematics of bats of the genus *Myotis* (Vespertilionidae) suggests deterministic ecomorphological convergences. *Mol. Phyl. Evol.* 21: 436–448.

105. Russo, D. & G. Jones (2002): Identification of twenty-two bat species (Mammalia: Chiroptera) from Italy by analysis of time-expanded recordings of echolocation calls. *J. Zool.* 258: 91–103.

106. Russo, D., G. Jones & M. Mucedda (2001): Influence of age, sex and body size on echolocation calls of Mediterranean and Mehely's horseshoe bats, *Rhinolophus euryale* and *R. mehelyi* (Chiroptera: Rhinolophidae). *Mammalia* 65: 429–436.

107. Ryberg, O. (1947): *Studies on bats and bat parasites*. Bokförlaget Svensk Natur, Stockholm.

108. Rydell, J. & J. Eklöf (2003): Vision complements echolocation in an aerial-hawking bat. *Naturwissenschaften* 90: 481–483.

109. Rydell, J. & J.R. Speakman (1995): Evolution of nocturnality in bats: Potential competitors and predators during their early history. *Biol. J. Linn. Soc.* 56: 183–191.

110. Sachanowicz, K., M. Ciechanowski & K. Piksa (2006): Distribution patterns, species richness and status of bats in Poland. *Vespertilio* 9–10: 151–173.

111. Sachanowicz, K., A. Wower & A.-T. Bashta (2006): Further range extension of *Pipistrellus kuhlii* in central and eastern Europe. *Acta Chiropterologica* 8: 543–548.

112. Saint Girons, M.-C. (1981): Notes sur les mammifères de France. XV. Les Pipistrelles et la circulation routière. *Mammalia* 45: 131.

113. Schmidt, A. (1994): Phänologisches Verhalten und Populationseigenschaften der Rauhhautfledermaus, *Pipistrellus nathusii*, in Ostbrandenburg (Teil 1). *Nyctalus* (N.F.) 5: 77–100.

114. Schmidt, A. (1994): Phänologisches Verhalten und Populationseigenschaften der Rauhhautfledermaus, *Pipistrellus nathusii*, in Ostbrandenburg (Teil 2). *Nyctalus* (N.F.) 5: 123–148.

115. Schmidt, A. (2004): Beitrag zum Ortsverhalten der Rauhhautfledermaus (*Pipistrellus nathusii*) nach Beringungs- und Wiederfundergebnissen aus Nordost-Deutschland. *Nyctalus* (N.F.) 9: 269–294.

116. Schnetter, W. (1960): Beringungsergebnisse an der Langflügelfledermaus (*Miniopterus schreibersii*) im Kaiserstuhl. *Bonner Zool. Beitr., Sonderheft* 11: 150–165.

117. Schnitzler, H.-U. (1968): Die Ultraschall-Ortungslaute der Hufeisen-Fledermäuse (Chiroptera, Rhinolophidae) in verschiedenen Orientierungssituationen. *Z. Vergl. Physiol.* 57: 376–408.

118. Schnitzler, H.-U., C.F. Moss & A. Denzinger (2003): From spatial orientation to food acquisition in echolocating bats. *Trends in Ecology and Evolution* 18: 386–394.

119. Schober, W. & E. Grimmberger (1998): *Die fledermäuse Europas*. Kosmos-Naturführer, Stuttgart.

120. Sendor, T. & M. Simon (2003): Population dynamics of the pipistrelle bat: effects of sex, age and winter weather on seasonal survival. *J. Anim. Ecol.* 72: 308–320.

121. Siemers, B.M., E. Baur & H.-U. Schnitzler (2005): Acoustic mirror effect increases prey detection distance in trawling bats. *Naturwissenschaften* 92: 272–276.

122. Siemers, B.M., C. Dietz, D. Nill & H.-U. Schnitzler (2001): *Myotis daubentonii* is able to catch small fish. *Acta Chiropterologica* 3: 71–75.

123. Siemers, B.M. & R. Güttinger (2006): Prey conspicousness can explain apparent prey selectivity. *Current Biology* 16: 157–159.

124. Siemers, B. & D. Nill (2000): *Fledermäuse*. Das Praxisbuch, BLV Verlagsgesellschaft.

125. Siemers, B.M. & H.-U. Schnitzler (2004): Echolocation signals reflect niche differentiation in five sympatric congeneric bat species. *Nature* 429: 657–661.

126. Simmons, N.B. (2005): Order Chiroptera. In: D.E. Wilson & D.M. Reeder (eds) *Mammal species of the world. A taxonomic and geographic reference.* John Hopkins University Press.

127. Simmons, N.B. (2005): An Eocene big bang for bats. *Science* 307: 527–528.

128. Skiba, R. (2003): *Europäische fledermäuse*. Die Neue Brehm-Bücherei, Westarp Wissenschaften.

129. Skiba, R. (2004): Möglichkeiten und Grenzen der Artbestimmung von Fledermäusen mit Hilfe von Kot. *Nyctalus* (N.F.) 9: 477–488.

130. Sluiter, J.W., P.F. van Heerdt & J.J. Bezem (1956): Population statistics of the bat *Myotis mystacinus*, based on the marking-recapture method. *Archives Néerlandaises de Zoologie* 12: 63–88.

131. Sluiter, J.W., P.F. van Heerdt & A.M. Voûte (1971): Contribution to the population biology of the pond bat, *Myotis dasycneme*. *Decheniana-Beihefte* 18: 1–44.

132. Speakman, J.R. & G.C. Hays (1992): Albedo and transmittance of short-wave radiation for bat wings. *J. Therm. Biol.* 17: 317–321.

133. Speakman, J.R., P.A. Racey, C.M.C. Catto, P.I. Webb, S.M. Swift & A.M. Burnett (1991): Minimum summer populations and densities of bats in N.E. Scotland, near the northern borders of their distributions. *J. Zool.* 225: 327–345.

134. Speakman, J.R. & A. Rowland (1999): Preparing for inactivity: how insectivorous bats deposit a fat store for hibernation. *Proceedings of the Nutrition Society* 58: 123–131.

135. Speakman, J.R. & D.W. Thomas (2003): Physiological ecology and energetics of bats. In: T.H. Kunz & M.B. Fenton (eds) *Bat ecology*. The University of Chicago Press.

136. Spitzenberger, F. (2001): *Die Säugetierfauna Österreichs*. Graz.

137. Spitzenberger, F., J. Pialek & E. Haring (2001): Systematics of the genus *Plecotus* (Mammalia, Vespertilionidae) in Austria based on morphometric and molecular investigations. *Folia Zool.* 50: 161–172.

138. Spitzenberger, F., P.P. Strelkov, H. Winkler & E. Haring (2006): A preliminary revision of the genus *Plecotus* (Chiroptera, Vespertilionidae) based on genetic and morphological results. *Zoologica Scripta* 35: 187–230.

139. Steffens, R., U. Zöphel & D. Brockmann (2005): *40 Jahre Fledermausmarkierungszentrale Dresden – methodische Hinweise und Ergebnisübersicht*. Materialien zu Naturschutz und Landschaftspflege, Sächsisches Landesamt für Umwelt und Geologie.

140. Strelkov, P.P. (1969): Migratory and stationary bats of the European part of the Soviet Union. *Acta Zoologica Cracoviensia* 16: 393–439.

141. Teeling, E.C., M.S. Springer, O. Madsen, P. Bates, S.J. O'Brien & W.J. Murphy (2005): A molecular phylogeny for bats illuminates biogeography and the fossil record. *Science* 307: 580–584.

142. Toschi A. & B. Lanza (1959): *Fauna d'Italia Vol. IV Mammalia: Generalita – Insectivora – Chiroptera.* Edizioni Calderini, Bologna.

143. Trujillo, D. (1991): *Murciélagos de las Islas Canarias.* Coleccion Tecnica, Instituto Nacional para la Conservacion de la Naturaleza, Icona.

144. Voigt, C.C. & Y. Winter (1999): Energetic cost of hovering flight in nectar feeding bats (Phyllostomidae: Glossophaginae) and its scaling in moths, birds and bats. *J. Comp. Physiol.* B 169: 38–48.

145. Weid, R. & O. von Helversen (1987): Ortungsrufe europäischer Fledermäuse beim Jagdflug im Freiland. *Myotis* 25: 5–27.

146. Willig, M.R. & K.W. Selcer (1989): Bat species density gradients in the New World: a statistical assessment. *Journal of Biogeography* 16: 189–195.

147. Willis, C.K.R. & R.M. Brigham (2005): Physiological and ecological aspects of roost selection by reproductive female hoary bats (*Lasiurus cinereus*). *J. Mammal.* 86: 85–94.

148. Winter, Y. & O. von Helversen (1998): The energy cost of flight: do small bats fly more cheaply than birds? *J. Comp. Physiol.* B 168: 105–111.

149. Wolz, I. (1993): Untersuchungen zur Nachweisbarkeit von Beutetierfragmenten im Kot von *Myotis bechsteini. Myotis* 31: 5–25.

150. Wolz, I. (1993): Das Beutespektrum der Bechsteinfledermaus *Myotis bechsteini* ermittelt aus Kotanalysen. *Myotis* 31: 27–68.

GENERAL LITERATURE FOR THE ENGLISH EDITION

151. Altringham, J.D. (1996): *Bats: Biology and Behaviour.* Oxford University Press, Oxford.

152. Baker, A.S. & J.C. Craven (2003): Checklist of the mites (Arachnida: Acari) associated with bats (Mammalia: Chiroptera) in the British Isles. *Systematic & Applied Acarology Special Publications* 14: 1–20.

153. Battersby, J. (ed.) & Tracking Mammals Partnership (2005): *UK Mammals: species status and population trends.* First report by the Tracking Mammals Partnership. Joint Nature Conservation Committee/Tracking Mammals Partnership, Peterborough.

154. Briggs, B & D. King (1998): *The Bat Detective: A field guide for bat detection* (includes CD of bat sounds). Stag Electronics, Shoreham-by-Sea.

155. Harris, S. & D.W. Yalden (eds) (2008): *Mammals of the British Isles: Handbook, 4th edition.* The Mammal Society, Southampton.

156. Hutson, A.M. (1984): Keds, flat-flies and bat-flies: Diptera Pupipara (families Hippoboscidae and Nycteribiidae). *Handbk. Ident. Br. Insects* 10(7): 1–40.

157. Hutson, A.M., S.P. Mickleburgh & P.A. Racey (2001): *Microchiropteran Bats – global status survey and conservation action plan.* IUCN, Gland.

158. Kunz, T.H. ed. (1988): *Ecological and Behavioral Methods for the Study of Bats.* Smithsonian Institution Press, Washington. (Revised edition due 2009.)

159. Lanza, B. (1999): I parassiti dei pipistrelli (Mammalia, Chiroptera) della fauna italiana. *Museo Regionale di Scienze Naturali Torino, Monographie* 30: 1–318.

160. Robinson, R.A., J.A. Learmouth, A.M. Hutson, C.D. MacLeod, T.H. Sparks, D.I. Leech, G.J. Pierce, M.M. Rehfisch & H.Q.P. Crick (2005): *Climate Change and Migratory Species. British Trust for Ornithology Research Report 414.* Defra, London.

161. Rodrigues, L., L. Bach, M.J. Dubourg-Savage, J. Goodwin, & C. Harbusch, (2008): *Guidelines for the consideration of bats in wind farm projects.* Eurobats Publications Series No. 3. UNEP/EUROBATS Secretariat, Bonn.

162. Shiel, C., C. McAney, C. Sullivan, & J. Fairley (1997): *Identification of Arthropod Fragments in Bat Droppings.* Mammal Society, London, Occasional Publication No. 17.

163. Vaughan, N. (1997): The diets of British bats (Chiroptera). *Mammal Review* 27: 77–94.

164. Walsh, A., C. Catto, A.M. Hutson, P. Racey, P. Richardson, & S. Langton, (2001): *The UK's National Bat Monitoring Programme, Final Report 2001.* Defra, Bristol (plus annual reports from the Bat Conservation Trust to 2006).

165. Whitaker. A.P. (2007): Fleas (Siphonaptera) (2nd edition). *Handbk. Ident. Br. Insects* 1(16): 1–178.

FURTHER REFERENCES

166. Holland, R.A., K. Thorup, M.J. Vonhof, W.W. Cochran & M. Wikelski (2006): Bat orientation using Earth's magnetic field. *Nature* 444: 702.

167. Ibáñez, C., J.L. García-Mudarra, M. Ruedi, B. Stadelmann & J. Juste (2006): The Iberian contribution to cryptic diversity in European bats. *Acta Chiropterologica* 8: 277–297.

168. Lacki, M.J., J.P. Hayes & A. Kurta (2007): *Bats in forests, conservation and management.* The Johns Hopkins University Press, Baltimore.

INTERNET SITES

169. EUROBATS: www.eurobats.org

170. Natura 2000 categories and the EU Habitats Directive Annexes II and IV: www.ec.europa.eu

171. Red list of the IUCN: www.iucnredlist.org

172. Red list of the European Union: www.eunis.eea.europa.eu

173. The Bat Conservation Trust: www.bats.org.uk

Index

Bold page numbers refer to the species accounts.
Italicised page numbers refer to figures (photos, diagrams etc.) in the main text.

English edition published 2009 by A & C Black Publishers Ltd., 36 Soho Square, London W1D 3QY
www.acblack.com

First published in German in 2007 by Franckh-Kosmos Verlags

© Franckh-Kosmos Verlags GmBh & Co. KG, Stuttgart, 2007

Reprinted with corrections 2011

ISBN 978 1 4081 0531 3

A CIP catalogue record for this book is available from the British Library.

This book is produced using paper that is made from wood grown in managed, sustainable forests. It is natural, renewable and recyclable. The logging and manufacturen processes conform to the environmental regulators of the country of origin.

Original German text by Christian Dietz (species descriptions and parts of general chapters), Otto von Helversen (general chapters) and Irmhild Wolz (Food of bats).

English translation and revision: Peter H. C. Lina
Editing and additional English texts: Anthony M. Hutson

Project editor (English edition): Julie Bailey
Layouts (English edition): Julie Dando, Fluke Art

Maps by Melanie Weigand

Printed in Germany by aprinta Druck GmbH & Co. KG

10 9 8 7 6 5 4 3 2

TM
MIX
Paper from
responsible sources
FSC
www.fsc.org
FSC™ C004592

Photo, front cover: Alpine Long-eared Bat (*Plecotus macrobullaris*) © D. Nill.
Photos, back cover: main, Sardinian Long-eared Bat (*Plecotus sardus*) © D. Nill; top, Brown Long-eared Bat (*Plecotus auritus*) © D. Nill; middle, Bechstein's Bat (*Myotis bechsteinii*) © D. Nill; bottom, Soprano Pipistrelle (*Pipistrellus pygmaeus*) © D. Nill.
Photo, spine: Lesser Horseshoe Bat (*Rhinolophus hipposideros*) © D. Nill
Photo, pages 2–3: Greater Mouse-eared Bat (*Myotis myotis*). © D. Nill.